CORPORATE FINANCE

ASPEN CASEBOOK SERIES

CORPORATE FINANCE

STEPHEN J. LUBBEN

Harvey Washington Wiley Chair in Corporate Governance & Business Ethics
Seton Hall University School of Law

Wolters Kluwer

Law & Business

ISBN 978-1-4548-3387-1

Library of Congress Cataloging-in-Publication Data

Lubben, Stephen J., 1971- author.
    Corporate finance / Stephen J. Lubben, Harvey Washington Wiley Chair in Corporate Governance & Business Ethics, Seton Hall University School of Law.
        pages cm
    Includes index.
    ISBN 978-1-4548-3387-1 1.
1. Corporations–Finance–Law and legislation–United States. I. Title.

KF1428.L83 2013
346.73'0664–dc23

                                                                        2013035302

SUSTAINABLE FORESTRY INITIATIVE

Certified Sourcing
www.sfiprogram.org
SFI-01234

SFI label applies to the text stock

About Wolters Kluwer Law & Business

Wolters Kluwer Law & Business is a leading global provider of intelligent information and digital solutions for legal and business professionals in key specialty areas, and respected educational resources for professors and law students. Wolters Kluwer Law & Business connects legal and business professionals as well as those in the education market with timely, specialized authoritative content and information-enabled solutions to support success through productivity, accuracy and mobility.

Serving customers worldwide, Wolters Kluwer Law & Business products include those under the Aspen Publishers, CCH, Kluwer Law International, Loislaw, ftwilliam.com and MediRegs family of products.

CCH products have been a trusted resource since 1913, and are highly regarded resources for legal, securities, antitrust and trade regulation, government contracting, banking, pension, payroll, employment and labor, and healthcare reimbursement and compliance professionals.

Aspen Publishers products provide essential information to attorneys, business professionals and law students. Written by preeminent authorities, the product line offers analytical and practical information in a range of specialty practice areas from securities law and intellectual property to mergers and acquisitions and pension/benefits. Aspen's trusted legal education resources provide professors and students with high-quality, up-to-date and effective resources for successful instruction and study in all areas of the law.

Kluwer Law International products provide the global business community with reliable international legal information in English. Legal practitioners, corporate counsel and business executives around the world rely on Kluwer Law journals, looseleafs, books, and electronic products for comprehensive information in many areas of international legal practice.

Loislaw is a comprehensive online legal research product providing legal content to law firm practitioners of various specializations. Loislaw provides attorneys with the ability to quickly and efficiently find the necessary legal information they need, when and where they need it, by facilitating access to primary law as well as state-specific law, records, forms and treatises.

ftwilliam.com offers employee benefits professionals the highest quality plan documents (retirement, welfare and non-qualified) and government forms (5500/PBGC, 1099 and IRS) software at highly competitive prices.

MediRegs products provide integrated health care compliance content and software solutions for professionals in healthcare, higher education and life sciences, including professionals in accounting, law and consulting.

Wolters Kluwer Law & Business, a division of Wolters Kluwer, is headquartered in New York. Wolters Kluwer is a market-leading global information services company focused on professionals.

For J. and V.

SUMMARY OF CONTENTS

CONTENTS

3

DISCOUNT RATES   35

4

THE NET PRESENT VALUE RULE AND SOME
COMPETITORS   51

5

6

7

18

DERIVATIVES   315

19

ASSET SECURITIZATION   339

23

TENDER OFFERS   487

24

ASSET SALES   515

27

PREPACKAGED CHAPTER 11 CASES	**603**

28

INTRODUCTION TO CHAPTER 11	**649**

29

SELL AND LIQUIDATE REORGANIZATIONS   675

30

CHAPTER 11 PLANS   711

ACKNOWLEDGEMENTS

The author is grateful to the following authors, journals, and periodicals that granted permission to excerpt their work:

John D. Ayer et. al., *Welcome to the Jungle*, Am. Bankr. Inst. J., July/August 2003, at 24.

Robert P. Bartlett, III, *Venture Capital, Agency Costs, and the False Dichotomy of the Corporation*, 54 UCLA L. Rev. 37 (2006).

Stephanie Ben-Ishai & Stephen J. Lubben, "Involuntary Creditors and Corporate Bankruptcy" (2012) 45:2 UBC L Rev 253.

William W. Bratton, *The New Dividend Puzzle*, 93 Geo. L.J. 845 (2005).

Brian R. Cheffins & John Armour, *The Past, Present, and Future of Shareholder Activism by Hedge Funds*, 37 J. Corp. L. 51 (2011).

Lawrence A. Cunningham, *From Random Walks to Chaotic Crashes: The Linear Genealogy of the Efficient Capital Market Hypothesis*, 62 Geo. Wash. L. Rev. 546 (1994).

Ronald J. Gilson, *Engineering a Venture Capital Market: Lessons from the American Experience*, 55 Stan. L. Rev. 1067 (2003). Reproduced with permission of School of Law, Stanford University in the format republish in a book via Copyright Clearance Center.

Zohar Goshen, *Shareholder Dividend Options*, 104 Yale L.J. 881 (1995). Reproduced under license from The Yale Law Journal Company, Inc.

Michelle M. Harner, *The Search for an Unbiased Fiduciary in Corporate Reorganizations*, 86 Notre Dame L. Rev. 469 (2011).

Michelle M. Harner, *Trends in Distressed Debt Investing: An Empirical Study of Investors' Objectives*, 16 Am. Bankr. Inst. L. Rev. 69 (2008).

Espen Gaarder Haug & Nassim Nicholas Taleb, *Option Traders Use (Very) Sophisticated Heuristics, Never the Black–Scholes–Merton Formula*, J. Economic Behavior & Organization, Volume 77, Issue 2, February 2011, Pages 97-106. Reproduced with permission of Elsevier BV in the format reuse in a book/textbook via Copyright Clearance Center.

Claire A. Hill, *Securitization: A Low-Cost Sweetener for Lemons*, 74 Wash. U. L.Q. 1061 (1996).

Marcel Kahan, *Rethinking Corporate Bonds: The Trade–Off Between Individual and Collective Rights*, 77 NYU L. Rev. 1040 (2002).

Kenneth C. Kettering, *Securitization and Its Discontents: The Dynamics of Financial Product Development*, 29 Cardozo L. Rev. 1553 (2008).

Stephen J. Lubben & Rajesh P. Narayanan, *CDS and the Resolution of Financial Distress*, 24 J. Applied Corp. Fin. 129 (2012). © 2012 Morgan Stanley.

Stephen J. Lubben, *In Exit, Dynegy Shareholders Look to Eke Out Something*, New York Times Dealb%k, August 29, 2012. © 2012 The New York Times. All rights reserved.

Daniel J. Morrissey, *Another Look at the Law of Dividends*, 54 U. Kan. L. Rev. 449 (2006).

Katherine Pratt, *The Debt-Equity Distinction in a Second-Best World*, 53 Vand. L. Rev. 1055 (2000).

Nicholas P. Saggese, et al., *A Practitioner's Guide to Exchange Offers and Consent Solicitations*, 24 Loy. L.A. L. Rev. 527 (1991).

Elizabeth Warren, *A Theory of Absolute Priority*, 1991 Ann. Surv. Am. L. 9, 37-38 (1992).

Charles K. Whitehead, *Destructive Coordination*, 96 Cornell L. Rev. 323, 353-56 (2011).

Harry Wilson, *Budget 2012: Perpetual bonds issue examined*, The Telegraph, 21 Mar. 2012. © Telegraph Media Group Limited 2012, used under license.

Sarah Pei Woo, *Regulatory Bankruptcy: How Bank Regulation Causes Fire Sales*, 99 Geo. L.J. 1615 (2011), used with the permission of Kenneth Wee.

In addition, several Bloomberg news articles appear throughout the book under license from Bloomberg L.P., who retains the copyright therein.

Finally, while in practice I took a year off from the firm to earn an LL.M at Harvard. While there, I took Corporate Finance with Reinier Kraakman, and I would be remiss if I did not acknowledge the undoubted influence that course, as taught by him, had on my approach to this subject. Indeed, in my early years in academia our two courses were virtually identical. Many thanks are due.

INTRODUCTION: WHY CORPORATE FINANCE?

In many ways, the Corporate Finance class can be seen as a collection of bits that were left out of other courses. The Trust Indenture Act of 1939 (Chapter 14) falls by the wayside for want of time in Securities Regulation. The more sophisticated corporate reorganization techniques (Chapters 27 & 29) tend to similarly get little treatment in the general Bankruptcy class that often barely has time to introduce chapter 11.

Now you might think that there is a reason why these things get dropped from other courses: maybe they're not so important?[1]

But I have repeatedly started my first class by explaining that Corporate Finance teaches topics that I wished I had learned before I became a first-year associate in New York. I learned these topics on the job, but this course gives you a chance to learn them in advance, so you can "hit the ground running." Given the current job market, that can't be a bad thing.

In short, this is a very functional course that teaches a collection of advanced skills that are useful for corporate lawyers of both the transactional and litigation variety. It also provides some useful skills for noncorporate lawyers, too, as I explain below.

This book is organized around four basic units: valuation (Chapters 1–11), finance (Chapters 12–21), mergers and acquisitions (Chapters 22–25), and financial distress (Chapters 26–30).

Valuation is the math-heavy part of the course, but it also introduces some finance theory. Understanding both the basics of the math and theory as taught in MBA programs will help you interact with bankers and accountants in practice.

Understanding the math is also helpful in several noncorporate contexts as well. For example, you need to understand how to value a business if you are going to practice family law. Families, you see, often own businesses. The same goes for any sort of estate planning or tax practice.

The goal is to help you understand the math, not necessarily to help you set up shop as an investment banker. Rather, when you find yourself

---

1. *Cf.* 1 William Blackstone, *Commentaries on the Laws of England* 6 (1765).

negotiating a deal in the future, some intuitive understanding of how the other side's banker got to a particular figure will help you do your job as a lawyer.

The second unit turns to specific financial instruments. Some, like common shares, are apt to be familiar; others — like swaps and CDOs — probably less so. But a working knowledge of the instruments covered in this section is vital to anyone who intends to practice with a big law firm anywhere in the world. Many of you might not practice on Wall Street, but your clients will inevitably have many, many interactions with Wall Street.

The third unit covers mergers and acquisitions, or M&A.

You might have covered the case law regarding mergers in your Business Associations class, but the aim of these chapters is to focus on the negotiation of the actual contracts involved in deals. You might have already studied *Revlon* and *Unocal*, but did you cover covenants, reps, and warranties? How about the choice between a merger and a sale of all of the company's assets?

The final unit covers financial distress, and examines the ways in which a corporation can work out of financial difficulties. This could mean bankruptcy, and several chapters examine chapter 11 as used by very large corporations like American Airlines and General Motors, but it might involve some sort of out-of-court workout, too. Chapter 26 in particular covers nonbankruptcy exchange offers, which involves the exchange of existing debt for new securities in an attempt to avoid bankruptcy. Chapter 27 examines prepackaged bankruptcy cases, which involves an attempt to use the Bankruptcy Code's power while only interacting with the bankruptcy process to a very minimal extent.

This material reflects the area where your author practiced, and thus is of special interest. But it should be of interest to any corporate lawyer, especially those who expect to have a transactional practice. By and large, corporate transactions are driven by either taxes or bankruptcy. Lawyers aim to structure the deal to avoid both.

A NOTE ON EDITING

While I like to provide a bit more of a case than many authors, entire sections have been chopped. Many citations have been removed to increase readability, and footnotes have often been removed. When retained, footnotes have been renumbered to conform to the chapter's numbering scheme.

I

VALUATION

1

CORPORATE FINANCE, ACCOUNTING, AND CASH FLOWS

Corporate Finance texts, and finance articles, spend much time discussing "firms." For a law student, a firm is the source of a job, hopefully. But for purposes of this text and this class, firm means something more than law firm.

In finance a firm is any of the entities you studied in your Business Associations or Corporations class: sole proprietorships, partnerships, limited liability companies, and corporations. The firm is a way of organizing business and economic activity. The specific nature of each type of firm is a function of the law that created it.

There are many different types of businesses and each has its own unique set of transactions, but the fundamentals of all firms are basically the same. First, all firms have assets and liabilities. Assets are the things the firm *owns*, and liabilities are the things the firm *owes*. A factory is an asset — no matter how old and decrepit it might be — and a bank loan, a tort judgment against the firm, or a promise to pay employees is a liability.

But notice that for the bank, the loan to the firm is an asset. The bank has received a contract that will generate periodic interest payments, along with the return of the principal amount the bank lent. Most liabilities have this property: a liability for one firm is an asset to another.

Also notice that the only assets and liabilities that are shown on the balance sheet are those that can be reduced to dollar figures. The firm's good reputation might be thought of as an asset, but you won't find it on the balance sheet.

Next, all firms — at least all the firms covered in this class — have owners.[1] The owners' interest in the firm is called *equity*. It has nothing to do with justice. Equity can take the form of shares (in corporations), membership interests (LLCs), or any other ownership claim.

---

1. Not-for-profit firms have no owners, but do have beneficiaries.

With that background, you are ready to learn some basic accounting. Accounting is important, because much of corporate finance is based on an understanding of the firm's financial situation. The way to get that understanding is through the accounting statements.[2]

1. BALANCE SHEETS

A balance sheet is a picture of a firm's assets, liabilities, and equity at a point in time. As such, the balance sheet is often out of date one minute after it is prepared. The static nature of balance sheets can also be abused, as noted in the following excerpt from the Lehman Brothers examiner's report. An examiner is a neutral party appointed by a bankruptcy court to investigate some aspect of a company that has ended up in chapter 11.[3] In this case, the examiner was appointed to investigate the collapse of Lehman during the financial crisis of 2008.

IN RE LEHMAN BROTHERS HOLDINGS, INC.,
(BANKR. S.D.N.Y. 2010)
Report of Anton R. Valukas, Examiner, pages 732–735

Lehman employed off-balance sheet devices, known within Lehman as "Repo 105" and "Repo 108" transactions, to temporarily remove securities inventory from its balance sheet, usually for a period of seven to ten days, and to create a materially misleading picture of the firm's financial condition in late 2007 and 2008.[4] Repo 105 transactions were nearly identical to standard repurchase and resale ("repo") transactions that Lehman (and other investment banks) used to secure short-term financing, with a critical difference: Lehman accounted for Repo 105 transactions as "sales" as opposed to financing transactions based upon the overcollateralization or higher than normal haircut in a Repo 105 transaction.[5] By recharacterizing the Repo 105 transaction as a "sale," Lehman removed the inventory from its balance sheet.

---

2. If offered at your school, a full accounting for lawyers class can be invaluable.

3. 11 U.S.C. §1104(c).

4. Unless otherwise noted, the Report uses the term "Repo 105" to refer to both Repo 105 and Repo 108 transactions. Lehman treated the two transactions identically under the same internal accounting policy and both transactions shared the same anatomy. They differed only in that Repo 105 transactions utilized fixed income securities and required a minimum five percent overcollateralization amount (i.e., a minimum of $105 worth of securities in exchange for $100 cash borrowed), while Repo 108 transactions utilized equities securities and required a minimum eight percent overcollateralization amount (i.e., a minimum of $108 worth of securities in exchange for $100 cash borrowed).

5. Sale and repurchase agreements ("repos") are agreements where one party transfers an asset or security to another party as collateral for a short-term borrowing of cash, while simultaneously agreeing to repay the cash and take back the collateral at a specific point in time. When the repo transaction matures, the borrower repays the funds plus an agreed upon interest rate and takes back its collateral. . . . Overcollateralization amounts, or haircuts, in Repo 105 transactions were higher than the typical haircut applied to ordinary repos using similar securities.

Lehman regularly increased its use of Repo 105 transactions in the days prior to reporting periods to reduce its publicly reported net leverage and balance sheet. Lehman's periodic reports did not disclose the cash borrowing from the Repo 105 transaction — i.e., although Lehman had in effect borrowed tens of billions of dollars in these transactions, Lehman did not disclose the known obligation to repay the debt. Lehman used the cash from the Repo 105 transaction to pay down other liabilities, thereby reducing both the total liabilities and the total assets reported on its balance sheet and lowering its leverage ratios. Thus, Lehman's Repo 105 practice consisted of a two-step process: (1) undertaking Repo 105 transactions followed by (2) the use of Repo 105 cash borrowings to pay down liabilities, thereby reducing leverage. A few days after the new quarter began, Lehman would borrow the necessary funds to repay the cash borrowing plus interest, repurchase the securities, and restore the assets to its balance sheet.

Lehman never publicly disclosed its use of Repo 105 transactions, its accounting treatment for these transactions, the considerable escalation of its total Repo 105 usage in late 2007 and into 2008, or the material impact these transactions had on the firm's publicly reported net leverage ratio. According to former Global Financial Controller Martin Kelly, a careful review of Lehman's Forms 10-K and 10-Q [annual and quarterly reports filed with the SEC] would not reveal Lehman's use of Repo 105 transactions. Lehman failed to disclose its Repo 105 practice even though Kelly believed "that the only purpose or motive for the transactions was reduction in balance sheet;" felt that "there was no substance to the transactions;" and expressed concerns with Lehman's Repo 105 program to two consecutive Lehman Chief Financial Officers — Erin Callan and Ian Lowitt — advising them that the lack of economic substance to Repo 105 transactions meant "reputational risk" to Lehman if the firm's use of the transactions became known to the public. In addition to its material omissions, Lehman affirmatively misrepresented in its financial statements that the firm treated all repo transactions as financing transactions — i.e., not sales — for financial reporting purposes.

Starting in mid-2007, Lehman faced a crisis: market observers began demanding that investment banks reduce their leverage. The inability to reduce leverage could lead to a ratings downgrade, which would have had an immediate, tangible monetary impact on Lehman.

Despite the potential for abuse, the balance sheet provides useful information about the company. From a lender's perspective, the balance sheet provides some insight into the firm's ability to repay. From a supplier's perspective, the balance sheet's discussion of liabilities reveals the degree to which other creditors have claims against the same firm, and the accounts payable line, over time, might offer the first sign of liquidity problems at the firm. When firms approach bankruptcy they often begin to "stretch the trade," which involves paying bills more slowly than in the past.

The balance sheet is said to comprise two sides: the left-hand side (assets) and the right-hand side (liabilities and equity). Visually you can think of an old-fashioned ledger that looks something like Table 1-1, even if modern balance sheets are rarely presented in this manner.

TABLE 1-1
Basic Balance Sheet

Assets	Liabilities
	Equity

The right side of the balance sheet is where most of the finance that is the subject of this class happens. But the asset side of the balance sheet can influence the financing choices that are made on the right side.

Table 1-2 puts some numbers on the balance sheet to make it a bit more realistic. Here is something you should notice right off the bat:

$$\text{Assets} = \text{Liabilities} + \text{Equity, and}$$
$$\text{Assets} - \text{Liabilities} = \text{Equity}$$

That is, the right side of the balance sheet balances with the left; hence the name.

TABLE 1-2
Bogartco, Inc. Balance Sheet

Bogartco, Inc., A Leading Making of Trenchcoats and Fedoras

(In millions)

	Year Ended December 31,	
	2012	2011
Assets		
Current assets:		
Cash and cash equivalents	**$8,161**	$5,505
Short-term investments (including securities loaned of $683 and $62)	**36,012**	31,283
Total cash, cash equivalents, and short-term investments	**44,173**	36,788
Accounts receivable, net of allowance for doubtful accounts		
of $312 and $375	**9,646**	13,014
Inventories	**1,242**	740
Deferred income taxes	**2,344**	2,184
Other	**2,176**	2,950
Total current assets	**59,581**	55,676
Property and equipment, net of accumulated depreciation		
of $8,942 and $8,629	**7,771**	7,630
Equity and other investments	**9,211**	7,754
Goodwill	**12,471**	12,394
Intangible assets, net	**1,077**	1,158
Other long-term assets	**1,429**	1,501
Total assets	**$91,540**	$86,113

	Year Ended December 31,	
	2012	2011
Liabilities and stockholders' equity		
Current liabilities:		
Accounts payable	**$3,654**	$4,025
Short-term debt	**1,000**	1,000
Accrued compensation	**2,252**	3,283
Income taxes	**2,136**	1,074
Short-term unearned revenue	**12,767**	13,652
Securities lending payable	**909**	182
Other	**3,139**	2,931
Total current liabilities	**25,857**	26,147
Long-term debt	**9,665**	4,939
Long-term unearned revenue	**1,152**	1,178
Deferred income taxes	**540**	229
Other long-term liabilities	**7,384**	7,445
Total liabilities	**44,598**	39,938
Commitments and contingencies		
Stockholders' equity:		
Common stock and paid-in capital—shares authorized 24,000; outstanding 8,562 and 8,668	**61,935**	62,856
Retained deficit, including accumulated other comprehensive income of $1,519 and $1,055	**(14,993)**	(16,681)
Total stockholders' equity	**46,942**	46,175
Total liabilities and stockholders' equity	**$91,540**	$86,113

Notice that some categories are now subdivided. Current assets are cash and things that can be turned into cash relatively quickly. Cash here means not only currency, but also bank account balances and other relatively riskless things like U.S. Treasury obligations.

Fixed or long-term assets are things than can only be turned into cash with some effort: Real estate is a classic example. Other less obvious examples include intellectual property, like trademarks. In normal times, these assets will not be turned into cash. Likewise, liabilities have been similarly subdivided among current liabilities (those due within a year) and long-term liabilities.

Total equity is equal to paid-in capital, the original price paid for stock at issuance, plus retained earnings. Paid-in capital is often further subdivided between par value, a concept that you probably remember used to have some legal meaning, and additional paid-in capital. Retained earnings is money the company has earned, but not paid out as dividends to shareholders. When a company loses money in a year, retained earnings is the first item to absorb the loss.

Equity on the balance sheet has no direct relationship with the current market value of the firm's shares.

Every entry on the right side of the balance sheet must have a corresponding entry on the left to maintain the basic equality or balance we already discussed. This is what is often referred to as *double-entry bookkeeping*. If the company adds more money to the retained earnings line, what entry would it make on the left side of the balance sheet?

Because firms only prepare balance sheets periodically — maybe once per quarter — transactions occurring in between the balance sheets are recorded on a ledger known as a journal. By convention, additions to the left side of the balance sheet are recorded as "debits" in the journal, and additions to the right side of the balance sheets are recorded as "credits." Don't even try to make linguistic sense of the terms, and simply remember this:

$$\text{Debits} = \text{left increases}$$
$$\text{Credits} = \text{right increases}$$

Because of the double-entry system used on the balance sheet, which carries over to the journal, a debit entry is paired with a corresponding credit entry, and vice versa. A $5 million credit, increasing liabilities to reflect a loan taken out from the bank, would be matched with a $5 million debit that reflects the increase in cash on the asset side of the balance sheet.

When the firm prepares its next balance sheet the journal will be used to update the prior balance sheet.

PROBLEM SET 1.1

1. If assets minus liabilities equals equity, as noted earlier, how would you interpret negative equity?
2. Under generally accepted accounting practices (GAAP) in the United States, balances sheets like the one seen in Table 1-2 value assets at cost. What risks arise from such a valuation of Bogartco's plant (included in "property and equipment")? In particular, what is the likely difference between the value on the balance sheet and market value?
3. Bacall Tin Whistles, Inc. has current assets of $5.7 million, fixed assets of $4.3 million, current liabilities of $3.9 million, and long-term debt of $1.1 million. Construct a simple balance sheet. What is the shareholder equity?

2. INCOME STATEMENTS

Income or net income refers to the total revenue that a firm takes in, less the cost of generating that revenue. That is

$$\text{Revenues} - \text{Expenses} = \text{Net Income}$$

Income statements partially make up for the weaknesses of a static balance sheet. In particular, an income statement shows the flow of money into and out

TABLE 1-3
Simple Income Statement

Spade & Marlowe Corporation

For the Year Ending December 31, 1937

Revenues	$100
Less Expenses	24
Net Income	$76

of a firm during a particular year. These flows will have an effect on the overall balance sheet, with positive income items increasing the equity and negative income items decreasing it, but the income statement, a sample of which is shown in Table 1-3, shows how the balance sheet came to be.

The accuracy of the foregoing statement is tempered by the GAAP notion that revenues should be matched with their corresponding expenses. This is known as *accrual accounting*, as contrasted with *cash accounting*, which is the kind of accounting your bank uses for your checking account (cash in, cash out). All of the firms studied in this course will use accrual accounting.

Thus, under accrual accounting, income is reported when a sale is made — even if the sale is on credit and the firm receives no actual cash until some point in the future. A firm could have lots of income and still be unable to pay its electricity bill. The utility company likes cash.

The most important concept related to this principle is *depreciation*. When an asset is depreciated, the cost of the asset is incurred over the life of the asset. This represents an attempt to match the cost with the revenue resulting from the asset. But depreciation is merely an estimate of how much a thing is used up, and a variety of tax policies might permit deviations for this norm.

Thus, Bogartco might purchase a new fedora-creasing machine for $100,000. It expects the machine to last for ten years, after which it will have no value at all. Casually we might think that Bogartco will incur a cost of $100,000 in year one, and revenues but no cost in the nine years thereafter.[6] But such straightforward thinking would put legions of attorneys and accountants out of work.

Instead, under GAAP, Bogartco will incur part of the $100,000 over each of next ten years. If Bogartco uses "straight line" depreciation, it will incur a $10,000 cost each year. From a cash flow perspective, it has spent $100,000 in year one. From an accounting perspective, it has spent $10,000.

Amortization is the same idea applied to nontangible assets — in particular, goodwill.[7]

---

6. If Bogartco were to do this, it would be engaging in "cash" accounting. Sole proprietorships often use this method.

7. Goodwill is a kind of accounting catchall that covers the "intangibles" of a business. For example, if a company buys another company for $100 over book value, that extra $100 will appear as "goodwill" on the acquiring company's balance sheet.

Because accounting and "real" cash flows are often out of sync, a similar issue develops with regard to taxes. Namely, the amount of tax actually owed in a particular year might not match with the amount of tax that would seem to be due based on the accounting income. This is because actual income might be more or less than accounting income.

To adjust for this, income statements (see Table 1-4) typically report taxes as the sum of the "current" taxes, which represents the actually paid amount, and deferred taxes, which represents taxes that would be due based on the accounting income reported. In theory, the deferred and current taxes will balance out over the long term.[8]

TABLE 1-4
Bogartco, Inc. Income Statement

Bogartco, Inc., *A Leading Making of Trenchcoats and Fedoras*

Income Statement

(In millions, except per share amounts)

	Year Ended December 31,
	2012
Revenue	**$16,195**
Operating expenses:	
Cost of revenue	**3,139**
Research and development	**2,196**
Sales and marketing	**2,806**
General and administrative	**938**
Total operating expenses	**9,079**
Operating income	**7,116**
Other income	**114**
Income before income taxes	**7,230**
Provision for income taxes	**1,820**
Net income	**$5,410**
Earnings per share:	
Basic	**$0.63**
Diluted	**$0.62**
Weighted average shares outstanding:	
Basic	**8,614**
Diluted	**8,695**
Cash dividends declared per common share	**$0.16**

8. *Cf.* John Maynard Keynes, *A Tract on Monetary Reform* 80 (1923) ("[T]his *long run* is a misleading guide to current affairs. *In the long run* we are all dead. Economists set themselves too easy, too useless a task if in tempestuous seasons they can only tell us that when the storm is long past the ocean will be flat again.").

Net income is often expressed per share of stock outstanding — that is, as earnings per share. This allows for easy comparison of companies in similar industries. This is calculated as

$$EPS = Net\ Income/Shares\ Outstanding$$

As discussed later, EBITA is an even more useful measure of the firm's cash flow.

3. CASH FLOW STATEMENTS

The income statement shows how the firm made or lost money over a specific period of time — typically, a quarter or a year. The balance sheet shows the firm's overall financial condition at the end of that same period of time.

A cash flow statement, shown in Table 1-5 on the next page, then reconciles the firm's opening and closing cash balance for the same period of time. The focus here is specifically on cash, rather than income. The use of cash is detailed, then that use is compared to the prior cash balance to then calculate the final, end-of-period cash balance.

In the case of cash flows from operations, the cash flow statement starts with net income and then adjusts for noncash changes in net income that come from depreciation and amortization. Likewise, the cash flow statement will reflect changes in the type of assets and liabilities the firm shows on its balance sheet — for example, a reduction in accounts receivable is typically reflected in an increase in cash, assuming the reduction is a result of getting paid. An increase in inventory will likely reflect a corresponding decrease in cash, as the cash is used to pay for the inventory.

For nonoperating activities the process works in a similar way. If the company pays off debt, it uses cash. If it issues new debt, the proceeds become new cash on the balance sheet. An increase in plant, property, and equipment is a use of cash, and new equity issuance is a source of cash.

4. CONSOLIDATED REPORTS

In casual conversation, it is common to speak of a firm, when legally we really mean a group of firms. For example, normal people (i.e., nonlawyers) often speak of "Bank of America." But in fact, the thing known as Bank of America is comprised of more than 2,000 separate legal entities, grouped under a single Delaware holding company based in North Carolina.

Although corporate law might treat Bank of America as thousands of entities, as a matter of securities and tax law it is treated as a single legal entity, and Bank of America will prepare a single set of consolidated financial statements under the accounting rules. Essentially a new, hypothetical entity is created as a matter of accounting, and it is this entity that files Securities and Exchange Commission (SEC) reports and pays taxes.

TABLE 1-5
Bogartco, Inc. Cash Flow Statement

Bogartco, Inc., A Leading Making of Trenchcoats and Fedoras

Cash Flow Statement

(In millions)

	Year Ended December 31,
	2012
Operations	
Net income	**$5,410**
Adjustments to reconcile net income to net cash from operations:	
Depreciation, amortization, and other noncash items	694
Stock-based compensation	528
Net recognized losses (gains) on investments and derivatives	(29)
Excess tax benefits from stock-based compensation	(5)
Deferred income taxes	(148)
Deferral of unearned revenue	5,881
Recognition of unearned revenue	(6,862)
Changes in operating assets and liabilities:	
Accounts receivable	3,674
Inventories	(468)
Other current assets	208
Other long-term assets	62
Accounts payable	(400)
Other current liabilities	(911)
Other long-term liabilities	560
Net cash from operations	8,194
Financing	
Short-term borrowings, maturities of 90 days or less, net	814
Proceeds from issuance of debt, maturities longer than 90 days	4,721
Repayments of debt, maturities longer than 90 days	(814)
Common stock issued	177
Common stock repurchased	(4,399)
Common stock cash dividends paid	(1,118)
Excess tax benefits from stock-based compensation	5
Other	(25)
Net cash used in financing	(639)
Investing	
Additions to property and equipment	(564)
Acquisition of companies, net of cash acquired	0
Purchases of investments	(7,417)
Maturities of investments	870
Sales of investments	1,427
Securities lending payable	727
Net cash used in investing	(4,957)
Effect of exchange rates on cash and cash equivalents	58
Net change in cash and cash equivalents	2,656
Cash and cash equivalents, beginning of period	5,505
Cash and cash equivalents, end of period	$8,161

Every subsidiary that the parent company owns more than a 50 percent interest in will be consolidated within the consolidated entity. As a result, the parent company must eliminate transactions between the parent and its subsidiaries for accounts receivable and accounts payable to avoid counting revenue twice and giving the impression that the consolidated entity has more profits or owes more money than it actually does.

If the parent company owns all of the equity interests of its subsidiaries, the consolidated revenues will be equal to the aggregate revenues of the group, less intercompany sales, and net income should equal the aggregate net income of the group, less the effect of intercompany transactions. It is slightly more complicated if the subsidiary is majority owned, but not wholly owned. Than an adjustment must be made to account for the cash flows that belong to the minority shareholders.

If a parent company owns between 20 percent and 50 percent of another company, a proportional share of the subsidiary's net income will appear in the net income of the parent company. This proportional treatment is called the equity method of accounting.

5. LIQUIDITY, CASH FLOW, AND MEASURES OF FIRM HEALTH

The following press release from 2002 relates to Dynegy, an energy company that is used as an example throughout the textbook. Apparently Dynegy was concerned that stock analysts, who typically work for brokerage houses and make recommendations to clients about whether a particular stock should be bought or sold, were penalizing the company for the gap between reported net income and actual operating cash flow. Dynegy set out to close the gap with a corporate finance transaction that had no real economic substance.

SEC PRESS RELEASE
DYNEGY SETTLES SECURITIES FRAUD CHARGES
INVOLVING SPES, ROUND-TRIP
ENERGY TRADES
FOR IMMEDIATE RELEASE
2002–140
COMPANY WILL PAY $3 MILLION CIVIL PENALTY,
CEASE AND DESIST FROM
VIOLATING ANTI-FRAUD PROVISIONS OF
FEDERAL SECURITIES LAWS

Washington, D.C., September 24, 2002 — The Securities and Exchange Commission filed a settled enforcement action today against Dynegy Inc., in connection with accounting improprieties and misleading statements by the

Houston-based energy production, distribution and trading company. The Commission's case arises from (i) Dynegy's improper accounting for and misleading disclosures relating to a $300 million financing transaction, known as Project Alpha, involving special-purpose entities (SPEs), and (ii) Dynegy's overstatement of its energy-trading activity resulting from "round-trip" or "wash" trades — simultaneous, pre-arranged buy-sell trades of energy with the same counter-party, at the same price and volume, and over the same term, resulting in neither profit nor loss to either transacting party.

The Commission found that Dynegy engaged in securities fraud in connection with its disclosures and accounting for Project Alpha, and negligently included materially misleading information about the round-trip energy trades in two press releases it issued in early 2002. In settlement of the Commission's enforcement action, Dynegy, without admitting or denying the Commission's findings, has agreed to the entry of the cease-and-desist order and to pay a $3 million penalty in a related civil suit filed in U.S. district court in Houston. The Commission's investigation is continuing as to others.

More specifically, the Commission's Order finds as follows.

PROJECT ALPHA

By 2000, some energy analysts following Dynegy had noticed a widening gap between Dynegy's net income and operating cash flow. The gap resulted from Dynegy's recognition of net income in the form of unrealized gains from net forward positions,[9] and the fact that the net forward positions generate no current cash flow. This treatment of unrealized gains as net income was required under "mark-to-market" accounting principles. In April of 2001, Dynegy closed on Project Alpha, a complex web of transactions involving SPEs, to boost its 2001 operating cash flow by $300 million, or 37%, and thereby reduce the gap between its net income and operating cash flow, as well as to achieve a $79 million tax benefit.

Dynegy defrauded the investing public by failing to disclose in its 2001 Form 10-K the true financing, as opposed to operating, nature of the $300 million. In reality, the $300 million was a loan masquerading as operating cash flow on Dynegy's 2001 Statement of Cash Flows. This is particularly significant for two reasons: first, analysts view operating cash flow as a key indicator of the financial health of energy trading firms such as Dynegy; and second, historically, the Statement of Cash Flows has been considered immune from cosmetic tampering.

In addition, Dynegy's accounting in its financial statements for the $300 million failed to conform to GAAP in at least two respects. Under Financial Accounting Standard 95, Dynegy should have accounted for the Alpha-related cash flow as financing, rather than operating, cash flow. Moreover, Dynegy failed to comply with the 3% at-risk requirement for SPEs. Consequently, Dynegy overstated net income in 2001 by 12% — the amount of the purported $79 million Alpha-linked tax benefit.

9. A forward is a contract for purchase or sale of an item at some point in the future. *See* Chapter 17. — AUTHOR

ROUND-TRIP ENERGY TRADES

Dynegy issued materially misleading information to the investing public about the amount of trading on its electronic trading platform, Dynegydirect. On November 15, 2001, Dynegy entered into two massive "round-trip" electricity transactions. In a January 2002 press release, Dynegy included the notional trading value (multiple of volume, price and term) from one of these trades in a discussion of an increase in trading traffic on Dynegydirect. In an April 2002 press release, Dynegy included the results of these trades in its reported energy trading volume and in its first quarter 2002 revenues and cost of sales.

In both releases, Dynegy negligently failed to disclose that the resulting increases in energy trading volume, revenue and notional trading value were materially attributable to the round-trip trades. The contents of the press releases were also used in the offer and sale of securities. Because the round-trip trades lacked economic substance, Dynegy's statements were materially misleading to the investing public. This case is the first enforcement action resulting from an energy trading company's misleading disclosures regarding use of "round-trip" or "wash" trades.

DYNEGY'S CONDUCT AFTER CONTACT BY COMMISSION STAFF

Dynegy disclosed Alpha's impact on its financial performance in a Form 8-K that the company filed with the Commission on April 25, 2002, only after the Commission staff expressed to Dynegy concerns about Alpha. After those concerns were first raised, but before the filing of the Form 8-K, Dynegy's former Chief Financial Officer falsely stated to the public that Alpha's "primary purpose" was to secure a long-term natural gas supply, and Dynegy continued to assert that its obtaining a long-term gas supply was a principal purpose of Alpha. Dynegy officials did not, prior to Dynegy's filing of the Form 8-K, acknowledge that Alpha's principal purposes were, in fact, to minimize the gap between Dynegy's reported net income and reported operating cash flow and to realize an associated tax benefit.

As the foregoing indicates, net income is a widely reported measure that is often of limited practical value.[10]

EBITDA is a considerably more important measure than net income, and one that is often referenced in corporate finance transactions. EBITDA is pronounced exactly as it is spelled — E-BIT-DA. It stands for earnings before interest, taxes, depreciation, and amortization. The idea is to get a measure of the firm's cash flow that does not depend on accounting entries that often reflect noncash events. In the debt context in particular, documents will often demand a certain level of EBITDA, which gives the lender confidence that the debt will actually be paid. EBITDA is also often used as part of financial ratio — for example, EBITDA over total debt is a commonly used measure of the viability of a company.

10. The excerpt also introduces a series of SEC reports, which are discussed in the next section.

TABLE 1-6
Common Financial Ratios

Name	Formula
Earnings per share	Net earnings/# of shares
Debt ratio	Liabilities/Assets
Debt/equity ratio	Liabilities/Equity
Quick ratio	Current assets–(Inventory & Prepayments)/ Current liabilities
Current ratio	Current assets/Current liabilities
Cash ratio	Cash/Current liabilities
Profit or operating margin	Net income/Sales
EBITDA margin	EBITDA/Sales
Return on equity (ROE)	Net income/Total equity

Myriad other ratios are used to measure a firm's health. Each ratio measures something slightly different, and which ratio is appropriate depends on the goal. Table 1-6 summarizes some of the most common financial ratios; think about their purpose as you read the table. One — EPS — you have already seen. Other ratios will be introduced later — like the dividend yield calculation we do in Chapter 12.

You should now be ready to understand this in the real world. Give it a try.

HERMES RAISES GROWTH TARGET
AS CHINA DEMAND BOOSTS SALES

By Andrew Roberts — Aug 31, 2012, Bloomberg.com[11]

Hermes International SCA (RMS), the French maker of silk scarves and leather goods, raised this year's sales-growth target after first-half earnings beat estimates on Asian demand for luxury products.

The maker of Birkin and Kelly bags' annual sales growth excluding currency shifts "could be around 12 percent," it said today in a statement. The Paris-based company last month said it targeted annual revenue growth of 10 percent.

Hermes, in which LVMH Moet Hennessy Louis Vuitton SA (MC) owns a 22.3 percent stake, is seeking to tap growing demand for luxury goods in Asia, where wealthy clients continue to increase spending on items such as Birkin bags. Sales in the region, other than Japan, rose 25 percent in the half-year, led by China, Singapore and Hong Kong, the company said.

The report was "good and reassuring," said Thomas Mesmin, an analyst at Cheuvreux in Paris. A 0.1 percentage point improvement in the operating profit margin to 32.1 percent of sales was "a very strong performance," Mesmin said in a note.

Hermes rose as much as 4.1 percent in Paris trading and was up 2.1 percent at 228.45 euros as of 9:36 a.m. The gain erased the stock's decline this year, which had followed surges of 47 percent in 2011 and 68 percent in 2010.

CHINA BOOM

Hermes got about 47 percent of sales from Asia in the second quarter, compared with 35 percent from Europe and 16 percent from the Americas. Sales of discretionary goods in China will grow by a compounded annual rate of 13.4 percent between 2010 and 2020 to reach $1.88 trillion as shoppers in the world's second-largest economy become more affluent, according to data in a McKinsey & Co. report in March.

Hermes last month reported second-quarter sales rose 22 percent to 814.5 million euros ($1.02 billion), exceeding the 799.3 million-euro average of three analysts' estimates compiled by Bloomberg.

Operating margin for the year should be between that achieved in 2010 and 2011, the company said today.

Operating income climbed to 510.9 million euros from 418.1 million euros a year earlier, higher than the 502 million-euro average of three analysts' estimates. Net income gained 15 percent to 335.1 million euros, beating the 320.7 million-euro average of three estimates compiled by Bloomberg.

---

6. SEC REPORTS

If a firm's shares are traded on a regulated stock exchange — like the New York Stock Exchange — the firm must file a series of reports with the SEC. These forms include the following:

Form 10-K — Annual report, must be filed by companies that have registered securities under Section 12 of the 1934 Act.

Form 10-Q — Quarterly report required for each of the first three quarters of the fiscal year.

Form 8-K — Current report required to be filed when certain key events occur.

Basically the 10-K and 10-Qs are routine forms, and the 8-K is used to report something exciting. 10-K and 10-Qs contain much of the accounting information discussed early in the chapter. The SEC's web page (*www.sec.gov*) allows you to search and find these forms for all publicly traded companies.

Typically a company will file the 10-K sometime around March of the following year. For example, the Dynegy 2010 10-K, discussed in the next section, was filed in March 2011.

7. DYNEGY's 2010 FORM 10-K

Corporate documents from Dynegy are used throughout this text to illustrate many of the transactions. On its web page, Dynegy explains itself as follows:

> Dynegy provides wholesale power, capacity and ancillary services to utilities, cooperatives, municipalities and other energy companies in six states in our key U.S. regions of the Midwest, the Northeast and the West Coast. The company's power generation portfolio consists of approximately 11,600 megawatts of baseload, intermediate and peaking power plants fueled by a mix of coal, fuel oil and natural gas. Our geographic, dispatch and fuel diversity contribute to a portfolio that is well-positioned to capitalize on regional differences in power prices and weather-driven demand.[12]

Or as the company states more concisely on another part of the web page:

> We are a power generation company producing approximately 11,800 megawatts of electricity in 6 states.

For a junior associate tasked with reading the company's 10-K, terms like "baseload, intermediate and peaking" are apt to be quite foreign. That will be the case whenever you begin to learn about a new client, in a new industry. But hopefully the foregoing gives you at least some sense that Dynegy is an energy company that operates pretty much across the country, with the exception of the South.[13]

A common assignment for newly minted attorneys is to write a memo summarizing a new client's business, or for the associate to "get smart" on the client's business.

The easiest way to do this is to get your hands on a copy of the company's most recent 10-K. Maybe you will also pull a copy of the most recent 10-Q, especially if your assignment comes several months after March, and some recent 8-Ks, too.

Please read the Dynegy 2010 10-K, which is available on the course web page. When reading the 10-K, focus especially on the following sections that are apt to be of importance to lawyers:

- Item 1: Business
- Item 1A: Risk Factors
- Item 3: Legal Proceedings

---

12. http://www.dynegy.com/about_dynegy/about_dynegy.asp
13. Somewhat ironically, since the company has its headquarters in Texas.

- Item 7: Management's Discussion and Analysis of Financial Condition and Results of Operations
- Item 8: Financial Statements and Supplementary Data
- Notes to Consolidated Financial Statements

The Notes are especially important for lawyers. All of the nuances — the stuff of lawyers — will appear there.

For those of you who are disinclined to read a very long document this early in the class, keep in mind that we will return to Dynegy throughout the course. The better you understand the business now, the easier it will be to understand the company's bond indenture or merger agreement in the future. And how would your client — and your supervising partner — take it if you showed up to the meeting unprepared?

2

THE TIME VALUE OF MONEY

Intuitively you probably understand that getting $100 today is different from getting $100 one year from today. For one, you might worry that you will not actually receive the money one year from now. We will ignore the issue of risk for now, but it certainly plays an important role in all corporate finance and will be the subject or subtext of many future chapters.

What other differences are there between $100 today and the same in one year? Having taken the risk of nonpayment off the table, you might be somewhat stumped. After all, $100 is $100, right?

Well, no. If you get $100 today, you can put it in the bank and earn a little interest on it over the next year. That lost interest—which you can think of as the value of getting to use the $100 for a year, in this case you are letting the bank use it and they are paying you—is the heart of the difference between the two payments of $100.

This chapter looks at various ways of accounting for the time value of money. It recognizes that $100 today is not the same as $100 in the future. This chapter is also the first of a few chapters that involve some math. The point is not to review your high school math course, or to make you into a math whiz. Rather, having at least a basic understanding of the math behind valuation techniques will aid you in future interactions with accountants and investment bankers. For example, how can you possibly cross-examine investment bankers if your eyes glaze over when they present their valuation of a company?

Take a deep breath, and if it is of any comfort, know that your author was a history major in college.

1. ONE PERIOD PRESENT AND FUTURE VALUES

Suppose you take the $100 today, and put it in the bank. How much will you have in a year if the interest rate is 5 percent? Intuitively you probably understand that you will have $5 in interest,[1] and $100, representing the return of your principal.

Mathematically this can be expressed as:

$$C_1 = C_0 \times (1 + r)$$

where r is the interest rate and C_0 represents the principal amount in question. C_1 is the total value one period in the future—one year in this case.

This is known as a future value calculation. Such formal math probably seems overdone in this case, but understanding this basic form now will make it easier to understand some of the topics addressed in the next section. The future value formula also helps us understand present value calculations. To figure out how much the $100 you get in one year is worth today, we use the following formula:

$$C_0 = C_1 / (1 + r)$$

Note that this is just an algebraic transformation of the future value formula, achieved by dividing each side of the first equation by $(1 + r)$. In short, the current or present value (C_0) is equal to the future payment (C_1) divided by the interest rate (r) added to the full principal (here represented by 1, which means 100 percent).

Because r is used to reduce the value of the sum to today's value, it is often referred to as the *discount rate*.[2] The process of calculating the reduced present value of a future payment is known as *discounting*.

Using the numbers from before, imagine you will get $100 in one year, and if you had the money today you could earn 5 percent on it from the bank. How much is that future payment worth today?

$$C_0 = C_1 / (1 + r)$$
$$PV = \$100 / (1.05) = \$95.24$$

Whereas $100 today is worth $100, $100 in one year is worth just over $95. Which would you rather have?

Note also that the utility of this comparison is highly dependent on the interest rate. If 5 percent is not a useful or relevant interest rate, the result ($95.24) is largely meaningless. For example, if banks are really paying 2 percent on savings accounts

$$C_0 = C_1 / (1 + r)$$
$$PV = \$100 / (1.02) = \$98.04$$

This is a much smaller difference, although if the sum in question is $100 million, rather than just $100, the different between $100 million and $98 million can hardly be ignored.

---

1. $100 × 0.05 = $5. Remember that .05 represents 5 percent in decimal form.
2. In the financial press you will often hear mention of the discount rate, but in that context it refers to the rate at which the local Federal Reserve Bank will lend to commercial banks.

The goal here is to translate all future cash flows into "today dollars." Only by making this adjustment can you directly compare the amounts. But the translation has to be done correctly.

When we introduce risk into the calculation in subsequent chapters, picking the appropriate discount rate becomes even more challenging.

PROBLEM SET 2.1

1. The preferred stock of Bogartco offers an 8.5 percent rate of return. The stock is currently priced at $200 per share. What is the amount of the annual dividend?
2. Suppose your client P sues D for breach of contract. D agrees to settle the suit for a payment of $1,000 in one year, which D asserts has a value of $943. What would you want to know?
3. Given a 10 percent interest rate, why should an investor be indifferent between $100 today and $110 in one year?
4. What happens to a future value when you decrease r? A present value?
5. One year ago, you invested $3,000. Today it is worth $3,142.50. What rate of interest did you earn?
6. You list your apartment for sale and receive two offers. The first offer is for $189,000 in cash. The second offer is for $100,000 today and an additional $100,000 a year from today. If the applicable discount rate is 8.75 percent, which offer should you accept and why?

2. MULTIPLE PERIOD PRESENT AND FUTURE VALUES

What if you are offered your choice of $100 today or $1,000 in five years? Which is the better choice?

First, start with the question of how much $100 might be worth five years from now, if the bank pays 5 percent. Your first answer might be $125. That is, $5 times five years, plus the original $100.

That calculation is known as *simple interest*. Almost no real world transaction uses simple interest. Instead interest is usually *compounded*—that is, interest is earned on interest. Interest earned in year one is added to principal and then all subsequent years' interest is based on that larger principal amount. For example, in year two you would earn 5 percent interest on $105 in your account, assuming annual compounding.

The formula to calculate compound interest should look very familiar:

$$C_t = C_0 \times (1 + r)^t$$

Other than that pesky little *t*, this is just the future value formula you saw earlier. Indeed, the exponent added to the 1 + r was there in section 1, but we could safely ignore it because it was equal to 1.[3] The t is just the number of time periods involved in the calculation.

So if $100 is worth $125 in five years with simple interest, how much is it worth with annual compounding?

$$C_t = C_0 / (1 + r)^t$$
$$C_t = \$100 \times (1.05)^5 = \$127.63$$

In short, annual compounding would result in an extra return of $2.63.

An important thing to note and understand right at the beginning is this: The formulas in this chapter all involve a payment one period in the future. That is, in the foregoing problem we assumed that the first interest payment would be made one year hence. If there is an interest payment made today, and then every year for five years going forward, you have to add the first interest payment into the first cash flow:

$$C_t = \$105 \times (1.05)^5 = \$134.01$$

Notice that having that extra $5 in there at the start results in an extra $1.38 at the end.

What if compounding happened more frequently, say monthly? Here you have to remember that t can represent any time period — but you have to be consistent and only compare like time periods to like time periods, both in terms of t and r. In particular, 5 percent is an annual interest rate, but if we are going to use a monthly time period, we need to adjust the rate accordingly. Thus, we get something that looks like this:

$$C_t = \$100 \times (1.0042)^{60} = \$128.34$$

where 0.0042 is equal to .05/12, and 60 is equal to 12×5.

We get about 70 cents more with monthly compounding than with annual compounding.

What if the bank offered continuous compounding? Take a deep breath. The equation looks like this:

$$C_T = C_0 \times e^{rT}$$

Back in the far reaches of your mind you probably remember the imaginary number e, which equals 2.718. And we use capital T here to indicate the number of years involved. Once you understand that, this is actually an easily solvable equation — so long as you don't try to do it with pencil and paper, or fingers and toes.

What if the $100 in question were repayment on a loan, in millions of dollars, due in 30 years. Which would the bank rather have, monthly or continuous compounding of interest?

3. Recall that $x^1 = x$.

$$C_t = \$100 \times (1.0042)^{360} = \$446.77 \text{ million}$$
$$C_T = \$100 \times e^{.05*30} = \$448.17 \text{ million}$$

If there is any doubt in your mind, the bank would rather have the extra $2 million offered by continuous compounding.

Once you understand how to calculate future values with compound interest, you are ready to calculate present values of payments that will be made several periods into the future. Notice the intentional use of "periods," instead of "years." Any time period will work here, too, you just need to remember to keep your periods and rates in the same units.

The present value formula, and the calculation of the present value of $100 received in five years then is:

$$C_t = C_0/(1 + r)^t$$
$$C_t = \$100/(1.05)^5 = \$78.35$$

$100 in five years is worth just over $78 today.

PROBLEM SET 2.2

1. If you want to put some money in the bank today so that you will have $10,000 in ten years, and the bank will pay you 4 percent on a ten-year certificate of deposit (CD), how much should you deposit?
2. What is the difference between $100 in a five-year CD that pays 2 percent and the same CD that pays 2.5 percent, assuming monthly compounding?
3. You are comparing two investments that cost the same. Both will provide you with $30,000 of income. Investment 1 pays five annual payments starting with $10,000 the first year followed by four annual payments of $5,000 each. Investment 2 pays five annual payments of $6,000 each. Which is better?
4. If you have a choice to earn simple interest on $100,000 for three years at 10 percent or annually compounded interest at 9.5 percent for three years, which one will pay more and by how much?
5. You are considering a side job that will pay you $5,000 next year, $7,000 the following year, and $6,000 the third year. What is the present value of these cash flows, given a 7 percent discount rate?

3. PERPETUITIES

BUDGET 2012: PERPETUAL BONDS ISSUE EXAMINED
Harry Wilson, *The Telegraph*, 21 March 2012

The [UK] Treasury is consulting with investors on issuing gilts [government bonds] with maturities of more than 50 years and potentially looking at selling the first perpetual government bond — which pays a coupon but has no redemption date — in more than 60 years.

UK government perpetual bonds are extremely rare and are the oldest gilts still in issue. One bond dates back as far as 1853, though just £900,000 of this issue remains outstanding. In total eight perpetual bonds, worth a combined £2.7bn, remain out of a total gilt stock of £1 trillion.

Anthony Peters, a strategist at SwissInvest, said he thought there would be strong investor demand for a new perpetual gilt if it offered a coupon of 4.5pc, but that below this level the bond would not be attractive. Mr Osborne's [the Chancellor of the Exchequer] decision to look again at issuing perpetual debt is likely to have come after demand from pension funds for longer-dated bonds and comes as UK interest rates are at a historic low.

"I think the Treasury has probably had a lot of enquiries from investors," said one banker.

As you will learn in subsequent chapters, a bond is simply a debt contract. The borrower agrees to pay back the principal borrowed at some point in the future, and agrees to pay interest on the amount borrowed during the life of the loan.

But note that the article mentions £900,000 of British government debt outstanding from 1853 — the year the Crimean War started. When precisely is the bond due? Never.

The British Consols are the most famous real world example of a perpetuity; some were issued in the mid-1700s, but those from the nineteenth century are the oldest currently outstanding.[4] The British government can pay off the debt at its option. Otherwise, the debt remains outstanding and the holder receives periodic interest payments. Obviously no individual buyer from 1853 is still holding the debt, but holders who bought from an original holder or who inherited the bonds are holding the debt and receiving the payments.

How much should you expect to pay to buy an 1853 Consol today? Under the Consol, Her Majesty's Government promises to repay the principal — we will assume £1,000 — at some indefinite point in the future.

If we assume the interest rate on the debt is 3 percent, and interest is paid annually, you could do a present value calculation. To keep the math somewhat manageable, we will start with 100 years as our duration.

$$C_t = C_0/(1 + r)^t$$
$$C_t = £1,000/(1.03)^{100} = £52.03$$

What if we had wanted to be a bit more precise, and use 1,000 years in our calculation? Given the size of the exponent, it will be easier to do this calculation with Excel, if you know how to use it.[5]

$$C_t = C_0/(1 + r)^t$$
$$C_t = £1,000/(1.03)^{1,000} = £0$$

---

4. Mentions of Consols can be found in *David Copperfield*, *Howards End*, and other classic British works.
5. If not, don't worry, it will be covered in a coming chapter.

What happened? Remember that this calculation measures the value of getting our £1,000 principal back at some point (t) in the future. If you go out long enough, the value of getting your money back begins to approach zero. For example, using these numbers at 350 years out, the Consol is worth about 3 pence.

This makes some sense. If you were an investor in 1853, would you have ever given the British government £1,000 for 350 years — with instructions to repay your great-great grandchildren with interest in 2203? Given all the important historical events that have already happened since 1853 — two World Wars, and the collapse of the British Empire, among other things — can you really know if the British government will be in a position to repay at a date that is still some 190 years in the future? It makes some sense that you might have been willing to pay 3 pence, and not much more, for the chance your distant relations would realize £1,000.

Does that mean a perpetuity is worthless? No. At least not if the perpetuity pays the interest during its life, rather than holding it until some unknown maturity at the end.

For a perpetuity that pays periodic interest and then returns principal at the end, the proper way to value the perpetuity is actually to do a series of present value calculations that separate out the interest payments from the principal; for example, 1,000 present value calculations to find the value of the interest payment (£30) over the next ten centuries, then another calculation to value the return of the principal. And then add the whole lot together:

$$PV = \sum \left[\frac{C_t}{(1 + r)^t} \right] \qquad \text{where } t \text{ ranges from 1 through } \infty$$

Needless to say, this would be quite cumbersome.

The calculations we originally did provide an important insight: namely, most of the value of a perpetuity resides in the early years. For example, we already discovered that at 100 years the principal is worth £52.03. At 50 years it would be worth £228.11, so you can see how quickly the value drops after even the 50th year.

Thus we can value the perpetuity based on the early interest payments alone, and ignore the return of principal at the end. Moreover, only the interest payments in the near term really matter, because anything beyond 50 years or so is of increasingly lesser importance. The formula looks like this:

$$C_t = C_0 / r$$

Here C_0 is the periodic interest payment, and C_t gives you the current value of the perpetuity. One way to think about this that makes it tangible is to consider that you are one person in a long chain of people who have bought a specific Consol since 1853. Each of you holds it for about 50 years or so, and then sells it to a new young person who continues the cycle. It goes on like that forever, or at least until the British government decides to redeem the debt just prior to joining the United Federation of Planets.

The calculation for our 1853 Consol looks like this:

$$C_t = C_0 / r$$
$$C_t = £30 / .03 = £1,000$$

£30 is just the principal amount multiplied by 3 percent. So today you should expect to pay about £1,000 for your right to take your turn with the 1853 Consol.

Other than British governmental bonds, there are few actual examples of perpetuities in the real world. But an important insight from this exercise is that if something pays a steady cash flow for enough years — approximately 50 or more — we can treat it as if it were a perpetuity, because the back end does not really affect that math all that much. So, for example, if you win a lottery that promises to pay you $1,000 per year for life, we can treat it as if it were a perpetuity, assuming you are less than 40 years old.[6] If we use a 3 percent discount rate again, your payment stream is worth just over $33,000.

What if your lottery winnings include an adjustment to account for expected increases in the cost of living? For example, what if payout starts at $1,000 and increases by 2 percent each year? This is known as a growing perpetuity, for obvious reasons, and the formula you can use to value it is as follows

$$C_t = C_0/r - g$$

One qualification: The growth rate must be less than the initial discount rate. If the growth rate equals r, you will end up with zero on the bottom. You also cannot get sensible results if you have a negative number on the bottom. Finally, remember that this assumes a constant rate of growth.

Plugging in the numbers in the example, we get

$$C_t = C_0/r - g$$
$$C_t = 1,000/0.03 - 0.02 = 1,000/0.01 = \$100,000$$

In short, you lottery winnings are worth a lot more with the inflation adjustment built into the payment.

PROBLEM SET 2.3

1. A friend who owns a perpetuity that promises to pay $10,000 at the end of each year, forever, comes to you and offers to sell you all of the payments to be received after the 25th year for a price of $10,000. At an interest rate of 10 percent, should you pay the $10,000 today to receive payment numbers 26 and onward? What does this suggest to you about the value of perpetual payments?

2. Your grandmother establishes a trust in your name and deposits $1 million in it. The trust pays a guaranteed 3 percent rate of return. How much will you receive each year if the trust is required to pay you all of the interest earnings on an annual basis?

3. You are to receive $20,000 per year indefinitely. The market rate of interest for these types of payments is 6 percent. What is the value of your payment stream?

---

6. Even better if you are less than 30, but textbook authors who have just turned 40 are sensitive to this sort of thing.

4. Following an unfortunate incident involving your laptop, the manufacturer promises to pay you $25,000 a year for life. You further negotiate to have the payment increased by 3 percent per year, which represents the average inflation rate over the past decade. If you want to sell this payment stream to get some immediate cash, how should you price it? You estimate that an appropriate discount rate would be 5 percent.

5. If the relevant interest rate is 5 percent, and a perpetuity pays $100 per year, what is the difference between a 3 percent and 4 percent growth rate?

4. ANNUITIES

You might have some vague notion that an annuity has something to do with insurance. Insurance companies do offer contracts called annuities, but these are just one example of the larger group of cash flows that can be considered annuities.[7]

Essentially an *annuity* is any regular, periodic payment that does not constitute a perpetuity. For example, suppose you want to borrow money to buy a house. You are considering a 15-year or a 30-year loan. From the lender's perspective, the payments you make on these loans can be seen as 15- or 30-year annuities. Likewise, if you buy a Treasury bond from the U.S. Government, you will receive a series of interest payments and then the return of your principal at the end. As you will see later, this can be valued as an annuity (interest payments) plus the present value of the return of the principal.

In all cases these are perpetuities with the end years cut off. If you understand an annuity in this way, the following equation for the present value of an annuity will be a bit less intimidating:

$$\text{PV of annuity} = \frac{C}{r} \times \left[1 - \frac{1}{(1 + r)^i} \right]$$

The first term is the present value of a perpetuity. Hopefully you already know all about that. If not, get some coffee and read the prior section again.

The second term, which is always less than one, tells you how much less the annuity is worth because it doesn't continue forever — because you don't get the payments from year n + 1 to infinity. For example, if the second term is equal to 0.40, you know that the annuity is worth 60 percent less than a perpetuity with the same basic terms.[8] In short, the present value of an annuity is the value of the perpetuity less the part you do not receive, because the annuity does not go on forever.

For example, suppose you decide to lease a car for five years, at $400 per month, at a time when annual interest rates are 4 percent. What is the cost of the lease?

---

7. *See http://www.sec.gov/answers/annuity.htm*

8. 60 percent less, because you are multiplying the perpetuity value by .4, which means you are "keeping" 40 percent of the total value.

$$\text{PV of annuity} = \frac{C}{r} \times \left[1 - \frac{1}{(1+r)^t} \right]$$

$$\text{PV of lease} = \frac{\$400}{0.0033} \times \left[1 - \frac{1}{(1+0.0033)^{60}} \right]$$

Solving the equation, we get a total cost of $21,719.63. Notice that the 4 percent interest rate has been converted into a monthly interest rate, to correspond with the monthly payments reflected in the exponent (t).

We should also consider the future value of an annuity. For example, what if you put $20,000 into a bank account at the end of every year, and the bank pays you 8 percent. What is the value at the end of year five?

Notice this is a different question from that in section 2, where we considered a lump sum placed in a bank account at the beginning of our time period. Here there are a series of sums that go into the account over time. The formula for the future value of an annuity is as follows:

$$\text{FV of annuity} = C \times \left[\frac{(1+r)^t - 1}{r} \right]$$

Plugging in the numbers from the hypothetical, we get

$$\text{FV of account} = 20,000 \times \left[\frac{(1+.08)^5 - 1}{.08} \right] = \$117,332$$

You will have saved just over $117,000 by the end of the fifth year, about $17,000 more than the principal you have put into the account.

If you are beginning to think all this valuation stuff is entirely too hypothetical, we interrupt the chapter to present a case. This involves annuities of the insurance company variety, and the question of how to properly value them for estate tax purposes.

ESTATE OF JOHN A. HANCE, PERCY L. HANCE, EXECUTOR, PETITIONER, v. COMMISSIONER OF INTERNAL REVENUE, RESPONDENT

18 T.C. 499
Tax Court of the United States
June 11, 1952

OPPER, Judge:

Respondent determined a deficiency in estate tax of $125,580.69, based on a number of adjustments of which only one now remains in controversy. An overpayment of $14,791.55 is claimed. The single issue relates to the valuation of seven survivorship annuities taken out by decedent during his life. All of the facts have been stipulated and are hereby so found. The estate tax return was filed with the collector for the third district of New York.

The factual background and the question presented are well summarized in petitioner's brief from which we quote verbatim (pp. 2–3):

* * * Decedent John A. Hance died February 22, 1947, survived by his widow. The estate tax return was duly filed and the executor elected to have the gross estate valued as of the optional date in accordance with Section 811 (j) of the Internal Revenue Code. Among the assets reported in the return were seven single premium annuity contracts issued by five life insurance companies. Each of these contracts provided for the payment of a specified annuity to decedent during his lifetime and thereafter to his widow for her life. The widow died May 15, 1947, at the age of 83 years and 9 months. In the estate tax return these contracts were valued at an aggregate amount of $44,632.92. This valuation was arrived at by discounting at the rate of 4% the total payments which would have been received by the widow on the basis of her life expectancy at the time of decedent's death, without regard for the fact that she died on May 15, 1947. For present purposes it is conceded that this method of valuation was incorrect.

The Commissioner has determined that these contracts should be valued on the basis of the cost of similar policies issued on the date of decedent's death to a female applicant of the same age as the surviving widow. It has been stipulated that the total cost of such policies would be $121,905.27. This increase in the valuation of the annuities, coupled with several minor changes not in issue, results in the assessed deficiency of $125,580.69.

Petitioner concedes that the Commissioner has correctly valued the annuity policies as of the date of decedent's death but contends that, because of the election to have the estate valued as of the date one year after death, the Commissioner erred in failing to allow an adjustment for the difference in value as of the later date not due to mere lapse of time.

The point where the parties are really at odds is the correct interpretations of section 811(j), Internal Revenue Code, [which allows the estate to make] "adjustment for any difference in its value as of [one year after death] not due to mere lapse of time."

The error of respondent's position may be described as his insistence that the widow's actual intervening death did not affect the value of the annuities on the optional date because the possibility of her death within that period was one of the factors taken into account in appraising the property as of the date of decedent's death.

But possibility is all that an actuarial computation can deal with. Actuality is an opposite concept. If we were confined to an appraisal of the facts as they existed at decedent's death, the possibility would be the limit of our concern . . .

The present situation was, however, envisioned, and we think correctly dealt with, in the *Welliver* case, where we said, referring to the actual intervening death of an annuitant: ' * * * by such event the interest or estate would not be affected merely by the lapse of time and express provision is made for adjustment on the later date because of a contingency other than the lapse of time.'

Respondent in fact expressly a disavows any contention 'that death is an event due to mere lapse of time.' But it was precisely the widow's death which made the annuities totally worthless by the time the optional date arrived. The statute requires 'adjustment for (such) difference in its value as of the later date * * *,' and there is of course nothing in respondent's regulations to the contrary.

Petitioner proposes to make the requisite adjustment by comparing the cost of annuities of the character involved on the date of decedent's death and of that of the widow. The difference, slightly over $5,000, which is in effect the value of the payments during the interval, is treated as the amount due to mere lapse of time. This appears reasonable considering that an annuitant situated as was decedent's widow would collect the differential by merely remaining alive.

The ultimate effect of this process is to include in the estate the figure representing in substance the payments actually received by the widow, notwithstanding that as of the optional date the annuities were entirely worthless. It is a reasonable result, since that is what turned out to be the dimensions of the property which decedent actually left, and it neither excludes the entire amount nor includes all of an item which by the optional date had ceased to exist. That is exactly what Congress said and we see no reason why they should not also have meant it.

—————————

The court ultimately rejects both parties' valuation of the annuities. What value does it use? Why was the IRS's valuation of the annuities rejected? What is the relationship between the IRS's proffered valuation and those just discussed in this text?

—————————

Just as with perpetuities, annuities can have growth features built into the periodic payments. As before, to calculate the present value of a growing annuity, we need to introduce the growth rate (g) at various points in the formula

$$PV = \frac{C}{r-g} \times \left[1 - \left(\frac{1+g}{(1+r)}\right)^t\right]$$

Be careful to note that sometimes you need to subtract g, but sometimes you are adding g.

For example, a pension might pay $40,000 per year for 30 years with a 5 percent cost of living increase each year. If current interest rates are 8 percent, then

$$PV = \frac{C}{r-g} \times \left[1 - \left(\frac{1+g}{(1+r)}\right)^t\right]$$

$$PV = \frac{\$40,000}{.08 - .05} \times \left[1 - \left(\frac{1+.05}{1+.08}\right)^{30}\right]$$

$$PV = 1.33m \times 0.5705$$
$$PV = \$760,666.67$$

The recipient owns a stream of cash flows that is currently worth just over $760,000. In this example more of the steps are shown to highlight the fact that a growing perpetuity under these terms would be worth $1.33 million, whereas the 30-year annuity is worth about 60 percent as much.

PROBLEM SET 2.4

1. What is the present value of a four-year annuity of $100 per year that makes its first payment two years from today if the discount rate is 4 percent?
2. A settlement gave an accident victim four payments of $50,000 to be paid at the end of each of the next four years. Using a discount rate of 2 percent, what is the value of the settlement? What if the discount rate were 3 percent?
3. Goldman Sachs currently has notes outstanding that pay 5.95 percent interest on the $1,000 face amount of each note. Interest is paid every six months, and the notes mature January 16, 2027. What is the present value of the interest payments from January 15, 2013 until maturity?
4. There are three factors that affect the future value of an annuity. How will an increase in each affect the future value of the annuity?
5. You represent Nick in a divorce. He is married to Charles, who is retired and has a pension that entitles him to a monthly benefit of $1,200 on the date of separation. Charles has a life expectancy of 30 years. The pension company is well established, and you believe a reasonable rate of return would be 3.0 percent above 20-year Treasury bonds — or 6 percent compounded monthly. If the entire pension was earned during marriage, what is its current value as a marital asset?
6. An investment that costs $800,000 will pay you $170,000 a year for ten years. Investments with similar risk pay 14 percent interest. What is the value of the investment? What can you conclude by comparing the value of the investment to its cost?

3

DISCOUNT RATES

To this point we have used a discount rate that was stated in the problem, or assumed that the cash flows at hand could be discounted using a low-risk or risk-free interest rate, like the government bond rate, or a bank account rate. But the real world rarely works that way, so now that we have the basics of valuation under our belts, we need to examine the factors that go into a proper discount rate.

You can think of interest as the rent that a debtor has to pay a creditor for use of the creditor's money. If the creditor can get 5 percent by lending its money to the federal government, then you will have to pay something more than 5 percent to get the creditor to lend the money to you instead. Likewise, if you want to borrow money for five years, and the creditor can lend the money for two years and get 3 percent, you will likely have to pay something more than 3 percent to borrow for five years.

Imbedded in these and other questions are important issues of risk, capital structure, and inflation. But first we talk about two foundation issues: the concepts of expected return and opportunity cost of capital.

1. EXPECTED RETURN

Suppose you loan your friend $1,000 for a year, and she promises to pay you back with 5 percent interest. In friendly terms, you might say that you expect to get $1,050 from this transaction.

But is that really right? You might not think about it, but there is probably some chance, however slight, that your friend won't pay you back. It might be for "bad" reasons, like she decides she would rather use the money for a new boogie board. Or she might not pay for a "good" reason, like she ended up in the hospital after an "incident" while boogie boarding in Santa Monica (piers are hard).

In any event, there is some chance you will not get paid. Let's say that chance is 5 percent—in other words, your friend pays you back 95 percent of the time. Then the possible outcomes for this transaction are:

Paid back	$1,050
Not paid back	$0

Putting the outcomes together with the probability that each will happen, you could calculate a weighted average of the outcomes

$$ER = (.05)\$0 + (.95)\$1,050$$
$$ER = \$997.50$$

This is an expected return calculation as used in economics and finance. Your real expected return at the outset of this transaction is about $52 less than you thought it was.

Notice also that the expected return is not necessarily a return that will actually happen—instead, it's an average. In the current example the possible outcomes are rather binary—all or nothing—and there is no way to actually achieve a return of $997.

But as we discuss later in this chapter, the expected return might influence your decision about whether 5 percent is the right interest rate to charge on this loan. Notice that you are "buying" an investment for $1,000 that has an expected return of less than $1,000. That should give you pause.

And then there is the time value of money. You are paying $1,000 for an expected return of $997 in one year. As we saw in the prior chapter, it is very unlikely that $997 in one year is worth $1,000 today.

PROBLEM SET 3.1

1. Joe is considering an investment in London Calling, Inc. He expects that if the economy does poorly the investment will lose about 10 percent, but if the economy is booming it will make 10 percent. He thinks there is about an equal chance of either outcome. On the other hand, if the economy stays about as it is, which he thinks has a 50 percent chance of happening, his investment will return 4 percent. What is the expected return?

2. It is reported that in the early 1800s the Prince of Wales was short of cash, and thus offered, on his ascension to the throne, to give £10,000 and a lordship in Ireland to anyone who would give him £5,000 right away.[1] Assume you are a wealthy investor in 1800, how would you evaluate this "investment?"

---

1. See the second volume of J.F. Molloy, *Court Life Below Stairs* (rev ed. 1885).

2. OPPORTUNITY COST OF CAPITAL

As has been suggested before, one sensible way of evaluating investments is to consider the alternatives. If you can put your $1,000 in the bank for a year and earn 5 percent, there probably is no reason to lend the money to your friend at the same rate, unless you are a very good friend indeed. After all, the FDIC insures bank accounts in the United States for up to $250,000, so the probability of the bad outcome from that investment is 0 percent.[2]

That tells you that your loan should carry an interest rate of more than 5 percent, but it does not tell you what interest rate you should charge. For example, what if the proper comparison is the Standard & Poor's (S&P) 500, an index of the return of the 500 largest U.S. company stocks?

For the past three years that index returned 19.46 percent.[3] Of course, over the past five years the index returned only 1.01 percent, reflecting the inclusion of the period around the Lehman Brothers bankruptcy in September 2008.[4] If the loan carries similar risks as stocks of large corporations, the S&P 500 reflects an appropriate return for the loan.

In short, making the loan to your friend has a positive cost. If you have $1,000 available, you could invest it in a variety of projects, only one of which is the loan to your friend. Assuming your funds are finite — which they are for most everyone besides the Federal Reserve — choosing one project precludes another.

This is the concept of opportunity cost of capital. The corresponding rule is that the "opportunity cost of capital" is always the right rate at which to discount cash flows. Why?

If the bank pays 5 percent on one-year deposits, and your friend will also pay 5 percent, but with a chance of default, 5 percent is the minimum applicable discount rate because that is what you are giving up by making the loan. And the real cost or value of the loan is what your friend would pay if she obtained the loan in the market, in an arm's-length transaction. If you want to give your friend a break, that's fine. But the value of the loan is still measured by the opportunity cost of giving it.

PROBLEM SET 3.2

1. Ziggy has a chance to invest in his friend David's new startup company, Sound & Vision, Ltd. David has promised Ziggy that if he makes a $100,000 investment, Sound & Vision will begin paying a 10 percent return in five years. David expects this return to continue at that level for decades to come. Ziggy currently earns 5 percent on his account at Aladdin Bank, 6 percent on his investment in Scary Monsters Industries, a large NYSE traded company, and 7 percent on his investment in Major Tom Bakeries, a company started by another friend. Should Ziggy make the investment in David's new company?

---

2. If you've been burying gold in your backyard because of your fears of the size of the federal government's debts, feel free to replace 0 percent with "really, really small."

3. In all cases, measured from the end of April 2012.

4. http://goo.gl/cxYQU

MARVIN L. FISHMAN AND ILLINOIS BASKETBALL, INC.,
PLAINTIFFS-APPELLEES, V. ESTATE OF ARTHUR M. WIRTZ, ET AL.,
DEFENDANTS-APPELLANTS.

807 F.2d 520
United States Court of Appeals, Seventh Circuit.
Nos. 85–1453, 85–1545. | Argued Feb. 24, 1986. | Decided Nov. 21, 1986.

CUDAHY, Circuit Judge.

This appeal concerns the 1972 purchase by defendant Chicago Professional Sports Corporation ("CPSC") of the Chicago Bulls professional basketball team. Plaintiffs Illinois Basketball, Inc. ("IBI") and Marvin Fishman, who had also sought to purchase the Bulls, brought suit alleging that the Bulls had been acquired through violations of the Sherman Act and Illinois common law. The district court found that IBI and CPSC had been competing to control a natural monopoly market in the presentation of live professional basketball in Chicago. In the court's view, the plaintiffs had "won" when they executed a contract with the Bulls' former owners. The sale was, however, contingent upon the approval of the National Basketball Association ("NBA"), and the court found that the defendants had set out to destroy the plaintiffs' victory through anticompetitive acts. It ruled that they had violated sections 1 and 2 of the Sherman Act, 15 U.S.C. §§1, 2 (1982), by refusing the plaintiffs a lease at the Chicago Stadium and by participating, with certain NBA members, in a group boycott of IBI, and it awarded plaintiff IBI treble damages for these violations. The court also ruled that the defendants had interfered with IBI's contract rights and prospective advantage in violation of Illinois law and entered an alternative judgment for actual and punitive damages.

We agree with the district court that the refusal to lease the Chicago Stadium violated sections 1 and 2 and constituted tortious interference with prospective advantage, and we affirm its judgment as to liability on these bases . . .

[We] agree with the district court that some reasonable amount must be charged against plaintiffs' recovery as the opportunity cost of equity to represent the returns which may reasonably be imputed to IBI or its shareholders from investments made as alternatives to investment in the Bulls.

We believe [however] that it is necessary to vacate the damage award and remand this case to the district court to reconsider the question of an appropriate opportunity cost. The district court should bear in mind that, while undue risk may not be forced on a victim of wrongdoing, leaving equity funds indefinitely in treasury bills could discourage enterprise and would not be a proper assumption for the computation of the opportunity cost of equity in the long run. On remand an opportunity cost of equity must be established for the period *after* the initial term when funds could be quite justifiably left in treasury bills.

EASTERBROOK, Circuit Judge, dissenting in part.

The award of lost profits here is based on the proposition that CPSC's gain is IBI's loss. All the "profits" refer to CPSC's operating results. There would be an identity of gain and loss if CPSC's costs of doing business were computed accurately and subtracted from the cash flows, and if all elements of value attributable to CPSC's efforts were stripped from the computation. They have not been, however, and there lies the difference in the valuations produced by the two processes. There are several principal sources of differences . . .

Suppose the accounting profit on the Bulls' books includes items that are real costs of doing business — costs IBI also would have borne. This is what the "opportunity cost" and interest rate calculations are about. Capital must be hired, just like labor or any other input. It may be hired on the market (borrowed) or hired out of other uses the investors have (diverted). If CPSC had hired capital at 15% interest from a bank, the interest would have been an explicit cost of doing business. So if in 1975 CPSC had $10 million of a bank's money in use, it would have paid $1.5 million in return. This would have been subtracted from its income before a computation of profits.

What actually happened is that CPSC's investors supplied most of the money. They want to pay themselves for this money at the rate lenders charged for risky, arms' length investments. This is how "opportunity cost" has been used — the amount of the Bulls' income that is assigned as the "cost of capital" and subtracted from profits. If the investors had $10 million in the Bulls in 1975, they say, they are entitled to 15 or 20% return. The district court, on the other hand, allowed them only the rate of interest the United States was paying on Treasury Bills at the time. This risk-free rate was much lower than the rate paid to investors in high-risk businesses. So to keep the figures simple, in 1975 the district court allowed only $500,000 as the cost of capital, while CPSC says the allowance should have been $1.5 million. The difference between the risky rate of interest and the safe, T–Bill rate accounts for more than the entire award of lost profits in this case.

The district court's choice of rate was mistaken. The rate allowed to CPSC's investors should be almost the same rate that a bank would have charged to CPSC. Any supplier of capital is entitled to compensation, and the Bulls' full cost of capital must appear in the damages calculations as a subtraction.

If CPSC had hired all of its capital from banks or outside investors, the rate would have been very high. CPSC suggests a rate of prime plus 3%, which seems favorable to the plaintiffs. Sports teams are risky ventures. Part of their value lies in publicity for the owners and tax advantages. These elements of value cannot be used to secure the loan, so the outside investors must charge a higher rate to compensate. Banks might accept lower rates if the investors guarantee the loan with their other assets (as investors in both groups did), but the guarantee has opportunity costs of its own because assets used to secure this loan cannot be used to finance some other venture.

Because the use of personal assets creates an opportunity cost that offsets the reduction in the rate of interest, the correct rate is the one the bank will charge without personal guarantees.[5] This will turn out to be high, reflecting the risk of sports, the illiquidity of the assets, and the personal consumption value of ownership. The opportunity cost incurred by the owners in holding their own capital in the business is less than the rate a bank would have charged for a loan, because the

5. To put this a little differently, banks lent to CPSC, with guarantees, for prime plus one-half percent because if CPSC had gone belly up the guarantees would have made the banks whole. If CPSC had failed no one was going to make its investors whole; their risk (and the appropriate rate of interest) was therefore the same as the banks would have demanded without the guarantees.

owners get the recognition and tax benefits. But risk alone will make the opportunity cost high. The upshot of even a moderate opportunity cost for CPSC's capital, as the district court recognized, is no or low damages. The award of damages in this case is an artifact of the district court's assumption that the opportunity cost of CPSC's capital was the rate available on T–Bills, a riskless investment. It is a fantastic assumption. It has nothing to do with business reality or the economics of determining profits. The court properly reverses the use of the T–Bill rate, and although I think prime plus one-half percent is too low, it is a great improvement.

To put this somewhat differently, CPSC's owners supplied a service, much as labor is a service: risk-bearing. They are entitled to be paid for this service, which means that the value of the risk-bearing must be subtracted from CPSC's accounting profits. Gains resulting from defendants' efforts always are subtracted in computing lost profits. If CPSC had been a regulated utility under a profit constraint, it would have been allowed to subtract the market, risky rate of capital as an opportunity cost to determine whether it was making a profit. E.g., *Illinois Commerce Commission v. ICC*, 776 F.2d 355, 362–64 (D.C.Cir.1985) (Scalia, J.); *City of Charlottesville v. FERC*, 774 F.2d 1205, 1213–23 (D.C.Cir.1985) (Scalia, J.), *cert. denied*, 475 U.S. 1108, 106 S.Ct. 1515, 89 L.Ed.2d 914 (1986). This shows why opportunity cost here, too, goes into the computation of profit. It is not properly an item of "mitigation" — an analogy that has led my brethren to look at IBI's opportunities rather than CPSC's true costs.

Had IBI owned the Bulls, it would have supplied the risk-bearing service for itself. It did not, and it did not lose anything as a result. Payment for bearing risk is not a profit of any sort. It is simply a cost of doing business. Players' salaries were subtracted from the Bulls' income to get its profits; the implicit expense of risk-bearing also must be subtracted. IBI was of course free to bear risk if it wanted. It could have bought another pro sports team, or gone into another (risky) line of business. Then it could have reaped any rewards from bearing risk, but it didn't.

My colleagues say that the district court on remand should "err on the side of conservatism" because it is not appropriate to demand that IBI take substantial risks to mitigate its damages. This is where the choice between capital as a cost to CPSC and as an opportunity for IBI to reinvest has its bite. I agree with my colleagues that *if* this is a problem in "mitigation" the district court should be conservative. A disappointed bidder need not mitigate by taking risks greater than those it had planned to take if it purchased the assets. But it is not a problem in mitigation. We are simply trying to calculate CPSC's true "profits," net of its full costs of doing business. IBI gets the profits, trebled. The opportunity cost is a real cost. It is the largest difference between CPSC's gain and IBI's loss.

To sum up: The right way to compute damages is to determine the bargain element, if there was one, of which IBI was deprived in 1972. . . . If damages are to be computed from discounting cash flows . . . the calculation of the flows should use as the cost the interest CPSC would have paid, without guarantees, for all of its capital. Realistic cost computations also should allow CPSC to retain any elements of value that IBI could have duplicated (such as value attributable to a general increase in the popularity of NBA basketball).

Do you get the sense the majority and dissent are talking past each other? The penultimate paragraph of the dissent deserves a close read in this regard. What do you make of the dissent's treatment of the loan guarantees?

Although the dissent questions CPSC's argument that the appropriate discount rate should be the prime rate plus 3 percent, note that the rate comes from a loan offered to IBI at the time of the original transaction.

3. RISK

Up until now, we have largely skirted around the question of risk by either stipulating that the risk-free rate applied or by stating the amount of risk involved in a particular project. Not so anymore.

Risk is one of the biggest drivers of corporate finance transactions, but it is also an extremely broad concept. Take the prior problem, where Ziggy:

- Gives Sound & Vision $100,000 with no fixed promise of repayment.
- Waits five years to begin receiving returns.
- Receives a fixed return once the return begins.

Each of these elements presents risk. For example, the first bullet point highlights the liquidity risk associated with this investment. We are not told if the investment takes the form of a loan or equity (shares), but in any event there is no obvious way for Ziggy to get his money out if he needs it. The second bullet point reminds us that Ziggy turns over his money to Sound & Vision and then has to trust that the company will honor its end of the bargain. In your first year of law school you took an entire class about people breaching their contracts — investment contracts are no different. And the final bullet point reminds us that Ziggy is locking in a return that looks good today, but might look very bad in the future.

In general, risk in finance relates to future changes that will cause a particular deal to become more expensive or otherwise less attractive. These changes will alter the return of the project.

The other thing to understand about risk and corporate finance is that risk comes with a price. The United States currently borrows money for five years at less than 1 percent interest — in May 2012 it was about 0.8 percent. The highest rated corporations currently borrow for the same term at about 1.14 percent.[6] That is, although these highly regarded corporations are considered essentially risk free — they have the same credit ratings as Norway and Switzerland — the market perceives there is slightly more risk lending to a corporation rather than the U.S. government. Perhaps this reflects the ability of the U.S. government to raise taxes, or even "print" money, to satisfy its obligations. Whatever the reason, the corporation pays 0.34 percent more to borrow money.

---

6. This specifically refers to the yield on a Johnson & Johnson note as of May 2012.

As you will see throughout this book, risk and return are closely related. In May 2012 another five-year debt obligation was paying a return of 9.95 percent. Why so much more? The debt was issued by Banco Macro SA, a large Argentinian bank. Argentina, as you might know, has experienced its share of financial problems since defaulting on its own sovereign debt a few years ago, and as of this writing the country is also engaged in a series of testy exchanges with the United Kingdom regarding the ownership of the Falkland Islands. The United Kingdom and Argentina went to war over the Falklands about 30 years ago, following an Argentinian invasion, and now there are indications the islands might have rich oil and gas deposits offshore. In short, there is more doubt about this bank's ability to repay five years down the road.

A lesson to learn now is that if five-year U.S. government debt is paying 0.8 percent, the only way to earn more than that is to take on more risk.[7] You might lend the money for a longer time period, or you might lend it to a riskier borrower. But you will take on more risk. Anybody who tells you otherwise is lying.

4. CAPITAL STRUCTURE AND THE ABSOLUTE PRIORITY RULE

One key element of risk in corporate finance involves the investor's standing on default. For example, imagine a simple company that defaults on its debts with a balance sheet as follows:

Assets	Liabilities & Equity
$100	$100 unsecured loan
	100 shares of common stock

Who gets what? The short answer is that the creditors — who gave the loan — take the assets and the shareholders get nothing. In bankruptcy this ordering of claimants is known as the absolute priority rule.[8]

ELIZABETH WARREN, *A THEORY OF ABSOLUTE PRIORITY*
1991 Ann. Surv. Am. L. 9, 37–38 (1992)

The legal rule of absolute priority had its genesis in the long-standing common law maxim that creditors would be paid ahead of equity. This rule assured those who did business with the corporation that if the business were dissolved the creditors would be paid before the insiders would recover their

---

7. The assumption here is that we are dealing with efficient or liquid markets — like the market for U.S. government debt. In some less efficient markets it might be possible to find mispriced assets, but the price will still be higher than the corresponding U.S. government interest rate.

8. Case v. Los Angeles Lumber Products Co., 308 U.S. 106, 117, 60 S. Ct. 1, 8, 84 L. Ed. 110 (1939).

investments. In the case of collapse, the creditors could count on payment in full before equity collected anything from the business assets.

The provision is a form of creditor protection, one of many that attempt to restrict the ability of corporate owners and insiders from depleting a failing business for their own benefit, leaving the creditors with only the empty shell of a business. In part, the rule is designed to offset some of the consequences of superior information and control necessarily available to equity owners when they manage the business or exercise close supervision over the nominal managers. The rules of absolute priority satisfy concerns similar to those of state law rules of dividend distribution, for example, which require that the corporation only distribute stock dividends from earned surplus rather than from general assets of the business. As any good law-and-economics devotee could point out, creditors could have insisted on such provisions in advance, but the law provides an off-the-rack ordering among the parties that is nearest to what the parties would likely have negotiated for themselves, requiring that the owners/insiders restrict their abilities to take assets from the business to the injury of the creditors.

The basic idea is that secured creditors (creditors with liens or mortgages) get paid before unsecured creditors who get paid before shareholders.

Each of these financial instruments is examined in greater detail in subsequent chapters, but the basic idea now is to understand how the rule affects the cost of financing. Return to the simple example of the $100 asset firm at the start of this section — once you understand the absolute priority rule you can understand why the company will have to pay a greater return to its shareholders than it pays to unsecured creditors. Unless the firm can dupe its investors. But that is a trick that typically only works once; thereafter, investors get wise.

OVERSEAS SHIPHOLDING OWES $463 MILLION TAXES; BONDS DROP

By Steven Church and Alaric Nightingale — February 13, 2013, Bloomberg.com[9]

Overseas Shipholding Group Inc., the largest U.S. tanker operator, owes $463 million in U.S. taxes and interest, the Internal Revenue Service said. The bankrupt company's bonds plunged.

The company owes $27.9 million in interest on $435.1 million of taxes, the IRS said in papers filed Feb. 11 with Kurtzman Carson Consultants LLC, the agent processing claims for Overseas. The IRS labeled it an unsecured priority claim, meaning that the agency wants it paid ahead of other unsecured and lower-ranking debts.

"The bonds could be worth zero or very little if that claim were sustained," Oliver Corlett, an analyst at RW Pressprich & Co. in New York, said by phone.

Overseas, based in New York, filed for bankruptcy last year after global shipping rates fell and the company gave up trying to win a federal loan guarantee.

Overseas listed assets of $4.15 billion and debt of $2.67 billion in its Chapter 11 petition in U.S. Bankruptcy Court in Wilmington, Delaware.

The company's 8.125 percent senior unsecured bonds due in March 2018 fell as much as 8.9 cents to 30 cents on the dollar in New York, according to Trace, the bond-price reporting system of the Financial Industry Regulatory Authority. The price was the lowest since the securities traded at 23 cents on Nov. 14.

Daniel H. Golden, an attorney for Overseas, and Chuck Burgess, a company spokesman, didn't immediately return calls seeking comment on the claim.

FEDERAL RULES

Grant Williams, a spokesman for the IRS, declined to comment, citing federal rules prohibiting the agency from publicly talking about individual taxpayers. In bankruptcy, companies have the right to challenge claims filed by creditors. In the Overseas case, should the IRS prevail, the claim would outrank the claims of bondholders, Corlett said.

"That's the worst-case scenario," Ken Luskin, President of Intrinsic Value Asset Management Inc. in Santa Monica, California, said of the size of the IRS claim. "You are going to put in the largest claim you can consider." The claim will help investors value Overseas securities by making the company's liabilities more certain, Luskin said.

CEO REPLACED

Overseas announced Feb. 11 that it replaced Morten Arntzen, who had been chief executive officer for nine years. Robert Johnston, head of the company's U.S.-flag business, took over as CEO, the company said in a statement.

Last year, Overseas withdrew an application for a $241.8 million loan guarantee to help pay for two tankers built at U.S. shipyards after Bloomberg News reported that the company's ships were calling at Iran's largest oil terminal and U.S. House Majority Leader Eric Cantor asked the Transportation Department to reject the application.

After that, the company was shut out of credit markets, partly because it said in an Oct. 22 regulatory report that investors couldn't rely on its financial statements for the past three years, Overseas said in court papers.

It is a simple matter of risk, opportunity costs, and expected return: The shareholders face a higher risk of losing their investment, so they will demand a higher return on their investment. Otherwise they might as well put their money in the bank. Or U.S government debt.

As a result of the absolute priority rule, investors higher in the capital structure face lower risks and get correspondingly lower returns. Of course, this does not mean that there is no risk—if there are no assets to liquidate, the pain will quickly move up the capital structure.

Imagine, for example, the investors in a manual typewriter manufacturer. How much will the machinery in the factory sell for?

PROBLEM SET 3.3

1. Siouxsie & Banshees, Inc. has 100 shareholders, each holding one share, and the following creditors: a $10 million secured bank loan, $400,000 owed to various trade creditors, $500,000 owed to unsecured bond-holders, and $300,000 owed on a tort judgment. If its assets equal $11 million, who gets what on liquidation? Would you expect the bank loan or the unsecured bonds to have the higher interest rate? What about the trade creditors and the tort judgment?

5. THE ROLE OF INFLATION

If you took a history class in college you probably associate inflation with Germany of the 1920s, when people had to bring wheelbarrows full of bills to the store just to buy a lamb chop.[10] Strictly speaking, that is an example of hyperinflation: The money lost so much value that German Marks were sold in London's East End as decorative paper to line kitchen shelves. The notes were sold by weight.

Inflation is the rate at which prices are rising and purchasing power is falling. For example, if inflation is 3 percent, a bottle of soda that costs $1 now will cost $1.03 in a year.[11] Conversely, for every dollar in wages you can buy increasingly less soda each year (which is probably for the best, anyway).

One of the most common measures of inflation is the Consumer Price Index (CPI), which measures the average change over time of prices paid by urban consumers for a basket of several hundred consumer goods and services. There are actually several versions of the CPI. One of the most common, shown in Figure 3-1, is called the All Items Consumer Price Index for All Urban Consumers (CPI-U) for the U.S. City Average. Another commonly used measure, which is also shown on the chart, is the same measure less food and energy costs. This is often referred to as "core" inflation, as the items that are removed tend to be more volatile than inflation generally.

As shown, the United States briefly experienced deflation in the immediate aftermath of the recent financial crisis. Typically central banks — like the U.S. Federal Reserve — try to manage inflation to keep it from getting too high, while also avoiding deflation, which can have serious economic consequences. An inflation rate of 2 to 3 percent is often said to be ideal. As you can see, the core rate of inflation only recently returned to those levels.

In finance inflation (or deflation) is a key risk factor, especially in transactions that involve a fixed rate of return. Inflation is a risk here because the investor

---

10. *http://en.wikipedia.org/wiki/German_reichsmark*
11. For those of you wondering about the realism of this example, we can concede that the manufacturer likely will absorb the price increase for a year or two, and then raise the price to some nice round number, say $1.25.

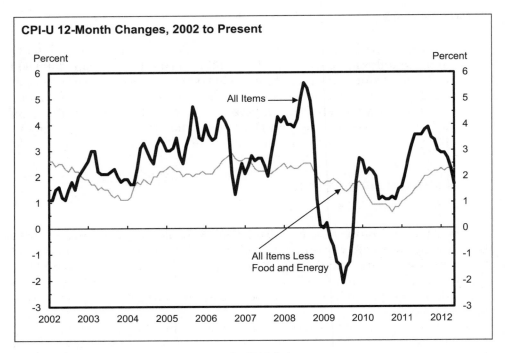

FIGURE 3-1
CPI-U 12-Month Changes, 2002 to Present.
Source: **U.S. Bureau of Labor Statistics.**

does not know what its *real rate of return* will be. For example, if you loan your friend $1,000 at 5 percent for a year, and inflation rate is currently 3 percent per year, then the real return on your loan would be 2 percent at year's end. And if the Federal Reserve stumbles a bit, and inflation goes to 5 percent, you have received no real return whatsoever — you've essentially treaded water.

Thus when we speak of inflation as a risk, we are referring to the uncertainty over the future real value of an investment. The risk increases the longer the term of the investment, simply because if there is some uncertainty about inflation next year, there is even more uncertainty regarding the level of inflation in years thereafter.

PROBLEM SET 3.4

1. Bauhaus Bank is considering making a ten-year loan to Peter. Peter would like a fixed-rate loan. The bank wants to make a floating-rate loan, where Peter would pay interest equal to the U.S. government bond rate plus a spread. What risks do Peter and Bank face with either approach?
2. Explain how inflation and deflation affect the interests of debtors and creditors.

6. THE YIELD CURVE

The *term structure of interest rates*, also known as the *yield curve*, refers to the typical pattern of interest rates where rates get progressively higher the longer the term of the lending. Table 3-1 illustrates this with U.S government bond rates at the beginning of May 2012.[12]

TABLE 3-1
U.S. Government Bond Rates

	1 Mo	3 Mo	6 Mo	1 Yr	2 Yr	3 Yr	5 Yr	7 Yr	10 Yr	20 Yr	30 Yr
5/1/12	0.07	0.09	0.15	0.19	0.27	0.39	0.84	1.35	1.98	2.76	3.16

When the yield curve displays this pattern it is said to be upward sloping, because if you graphed the rates the result would be an upward sloping curve. The longer the money is lent to the government, the greater the return.

This is a normal situation because short-term debts generally hold less risk than long-term debts; the further into the future a debt's maturity, the more time and, therefore, uncertainty the creditor faces before being paid back its principal. There is risk of nonpayment and risk of unforeseen inflation. To invest in one instrument for a longer period of time, an investor needs to be compensated for undertaking the additional risk.

Other situations can arise. For example, sometimes the yield curve will "flatten." In these situations, long-term interest rates are very close to short-term interest rates. This often indicates periods of market uncertainty. For example, the U.S. government bond rates shown in Table 3-2 were quoted at the beginning of 2008. Notice how close the three-month and five-year rates are.

TABLE 3-2
U.S. Government Bond Rates, 2008

	1 Mo	3 Mo	6 Mo	1 Yr	2 Yr	3 Yr	5 Yr	7 Yr	10 Yr	20 Yr	30 Yr
1/2/08	3.09	3.26	3.32	3.17	2.88	2.89	3.28	3.54	3.91	4.39	4.35

In especially rare situations, the yield curve can invert. One reason why this might happen could be a rush of investors locking in long-term rates, because they expect rates to decline because the economy is entering recession (or worse). Table 3-2 shows some evidence of inversion — compare the one-, three-, and six-month rates with the two- and three-year rates. Recall that Lehman Brothers filed its bankruptcy petition in September of that year.

---

12. For the current rates, see *http://goo.gl/BLjf1*

If you had correctly interpreted the yield curve in January, you might have made a lot of money (or at least avoided some losses).

The key lesson here is that interest rates — and thus discount rates — vary a good deal based on their term. Thus, when discounting it is vital to use an interest rate that reflects the term of the project you are discounting. For example, it would make no sense to discount the one-year loan to your friend using the five-year government bond rate.[13] Inasmuch as the term structure of rates reflects the risks involved lending over various periods of time, you can think of this rule as a subset of the larger rule that you should always discount at the opportunity cost of capital.

PROBLEM SET 3.5

1. Andrew wants to borrow some money from Floodland Bank so he can buy a drum machine for his new gothic rock band. As it happens, Andrew is so very wealthy that the bank considers the loan nearly risk free, and they will charge Andrew the government bond rate plus 0.05 percent. If the loan is made in May 2012, how much interest would Andrew pay if he borrowed $5,000 for three, five, or seven years? What is the present value of these loans? Be ready to discuss the implications of these calculations.

7. DISCOUNTING WITH RISK

As we have seen in this chapter, calculating present or future values in a meaningful way requires the use of an appropriate discount rate. By "appropriate" we have shown that to mean a discount or interest rate that takes into account the risk of nonpayment (the default risk), the inflation risk, and the duration risk. As part of duration, you might also consider liquidity risk — how easy will be it for one party to sell their position if they need quick cash?

Considering the expected return of a particular project will lead you to understand the actual return for a project, assuming that you correctly weight each of the possible outcomes. In the real world, assigning probabilities to outcomes is much less precise than it is in a law school classroom.

That expected return then needs to be expressed in present value terms by discounting using the opportunity cost of capital, which will encapsulate all the risks discussed in this chapter. Note also how the decisions made in the expected value calculation — for example, what is the probability of nonpayment? — will tend to influence the choices made with regard to the appropriate opportunity cost of capital.

For example, remember that we decided at the beginning of the chapter that the $1,000 loan to your friend had a 5 percent chance of default, resulting in an expected return of $997 on your $1,000 investment. You would then look

---

13. That actually involves two errors, as we have discussed: the term is wrong, and lending to your friend entails greater default risk than lending to the U.S. government.

around for a comparable investment: a one-year investment, with similar risk of nonperformance. But the latter exercise presupposes that we correctly estimated your friend's likelihood of default — if the probability the friend will not repay is instead 8 percent, we need to consider a different opportunity cost of capital.

PROBLEM SET 3.6

1. Review pages 95 to 96 of the Dynegy 10-K (regarding the pension obligations) and be prepared to discuss.

4

THE NET PRESENT VALUE RULE
AND SOME COMPETITORS

Given an investment opportunity, a firm needs to decide whether undertaking the investment will generate net economic profits or losses for the company. To do this, the firm estimates the future cash flows of the project and discounts them using a discount rate that represents the project's opportunity cost of capital. Subtracting this number from the initial cash outlay required for the investment provides the net present value of the investment.

In short, return minus cost gives you the value of the investment. If the value is positive, it's a good investment. If the value is negative, you are losing money on the deal. That's the essence of the net present value (NPV) rule.

For example, remember your loan to a friend. The net present value of that loan is the difference between the present value of its benefits (e.g., the interest the friend will pay you) and the present value of its costs (e.g., the loss of use of the money for a year, or the risk of nonpayment).

$$NPV = PV(Benefits) - PV(Costs)$$

But traditionally we actually write the formula this way

$$NPV = PV(Costs) + PV(Benefits)$$
$$or$$
$$NPV = C_0 + C_1 ... + C_t$$

The reason is that this puts the cash flows in time order: The costs typically come before the benefits. The trick is to remember that costs are a *negative* cash flow, as you are paying money out.

If the NPV of a prospective project is positive, it should be accepted. However, if the NPV is negative, the project should be rejected because cash flows will also be negative. This is the NPV rule.

So you loan your friend $1,000 for a year, and she promises to pay you back with 5 percent interest. You now know about expected return, and the opportunity cost of capital, so after thinking about it for a while you decide that an appropriate discount rate is 10 percent for this investment.

51

Now right off the bat you should intuitively see the problem: When the discount rate is higher than the return on the project, the project can never have a positive NPV. But it is very important not to solve this problem by fooling yourself, and rationalizing your way into a discount rate that is below 5 percent.

This is also why understanding the role of the discount rate is vital. When you find yourself cross-examining a witness who is explaining why the defendant bank manager's loan to his friend was perfectly proper based on an NPV calculation, that witness is never going to say "and I used a 4 percent discount rate because that's the only way I could get the numbers to 'work.'" You have to be able to show the judge or jury that the witness manipulated the NPV formula to achieve a desired result.

Just to confirm that you understand this, let's prove what we already intuitively know. Here is the NPV calculation for the loan to your friend:

$$NPV = C_0 + C_1$$
$$NPV = -1,000 + \frac{997}{1.07}$$
$$NPV = -68.22$$

Notice that we used the expected cash flow here, not the "best case" cash flow. If your discount rate already accounts for the risk of default, you could argue that this overpenalizes your friend for the risk of nonpayment. If you are comfortable with your discount rate assumptions, you might use $1,000 instead of $997 for the final cash flow.

In either case, the project has a negative NPV, and thus should be rejected under the "NPV rule." Of course, this is your friend, and maybe the amorphous benefits of helping your friend make up the difference.

But in most business transactions, conducted at arm's length, the lender has no desire to subsidize the other side of the deal. And that makes sense: Why should the shareholders of JP Morgan Chase subsidize the shareholders of some other big corporation that borrows from the bank? Indeed, if you see one firm making a negative NPV investment in another firm, you should immediately question why this is happening. Maybe there is a common controlling shareholder? Or maybe the officers of one of the corporations are breaching their duty of loyalty?

PROBLEM SET. 4.1

1. In exchange for $500 today, you will receive $550 in one year with certainty. If the risk-free rate is 3 percent, what is the NPV of this investment? What if the risk-free rate were 8 percent?
2. A company can spend $28,000 today for a machine that it expects will help the company make $12,500 next year and $19,500 the following year, but only $3,000 in the third year, as the machine begins to break down and needs to be replaced. If the company's discount rate is 12 percent, should the company buy the machine?

1. COMPARING COMPETING PROJECTS: MORE ON THE NPV RULE

For the most part, clients do not typically sit around with infinite piles of money, considering possible investments. Instead, a decision to invest in one project necessarily precludes another project.

How does the NPV rule work here? It works quite well, thanks for asking. This is also a good place to introduce Excel, the big green X on your computer that you've probably only opened by mistake and then quickly closed. Open it up now and follow along, because it is important to get over your fears about the program. After all, many of your clients will use it, and they are not apt to be too impressed if you will not even open a spreadsheet they send you.

Imagine that you have created a small business while in law school that delivers coffee, tea, and other caffeinated products to students throughout the law school based on orders placed via text message or Twitter. Business is booming, and you think you could sell the operation to the dean or a 1L for $300,000.

It costs you about $20,000 per year to run the business, which generates $70,000 a year in income, and you could still sell the business in two years when you graduate. If you did not have to study so much, you think the business could generate more income — maybe $100,000. You could hire an employee to run the business for you, but that would increase costs up to $50,000. The advantage of this approach is that you suspect you could keep the business operating for about 11 years with very little day-to-day involvement. In the background is your belief that you could receive a 5 percent return, with similar risk, if you invested your money elsewhere. How do you compare your various options?

First, we will make a simplifying assumption: All costs are incurred in full now, but any income is received only at the end of the year. We also assume that the decision takes place at the beginning of the year.

Consider three options that appear in the problem:

- Sell the business now and use the $300,000 to pay off student loans.
- Continue to operate the business and sell it at the end of the year you graduate.
- Continue to own the business, but not operate it personally, for 11 years.

Each option can then be valued and considered with the NPV rule. The cash flows look like this:

	Today	End 2L	End 3L
Sell	$300,000	$0	$0
Operate	–$20,000	$70,000	$370,000
Own	–$50,000	$50,000	$50,000 . . .

Notice that if you retain ownership of the business, but delegate operations to an employee, you simply hold an annuity that generates $100,000 per year, but to keep it going you have to incur $50,000 of cost for the next 11 years.[1] And the basic question is whether $300,000 in hand is worth more than $370,000 next year or the annuity.

If you open the spreadsheet for this chapter, you will see something that looks like this:

	Today	End 2L	End 3L	NPV	Excel Formula
Sell	$300,000	$0	$0	**300,000.00**	
Operate	($20,000)	$70,000	$370,000	**382,267.57**	=B3+NPV(5%, C3:D3)
Own	($50,000)	$50,000	$50,000 ...	**336,086.75**	=B4+PV(5%, 10, -C4)

The left side looks just like this table, but on the right we have added two new columns. The first, helpfully entitled "NPV," provides the answers to this problem. More on that in a moment.

First, note the column on the far right. This shows the formula that you can also see if you click on the answer in the NPV column. That is, $382,267.57 is the answer provided by the formula =B3+NPV(5%, C3:D3). What does this mean in English?

Excel's NPV formula is essentially not an NPV formula, but rather a present value formula, as it leaves out the "net" bit. It assumes that the first cash flow starts in one time period in the future. That means to actually do an NPV calculation you have to manually enter the first payment, which is typically a negative. That explains the "B3+" part of the formula, as that tells Excel to add the contents of box (or cell) B3 to the results of the NPV formula.

The Excel NPV formula itself generates the present value of a range of numbers — here the numbers in cells C3 through D3 — at a specified interest rate, which in this problem is given as 5 percent.

As you might expect given the confusing nature of the NPV formula, the PV formula is also not quite a present value formula. It is a present value of an annuity formula. Thus, "PV(5%, 10, -C4)" provides the present value of an annuity at a 5 percent discount rate, with ten periods (starting one year from today, to get us 11 years out), paying the negative of the amount shown in cell C4.

The formula is set up for outbound cash flows — that is, there is an implied negative in the formula — so if you omit the negative sign, your result will be negative and you will get the wrong answer once you do the addition to reach the NPV. If you are using the formula to find the present value of a loan — or any other transaction with periodic cash payments — the formula works "as is" and does not require the negative sign.

Despite these quirks, using Excel is obviously much easier than using the manual formulas discussed in Chapter 2. Of course, only by looking at the formulas can you understand the intuitions involved, which is likely to be of

---

1. There is an unrealistic assumption about inflation here — do you see it?

greater use in your future career. That, in short, is why the mean old author is only introducing Excel now.

Returning to the problem, you can see that operating the business for two more years and then selling it is the highest value option, worth almost $50,000 more than the next best option.

But there is one thing missing from the table. What if you can sell the business for a positive value in 11 years under the third option? How big would the sale price have to be to make the third option the most attractive?

PROBLEM SET 4.2

1. How would the hypothetical above change if the discount rate were 19 percent. Or 1 percent?
2. Bogartco is considering expanding from its traditional trenchcoats and fedoras into a new product line. It can fund up to $400,000 in new projects, and its cost of capital is 8 percent. Bogartco will liquidate whatever project it chooses at year four. Which of the following should it choose?

	Initial Cost	Year 1 Cash Flow	Year 2 Cash Flow	Year 3 Cash Flow	Value at end of Year 4
Lead falcon statues	$100,000	$50,000	$50,000	$50,000	$60,000
Piano covers	$200,000	$20,000	$20,000	$20,000	$100,000
High Sierra brand tonic water	$300,000		$50,000	$50,000	$250,000
Badges	$400,000	$10,000	$10,000	$10,000	$100,000

2. COMPARING COMPETING PROJECTS: INTERNAL RATE OF RETURN

As the last problem of the foregoing problem set shows, NPV can help you choose among competing projects. But the results are often somewhat less than intuitive. For example, how would you explain in plain English your decision to pick a certain project over another in the prior problem?

The internal rate of return (IRR) rule provides more intuitive results, but it would not be easy to use it for Problem 2, for reasons that will soon become clear. First, we need to understand IRR.

IRR is defined as the interest rate that will set a particular NPV calculation to zero. Finding the IRR of a particular project thus involves solving the NPV equation for r. You could probably do the math for a simple, two-cash-flow NPV equation. But with multiple cash flows, the math becomes cumbersome.

Business school textbooks typically describe three ways to find an IRR without higher math. Only one of these is likely to be of relevance to you.

First, you can graph an NPV profile — basically just the graph of the NPV values (on the y axis) that result from a range of discount rates (on the x axis). The point at which the graph crosses zero is your IRR. Better find that graph paper you have left over from junior high school! The other method involves trial and error. In short, start plugging in possible discount rates, narrowing down the range until you get an NPV close to zero.

Both of these methods are useful if you find yourself transported back to the 1940s (and forget to take your laptop). But for at least 30 years, the only likely way that you would calculate an IRR is with a spreadsheet, which today probably means Excel, unless you're an anti-Microsoft fanatic.

Take the example of Bogartco's badge manufacturing business from Problem Set 4.2. The cash flows looked like this:

($400,000) $10,000 $10,000 $10,000 $200,000

To calculate the IRR, you simply put these numbers into a spreadsheet and use the IRR formula in reference to them. For example, in a new spreadsheet your formula would look like this:

$$= IRR(A1 : E1)$$

That returns a result of −27 percent. Negative 27 percent sounds bad. Much more intuitive than the negative dollars you obtained in the NPV calculation.

Beyond its intuitive appeal, the IRR also provides a good check on how sensitive a particular NPV calculation is to the assumed discount rate. Namely, because IRR is the point at which NPV crosses over to a negative number, we can subtract the assumed cost of capital from the IRR to find the margin of error in our estimate.

So if we have a particular project with an IRR of 37 percent, and we subtract our discount rate of 8 percent from that, we know that even if our discount rate is seriously in error, the project will still have a positive NPV. On the other hand, if you calculate that the IRR is very close to the discount rate, you know that a small change in the discount rate could tip the project from one you should accept to one you should reject.

This also leads us to a clear statement of the IRR rule: Take any project where the IRR exceeds the cost of capital, and reject any project where the IRR is less than the cost of capital.

The IRR rule is predicated on a traditional pattern of cash flows, where cash is paid out at the beginning and returned at various periods thereafter. If you reverse the pattern — say you receive $1,000 today, but pay out $100 over the next five years — what you are really examining is a loan. In that case, the rule must be flipped: Only accept the project if the IRR is *less than* the cost of capital.

Indeed, the IRR method really only works with the prototypical example of cash paid out at T_0 and cash paid back over several periods. For example, if cash is paid into the project at several points — after the project has begun to return cash — there will be several possible IRRs, as the plot of NPV values crosses zero every time the project's cash flows change their sign.

There can also be instances where there is no IRR for a particular project — imagine a project with NPV values that are uniformly positive or uniformly negative. The plot never crosses the x-axis in either case.

Most important, you cannot directly compare IRRs when projects differ in their scale (different amounts of money are involved), their timing (cash flows come at different times), or their riskiness. To examine this, let's return to your law school business from the beginning of the chapter. Recall that you had the following opportunities:

- Sell the business now and use the $300,000 to pay off student loans.
- Continue to operate the business and sell it at the end of the year before you graduate.
- Continue to own the business, but not operate it personally, for 11 years.

These resulted in the following cash flows:

	Today	End 2L	End 3L	NPV
Sell	$300,000	$0	$0	300,000.00
Operate	($20,000)	$70,000	$370,000	382,267.57
Own	($50,000)	$50,000	$50,000 ...	336,086.75

Under the NPV rule, and using a 5 percent discount rate, we decided you would be best off operating the business until graduation and then selling it. How would this analysis look under IRR?

Let's focus our analysis on the decision between "operate" and "sell," because once you pick between those, you can then decide if the return from the better project beats what you could do with $300,000 (the "sell" option) over the same time period.

You might be tempted to do something like this, especially if you have not been reading very closely:

	Today	End 2L	End 3L	IRR
Operate	($20,000)	$70,000	$370,000	539%
Own	($50,000)	$50,000	$50,000 ...	100%

Then you say *voilà!* Only a moron would turn down 539 percent! Especially when compared to 100 percent, which you are quite sure is less than 539 percent.

In this case you will end up picking the right project, but for the wrong reasons. And the NPV calculations should give you some pause, as they are not nearly as far apart as the IRR calculations would suggest.

To see an example where using IRR would lead to the completely wrong result, look at the following table, which involves comparison of projects with a 5 percent discount rate:

	Today	Year One	Year Two	Year Three	IRR	NPV
Monty's Project	(750,000.00)	310,000.00	430,000.00	330,000.00	0.1983	220,327.18
Pat's Project	(2,100,000.00)	1,200,000.00	760,000.00	850,000.00	0.1736	466,461.51

If you are an IRR fanatic, you would take Monty's project, which has the higher rate of return. But what about Pat's project, with the higher NPV? The problem is that Monty's project offers a higher rate of return on a smaller amount of money. Is it really better to get 19.8 percent on an investment of $750,000, or should you take 17.36 percent on an investment of nearly three times as much money?

To answer this question, you need to calculate an incremental IRR and compare that to the relevant cost of capital (sometimes also referred to as a "hurdle rate"—5 percent in this case).

This involves creating a hypothetical project where you give up the seemingly higher returning project but smaller project by subtracting it from the larger, but seemingly lower returning project. You then calculate the IRR for that new project.

	Today	Year One	Year Two	Year Three	IRR	NPV
Monty's Project	(750,000.00)	310,000.00	430,000.00	330,000.00	0.1983	220,327.18
Pat's Project	(2,100,000.00)	1,200,000.00	760,000.00	850,000.00	0.1736	466,461.51
P-M	(1,350,000.00)	890,000.00	330,000.00	520,000.00	0.1578	

The result—15 percent—is well above our 5 percent hurdle rate, so we should take Pat's project and reject Monty's.

The same basic rule applies for projects of unequal duration. Which project would you rather invest in?

- Franklin's project lasts for one year, and offers a 100 percent IRR. Your money doubles.
- Winston's project lasts for five years, and offers a lower IRR of 58 percent, but a higher NPV.

Franklin's project would indeed be better, if you could reinvest the proceeds for four more years at a 100 percent annual rate of return. If you can only reinvest at a lower market rate, say 10 percent, Winston's project is better. Only by calculating an incremental IRR, where you consider if Winston's project is still attractive even after giving up the gains of Franklin's project, can you really understand which project is the better investment.

PROBLEM SET 4.3

1. Calculate the incremental IRR for the "own" versus "operate" decision discussed earlier:

	Today	End 2L	End 3L	IRR
Operate	($20,000)	$70,000	$370,000	539%
Own	($50,000)	$50,000	$50,000 . . .	100%

2. Compare the IRR for two projects. In Project 1 you invest $100 and receive $150 back in year. In Project 2, you invest $100 and receive $750.38 back in five years. If the cost of capital is 10 percent, which project do you choose? What is the IRR and NPV for each project?

3. Assume we have the following two projects, with the following payouts:

	Project A	Project B
2012	–$100,000	–$100,000
2013	+$50,000	0
2014	+$50,000	0
2015	+$50,000	+$152,087.50

The cost of capital for both projects is 10 percent. Find the NPV and IRR for each. Which project should you choose?

3. PAYBACK AND HURDLE RATES

Payback rules and hurdle rates are largely tangential to understanding finance from a legal perspective. Because your client might mention them, though, it helps to know what they are. After all, blank stares don't inspire confidence.

Hurdle rates were mentioned in passing before, but warrant a fuller discussion. Virtually all businesses have some sort of hurdle rate, even if it is implicit, but the easiest way to understand this idea is to look at financial institutions. If a bank has to pay 5 percent to its depositors, then the "hurdle rate" for its projects (i.e., loans) must be at least 5 percent. That is, unless it wants to experience insolvency, it has to take in more than it pays out.

That's the basic ideal with a hurdle rate: The firm sets some minimal bar over which all projects must pass.[2] At the very least this hurdle rate should be the opportunity cost of capital—for the reasons we discussed in prior chapters.

Payback rules are similar rules of thumb that companies use when evaluating projects. The idea is that all projects must "pay back" their initial investment within a specified period of time. This does tend to reject long-term projects, but

---

2. In the hedge fund context, it has the related meaning of the minimum return that the fund must earn before the manager starts to collect management fees. *See* Chapter 20.

it also preserves liquidity for the firm, because the firm's cash must come back within the specified period.

To calculate the payback period for a particular project, simply add up the number of cash flows needed to return the nominal amount of cash originally invested in the project. For example, if a project involves a $50,000 investment and returns $10,000 per year, the payback period is five years.

Rarely will the calculation be this tidy, and thus calculation of a payback period often involves prorating the final payment over the final year. If we again take the $50,000 investment, but posit $12,000 per year cash flows, the calculation becomes

$$PP = 4 + \left[\frac{50,000 - 48,000}{12,000} \right]$$
$$PP = 4 + 0.167$$
$$PP = 4.167$$

where PP is the payback period, which we find is 4.167 years.

Neither of these rules is a substitute for the NPV or IRR analysis described earlier, but rather you will tend to see them used in conjunction with other tools for evaluating projects.

PROBLEM SET 4.4

1. Consider the projects outlined in Problem 3 of Problem Set 4.3. What is the payback period for each? If Bogartco uses a two-year payback rule, which project will it pick?
2. If Bogartco has an internal hurdle rate of 10 percent and finds that a particular new project has an IRR of 12 percent, should it necessarily go forward with the project?

5

VALUING BONDS

CORPORATE BOND SALES TOP $237 BILLION IN RECORD AUGUST

By Sarika Gangar — August 30, 2012, Bloomberg.com[1]

Sales of corporate bonds globally surged to the most on record for August as issuers rushed to lock in record-low borrowing costs.

Siemens AG (SIE), Europe's largest engineering company, and JPMorgan Chase & Co. (JPM) led borrowers selling $237.6 billion of debt this month, exceeding the $235.3 billion raised in August 2010, according to data compiled by Bloomberg. Yields fell to an unprecedented low of 3.72 percent on Aug. 28, according to Bank of America Merrill Lynch index data.

Offerings are increasing as issuers take advantage of demand with default rates below historic averages and optimism rising that Europe's leaders may contain the region's fiscal strains. While yields on corporate bonds average less than 4 percent, the spread to U.S. Treasuries is higher than before the credit crisis. Government bond yields have been suppressed by central banks easing monetary policy to stimulate growth.

Sales in the U.S. reached $94.6 billion, split between $63.9 billion in investment-grade debt and $30.7 billion in high-yield, while issuance in Europe totaled 33.6 billion euros ($42 billion), Bloomberg data show.

Siemens sold $3.3 billion of bonds denominated in pounds and euros yesterday in Europe's biggest corporate fundraising since May, the data show. The Munich-based company's offering included 350 million pounds ($553 million) of 2.75 percent, 13-year debt and 650 million pounds of 3.75 percent, 30-year securities, Bloomberg data show.

JPMorgan sold $2.5 billion of 2 percent, five-year bonds on Aug. 13 and $1.1 billion of 5.5 percent, perpetual preferred shares on Aug. 20, Bloomberg data show. The New York-based bank's offering of shares, rated the highest level

---

1. Used with permission of Bloomberg L.P. © 2013. All rights reserved.

of speculative grade at Ba1 by Moody's Investors Service, was increased from an initial $500 million amid demand from investors.

A *bond* is a security sold by a government or corporation. In essence, it is a contract whereby an investor (the creditor) gives the government or corporation (the debtor) some money, and the borrower promises to repay that money at some point in the future.

The bond markets are massive in the United States, representing almost $35 trillion of investments — about three and a half times the size of the better known stock market. The largest single borrower in that market is the U.S. government. As of this writing, there was approximately $7 trillion of U.S. Treasury debt outstanding.

Bonds will be the subject of several classes in this course, but for now we consider bonds from a valuation perspective.[2] Of course, to value bonds you first have to understand them, so we begin with a basic primer of bond types and how they "work."

1.   TYPES OF BONDS

In North America, corporate bonds typically come in $1,000 increments and pay interest semiannually.[3] Thus, if you hold a single "Goldman Sachs Group 5.95% Note due 01/15/27," the company owes you $1,000 in 2027, and will pay you 2.975 percent interest on $1,000 every six months.[4] The 5.95 percent in the bond's title is simply the semiannual interest rate multiplied by two, as by convention bonds quote annual interest rates.

Each interest payment is referred to as a *coupon*. In the old days — and still today with respect to some European bonds — bonds were bearer instruments. Whoever had physical possession of the bond was the owner. To get an interest payment, the holder had to cut off a coupon attached to the bond and send it in to the issuer or the issuer's agent (often a bank).

The $1,000 value of the bond is the principal lent to the issuer. It is also referred to as the bond's par value. Zero coupon bonds are bonds that make no periodic interest payments during their life. Instead, they are issued at a discount to par.

For example, a company might sell a one-year zero coupon bond to an investor for $960. The investor gets $1,000 in 12 months. The difference between the face value of the bond and the purchase price is effectively interest, and the IRS will treat it as such for tax purposes. U.S. government Treasury Bills — which have a maturing of less than one year — and U.S. Savings Bonds are common examples of zero coupon bonds.

Bonds that are issued at less than par are said to have "original issue discount" (OID). All zero coupon bonds have OID by definition — but interest-paying

---

2. *See also* Chapters 14 and 15.

3. In other jurisdictions you might find that bonds pay interest quarterly or annually.

4. These bonds — or notes — were issued in November 2006. The issuer is the parent holding company of the bank with the same name.

bonds might also be issued with OID. Can you describe what the effect is of combining OID and a stated interest rate?

As noted before, bonds can be issued by corporations or governments, and the issuing entity could be either foreign or domestic. For example, you might have heard that Greece recently engaged in a restructuring of its debt — bonds that it had issued to borrow money for various governmental purposes.

PRELIMINARY REOFFERING CIRCULAR DATED JULY 15, 2013

<u>**Existing Issues Reoffered**</u>

On the date of original issuance of the Bonds, Sidley Austin LLP, Bond Counsel, delivered its opinion that interest on the Bonds would be exempt from personal income taxes imposed by the State of New York or any political subdivision thereof, including the City, and assuming continuing compliance with the provisions of the Internal Revenue Code of 1986, as amended (the "Code"), interest on the Bonds is not includable in the gross income of the owners thereof for federal income tax purposes. In connection with the reoffering, Fulbright & Jaworski LLP, Bond Counsel to the City for Tax Matters, will deliver its opinion (i) with respect to any of the Bonds that are not treated as reissued under the Code, that the conversion to a fixed rate to maturity of the interest rate will not in and of itself adversely affect the exclusion of interest on such Bonds from gross income for purposes of federal income taxation and (ii) with respect to any of the Bonds that are treated as reissued under the Code, that interest on such Bonds will be exempt from personal income taxes imposed by the State of New York or any political subdivision thereof, including the City, and assuming compliance with the provisions of the Code, interest on such Bonds is not includable in the gross income of the owners thereof for federal income tax purposes. See "SECTION III: MISCELLANEOUS — Tax Matters" herein for further information.

$135,000,000*

The City of New York

Tax-Exempt General Obligation Bonds
Fiscal 2014 Subseries 1

Conversion Date: August 15, 2013*   Due: As shown on the inside cover page

The outstanding bonds of (i) Fiscal 1994 Series A, Subseries A-8, A-9 and A-10 that are scheduled to mature in the years 2016 through 2018, inclusive, (ii) Fiscal 1994 Series B, Subseries B-3 that are scheduled to mature in the years 2017 and 2018, (iii) Fiscal 1994 Series H, Subseries H-3 that are scheduled to mature in 2014 and (iv) Fiscal 2006 Series E, Subseries E-2, E-3 and E-4 that would have been mandatorily redeemed in the years 2017 through 2021, inclusive, will be converted to the Fixed Rate Mode. To the extent such conversions constitute a reissuance under the Code, the related Bonds will be redesignated Fiscal 2014, Subseries 1 and, to the extent such conversions do not constitute a reissuance under the Code, the related Bonds will retain their original designation.

The Bonds are registered in the nominee name of The Depository Trust Company, New York, New York, which acts as securities depository for the Bonds.

Interest on the Bonds will be payable on each February 1 and August 1, commencing February 1, 2014. The Bonds can be purchased in principal amounts of $5,000 or any integral multiple thereof. Other terms of the Bonds are described herein. *A detailed schedule of the Bonds is set forth on the inside cover page.*

Effective upon the conversion of the Bonds to the Fixed Rate Mode, the Bonds will not be subject to tender for purchase and the former liquidity and letter of credit providers, as applicable, will have no liability with respect to the Bonds. The Bonds are subject to redemption as set forth herein.

In connection with the change in the method of determining the interest rates and other modifications of the Bonds, certain legal matters will be passed upon by Sidley Austin LLP, New York, New York, Bond Counsel to the City. Certain legal matters will be passed upon for the City by Fulbright & Jaworski LLP, a member of Norton Rose Fulbright, New York, New York, Bond Counsel to the City for Tax Matters. Certain legal matters in connection with the preparation of this Reoffering Circular will be passed upon for the City by Orrick, Herrington & Sutcliffe LLP, New York, New York, Special Disclosure Counsel to the City. Certain legal matters will be passed upon for the Underwriters by Squire Sanders (US) LLP, New York, New York, and D. Seaton and Associates, New York, New York, Co-Counsel to the Underwriters. It is expected that the Bonds will be available for delivery in New York, New York, on their date of conversion which is expected to be on or about August 15, 2013.

J.P. Morgan

BofA Merrill Lynch		**Citigroup**
Jefferies	**Morgan Stanley**	**Siebert Brandford Shank & Co., L.L.C.**
Barclays Capital	**M.R. Beal & Company**	**Fidelity Capital Markets**
Goldman, Sachs & Co.	**Janney Montgomery Scott LLC**	**Lebenthal & Co., LLC**
Loop Capital Markets LLC	**PNC Capital Markets LLC**	**Ramirez & Co., Inc.**
Raymond James	**RBC Capital Markets**	**Rice Financial Products Company**
Roosevelt & Cross Incorporated	**Southwest Securities, Inc.**	**Wells Fargo Securities**
Blaylock Robert Van, LLC	**Cabrera Capital Markets, LLC**	**Drexel Hamilton LLC**
	TD Securities (USA) LLC	

July   , 2013

---

*   Subject to change.

Bonds are also issued by cities, counties, and states within the United States. Under U.S. tax law, interest paid on this state and municipal debt is not subject to federal tax, and interest paid by the investor's "home state" is typically exempt from state tax, too. This gives these *municipal bonds* a special advantage in the marketplace.[5]

For example, assume a corporate bond has a yield of 8 percent, and a municipal bond has a yield of 6 percent. If your tax rate is 40 percent, which would you prefer?

It should also be noted that cities and counties can file for bankruptcy under chapter 9 of the Bankruptcy Code—Detroit being a recent example—whereas states are not presently eligible to file (and some argue could never be for Constitutional reasons). How would this affect the value of a California bond as compared with a bond issued by the City of Los Angeles?

2. BOND PRICING AND THE PRICE/YIELD RELATIONSHIP

As noted previously, corporate bonds are typically issued in $1,000 increments. Nonetheless, bond prices are quoted in the market in terms of 100. You can either think of this as a percentage, or the price without one of the trailing zeros. Thus, a bond priced at 100 is trading at par value — its original $1,000 issued price. But bonds don't necessarily trade at par. Instead, bonds can trade at a premium or a discount to par, and movements away from par are particularly common with long-term debt instruments. For example, the Goldman Sachs notes discussed earlier were issued in late 2006 at par, but in July 2012 were priced at 103.93800, meaning you could sell the note for more than the face value the holder will receive when the note matures in 2027. Why might that be?

Remember back in Chapter 3, when we talked about interest rates? There we noted that ten-year U.S. government bonds were paying 1.98 percent interest and 20-year government bonds were paying 2.76 percent. The Goldman Sachs bonds — which are due in 15 years — have a 5.95 percent coupon.

Although Goldman Sachs plainly presents more risk than the U.S. government — the financial crisis made that clear — in the present environment the 5.95 percent coupon is so desirable that investors are willing to pay more than par to buy the bonds.

What is the effect of paying more than par? In short, it reduces the return or yield the bondholder receives. Rather than receiving 5.95 percent, as a par buyer would, a Goldman Sachs noteholder who buys at 103.93800 will receive a lower yield — closer to 5.5 percent.

---

5. Municipal bonds are often issued in increments of $5,000, unlike corporate bonds.

When a bond's interest rate is higher than prevailing rates, the bond's price will go up—beyond par value. When a bond's interest rate is lower than prevailing rates, the bond price will go down. In short, this is the fundamental law of bond prices: Prices and yields move in opposite directions. If market interest rates go up, prices will go down, and vice versa.

Final Term Sheet
USD 3,000,000,000 4.75% Global Notes due May 15, 2012

Terms:	
Issuer:	KfW
Guarantor:	Federal Republic of Germany
Aggregate Principal Amount:	USD 3,000,000,000
Denomination:	USD 1,000
Maturity:	May 15, 2012
Redemption Amount:	100%
Interest Rate:	4.75% per annum, payable semiannually in arrears
Date of Pricing:	April 24, 2007
Closing Date:	April 30, 2007
Interest Payment Dates:	May 15 and November 15 in each year
First Interest Payment Date:	November 15, 2007
Interest Payable on First Payment Date:	USD 77,187,500
Currency of Payments:	USD
Price to Public/Issue Price:	99.665%
Underwriting Commissions:	0.10%
Proceeds to Issuer:	99.565%
Format:	SEC-registered global notes
Listing:	Luxembourg Stock Exchange (regulated market)
Business Day:	New York
Business Day Convention:	Following, unadjusted
Day Count Fraction:	30/360
Governing Law/Jurisdiction:	German Law; District Court Frankfurt am Main

FIGURE 5-1
KfW Bond Sheet

PROBLEM SET 5.1

1. Review and explain the following table, which shows actual bonds as of July 2012:

	Coupon	Maturity	Qty	Price	Min	Max	Accrued Interest	Estimated Total Cost
JOHNSON & JOHNSON NOTES	6.95	9/1/29	25	150.541	1	372	$661.22	$38,296.47
WAL-MART NOTES	5.875	4/5/27	25	132.29302	2	50	$420.23	$33,493.49
GEN ELEC CAP CP MED TRM NT	5.1	2/15/19	6	111.66667	6	6	$130.05	$6,830.05
GE CAPTAL BONDS	5.55	5/4/20	25	116.459	1	104	$285.21	$29,399.96
GEN ELEC CAP CP MED TRM	3.5	4/15/22	25	102.8	1	541	$221.18	$25,921.18
RALSTON PURINA DEBENTURE	8.625	2/15/22	5	144.772	1	5	$183.28	$7,421.88
MERCK & CO INC DEB	6.4	3/1/28	25	138.72202	10	44	$608.89	$35,289.39
GENL ELEC CAP CP	6.75	4/15/18	12	118.49	1	12	$209.25	$14,428.05

3. VALUING A BOND AS AN ANNUITY

The value of a bond is the sum of the present values of all coupon payments plus the present value of the returned par value at maturity of the bond. In short, you need to value (1) a stream of cash flows (semiannual interest payments), and (2) the return of $1,000 at some point in the future, and then add the two together.

Valuing a stream of cash flows we already know how to do — that's an annuity. And you know how to value the return of a lump sum at some point in the future. Putting it together, the formula for valuing a bond is then

$$\text{PV of bond} = \frac{I}{r}\left[1 - \frac{1}{(1+r)^t}\right] + \frac{\$1,000}{(1+r)^t}$$

where I is equal to the periodic interest payment. Remember that you will typically have to divide the stated interest rate by two and multiply that by $1,000 to calculate I. Also remember that the entire formula here will have to be based on a t of some number of six-month periods. For example, if you are valuing a ten-year bond, t will equal 20, and your discount rate (r) will have to be a six-month interest rate as well.

This assumes that you find yourself valuing a bond one day after an interest payment. Quite often, that will not be the case. Instead, some amount of interest will have accrued and the valuation will need to take that into account.

You saw an example of this in Problem Set 5.1. The price with the extra accrued interest is referred to as the "dirty" price for the bond, and you see that price listed in the column on the far right.

Figuring out how much interest is accrued but unpaid since the last interest payment is somewhat trickier than it might appear at first blush. The problem arises because you need to know how many days are in a year—as calculated under the terms of the bond in question. That is, although we all know that most years have 365 days, unless it's a leap year with 366, any sort of corporate finance document is free to adopt a different day count convention.

U.S. government debt uses the actual days of the year to calculate interest payments, but most corporate bonds do not. The actual day count convention might appear easier—it's certainly more intuitive—but remember that for any fraction of a year you have to account for months with 30 days, others have 31 days, and then there is the oddness that is February. Because of this, most bonds instead provide that all months are deemed to have 30 days, and all years are deemed to have 360 days. Then, a bond sold between semiannual interest payments accrues interest at the rate of 1/180th of the six-month interest payment per day.

Look at the KfW term sheet on page 65. What was the day count convention used there?

Next, recall the Goldman Sachs Group 5.95 percent notes. The semiannual interest is calculated as 0.0595 divided by two, or 0.02975, times $1,000. That results in a semiannual interest payment of $29.75. If we are now two months past the last interest payment, we know that $9.917 of interest has accrued. Do you see why?

PROBLEM SET 5.2

For all problems in this set, assume the market rate of interest is 6 percent per year.

1. Value the Goldman Sachs notes described in the prior section as of January 1, 2013, assuming that there is no accrued interest. Then assume that two months of interest have accrued (see above). What is the total value of the bond? What price would you expect to pay for the bond?
2. Value a ten-year zero coupon bond. What price would you expect it to sell for today? Would a zero coupon bond ever trade at a premium?

4. YIELD TO MATURITY

Yield to maturity (YTM) is a useful concept for comparing various bonds of different durations and prices in the market. YTM calculates the yield for a particular bond, given its current market price, if held to maturity. In other words, what r will give you a value for the bond that is equal to its current price? This should sound very familiar.

YTM is essentially an application of internal rate of return (IRR) to bonds. By finding the r that sets the bond's present value equal to its price, we are also finding the *r* that gives us a zero NPV if we were evaluating a project comprised of investing in the bond.

As with IRR, calculating YTM by hand would be quite burdensome, and after about 1980 only a math fanatic would do such a thing. Instead, use the "Yield" function in Excel.

For example, to calculate the YTM for the Goldman Sachs Group 5.95 percent notes discussed earlier (which mature on January 15, 2027), and using July 13, 2012 as "today," when the notes were trading at just over 105, you would enter the following into Excel:

$$= \text{YIELD (Start, Maturity, Rate, Price, Redemption, Frequency)}$$
$$= \text{YIELD (``7/13/2012'', ``1/15/2027'', 0.0595, 105.139, 100, 2)}$$

which gives you a YTM of 5.4 percent. Note that the interest rate is put in at its annual rate, and then the "2" toward the end of the formula tells Excel to use semiannual payments. The number corresponds to the number of annual payments — for example, 12 would indicate monthly payments.

While we're at it, you should also know about another useful formula, the "Price" function in Excel. This allows you to calculate the price or value of a bond, given certain pieces of information. Wouldn't that have been helpful in the prior section?

Again, consider the Goldman Sachs notes:

$$= \text{PRICE (Settlement, Maturity, Rate, Yield, Redemption, Frequency)}$$
$$= \text{PRICE (``7/13/2012'', ``1/15/2027'', 0.0595, 0.0543, 100, 2)}$$

As you can see, this function works much like the yield function, but here we are solving for price given the *required* yield (i.e., market yield) or a YTM. The formula above refers to the YTM we previously calculated, and we see that the result is the same as the actual market price used in the yield calculation earlier.

PROBLEM SET 5.3

1. Schnoodleman Ltd. issued a 30-year bond on March 15, 2003 with a 5 percent coupon. The bond currently trades at 120. What is the bond's YTM? What is the YTM if the bond currently trades at 85?
2. B. B. Worth, Inc. issued some bonds that have 20 years to go until maturity. The bonds have a 4 percent coupon, but similar companies are issuing new 20-year debt with 5 percent coupons. What is the current price of the bonds?
3. Hugo & Monkey Newspapers, Inc. just issued 30-year bonds, with a 3.5 percent coupon. Find the price for these bonds at years 3, 5, 10, 20, 25, and 29 if similar bonds yield 4.5 percent throughout. What if similar bonds instead yield 3 percent?

5. BOND RATINGS

Bond ratings are an assessment of an issuer's ability to repay its debt, based on its history of borrowing, repayment, and other factors. Currently three companies dominate the ratings business: Fitch, Moody's, and Standard & Poor's. S&P uses letters ranging from AAA — the highest rated companies, like Microsoft — to D, which means the company is in default (e.g., Kodak or American Airlines). The corresponding Moody's ratings are Aaa and C.

Ratings reflect an assessment of an issuer's creditworthiness, and thus lower ratings should correspond with higher yields. Bonds in the lower range, but not in default, are referred to as "junk" or high-yield bonds.[6] This, of course, assumes that the rating agencies are doing a good job.

S&P RATINGS DEBATE DOESN'T SHOW FRAUD, PETERSON SAYS
By Alan Goldstein — March 7, 2013, Bloomberg.com[7]

Analysts at Standard & Poor's, the ratings firm accused by the U.S. of misleading investors about the risks of mortgage bonds that helped ignite the financial crisis, were arguing the merits of their views on debt opinions, not committing fraud, President Doug Peterson said.

"Our culture has always been characterized by vigorous debate and robust analysis," Peterson said yesterday in a video message that the world's largest ratings firm sent to clients. "There may have been differing opinions within S&P and some were strongly held but that is not evidence of fraud."

The Justice Department sued S&P and its parent, New York-based McGraw-Hill Cos. (MHP), in federal court in Los Angeles on Feb. 4, alleging analysts inflated ratings on mortgage securities and collateralized debt obligations leading up to the seizure in credit markets to win business from Wall Street banks. The civil lawsuit seeks about $5 billion in penalties, equivalent to more than five years of McGraw-Hill profit. S&P said on Feb. 5 the lawsuit is without merit.

S&P rated more than $2.8 trillion of residential mortgage-backed securities and about $1.2 trillion of CDOs from September 2004 through October 2007, according to the Justice Department complaint. When the U.S. housing boom collapsed, the world's largest banks reported $2.1 trillion in losses and write-downs, triggering the worst financial crisis since the Great Depression and costing 8.8 million people their jobs.

"DEEPLY REGRET"

The Justice Department accuses S&P in its complaint of falsely representing to investors that its ratings were objective, independent and uninfluenced by any

---

6. From BB (S&P) or Bb (Moody's), to C or Ca.
7. Used with permission of Bloomberg L.P. © 2013. All rights reserved.

conflicts of interest. The company shaped its ratings to suit its business needs by weakening adjustments to its analytical models and by issuing inflated rankings on CDOs collectively worth hundreds of billions of dollars, according to the complaint.

In the 128-page civil complaint, the U.S. cites internal e-mail exchanges to bolster its case, including one in which an S&P analyst allegedly told a colleague in April 2007 that deals "could be structured by cows and we would rate it."

"In hindsight, our rating opinions turned out to be insufficient in anticipating the speed, depth and duration of the housing crisis," Peterson said in the video. "This is something we deeply regret. But we do not believe the government can prove that this was the product of intentional misconduct by anyone at S&P."

"Key Enablers"

S&P, Moody's Investors Service (MCO) and Fitch Ratings were "key enablers of the financial meltdown," the Financial Crisis Inquiry Commission, created by Congress with a 10-member bipartisan board, said in its January 2011 report. "This crisis could not have happened without the rating agencies."

The government didn't sue Moody's or Fitch. Peterson said in the video that S&P's ratings on CDOs cited in the complaint were "identical" to those from rival firms, and that its underlying assumptions about the U.S. real estate market were "consistent" with the opinions expressed at the time by the Treasury Department and the Federal Reserve.

"Our ratings were independent and issued by us in good faith, based upon the views of our rating committees at the time," Peterson said.

The FCIC's report also blamed the crisis on lenders' irresponsible and sometimes fraudulent practices; regulators' inattention and overconfidence; and the recklessness of borrowers and investors.

State Lawsuits

McGraw-Hill faces lawsuits from 16 states and the District of Columbia in addition to the federal case, which may not go to trial for "two to three years," Kenneth Vittor, the company's chief counsel, said on a conference call Feb. 12.

The company is asking for those lawsuits to be moved to federal court, where it may claim S&P is protected by the U.S. Constitution's guarantee of free speech. McGraw-Hill filed so-called notices of removal in several courts to put the cases under federal jurisdiction and combine them for pretrial matters, such as the exchange of evidence and questioning of witnesses.

In federal court, the cases will be "adjudicated in a manner that takes into account the significant federal regulatory and constitutional issues that are necessarily and directly implicated," the company said in papers filed this week in U.S. District Court in Wilmington, Delaware.

The mortgage-backed securities discussed in the article are the subject of Chapter 19.

6

RISK AND RETURN

This chapter begins the transition from some basic, building block segments on valuation to the final chapters in the valuation unit, which put these building blocks together to provide a more sophisticated discussion of valuation. To complete that transition, you need to understand five more concepts that will undergird the coming chapters.

We begin first with *diversification*, a concept that you might have some intuitive understanding of, but that we need to solidify before moving on to portfolio theory, the Modigliani-Miller theorems, and the Capital Asset Pricing Model (CAPM) in coming chapters. Closely related to diversification are the ideas of separating risk into systematic and firm-specific risk, and then measuring a firm's relationship to systematic or market risk with beta (β). Integral to this entire analysis is some understanding of the law of one price — the idea that an asset should have but one price, no matter how many forms or locations it might be sold in — and the limits to this theoretical law that exist in reality.

1. DIVERSIFICATION

At its most basic level, the idea behind diversification is that spreading out investments across several projects will reduce risk, and might even increase return. For example, if there are ten large, high-quality companies you might invest in, each of which looks equally good now, but only one of which will do really well over the next few years, putting all of your money in a single company constitutes a high-risk, potentially high-return strategy. If you correctly guess the high-performing company, you win. But you have a 90 percent chance of selecting a disappointment.

In re JP MORGAN CHASE BANK

27 Misc. 3d 1205(A), 910 N.Y.S.2d 405
Unreported Disposition
Surrogate's Court, Westchester County, New York
March 31, 2010

Opinion

ANTHONY A. SCARPINO, JR., J.

This is a contested proceeding to judicially settle the final accounting of JP Morgan Chase Bank, N.A. (formerly Lincoln First Bank of Rochester [the Bank]), as co-trustee of a trust created under the will of Blanche D. Hunter (decedent) for the benefit of Pamela Townley Creighton (Pamela), decedent's granddaughter, for the periods March 27, 1973 through August 13, 1996 (the intermediate account) and August 14, 1996 through January 17, 2003.

From June 22, 2009 through July 1, 2009, the court conducted a trial on the amended verified objections to the accounting which were filed and/or adopted by Margaret Hunter (Pamela's mother) and Pomona College, as testamentary appointees under Pamela's will, and the Office of the New York State Attorney General (the AG), on behalf of the charitable beneficiaries (collectively, objectants).

BACKGROUND

[Under her will the decedent created two trusts for the benefit of her grand-daughters Alice and Pamela. The decedent passed away in 1972, and the two trusts were funded with large blocks of Kodak stock—in Pamela's case, she received more than 13,000 shares of Kodak.]

In March 1980, Alice died ... [and] the Bank ... transferred all of [her trust's] assets, including 12,981 Kodak shares with a value, as of that date, of $598,424.10 ($46.10 per share), to [Pamela's] Trust, bringing the total number of Kodak shares in [Pamela's] Trust to 26,016 with a value of $1,560,498.13

In May 2002, Pamela filed objections to the [Bank's request for approval of its fees], claiming, that the Bank had acted improperly, as co-executor and as co-trustee of the [two trusts]. She alleged that the Bank should not have retained such a high concentration of Kodak shares in the estate and the trusts from 1973 through the early 1980's, when there was a precipitous decrease in the value of those shares. Pamela sought a surcharge against the Bank for breaching multiple fiduciary duties ...

By decision and order dated December 31, 2002 (December 2002 order), this court dismissed certain of Pamela's objections which sought to surcharge the Bank for improprieties as co-executor of decedent's estate and/or as co-trustee of the A Trust. However, the court did not dismiss those of Pamela's objections which sought to surcharge the Bank for its failure, as co-trustee of [Pamela's] Trust, to object to any of its actions as co-executor of the estate and as co-trustee of the A Trust.

... the primary issue at trial was the Bank's liability for the alleged retention of a concentration of common stock in Eastman Kodak Company (Kodak shares) in the trust. At the trial, objectants and the AG called James Lieb, the Bank's administrative officer for [Pamela's] Trust from 1993 through mid-1997 (Lieb), and John Teegardin, the Bank's investment officer for [Pamela's] Trust from 1977 to 1997 (Teegardin) as adverse witnesses; Loren Ross, as their liability expert (Ross), and Frank Torchio, as their damages expert. The Bank called two witnesses: William J. Wilkie, the Chief Fiduciary Officer for Banker's Trust Company, as its liability expert (Wilkie) and William Schwert, as its damages expert . . .

DIVERSIFICATION/RETENTION OF KODAK SHARES

Objectants contend that, as a result of the Bank's imprudence, they have sustained compensatory damages in a sum not less than $9 million as of January 17, 2003, plus prejudgment statutory interest, compounded annually.

[The court then reviews the testimony, concluding with] Ross's opinion, under the circumstances here where the Bank had already held onto a concentration of Kodak shares for more than 10 years, a prudent fiduciary would have sold 95% of Kodak stock in the summer of 1987. The court accepts and credits Ross's testimony.

The foregoing proof demonstrates that at no time during the administration of the trust did the Bank formulate any investment plan, let alone establish a plan to diversify its concentration of Kodak. The Bank acted contrary to its internal policies to restrict its holding of any one stock to certain circumstances, none of which were presented here. Following the enactment of the Prudent Investor Act, on January 1, 1995, the Bank continued to hold a concentration of Kodak shares in violation of the statutory requirement to "diversify assets unless the trustee reasonably determines that it is in the interests of the beneficiaries not to diversify, taking into account the purposes and terms and provisions of the governing instrument" (EPTL 11–2.3[b][3][C]). The record is clear that, after January 1, 1995, the Bank continued to hold a concentration of Kodak shares in the trust. The Bank failed to rebut such proof and establish that it took steps to determine whether it was in the interests of the beneficiaries not to diversify in relation to the purposes and terms of the trust and under the provisions of the governing instrument.

In addition, the Bank failed to consider the best interests of the persons interested in the trust. The proof establishes that the Bank paid limited attention to the needs of the income beneficiary and virtually no attention to the remainder interests.

Teegardin makes reference to the income beneficiary, the family's purported desire to hold onto the stock, and in one letter, noted the existence of potential tax consequences. The record is devoid of any proof that the Bank was proactive by assessing the volatility resulting from the concentration of Kodak and the benefit to selling and diversifying the portfolio, obtaining Pamela's written consent to retaining Kodak stock, ascertaining the tax consequences, if any, to Pamela and determining whether the concentration jeopardized the remainder interest.

As in *Janes* [a NY Court of Appeals case on diversification], notably absent here is any proof that the Bank considered the increased risk to the trust portfolio by its continued concentration of one security in the portfolio. Also consistent with *Janes*, the record here establishes that the Bank: 1) failed to undertake a formal analysis of the trust by creating an investment plan; and 2) failed to conduct more than a superficial review of its holding of Kodak shares and consider alternative investments.

Introduced into evidence is a graph upon which the market price for Kodak stock during the period 1960 through August 2008 is shown on one side together with the dates when the trust was funded with the stock and the dates when the Bank sold its Kodak shares. The graph provides a useful depiction of the volatility of Kodak stock.

Between the initial funding of the trust in 1977, and the distribution from [Alice's trust] in 1980, the value of Kodak shares fell. Thereafter, the stock experienced an increase in its value in the early 1980s followed by another decrease in value in the mid-1980s and then began a steady climb to a peak in July, 1987. Teegardin acknowledged that in mid 1987, the Bank was aware that the price of Kodak was on the rise and testified that in July and August, 1987, the stock was "fairly valued." Yet, Teegardin made a deliberate decision in the summer of 1987 not to sell the Kodak shares.

Kodak suffered significant losses in value when the market turned in October, 1987. Not until August 17, 1989, did the Bank next sell stock, 5,000 shares and then on November 20, 1991, the Bank sold 6,100 shares. Thereafter, the Bank sold shares of Kodak during most of the years from 1989 through October 25, 2000, during which period there were gains and some losses.

Contrary to the Bank's assertions, the proof demonstrates that it considered the price of Kodak stock to be the determinative factor on whether to sell. Essentially, the Bank asks the court to consider the net gain to find that there is no liability. While the Bank repeatedly characterizes objectants' arguments as hindsight, it is the Bank that has engaged in hindsight by suggesting that an overall gain in the trust corpus protects it from surcharge . . .

Under the circumstances here, an experienced, careful investor should have seen that in the early summer of 1987, the market for the sale of Kodak shares had improved to the point that it was prudent to sell at least 95% of the Kodak shares, in order to eliminate the concentration in the portfolio and recoup the unrealized loss in the trust . . . Giving the Bank a reasonable period to implement the sale of Kodak, the court finds that the Bank should have sold 95% of the Kodak shares on July 30, 1987.

The record here demonstrates a pattern of neglect which rises to a breach of fiduciary duty by the Bank for over a 20 year period. Based upon such facts the court awards statutory interest [9%], compounded annually . . .

Accordingly, the proper measure of damages for "lost capital" shall be calculated by: (1) determining the gross value of 95% of the Kodak shares remaining in the B Trust on July 31, 1987, measured by the average of the high and low value of the stock on that day, (2) less any capital gains tax which would have been incurred upon the sale of such shares to obtain the net value of those shares on that date (the rolling balance). (On July 31, 1987, the trust held 22,686 Kodak shares, of which 95% equaled 21,552 shares.).

FIGURE 6-1
Share Prices of JP Morgan Chase and Wells Fargo.

Eastman Kodak Company filed for chapter 11 bankruptcy in January 2012, a victim of the growth of digital cameras and smartphones. Unfortunately, Pamela had also passed away by the time of the court's opinion, and thus her heirs were the primary beneficiaries of the court's decision.

The basic idea behind diversification is one you already know: "Don't put all your eggs on one basket." There is also an additional idea imbedded in diversification that turns on the concept of *correlation*. Correlation is a concept that you might have encountered if you took a college statistics class — if the values of two variables line up on a plot, they are correlated.

Investments can also be correlated: For example, you might expect that the share prices of similarly sized companies in the same industry will be highly correlated. For example, Figure 6-1 shows the share prices of JP Morgan Chase and Wells Fargo over the five years from the start of 2007 to the end of 2012. Until 2012 — when Chase was the subject of some specific concerns, concerning its "London Whale" trade — the two shares were quite correlated.

If an investor assembles a portfolio that spreads investments across various, uncorrelated investments, then they are said to be well diversified.

PROBLEM SET 6.1

1. On July 31, 1987 Kodak shares closed at $93.87. On March 31, 2010, when the court's decision was issued, the shares closed at $5.79. On July 16, 2012, when this chapter was written, the shares closed at $0.28. How much damages were Pamela's heirs entitled to? What amounts should be offset against that figure (beyond capital gains taxes, as noted in the earlier excerpted opinion)?

2. Which five of the following investments would achieve the greatest degree of diversification?

East Coast Railroad	East Coast Coal Mining Co.	Midwestern Utility Co.	FedEx	Nestle SA
West Coast Railroad	West Coast Coal Mining Co.	California Tech. Co.	UPS	Pfizer, Inc.
Chevron Corp.	Wal-Mart Stores, Inc.	British Petroleum	Royal Dutch Shell PLC	France Telecom SA

2. FIRM-SPECIFIC AND SYSTEMATIC RISK

Postwar finance theory (sometimes called "modern" finance) slices investments across several dimensions, two of which are particularly relevant for lawyers to understand. First, investments can be either "risk-free" or risky. Although an utterly risk-free investment is more of an academic invention, typically the debt of stable countries that borrow in their own currency are treated as risk free for these purposes. This includes not only the United States, but countries like Canada, Japan, Norway, Switzerland, Australia, and the like. Germany and the Netherlands, even though they do not borrow in their own currency, undoubtedly belong in this group, too.

Risky assets are everything else, be it Belgian debt, gold bars, or shares in ExxonMobil or Pets.com.[1] To varying degrees, each of these investments could return less than the investor originally paid. Hence, they are risky investments.

Of course, as we noted in the prior chapter, there are degrees of risk. Shares in Exxon are clearly less risky than Pets.com shares (20/20 hindsight being what it is).

The risks faced by risky assets are then divided into two forms: systematic risk and firm-specific risk. *Systematic risk* is the risk that the value of an investment will go up or down as "the market" goes up or down. Inflation, war, and general economic conditions are all examples of systematic risk. In short, it is the risk that all investments face. To some degree, the definition of systematic risk depends on your frame of reference. For example, are the relevant economic conditions global or simply with regard to the U.S. economy?

To use a U.S. example, consider that Goldman Sachs' shares were down during the recent financial crisis by about 60 percent. During that time the entire S&P 500 went down about 13 percent. You might consider 13 percent to be a reflection of systemic risk, and the additional decline in Goldman's share price might be attributed to firm-specific risk.

As this implies, *firm-specific risks* are those that are unique to a particular firm or investment. These risks include the risk that Exxon will spill oil and incur

---

1. *http://en.wikipedia.org/wiki/Pets.com*

cleanup costs, that Pets.com will try to gain market share by offering free shipping on heavy boxes of dog food, or that a new gold vein will be discovered in the rocks under Central Park. Each of these affects the specific investment in question, lowering its value, but the money Pets.com loses offering free shipping has little effect on the price of gold, and vice versa.

This conception of risk leads to a couple of important insights. First, by diversifying, an investor can reduce his or her exposure to firm-specific risk. But diversification will not resolve systemic risk. Specifically, by splitting your money between Chase and Wells Fargo, you hedge against the chance that one of them will fail, but you don't avoid a general decline in U.S. financial institutions. In short, you have not done a very good job at diversification.

Spreading your money between Chase and the Union Pacific Railroad takes care of the risk specifically associated with financial institutions, but still leaves you exposed to general declines in the U.S. economy. Buying Chase and Nestle takes care of the concentrated exposure to the domestic economy — although both firms have some large degree of exposure to the U.S. economic climate — but you are still exposed to global economic slowdowns, and the United States is the largest single economy.

The other insight comes from considering assets or investments as risk-free or risky. Namely, the price that risk-free assets pay investors must operate as a kind of floor to what risky assets will pay. Or, stated another way, if investors are even somewhat rational, they will demand that risky assets pay the risk-free rate of return plus some premium.

Otherwise the expected return of the risky asset will be lower than the expected return of the risk-free asset, and who would take a lower expected return?

3. MEASURING SENSITIVITY TO SYSTEMIC RISK — BETA

Once we realize that systemic risk — at least if measured broadly — is largely unavoidable, it becomes important to understand how a particular investment reacts to such risk. For example, when the world economy slows, if one investment will decline by 5 percent and another by 10 percent, an investor would like to know that before investing. Indeed, the sensitivity to systemic risk must be accounted for when valuing the investment.

The most common way to measure this sensitivity is through something called beta (β) — because using a Greek letter makes the concept more approachable.

Beta is a ratio. As such, it measures a particular investment relative to something else. As a matter of theory, the appropriate comparison is the "market." Measuring the performance of all investments worldwide is quite difficult — think not only stocks and bonds, but also commodities broadly defined — and thus more often investments are compared to their relevant submarket.

For equity investments in large U.S. companies, the point of comparison is the Standard & Poor's 500 Index. For bonds, the Lehman Aggregate Bond Index which tracks U.S. Treasury securities, U.S. government agency bonds, mortgage-backed bonds, corporate bonds, and foreign bonds traded in the United States, has been used for a long time. (But, for obvious reasons, the index is now called the *Barclays Capital* Aggregate Bond Index.)

Beta is typically calculated historically, comparing the investment's volatility relative to the index over the past three or five years. Mathematically, beta is calculated as the ratio of the covariance of the stock with the market (or index being used as a proxy for the market) to the variance of the market:

$$\beta_i = \frac{Cov\ (Investment,\ Market)}{Var\ (Market)}$$

Variance and covariance are statistical terms that you probably forgot from your college statistics course. Variance is squared standard deviation. I'm sure that was helpful.

Perhaps more helpful is to remember that variance is the average of all squared deviations from the mean (average). So if a particular investment returns, on average $5, but one year it returns $10, another year it returns $0, and another year it returns $5, you calculate variance as

$$(10 - 5)^2 + (0 - 5)^2 + (5 - 5)^2$$
$$25 + 25 + 0 = \$^2 50$$

That is, the variance is 50 squared dollars, whatever that means.

You are probably now remembering why standard deviation is useful — you take the square root of 50 squared dollars and then say, "This investment has a standard deviation of $7.07."

If you remember some rules from your college stats — and make the grand assumption that the investment's returns are "normally" distributed[2] — you can make some bold pronouncements like, "95 percent of the time this investment will return $5 ± $14. You could earn up to $19."[3] Hopefully your audience won't notice that standard deviations work in both directions, and that the returns might not be normally distributed, and you are ready to sell mortgage-backed securities.[4]

Covariance, the top part of the beta calculation, is the sum of the investment's deviation from the mean multiplied by the market's deviation from the mean, for each year, divided by the number of years less one. That's a bit much, but the basic idea is that this measures the degree to which two items move in tandem.[5]

---

2. That is, the historical returns fall into a bell-shaped curve.

3. For those of you who don't remember, the shorthand, rule of thumb is that if you have a bell-shaped curve, 95 percent of the data will be within two standard deviations of the mean (average).

4. Don't worry; this will make more sense once you have covered asset securitization in Chapter 19.

5. For those of you interested in the math, let's use the numbers from above, and assume a market return of $2, $3, and $5 for each of the three years. That gives us an average market return of $3.33. For year one you have (10 – 5), the investment calculation, multiplied by (2 – 3.33), the market calculation. You add that to the same calculations for years two and three, and divide by two (three years minus one). Or you use the "COVAR" function in Excel. That would look like this:

= COVAR ({refer to range of market numbers}, {refer to range of investment numbers})

A positive covariance means that asset returns move together. A negative covariance means returns move inversely; in short, the ratio of the degree to which the investment moves with the market over the overall market movement. By definition, the beta of the S&P 500 is 1.0 — after all, it is used as the proxy for the "market" and x over x always equals one.

An investment with a beta of 1.10 tends to perform 10 percent better than the market in up markets and 10 percent worse in down markets. Often high betas are deemed riskier investments, although a low beta might only indicate that the investment's volatility relative to the market is low, not that the investment has low risk.

You could calculate beta with Excel,[6] but more often you would probably look it up on a commercial service like Bloomberg, because the calculation requires three to five years of relevant market data. For casual use, Yahoo! Finance, MSN Money, and Google Finance all report stock beta values, too.[7]

PROBLEM SET 6.2

1. How would you interpret a beta of 1, 2, 3? How about −1, −2, −3?
2. Compare Coca-Cola's beta to that for Dow Chemical (DOW).[8] What can you conclude?
3. What are the limitations of beta when calculated on historical data?
4. What would you expect to find if you examined the relationship between price and beta?

4. THE LAW OF ONE PRICE (AND A BIT ON SHORT SELLING)

The law of one price is an implicit assumption in much of the finance theory we are about to encounter, so it bears making it explicit and exploring its limitations.

The law of one price holds that in an efficient market[9] all oranges of equal quality must have equal prices.

We have already assumed something like this was at work. Think back to the last chapter on bond valuation — remember how we equated the value of a bond with its price? The reason for doing that is an assumption — the law of one

---

6. = COVAR({refer to range of market numbers}, {refer to range of investment numbers})/ VARP ({refer to range of market numbers}).

7. For example, go to *https://www.google.com/finance?client=ob&q=NYSE:KO* to see the report for The Coca-Cola Company (or just Google "KO," and click over to Google Finance). What is its beta? How would you interpret that?

8. Google "NYSE:DOW."

9. This is a concept that itself will be explored in coming chapters. In short, this means a market where buyers do not face any hindrances in examining goods and comparing prices; that is, information is freely available and costs of moving among sellers is low.

price — that large deviations between price and value will not be long tolerated in liquid markets.

Of course, the rule applies to things other than oranges. For example, imagine a company (Bogartco Ltd.) that owns half of another company (High Sierra, Inc.) and has no other assets. And let's further assume that High Sierra's only asset is a bank account with a $100,000 balance. If both companies' shares are traded on the stock exchange, and Bogartco gets no special benefits from owning a large block of High Sierra shares, what should we expect regarding the value of these two companies?

Bogartco should be worth exactly half of High Sierra, or $50,000. What if instead Bogartco was trading at a price that implied it was worth $60,000? Smart investors should sell Bogartco shares and buy High Sierra shares, because they amount to the same thing. In short, the equivalent assets will have the same price before long.

What if we only had High Sierra, Inc., without Bogartco, and the price of High Sierra implied its value was $110,000? That is, the price implied a value $10,000 higher than reality. If you already own the High Sierra shares, now is a good time to sell. But what if the High Sierra shareholders are all blockheads, who can't see what is readily apparent to everyone else? Does the law of one price get suspended? (Maybe we call it the Blockhead Exception?)

Not really, because at least according to the theory, arbitrage will come into play. *Arbitrage* refers to an opportunity to make money with little or no risk. Typically it involves the selling of overpriced assets or the buying of underpriced assets, with the effect that prices and value come together.

For example, if oranges are selling in Los Angeles for $10 a bag, but in New York City for $20 a bag, there is a potential arbitrage opportunity. Namely, so long as I can transport oranges to New York for less than $10 per bag, I can sell LA oranges in New York City. Eventually the price in New York should approach the LA price plus the cost of transport.

In the case of High Sierra, the arbitrage would take the form of short sales. Namely, an investor borrows High Sierra shares and then sells them, promising to return the borrowed shares at some point in the future. The expectation, of course, is that the share price will go down and the investor will be able buy them back on the cheap. The investor then makes money on the difference between the sale proceeds and the cost of buying the replacement shares.

Arbitrage is an important element in the law of one price. As we consider finance theory going forward, we must be mindful of instances where arbitrage is not possible. For example, if you believe that your neighbor is overvaluing the shares of the local dry cleaners they own, there is not much you can do about it. Nobody is going to lend you dry cleaners shares to short. More often the limits to arbitrage are less obvious, and thus require deeper consideration of the issue.

For example, the noted economist John Maynard Keynes is reported to have said "[m]arkets can remain irrational a lot longer than you and I can remain solvent." The next case examines the truth of that pronouncement.

ZLOTNICK, ALBERT M., APPELLANT, v.
TIE COMMUNICATIONS & L.W. KIFER

836 F.2d 818
United States Court of Appeals, Third Circuit
No. 87–1370.
| Argued Dec. 7, 1987 | Decided Jan. 6, 1988 | As Corrected Jan. 14, 1988

JAMES HUNTER, III, Circuit Judge:

Appellant Albert Zlotnick filed this class action against Appellees TIE Communications, Inc. ("TIE") and L.W. Kifer, alleging violations of §§9 and 10(b) of the Securities Exchange Act of 1934 and of the RICO Act. Zlotnick claims that appellees' misrepresentations artificially inflated the price of a stock which he had sold short, causing him to lose money when he made the purchase necessary to cover the short sale. The District Court dismissed for failure to state a claim, 665 F.Supp. 397. Zlotnick now seeks a reversal and the reinstatement of his complaint.

I. BACKGROUND

A. THE ALLEGATIONS

In reviewing a dismissal under Fed.R.Civ.P. 12(b)(6), the court must accept as true both the factual allegations contained in the complaint and all the reasonable inferences that can be drawn from those allegations. We therefore accept the facts as presented in Zlotnick's allegations.

In 1981, appellees TIE and Kifer formed Technicom International, Inc. ("Technicom"), a manufacturer of systems to monitor and control the moisture level of communication cables. At all relevant times in this case, TIE was the parent of Technicom and owned a majority of its stock, and Kifer was the Chairman and CEO of Technicom and held a significant equity interest in the company. In March, 1982, TIE and Technicom entered into a "distribution agreement" whereby each would distribute the products of the other. Shortly thereafter, Technicom made a public offering of its common stock, selling approximately 625,000 shares at a price of $9.75 per share. The price of Technicom stock rose steadily throughout 1982, selling at six times its offering price by the end of the year.

On January 6, 1983, Zlotnick sold short 1,000 shares of Technicom at $16.875 per share. Five days later he sold short another 1,000 shares at an average price of $19.30. Zlotnick sold the stock short because he concluded that the stock was overvalued. He based this conclusion in part on his analysis of the company's earnings and prospects, finding that the stock was then selling at a ratio of approximately 50 times current annualized earnings. Zlotnick also based his conclusion on his belief that Technicom faced increasing competition that would diminish its profit margins and depress future earnings. At the time of his short sale Zlotnick was unaware of any wrongdoing or misrepresentations by appellees; and he did not base his decision to sell short on a belief that appellees were deceiving investors.

In early 1983, subsequent to Zlotnick's short sales, appellees undertook to inflate artificially the price of Technicom stock. Specifically, TIE and Kifer caused Technicom to issue several press releases which misrepresented the company's sales agreements and earnings prospects. They also caused Technicom to engage in illusory sales to TIE. Both misrepresentations falsely inflated the company's reported sales and earnings for the fourth quarter and entire fiscal year of 1982 to record levels. By March 14, 1983, the price of Technicom stock had risen to approximately $33.00 per share. Zlotnick, unaware of any deceptive practices by appellees, decided to cut his losses by making the purchases necessary to cover his short position; ultimately, he realized a loss of about $35,000.

The price of Technicom stock did not begin to fall until the summer of 1983. Thereafter, due in part to more realistic statements by Technicom, the value of the stock dropped sharply. On June 30, 1984, the stock was trading at $4.12 per share. Following further reported losses, Technicom merged with its parent TIE via a transaction in which Technicom stockholders received .29 shares of TIE stock for every share of Technicom; the value to shareholders of this transaction was approximately $2.50 per share of Technicom. This represented a drop in value of approximately 90% from the high of the previous year.

Zlotnick instituted this action on March 13, 1985 by filing a complaint on behalf of himself and all similarly situated investors. The complaint was amended on June 6, 1985. Appellees moved for dismissal on September 16, 1985 . . . [and the District Court] held that Zlotnick had not sufficiently alleged reliance on appellees' deception, and therefore had not stated a claim upon which relief could be granted. Zlotnick filed a notice of appeal on June 26, 1987.

B. SHORT SELLING

Because this case turns to some extent on the nature of short selling as an investment strategy, we set out here our understanding of that process. Where the traditional investor seeks to profit by trading a stock the value of which he expects to rise, the short seller seeks to profit by trading stocks which he expects to decline in value. A typical short seller expects decline because, based on his view of the underlying strengths and weaknesses of a business, he concludes that the market overvalues the business' stock. As demonstrated by the allegations, these underlying facts can concern the present — such as the fact that a stock trades at fifty times its earnings — or they can concern the future — such as the fact that a business will face increased competition.

Short selling is accomplished by selling stock which the investor does not yet own; normally this is done by borrowing shares from a broker at an agreed upon fee or rate of interest. At this point the investor's commitment to the buyer of the stock is complete; the buyer has his shares and the short seller his purchase price. The short seller is obligated, however, to buy an equivalent number of shares in order to return the borrowed shares. In theory, the short seller makes this covering purchase using the funds he received from selling the borrowed stock. Herein lies the short seller's potential for profit: if the price of the stock declines after the short sale, he does not need all the funds to make his covering purchase; the short seller then pockets the difference. On the other hand, there is no limit to the short seller's potential loss: if the price of the stock rises, so too does the short seller's loss, and since there is no cap to a stock's price, there is no limitation on the short seller's risk. There is no time limit on this obligation to cover.

"Selling short," therefore, actually involves two separate transactions: the short sale itself and the subsequent covering purchase. We reject appellees' suggestion that the two components of selling short be considered one transaction. When the short seller transfers borrowed stock to a buyer, its obligations to that buyer are ended.

His only obligation is an open-ended one to the person who loaned him the stock. A short seller's default on this obligation will not affect the prior transfer. Also, the short seller exercises real discretion in choosing when to purchase shares, and this latter transaction actually determines his profit or loss. Thus, this investment, like most investments, involves two transactions: a purchase and a sale. That the sale occurs "before" the purchase does not affect our consideration of each separate transaction for the possible effects of fraud.

II. Standing

Appellees challenge Zlotnick's standing to bring suit under the securities laws. They claim that since Zlotnick, in effect, sold his stock before he purchased it, he never owned any Technicom stock. Therefore, they argue, he has no standing under the Supreme Court's ruling in *Blue Chip Stamps v. Manor Drug Stores*, 421 U.S. 723, 95 S. Ct. 1917, 44 L.Ed.2d 539 (1975). Appellees also seek to distinguish the short seller from the traditional investor, arguing that while the traditional investor hopes to profit from the company's good fortune, the short seller gains his profit from the company's decline. In effect, the short seller "bets against" the company, and so should not be treated as an investor in it. Appellees also analogize the short seller to the options trader, whom several courts have found unprotected by the anti-fraud provisions of the securities acts.

Appellees' standing arguments are without merit . . .

B. The Integrity of the Market

Zlotnick argues that, as a short seller, he relied upon the integrity of the market. Though he believed the price of the stock overvalued at the time of the short sale, he relied on the market's ability, given accurate information, to correct its valuation of the stock and set a better price. By falsely inflating the price of the stock, defendants interfered with the market's ability to correct itself. Once he had sold short, Zlotnick was unable to protect himself from this fraud. Therefore, he argues, requiring him to prove individual reliance on defendant's misrepresentations "'imposes an unreasonable and irrelevant evidentiary burden.'" *Peil*, 806 F.2d at 1160 (quoting *Blackie v. Barrack*, 524 F.2d 891, 907 (9th Cir. 1975), *cert. denied*, 429 U.S. 816, 97 S. Ct. 57, 50 L.Ed.2d 75 (1976)).

Reliance on the integrity of the *market* in a stock differs from reliance on the integrity of the market *price* in that stock. An investor relying on the integrity of a market price in fact relies on other investors to interpret the relevant data and arrive at a price which, at the time of the transaction, reflects the true worth of the company. By contrast, an investor relying on the integrity of the market relies on the continuing ability of investors to interpret data subsequent to the transaction; he relies on future conditions. In the context of a short sale, the difference between these two types of reliance is more pronounced. The traditional purchaser depends on the "market" to determine a present value for the stock that allows the purchaser an adequate return on his investment. On the other hand, the short seller depends for a return on his investment on the "market" realizing that the value of the stock at the time of the short sale does not allow for an adequate return on the investment. This realization is what drives the price of the stock down and allows the short seller his profit.

More important, reliance on the integrity of the market price is actual, if indirect, reliance. The short seller is not injured because he knew of or depended on the misrepresentation; he is injured because others investing in the stock so relied. The fraud of which Zlotnick complains was truly perpetrated "on the market," and not, even indirectly, on Zlotnick as an investor in the market. We are mindful that reliance is not an abstract requirement in the securities laws: plaintiff must prove reliance in order to prove that the misrepresentation caused actual injury. "Reliance is therefore one aspect of the ubiquitous requirement that losses be causally related to the defendant's wrongful acts." *Sharp v. Coopers & Lybrand*, 649 F.2d 175, 186 (3d Cir. 1981), *cert. denied*, 455 U.S. 938, 102 S. Ct. 1427, 71 L.Ed.2d 648 (1982). Zlotnick may, as discussed above, be able to prove his own actual, indirect reliance upon the market price. However, to the extent Zlotnick argues he is entitled to recover for the reliance of third parties, we reject his claim.

Zlotnick alleges that defendants misrepresented the truth, and that such misrepresentations caused the price of the stock to rise at the time he sold short. He concludes that since the fraudulently-induced rise in the stock caused him to lose money, he is entitled to recover. Under Zlotnick's theory, he would be allowed to recover even if he purchased after deciding, based solely on accurate information, that the stock was not overvalued and his short sale was ill-conceived. Yet, in such a case, Zlotnick is no different from the traditional purchaser who buys at a fraudulently-inflated price but actually relies solely on accurate information in purchasing: both have made bad valuations of the stock, but those valuations were independent of any alleged fraud. Zlotnick cannot recover his loss on his covering purchase unless he shows that his decision to cover was somehow connected with the fraud.

C. INDIRECT RELIANCE

That Zlotnick states his claim in terms of reliance on the market's integrity does not preclude the conclusion that a fraudulent market price was a material factor in his decision to cover. Zlotnick might have changed his investment strategy and actually relied on the "integrity" of the inflated market price. The rise in price itself may have changed his opinion of the stock's value. The rise may also have increased his risk of loss beyond acceptable levels, causing him to purchase. It may have led him to conclude that the stock would take so long to decline in value that the cost of maintaining his short position would exceed his potential gain. In *Peil*, this court accepted that a market price which reflects a defendant's misrepresentation may pass that misrepresentation on to potential purchasers. It is only logical to hold that the same price which may communicate a misrepresentation to the traditional investor may also communicate a misrepresentation to the short seller.

Zlotnick is entitled to have this court consider as true both his allegations and all reasonable inferences from those allegations. *Wisniewski, supra.* We find Zlotnick's amended complaint sufficient to support a reasonable inference of actual, if indirect, reliance.[10] Defendants, on the other hand, have not made sufficient proof of either the reason for Zlotnick's decision to cover or the materiality of the price in these circumstances to entitle them to dismissal. We will therefore vacate the District Court's order dismissing the complaint and remand for further proceedings. However, unlike the plaintiff in *Peil*, Zlotnick is not entitled to a presumption at trial that the market price did actually pass defendants' misrepresentations on to him, or that he did actually rely on the inflated market price in making his decision to cover. We hold no more than that Zlotnick is entitled to a chance to prove such actual reliance to a finder of fact.

CONCLUSION

For the reasons stated above, this court will vacate the order of the District Court dismissing the complaint, and remand for further proceedings consistent with this opinion.

———————————

What other ways might the law of one price break down?

---

10. Zlotnick does not allege facts sufficient to establish fraud in his initial decision to sell short. He does not allege misrepresentation of the underlying strength of the business that induced his short sale: false inflation of the company's earnings would discourage his short sale by reducing the price/earnings ratio. Also, false inflation of the market price prior to his short sale would act to increase his potential profit.

7

THE CAPITAL ASSET PRICING
MODEL

You now have a basic understanding of the time value of money, valuation, and the ideas that go into consideration of investments.[1]

This chapter begins to put together the lessons of prior chapters to explain the key elements of "modern" (post–World War II) finance theory. This chapter explains portfolio theory, the efficient capital markets hypothesis, and then the capital asset pricing model (CAPM), which is a common method for finding the "r" used in many valuation calculations. The final section of this chapter notes some of the alternatives to CAPM, which you will see has some flaws. Namely, CAPM gives but a very rough estimate of the return of any particular investment. Unfortunately, so do most of the alternatives.

Nonetheless, CAPM combined with the weighted average cost of capital (WACC, covered in Chapter 11) are some of the valuation methods you are most apt to encounter in practice, probably because most corporate lawyers and judges understand them.

1. PORTFOLIO THEORY

Accordingly to lore, before Harry Markowitz came along in the 1950s, investors looked at individual stocks and considered a particular company's risk and return in isolation before investing. If this resulted in a portfolio of all railroads, so be it. If you find it hard to believe that investors before World War II were quite this dopey, join the club. As one profile of Professor Markowitz notes, "[i]nvestors already had been spreading their risks ever since the first bull market on Wall Street in 1792."[2]

---

1. Assuming, of course, you've done the reading and attended class.
2. *http://goo.gl/SVAvC*

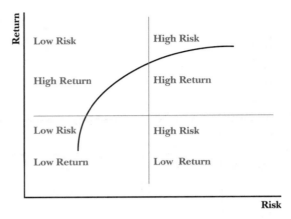

FIGURE 7-1
The Efficient Frontier.

The real insight that Markowitz provided was that investors would be better served by looking at the correlation of their entire portfolio, moving away from the risk and return of individual investments.[3] He explained that all the possible investment portfolios could be graphed with their expected return plotted against standard deviation or variance, which Markowitz proposed as a measure of risk. Essentially, volatility and expected return stand in for the basic concepts of risk and return.

Out of the entire universe of possible portfolios, certain portfolios will best balance risk and reward. These comprise what Markowitz called an efficient frontier of portfolios — the portfolios that lay along the upper left-hand edge of the graph of all portfolios (see Figure 7-1). According to Markowitz, a rational investor should pick a portfolio that lies on the efficient frontier.

Although the tendency is to think of this in terms of stock market investments, the following excerpt makes clear that Professor Markowitz's insights work with regard to most any sort of investment.

SARAH PEI WOO, *REGULATORY BANKRUPTCY: HOW BANK REGULATION CAUSES FIRE SALES*
99 Geo. L.J. 1615, 1631–1632 (2011)

Every bank maintains a portfolio of loans and assets whose value and risk profile is not simply the sum of its parts. The assessment of the risk of a loan within a portfolio is different from an assessment of that same loan in isolation, due to portfolio composition effects such as diversification of risk.[4]

---

3. His book is available online at *http://goo.gl/FxGHz*

4. The concept of "Markowitz diversification" is used in this Article, being commonly used in portfolio risk management in the United States by banks and regulators. A "key contribution of Markowitz diversification is the formulation of an asset's risk in terms of a portfolio," rather than in isolation. *See* Frank J. Fabozzi, Harry M. Markowitz & Francis Gupta, *Portfolio Selection*, in The Theory and Practice of Investment Management 15, 29 (Frank J. Fabozzi & Harry M. Markowitz eds., 2002).

Of particular interest to regulators is whether a bank's portfolio composition will cause, over the short or long term, uncompensated losses that will threaten the bank and require outside intervention to protect depositors or the economy. [There are] complex interlinkages among capital adequacy, portfolio composition, and the debtor-creditor relationship.

Another professor—James Tobin—came along next and extended Markowitz's work to develop the Capital Market Line (CML). Basically, Tobin asked "What if we consider that investors can invest in a risk free asset, and they can borrow money to invest, too?"

You can think of the "risk-free asset" as a Treasury Bill to make it more tangible. And borrowing to invest has existed for a long time: Stockbrokers allow customers to borrow on "margin" so that they can buy many more shares than they might be able to with their cash on hand. Brokers, of course, get paid interest for offering this service.

Tobin then showed that investors should then want to invest in some combination of one portfolio (M) on the efficient frontier and the risk-free asset, because of higher returns for a given level of risk everywhere except at the tangential point. You can see this in Figure 7-2.

By mixing in the risk-free asset, investors can move along the CML, which provides higher expected returns with equal or lower risk. The tangential point reflects investing 100 percent of your money in the portfolio. Anywhere to the left of that point reflects a lower percentage of the portfolio, with the balance made up of the risk-free asset. When you hit the axis, you have reached 100 percent risk-free asset.

Moving to the right of the tangential point, you are investing in more than 100 percent of the Markowitz portfolio. How is that possible? You borrow money and use it to buy more of the portfolio.

Note a couple of unrealistic points here: First, the CML assumes you are borrowing at the same rate as you are lending. That is, the only reason the line is straight is that it assumes you can borrow from your stockbroker to move to the right of the tangential point at the same interest rate (r_f) that you lend money to the government at. Most people can't borrow from their stockbroker at the same rate as the U.S. Treasury—for the simple reason that your stockbroker has figured out that you're not as good of a credit risk.

FIGURE 7-2
Capital Markets Line.

Similarly, although the graph implies that you can go off to the right side into infinity, since the 1929 stock market crash, when lots of investors got in trouble buying stocks on margin, the Federal Reserve has limited margin lending.[5] The initial margin requirement represents the minimum amount of funds that investors must put up to purchase stocks on credit. The current rate, set in 1974, is 50 percent, which means that an investor can only borrow up to half the value of a share from the broker.[6]

And also note the oddity of using variance or standard deviation as a measure of risk. Under this approach, both downside and upside movements count as risk.[7] Are most investors all that concerned with unexpected upside movements? Oh darn, my investment went up more than I expected it to!

This is part of a larger problem of assuming that risk and return are symmetric, and could equally go in either direction. It bakes in the idea that investors can never beat the market, a concept that in turn becomes the foundation of the efficient capital markets hypothesis we discuss later. Moreover, symmetric returns are simply not true for most mainstream investments.[8] As you learned in your Business Associations class, corporate shareholders benefit from limited liability. Thus, share prices can never go below zero, meaning that returns on the left side of the distribution are artificially truncated.

Nonetheless, from the combination of Markowitz and Tobin we can get the *one-fund theorem,* which says that the investors will trade only in the risk-free asset and one portfolio (consisting of only risky assets). And this work provides the foundation for CAPM. But first, we have to pick up one other theory.

Think about something before we move on, though: What is the relationship between portfolio theory and the separation of risk into systematic and non-systematic risk, discussed in the prior chapter?

2. THE EFFICIENT CAPITAL MARKETS HYPOTHESIS

Recall both in the prior chapter and the first part of this chapter that passing mention was made to "efficient" or well-functioning capital markets and "rational" investors. Now is the time to formalize these ideas.

French mathematician Louis Bachelier performed the first notable analysis of stock market returns in his 1900 dissertation. He documented the statistical independence of stock returns — meaning that today's return signals nothing

---

5. Timothy A. Canova, *Financial Market Failure as a Crisis in the Rule of Law: From Market Fundamentalism to a New Keynesian Regulatory Model,* 3 Harv. L. & Pol'y Rev. 369, 374 (2009).

6. Federal Reserve Regulations T and U. The Fed only sets the initial margin. After purchase, the minimum margin required as a result of price fluctuations, typically 25 percent, is set by stock exchange rules. Brokers, of course, can set higher limits as part of their normal risk management.

7. Michael C. Macchiarola, *Beware of Risk Everywhere: An Important Lesson from the Current Credit Crisis,* 5 Hastings Bus. L.J. 267, 277 (2009).

8. But remember, this only applies to mainstream investments like stocks and bonds. As you will see in Chapter 18, derivatives can be quite different.

about the direction or magnitude of tomorrow's return—and this led him to model stock returns as a "random walk."

This view was not prevalent, however. Instead, most prewar investors probably agreed with John Maynard Keynes's beauty contest analogy, in which each analyst recommends not the stock he thinks best, but rather the stock he thinks most other analysts think is best. In Keynes's view, stock prices are based more on speculation, and analysts' fears about being wrong, than on economic fundamentals.[9]

In the 25 years following the war, financial theory began to return to Bachelier's approach, which fit nicely with other developments in the field. By 1978, well-known economist Michael Jensen would famously say that "there is no other proposition in economics which has more solid empirical evidence supporting it than the Efficient Market Hypothesis."

LAWRENCE A. CUNNINGHAM, *FROM RANDOM WALKS TO CHAOTIC CRASHES: THE LINEAR GENEALOGY OF THE EFFICIENT CAPITAL MARKET HYPOTHESIS*

62 GEO. WASH. L. REV. 546, 559–563 (1994)

The perfect market is a heuristic invented by stipulating the following assumptions concerning a market: there are a large number of participants such that the actions of any individual participant cannot materially affect the market; participants are fully informed, have equal access to the market, and act rationally; the commodity is homogeneous; and there are no transaction costs. Under these assumptions, the perfect market model would predict precisely what the random walk model was implying: that prices of goods (securities) in the public capital markets should adjust instantaneously and accurately to new information concerning them. That prediction was embodied in the ECMH as first propounded: in its broadest terms, the ECMH held that the prices of securities traded in public capital markets fully reflect all information concerning those securities.

1. THREE FORMS OF EFFICIENCY

Under this broad statement, the ECMH explains more than the random walk model required: the random walk model holds simply that successive price changes are independent or uncorrelated, whereas the ECMH explains that holding by saying that public security prices fully reflect all information—not just price histories—about a security. As a result, virtually since the emergence of the ECMH as an explanation of the random walk model, the ECMH has been divided into three forms, defined in terms of specified categories of information. The three forms were first proposed to classify empirical tests of price behavior given specified kinds of information. The weak form tested the random

---

9. *http://goo.gl/xj0JFg.*

walk model itself, using autocorrelation tests and run analysis to investigate whether past prices indicate anything about future prices. Semi-strong form testing investigated whether publicly available information other than prices was reflected in prevailing prices, and strong-form testing investigated whether private information was reflected in prevailing prices.

As the wealth of tests and discussion proceeded in the 1970s, the three forms of the ECMH came to be used to refer to the conclusions those tests suggested. Thus, the forms of the ECMH are now specified as follows: the weak form holds that current security prices fully reflect all information consisting of past security prices; the semi-strong form holds that current security prices fully reflect all information that is currently publicly available; and the strong form holds that current security prices fully reflect all currently existing information, whether publicly available or not. Finally, each of these three forms may be respecified in terms of their implications: a market is efficient with respect to an information set (defined, for example, as price histories, publicly available information, or private information) when it is not possible to generate above-normal returns by trading on the basis of that information set.

There is thus a direct and logical link between the random walk model and weak-form efficiency and a more attenuated and contingent link between the random walk model and stronger forms of the ECMH. Recall that the random walk model held that price changes are independent of or uncorrelated with prior price changes. That means that technical analysis of past price changes — sometimes called chartist analysis — cannot aid prediction of future price changes in any systematic way. Weak-form efficiency explains this independence and its implications for prediction by hypothesizing that the current price impounds all information contained in prior prices. Thus, any price change can only be the result of new information, the production of which is itself assumed to be random. This process of information absorption continues and thus explains the absence of substantial linear dependence in successive price changes discovered in the autocorrelation and run tests described above. It also leads to the stronger forms of the hypothesis.

The semi-strong form of the ECMH posits not only that current security prices reflect all information consisting of prior security prices but also that they reflect all publicly available information about the security in question. Testing this more ambitious claim requires a focus not on correlation analysis of price changes but on the relative swiftness with which prices change given new information. Despite this different testing methodology, semi-strong efficiency depends on the validity of the random walk model, which depends in turn on empirical conclusions concerning the absence of statistical dependence in security price data. In other words, if future price changes are dependent on prior price changes, then any price change the semi-strong form tests cannot be attributable solely to new information the test is evaluating. Thus, weak-form and semi-strong-form efficiency each depend on the proof provided by linear testing models.

The strong form of the ECMH extends much further than the random walk model suggested. Indeed, the strong form is a theological proposition, holding that public capital markets are infinitely wise: even non-public information is reflected in public security prices. Numerous studies have investigated whether persons possessing non-public information could, by using that information as a basis for trading decisions, achieve abnormal market returns. The theory is that, if market prices reflect less than all information, then those with the excess (private) information should be able to outperform the rest of the market. The insider trading scandals of the 1980s are among the many proofs that the strong form of the ECMH is invalid.

Because the strong form of the ECMH is widely discredited, debate concerning the ECMH centers on the semi-strong and weak forms. Debate over the weak form generally is defined by analysis of the random walk model itself, usually in terms of linear empirical models used to test the relationship between successive price changes, although more recent attention is being paid to nonlinear testing and nonlinear models. Debate over the semi-strong form traditionally has been defined in terms of anomaly studies — empirical models demonstrating that above-normal returns can be achieved by using specified information sets that are publicly available.

———————————

Although the theory applies to all types of investment assets, most of the testing has been done on common stocks. After all, stocks have the most liquid and transparent trading markets, so if the theory applies anywhere, it should apply to stocks.

As noted in the excerpt, most of the battle of the utility of ECMH has taken place at the point of semistrong efficiency. This version of the doctrine holds that it is (generally) impossible to make money from publicly available information. And if any small deviations in price do exist, sophisticated traders will quickly remove them via arbitrage.

Noted economist Joseph Stiglitz has observed that this is kind of impossible. Namely, if it really were impossible to beat the markets with public information, why would sophisticated investors spend any time trying to find mispricings? Indeed, there would not be any need for market analysts at all if the markets are highly efficient.

There is also little discussion of the reality of investing: namely, most people do not invest directly into the stock market. Instead, they invest through agents like pension fund managers, mutual fund managers, hedge fund managers, or stockbrokers. Even a big investor like a bank invests through its agents — the bank employees. These agents have their own incentives — namely, getting paid — that could sometimes conflict with the interests and rationality of the investor.

Perhaps most puzzling, in the early 1990s Eugene Fama, often credited as the father of ECMH, and Kenneth French published a large empirical survey of stock market returns since 1940 and found several ways in which returns were not random.[10] Small company stocks returned more than they "should," and value investing, which involves buying stocks that appear "cheap" relative to asset value, could get an investor "excessive" returns for long periods of time. Sometimes an investor could make money simply by buying a stock whose share price had recently been on the upswing.

10. There are other assumptions built into the model, too, but we will save the rest for our discussion of CAPM, which is codependent on ECMH.

There are other assumptions built in here, too, that we will look at again in connection with CAPM, which is codependent on ECMH. For example, there is an assumption that returns are normally distributed — that is, they fall out in a bell-shaped curve pattern. And remember that all of this is tested with historical data, but how much of the historical data should you use? Market data in the United States goes back to the 1890s — although the number of stocks traded back then was small (mostly railroads). Should the models be tested using all that data, or just the data after 1945? After all, is data from 1904 really comparable to data from today?

Despite this ongoing debate, there was and is some faith that markets function efficiently most of the time, aggregating vast amounts of disparate information into a single number — the price — on the basis of which millions of decisions are made.

But the recent financial crisis has called into question how often "most of the time" might be. In late 2011, a survey of sophisticated investors by RBC Capital Markets and the *Economist* Intelligence Unit found that

> More than half (56%) now have doubts about such tenets of modern finance as efficient markets hypothesis, the capital asset pricing model and portfolio theory; only one in four (27%) accept these concepts unquestioningly. More than half of fund managers (53%) question the value of diversification in mitigating portfolio risk. While the basic theory seems sound, there is uncertainty about how to apply it as assets become more closely correlated.

PROBLEM SET 7.1

1. On May 13, 2009, your author was quoted as a corporate bankruptcy expert in the *Wall Street Journal*, where I said that General Motors' share price of about $1.50 per share "might be about $1.45 a share too much."[11] On June 1, 2009, GM filed its chapter 11 petition, and soon thereafter it filed a reorganization plan that provided for no recovery by shareholders. Its share price was about 75 cents the Friday before the bankruptcy petition. What does this tell us about the ECMH? Does it matter that GM was part of the Dow Jones Industrial Index, an index of the largest U.S. companies, until June 8?

2. A study by the London Business School found that, since 1900, buying British stocks with the best performance the prior year would have turned £1 into £1.95m (before costs and tax) by the end of 2008; the same sum invested in the worst performers would have grown to just £31. Is this consistent with the ECMH?

3. Bernard Madoff promised his investors returns that beat the S&P 500 with less volatility. Indeed, he provided such returns (no negative returns for months!) for many years. Even if you are an ECMH skeptic, explain why investors might have been suspicious sooner.

4. The following question was asked by the Buttonwood columnist for *The Economist* in March 2009:

---

11. *http://goo.gl/fE9WQ*

> If regulators thought markets were too efficient to interfere with, how come they allowed banks to get involved in an activity which, after bonuses, was a game they collectively could not win?

Do you have an answer? (No, "I have not taken Banking Regulation/ Financial Institutions" does not count.).[12]

5. One of the implications of portfolio theory and the ECMH is that most investors would be better off buying an index fund, thus buying "the market," rather than attempting to pick specific stocks that will provide extra return. But portfolio theory also describes the benefits of diversification, and at present, about 20 percent of the S&P 500 index is made up of ten really big companies.[13] An investor who buys the index invests more in Apple alone than in the smallest 100 companies in the index. Can these ideas be reconciled?

3. THE CAPITAL ASSETS PRICING MODEL

CAPM is a model for determining what the expected return (r) should be on any given security. As such, it puts together many of the concepts we have covered both in this chapter and prior chapters. As you will see in subsequent chapters, CAPM is often used along with the WACC method to value a company.

CAPM is the result of work done in the early 1960s by William F. Sharpe, which builds on the work of Markowitz, Tobin, and others, including an early version of the ECMH, which Fama wrote about later.

CAPM states that the risk of an asset and its expected return are a function of beta, which you will recall is a measure of an asset's variance in relation to the market's variance.

The model begins with some strong assumptions, which we will come back to at the end. First, it assumes that all investors are mean-variance investors. That means that all investors simply slide along Tobin's line, deciding how much variance (risk) they are willing to tolerate.

That is, mean-variance analysis assumes that all investors have the same beliefs about the market and the relationship among different assets. And as we discussed before, mean-variance analysis assumes all investors can borrow at the risk-free rate, without transactions costs. For example, your stockbroker does not charge you anything to buy or sell. Finally, all assets you might want to buy are liquid under this analysis — if you want to buy or sell, there is never a problem finding somebody who will take the other side of the trade.

Once we make these heady assumptions, then it becomes easy to say that all investors will thus own only mixtures of the portfolio at the intersection point of the Tobin line and the risk-free asset. We call that intersection portfolio M for convenience (see Figure 7-2).

---

12. *http://www.economist.com/node/13240822/print*
13. In order, ExxonMobil, Apple, Microsoft, Wal-Mart, IBM, General Electric, Google, Chevron, AT&T, and Berkshire Hathaway.

Notice then that if a security is traded, it has to be one of the securities that makes up M, because this is the only portfolio the investors will even consider. Stated another way, all securities must be in M, because otherwise they would not even be looked at by investors and wouldn't really count as securities.

That means that the sum of all traded securities is M, and M is therefore "the market." Thus, according to CAPM, all investors should hold the market portfolio, complemented with greater or lesser positions in the risk-free asset, as Tobin described. Under Sharpe's CAPM analysis, not only does the market portfolio (M) sit on the efficient frontier, but it *is* Tobin's efficient portfolio.

CAPM thus relates the return that an individual security must provide to the entire market, as Professor Sharpe concluded that most of an investment's risk comes from its sensitivity to the market. After all, remember that Markowitz had already shown that firm-specific risks could be diversified away. An investor with low risk tolerance will have most of her money in the risk-free security, whereas a person with high risk tolerance will borrow to finance the purchase of extra investments in the market portfolio.

Thus, the value of any asset is a function of the return on the risk-free asset plus a return that is tied to how that asset responds to movements in the overall market. You already know how to measure the relationship between an asset's return and the market return, that's beta. CAPM is thus written as

$$r = r_f + \beta(r_m - r_f)$$

where r_f is the risk-free rate, and the term $(r_m - r_f)$ is often referred to as the spread, as its reflects the return on the market portfolio (r_m) beyond the risk-free rate.

Now the CAPM formula might seem very mysterious and "mathy," but I'm sure that somewhere deep in the recesses of your brain, you can remember some school teacher incanting

$$y = ax + b$$

Move the b to the other side and compare that formula with CAPM:

$$y = b + ax$$
$$r = r_f + \beta(r_m - r_f)$$

CAPM is just the formula for a line, often referred to as the Security Market Line (which you should not confuse with the CML). The risk-free rate of return is the intercept, and beta acts as the slope of the line. That is, it assumes that there is a linear relationship between risk (measured by variance) and return for all investments.

In prior chapters we talked about how investors need to be compensated for the time value of money. To paraphrase the old cartoon, a hamburger today is worth more than a hamburger tomorrow. If I'm going to let you use my money, so that I can't buy a hamburger today, I want something in return.

But investors also need to be compensated for risk, otherwise the expected return on lending out or investing the money is not the same as just keeping it or

putting in a government-insured bank account, where I hopefully make enough
to at least keep pace with inflation.

Let's consider a simple example, to make all this more concrete. Assume that
one-year U.S. Treasury debt is paying 1 percent, and the S&P 500 has returned
an average of 3 percent over the past few years. Bogartco's stock has a beta of 2.3.
What rate should we use to discount an investment in Bogartco? This involves
plugging in the numbers to the CAPM formula, and because we have been given
all the relevant data, we can find the expected return for Bogartco:

$$r = r_f + \beta(r_m - r_f)$$
$$r = 0.01 + 2.3(0.03 - 0.01)$$
$$r = 0.056 \text{ or } 5.6\%$$

A risk-free investment returns 1 percent, the market returns 3 percent, and
Bogartco should return 5.6 percent, which makes sense given the beta of 2.3.

Now is a good time to go back and think about the assumptions built into
CAPM, and its foundations. In particular, ask yourself these questions:

1. What if returns are not normally distributed?
2. What if investors are not rational all the time?
3. What if markets are not fully efficient?

You might also consider how CAPM applies beyond the S&P 500. That is, do
the assumptions hold when applied to stocks traded not in New York or London,
but also Lagos?[14] How about real estate located in Nevada or Florida or
Damascus? Or the markets in the frozen concentrated orange juice,[15] or
autographed Don Ameche photographs?[16]

PROBLEM SET 7.2

1. Which of the following investments are correctly priced if the risk-free
   rate of return is 1.5 percent and the market rate of return is 3.5 percent?

Investment	Beta	Expected Return
A	0.85	3.5%
B	1.08	4.1%
C	1.69	5.1%
D	0.71	2.9%
E	1.45	4.4%

14. *See* Erb, Harvey and Viskanta, *Expected Returns and Volatility in 135 Countries,* J. Portfolio Management, Spring 1996 at 46. The authors find that CAPM has some problems when applied to nondeveloped markets.

15. *http://goo.gl/KP5iAJ.*

16. *http://en.wikipedia.org/wiki/Don_Ameche.*

2. Online,[17] you can find a chart that plots the share price of Apple Inc. against the return for all of NASDAQ, the stock market on which Apple shares trade, over the past year. At the top left of the chart, you'll find the return for both in numbers. Calculate the expected return for Apple using the information there and the current one-year U.S. Treasury rate[18] as the risk-free rate. What can you conclude?

3. Sam Spade is considering buying some shares in Bogartco, which trades on the market for $50 per share. He concludes that the expected rate of return on this investment is 10 percent per year. If the risk-free rate is 3 percent, the market return is 4 percent, and the stock's beta is 1.5, this a good buy or not? What if the risk-free rate changes to 5 percent? What are the limitations of this analysis?

4. ALTERNATIVES TO CAPM

In financial academia, CAPM lives on primarily in old articles and most researchers have moved on to newer asset pricing models. But in law, CAPM still plays an important role, in part because of its (relative) simplicity.

The fact that betas are scaled around one provides for a simple intuitive understanding: An investment with a beta of 1.2 is a bit more risky than the average investment in the market. Even math-phobic lawyers can understand that.

Because of all the simplifying assumptions built into the CAPM model, however, it provides but a rough estimate of a proper expected return or discount rate. As we have seen earlier, even small changes in discount rates can sometimes result in big differences in valuation.

And the CAPM model becomes even wobblier the further we get away from its core competence: namely, the valuation of very large company shares traded on well-developed stock exchanges. CAPM is also somewhat dependent on the ECMH, which itself is the subject of some skepticism.[19]

One commonly seen alternative is the Arbitrage Pricing Model, also called arbitrage pricing theory. It was developed by Steven Ross, a professor at MIT.[20] His basic idea was that several factors can affect return, and betas should be estimated for each of these factors.

If you took statistics in college, you will recognize that this moves from a univariate model, with CAPM, to a multivariate model. But it's still a linear model. And the hard part is specifically what factors should be included in the model. For example, the share price of the Union Pacific Railroad is probably very sensitive to diesel fuel prices, but the share price of JP Morgan Chase, not so much.

---

17. *http://goo.gl/M78UD*

18. *http://goo.gl/7ZFWv*

19. Claire A. Hill, *Why Financial Appearances Might Matter: An Explanation for "Dirty Pooling" and Some Other Types of Financial Cosmetics*, 22 Del. J. Corp. L. 141, 149 & n.22 (1997).

20. Edward S. Adams & David E. Runkle, *Solving a Profound Flaw in Fraud-on-the-Market Theory: Utilizing a Derivative of Arbitrage Pricing Theory to Measure Rule 10b-5 Damages*, 145 U. Pa. L. Rev. 1097, 1129 (1997).

Some newer versions of this, which tend to be called multifactor models, use historical data to develop relevant factors for future stock prices. Your statistics professor — if you had one — would have called it data mining, and frowned on it.[21]

In essence, the APM is simply an invitation to construct your own model. Not surprisingly, even sophisticated courts and corporate lawyers have tended to decline.

Many additional models have been developed, but none has been shown to be without faults. That, in addition to its simplicity, might be the ultimate reason why CAPM continues to prevail in legal circles.

21. Your statistics professor probably did not have any money on the line either.

8

CAPITAL STRUCTURE AS ECONOMIC DREAM

Companies have two basic choices when deciding on a financial structure: debt or equity. More realistically, the company (or its managers) needs to decide what portion of debt should be used to finance the firm — equity being something of the default choice.

As a theoretical matter, the optimal capital structure is easily explained. Namely, an optimal capital structure is one that minimizes the costs to the firm while maximizing the firm's ability to take on any project with a positive NPV that it desires.[1]

When the firm is first incorporated, its capital structure is made up of only equity. If it needs more funds — either to provide liquidity for daily operations or to purchase more assets — it then faces the choice. It could sell more shares. Doing so will reduce the ownership stake of existing shareholders, unless they are willing to buy the new shares. Or the company can borrow money. This could either take the form of a loan from a bank or the sale of bonds. In either case, the firm has contractually promised to repay the money with interest at some point in the future. That means that the company has committed to a fixed obligation, whereas shareholders have no contractual entitlement to dividends. If the company is uncertain about its ability to repay, this tips the balance in favor of issuing more shares.

Many investors look for "strong" balance sheets, which is typically taken to mean limited debt. On the other hand, using debt instead of equity to pursue profitable investments means that upside gains are shared with a smaller group of shareholders. Debt holders only get a fixed return; shareholders take the rest. This, of course, assumes that the firm makes more on its projects than it pays on its debts.

---

1. George S. Geis, *The Space Between Markets and Hierarchies*, 95 Va. L. Rev. 99, 114 (2009).

1.   THE MODIGLIANI AND MILLER CAPITAL STRUCTURE IRRELEVANCE THEOREM (PART I)

Given the practical concerns just outlined, you might be surprised to learn that Professors Modigliani and Miller promoted a widely discussed theory that all of this is a waste of time.[2] And one of them got a Nobel Prize for it.

M&M Proposition I, the first part of their capital structure irrelevance theorem, states that the value of a firm does *not* depend on its capital structure.[3] As explained by Professor Modigliani himself in 1990:

> With well-functioning markets (and neutral taxes) and rational investors, who can "undo" the corporate financial structure by holding positive or negative amounts of debt, the market value of the firm — debt plus equity — depends *only* on the income stream generated by its assets. It follows, in particular, that the value of the firm should not be affected by the share of debt in its financial structure or by what will be done with the returns — paid out as dividends or reinvested (profitably).[4]

There is a lot here. Here is how one lawyer unpacks the capital structure irrelevance theorem.

CLAIRE A. HILL, *SECURITIZATION: A LOW-COST SWEETENER FOR LEMONS*
74 Wash. U. L.Q. 1061, 1084-1085 (1996)

Modigliani and Miller's famous irrelevance theorem holds that capital structure does not affect firm value: a firm cannot increase its value by having one capital structure rather than another. But clearly, firms spend enormous time, energy and expense choosing among, and sometimes developing, different capital structures. This behavior can be seen as rational only in a world where the theorem's underlying assumptions are violated, and the theorem therefore does not hold.

The Modigliani and Miller assumptions can be stated as follows:

(1) Financing decisions are independent of investment decisions, broadly construed: a firm's capital structure decision will not affect its future receipts and expenditures (cash flows). Agency, regulatory, and other costs affect a firm's future cash flows; financing decision independence means that there are no such costs which a firm's capital structure can affect.

---

2. Robert P. Bartlett III, *Taking Finance Seriously: How Debt Financing Distorts Bidding Outcomes in Corporate Takeovers*, 76 Fordham L. Rev. 1975, 1981 (2008).

3. D. Bruce Johnsen, *The Quasi-Rent Structure of Corporate Enterprise: A Transaction Cost Theory*, 44 Emory L.J. 1277, 1278 (1995).

4. *Quoted in* Anne P. Villamil, *The Modigliani-Miller Theorem*, in The New Palgrave Dictionary of Economics.

(2) Financial markets are perfect. . . . This also means that there are no transaction costs to issue, buy, or sell.
(3) Financial markets are complete. For my purposes, this means principally that perfect substitutes for everything are available.
(4) Financial markets do not discriminate between those seeking financing and those providing financing: each has the same opportunities available to them on the same terms.

The first assumption, coupled with the traditional finance principle that a firm's value is the net present value of its expected future cash flows, implies that there is only one correct value for a firm, regardless of its capital structure. The remainder of the assumptions imply that a price difference between two equally valuable firms (or cash flow streams) should not persist as it would be arbitraged away. And it is not only differences between equally valuable firms or cash flow streams that will be arbitraged away. Each firm (and cash flow stream) has a correct price; if perfect arbitrage is possible, it also will assure that the relationship between the price of any two firms or cash flow streams is correct.

The world of Modigliani and Miller's theorem is, of course, not our world. In our world, there are many costs, including information costs, agency costs, regulatory costs, and transaction costs. And there are benefits which particular capital structures can provide.

In short, in a *very* stylized world, it does not matter what mix of equity and debt a firm uses, the value of the firm will be the same. Under these special conditions, firm value is like a pie (or a pizza, if you prefer): It does not matter how you slice it, the overall size of the pie stays the same. That is, there is no benefit to the firm of separating cash flows into different types of claims on the firm as that just concerns distribution, not overall value.

If debt could increase the value of the corporation, investors would create "homemade" debt, and would rather purchase a less expensive comparable company with money borrowed from their broker.

Nobody, probably not even the authors of the theory, thought that M&M Proposition I described reality. But by understanding M&M's theory, we can better understand kinds of market imperfections we need to look for and pay attention to.[5] As we'll see in coming chapters, the issues that are most likely to make a difference are taxes, the costs of insolvency or bankruptcy, and the costs of writing and enforcing complicated investment contracts.

PROBLEM SET 8.1

1. Bogartco, a leading manufacturer of trenchcoats and fedoras, as you know, has a capital structure of 1,000 common shares. The firm earns

---

5. Peter H. Huang & Michael S. Knoll, *Corporate Finance, Corporate Law and Finance Theory*, 74 S. Cal. L. Rev. 175, 179 (2000).

$1,000 per year in profits. Then HB, the chief executive, decides Bogartco should issue $10,000 of debt to fund a new project. Bogartco will pay 10 percent interest per year on this debt. If we are in an "M&M world," what is the value of the firm before and after the debt is issued? Why? (Hint: Start by considering what the share price should be, with and without debt.)

2. Problem 1 gives us a chance to talk about another aspect of Modigliani and Miller, their "dividend irrelevance" proposition. The idea is that what a firm pays in dividends is irrelevant and that stockholders are indifferent about receiving dividends, given the same assumptions as we have thus far made regarding capital structure. Why might this be?

2. THE MODIGLIANI AND MILLER CAPITAL STRUCTURE IRRELEVANCE THEOREM (PART II)

The second part of the capital structure irrelevance theorem is called M&M Proposition II. It holds that the greater the percentage of debt in the capital structure, the greater the rate of return required by equity holders.[6] This is the natural corollary of the first M&M proposition: If firm value stays the same after the addition of a senior claim on the firm, something must have happened elsewhere in the capital structure.

M&M Proposition II essentially views firm capital structure as a zero-sum game, where additions of senior claims will result in lower claimants demanding greater returns to compensate for greater risks to their returns.

That is, the expected return on equity of the firm is positive and a function of the debt-to-equity ratio. The increase in expected equity return reflects increased risk. The increase in debt increases the degree of variation in cash flows available to shareholders, as the debt holders have first claim on the cash flows.[7]

Assume Bogartco has a discount rate (and thus required return) of 12.5 percent and 100 shares outstanding. It earns $250 per year. Bogartco decides that it wants to try to increase value by issuing $1,000 of debt and using the proceeds to repurchase shares. Bogartco can issue debt at a risk-free rate of 10 percent. With the $1,000, Bogartco is able to purchase 50 shares, so there are 50 shares outstanding. What is the required rate of return on its shares, assuming the M&M assumptions are in place?

M&M Proposition I tells us that the firm value will not change, despite Bogartco's best efforts. That is, the overall return on this firm will remain 12.5 percent. But M&M Proposition II tells us that to achieve this result, the return to equity will have to go up. That is, although the average return of the

---

6. Herwig J. Schlunk, *The Zen of Corporate Capital Structure Neutrality*, 99 Mich. L. Rev. 410, 436 (2000).

7. Note that the risk to shareholders here is not the risk of default, as M&M Proposition II is based on the idea that small amounts of debt are virtually risk free, and thus they treated the debt in their model as risk free. Of course, in reality even a company with an AAA credit rating pays slightly more for its debt than the U.S. government (which we treat as risk free, despite the reality of some political risk).

firm remains 12.5 percent, the return to shareholders has to increase because their expected return decreases as some of the firm's cash flows are now promised elsewhere.

In numbers, we can find this required return by using the formula that M&M provided. Remember that they said that return to equity increases in a linear fashion as the proportion of debt in the firm increases. Taking what we already know from CAPM, we can say that the return on equity in this firm would then look like this:

$$r_e = r_f + \frac{Debt}{Equity}(r_f - r_d)$$

Note that r_f represents the firm rate of return without debt. Like CAPM, the equation is for a line, with the basic rate of return for the firm, plus a spread that increases as the amount of debt increases in the firm, giving the return on equity. Using the numbers, we get

$$r_e = 12.5\% + \frac{1{,}000}{1{,}000}(12.5\% - 10\%)$$
$$r_e = 15\%$$

We can check our result in this case quite easily, as debt and equity are balanced. Thus, the average of the two returns should equal the firm rate of return, 12.5 percent.

PROBLEM SET 8.2

1. Describe the range of outcomes for shareholder's returns in (a) an all-equity financed firm, and (b) a firm with 50 percent debt and 50 percent equity.
2. If in the preceding hypothetical, Bogartco instead had $1,500 of debt or $500 of debt, how would this change the results?
3. A company is currently an all-equity firm that pays no taxes. The market value of the firm's equity is $3 million. The return on this company's shares is 15 percent per year. The company plans to issue $600,000 in debt and use the proceeds to repurchase stock. The cost of debt is 4 percent annually. After the repurchase, what will the cost of equity be? Explain.

9

SOME REAL-WORLD
CONSIDERATIONS (PART 1)

In this chapter and the next, we examine the reasons why the M&M propositions do not hold in the real world. If you understand these considerations, you can often discover the motives for many of the financial instruments and transactions we cover in subsequent chapters.

In this chapter we look at not only M&M Propositions I and II, but also their claim that a firm's dividend policy does not matter. Recall that this was related to their larger points that capital structure is irrelevant. If capital structure is irrelevant, it also makes sense that details about the securities that make up the capital structure also do not matter. In particular, M&M argued that shareholders could create their own "dividends" by selling some shares if they need cash — and that managers should simply focus on increasing the value of the firm.

Of course, in the real world managers do spend a good bit of time thinking about dividends. And historically the taxation of dividends meant that there was some difference between selling shares and paying dividends.[1]

Moreover, much of the M&M propositions were based on perfectly functioning financial markets. Later, we examine how more realistic assumptions in this regard make the financing and cash retention decisions of actual corporations more understandable. In the final section we look at the creation of corporate conglomerates and the spinoff of parts of corporations. Both should not matter in the idealized world of M&M, but reality is somewhat different.

1. DIVIDEND POLICY

Once the firm has decided on a mix of debt and equity, it also faces the question of whether it should pay dividends to shareholders.[2] Some firms

---

1. And such a situation might return with changes to the tax code.
2. A dividend payment is a payout of portion of a company's profits or retained earnings to stockholders.

have paid dividends since time immemorial, and if they stop paying dividends, it becomes big news. General Motors is an obvious example. Other firms pay dividends reluctantly, if at all. Apple, Inc. is a good example here. It only recently started to pay dividends, despite a growing amount of cash on its balance sheet.

Some investors favor dividend-paying stocks, which are seen as safer investments. The thinking is that even in a down market, these stocks provide income, if not share appreciation. Moreover, dividend-paying companies are often seen as "stable" firms.

Of course, AIG was considered just such a firm in 2007. And during the most recent financial crisis, many such stable firms — like Bank of America, General Motors, Pfizer, and GE — either suspended or cut their dividends.

From the company's perspective, returning money to shareholders only makes sense if there is not a better use for the funds. Nonetheless, many managers feel pressure to return cash to shareholders, particularly if, as in Apple's case, there is no immediate need for the funds that managers can point to.

DANIEL J. MORRISSEY, *ANOTHER LOOK*
AT THE LAW OF DIVIDENDS

54 U. Kan. L. Rev. 449, 453, 461-468 (2006)

A.   THE CURRENT LAW OF DIVIDENDS

Dividends are the conventional vehicle by which corporations distribute their profits to shareholders. Those equity stakeholders, however, have no direct control over the firms in which they invest. Corporations exist as separate legal entities run by their directors. Among other powers vested in those managers is the authority to declare and set the amount of dividend payments . . .

IV.   THE HISTORY OF DIVIDEND POLICY

A.   THE EARLY DAYS OF LIBERAL DIVIDENDS

The corporation developed in nineteenth-century America as the premier form of business organization that could gather capital from numerous and widespread investors. Through the early part of the twentieth century, those entities retained little of their earnings, and paid out almost all of them regularly as dividends. There were two principal reasons for that early practice.

First, corporations in the nineteenth century typically made few financial disclosures to their public shareholders. Dividends were thus the only real way a firm would keep its shareholders' faith and provide them income from its operations. Second, such payments were the only viable means for shareholders to make a return on their investments because trading markets for those instruments were either nonexistent or in their infancy.

C.   THE MOVE TO MORE CONSERVATIVE DIVIDEND POLICIES

[L]egal reluctance to second-guess management coincided with the increasing separation of ownership from corporate control that occurred in the early decades of the twentieth century. As Berle and Means famously found, by the 1930s equity investment in most large corporations had become so widely dispersed that hardly any shareholders had effective power in their enterprises. Governance of public firms had been ceded to a managerial class.

As business boomed after World War I, industrial leaders used the earnings of their firms to expand their operations . . .

In those times, shareholders also began to favor a steady pattern of regular, if reduced, dividends over the boom-or-bust payouts of the nineteenth century.

D. THE ERA OF THE DIVIDEND PUZZLE

[D]uring the past seventy-five years, dividends have easily accounted for more than half of the long-term returns on the stocks of large, publicly held companies.

Through the 1960s, '70s, and '80s, companies listed in the Standard and Poors 500 (S&P 500) annually paid dividends in the range of three to five percent of their stocks' prices. The approach peaked in 1980 when more than ninety percent of firms listed in the S&P 500 paid dividends in that range.

Influential financial experts found this inclination to declare dividends puzzling, and they argued that dividend payment was really irrelevant. Not only were there substantial disincentives in the tax code to pay dividends, but shareholders of publicly traded companies really did not need them. Instead, those shareholders could get a cash equivalent whenever they wanted by selling some of their shares or borrowing against them.

Shareholders, said these economists, really should be "indifferent" to a firm's dividend policy. From a wealth-generating perspective, it should not matter whether a firm pays out its income directly to shareholders or redeploys it in a way that will grow the business and thus build up the price of its shares. So long as the firm's expected rate of return is greater than its opportunity costs, such an investment will be productive. And because a trading market exists, any shareholders who believe they can put those funds to better use can access that gain by selling their shares.

Even more incongruous, according to those theorists, was the practice of many firms to pay dividends while at the same time going to the public market to finance new ventures. Such companies could easily and cheaply fund their projects with internally generated cash instead of bearing all the transaction costs of those offerings.

Various explanations were put forward to justify the seemingly illogical approach of those firms. Shareholders were said to value cash received in hand by way of dividends more highly than the mere "paper" appreciation of their shares. Others theorized that dividends sent favorable signals to skeptical shareholders that their firms were prospering. Studies seemed to bear out this second theory. Management distributed dividends out of sensitivity to a perceived shareholder preference for steady payments. According to conventional wisdom, it was better to follow such a systematic, if conservative, pattern than to vary dividends with fluctuations in earnings. Many believed firms should not even raise dividends in good times for fear that they might anger shareholders by cutting them back when conditions reversed. A fortiori, corporate officials were reluctant to lower them in hard times for fear of adverse publicity and would even seek alternate funding to keep paying them when profits fell off.

Another justification for the payment of dividends was the so-called "clientele" theory. It postulated that different groups of investors would gravitate toward firms that met their particular needs. For instance, tax-exempt institutions or conservative investors who preferred steady payments would place their funds with companies that paid ample dividends. Others, more concerned about long-term growth and tax deferral, would opt for firms that offered little or no such yields.

Given such diverse corporate practices and shareholder expectations, Professor Victor Brudney wrote an influential article in 1980 arguing that federal law ought to compel publicly traded firms to make meaningful disclosures about how they planned to use their income streams. Dividend decisions would thus be open to public scrutiny. Not only would such transparency, he said, give investors a better idea of what to expect in the deployment of corporate earnings, but it also would provide a check on the inherent tendency of management to make suboptimal use of a firm's earnings in ways that advanced their own interests to the detriment of their shareholders.

Several years later Professor (now Judge) Frank Easterbrook continued that theme in a scholarly piece that offered two justifications for the puzzling tendency of shareholders to favor dividends over the reinvestment of corporate earnings. First, corporate officials are agents of shareholders and thus at all times should act to further their interests. But because opportunities often arise that can lead management to favor themselves at the expense of their shareholders, vigilance is needed to restrain corporate officials from such behavior. A commitment to regular dividends, Easterbrook argues, disciplines management by forcing it to go to the public market to finance new projects. This process monitors management activity in a way that no individual shareholder has sufficient incentive to do. Second, the payment of dividends helps overcome management's natural inclination to risk-adverse behavior and forces it to adhere to its profit-maximizing mission. Taking funds out of the firm's net worth account increases the level of debt over equity. Such higher leveraging benefits shareholders because debt holders are owed only their interest fixed by contract. Any gain over and above those payments goes to the shareholders. Shareholders thus make more with the same amount of their money at risk.

E.   THE DISAPPEARING DIVIDEND AND THE ALTERNATIVE OF SHARE REPURCHASES

In the booming market of the 1990s, dividend payments tailed off substantially. As one observer put it, "[d]uring the last decade, dividends were scarcely a market focal point. Investors sought growth, and companies plowed profits back into their businesses to achieve it, especially in the heady days of the late 1990s." By 2000, the average dividend yield of stocks in the S&P 500 was down to 1.1%.

───────────────

By mid 2013, the S&P 500 dividend yield was 1.98 percent. The foregoing primarily discusses dividends from the investor perspective, which of course influences the behavior of firms to the extent they cater to investor wants and desires. The basic point is that firms *do* spend time worrying about dividends despite finance theory.

Finance theory itself was slow to develop any theory of dividends. Arthur Stone Dewing (a big name in finance from about 1900 to the 1950s, and the author of a leading corporate finance text) had done some descriptive papers on dividends, but there was not really any theory. The one exception was John Lintner, who interviewed a sample of corporate managers in the mid-1950s. From those interviews he came up with some basic facts about dividend policy, and they are generally a good description of real-world practice even today.

One of the primary findings of the interviews was that a high portion of managers wanted — above all else — to maintain a stable, regular dividend. As Professor Lintner put it, managers demonstrate "a reluctance (common to all companies) to reduce regular rates once established and a consequent conservatism in raising regular rates."

But companies that lock themselves into fixed dividends are in effect turning their equity into bonds and taking away the primary benefit of using equity, namely the flexibility that comes from not having a fixed payment obligation.

As noted in the preceding excerpt, there are some defenders of this approach. The drawbacks include dividend payments that are lower than they could be and the potential that some firms might get locked into unsustainable dividends and end up in much worse trouble.

PROBLEM SET 9.1

1. In some countries, firms pay a percentage of their net income as dividends each year. Is there an advantage to this approach? If so, why might it be that large U.S. companies have been slow to adopt it?
2. Can you think of other, objective measures that a company might use to commit to return cash to shareholders, without locking itself into an unsustainable dividend policy?

2. DIVIDENDS AND THE ROLE OF SHARE BUYBACKS

For many years, the big American automakers would maintain a low regular dividend, but declare "special" dividends whenever they had extra cash. But the U.S. Tax Code changed to provide that capital gains would be taxed at a lower rate than income and dividends, which were treated as regular income. This provided a justification for companies to buy back their own shares instead of paying extra dividends, although one that came late to the game — the tax difference long predated the move to buybacks.[3] Then the law changed yet again.

3. Steven A. Bank, *Is Double Taxation A Scapegoat for Declining Dividends? Evidence from History*, 56 Tax L. Rev. 463, 464 (2003).

WILLIAM W. BRATTON, *THE NEW DIVIDEND PUZZLE*
93 Geo. L.J. 845 (2005)

The Jobs and Growth Tax Relief Reconciliation Act of 2003 (the "JGTRRA") aligns tax rates on shareholder capital gains and dividend income at a maximum fifteen percent, departing from the classical rate preference for capital gains and ameliorating the tax system's longstanding bias against dividends. According to the JGTRRA's proponents, this adjustment will help jumpstart a staggering economy, jolt stock prices upward, and release a cascade of corporate cash into the pockets of upscale consumers. Several high profile dividend increases since the JGTRRA's enactment and an increase in the overall amount paid out create an appearance of immediate success. Cooler heads point out that these increases fail to impress when viewed in historical context. This Article joins the cooler heads to predict that no fundamental shift in payout practice should be expected in the wake of the JGTRRA. But it simultaneously enters a governance objection: Corporate boards should take the occasion of the JGTRRA to reconsider prevailing assumptions about payouts, in particular the relative advantages of dividends and stock repurchases.

During the two decades preceding the JGTRRA, corporate boards steadily moved away from the dividend — the traditional vehicle for distributing profits to shareholders — diverting about half of the cash they distribute to shareholders to open-market repurchases of their firms' own common stock ("OMRs"). The shift seemed desirable for four reasons. First, OMRs offered the lower capital gains rate to the selling shareholders, along with a tax deferral and the same lower rate for nonselling shareholders. Second, OMRs increased earnings per share by reducing the number of shares outstanding. Third, OMRs signaled good news and supported the firm's stock price in the market. Fourth, because OMRs suited management's preferences, they facilitated payout and reduced the risk of suboptimal earnings retention. Old-fashioned dividends, in contrast, carried a tax disadvantage for most shareholders, did nothing for earnings per share, did less than OMRs to support the stock price, and overly constrained cash flow management. Rate parity under the JGTRRA substantially removes the first of the four justifications, inviting reconsideration of the emphasis accorded the second, third, and fourth.

This Article moots the proposition that, given tax-rate parity under the JGTRRA, dividends could rise to relative superiority over repurchases for shareholders of many firms. Prior to rate parity, straightforward reasoning supported a preference for repurchases over dividends. Rate parity brings the relative advantages of dividends and OMRs into much closer balance, turning the choice into a puzzle. In addition to tax-rate parity, four factors favor dividends. First, dividends are transparent, but OMRs can fly under the radar of the disclosure system. Second, dividends treat all shareholders equally, but OMRs can divide shareholders into groups of winners and losers. Third, dividends discipline managers, but OMRs augment management discretion respecting the marginal dollar's payout. Fourth, repurchases help managers line their own pockets by supporting the value of their stock options even as they obscure the options' cost.

Corporate boards should confront the puzzle, reviewing payout policy de novo and actively monitoring it on an ongoing basis. Unfortunately, in the corporate governance system's present posture, boards are unlikely to confront the puzzle, much less to attempt to solve it from the shareholder's point of view. Managers retain a bias in favor of OMRs, stemming in part from their interest in their own stock option compensation and from their dislike of the disciplinary effect of dividends. Corporate and securities law inadvertently support this bias.

As this excerpt notes, the most obvious reason for favoring buybacks disappeared once the taxation of dividends was equalized with that for capital gains.

PROBLEM SET 9.2

1. Based on your knowledge of corporate law, which do you think the author is alluding to at the end of the excerpt?
2. Would a shareholder be indifferent as between a dividend or a share buyback?

3. CORPORATE CASH RETENTION

One of the key assumptions of the M&M theories is that the financial markets work perfectly. Thus, if a firm has a good project, it does not matter if it pays out its cash as a dividend or uses it to the fund the project, because in the first case the firm can always borrow the needed funding from the markets. Likewise, the flexibility embedded in the use of equity in place of debt is unneeded, because the financial markets stand ready to provide for the firm's liquidity needs.

Managers often object that some amount of cash must be retained within a firm to provide for a potential rainy day. In recent decades, scholars have been skeptical.

ZOHAR GOSHEN, *SHAREHOLDER DIVIDEND OPTIONS*
104 Yale L.J. 881, 882-883 (1995)

A firm's dividend policy reflects management's decision as to what portion of accumulated earnings will be distributed to shareholders and what portion will be retained for reinvestment.[4] A firm's retained earnings represent the amount

---

4. The result of this decision is referred to as the firm's dividend payout ratio: the ratio between earnings distributed as dividends and total earnings (dividends/total earnings = payout ratio).

of financing that the firm can utilize without having to compete against other firms in the capital markets. Because dividend policy wholly determines the amount of earnings that a firm retains, dividend policy also determines the extent to which a firm can escape the scrutiny of participants in the capital markets.

Retained earnings are the greatest source of capital for firms. The typical U.S. industrial corporation finances almost seventy-five percent of its capital expenditures from retained earnings, whereas new equity issues provide a negligible fraction of corporate funding.[5] Scholars have long recognized firms' significant dependence on retained earnings and negligible dependence on equity financing.[6] This phenomenon led Professor Baumol to the inescapable conclusion that a substantial proportion of firms "manage to avoid the *direct* disciplining influences of the securities market, or at least to evade the type of discipline which can be imposed by the provision of funds to inefficient firms only on extremely unfavorable terms."[7] Unfortunately for the sake of allocative efficiency, in recent years, most firms have also managed to avoid even the *indirect* disciplining influences of the market for corporate control.[8]

Inefficient managers might try to escape a market inspection of their performance by adopting a low-payout dividend policy and avoiding the competitive external market for financing.[9]

But perhaps this skeptical view might change in light of recent events.

---

5. From 1981 to 1991, U.S. corporations financed 74.7% of their new investments from internally generated cash flow. The figure of 74.7% represents net income plus depreciation minus dividends. Between 1981 and 1991, average new equity financing was about −11%, as firms repurchased more shares than they issued. *See* Stephen A. Ross et al., *Corporate Finance* 406 tbl. 14.1 (3d ed. 1993). Moreover, on average, publicly traded firms issue "seasoned" equity—additional equity issued by a firm whose shares are already traded in public markets—only once every 18.5 years. *See* Lynn A. Stout, *The Unimportance of Being Efficient: An Economic Analysis of Stock Market Pricing and Securities Regulation*, 87 Mich. L. Rev. 613, 647 n.186 (1988). The portion of corporate funding that does not come from either retained earnings or equity is raised through debt financing. *See id.* at 648.

6. *See, e.g.*, William J. Baumol, *The Stock Market and Economic Efficiency* 69 (1965); Gordon Donaldson, *Corporate Debt Capacity* 56 (1961). The proclivity of U.S. firms to finance their capital expenditures from internally generated cash flows is almost without parallel in the world of international corporate finance. Compared to U.S. corporations, firms in other countries finance much less of their capital expenditures from internal cash flow and much more of their capital expenditures from new equity issues. Germany is the only major industrial country whose firms generate as much financing internally as do U.S. firms.

7. Baumol, *supra*, at 70. For this reason, Baumol noted that "[o]ne might almost venture to conclude . . . that the market in fact does not allocate much of the economy's capital." *Id.* at 79. Market pricing of new stock issues directly influences the allocative efficiency of the economy by determining firms' cost of capital. The fact that the market allocates so little capital, however, has provided grounds for doubting the importance of capital markets efficiency. *See* Stout, *supra* note 2, at 617-618.

8. *See* Stout, *supra*, at 691 (contending that managerial defensive tactics and state antitakeover legislation have raised costs of hostile takeover significantly above that which would be incurred in free market for corporate control).

9. The risk of managerial abuse of discretion is known as agency cost. *See* Michael C. Jensen & William H. Meckling, *Theory of the Firm: Managerial Behavior, Agency Costs and Ownership Structure*, 3 J. Fin. Econ. 305, 310-311 (1976). Indeed, as some of the literature on takeovers suggests, many managers do abuse their discretion and retain excessive earnings. *See, e.g.*, Michael C. Jensen, *Agency Costs of Free Cash Flow, Corporate Finance, and Takeovers*, 76 Am. Econ. Rev. 323 (1986).

In re LEHMAN BROTHERS HOLDINGS INC., ET AL., DEBTORS.
In re LEHMAN COMMERCIAL PAPER, INC., DEBTORS.
LH 1440 L.L.C., PLAINTIFF,

v.

LEHMAN COMMERCIAL PAPER, INC., LEHMAN BROTHERS
HOLDINGS, INC., AND STATE STREET BANK AND
TRUST COMPANY, DEFENDANTS

416 B.R. 392
United States Bankruptcy Court, S.D. New York
Bankruptcy Nos. 08–13555(JMP), 08–13900(JMP) | Adversary
No. 09–01138(JMP) | Sept. 25, 2009

JAMES M. PECK, Bankruptcy Judge.

INTRODUCTION

This dispute involves one of the loans held by State Street Bank and Trust Company ("State Street") that is part of a pool of commercial loans transferred pursuant to the terms of a master repurchase agreement (the "MRA").[10] Under the MRA, State Street paid approximately $1 billion to purchase this portfolio of financial assets from Lehman Commercial Paper, Inc. ("LCPI"). The transaction evidenced by the MRA contemplated that LCPI would repurchase these assets and repay State Street in accordance with the agreement, but LCPI filed for relief under chapter 11 and has defaulted under the MRA. The result is that State Street now owns these assets, including the loan in question made to LH 1440 LLC ("LH 1440") as borrower.

Plaintiff LH 1440 complains that the transfer of this loan to State Street adversely impacted its rights under other contemporaneous loan documentation. In substance, LH 1440 contends that it entered into three integrated loans that were intended to function as a unified financing package for the acquisition and improvement of certain commercial real estate. It claims that its expectations have been frustrated due to the sale of only one of these loans to State Street under the terms of the MRA. The splitting up of the financing and the selection of one loan for inclusion in the pool of loans sold to State Street allegedly has exposed Plaintiff to the risk of a mortgage foreclosure action at a time when it is unable to obtain advances needed to support the project under the remaining loans still held by LCPI. Plaintiff argues that State Street, as purchaser of this pool of assets, should be placed in the shoes of the original lender and be required to advance funds to LH 1440 even though financing documents for these other loans were not included within the pool of assets acquired by State Street. . . .

On June 8, 2007, LH 1440, as borrower, and LBHI, as lender, entered into real estate financing arrangements documented by means of two separate loan

---

10. Recall the discussion of "repo" agreements in Chapter 1 with regard to Lehman's "Repo 105" transactions. — AUTHOR

agreements, the Acquisition and Project Loan Agreement and the Building Loan Agreement. In addition, the parties executed a Consolidated, Amended and Restated Acquisition Loan Mortgage and Security Agreement, and an Option Agreement referencing three loans: 1) the Acquisition Loan of $15,649,568.31; 2) the Project Loan of $6,232,323.69; and 3) the Building Loan of $4,875,819.00. The loans were secured by three separate promissory notes. A single Participation Fee of 28.5% and a single Interest Rate Cap of $26,757,711.00 applied to the loans.

The Acquisition Loan was used to acquire certain real property located at 1440 Story Avenue in the Bronx, New York. The Project and Building Loans have been used to maintain and improve the acquired property and to fund interest payments on the Acquisition Loan. The Acquisition Loan is fully funded, and the Project and Building Loans have future funding obligations. Thus, the holder of the Acquisition Loan is under no direct obligation to advance funds to LH 1440. At some point, LCPI acquired the above referenced loans from LBHI.

On May 1, 2007, State Street entered into the MRA with LCPI, and as evidenced by a July 2007 confirmation letter, purchased a pool of commercial loans for $1 billion. Pursuant to the MRA, LCPI was entitled to substitute loans, as long as the value of those assets, in the aggregate, exceeded $1 billion. On September 17, 2008, State Street gave LCPI a notice of default under the MRA. When LCPI failed to repurchase the loans, State Street took possession of the mortgages and promissory notes for those assets. At that time, the promissory note for the Acquisition Loan was one of thirty-six commercial loans within the pool of assets held by State Street, but the promissory notes for the Project Loan and the Building Loan were not included among those assets.

On March 31, 2009, LH 1440 filed this adversary proceeding to obtain a declaratory judgment that the loan agreements together constitute an integrated loan to LH 1440 and that State Street necessarily acquired the Acquisition Loan, Project Loan, and Building Loan when it exercised its rights as counterparty under the MRA and took possession of the commercial loans described in the MRA. Thereafter, on May 1, 2009, State Street filed the Motion based on the failure to state a claim upon which relief may be granted. LBHI and LCPI have joined in the Motion. Following oral argument, the Court reserved judgment. . . .

The Court concludes that it would be inconsistent with customary market practices to expect the counterparty in a repo transaction to conduct a time consuming investigation regarding the assets that are included in the transaction. This is particularly true in consideration of the fact that other assets often can be substituted, and the focus of the transaction is on the aggregate value of the assets, rather than the specific assets within the pool. LH 1440 has not alleged that State Street as repo counterparty had any reason to know about or a duty to discover the alleged connection between the Acquisition Loan Note and other instruments executed by LH 1440 and LBHI. The complaint as to State Street seeks a remedy from a party that owes no duty to LH 1440 and fails to state a claim that rises above the speculative level. For that reason, the Motion is granted as to State Street, but LH 1440 shall be granted the opportunity to reformulate its allegations in an amended complaint.

The Motion is denied as to LBHI and LCPI. While the transfer provisions and the splitting clause establish that the loans were separately transferable, the underlying documents indicate that the transaction appears to have been intended to function as an interrelated loan. The loans were to be used in tandem; the Acquisition Loan, now fully funded, provided funds to purchase the property, while the Project and Building Loans, with ongoing funding obligations, would allow the borrower to maintain and improve the acquired property. The single Participation Fee and the single Interest Rate Cap Agreement also may be indicative of a single loan transaction . . .

Even in late 2012, long after Lehman's bankruptcy filing in 2008, the company continued to hold more than $3 billion in loans it had made to other corporations.

PROBLEM SET 9.3

1. The text suggests that the recent failures of financial institutions might change attitudes toward companies that finance expansion with retained earnings. How so?
2. Why would a shareholder object to a corporation that kept a large cash balance in its bank account (or money market fund)?
3. In 1968 the Pennsylvania Railroad and the New York Central Railroad merged to form the PennCentral Railroad. Two years later, PennCentral unexpectedly filed what was then the largest corporate bankruptcy case in American history. PennCentral had financed its operations with more than $70 million in money market paper, and the default had the effect of dislocating the money markets in the United States for several weeks. Investors lost confidence in other corporate issuers and stopped refinancing maturing commercial paper. Within three weeks of PennCentral's bankruptcy, the amount of corporate commercial paper outstanding had dropped almost 10 percent. As a result, most large corporations began to keep lines of credit with large banks as a "backup" in case such an event happened again. Does the case above suggest the limitations to that strategy?

4. CONGLOMERATES

The diversified corporation or conglomerate, was the way big business was done until the 1980s. There were several reasons for this:

The diversified corporation became the dominant form of industrial firm in the United States over the course of the twentieth century. During the 1920s, DuPont and General Motors pioneered the use of the multi-divisional form (or M-form) to produce and market a number of related products through separate divisions, and this organizational structure subsequently spread (Chandler 1962). The M-form also allowed easy integration of acquired businesses, which enabled firms to grow through acquisition. Following the enactment of the Celler-Kefauver Act in 1950, horizontal and vertical acquisitions (buying competitors, buyers, or suppliers) fell out of regulatory favor, and firms seeking to grow through acquisition were forced to diversify into other industries. This fueled the conglomerate mergers of the late 1960s and 1970s (Fligstein 1991). The strategy of growth through acquiring firms in unrelated lines of business and structuring them as a collection of separate business units reflected an under-lying model of appropriate corporate practice-the "firm-as-portfolio" model. By 1980, the triumph of the firm-as-portfolio model seemed complete, as growth through diversification was perhaps the most widely used corporate strategy among large firms (Porter 1987), and fewer than 25 percent of the *Fortune* 500 largest industrial corporations made all their sales within a single broadly-defined (2-digit SIC) industry.[11]

In short, antitrust law discouraged buying firms within a related industry, so managers began buying unrelated firms. The prototypical example was ITT, which began life as International Telephone & Telegraph in 1920, but ended up owning the Sheraton Hotel chain, the ITT Technical Institutes of afternoon TV fame, a major insurance company, the maker of Wonder Bread, and the Avis rental car company. All while becoming heavily involved in South American politics along with the CIA.[12]

The key justification for this hodge-podge of companies was diversification.[13] When one part of the firm was in the dumps, another would be doing well and overall the arrangement would provide for slow and steady corporate profits.

Today it seems incredible that managers would be allowed to assemble what amounts to a mutual fund, when they were typically paid based on the size of the company they managed. But it is important to remember that in the 1960s and early 1970s mutual funds were expensive, and brokerage fees were high. That is, it was not cheap or easy to assemble a diversified portfolio, despite what finance theory at the time suggested.

By the 1980s neither of these two factors were at play, as brokerage fees had become deregulated, and mutual funds were going mainstream. In short, the notion that investors needed managers to achieve diversification — which conflicted with much of modern finance theory, and represented a rather extreme attempt to finance projects "internally" — largely came to an end.

The key exception is in the financial industry, where even after the recent financial crisis conglomerates control increasingly large parts of finance.[14] Widely admired companies like General Electric and United Technologies Corporation, and international firms like Unilever and Siemens, also suggest that the conglomerate is not completely gone.

---

11. Gerald F. Davis, et al., *The Decline and Fall of the Conglomerate Firm in the 1980s: The Deinstitutionalization of an Organizational Form*, 59 American Sociological Rev. 547 (1994).

12. *http://foia.state.gov/reports/churchreport.asp*

13. Richard A. Booth, *Five Decades of Corporation Law: From Conglomeration to Equity Compensation*, 53 Vill. L. Rev. 459, 464 (2008).

14. Arthur E. Wilmarth, Jr., *The Dark Side of Universal Banking: Financial Conglomerates and the Origins of the Subprime Financial Crisis*, 41 Conn. L. Rev. 963 (2009).

But were the conglomerates justified by their times? Even that is a bit unclear. For example, one author found

> [N]o evidence that diversified firms are valued more than single segment firms in the 1960s and early 1970s; on the contrary, for several years diversified firms sell at a substantial discount when compared to single segments firms. This discount is large and significant over the 1961-1970 period, but it becomes small and insignificant in 1973-1976. These results hold after controlling for industry effects and for differences between diversified and undiversified firms in profitability, leverage, and investment policy. The largest increase in diversification takes place over the 1970-1976 period when the penalty imposed by capital markets is small. Thus, the firms that diversified at that time did not impose a cost on their shareholders.[15]

In short, originally the conglomerates did seem to impose a cost on shareholders — the parts were worth more than the whole — but eventually the harm seems to have gone away. Why is unclear.

PROBLEM SET 9.4

1. GE and United Technologies shares do not tend to exhibit the conglomerate discounts referred to in the article. Why might that be? Does it suggest the anti-conglomerate wave of the 1980s and 1990s was overdone?
2. During the 1960s it was thought that conglomerates added value, by providing shareholders with a diversified return that reduced overall risk. More recently, it has been suggested that "spinoffs," which involve the separation of large corporations into smaller, more coherent parts, might create real value for shareholders. Is either view consistent with the M&M propositions?

15. Henri Servaes, *The Value of Diversification During the Conglomerate Merger Wave*, 51 J. Fin. 1201, 1203 (1996).

10

SOME REAL-WORLD CONSIDERATIONS (PART 2)

In Chapter 9 we examined some of the reasons why the M&M propositions, and some other related elements of finance theory, do not hold in the real world. For example, if a company favors "internal" financing instead of paying dividends and financing in the market, this violates M&M dividend irrelevance. But it could also be seen as a violation of the ECMH, to the extent the firm makes this choice because it believes that the market will not appreciate the value of its new project.

Our focus in Chapter 9 was largely on issues affecting the firm's equity. Now we turn to debt, and the issues that influence the firm's use of debt despite the M&M propositions.

1. DEBT AND TAXES

Although the choice between debt and equity does not matter in the M&M world, in a world with a tax code, the choice matters very much.

KATHERINE PRATT, *THE DEBT-EQUITY DISTINCTION IN A SECOND-BEST WORLD*
53 Vand. L. Rev. 1055, 1059-1065 (2000)

Our federal income tax system treats corporations as taxpaying entities.[1] Each year, a corporation must pay tax on its income for the year. The tax is on net

---

1. I.R.C. §11 imposes tax on "C" corporations. *See* I.R.C. §11 (1994). For purposes of this Article, assume that the corporation is a "C" corporation, which is any corporation that has not elected to be treated as an "S" corporation. C corporations and S corporations are named for the subchapters of the

income, not gross income, so corporations can deduct the costs of earning their income.

Corporations finance their operations by raising debt and equity capital. A corporation, acting as a borrower, can issue debt (e.g., bonds) to debtholders, the creditors, in exchange for cash or other property. The corporation can also issue stock to shareholders in exchange for cash or other property.[2] As compensation for the use of the debtholders' money, the corporation pays the debtholders interest.[3] As compensation for the use of the shareholders' money, the corporation pays the shareholders distributions in the form of dividends.

Although, for reasons discussed later, the Internal Revenue Code (the "Code") should treat debt and equity similarly for tax purposes, the Code has always distinguished between debt and equity. There are numerous tax differences between debt and equity. Some of these differences relate to the tax consequences to the corporate issuer of the debt or equity.[4]

Code that apply to those types of corporations. A corporation can be an S corporation only if it has 75 or fewer shareholders, no foreign or entity shareholders, and only one class of stock. *See id.* §1361(b)(1) (1994) (amended 1998). S Corporations are not taxpaying entities; instead S Corporation income and other tax items pass through to the shareholders and each shareholder reports her allocable share of those items on her individual tax return. *See id.* §1366 (1994) (amended 1996).

2. The stock proceeds the corporate issuer receives from the shareholder are not included in the corporation's income. *See* I.R.C. §1032(a) (1994).

3. The corporate borrower also eventually returns to the bondholders the amount they loaned the corporation. Interest paid on the bond includes a pure time value of money element (with an inflation component) and compensation for the risk that the issuer will default.

4. For example, the tax consequences of a corporation retiring its stock or debt differ. A corporation does not have income when it receives cash or other property in exchange for its stock. *See* I.R.C. §1032(a) (1994). If the corporation later repurchases the stock for an amount of cash less than the amount for which the stock was issued, the corporation recognizes no income. See I.R.C. §311(a) (1994). Section 1032(a), which insulates the corporate issuer from gain on the issuance of stock in exchange from property, does not technically apply to the issuer's repurchase of the stock. *See id.* §1032(a) (1994). Treasury Regulations provide that §1032 does not apply to a corporation's acquisition of its own shares unless the corporation acquires the shares in exchange for its own stock (although the regulation cross references the §311 regulations). *See* Treas. Reg. §1.1032-1(b). Section 311(a) provides that a corporation does not recognize gain on the distribution of property with respect to its stock. *See* I.R.C §311(a) (1994). Property includes cash under I.R.C. §317(a). *See id.* §317 (a) (1994); *see also* Bittker & Eustice, *supra*, at 4-71 (6th ed. 1998) ("Upon redeeming or repurchasing its own stock, a corporation recognizes no gain, even if the amount paid is less than the stock's par or stated value or the amount received when it was issued; any corporate level gain on the transaction is instead treated as a tax-free capital contribution under I.R.C. §118(a), as a distribution covered by I.R.C. §311(a)(2), or simply as a nontaxable capital adjustment.") (footnote omitted).

A corporation does not have to include proceeds from the issuance of debt in income. If a corporation retires debt for less than the amount owed on the debt, however, the corporation must generally include in income the difference between the amount owed on the debt and the amount paid to discharge the debt. *See* I.R.C. §61(a)(12) (1994); United States v. Kirby Lumber Co., 284 U.S. 1, 3 (1931). If the debt discharge occurs in a bankruptcy proceeding, I.R.C. §108(a)(1)(A) permits the corporation to exclude the debt discharge income completely. *See* I.R.C. §108(a)(1)(A) (1994). If the debt discharge does not occur in a bankruptcy proceeding, I.R.C. §108(a)(1)(B) and (3), and (d)(3) permit the corporation to exclude the debt discharge income to the extent of the corporation's insolvency (the corporation's liabilities less assets) prior to the discharge. *See id.* §§108(a)(1)(B), (a)(3), (d)(3) (1994). Section 108(a) often just defers the tax on debt discharge income because debt discharge income excluded under I.R.C. §108(a) reduces the corporation's net operating losses. *See id.* §108(b)(2)(A) (1994). A net operating loss for one tax year can be used to reduce the corporate taxpayer's tax liability for other profitable years. Net operating losses can be carried back two years and forward 20 years. *See id.* §172(b) (1994). If the corporation that has excluded debt discharge income later begins earning income again, the §108(b) reduction in its net operating losses will increase its tax liability because the net operating losses would otherwise have reduced the corporation's income.

Some relate to the tax consequences to the holder of the debt or equity.[5]

This Article will focus on the most important difference between debt and equity at the level of the corporate issuer: a corporation can deduct interest paid or accrued on the debt it issues but cannot deduct the dividends it pays on the shares it issues.[6] It will also consider investor level character and timing differences between debt and equity because these differences affect the amount of debt and equity in corporate capital structures.

First consider the character differences. Debtholders pay tax at ordinary income tax rates on interest paid or accrued on the corporate debt they own . . . If a corporation retains earnings, instead of distributing them as dividends, the value of the assets of the corporation will increase, which will in turn increase the value of the stock of the corporation held by its shareholders. If a shareholder sells stock that has appreciated, the shareholder will realize gain equal to the amount for which the stock was sold less the amount the shareholder paid for the stock. (The gain from the sale of the stock [and now dividends are] usually taxed at preferential capital gains rates.) In summary, shareholders typically pay tax on undistributed corporate earnings when they sell their stock.

Second, consider the timing differences between the investor level tax consequences of stock and debt. Shareholders typically include dividends when they receive the dividends and include gain from the sale of stock when they sell the stock. In other words, corporate earnings are not typically taxed at the shareholder level until the corporation pays a dividend or the shareholder sells appreciated stock. Stock is therefore taxed using what is sometimes called a "wait-and-see" method.

Debtholders include (and the issuer deducts) interest as it is paid or as it accrues. Interest on corporate debt may be stated interest or unstated interest. If all of the interest is stated, the debtholders include the interest and the issuer deducts the interest as it is paid. If the debt instrument bears unstated interest, which the Code refers to as original issue discount ("OID"), the debtholder includes the OID and the issuer deducts the OID as it accrues. In other words, the bondholder's interest inclusion and corporate issuer's interest deduction may precede the payment of that interest . . .

To summarize, the corporate earnings distributed or allocable to the debtholders as interest are taxed once at the debtholder level because the corporate issuer deducts the interest and the bondholder includes the interest. On the

---

5. Stock and debt instruments are generally "capital assets," so that gain from the sale of such securities qualifies for preferential capital gain rates and loss from the sale of such securities is subject to special loss limitation rules. *See* I.R.C. §§1(h) (amended 1997), 1201 amended 1997), 1211, 1221, 1222 (1994); Van Suetendael v. Commissioner, 13 T.C.M. 1071, 1075-76 (T.C. 1944), aff'd, 152 F.2d 654 (2d Cir. 1945) (holding that sale by an individual who traded securities generated capital gain, not ordinary income).

Special rules may apply, however, that distinguish between stock and debt instruments in certain circumstances. For example, I.R.C. §306, which recharacterizes all or a part of the capital gain from the sale of preferred stock as ordinary income, does not apply to debt instruments. *See* I.R.C. §306(a)(1) (1994).

6. *See* I.R.C. §163(a) (1994) (amended 1998).

other hand, corporate earnings distributed to shareholders as dividends are taxed twice, first at the corporate level (since the corporation cannot deduct the dividends paid to shareholders) and second at the shareholder level when the dividends are paid. The corporate earnings that are not distributed are also taxed twice, first at the corporate level, and second at the shareholder level when the shareholder sells the stock, which has appreciated to reflect the earnings retained by the corporation.

From the firm's perspective, the deductibility of interest payments makes debt more attractive than equity. The value of the extra benefit of debt is equal to the corporation's tax rate multiplied by the amount of interest it pays in any year. For example, if Bogartco pays $1,000 per year in interest on its debt, and has a tax rate of 30 percent, the benefit of using debt would be $300 per year. Over a period of several years, we can assume the value of the tax deduction is either a perpetuity or an annuity and value accordingly.

This extra value to debt that results from corporate tax law is referred to as the "tax shield." In the preceding example, Bogartco can "protect" up to $1,000 of corporate income from taxation because of the deductibility of its interest payments.

M&M recognized the effect of taxes and revised their propositions to take taxes into account. First, recall the M&M Proposition I original provided that firm value does not change with changes in the capital structure ($V_L = V_U$). In the revised M&M world with taxes, Proposition I now holds that firm value increases with leverage (i.e., the use of debt). Mathematically, we would write this new Proposition I as

$$V_L = V_U + T_C B$$

The initial terms are the old Proposition I, but now the value of the "leveraged" firm is the value of the unleveraged firm plus the value of the tax shield.

Similarly, M&M modified their Proposition II to account for taxes. Remember that originally this proposition had described efforts to "slice up" the capital structure as a zero-sum game: Increased use of debt simply resulted in higher costs of equity. But when we add in taxes, the new Proposition II instead holds that some of the increase in equity risk and return is offset by the interest tax shield.

PROBLEM SET 10.1

1. What might be the policy justification for allowing corporations to deduct interest payments but not dividend payments?
2. You own all the equity in a company. The company has no debt. The company's annual cash flow is $1,000, before interest and taxes. The corporate tax rate is 40 percent. You have the option to exchange half of your equity position for $1,000 in 10 percent debt. Should you do this and why?

2. THE EFFECTS OF LEVERAGE

Online,[7] you can find a chart that compares the return of two exchange traded funds (ETFs).[8] One (SPY[9]) tracks the S&P 500 index and the other (UPRO[10]) aims to provide three times the return of the index. How could the second fund do that?

If your answer is "by buying three times as many stocks" take a moment and think about that. If the S&P 500 returns 10 percent, do I get a three times greater return by investing $300 instead of $100? Nope. I still get a 10 percent return, it's just on a bigger amount now.

The ProShares UltraPro S&P 500 Fund's (UPRO) disclosures give us some indication of how it achieves its returns:

> The fund invests in equity securities and derivatives that [the fund manager] believes, in combination, should have similar daily return characteristics as three times (3x) the daily return of the index.

Derivatives, which we cover in a later chapter, are one way of achieving leverage. But the more traditional way of achieving leverage is by using debt. A home mortgage loan is a common example of the use of leverage. If you have $100,000 to spend on a house, without leverage that is the maximum value of the house you can buy. But if a bank will lend you 80 percent of the purchase price of a house, you can buy a $500,000 house. That means you have five times as much exposure to the local real estate market.

In good times, the use of the loan benefits you tremendously. For example, if home prices double you would now have a $100,000 gain if you had bought your house with cash ($100,000 $\times$ 2). But with the loan, you have a $500,000 gain — your house is worth $1 million, less the $400,000 you owe to the bank and your $100,000 investment. With the same initial investment, you have obtained a 500 percent return as opposed to a 100 percent return if you used only cash.

But, leverage also works the other way around too. If home prices decline, cutting values in half, your cash-purchased home is worth $50,000 and you have a $50,000 loss. But your finer home, purchased with the help of the bank, is now worth $250,000. Your initial investment is gone and you owe the bank $150,000 beyond the value of the home. In the vernacular, you are "underwater" by $150,000. The lesson is that leverage magnifies returns–in both directions.

It works with corporations, too. And given the tax benefits already described, it provides a strong temptation for managers to use at least some leverage to amplify their returns. After all, shareholders are diversified (or they should be)

---

7. *http://goo.gl/PKE0G*

8. An ETF is a mutual fund that trades throughout the day like a stock. A mutual fund is a fund that investors buy to get exposure to a portfolio of securities. For example, if you have $1,000 to invest, it would be hard to obtain a diversified portfolio by buying individual stocks. But if you bought shares in a mutual fund that itself owned a diversified portfolio, you get the benefits of diversification. Of course, it is more costly to buy shares through a mutual fund (the manager gets paid) than to buy them directly.

9. *http://goo.gl/ScL33*

10. *http://goo.gl/WCHIz*

and limited liability means that at most shareholders will lose their investment (unlike the mortgage example, involving an individual borrower).

On the eve of the financial crisis, Merrill Lynch led all financial institutions with a leverage ratio of 40 to 1.

PROBLEM SET 10.2

1. Consider the following table. If it had been around, how much would the ProShares UltraPro S&P 500 fund (UPRO) have returned in the two best and worst years for the index?

	S&P 500 Annual Returns		
Year Ending	*Price Close*	*Price Change*	*Change*
12/30/11	1257.60	−0.03	−0.0025%
12/31/10	1257.64	142.53	12.78%
12/31/09	1115.10	211.85	23.45%
12/31/08	903.25	−565.10	−38.49%
12/31/07	1468.36	50.05	3.53%
12/29/06	1418.30	170.01	13.62%
12/31/05	1248.29	36.37	3.00%
12/31/04	1211.92	100.00	8.99%
12/31/03	1111.92	232.10	26.38%
12/31/02	879.82	−268.26	−23.37%
12/31/01	1148.08	−172.20	−13.04%
12/29/00	1320.28	−148.97	−10.14%
12/31/99	1469.25	240.02	19.53%
12/31/98	1229.23	258.80	26.67%
12/31/97	970.43	229.69	31.01%
12/31/96	740.74	124.81	20.26%
12/29/95	615.93	156.66	34.11%
12/30/94	459.27	−7.18	−1.54%
12/31/93	466.45	30.74	7.06%
12/31/92	435.71	18.62	4.46%
12/31/91	417.09	86.87	26.31%
12/31/90	330.22	−23.18	−6.56%
12/29/89	353.40	75.68	27.25%
12/30/88	277.72	277.72	12.40%

2. Why might managers decline to use as much leverage as shareholders might like? Alternatively, recall the Bratton article in Chapter 9 and the discussion of manager compensation. Why might managers decide to use lots of leverage?
3. What are the systematic risks that might occur for the use of high levels of leverage?

3.   THE COSTS OF DEBT

Recall that one of the M&M assumptions was that debt was essentially risk free. In the real world, of course, corporate debt is not risk free. American Airlines (and every other major U.S. airline), Lehman Brothers, Kodak, Blockbuster Video, Border's Books, and the Los Angeles Dodgers all remind us that sometimes corporations do not pay their debts.

STEPHEN J. LUBBEN, *WHAT WE "KNOW" ABOUT CHAPTER 11 COST IS WRONG*
17 FORDHAM J. CORP. & FIN. L. 141, 147-167 (2012)

The costs of corporate reorganization are compelling in any recession, and particularly so in a financial crisis, such as the one we are currently experiencing. To the casual reader of the *Wall Street Journal* who still thinks of bankruptcy as the equivalent to corporate death, the millions of dollars paid by "bankrupt" or "insolvent" firms like Lehman Brothers, or Enron before it, often seems quite extreme.

A similar phenomenon can be seen in academic literature, dating back to Modigliani and Miller in 1958, and the notion that a firm's capital structure amounts to little more than slices in a pie. In this world, debtor-firms are typically discussed relative to a backdrop of complete contracts and zero transaction costs. Accordingly, firms that encounter financial distress — that is, having liquid assets insufficient to meet current fixed claims — simply renegotiate their obligations and proceed accordingly. Slight deviations from the background assumptions can be assumed and then addressed by neatly automated contractual responses. That Kmart, a large discount store chain, would pay more than $134 million to professionals to do so is inconsistent with this idealized understanding of the world, and thus each dollar spent is evidence of inefficiency.

Of course, both views of "bankruptcy" are based on basic misunderstanding or oversimplification. Both assume that financial distress is costless, whereas even liquidation does not happen by itself. Indeed, only abandonment of a distressed firm might be costless — if we limit our conception of cost to actual "out of pocket" expenditures by the debtor-firm. More broadly, understanding the cost of a corporate reorganization system is important because debtor-firms face the reality of a world with incomplete contracts, incomplete information, uncertain asset values, and complex capital structures that highlight the many ways in which assumptions about capital structure irrelevance or managerial rationality, or both, fail. Given these truths, and the added reality of asset market disruptions, it is generally thought that reorganization structures are important tools to avoid excessive and economically disruptive liquidation of assets. If given a choice of possible approaches to reorganization, the cost of any particular system, weighed against its benefits, provides an obvious metric for evaluation. . . .

[My] dataset is non-random, comprising all 2004 bankruptcy cases listed in the "Major Bankruptcies" database on www.bankruptcydata.com (published by New Generation Research, Inc.) except for cases initially filed under chapter 7 and not converted to chapter 11 and cases filed under former section 304 of the Bankruptcy Code.[11]

. . . In a chapter 11 case, all professionals that are to be paid with estate funds are required to have their retention approved at the start of the case.[12] And the bulk of those professionals are also required to have their fees and expenses approved by the bankruptcy court before being paid from the estate.[13] In short, there is both *ex ante* and *ex post* oversight of most professionals by the bankruptcy court.

The debtor's bankruptcy estate is responsible for paying for all professionals it retained in the case. In addition, the estate is responsible for paying the expenses of any professionals retained by official — that is, court appointed — committees in the case.[14] Finally, the estate is also responsible for paying any court appointed "neutrals," and their professionals, including trustees and examiners. All of these expenses count as costs of administration of the estate, and are thus entitled to priority payment.[15] . . .

Throughout the literature, it has become common to report fees as a percentage of debtor size. The advantage of such a measure is obvious — namely it provides an easy "rule of thumb" for considering whether a particular case is above or below the average cost. But as Professor LoPucki has noted, the relationship between debtor size and cost is highly sensitive to the size of the cases under study, meaning that use of such "rules of thumb" will often result in substantial errors.

This same effect is evident in the present study, where the average cost of the smallest quartile of cases is 10% of size,[16] while in the largest cases cost is 2% of size. Based on the ratios of cost to size shown on Table 7B, it appears that there are substantial economies of scale to chapter 11 cases, a relationship that is also examined in Figure 7A.[17] The relationship between size and standardized cost demonstrates a strong downward trend, further suggesting that there may be significant fixed costs to chapter 11, and thus a declining cost for the largest of debtors.

---

11. Section 304 was repealed in 2005 as part of the enactment of new chapter 15. Both section 304 and new chapter 15 deal with the recognition of foreign bankruptcy proceedings in the United States. *See* Jay Lawrence Westbrook *Chapter 15 at Last*, 79 Am. Bankr. L. J. 713 (2005).

12. 11 U.S.C. §327(a).

13. *See* 11 U.S.C. §§327, 330, 331.

14. 11 U.S.C. §§1103; 330

15. 11 U.S.C. §§507(a)(2); 503(b)(2).

16. Defined as the average of assets and debts . . .

17. The outlier at the top of the graph represents the chapter 11 case of Mid-State Raceway, Inc., the owner of a horse-racing track and affiliated hotel in northern New York State. In re Mid-State Raceway, Inc., 04-65746, 2006 BL 27793 (Bankr. N.D.N.Y. Feb. 10, 2006) (opinion confirming chapter 11 plan). It is unclear from reviewing the case file why the case appears so relatively expensive, although gambling is heavily regulated in the United States and it could be that this extra regulation resulted in additional cost.

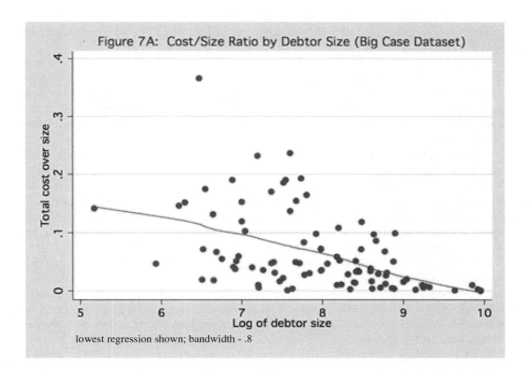

Figure 7A: Cost/Size Ratio by Debtor Size (Big Case Dataset)

lowest regression shown; bandwidth - .8

TABLE 7B
Standardized Chapter 11 Cost by Size Quartiles (Big Case Dataset)

	Mean	Std. Err.	[95% Conf.	Interval]
Total cost over size				
1 (smallest)	0.101	0.017	0.067	0.135
2	0.089	0.015	0.059	0.119
3	0.042	0.006	0.029	0.055
4	0.021	0.006	0.010	0.033
Mean debtor size (USD)				
1	7,080,907.00	981,618.40	5,131,608.00	9,030,207.00
2	44,700,000.00	4,120,754.00	36,500,000.00	52,900,000.00
3	242,000,000.00	21,800,000.00	198,000,000.00	285,000,000.00
4	2,410,000,000.00	609,000,000.00	1,200,000,000.00	3,620,000,000.00
n = 94				

The costs of corporate bankruptcy or reorganization are often considered to encompass two concepts. First, there are the direct costs, made up chiefly of the professional fees associated with reorganization, but also including other lesser costs like court filing fees and, in the United States, quarterly fees due to the U.S. Trustee's office.[18] The excerpt examines these costs.

In addition, there are also indirect costs of a firm's bankruptcy, which are more abstract but include things like lost revenues, lost opportunities, and lost goodwill. Some of these costs might be of concern to the firm's stakeholders, but not to policymakers if, for example, financial distress simply results in the shifting of sales from the distressed firm to a competitor firm — unless the competitor is abroad.

Although there have been some efforts to study indirect costs empirically, and one recent study suggests that the total expected cost of financial distress might be as high as 4.5 percent of the firm's predistress assets,[19] more often efforts to examine these costs have been theoretical, particularly in the legal literature.[20] In addition, studies of indirect costs have been limited to publicly held companies, and it is unknown if the results found in that context will translate to privately held firms, which make up the vast majority of debtors.

In addition, there might be "agency costs" associated with the use of debt. For example, managers and shareholders might collude to take extra risks, knowing that limited liability will protect them from the downside, while all the upside will result in extra return for them. Creditors suffer when this happens, and in Chapters 14 and 15 of this text we will talk about how creditors protect themselves against these costs.

The more debt a firm has, the greater the probability that they will encounter financial distress, and thus, the greater the probability that the firm will incur the direct and indirect costs associated with financial distress. Whereas taxes suggest a firm should use as much debt as it managers and shareholders can stand, the risk of bankruptcy pushes in the other direction, particularly if creditors are able to pass on the projected costs of bankruptcy to the borrower in the form of higher interest rates.

PROBLEM SET 10.3

1. How might you integrate taxes and financial distress costs into an overall theory of firm value?
2. How could it be that chapter 11 is efficient if it costs millions of dollars to complete a case?
3. If the taxation of debt and equity were equalized, how might bankruptcy costs affect the use of debt?

---

18. The U.S. Trustee Program is a component of the Department of Justice that monitors bankruptcy cases for fraud and the like. It is distinct from the bankruptcy trustee appointed in all chapter 7 and some chapter 11 cases.

19. Heitor Almeida & Tomas Philippon, *The Risk-Adjusted Cost of Financial Distress*, 62 J. Fin. 2557 (2007).

20. Barry E. Adler, *Bankruptcy and Risk Allocation*, 77 Cornell L. Rev. 439 (1992); James J. White, *Harvey's Silence*, 69 Am. Bankr. L.J. 467 (1995).

11

VALUING A FIRM

CONSOLIDATED ROCK PRODUCTS CO. ET AL. V. DU BOIS

312 U.S. 510 Supreme Court of the United States
Argued Feb. 13, 14, 1941 | Decided March 3, 1941

Mr. Justice Douglas delivered the opinion of the Court.

This case involves questions as to the fairness under §77B of the Bankruptcy Act [a predecessor to today's chapter 11], of a plan of reorganization for a parent corporation (Consolidated Rock Products Co.) and its two wholly owned subsidiaries — Union Rock Co. and Consumers Rock and Gravel Co., Inc. The District Court confirmed the plan; the Circuit Court of Appeals reversed. We granted the petitions for certiorari because of the importance in the administration of the reorganization provisions of the Act of certain principles enunciated by the Circuit Court of Appeals.

The stock of Union and Consumers is held by Consolidated. Union has outstanding in the hands of the public $1,877,000 of 6% bonds secured by an indenture on its property, with accrued and unpaid interest thereon of $403,555 — a total mortgage indebtedness of $2,280,555. Consumers has outstanding in the hands of the public $1,137,000 of 6% bonds secured by an indenture on its property, with accrued and unpaid interest thereon of $221,715 — a total mortgage indebtedness of $1,358,715. Consolidated has outstanding 285,947 shares of no par value preferred stock and 397,455 shares of no par common stock.

The plan of reorganization calls for the formation of a new corporation to which will be transferred all of the assets of Consolidated, Union, and Consumers free of all claims.[1] The securities of the new corporation are to be distributed as follows:

Union and Consumers bonds held by the public will be exchanged for income bonds and preferred stock of the new company. For 50 per cent of the principal amounts of their claims, those bondholders will receive income bonds secured by a mortgage on all of the property of the new company; for the balance they will receive an equal amount of par value preferred stock.

---

1. The claims of general creditors will be paid in full or assumed by the new company.

Their claims to accrued interest are to be extinguished, no new securities being issued therefor. Thus Union bondholders for their claims of $2,280,555 will receive income bonds and preferred stock in the face amount of $1,877,000; Consumers bondholders for their claims of $1,358,715 will receive income bonds and preferred stock in the face amount of $1,137,000. Each share of new preferred stock will have a warrant for the purchase of two shares of new $2 par value common stock at prices ranging from $2 per share within six months of issuance, to $6 per share during the fifth year after issuance.

Preferred stockholders of Consolidated will receive one share of new common stock ($2 par value) for each share of old preferred or an aggregate of 285,947 shares of new common.

A warrant to purchase one share of new common for $1 within three months of issuance will be given to the common stockholders of Consolidated for each five shares of old common.

The bonds of Union and Consumers held by Consolidated, the stock of those companies held by Consolidated, and the intercompany claims (discussed hereafter) will be cancelled.

In 1929 when Consolidated acquired control of these various properties, they were appraised in excess of $16,000,000 and it was estimated that their annual net earnings would be $500,000. In 1931 they were appraised by officers at about $4,400,000, "exclusive of going concern, good will and current assets." The District Court did not find specific values for the separate properties of Consolidated, Union, or Consumers, or for the properties of the enterprise as a unit. The average of the valuations (apparently based on physical factors) given by three witnesses at the hearing before the master were $2,202,733 for Union as against a mortgage indebtedness of $2,280,555; $1,151,033 for Consumers as against a mortgage indebtedness of $1,358,715. Relying on similar testimony, Consolidated argues that the value of its property, to be contributed to the new company, is over $1,359,000, or exclusive of an alleged good will of $500,000, $859,784. These estimated values somewhat conflict with the consolidated balance sheet (as at June 30, 1938) which shows assets of $3,723,738.15 and liabilities (exclusive of capital and surplus) of $4,253,224.41. More important, the earnings record of the enterprise casts grave doubts on the soundness of the estimated values. No dividends were ever paid on Consolidated's common stock; and except for five quarterly dividends in 1929 and 1931, none on its preferred stock. For the eight and a half years from April 1, 1929, to September 30, 1937, Consolidated had a loss of about $1,200,000 before bond interest but after depreciation and depletion. And except for the year 1929, Consolidated had no net operating profit, after bond interest and amortization, depreciation and depletion, in any year down to September 30, 1937. Yet on this record the District Court found that the present fair value of all the assets of the several companies, exclusive of good will and going concern value, was in excess of the total bonded indebtedness, plus accrued and unpaid interest. And it also found that such value, including good will and going concern value, was insufficient to pay the bonded indebtedness plus accrued and unpaid interest and the liquidation preferences and accrued dividends on Consolidated preferred stock. It further found that the present fair value of the assets admittedly subject to the trust indentures of Union and Consumers was insufficient to pay the face amount, plus accrued and unpaid interest of the respective bond issues. In spite of that finding, the District Court also found that "it would be physically impossible to determine and segregate with any degree of accuracy or fairness properties which originally belonged to the companies separately"; that as a result of unified operation properties of every character "have been commingled and are now in the main held by Consolidated without any way of ascertaining what part, if any thereof, belongs to each or any of the companies separately"; and that, as a consequence, an appraisal "would be of such an indefinite and unsatisfactory nature as to produce further confusion."

We agree with the Circuit Court of Appeals that it was error to confirm this plan of reorganization.

On this record no determination of the fairness of any plan of reorganization could be made. Absent the requisite valuation data, the court was in no position to exercise the "informed, independent judgment" (National Surety Co. v. Coriell, 289 U.S. 426, 436, 53 S.Ct. 678, 681, 682, 77 L.Ed. 1300, 88 A.L.R. 1231) which appraisal of the fairness of a plan of reorganization entails. Case v. Los Angeles Lumber Products Co., 308 U.S. 106, 60 S.Ct. 1, 84 L.Ed. 110. And see First National Bank v. Flershem, 290 U.S. 504, 525, 54 S.Ct. 298, 306, 78 L.Ed. 465, 90 A.L.R. 391. There are two aspects of that valuation problem.

In the first place, there must be a determination of what assets are subject to the payment of the respective claims. This obvious requirement was not met . . .

In the second place, there is the question of the method of valuation. From this record it is apparent that little, if any, effort was made to value the whole enterprise by a capitalization of prospective earnings. The necessity for such an inquiry is emphasized by the poor earnings record of this enterprise in the past. Findings as to the earning capacity of an enterprise are essential to a determination of the feasibility as well as the fairness of a plan of reorganization. Whether or not the earnings may reasonably be expected to meet the interest and dividend requirements of the new securities is a sine qua non to a determination of the integrity and practicability of the new capital structure. It is also essential for satisfaction of the absolute priority rule of Case v. Los Angeles Lumber Products Co., supra. Unless meticulous regard for earning capacity be had, indefensible participation of junior securities in plans of reorganization may result.

As Mr. Justice Holmes said in Galveston, Harrisburg & San Antonio Ry. Co. v. Texas, 210 U.S. 217, 226, 28 S.Ct. 638, 639, 52 L.Ed. 1031, "the commercial value of property consists in the expectation of income from it." Such criterion is the appropriate one here, since we are dealing with the issue of solvency arising in connection with reorganization plans involving productive properties. It is plain that valuations for other purposes are not relevant to or helpful in a determination of that issue, except as they may indirectly bear on earning capacity. The criterion of earning capacity is the essential one if the enterprise is to be freed from the heavy hand of past errors, miscalculations or disaster, and if the allocation of securities among the various claimants is to be fair and equitable. Since its application requires a prediction as to what will occur in the future, an estimate, as distinguished from mathematical certitude, is all that can be made. But that estimate must be based on an informed judgment which embraces all facts relevant to future earning capacity and hence to present worth, including, of course, the nature and condition of the properties, the past earnings record, and all circumstances which indicate whether or not that record is a reliable criterion of future performance. A sum of values based on physical factors and assigned to separate units of the property without regard to the earning capacity of the whole enterprise is plainly inadequate. But hardly more than that was done here.

———————

The case should dispel any notion that the concepts of valuation that we have discussed in prior chapters are a new invention. In this chapter we apply these concepts to value an entire company, as the Supreme Court did in the *Consolidated Rock* case.

1. WACC

In prior classes we have noted that the proper discount rate to use when valuing any project is the opportunity cost. As Justice Douglas notes, a firm can be valued as a project, too. Here the opportunity cost is the firm's own cost of capital. That is, how much return does it have to promise investors to get them to invest?

For an all equity firm, at least one that is publicly traded, you already know how to do this. The capital assets pricing model (CAPM) provides the expected return on shares in such a firm.

But what if the firm has some debt? CAPM still provides the return for the equity, but M&M have already shown us, the cost of equity is influenced by amount of debt outstanding. What we really need to find is the firm's cost of capital, which is the blended rate of its entire capital structure, taking into account both debt and equity.

The conventional technique for obtaining this weighted average is known as the weighted average cost of capital (WACC). The method relies on M&M principles and makes use of CAPM to find the cost of equity, which is then weighted along with the cost of debt. In short

$$WACC = \left[\frac{Equity}{Equity + Debt} \times R_E \right] + \left[\frac{Debt}{Equity + Debt} \times R_D \times (1 - T) \right]$$

The first term in each bracket represents the proportion of the overall capital structure that is equity or debt, respectively. These terms weight the returns paid on equity (R_E) and debt (R_D) by the proportion of each in the capital structure.

The second bracket also includes the term $(1-T)$, which is just one minus the corporation's tax rate. This accounts for the tax-privileged status of debt — namely, the firm does not ultimately pay for the entire cost of debt. For example, if the tax rate is 25 percent, then the firm only pays 75 percent of the cost of its debt, as the remainder offsets taxes that would otherwise be due.

We have already noted that CAPM can be used to find the firm's cost of equity (R_E). What about the cost of debt? Yield to maturity (YTM) of the firm's outstanding debt can provide an estimate of how much it would cost the firm to issue debt today.

The result of this calculation is the rate that should be used to discount any project where one believes that the project's risk is equal to the risk of the firm as a whole (and the project has the same leverage as the firm as a whole), or to value the firm, as described in the next section.

But first, we need some practice on WACC. The problems that follow are best done in a spreadsheet (remember, for example, the Yield function in Excel if you need to find YTM).

PROBLEM SET 11.1

1. Bogartco has 80,000 bonds outstanding. Bonds with similar characteristics are yielding 10.5 percent. The company also has 10 million shares of common stock outstanding. The stock has a beta of 1.1 and sells for $40 a share. The U.S. Treasury bill is yielding 4 percent and the market risk premium is 8 percent. Bogartco's tax rate is 35 percent. What is Bogartco's weighted average cost of capital?

2. Merciful Release, Inc. is considering financing a new band called Doktor Avalanche. Merciful expects to spend about $72 million up front promoting the band and estimates the band will return $13.5 million a year for five years. Merciful has a debt/equity ratio of one. The firm's cost of equity is 13 percent, the cost of debt is 9 percent, and the tax rate is 34 percent. What is the appropriate discount rate? What assumptions about Doktor Avalanche does your calculation entail? Should Merciful undertake the investment in Doktor Avalanche?

2. DCF

Discounted cash flow (DCF) valuation is essentially the valuation referred to by Justice Douglas in the *Consolidated Rock* case. It is the most common valuation method used in many legal settings.[2]

The basic idea is to find the present value of the company's projected earnings. Earnings are projected over a number of years — often five or ten — and then the value of the firm at the end of this income stream is added onto the equation. Typically for this final or terminal value the firm will be valued as a perpetuity, or, more precisely, a growing perpetuity, based on projected earnings at that final time period and some projected growth rate.

In short, DCF valuation involves an annuity (the projected cash flows for five years) plus a perpetuity, which reflects the "terminal value" of the company. The WACC provides the appropriate discount rate for these present value

2. *E.g.*, Bernard Trujillo, *Patterns in a Complex System: An Empirical Study of Valuation in Business Bankruptcy Cases*, 53 UCLA L. Rev. 357, 384 (2005).

calculations. In practice, you will often see DCF combined with some other valuation model.

CEDE & CO., PETITIONER, V. JRC ACQUISITION CORP., L & LR, INC., AND 800-JR CIGAR, INC., RESPONDENTS

29 Del. J. Corp. L. 887
Court of Chancery of Delaware
No. Civ.A. 18648-NC. | Submitted Dec. 5, 2003 | Decided Feb. 10, 2004

CHANDLER, J.

This action, brought under 8 *Del. C.* §262, seeks an appraisal of 652,400 shares of 800-JR Cigar, Inc. ("Respondent," "JR Cigar" or the "Company") held of record by Cede & Co. ("Petitioner" or "Cede") for the benefit of various investment funds. This Opinion determines the fair value of those shares, together with an appropriate rate of interest. For the reasons set forth in greater detail below, I conclude that the fair value of JR Cigar stock as of the merger date is $13.58 per share. The Company must pay Petitioner $8,859,592. In addition, I award Petitioner 4.73% interest on the principal, compounded monthly, from October 4, 2000 to the date of payment.

I. BACKGROUND

A. THE STIPULATED FACTS

On August 29, 2000, pursuant to a merger agreement dated the day before, the Rothman family commenced an offer to purchase all shares of common stock of JR Cigar that they did not already own. The Rothmans, before the offer, owned 78% of the outstanding common shares of JR Cigar. After the offer closed on September 26, 2000, the Rothmans, through an acquisition corporation owned by them, beneficially owned over 90% of the outstanding shares of JR Cigar. Because the Rothmans owned more than 90% of the outstanding shares following the offer, the merger was accomplished pursuant to 8 *Del. C.* §253. The merger became effective on October 4, 2000.

Under the merger agreement, each share of common stock outstanding immediately before the merger was converted into the right to receive $13.00 per share in cash.

The only issue in this case is the fair value of Petitioner's shares, together with the appropriate rate of interest.

B. THE EXPERTS

Cede's expert, Charles DeVinney, has his MBA in Finance, is Vice President of Curtis Financial Group, Inc., an Accredited Senior Appraiser, and a Chartered Financial Analyst. DeVinney is in the business of appraising companies. He used two methods to value JR Cigar. First, he looked at transactions comparable to the acquisition of JR Cigar. Based on these purportedly comparable transactions,

DeVinney found that JR Cigar was worth $16.80 per share as of October 4, 2000, the date the merger became effective. Second, DeVinney performed a discounted cash flow ("DCF") analysis. His DCF analysis resulted in an estimated fair value of $19.80 per share. Placing equal weight on the two valuation methods, DeVinney opined that JR Cigar was worth between $16.80 and $19.80 per share.

JR Cigar's expert, Dr. Gregg Jarrell, is a Professor of Economics and Finance at the University of Rochester's William E. Simon Graduate School of Business. Jarrell holds a Ph.D. in Business Economics and was formerly the Chief Economist for the SEC. He teaches graduate courses in finance, is well-published, and has served as an expert witness in several valuation cases. In rendering his opinion, Jarrell relied principally on a DCF analysis, but he also conducted two market-based analyses to verify his DCF analysis. First, he performed what he referred to as a "market check," which consisted of a determination of whether other reasonably *bona fide* offers were made for JR Cigar. Second, Jarrell conducted an analysis of the control premium in this case as compared to control premiums obtained in over 2,000 other deals during a five-year period. He concluded that the fair value of JR Cigar was $12.67 per share.

[B]oth experts testified at trial. Additionally, both experts prepared a report shortly before trial summarizing their valuation work. Those reports, along with numerous other documents, were introduced as exhibits at trial.

II.   LEGAL FRAMEWORK

Under 8 *Del. C.* §262, dissenting stockholders are entitled to their *pro rata* share of the "fair value" of the corporation in which they held stock before the merger. "Accordingly, the Court of Chancery's task in an appraisal proceeding is to value what has been taken from the shareholder, *i.e.*, the proportionate interest in the going concern."[3] "The application of a discount to a shareholder is contrary to the requirement that the company be viewed as a 'going concern.'" But the valuation is "exclusive of any element of value arising from the accomplishment or expectation of the merger," although it may "encompass known elements of value" not the product of speculation.[4]

The corporation may be valued "by any techniques or methods which are generally considered acceptable in the financial community and otherwise admissible in court."[5] In recent years, the DCF valuation methodology has featured prominently in this Court because it "is the approach that merits the greatest confidence" within the financial community. In appropriate cases, this Court has relied exclusively on DCF models. Regardless of the methodology, however, this Court prefers valuations based on management projections available as of the date of the merger and holds a healthy skepticism for post-merger adjustments to management projections or the creation of new projections

3. *Cede & Co. v. Technicolor, Inc.*, 684 A.2d 289, 298 (Del.1996) (citing *Cavalier Oil Corp. v. Harnett*, 564 A.2d 1137, 1145 (Del.1989)).

4. *Cede & Co.*, 684 A.2d at 299 (citing *Weinberger v. UOP*, 457 A.2d 701, 713 (Del.1983)).

5. *Weinberger*, 457 A.2d at 713.

entirely. Expert valuations that disregard contemporaneous management projections are sometimes completely discounted.

In this proceeding, "both sides have the burden of proving their respective valuation positions by a preponderance of the evidence." If neither party satisfies its burden, however, the Court must use its own independent judgment to determine fair value. The Court can reject the views of both experts.

III. ANALYSIS

In this section, I evaluate the respective valuations of the parties' experts. I begin with DeVinney's comparable transactions analysis, turn to the dueling DCF models, assess Jarrell's "market checks," and then reach the Court's determination as to the fair value of JR Cigar as of October 4, 2000.

A.   DEVINNEY'S COMPARABLE TRANSACTIONS ANALYSIS

DeVinney used the comparable transactions found in Merrill Lynch's "Presentation to the Special Committee of the Board of Directors of Leaf."[6] A special committee of JR Cigar's Board of Directors retained Merrill Lynch to advise them in connection with the then-proposed merger, and it rendered a fairness opinion dated August 28, 2000. "Merrill Lynch noted that nearly all of the Comparable Transactions represent the acquisition of control of the target company which may not be directly comparable to the acquisition of a minority stake of a target company, as in the Offer and the Merger." Nonetheless, "Merrill Lynch determined a reference multiple range LTM [latest twelve months] EBITDA [earnings before interest, taxes, depreciation, and amortization] for the Company of 6.0x to 7.5x, resulting in a reference range for an implied value per Share of $12.00 to $15.50." Merrill Lynch found that "the most comparable transaction," one involving Swisher International, "represents 6.2x LTM EBITDA or $12.00 per share." The Swisher International transaction was the most comparable because, like the JR Cigar deal, it did not involve a change of control. But even that transaction, as well as all the other "comparable" transactions, involved companies that manufacture cigars and related products. JR Cigar is not a manufacturer; it only sells cigars, cigarettes, and related products.

DeVinney looked at the same set of transactions as Merrill Lynch, but altered their calculations in one significant respect. One of the transactions reviewed by Merrill Lynch was Swedish Match's acquisition of General Cigar. Merrill Lynch calculated the LTM EBITDA multiple in that transaction at 10.4x. DeVinney calculated the multiple at 12.8x because he included EBITDA of General Cigar for a 13-week period ending after the transaction was announced. During this period, General Cigar's EBITDA declined, which has the effect of inflating the transaction multiple. I cannot discern any principled basis for this alteration of General Cigar's EBITDA. As DeVinney admitted on cross-examination, Swedish Match did not use the post-transaction EBITDA data in arriving at its offer price.

---

6. Leaf was the codename for JR Cigar.

Moreover, Merrill Lynch did not use the post-transaction EBITDA data, even though it advised Swedish Match on the transaction and had "expertise in evaluating similar transactions."

Moreover, contrary to DeVinney's expert report, the Swedish Match transaction is not comparable to the transaction in this case. Swedish Match's acquisition of General Cigar was, unlike the going private merger here, a strategic acquisition. The synergistic nature of the deal accounts for some of the premium, which DeVinney conceded on cross-examination. Additionally, Swedish Match was acquiring 64% of the equity of General Cigar. Again, DeVinney testified on cross-examination that this "may explain some of the premium." Merrill Lynch, also Swedish Match's advisor, determined that the transaction in that case was not the most comparable to the JR Cigar merger. Merrill Lynch's opinion was that the Swisher International transaction was the most comparable. The Swisher transaction multiple was 6.2x, less than half of the "adjusted" multiple DeVinney derived for the Swedish Match transaction.

The problems identified above render DeVinney's comparable transactions analysis unreliable. Most of these errors were exposed on cross-examination, as he was unable to fully defend his methodology. Witnessing DeVinney's testimony first-hand convinces me once again that "no substitute has ever been found for cross-examination as a means of . . . reducing exaggerated statements to their true dimensions."[7]

B. DISCOUNTED CASH FLOW ANALYSIS OF DEVINNEY AND JARRELL

The DCF method estimates the value of a business such as JR Cigar based on projected future free cash flows that are discounted to present value, Based on a DCF analysis, DeVinney concluded that the fair value of JR Cigar was $19.80 per share. Jarrell, using the same basic DCF methodology, concluded that the range of fair value of JR Cigar was from $11.76 to $13.58 per share. By way of comparison, Merrill Lynch performed a DCF analysis in connection with its fairness opinion that produced a reference range for an implied value per share of $9.49 to $12.63.

The parties agree that most of the difference between the experts' DCF calculations is the result of four variables: (1) JR Cigar's estimated growth rate in perpetuity; (2) the Company's debt-to-equity ratio; (3) the *Ibbotson* equity size premium applied in the capital asset pricing model (CAPM); and (4) JR Cigar's tax rate. The latter three factors collectively contribute to JR Cigar's weighted average cost of capital (WACC), which is used to discount future cash flows. I will discuss each variable in turn.

1. Growth Rate in Perpetuity

In a DCF valuation, the cash flow is projected for each year into the future for a period of years, typically five. After that point, one uses a single value representing all subsequent cash flows to calculate a company's terminal value. The terminal value may be determined by using multiples from comparable

---

7. Francis L. Wellman, *The Art of Cross-Examination* 7 (4th rev. ed. 1948).

transactions, referred to as an exit multiple, or may be ascertained by assuming a constant growth rate after the initial five year forecast period, *i.e.*, the growth rate in perpetuity. The terminal value calculation is critical here because it represents well over half of JR Cigar's total estimated present value.

Jarrell used the perpetuity growth approach and computed a range of values based on growth rates of 2.5% to 3.5%, rates equal to or exceeding the long-term rate of inflation. DeVinney used both the comparable transactions approach and the perpetuity growth approach to calculate JR Cigar's terminal value. DeVinney used the multiple of 8.5x (ascertained in his comparable transaction analysis) and applied that multiple to JR Cigar's estimated 2004 EBITDA. DeVinney also used a perpetuity growth rate of 5%. DeVinney opined that each method of calculating terminal value is equally appropriate and averaged the two indications of value.

Regardless of whether ascertaining a company's terminal value by applying a transaction multiple is appropriate as a matter of finance theory, I have already determined that the 8.5x multiple derived by DeVinney is unreliable and should not be used in any DCF analysis. As such, in determining the terminal value of JR Cigar, the analysis is necessarily limited to the appropriate perpetual growth rate. DeVinney on cross-examination agreed that this was the appropriate route if the Court concluded that his comparable transaction analysis was not valid.

Although DeVinney's report is silent as to the rationale for using a 5% growth rate into perpetuity, at trial he indicated reliance on a document prepared by Fleet Bank, N.A.[8] DeVinney testified on direct examination that "it appears that there were management projections provided to Fleet that utilized a five percent growth rate through 2009." The document at issue does in fact show 5% growth from 2000 through 2009 and includes small type in the lower left that reads "Management Case." Jarrell testified, however, that upon conversation with JR Cigar's CFO Michael Colleton, he understood that JR Cigar had not prepared projections beyond five years. Moreover, he testified that it appeared from the face of the document that Fleet merely extrapolated upon management's five-year projections. This conclusion is sustainable given that only five-year projections are shown in another portion of the document that discusses the "Management Case."

Petitioner is anxious to have the Fleet document characterized as a "management projection" because of the Court's preference for such projections. After reviewing the document and after considering the testimony of both experts, however, I cannot conclude with confidence that the projections in the Fleet document for the years 2004 to 2009 are actually "management projections." Petitioner attempts to create the inference that the later year projections were management's with several novel arguments that, to be candid, are mostly sophistry. The bottom line is that nothing in the document states affirmatively that JR Cigar provided Fleet with ten-year projections *and* Colleton stated that this was because JR Cigar did not give Fleet such projections.

---

8. Fleet provided part of a $55 million loan to finance the merger.

Because I cannot safely conclude that management projected growth of 5% after 2004 does not mean that calculating JR Cigar's terminal value based on such a growth rate is inaccurate. Nor does it mean, presumptively, that Jarrell's lower perpetual growth rate of 2.5% to 3.5% is accurate. The lack of definite, long-term management projections simply means that the experts, and ultimately this Court, must ascertain some independently justifiable growth rate with which to calculate JR Cigar's terminal value.

In Jarrell's opinion, JR Cigar's likely growth rate in the long-term was only at or slightly above the rate of inflation. Jarrell based this opinion initially on the fact that the management forecasted growth rate of 5% for 2000 to 2004 was modest and that it is "quite common and normal in discounted cash flow analysis to observe a higher growth rate in the forecast period than in the perpetuity period." Jarrell buttressed this opinion with empirical and contemporaneous evidence that sales of JR Cigar's two main products, cigars and cigarettes, were on the decline. Merrill Lynch's presentation to JR Cigar shows that sales of premium cigars were on the decline. Rothman testified in his deposition that sales of premium cigars were on the decline. And since the early 1980s, there has been a "steep and steady" decline in the domestic consumption of cigarettes. Based on the foregoing, Jarrell testified that it was "conservative on behalf of the petitioners, to assume that over the long haul after 2004 that this company's sales, dollar sales, will keep up with the inflation rate."

In support of using a 5% perpetual growth rate, Petitioner turns back to the Fleet document. In that document, prepared as part of a credit offering, Fleet notes JR Cigar's impressive pre-2000 results and that "the U.S. cigar market [was] expected to grow by 2.0% to 5.0% in the medium to long term." Additionally, in his deposition, Rothman noted that, although cigar prices were declining, JR Cigar's revenues grew by 10.6% in 1999 and that the Company increased its market share. Perhaps realizing that JR Cigar's performance before 2000 was no indication of growth beyond the year 2004, especially given the declining state of the domestic market, Petitioner offered a couple of other rationales for a 5% perpetual growth rate. First, DeVinney testified that JR Cigar could eliminate competitors in a declining market due to its advantageous distribution systems. Second, Petitioner hypothesized that JR Cigar could have seized upon international sales, sales over the internet, and sales in non-tobacco related products to grow at 5% in perpetuity in spite of a declining domestic market.

As to international expansion, there is simply no record support for this theory. It is the product of speculation. As to the sale of non-tobacco related products, again, there is no record support that JR Cigar had any plans to enhance revenue in this fashion. In fact, JR Cigar's already minimal sales of fragrances and other merchandise declined in 2000 from the previous year.

The most compelling rationale offered by Petitioner for JR Cigar's ability to maintain growth at 5% is through the elimination of competitors. This rationale has some historical support. Rothman testified that JR Cigar increased revenues and market share in the late 1990s even though the tobacco market was beginning to contract. Notwithstanding Rothman's testimony, there is no persuasive evidence that JR Cigar's ability to sustain growth in the face of an initial market decline would have translated into long-term growth prospects.

Increased market share could explain the 5% growth forecasted by management in years 2000 to 2004, but it does not follow that JR Cigar would grow by 5% per year into perpetuity. Additionally, increasing market share when the market is declining overall is not a recipe for growth: half of two is one, but all of one is still one.

The problem with ascertaining a growth rate in perpetuity is that it is an inherently speculative enterprise, Jarrell, under questioning by the Court, was refreshingly candid when he stated: "Who knows what the growth rate in perpetuity is going to be. It's a judgment call." The experts, and ultimately the Court, are asked to surmise what rate a company will grow at five years into the future. This is hardly an exact science. In this type of circumstance it is difficult (if not impossible) for litigants to "prov[e] their respective valuation positions by a preponderance of the evidence." Nevertheless, the Court must assess whether one expert's judgment is more defensible than the other. And, on this record, it appears that Jarrell's judgment that JR Cigar's growth rate in perpetuity is at or slightly above the rate of inflation is more credible. Jarrell used a range of 2.5% (roughly equal to the long-term rate of inflation in 2000) to 3.5% in his DCF analysis. In my opinion, the upper end of that range is appropriate and fair. Using a rate of 3.5% accounts for the possibility, however marginal, that JR Cigar may be able to expand in an otherwise declining domestic market for cigars and cigarettes.

2.   Debt-to-Equity Ratio

Under a DCF analysis, JR Cigar's future cash flows must be discounted to present value. DeVinney and Jarrell based their discount rates on the weighted average cost of capital ("WACC") methodology. DeVinney explained WACC quite concisely at trial: "It's the cost of equity times the percentage of equity in the capital structure plus the cost of debt times that percentage of debt." The parties dispute the "percentage of debt" part of this equation, primarily because the more weight one gives to debt, the lower the discount rate and the higher the valuation. Petitioner argues that the appropriate percentage of debt to ascribe to JR Cigar is 25%. Respondent urges a debt percentage of 10% or less.

Respondent's position that 10% debt is appropriate is based on three factors. First, before the merger, JR Cigar had no debt. Second, Jarrell testified that at the time of the transaction JR Cigar did not anticipate any large capital expenditures and that management believed that the Company optimally was run with minimal debt. Third, Jarrell noted that the only other publicly-traded retail cigar company operated with no debt.

Petitioner's support for 25% debt-allocation is based on four factors. First, Petitioner points to JR Cigar's pre-IPO capital structure, which was approximately 17% debt. Second, DeVinney opined that 25% debt was similar to that of comparable companies. Third, Petitioner argues that JR Cigar had expansion opportunities that would require additional capital. And, fourth, Petitioner notes that JR Cigar borrowed $55 million for the merger.

Reviewing the record and submissions by the parties, I am convinced that the appropriate percentage of debt for the WACC calculation is 10%. The pre-IPO structure is not indicative of JR Cigar's going-forward capital structure precisely because it was "pre-IPO." The IPO was in 1997, three years before the valuation date, and the IPO was used to reduce JR Cigar's debt. Moreover, the comparable companies relied upon by Petitioner are not comparable. The companies used as reference points by DeVinney are manufacturing companies, not retailers. DeVinney conceded on cross-examination that the capital structure of those companies "would be different most likely." As noted above, the only other publicly-traded retail cigar company had no debt. Finally, although I agree that JR Cigar may have pursued expansion opportunities, no evidence exists to suggest that those opportunities would have required such debt as to justify a 25% capital allocation, especially since management did not plan on incurring significant debt and since the Company already had over $13 million in cash and equivalents as of June 30, 2000.

Petitioner's final justification for a 25% debt allocation is that JR Cigar incurred $55 million of debt to finance the merger. Petitioner's argument is that "[t]he merger did not enhance JR Cigar's ability to borrow; therefore valuing it based on its optimal capital structure instead of its actual capital structure does not contravene, but instead comports with, 8 *Del C.* 262(h)."

[T]he fact that the merger did not enhance JR Cigar's ability to borrow does not condone ignoring its actual capital structure in favor of some "optimal capital structure." In *In re Radiology Assocs., Inc.*, the petitioner argued that the respondent's debt to equity ratio should mimic the overall industry's debt-to-equity ratio because it was more efficacious than the respondent's actual debt-to-equity ratio. The Court dismissed this effort because an appraisal proceeding does "not attempt [. . .] to determine the potential maximum value of the company." I must value JR Cigar, "not some theoretical company."

JR Cigar had no debt before the merger. Petitioner has introduced no evidence of non-speculative plans to incur significant debt that is not due to the accomplishment of the merger. Therefore, a capital structure of 25% debt is not appropriate. A debt ratio of 10% is, however, reasonable and accounts for the probability that JR Cigar may seek to incur limited debt to pursue expansion opportunities.

3. Ibbotson Equity Size Premium

The parties also disagree about another component of the WACC formula — the cost of equity. A standard method of ascertaining the cost of equity is CAPM. CAPM is based on the premise that the expected return of a security equals the rate on a risk-free security plus a risk premium. Under CAPM the cost of equity is equal to the risk-free rate (the yield on 20 year Treasury bonds) plus a large company equity risk premium multiplied by the specific company adjusted beta for JR Cigar. Added to this figure is an equity size premium. An equity size premium is added because smaller companies have higher returns on average than larger ones,[9] *i.e.*, small companies have a higher cost of equity. The equity size premium for all sized companies is published by Ibbotson Associates.

Both experts used CAPM to derive JR Cigar's cost of equity, but applied different equity size premiums. Both used a chart published in *Ibbotson* to find the premium. The *Ibbotson* chart indicates that the size premium for

9. Ibbotson Associates, *Ibbotson, Stocks, Bonds, Bills and Inflation: Valuation Edition 2001 Yearbook* 107 (2001) ("Ibbotson").

companies with capitalization between $192 and $840 million is 1.1%, the "low-cap" category. The premium is 2.6% for companies with capitalization below $192 million, the "micro-cap" category. DeVinney added an equity size premium of 1.1%, while Jarrell added 2.6%. Jarrell placed JR Cigar in the micro-cap category because its market capitalization, based on the traded price of the stock before the announcement of the merger (or based on the merger price), was well below $192 million. On the other hand, DeVinney placed JR Cigar in the low-cap category because he "determined that the value, the market capitalization, should be more at the fair value implied market capitalization." DeVinney made this determination because the stock price was, in his opinion, depressed.

Respondent argues that basing the equity size premium on JR Cigar's implied fair value contravenes finance theory. When asked on cross-examination if the *Ibbotson* text suggested that his methodology was sound, DeVinney answered in the negative. Jarrell testified that implying the fair value, rather than using a market measurement, is somewhat circular because the whole purpose of the DCF analysis is to ascertain JR Cigar's fair value. Additionally, Jarrell testified that the *Ibbotson* data already incorporates illiquidity and depressed values since it is derived exclusively from traded stock prices. Although one valuation textbook suggests that simply estimating the market value of the equity is appropriate for some WACC calculations, it does not state whether it is appropriate to imply a fair value to determine the equity size premium, a number derived from actual market prices.

Regardless of whether or not adjusting the equity size premium based on implied fair value is appropriate in some circumstances, I ultimately determine that the record in this case does not support DeVinney's methodology. According to Petitioner, JR Cigar's stock was depressed because Rothman held an abnormally large majority position and because the minority portion of the stock was very illiquid. In order for Petitioner's argument to stand, JR Cigar's stock would have needed to be depressed by over five dollars per share-over half its value. Petitioner cites to two First Union presentations as support for this position. These documents reveal that First Union believed JR Cigar's shares were discounted in the public markets because of Respondent's "[s]mall public float," i.e., the number of shares available for trading, "[s]ignificant inside ownership," and "[l]ack of research coverage." But the same documents indicate that the stock was also depressed because of JR Cigar's small market capitalization and "[n]egative public, legal and governmental sentiment toward tobacco." These documents offer mixed support for the position that JR Cigar's stock was significantly depressed because they do not quantify the extent to which the stock was depressed by illiquidity as opposed to generalized industry factors. The sour state of the tobacco market would undoubtedly depress JR Cigar's stock price, but would also depress JR Cigar's fair value.

The failure to isolate the specific impact of JR Cigar's illiquidity on its stock price undermines Petitioner's analysis. The illiquidity of a particular security is usually measured by the size of the bid/ask spread. In general, the lower the liquidity, the higher the bid/ask spread. And when the spread is higher, the "discount" to a firm's fundamental value increases. Petitioner introduced no evidence regarding JR Cigar's bid/ask spread. The only evidence introduced related to JR Cigar's trading volume. That evidence shows that 7.9 million shares of JR Cigar were traded during the 12 months preceding the announcement of the merger — more than double the number of shares not controlled by Rothman. During this period, JR Cigar's stock price never rose above $12.75 per share — well within the *Ibbotson* micro-cap category.

Even assuming that JR Cigar's stock price was depressed because of its illiquidity, Petitioner cannot justify categorizing JR Cigar as a low-cap, rather than micro-cap, company (for the purposes of CAPM) based on this fact. CAPM identifies the expected return on a particular security, an expected return that is inputted into the WACC and used to discount JR Cigar's future cash flows to present value. The *Ibbotson* size premium number reflects the empirical evidence that smaller firms have higher returns than larger firms. Petitioner's position that JR Cigar is a low-cap company (rather than a micro-cap company) decreases the expected rate of return on JR Cigar's stock by lowering the "size premium" applied. The problem with using liquidity as a basis for justifying a lower expected return, however, is that low liquidity is associated with higher expected returns. Investors seek compensation for the high transaction costs of illiquid securities, *e.g.*, the bid/ask spread. In other words, even if JR Cigar had a higher market capitalization than the market price of its stock suggested *because of its illiquidity*, investors would still expect higher returns *because of its illiquidity*.

Petitioner also seeks to justify the categorization of JR Cigar as a low-cap company based on its beta. A company's beta is the measure of its volatility in relation to the overall market, in this case the S & P 500. Petitioner's argument is that JR Cigar's adjusted beta, calculated by DeVinney at .62, is much lower than the betas of the other companies in its *Ibbotson* micro-cap group.[10] This argument is unavailing for several reasons. First, there is no evidence that DeVinney categorized JR Cigar as a low-cap company based on its low beta. DeVinney only testified that he thought that JR Cigar's stock was "depressed." Second, Petitioner did not introduce evidence that JR Cigar's beta is outside the ranges of betas for the micro-cap category. Lastly, the size premium is not dependent on the beta of the firm. In fact, it is because the beta does not capture all the systemic risk that a size premium is included. "[E]ven after adjusting for the systematic (beta) risk of small stocks, they outperform large stocks."

4. Tax Rate

Petitioner argues that JR Cigar's tax rate is 36%. DeVinney arrived at this figure after reviewing JR Cigar's income statement contained in Merrill Lynch's August 28, 2000 presentation to the JR Cigar Board. The income statement does not actually list JR Cigar's tax rate, but the rate used by Merrill Lynch can be deduced by calculating the difference between the yearly EBIT and net income figures over the historical and forecast period. Merrill Lynch's figures imply a tax

10. DeVinney calculated a beta of .62 based on a period beginning six months after JR Cigar's IPO. Tr. at 84–85. Jarrell calculated a beta of .67 based on a period beginning a week after the IPO. *Id.* Neither period is presumptively valid. A longer period of time, such as the period used by Jarrell, is generally preferred. A five-year period, longer than the period used by either expert, is the most common. Shannon P. Pratt, *Cost of Capital: Estimations and Applications* 82 (2d ed. 2002). Petitioner's argument that the stock should be given time to "season" after an IPO is understandable, but I am unsure why this takes six months.

rate near the 36% rate used by DeVinney. The August 28, 2000 presentation, as well as other documents, indicate that Merrill Lynch's income statement was based on management forecasts and estimates. It is unclear from the face of these documents, however, what exactly JR Cigar management provided to Merrill Lynch. Merrill Lynch's due diligence request list does not show that Merrill Lynch ever asked for JR Cigar's effective tax rate. No evidence indicates that Merrill Lynch ever received such information.

Even if management did provide Merrill Lynch with information regarding its effective tax rate, the presentation upon which Petitioner relies does not imply that management gave Merrill Lynch the 36% figure that DeVinney used for his calculations. A colloquy between DeVinney and Respondent's counsel on cross-examination demonstrated that the Merrill Lynch presentation may have included other items in JR Cigar's net income, resulting in an implied tax rate lower than the actual tax rate. DeVinney could have made some inquiry, but did not speak to anybody at Merrill Lynch or JR Cigar to identify the actual effective tax rate.

Fortunately, the Court does not need to engage in guesswork to determine JR Cigar's tax rate. Note 6 to JR Cigar's financial statements in its 1999 Annual Report explicitly states that the tax rate was 40.9% in 1997, 40.1% in 1998, and 40.2% in 1999. This information came from management. Nothing indicates that management understood that the 40% tax rate would decline. JR Cigar's CFO indicated that the tax rate was 40% and, generally, 40% is a common tax rate to use. At the end, JR Cigar's historical tax rate published in its annual report is more reliable than speculation regarding Merrill Lynch's analysis.

5.   *Reconciling the Differences in the DCF Analyses*

The parties anticipated that the validity of the DCF calculations would hinge on the four differing assumptions examined above. Respondent introduced a demonstrative exhibit at trial that purported to recast DeVinney's DCF analysis by integrating Jarrell's assumptions. Respondent, for example, introduced a demonstrative exhibit that showed the impact that changing the tax rate had on DeVinney's DCF calculations. According to Respondent, changing the four variables discussed at length in this section has the effect of reducing DeVinney's imputed fair value by $9.95 per share. In its opening brief, Petitioner took issue with these calculations and stated that the composite effect of the four variables is to decrease DeVinney's DCF value per share by $8.03. In other words, the parties put Jarrell's assumptions into DeVinney's model and came up with *two different values.*[11]

Failing to adhere to elementary principles and to "show your work," the Court was unable to ascertain the nature of the $1.92 (the difference between $9.95 and $8.03) discrepancy. Nonetheless curious as to why the DCF estimates were off by almost two dollars per share, I sought the parties input on this issue. The parties' responses were less than satisfactory as they largely regurgitated exhibits already submitted at trial. Although Respondent was able to ascertain some of the discrepancy, it was ultimately unable to reconcile $0.69 per share

---

11. This discrepancy is in addition to the fact that Jarrell's model generates a fair value per share that is different from using his assumptions in DeVinney's model.

difference. Despite having the benefit of Respondent's submission, Petitioner was unable to explain the reason for *any* of the discrepancy.[12] As such, insufficient evidence has been presented to enable the Court to integrate Jarrell's assumptions (those largely accepted by the Court) into DeVinney's DCF model.[13] Consequently, the Court must rely on Jarrell's DCF model exclusively.

C.   JARRELL'S MARKET-BASED ANALYSIS

1.   *Measurement of Control Premiums*

Jarrell, in addition to his DCF analysis, looked at how the premium paid in the JR Cigar merger compared with control premiums paid in 2,077 deals between January 1995 and August 2000. For that sample, the median one-day control premium was 25% and the mean one-day control premium was 30.4%. Isolating the 31 mergers out of 2,077 where the buyer already owned 75% or more of the stock (as is the case here), Jarrell found that the median one-day control premium for those 31 transactions was 17%, as compared with the 21% premium paid by the Rothmans. Petitioner argues, among other things, that this analysis "violate[s] any concept of comparability, including the 'law of one price.'" I agree.

The only thing that the transactions in Jarrell's sample have in common are that they are all transactions. The data is not segmented by industry or date. The one-day premiums vary considerable; the standard deviation is 32%. Additionally, it is not clear that any analysis of premiums over all transactions has any bearing on "fair value" in an appraisal action, even if it may bear on how efficiencies arising from a merger could equitably be apportioned between the buyer and the sellers.

2.   *"Market Check"*

Jarrell considered the fact that First Union was unable to find any interested potential acquirers and that none emerged once the deal was publicly announced at $13 per share. He testified that "in my judgment, the evidence clearly indicated that there were no such offers and that there were no such folks out there willing to pay that, because if there were, they would have shown up."

Although Jarrell's testimony has a certain intuitive appeal, there is insufficient record support from which a reliable conclusion can be drawn about this "market check." First Union, JR Cigar's financial advisor at the time, was only authorized to conduct a "limited market check." As such, First Union only contacted two possible buyers. Little can be drawn from the fact that these two buyers declined to make an offer. Additionally, simply because no rival bidders appeared after the announcement of the going private proposal does not help the Court ascertain the fair value of JR Cigar.

---

12. Petitioner's submission was a day late and (almost literally) a dollar short. Letter from Mondros to Chandler, C. of 1/13/04. Importantly, Petitioner did not deny that DeVinney made calculation errors.

13. This problem was compounded by Petitioner's decision to not comply with my request to "provide the Court with electronic versions (Microsoft Excel compatible) of the DCF worksheets," *e.g.*, "Exhibit 4 of Prof. Jarrell's report." Letter from Chandler, C. to Counsel of 1/2/04, at 2. Only Respondent complied with this request.

D.   THE COURT'S DETERMINATION

The comparable transactions looked at by DeVinney are not reliable indicators of the fair value of JR Cigar. The only transaction worth noting is the Swisher International transaction that was, in the opinion of Merrill Lynch, the most comparable to the JR Cigar transaction. That transaction implies a fair value of $12.00 per share. Jarrell's market based analysis, the measurement of control premiums and his "market check," are not reliable indicators of JR Cigar's fair value. In my opinion, the more "reliable" indicator of JR Cigar's fair value is a DCF analysis.

The four key DCF variables identified by the parties are JR Cigar's growth rate in perpetuity, its debt to equity ratio, the equity size premium, and JR Cigar's tax rate. As discussed earlier in the Court's analysis, the appropriate growth rate in perpetuity is 3.5%, the WACC calculation should reflect a 10% debt ratio, the equity size premium included in the CAPM calculation should be 2.6, and JR Cigar's effective tax rate is 40%. Jarrell's DCF calculations include an equity size premium of 2.6 and a tax rate of 40%. Jarrell uses a range of growth rates (2.5% to 3.5%) and a range of discount rates (13% to 15%). The range of discount rates reflect a debt weighting of 0% to 10% (13% discount rate reflecting 10% debt). Looking at the upper end of Jarrell's ranges, *i.e.*, 10% debt and 3.5% growth, his DCF model produces a value of $13.58 per share ...

The last matter for consideration is the form of interest. "The compounding interval should ... reflect the interval available to the petitioners had they the use of their funds as well as, if possible, the interval actually received by the corporation." Petitioner requests that interest be compounded daily. Although I have commented that daily compounding may be appropriate in some cases, Petitioner has not introduced evidence that daily compounding is appropriate in this case. In fact, DeVinney compounded interest annually in his report. JR Cigar's post-trial brief is silent regarding the compound interval, as is Jarrell's report. Jarrell does, however, compound the prime rate on a monthly basis in order to determine JR Cigar's annual borrowing costs. Ultimately, given that neither side has provided evidence as to the appropriate interval, "I find that the dual purposes of compensation and restitution may only be served by a compounding interval at least as frequent as one month."

PROBLEM SET 11.2

1. What was the net gain to the petitioners by bringing this action?
2. How hard would it have been for the petitioner to introduce evidence of an alternative investment that paid daily compound interest? Could the court have taken judicial notice of such an investment? Should it have done so?
3. As we discuss in the next chapter, Cede & Co. was acting as an agent for the true shareholders in this case. Those shareholders were a group of well-known small cap mutual funds.

II

FINANCE

12

COMMON SHARES

By the time you get to this chapter, it is likely that you have either already taken or are well into a Corporations or Business Associations class. Thus you already know lots about corporations, and a fair amount about the rights of their common shareholders. If a corporation contains nothing else in its capital structure, it has common shares.

Shares measure the investor's stake in the corporation. That stake often, but not always, entitles the shareholder to vote and receive dividends.[1] It also entitles the shareholder to receive a proportionate distribution upon dissolution of the corporation, subject to the absolute priority rule and firm not being insolvent.

AMERICA ASCENDS IN BIGGEST STOCKS
By Lu Wang and Rita Nazareth — August 27, 2012, Bloomberg.com[2]

American stocks are dominating global equities by the most in a decade, taking a majority of the spots in a ranking of the 20 biggest companies, after earnings rose faster than the rest of the world as the global economy rebounded.

Apple (AAPL) Inc., International Business Machines Corp. (IBM), Wells Fargo (WFC) & Co. and four more U.S. companies joined the top 20 since stocks peaked in 2007, bringing the total to 14, according to data compiled by Bloomberg. They replaced Moscow-based Gazprom OAO (GAZP), China Petroleum & Chemical Corp. (600028) in Beijing, Petroleo Brasileiro SA (PETR4) of Rio de Janeiro and six others from Europe and Asia. Of the nine added, only BHP Billiton (BHP) Ltd. and Nestle SA (NESN) are based outside the U.S.

More U.S. corporations are represented than any time since 2003 after 10 quarters of economic expansion and profit growth lifted the Standard & Poor's 500 Index 109 percent since shares bottomed in March 2009. The shift reflects volatility in emerging markets and shows how innovation builds value in the U.S. . . .

---

1. *See* Del. Code Ann. tit. 8, §211(b).
2. Used with permission of Bloomberg L.P. © 2013. All rights reserved.

RELATIVE STRENGTH

American companies are gaining strength in part because of Europe's sovereign debt crisis. While the S&P 500 fell 0.5 percent last week, retreating from a four-year high, amid concern European leaders will fail to preserve the 17-nation currency union, the Euro Stoxx 50 Index slid 1.5 percent. The S&P 500 fell less than 0.1 percent to 1,410.44 at 4 p.m. in New York today.

Computer and software makers became the top industry in the S&P 500, overtaking financial companies, as Apple and IBM joined Google Inc. (GOOG) and Microsoft (MSFT) Corp. among the biggest stocks. The last time a non-U.S. technology producer made the global ranking was in 2001, when Espoo, Finland-based Nokia Oyj was the world's largest mobile-phone maker. Nokia's market value has fallen by 92 percent since Apple introduced the iPhone in 2007.

The Cupertino, California-based maker of iPad computers last week became the most valuable U.S. company ever as the stock rose to $668.87 on Aug. 22, giving the company a value of $627 billion. Apple, which approached bankruptcy in 1997, has jumped more than 80-fold in the past decade.

IBM, MICROSOFT

IBM's market value more than doubled over the decade as the company shifted its strategy toward more-profitable software sales and away from hardware and consulting. The Armonk, New York-based company, with a market capitalization of $226 billion, closed the gap with Microsoft, valued at $256.2 billion, to become the No. 3 technology maker and the world's seventh-biggest company.

Microsoft, based in Redmond, Washington, was worth four times as much as IBM in 1999. Mountain View, California-based Google, owner of the world's most popular search engine, is valued at $222.6 billion.

"There are not a lot of other companies that can compete with the Googles and the Apples of the world," Jeffrey Saut, chief investment strategist at Raymond James & Associates in St. Petersburg, Florida, said in an Aug. 23 phone interview. His firm oversees $350 billion. "We have probably the most cutting-edge companies in the technology space that exist today. Who can match Apple? I can't think of anybody."

Computer and software makers represent 20 percent of the S&P 500. The industry's weighting outside the U.S. is 4 percent, as measured by the MSCI World ex-U.S. Index . . .

GLOBAL RECESSION

China is projected to expand by 8.1 percent, compared with its mean rate of 11.2 percent before the global recession. Brazil's GDP may increase 1.9 percent, down from an average of 3.8 percent. Russia may grow by 3.8 percent, next to 7.1 percent in the five years before the credit crisis.

"People perceive not only better growth for the U.S., but also less risk," Chris Leavy, the chief investment officer of fundamental equities at New York-based BlackRock Inc., which oversees $3.56 trillion as the world's biggest money manager, said in an Aug. 22 interview.

Investors are demanding more profit to reward companies with higher stock prices than before the credit crisis shattered confidence in equities. The average capitalization of the largest 20 companies shrunk 17 percent to $242.5 billion since 2007 even as profits surged almost fourfold to $18.8 billion, data compiled by Bloomberg show.

COMMODITIES, CHINA

The biggest companies, dominated in 2007 by commodity explorers and enterprises controlled by China's government, traded at an average price-earnings ratio of 57.6, the data show. Today, after the addition of two American technology developers and a California bank, the average valuation is 12.9, according to the data . . .

PETROCHINA, EXXON

PetroChina Co. (857) surpassed Exxon (XOM) Mobil Corp. to become the world's biggest company after shares of the Beijing-based oil producer almost tripled on the first day of Shanghai trading on Nov. 5, 2007. The same year, Industrial & Commercial Bank of China Ltd. overtook Citigroup Inc. as the world's largest bank while Gazprom and Petrobras eclipsed Procter & Gamble Co. (PG) and Berkshire Hathaway Inc. (BRK/A).

The number of Chinese companies has since fallen to three from six while those from Brazil, Russia, U.K. and France have disappeared from the top 20 amid the weakest Chinese growth since 2009 and an economic contraction in Europe.

PetroChina, which became the world's first $1 trillion company five years ago, has dropped to No. 4 with a market capitalization of $251.7 billion. Irving, Texas-based Exxon, the second-biggest company, is valued at $406.4 billion.

While America's expansion is "impressive," companies need to boost sales rather than counting on cost cuts to increase profits, according to Mike Ryan, the New York-based chief investment strategist at UBS Wealth Management Americas.

SALES GROWTH

"I would be careful not to over-interpret that and say that this is now validation that the U.S. corporate sector will continue to dominate," Ryan, whose firm oversees $797 billion, said in an Aug. 22 phone interview. "You still need to see U.S. companies continue to do the things that they've done well, i.e. improving efficiency, but also finding ways of trying to grow the top line."

Sales at S&P 500 companies are forecast to rise 0.4 percent in the current quarter, the slowest growth since 2009, according to analyst estimates compiled by Bloomberg.

Three other energy stocks ceded their top spots along with Gazprom and Petrobras. Total SA (FP) in France, BP Plc (BP/) in U.K. and China Petroleum exited as their market value shrank at least 41 percent since 2007.

Chevron Corp. (CVX), an oil and natural gas producer based in San Ramon, California, and BHP Billiton, a mining company based in Melbourne, entered the list, valued $219.8 billion and $175.8 billion, respectively.

BIGGEST BANKS

Wells Fargo, based in San Francisco, is catching up with Beijing-based ICBC, whose $206.5 billion makes it the world's most valuable bank. The largest U.S. home lender, which posted annual profits for more than a decade, is worth $179.8 billion and ranks No. 18 in the top 20 list.

Wal-Mart Stores Inc. (WMT), the discount retailer in Bentonville, Arkansas, and health-care companies Johnson & Johnson (JNJ) and Pfizer Inc. (PFE) joined the group as investors favored stocks whose earnings are less tied to economic swings.

Wal-Mart rose to the fifth spot with a market capitalization of $244 billion. J&J and Pfizer, ranked 16th and 19th, are valued $186.4 billion and $179.3 billion, respectively.

Nestle, a food company based in Vevey, Switzerland, is the only addition from Europe, valued $202.8 billion.

1.   THE STOCK MARKET AND IPOs

The preceding excerpt deals with the trading of shares in the secondary market, as opposed to the primary market, which involves the initial sale of shares by a firm to the public.

When a firm enters the primary market, it typically does so by way of an *initial public offering* (IPO). When companies that already have publicly traded shares sell more shares into the market, it is termed a *secondary offering*.

In the first case, this involves compliance with the "33 Act," the Securities Act of 1933. Issuers must register their securities by filing the registration statement with the Securities and Exchange Commission (SEC) before selling or advertising the securities in ways that implicates interstate commerce. This is covered in more detail in the Securities Regulation course.

Once the securities are sold to the public, the firm becomes subject to the "34 Act," the Securities Exchange Act of 1934. This requires ongoing disclosure — an example of which you saw in Chapter 1 when we reviewed the Dynegy 10-K.

Trading in the secondary market typically does not implicate the issuing firm. For example, if you want to buy shares of Apple, you would place a trade with a broker, who in turn would send the order to a stock exchange for execution. The stock exchange would match your order with a willing seller of Apple shares.

In the case of Apple, this exchange would be NASDAQ, the second largest stock exchange in the world, and home to many California-based tech firms. NASDAQ is a computerized exchange, in which multiple market makers post bids on a computer system indicating the prices at which they are willing to buy and sell Apple and other NASDAQ listed shares. When an order is submitted, the system automatically matches the order with the best offer. Apple would have no involvement in the transaction.

The largest stock exchange in the world is the New York Stock Exchange (NYSE), which operates more traditionally and is where many traditional companies list their shares (e.g., Exxon, General Electric, and Wells Fargo).[3] The NYSE is a physical place in lower Manhattan where orders from buyers and sellers are routed to dedicated market makers in a particular stock. Unlike NASDAQ, the NYSE only has one market maker per listed company.

Both of the exchanges have various requirements for listing shares. Oscala's Roast Beef & Smoothie Palace, Inc. is not going to be traded on the "Big Board," as the NYSE is sometimes called, or NASDAQ anytime soon. Moreover, companies on the decline could be involuntarily delisted from an exchange.

Shares that are not listed on a market, or those that have become delisted, trade "over the counter." There are two electronic quotation services on the OTC Market, the OTC Bulletin Board (OTCBB) and the Pink Sheets.

In the case of exchange listed shares, market makers provide two price quotes for each share — a *bid price* (the price at which they are willing to buy) and the *ask price* (the price at which they are willing to sell). Ask prices are always higher than bid prices, resulting in the bid-ask spread. This is how market makers earn a profit. The size of the bid-ask spread also provides some information on market efficiency, as lower spreads indicate more liquid, efficient markets.

From an investor's perspective, the bid-ask spread is a transaction cost in addition to any brokerage fees associated with the trade.

PROBLEM SET 12.1

1. Why is the bid-ask spread a transaction cost?
2. In the article excerpted in the introduction, it is noted regarding Apple that:

> The Cupertino, California-based maker of iPad computers last week became the most valuable U.S. company ever as the stock rose to $668.87 on Aug. 22, giving the company a value of $627 billion. Apple, which approached bankruptcy in 1997, has jumped more than 80-fold in the past decade.

---

3. The next largest stock exchanges are London and Tokyo, respectively. Together these four exchanges account for about 75 percent of the total stock trade volume worldwide.

The total market capitalization is simply computed by multiplying the number of shares outstanding by the current price. Based on that calculation, how many shares would you have to buy to own 51 percent of Apple and realize your dream of having them produce a tartan iPad cover? As for the last sentence in the quote, on January 1, 1998, you could have bought an Apple share for $3.41.[4]

2. LEGAL ASPECTS OF SHARE OWNERSHIP

Consider the story of SJL, as we'll call him, to protect him from shame. He's a young associate, the first week on the job in the mid-1990s. A partner asks him to pull a client's shareholder list in anticipation of a possible restructuring. He does so, and finds three entries on the list. "It seems that Cede & Co. owns almost 95 percent," he reports to the partner.

You'll understand the humor at the end of this section.

Shares are commonly held in one of two ways. First, a shareholder might have possession of a physical certificate. That's increasingly rare, but does sometimes happen. For example, if you want to give your spouse 1,000 shares of Hermes[5] (he really likes their purses), presenting the certificate is much nicer than a brokerage statement.[6]

But most shareholders, whether individuals or institutions, like mutual funds, hold shares through their brokerage account. This is more convenient if the investor intends to trade the securities, and avoids the problem of losing or damaging a physical certificate.

In this case, the shares are typically held in "street name," that is, all shares in a particular company are kept in the name of the broker. The broker then internally allocates the shares to individual customers. For a large brokerage, some of those individual customers might be smaller brokerage firms that use the big brokerage to execute trades. In these instances, street name registration of the shares obscures multiple layers of claims on the shares.

The true, ultimate owner of a share is called the *beneficial owner*. To further confuse the issue, even the big brokerage firm that is the top-level street name holder probably does not hold the shares in its own name. Rather, to facilitate easy transfers of shares among brokerage firms, most register their shares with the Depository Trust Company (DTC).[7] The actual holder of these shares is Cede & Co., a DTC subsidiary.

Thus, when Brokerage A's clients sell Apple shares and Brokerage B's clients buy, the actual exchange of ownership will take place on the books of DTC, rather than on the shareholder list of the company, which, by the way, is also provided by DTC.

---

4. *http://goo.gl/QU3sa*

5. More formally, Hermes International SCA: *http://goo.gl/GxsDW*

6. Assuming you can get a certificate. Companies are increasingly providing shares in "book entry" form only, which means the shares exist only as a computer file somewhere. Even if you can get a certificate, there typically will be an extra charge associated with preparing it.

7. DTC's parent company is DTCC, Depository Trust & Clearing Corporation.

The list DTC provides, and which SJL obtained in the story above, is a list of registered owners. Registered owners correspond with beneficial owners only to the limited degree that shareholders hold in their own name — which is largely comprised of those few shareholders who hold physical certificates. In most cases Cede & Co. will instead be the record holder, but obviously not the beneficial holder.

Thus, to get in touch with the actual "owners" of the securities, you have to drill through many layers: DTC/Cede — Big Broker — Small Broker — Customer. And note that there is ambiguity here, in that Big Broker might be holding for a customer or it might be holding for its own trading purposes.

To address the distinction between record and beneficial ownership, the SEC has created rules to allow firms to communicate with beneficial owners through broker or other intermediaries.[8] The rules allow brokers to disclose to a company the identity of those beneficial owners who do not object to such disclosure. Those who object are known as "objecting beneficial owners" (OBOs) under the SEC's rules. The company cannot contact OBOs directly.

The company may, however, have direct contact with shareowners who have designated themselves "non-objecting beneficial owners" (NOBOs), owners who do not object to having their identity known to the issuing company.

To get a list of NOBOs, you might think you would have to go to each and every broker. Most brokers, but not all, delegate this responsibility to an agent, in almost all cases Broadridge Financial Solutions, Inc.[9] Broadridge provides a single list of all NOBOs. The NOBO list includes the name, address, and securities position for each NOBO. Because Broadridge does not disclose the identity of a NOBO's broker or bank intermediary, brokers like this approach because it prevents outsiders from figuring out who their customers are.

The NOBO list from Broadridge provides some insight into the beneficial owners, but remember not all brokers participate. You (or, more likely, the client issuer) would have to get lists from those brokerages individually.

And let's not forget the OBOs. All indications are that the bulk of brokerage customers are OBOs, so they will remain behind the veil of a brokerage name — so even if you see the name of a big brokerage house on a list from Broadridge, you still do not know if that broker holds for itself, for one customer, or for a million customers.

Working with a firm that specializes in these matters, you can pass information to the shareholders through the brokerages. But you will still never know if the broker's 100 customers all hold roughly equal amounts of shares, or if one customer holds the vast bulk of the client's shares.

To make matters more confusing, state corporate law provides for voting by the record holder. As a result, the company cannot send a proxy card and proxy materials directly to each beneficial owner, but must provide the proxy card to the record holder. To delegate voting authority under state law to the beneficial owner, first, as the record holder of shares held in street name, DTC executes an

---

8. *See* Rules 14b-1 and 14b-2 under the 34 Act.
9. Before 2007 Broadridge was a subsidiary of a company called ADP, so many older attorneys will still refer to it as "getting the NOBO list from ADP."

"omnibus" proxy in favor of all brokers and banks who hold the company's shares through DTC's facilities.

In turn, after being vested with voting authority by DTC, the broker requests voting instructions from the beneficial owner. Typically Broadridge sends the requests for voting instructions on behalf of the broker and beneficial owners return instructions as to how the proxies should be voted to Broadridge, which then tabulates the voting instructions received and fills out a proxy for each intermediary broker for which it acts as agent, aggregating the voting instructions received from all beneficial owners from a particular broker.

The issuing company pays brokers and Broadridge for the services they provide under this system at levels fixed by the NYSE.

PROBLEM SET 12.2

1.   What is the consequence of this foregoing system for the issuing firm? For those who would like to mount a takeover of the firm? What justification might there be for the existing system? Note that in most other countries, issuing firms can and do communicate directly with their investors. *See* Del. Gen. Corp. Law §113.
2.   Take another look at the *JRC Acquisition Corp* in Chapter 11. Does the opening paragraph make more sense now?
3.   Some institutional investors — like mutual funds and pension funds — outsource their voting rights to a firm that researches and analyzes various corporate proposals. How does this development interact with the information provided in this section?

3.   VALUING SHARES

As we have learned in prior chapters, the value of an asset is the expected cash flows it will generate — including any cash flows generated by sale of the asset. For a common share, you might think it easiest to simply value the shares based on the earnings of the company, with earnings being a kind of proxy for cash flows.

But we have already discussed how some investors might have prior claims on the cash flows, claims that are fixed and thus not subject to the board's discretion.

Additionally, the firm might decide to provide cash flows (i.e., dividends) to shareholders even in the absence of earnings. We have already discussed why that might be, too.

The dividends thing might give you an idea: What about valuing the shares like an annuity? After all, this is essentially what we did when we valued companies using the DCF method. In particular, if a company pays dividends, you could value the company as a string of dividends followed by the money you receive upon sale of the shares.

That works, but what will you receive when you sell the share? That is, how to value the terminal value? Well, if you were buying the shares, you might value it based on the future dividends you will receive. That is, if you value the shares as an annuity, you might end up valuing it as a series of dividend payments you will receive, and then the value of a series of dividend payments the next owner will receive.

This is beginning to look less like an annuity and more like a perpetuity. And if you want to get fancy, you might consider valuing the shares as a growing perpetuity to account for the trend of future dividend payments.

This is the essence of the dividend discount model (DDM). Dividend-paying shares are valued as a growing perpetuity:

$$P_t = D_t \times (1 + g) / (r - g)$$

You should have two questions immediately: How do I estimate the r and the g? The r used in this calculation is typically calculated as the shares' dividend yield plus the growth rate (g). Dividend yield is a simple ratio of the annual dividend payment over the current share price. It is also widely reported, if you are fully "mathed out" at this point in the class.

Then how do we find g, which figures so importantly in our growing perpetuity formula? That's a bit more complex, and even small changes in the assumed g can have big effects on the estimated share price under the DDM.

In short, g is frequently estimated as the firm's retention ratio[10] multiplied by the firm's return on retained earnings; that is, how much the firm keeps (the retention ratio) and what it earns on what it keeps (the return on retained earnings).

Because return on retained earnings is very difficult for an outside observer to project, most often it will be replaced with the historical return on equity (ROE), which is widely reported and easily calculated. This, of course, assumes that today's managers will do just as good of a job as past managers.

$$g = ROE \times RR$$

with *RR* being the retention ratio.

ROE is calculated as net income over shareholder equity. You can find net income on the income statement. Shareholder equity, meanwhile, is located on the balance sheet, in both cases as we saw in Chapter 1.

PROBLEM SET 12.3

1. Review the financial information for Exxon Mobil[11] and calculate its per share value using the DDM. Note the "Financials" tab on the left side of the Google page, but be sure to note whether you are looking at annual or

---

10. The ratio of retained earnings to total earnings.
11. *https://www.google.com/finance?q=NYSE:XOM*

quarterly numbers. And you can find the risk free rate here[12] — use the
20-year rate.

2. Given your understanding of balance sheets, what problems might you
   foresee with ROE and its use in the DDM?

3. What other limitations might there be to DDM beyond those discussed in
   the text?

4.   A NOTE ON THE P/E RATIO AND "MULTIPLES"

In Chapter 1 we introduced a variety of ratios that are derived from a firm's
balance sheet and other financial statements. ROE is one example we have seen
in this chapter.

Another share valuation ratio that is tied to the financial statements is the
price/earnings (P/E) ratio. Thus, the ratio is calculated as the current share
price over the earnings per share, or alternatively, total market value over net
income.

This is a simple measure that reports the cost of the firm's shares in relation to
its earnings. Thus, if Exxon's shares are trading at $87.90 and its EPS is 9.23, it
has a P/E ratio of 9.52. That is, its current share price is 9.52 times its current
EPS.

Whether that means the share price is low or high depends on your point of
reference. Most important, particular industries tend to have particular P/E
ratios. Thus, if you compared Exxon to Google — which as of August 2012
had a P/E ratio of 20.4 — you might think that Exxon is massively underpriced.
But then note that Apple has a ratio of 15.83, Hermes is at 39.57, and Chevron
has a ratio of 9.23.

More broadly, a particular multiple can be used to compare firms of different
sizes. For example, Exxon is extremely large, but when valuing a smaller oil
company we might consider what share price would be implied by using a similar
9.52 P/E ratio.

Of course, none of this takes into account firm-specific differences. For
example, British Petroleum currently trades at a multiple of 7.8. Before assuming it is cheap relative to Exxon and Chevron, one might want to consider the
effects of a certain oil spill in 2010.[13] Similarly, if two firms have different
accounting policies, comparing multiples might lead to misleading results, especially for those multiples (like P/E ratio) that do not take into account capital
structure.[14]

---

12. *http://goo.gl/BLjf1*

13. *http://en.wikipedia.org/wiki/Deepwater_Horizon_oil_spill*

14. EBITDA-based multiples are popular because they are less affected by these issues, as they measure
firm cash flows before depreciation and amortization, which underlay many differences among firms.

13

PREFERRED SHARES

It is often noted that preferred shares are a hybrid between debt and equity. A less polite observer might note that a preferred shareholder is a shareholder without voting power or a deeply subordinated debtholder.[1]

Financial institutions are some of the biggest issuers of preferred shares in the United States, as preferred shares' equity status provides regulatory benefits under the applicable capital requirements. Before the recent financial crisis, financial institutions experimented with a wide variety of instruments that appeared to be equity for regulatory purposes, while acting as debt for tax purposes. Although these instruments had lots of clever names, in the financial industry it was widely thought that these instruments were more often sold rather than bought. Large, staid businesses historically also issued a good bit of preferred stock, often to meet the putative demand from retirees seeking steady income.[2]

Other specialized uses of preferred stock include the U.S. Treasury's bailout of financial institutions in late 2008 — its investment in AIG, for example, came in the form of convertible preferred shares — and venture capitalists, who often invest in companies by way of convertible preferred shares.[3] Convertible shares, which allow the holder to transform their investment into some number of common shares, are covered in the subsequent chapter on options and convertible instruments. Venture capital investments are also the subject of a separate chapter.

The term *preferred* means that a firm must pay the dividends due on its preferred shares before it pays any common stock dividends. Also, in theory, if a company goes bankrupt, preferred holders have priority over common stock shareholders. In many cases, the liquidation preference might entitle the

---

1. *See* Melissa M. McEllin, Note, *Rethinking Jedwab: A Revised Approach to Preferred Shareholder Rights*, 2010 Colum. Bus. L. Rev. 895 (2010); Noelle M. Holladay, Note, *The Limited Fiduciary Duties Owed by Corporate Managers to Preferred Shareholders: A Need for Change*, 88 Ky. L.J. 87 (2000).

2. Whether this demand was actually the result of investors' demands or the result of marketing efforts by the banks that underwrote the preferred shares remains uncertain.

3. *See* Chapter 21.

preferred shareholders to be first in line to receive nothing. The absolute priority still applies, and thus means creditors first.

1. STRUCTURAL ISSUES (THE TERMS OF THE DEAL)

As a matter of general corporate law, simply calling a particular class of "preferred" shares does nothing.[4] The shares remain common shares, entitled to all the normal rights of shareholders that are the subject of your basic Business Associations class.[5]

Any special rights, therefore, must be specified by some other document.[6] Typically this other document is either the firm's certificate of incorporation itself, or a document known as a certificate of designation.

CERTIFICATE OF DESIGNATION OF TERMS OF
6.75% NON-CUMULATIVE PREFERRED STOCK, SERIES Q
CUSIP Number: 313586778

1. DESIGNATION, PAR VALUE AND NUMBER OF SHARES.

The designation of the series of preferred stock of the Federal National Mortgage Association ("Fannie Mae") created by this resolution shall be "6.75% Non-Cumulative Preferred Stock, Series Q" (the "Series Q Preferred Stock"), and the number of shares initially constituting the Series Q Preferred Stock is 15,000,000. Shares of Series Q Preferred Stock will have no par value and a stated value of $25 per share. Shares of Series Q Preferred Stock will have no stated maturity date, and, subject to Section 3 below, will be perpetual. The Board of Directors of Fannie Mae, or a duly authorized committee thereof, in its sole discretion, may reduce the number of shares of Series Q Preferred Stock, provided such reduction is not below the number of shares of Series Q Preferred Stock then outstanding.

2. DIVIDENDS.

(a)   Holders of record of Series Q Preferred Stock (each individually a "Holder," or collectively the "Holders") will be entitled to receive, when, as and if declared by the Board of Directors of Fannie Mae, or a duly authorized committee thereof, in its sole discretion out of funds legally available therefor, non-cumulative quarterly dividends . . .

---

4. *Shanghai Power Co. v. Del. Trust Co.*, 316 A.2d 589, 593 (Del. Ch. 1974).
5. Del. Gen. Corp. Law §212(a).
6. Richard M. Buxbaum, *Preferred Stock and Draftsmanship*, 42 Cal. L. Rev. 243, 303 (1954).

(b)   No dividend (other than dividends or distributions paid in shares of, or options, warrants or rights to subscribe for or purchase shares of, the common stock of Fannie Mae or any other stock of Fannie Mae ranking, as to the payment of dividends and the distribution of assets upon dissolution, liquidation or winding up of Fannie Mae, junior to the Series Q Preferred Stock) may be declared or paid or set apart for payment on Fannie Mae's common stock (or on any other stock of Fannie Mae ranking, as to the payment of dividends, junior to the Series Q Preferred Stock) unless dividends have been declared and paid or set apart (or ordered to be set apart) on the Series Q Preferred Stock for the then-current quarterly Dividend Period; provided, however, that the foregoing dividend preference shall not be cumulative and shall not in any way create any claim or right in favor of the Holders of Series Q Preferred Stock in the event that dividends have not been declared or paid or set apart . . .

(c)   The Board of Directors of Fannie Mae, or a duly authorized committee thereof, may, in its discretion, choose to pay dividends on the Series Q Preferred Stock without the payment of any dividends on Fannie Mae's common stock (or any other stock of Fannie Mae ranking, as to the payment of dividends, junior to the Series Q Preferred Stock).

(d)   No full dividends shall be declared or paid or set apart for payment on any stock of Fannie Mae ranking, as to the payment of dividends, on a parity with the Series Q Preferred Stock for any period unless full dividends have been declared and paid or set apart for payment on the Series Q Preferred Stock for the then-current quarterly Dividend Period. When dividends are not paid in full upon the Series Q Preferred Stock and all other classes or series of stock of Fannie Mae, if any, ranking, as to the payment of dividends, on a parity with the Series Q Preferred Stock, all dividends declared upon shares of Series Q Preferred Stock and all such other stock of Fannie Mae will be declared pro rata so that the amount of dividends declared per share of Series Q Preferred Stock and all such other stock will in all cases bear to each other the same ratio that accrued dividends per share of Series Q Preferred Stock (but without, in the case of any noncumulative preferred stock, accumulation of unpaid dividends for prior Dividend Periods) and such other stock bear to each other.

(e)   No dividends may be declared or paid or set apart for payment on any shares of Series Q Preferred Stock if at the same time any arrears exist or default exists in the payment of dividends on any outstanding class or series of stock of Fannie Mae ranking, as to the payment of dividends, prior to the Series Q Preferred Stock.

(f)   Holders of Series Q Preferred Stock will not be entitled to any dividends, whether payable in cash or property, other than as herein provided and will not be entitled to interest, or any sum in lieu of interest, in respect of any dividend payment.

3.   OPTIONAL REDEMPTION.

(a)   The Series Q Preferred Stock shall not be redeemable prior to September 30, 2010. On and after that date, subject to (x) the notice provisions set forth in Section 3(b) below, (y) the receipt of any required regulatory approvals and (z) any further limitations which may be imposed by law, Fannie Mae may redeem the Series Q Preferred Stock, in whole or in part, at any time or from time to time, out of funds legally available therefor, at the redemption price of $25 per share plus an amount equal to the amount of the dividend (whether or not declared) for the then-current quarterly Dividend Period accrued to but excluding the date of such redemption, but without accumulation of unpaid dividends on the Series Q Preferred Stock for prior Dividend Periods.

(d)   The Series Q Preferred Stock will not be subject to any mandatory redemption, sinking fund or other similar provisions. In addition, Holders of Series Q Preferred Stock will have no right to require redemption of any shares of Series Q Preferred Stock.

4.   LIQUIDATION RIGHTS.

(a)   Upon any voluntary or involuntary dissolution, liquidation or winding up of Fannie Mae, after payment or provision for the liabilities of Fannie Mae and the expenses of such dissolution, liquidation or winding up, the Holders of outstanding shares of the Series Q Preferred Stock will be entitled to receive out of the assets of Fannie Mae or proceeds thereof available for distribution to stockholders, before any payment or distribution of assets is made to holders of Fannie Mae's common stock (or any other stock of Fannie Mae ranking, as to the distribution of assets upon dissolution, liquidation or winding up of Fannie Mae, junior to the Series Q Preferred Stock), the amount of $25 per share plus an amount, determined in accordance with Section 2 above, equal to the dividend (whether or not declared) for the then-current quarterly Dividend Period accrued to but excluding the date of such liquidation payment, but without accumulation of unpaid dividends on the Series Q Preferred Stock for prior Dividend Periods.

(b)   If the assets of Fannie Mae available for distribution in such event are insufficient to pay in full the aggregate amount payable to Holders of Series Q Preferred Stock and holders of all other classes or series of stock of Fannie Mae, if any, ranking, as to the distribution of assets upon dissolution, liquidation or winding up of Fannie Mae, on a parity with the Series Q Preferred Stock, the assets will be distributed to the Holders of Series Q Preferred Stock and holders of all such other stock pro rata, based on the full respective preferential amounts to which they are entitled (but without, in the case of any noncumulative preferred stock, accumulation of unpaid dividends for prior Dividend Periods).

(c)   Notwithstanding the foregoing, Holders of Series Q Preferred Stock will not be entitled to be paid any amount in respect of a dissolution, liquidation or winding up of Fannie Mae until holders of any classes or series of stock of Fannie Mae ranking, as to the distribution of assets upon dissolution, liquidation or winding up of Fannie Mae, prior to the Series Q Preferred Stock have been paid all amounts to which such classes or series are entitled.

(d)   Neither the sale, lease or exchange (for cash, shares of stock, securities or other consideration) of all or substantially all of the property and assets of Fannie Mae, nor the merger, consolidation or combination of Fannie Mae into or with any other entity or the merger, consolidation or combination of any other entity into or with Fannie Mae, shall be deemed to be a dissolution, liquidation or winding up, voluntary or involuntary, for the purposes of this Section 4.

(e)   After payment of the full amount of the distribution of assets upon dissolution, liquidation or winding up of Fannie Mae to which they are entitled pursuant to paragraphs (a), (b) and (c) of this Section 4, the Holders of Series Q Preferred Stock will not be entitled to any further participation in any distribution of assets by Fannie Mae.

7.   VOTING RIGHTS; AMENDMENTS.

(a)   Except as provided below, the Holders of Series Q Preferred Stock will not be entitled to any voting rights, either general or special.

(c)   Except as set forth in paragraph (b) of this Section 7, the terms of this Certificate or the Series Q Preferred Stock may be amended, altered, supplemented, or repealed only with the consent of the Holders of at least two-thirds of the shares of Series Q Preferred Stock then outstanding, given in person or by proxy, either in writing or at a meeting of stockholders at which the Holders of Series Q Preferred Stock shall vote separately as a class. On matters requiring their consent, Holders of Series Q Preferred Stock will be entitled to one vote per share.

8.   ADDITIONAL CLASSES OR SERIES OF STOCK.

The Board of Directors of Fannie Mae, or a duly authorized committee thereof, shall have the right at any time in the future to authorize, create and issue, by resolution or resolutions, one or more additional classes or series of stock of Fannie Mae, and to determine and fix the distinguishing characteristics and the relative rights, preferences, privileges and other terms of the shares thereof. Any such class or series of stock may rank prior to, on a parity with or junior to the Series Q Preferred Stock as to the payment of dividends or the distribution of assets upon dissolution, liquidation or winding up of Fannie Mae, or otherwise.

PROBLEM SET 13.1

1. What are the dividend, voting, and preference rights of a holder of the Series Q Preferred Stock? What risks does the holder face based on the terms presented?
2. Contrast the dividends in the foregoing shares to those provided by the following provision:

    The holders of shares of the outstanding Preferred Stock shall be entitled, when, as and if declared by the Board of Directors out of funds of the

Corporation legally available therefor, to receive cumulative cash dividends at the rate per annum of 4.50% per share on the Liquidation Preference (equivalent to $2.25 per annum per share), payable quarterly in arrears (the "Dividend Rate") ... Such dividends shall be cumulative ... (whether or not in any dividend period or periods the Board of Directors shall have declared such dividends or there shall be funds of the Corporation legally available for the payment of such dividends) and shall accumulate on a day-to-day basis, whether or not earned or declared, from and after the Issue Date. Dividends payable for any partial dividend period shall be computed on the basis of days elapsed over a 360-day year consisting of twelve 30-day months. Accumulated unpaid dividends accrue and cumulate dividends at the annual rate of 4.50% and are payable in the manner provided in this Section 3.

3.   Unlike common shares, preferred shares typically remain close to their initial issue price, and rarely go over their initial issue price. Why?

2.   INTERPRETING THE TERMS

ELLIOTT ASSOCIATES, L.P., A DELAWARE LIMITED PARTNERSHIP, V. AVATEX CORPORATION, A DELAWARE CORPORATION

715 A.2d 843, Supreme Court of Delaware.
Nos. 279, 1998, 282, 1998 | Submitted: July 21, 1998 | Decided: Aug. 28, 1998

VEASEY, Chief Justice:

In this case of first impression, we hold that certain preferred stockholders have the right to a class vote in a merger where: (1) the certificate of incorporation expressly provides such a right in the event of any "amendment, alteration or repeal, whether by merger, consolidation or otherwise" of any of the provisions of the certificate of incorporation; (2) the certificate of incorporation that provides protections for the preferred stock is nullified and thereby repealed by the merger; and (3) the result of the transaction would materially and adversely affect the rights, preferences, privileges or voting power of those preferred stockholders. In so holding, we distinguish prior Delaware precedent narrowly because of the inclusion by the drafters of the phrase, "whether by merger, consolidation or otherwise."

FACTS

Defendant Avatex Corporation ("Avatex") is a Delaware corporation that has outstanding both common and preferred stock. The latter includes two distinct series of outstanding preferred stock: "First Series Preferred" and "Series A Preferred." Plaintiffs in these consolidated cases are all preferred stockholders of defendant Avatex. The individual defendants are all members of the Avatex board of directors.

Avatex created and incorporated Xetava Corporation ("Xetava") as its wholly-owned subsidiary on April 13, 1998, and the following day announced its intention to merge with and into Xetava. Under the terms of the proposed merger, Xetava is to be the surviving corporation. Once the transaction is consummated, Xetava will immediately change its name to Avatex Corporation. The proposed merger would cause a conversion of the preferred stock of Avatex into common stock of Xetava. The merger will effectively eliminate Avatex' certificate of incorporation, which includes the certificate of designations creating the Avatex preferred stock and setting forth its rights and preferences.[7] The terms of the merger do not call for a class vote of these preferred stockholders. Herein lies the heart of the legal issue presented in this case.

Plaintiffs filed suit in the Court of Chancery to enjoin the proposed merger, arguing, among other things, that the transaction required the consent of two-thirds of the holders of the First Series Preferred stock. Defendants responded with a motion for judgment on the pleadings, which the Court of Chancery granted, finding that the provisions governing the rights of the First Series Preferred stockholders do not require such consent.

The plaintiffs allege that, because of Avatex' anemic financial state, "all the value of Avatex is [currently] in the preferred stock." By forcing the conversion of the preferred shares into common stock of the surviving corporation, however, the merger would place current preferred stockholders of Avatex on an even footing with its common stockholders. In fact, the Avatex preferred stockholders will receive in exchange for their preferred stock approximately 73% of Xetava common stock, and the common stockholders of Avatex will receive approximately 27% of the common stock of Xetava.

Under the terms of the Avatex certificate of incorporation, First Series stockholders have no right to vote except on:

(a) any "amendment, alteration or repeal" of the certificate of incorporation "whether by merger, consolidation or otherwise," that

(b) "materially and adversely" affects the rights of the First Series stockholders.

The text of the terms governing the voting rights of the First Series Preferred Stock is set forth in the certificate of designations as follows:

> Except as expressly provided hereinafter in this Section (6) or as otherwise . . . required by law, the First Series Preferred Stock shall have no voting rights. . . .
>
> So long as any shares of First Series Preferred Stock remain outstanding, the *consent* of the holders of at least two-thirds of the shares of the *First Series Preferred Stock* outstanding at the time (voting separately as a class . . .) . . . *shall be necessary to permit, effect or validate* any one or more of the following:
>
> . . .
>
> (b) *The amendment, alteration or repeal, whether by merger, consolidation or otherwise, of any of the provisions of the* Restated *Certificate* of Incorporation or of [the certificate of

---

7. When certificates of designations become effective, they constitute amendments to the certificate of incorporation so that the rights of preferred stockholders become part of the certificate of incorporation. Accordingly, we will use the term "certificate" to refer to the certificate of designations as integrated into the certificate of incorporation. See Kaiser Aluminum Corp. v. Matheson, Del.Supr., 681 A.2d 392, 394 n. 3 (1996) (citing 8 Del. C. §§102(a)(4), 151(g)).

designations] which would *materially and adversely affect any right, preference, privilege or voting power of the First Series Preferred Stock* or of the holders thereof. . . .

These are the operative terms of Section 6 of the certificate of designations (with emphasis supplied) setting forth the rights and preferences of the First Series Preferred stock that became effective March 18, 1983. On September 14, 1983 a new certificate of designations became effective with respect to the Second Series Preferred stock. There is, however, no Second Series Preferred stock outstanding. Unlike the First Series certificate, Section 6 of the Second Series certificate expressly provides the Second Series Preferred stock with a right to vote on any consolidation or merger (with certain exceptions not relevant here) to which Avatex is a party:

> So long as any shares of the Second Series Preferred Stock remain outstanding, the consent of the holders of at least a majority of the shares of the Second Series Preferred Stock outstanding at the time . . . shall be necessary to permit or approve any of the following:
> . . .
> (b) The consolidation or merger of the Corporation with or into any other corporation unless. . . .

We discuss this provision further in our analysis of the legal issue involved.

Analysis

Delaware law permits corporations to create and issue stock that carries no voting power. Professor Buxbaum, in his seminal article on preferred stock nearly 45 years ago, noted, among many other cogent observations, that: (a) statutes often permit alteration of preferred stock rights and preferences by merger; (b) the merger may be with a "paper subsidiary created for that purpose with no independent business validity"; (c) "corporate articles [often] require consent of two-thirds (or a majority) of the preferred share-holders as a class for the consummation of any merger . . ."; and (d) courts have struggled with "controls in the name . . . of 'fairness' and generally abandoned them [, which] is as it should be [since the] issue is one of corporate power."

The Avatex certificate of incorporation provides that Avatex preferred shares have no right to vote except on matters set forth therein or required by law. This denial of the right to vote is subject to an exception carved out for any "amendment, alteration or repeal" of the certificate "whether by merger, consolidation or otherwise" that "materially and adversely" affects the rights of the preferred stockholders. Such an event requires the consent of two-thirds of the First Series Preferred stockholders voting as a class.

This appeal, then, reduces to a narrow legal question: whether the "amendment, alteration or repeal" of the certificate of incorporation is caused "by merger, consolidation or otherwise" thereby requiring a two-thirds class vote of the First Series Preferred stockholders, it being assumed for purposes of this appeal that their rights would be "materially and adversely" affected. The Court of Chancery answered this question in the negative. Although we respect that Court's craftsmanlike analysis, we are constrained to disagree with its conclusion.

Relying primarily on *Warner Communications Inc. v. Chris-Craft Industries Inc.*, the Court of Chancery held that it was only the *conversion* of the stock as a result of the merger, and not the *amendment, alteration or repeal* of the certificate, that would adversely affect the preferred stockholders. It is important to keep in mind, however, that the terms of the preferred stock in *Warner* were significantly different from those present here, because in *Warner* the phrase "whether by merger, consolidation or otherwise" was not included. The issue here, therefore, is whether the presence of this additional phrase in the Avatex certificate is an outcome-determinative distinction from *Warner*.

In *Warner*, the question was whether the Series B preferred stock of Warner Communications, Inc. had the right to a class vote on a proposed merger of Warner with Time, Inc. (renamed Time Warner Inc.) and TW Sub, its wholly-owned subsidiary. As the first step in a two-step transaction, Time had acquired approximately 50% of Warner's common stock in a tender offer. The second step was the "back-end" merger in which TW Sub was merged into Warner, which survived as a wholly-owned subsidiary of Time. The Warner common stock not held by Time was converted into cash, securities and other property. In the merger, the Warner Series B preferred would be converted into Time Series BB preferred stock. The parties stipulated that the Warner Series B stockholders would thereby be adversely affected.

The Chancellor held that the drafters of the Warner Series B certificate of designations did not intend for two-thirds of the Series B stockholders to have a veto over every merger in which their interest would be adversely affected because the right to vote was conferred expressly (as it must under Delaware law), and "only in narrowly defined circumstances . . . not present here."

Here the First Series Preferred stock of Avatex is converted to common stock of the surviving corporation, Xetava, a newly formed corporation admittedly a wholly owned subsidiary of Avatex created for the sole purpose of effecting this merger and eliminating the rights of the Avatex First Series Preferred. In *Warner*, the Warner, Series B Preferred also received a new security—Time Series BB Preferred—a senior security issued by the surviving corporation, Time (renamed Time Warner). This was accomplished by using TW Sub, Time's wholly-owned subsidiary, as the merger partner of Warner. Since we do not reach the question of the economic quality of the transaction, it makes no difference for purposes of this analysis (as plaintiffs argue) that in *Warner* there were two distinct acts that operated independently—that the substitution of charters was between Warner and TW Sub and the exchange of shares was between Warner and Time. The operative events here are that the proposed downstream merger of Avatex into Xetava results in the conversion of Avatex stock to Xetava stock and the elimination "by merger" of the certificate protections granted to the Avatex First Series Preferred. Thus, it is *both* the stock conversion *and* the repeal of the Avatex certificate that causes the adverse effect to the First Series Preferred. In *Warner*, it was only the stock conversion that caused the adverse effect because the phrase, "whether by merger, consolidation or otherwise" was not present.

The relevant statutory provisions are found in Sections 251(b) and 251(e) of the Delaware General Corporation Law ("DGCL") . . .

Avatex argued below, and the Court of Chancery appears to have agreed, that *only* a Section 251(b)(3) Amendment to the surviving corporation's charter amounts to an "amendment, alteration or repeal" within the meaning of the provisions defining the voting rights of the preferred stockholders. Accordingly, the argument runs, these provisions would apply *only* in the circumstance (not present here) where Avatex survives the merger and its certificate is amended thereby. Since the proposed merger with Xetava does not contemplate any such amendments to the disappearing Avatex certificate, the argument goes, the transaction can go forward without a First Series class vote.

The first question is: What will happen as a result of the merger to the "rights, preferences, privileges or voting power" of the Avatex First Series Preferred stock as set forth in the existing Avatex certificate? They disappear when the preferred stockholders of Avatex become common stockholders of Xetava under its certificate that does not contain those protections. We assume, as did the trial court, that their elimination would affect the First Series Preferred stockholders adversely.

The second question is: What act or event will cause this adverse effect if the merger is consummated? The trial court held that, "[a]s in *Warner*," the adverse effect on the plaintiffs "will not flow from any 'amendment, alteration or repeal' of the First Series Certificate (however accomplished) but from the conversion into common stock of the First Series Preferred in the Proposed Merger." The Court so held notwithstanding that it had noted the distinguishing language of the certificate here—not present in *Warner*—"whether by merger, consolidation or otherwise." But the Court dismissed this distinction by concluding that this "language only modifies the phrase 'amendment, alteration and repeal' and does not independently create a right to a class vote in the case of *every merger*." But that is not the issue here where there is no contention that the First Series Preferred have a right to a class vote on *every merger*.

In our view, the merger does cause the adverse effect because the merger is the corporate act that renders the Avatex certificate that protects the preferred stockholders a "legal nullity," in defendants' words. That elimination certainly fits within the ambit of one or more of the three terms in the certificate: *amendment* or *alteration* or *repeal*. The word *repeal* is especially fitting in this context because it contemplates a nullification, which is what defendants concede happens to the Avatex certificate.

Articulation of the rights of preferred stockholders is fundamentally the function of corporate drafters. Construction of the terms of preferred stock is the function of courts. This Court's function is essentially one of contract interpretation against the background of Delaware precedent. These precedential parameters are simply stated: Any rights, preferences and limitations of preferred stock that distinguish that stock from common stock must be expressly and clearly stated, as provided by statute. Therefore, these rights, preferences and limitations will not be presumed or implied. The other doctrine states that when there is a hopeless ambiguity attributable to the corporate drafter that could mislead a reasonable investor such ambiguity must be construed in favor of the reasonable expectation of the investor and against the drafter. This latter doctrine is not applicable here because there is no ambiguity.

In our view, the rights of the First Series Preferred are expressly and clearly stated in the Avatex certificate. The drafters of this instrument could not reasonably have intended any consequence other than granting to the First Series Preferred stock the right to consent by a two-thirds class vote to any merger that would result in the elimination of the protections in the Avatex certificate if the rights of the holders of that stock would thereby be adversely affected. The First Series Preferred stock rights granted by the corporate drafters here are the functional equivalent of a provision that would expressly require such consent if a merger were to eliminate any provision of the Avatex certificate resulting in materially adverse consequences to the holders of that security.

The drafters were navigating around several alternatives. First, all parties agree that pure amendment protection available to the First Series Preferred stockholders as granted by Section 242(b)(2) of the DGCL and Section 4 of the certificate does not — absent the very phrase at issue here — apply to this merger. Although *Warner* was decided after the Avatex certificate of designations became effective, *Warner* clearly supports this view and it continues to be valid precedent for that proposition. Second, all parties agree that if Avatex would have been the survivor, and its certificate were amended in the merger as contemplated by 8 *Del.C.* §251(c)(3), the First Series Preferred would have the right to consent by two-thirds class vote. Third, all parties agree that the right to consent to *any* merger that was granted (subject to certain exceptions not relevant here) to the Second Series Preferred stock (of which none is outstanding) was not intended to be granted to the First Series holders whose rights are more narrowly circumscribed. In their case: (a) the merger must be the cause of an "amendment alteration or repeal" of the certificate (not all mergers do this); and (b) their rights must be adversely affected (which does not inevitably occur in a merger).

If Section 6 of the certificate does not guarantee a class vote to the First Series Preferred in this merger, what could it conceivably be interpreted to mean? Defendants argue that the certificate can be construed to apply *only* in the second instance noted above-namely, in the case where Avatex is the survivor and its certificate is amended, altered or repealed, as contemplated by Section 251(b)(3). But, as plaintiffs point out, this cannot be the *only* outcome the drafters intended because the certificate grants the First Series Preferred this protection in a consolidation where Section 251(b)(3) does not apply. Because the word *consolidation* is included, it cannot reasonably be argued that the protections of Section 6 of the certificate applicable to the First Series Preferred are confined to a Section 251(b)(3) amendment. Therefore, the term *consolidation* cannot be ignored or wished away as surplusage, as defendants argue. It is well established that a court interpreting any contractual provision, including preferred stock provisions, must give effect to all terms of the instrument, must read the instrument as a whole, and, if possible, reconcile all the provisions of the instrument.

PROBLEM SET 13.2

1. The preferred shareholders won in this case, but should preferred shareholders generally look to the Delaware courts for protection?
2. Does DGCL §242(b) provide greater protection for preferred shareholders if the company instead proceeds by way of charter amendment?
   See Hartford Accident & Indemnity Co. v. W.S. Dickey Clay Mfg. Co., 24
   A.2d 315 (Del. 1942). Would preferred shareholders be better off under
   California law? California Corporations Code §903.

3. APPRAISAL RIGHTS OF PREFERRED SHARES

IN RE APPRAISAL OF METROMEDIA INTERNATIONAL GROUP, INC.
971 A.2d 893, Court of Chancery of Delaware
Civil Action No. 3351–CC. | Submitted: Jan. 30, 2009 |
Decided: April 16, 2009

CHANDLER, Chancellor.

In this consolidated appraisal proceeding, dissenting petitioners seek a judicial
determination of the "fair value" of the 7.25% Cumulative Convertible Preferred Stock of respondent Metromedia International Group, Inc. ("MIG").
This litigation arises from the August 22, 2007 merger of CaucusCom Mergerco
Corp. ("MergerSub"), a wholly-owned subsidiary of CaucusCom Ventures, L.P.
("CaucusCom"), with MIG, in which MIG was the surviving entity. The merger
occurred after MergerSub had already acquired in a tender offer approximately
77% of MIG's outstanding common shares. After the tender offer, the merger
agreement between MIG, CaucusCom, and MergerSub granted MergerSub the
option (referred to as the "Top-Up Option"), which MergerSub exercised, to
obtain additional common shares from MIG in order to raise MergerSub's ownership stake to 90%. The Top-Up Option was followed by a short-form merger
under 8 *Del. C.* §253 in which the remaining common shares were cashed out,
and which led to this appraisal proceeding.

MIG asserts that the highest value of the preferred shares is based on the
preferred's being converted into common shares under the certificate of designation. According to MIG, the certificate of designation imposed limitations
on the consideration that preferred holders would receive upon conversion,
which tops out at $18.07 for each preferred share. In contrast, petitioners rely
upon three different valuation approaches, which yield a range of values from
$67.50 per share to $79.76 per share. They view their methodologies as vindi-
cated by virtue of their "convergence" on the preferred stock's $79.76 redemp-
tion price under the certificate of designation, even though (as I determine) no
redemption has ever occurred.

The case was tried before the Court on December 12, 15, 16, and 17, 2008.
This is the Court's post-trial decision. After considering the record of over 220
exhibits, the testimony of one fact and three expert witnesses, and having
weighed all of the evidence, I determine the fair value of MIG preferred shares

on August 22, 2007 to be $38.92 for each share. I also award interest on this amount at the statutorily prescribed rate.

In September 1997, when MIG issued the preferred shares, MIG's total enterprise value was approximately $1 billion. MIG owned all or part of telecommunications businesses in fourteen countries throughout Eastern Europe, the republics of the former Soviet Union, and other emerging markets . . . As of the time of the Merger, the accrued and unpaid dividends totaled $121,732,028, or $29.40 for each preferred share . . . Salford Capital Partners Inc. ("Salford")] is a private equity investment management firm that specializes in the former Soviet Union and other Central and Eastern European countries . . . Sun Capital Partners Ltd., a United Kingdom principal investment group ("Sun"), joined Salford as a partner in the discussions with MIG regarding a tender offer . . . Salford and Sun agreed with MIG to include a back-end merger as part of the transaction

II. ANALYSIS

A preferred shareholder's rights are defined in either the corporation's certificate of incorporation or in the certificate of designation, which acts as an amendment to a certificate of incorporation. Thus, rights of preferred shareholders are contractual in nature and the "construction of preferred stock provisions are matters of contract interpretation for the courts."

This proposition of contract interpretation for preferred stock is interwoven with a stockholder's statutory right of appraisal. Generally, in an appraisal action, this Court has broad discretion and uses a "liberal approach" in considering "all relevant factors involving the value of a company," to independently determine the "fair price" of the stock. Narrowly interpreted "speculative elements of value," usually contemplated synergies or speculative *pro forma* projections, are eliminated from consideration. Moreover, this Court will consider "proof of value by any techniques or methods which are generally considered acceptable in the financial community and otherwise admissible in court." Methods approved by this Court in determining fair value include the discounted cash flow valuation methodology, the comparable transactions approach, and the comparable company analysis. Each approach is dependent on the reliability of its inputs and is limited by the similarities between the companies or transactions being compared.

The law of Delaware governing contracts is clear: a valid contract will be enforced unless the contract violates public policy or positive law, or unless a party's non-performance is excused. Given the contractual nature of preferred stock, a clear contractual provision that establishes the value of preferred stock in the event of a cash-out merger is not inconsistent with the language or the policy of §262. Thus, the most critical question in this action is whether the certificate of designation, which establishes the rights of MIG's preferred shares, contractually establishes the metric for valuing the preferred shares in the event of a merger. I conclude that it does, which effectively renders irrelevant many of the underlying disputes among the testifying experts over the competing valuation models.

Unlike common stock, the value of preferred stock is determined solely from the contract rights conferred upon it in the certificate of designation. The only reported post-*Weinberger* opinion involving an appraisal of preferred stock, *In re Appraisal of Ford Holdings, Inc. Preferred Stock*, demonstrates the primacy of contract as the measure of the preferred's value. There, former-Chancellor Allen analyzed the rights conferred upon preferred shareholders by the certificate of designation because, "[t]o the extent it possesses any special rights or powers and to the extent it is restricted or limited in any way, the relation between the holder of the preferred and the corporation is contractual." When determining the fair value of preferred stock, therefore, I must first look to the contract upon which the preferred stock's value is based. In other words, the valuation of preferred stock must be viewed through the defining lens of its certificate of designation, unless the certificate is ambiguous or conflicts with positive law. As former-Chancellor Allen recognized in *Ford Holdings*, statutory appraisal rights can be modified or relinquished by contract, but in the case of unclear or indirect drafting, this Court will not "cut stockholders off from a statutory right" to judicial appraisal of their preferred shares.

Turning to the facts of this case, I conclude that MIG's certificate of designation clearly and unambiguously delimits the value to which preferred stockholders are entitled in the event of a merger. The certificate fixes the precise value to be paid to the preferred holders upon a merger event. I begin with Section 8(a) of the certificate of designation, which provides:

> Each holder of Preferred Stock shall have the right, at its option, at any time and from time to time from the Issue Date to convert, *subject to the terms and provisions of this Section 8*, any or all of such holder's shares of Preferred Stock. In such a case, the shares of Preferred Stock shall be converted into such number of fully paid and nonassessable shares of Common Stock as is equal, *subject to Section 8(g)*, to the product of the number of shares of Preferred Stock being so converted multiplied by the quotient of (i) the Liquidation Preference plus any Accumulated Dividends and any Accrued Dividends to and including the date of conversion divided by (ii) the Conversion Price (as defined below) then in effect, except that with respect to any share which shall be called for redemption such right shall terminate at the close of business on the date of redemption of such share, unless the Company shall default in performance or payment due upon exchange or redemption thereof. The Conversion Price shall be $15.00, subject to adjustment as set forth in Section 8(c).

The rights granted to the preferred shares in Section 8(a), however, are "subject to" the provisions of Section 8(g). Turning to Section 8(g), it states in part:

> In case of any capital reorganization or reclassification or other change of outstanding shares of Common Stock (other than a change in par value . . .) or *in case of any consolidation or merger* of the Company with or into another Person . . . *each share of Preferred Stock then outstanding shall, without the consent of any holder of Preferred Stock, become convertible only into* the kind and amount of shares of stock or other securities (of the Company or another issuer) or *property or cash receivable upon such [merger] by a holder of the number of shares of Common Stock into which such share of Preferred Stock could have been converted immediately prior to such [merger]* after giving

effect to any adjustment event. The provisions of this Section 8(g) and any equivalent thereof in any such certificate similarly shall apply to successive [mergers]. *The provisions of this Section 8(g) shall be the sole right of holders of Preferred Stock in connection with any [merger]* and such holders shall have no separate vote thereon.

Section 8(g) effectively determines the value to be paid to preferred holders upon certain events. It is triggered by a merger, and the preferred holders' shares, without their consent, are to be valued as if they had been converted immediately before the merger. Here, a short-form merger followed immediately after the tender offer closed. Thus, the "sole right" available to MIG's preferred holders under the certificate of designation was the non-consensual conversion procedure under Section 8(g).

Section 8(g) also defines the formula for determining the value of preferred shares upon a merger or like transaction:

> [E]ach share of Preferred Stock then outstanding *shall, without the consent of any holder of Preferred Stock, become convertible only into* the kind and amount of shares of stock or other securities . . . or property or *cash receivable upon such [merger] by a holder of the number of shares of Common Stock into which such share of Preferred Stock could have been converted* immediately prior to such [merger] after giving effect to any adjustment event.

This language defines the consideration to which preferred shares are entitled in a merger because it stipulates that the preferred "becomes convertible" into the cash received in the merger by the number of common shares into which the preferred holder "could have been converted" immediately before the merger. In this case, pursuant to Section 8(a), every preferred holder immediately before the merger could have converted each preferred share into 5.29 shares of common stock.

Importantly, Section 8(g) operates as a non-consensual conversion provision, treating the preferred on a merger event as though they have converted ("become convertible" and "which could have been converted"). It could not be more clear on this point: if there is a merger, the preferred holder must accept ("without consent") a conversion into common stock, calculated pursuant to the certificate's formula in Section 8(a).

Therefore, because the cash receivable upon the merger for each common share was $1.80, Section 8(a) sets the amount receivable after the merger for each preferred holder to $9.52 per share (1.80 × 5.29). Section 8(g), however, is not the only value-adding contractual provision triggered by the merger. Section 8(b) also mandates that:

> When shares of Preferred Stock are converted *pursuant to this Section 8, all Accumulated Dividends and all Accrued Dividends* (whether or not declared or currently payable) on the Preferred Stock so converted to (and not including) the date of conversion *shall be immediately due and payable,* at the Company's option, (i) in cash; (ii) in a number of fully paid and nonassessable shares of Common Stock equal to the quotient of (A) the amount of Accumulated Dividends and Accrued Dividends payable to the holders of Preferred Stock hereunder, divided by (B) the Market Value for the period ending on the date of conversion; or (iii) a combination thereof.

Since 8(g) is triggered by the merger, mandating the conversion of each preferred share into 5.29 common shares, 8(b) is also triggered, mandating the payment of the $29.40 in accumulated and accrued dividends. This provision 8(b) is applicable to Section 8 in its entirety and is not subordinate to Section 8(g). Section 8(b) is incorporated into the calculation of value under 8(g) by the clear provision that Section 8(b) applies to *all* of Section 8.

Turning briefly to the gist of petitioners' arguments, they insist that there are alternative value-adding provisions in the certificate of designation (other than Sections 8(g) and 8(b)) that were triggered by the merger. Specifically, they point to: (1) Section 7, granting the preferred shares a liquidation preference amounting to $50.00 for each preferred share, and (2) Section 3, granting MIG the right to redeem each preferred share at $50.00. Petitioners essentially ask this Court to award an appraisal value based on "hypothetical" scenarios — what preferred holders would have been entitled to had their stock been redeemed or had there been a liquidation event. Their expert's valuation models turn on assumptions about what an economically rational MIG board "ought" to do in the future — whether redeem or liquidate — in order to meet notions of an efficient capital market. These views are based on a fundamental misconception of the contractual obligations imposed by the certificate, a few examples of which should illustrate the fallacy of petitioners' position.

I turn first to the fallacy that the merger constituted a redemption under Section 3 of the certificate of designation. Section 3 defines the redemption value of the preferred shares by setting the redemption price at $50.00 for each share. Section 3.1 grants MIG the option to redeem the preferred shares. Under the certificate of designation, redemption would also trigger payment of the $29.40 in accrued and unpaid dividends.

Petitioners argue that redemption of the preferred shares will occur because it is likely that Salford will seek a liquidity event for MIG in the next three to five years. Salford is a private equity investor. Robert Brokaw, petitioners expert witness, testified that a redemption period of three to five years is industry standard for private equity investors and provides the best internal rates of return on investments. Brokaw also opined that in the event Salford exits its investment in MIG, it would make no sense to keep the preferred shares in perpetuity and not pay dividends because defaulted securities in the capital structure will impair Salford's ability to achieve the highest multiple in a sale. Thus, the theory goes, Salford will leave money on the table when it attempts to exit its investment in MIG unless it voluntarily redeems the preferred shares and becomes current on the accumulated and accrued dividends.

The problem with this argument is that petitioners assume that Salford's exit will result in a redemption. In so assuming, they fail to consider various exit strategies available to Salford that would not require redemption of the preferred shares. For example, a potential buyer could enter into a transaction similar to the transaction Salford and MIG effectuated in this case, such as a tender offer and the purchase of the common shares directly from Salford. Alternatively, MIG could conduct an IPO of MIG or sell its shares in Magticom. Brokaw's assumption is thus speculative in that it assumes the probability of a future event, that is not certain to occur, and that has not occurred as of the appraisal date. Salford has every incentive to avoid entering into a transaction that would cause redemption of the preferred shares. Moreover, the preferred holders are only entitled to the value provided for in the certificate of designation. The certificate does not contemplate the probability of future events, regardless of the industry standard or what would amount to Salford's optimal outcome. The probability that redemption will occur seems remote, is at least speculative, and is not supported by the certificate of designation. Thus, it is no basis on which I may determine "fair value" in this appraisal proceeding.

Petitioners further contend that the events of the merger constituted an effective redemption because the common shareholders received value ahead of the preferred holders in violation of the preferred's seniority in MIG's capital structure. As I stated above, the events of the merger complied with the provisions of the certificate of designation. The common shareholders did not receive any value that violated any expressly contemplated rights granted to the preferred under the certificate. If the parties had intended that a transaction, such as the merger, constituted an "effective redemption" of the preferred holders then they should have included language to that effect in the contract. The absence of such language in an otherwise clear and unambiguous contract leads me to the opposite conclusion — the events of the merger did not operate as an effective redemption of the preferred shares.

I turn finally, and briefly, to the liquidation value of the preferred shares under Section 7 of the certificate of designation. Section 7.1 provides:

> In the event of any liquidation, dissolution or winding-up of the Company, whether voluntary or involuntary, the holders of the shares of Preferred Stock shall be entitled to receive out of the assets of the Company available for distribution to stockholders up to the Liquidation Preference plus Accumulated Dividends and Accrued Dividends thereon in preference to the holders of, and before any distribution is made on, any Junior stock, including, without limitation, on any Common Stock.

Petitioners argue that the merger resulted in a liquidation of MIG entitling the preferred shares to the liquidation preference of $50.00 for each share plus the accumulated and accrued dividends. This argument is equally without merit. "The right to be paid the amount due in the event of a liquidation or a redemption arises only in the circumstances specified in the preferred stock terms." Section 7.2 of the certificate of designation specifically states that:

> Neither the sale, conveyance, exchange or transfer . . . of all or substantially all the property and assets of the Company nor the merger or consolidation of the Company into or with any other corporation . . . shall be deemed to be a liquidation, dissolution or winding up, voluntary or involuntary, for the purposes of this Section 7.

Salford purchased the common shares of MIG pursuant to a tender offer, a Top-Up Option, and a §253 short-form merger. Under a plain reading of the certificate of designation, these events have not resulted in a "liquidation," "dissolution" or "winding-up" of MIG. To the contrary, MIG continues as a going concern. No event triggering the liquidation provision has occurred, and thus to base valuation decisions on assumptions that it did would be error.

None of the alternative value-adding sections of MIG's certificate of designation have been triggered and, thus, these untriggered contract rights offer no non-speculative value upon which this Court is entitled to rely in an appraisal proceeding. Accordingly, the "sole right" available to the preferred holders in the event of merger, as explicitly set forth in the certificate of designation, is the nonconsensual conversion right under Section 8(g), which also triggered payment of the accumulated and accrued dividends under Section 8(b). As described above, that right, the preferred holders "sole right" under the certificate, yields a value of $38.92 per share of preferred stock. Preferred holders who acquired their stock in 1997 for $50 may be disappointed that ten years later their stock was worth only 78% of its original issuance price, just as common stockholders who paid $12 in 1997 are no doubt disappointed to realize only 15% of their purchase price, but these consequences flow from the certificate and the market, not from the vagaries of financial methodologies applied in appraisal proceedings. Where the rights of preferred shareholders in the event of a merger are clearly stated in the certificate of designation, those shareholders cannot come to this Court seeking additional consideration in the merger through the appraisal process.

PROBLEM SET 13.3

1. The court interprets section 8(g) — *each share of Preferred Stock then outstanding shall, without the consent of any holder of Preferred Stock, become convertible only into the kind and amount of shares of stock or other securities* — as effectively requiring conversion of the shares. What is the effect of this interpretation, and what other interpretation might the preferred shareholders have argued for?
2. Why might the preferred shareholders wanted to have exited the firm after the merger? Dalton v. Am. Inv. Co., 501 A.2d 1238 (Del. 1985).
3. The appraisal remedy is often thought to have its roots in the historic ability of shareholders to veto mergers — throughout most of the nineteenth century mergers required unanimous shareholder approval. Appraisal rights were given in exchange for loss of these strong voting rights. In this context, does it make sense to allow preferred shareholders to bring appraisal actions?
4. Note that appraisal rights can be modified or waived by the terms of the preferred shares. *Matter of Appraisal of Ford Holdings, Inc. Preferred Stock*, 698 A.2d 973 (Del. Ch. 1997).

4. FIDUCIARY DUTIES TO PREFERRED SHAREHOLDERS

As you no doubt remember from Business Associations, or earlier in this course, the primary protections for shareholders under state corporate law are voting rights and fiduciary duties. Because preferred shareholders often have given up their voting rights by contract, fiduciary duties remain their only possible means of protection if the terms of the contract come up short.

MARILYN JEDWAB, PLAINTIFF, V. MGM GRAND HOTELS, INC., TRACINDA CORPORATION, KIRK KERKORIAN, JAMES D. ALJIAN, ALVIN BENEDICT, FRED BENNINGER, BARRIE K. BRUNET, CARY GRANT, PETER M. KENNEDY, FRANK E. ROSENFELT, BERNARD J. ROTHKOPF, WALTER M. SHARP, ROBERT VAN BUREN, BALLY MANUFACTURING CORPORATION, AND BALLY MANUFACTURING CORPORATION INTERNATIONAL, DEFENDANTS

509 A.2d 584, Court of Chancery of Delaware, New Castle County
No. 8077 | Submitted: March 31, 1986 | Decided: April 11, 1986

ALLEN, Chancellor.

MGM Grand Hotels, Inc., a Delaware corporation ("MGM Grand" or the "Company") that owns and operates resort hotels and gaming establishments in Las Vegas and Reno, Nevada, has entered into an agreement with Bally Manufacturing Corporation, also a Delaware corporation, ("Bally") contemplating a merger between a Bally subsidiary and the Company. On the effectuation of such merger, all classes of the Company's presently outstanding stock will be converted into the right to receive cash.

Defendant Kerkorian individually and through Tracinda Corporation, which he wholly owns, beneficially owns 69% of MGM Grand's issued and outstanding common stock and 74% of its only other class of stock, its Series A Redeemable Preferred Stock (the "preferred stock" or simply the "preferred"). Mr. Kerkorian took an active part in negotiating the proposed merger with Bally and agreed with Bally to vote his stock in favor of the merger. Since neither the merger agreement nor the Company's charter contains a provision conditioning such a transaction on receipt of approval by a greater than majority vote, Mr. Kerkorian's agreement to vote in favor of the merger assured its approval.

Neither Kerkorian nor any director or officer of MGM Grand is affiliated with Bally either as an owner of its stock, or as an officer or director. Nor, so far as the record discloses, has any such person had a business or social relationship with Bally or any director, officer or controlling person of Bally. Bally—at least prior to its obtaining an option on Kerkorian's shares as part of the negotiation of the agreement of merger—has owned no stock in MGM Grand.

Plaintiff is an owner of the Company's preferred stock. She brings this action as a class action on behalf of all owners of such stock other than Kerkorian and Tracinda and seeks to enjoin preliminarily and permanently the effectuation of the proposed merger. The gist of the theory urged as justifying the relief sought is that the effectuation of the proposed merger would constitute a breach of a duty to deal fairly with the preferred shareholders owed to such shareholders by Kerkorian, as a controlling shareholder of MGM Grand, and by the directors of the Company. The merger is said to constitute a wrong to the preferred shareholders principally in that it allegedly contemplates an unfair apportionment among the Company's shareholders of the total consideration to be paid by Bally upon effectuation of the merger. Pending is plaintiff's motion for a preliminary injunction.

II.

Plaintiff claims that the proposed merger constitutes a breach of a fiduciary duty owed by the directors of MGM Grand and its controlling shareholder to the preferred stockholders. As developed at oral argument, the central aspect of plaintiff's theory of liability involves a breach of the duty of loyalty, although plaintiff contends as well that the manner in which the merger was negotiated and approved constitutes a breach of a duty of care.

The main argument advanced by plaintiff is premised upon the assertion that the directors of a Delaware corporation have a duty in a merger transaction to negotiate and approve only a merger that apportions the merger consideration fairly among classes of the company's stock. To unfairly favor one class of stock over another is, on this view, a breach of the duty of loyalty that a director owes to the corporation and, by extension, that he owes equally to all of its shareholders. Asserting factually that under all the circumstances the two outstanding classes of MGM Grand's stock represent equivalent values, plaintiff contends that the proposed Bally merger which does not apportion the merger consideration equally breaches this duty.

Intertwined with this central contention, are a host of other liability theories, including arguments (1) that the board of MGM Grand violated its duty of care in negotiating and approving the merger (relying heavily in that connection on the recent holding of our Supreme Court in *Smith v. Van Gorkom*, Del.Supr., 488 A.2d 858 (1985)); (2) that in instigating the merger at this time and in arrogating to himself the power to negotiate the terms of the merger on behalf of the corporation, Kerkorian (without regard to the specific terms ultimately agreed upon) acted without legal authority and in breach of duties to the preferred; and (3) that the merger constitutes a manipulation of the corporate machinery of the Company in order to avoid paying the preferred a $20 redemption price.

IV.

Initially I address two preliminary although critical legal questions: first, whether, in these circumstances, defendants owe any fiduciary duties to the preferred at all and, second, what standard — entire fairness or business judgment — is appropriate to assess the probability of ultimate success.

A.

Issue on the merits of claims alleged is first joined on the fundamental question whether the directors of MGM Grand owe *any* duty to the holders of the preferred stock other than the duty to accord to such holders the rights, powers and preferences set out in the certificate designating and defining the legal rights of the preferred. As I understand plaintiff's principal theories of liability each is premised upon the existence of a supervening fiduciary duty recognized in equity that requires directors and controlling shareholders to treat shareholders fairly. *See, Weinberger v. UOP, Inc.*, Del.Supr., 457 A.2d 701 (1983); *Sterling v. Mayflower Hotel Corp.*, Del.Supr., 93 A.2d 107 (1952);

Guth v. Loft, Inc., Del.Supr., 5 A.2d 503 (1939). If there is no such duty insofar as preferred stockholders are concerned plaintiff's theories of liability would seem fatally flawed.

Defendants contend there is no broad duty of fidelity owed to preferred stock if that duty is understood to extend beyond the specific contractual terms defining the special rights, preferences or limitations of the preferred. In support of its position on this point defendants cite such cases as *Rothschild International Corp. v. Liggett Group, Inc.*, Del.Supr., 474 A.2d 133 (1984); *Wood v. Coastal States Gas Corp.*, Del.Supr., 401 A.2d 932 (1979) and *Dart v. Kohlberg, Kravis, Roberts & Co.*, Del.Ch., C.A. No. 7366, Hartnett, V.C. (May 6, 1985). Broadly speaking these cases apply the rule that "preferential rights are contractual in nature and therefore are governed by the express provisions of a company's certificate of incorporation" *Rothschild, supra*, 474 A.2d at 136. Defendants restate this accepted principle as meaning "all rights of preferred shareholders are contractual in nature." They then go on to argue (analogizing to the wholly contractual rights of bondholders — as to which no "fiduciary" duties extend) that the only duties directors have to preferred shareholders are those necessary to accord the preferred rights set out in their contract, i.e., the document designating the rights, preferences, etc., of their special stock.

The flaw in this argument lies in a failure to distinguish between "preferential" rights (and special limitations) on the one hand and rights associated with all stock on the other. At common law and in the absence of an agreement to the contrary all shares of stock are equal. *Shanghai Power Co. v. Delaware Trust Co.*, Del. Ch., 316 A.2d 589 (1974). Thus preferences and limitations associated with preferred stock exist only by virtue of an express provision (contractual in nature) creating such rights or limitations. But absent negotiated provision conferring rights on preference stock, it does not follow that no right exists. The point may be conclusively demonstrated by two examples. If a certificate designating rights, preferences, etc. of special stock contains *no* provision dealing with voting rights or *no* provision creating rights upon liquidation, it is not the fact that such stock has no voting rights or no rights upon liquidation. Rather, in such circumstances, the preferred stock has the same voting rights as common stock (8 *Del.C.* §212(a); *Rice & Hutchins, Inc. v. Triplex Shoe Co.*, Del.Ch., 147 A. 317 (1929) *aff'd.*, 152 A. 342 (1930)) or the same rights to participate in the liquidation of the corporation as has such stock (11 W. Fletcher Cyclopedia of the Law of Private Corporations §5303 (rev. perm. ed. 1971); *Continental Insurance Company v. Reading Company*, 259 U.S. 156, 42 S.Ct. 540, 66 L.Ed. 71, 871 (1922)).

Thus, with respect to matters relating to preferences or limitations that distinguish preferred stock from common, the duty of the corporation and its directors is essentially contractual and the scope of the duty is appropriately defined by reference to the specific words evidencing that contract; where however the right asserted is not to a preference as against the common stock but rather a right shared equally with the common, the existence of such right and the scope of the correlative duty may be measured by equitable as well as legal standards.

With this distinction in mind the Delaware cases which frequently analyze rights of and duties towards preferred stock in legal (i.e., contractual) terminology (*e.g., Wood v. Coastal States Gas Corp., supra; Judah v. Delaware Trust Company*, Del.Supr., 378 A.2d 624 (1977); *Rothschild International Corp. v. Liggett Group, Inc., supra*) may be made consistent with those cases that apply fiduciary standards to claims of preferred shareholders (*e.g., David J. Greene & Co. v. Schenley Industries, Inc.*, Del.Ch., 281 A.2d 30 (1971); *Lewis v. Great Western United Corporation*, Del.Ch., C.A. No. 5397, Brown, V.C. (September 15, 1977)).

Accordingly, without prejudging the validity of any of plaintiff's liability theories, I conclude that her claim (a) to a "fair" allocation of the proceeds of the merger; (b) to have the defendants exercise appropriate care in negotiating the proposed merger and (c) to be free of overreaching by Mr. Kerkorian (as to the timing of the merger for his benefit) fairly implicate fiduciary duties and ought not be evaluated wholly from the point of view of the contractual terms of the preferred stock designations.

B.

Assuming that plaintiff and the other preferred shareholders have a "right" recognized in equity to a fair apportionment of the merger consideration (and such a right to require directors to exercise appropriate care) it becomes material to know what legal standard is to be used to assess the probability that a violation of that right will ultimately be proven. Plaintiff asserts that the appropriate test is one of entire or intrinsic fairness. That test is the familiar one employed when fiduciaries elect to utilize their power over the corporation to effectuate a transaction in which they have an interest that diverges from that of the corporation or the minority shareholders. *See, Weinberger v. UOP, Inc., supra; Gottlieb v. Heyden Chemical Corp.*, Del.Supr., 91 A.2d 57 (1952).

Our Supreme Court has made it quite clear that the heightened judicial scrutiny called for by the test of intrinsic or entire fairness is not called forth simply by a demonstration that a controlling shareholder fixes the terms of a transaction and, by exercise of voting power or by domination of the board, compels its effectuation. (The apparent situation presented in this action.) It is in each instance essential to show as well that the fiduciary has an interest with respect to the transaction that conflicts with the interests of minority shareholders. *Aronson v. Lewis*, Del.Supr., 473 A.2d 805, 812 (1984). Speaking in the context of a parent dealing with a controlled but not wholly-owned subsidiary our Supreme Court has said:

> The basic situation for the application of the rule [requiring a fiduciary to assume the burden to show intrinsic fairness] is the one in which the parent has received a benefit to the exclusion and at the expense of the subsidiary.

A parent does indeed owe a fiduciary duty to its subsidiary when there are parent-subsidiary dealings. However, this alone will not evoke the intrinsic fairness standard. This standard will be applied only when the fiduciary duty is accompanied by self-dealing — the situation when a parent is on both sides of a transaction with its subsidiary. Self-dealing occurs when the parent, by virtue of its domination of the subsidiary, causes the subsidiary to act in such a way that

the parent receives something from the subsidiary to the exclusion of, and detriment to, the minority stockholders of the subsidiary.
Sinclair Oil Corporation v. Levien, Del.Supr., 280 A.2d 717, 720 (1971).
As to what appears to be the material element of the negotiation of the Bally merger — the $440,000,000 cash price — Mr. Kerkorian had no conflicting interest of a kind that would support invocation of the intrinsic fairness test. With respect to total price, his interest was to extract the maximum available price. Moreover, as to the apportionment of the merger consideration between the two classes of the Company's stock, Mr. Kerkorian's interest again appears to create no significant bias on his part since his ownership of each class is not only great but substantially equal. Indeed, as indicated, Kerkorian's ownership of the preferred is proportionately somewhat greater.

Thus, had Kerkorian apportioned the merger consideration equally among members of each class of the Company's stockholders (as distinguished from equally between classes of stock on a per share basis), then the fact of his sub-stantially equivalent ownership of each class of stock would have supported invocation of the legal test known as the business judgment rule. *Aronson v. Lewis*, Del.Supr., 473 A.2d 805 (1984). The fact that each class was treated differently would not itself require application of the intrinsic fairness test. *See, MacFarlane v. North American Cement Corp.*, Del.Ch., 157 A. 396 (1928); *Bodell v. General Gas & Electric Corp.*, Del.Supr., 140 A. 264 (1927).

But Kerkorian directed the apportionment of merger consideration in a way that treated himself differently from other holders of common stock. He accorded to himself less cash per common share ($12.24) but, in the License Agreement, arrogated to himself the right to use or designate the use of the MGM Grand name and, under the Price Adjustment Agreement, he is to assume certain obligations and acquire certain rights with respect to pending property insurance claims of the Company.

I conclude [...] that, in apportioning that element of consideration wholly to his own shares to the exclusion of others Kerkorian was exercising power of a kind and in circumstances justifying invocation of the heightened standard of judicial review.

V.

I also conclude that, as to the claim of the preferred to an equal or fair share of the merger proceeds, the defendants are likely to meet the burden thus imposed upon them. It follows that plaintiff has failed to demonstrate a reason-able probability of success on this issue.

First, it seems elementary that the preferred has no *legal* right to equivalent consideration in the merger. Neither the certificate of incorporation nor the certificate of designation of the preferred stock expressly creates such a right. Nor does it appear that such a right may be fairly implied from those documents when read in the light of the terms of the 1982 Exchange Offer. *Cf., Katz v. Oak Industries, Inc.*, Del.Ch., 508 A.2d 873 (1986). Nor do I perceive any basis to recognize an *equitable* right to mathematically equal consideration based upon the conduct of Kerkorian as a fiduciary. Some of what is said below supports this conclusion.

As to a right of the preferred to have the total consideration fairly (as distinguished from equally) apportioned, the current record provides no persuasive basis to conclude that the allocation contemplated by the Bally merger is unfair.

Plaintiff's claim of unfairness in an apportionment of $18 per share to the common stockholders and $14 a share to the preferred, in my opinion, involves a fundamental defect: it rests upon an invalid comparison. The pertinent comparison, if one is treating a right to fair apportionment among classes of stock, is between what those *classes* receive in the merger, on a per share basis, not between what the class of preferred receive per share and what the public holders of common stock are to receive ... when the financial value of the appropriate comparison is developed (to the extent the current record permits the development and evaluation of that comparison) it does not appear very great and certainly does not at this stage appear unsustainable in light of the differences in the rights of common and preferred stockholders and the historical treatment of both classes of stock by the market.

The foregoing evaluation of the probabilities of ultimate success forecloses the necessity for an evaluation of plaintiff's claim of irreparable injury. However, in denying the pending motion, I am sensitive to the interests of the public common stockholder and of Bally to have the proposed merger effectuated without judicial interference. While the complaint in conclusory language alleges that Bally knowingly participated in a breach of fiduciary duty, no specific facts are alleged — nor so far as the present record discloses have facts been uncovered in discovery — that would support that conclusion. In these circumstances, Bally's contract rights — while not dispositive — present an additional circumstance supporting the denial of the pending motion.

PROBLEM SET 13.4

1. What precisely is Chancellor Allen's approach to the duties owed to preferred shareholders?
2. One noted corporate law scholar has argued that preferred shareholder's rights should start and end with the terms of the preferred shares.[8] Beyond its ease of application, what arguments for and against such an approach can you think of?

---

8. *http://goo.gl/6sbhN*

14

BOND INDENTURES

Before Virginia's colonial economy was rooted in African slavery, it first experimented with labor provided by indentured servants. The term *indenture* here refers to the contract that bound the laborer to a term of otherwise unpaid service in exchange for their passage to the New World from England.[1]

In early English law, an indenture was often used for conditional contracts, the name apparently coming from the ability to split the agreement in two parts along a notch at the top, so that each party could retain a piece of the agreement. As explained by a legal historian, when parties agreed to a debt that was conditional on performance of a number of terms, a

> sophisticated method, which was very commonly employed in the case of bilateral agreements, was to set out the terms of the agreement in the form of covenants in an indenture under seal; both parties could then retain one part of the indenture which they had executed. They could then both execute bonds of even date with the indenture, binding themselves to pay a sum of money unless the covenants in the indenture were performed.[2]

Today these terms — indenture, covenant, and bond — are all still used with regard to corporate and sovereign debt, but the agreements have been collapsed to a single, if still formidable, writing.

---

1. *See generally* Edmund S. Morgan, *American Slavery American Freedom: The Ordeal of Colonial Virginia* (1975).

2. A.W. Brian Simpson, *A History of the Common Law of Contract* 91 (1975).

MARCEL KAHAN, *RETHINKING CORPORATE BONDS: THE TRADE–OFF BETWEEN INDIVIDUAL AND COLLECTIVE RIGHTS*

77 NYU L. Rev. 1040, 1044–1047 (2002)

I.   THE STRUCTURE OF BONDHOLDER RIGHTS

With few exceptions, the bond indenture must comply with the provisions in the Trust Indenture Act. The Trust Indenture Act requires that a trustee be appointed as representative of the bondholders and specifies certain ground rules relating to eligibility and disqualification of the trustee. Most aspects of bondholder rights, however — including the substantive content of bondholder rights and most provisions relating to the modification and enforcement of these rights — are not regulated by the Trust Indenture Act and are thus left open to contracting. Though this means that each bond indenture could contain widely varying provisions, many bond provisions are standardized and included in a virtually identical form in each indenture.

A.   AN OVERVIEW OF SUBSTANTIVE BONDHOLDER RIGHTS

The contractual rights of bondholders fall into three categories: financial terms, protective covenants, and miscellaneous provisions. Beyond their contractual rights, bondholders — as creditors and security holders — have rights that arise under statutory and common law.

The most important right of bondholders is the right to receive payments of interest at stated intervals and payment of principal when the bonds mature. In addition, corporate bonds often contain other financial terms, the most important of which are optional redemption rights, sinking funds, put rights, conversion rights, and subordination clauses. Optional redemption (or call) provisions grant the company a right to repay its bonds prior to their maturity. By contrast, sinking fund (or mandatory redemption) provisions obligate the company to repay a specified portion of a bond issue prior to the final maturity of all bonds in that issue. Put rights, in turn, obligate the company, in specified circumstances, to repay the bonds of those bondholders who have elected to exercise their rights. Conversion rights permit bondholders to exchange their bonds for other securities, usually common stock, of the issuing company. Subordination clauses contain an agreement by bondholders to subordinate their right to receive payments from the company to the rights of other specified creditors.

Protective covenants are a second important set of bondholder rights. Designed to protect the bondholders' entitlement to receive payments from the company, protective covenants are limitations on the company's conduct of its business. The most common types of protective covenants in publicly issued bonds are debt restrictions, dividend restrictions, asset sale restrictions, investment restrictions, restrictions on mergers, restrictions on liens and sale/leasebacks, and restrictions on transactions with affiliates.

Beyond financial terms and protective covenants, and beyond the provisions related to amendment and enforcement . . . , bond indentures provide for a host of other bondholder rights. These provisions relate to matters such as the right to receive a replacement bond certificate should one's certificate get lost or stolen; the right to receive notice of a special payment date for the payment of defaulted interest; the right to receive notice of a redemption of bonds or of the fact that a put right has become exercisable; the right to have the conversion price adjusted in certain events; or the right of holders of subordinated bonds to be subrogated to the rights of holders of senior debt once all senior debt is paid in full.

In addition to these contractual rights, bondholders have rights that result from their status as creditors and securityholders. These include rights under fraudulent conveyance law, under provisions of corporation law designed to protect creditors, under federal securities laws and state blue-sky laws, under federal bankruptcy law, and under the common law of fraud.

1. THE TRUST INDENTURE ACT

Until the New Deal, the terms of a bond indenture were subject to the normal rules of contract, supplemented by whatever moral obligation was felt by the key parties — namely the issuer and its underwriter bank. Following the 1929 Crash, and the subsequent Depression, this began to change.

In particular, future Supreme Court justice William O. Douglas led a series of SEC hearings into the treatment of bondholders in "equity receiverships," the corporate bankruptcy proceedings of the times.[3] Ultimately these hearings led to the federalization of corporate bankruptcy, and the enactment of the Trust Indenture Act.[4]

IN THE MATTER OF J.P. MORGAN & CO.
INCORPORATED FILE NO. 25-1
SECURITIES AND EXCHANGE COMMISSION

1941 SEC LEXIS 1210; 10 S.E.C. 119
September 19, 1941

FINDINGS AND OPINION OF THE COMMISSION

The questions before us in this proceeding concern the eligibility, under the Trust Indenture Act of 1939, of J.P. Morgan & Co. Incorporated to serve as indenture trustee for securities which may be issued and sold in the future by an obligor or obligors, at present unknown, for which Morgan Stanley & Co. Incorporated is or may be an underwriter.

---

3. Stephen J. Lubben, *Railroad Receiverships and Modern Bankruptcy Theory*, 89 Cornell L. Rev. 1420 (2004). *See also* Report on the Study and Investigation of the Work, Activities, Personnel and Functions of Protective and Reorganization Committees (1936).

4. 15 U.S.C. §§77aaa-77bbbb.

By Sections 305(b) and 307(c) of the Act it is provided that this Commission, in an appropriate proceeding, shall issue an order refusing to permit a registration statement or application for the qualification of an indenture to become effective if the Commission finds, among other things, that any person designated as trustee under the indenture has any "conflicting interest," as that term is defined in Section 310(b) of the Act. As will be more fully developed further on in this opinion, one of the primary objectives of the Act is to ensure that the holders of bonds, debentures, notes, and other debt securities (referred to as "indenture securities") issued subject to the Act shall have the services of an effective and independent trustee. Among the conflicting interests which the Congress deemed detrimental to that objective, and which the Act provides shall render a person ineligible to serve as trustee under an indenture, are those which exist if — "(3) such trustee directly or indirectly controls or is directly or indirectly controlled by or is under direct or indirect common control with an obligor upon the indenture securities *or an underwriter for such an obligor;*" or if — "(6) such trustee is the beneficial owner of . . . (A) 5 per centum or more of the voting securities, or 10 per centum or more of any other class of security, of an obligor upon the indenture securities . . . or (B) *10 per centum or more of any class of security of an underwriter for any such obligor;* . . . "

The partnership of J.P. Morgan & Co., formed in 1894 as successor to the partnership of Drexel, Morgan & Co., carried on a commercial banking and agency business until 1940 and, until 1934, also a securities underwriting business. These businesses were carried on in New York under the name of J.P. Morgan & Co., and in Philadelphia under the name of Drexel & Co.

The requirement of the Banking Act of 1933 [commonly known as Glass-Steagall] that the business of underwriting securities be separated from the business of commercial banking became effective in June of 1934. The major part of the business of J.P. Morgan & Co. had always been in the commercial banking and agency fields, and in addition, the securities markets had then been dormant for some time. Thus, when faced with the necessity of electing between commercial banking and the underwriting business, the partnership elected to continue its commercial banking activities.

3. OBJECTIVES OF THE TRUST INDENTURE ACT.

The facts bearing on the relationship between the trust company and underwriter here involved must be considered in the light of the purposes and history of the Trust Indenture Act, with particular reference to the objectives Congress had in mind when it defined the conflicts of interest disqualifying the indenture trustee.

Among the primary purposes of the Act was the purpose to "assure that the security holders [holders of bonds, notes, debentures, and similar securities] will have the services of a *disinterested indenture trustee.* . . .

With this end in view, it is obvious why an indenture trustee should not be permitted to have a community of interest with an obligor on the indenture securities: for the creditor interests represented by the trustee will clearly be adverse to the interests of the obligor and its stockholders in the event of a default, or in a period when default is near. Moreover, their interests will be adverse in many ways throughout the life of the indenture securities, in respect of such matters as substitution of collateral, compliance with negative pledge clauses, disclosure of financial condition, declaration and payment of dividends, wasting or diversion of assets, and other matters.

It is equally true that there is danger in a community of interest between the indenture trustee and an underwriter for the obligor. Significantly, the Act treats such relationships as a problem to be met and a practice to be eliminated on virtually the same basis as a community of interest between the trustee and the obligor itself. Section 302 declares that

> "the national public interest and the interest of investors in notes, bonds, debentures . . . [etc.], which are offered to the public, are adversely affected —
> "(1) when the obligor fails to provide a trustee to protect and enforce the rights and to represent the interests of such investors . . .
> "(2) when the trustee does not have adequate rights and powers, or adequate duties and responsibilities, in connection with matters relating to the protection and enforcement of the rights of such investors . . .
> "*(3) When the trustee . . . has any relationship to or connection with the obligor or any underwriter of any securities of the obligor, or holds, beneficially or otherwise, any interest in the obligor or any such underwriter, which relationship, connection, or interest involves a material conflict with the interests of such investors;*
> "(b) Practices of the character above enumerated have existed to such an extent that, unless regulated, the public offering of notes, bonds, debentures, evidences of indebtedness, and certificates of interest or participation therein, by the use of means and instruments of transportation and communication in interstate commerce and of the mails, is injurious to the capital markets, to investors, and to the general public; *and it is hereby declared to be the policy of this title, in accordance with which policy all the provisions of this title shall be interpreted, to meet the problems and eliminate the practices, enumerated in this section, connected with such public offerings.*" (Italics supplied.)

Under clauses (2) to (6), inclusive, of Section 310(b), which defines various situations in which the indenture trustee shall be deemed to have a conflicting interest, various relationships with the underwriter are treated in exactly the same manner as relationships with the obligor. Thus a trustee is disqualified: if the trustee or any of its directors or executive officers is an *obligor* on the indenture securities or an *underwriter* for such an obligor (310(b)(2)); if the trustee controls, or is controlled by, or is under common control with, such an *obligor* or an *underwriter* for such an obligor (310(b)(3)); if the trustee or any of its directors or executive officers is a director, officer, partner, employee, appointee, or representative of such an *obligor* or of an *underwriter* for such an obligor (with certain exceptions favoring limited representation of the trustee in the management of the obligor) (310(b)(4)); if specified percentages of the trustee's voting securities are beneficially owned by such an *obligor*, its directors, partners or executive officers, or by an *underwriter* for such an obligor or by its directors, partners or executive officers (the test being more stringent with respect to the underwriter) (310(b)(5)); and if the trustee beneficially owns 5% of the voting securities or 10% of any other class of security of such an *obligor,* or 10% of any class of security of an *underwriter* for such an obligor (310(b)(6)).

The reasons impelling Congress to treat relationships with an underwriter on the same basis as relationships with the obligor are declared in the legislative history of the Act. It was, of course, recognized that indenture trustees must be given not only the power but also the duty to take affirmative action promptly for the benefit of their beneficiaries, and "should be made to live up to the responsibility which nearly every purchaser assumes it has, and which it represents to the public as having undertaken, in a sense, by the very advertisement of the designation 'trustee.'" Yet conferring adequate powers and imposing necessary duties upon the trustee in the indenture was not considered enough for the purpose. "Few of the indentures examined contained any restrictions upon the possession or acquisition by the trustee of interests materially conflicting with those of the bondholders. Some of the indentures specifically permitted them. It is difficult in many cases quantitatively to estimate the effect of too close affiliations with the obligor *or with the underwriters* of its outstanding securities . . . *It is clear, however, that the existence of such relationships does have a tendency to dilute the loyalty of the indenture trustee.*"

As was said by Commissioner (now Mr. Justice) Douglas, testifying before a subcommittee of the Senate:

"A further danger lurks in affiliations which a corporate trustee may have with the underwriters of the bonds under its indenture . . .

"*Such affiliations of the trustee with the underwriter, whose objectives in reorganizations are frequently incompatible with those of investors, tend to submerge the interests of the security holders and to make them subordinate to the wishes, desires, and possible selfish interests of the underwriter. The trustee will be either unable or unwilling to look at the situation coldly and objectively with a single eye to the protection of his beneficiaries.*"

Situations in which the interests of the underwriter were found to be incompatible with those of the security holders represented by the indenture trustee included default situations, in which the underwriters found it to their interest to conceal defaults and delay action thereon by the trustee at least long enough to permit them to set the stage for reorganization and obtain control of reorganization committees:

"In the minds of bondholders, default itself creates distrust and suspicion of the houses which originated and sold the bonds. Not much is required to fan this feeling of growing distrust and suspicion into a blazing fire of resentment against the houses of issue which may result in adverse publicity, litigation, and damage to any future business. In every default situation, regardless of the guilt or innocence of the houses of issue, there is present the possibility that a committee not controlled by the houses may take aggressive action of this sort. On the other hand, control of the committee — whether exerted by placing members of the house of issue directly on the committee or by insuring the selection of men acceptable to the house of issue — means control over the version of the situation presented to the bondholders through committee circulars, advertisements and answers to inquiries. It also means that if a friendly and cooperative plan of reorganization were worked out, the true facts as to the value of the property and the relation of the houses of issue to it could be kept permanently in their possession and not brought to light. It also means that there will not be a thorough investigation of possible causes of action against the houses of issue nor will there be litigation by the committees against them.

"In this manner the houses of issue will minimize the risk of their own liability to bondholders. In this manner they will also "save face." Through their mouthpiece — the protective committee — they can minimize the seriousness of the situation. They can blame mortgagors, depressions, and business cycles. They can divert criticism to those causes. They can, perhaps completely prevent the searching light of publicity being cast on their own misdeeds. They can, perhaps, lull bondholders into some sense of security by virtue of the fact that they, the houses of issue, are working assiduously in the cause of the investor. In this manner they can perhaps avoid facing the clamor of bondholders. By this method of control the bondholders may not get scent of the facts surrounding the issuance and sale of the securities. In this way perhaps vast majorities of bondholders can be induced to deposit their securities with the house of issue. Once that is accomplished effective control over foreclosure and reorganization has been attained. Minorities are rendered quite impotent. They cannot marshal enough support to make up the percentage necessary under the trust indenture to demand foreclosure or other enforcement of the security under-lying the bonds by the trustee. Likewise, the trust indenture may prohibit suit on their non-deposited bonds unless the trustee refuses to act after demand by holders of a specified percentage of bonds. Thus dissenting groups are slowed up and made ineffective, if not completely stilled and rendered impotent. . . .

"In such a manner do protective committees controlled or dominated by houses of issue stand in a peculiarly strategic position to protect the house of issue against its own misdeeds. In such a manner do deposit agreements serve as insulation for trustees (or their principals) against assertions of fraud, duress, and deception practiced on their beneficiaries."[5] . . .

"*To obtain such control over the reorganization the underwriter normally needs a friendly or complacent trustee — a trustee who will not sound a cry of warning to the security holders; a trustee who by inaction or by compliance with the wishes of the underwriter will take no steps contrary to the desires of the underwriter.* The underwriter had such a trustee in the real estate bond field. He will be likely to have such a trustee in any field if it is an affiliated interest. In such cases the interests of the underwriter and security holder frequently become antithetical. In the same manner the interests of the affiliated trustee become incompatible with those of its beneficiaries."

Under all the circumstances of this case, we are of the opinion that the persons in control of the two corporations have such a community of interest as to preclude a finding by us that the trust company is not "under direct or indirect common control" with the underwriter. The provisions and intent of Section 310(b)(3) of the Act are such that under existing circumstances, for the purposes of Sections 305(b) and 307(c), we are unable to conclude that the applicant trust company is eligible to act as indenture trustee in respect of

---

5. *Report on the Study and Investigation of the Work, Activities, Personnel and Functions of Protective and Reorganization Committees* (Government Printing Office, 1936), Part III, at 85–87, 90; quoted *id.*, Part VI, at 105–106. Such report was made by this Commission to Congress pursuant to Section 211 of the Securities Exchange Act of 1934. In the Trust Indenture Act, Section 302(a) entitled "Necessity for Regulation" begins with the recitation: "Upon the basis of facts disclosed by reports of the Securities and Exchange Commission made to Congress pursuant to Section 211 of the Securities Exchange Act of 1934 and otherwise disclosed and ascertained, it is hereby declared . . ." etc.

securities of any obligor for which Morgan Stanley & Co. Incorporated is or may be an underwriter

---

The Trust Indenture Act of 1939 was amended in 1990 with the stated goal of recognizing changes in debt-financing techniques that had evolved in the more than 50 years since the TIA's original adoption.

Sections 310–318 of the Trust Indenture Act set forth indenture provisions that are mandatory, and they apply as a matter of federal law and those that impose duties on any person are automatically deemed included in every qualified indenture whether or not actually set forth therein.

The most important mandatory provisions can be briefly summarized as follows:

- Section 310, the subject of the SEC opinion excerpted above, sets standards of eligibility for trustees and lists the conflicts of interest that will result in disqualification of trustees.
- Section 315(b) requires the trustee to notify holders of defaults of which the trustee is aware.
- Upon default, section 315(c) requires the trustee to exercise its rights and powers under the indenture according to a "prudent-person" standard.
- Section 316(b) states that the right of any bondholder to receive payment of principal and interest on his indenture securities, and to institute suit for enforcement of such payment, shall not be impaired without her consent.
- Section 317 authorizes the trustee, in case of a default in payment of principal or interest on the indenture securities, in its own name as trustee, to recover judgment against the obligor on the indenture securities and to file proofs of claim in any bankruptcy proceedings.
- Finally, section 318 provides that the mandatory provisions of the TIA will override any conflicting provision of the indenture.

The TIA also requires the "qualification" of most indentures before they can become effective. Since adoption of the 1990 amendments, the SEC no longer reviews indentures to determine their conformity with the TIA. The SEC's role is confined to determining that the debt securities being registered will be issued under an indenture and that the designated trustee is eligible to serve as such and not disqualified.

The SEC has no enforcement authority over the terms of the indenture once the registration statement becomes effective, but the TIA contains criminal liability for certain willful violations and misrepresentations and express civil liability for any omission or misstatement in the filing documents. Courts have also implied a federal private right of action against indenture trustees for violations of the TIA and the terms of indentures issues thereunder.[6]

One final note of relevance to future chapters: Section 304 of the TIA and section 1145 of the Bankruptcy Code[7] contain certain exemptions from the requirements of the TIA. For example, under section 1145(d) of the Bankruptcy

---

6. Zeffiro v. First Pennsylvania Banking & Trust Co., 623 F.2d 290, 298 (3d Cir. 1980).
7. 11 U.S.C. §1145.

Code, a note issued under a reorganization plan that matures no later than one year after the effective date of the plan is exempt from compliance with the TIA.

PROBLEM SET 14.1

1. What is the purpose of section 316(b)'s prohibition on changes to the indenture? Note that sovereign debt, which is not subject to the TIA, often contains a "collective action clause" that allows these terms to be changed by majority or supermajority vote.
2. Review the TIA in your statutory supplement and be prepared to discuss in class.

2. NEGOTIATING THE INDENTURE

RACEPOINT PARTNERS, LLC, ET AL., APPELLANTS, V. JP MORGAN CHASE BANK, N.A., RESPONDENT

14 N.Y.3d 419
Court of Appeals of New York
April 1, 2010

PIGOTT, J.

On February 7, 2001, the energy company Enron executed an indenture agreement with Chase Manhattan Bank (Chase), naming Chase as the indenture trustee for the holders of certain Enron notes. The agreement contained, in section 4.02, a standard provision setting forth a covenant by Enron

> "[to] file with the Trustee [i.e. Chase], within 15 days after it files the same with the SEC [Securities and Exchange Commission], copies of its annual reports and of the information, documents and other reports . . . which the Company [i.e. Enron] is required to file with the SEC pursuant to Section 13 or 15(d) of the [Securities] Exchange Act. Delivery of such reports, information and documents to the Trustee is for informational purposes only and the Trustee's receipt of such shall not constitute constructive notice of any information contained therein or determinable from information contained therein, including the Issuer's compliance with any of its covenants hereunder (as to which the Trustee is entitled to rely exclusively on Officers' Certificates). The Issuer also shall comply with any other provisions of Trust Indenture Act Section 314(a)."

The agreement also set forth various circumstances or events that would constitute default by either party, including failure by Enron to comply with this provision, if not corrected within 60 days of notification by Chase.

In December 2001, in the wake of the major accounting fraud scandal with which it has become synonymous, Enron filed for bankruptcy. Thereafter, plaintiffs Racepoint Partners, LLC, and Willow Capital–II, L.L.C., bought approximately $1 billion of the notes from their holders. Plaintiffs, which, as secondary holders of the notes, are vested with the claims and demands of the sellers, then brought this common-law action against Chase alleging, among other things, breach of contract. Plaintiffs claim, first, that Enron defaulted under the indenture agreement and, second, that Chase had actual knowledge of this default and that its failure to notify Enron and the noteholders of the default constituted breach of the agreement. The issue in this appeal is the allegation of contractual default by Enron in filing reports that were false.

Plaintiffs point to the fact that Enron agreed in section 4.02 to file with Chase copies of all reports that it was "required to file with the SEC pursuant to Section 13 or 15(d) of the [Securities] Exchange Act." Section 13 of the Act requires publicly traded companies to keep records accurately reflecting their transactions and assets, and to file annual and quarterly reports with the Securities and Exchange Commission (*see* 15 USC §78m). Plaintiffs argue that because the financial reports filed by Enron with Chase were inaccurate and did not comply with federal securities law, they were not the reports Enron was "required to file with the SEC." Plaintiffs posit that, by filing these same fraudulent reports with Chase, Enron failed to satisfy its section 4.02 covenant, and thus defaulted.

Chase moved to dismiss the complaint under CPLR 3211. Supreme Court denied Chase's motion. The Appellate Division reversed, granting the motion (57 A.D.3d 378, 869 N.Y.S.2d 489 [2008]). We granted leave to appeal (12 N.Y.3d 706, 879 N.Y.S.2d 52, 906 N.E.2d 1086 [2009]), and now affirm.

Section 4.02 of the indenture agreement is a mandated provision based on the requirements of section 314(a)(1) of the Trust Indenture Act of 1939:

> "Each person who, as set forth in the registration statement or application, is or is to be an obligor upon the indenture securities covered thereby shall . . .
>
> "file with the indenture trustee copies of the annual reports and of the information, documents, and other reports (or copies of such portions of any of the foregoing as the [Securities and Exchange] Commission may by rules and regulations prescribe) which such obligor is required to file with the Commission pursuant to section 13 or section 15(d) of the Securities Exchange Act of 1934 [15 USC §78m or §78o(d)]; or, if the obligor is not required to file information, documents, or reports pursuant to either of such sections, then to file with the indenture trustee and the [Securities and Exchange] Commission, in accordance with rules and regulations prescribed by the Commission, such of the supplementary and periodic information, documents, and reports which may be required pursuant to section 13 of the Securities Exchange Act of 1934 [15 USC §78m], in respect of a security listed and registered on a national securities exchange as may be prescribed in such rules and regulations" (codified at 15 USC §77nnn [a][1]).

Plaintiffs concede that the parties' intent in section 4.02 may be equated with congressional intent with respect to section 314(a) of the Trust Indenture Act of 1939. In drafting the Trust Indenture Act, Congress intended simply to ensure that an indenture trustee was provided with up-to-date reports on a company's financial status, by requiring the company to send the trustee a copy of filed financial reports. In the 1930s, when section 314(a) was drafted, computer-based technologies, whereby copies of SEC reports can now be obtained, did not exist.

The legislative history of section 314(a) suggests that Congress intended to create a delivery requirement and no more. The 1939 House Report highlighted the legislators' concern that trustees and bondholders at the time did not receive periodic reports from companies issuing bonds.

"In a substantial portion of the indentures . . . the issuer was under no obligation to file an annual report with the indenture trustee. None of the indentures . . . required the transmission to the bondholders of periodic reports, such as stockholders customarily receive. None of them established machinery for the transmission of such reports . . . . " (HR Rep. 1016, 76th Cong., 1st Sess., at 35 [1939].)

It is apparent that section 314(a) was designed to mandate such a mechanism of delivery of reports to indenture trustees. The same House Report, observing that in many cases a company "will already be required to file periodic reports with the [Securities and Exchange] Commission under section 13 or section 15(d)," stated that the bill under consideration "merely requires that copies of such reports . . . be filed with the indenture trustee" (HR Rep. 1016, 76th Cong., 1st Sess., at 35).

As federal courts have observed, when considering indenture agreement provisions very similar to the one at issue here,

"the provision merely requires the company to transmit to the trustee copies of whatever reports it *actually* files with the SEC . . .
"[A]ny duty actually to file the reports is imposed 'pursuant to Section 13 or 15(d) of the Exchange Act' and *not* pursuant to the indenture itself. The provision does not incorporate the Exchange Act; it merely refers to it in order to establish which reports must be forwarded. . . .
"[It] impose[s] nothing more than the ministerial duty to forward copies of certain reports, identified by reference to the Exchange Act, within fifteen days of actually filing the reports with the SEC" (*UnitedHealth Group Inc. v. Wilmington Trust Co.*, 548 F.3d 1124, 1128–1130 [8th Cir.2008]; *see also e.g. Affiliated Computer Servs., Inc. v. Wilmington Trust Co.*, 565 F.3d 924, 930–931 [5th Cir.2009]; *American Stock Transfer & Trust Co. v. Par Pharm. Cos., Inc.*, 2009 WL 1754473, *4–5, 2009 U.S. Dist LEXIS 52602, *10–13 [SD N.Y.2009]).

It is clear therefore that indenture agreements containing the required delivery provisions pursuant to section 314(a) refer to the Securities Exchange Act only to identify the types of report that should be forwarded to indenture trustees. They do not create contractual duties on the part of the trustee to assure that the information contained in any report filed is true and accurate. That is simply not the mission or purpose of the trustee or the contract under which it undertakes its duties.

Of course, companies have a duty to file accurate reports with the SEC. That obligation, however, derives from the Securities Exchange Act, not from indenture agreements.

Our holding that section 4.02 of the indenture agreement simply embodies a delivery requirement, and does not imply a duty on the part of the trustee to assure the filing of accurate reports or risk default, is consistent with the limited, "ministerial" functions of indenture trustees (*AG Capital Funding Partners, L.P. v. State St. Bank & Trust Co.*, 11 N.Y.3d 146, 157, 866 N.Y.S.2d 578, 896 N.E.2d 61 [2008]), and with the plain language of section 4.02, which states that "[d]elivery of such reports, information and documents [filed with the SEC] to the Trustee is for informational purposes only." Plaintiffs' proposed interpretation, on the other hand, would require indenture trustees to review the substance of SEC filings, so as to reduce the risk of liability, greatly expanding indenture trustees' recognized administrative duties far beyond anything found in the contract.

Accordingly, the order of the Appellate Division should be affirmed, with costs.

Order affirmed, with costs.

The case reaffirms the basic notion in corporate finance that if you want something, you had better negotiate for it in the contract. And it had better be expressly set forth in the contract. This point will be the subject of the next chapter.

Actually, the terms of the indenture are not so much negotiated; rather the parties negotiate the section of the offering memorandum entitled "Description of Notes" or "Bond" or whatever debt instrument is being issued.[8] That section will set forth, verbatim, the desired covenants of the indenture, with the remainder of the indenture consisting of so-called "boilerplate" that the junior associate cuts and pastes in from a prior deal.[9]

Often bonds or notes are first sold privately, under exemptions from the securities laws like Rule 144A, and later exchanged for public bonds in an "A/B" exchange offer registered with the SEC.[10] Sometimes bonds or notes are sold without registration rights, as "144A for life."

In all cases the investors are bargaining about the terms of a relationship that will last from 10 to 30 years, if not longer. The covenants in the indenture not only act directly, by prohibiting certain conduct, but also by triggering opportunities for renegotiation during the life of the agreement. The issuer-debtor would like to limit those events, to allow maximum flexibility when running its business. The investor-creditors worry that they will be abused by the debtor at a point when their leverage over the debtor might be quite minimal.[11]

Before 1980, there was a relatively standard set of traditional protective covenants that were included in most bond indentures. Since then the strength of covenants has ebbed and flowed with the bond markets. Before the recent financial crisis, some issuers were able to place "covenant light" debt, meaning debt that had few if any covenants. Following the crisis, there is some sense that covenants that had been forgotten are reappearing in indentures. But low interest rates and high demand for bond debt has also pushed the other direction in recent years, and more stories about "Cov Light" appear in the financial press each day.

As a general rule, high-yield (junk) debt will contain more covenants than investment-grade debt.

---

8. This difference in terms relates to their duration — notes are issued for ten years or less.

9. *See* Stephen J. Choi and G. Mitu Gulati, *Innovation in Boilerplate Contracts: The Case of Sovereign Bonds*, 53 Emory L. J. 929 (2004).

10. Exchange offers are discussed later in the course.

11. Marcel Kahan, *The Qualified Case Against Mandatory Terms in Bonds*, 89 Nw. U. L. Rev. 565, 572 (1995).

3. CALL PROVISIONS AND OTHER COVENANTS

Callable or redeemable bonds are bonds that can be redeemed or paid off by the issuer prior to the bonds' maturity date. When an issuer calls its bonds, it pays investors the call price, which may simply be the face value of the bonds, together with accrued interest to date. In many respects this is the corporate equivalent of refinancing your house (or your parents refinancing their house) — the old debt is paid off, often with the proceeds of a new loan.

Call provisions are often part of corporate and municipal bonds, but not bonds issued by the federal government. Even bonds with call provisions are typically not callable during the early years of the bond's term.

PROBLEM SET 14.2

1. A call option is an advantage for the issuer and a disadvantage to the investor. Why is this?
2. In what situations might the issuer want to exercise the call?
3. A make-whole call feature allows the issuer to call the security prior to the stated maturity date at the greater of par or par plus the "make whole premium." Here is the description of the clause from a Goldman Sachs offering memorandum:

> We will have the option to redeem the subordinated notes, in whole or in part, at our option at any time, at a redemption price equal to the greater of (1) 100% of the principal amount of the subordinated notes to be redeemed or (2) as determined by the quotation agent described below, the sum of the present values of the remaining scheduled payments of principal and interest on the subordinated notes to be redeemed, not including any portion of these payments of interest accrued as of the date on which the subordinated notes are to be redeemed, discounted to the date on which the subordinated notes are to be redeemed on a semi-annual basis assuming a 360-day year consisting of twelve 30-day months, at the adjusted U.S. treasury rate described below plus 20 basis points, plus, in each case, accrued interest on the subordinated notes to be redeemed to the date on which the subordinated notes are to be redeemed.

What is the purpose of this clause? What is the effect of the interest rate described in this text? How does this clause compare to a straight call provision?

A *change of control covenant* is designed to protect bondholders most directly from leveraged buyouts or other transactions where a change in ownership of the firm could impair the firm's creditworthiness. The covenant generally gives bondholders the opportunity to put their bonds back to the issuer before a change at 101 percent of the face amount. This commonly applies following a transaction that affects "all or substantially all," of the firm and, sometimes, its subsidiaries.[12]

The covenants often have an exception to their operation if the surviving corporation assumes the debt, and there is no immediate event of default. Other limitations of this covenant include uncertainty about when a sale of all or substantially all assets has occurred. This is especially true if the firm has engaged in a series of transactions.

BEST BUY POISON PUT ELUSIVE IN SCHULZE OFFER: CORPORATE FINANCE

By Mary Childs — August 29, 2012, Bloomberg.com[13]

Best Buy (BBY) Co. founder Richard Schulze says his takeover offer gives the world's largest electronics retailer its best shot at competing with Amazon.com Inc. (AMZN) and Wal-Mart Stores Inc. (WMT). Bondholders aren't convinced.

Best Buy has $1.5 billion of securities that have a so-called poison put, which requires the company to purchase the notes at 101 cents on the dollar in the event of an acquisition combined with a ratings downgrade. A total of $1 billion of that debt is trading as much as 11 cents below that repurchase price, indicating bondholders believe a buyout isn't imminent.

Talks between Schulze, 71, and Richfield, Minnesota-based Best Buy broke down on Aug. 19 and resumed two days later after the company posted quarterly earnings that trailed analysts' estimates. The retailer has been closing big-box stores and paring jobs to generate savings for promotions and training store employees as it struggles to convince investors that its strategy is still relevant.

"We don't think the credit market is putting much stock in the transaction," Joscelyn MacKay, a credit analyst at Morningstar Inc. (MORN) in Chicago, said in a telephone interview. "There are just a lot of outside issues that we think are hurdles to get this deal done."

Online retailers like Amazon are willing to accept lower margins than its brick and mortar counterparts, putting pressure on companies like Best Buy to defend market share and reduce costs through closing stores, MacKay said.

Bruce Hight, a Best Buy spokesman, and David Reno, a spokesman for Schulze, both declined to comment.

"Further Downgrades"

Best Buy's $650 million of 5.5 percent senior unsecured bonds due in March 2021 traded at 90 cents on the dollar to yield 7.08 percent yesterday, according to Trace, the bond-price reporting system of the Financial Industry Regulatory Authority. Its $350 million of 3.75 percent notes due March 2016 are at 93 cents, yielding 5.978 percent.

---

12. *Cf.* DGCL §271.
13. Used with permission of Bloomberg L.P. © 2013. All rights reserved.

"Any Schulze-led buyout would require incurring a large amount of debt that would require further ratings downgrades," Alexander Diaz-Matos, an analyst at the credit research firm Covenant Review LLC, said in a telephone interview. "Even if the bonds are rated below investment-grade by all three ratings agencies prior to a buyout, it's extremely likely given the leverage required, a further downgrade would take place."

Without the buyout, "you're left without a 101 percent change of control right and a deteriorating business," he said.

BOND COUPONS

Best Buy's $500 million of 6.75 percent bonds due in July 2013 compensate investors for downgrades, with the interest rate increasing 25 basis points for every level below junk the rating falls until it reaches B, according to a Dec. 15, 2008, prospectus. Those bonds are trading at 103.1 cents, from as high as 107.3 cents on Oct. 11, Trace data show. Investors in that debt are less concerned with buyout speculation as the maturity date ticks closer, according to Diaz-Matos.

Once a $29 billion company, Best Buy has wiped out almost 80 percent of its market value as it lost sales to Internet-based retailers such as Amazon.com and discount stores like Wal-Mart. It posted a net loss of $1.23 billion on revenue of $50.7 billion for the year that ended in March, its first annual loss since 1991, data compiled by Bloomberg show.

Best Buy and Schulze reached an agreement Aug. 27 allowing him to conduct due diligence and bring a fully financed, definitive proposal to the company within 60 days. If that offer is rejected, he must wait until January to pursue an acquisition through other means, the company said in a statement.

PRIVATE EQUITY

"The board probably was frightened by the falling stock price and felt that to cover itself it had to agree to allow Mr. Schulze to make an offer," Carol Levenson, an analyst at debt-research firm Gimme Credit LLC in Chicago, said in an e-mail. "Perhaps they are calling his bluff about his ability to raise the cash."

The agreement gave Schulze access to financial data that may help him line up private-equity firms he needs to fund a takeover of the company he founded more than four decades ago and left in June.

Best Buy fell to $17.72 as of 11:09 a.m. in New York. The shares have declined 24 percent this year and trade below Schulze's Aug. 6 offer of as much as $26 a share, or about $9 billion. That "tells you folks don't think it's likely," Noel Hebert, chief investment officer at Bethlehem, Pennsylvania- based Concannon Wealth Management LLC, said in an e-mail.

LIKE JUNK

Traders already are treating some Best Buy debt like junk. At 7.08 percent, the yield on the 5.5 percent notes due March 2021 was higher than the average yield on BB rated bonds at 5.63 percent on Aug. 28, according to Bank of America Merrill Lynch index data.

Standard & Poor's lowered Best Buy's credit rating to BB+ from BBB− on Aug. 6, as a result of Schulze's pitch. Moody's Investors Services gives the company a Baa2 grade, two steps above high-yield.

"The transaction, if completed, would materially weaken Best Buy's credit protection metrics because we believe it will add a significant amount of debt," S&P analysts Jayne Ross and Charles Pinson-Rose wrote in the note. Even without the buyout, "management still hasn't been able to keep the leverage in line," MacKay said. "This is a company that is going south. Yes, this company is investment-grade right now, but in 2016, this paper might be more like a single B."

NEW CEO

The average yield on single B bonds was 7.196 percent Aug. 28, according to Bank of America Merrill Lynch index data.

Best Buy named Hubert Joly as its new chief executive officer on Aug. 20 to oversee a turnaround plan that entails shifting to smaller locations in a bid to fend off rivals.

The next day, the company reported second-quarter profit that trailed analysts' estimates and will no longer provide an earnings forecast as sales of computers and televisions dropped. Excluding restructuring charges and other items, profit was 20 cents a share, the company said, missing analysts' average estimate of 31 cents. Revenue of $10.5 billion last quarter is down from $11.3 billion in the same period last year.

The company's leverage, or adjusted total debt to earnings before interest, taxes, depreciation and amortization, was 1.9 times May 5, according to the S&P rating report. That will increase to 3.8 times after a $9 billion transaction, the rating company wrote.

A *negative pledge clause* is quite common and often quite useless. The basic idea is to prevent the issuer from granting liens on its assets. In short, the goal is to prevent the insertion of senior debt into the capital structure. Typically there are exceptions for small liens and mortgages on real property.

PROBLEM SET 14.3

1. Bogartco, Inc. has a clause in its 20 Year Senior Unsecured Floating Rate Notes that prohibits the granting of "any lien, security interest, charge, mortgage, pledge or other encumbrance of any kind including any conditional sale or other title retention agreement, any lease in the nature thereof, and any agreement to give any security interest other than an agreement to secure indebtedness equally and ratably upon

the incurrence of other secured indebtedness." What risks does this leave open? For example, would it prohibit Bogartco's plans to issue $200 million in new Senior Unsecured Floating Rate Notes?

2. Many negative pledge clauses contain exceptions for new borrowing under existing bank loans and borrowing at the subsidiary level. What risks do these exceptions present to the bondholder?

Limitations on debt are meant to restrict the total claims on a company. They solve some of the problems of negative pledge clauses. What the definition of "debt" is will make or break the utility of this kind of clause.

Typically the clause allows for the incurrence of debt so long as a specified financial ratio is satisfied. Often this is a ratio of EBITDA to interest expense or debt to EBITDA. Once the ratio no longer meets the standard, new debt (however defined) is no longer permitted. You knew there was a reason to learn what EBITDA was.

A *subordination provision* is a contractual agreement by one group of bond-holders to defer getting paid until another group of bondholders gets paid in full. Importantly, such a provision is enforceable under the Bankruptcy Code.[14]

Such a provision does not, however, guarantee that the senior bondholders will get paid in full. Why not? If a company has senior and subordinated debt, what would you assume about the coupons on the respective bonds?

A *restricted payment covenant* typically restricts an issuer's ability to make distributions to shareholders or pay off subordinated debt. Such a covenant also constrains an issuer's ability to make "restricted investments." These are investments in "unrestricted subsidiaries" — that is, subsidiaries not subject to the indenture covenants — as well as other investments that are not "permitted investments," such as joint ventures with other companies.

Finally, consider who is borrowing the money under an indenture. Often an indenture will require guarantees by all key subsidiaries. These guarantees mean that the corporate group is liable for the debt, and not just the specific parent company corporate entity. Why include such a provision?

4. THE DYNEGY BOND INDENTURE AND NOTE

Please read the sample bond indenture provided online, especially Articles II and III. Look for the clauses discussed earlier. Consider the definitional questions raised in the preceding discussion.

How much is being borrowed? What are the rights of the creditors? Who is obligated to repay the amounts borrowed and when? What remedies (beyond a suit for breach of contract) are contained in this indenture?

---

14. 11 U.S.C. §510(a).

15

BONDS AFTER THE INDENTURE

Once the bond indenture is signed, it can be the beginning of what might be a long-term relationship between issuer and bondholder, and a very long-term relationship if you buy into the century-long debt once commonly issued by railroads, and recently issued by companies like Disney to take advantage of low interest rates.

One should not be too literal about this. After all, bondholders always have the ability to sell their bonds if they no longer believe in their earlier investment. Of course, the new owner of the bond will at least partially base the price they are willing to pay on the terms of the indenture.

In all events, the primary avenue for subsequent change, or to resolve disagreements about the terms of the previously negotiated indenture, is through negotiation. Typically these negotiations will happen between a group of large bondholders — that is, bondholders who hold many bonds, not linebacker bondholders — and the issuer.

These negotiations take place in the shadow of the existing case law regarding bond indentures. That is, the parties will argue about which prior case is more like the current situation, and beliefs regarding that case law will dictate who has power in the negotiations.

Thus, case law is important here even if most indentures will never result in litigation. Because most bonds sold in the United States have a New York choice of law clause — and bonds worldwide tend to have either a New York or English choice of law clause — cases from New York, including the federal courts therein, are especially important. Delaware sees a lot of these cases, too, although often it finds itself applying New York law.[1]

---

1. Bankruptcy courts in New York and Delaware, where most of the big chapter 11 cases are filed, also end up interpreting a lot of indentures after default.

1. INTERPRETING THE INDENTURE

SHARON STEEL CORPORATION v. THE CHASE MANHATTAN BANK, N.A., AND MANUFACTURERS HANOVER TRUST COMPANY

691 F.2d 1039
United States Court of Appeals, Second Circuit

Ralph K. Winter, Circuit Judge

Background

1. THE INDENTURES

Between 1965 and 1977, UV issued debt instruments pursuant to five separate indentures, the salient terms of which we briefly summarize. In 1965, UV issued approximately $23 million of 5⅜% subordinated debentures due in 1995, under an indenture naming The Chase Manhattan Bank, N.A. ("Chase") as the trustee ("First Chase Indenture"). The current principal amount of the debentures outstanding under that indenture is approximately $14 million.

In 1968, the City of Port Huron, Michigan, issued approximately $22 million in Industrial Development Revenue Bonds, bearing 6 ¼% interest and due in 1993, under an indenture also naming Chase as the trustee ("Second Chase Indenture"). These bonds were issued by Port Huron to raise funds for the construction of a facility to be leased by Mueller Brass Company, a UV subsidiary. The rent paid by Mueller Brass covers the principal and interest on the bonds. Moreover, UV executed an unconditional guaranty of these obligations of its subsidiary ("Chase Lease Guaranty"). The principal amount presently outstanding is approximately $16.5 million.

Similarly, in 1968, the County of Itawamba, Mississippi, issued approximately $13 million in Industrial Development Revenue Bonds due in 1993, under an indenture naming Union Planters National Bank of Memphis as the trustee ("Union Planters Indenture"). These bonds were also issued to fund construction of facilities to be leased by Mueller Brass, the rent payments being sufficient to satisfy the debt service on the bonds. Again, UV guaranteed Mueller Brass' lease obligations ("Union Planters Lease Guaranty"). Approximately $9.78 million principal amount of these Itawamba County bonds remains outstanding.

In 1977, UV issued $75 million of 8 ⅞% debentures due in 1997 under an indenture naming Manufacturers Hanover Trust Company ("Manufacturers") as the trustee ("Manufacturers Indenture"). The principal amount of these debentures has been reduced to approximately $66.78 million. At the same time, UV issued $25 million of 9 ¼% senior subordinated notes due in 1987 pursuant to an indenture under which United States Trust Company of New York ("U.S. Trust") is the trustee ("U.S. Trust Indenture"). Approximately $16 million principal amount of these notes remains outstanding.

The debentures, notes and guaranties are general obligations of UV. Each instrument contains clauses permitting redemption by UV prior to the maturity date, in exchange for payment of a fixed redemption price (which includes principal, accrued interest and a redemption premium) and clauses allowing acceleration as a non-exclusive remedy in case of a default. The First Chase Indenture,[2] the Port Huron Lease Guaranty, the Union Planters Lease Guaranty, the Manufacturers Indenture and the U.S. Trust Indenture each contains a "successor obligor" provision allowing UV to assign its debt to a corporate successor which purchases "all or substantially all" of UV's assets. If the debt is not assigned to such a purchaser, UV must pay off the debt. While the successor obligor clauses vary in language, the parties agree that the differences are not relevant to the outcome of this case.

2. THE LIQUIDATION OF UV

During 1977 and 1978, UV operated three separate lines of business. One line, electrical equipment and components, was carried on by Federal Pacific Electric Company ("Federal"). In 1978, Federal generated 60% of UV's operating revenue and 81% of its operating profits. It constituted 44% of the book value of UV's assets and 53% of operating assets. UV also owned and operated oil and gas properties, producing 2% of its operating revenue and 6% of operating profits. These were 5% of book value assets and 6% of operating assets. UV also was involved in copper and brass fabrication, through Mueller

---

2. Section 13.01 of the First Chase Indenture reads as follows:

Nothing in this Indenture or any of the Debentures contained shall prevent any merger or consolidation of any other corporation or corporations into or with the Company, or any merger or consolidation of the Company (either singly or with one or more corporations), into or with any other corporation, or any sale, lease, transfer or other disposition of all or substantially all of its property to any corporation lawfully entitled to acquire the same or prevent successive similar consolidations, mergers, sales, leases, transfers or other dispositions to which the Company or its successors or assigns or any subsequent successors or assigns shall be a party; provided, however, and the Company covenants and agrees, that any such consolidation or merger of the Company or any such sale, lease, transfer or other disposition of all or substantially all of its property, shall be upon the condition that the due and punctual payment of the principal of, interest and premium, if any, on, all of the Debentures, according to their tenor, and the due and punctual performance and observance of all the terms, covenants and conditions of this Indenture to be kept or performed by the Company shall, by an indenture supplemental hereto, executed and delivered to the Trustee, be assumed by any corporation formed by or resulting from any such consolidation or merger, or to which all or substantially all of the property of the Company shall have been sold, leased, transferred or otherwise disposed of (such corporation being herein called the "successor corporation"), just as fully and effectively as if the successor corporation had been the original party of the first part hereto, and such supplemental indenture shall be construed as and shall constitute a novation thereby releasing the Company (unless its identity be merged into or consolidated with that of the successor corporation) from all liability upon, under or with respect to any of the covenants or agreements of this Indenture but not, however, from its liability upon the Debentures.

After the execution and delivery of the supplemental indenture referred to in the preceding paragraph, any order, certificate, resolution or other instrument of the Board of Directors or officers of the Company may be made by the like board or officers of the successor corporation. The Trustee shall receive an Officers' Certificate that the foregoing conditions are complied with, and an Opinion of Counsel that any such indenture supplemental hereto complies with the foregoing conditions and provisions of this Section 13.01. Subject to the provisions of Section 10.01, such Officers' Certificate and Opinion shall be full warrant to the Trustee for any action taken in reliance thereon.

Brass, and metals mining, which together produced 13% of profits, 38% of revenue and constituted 34% of book value assets and 41% of operating assets. In addition to these operating assets, UV had cash or other liquid assets amounting to 17% of book value assets.

On December 19, 1978, UV's Board of Directors announced a plan to sell Federal. On January 19, 1979, the UV Board announced its intention to liquidate UV, subject to shareholder approval. On February 20, 1979, UV distributed proxy materials, recommending approval of (i) the sale of Federal for $345,000,000 to a subsidiary of Reliance Electric Company and (ii) a Plan of Liquidation and Dissolution to sell the remaining assets of UV over a 12-month period. The proceeds of these sales and the liquid assets were to be distributed to shareholders.

On March 26, 1979, UV's shareholders approved the sale of Federal and the liquidation plan. The following day, UV filed its Statement of Intent to Dissolve with the Secretary of State of Maine, its state of incorporation. On March 29, the sale of Federal to the Reliance Electric subsidiary for $345 million in cash was consummated. On April 9, UV announced an $18 per share initial liquidating distribution to take place on Monday, April 30.

The Indenture Trustees were aware that UV contemplated making an $18 per share liquidating distribution since at least February 20, 1979 (the date the proxy materials were distributed). On April 26, representatives of Chase, Manufacturers and U.S. Trust met with UV officers and directors and collectively demanded that UV pay off all the debentures within 30 days or, alternatively, that UV establish a trust fund of $180 million to secure the debt. There was testimony that at least one of the Indenture Trustees threatened to sue to enjoin UV from paying the $18 liquidating distribution on the grounds that a liquidating distribution prior to payment of UV's debts would violate Maine law,[3] which provides, as to a liquidating corporation, that:

> *After* paying or adequately providing for the payment of all its obligations, the corporation shall distribute the remainder of its assets . . . among its shareholders . . .
>
> Me.Rev.Stat.Ann.Tit. 13-A, §1106(4) (1971) (emphasis added).

---

3. The Indenture Trustees apparently concede that as of the April 26 meeting none of the Indentures was in default and the forthcoming $18 distribution would not be a default under any of the indentures. Such an interpretation by the Trustees is evidenced by two letters written by Manufacturers and U. S. Trust, respectively, to debentureholders. The letter from Manufacturers to one of its debentureholders, dated June 22, 1979, states, in pertinent part:

> In our opinion and in the opinion of our counsel, neither the approval by stockholders [of UV] of the Plan of Liquidation and Dissolution, nor the initial liquidating dividend constitutes a default under the Indenture. Nor are we aware of any other act or omission on the part of UV which constitutes a default under the Indenture. Absent a default under the Indenture, neither the Trustee nor the Debentureholders can, in our opinion, require UV to call the Debentures or in any other way compel payment of the Debentures other than in accordance with the terms of the Debentures and of the Indenture.

A similar conclusion was expressed by U. S. Trust in a letter to a debentureholder dated June 13, 1979, which reads in part:

> We advise, as Trustee, less complete Liquidation and Dissolution, that nothing has come to our attention that caused us to believe that [UV] was not in compliance with any of the covenants or agreements of the governing Indenture.

The outcome of this meeting was an "Agreement for Treatment of Certain Obligations of UV Industries, Inc.," dated April 27, 1979, between UV and the Indenture Trustees ("April Document"). Under the April Document, UV agreed, *inter alia*, to set aside a cash fund of $155 million to secure its public debt and to present a proposal for the satisfaction and discharge of that debt to the Indenture Trustees within 90 days. The Indenture Trustees agreed not to seek an injunction against the payment of the $18 per share liquidating distribution. The April Document provided that all obligations thereunder would terminate upon the payment of UV's public debt or upon UV's abandonment of the plan of liquidation.

On July 23, 1979, UV announced that it had entered into an agreement for the sale of most of its oil and gas properties to Tenneco Oil Company for $135 million cash. The deal was consummated as of October 2, 1979 and resulted in a net gain of $105 million to UV.

3. THE SALE TO SHARON STEEL

In November, 1979, Sharon proposed to buy UV's remaining assets. Another company, Reliance Group (unrelated to Reliance Electric), had made a similar offer. After a brief bidding contest, UV and Sharon entered into an "Agreement for Purchase of Assets" and an "Instrument of Assumption of Liabilities" on November 26, 1979. Under the purchase agreement, Sharon purchased all of the assets owned by UV on November 26 (*i.e.*, Mueller Brass, UV's mining properties and $322 million in cash or the equivalent) for $518 million ($411 million of Sharon subordinated debentures due in 2000 — then valued at 86% or $353,460,000 — plus $107 million in cash). Under the assumption agreement, Sharon assumed all of UV's liabilities, including the public debt issued under the indentures. UV thereupon announced that it had no further obligations under the indentures or lease guaranties, based upon the successor obligor clauses.

On December 6, 1979, in an attempt to formalize its position as successor obligor, Sharon delivered to the Indenture Trustees supplemental indentures executed by UV and Sharon. The Indenture Trustees refused to sign. Similarly, Sharon delivered an assumption of the lease guaranties to both Chase and Union Planters but those Indenture Trustees also refused to sign.

4. THE PROCEEDINGS IN THE DISTRICT COURT

By letters dated December 24, 1979, Chase, U.S. Trust and Manufacturers issued virtually identical notices of default as a result of UV's purported assignment of its obligations to Sharon. Each demanded that the default be cured within 90 days or that the debentures be redeemed. Chase and U.S. Trust brought separate actions in New York County Supreme Court against UV and Sharon for redemption of the debentures; Manufacturers subsequently initiated a similar lawsuit. On December 26, 1979, Sharon initiated this action against Chase, U.S. Trust and Manufacturers. The state court actions have been stayed pending disposition of this case.

Chase, U. S. Trust and Manufacturers sought specific performance of the redemption provisions by counterclaim.

[The district court largely ruled in favor of the indenture trustees.]

DISCUSSION

1.   THE SUCCESSOR OBLIGOR CLAUSES

Sharon Steel argues that Judge Werker erred in not submitting to the jury issues going to the meaning of the successor obligor clauses. We disagree. Successor obligor clauses are "boilerplate" or contractual provisions which are standard in a certain genre of contracts. Successor obligor clauses are thus found in virtually all indentures. Such boilerplate must be distinguished from contractual provisions which are peculiar to a particular indenture and must be given a consistent, uniform interpretation. As the American Bar Foundation *Commentaries on Indentures* (1971) (*"Commentaries"*) state:

> Since there is seldom any difference in the intended meaning [boilerplate] provisions are susceptible of standardized expression. The use of standardized language can result in a better and quicker understanding of those provisions and a substantial saving of time not only for the draftsman but also for the parties and all others who must comply with or refer to the indenture, including governmental bodies whose approval or authorization of the issuance of the securities is required by law.

Id.

Boilerplate provisions are thus not the consequence of the relationship of particular borrowers and lenders and do not depend upon particularized intentions of the parties to an indenture. There are no adjudicative facts relating to the parties to the litigation for a jury to find and the meaning of boilerplate provisions is, therefore, a matter of law rather than fact.

Moreover, uniformity in interpretation is important to the efficiency of capital markets. . . .

We turn now to the meaning of the successor obligor clauses. Interpretation of indenture provisions is a matter of basic contract law. As the *Commentaries* at 2 state:

> The second fundamental characteristic of long term debt financing is that the rights of holders of the debt securities are largely a matter of contract. There is no governing body of statutory or common law that protects the holder of unsecured debt securities against harmful acts by the debtor except in the most extreme situations . . . [T]he debt securityholder can do nothing to protect himself against actions of the borrower which jeopardize its ability to pay the debt unless he . . . establishes his rights through contractual provisions set forth in the . . . indenture.

Contract language is thus the starting point in the search for meaning and Sharon argues strenuously that the language of the successor obligor clauses clearly permits its assumption of UV's public debt. Sharon's argument is a masterpiece of simplicity: on November 26, 1979, it bought everything UV owned; therefore, the transaction was a "sale" of "all" UV's "assets." In Sharon's view, the contention of the Indenture Trustees and Debenture holders that proceeds from earlier sales in a predetermined plan of piecemeal liquidation may not be counted in determining whether a later sale that involves "all assets" must be rejected because it imports a meaning not evident in the language.

Sharon's literalist approach simply proves too much. If proceeds from earlier piecemeal sales are "assets," then UV continued to own "all" its "assets" even after the Sharon transaction since the proceeds of that transaction, including the $107 million cash for cash "sale," went into the UV treasury. If the language is to be given the "literal" meaning attributed to it by Sharon, therefore, UV's "assets" were not "sold" on November 26 and the ensuing liquidation requires the redemption of the debentures by UV. Sharon's literal approach is thus self-defeating.

The words "all or substantially all" are used in a variety of statutory and contractual provisions relating to transfers of assets and have been given meaning in light of the particular context and evident purpose.

Sharon argues that such decisions are distinguishable because they serve the purpose of either shareholder protection or enforcement of the substance of the Internal Revenue Code. Even if such distinctions are valid, these cases nevertheless demonstrate that a literal reading of the words "all or substantially all" is not helpful apart from reference to the underlying purpose to be served. We turn, therefore, to that purpose.

Sharon argues that the sole purpose of successor obligor clauses is to leave the borrower free to merge, liquidate or to sell its assets in order to enter a wholly new business free of public debt and that they are not intended to offer any protection to lenders. On their face, however, they seem designed to protect lenders as well by assuring a degree of continuity of assets. Thus, a borrower which sells all its assets does not have an option to continue holding the debt. It must either assign the debt or pay it off. As the *Commentaries* state at 290:

> The decision to invest in the debt obligations of a corporation is based on the repayment potential of a business enterprise possessing specific financial characteristics. The ability of the enterprise to produce earnings often depends on particular assets which it owns. Obviously, if the enterprise is changed through consolidation with or merged into another corporation or through disposition of assets, the financial characteristics and repayment potential on which the lender relied may be altered adversely.

The single reported decision construing a successor obligor clause, *B. S. F. Company v. Philadelphia National Bank*, 42 Del.Ch. 106, 204 A.2d 746 (1964), clearly held that one purpose of the clause was to insure that the principal operating assets of a borrower are available for satisfaction of the debt.

Sharon seeks to rebut such inferences by arguing that a number of transactions which seriously dilute the assets of a company are perfectly permissible under such clauses. For example, UV might merge with, or sell its assets to, a company which has a miniscule equity base and is debt heavy. They argue from these examples that the successor obligor clause was not intended to protect borrowers from the kind of transaction in which UV and Sharon engaged.

We disagree. In fact, a substantial degree of protection against diluting transactions exists for the lender. Lenders can rely, for example, on the self-interest of equityholders for protection against mergers which result in a firm with a substantially greater danger of insolvency. So far as the sale of assets to such a firm is concerned, that can occur but substantial protection exists even there since the more debt heavy the purchaser, the less likely it is that the seller's equityholders would accept anything but cash for the assets. A sale to a truly crippled firm is thus unlikely given the self-interest of the equityholders. After a sale, moreover, the lenders would continue to have the protection of the original assets. In both mergers and sales, complete protection against an increase in the borrower's risk is not available in the absence of more specific restrictions, but the self-interest of equityholders imposes a real and substantial limit to that increase in risk. The failure of successor obligor clauses to provide even more protection hardly permits an inference that they are designed solely for the benefit of borrowers.

We hold, therefore, that protection for borrowers as well as for lenders may be fairly inferred from the nature of successor obligor clauses. The former are enabled to sell entire businesses and liquidate, to consolidate or merge with another corporation, or to liquidate their operating assets and enter a new field free of the public debt. Lenders, on the other hand, are assured a degree of continuity of assets . . .

We hold, therefore, that boilerplate successor obligor clauses do not permit assignment of the public debt to another party in the course of a liquidation unless "all or substantially all" of the assets of the company at the time the plan of liquidation is determined upon are transferred to a single purchaser.

The application of this rule to the present case is not difficult. The plan of liquidation was approved by UV's shareholders on March 26, 1978. Since the Indenture Trustees make no claim as to an earlier time, *e.g.*, the date of the Board recommendation, we accept March 26 as the appropriate reference date. The question then is whether "all or substantially all" of the assets held by UV on that date were transferred to Sharon. That is easily answered. The assets owned by UV on March 26 and later transferred to Sharon were Mueller Brass, certain metals mining property, and substantial amounts of cash and other liquid assets. UV's Form 10-K and Sharon's Form S-7 state that Mueller Brass and the metals mining properties were responsible for only 38% of UV's 1978 operating revenues and 13% of its operating profits. They constitute 41% of the book value of UV's operating properties. When the cash and other liquid assets are added, the transaction still involved only 51% of the book value of UV's total assets.

Since we do not regard the question in this case as even close, we need not determine how the substantiality of corporate assets is to be measured, what percentage meets the "all or substantially all" test or what role a jury might play in determining those issues. Even when the liquid assets (other than proceeds from the sale of Federal and the oil and gas properties) are aggregated with the operating properties, the transfer to Sharon accounted for only 51% of the total book value of UV's assets. In no sense, therefore, are they "all or substantially all" of those assets. The successor obligor clauses are, therefore, not applicable. UV is thus in default on the indentures and the debentures are due and payable. For that reason, we need not reach the question whether the April Document was breached by UV.

3. THE REDEMPTION PREMIUM

Judge Werker held that the redemption premium under the indentures need not be paid by UV. His reasoning was essentially that UV defaulted under the indenture agreement and that the default provisions provide for acceleration rather than a redemption premium. We do not agree. The acceleration provisions of the indentures are explicitly permissive and not exclusive of other remedies. We see no bar, therefore, to the Indenture Trustees seeking specific performance of the redemption provisions where the debtor causes the debentures to become due and payable by its voluntary actions.

Sharon Steel has become the leading case on interpretation of bond indentures, and its discussion of how such indentures should be read in light of their "boilerplate" nature is quoted in many of the opinions in this chapter.

PROBLEM SET 15.1

1. What precisely is the protection provided by the successor clause in this case?
2. Can you reconcile Judge Winter's discussion of boilerplate with his subsequent interpretation of the clause? In particular, do you find it odd that he investigates the background and meaning of the clause rather than simply read the "four corners" of the text?
3. Why did Sharon and UV want to avoid paying off these bonds and notes?

IN RE DURA AUTOMOTIVE SYSTEMS, INC., ET. AL., DEBTORS

379 B.R. 257
United States Bankruptcy Court, D. Delaware
Bankruptcy No. 06-11202-KJC | Adversary No. 07-51715-KJC | Dec. 7, 2007

Kevin J. CAREY, Bankruptcy Judge.
On October 30, 2006 (the "Petition Date"), Dura Automotive Systems, Inc. and related entities (the "Debtors") filed voluntary petitions for relief under chapter 11 of title 11 of the United States Code in the United States Bankruptcy Court for the District of Delaware. The Debtors are operating their businesses and managing their properties as debtors-in-possession pursuant to Bankruptcy Code sections 1107(a) and 1108.

The Debtors filed a proposed plan of reorganization (as amended, the "Plan") and corresponding disclosure statement (as amended, the "Disclosure Statement") on August 22, 2007. Revised versions of the Plan and Disclosure Statement were filed on September 28, 2007 and October 4, 2007. The Disclosure Statement was approved by the Court on October 4, 2007. The deadline for filing objections to the Plan was November 5, 2007 and the deadline for creditors to vote whether to accept or reject the Plan was November 15, 2007. Hearing on confirmation of the Plan is now scheduled for December 11, 2007.

Thomas A. and Pattiann Kurak (the "Plaintiffs") assert that they are beneficial holders of $81.5 million of certain subordinated notes issued by Debtor Dura Operating Corp. ("Dura OpCo") pursuant to the Subordinated Note Indenture (described in more detail below), who argue that the Debtors'

Plan improperly excludes them from all distributions and recovery. On September 19, 2007, the Plaintiffs filed this adversary proceeding against the Debtors, seeking a declaratory judgment that the Debtors' Plan violates applicable law by failing to provide for a distribution to Plaintiffs of New Common Stock (as defined below) and by failing to allow the Plaintiffs to participate in the Rights Offering (as defined below).

By order dated October 15, 2007, the Bank of New York Trust Company, N.A. ("BNY" or the "Senior Notes Trustee") was authorized to intervene as a defendant in this adversary proceeding.

UNDISPUTED FACTS

From the parties' respective submissions, I discern the following undisputed facts, upon which I rely in my analysis of the Motions.

A.   THE INDENTURES.

In April 1999, Series A and Series B of the 9% Notes, denominated $300 million (U.S.) and $100 million, respectively, were issued pursuant to two indentures, each dated as of April 22, 1999 (as amended or supplemented, the "April 1999 Indentures"), among Dura OpCo, as issuer, U.S. Bank Trust National Association ("US Bank"), as indenture trustee, and certain of the Defendants listed on the signature pages thereto as guarantors (the "Guarantors"). Subsequently, Dura OpCo issued an additional $158.5 million in 9% Notes, Series C and D, pursuant to that certain indenture, dated as of June 22, 2001 (as amended or supplemented, the "June 2001 Indenture" and, together with the April 1999 Indentures, the "Subordinated Note Indenture"), among Dura OpCo, as issuer, U.S. Bank, as indenture trustee, and the Guarantors, as guarantors. The holders of notes issued under the Subordinated Note Indenture are known herein as the "Subordinated Noteholders" or the "9% Noteholders."

In April of 2002, Dura OpCo issued the 8 5/8% Senior Notes (the "Senior Notes") in the aggregate principal amount of $400 million, pursuant to that certain indenture dated as of April 18, 2002 (as amended or supplemented, the "Senior Notes Indenture") among Dura OpCo, as issuer, BNY, as indenture trustee, and certain Defendants listed on the signature pages thereto as guarantors.

Article 10 of the Subordinated Note Indenture is entitled "Subordination" and contains the following provision:

Section 10.01 Agreement to Subordinate.
The Company agrees, and each Holder by accepting a Note agrees, that the Indebtedness evidenced by the Notes is subordinated in right of payment, to the extent and in the manner provided in this Article 10, to the prior payment in full of all Senior Debt of the Company, including Senior Debt incurred after the date of this Indenture, and that the subordination is for the benefit of the holders of Senior Debt.

The term "Company" is defined in the Subordinated Notes Indenture as "Dura Operating Corp., and any and all successors thereto." The Subordinated

Note Indenture also provides a specific provision addressing the subordination in the event of a chapter 11:

> Section 10.02. Liquidation; Dissolution; Bankruptcy.
> Upon any distribution to creditors of the Company in a liquidation or dissolution of the Company, in a bankruptcy, reorganization, insolvency, receivership or similar proceeding relating to the Company or its property, in an assignment for the benefit of creditors or in any marshalling of the Company's assets and liabilities:
> (i) holders of Senior Debt shall be entitled to receive payment in full of all Obligations due in respect of such Senior Debt (including interest after the commencement of any such proceeding at the rate specified in the applicable Senior Debt) before Holders of the Notes shall be entitled to receive any payment with respect to the Notes (*except that Holders may receive (i) Permitted Junior Securities* and (ii) payments and other distributions made from any defeasance trust created pursuant to Section 8.01 hereof); and
> (ii) until all Obligations with respect to Senior Debt (as provided in subsection (i) above) are paid in full, any distribution to which Holders would be entitled but for this Article 10 shall be made to the holders of Senior Debt (*except that Holders of Notes may receive (i) Permitted Junior Securities* and (ii) payments and other distributions made from any defeasance trust created pursuant to Section 8.01 hereof), as their interests may appear.

See Subordinated Notes Indenture, §10.03 (adding emphasis to the language at issue, known as the "X–Clause"). The term "Permitted Junior Securities" is defined in Section 1.01 as follows and is reproduced here precisely as it appears in the Subordinated Notes Indenture:

> "*Permitted Junior Securities*" means:
> (1) Equity Interests in the Company, DASI or any Guarantor; or
> (2) debt securities that are subordinated to all Senior Debt and any debt securities issued in exchange for Senior Debt to substantially the same extent as, or to a greater extent than, the Notes and the Guaranties are subordinated to Senior Debt under this Indenture.

B. THE PLAN.

The Debtors' prepetition non-current debt structure is approximately $1.3 billion and comprised of: (a) credit facilities secured by first and second liens providing for aggregate borrowings of $325 million; (b) the Senior Notes, in principal face amount of $400 million; (c) the Subordinated Notes, in principal face amount of approximately $536.6 million (using the exchange rate applicable on the Petition Date for those Subordinated Notes denominated in Euros), and (d) certain convertible subordinated debentures, in principal face amount of $55.2 million (the "Convertible Notes").

The Plan contemplates a rights offering ("Rights Offering") of between $140 million and $160 million in new cash investments in exchange for between 39.3% and 42.6% of the common stock of the reorganized company (the "New Common Stock"), with the balance of the New Common Stock being distributed to holders of the Senior Notes and certain large trade creditors. Based on the valuations set forth in the Disclosure Statement, the Plan provides for holders of Senior Notes and other unsecured claimants to receive substantially less than full recovery on their claims.

The Plan provides the following classification and treatment of the Debtors' unsecured notes:

Class 3 — Senior Notes Claims. The Plan provides that claims in Class 3, the Senior Notes claims, will receive their pro rata share of New Common Stock (including the New Common Stock that would otherwise be distributable to the holders of the Subordinated Notes and the Convertible Notes but for the subordination provision) and be afforded the right to participate in the rights offering. (*See* Plan at III.B.3). Even with the enforcement of the subordination provisions, it is estimated that holders of Senior Notes Claims will receive a recovery of only approximately 55% of the value of their claim. (*See* Disclosure Statement at xiii).

Class 4 — Subordinated Notes Claims. With respect to claims in Class 4, the 9% Subordinated Notes claims, the Plan provides that "Holders of Subordinated Notes Claims shall neither receive nor retain any property under the Plan, pursuant to the Subordinated Notes Indenture, which subordinate their right to payment to the right of holders of Senior Notes Claims to payment in full prior to any distribution being made to holders of 9% Subordinated Notes Claims." (*See* Plan at III.B.4). The Plan further provides that holders of 9% Subordinated Notes claims are not entitled to vote, as they are "conclusively deemed to reject the Plan." (*Id*).

Class 6 — Convertible Notes Claims. Similarly, with respect to claims in Class 6, the Convertible Notes claims, the Plan provides that "Holders of Convertible Subordinated Debentures Claims shall neither receive nor retain any property under the Plan, pursuant to the Convertible Subordinated Indenture, which subordinates their right to payment to the right of holders of Senior Notes Claims to payment in full prior to any distribution being made to holders of Convertible Subordinated Debentures Claims." (*See* Plan at III.B.6). The Plan further provides that holders of Convertible Notes claims are not entitled to vote, as they are "conclusively deemed to reject the Plan." (*Id.*)

The Subordinated Notes are not permitted to participate in the Rights Offering. Any New Common Stock otherwise distributable to the Subordinated Noteholders will instead be distributed to the 8 5/8% Noteholders.

DISCUSSION

A.   BNY'S MOTION TO DISMISS.

As a threshold issue, BNY argues that the Plaintiffs do not have standing to bring this adversary proceeding because the Plaintiffs failed to allege in their complaint that they satisfied the procedural requirements of Section 6.06 of the Subordinated Notes Indenture, which provides as follows:

A Holder of a Note may pursue a remedy with respect to this Indenture or the Notes only if:
    (a) the Holder of a Note gives to the Trustee written notice of a continuing Event of Default;

(b) the Holders of at least 25% in principal amount of the then outstanding Notes make a written request to the Trustee to pursue the remedy;

(c) such Holder of a Note or Holders of Notes offer and, if requested, provide to the Trustee indemnity satisfactory to the Trustee against any loss, liability or expense;

(d) the Trustee does not comply with the request within 60 days after receipt of the request and [*sic*] the offer and, if requested, the provision of indemnity; and

(e) during such 60-day period the Holders of a majority in principal amount of the then outstanding Notes do not give the Trustee a direction inconsistent with the request.

In response, the Plaintiffs argue that this section (known as a "no-action clause") only applies to pursuit of a default remedy and, therefore, is not applicable to their declaratory judgment action. The term "remedy" is not defined in the Subordinated Notes Indenture and I disagree that the language in the indenture necessarily limits application of this provision to specific types of remedies. Furthermore, the Plaintiffs argue that they were not required to ask the indenture trustee (U.S. Bank) to bring the action because such a demand would be futile, since the deadlines for Plan confirmation prevent the Plaintiffs from waiting sixty days for the indenture trustee's response. Finally, the Plaintiffs also argue that the Court should hear this action under principles of judicial economy because they have asserted the same issue as a confirmation objection.

A no-action clause is a bargained-for contractual provision that inures to the benefit of both the issuer and the investors. The main purpose of a no-action clause is:

to deter individual debentureholders from bringing independent law suits for unworthy or unjustifiable reasons, causing expense to the Company and diminishing its assets. The theory is that if the suit is worthwhile, [a significant percent] of the debentureholders would be willing to join in sponsoring it. . . . An additional purpose is the expression of the principle of law that would otherwise be implied that all rights and remedies of the indenture are for the equal and ratable benefit of all holders.

Courts have recognized, however, that asking a trustee to take action may be excused if such a demand would be futile.

Parties should not be readily freed from the constraints of a clearly written no-action clause. However, dismissing the complaint at this juncture to allow the Plaintiffs to comply with the procedural requirements would only cause further delay. Moreover, at oral argument the parties indicated that the indenture trustee was unlikely to pursue this action, due to a failure to reach a satisfactory indemnification agreement.

The Plaintiffs argue correctly that, regardless of the no-action clause, they have a right to be heard on this issue at confirmation under Bankruptcy Code §1109(b). The no-action clause's main purpose — to prevent the expense of unwarranted litigation — is not applicable to this adversary proceeding. As a practical matter, all of the parties consented to scheduling oral argument on this issue prior to the confirmation hearing and, further, expressed their interest in having this matter decided prior to confirmation, since a judgment against the Debtors on this issue would likely require — at the least — major revisions to the Debtors' Plan. Because dismissal of the complaint would not advance the interests of any party or further the purposes of the no-action clause, BNY's Motion to Dismiss, under these specific circumstances, will be denied.

B.   THE MOTIONS FOR SUMMARY JUDGMENT.

(2)   The "X-Clause."

All of the parties agree on the following principles:

1.   The Subordinated Notes Indenture should be enforced in accordance with its terms;
2.   The X-Clause is enforceable in bankruptcy. Bankruptcy Code §510(a);
3.   The Court must look to state law — in this case the law of New York state — to interpret the Subordinated Notes Indenture and to determine the intent of the parties; and
4.   The contract provisions at issue here are not ambiguous.

It is also not disputed that the purpose of subordination provisions in the Subordinated Notes Indenture is to assure payment in full of the Senior Notes before there is any recovery on the Subordinated Notes.

Plaintiffs' argument is straightforward: they are entitled to receive New Common Stock because, by operation of the unconditional and absolute obligation of the Debtors to repay the 9% Notes and Section 1129(b) of the Bankruptcy Code, the 9% Notes must receive the same distribution as any other general unsecured creditor of the Debtors, unless there is some basis for disparate treatment of the 9% Notes. The subordination provisions of the 9% Indenture provides this basis in most circumstances; however, Permitted Junior Securities are unambiguously excepted from the subordination provisions by the X-Clause, and therefore holders of the 9% Notes may receive such securities *even if the 8 5/8% Notes have not yet received payment in full.* Because New Common Stock and the Rights Offering clearly fall within the definition of Permitted Junior Securities, Plaintiffs and all other holders of the 9% Notes must share in the distribution of New Common Stock and be permitted to participate in the Rights Offering on a *pari passu* basis with holders of the 8 5/8% Notes. Otherwise, the Plan is in clear violation of section 1129(b) of the Bankruptcy Code [prohibiting unfair discrimination between classes of creditors of equal priority].

The key to this position rests upon the Plaintiffs' assertion that the Subordinated Notes Indenture's definition of "Permitted Junior Securities" sets forth phrases (1) and (2) as independent clauses. This interpretation rests on the use of a semi-colon and the word "or" at the end of phrase (1), a blank line, and the break which separates phrase (2). The consequence of this reading places "Equity Interests" within the definition without qualification, while "debt securities," the subject of phrase (2), are "Permitted Junior Securities" only if subordinated to the Senior Notes. Since the term "Equity Interests" would include, in this case, the distribution of New Common Stock and the right to participate in the Rights Offering, the Plaintiffs claim that the X-Clause exception to subordination applies, and the Subordinated Noteholders are entitled to retain their share of the Plan's distribution to general unsecured creditors.

The Defendants respond to this by pointing out that "every subordinated noteholder that has litigated this issue has made precisely the same argument . . ." and lost. *See* Reply Memorandum of BNY (docket no. 42) at p. 23. The Defendants cite to three reported decisions (and one unreported decision) in support of this view. All three reported decisions are by circuit courts of appeals.

Despite an invitation extended by this Court at oral argument, neither BNY nor the Debtor would acknowledge that the X-Clause at issue here was poorly drafted. However, like the X-clause in [the Seventh Circuit's opinion in *In re Envirodyne Industries, Inc.,* 29 F.3d 301 (7th Cir.1994) (Posner, J.)] the X-Clause here, while not legally ambiguous, lacks the utter clarity that BNY and the Debtor would now surely prefer.

But, like the *Envirodyne* courts, in interpreting the contract language before me, I will: "*read the contract as a whole* and consider all parts of the whole and not give undue force to certain words or phrases that would distort or confuse the primary and dominant purpose of the contract." *Envirodyne,* 161 B.R. at 445 (*citing Empire Props. Corp. v. Mfrs. Trust Co.,* 288 N.Y. 242, 248, 43 N.E.2d 25, 28 (1942)) (emphasis added). *See also id.* at 445–46. (noting that "courts should construe an indenture as a whole to carry out the plain purpose and object of the indenture and *not limit itself to literal interpretations.*")(emphasis added). The *Envirodyne* courts were also applying the rules of New York contract interpretation that this Court must apply here. *See id.* at 445 (noting applicability of New York law).

The X-Clause must be read in context. When read as a whole, the Subordinated Note Indenture clearly manifests the intent to assure payment in full of the Senior Notes before permitting payment (in whatever form) to the Subordinated Noteholders. The Plaintiffs argue, in counterpoint, that the purpose of an x-clause is to carve out certain distributions from the otherwise applicable subordination provisions. Therefore, the X–Clause should be read generously in favor of those who are its intended beneficiaries so as to give the fullest effect to this intention. This argument must fail because an x-clause, as a general proposition, creates only limited exceptions to the otherwise applicable subordination provisions and, therefore, must be read narrowly, and in harmony, with the entire contract. This principle applies equally to the X–Clause at issue here.

In an opinion authored by the late Chief Judge Becker, the Third Circuit Court of Appeals followed *Envirodyne. In re PWS Holding Corp.,* 228 F.3d 224 (3d Cir.2000).

In *PWS,* the debtor's plan provided no distribution to a subordinated noteholder. The subordinated noteholder argued that the x-clause created an affirmative obligation by the debtor to distribute securities, so long as the securities distributed to the subordinated noteholder were junior to those issued to senior debt. *Id.* at 244–245. The x-clause in *PWS* provided:

> [u]ntil all Obligations with respect to Senior Indebtedness (as provided in Subsection above) are paid in full in cash or cash equivalent, any distribution to which holders would be entitled but for this article shall be made to holders of Senior Indebtedness (except that Holder may receive . . . securities that are subordinated to at least the same extent as the Securities to (a) Senior Indebtedness and (b) any securities issue [sic] in exchange for Senior Indebtedness), as their interests may appear.

The Court, citing the *Envirodyne* decision, explained that the purpose of the x-clause was to avoid the cumbersome procedure that would require junior creditors to pay over securities received pursuant to a plan of reorganization and then take the securities back once the senior creditors were paid in full.

The Plaintiffs contend that *PWS* is not dispositive of this dispute because *PWS* involved a dispute over whether the x-clause at issue there *required* the debtor, when making a distribution to senior debt that was not excluded by the x-clause from the subordination provisions, to make a separate and distinct subordinated distribution to the junior creditors of a different class of security.

Plaintiffs argue, correctly, that each x-clause is different and must be considered only in the specific context of the applicable contract. Considering the X–Clause before me, I conclude that it must not be considered based upon its grammatical structure alone, but also within the context of the entire agreement, which, here, is more reflective of the parties' intent: that except in very limited circumstances, no payment can be made to the Subordinated Noteholders until (1) the Senior Notes are paid in full, or (2) the Senior Noteholders consent. Neither circumstance is present here. I conclude that the language which follows the words "debt securities" in phrase (2) of the "Permitted Junior Securities" definition modifies both phrase (1) and phrase (2). To interpret the X–Clause to include the New Common Stock and the Rights Offering in the definition of "Permitted Junior Securities" would eviscerate the purpose of the subordination provisions in the Subordinated Notes Indenture and expand the limited carve out beyond its intended scope. As the bankruptcy court in *Envirodyne* said, the interpretation advanced by the Subordinated Noteholders "defies explanation and logic. A senior creditor simply would not agree to a subordination agreement in which its priority depended upon the form of consideration chosen by the debtor." *Envirodyne*, 161 B.R. at 448.10

PROBLEM SET 15.2

1. Why might you want a "no action clause" in an indenture? What are the risks of such a clause?
2. In the *Envirodyne* case, Judge Posner noted that the x-clause was poorly drafted. So did this court, even though the indenture in this case was drafted five years after the *Envirodyne* opinion. Are bond lawyers ignoring Circuit Court opinions?

3. Notice that the plaintiff bondholders in this case were not originally subordinated, but agreed to future subordination. Why might the issuer-debtor have sought to subordinate bondholders from inception?

2. IMPLIED RIGHTS OF BONDHOLDERS

METROPOLITAN LIFE INSURANCE COMPANY v. RJR NABISCO, INC.

716 F.Supp. 1504
United States District Court, S.D. New York
No. 88 Civ. 8266 (JMW) | June 1, 1989

WALKER, District Judge:

I. INTRODUCTION

The corporate parties to this action are among the country's most sophisticated financial institutions, as familiar with the Wall Street investment community and the securities market as American consumers are with the Oreo cookies and Winston cigarettes made by defendant RJR Nabisco, Inc. (sometimes "the company" or "RJR Nabisco"). The present action traces its origins to October 20, 1988, when F. Ross Johnson, then the Chief Executive Officer of RJR Nabisco, proposed a $17 billion leveraged buy-out ("LBO") of the company's shareholders, at $75 per share.[4] Within a few days, a bidding war developed among the investment group led by Johnson and the investment firm of Kohlberg Kravis Roberts & Co. ("KKR"), and others. On December 1, 1988, a special committee of RJR Nabisco directors, established by the company specifically to consider the competing proposals, recommended that the company accept the KKR proposal, a $24 billion LBO that called for the purchase of the company's outstanding stock at roughly $109 per share.

The flurry of activity late last year that accompanied the bidding war for RJR Nabisco spawned at least eight lawsuits, filed before this Court, charging the company and its former CEO with a variety of securities and common law violations. The Court agreed to hear the present action — filed even before the company accepted the KKR proposal — on an expedited basis, with an eye toward March 1, 1989, when RJR Nabisco was expected to merge with the KKR holding entities created to facilitate the LBO. On that date, RJR Nabisco was also scheduled to assume roughly $19 billion of new debt. After a delay unrelated to the present action, the merger was ultimately completed during the week of April 24, 1989.

---

4. A leveraged buy-out occurs when a group of investors, usually including members of a company's management team, buy the company under financial arrangements that include little equity and significant new debt. The necessary debt financing typically includes mortgages or high risk/high yield bonds, popularly known as "junk bonds." Additionally, a portion of this debt is generally secured by the company's assets. Some of the acquired company's assets are usually sold after the transaction is completed in order to reduce the debt incurred in the acquisition.

Plaintiffs now allege, in short, that RJR Nabisco's actions have drastically impaired the value of bonds previously issued to plaintiffs by, in effect, misappropriating the value of those bonds to help finance the LBO and to distribute an enormous windfall to the company's shareholders. As a result, plaintiffs argue, they have unfairly suffered a multimillion dollar loss in the value of their bonds.[5]

On February 16, 1989, this Court heard oral argument on plaintiffs' motions. At the hearing, the Court denied plaintiffs' request for a preliminary injunction, based on their insufficient showing of irreparable harm. An exchange between the Court and plaintiffs' counsel, like the submissions before it, convinced the Court that plaintiffs had failed to meet their heavy burden:

> THE COURT: How do you respond to [defendants'] statements on irreparable harm? What we're looking at now is whether or not there's a basis for a preliminary injunction and if there's no irreparable harm then we're in a damage action and that changes . . . the contours of the suit. . . . We're talking about the ability . . . of the company to satisfy any judgment.
> PLAINTIFFS: That's correct. And our point . . . is that if we receive a judgment at any time, six months from now, after a trial for example, that judgment will almost inevitably be the basis for a judgment for everyone else . . . But if we get a judgment, everyone else will get one as well . . .
> THE COURT: [Y]ou're . . . asking me . . . [to] infer a huge number of plaintiffs and a lot more damages than your clients could ever recover as being the basis for deciding the question of irreparable harm. And those [potential] actions aren't before me.
> PLAINTIFFS: I think that's correct . . .

Plaintiffs failed to respond convincingly to defendants' arguments that, although plaintiffs have invested roughly $350 million in RJR Nabisco, their potential damages nonetheless remain relatively small and that, upon completion of the merger, the company will retain an equity base of $5 billion. *See, e.g.,* Tr. at 32, 35; D. Opp. at 48, 49. Given plaintiffs' failure to show irreparable harm, the Court denied their request for injunctive relief. This initial ruling, however, left intact plaintiffs' underlying motions, which, together with defendants' cross-motions, now require attention.

Although the numbers involved in this case are large, and the financing necessary to complete the LBO unprecedented,[6] the legal principles nonetheless remain discrete and familiar. Yet while the instant motions thus primarily

---

5. Agencies like Standard & Poor's and Moody's generally rate bonds in two broad categories: investment grade and speculative grade. Standard & Poor's rates investment grade bonds from "AAA" to "BBB." Moody's rates those bonds from "AAA" to "Baa3." Speculative grade bonds are rated either "BB" and lower, or "Ba1" and lower, by Standard & Poor's and Moody's, respectively. *See, e.g., Standard and Poor's Debt Rating Criteria* at 10–11. No one disputes that, subsequent to the announcement of the LBO, the RJR Nabisco bonds lost their "A" ratings.

6. On February 9, 1989, KKR completed its tender offer for roughly 74 percent of RJR Nabisco's common stock (of which approximately 97% of the outstanding shares were tendered) and all of its Series B Cumulative Preferred Stock (of which approximately 95% of the outstanding shares were tendered). Approximately $18 billion in cash was paid out to these stockholders. KKR acquired the remaining stock in the late April merger through the issuance of roughly $4.1 billion of pay-in-kind exchangeable preferred stock and roughly $1.8 billion in face amount of convertible debentures.

require the Court to evaluate and apply traditional rules of equity and contract interpretation, plaintiffs do raise issues of first impression in the context of an LBO. At the heart of the present motions lies plaintiffs' claim that RJR Nabisco violated a restrictive covenant — not an explicit covenant found within the four corners of the relevant bond indentures, but rather an *implied* covenant of good faith and fair dealing — not to incur the debt necessary to facilitate the LBO and thereby betray what plaintiffs claim was the fundamental basis of their bargain with the company. The company, plaintiffs assert, consistently reassured its bondholders that it had a "mandate" from its Board of Directors to maintain RJR Nabisco's preferred credit rating. Plaintiffs ask this Court first to imply a covenant of good faith and fair dealing that would prevent the recent transaction, then to hold that this covenant has been breached, and finally to require RJR Nabisco to redeem their bonds.

RJR Nabisco defends the LBO by pointing to express provisions in the bond indentures that, *inter alia*, permit mergers and the assumption of additional debt. These provisions, as well as others that could have been included but were not, were known to the market and to plaintiffs, sophisticated investors who freely bought the bonds and were equally free to sell them at any time. Any attempt by this Court to create contractual terms *post hoc*, defendants contend, not only finds no basis in the controlling law and undisputed facts of this case, but also would constitute an impermissible invasion into the free and open operation of the marketplace.

For the reasons set forth below, this Court agrees with defendants. There being no express covenant between the parties that would restrict the incurrence of new debt, and no perceived direction to that end from covenants that are express, this Court will not imply a covenant to prevent the recent LBO and thereby create an indenture term that, while bargained for in other contexts, was not bargained for here and was not even within the mutual contemplation of the parties.

II. BACKGROUND

A. THE PARTIES:

Metropolitan Life Insurance Co. ("MetLife"), incorporated in New York, is a life insurance company that provides pension benefits for 42 million individuals. According to its most recent annual report, MetLife's assets exceed $88 billion and its debt securities holdings exceed $49 billion. MetLife is a mutual company and therefore has no stockholders and is instead operated for the benefit of its policyholders. MetLife alleges that it owns $340,542,000 in principal amount of six separate RJR Nabisco debt issues, bonds allegedly purchased between July 1975 and July 1988. Some bonds become due as early as this year; others will not become due until 2017. The bonds bear interest rates of anywhere from 8 to 10.25 percent. MetLife also owned 186,000 shares of RJR Nabisco common stock at the time this suit was filed.

RJR Nabisco, a Delaware corporation, is a consumer products holding company that owns some of the country's best known product lines, including LifeSavers candy, Oreo cookies, and Winston cigarettes. The company was formed in 1985, when R.J. Reynolds Industries, Inc. ("R.J. Reynolds") merged with Nabisco Brands, Inc. ("Nabisco Brands"). In 1979, and thus before the R.J. Reynolds-Nabisco Brands merger, R.J. Reynolds acquired the Del Monte Corporation ("Del Monte"), which distributes canned fruits and vegetables. From January 1987 until February 1989, co-defendant Johnson served as the company's CEO. KKR, a private investment firm, organizes funds through which investors provide pools of equity to finance LBOs.

B.   THE INDENTURES:

The bonds implicated by this suit are governed by long, detailed indentures, which in turn are governed by New York contract law. No one disputes that the holders of public bond issues, like plaintiffs here, often enter the market after the indentures have been negotiated and memorialized. Thus, those indentures are often not the product of face-to-face negotiations between the ultimate holders and the issuing company. What remains equally true, however, is that underwriters ordinarily negotiate the terms of the indentures with the issuers. Since the underwriters must then sell or place the bonds, they necessarily negotiate in part with the interests of the buyers in mind. Moreover, these indentures were not secret agreements foisted upon unwitting participants in the bond market. No successive holder is required to accept or to continue to hold the bonds, governed by their accompanying indentures; indeed, plaintiffs readily admit that they could have sold their bonds right up until the announcement of the LBO. Instead, sophisticated investors like plaintiffs are well aware of the indenture terms and, presumably, review them carefully before lending hundreds of millions of dollars to any company.

Indeed, the prospectuses for the indentures contain a statement relevant to this action:

> The Indenture contains no restrictions on the creation of unsecured short-term debt by [RJR Nabisco] or its subsidiaries, no restriction on the creation of unsecured Funded Debt by [RJR Nabisco] or its subsidiaries which are not Restricted Subsidiaries, and no restriction on the payment of dividends by [RJR Nabisco].

Further, as plaintiffs themselves note, the contracts at issue "[do] not impose debt limits, since debt is assumed to be used for productive purposes."

2.   The elimination of restrictive covenants:

In its Amended Complaint, MetLife lists the six debt issues on which it bases its claims. Indentures for two of those issues — the 10.25 percent Notes due in 1990, of which MetLife continues to hold $10 million, and the 8.9 percent Debentures due in 1996, of which MetLife continues to hold $50 million — once contained express covenants that, among other things, restricted the company's ability to incur precisely the sort of debt involved in the recent LBO. In order to eliminate those restrictions, the parties to this action renegotiated the terms of those indentures, first in 1983 and then again in 1985.

MetLife acquired $50 million principal amount of 10.25 percent Notes from Del Monte in July of 1975. To cover the $50 million, MetLife and Del Monte entered into a loan agreement. That agreement restricted Del Monte's ability, among other things, to incur the sort of indebtedness involved in the RJR Nabisco LBO. Reynolds — the corporate predecessor to RJR Nabisco — purchased Del Monte and assumed its indebtedness. Then, in December of 1983, R.J. Reynolds requested MetLife to agree to deletions of those restrictive covenants in exchange for various guarantees from R.J. Reynolds. A few months later, MetLife and R.J. Reynolds entered into a guarantee and amendment agreement reflecting those terms. Pursuant to that agreement, and in the words of Robert E. Chappell, Jr., MetLife's Executive Vice President, MetLife thus "gave up the restrictive covenants applicable to the Del Monte debt . . . in return for [the parent company's] guarantee and public covenants."

MetLife acquired the 8.9 percent Debentures from R.J. Reynolds in October of 1976 in a private placement. A promissory note evidenced MetLife's $100 million loan. That note, like the Del Monte agreement, contained covenants that restricted R.J. Reynolds' ability to incur new debt. In June of 1985, R.J. Reynolds announced its plans to acquire Nabisco Brands in a $3.6 billion transaction that involved the incurrence of a significant amount of new debt. R.J. Reynolds requested MetLife to waive compliance with these restrictive covenants in light of the Nabisco acquisition.

In exchange for certain benefits, MetLife agreed to exchange its 8.9 percent debentures — which *did* contain explicit debt limitations — for debentures issued under a public indenture — which contain no explicit limits on new debt. An internal MetLife memorandum explained the parties' understanding:

> [MetLife's $100 million financing of the Nabisco Brands purchase] had its origins in discussions with RJR regarding potential covenant violations in the 8.90% Notes. More specifically, *in its acquisition of Nabisco Brands, RJR was slated to incur significant new long-term debt, which would have caused a violation in the funded indebtedness incurrence tests in the 8.90% Notes.* In the discussions regarding [MetLife's] willingness to consent to the additional indebtedness, *it was determined that a mutually beneficial approach to the problem* was to 1) agree on a new financing having a rate and a maturity desirable for [MetLife] and 2) modify the 8.90% Notes. The former was accomplished with agreement on the proposed financing, while the latter was accomplished by [MetLife] agreeing to substitute RJR's public indenture covenants for the covenants in the 8.90% Notes. In addition to the covenant substitution, RJR has agreed to "debenturize" the 8.90% Notes upon [MetLife's] request. This will permit [MetLife] to sell the 8.90% Notes to the public.

3. The recognition and effect of the LBO trend:

Other internal MetLife documents help frame the background to this action, for they accurately describe the changing securities markets and the responses those changes engendered from sophisticated market participants. . . . At least as early as 1982, MetLife recognized an LBO's effect on bond values.[7] In the

---

7. MetLife itself began investing in LBOs as early as 1980. *See* MetLife Special Projects Memorandum, dated June 17, 1989, attached as Bradley Aff.Exh. V, at 1 ("[MetLife's] history of investing in leveraged buyout transactions dates back to 1980; and through 1984, [MetLife] reviewed a large number of LBO investment opportunities presented to us by various investment banking firms and LBO specialists. Over

spring of that year, MetLife participated in the financing of an LBO of a company called Reeves Brothers ("Reeves"). At the time of that LBO, MetLife also held bonds in that company. Subsequent to the LBO, as a MetLife memorandum explained, the "Debentures of Reeves were downgraded by Standard & Poor's from BBB to B and by Moody's from Baa1 to Ba3, thereby lowering the value of the Notes and Debentures held by [MetLife]."

MetLife further recognized its "inability to force any type of payout of the [Reeves'] Notes or the Debentures as a result of the buy-out [which] was somewhat disturbing at the time we considered a participation in the new financing. However," the memorandum continued,

> our concern was tempered since, as a stockholder in [the holding company used to facilitate the transaction], we would benefit from the increased net income attributable to the continued presence of the low coupon indebtedness. The recent downgrading of the Reeves Debentures and the consequent "loss" in value has again raised questions regarding our ability to have forced a payout. *Questions have also been raised about our ability to force payouts in similar future situations, particularly when we would not be participating in the buy-out financing.*

Id. (emphasis added). In the memorandum, MetLife sought to answer those very "questions" about how it might force payouts in "similar future situations."

> *A method of closing this apparent "loophole," thereby forcing a payout of [MetLife's] holdings, would be through a covenant dealing with a change in ownership.* Such a covenant is fairly standard in financings with privately-held companies . . . It provides the lender with an option to end a particular borrowing relationship via some type of special redemption . . .

(emphasis added).

A more comprehensive memorandum, prepared in late 1985, evaluated and explained several aspects of the corporate world's increasing use of mergers, takeovers and other debt-financed transactions. That memorandum first reviewed the available protection for lenders such as MetLife:

> Covenants are incorporated into loan documents to ensure that after a lender makes a loan, the creditworthiness of the borrower and the lender's ability to reach the borrower's assets do not deteriorate substantially. *Restrictions on the incurrence of debt,* sale of assets, mergers, dividends, restricted payments and loans and advances to affiliates *are some of the traditional negative covenants that can help protect lenders in the event their obligors become involved in undesirable merger/takeover situations.*

MetLife Northeastern Office Memorandum, dated November 27, 1985 (emphasis added). The memorandum then surveyed market realities:

> Because almost any industrial company is apt to engineer a takeover or be taken over itself, *Business Week* says that investors are beginning to view debt securities of

---

this five-year period, [MetLife] invested, on a direct basis, approximately $430 million to purchase debt and equity securities in 10 such transactions . . .").

high grade industrial corporations as Wall Street's riskiest investments. In addition, *because public bondholders do not enjoy the protection of any restrictive covenants,* owners of high grade corporates face substantial losses from takeover situations, if not immediately, then when the bond market finally adjusts. . . . [T]here have been 10–15 merger/takeover/LBO situations where, *due to the lack of covenant protection, [MetLife] has had no choice but to remain a lender to a less creditworthy obligor.* . . . The fact that the quality of our investment portfolio is greater than the other large insurance companies . . . may indicate that we have negotiated better covenant protection than other institutions, thus generally being able to require prepayment when situations become too risky . . . [However,] a problem exists. And *because the current merger craze is not likely to decelerate* and because there exist vehicles to circumvent traditional covenants, the problem will probably continue. Therefore, *perhaps it is time to institute appropriate language designed to protect Metropolitan from the negative implications of mergers and takeovers.*

Id. at 2–4 (emphasis added).

Indeed, MetLife does not dispute that, as a member of a bondholders' association, it received and discussed a proposed model indenture, which included a "comprehensive covenant" entitled "Limitations on Shareholders' Payments." As becomes clear from reading the proposed-but never adopted-provision, it was "intend[ed] to provide protection against all of the types of situations in which shareholders profit at the expense of bondholders." *Id.* The provision dictated that the "[c]orporation will not, and will not permit any [s]ubsidiary to, directly or indirectly, make any [s]hareholder [p]ayment unless . . . (1) the aggregate amount of all [s]hareholder payments during the period [at issue] . . . shall not exceed [figure left blank]." The term "shareholder payments" is defined to include "restructuring distributions, stock repurchases, debt incurred or guaranteed to finance merger payments to shareholders, etc."

These documents must be read in conjunction with plaintiffs' Amended Complaint. That document asserts that the LBO "undermines the foundation of the investment grade debt market . . . ,"; that, although "the indentures do not purport to limit dividends or debt . . . [s]uch covenants were believed unnecessary with blue chip companies . . . ,"; that "the transaction contradicts the premise of the investment grade market . . . ,"; and, finally, that "[t]his buyout was not contemplated at the time the debt was issued, contradicts the premise of the investment grade ratings that RJR Nabisco actively solicited and received, and is inconsistent with the understandings of the market . . . which [p]laintiffs relied upon."

Solely for the purposes of these motions, the Court accepts various factual assertions advanced by plaintiffs: first, that RJR Nabisco actively solicited "investment grade" ratings for its debt; second, that it relied on descriptions of its strong capital structure and earnings record which included prominent display of its ability to pay the interest obligations on its long-term debt several times over, and third, that the company made express or implied representations not contained in the relevant indentures concerning its future creditworthiness. In support of those allegations, plaintiffs have marshaled a number of speeches made by co-defendant Johnson and other executives of RJR Nabisco. In addition, plaintiffs rely on an affidavit sworn to by John Dowdle, the former Treasurer and then Senior Vice President of RJR Nabisco from 1970 until 1987.

In his opinion, the LBO "clearly undermines the fundamental premise of the [c]ompany's bargain with the bondholders, and the commitment that I believe the [c]ompany made to the bondholders . . . I firmly believe that the company made commitments . . . that require it to redeem [these bonds and notes] before paying out the value to the shareholders."

III. DISCUSSION

At the outset, the Court notes that nothing in its evaluation is substantively altered by the speeches given or remarks made by RJR Nabisco executives, or the opinions of various individuals — what, for instance, former RJR Nabisco Treasurer Dowdle personally did or did not "firmly believe" the indentures meant. *See supra*, and *generally* Chappell, Dowdle and Howard Affidavits. The parol evidence rule bars plaintiffs from arguing that the speeches made by company executives prove defendants agreed or acquiesced to a term that does not appear in the indentures.

The indentures at issue clearly address the eventuality of a merger. They impose certain related restrictions not at issue in this suit, but no restriction that would prevent the recent RJR Nabisco merger transaction. The indentures also explicitly set forth provisions for the adoption of new covenants, if such a course is deemed appropriate. While it may be true that no explicit provision either permits or prohibits an LBO, such contractual silence itself cannot create ambiguity to avoid the dictates of the parole evidence rule, particularly where the indentures impose no debt limitations.

Under certain circumstances, however, courts will, as plaintiffs note, consider extrinsic evidence to evaluate the scope of an implied covenant of good faith. However, the Second Circuit has established a different rule for customary, or boilerplate, provisions of detailed indentures used and relied upon throughout the securities market, such as those at issue. Thus, in *Sharon Steel Corporation v. Chase Manhattan Bank, N.A.*, 691 F.2d 1039 (2d Cir.1982), Judge Winter concluded that

> [b]oilerplate provisions are . . . not the consequences of the relationship of particular borrowers and lenders and do not depend upon particularized intentions of the parties to an indenture. There are no adjudicative facts relating to the parties to the litigation for a jury to find and the meaning of boilerplate provisions is, therefore, a matter of law rather than fact. Moreover, uniformity in interpretation is important to the efficiency of capital markets . . . Whereas participants in the capital market can adjust their affairs according to a uniform interpretation, whether it be correct or not as an initial proposition, the creation of enduring uncertainties as to the meaning of boilerplate provisions would decrease the value of all debenture issues and greatly impair the efficient working of capital markets . . . . Just such uncertainties would be created if interpretation of boilerplate provisions were submitted to juries sitting in every judicial district in the nation.

Id. at 1048. *See also Morgan Stanley & Co. v. Archer Daniels Midland Co.*, 570 F.Supp. 1529, 1535–36 (S.D.N.Y.1983) (Sand, J.) ("[Plaintiff concedes that the legality of [the transaction at issue] would depend on a factual inquiry . . . This case-by-case approach is problematic . . . [Plaintiff's theory] appears keyed to the subjective expectations of the bondholders . . . and reads a subjective element into what presumably should be an objective determination based on the language appearing in the bond agreement."). Ignoring these principles, plaintiffs would have this Court vary what they themselves have admitted is "indenture boilerplate," of "standard" agreements, to comport with collateral representations and their subjective understandings.

A. PLAINTIFFS' CASE AGAINST THE RJR NABISCO LBO:

1. *Count One: The implied covenant:*

In their first count, plaintiffs assert that

> [d]efendant RJR Nabisco owes a continuing duty of good faith and fair dealing in connection with the contract [i.e., the indentures] through which it borrowed money from MetLife, Jefferson-Pilot and other holders of its debt, including a duty not to frustrate the purpose of the contracts to the debtholders or to deprive the debtholders of the intended object of the contracts-purchase of investment-grade securities.
>
> In the "buy-out," the [c]ompany breaches the duty [or implied covenant] of good faith and fair dealing by, *inter alia*, destroying the investment grade quality of the debt and transferring that value to the "buy-out" proponents and to the shareholders.

In effect, plaintiffs contend that express covenants were not necessary because an *implied* covenant would prevent what defendants have now done. A plaintiff always can allege a violation of an express covenant. If there has been such a violation, of course, the court need not reach the question of whether or not an *implied* covenant has been violated. That inquiry surfaces where, while the express terms may not have been technically breached, one party has nonetheless effectively deprived the other of those express, explicitly bargained-for benefits. In such a case, a court will read an implied covenant of good faith and fair dealing into a contract to ensure that neither party deprives the other of "the fruits of the agreement." Such a covenant is implied only where the implied term "is consistent with other mutually agreed upon terms in the contract." In other words, the implied covenant will only aid and further the explicit terms of the agreement and will never impose an obligation "'which would be inconsistent with other terms of the contractual relationship.'" Viewed another way, the implied covenant of good faith is breached only when one party seeks to prevent the contract's performance or to withhold its benefits. As a result, it thus ensures that parties to a contract perform the substantive, bargained-for terms of their agreement.

In contracts like bond indentures, "an implied covenant . . . derives its substance directly from the language of the Indenture, and 'cannot give the holders of Debentures any rights inconsistent with those set out in the Indenture.' *[Where] plaintiffs' contractual rights [have not been] violated, there can have been no breach of an implied covenant.*"

The appropriate analysis, then, is first to examine the indentures to determine "the fruits of the agreement" between the parties, and then to decide whether those "fruits" have been spoiled—which is to say, whether plaintiffs' contractual rights have been violated by defendants.

A review of the parties' submissions and the indentures themselves satisfies the Court that the substantive "fruits" guaranteed by those contracts and relevant to the present motions include the periodic and regular payment of interest and the eventual repayment of principal. According to a typical indenture, a default shall occur if the company either (1) fails to pay principal when due; (2) fails to make a timely sinking fund payment; (3) fails to pay within 30 days of the due date thereof any interest on the date; or (4) fails duly to observe or perform any of the express covenants or agreements set forth in the agreement. Plaintiffs' Amended Complaint nowhere alleges that RJR Nabisco has breached these contractual obligations; interest payments continue and there is no reason to believe that the principal will not be paid when due.

It is not necessary to decide that indentures like those at issue could never support a finding of additional benefits, under different circumstances with different parties. Rather, for present purposes, it is sufficient to conclude what obligation is *not* covered, either explicitly or implicitly, by these contracts held by these plaintiffs. Accordingly, this Court holds that the "fruits" of these indentures do not include an implied restrictive covenant that would prevent the incurrence of new debt to facilitate the recent LBO. To hold otherwise would permit these plaintiffs to straightjacket the company in order to guarantee their investment. These plaintiffs do not invoke an implied covenant of good faith to protect a legitimate, mutually contemplated benefit of the indentures; rather, they seek to have this Court create an additional benefit for which they did not bargain.

Although the indentures generally permit mergers and the incurrence of new debt, there admittedly is not an explicit indenture provision to the contrary of what plaintiffs now claim the implied covenant requires. That absence, however, does *not* mean that the Court should imply into those very same indentures a covenant of good faith so broad that it imposes a new, substantive term of enormous scope. This is so particularly where, as here, that very term—a limitation on the incurrence of additional debt—has in other past contexts been expressly bargained for; particularly where the indentures grant the company broad discretion in the management of its affairs, as plaintiffs admit, particularly where the indentures explicitly set forth specific provisions for the adoption of new covenants and restrictions, and *especially* where there has been no breach of the parties' bargained-for contractual rights on which the implied covenant necessarily is based. While the Court stands ready to employ an implied covenant of good faith to ensure that such bargained-for rights are performed and upheld, it will not, however, permit an implied covenant to shoehorn into an indenture additional terms plaintiffs now wish had been included.

Plaintiffs argue in the most general terms that the fundamental basis of all these indentures was that an LBO along the lines of the recent RJR Nabisco transaction would never be undertaken, that indeed *no* action would be taken, intentionally or not, that would significantly deplete the company's assets. Accepting plaintiffs' theory, their fundamental bargain with defendants dictated that nothing would be done to jeopardize the extremely high probability that the company would remain able to make interest payments and repay principal over the 20 to 30 year indenture term — and perhaps by logical extension even included the right to ask a court "to make sure that plaintiffs had made a good investment." *Gardner*, 589 F.Supp. at 674. But as Judge Knapp aptly concluded in *Gardner*, "Defendants . . . were under a duty to carry out the terms of the contract, but not to make sure that plaintiffs had made a good investment.

To respond to changed market forces, new indenture provisions can be negotiated, such as provisions that were in fact once included in the 8.9 percent and 10.25 percent debentures implicated by this action. New provisions could include special debt restrictions or change-of-control covenants. There is no guarantee, of course, that companies like RJR Nabisco would accept such new covenants; parties retain the freedom to enter into contracts as they choose. But presumably, multi-billion dollar investors like plaintiffs have some say in the terms of the investments they make and continue to hold. And, presumably, companies like RJR Nabisco need the infusions of capital such investors are capable of providing.

Whatever else may be true about this case, it certainly does not present an example of the classic sort of form contract or contract of adhesion often frowned upon by courts. In those cases, what motivates a court is the strikingly inequitable nature of the parties' respective bargaining positions. *See generally*, Rakoff, *Contracts of Adhesion: An Essay in Reconstruction*, 96 Harv.L.Rev. 1173 (1982). Plaintiffs here entered this "liquid trading market," with their eyes open and were free to leave at any time. Instead they remained there notwithstanding its well understood risks.

Ultimately, plaintiffs cannot escape the inherent illogic of their argument. On the one hand, it is undisputed that investors like plaintiffs recognized that companies like RJR Nabisco strenuously opposed additional restrictive covenants that might limit the incurrence of new debt or the company's ability to engage in a merger. Furthermore, plaintiffs argue that they had no choice other than to accept the indentures as written, without additional restrictive covenants, or to "abandon" the market.

Yet on the other hand, plaintiffs ask this Court to imply a covenant that would have just that restrictive effect because, they contend, it reflects precisely the fundamental assumption of the market and the fundamental basis of their bargain with defendants. If that truly were the case here, it is difficult to imagine why an insistence on that term would have forced the plaintiffs to abandon the market. The Second Circuit has offered a better explanation: "[a] promise by the defendant should be implied only if the court may rightfully assume that the parties would have included it in their written agreement had their attention been called to it . . . *Any such assumption in this case would be completely unwarranted.*"

2. *Count Five: In Equity:*

Count Five substantially restates and realleges the contract claims advanced in Count I.

In their papers, plaintiffs variously attempt to justify Count V as being based on unjust enrichment, frustration of purpose, an alleged breach of something approaching a fiduciary duty, or a general claim of unconscionability. Each claim fails.

[P]laintiffs advance a claim that remains based, their assertions to the contrary notwithstanding, on an alleged breach of a fiduciary duty. Defendants go to great lengths to prove that the law of Delaware, and not New York, governs this question. Defendants' attempt to rely on Delaware law is readily explained by even a cursory reading of *Simons v. Cogan*, 549 A.2d 300, 303 (Del.1988), the recent Delaware Supreme Court ruling which held, *inter alia*, that a corporate bond "represents a contractual entitlement to the repayment of a debt and does not represent an equitable interest in the issuing corporation necessary for the imposition of a trust relationship with concomitant fiduciary duties." Before such a fiduciary duty arises, "an existing property right or equitable interest supporting such a duty must exist." A bondholder, that court concluded, "acquires no equitable interest, and remains a creditor of the corporation whose interests are protected by the contractual terms of the indenture." Defendants argue that New York law is not to the contrary, but the single Supreme Court case they cite — a case decided over fifty years ago that was not squarely presented with the issue addressed by the *Simons* court — provides something less than dispositive support. For their part, plaintiffs more convincingly demonstrate that New York law applies than that New York law recognizes their claim.

Regardless, this Court finds *Simons* persuasive, and believes that a New York court would agree with that conclusion. In the venerable case of *Meinhard v. Salmon*, 249 N.Y. 458, 164 N.E. 545 (1928), then Chief Judge Cardozo explained the obligations imposed on a fiduciary, and why those obligations are so special and rare:

> Many forms of conduct permissible in a workaday world for those acting at arm's length, are forbidden to those bound by fiduciary ties. A trustee is held to something stricter than the morals of the market place. Not honesty alone, but the punctilio of an honor the most sensitive, is then the standard of behavior. As to this there has developed a tradition that is unbending and inveterate. Uncompromising rigidity has been the attitude of courts of equity when petitioned to undermine the rule of undivided loyalty . . . Only thus has the level of conduct for fiduciaries been kept at a level higher than that trodden by the crowd.

Before a court recognizes the duty of a "punctilio of an honor the most sensitive," it must be certain that the complainant is entitled to more than the "morals of the market place," and the protections offered by actions based on fraud, state statutes or the panoply of available federal securities laws. This Court has concluded that the plaintiffs presently before it — sophisticated investors who are unsecured creditors — are not entitled to such additional protections.

PROBLEM SET 15.3

1. *MetLife* is often cited for the proposition that bondholders have no rights beyond the terms expressly set forth in the indenture. Do you agree with that interpretation of the case?

2. Would an individual bondholder have made a better plaintiff in this case?
3. From MetLife's perspective, how has it been harmed? After all, it obtained full payment on its bonds (as we now know that RJR did not enter bankruptcy).[8]

3. FIGHTS WITHIN THE CAPITAL STRUCTURE

Whereas MetLife was involuntary forced into holding junk bonds, sometimes investors know what they are buying from inception. That does not mean the indenture will necessarily anticipate all the wants and desires of the bondholders.

HARRIS TRUST AND SAVINGS BANK v. E-II HOLDINGS, INCORPORATED

926 F.2d 636
United States Court of Appeals, Seventh Circuit
No. 90–1095 | Argued Oct. 30, 1990 | Decided Feb. 21, 1991 |
Rehearing and Rehearing In Banc Denied May 3, 1991

Harrington WOOD, Jr., Circuit Judge.
Technically, they are high yield debt securities, but in common parlance we call them junk bonds. It is an unflattering and unwelcome appellation, due in no small part to the fact that oftentimes the securities are, quite literally, junk. *See* Kuhn, *Junk: The Weak and the Strong*, Fortune, Oct. 23, 1989, at 17. The appellants, trustees of high yield debt securities with a face value of $1.5 billion, are before this court in an attempt to assuage their fears that the worst has occurred. We cannot provide the reassurance they seek, however; we lack subject matter jurisdiction over most of the complaint and the remainder fails to state a claim.

The facts are straightforward and, for purposes of this decision, undisputed. In 1987, BCI Holdings Corp. ("BCI") engineered a $6.2 billion leveraged acquisition of Beatrice Companies, Inc ("Beatrice"). During the reshuffling that ensued, BCI created E-II Holdings, Inc. ("E-II"), and capitalized it with an initial portfolio of fifteen business concerns that were once part of Beatrice. Soon thereafter, E-II made a registered public offering of $1.5 billion in high yield debt securities: $750,000,000 of 12.85% senior subordinated notes and $750,000,000 of 13.05% subordinated debentures. The trustee under the note indenture was Harris Trust and Savings Bank ("Harris"). The trustee under the debenture indenture was LaSalle National Bank ("LaSalle") (collectively, the "Trustees").

E-II was not immune to the takeover mania that victimized the 1980s, and in December 1987 it launched a hostile takeover bid for American Brands, Inc. ("American Brands"). American Brands countered with a bid for E-II-the so-

---

8. *http://www.businessweek.com/archives/1991/b322820.arc.htm*

called "pac man" defense. And when the dust settled, it was American Brands, and not E-II, that prevailed.

Following its unsuccessful takeover attempt, E-II was involved in a number of business transactions that gave rise to uneasiness on the part of the Trustees. For example, on February 29, 1988, E-II became a wholly owned direct subsidiary of American Brands. On July 1, 1988, American Brands sold E-II to McGregor Acquisition Corp. ("McGregor"). And one day after that sale, McGregor made a "capital contribution" to E-II of all of the issued and outstanding stock of its subsidiary, Faberge, Inc. ("Faberge"), in exchange for 840 shares of E-II and a "dividend" of $925,000,000. In all, the Trustees have concerns about some fourteen different transactions (the parties refer to them as "Extraordinary Transactions") occurring between February and December of 1988.

The Trustees were not alone in their concern. A significant number, though not a majority, of investors filed notices of default with the Trustees during the summer and fall of 1988. These notices alleged that a default had occurred because the transaction involving Faberge was in violation of the Indentures.[9]

The Trustees sought to quell their own concerns, as well as those of the investors, by going directly to the source. In addition to the officers' certificates and opinions of counsel required under the Indentures, the Trustees demanded that E-II provide additional information about the Extraordinary Transactions. In particular, the Trustees asked E-II to disclose the factual information on which the certificates and opinions were based. E-II was not accommodating, however; it provided the certificates and opinions required under the Indentures but did not disclose the factual bases of those certificates and opinions. E-II refused to provide the additional information on the ground that the Indentures did not provide such a right.[10]

In the Trustees' view, E-II's failure to cooperate placed them in a quandary the likes of Scylla and Charybdis. If they acted immediately and declared E-II in default, then the declaration could trigger cross-default provisions in other loan agreements and thereby catapult E-II into involuntary bankruptcy. And if it was later discovered that the Trustees were wrong and that E-II had not been in default, then the disgruntled investors would likely sue the Trustees. On the other hand, the Trustees were also amenable to suit if they failed to act and the investors later discovered that, in fact, E-II's actions had breached the Indentures' covenants. Neither course of action seemed prudent in view of what the Trustees perceived as the insufficient nature of the information in their possession.

Paralyzed by indecision, the Trustees searched for someone to make their decision for them. On January 10, 1989, the Trustees filed a declaratory

---

9. Under section 6.01(3) of the Indentures, a "Default" occurs if E-II "fails to comply in any respect with any of its other agreements contained in the Securities or this Indenture." This "Default" does not become an "Event of Default" (allowing the Trustees to accelerate payment, etc.) until E-II (1) receives written notice from the Trustees or a majority of the investors and (2) fails to correct the Default within 30 days of receiving the notice. Indentures §6.01.

10. E-II apparently would have provided some of the information on a confidential basis, but the Trustees did not believe that their fiduciary duties would allow them to withhold information from the investors and they declined E-II's offer.

judgment action against E-II and asserted that the following issues were "matter[s] in dispute":

a. Whether the acquisition of E-II by American Brands was in compliance with the terms of the Indentures and principles of applicable law and equity, including the implied covenants of good faith and fair dealing;

b. Whether the post-acquisition Extraordinary Transactions . . . were in compliance with the terms of the Indentures and principles of applicable law and equity, including the implied covenants of good faith and fair dealing;

c. Whether E-II has complied with the provisions of the [Trust Indenture Act ("Act"), 15 U.S.C. §§77aaa-bbbb,] including but not limited to Section 314, [*id.* §77nnn,] which requires evidence of compliance with indenture provisions;

d. Whether an Event of Default has occurred on the Notes or the Debentures within the meaning of Section 315 of the [Act, 15 U.S.C. §77000];

e. What action the Trustees should take with respect to the Notices of Default . . . received . . . ;

f. Whether or not the assets remaining in E-II are sufficient to generate sufficient revenues to ensure payment of principal, interest, and sinking fund obligations of the Notes and Debentures;

g. Whether any future asset sales by E-II can be permitted and, if so, under what circumstances; and

h. To what information are the Trustees entitled in order to determine if unusual occurrences, such as the Extraordinary Transactions, violate the terms of the Indentures.

The Trustees closed their complaint with a request for a judicial declaration concerning each of these "matter[s] in dispute."

E-II, however, and subsequently the district court, were hard pressed to determine the Trustees' positions with respect to the alleged "matter[s] in dispute." And in fact, the Trustees had failed to take a position with respect to virtually every one of the issues for which they sought a judicial declaration. The Trustees did argue that they were entitled to more information than E-II was giving them (the eighth "matter in dispute"), but otherwise peppered their submissions with qualifiers — "may," "could," and other verbalisms that failed to indicate a stance.

On E-II's motion to dismiss under rules 12(b)(1) and 12(b)(6) of the Federal Rules of Civil Procedure, the district court held that it had no subject matter jurisdiction to decide those issues for which the Trustees failed to take a position. That failure, the district court concluded, precluded jurisdiction because it evidenced the lack of a case or controversy. As to the dispute over the Trustees' entitlement to additional information, the district court concluded that a case or controversy existed because the parties disputed the quantity and quality of disclosure required of E-II. The district court then found no legal basis to support the Trustees' claim that they were entitled to more information than E-II was willing to disclose. As such, it dismissed the request for information on the ground that it failed to state a cause of action. The district court also denied a subsequent motion by the Trustees to alter or amend the judgment.

On appeal, the Trustees continue to assert that it is neither necessary nor appropriate for them to commit to a position. Indeed, they assert that their request for "judicial guidance" and "judicial instruction" is the paradigm on which all declaratory judgment cases are built. And in so doing, they seal their fate: "Frequently, an issue of this sort will come before [this court] clad, so to speak, in sheep's clothing: the potential of the asserted principle to effect important change . . . is not immediately evident, and must be discerned by a careful and perceptive analysis. But this wolf comes as a wolf."[11]

As a predicate to relief, the Declaratory Judgment Act requires that the case be one of "actual controversy." 28 U.S.C. §2201(a). That predicate, which tracks the "cases" or "controversies" requirement of article III, saves the statute from unconstitutionally expanding the federal courts' jurisdiction. *See Aetna Life Ins. Co. v. Haworth*, 300 U.S. 227, 57 S.Ct. 461, 81 L.Ed. 617 (1937) (upholding Act); U.S. Const. art. III, §2.10 The often unspoken, but yet obvious, corollary of the "actual controversy" predicate is that the dispute must exist *between the parties to the declaratory judgment action. See Aetna Life*, 300 U.S. at 242, 57 S.Ct. at 464 ("There is here a dispute between parties who face each other in an adversary proceeding.").

The only issue in the Trustees' complaint that does appear to present a case or controversy is the dispute over the quantity and quality of information that the Trustees are entitled to receive from E-II. This dispute fails to clear a different hurdle, however; the Trustees have not put forth a cognizable legal basis under which they might be entitled to the information that they seek. Of the three bases offered — express covenant, implied covenant, and the Act — not one can support the Trustees' demand for additional information.

The first potential basis for relief — the express language of the Indentures — is a latecomer to this litigation; the Trustees failed to raise this argument until they filed a motion to alter or amend the judgment.

Even if we were to reach the merits on this issue, we would feel compelled to agree with the district court. The argument that section 11.05 expressly requires E-II to provide the requested information is more wishful thinking than anything else. As the district court observed, section 11.05 is limited by its express terms to a "certificate" or "opinion." Nowhere does it require E-II to disclose the facts underlying these documents. Indeed, when more disclosure is necessary, the Indentures make express provisions for that disclosure. *See, e.g.*, Indentures §4.07 (if E-II knows of a "Default" or "Event of Default," "the certificate shall describe any such Default or Event of Default and its status"); *Id.* §5.01(5) (certificate shall contain a statement of compliance and have attached "arithmetic computations" demonstrating compliance with the Consolidated Interest Expense Ratio).

The second potential basis for relief — the implied covenant of good faith and fair dealing — presents a more difficult question. The parties agree that New York law applies and that every contract governed by New York law contains an implied covenant to perform the contract fairly and in good faith. The parties are in relatively sharp disagreement, however, as to what that implied covenant requires in this case.

---

11. *Morrison v. Olson*, 487 U.S. 654, 699, 108 S.Ct. 2597, 2623, 101 L.Ed.2d 569 (1988) (Scalia, J., dissenting).

Courts often use broad and unqualified language in describing the content of the implied covenant of good faith. *See, e.g., Metropolitan Life Ins. Co. v. RJR Nabisco, Inc.*, 716 F.Supp. 1504, 1516–18 (S.D.N.Y.1989). In contrast to their broad definitional language, however, their analyses indicate that the "party who asserts the existence of an implied-in-fact covenant bears a heavy burden." And from these analyses, we discern that New York law appears to invoke the implied covenant of good faith and fair dealing only in those instances where one party has violated the spirit, although not the letter, of a contract. *See Metropolitan Life*, 716 F.Supp. at 1517 (implied covenant appropriate where, while the express terms of the contract "may not have been technically breached, one party has nonetheless effectively deprived the other of those express, explicitly bargained-for benefits.").

Here, as in *Metropolitan Life*, the relevant contracts do not support the interpretation that the Trustees now advocate. The Trustees allude to the "fruits" of the investors' bargain but fail to demonstrate, especially in light of the limited requirements of section 11.05, how a reasonable investor would be justified in assuming that E-II promised to disclose the factual bases underlying its certificates and opinions. Indeed, their language suggests, without basis, that E-II has a continuing duty to reassure the investors that they have made a good investment — the same type of argument rejected in *Metropolitan Life*. New York law does not, as the Trustees would have us believe, imply a covenant merely on the basis of strong societal concerns; the foundation of the implied covenant is the express covenant, and the Trustees' claim simply fails to provide that foundation.

True, the Indentures do not preclude the Trustees from obtaining the information they now seek, but that does not mean that we should imply such a right of access.

Implying the covenant requested by the Trustees would also be "troublesome" in view of the fact that the Indentures "could easily have been drafted to incorporate expressly the terms the [Trustees] now urge this court to imply." Section 603(f) of the Model Debenture Indenture Provisions even provides a basic model for such a provision:

> Except as otherwise provided in Section 601: . . .
> (f) the Trustee shall not be bound to make any investigation into the facts or matters stated in any resolution, certificate, statement, instrument, opinion, report, notice, request, direction, consent, order, bond, debenture, coupon or other paper or document but the Trustee, in its discretion, may make such further inquiry or investigation into such facts or matters as it may see fit, and, if the Trustee shall determine to make such further inquiry or investigation, it shall be entitled to examine the books, records and premises of the Company, personally or by agent or attorney. . . .

The third potential basis for relief — the Act — fares no better than its predecessors. Section 314(e) of the Act specifies the "evidence of compliance" (with a condition or covenant) that an issuer must furnish to an indenture trustee. 15 U.S.C. §77nnn(e). That section (like section 11.05 of the Indentures) requires certificates and opinions but does not require issuers to disclose the factual bases of certificates or opinions. Moreover, although section 314(a)(2) of the Act, 15 U.S.C. §77nnn(a)(2), allows the SEC to promulgate rules or regulations that could require E-II to provide additional "evidence of compliance," the SEC to date has failed to promulgate any such rule or regulation. *See* 17 C.F.R. §§260.0-1 to 260.14a-1. Last, section 314(f) dispositively states:

> Nothing in this section shall be construed either as requiring the inclusion in the indenture to be qualified of provisions that the obligor upon the indenture securities shall furnish to the indenture trustee any other evidence of compliance with the conditions and covenants provided for in the indenture than the evidence specified in this section, or as preventing the inclusion of such provisions in such indentures, if the parties so agree.

Id. §77nnn(f). This freedom-of-contract mentality leaves no room for the interpretation that the Trustees would thrust upon the Act.

The doors to the federal courthouse remain open to the Trustees as they remain open to all litigants: subject to such prerequisites as subject matter jurisdiction and stating a cognizable claim. Until the Trustees are willing and able to meet those prerequisites, however, we must turn them away.

PROBLEM SET 15.4

1. How could this problem have been avoided? Is it a problem?
2. What would you advise a trustee in a similar position in the future do in these circumstances?

IN THE MATTER OF CHICAGO, MILWAUKEE, ST. PAUL AND PACIFIC RAILROAD COMPANY, DEBTOR

791 F.2d 524
United States Court of Appeals, Seventh Circuit
Nos. 85–2364, 85–2428 | Argued Feb. 25, 1986 | Decided May 20, 1986

POSNER, Circuit Judge.

In 1955 the Chicago, Milwaukee, St. Paul and Pacific Railroad Company, known as the Milwaukee Road, issued $56 million in income debentures. The debenture indenture provided that the railroad would pay the holders of the debentures interest installments every year, at the rate of 5 percent, provided that the railroad had "available net income" — income in excess of various fixed expenses, in particular interest due secured creditors. This was to continue for 100 years, at the end of which time the principal would be repaid. In 1977 the railroad petitioned for reorganization under section 77 of the Bankruptcy Act, 11 U.S.C. §205 (1952 ed.) (which has since been repealed but remains applicable to this proceeding, see Bankruptcy Reform Act of 1978, Pub.L. 95-598, §403(a), 92 Stat. 2683), precipitating an avalanche of litigation unnecessary to recount here; for a thumbnail sketch see *In re Chicago, Milwaukee St. Paul & Pac. R.R.*, 713 F.2d 274, 277–78 (7th Cir.1983). A month later the indenture trustee declared the debentures in default.

After selling off many of the railroad's lines the Milwaukee Road's trustee in bankruptcy in 1985 sold the remaining lines to the Soo Railroad, see *In re Chicago, Milwaukee, St. Paul & Pac. R.R.*, 756 F.2d 508 (7th Cir.1985), and turned over the proceeds to the CMC Real Estate Corporation, as the debtor has been renamed. CMC Real Estate Corporation is a wholly owned subsidiary of Chicago Milwaukee Corporation; to simplify exposition, we shall refer to parent and subsidiary interchangeably as CMC. With the proceeds of the various sales, and the nonrail assets (chiefly real estate) that have never been sold, CMC will emerge from bankruptcy with a net worth of more than $400 million after paying off all of the Milwaukee Road's creditors, including the debenture holders, at the highest valuation of their claims.

The issue is how much the debenture holders should receive. The district judge presiding over the reorganization held that they should receive the $56 million principal, plus interest on that principal for every year during which the debentures were in default—even though there was available net income sufficient to pay interest during only two of them—plus interest on this interest. The total is $92 million. CMC has appealed, contending that repayment of the principal should not be accelerated, that no interest is due for the years in which there was no available net income, and that interest on interest should not be allowed. The interest for the two years in which there was available net income comes to $6 million. The present value of $56 million in 2055, when added to the present value of 5 percent interest for 70 years (2055–1985), is $24 million. (The discount rate used to make this calculation was 12 percent; its correctness is not an issue in this appeal.) Hence CMC is arguing that the debenture holders should get the equivalent of $30 million ($24 million plus $6 million), rather than the $92 million that the judge awarded.

The debenture holders have cross-appealed, making two arguments. One, which we shall not have to address, is that the judge used too low an interest rate in computing the interest due on interest. The other is that the debenture holders are entitled to interest on the overdue principal at a rate higher than 5 percent. We shall have to decide only four issues: whether repayment of the principal should have been accelerated, whether interest should have been allowed in years in which there was no available net income, whether if so 5 percent was the proper rate, and finally whether interest on interest should have been allowed.

The indenture provides that in the event of a default the indenture trustee shall be entitled to declare the principal immediately due and payable. There was a default; the trustee made the required declaration; hence the indenture by its terms entitled the debenture holders to receive the full $56 million in principal immediately rather than having to wait till the year 2055. Nevertheless they concede that the reorganization court had the power to make them wait ("decelerate"). CMC argues that the court should have exercised this power— that because of the rise in interest rates since 1955, acceleration will confer an enormous windfall on the debenture holders, giving them $56 million when, but for the default, the present value of the debentures would be as we said only $24 million (and that only if they could be sure of receiving 5 percent interest every year from now to then). Many of the debenture holders bought the debentures at a tremendous discount from face value, after the inflationary rise in interest rates had reduced the debentures' market value — though the risk of nonpayment of principal or interest or both may have been an even larger factor in the reduction. CMC has offered to give the debenture holders an ironclad guarantee that they will get 5 percent a year until 2055 and the full principal then; and given CMC's net worth, such a guarantee should not be hard to arrange. So the debenture holders will do no worse than if there had been no default.

Nevertheless, the district judge did not err in allowing acceleration. The only good reason for refusing to give a creditor in reorganization all that he bargained for when he extended credit is to help other creditors, the debtor's assets being insufficient to pay all creditors in full. All of the Milwaukee Road's creditors will be paid in full, even if the debenture holders are paid out at the highest valuation of their claim. The only competing equities are those of CMC's shareholders, and are weak, quite apart from the fact that many or for that matter all of them may have bought their shares after the Milwaukee Road went into bankruptcy and may therefore have lost nothing because of the bankruptcy — admittedly a fact that does not distinguish them from the debenture holders.

The important point is that back in 1955 the Milwaukee Road unequivocally promised to repay the principal of the debentures immediately in the event of a default (provided, for some forms of default, that the indenture trustee demanded immediate repayment, but he did so here, as we shall see), and the Milwaukee Road did default, and it can honor its promise without hurting any other creditor. In these circumstances the presumption in favor of acceleration is a strong one, perhaps conclusive, and certainly is not overcome by pointing out that some or even all of the debenture holders are speculators. The provision for acceleration was part of the consideration for the Milwaukee Road's being able to borrow money for 100 years without having to amortize the loan. The debenture holders got in exchange a distribution of possible outcomes: probably they would receive interest for 100 years and the principal at the end of that time, but possibly they would get their principal back sooner. CMC proposes to truncate that distribution.

What it describes as a windfall gain to the debenture holders is simply the coming to pass of one of the contingencies for which they or their predecessors bargained. If you pay $1 for a lottery ticket and win $1,000 in the lottery, your winnings are not a windfall; you bought the chance to get them. The debenture holders bought the chance to get the principal back early, at a time when a rise in interest rates might enable them to reinvest it more advantageously elsewhere, as they will now be able to do. This chance was a hedge against the risk of lending money for 100 years at a fixed interest rate. A sharp rise in interest rates might (as it did) signify a general disturbance of business conditions which would make the Milwaukee Road more likely to default; and if it did default, the debenture holders would be able to reinvest the principal of the debentures at the then higher rates. If the original debenture holders bought this right, then the current holders acquired it, for value, when they bought the debentures; enforcing the right will therefore confer no windfall on the current holders either.

The indenture provided for acceleration not only if there was a default but also if there was a purely voluntary liquidation. The Milwaukee Road's stockholders might well have decided to liquidate the corporation after the sale of its remaining assets to the Soo; for what remained was not an enterprise but a portfolio. If they had liquidated they would have had to repay the $56 million immediately. Maybe they did not liquidate because if the principal is not accelerated they will have 70 years of 5 percent money to play with (admittedly, tax considerations may also have played a role in this decision). It is not the objective of the bankruptcy laws to confer windfalls on debtors. See Blum, *Full Priority and Full Compensation in Corporate Reorganizations: A Reappraisal*, 25 U.Chi.L.Rev. 417, 423 (1958).

CMC's appeal to equity is misplaced for another reason. The fact that a proceeding is equitable does not give the judge a free-floating discretion to redistribute rights in accordance with his personal views of justice and fairness, however enlightened those views may be. The function of equitable considerations in a bankruptcy proceeding is to guide the division of a pie that is too small to allow each creditor to get the slice for which he originally contracted. Hence if the bankrupt is solvent the task for the bankruptcy court is simply to enforce creditors' rights according to the tenor of the contracts that created those rights; and one of those rights in this case was the right to accelerate the repayment of principal.

The issue with regard to interest in years when the railroad had no available net income requires close consideration of several provisions of the indenture. Article V sets forth the method of determining available net income. Section 6 thereof states: "The provisions of this Article V are hereby made expressly subject to each and all of the remedies of the Trustee or the Debenture holders as set forth in Article XI, and the operation of the provisions of this Article V shall be suspended during the continuance of either of the Events of Default specified in clause (a) or clause (b) of Section 2 of Article XI." We go to Article XI, and find that clause (a) relates to defaults in the payment of the principal of the debentures "when the same shall become due and payable either by the terms thereof or otherwise as herein provided," while clause (b) relates to defaults in the payment of any installment of interest "when and as such interest shall become due and payable as therein and in the Indenture expressed and such default shall continue for 60 days." The indenture trustee, however, declared the Milwaukee Road's default under another clause of Article XI, clause (f), which relates to the institution of bankruptcy proceedings, and which is not mentioned in Article V. CMC argues that since the default was declared under clause (f), the provisions regarding available net income were not suspended, and hence the debenture holders are not entitled to income during any year of reorganization in which the railroad lacked available net income.

Notice that section 6 of Article V, quoted above, has two clauses. The second (beginning "and the operation . . .") provides for automatic suspension of the provisions on available net income if the railroad defaults in paying either principal or (for 60 days) interest; the suspension begins at the moment of default in the case of a default in principal and on the 61st day following default in the case of a default in interest. The first clause of section 6, however, merely subjects Article V to the remedies that the trustee and the debenture holders have under Article XI, and thus is not self-executing. Article XI provides that in the event of a default other than in the payment of principal, the trustee may, and if the holders of at least 25 percent of the face amount of the debentures so request must, declare the principal to be due and payable immediately. This is the acceleration clause, on which the district judge based his ruling that CMC must repay the principal without waiting till the year 2055.

A month elapsed between the petition for bankruptcy and the indenture trustee's demand for repayment of principal on the ground of a clause (f) default, and the debenture holders concede that the provisions on available net income were not suspended until that demand was made. They argue, however, correctly in our view, that when the Milwaukee Road did not repay the principal in response to the demand made pursuant to clause (f), this placed the Milwaukee Road in default under clause (a) (refusal to repay principal "when the same shall become due and payable either by the terms thereof or otherwise as herein provided"); the second clause of Article V, section 6 therefore kicked in; and from that moment on, the provisions on available net income were suspended by the express terms of section 6. The indenture trustee could not have invoked clauses (a) or (b) in the first instance, because until the Milwaukee Road declared bankruptcy the principal of the debentures was not due and neither was interest, for the railroad had no available net income at the time. But once the Milwaukee Road petitioned for bankruptcy, the trustee could and did declare a default under clause (f), which accelerated the principal, thereby precipitating a default under (a), which caused the provisions on available net income to be suspended.

It is not a good answer that, once bankruptcy was declared, a default under (a) was impossible because the debtor could not have repaid the principal immediately even if it had wanted to do so. Defaults often are involuntary. The purpose of clause (a) is not to guarantee that the principal will be repaid immediately, because that might be impossible, but to accelerate repayment as much as possible. The indenture contemplates that repayment may indeed not follow immediately upon default: Article XI provides that in the event of a default in principal, interest shall be payable on the overdue principal at the rate of 5 percent. There is no reference to available net income. When the trustee exercised his right under Article XI to declare the principal immediately due and payable, the principal began to accrue interest at 5 percent regardless of available net income; and that is the interest which the district judge awarded for the period until the principal is repaid.

All this seems eminently sensible. Once the principal is accelerated by the declaration of a default, it becomes a matter of very little interest to the debenture holders whether the railroad has available net income. The contract has been broken, they want out, and they negotiated for 5 percent interest on their overdue principal until they got out.

We have not forgotten the venerable principle that a bankruptcy court can refuse to award interest that accrues on a creditor's claim after the petition for bankruptcy is filed. See, e.g., *Sexton v. Dreyfus*, 219 U.S. 339, 31 S.Ct. 256, 55 L.Ed. 244 (1911) (Holmes, J.); *New York v. Saper*, 336 U.S. 328, 330-32, 69 S.Ct. 554, 555-57, 93 L.Ed. 710 (1949). But it is designed for cases where there is not enough money to pay all the creditors — so that there is a question whether one creditor should get interest while another doesn't even recover principal — and not for cases like this, where the debtor is solvent. It can be argued that the principle casts light on the question whether the contract was intended to apply to a default that ends up in bankruptcy court. But we think it was. The parties provided expressly for interest on overdue principal, and though the debenture holders must have known there was a chance that this contractual right would not be enforced in bankruptcy, they did everything they could to maximize the likelihood that it would be.

The debenture holders want more than 5 percent, but we think the district court was right to reject this request. The contract is the measure of their rights. Whatever rights to prejudgment interest they might otherwise have are merged in their contractual understanding. As will become clear from our analysis of the fourth issue, the fact that if the default had occurred outside of bankruptcy the debenture holders might have collected the overdue principal faster and therefore have been able to invest it at a higher interest rate (the current market rate) does not alter this conclusion.

The district judge awarded the debenture holders interest on the 5 percent interest installments that had accrued but had not been paid, from the date of accrual. (Interest on interest may seem a detail, but is not; it could be as much as $15 million if the debenture holders' contentions with regard to the proper rate of interest were accepted.) His analysis of this question was exceedingly terse; essentially he treated the date of accrual of each installment as if it were the date on which a judgment or its equivalent had been entered against the Milwaukee Road. Actually they were just the due dates of the installments.

PROBLEM SET 15.5

1. Does this case actually involve bonds?
2. When discussing potential deacceleration of the bonds, Judge Posner argues that as between the bondholders and the shareholders, the bondholders should win, especially given that "many or for that matter all of them may have bought their shares after the Milwaukee Road went into bankruptcy." How convincing is this argument?
3. Further on in the opinion, he argues that the acceleration clause should be seen as one outcome that the bondholders bargained for, noting that the "debenture holders bought the chance to get the principal back early, at a time when a rise in interest rates might enable them to reinvest it more advantageously elsewhere." How plausible is this interpretation?

4. DISTRESSED DEBT INVESTORS

Debt investing was once seen as the safe part of the investing market, reserved for retirees and life insurance companies. That, of course, changed with the growth of the junk bond market in the 1980s, and the intentional issuance of debt that offered high yield in exchange for high risk.

Recent years have also seen the growth of investors that intentionally target the debt of underperforming companies. Indeed, these sorts of investors are important clients of all the major law firms.[12]

MICHELLE M. HARNER, *TRENDS IN DISTRESSED DEBT INVESTING: AN EMPIRICAL STUDY OF INVESTORS' OBJECTIVES*
16 Am. Bankr. Inst. L. Rev. 69, 75-77 (2008)

A distressed debt investor is an entity that purchases the debt of a financially troubled company at a discount against the face value of the debt. The amount of the discount varies by situation, but can range from a low discount of 20% to a high discount of 60% or perhaps even 80%. The investor seeks to make a profit on its investment primarily by reselling the debt, through recoveries on the debt in the restructuring process or by converting the debt into an equity position in the reorganized debtor.

The practice of distressed debt investing is not new; however, the market for distressed debt has expanded significantly since its inception.[13] Trade vendors no longer are the only creditors that desire to liquidate their claims against a debtor quickly. Rather, traditional financial institutions and long-term institutional investors, such as banks and insurance companies, are now quick to sell troubled credits. Banks and other traditional lenders also are increasingly syndicating commercial loans at the outset. These practices make it easy for traditional lenders and investors to exit, and hedge funds, private equity firms and other nontraditional lenders to enter, troubled situations.

The presence of nontraditional lenders in troubled situations changes the dynamics of corporate restructurings, including corporate chapter 11 cases. As one commentator observed, most distressed debt investors are "far less image conscious — they do not have the white-shoe, gentlemanly workout orientation of commercial banks, previously the biggest creditors in bankruptcies." The concept of "relationship lending," where a bank would work with a troubled company to develop a mutually-agreeable restructuring plan to foster repeat business with the company, is now the rare exception rather than the rule. Most distressed debt investors are repeat players in the market, but not with respect to a particular company or management team.

---

12. For an interview with one prominent distressed investor, see *http://goo.gl/wPNMm*

13. For a discussion of the history of the distressed debt market, see Hilary Rosenberg, *The Vulture Investors* 16–19 (John Wiley & Sons, Inc., 2000) (detailing growth of "vultures" during 1980s, and how they had an increased role in "restructuring of corporate America . . ." and changed "dynamics of bankruptcy" so creditors have increased influence. By the late 1990s, the "vulture market had matured" so "new activist" players were raising money to invest in these "downtrodden companies . . ."). *See also* Jay Krasoff & John O'Neill, *The Role of Distressed Investing and Hedge Funds in Turnarounds and Buyouts and How this Affects Middle-Market Companies*, J. Private Equity, Spring 2006, at 17 (explaining how distressed debt investing has a long history, stretching as far back as moneychangers in Bible, and noting changes accompanying "credit-oriented hedge funds" becoming more "proactive in the distressed investing market and the accompanying restructuring process"). For a discussion of the growth in the market, see Heidi Moore, *Distressed Debt Fundraising Hits Record*, Fin. News (Online US), July 13, 2007. Ms. Moore's article states that "high leverage levels and sub-prime downgrades" created doubt with respect to credit markets, noting that distressed-debt firms raised more in the first six months of 2007 than at the end of 2006, and observing that some "firms are rushing to get part of the distressed-debt markets." *Id.*

The upshot for troubled companies is that they now face increasing demands and pressures from their debt holders. Even before the filing of a chapter 11 case, the company may lose control of its restructuring process to one or more distressed debt investors. Investors may obtain this type of leverage over a company through contractual covenants, promises of post-bankruptcy financing, statutory rights under Article 9 of the Uniform Commercial Code or chapter 11 of the Bankruptcy Code or some combination of the foregoing. The end result is a more creditor-controlled restructuring process.

At its simplest, distressed debt investing involves purchasing debt obligations trading at a distressed level — for example at 30 percent of par value — with the expectation that the true value is somewhat higher. In short, distressed debt traders are looking for investments where the debt obligations are fundamentally mispriced and will rebound in value.

This involves a variety of legal issues as these investors explore their legal rights under the debt instrument and how those rights might allow them to obtain value from the instrument, especially if the market price for the debt does not rebound or the debtor decides to restructure its debt obligations before such rebound.

16

SYNDICATED LOAN AGREEMENTS

Corporations often borrow from banks, just like real people. Corporations' lending needs are quite a bit larger than yours or mine — even if you are quite wealthy (textbook authors are not).

Accordingly, specialized legal and financial structures have developed around large loans to corporations.[1] Moreover, a secondary market in these loans has developed, and a trade association, The Loan Syndications and Trading Association, has established standardized documentation for loan trading and model credit agreement provisions to facilitate trading.[2]

We start by considering structural issues, which once again bring us into a world of complex contracts. The subsequent sections deal with the legal issues that arise from these contracts.

1. LOAN STRUCTURES

Large corporate loans typically take one of two forms. First, a loan might be syndicated. Syndication just means that the loan is made by a group of lenders.

Thus, a $100 million loan to Bogartco might be made under a single loan agreement whereby ten lenders agree to contribute $10 million to the whole. You can think of this as a kind of diversification strategy by the lending financial institutions.

In a syndication, each lender has a legal relationship with the borrower. Essentially a syndication is either a joint loan or an assignment of an interest in the loan, which means that the lead bank who may have organized the loan no longer has any performance obligation on the syndicated pieces of the

---

1. Douglas G. Baird & Robert K. Rasmussen, *Antibankruptcy*, 119 Yale L.J. 648, 667 (2010).
2. Stephen J. Lubben, *Credit Derivatives and the Future of Chapter 11*, 81 Am. Bankr. L.J. 405, 426 (2007).

loan.[3] The following case gives an example of an actual syndicated loan agreement.

DEUTSCHE BANK AG, PLAINTIFF-COUNTERCLAIM-DEFENDANT, v. JPMORGAN CHASE BANK (F/K/A THE CHASE MANHATTAN BANK), DEFENDANT-COUNTERCLAIM-PLAINTIFF

2007 WL 2823129
United States District Court, S.D. New York
No. 04 Civ. 7192 (SHS) | Sept. 27, 2007

II.   Background

The following facts are either undisputed or, where disputes exist, they are set forth and do not create a genuine issue of material fact.

Genuity, Inc. is an internet company that had been "spun off" in June 2000 by Verizon Communications, Inc. as a requirement for Federal Communications Commission approval of the merger between GTE and Bell Atlantic that led to Verizon's formation.

On September 5, 2000, Genuity and ten banks — The Chase Manhattan Bank, Credit Suisse First Boston, Citicorp USA, Inc., BNP Paribas, Morgan Guaranty Trust Co. of New York, The Bank of New York, The Industrial Bank of Japan, Toronto Dominion (Texas) Inc., Wachovia Bank, N.A., and Deutsche Bank AG — entered an agreement ("the Original Credit Agreement") to establish a $2 billion unsecured credit facility in favor of Genuity. Pursuant to the Original Credit Agreement, the loan commitments of each of the ten banks were as follows:

- The Chase Manhattan Bank committed $300,000,000, which represented 15% of the total.
- Citicorp USA, Inc. committed $300,000,000, which represented 15% of the total.
- Credit Suisse First Boston committed $300,000,000, which represented 15% of the total.
- Deutsche Bank AG committed $300,000,000, which represented 15% of the total.
- BNP Paribas committed $200,000,000, which represented 10% of the total.
- Morgan Guaranty Trust Co. of New York committed $200,000,000, which represented 10% of the total.
- The Bank of New York committed $100,000,000, which represented 5% of the total.
- The Industrial Bank of Japan committed $100,000,000, which represented 5% of the total.
- Toronto Dominion (Texas) Inc. committed $100,000,000, which represented 5% of the total.

---

3. Loan syndications have been around for a while. *E.g.*, Coffin v. President, etc., of Grand Rapids Hydraulic Co., 18 N.Y.S. 782, 783 (Super. 1892) *aff'd*, 136 N.Y. 655, 32 N.E. 1076 (1893).

- Wachovia Bank, N.A. committed $100,000,000, which represented 5% of the total.

The banks appointed The Chase Manhattan Bank — a predecessor in interest to JPMorgan Chase — to act as their Administrative Agent ("Agent") pursuant to the Original Credit Agreement. In exchange for the committed revolving credit facility, Genuity paid the banks an annual commitment fee of approximately $2.5 million. Under the Original Credit Agreement, Genuity had the right to draw on the facility at any time by issuing to the Agent a "Notice of Revolving Credit Borrowing" (or "Notice") by telephone, confirmed immediately in writing, in the form annexed to the Original Credit Agreement. The Notice was to specify the date and amount of the draw, confirm the continued correctness of Genuity's representations and warranties, and certify that no "Event of Default" had occurred, was continuing, or would result from the borrowing. The Original Credit Agreement required that Genuity give this Notice no later than 11:00 a.m. "New York City time", and it allowed Genuity the option of demanding the advance of funds by 12:00 noon on the third business day after the Notice and pay one particular interest rate, or to demand the funds by 12:00 noon on the same business day and pay a higher interest rate.

[T]he Original Credit Agreement also set forth certain "Events of Default", which would terminate the obligation of the banks to make advances to Genuity.

Approximately one year after executing the Original Credit Agreement — on September 24, 2001 — Genuity and nine banks — JPMorgan Chase, Credit Suisse First Boston, Citibank, N.A., BNP Paribas, The Bank of New York, The Industrial Bank of Japan, Toronto Dominion (Texas) Inc., Wachovia Bank, N.A., and Deutsche Bank AG — entered into an Amended and Restated Credit Agreement (the "Amended Credit Agreement"). The lending banks retained the same percentage commitments as under the Original Credit Agreement; however, because the Chase Manhattan Bank and Morgan Guaranty Trust Co. of New York had merged in June 2000, the combined entity — JPMorgan Chase — now became the Agent and the holder of a $500,000,000 commitment to Genuity, representing 25% of the total credit facility.

This Amended Credit Agreement still provided for $2 billion of financing to Genuity, but whereas the Original Credit Agreement provided only for "Revolving Credit Advances" (also known as "Revolver Advances"), the new agreement provided for both "Revolving Credit Advances" and "Letter of Credit" advances. The new "Letter of Credit" option allowed Genuity to use the credit facility to obtain funds without actually drawing down on the facility.

On September 27, 2001 — three days after the parties ratified the Amended Credit Agreement — JPMorgan Chase issued a Letter of Credit pursuant to the Amended Credit Agreement to Genuity in the amount of $1.15 billion in order to support a bond offering by Genuity in that amount. In the event of default on the Genuity bonds, the bondholders could draw on the Letter of Credit, and the other bank lenders were obligated to reimburse JPMorgan Chase in proportion to their commitments under the Amended Credit Agreement.

———————

In a loan participation, as contrasted with a syndication, the participant will have no direct relationship with the borrower. Instead, the buyer of a loan participation simply obtains an interest in a relationship that the lender has already established with the borrower — somewhat like a sublease.[4]

Unfunded loan commitments, whether syndications or participations, are often in the form of a revolving credit agreement — ominously termed the "revolver", in industry slang.[5] Revolving credit is like your credit card: The company can borrow, and pay, and borrow and pay against the same loan for the entire term of the agreement.

A term loan, on the other hand, is more like a bond. The loan is typically funded at the outset, and repayable on a set schedule. One key distinction from a bond, however, is that bank loans typically have floating interest rates, whereas bonds are most often fixed rate instruments. Thus, whereas bonds involve both credit risk and interest rate risk, investments in loans arguably involve only credit risk.

In addition to the floating interest rate, most credit facilities charge a variety of fees. A commitment fee, or unused credit line fee, is the amount paid on the unused portion of the loan commitment. This is specified as a percentage of the undrawn amount, and is paid on a schedule similar to interest. Because banks are required by bank regulators to maintain reserves against their commitments, these fees essentially pass the cost of these reserves on to the potential borrowers.

If the loan is syndicated, the borrower often pays an annual fee to compensate the agent bank for its duties. Typically the borrower will also have to pay the agent bank's expenses in connection with the loan.

The borrower also often does its banking with the lead bank on the loan. This may provide the lender with an ability to seize the debtor's cash upon bankruptcy, and it provides the lead bank with another benefit from managing the loan.

IN RE FONTAINEBLEAU LAS VEGAS HOLDINGS, LLC, ET AL., DEBTORS. FONTAINEBLEAU LAS VEGAS, LLC, PLAINTIFF, v. BANK OF AMERICA, N.A., ET AL., DEFENDANTS

417 B.R. 651

United States District Court, S.D. Florida

No. 09–21879–CIV | Aug. 26, 2009

Alan S. GOLD, District Judge.

1. THE CREDIT AGREEMENT AND DISBURSEMENT AGREEMENT

On June 9, 2009, Plaintiff Fontainebleau Las Vegas, LLC ("Fontainebleau" or the "Borrower") and other affiliated entities filed a voluntary Chapter 11 petition in the United States Bankruptcy Court for the Southern District of Florida. On the same day, Fontainebleau commenced the instant [] proceeding

---

4. In re Okura & Co. (Am.), Inc., 249 B.R. 596, 604 (Bankr. S.D.N.Y. 2000).

5. Another common unfunded loan interest relates to letters of credit, as seen in the prior case.

against Defendants, a group of banks with whom Fontainebleau had entered into a Credit Agreement and Disbursement Agreement on June 6, 2007 for loans to be used for the construction and development of a casino resort in Las Vegas, Nevada (the "Project"). Under the Credit Agreement and the Disbursement Agreement, a syndicate of lenders were to loan, contingent on a variety of conditions set forth in the parties' various agreements, funds under three credit facilities, the Term Loan, the Delay Draw Term Loan, and the Revolving Loan facilities. Each facility respectively provided for a total commitment of $700 million, $350 million, and $800 million, with the Revolving Loan facility permitted reborrowing.[6] Defendants in this case are those banks that have agreed to lend money under the Revolving Loan facility (the "Revolver Banks").[7] Bank of America, N.A., in addition to being one of the Revolver Banks, was the Administrative Agent for all loans made under the Credit Agreement and the Disbursement Agreement, among other loan documents.

The Initial Term Loan of $700 million was funded in full upon execution of the Credit Agreement. With respect to loans under the Delay Draw Term Loan and Revolving Loan facilities, the agreements provide for a two-step borrowing process. First, per the Credit Agreement, the Borrower submits a Notice of Borrowing to the Administrative Agent. Upon receipt of the Notice of Borrowing, the Administrative Agent is required to promptly notify "each Delay Draw Lender and/or Revolving Lender, as appropriate", that the Notice has been received. After the respective lenders have been notified, they "will make the amount of its pro rata share of each borrowing available to Administrative Agent . . . prior to 10:00 am on the Borrowing Date", which is typically the next business day. "Upon satisfaction or waiver of the applicable conditions precedent specified in Section 2.1, the proceeds of the loans will be made available by the Administrative Agent, in like funds as received by Administrative Agent from the Lenders, not later than noon on the Borrowing Date." These loans are remitted to the Bank Proceeds Account. As a second step, Fontainebleau is required to fulfill certain conditions set forth in the Disbursement Agreement, including the submission of an "Advance Request" and the satisfaction of an "In-Balance Test", at which point the money is moved to various Funding and Payment Accounts for disbursement to Fontainebleau.

Historically term and revolving loans would be combined in a single agreement, with the lenders having equal rights against any collateral given under the agreement. In the years immediately before the 2008 financial crisis, there was some move to combine a series of loans, each of different priority, in a single loan agreement.

These so-called A/B or senior/subordinate loan structures, where the senior and subordinate loan are documented in a single set of loan documents and are

---

6. The Project was also financed by $675 million in second-mortgage notes, along with separate financing for development of the Project's retail space.

7. The Defendants in this action are Bank of America, N.A., Merrill Lynch Capital Corporation, JP Morgan Chase Bank, N.A., Barclays Bank PLC, Deutsche Bank Trust Company Americas, The Royal Bank of Scotland PLC, Sumitomo Mitsui Banking Corporation, Bank of Scotland PLC, HSH Nordbank AG (New York Branch), and MB Financial Bank, N.A.

secured by the same security, give rise to additional complexities regarding inter-creditor relationships. Sometimes these loans are documented from inception with different "tranches" or they may be created by a lender that has made a whole loan to a firm, and then sells off slices to investors.

PROBLEM SET 16.1

1. Diagram both transactions described in the cases above and be prepared to discuss them in class. How do the two transactions differ? What is the effect of the letter of credit on the Genuity bonds?
2. The Genuity loan features a "swing line" that allows the borrower to obtain funds on short notice. What are the costs and benefits of this feature to both Genuity and its banks?
3. As noted, one distinction between a large corporate loan and a bond is the floating interest rate typically seen in a loan. Another distinction is that loan agreements are often secured, although there is no require-ment that they be secured — and some highly rated borrowers do obtain unsecured syndicated loans. What are the trade-offs from the borrowing firm's perspective when deciding whether or not to obtain a secured loan, and unsecured loan, or issue bond debt?

2. DECISION MAKING

Loan agreements typically come with more covenants and disclosure obliga-tions than bond debt. But if the lenders are to exercise these extra rights in a meaningful way, they need to provide for some internal governance structures to resolve disputes amongst lenders. These governance issues become even more acute if loans of differing priorities are combined within a single agreement, as discussed earlier.

When buying a loan participation, the participant will typically not receive its own note and have but limited rights to control the lending relationship.

PARTICIPATION AGREEMENT

This PARTICIPATION AGREEMENT (this "**Agreement**") is entered into as of _____, 20__ by and between _____, a [n] _____ ("**Lead Lender**") and _____, a _____ ("**Participant**").

A. Lead Lender has made or is making the loan (the "**Loan**") identified in the Summary of Terms (defined below) (1) to the borrower indicated in the Sum-mary of Terms ("**Borrower**"), (2) in the principal amount indicated in the Summary of Terms and (3) secured by a mortgage, deed of trust or similar instrument ("**Mortgage**") on the project indicated in the Summary of Terms ("**Project**").

B. Lead Lender and Participant have agreed that Lead Lender shall sell and transfer, and Participant shall purchase and assume, an undivided participation interest in the Loan on the terms and conditions set forth herein.

IN CONSIDERATION of the agreements, provisions and covenants herein contained, the parties hereto agree as follows:

SECTION 4
LOAN ADMINISTRATION

4.1 <u>Loan Administration</u>. Subject to the provisions of <u>Section 4.2</u>, Participant hereby authorizes Lead Lender to: (a) negotiate, manage and administer the Loan, (ii) give consents, approvals or waivers in connection with the Loan Documents, (c) amend the Loan Documents; (c) take or refrain from taking any action and make any determination provided for herein or in the Loan Documents, (d) retain the original Loan Documents, (e) collect all payments made under the Loan Documents, (f) require funding by the parties hereto (in their respective Percentages) of Protective Advances or other Costs (to the extent not paid by Borrower); (g) realize or manage and dispose of Collateral; and (g) exercise all other powers as are available to the holder of the Loan. Lead Lender shall administer the Loan in a manner consistent with the standard of care applied by Lead Lender in administering loans owned entirely for its own account.

4.2 <u>Major Decisions</u>. Notwithstanding <u>Section 4.1</u>, Lead Lender shall not take the following actions (each a "Major Decision") with respect to the Loan without the prior written consent of Participant (provided, however, Lead Lender shall be authorized to take any of the following actions without the consent of Participant if Participant has defaulted in funding an Advance and failed to cure such default within the period set forth in Section 2.4):

> (a) Release the Mortgage, in any material respect, or release any guaranty of the Loan, except in connection with the full repayment of the Loan or pursuant to the express terms of the Loan Documents;
> (b) Subordinate the Mortgage to other indebtedness;
> (c) Amend, modify or waive any provision of the Loan Documents so as to (a) reduce or forgive the amount of any interest or principal payable required under the Loan Documents; (b) change or modify the interest rate under the Loan Documents; (c) extend the maturity date of the Loan; (d) postpone or defer any date for payment of principal or interest under any Loan Document; or (e) increase the principal amount of the Loan except for (x) Advances to be made after the date hereof pursuant to the Loan Documents, and (y) any Protective Advances; or
> (d) Approve a sale of the Project by Borrower.

In no event shall the decision to assess or waive late charges or default interest be a Major Decision.

4.3 <u>Response to Requests</u>. Participant shall respond to a written request for approval or consent from Lead Lender within five (5) Business Days after such request. A failure to respond within such time period shall be deemed an approval or consent. If Lead Lender and Participant are unable to reach an agreement on any Major Decision within five (5) Business Days following the disapproval of the request, then Lead Lender shall have the option to exercise its rights under Section 6.1.

A syndicated loan agreement is an agreement between the borrower and every bank in the credit line. As such, the syndicate banks may be less inclined to delegate to the lead or agent bank. But the borrower will want to make sure that the lead lender can make as many decisions as possible without having to go to all the other lenders for approval, which may prove time consuming and burdensome. Thus the agreement typically provides that the lead bank can make certain decisions, other decisions can be made only upon majority vote of the lenders, and other decisions require unanimous consent.

IN RE CHRYSLER LLC, ET AL., DEBTORS
405 B.R. 84
United States Bankruptcy Court, S.D. New York
No. 09 B 50002(AJG) | May 31, 2009

Arthur J. GONZALEZ, Bankruptcy Judge.
Before the Court is a motion seeking authority to sell substantially all of the debtors' operating assets, free and clear of liens, claims, interests and encumbrances to a successful bidder and to authorize the assumption and assignment of certain executory contracts and unexpired leases in connection with the sale, as well as certain other related relief. The sale transaction for which authorization is sought (the "Sale Transaction" or "Fiat Transaction") is similar to that presented in other cases in which exigent circumstances warrant an expeditious sale of assets prior to confirmation of a plan. The fact that the U.S. government is the primary source of funding does not alter the analysis under bankruptcy law.

The Debtors and their non-debtor direct and indirect subsidiaries (collectively, the "Chrysler Companies") comprise one of the largest manufacturers and distributors of automobiles and other vehicles, together with related parts and accessories. At the Petition Date[8], Chrysler had 32 manufacturing and assembly facilities and 24 parts depots worldwide; and in addition, at the Petition Date, it had a network of 3,200 independent dealerships in the United States, with 72% of Chrysler sales occurring in the United States.

Chrysler's ultimate parent company is Chrysler Holding LLC ("Holding"). The owners of Holding are Cerberus Capital Management L.P. ("Cerberus") and Daimler AG ("Daimler"). As of the Petition Date, Cerberus or its affiliates held 80.1% of the membership interests in Holding, and Daimler or its affiliates held 19.9% of its membership interests.

Pursuant to an Amended and Restated First Lien Credit Agreement dated as of November 29, 2007 (the "First Lien Credit Agreement") a $10 billion term loan that matures on August 2, 2013 was made available to Chrysler. JP Morgan

---

8. The date the bankruptcy case was commenced; the date the bankruptcy petition was filed with the court. — AUTHOR

Chase Bank N.A. is the administrative agent (the "Administrative Agent") under the First Lien Credit Agreement. Chrysler's obligations under the First Lien Credit Agreement are secured by a security interest in and first lien on substantially all of Chrysler's assets. In addition, those obligations are guaranteed by certain other Debtors. The guarantees by these "other" Debtors are secured by a first priority lien on substantially all of such Debtors' respective assets. On the Petition Date, Chrysler owed the first-lien prepetition lenders (the "First–Lien Lenders") approximately $6.9 billion under that term loan.

In the fall of 2008, a global credit crisis affecting the liquidity markets impacted the availability of loans both to dealers and consumers, resulting in the erosion of consumer confidence and a sharp drop in vehicle sales. Chrysler was forced to use cash reserves to compensate for the reduction in cash flow and the resulting losses. The losses eliminated the gains that Chrysler had made early in its restructuring effort. Moreover, other OEM's were impacted, forcing them to confront their own liquidity issues.

As a result, in late 2008, Chrysler and other entities sought assistance from the government to obtain new financing to fund their operations to carry them through the liquidity crunch. In response, the TARP Financing was provided. Chrysler sought $7 billion and they were given $4 billion. Pursuant to the terms of the loan, Chrysler was required to submit a plan showing that it was able to achieve and sustain long-term viability, energy efficiency, rationalization of costs and competitiveness in the U.S. marketplace (the "Viability Plan"), which would indicate Chrysler's ability to repay the TARP Financing.

The Debtors used the $4 million TARP Loan to operate their business, including paying vendors and other ordinary course payables, and to fund their effort to pursue the Viability Plan. At the same time, Chrysler continued to pursue an alliance with Fiat; Chrysler considered Fiat to be a good prospect because it viewed Fiat's products and distribution network as complementary to those of Chrysler.

On January 16, 2009, Chrysler entered into a term sheet with Fiat for a strategic alliance (the "Fiat Alliance") pursuant to which Fiat would acquire 35% of the equity of Chrysler and would provide access to competitive fuel-efficient vehicle platforms, distribution capabilities in key growth markets and substantial cost-saving opportunities. The Fiat Alliance also would provide Chrysler with a distribution network outside of the North American region.

On May 19, 2009, the Indiana State Teachers Retirement Fund, Indiana State Police Pension Trust, and Indiana Major Moves Construction (the "Indiana Funds"), which oversee the investment of retirement assets for certain civil servants in the state of Indiana, filed an objection to the Sale Motion. The Indiana Funds hold approximately $42 million of the $6.9 billion in first priority secured claims, which represents less than 1% of the first-lien debt. In their objection, the Indiana Funds argue that pursuant to the Sale Motion, the First–Lien Lenders' collateral would be stripped and, in return, those lenders would be paid 29 cents on the dollar. The collateral would then be transferred to New Chrysler, where, according to the Indiana Funds, it would be worth significantly more than the money paid to the First-Lien Lenders. The Indiana Funds further argue that unsecured deficiency claims would not be paid while unsecured trade debt would be paid in full. In addition, the Indiana Funds contend that their senior claims will be impaired while the Governmental Entities, as junior lienholders and VEBA and the UAW, as unsecured creditors, will receive value . . .

The Indiana Funds are parties to the First Lien Credit Agreement as assignees to a portion of the debt. As previously noted, Chrysler's obligation to repay the loans under the First Lien Credit Agreement is secured by liens on most of its assets. Consequently, two additional documents are relevant: an Amended and Restated Collateral Trust Agreement, dated November 29, 2007 (as amended, the "CTA"), pursuant to which Wilmington Trust Company is the collateral trustee (the "Collateral Trustee"); and the Security Agreement, pursuant to which Chrysler grants a security interest in most of its assets, and the proceeds thereof, to the Collateral Trustee. *Security Agreement*, §2(a). Thus, while the liens are for the benefit of the lenders under the First Lien Credit Agreement, the liens themselves were granted to and are held by the Collateral Trustee. *See CTA* at p. 1.

Each lender under the First Lien Credit Agreement irrevocably designated the Administrative Agent to act as such lender's agent in exercising the powers delegated to the Administrative Agent and to be bound by its action. *First Lien Credit Agreement*, §§8.1, 8.4. The lenders, including the Indiana Funds, agreed to be bound by the Administrative Agents' action made at the request of lenders holding a majority of the indebtedness under the First Lien Credit Agreement (the "Required Lenders"). *Id.* at §1.1 & §8.4.

The commencement of the Debtors' bankruptcy cases was an event of default under the First Lien Credit Agreement, *Id.* at §7(e)(i)(A). The CTA defines the Administrative Agent as the "Controlling Party" as long as the first and second secured obligations have not been paid. *CTA* §1.1. Upon receipt of a "notice of event of default", the Collateral Trustee exercises the rights and remedies provided for in the CTA, and related security documents, "subject to the direction of the Controlling Party." *CTA* §2.1(a). A notice of event of default is deemed to be in effect whenever there is a bankruptcy filing. *CTA* §2.1(b). While such notice of an event of default is in effect, the Collateral Trustee has power to take any Collateral Enforcement Actions permitted under the security documents or any action it "deems necessary to protect or preserve the Collateral and to realize upon the Collateral", including selling all or any of the Collateral. CTA §§2.2. & 2.3. A Collateral Enforcement Action is defined, with respect to any secured party, as exercising, instituting or maintaining or participating "in any action or proceeding with respect to, any rights or remedies with respect to any Collateral, including . . . exercising any other right or remedy under the Uniform Commercial Code or any applicable jurisdiction or under any Bankruptcy Law or other applicable law." CTA §1.1.

Further, section 2.5(b) of the CTA provides that the Administrative Agent, as Controlling Party, has the right to direct, among other things, "the taking or the refraining from taking of any action authorized by this Collateral Trust Agreement or any Trust Security Document." Further, section 2.5(c) of the CTA provides, in relevant part:

Whether or not any Insolvency Proceeding has been commenced by or against any of the [Chrysler parties to the CTA], no . . . [secured party] shall do. any of the following without the consent of the Controlling Party; (i) take any Collateral Enforcement Action . . . or (ii) object to, contest or take any other action that is reasonably likely to hinder (1) any Collateral Enforcement Action initiated by the Collateral Trustee, (2) any release of Collateral permitted under Section 6.12, whether or not done in consultation with or with notice to such Secured Party or (3) any decision by the Controlling Party to forbear or refrain from bringing or pursuing any such Collateral Enforcement Action or to effect any such release.

Thus, section 2.5, concerning the exercise of powers, gives the Collateral Trustee the exclusive right to pursue all of the lenders' rights and remedies concerning the Collateral and, further, gives the Administrative Agent, as Controlling Party, the exclusive authority to direct the Collateral Trustee's action concerning the Collateral.

In accordance with the direction of the Administrative Agent, the Collateral Trustee, who is the holder of the liens, has consented to the Fiat Transaction. The right to consent to the sale of the Debtors' assets that constitute Collateral is a Collateral Enforcement Action. It is an exercise of a right pursuant to Bankruptcy Law concerning the Collateral. *CTA*, §1.1. The Administrative Agent has received the concurrence of 92.5% of the outstanding principal amount of the loans under the First Lien Credit Agreement. Thus, the Administrative Agent has obtained the needed support of the Required Lenders. Consequently, pursuant to the CTA, the Administrative Agent properly directed the Collateral Trustee, who holds the liens, to consent to the section 363 sale of the Collateral. Moreover, the Administrative Agent acted as agent to the Indiana Funds and on their behalf. Thus, the Indiana Funds are bound by the Administrative Agent's action in that regard. *First Lien Credit Agreement*, §§8.1(a), 8.4. Therefore, the Administrative Agent's consent to the sale of the assets and its direction to the Collateral Trustee to consent, under section 363(f)(2) of the Bankruptcy Code, satisfies that section and allow for the purchased assets to be sold free and clear of the liens on the property held by the Collateral Trustee.

The Indiana Funds direct the Court's attention to section 9.1(a)(iii) of the First Lien Credit Agreement and argue that it requires the Administrative Agent to receive the consent of all Lenders before it can release collateral. The section referenced by the Indiana Funds, however, concerns waivers, amendments, supplements or modifications to the First Lien Credit Agreement and related documents. The transfer of the purchased assets to New Chrysler pursuant to section 363 of the Bankruptcy Code does not require any amendment, supplement or modification to the loan documents. *See In re GWLS Holdings, Inc.*, No. 08–12430, 2009 WL 453110, 2009 Bankr. LEXIS 378 (Bankr.D.Del. Feb. 23, 2009) (concluding that a provision concerning waivers, amendments, supplements or modifications after execution of certain related credit agreements did not override the provision concerning the right of the lenders' agent to credit bid). *See also Beal Sav. Bank v. Sommer*, 8 N.Y.3d 318 328–29, 834 N.Y.S.2d 44, 865 N.E.2d 1210 (2007) (concluding that provisions in a syndicate loan arrangement requiring unanimous consent by participating lenders in order to amend, modify or waive terms of related loan agreements did not preclude application of specific provisions which accomplished the parties' agreed-upon intent for collective action through an agent upon default by borrower). The purpose of section 9.1(a)(iii) of the First Lien Credit Agreement is to ensure that, unless there is unanimous consent by all lenders under the related loan agreements, the terms of those agreements cannot be altered in a manner that is inconsistent with the terms originally agreed to by the parties. *See id.* It does not concern collective action to enforce rights as authorized under the agreed-upon specific provisions of the parties' loan agreements.

Upon an Event of Default, the CTA expressly granted the Collateral Trustee the right to sell any or all of the Collateral. Thus, the loan documents authorized the Collateral Trustee to consent to the sale without the need to amend or modify the loan documents. Further, the Administrative Agent and Collateral Trustee are operating under their exclusive authority to take any Collateral Enforcement Action necessary to realize upon the Collateral. Moreover, it is not a "release" of collateral because the lien attaches to the proceeds of the sale, which remain as collateral to secure the loan made by the Lenders. Finally, even if the action were viewed as an amendment to the loan documents, the prohibition against releasing collateral without the consent of all lenders under section 9.1(iii) of the First Lien Credit Agreement, itself has an exception where the action is otherwise provided for in the loan documents. Here, the loan documents expressly provide for the Administrative Agent to direct the Collateral Trustee to take Enforcement Actions, including the sale of all or any of the Collateral.

The Court concludes that the purpose of the relevant provisions of the First Lien Credit Agreement, the CTA, and the Security Agreements is to have the Administrative Agent and Collateral Trustee act in the collective interest of the lenders. Restricting enforcement to a single agent to engage in unified action for the interests of a group of lenders, based upon a majority vote, avoids chaos and prevents a single lender from being preferred over others. Pursuant to the CTA, the Indiana Funds are bound by the Administrative Agent's direction to the Collateral Trustee to consent to the sale of its collateral free and clear of liens and other interests in exchange for the $2 billion cash payment.

Finally, with respect to the consenting First-Lien Lenders, the Indiana Funds question their independence in entering into the compromise to allow the sale of the assets free and clear of the lien. Inasmuch as certain of the individual-consenting lenders were recipients of government loans under the TARP program, the objecting lenders seek to portray the TARP-recipient lenders as being intimidated by the government. A compromise that is not based upon business considerations, including an assessment of litigation risks, would raise issues regarding the Administrative Agent's obligations, if any to the Indiana Funds, under the agreement. Clearly, that issue is not before this Court.

The Indiana Funds seem to be asking that, if the Court finds that they are bound under the governance provisions of the First Lien Credit Agreement, the Court should nullify the consent given because it was brought about by undue pressure by the U.S. government on the TARP-recipient lenders, who voted to give consent to the transaction before the Court.

In the first instance, it is not clear that this Court would even have jurisdiction over this inter-creditor dispute. However, the suggestion that the TARP-recipient lenders have been pressured to the point that they would breach their fiduciary duty and capitulate to the settlements presented is without any evidentiary support. It is mere speculation and without merit.

The Indiana Funds contracted away their right to act inconsistently with the determination of the Required Lenders. In that regard, if they did not want to waive such rights, they should not have invested in an investment with such restrictions. The fact that they do not like the outcome is not a basis to ignore the governance provisions of the relevant agreements.

The First-Lien Lenders had limited options: demand a liquidation of the collateral, negotiate with the only available source of funding, i.e., the Governmental Entities, or provide funding to sustain the Debtors on a stand-alone basis. The First-Lien Lenders, operating under their governance structure, decided to concentrate their efforts on negotiating with the only available source of funding, the Governmental Entities, and to accept their proposal.

If governance amongst lenders in traditional loans is complex, it becomes even more challenging in A/B structure where lenders at various priority levels have conflicting interests from inception. Typically there is a separate co-lender agreement between the various lenders.

And where there are multiple loans of varying priorities, an intercreditor agreement is typically used. The following case looks at intercreditor agreements in the related context of real estate lending.

Unreported Disposition
29 Misc.3d 1216(A), 918 N.Y.S.2d 396 (Table), 2010 WL 4243437
(N.Y. Sup.), 2010 N.Y. Slip Op. 51848(U)

Bank of Am., N.A. v. PSW NYC LLC

651293/10
Supreme Court, New York County
Decided on September 16, 2010

OPINION OF THE COURT

Richard B. Lowe, J.

In this action, plaintiffs Bank of America, N.A. and U.S. Bank National Association seek to enforce their rights under an Amended and Restated Intercreditor Agreement dated February 16, 2007 (Intercreditor Agreement). The two-count complaint asserts one cause of action for a declaration of plaintiffs' rights under the Intercreditor Agreement, and one cause of action for injunctive relief preventing defendant PSW NYC LLC (PSW) from acquiring or selling certain equity collateral without first paying plaintiffs outstanding indebtedness under a senior loan, and from causing the commencement of bankruptcy proceedings while the senior loan is outstanding.

Plaintiffs now move, by order to show cause, for a preliminary injunction that enjoins PSW from the conduct complained of in the second cause of action.

FACTS

In 2007, non-party Tishman Speyer Development Corp. (Tishman) purchased from non-party Metropolitan Tower Life Insurance Company the residential housing development known as Peter Cooper Village and Stuyvesant Town (Property) for $5.4 billion. Tishman created various related entities to complete the transaction, with PCV ST Owner LP and ST Owner LP (together, Borrowers) serving as the entities holding title to the Property. To finance the purchase, the Borrowers secured a loan in the amount of $3 billion (Senior Loan) from Wachovia Bank, N.A. (Wachovia) and Merrill Lynch Mortgage Lending, Inc. (Merrill). The terms of the Senior Loan are stated in an Amended and Restated Loan and Security Agreement, dated February 16, 2007 (Senior Loan Agreement), entered into by Borrowers, and by Wachovia and Merrill as co-lenders (together, Senior Lenders). On the same day, the Borrowers executed and delivered to the Senior Lenders six notes evidencing their indebtedness of $3 billion under the Senior Loan (Notes), each of which is currently held in a mortgage securitization trust (Trust). The plaintiffs are the trustees of those Trusts. The Borrowers also executed a First Amendment to Mortgage, Security Agreement, Assignment of Rents and Fixture Filing, whereby they granted to the Senior Lenders a security interest in the Property (Amended Mortgage).

In order to secure an additional $1.4 billion in financing, the direct and indirect parents of the Borrowers (Junior Borrowers) pledged their direct and indirect ownership interests in the Borrowers and their respective general partners in exchange for 11 mezzanine loans (Junior Loans) issued by various lenders (Junior Lenders), with priority running in sequential order from Junior 1 Loan, as most senior, to Junior 11 Loan, as most junior.[9] Each of the Junior Loans was governed by a separate Mezzanine Loan Agreement (Mezzanine Loan Agreement), dated February 16, 2007. In addition, pursuant to separate Pledge and Security Agreements, also dated February 16, 2007, each Junior Lender was granted a first priority security interest in the corresponding Junior Borrower's ownership interest in the respective subsidiary Borrower or Junior Borrower and that entity's general partner (Equity Collateral). The Junior Lenders were not granted a security interest in the Property and are not creditors of the Borrowers.

Also on February 16, 2007, Wachovia and Merrill, in their capacities as Senior and Junior Lenders, entered into the Intercreditor Agreement. Plaintiffs identify several provisions of the Intercreditor Agreement that are relevant to their motion for a preliminary injunction. Section 9 is titled "*Subordination of Junior Loans and Junior Loan Documents.*" Subsection 9(a) provides, in pertinent part, as follows:

> Each Junior Lender hereby subordinates and makes junior the Junior Loan held by such Junior Lender, the related Junior Loan Documents and the liens and security interests created thereby, and all rights, remedies, terms and covenants contained therein to (i) the Senior Loan and the applicable Senior Junior Loans,

---

9. Under the Intercreditor Agreement, Wachovia, Merrill and non-party Gramercy Warehouse Funding I LLC were "Junior Lenders." Intercreditor Agreement, Hundertmark Aff., Ex. E, at 1 and 11. Wachovia and Merrill were the original Junior Lenders on, among others, Junior Loans 1–3, each of which was in the original principal amount of $100 million. Thus, Wachovia and Merrill were both Senior Lenders and Junior Lenders. Hundertmark states that Junior Loans 1–3 were owned by non-parties AIB Debt Management Limited, Deutsche Genossenschafts-Hypothekenbank AG, Hartford Fire Insurance Company, Hartford Life Insurance Company, Concord Real Estate CDO 2006–1 LTD, and Wachovia.

(ii) the liens and security interests created by the Senior Loan Documents and the applicable Senior Junior Loan Documents . . . .

Section 6 is titled *"Foreclosure of Separate Collateral."* (emphasis in original). Subsection 6(d) provides as follows:

> *To the extent that any Qualified Transferee acquires the Equity Collateral pledged to a Junior Lender pursuant to the Junior Loan Documents in accordance with the provisions and conditions of this Agreement* (including, but not limited to *Section 12* hereof), *such Qualified Transferee shall acquire the same subject to (i) the Senior Loan and the terms, conditions and provisions of the Senior Loan Documents* and (ii) the applicable Senior Junior Loans and the terms, conditions and provisions of the applicable Senior Junior Loan Documents, in each case for the balance of the term thereof, which shall not be accelerated by Senior Lender or the related Senior Junior Lender solely due to such acquisition and shall remain in full force and effect; *provided, however, that* (A) such Qualified Transferee shall cause, within ten (10) days after the transfer, (1) Borrower and (2) the applicable Senior Junior Borrowers, in each case to reaffirm in writing, subject to such exculpatory provisions as shall be set forth in the Senior Loan Documents and the related Senior Junior Loan Documents, as applicable, all of the terms, conditions and provisions of the Senior Loan Documents and the related Senior Junior Loan Documents, as applicable, on Borrower's or the applicable Senior Junior Borrower's, as applicable, part to be performed and *(B) all defaults under (1) the Senior Loan and (2) the applicable Senior Junior Loans, in each case which remain uncured or unwaived as of the date of such acquisition have been cured by such Qualified Transferee* or in the case of defaults that can only be cured by the Junior Lender following its acquisition of the Equity Collateral, the same shall be cured by the Junior Lender prior to the expiration of the applicable Extended Non-Monetary Cure Period.

(emphasis added).

Section 11(d) is titled *"Bankruptcy"* (*id.* at 66 [emphasis in original]), and subsection (ii) provides, in pertinent part, as follows:

> *For as long as the Senior Loan shall remain outstanding, none of the Junior Lenders shall solicit, direct or cause Borrower or any other entity which Controls Borrower . . . or any other Person to: (1) commence any Proceeding against Borrower* or any SPE Constituent Entity; (2) institute proceedings to have Borrower or any SPE Constituent Entity adjudicated a bankrupt or insolvent; (3) consent to, or acquiesce in, the institution of bankruptcy or insolvency proceedings against Borrower . . . or (9) *take any action in furtherance of any of the foregoing.* The terms and provisions of this *Section 11(d)* apply to each Junior Lender solely in its respective capacity as a Junior Lender. If any Junior Lender commences an Equity Collateral Enforcement Action against any Junior Borrower, and pursuant to such Equity Collateral Enforcement Action, such Junior Lender takes title to the Equity Collateral of such Junior Borrower, from and after the date title to such Equity Collateral is vested in such Junior Lender (as applicable), such Junior Lender shall be bound by the terms and provisions of the respective organizational documents of such Junior Borrower regarding bankruptcy and all matters requiring the vote of the independent directors/managers/members of such Junior Borrower.

(emphasis added).

On January 8, 2010, the Borrowers defaulted on the Notes by failing to pay the monthly installments required thereunder (Default). By letter dated January 8, 2010, CWCAM notified the Borrowers of the Default and demanded that they pay all unpaid amounts then due. Also on January 8th, CWCAM notified the Junior Lenders of the Default, which afforded the Junior Lenders the opportunity to cure under section 12(a) of the Intercreditor Agreement, but none of the Junior Lenders exercised their rights to cure the Default. By letter dated January 29, 2010, CWCAM notified the Borrowers and the Junior Lenders that the unpaid debt outstanding under the Notes was accelerated, making all amounts immediately due and payable, for failure to cure the Default (Acceleration). As a result of the Default and Acceleration, the full outstanding principal balance of the Senior Loan, all accrued and unpaid interest thereon and all other sums owing under the Senior Loan documents became due and payable.

On February 16, 2010, CWCAM, on behalf of the Senior Lenders, filed a complaint (as amended by the filing of an amended complaint on February 18th) in the United States District Court for the Southern District of New York, seeking foreclosure of the Property. On June 21, 2010, the District Court entered a Judgment of Foreclosure and Sale of the Property, in favor of the Senior Lenders, in the amount of $3,666,734,464.70, which is the amount due and owing to plaintiffs under the Notes, the Amended Mortgage, and the related Senior Loan documents (Indebtedness). *Bank of America, N.A. et al. v PCV ST Owner LP et al.*, 10-Civ-1178 (SD NY, June 21, 2010).

By letter dated August 6, 2010, Wells Fargo, as successor by merger to Wachovia, notified, among others, the Senior Lenders, that it transferred its interest in Junior Loans 1–3 to PSW, thereby placing PSW directly behind the Senior Lenders in structural priority and entitling PSW to receive any value of the Property above the amounts owed on the Senior Loan. The Wells Fargo notice certified that PSW is a "Qualified Transferee" as that term is defined in the Intercreditor Agreement. As discussed above, these loans have a combined face value of $300 million but were acquired by PSW for $45 million. Also on August 6th, PSW executed a "REPRESENTATION CERTIFICATE", whereby it notified, among others, the Senior Lenders, that it "agree[d] to be bound by [the] Intercreditor Agreement" with respect to Junior Loans 1–3, stating that PSW "does hereby remake, for the benefit of the Senior Lenders and the Junior Lenders, each of the representations in the Intercreditor Agreement which are applicable to the Mezzanine 1 Loan, Mezzanine 2 Loan and Mezzanine 3 Loan. . . ."

The next day, August 7th, PSW notified, among others, the Senior Lenders, that it intended to sell the Equity Collateral at a UCC public sale on August 25, 2010. On August 8th, the New York Times published a "NOTICE OF PUBLIC SALE OF COLLATERAL" for Junior Loans 1–3, scheduled for August 25, 2010, and in these notices PSW "reserve[d] the right to credit bid at the auction and to assign its bid", and "to adjourn, continue or cancel the auction without further notice" (UCC Sale). *Id.*, Ex. Q.

By letter dated August 10, 2010, counsel for the Senior Lenders requested that PSW provide support for its conclusion that it is a "Qualified Transferee" under the Intercreditor Agreement, and that PSW confirm that it will cure the Senior Loan Default as a condition to any acquisition or transfer of the Equity Collateral, as required under section 6(d) of the Intercreditor Agreement. In a response letter dated August 11th, PSW characterized the Senior Lenders' statements about section 6(d) as "ludicrous", and informed the Senior Lenders that section 6(d) "of the Intercreditor Agreement does not require the payment of the Senior Loan as a condition to a transferee acquiring the Equity Collateral." Thereafter, plaintiffs filed the instant motion for a preliminary injunction.

DISCUSSION

"The three prerequisites for obtaining a preliminary injunction are likelihood of success on the merits, irreparable injury in the absence of such injunctive relief, and balancing of the equities." *Seitzman v Hudson Riv. Assoc.*, 126 AD2d 211, 213 (1st Dept 1987); *Alexandru v Pappas*, 68 AD3d 690, 691 (2d Dept 2009) (plaintiffs need only make "a prima facie showing" of their right to relief).

LIKELIHOOD OF SUCCESS

Plaintiffs seek a declaration that, pursuant to sections 6(d)(B)(1) and (2) of the Intercreditor Agreement, PSW, or any purchaser of the auctioned Equity Collateral, is required to cure all Senior Loan defaults prior to acquiring the Equity Collateral. Plaintiffs also seek a declaration that section 11(d)(ii) of the Intercreditor Agreement prohibits PSW from orchestrating a Borrower's bankruptcy unless the Senior Loan is paid off in full. PSW counters that section 6(d) does not impose a pre-condition to the acquisition of Equity Collateral, but rather, applies only after the acquisition; that section 6(d) pertains to acceleration of the Senior Loan, which is irrelevant because that loan has already been accelerated and PSW is not seeking to prevent acceleration; and that the collateral it intends to sell at the UCC Sale consists of its equity ownership in the Senior Borrowers, which is different from the collateral—that is, the Property itself—that secures the Senior Loan, and that because there is no overlap in collateral, there can be no breach of the Intercreditor Agreement.

"[W]here the language [of a contract] is clear, unequivocal and unambiguous, the contract is to be interpreted by its own language", and the "writing should as a rule be enforced according to its terms." *R/S Assoc. v New York Job Dev. Auth.*, 98 NY2d 29, 32 (2002) (internal quotation marks and citations omitted).

Here, the Intercreditor Agreement is unambiguous. Its plain language obligates PSW to cure all Senior Loan defaults if PSW acquires the Equity Collateral, which includes the $3.6 billion Indebtedness resulting from the Default. Specifically, section 6(d) provides that,

[t]o the extent that any Qualified Transferee acquires the Equity Collateral pledged to a Junior Lender pursuant to the Junior Loan Documents in accordance with the provisions and conditions of this Agreement . . . , *such Qualified Transferee shall acquire the same subject to (i) the Senior Loan and the terms, conditions and provisions of the Senior Loan Documents.* . . . Subsection (ii) goes on to require that any such acquisition is also subject to any applicable Senior Junior Loans, and states that

neither the Senior Lender nor any Senior Junior Lender may accelerate outstanding loans solely as a result of a Qualified Transferee's acquisition of Equity Collateral. *Id.* Subsection 6(d)(A) conditions the acquisition of Equity Collateral upon the Qualified Transferee affirming that it is bound by the Senior and related Senior Junior Loan Documents. Subsection 6(d)(B) conditions the acquisition of Equity Collateral upon the Qualified Transferee curing "*all defaults under (1) the Senior Loan and (2) the applicable Senior Junior Loans, in each case which remain uncured or unwaived as of the date of such acquisition*", but allowing "defaults that can *only* be cured by the Junior Lender following its acquisition of the Equity Collateral" to "be cured by the Junior Lender prior to the expiration of the applicable Extended Non-Monetary Cure Period." (emphasis added).

Because the Default existing under the Senior Loan is not a default that can "*only* be cured . . . following [PSW's] acquisition of the Equity Collateral", PSW must cure the Default "as of the date of [its] acquisition" of the Equity Collateral. Thus, PSW's argument that section 6(d) is not a pre-condition to acquisition of Equity Collateral is undermined by the plain language of the contract.

This interpretation is confirmed by section 10 of the Intercreditor Agreement. Section 10 is titled "*Payment Subordination*", and section 10(d) states that "a Junior Lender may, in its sole and absolute discretion without Senior Lender's or any Senior Junior Lender's consent, take any Equity Collateral Enforcement Action or Separate Collateral Enforcement Action", but this provision is expressly "[s]ubject to the terms and provisions of *Section 6*", above.

PSW, a Junior Lender under the Intercreditor Agreement, has made clear its intention to acquire the Equity Collateral at the UCC Sale. In addition, in its letter dated August 11, 2010, counsel for PSW characterized its obligations under section 6(d) as "ludicrous" and expressly notified plaintiffs' counsel that "the Intercreditor Agreement does not require the payment of the Senior Loan as a condition to a transferee acquiring the Equity Collateral." This letter evidences PSW's renouncement of any intent to cure the Senior Loan defaults. Therefore, plaintiffs have "show[n] a likelihood of success on the merits by showing that [their] claims have prima facie merit."

PSW's argument that section 6(d) is designed to prevent the Senior Lenders from accelerating the Senior Loans due to a transfer of the Equity Collateral is not grounded in the terms of the Intercreditor Agreement. The last clause of section 6(d)(ii) prevents the Senior Lender and the related Senior Junior Lender from accelerating the Senior Loan or outstanding Senior Junior Loans solely due to a Qualified Transferee's acquisition of Equity Collateral. However, nothing in section 6(d) suggests that this provision is focused solely, or even primarily, upon acceleration. Rather, the clause relating to acceleration in section 6(d) merely harmonizes the Intercreditor Agreement with the Senior Loan Agreement, which provides in section 9.02 that "a Transfer in connection with an exercise of remedies by a Mezzanine Lender shall not be prohibited hereunder, provided such Transfer is done in accordance with any intercreditor agreement that such Mezzanine Lender and Lender are party to in connection with the Loan and the Mezzanine Loan." Contrary to PSW's argument, this interpretation is consistent with the plain language of the Intercreditor Agreement, and it is the only reasonable interpretation of this agreement.

PSW's argument concerning the doctrine of the last antecedent does not support a different result. The last antecedent doctrine provides that "[r]elative or qualifying words or clauses . . . ordinarily are to be applied to words or phrases immediately preceding, and are not to be construed as extending to others more remote, unless the intent clearly indicates otherwise." *Duane Reade, Inc. v Cardtronics, LP*, 54 AD3d 137, 141 (1st Dept 2008). PSW argues that the acceleration language in section 6(d) immediately precedes the conditions of reaffirmation in section 6(d)(A) and cure in 6(d)(B), and that, therefore, these conditions are limited in applying solely to acceleration. In other words, PSW argues that "cure is a pre-condition to *preventing acceleration* and is not a pre-condition to acquisition of the Equity Collateral. However, section 6 pertains to" *Foreclosure of Separate Collateral*, "as its heading suggests, not to acceleration. PSW's reading of section 6(d) cherry-picks the acceleration language while ignoring all of the additional language preceding the semicolon, which applies more generally to an acquisition of Equity Collateral. PSW's interpretation of section 6(d) was clearly not intended by the parties.

PSW argues that subsection 6(d)(A), which allows a Qualified Transferee to wait 10 days after the transfer to reaffirm its obligations under the Senior Loan Documents, supports the conclusion that section 6(d) is not a pre-condition to the UCC Sale. However, subsections 6(d)(A) and (B) are written in the conjunctive, requiring that both provisions be satisfied. In other words, the fact that (A) allows a Qualified Transferee 10 days to reaffirm does not vitiate the past-tense requirement in (B) that all defaults under the Senior Loan "as of the date of such acquisition *have been* cured." Therefore, PSW's argument is unpersuasive.

While the Senior Loan and PSW's Junior Loan are secured by different collateral, nothing contained in the Intercreditor Agreement permits PSW to acquire its Equity Collateral without complying with section 6(d). For example, PSW cites the Intercreditor Agreement in support of its argument that its "right . . . to foreclose on [its] separate collateral finds expression in many provisions, including Sections 2(n) and 9(a)(A)." However, section 2(n) merely prohibits the Senior Loan from constituting a lien on the separate collateral that secures a Junior Loan, and prevents a Senior Lender from declaring any such interest in the separate collateral. In this regard, section 2(n) confirms that the Senior and Junior Loans are secured by different collateral. However, plaintiffs are not asserting a lien on, or a security interest in, PSW's collateral. Significantly, nothing contained in section 2(n) exempts PSW from section 6(d). Section 9(a) generally reinforces that Junior Lenders' loans are subordinate to the Senior Loan. And although section 9(a)(A) permits a Junior Lender to "exercise . . . remedies and realization upon such Separate Collateral", this subsection is expressly subject to section 6(b), which states that "[n]othing contained herein shall limit or restrict the right of any Junior Lender to exercise its rights and remedies, in law or in equity, or otherwise, in order to realize on any of its Separate Collateral *that is not Equity Collateral*" [emphasis added]. Here, PSW seeks to foreclose on its Equity Collateral, which is governed by section 6(d), as discussed above.

PSW argues that section 6(a) of the Intercreditor Agreement recognizes the right of a Junior Lender to foreclose upon its Equity Collateral, and that, if the parties had so intended, section 6(a) would have expressly stated that curing a default on the Senior Loan was a pre-condition to a Junior Lender's foreclosure. Section 6(a) requires a Junior Lender to comply with seven requirements before "complet[ing] a foreclosure or otherwise realiz[ing] upon any of its Equity Collateral. . . ." However, as discussed above, section 6 pertains to "*Foreclosure of Separate Collateral*", and none of the subsections to section 6 are individually titled. In substance, all of these subsections relate to foreclosure of separate collateral, and each subsection includes different obligations, conditions and rights. The fact that the requirements of subsection (d) are stated in their own subsection, rather than in subsection (a), does not serve to vitiate subsection (d). If anything, the implication is that the parties considered subsection (d) worthy of treatment in its own subsection. Therefore, PSW's argument is contradicted by the plain language of the Intercreditor Agreement.

PSW also argues that sections 10(a) and (d) "provide that a Junior Lender's rights to foreclose upon its own Equity Collateral is exempted from the general provisions regarding payment subordination that CWCAM cites in its papers." However, the first clause of section 10(a) states, "Except (i) as otherwise expressly provided in this Agreement", and, as discussed above, the first clause of section 10(d) makes this subsection "[s]ubject to the terms and provisions of *Section 6*", thereby undermining PSW's argument. PSW also ignores that section 10 deals generally with "*Payment Subordination*", as its title suggests, and section 10(b)(ii) provides, in pertinent part, as follows:

> *If . . . there shall have occurred and be continuing an Event of Default under the Senior Loan Documents,* after giving effect to Junior Lender's cure rights pursuant to *Section 12,* except as expressly otherwise provided herein, *Senior Lender shall be entitled to receive payment and performance in full of all amounts due or to become due to Senior Lender before any Junior Lender is entitled to receive any payment* (including any payment which may be payable by reason of the payment of any other indebtedness of Borrower being subordinated to the payment of the Junior Loans) on account of any Junior Loan.

(emphasis added). Here, the Senior Loan is indisputably in default. The court recognizes the distinction between the separate collateral securing the parties' investments, and that the Intercreditor Agreement permits PSW to foreclose on its own collateral. However, plaintiffs have made a prima facie showing that PSW must comply with section 6(b) of the Intercreditor Agreement before doing so . . .

With respect to plaintiffs' cause of action for a declaration that section 11(d)(ii) of the Intercreditor Agreement prohibits PSW from orchestrating a Borrower's bankruptcy unless the Senior Loan is paid off in full, plaintiffs claim that PSW has retained Kirkland & Ellis LLP as bankruptcy counsel to represent the Borrowers once the UCC Sale is complete. However, PSW admits in its opposition brief that "presently, and so long as it is a Junior Lender, its ability to solicit, direct or cause the Senior Borrowers to institute bankruptcy proceedings is restricted by Section 11(d)(ii). . . ." This is consistent with the last sentence of section 11(d)(ii), which pertains to the situation where a Junior Lender acquires title to the Equity Collateral of a Junior Borrower, thereby becoming "bound by the terms and provisions of the respective organizational documents of such Junior Borrower regarding bankruptcy and all matters requiring the vote of the independent directors/managers/members of such Junior Borrower." In other words, PSW's argument focuses on what it could do as an owner of the Borrowers once a transfer of the Equity Collateral occurs, claiming that, thereafter, "PSW would no longer be subject to the restrictions set forth in Section 11(d)(ii)" and that, "if PSW were to successfully complete the UCC Sale and thereby acquire title to the Equity Collateral, the Intercreditor Agreement would terminate with respect to PSW." Moreover, according to Ashner, PSW has not retained Kirkland & Ellis, but has merely "communicated with K & E's attorneys about this matter." The Intercreditor Agreement does not prevent PSW, as a Junior Lender, from seeking legal advice or planning for future contingencies. Plaintiffs fail to make a prima facie showing that PSW has taken any action in violation of section 11(d)(ii).

Furthermore, there has been no transfer of Equity Collateral. Nor could there be without PSW's compliance with section 6(d), as discussed above. In short, PSW concedes that, as a Junior Lender, it must comply with the restrictions set forth in section 11(d)(ii) of the Intercreditor Agreement. Given PSW's admission, and the fact that the court is granting plaintiffs' motion for preliminary injunctive relief with respect to section 6(d), plaintiffs' request to enjoin PSW concerning section 11(d)(ii) of the Intercreditor Agreement is moot, and the purported hazard posed by plaintiffs is "speculative and abstract", and, therefore, nonjusticiable.

Accordingly, plaintiffs' motion for a preliminary injunction is denied with respect to section 11(d)(ii) of the Intercreditor Agreement . . .

The Senior Lenders bargained for the right to control the management of the Property, and they have spent the last nine months working with the Borrowers to transition management of the Property, which impacts tens of thousands of New York City residents. As discussed above, section 9.02 of the Senior Loan Agreement expressly acknowledges the Senior Lenders' reliance upon "the expertise of the Borrower . . . in owning and operating properties such as the Property in agreeing to make the Loan" and acknowledges plaintiffs' continuing reliance "on Borrower's ownership of the Property as a means of maintaining the value of the Property as security for repayment of the Debt. . . ." Indeed, the element of irreparable harm dovetails with the analysis of section 6(d) of the Intercreditor Agreement, above, in that the Senior Lenders expressly bargained for this contractual provision, which prohibits Junior Lenders like PSW from acquiring ownership and control of the Equity Collateral unless they pay any outstanding indebtedness under the Senior Loan, thereby ensuring that ownership and control over the Equity Collateral is not transferred from the Junior Borrowers to the Junior Lenders at a time when the Senior Loan is in default. Any loss of control is in violation of the Intercreditor Agreement and would constitute irreparable harm to plaintiffs.

Section 34 of the Intercreditor Agreement reinforces this conclusion. This section is titled "*Injunction*" and provides as follows:

> Each party to this Agreement acknowledges (and waives any defense based on a claim) that monetary damages are not an adequate remedy to redress a breach by the other hereunder and that a breach by any party hereunder would cause

irreparable harm to any other party to this Agreement. Accordingly, each party to this Agreement agrees that upon a breach of this Agreement by any other party, the remedies of injunction, declaratory judgment and specific performance shall be available to such non-breaching party.

(emphasis in original). PSW's "REPRESENTATION CERTIFICATE" expressly notified, among others, the Senior Lenders, that PSW "agree[d] to be bound by Intercreditor Agreement" with respect to Junior Loans 1–3 (Hundertmark Aff., Ex. M), thereby evidencing that PSW contemplated the irreparable harm that would result from a breach of the Intercreditor Agreement and agreed that monetary damages would not serve as an adequate remedy at law. Thus, the parties "set down their agreement in a clear, complete document", and, therefore, "their writing should . . . be enforced according to its terms." *Vermont Teddy Bear Co. v 538 Madison Realty Co.*, 1 NY3d 470, 475 (2004).

PSW argues that, if the preliminary injunction motion is granted, the court should require CWCAM to agree to stay its mortgage foreclosure action pending final adjudication of the instant action, and to post a bond in the full principal amount of $300 million that is owed to PSW. PSW's request for a stay of foreclosure is contained on page 23 of its opposition brief. PSW has not moved for any such relief. Therefore, PSW's request is not properly before the court. In any event, PSW fails to cite any legal authority in support of its request that this state court enjoin or stay a federal court judgment. Accordingly, PSW's request for a stay in the mortgage foreclosure action is denied.

PSW's request for a bond is governed by CPLR 6312, which provides that "the plaintiff shall give an undertaking in an amount to be fixed by the court, that the plaintiff, if it is finally determined that he or she was not entitled to an injunction, will pay to the defendant all damages and costs which may be sustained by reason of the injunction." CPLR 6312(b). "The fixing of the amount of an undertaking is a matter within the sound discretion of the court." *Lelekakis v Kamamis*, 303 AD2d 380, 380 (2d Dept 2003).

In the event that PSW is ultimately successful in demonstrating that plaintiffs are not entitled to injunctive relief, PSW is entitled to an undertaking that is "rationally related to the amount of the defendant's potential liability if the preliminary injunction later proves to be unwarranted, and not based upon speculation." Although the Junior Loans purchased by PSW — that is, Junior Loans 1, 2 and 3 — were each in the principal amount of $100 million, it is undisputed that PSW purchased these loans for only $45 million. Therefore, plaintiffs' undertaking is limited to the amount of this purchase price.

PROBLEM SET 16.2

1. Why might it make sense for syndicated loans to adopt majority rule for important changes? What are the risks?
2. In an A/B intercreditor agreement, it is common to provide that (a) the agent bank has control over routine matters, (b) the B lenders (the subordinated lenders) have control over all other decisions, (c) unless the collateral is appraised at a sufficient low level that the B lenders will either

have to guarantee the A lender claims or allow the A lenders to take control. Does it surprise you that the B lenders have control even though they are subordinated?

3. Would the Indiana Pension Funds have had a better argument in *Chrysler* if their investment was made under the loan participation agreement set forth above?

4. The court notes that "the suggestion that the TARP-recipient lenders have been pressured to the point that they would breach their fiduciary duty and capitulate to the settlements presented is without any evidentiary support." There are some indications that there was some pressure applied to TARP recipients. For example, some regulators conducting the "stress tests" of a major financial institution allegedly suggested that the institution "would be crazy vote against the Chrysler sale." Should that have influenced the court's decision?

5. Looking at that loan participation agreement excerpted earlier, what are the risks the original lender faces in selling participations in an unfunded loan? What are its remedies?

3. DUTIES OF THE LEAD BANK

Given that many loan agreements delegate considerable powers to the lead or agent bank, other participants in the loan have to trust that the agent bank's incentives are properly aligned. Yet often these large financial institutions interact with the borrower on a variety of levels beyond the loan agreement.

UNICREDITO ITALIANO SPA, AND BANK POLSKA KASA OPIEKI SA, PLAINTIFFS, v. JPMORGAN CHASE BANK, J.P. MORGAN CHASE & CO., J.P. MORGAN SECURITIES INC., CITIBANK, N.A., CITIGROUP, INC., AND SALOMON SMITH BARNEY INC.

288 F.Supp.2d 485
United States District Court, S.D. New York
No. 02Civ.5328(KTS)(JCF) | Oct. 14, 2003

SWAIN, District Judge.

This action concerns loans, made by Plaintiffs to or for the benefit of the Enron Corporation, that were administered by JP Morgan Chase Bank and Citibank. Plaintiffs contend that Defendants defrauded them in connection with the formation of certain syndicated credit facilities and payments under those facilities.

Defendants now move pursuant to Rules 12(b)(6) and 9(b) of the Federal Rules of Civil Procedure for an order dismissing the Second Amended Complaint. The Court has considered thoroughly all arguments and submissions in connection with the instant motions. For the following reasons, Defendants' motions are granted in part and denied in part.

BACKGROUND

The following factual recitation is drawn from the Second Amended Complaint (the "Complaint"), statements or documents incorporated in the Complaint by reference, public disclosure documents filed with the SEC, and/or documents that Plaintiffs either possessed or knew about and upon which they relied in bringing this action. All of Plaintiffs' allegations are taken as true for the purposes of this recitation.

Plaintiff UniCredito Italiano SpA ("UCI") is an Italian financial institution with headquarters in Milan, Italy. Plaintiff Bank Polska Kasa Opieki SA, also known as Bank Pekao SA ("Pekao") is a Polish financial institution with headquarters in Warsaw, Poland.

Defendant JP Morgan Chase & Co. ("JPMC & Co.") is a Delaware corporation with its principal place of business in New York. Its primary banking subsidiary is Defendant JP Morgan Chase Bank; its primary investment banking or securities subsidiary is Defendant J.P. Morgan Securities Inc. Defendant JP Morgan Chase Bank is a New York corporation, with its principal place of business in New York. Defendant J.P. Morgan Securities Inc. is a Delaware corporation with offices in New York.

Defendant Citigroup, Inc. ("Citigroup") is a Delaware corporation with its principal place of business in New York. Citigroup's primary banking subsidiary is Defendant Citibank, N.A. ("Citibank"); its primary investment banking or securities subsidiary is Defendant Salomon Smith Barney. Citibank is a national banking association with its principal place of business in New York. Defendant Salomon Smith Barney is a New York corporation with its principal place of business in New York.

[The Defendants were involved in a series of transactions designed to hide the true financial conditional of Enron]

THE CREDIT FACILITIES

The bulk of Plaintiffs' damages claims in this action arise from losses sustained on investments in credit facilities for Enron for which the Defendant banks served as Administrative and/or Paying Agents or, in the case of JP Morgan Chase Bank with respect to a 2001 letter of credit facility, the Issuing Bank, and which were marketed by the Defendant securities subsidiaries.

Defendants JP Morgan Chase Bank (through its predecessor in interest, The Chase Manhattan Bank) and Citibank were the Co-Administrative Agents for three Enron credit facilities in which Plaintiffs participated: 1) a $1.25 billion medium-term credit facility entered into on May 18, 2000 (the "2000 Credit Facility"), 2) a $1.75 billion short-term facility entered into on May 14, 2001 (the "2001 Credit Facility"), and 3) a $500 million letter of credit facility entered into on May 14, 2001 (the "2001 L/C Facility) (collectively, the "Syndicated Facilities"). Citibank was also the Paying Agent for the 2000 and 2001 Credit Facilities, and The Chase Manhattan Bank was the Paying Agent and Issuing Bank for the 2001 L/C Facility.

The agreements establishing each of the Syndicated Facilities contained disclaimer, covenant, and acknowledgment provisions identical in all relevant respects to the following provisions of the 2000 Credit Facility:

Section 7.02 *Paying Agent's Reliance, Etc.*
[T]he Paying Agent shall not have, by reason of this Agreement or any other Loan Document a fiduciary relationship in respect of any Bank or the holder of any Note; and nothing in this Agreement or any other Loan Document, expressed or implied, is intended or shall be so construed as to impose upon the Paying Agent any obligations in respect of this Agreement or any other Loan Document except as expressly set forth herein. Without limitation of the generality of the foregoing, the Paying Agent . . . (iii) makes no warranty or representation to any Bank for any statements, warranties or representations (whether written or oral) made in or in connection with any Loan Document or any other instrument or document furnished pursuant hereto or in connection herewith; (iv) shall not have any duty to ascertain or to inquire as to the performance or observance of any of the terms, covenants or conditions of any Loan Document or any other instrument or document furnished pursuant hereto or in connection herewith on the part of the Borrower or to inspect the property (including the books and records) of the Borrower;

Section 7.03 *Paying Agent and Its Affiliates*
With respect to its Commitment, the Advances made by it and the Note issued to it, each Bank which is also the Paying Agent shall have the same rights and powers under the Loan Documents as any other Bank and may exercise the same as though it were not the Paying Agent; the term "Bank" or "Banks" shall, unless otherwise expressly indicated, include any Bank serving as the Paying Agent in its individual capacity. Any Bank serving as the Paying Agent and its affiliates may accept deposits from, lend money to, act as trustee under indentures of, accept investment banking engagements from and generally engage in any kind of business with, the Borrower, any of the Subsidiaries and any Person who may do business with or own securities of the Borrower or any Subsidiary, all as if such Bank were not the Paying Agent and without any duty to account therefor to the Banks.

Section 7.04 *Bank Credit Decision*
Each Bank acknowledges that it has, independently and without reliance upon the Paying Agent or any other Bank and based on the financial statements referred to in Section 4.01(d) and such other documents and information as it has deemed appropriate, made its own credit analysis and decision to enter into this Agreement. Each Bank also acknowledges that it will, independently and without reliance upon the Paying Agent or any other Bank and based on such documents and information as it shall deem appropriate at the time, continue to make its own credit decisions in taking or not taking action under this Agreement and the other Loan Documents. The Paying Agent shall not have any duty or responsibility, either initially or on a continuing basis, to provide any Bank or the holder of any Note with any credit or other information with respect thereto, whether coming into its possession before the making of the Advances or at any time or times thereafter.

As noted above, JP Morgan Chase Bank was also designated as the "Issuing Bank" under the 2001 L/C Facility Agreement, which provided that the "Issuing Bank", in selling to the participating banks their pro rata share of the obligation under any letter of credit issued pursuant to the agreement, "represents and warrants to [the participating bank] that the Issuing Bank is the legal and beneficial owner of such interest being sold by it, free and clear of any liens, but makes no other representation or warranty. The Issuing Bank shall have no responsibility or liability to any other [participating bank] with respect to any [letter of credit obligation] or any such participation [.]" Section 7.03 of the 2001 L/C Facility Agreement provided that the Issuing Bank and its affiliates had the right to engage in transactions with Enron "with no duty to account therefor" to the participating banks, and section 7.04 contains the acknowledgment of participating banks that they had not relied on the Issuing Bank in making the decision to enter into the agreement and that they would make their continuing decisions as to whether or not to take action under the agreement or letters of credit issued under the agreement "independently and without reliance upon . . . the Issuing Bank[.]"

In each of the agreements for the Syndicated Facilities, Enron (which was referred to in the agreements as the "Borrower") entered into certain covenants concerning the participating banks' due diligence rights. These covenants were identical in all relevant respects to the covenants in the 2000 Credit Facility Agreement, the pertinent provisions of which follow:

> Section 5.01 *Affirmative Covenants.*
>   (a) Reporting Requirements [the Borrower will furnish to each Bank:]
>   (viii) such other information respecting the condition or operations, financial or otherwise, of the Borrower or any of its Subsidiaries as any Bank through the Paying Agent may from time to time reasonably request.
>   . . .
>   (f) *Visitation Rights* At any reasonable time and from time to time, after reasonable notice, [the Borrower will] permit the Paying Agent or any of the Banks or any agents or representatives thereof, to examine the records and books of account of, and visit the properties of, the Borrower and any of its Principal Subsidiaries, and to discuss the affairs, finances and accounts of the Borrower and any of its Principal Subsidiaries with any of their respective officers or directors.

Defendants Salomon Smith Barney and J.P. Morgan Securities (the "Securities Subsidiaries") were co-lead arrangers of the Syndicated Facilities. They distributed to participant banks offering memoranda and invitations to offer in connection with the Syndicated Facilities. Those documents contained and referred to publicly filed financial information about Enron. (*Id.*) The offering memoranda contained the following section entitled "Disclaimer":

> The information contained in this Information Memorandum has been supplied by or on behalf of Enron Corp. (the "Company"). Neither Salomon Smith Barney Inc. and Chase Securities Inc. (as "Co-Lead Arrangers") nor any of their affiliates has independently verified such information and the same is being provided by the Co-Lead Arrangers for informational purposes only. The Co-Lead Arrangers do not make any representation or warranty as to the accuracy or completeness of such information and does not [sic] assume any undertaking to supplement such information as further information becomes available or in light of changing circumstances. The Co-Lead Arrangers shall not have any liability for any

representations or warranties (express or implied) contained in, or any omissions from, the Information Memorandum or any other written or oral communication transmitted to the recipient in the course of its evaluation of the proposed financing or otherwise.

The information contained herein has been prepared to assist interested parties in making their own evaluation of the proposed financing for the Company and for no other purpose. The information does not purport to be all-inclusive or to contain all information that a prospective lender may desire. It is understood that each recipient of this Information Memorandum will perform its own independent investigation and analysis of the proposed financing and the creditworthiness of the Company, based on such information as it deems relevant and without reliance on Co-Lead Arrangers. The information contained herein is not a substitute for the recipient's independent investigation and analysis.

Plaintiff UCI contributed $10,416,667.67 under the 2000 Credit Facility, $11,666,666.67 under the 2001 Credit Facility, and $3,333,333.33 under the 2001 L/C Facility. Plaintiff Pekao purchased a participating interest in the 2000 Credit Facility in the amount of $6.25 million.

THE OCTOBER 25, 2001 BORROWING REQUESTS

Under the credit agreements governing the 2000 and 2001 Credit Facilities, Enron had to satisfy certain conditions before it could receive loan funds, including compliance with all laws and the maintenance of a 65% debt-to-capitalization ratio. On October 25, 2001, Plaintiff UCI received borrowing demands at 11:48 a.m. and 12 noon, conveyed through Citibank, for immediate payment of its shares of the 2000 and 2001 Credit Facilities, and Plaintiff Pekao received a demand at 12 noon, conveyed through Citibank, to fund immediately its share of the 2000 Credit Facility.

At 2:45 p.m., the Managing Director of JP Morgan Chase Securities, Claire O'Connor, notified UCI that Enron would explain its need for cash to redeem its commercial paper at a conference call at 3:00 p.m. The Defendant banks helped manage Enron's commercial paper program, but O'Connor did not mention their role. O'Connor falsely stated that Enron was drawing down the funds to reestablish market confidence. At the 3:00 p.m. conference call, Enron's CFO explained that Enron needed the full amounts of the 2000 and 2001 Credit Facilities so that Enron could redeem its commercial paper. The Defendant banks participated in the conference call, but said nothing about Enron's defaults under the credit agreements, defaults of which they were aware.

At 4:06 p.m., UCI received a facsimile from Citibank conveying Enron's certification that its representations and warranties, including those in the credit agreements, continued to be correct, and that there was no default or event of default under the credit agreements. UCI and Pekao subsequently forwarded their respective contributions under the credit facilities to Citibank, to be conveyed to Enron.

Pursuant to section 6.01 of the credit agreements governing the 2000 and 2001 Credit Facilities, if a majority of the participating banks had determined that a default or event of default had occurred that relieved them of their obligations under the agreements, the banks could have instructed Citibank to declare the termination of each bank's obligation to make advances. Defendants knew that Enron's debt-to-capitalization ratio put it in breach of the credit agreements, and their concealment of that breach prevented Plaintiffs from exercising their rights under section 6.01.

The Defendant banks, who were also participants in the 2000 and 2001 Credit Facilities, contributed their shares of the October 25, 2001 funding. The credit facilities enabled the banks to reduce their aggregate exposure and take a "smaller hit" with respect to Enron.

On November 1, 2001, the Defendant banks announced that they were negotiating to extend $1 billion in secured loans to Enron. Citibank conditioned its participation in that secured loan on Enron's payment of an earlier $250 million unsecured Citibank loan.

UCI AND THE 2001 L/C FACILITY

After its October 25, 2001 payments, UCI sought from JP Morgan Chase Bank the identification of all letters of credit that had been issued under the 2001 L/C Facility and information as to the current status of those letters of credit. On November 26, 2001, JP Morgan Chase Bank identified eleven letters of credit that it said had been issued under the 2001 L/C Facility, two of which had expired. On Friday, November 30, 2001, UCI received a request to fund $1,050,000 under a letter of credit for Enron, and made the requested payment to JP Morgan Chase Bank.

Enron filed for bankruptcy protection on Sunday, December 2, 2001. On December 3, 2001, UCI received a different list from JP Morgan Chase of letters of credit purportedly issued under the 2001 L/C Facility. The second list included a $150 million letter of credit dated October 9, 2001 in favor of an entity called Mahonia. The Mahonia letter of credit was drawn down on December 11, 2001.

Under the agreement governing the 2001 L/C Facility, Enron's breach of its covenants, representations, and warranties would have permitted a majority of the participating banks in that facility to demand security from Enron, including requiring Enron to deposit an amount equal to the undrawn letter of credit amounts into a cash collateral account.

Defendant JP Morgan Chase Bank has continued to demand payments from UCI under the 2001 L/C Facility, including a demand in May 2002. Plaintiff has refused to make any further payments under the 2001 L/C Facility. On June 4, 2002, JP Morgan Chase Bank advised UCI and other participating banks that JP Morgan Chase Bank had erroneously applied letters of credit in an aggregate amount exceeding the maximum authorized under that facility. UCI was advised that it would be paid its proportionate share of such excess. To date, no such payment has been made.

UCI has made repeated requests of JP Morgan Chase Bank for information, to which UCI is entitled to as a participant in the 2001 L/C Facility and which JP

Morgan Chase Bank has made available to other participating banks, about the letters of credit that have been issued under that Facility; those requests have been refused. JP Morgan Chase Bank has failed to allow UCI to have access to a repository or central file of documents relating to the 2001 L/C Facility, including documents that UCI has specifically requested.

JP Morgan Chase Bank has submitted and continues to submit bills for legal expenses to UCI that JP Morgan Chase Bank claims are subject to indemnification under the 2001 L/C Facility.

THE 2000 L/C FACILITY

In May 2000, the same month UCI approved its participation in the 2000 Credit Facility, it also, under a separate agreement with Enron, approved a $10 million letter of credit facility for Enron, which was increased to $30 million in August 2000 (the "2000 L/C Facility"). UCI would not have taken part in the 2000 L/C Facility had it not been for Defendants' participation in falsifying Enron's financial statements, including its Form 10-K and 10-Q, specifically the disclosures concerning revenues, earning, liabilities, and debt. Defendants knew that UCI had established the 2000 L/C Facility, but they did not advise UCI of Enron's actual financial condition.

On August 31, 2000, at the direction of Enron, UCI issued a standby letter of credit in favor of CalPX Trading Services in the amount of $10 million. On December 12, 2000, that amount was increased to $25 million at the direction of Enron. The maturity date was extended several times at Enron's request, including by an agreement on October 24, 2001, to extend the maturity date to November 30, 2001. After the October extension, UCI and Enron began negotiations concerning Enron providing collateral for the letters of credit that UCI had issued. By the third week of November 2001, Enron had delivered to UCI a form of agreement under which Enron was to provide the collateral.

On or about November 26, 2001, UCI received a phone call from Claire O'Connor. O'Connor asked UCI if it would be interested in contributing its $25 million exposure on the 2000 L/C Facility to a new letter of credit facility for the benefit of Enron that JP Morgan Chase Bank was proposing to arrange. UCI declined to participate, and explained that it expected to enter an agreement under which it would receive cash collateral from Enron for its 2000 L/C Facility exposure.

UCI and Enron never executed the proposed agreement for collateral. On November 30, 2001, the letter of credit was drawn down in the full amount of $25 million.

CHOICE OF LAW

The credit agreements for the Syndicated Facilities provide that they are governed by New York law.

PLAINTIFFS' CAUSES OF ACTION

Plaintiffs UCI and Pekao assert common law claims against all Defendants for fraudulent concealment (Count I), fraudulent inducement (Count II), aiding and abetting fraud by Enron (Count III), negligent misrepresentation (Count IV), civil conspiracy (Count V), and unjust enrichment (Count VII). Plaintiffs assert a claim against JP Morgan Chase Bank and Citibank for breach of an implied duty of good faith in connection with the Syndicated Facilities (Count VI). Plaintiff UCI also seeks declaratory relief against Defendant JP Morgan Chase Bank with respect to the 2001 L/C Facility (Count VIII).

PLAINTIFFS' FRAUD AND NEGLIGENT MISREPRESENTATION CLAIMS

... Plaintiffs' fraud and misrepresentation claims must be dismissed because the contracts pursuant to which they made their Enron loan investments preclude them from establishing essential elements of those claims, namely, that the Defendant banks had a duty to disclose information regarding or gained from their business dealings with Enron, and that any reliance by Plaintiffs on misrepresentations by the Defendants was reasonable ...

The operative documents also, on their face, preclude Plaintiffs from claiming that they relied reasonably on any alleged representations by the Defendants ...

PLAINTIFFS' AIDING AND ABETTING FRAUD CLAIM

Plaintiffs have stated a claim for aiding and abetting fraud. Plaintiffs allege that Defendants knowingly participated in and helped structure the transactions ... that enabled Enron to distort its public financial statements, specifically with respect to Enron's revenues and its ratio of balance sheet debt to balance sheet capital. Furthermore, Plaintiffs allege that Defendant's participation in those transactions contributed to Enron's collapse, and thus its inability to meet its obligations under the credit agreements. In addition, by identifying Enron's fraudulent statements, that is, the revenue and debt-to-equity figures in Enron's public financial statements, and specifying the way in which those figures misrepresented the reality of Enron's revenues and liabilities, Plaintiffs have plead Enron's fraud with sufficient particularity to satisfy the requirements of Rule 9(b) of the Federal Rules of Civil Procedure. Accordingly, Defendants' motions are denied to the extent they seek dismissal of Count III.

PLAINTIFFS' CLAIM FOR BREACH OF THE IMPLIED DUTY OF GOOD FAITH AND UCI'S CLAIM FOR DECLARATORY RELIEF

The express disclaimers in the credit agreements preclude Plaintiffs' claim for breach of the implied duty of good faith in those agreements to the extent that claim is premised on the allegedly fraudulent conduct addressed above. Plaintiffs allege that the failure of Defendant banks to disclose Enron's true financial condition in connection with the credit transactions prevented Plaintiffs from taking advantage of their various rights under the credit agreements. Although New York law implies a duty of good faith and fair dealing in every contract, "no obligation can be implied that would be inconsistent with other terms of the contractual relationship." Here, as explained above, the operative contracts specifically absolve the Defendant banks from any duty to disclose financial information regarding Enron and contain Plaintiffs' undertakings to rely on their own credit analyses in making the relevant decisions. Implication of a duty, notwithstanding these provisions, of the banks to make disclosures regarding Enron's financial conditions would clearly be inconsistent with the governing contracts . . .

PROBLEM SET 16.3

1. Is the opinion's treatment of the Defendant's as agents consistent with the agency law you learned in Business Associations?
2. Given the many hats worn by large financial institutions, why do buyers of loan interests and participations agree to exculpatory clauses like those seen in this case?

4. DEFAULTING AND UNWANTED LENDERS

One consequence of the increasing trend toward sale of bits of corporate loans is that the borrower is less apt to know who its lender is, and could end up with a group of lenders that it finds it is unable to work with. This might be especially likely to occur as the debtor's credit quality changes over time — for example, the group of staid insurance companies and banks that once owned the loan might be replaced by a new group of distressed debt investors who have very different goals and interests.

Short of refinancing the loan, the borrower has limited recourse. One potentially relevant provision is known as the "yank-a-bank" clause. It typically provides something like this:

12.24 REPLACEMENT OF LENDERS

If any Lender requests compensation under **Section 3.3**, or if the Borrowers are required to pay any additional amount to any Lender or any Governmental Authority for the account of any Lender pursuant to **Section 3.1**, or if any Lender is a Defaulting Lender or under the circumstance set forth in the last paragraph of **Section 11.1** [refusal to consent to a loan amendment, that has been agreed to a majority of lenders], then the Borrowers may, at their sole expense and effort, upon notice to such Lender and the Agent, require such Lender to assign and delegate, without recourse (in accordance with and subject to the restrictions contained in, and consents required by, **Section 11.2**), all of its interests, rights and obligations under this Agreement and the related Loan Documents to an assignee that shall assume such obligations (which assignee may be another Lender, if a Lender accepts such assignment); provided that:

(a) the Borrower shall have paid to the Agent the processing fee specified in **Section 11.2(a)**;
(b) such Lender shall have received payment of an amount equal to the outstanding principal of its Loans (including the L/C Loans), accrued interest thereon, accrued fees and all other amounts payable to it hereunder and under the other Loan Documents (including any amounts under **Section 3.5**) from the assignee (to the extent of such outstanding principal and accrued interest and fees) or the Borrowers (in the case of all other amounts);
(c) in the case of any such assignment resulting from a claim for compensation under **Section 3.3** or payments required to be made pursuant to **Section 3.1**, such assignment will result in a reduction in such compensation or payments thereafter; and
(d) such assignment does not conflict with Applicable Laws. A Lender shall not be required to make any such assignment or delegation if, prior thereto, as a result of a waiver by such Lender or otherwise, the circumstances entitling the Borrowers to require such assignment and delegation cease to apply.

This clause might also become relevant if a particular lender in the bank line fails to perform. Before 2008, the idea that a major financial institution would fail to fund a loan it had agreed to make was almost unthinkable. Then Lehman Brothers filed for bankruptcy, throwing into doubt financing for several major construction projects.

The issue of "defaulting lenders" also arises with regard to letters of credit outstanding on a bank loan. If and when a complying draw is made under the letter of credit (and the borrower does not reimburse the issuer), the issuing bank must turn to the other lenders to fund their part of these LCs.[10]

PROBLEM SET 16.4

1. How useful would the yank-a-bank clause set forth previously have been during the financial crisis, if Chrysler had wanted to replace the Indiana pension funds as a lender in its loan agreement? How about a borrower that wanted to replace Lehman as lender in an outstanding but unfunded loan agreement?
2. If an issuing bank sells participations in the credit risk to the other lenders, and those participations are in turn sold to other investors, what are the potential issues that might arise? In particular, what concerns should the issuing bank have?

---

10. R.J. Miles, et al., *Syndicated Lending Update: Defaulting Lender Issues*, 126 Banking L.J. 165 (2009).

5. THE DYNEGY LOAN AGREEMENT

Take a look at the materials regarding the 2007 Dynegy Credit Agreement that are available online. As you review it, the following points might help you structure your reading:

- Who are the lenders?
- What types of agents are there?
- Who are the borrowers?
- Is the loan secured or unsecured?
- What types of loans are being made?
- What interest rates and fees are associated with the loan?
- How much can the borrower(s) get under the loan, and when can they and when must they pay it back?
- What covenants have the borrower(s) agreed to? In particular, what financial covenants apply and what limitations on the borrower(s) apply?
- How can the borrower(s) default under the agreement? What are the implications of a default?

17

OPTIONS, WARRANTS, AND CONVERTIBLES

This chapter addresses three related instruments of long pedigree. If you encountered "rights of first refusal" in your 1L property class, you have already seen an option in action. Basically any contract that gives one party the choice to perform at some future date can be deemed an *option*.

As you will see, *warrants* and *convertible instruments* are simply options in other forms. For example, convertible instruments are often bonds or preferred stocks with options imbedded in their documentation.

1. OPTIONS

For the purchaser, an option represents the right, but not the obligation, to buy or sell the reference, or underlying, asset within a specified time period for a specified price, known as the strike price. The underlying asset could be almost anything: an individual security, a real asset, a market index, or a currency.

Options are divided into calls and puts. A *call* option gives the holder or buyer the right to buy the underlying asset, whereas a *put* option gives the holder the right to sell.

The option buyer is the party that has the "option" — the seller or writer of an option must perform if the holder exercises their option. That is, the choice is not bilateral in an option, because the seller always has to perform if requested.

At expiration, an option is either valuable or "out of the money." For example, a call option to buy shares of Bogartco at $5 per share is valuable only if Bogartco's shares are currently trading at more than $5 per share. And the ultimate value of the option depends on the degree to which the current price exceeds $5 per share, the call option's "strike price."

Note that the strike price or exercise price is distinct from any cost you incur to buy the option itself. The cost of the option is incurred up front, and sometimes periodically during the life of the option, and will always be incurred, whether the holder exercises the option or not.

If the share price is less than $5 per share, exercise of the option would be nonsensical, because the option holder could buy shares on the open market. Thus the option expires without being exercised, and the holder is out the cost of the option.

You can thus see that options, unlike many other securities we have discussed to date, are a zero sum game. Gain for the option holder in the given example is loss for the option writer. In theory, the losses to the option writer in a call option are unlimited—the greater the rise in Bogartco's share price, the bigger the losses. Even if Bogartco shares zoom up to $100,000,000,000,000 per share, the option writer is still obligated to sell for $5 per share.

Because of limited liability, the exposure is somewhat more limited for the writer of a put. Do you see why?

Most options used in financial transactions are so-called *American options*, a term that no longer has geographic significance, but instead refers to the holder's ability to exercise the option at any point up until expiration. This is in contrast with the so-called *European option*, which is only exercisable on the maturity date.

Thus, if your call option just described was a March 2016 Bogartco option, you could exercise it any time Bogartco's share price exceeded $5 per share before March 2016. More precisely, options typically expire on the Saturday following the third Friday of the expiration month. Practically, this means the option expires on the third Friday in March 2016 in our example, as brokerages are not typically open for business on Saturdays. If you want to exercise the option, you will have to pay the strike price by Friday.

Figure 17-1 shows the options available from a major brokerage firm with respect to Coca-Cola (a real company, unlike Bogartco).

At the top right of Figure 17.1, you see the then current (September 2012) market price for the shares. Below that you see prices for calls (on the left) and puts (on the right). The strike prices for each are in the column in the center. OI stands for open interest, which indicates the number of contracts outstanding at a particular strike price. The shading indicates options that are "in the money."

The options are to buy or sell round lots of shares—100 shares—but are quoted at their per share price. Thus, the put option priced at $6.45 (bottom right) would actually cost $645 to buy. Because it gives you the right to sell shares currently worth $3,740 for $4,125, for an instant profit of $385, the high cost is perhaps understandable. After all, you have until January 2014 to make even more profit if KO prices were to decline.

PROBLEM SET 17.1

1. If you had bought the put option priced at $6.45 (bottom right) in September 2012, and in early May 2013 the KO share price was $42.24, where would you stand?
2. If in September 2012 you bought a January 2014 put with a strike price of $32.50, and also owned 100 shares of KO, what have you achieved?

Coca Cola Company (KO)
Last Trade: 4:00:38PM ET

Last	Change	Bid	Ask	High	Low	Volume
37.40	+0.26	37.40	37.54	37.58	37.15	20,711,518

KO 2/16/2013 (Expires: 166 days from today)

Calls						Strike	Puts					
Last	Change	Bid	Ask	Volume	OI		Last	Change	Bid	Ask	Volume	OI
5.15	+0.05	5.00	5.10	19	215	32.50	0.51	-0.03	0.48	0.50	7	784
4.15	0.00	3.90	4.05	0	135	33.75	0.66	-0.06	0.68	0.70	33	2,639
2.97	-0.08	2.95	3.05	2	235	35.00	0.94	-0.08	0.98	1.00	76	6,464
2.14	+0.21	2.11	2.14	1,226	697	36.25	1.43	+0.13	1.39	1.42	97	1,966
1.41	-0.05	1.40	1.43	60	1,913	37.50	2.05	+0.14	1.94	1.98	1	767
0.88	+0.06	0.86	0.89	575	2,023	38.75	2.64	+0.08	2.66	2.69	25	627
0.50	0.00	0.49	0.51	366	9,702	40.00	3.52	0.00	3.50	3.60	0	556
0.27	0.00	0.26	0.28	13	3,522	41.25	4.60	+0.70	4.50	4.60	40	311

KO 1/18/2014 (Expires: 502 days from today)

Calls						Strike	Puts					
Last	Change	Bid	Ask	Volume	OI		Last	Change	Bid	Ask	Volume	OI
5.80	+0.20	5.65	5.75	10	28,399	32.50	1.90	0.00	1.89	1.95	0	12,930
4.90	+0.15	4.80	4.90	42	3,518	33.75	2.20	0.00	2.32	2.37	0	28,958
4.10	+0.20	4.00	4.05	275	14,916	35.00	2.93	0.00	2.81	2.87	0	12,927
3.30	0.00	3.25	3.35	46	6,682	36.25	3.45	0.00	3.35	3.45	0	1,344
2.74	+0.09	2.64	2.70	101	5,500	37.50	4.00	-0.06	4.00	4.10	4	105,243
2.09	-0.05	2.09	2.15	50	3,090	38.75	4.60	0.00	4.75	4.85	0	2,125
1.68	+0.06	1.65	1.70	122	4,763	40.00	5.55	-0.15	5.55	5.65	7	934
1.25	-0.01	1.26	1.31	2	1,594	41.25	6.45	0.00	6.40	6.55	0	306

FIGURE 17-1
Coca-Cola Options.

3. If in September 2012 you own 100 KO shares and sell a January 2014 call
    with a $41.25 strike price, what will you have in January 2014 if the share
    price is (a) $40.00, (b) $42.00, or (c) $60.00?
4. Compare the following investments
    A. Buy a $1,000 Bogartco bond and a call option on the company's shares
        with a strike price of $10 per share
    B. Buy 100 shares of Bogartco and a put option with a strike price of $10
        per share.
        How are these similar?

2. WARRANTS

In many respects a warrant is just like a call option. The distinction is that a
warrant is issued by the firm whose stock is the underlying asset.

For example, Coca-Cola might sell warrants to buy its own shares. Exercise of a
warrant thus increases the amount of outstanding shares, unless the company
takes action to buy back a corresponding amount of its own shares on the open
market.

Warrants tend to have longer maturity periods than exchange-traded
options. They also tend to be issued in specialized situations. For example,
in a bankruptcy case where it is unclear if the equity should receive any value,
the reorganization plan might give warrants to the old shareholders, with a
strike price that only puts them in the money if the company's post-bankruptcy
share price exceeds some level that will result in full payment of creditors. We
saw an example of this in the Supreme Court's *Consolidated Rock* opinion in
Chapter 11.

PAUL R. LOHNES, PLAINTIFF, APPELLANT, v. LEVEL 3 COMMUNICATIONS, INC., DEFENDANT, APPELLEE

272 F.3d 49
United States Court of Appeals, First Circuit
No. 01–1613 | Heard Nov. 5, 2001 | Decided Nov. 30, 2001

SELYA, Circuit Judge.
The primary issue raised in this appeal is whether the terms "capital reorganization" and/or "reclassification of stock", as used in a stock warrant, encompass
a stock split. Asserting the affirmative of this proposition, a warrantholder, plaintiff-appellant Paul R. Lohnes, claims that a stock split effectuated by defendant-
appellee Level 3 Communications, Inc. (Level 3) triggered an antidilution
provision in the warrant that automatically increased the number of shares of
stock to which he was entitled. Level 3 resists this claim. The district court
concluded that the language of the warrant could not reasonably be construed
to encompass a stock split and, accordingly, granted Level 3's motion for summary judgment. We affirm.

I. BACKGROUND

Consistent with the conventional summary judgment praxis, our account of the relevant facts construes the record in the light most favorable to the non-moving party (here, the appellant).

The appellant is both a trustee and a beneficiary of C.E.M. Realty Trust (the Trust). In February of 1998, the Trust leased 40,000 square feet of commercial space to XCOM Technologies, Inc. (XCOM). The details of the lease transaction need not concern us, save for the fact that, as part of the consideration, XCOM issued a stock warrant to the appellant. The parties negotiated the principal terms of the warrant—the number of shares, the exercise price, and the expiration date—and XCOM's lawyer then drafted the document. The warrant specified that its exercise would be governed by Massachusetts law. It empowered the holder to purchase, at his discretion but within a fixed period, 100,000 shares of XCOM common stock at $0.30 per share.

Unbeknownst to the appellant, XCOM's days as an independent entity were numbered. Shortly after the appellant executed the lease and accepted the warrant, Level 3 acquired XCOM in a stock-for-stock transaction and converted XCOM into a wholly-owned subsidiary. As part of this transaction, Level 3 agreed to assume XCOM's warrant obligations and satisfy them with shares of Level 3's common stock (using a designated share exchange formula). Following this paradigm, the appellant's unexercised warrant for XCOM shares was duly converted into a warrant to purchase 8,541 shares of Level 3's common stock. The appellant does not challenge this conversion (which took effect in April of 1998).

The next significant development occurred on July 14, 1998. On that date, Level 3's board of directors authorized a two-for-one stock split, to be effectuated in the form of a stock dividend granting common shareholders one new share of stock for each share held.[1] The board set the record date as July 30, 1998. On July 20, Level 3 issued a press release announcing the stock split, but it did not provide the appellant with personalized notice.

The split occurred as scheduled. Adhering to generally accepted accounting practices, Level 3 adjusted its balance sheet to account for the split by increasing its common stock account in the amount of $1,000,000 and reducing paid-in-capital by a like amount. These accounting entries had no net effect on either the retained earnings or the net equity of the company.

Despite the sharp reduction in the share price that accompanied the stock split, the appellant paid no heed until approximately three months after the record date. When his belated inquiry revealed what had transpired, the

---

1. A corporation effects a "stock split" by increasing the number of shares outstanding without changing the proportional ownership interests of each shareholder. Companies typically execute a stock split by issuing a "stock dividend" to current shareholders, i.e., "paid in stock expressed as a percentage of the number of shares already held by a shareholder." Black's Law Dict. 493 (7th ed.1999) (cross-referencing definition of "dividend"). Stock splits lower the price per share, thereby fostering increased marketability and wider distribution of shares.

Technically, not all stock dividends are stock splits, and the two may, in limited instances, receive different accounting treatment. In the instant matter, however, "stock split" and "stock dividend" are two sides of the same coin, and we use the terms interchangeably.

appellant contacted Level 3 to confirm that the stock split had triggered a share adjustment provision, thus entitling him to 17,082 shares (twice the number of shares specified in the warrant). Level 3 demurred on the ground that the warrant did not provide for any share adjustment based upon the occurrence of a stock split effected as a stock dividend.

Dissatisfied by Level 3's response, the appellant exercised the warrant and received 8,541 shares of Level 3's common stock. He then sued Level 3 in a Massachusetts state court alleging breach of both the warrant and the implied duty of good faith and fair dealing. Citing diversity of citizenship and the existence of a controversy in the requisite amount, Level 3 removed the action to the federal district court. The parties then engaged in a protracted period of pretrial discovery.

Discovery closed on October 30, 2000. Thereafter, Level 3 moved for summary judgment. *See* Fed.R.Civ.P. 56.

In due course, the district court ruled that, as a matter of law, a stock split, effected as a stock dividend, did not constitute a "capital reorganization" as that term was used in the warrant and, accordingly, granted the motion for summary judgment.

II. METHODOLOGY OF REVIEW

We begin our analysis by outlining the legal framework that governs our review. Next, we apply well-worn principles of contract interpretation to resolve the appellant's contention that the terms "capital reorganization" and "reclassification of stock" encompass a stock split implemented as a stock dividend. In this endeavor, our principal task is to determine the ambiguity *vel non* of the disputed terms. Thus, we investigate whether either term is reasonably susceptible to the interpretation urged by the appellant. As part of this exercise, we consider (and reject) the appellant's belated attempt to introduce expert testimony bearing on this question. We conclude by addressing the appellant's claim that Level 3 breached the implied duty of good faith and fair dealing inherent in the warrant.

III. THE CONTRACT INTERPRETATION CLAIMS

A stock warrant is an instrument that grants the warrantholder an option to purchase shares of stock at a fixed price. Against the backdrop of this well-established definition, we turn to the appellant's contract interpretation claims.

B. PARSING THE WARRANT.

The warrant at issue here contained a two-paragraph antidilution provision which, upon the occurrence of certain described events, automatically adjusted the number of shares to which the warrantholder would be entitled upon exercise of the warrant. In all, share adjustments were engendered by five separate contingencies: capital reorganization, reclassification of common stock, merger, consolidation, and sale of all (or substantially all) the capital stock or assets. However, the warrant did not explicitly provide for an adjustment of shares in the event of a stock split. The appellant attempts to plug this lacuna by equating a stock split with a capital reorganization and/or a reclassification of stock. This argument brings the following paragraph of the antidilution provision into play:

> *Reorganizations and Reclassifications.* If there shall occur any capital reorganization or reclassification of the Common Stock, then, as part of any such reorganization or reclassification, lawful provision shall be made so that the Holder shall have the right thereafter to receive upon the exercise hereof the kind and amount of shares of stock or other securities or property which such Holder would have been entitled to receive if, immediately prior to any such reorganization or reclassification, such Holder had held the number of shares of Common Stock which were then purchasable upon the exercise of this Warrant.

Building upon the premise that either "capital reorganization" or "reclassification of stock" encompasses a stock split, the appellant concludes that Level 3's stock split activated the share adjustment mechanism set forth in the quoted paragraph.

As said, the appellant bears the burden of establishing the existence of a genuine issue of material fact. Given the circumstances of this case, the only way for him to succeed in this endeavor is by showing that one of the disputed terms ("capital reorganization" or "reclassification of stock") is shrouded in ambiguity, that is, that reasonable minds plausibly could reach opposite conclusions as to whether either term extended to stock splits. To appraise the success of the appellant's efforts, we ponder each term separately.

C.   CAPITAL REORGANIZATION.

Since the warrant does not elaborate upon the meaning of "capital reorganization," we turn to other sources. Massachusetts law offers no discernible guidance . . .

Moving beyond the case law, the meaning of the term "capital reorganization" in common legal parlance seemingly belies the appellant's ambitious definition. The preeminent legal lexicon defines "reorganization," in pertinent part, as a "[g]eneral term describing corporate amalgamations or readjustments occurring, for example, when one corporation acquires another in a merger or acquisition, a single corporation divides into two or more entities, or a corporation makes a substantial change in its capital structure." *Black's Law Dict.* 1298 (6th ed.1990). The first two prongs of this definition are clearly inapposite here. That leaves only the question of whether a stock split entails a "substantial change in [a corporation's] capital structure." We think not.

First and foremost, the accounting mechanics that accompany a stock split are mere window dressing. To be sure, a stock split effected through the distribution of shares in the form of a stock dividend results in an increase in the common stock at par account and an offsetting decrease in additional paid-in capital, but this subtle set of entries has no effect on total shareholder equity or on any other substantive aspect of the balance sheet. Because a stock split does not entail a substantial change in a corporation's capital structure, the unelaborated term "capital reorganization" cannot plausibly include a stock split effected as a stock dividend.

D.   RECLASSIFICATION OF STOCK.

We turn next to the phrase "reclassification of stock." Two Massachusetts cases seem worthy of mention. In the first, a corporation took advantage of a new statute authorizing the issuance of preferred stock and amended its charter to divide its previously undifferentiated stock into common and preferred shares. *Page v. Whittenton Mfg. Co.*, 211 Mass. 424, 97 N.E. 1006, 1007–08 (1912). The Massachusetts Supreme Judicial Court approved the corporation's actions. It held that a corporation could classify stock into common and preferred shares (providing preferred shareholders with cumulative dividends and a liquidation preference) so long as that classification was effected through a charter amendment. *Id.* at 1007. Although *Page* uses the verb "classify," we view what transpired as a reclassification. *See* XIII *Oxford English Dict.* 339 (2d ed.1989) (defining "reclassify" as "[t]o classify again; to alter the classification of").

In *Boston Safe Deposit & Trust Co. v. State Tax Comm'n*, 340 Mass. 250, 163 N.E.2d 637 (Mass.1960), the court considered the tax implications of a reclassification of stock. The reclassification in question involved the partial substitution of redeemable, convertible, cumulative, nonvoting shares for nonredeemable, nonconvertible, noncumulative, voting shares. *Id.* at 642. The court held that the reclassification constituted a taxable event under Massachusetts law. *Id.* at 643.

Our reading of the Massachusetts cases leads us to conclude that the sine qua non of a reclassification of stock is the modification of existing shares into something fundamentally different. At the end of the day, the stockholders in *Page* held a different class of shares, while the stockholders in *Boston Safe* gained some privileges while losing the right to vote. Thus, *Page* and *Boston Safe*, respectively, illustrate two ways in which a security can be altered fundamentally: (a) by changing the class of stock, or (b) by modifying important rights or preferences linked to stock.

Stock splits effected as stock dividends do not entail any such fundamental alteration of the character of an existing security. For example, Level 3's stock split in no way altered its shareholders' proportionate ownership interests, varied the class of securities held, or revised any of the attributes associated with the stock. What is more, the stock split did not have a meaningful impact on either the corporation's balance sheet or capital structure. For those reasons, we perceive no principled basis on which to stretch the definition of "reclassification of stock" to encompass a stock split.

E.   THE OVERALL PLAN OF REORGANIZATION.

The appellant also makes a conclusory claim that the July 1998 stock split was part and parcel of a comprehensive corporate reorganization (and, thus, animated the warrant's antidilution provision). He did very little to develop this claim below, and he has not remedied that shortfall on appeal. For that reason, we deem the claim abandoned.

In any event, the claim lacks merit. As best we can understand it, the appellant hypothesizes that the stock split was an offshoot of a corporate reorganization launched by Level 3 in 1997. In that year, Level 3 shifted direction away from construction and mining activities in order to pursue its interests in communications and business services. Between August 1997 and May 1998, the company dramatically modified its capital structure by splitting off its construction business and eliminating two series of stock. Although none of these transactions involved XCOM or otherwise impacted the appellant, he implies that the July 1998 stock split, effected to increase the marketability of the company's shares as a prelude to raising capital in the public markets, should be viewed as an essential component of the company's overall capital reorganization and stock reclassification, thereby triggering the warrant's antidilution provision.

We reject the appellant's intimation that the stock split is magically transformed into a capital reorganization or reclassification of stock based upon its inclusion in a long-term business plan that also contains a number of more complex financial maneuvers. Taken to its logical extreme, the appellant's argument invites us to deem *any* corporate activity engaged in by Level 3 while in the midst of reorganizing its capital structure as a capital reorganization and reclassification of stock. We are unable to perceive any principled basis on which we could accept this invitation.

G. THE DENOUEMENT.

[T]he appellant plainly is fishing in an empty stream. We have found no legal usage of the terms "capital reorganization" or "reclassification of stock" that supports the proposition that a reasonable person plausibly could have believed that either term encompassed a stock split. This is made crystal clear when one contrasts the warrant received by the appellant with a warrant issued by XCOM approximately ten months earlier to a different party—a warrant that contained more than six full pages of antidilution protections (including explicitly-worded share adjustments for stock splits and stock dividends). Moreover, the appellant has failed to adduce any credible evidence that the parties here somehow intended to adopt such an unusually expansive interpretation of the terms "capital reorganization" and/or "reclassification of stock."

If more were needed—and we doubt that it is—the maxim *expressio unius est exclusio alterius* instructs that, "when parties list specific items in a document, any item not so listed is typically thought to be excluded." Here, the warrant's antidilution protection extended expressly to five designated contingencies: capital reorganizations, reclassification of the common stock, merger, consolidation, or sale of all (or substantially all) the capital stock or assets. Since nothing within the four corners of the warrant hints at additional contingencies, we apply this maxim and conclude that the parties intended stock splits to be excluded from the list of events capable of triggering the share adjustment machinery.

The appellant is left, then, with his reliance on the principle of *contra proferentum*—the hoary aphorism that ambiguities must be construed against the drafter of an instrument. This reliance is mislaid. In order to invoke this principle, the proponent first must demonstrate that there is an ambiguity. Here, the appellant has failed to show that the interpretation which he urges is, "under all the circumstances, a reasonable and practical one." *Id.* Accordingly, we have no occasion to apply the principle of *contra proferentum.*

IV.   THE IMPLIED COVENANT OF GOOD FAITH AND FAIR DEALING

Although the terms "capital reorganization" and "reclassification of stock," as they appear in the warrant, are inherently unambiguous and do not encompass stock splits, the appellant mounts one further attack. He posits that Level 3 had a legal obligation, under the implied contractual covenant of good faith and fair dealing, to provide him with personalized, advance warning of the stock split. The appellant further argues that Level 3 breached this obligation by failing to advise him specifically about the adverse impact that the stock split would have on the warrant if the appellant did not exercise it before the record date. This argument lacks force.

Under Massachusetts law, every contract includes an implied duty of good faith and fair dealing. *Anthony's Pier Four, Inc. v. HBC Assocs.*, 411 Mass. 451, 583 N.E.2d 806, 820 (1991). This implied covenant forbids a party from doing "anything which will have the effect of destroying or injuring the rights of the other party to receive the fruits of the contract."

The most prominent flaw in the appellant's attempt to wield this club is that he misperceives the fruits of the bargain that he struck. After all, a warrantholder does not become a shareholder unless and until he exercises his purchase option. Consequently, a warrantholder's right to insist that the corporation maintain the integrity of the shares described in the warrant, if it exists at all, must be found in the text of the warrant itself. Put another way, the fruits of the contract were limited to those enumerated in the warrant.

An examination of the warrant reveals quite clearly that Level 3 was not contractually bound to provide the appellant with individualized notice of the stock split. The warrant contained language stating that "[u]ntil the exercise of this Warrant, the Holder shall not have or exercise any rights by virtue hereof as a stockholder of the Company." This disclaimer hardly could have been written more plainly.

Furthermore, the warrant contained a notice provision which, by its terms, pertained to "notices, requests and other communications hereunder." Applying the settled definition of "hereunder," Level 3 was only obligated to provide notice for events contemplated in the warrant agreement. *See* VII *Oxford English Dict.* 165 (2d ed.1989) (defining "hereunder"). Because the warrant contained no provision that even arguably required Level 3 to furnish individualized notice of the stock split to the appellant, the failure to give such notice could not constitute a breach of the implied duty of good faith and fair dealing.[2]

---

2. We note in passing that Level 3's general press release announced the stock split ten days in advance of the record date and provided the appellant with constructive notice of the stock split. Thus, the appellant had ample opportunity to exercise the warrant and avoid the dilutive effects of which he now complains.

V. CONCLUSION

We need go no further. In light of the appellant's inability to show that a reasonable person plausibly could construe either "capital reorganization" or "reclassification of stock" to include stock splits, we conclude that these terms, as they appear in the warrant, were unambiguous and did not cover the contingency of a stock split effected as a stock dividend. It follows that the stock split in question here did not trip the warrant's antidilution provision. By like token, Level 3 did not breach the implied covenant of good faith and fair dealing by neglecting to give special notice beyond what the warrant itself required. The bottom line, then, is that the district court was correct in granting Level 3's motion for summary judgment.

PROBLEM SET 17.2

1.   Should the Appellant's original attorney be worried by this decision?
2.   The court suggests that the Appellant could have avoided his fate even given the shortcomings in the drafting of the warrant — how exactly?

3.   OPTION PRICING

Option pricing is a highly developed area of corporate finance theory that might or might not have real-world applications. The most famous theory of option pricing comes from work done by Fischer Black and Myron Scholes in the early 1970s, and expanded by Robert C. Merton. The original Black-Scholes option pricing formula prices European put or call options on a stock that does not pay a dividend or make other distributions. The formula assumes the underlying stock price follows a geometric Brownian motion with constant volatility. Merton and Scholes received the 1997 Nobel Prize in Economics for their work, Professor Black being ineligible due to his earlier death.
The original formula looks like this:

$$C_0 = S \times N(d_1) - Ee^{-Rt} \times N(d_2)$$

where $N(d)$ is a cumulative standard normal distribution function[3] and:

$$d_1 = \frac{\ln(S/E) + (R + \frac{\sigma^2}{2})t}{\sigma\sqrt{t}}$$

and:

$$d_2 = d_1 - \sigma\sqrt{t}$$

---

3. You can think of this as a probability calculation. It involves calculus, which if you took, you have likely forgotten. It involved things like calculating how many cows could fit into a two-dimensional pen.

S is the current stock price, R is the risk-free interest rate, e is your friend the imaginary number, t is the time until maturity, and the big E is the exercise price of the option. The lowercase sigma—as in, Ὀδυσσεύς—represents standard deviation, in this case of the underlying stock price. Think of that as a measure of the stock's volatility.

Brownian motion refers to the observations that English botanist Robert Brown made in 1828. While looking at pollen, he noticed that very small particles of pollen in water exhibited an incessant, irregular motion. Albert Einstein explained why this happens in a 1905 paper.

Assuming your math skills are somewhat less than Einstein's, even if he did work without a calculator or Excel, we will not dwell on the math behind Black-Scholes in this class, but you should understand its intuitions.

Moreover, you should understand that although Black-Scholes is the best-known option pricing theory, it provides at best an estimate of what an option's price should be, subject to a significant margin of error. It's a bit like CAPM in that regard. The next excerpt explores the limitations of Black-Scholes in detail.

First, a bit of terminology is in order. Dynamic hedging refers to the hedging of a nonlinear risk. For example, when a broker sells an option to a customer, the broker probably does not want to have risk exposure to the underlying stock. Even if the broker engages in "proprietary trading," or trading for its own account, it probably does that through a separate division of the brokerage.[4] For this reason, the broker will want to hedge (i.e., protect) its exposure under the option.

For an equity option, one way to hedge the option is to buy or sell the underlying shares. For example, if the broker sells a call option on Coca-Cola, it might buy some shares of KO. But if the broker wants to keep its losses to a minimum, it must buy more shares of KO as the price of KO increases, as the likelihood of the call being exercised will increase with the price of the underlying shares.[5] Then as the share price declines, and exercise becomes less likely, the broker will want to sell shares of KO.

This continual adjusting of the hedge is the dynamic part—specifically, the broker is engaged in dynamic delta hedging. More on delta (Δ) is presented in Chapter 18.

The broker removes the risk of changes in the value of the underlying, assuming it can hedge properly. If the stock moves in unexpected ways—imagine a dealer that had sold put options on Lehman, tying to hedge in late summer 2008 as Lehman approached bankruptcy—the cost of the hedge might exceed the option premium the broker has received from the customer, and the stock might decline faster than the broker can buy it to complete the hedge.

Nonetheless, as discussed next, Black-Scholes is based on a very robust theory of dynamic hedging that means that option prices are entirely free from supply and demand effects. This should sound somewhat similar to some of the assumptions made earlier in the course when discussing "modern" (post–World War II) finance.

---

4. And at least in theory, after the enactment of the Dodd-Frank Act, the largest brokers will soon cease to engage in such trading.

5. Follow this link for an example involving a put option: *http://goo.gl/e0h2L*

ESPEN GAARDER HAUG[6] & NASSIM NICHOLAS TALEB[7],
OPTION TRADERS USE (VERY) SOPHISTICATED HEURISTICS,
NEVER THE BLACK–SCHOLES–MERTON FORMULA
77 J. Economic Behavior & Organization 97 (February 2011)

Options, we will show, have been extremely active in the pre-modern finance world. Complicated, tacitly transmitted tricks and heuristically derived methodologies in option trading and risk management of derivatives books have been developed over the past century, and used quite effectively by operators. In parallel, many derivations were produced by mathematical researchers. The economics literature, however, did not recognize these contributions, substituting the rediscoveries or subsequent reformulations done by (some) economists. There is evidence of an attribution problem with Black–Scholes–Merton option "formula," which was developed, used, and adapted in a robust way by a long tradition of researchers and used heuristically by option market makers and "book runners." Furthermore, in a case of scientific puzzle, the exact formula called "Black–Sholes–Merton" was written down (and used) by Edward Thorp which, paradoxically, while being robust and realistic, has been considered unrigorous. This raises the following: (1) The Black–Scholes–Merton was, according to modern finance, just a neoclassical finance argument, no more than a thought experiment, (2) we are not aware of traders using their argument or their version of the formula.

Option traders call the formula they use the "Black–Scholes–Merton" formula without being aware that by some irony, of all the possible options formulas that have been produced in the past century, what is called the Black–Scholes–Merton "formula" (after [Black and Scholes, 1973] and [Merton, 1973]) is the one the furthest away from what they are using. In fact of the formulas written down in a long history it is the only formula that is fragile to jumps and tail events.

First, something seems to have been lost in translation: Black and Scholes (1973) and Merton (1973) actually never came up with a *new* option formula, but only a theoretical economic *argument* built on a new way of "deriving," rather re-deriving, an already existing — and well known formula. The argument, we will see, is extremely fragile to assumptions. The foundations of option hedging and pricing were already far more firmly laid down before them. The Black–Scholes–Merton argument, simply, is that an option can be hedged using a certain methodology called "dynamic hedging" and then turned into a risk-free instrument, as the portfolio would no longer be stochastic.[8] Indeed what Black, Scholes and Merton did was "marketing," finding a way to make a well-known formula palatable to the economics establishment of the time, little else, and in fact distorting its essence.

Such argument requires strange far-fetched assumptions: some liquidity at the level of transactions, knowledge of the probabilities of future events (in a

---

6. Independent Option Trader, London, United Kingdom.
7. NYU Poly, 6 Metrotech Center, Brooklyn, USA
8. Random and variable. — AUTHOR

neoclassical Arrow–Debreu style),[9] and, more critically, a certain mathematical structure that requires "thin-tails," or mild randomness, on which, [more] later. The entire argument is indeed, quite strange and rather inapplicable for someone clinically and observation-driven standing outside conventional neoclassical economics. Simply, the dynamic hedging argument is dangerous in practice as it subjects you to blowups; it makes no sense unless you are concerned with neoclassical economic theory. The Black–Scholes–Merton argument and equation flow a top-down general equilibrium theory, built upon the assumptions of operators working *in full knowledge* of the probability distribution of future outcomes — in addition to a collection of assumptions that . . . are highly invalid mathematically, the main one being the ability to cut the risks using continuous trading which only works in the very narrowly special case of thin-tailed distributions (or, possibly, jumps of a well-known structure). But it is not just these flaws that make it inapplicable: option traders do not "buy theories," particularly speculative general equilibrium ones, which they find too risky for them and extremely lacking in standards of reliability. A normative theory is, simply, not good for decision-making under uncertainty (particularly if it is in chronic disagreement with empirical evidence). Operators may take decisions based on heuristics under the impression of using speculative theories, but avoid the fragility of theories in running their risks.

Yet professional traders, including, initially, the authors (and, alas, the Swedish Academy of Science) have operated under the illusion that it was the Black–Scholes–Merton "formula" they actually used — we were told so. This myth has been progressively reinforced in the literature and in business schools, as the original sources have been lost or frowned upon as "anecdotal" (Merton, 1992). [S]imple random jumps represent too large a share of the variability of returns to make the Black-Schole-Merton argument scientifically acceptable — the Swedish Academy does not grant the Nobel in Medicine to works that are grounded in the assumption that men were mice . . .
There are indeed two myths:

- That we had to wait for the Black–Scholes–Merton options formula to trade the product, price options, and manage option books. In fact the introduction of the Black, Scholes and Merton argument increased our risks and set us back in risk management. More generally, it is a myth that traders rely on theories, even less a general equilibrium theory, to price options.
- That we "use" the Black–Scholes–Merton options "pricing formula." We simply don't.

In our discussion of these myths we will focus on the bottom-up literature on option theory that has been hidden in the dark recesses of libraries. And that

---

9. Of all the misplaced assumptions of Black–Scholes that cause it to be a mere thought experiment, though an extremely elegant one, a flaw shared with modern portfolio theory, is the certain knowledge of future delivered variance for the random variable (or, equivalently, all the future probabilities). This is what makes it clash with practice — the rectification by the market fattening the tails is a negation of the Black–Scholes thought experiment.

addresses only recorded matters — not the actual practice of option trading that has been lost.

It is assumed that the Black–Scholes–Merton theory is what made it possible for option traders to calculate their delta hedge (against the underlying) and to price options. This argument is highly debatable, both historically and analytically.

Options had been actively trading at least in 1600 as described by De La Vega (1688) — implying some form of *technë*; a heuristic method to price them and deal with their exposure. De La Vega describes option trading in the Netherlands, indicating that operators had some expertise in option pricing and hedging. He diffusely points to put-call parity, and his book was not even meant to teach people about the technicalities in option trading. De Pinto (1771) even more explicitly points out how to convert call options into put options. Our insistence on the use of put-call parity is critical for the following reason: the Black–Scholes–Merton's claim to fame is removing the necessity of a risk-based drift from the underlying security — to make the trade "risk-neutral." But one does not need dynamic hedging for that: simple put-call parity can suffice (Derman and Taleb, 2005), as we will discuss later. And yet it is this central removal of the "risk-premium" that apparently was behind the decision by the Nobel committee to grant Merton and Scholes the (then called) Bank of Sweden Prize in Honor of Alfred Nobel: "Black, Merton and Scholes made a vital contribution by *showing* that it is in fact not necessary to use any risk premium when valuing an option. This does not mean that the risk premium disappears; instead it is already included in the stock price." It is for having removed the effect of the drift on the value of the option, *using a thought experiment*, that their work was originally cited, something that was mechanically present by any form of trading and converting using far simpler techniques.

Options have a much richer history than shown in the conventional literature. Forward contracts seems to date all the way back to Mesopotamian clay tablets dating all the way back to 1750 B.C. Gelderblom and Jonker (2005) show that Amsterdam grain dealers had already used options and forward in 1550 (but Amsterdam is not the earliest, as even more sources document even earlier uses in Europe).

In the late 1800s and the early 1900s there were active option markets in London and New York as well as in Paris and several other European exchanges. Markets it seems, were active and extremely sophisticated option markets in 1870. Kairys and Valerio (1997) discuss the market for equity options in USA in the 1870s, indirectly showing that traders were sophisticated enough to price for tail events . . .

When Cyrus Field finally succeeded in joining Europe and America by cable in 1866, intercontinental arbitrage was made possible. Although American securities had been purchased in considerable volume abroad after 1800, the lack of quick communication placed a definite limit on the amount of active trading in securities between London and New York markets (see Weinstein, 1931). Furthermore, one extant source, Nelson (1904), speaks volumes: an option trader and arbitrageur, S.A. Nelson published a book "The A B C of Options and Arbitrage" based on his observations around the turn of the twentieth century. The author states that up to 500 messages per hour and typically 2000–3000 messages per day were sent between the London and the

New York market through the cable companies. Each message was transmitted over the wire system in less than a minute. In a heuristic method that was repeated in *Dynamic Hedging* by one of the authors (Taleb, 1997), Nelson describes in a theory-free way many rigorously clinical aspects of his arbitrage business: the cost of shipping shares, the cost of insuring shares, interest expenses, the possibilities to switch shares directly between someone being long securities in New York and short in London and in this way saving shipping and insurance costs, as well as many more similar tricks . . .

Herbert Filer was another option trader that was active from 1919 to the 1960s. Filer (1959) describes what must be considered a reasonable active option market in New York and Europe in the early 1920s and 1930s. Due to World War II, there was no trading on European Exchanges; the London markets did not resume until 1958. Since in the early 1900s, option traders in London were considered to be the most sophisticated, according to Nelson, it could well be that World War II and the subsequent shutdown of option trading for many years was the reason known robust arbitrage principles about options were forgotten and almost lost, to be partly re-discovered by finance professors such as Stoll (1969).

The put-call parity in the older literature seems to serve two main purposes:

1. As a pure arbitrage constrain,
2. but also as a tool to create calls out of puts, puts out of calls and straddles out of calls or puts for the purpose of hedging options with options. In other words more than simply arbitrage constraint, but a very important tool to transfer risk between options.

The original descriptions and uses of the put-call parity concept, unlike later theories, consider that supply and demand for options will affect option prices. Even if the Black, Scholes, Merton model in strict theoretical sense is fully consistent with the arbitrage constrain of the put-call parity, the model is actually not consistent with the original invention and use of the put-call parity.

In 1908, Vinzenz Bronzin published a book deriving several option pricing formulas, and a formula very similar to what today is known as the Black–Scholes–Merton formula, see [Hafner and Zimmermann, 2007] and [Hafner and Zimmermann, 2009]. Bronzin based his *risk-neutral* option valuation on robust arbitrage principles such as the put-call parity and the link between the forward price and call and put options — in a way that was rediscovered by Derman and Taleb (2005). Indeed, the put-call parity restriction is sufficient to remove the need to incorporate a future return in the underlying security — it forces the lining up of options to the forward price.

Again, in 1910 Henry Deutsch described put-call parity but in less detail than Higgins and Nelson. In 1961 Reinach again described the put-call parity in quite some detail. Traders at New York stock exchange specializing in using the put-call parity to convert puts into calls or calls into puts was at that time known as Converters, Reinach (1961):

"Although I have no figures to substantiate my claim, I estimate that over 60 per cent of all Calls are made possible by the existence of Converters."

In other words the *Converters* (dealers) who basically operated as market makers were able to operate and hedge most of their risk by "statically" hedging options with options. Reinach wrote that he was an option trader (Converter) and gave examples on how he and his colleagues tended to hedge and arbitrage options against options by taking advantage of options embedded in convertible bonds:

"Writers and traders have figured out other procedures for making profits writing Puts & Calls. Most are too specialized for all but the seasoned professional. One such procedure is the ownership of a convertible bond and then writing of Calls against the stock into which the bonds are convertible. If the stock is called converted and the stock is delivered."

Higgins, Nelson and Reinach all describe the importance of put-call parity and *hedging options with options*. Option traders were in no way helpless in hedging or pricing before the Black–Scholes–Merton formula. As already mentioned static market-neutral delta hedging was described by Higgins and Nelson in 1902 and 1904. Also, Gann (1937) discusses market neutral delta hedging for at-the-money options, but in much less details than Nelson (1904). Gann also indicates some forms of auxiliary dynamic hedging.

Mills (1927) illustrates how jumps and fat tails were present in the literature in the pre-Modern Portfolio Theory days. He writes: "A distribution may depart widely from the Gaussian type because the influence of one or two extreme price changes."

Which brings us to option pricing formulas. The first identifiable one was Bachelier (1900). Sprenkle (1961) extended Bachelier's work to assume lognormal rather than normally distributed asset price. It also avoids discounting (to no significant effect since many markets, particularly the U.S., option premia were paid at expiration) . . .

Now, delta hedging. As already mentioned static market-neutral delta hedging was clearly described by Higgins (1902) and Nelson (1904). Thorp and Kassouf (1967) presented market-neutral static delta hedging in more details, not only for at-the-money options, but for options *with any delta*. In his 1969 paper Thorp in shortly describing market-neutral static delta hedging, also briefly pointed in the direction of some dynamic delta hedging, not as a central pricing device, but a risk-management tool. Filer also points to dynamic hedging of options, but without showing much knowledge about how to calculate the delta. Another "ignored" and "forgotten" text is Bernhard (1970), a book/booklet published in 1970 by Arnold Bernhard & Co. The authors are clearly aware of market-neutral static delta hedging or what they name "balanced hedge" for any level in the strike or asset price. This book has multiple examples of how to buy warrants or convertible bonds and construct a market-neutral delta hedge by shorting the right amount of common shares. Arnold Bernhard & Co also published deltas for a large number of warrants and convertible bonds that they distributed to investors on Wall Street.

Referring to Thorp and Kassouf (1967), Black, Scholes and Merton took the idea of delta hedging one step further, Black and Scholes (1973):

"If the hedge is maintained continuously, then the approximations mentioned above become exact, and the return on the hedged position is completely independent of the change in the value of the stock. In fact, the return on the hedged position becomes certain. This was pointed out to us by Robert Merton."

This may be a brilliant mathematical idea, but option pricing is not mathematical theory.

Just after Black, Scholes and Merton published their papers, Thorp (1973) showed how there could not be risk-neutrality once one moved away from continuous delta hedging. And given that continuous delta hedging was obviously impossible in practice, the paper showed how a similar option formula derived under discrete time delta hedging in the limit (of continuous hedging) was equivalent with the Black, Scholes, Merton model. However, his point was that the continuous time delta hedging of the formula was not correct since continuous hedging is impossible and such hedging is very non-robust . . .

[O]perationally, a price is not quite "valuation." Valuation requires a strong theoretical framework with its corresponding fragility to both assumptions and structure of a model. For traders, a "price" produced to buy an option when one has no knowledge of the probability distribution of the future is not "valuation," but an expedient. Such price could change. Their beliefs do not enter such price. It can also be determined by his inventory.

This distinction is critical: traders are engineers, whether boundedly rational (or even non-interested in any form of probabilistic rationality), they are not privy to informational transparency about the future states of the world and their probabilities. So they do not need a general theory to produce a price . . .

. . . this thought experiment is a distortion: people would not trade options unless they are in the business of trading options, in which case they would need to have a book with offsetting trades. For without offsetting trades, we doubt traders would be able to produce a position beyond a minimum (and negligible) size as dynamic hedging not possible. (Again we are not aware of many non-blownup option traders and institutions who have managed to operate in the vacuum of the Black–Scholes–Merton argument.) It is to the impossibility of such hedging that we turn next.

It assumes, nay, requires all moments of the probability distribution to exist. [But "tail" events are not as rare as modern finance would like to think, leading to the likelihood of "fat" tails, that is, more frequent occurrence of high variance events than Black-Scholes would predict.[10]]

Furthermore, there is sampling error as we have less data for longer periods, hence fewer tail episodes, which give an in-sample illusion of thinner tails. In addition, the point that aggregation thins out the tails does not hold for dynamic hedging — in which the operator depends necessarily on high frequency data and their statistical properties . . .

The mechanics of dynamic hedging are as follows: Assume the risk-free interest rate of 0 with no loss of generality. The canonical Black–Scholes–Merton package consists in selling a call and purchasing shares of stock that provide a

---

10. Tail events refer to purportedly low-probability events that "reside" in the tails (far ends) of a normal distribution (bell curve). — AUTHOR

hedge against instantaneous moves in the security. Thus the portfolio π locally "hedged" against exposure to the first moment . . .

[But given certain real-world conditions] [s]uch policy does not match the call value: the difference remains stochastic (while according to Black Scholes it should shrink). Unless one lives in a fantasy world in which such risk reduction is possible.[11]

Further, there is an inconsistency in the works of Merton making us confused as to what theory finds acceptable: in Merton (1976) he agrees that we can use Bachelier-style option derivation in the presence of jumps and discontinuities — no dynamic hedging — but only when the underlying stock price is uncorrelated to the market. This seems to be an admission that dynamic hedging argument applies only to *some* securities: those that do not jump and are correlated to the market.

It is clear that option traders are not necessarily interested in probability distribution at expiration time — given that this is abstract, even metaphysical for them. In addition to the put-call parity constrains, we can hedge away inventory risk in options with other options. One very important implication of this method is that if you hedge options with options then option pricing will be largely demand and supply based. This is in strong contrast to the Black–Scholes–Merton (1973) theory in which demand and supply for options simply should not affect the price of options. If someone wants to buy more options the market makers can simply manufacture them by dynamic delta hedging that will be a perfect substitute for the option itself.

This raises a critical point: option traders do not "estimate" the odds of rare events by pricing out-of-the-money options. They just respond to supply and demand . . .

[T]here is evidence that while both the Chicago Board Options Exchange and the Black–Scholes–Merton formula came about in 1973, the model was "rarely used by traders" before the 1980s (O'Connell, 2001). When one of the authors (Taleb) became a pit trader in 1992, almost two decades after Black–Scholes–Merton, he was surprised to find that many traders still priced options heuristically . . . without recourse to any formula . . .

We conclude with the following remark. Sadly, all the equations, from the first (Bachelier), to the last pre-Black–Scholes–Merton (Thorp) accommodate a [simpler model]. The notion of explicitly removing the expectation [of the distribution of future outcomes] from the forward was present in Keynes (1924) and later by Blau (1944) — and long a Call short a put of the same strike equals a forward. These simple and effective arbitrage relationships appeared to be well known heuristics in 1904.

One could easily attribute the explosion in option volume to the computer age and the ease of processing transactions, added to the long stretch of peaceful economic growth and absence of hyperinflation. From the evidence (once one removes the propaganda), the development of scholastic finance appears to be an epiphenomenon rather than a cause of option trading. Once again, lecturing birds how to fly does not allow one to take subsequent credit.

---

11. We often hear the misplaced comparison to Newtonian mechanics. It supposedly provided a good approximation until we had relativity. The problem with the comparison is that the thin-tailed distributions are not approximations for fat-tailed ones: there is a deep qualitative difference.

This is why we call the equation Bachelier–Thorp. We have been using it all along and gave it the wrong name, after the wrong method and with attribution to the wrong persons. It does not mean that dynamic hedging is out of the question; it is just not a central part of the pricing paradigm. It led to the writing down of a certain stochastic process that may have its uses, some day, should markets "spiral towards dynamic completeness." But not in the present.

A difficult article, but an important one to remember if you ever find yourself negotiating against or cross-examining a finance professor.

Thus, to understand the pricing of options we need to understand not only the factors that affect price in a Black-Scholes world, but also those factors that affect price in the real world. Most important, an option's price will be greatly affected by the selling broker's ability to hedge the option, which means that supply and demand for a particular option, and the broker's assessment of the risks of its hedging strategy, will be important, too.

Returning to the Black-Scholes world, the formula provides that the following issues affect option price in the following ways:

		Call	Put
1.	Asset price	+	−
2.	Exercise price	−	+
3.	Interest rate	+	−
4.	Volatility in the asset price	+	+
5.	Expiration date	+	+

That is, rising asset prices increase the value of the call, and decrease the value of a put. Hopefully that is self-evident.

The other factors might be less intuitive, but think about them and be prepared to discuss in class why it might be that volatility, for example, is good for both types of option holder.

SECURITIES AND EXCHANGE COMMISSION (S.E.C.) IN THE MATTER OF DAVID J. LUBBEN, RESPONDENT

Administrative Proceeding File No. 3–13374
February 19, 2009
17 C.F.R.230; 240

ORDER INSTITUTING ADMINISTRATIVE PROCEEDINGS PURSUANT TO RULE 102(E) OF THE COMMISSION'S RULES OF PRACTICE, MAKING FINDINGS, AND IMPOSING REMEDIAL SANCTIONS

I.

The Securities and Exchange Commission ("Commission") deems it appropriate and in the public interest that public administrative proceedings be, and hereby are, instituted against David J. Lubben ("Respondent" or "Lubben") pursuant to Rule 102(e)(3)(i) of the Commission's Rules of Practice.[12]

II.

In anticipation of the institution of these proceedings, Respondent has submitted an Offer of Settlement (the "Offer") which the Commission has determined to accept. Solely for the purpose of these proceedings and any other proceedings brought by or on behalf of the Commission, or to which the Commission is a party, and without admitting or denying the findings herein, except as to the Commission's jurisdiction over him and the subject matter of these proceedings, and the findings contained in Section III. 3. below, which are admitted, Respondent consents to the entry of this Order Instituting Administrative Proceedings Pursuant to Rule 102(e) of the Commission's Rules of Practice, Making Findings, and Imposing Remedial Sanctions ("Order"), as set forth below.

III.

On the basis of this Order and Respondent's Offer, the Commission finds that:

1. Lubben, age fifty-six (56), is and has been an attorney licensed to practice in the State of Minnesota. From 1996 until late 2006, he served as General Counsel to UnitedHealth Group Inc. ("UnitedHealth").
2. UnitedHealth is and was, at all relevant times, a Minnesota corporation with its principal place of business in Minnetonka, Minnesota. United-Health is a diversified health and well-being company offering a variety of insurance and other products and services to approximately 70 million individuals through six operating businesses. UnitedHealth's securities are registered with the Commission pursuant to Section 12(b) of the Securities Exchange Act of 1934 ("Exchange Act") and are listed on the New York Stock Exchange.
3. On January 23, 2009, a final judgment was entered against Respondent in the civil action entitled *Securities and Exchange Commission v. David J. Lubben*, 08-cv-6454, in the United States District Court for the District of Minnesota. The final judgment permanently enjoined Lubben from future violations of Section 17(a) of the Securities Act of 1933 ("Securities Act") and Sections 10(b), 13(b)(5), 14(a) and 16(a) of the Exchange Act

---

12. Rule 102(e)(3)(i) provides, in relevant part, that:

The Commission, with due regard to the public interest and without preliminary hearing, may, by order, . . . suspend from appearing or practicing before it any attorney . . . who has been by name: (A) permanently enjoined by any court of competent jurisdiction, by reason of his or her misconduct in an action brought by the Commission, from violating or aiding and abetting the violation of any provision of the Federal securities laws or of the rules and regulations thereunder.

and Rules 10b-5, 13b2–1, 14a-9 and 16a-3 thereunder, and from aiding and abetting violations of Sections 13(a), 13(b)(2)(A), 13(b)(2)(B) and 16(a) of the Exchange Act and Rules 12b-20, 13a-1, 13a-11, 13a-13 and 16a-3 thereunder. The final judgment also ordered that Lubben is liable for $1,403,310 in disgorgement, plus $347,211 in prejudgment interest, and a $575,000 civil money penalty.

4. The Commission's complaint alleged, among other things, that Lubben participated in a stock options backdating scheme at UnitedHealth, in which hindsight was used to pick advantageous grant dates for the Company's nonqualified stock options, which dates corresponded to dates of historically low annual or quarterly closing prices for UnitedHealth's common stock. The complaint further alleged that various individuals, including Lubben or others acting at his direction, created false or misleading Company records indicating that the grants had occurred on the earlier dates when the Company's stock price had been at a low. According to the complaint, because of the undisclosed backdating, for fiscal years 1996 through 2005, UnitedHealth filed with the Commission and disseminated to investors quarterly and annual reports, proxy statements and registration statements that Lubben knew, or was reckless in not knowing, contained or incorporated by reference materially false and misleading statements pertaining to the true grant dates of UnitedHealth options and materially false and misleading financial statements, which underreported compensation expenses. In addition, the complaint alleged that Lubben received and exercised backdated options on shares of UnitedHealth stock, and thus personally benefited from the backdating.

IV.

In view of the foregoing, the Commission deems it appropriate and in the public interest to impose the sanction agreed to in Respondent Lubben's Offer.

Accordingly, it is hereby ORDERED, effective immediately, that:

Lubben is suspended from appearing or practicing before the Commission as an attorney for three (3) years. Furthermore, before appearing and resuming practice before the Commission, Lubben must submit an affidavit to the Commission's Office of General Counsel truthfully stating, under penalty of perjury, that he has complied with the Order; that he is not the subject of any suspension or disbarment as an attorney by a court of the United States or of any state, territory, district, commonwealth, or possession; and that he has not been convicted of a felony or misdemeanor involving moral turpitude as set forth in Rule 102(e)(2) of the Commission's Rules of Practice.

By the Commission.
Elizabeth M. Murphy
Secretary

What was the point of the conduct alleged in paragraph 4?

4. CONVERTIBLES

Convertible securities are stocks or bonds that have an option to convert built into them. Typically the securities are preferred shares or debt that have an option to convert into common shares.

The call option is exercised any time before the instrument either matures or is called. The holder exchanges the debt or preferred shares for common shares at an exchange rate that is set in the instrument.

JEFFERIES CONVERTS KNIGHT PREFERRED, BOOSTING SHARES OUTSTANDING

By Steve Chambers — September 6, 2012, Bloomberg.com[13]

Jefferies Group Inc. (KCG), the New York-based brokerage that helped arrange a $400 million bailout for Knight Capital Group Inc., has converted almost all of the preferred shares it acquired in the transaction to common stock.

The conversion almost doubled the outstanding stock of Knight, which was pushed to the brink of bankruptcy after its computers mistakenly bombarded U.S. markets with share orders on Aug. 1. Almost 182 million common shares were outstanding as of yesterday compared with 97.8 million on Aug. 31, according to data compiled by Bloomberg.

Jefferies helped assemble the group of investors that bought convertible securities representing a 73 percent stake. While the money enabled Jersey City, New Jersey-based Knight to remain solvent, it diluted existing stockholders whose ownership proportion will shrink as the convertibles are exercised.

"It's a moot point from a shareholder perspective, because if you were holding the stock back on July 31 you were diluted," said Chris Allen, an equity analyst at Evercore Partners in New York. "You lost money."

According to the SEC filing, Jefferies converted into common stock about 122,000 of the 125,000 preferred shares it held. The brokerage said it owns 81.25 million Knight common shares, making it the largest shareholder, in a filing with the Securities and Exchange Commission Aug. 30. Richard Khaleel, a spokesman for Jefferies, declined to comment.

CONVERSION ELIGIBLE

Under an agreement between Knight and the investors, the first preferred securities were eligible to be swapped for common on Aug. 13 at $1.50 a share. There were no restrictions on when members of the investor group, which also includes TD Ameritrade Holding Corp., Blackstone Group LP, Getco LLC, Stifel Nicolaus & Co. and Stephens Inc., could sell common shares.

Allen said the conversion doesn't necessarily mean Jefferies is preparing to sell to realize gains, though it gives it the flexibility to do so, he said.

Should Knight's stock trade at $3 a share for 60 trading days, all preferred shares will automatically be converted to common. The stock closed at $2.74 today.

―――――――――――

Assume that Bogartco issues 1 million, 4.5 percent convertible preferred shares priced at $100 per share. The shareholders are entitled to a 4.5 percent dividend before the common shareholders get anything, and they also have priority in liquidation, just like any other preferred share. But if Bogartco's common shares rise, so that the option to purchase common shares by trading in the preferred share goes "into the money," then preferred shareholders have an additional way to earn returns on their investment. For example, if the conversion ratio set forth in the Bogartco preferred shares is five, any price above $20 per share for the common stocks makes the conversion feature valuable.[14]

The same basic idea holds for convertible debt, except that debt typically involves trading in increments of $1,000 — or $5,000 in Europe — in exchange for the common shares.

Both instruments also operate under a kind of floor. That is, once the call option on the debt or preferred shares becomes sufficiently out of the money, you can treat the instrument as a straight bond or preferred stock, because the conversion feature likely will never be exercised.

WILLIAM F. LORENZ V. CSX CORPORATION (FORMERLY CHESSIE SYSTEMS, INC.); THE CHESAPEAKE AND OHIO RAILROAD; THE BALTIMORE AND OHIO RAILROAD COMPANY AND THE CHASE MANHATTAN BANK, N.A.

1 F.3d 1406
United States Court of Appeals, Third Circuit

COWEN, Circuit Judge.
Prior to December 13, 1977, the plaintiffs in these two related actions purchased convertible debentures issued by the defendant Baltimore and Ohio Railroad Company ("B & O"). At that time, 99.63% of the B & O's shares were owned by defendant Chesapeake and Ohio Railroad Company, which in turn was a wholly-owned subsidiary of Chessie Systems, Inc., the corporate predecessor to defendant CSX Corporation ("CSX"). The indenture trustee was defendant Chase Manhattan Bank. Plaintiffs allege that the defendants defrauded them from 1977 to 1986 by failing to disclose material information which would have enabled them to convert their debentures into B & O common stock and receive a lucrative dividend. Plaintiffs appeal the dismissal of their claims for breach of fiduciary duty, breach of the implied covenant of good faith and fair dealing, civil RICO, and violations of section 10(b) and Rule 10b-5 of the Securities Exchange Act of 1934 ("'34 Act"). We will affirm.

14. $100/5 = 20

I. FACTS AND PROCEDURAL HISTORY

The defendants have been involved in litigation against their debentureholders for the past fifteen years in a series of closely related actions. A detailed description of the facts and procedural history can be found in earlier district and circuit court opinions in the *Pittsburgh Terminal Corp./ Guttmann* litigation. *See, e.g., Pittsburgh Terminal Corp. v. Baltimore & Ohio R.R. Co.*, 509 F.Supp. 1002 (W.D.Pa.1981), *aff'd in part, rev'd in part*, 680 F.2d 933 (3d Cir.), *cert. denied*, 459 U.S. 1056, 103 S.Ct. 475, 74 L.Ed.2d 621 (1982); *Pittsburgh Terminal Corp. v. Baltimore & Ohio R.R. Co.*, 824 F.2d 249 (3d Cir.1987) (*PTC IV*). We will recite only those facts which are relevant to these appeals.

The plaintiffs were holders of debentures in the B & O Railroad as of December 13, 1977. The debentures were convertible into B & O common stock at any time before maturing in the year 2010. To avoid Interstate Commerce Commission regulations hindering the development of non-rail assets owned by railroads, B & O devised a plan to segregate its rail and non-rail assets. Non-rail assets were transferred to a wholly owned subsidiary, Mid Allegheny Corporation ("MAC"), and MAC common stock was distributed as a dividend on a share-for-share basis to B & O shareholders. B & O sought to avoid the registration of its shares with the Securities and Exchange Commission ("SEC"), a time-consuming process which would have required appraisals of the transferred assets. Because B & O had few shareholders, the company thought that the SEC would issue a "no-action" letter excusing the registration of MAC stock. This plan would have been foiled if large numbers of B & O debentureholders exercised their conversion option in order to receive the MAC dividend.

To avoid this occurrence, B & O transferred its non-rail assets to MAC on December 13, 1977 and declared the dividend in MAC stock on the same date, without prior notice. As a result, the debentureholders could not convert their shares in time to receive the MAC dividend. Some of the debentureholders brought actions, later consolidated, under section 10(b) of the '34 Act against B & O, C & O, and Chessie Systems.[15] This suit is known as the *PTC/Guttmann* litigation. In 1978 and 1979, B & O and Chase Manhattan Bank entered into a series of letter agreements, whereby B & O agreed that if the *PTC/Guttmann* plaintiffs prevailed or obtained a settlement, debentureholders would be allowed to participate equally in that judgment or settlement regardless of whether they had converted their debentures.

The *PTC/Guttmann* plaintiffs moved for class certification. The district court denied the motion, at least in part because Chessie Systems' general counsel, Robert F. Hochwarth, filed an affidavit dated May 2, 1980 memorializing the earlier letter agreements with Chase Manhattan Bank. The affidavit, known as the "Hochwarth Stipulation," states that if plaintiffs prevail or a settlement is reached, "all holders of debentures as of December 13, 1977, whether or not they were subsequently converted, will be permitted to participate in the Court judgment or settlement on the same terms as the plaintiffs." App. at 279.

---

15. Chessie Systems later merged into defendant CSX Corporation.

After a bench trial, the district court entered judgment in favor of the defendants. *Pittsburgh Terminal Corp.*, 509 F.Supp. at 1017–18. We reversed. A divided panel agreed only that the failure to provide the debentureholders with advance notice of the dividend violated Rule 10b-17 of the '34 Act. *Pittsburgh Terminal Corp. v. Baltimore & Ohio R.R. Co.*, 680 F.2d 933, 941–42 (3d Cir.) (*PTC II*), *cert. denied*, 459 U.S. 1056, 103 S.Ct. 475, 74 L.Ed.2d 621 (1982); *id.* at 945–46 (Garth, J., concurring in part and concurring in the judgment). We remanded to the district court to fashion an appropriate remedy. On May 8, 1984, the district court granted plaintiffs the opportunity to convert their debentures into shares and receive the MAC dividend plus dividend income accruing since December 13, 1977. *Pittsburgh Terminal Corp. v. Baltimore & Ohio R.R. Co.*, 586 F.Supp. 1297, 1304–05 (W.D.Pa.1984), *aff'd*, 760 F.2d 257 (3d Cir.), *cert. denied*, 474 U.S. 919, 106 S.Ct. 247, 88 L.Ed.2d 256 (1985). The district court, construing the Hochwarth Stipulation, described the scope of the remedy:

> The remedy ordered here is limited to those persons who owned the subject debentures at the time of the violation, December 13, 1977, and who still own those debentures. Those persons who owned debentures on December 13, 1977 and subsequently converted to B & O common stock may also elect to participate in this remedy, obtaining MAC and its dividends, offset by interest accruing on the debentures after December 13, 1977. . . . Those persons who owned B & O debentures on December 13, 1977 and subsequently sold their debentures are not within the scope of . . . this action. . . .

Id. at 1305. The defendants were ordered to give notice to the debentureholders of the district court's order. In December of 1986, after the denial of certiorari, defendants published notice of the remedy in the *New York Times* and *Wall Street Journal*. In a subsequent appeal, we held that under the terms of the Hochwarth Stipulation, the district court's remedy also included persons who held B & O debentures on December 13, 1977, converted them to B & O common stock, and subsequently sold the stock. *PTC IV*, 824 F.2d at 256.

The plaintiffs in the present actions are those persons who are outside the scope of the *PTC/Guttmann* remedy. They held debentures on December 13, 1977 but subsequently sold them without having ever converted them into stock. On July 25, 1986, plaintiff Ethel B. Savin filed her complaint in the United States District Court for the Southern District of New York on behalf of a class of similarly situated former B & O debentureholders. The case was transferred to the Western District of Pennsylvania because of the related litigation there. On April 23, 1987, the *Lorenz* plaintiffs filed their complaint in the United States District Court for the Western District of Pennsylvania on behalf of a class of similarly situated former B & O debentureholders. The complaint alleged . . . breach of fiduciary duty.

In July of 1987, the defendants moved to dismiss under Fed.R.Civ.P. 12(b)(6).

On November 3, 1992, the district court dismissed *Savin* for the reasons stated in its *Lorenz* opinion of August 18. Plaintiffs filed these appeals.

We accept all factual allegations in the complaints and all reasonable inferences to be drawn therefrom in the light most favorable to the plaintiffs. We may affirm only if it is certain that no relief could be granted under any set of facts which could be proven.

IV. BREACH OF IMPLIED COVENANT OF GOOD FAITH AND FAIR DEALING CLAIMS AGAINST DEFENDANT CHASE MANHATTAN BANK

The district court dismissed plaintiffs' claims against the indenture trustee Chase Manhattan Bank for breach of the implied covenant of good faith and fair dealing, allegedly arising from the bank's failure to inform them of the MAC dividend, the letter agreements with B & O, and the *PTC/Guttmann* judgment. Because the indenture specifies that the liability of the trustee shall be determined under New York law, we will apply New York law.

The courts of New York consistently have held that the duties of an indenture trustee, unlike those of a typical trustee, are defined exclusively by the terms of the indenture. The sole exception to this rule is that the indenture trustee must avoid conflicts of interest with the debentureholders.

The plaintiffs specifically claim that Chase Manhattan Bank violated the implied covenant of good faith and fair dealing which, under New York law, is contained in every contract. The implied covenant prohibits either party from doing anything which would prevent the other party from receiving the fruits of the contract. The covenant, however, cannot be used to insert new terms that were not bargained for. A covenant is implied only when it is consistent with the express terms of the contract.

An indenture is, of course, a contract. Unless the indenture trustee has deprived the debentureholders of a right or benefit specifically provided to them in the indenture, there is no violation of the implied covenant of good faith and fair dealing. *cf. Metropolitan Life Ins. Co. v. RJR Nabisco, Inc.*, 716 F.Supp. 1504, 1517–22 (S.D.N.Y.1989) (no breach of implied covenant under New York law where corporation's incurrence of debt to fund leveraged buyout depleted the value of its debentures, as the indenture lacked any terms prohibiting the transaction). We therefore will consider whether the indenture in this case contains provisions which entitled the debentureholders to receive notice of the MAC dividend, the letter agreements with B & O, or any of the remedies in the *PTC/Guttmann* action.

The indenture contains no provisions which explicitly require the trustee to provide notice of any kind to the debentureholders. Plaintiffs cite two provisions which they claim implicitly require notice. First, the indenture states:

> The Indenture permits the amendment thereof and the modification or alteration, in any respect, of the rights and obligations of the Company and the rights of the holders of the Debentures . . . at any time by the concurrent action of the Company and of the holders of 66 ⅔% in principal amount of the Debentures then outstanding affected by such amendment, modification or alteration (including, in the case of a modification of the terms of conversion of this Debenture into common stock of the Company or of payment of the principal of, or the premium or interest on, this Debenture, the consent of the holder hereof), all as more fully provided in the Indenture.

Plaintiffs claim that the letter agreements between B & O and Chase Manhattan Bank altered their rights under the Indenture. Those agreements provided that the debentureholders would be allowed to participate equally in any judgment against B & O or any settlement regardless of whether they converted their debentures to common stock. Because the quoted language gives the debentureholders the right to vote regarding any change in their or the company's rights and obligations under the indenture, the plaintiffs argue that they were entitled to notice of the letter agreements.

Second, the indenture provides:

> At any meeting at which there shall be a quorum the holders of the Affected Debentures shall have the power by resolution adopted as hereinafter provided:
> (*a*) to authorize the Trustee to join with the Company in making any modification, alteration, repeal of or addition to any provision of this Indenture or of the Debentures, and any modification of or addition to the rights and obligations of the Company or the rights of the holders of the Debentures . . . under this Indenture or under the Debentures. . . .

The plaintiffs claim that the letter agreements between B & O and Chase Manhattan Bank were supplemental indentures which modified or added to their rights under the indenture. Because the debentureholders have the right to vote on whether to permit the indenture trustee and company to execute a supplemental indenture, the plaintiffs argue that they were entitled to notice.

Both provisions cited by plaintiffs provide debentureholders with the right to vote, and arguably therefore to receive notice, only if there is some modification of the debentureholders' rights or the company's obligations under the indenture. We agree with the district court that the letter agreements did not affect their rights under the indenture and cannot be characterized as supplemental indentures. The agreements pertained only to the scope of a possible remedy under the federal securities laws in the *PTC/Guttmann* litigation, in the event of a judgment against the defendant corporations or a settlement. The plaintiffs' contractual rights under the indenture itself, including rights regarding conversion of shares, were never modified.

It would have been advantageous for the plaintiffs to have been informed of the letter agreements and thus of potential violations of securities laws committed by B & O. They may have sued the defendant corporations years earlier. However, so long as an indenture trustee fulfills its obligations under the express terms of the indenture, it owes the debentureholders no additional, implicit duties or obligations, except to avoid conflicts of interest. There is no provision in the indenture which obligated the trustee Chase Manhattan Bank to inform the debentureholders that they possibly had rights against B & O and its parent companies under the federal securities laws. Because the bank did not deprive the plaintiff of any right under the indenture, the bank could not have breached the implied covenant of good faith and fair dealing.

In the present case . . . the indenture does not have any provision which required the bank to provide notice regarding B & O's alleged violations of securities laws and the resulting litigation. To infer such a requirement would, in effect, add a new term to the indenture, and the implied covenant can never be used for that purpose. The district court correctly dismissed the claims against Chase Manhattan Bank for breach of the implied covenant of good faith and fair dealing.

V. Breach of Fiduciary Duty Claims Against Defendants CSX and C & O

Plaintiffs claim that defendants CSX and C & O, as controlling shareholders of B & O, breached a fiduciary duty to disclose material information. The district court concluded that the defendants owed no duties to the plaintiff debenture-holders aside from those specified in the indenture. Finding no breach of the indenture, the district court dismissed the breach of fiduciary duty claims.

It is well-established that a corporation does not have a fiduciary relationship with its debt security holders, as with its shareholders. The relationship between a corporation and its debentureholders is contractual in nature. Just as an indenture trustee's duties are strictly defined by the indenture, a corporation is under no duty to act for the benefit of its debentureholders, or to refrain from action which dilutes their interest, except as provided in the indenture. *Parkinson v. West End St. Ry. Co.*, 173 Mass. 446, 448, 53 N.E. 891, 892 (1899) (Holmes, J.). Even if the debentures are convertible, the debentureholder is merely a creditor who is owed no fiduciary duty until conversion takes place.

As we stated in Part IV *supra* with respect to the indenture trustee's liability, the indenture contains no provisions which entitled the debentureholders to receive notice of the Hochwarth Stipulation, the letter agreements between B & O and Chase Manhattan Bank, or events in the *PTC/Guttmann* litigation. Plaintiffs have not identified, nor have we found, any additional provisions which impose upon B & O or its controlling shareholders a duty to disclose such information. The district court, therefore, correctly dismissed the breach of fiduciary duty claims.

PROBLEM SET 17.3

1. Compare the opinion above to an earlier opinion involving the same bonds:

> Whatever may be the fiduciary duty of majority stockholders and corporate directors under Maryland law to general unsecured creditors, we are here dealing with securities having an equity option feature. Maryland follows the settled rule that a control stockholder owes a fiduciary obligation not to exercise that control to the disadvantage of minority equity partici-pants. . . . Similarly, Maryland directors must act as fiduciaries to all equity participants. Although no Maryland case has been called to our attention presenting the precise issue of fiduciary obligations to holders of securities containing stock options, we would be very much surprised if Maryland or any other state would today hold that no such obligations were owed by an issuer of such securities and its directors.

Pittsburgh Terminal Corp. v. Baltimore & Ohio R. Co., 680 F.2d 933, 941 (3d Cir. 1982). Notably, only Judge Gibbons joined in this part of the opinion.

Which is the better rule?

The opinion excerpted above, rather than Judge Gibbons's, probably reflects the majority approach. *E.g.*, Pittelman v. Pearce, 6 Cal. App. 4th 1436, 1444, 8 Cal. Rptr. 2d 359, 364 (1992) (decided under California law, but holding that there was no difference with Delaware law).

2. Sophisticated investors often purchase convertible bonds as a convertible arbitrage strategy (simultaneous purchase of a company's convertible bond and shorting of the company's stock). How could that work?

5. "DEATH SPIRAL" CONVERTIBLES

As the next case indicates, convertibles are not always the staid investments we have covered thus far.

LOG ON AMERICA, INC., PLAINTIFF, v. PROMETHEAN ASSET MANAGEMENT L.L.C., HFTP INVESTMENT L.L.C., FISHER CAPITAL LTD., WINGATE CAPITAL LTD., CITADEL LIMITED PARTNERSHIP, AND MARSHALL CAPITAL MANAGEMENT, INC., DEFENDANTS

223 F.Supp.2d 435
United States District Court, S.D. New York
No. 00 Civ. 6218(RMB) I Dec. 10, 2001

BERMAN, District Judge.

On or about August 18, 2000, Plaintiff Log On America, Inc. ("Plaintiff" or "LOA") filed this action against defendants Promethean Asset Management L.L.C. ("Promethean") and HFTP Investment L.L.C. ("HFTP" and, together with Promethean, the "Promethean Defendants"); Fisher Capital Ltd. ("Fisher"), Wingate Capital Ltd. ("Wingate") and Citadel Limited Partnership ("Citadel" and, together with Fisher and Wingate, the "Citadel Defendants"); and Marshall Capital Management, Inc. ("Marshall") (the Promethean Defendants, the Citadel Defendants and Marshall are collectively, the "Defendants"), asserting claims under the Securities Exchange Act of 1934, as amended (the "1934 Act"), specifically Section 10(b), 15 U.S.C. §78j(b), Section 13(d), 15 U.S.C. §78m(d), and Section 16(b), 15 U.S.C. §78p(b); and claims for common law fraud, breach of contract, and breach of the covenants of good faith and fair dealing under New York law. Plaintiff seeks damages, injunctive relief, declaratory relief, rescission, disgorgement, and costs. Defendants now move to dismiss Plaintiff's claims pursuant to Rule 12(b)(6) of the Federal Rules of Civil Procedure ("Fed. R. Civ.P."). For the reasons stated below, Defendants' motion to dismiss is granted.

I. Background

Plaintiff is a Delaware corporation with its principal place of business in Providence, Rhode Island. Plaintiff provides telephone service, high-speed Internet access, and cable programming to homes and businesses throughout the Northeast of the United States.

Defendant HFTP is a limited liability company, organized and doing business in New York, engaged principally in the business of investments and financial services. Defendant Promethean, a New York company, is an affiliate of HFTP and also its investment advisor. Defendants Fisher and Wingate are limited partnerships organized under the laws of the Cayman Islands and have offices in Chicago, Illinois. Fisher and Wingate are venture capital lenders. Defendant Citadel, a limited partnership, is a registered broker-dealer and is the trading manager of both Fisher and Wingate. Defendant Marshall, an Illinois (venture capital) investor corporation doing business in New York, is a wholly-owned subsidiary of Credit Suisse Group and an affiliate of Credit Suisse First Boston Corporation.

On February 23, 2000, LOA entered into the following financial agreements with HFTP, Fisher, Wingate, and Marshall: (i) Securities Purchase Agreement (the "Agreement"); (ii) Registration Rights Agreement ("Registration Agreement"); and (iii) Certificate of Designations, Preferences and Rights of Series A Convertible Preferred Stock of Log On America, Inc. (the "Certificate of Designations") (collectively, the "Transaction Documents"). Under the Transaction Documents, HFTP, Fisher, Wingate, and Marshall (cumulatively) paid to LOA $15 million in exchange for: (i) 15,000 shares of LOA's Series A Convertible Preferred Stock ("Preferred Stock");[16] and (ii) 594,204 warrants (the "Warrants") for the purchase of LOA common shares ("Common Stock").

Plaintiff acknowledged that "its obligation to issue Conversion Shares upon conversion of the Preferred Shares . . . is . . . absolute and unconditional regardless of the dilutive effect that such issuance may have on the ownership interests of other stockholders of [LOA]." The Certificate of Designations contains a "conversion cap" (or "blocker") limiting the beneficial ownership by any holder of Preferred Stock and its affiliates to 4.99% of the total outstanding shares of Plaintiff's common stock.

The Agreement provided that Defendants were acquiring the Preferred Stock and Warrants "for investment only." It did not by its terms constrain Defendants to hold the securities for any minimum period of time . . .

Defendants were granted the right to sell short LOA Common Stock. However, they agreed not to sell short more than 594,204 shares of Common Stock for a certain period of time . . .

Pursuant to the Agreement, Plaintiff was required to file a Registration Statement covering resale of the common stock underlying the Preferred Stock and

---

16. Defendants were granted the right to convert their Preferred Stock into Common Stock at a fixed discount to market at the time of conversion. Plaintiff states that this type of Preferred Stock, which is based on a "floating" conversion ratio, is known as "floorless convertible," "toxic convertible," or "death spiral convertible." According to Plaintiff, the lower the market price of the common stock at the time of conversion, the greater the number of shares Defendants would receive upon conversion of Preferred Stock.

Warrants and to request the Securities and Exchange Commission ("SEC") to declare the Registration Statement effective "as soon as practicable, but in no event later than 180 days after [February 23, 2000]." Plaintiff filed a Registration Statement with the SEC on or about April 26, 2000 to register shares of Common Stock on behalf of the holders of Preferred Stock, but the Registration Statement was not declared effective before the 180 day period expired on August 21, 2000.

Plaintiff alleges in the instant Complaint that Defendants "wrongfully utilized 'floorless' convertible stocks . . . to launch an unlawful scheme to 'short sell' Plaintiff's stock in sufficient volume to drive down its price knowing that they would be in a position to cover the short sales by converting their preferred stock at depressed market prices." Plaintiff maintains that Defendants violated the Federal Securities Laws and breached the terms of the Transaction Documents by artificially manipulating the market prices of LOA's common stock through massive and unlawful short sales while in possession of material non-public information concerning LOA's business."

Defendants state that "[t]he fundamental problem with Plaintiff's claims is that short selling was expressly contemplated and authorized under the Agreement" and that "what Plaintiff is really complaining of here is not fraud or breach of contract, but of having to live up to its obligations under the Agreement." "Indeed, Plaintiff admitted in its Registration Statement that the holders of Preferred Stock could engage in short sales as a legitimate hedging strategy."

1.   MISREPRESENTATION

Plaintiff alleges that Defendants' conduct was "manipulative" and "fraudulent" because it was allegedly contrary to written representations that Defendants would not engage in short sales and that they would hold the Preferred Stock as a long-term investment. The Court finds that these misrepresentation claims as currently stated are inadequate.

To maintain a misrepresentation claim under Section 10(b) of the 1934 Act and Rule 10b–5, "a plaintiff must plead that in connection with the purchase or sale of securities, the defendant, acting with scienter, made a false representation or omitted to disclose material information and that the plaintiff's reliance on the defendant's action caused the plaintiff injury."

Short Sales

Section 4(*o*) of the Agreement explicitly authorizes Defendants to make short sales of up to 594,204 shares of Common Stock. **"[E]ach Buyer and its Affiliates are entitled to engage in transactions which constitute Short Sales to the extent that following such transaction the aggregate net short position of such Buyer and its Affiliates does not exceed . . . the number of shares of Common Stock equal to the aggregate number of Warrant Shares which such Buyer and its Affiliates have the right to acquire upon exercise of the Warrants held by such Buyer and its Affiliates (without regard to limitations on exercises of the Warrants)."** (emphasis added). Plaintiff contends that this "'carve out,' upon which Defendants rely [for the right to sell short] never 'matured'" because "the Warrants were never 'in the money.'" Plaintiff cites no language in the

Agreement in support of its position. "[The Agreement] says nothing about being in the money or out of the money."

The Court finds that the language in Section 4(o) is plain and unambiguous. It authorizes the very activity Plaintiff says is impermissible, namely short sales. Plaintiff's interpretation, as noted by Defendants, "would strain the contract language beyond its reasonable and ordinary meaning."

Investment Intent

The Agreement (itself) makes clear that while they were purchasing for investment, Defendants were not obligated to hold the Preferred Stock for any specified period of time. **"[B]y making the representations herein, such Buyer does not agree to hold any of the securities for any minimum or other specific term and reserves the right to dispose of the securities at any time in accordance with or pursuant to a registration statement or an exemption under the 1933 Act."** (emphasis added). It is difficult to ascertain the basis for a misrepresentation claim upon the instant conclusory pleadings as to investment intent.

2. MARKET MANIPULATION

Preliminarily, the Court addresses Defendants' challenge to Plaintiff's "standing." Under Section 10(b) of the 1934 Act or Rule 10-b, a plaintiff must be a purchaser or seller of securities. *See Blue Chip Stamps*, 421 U.S. at 730–31, 95 S.Ct. 1917.18 In *Global Intellicom v. Thomson Kernaghan & Co.*, United States District Court Judge Denise J. Cote confronted a similar standing challenge and determined that the plaintiff (there) was neither a purchaser nor a seller: "[Plaintiff] has no standing to bring such a claim since it does not allege that it purchased or sold securities in connection with the alleged manipulation." *Global Intellicom*, 1999 WL 544708, at *9.

LOA does not here allege to have acted as a purchaser or seller with respect to the securities allegedly sold short by Defendants, apart from its view that the conversion feature of the Preferred Stock qualifies as a contract for the purchase or sale of a security. Neither *Pittsburgh Terminal* nor *FS Photo* stands for the proposition that the sale of a convertible security provides an issuer with standing to challenge the kinds of activity alleged here. *See Pittsburgh Terminal*, 680 F.2d at 938–40; *FS Photo*, 61 F.Supp.2d at 478.

C. COMMON LAW FRAUD

To support a claim of fraud where, as here, a contract exists, a plaintiff must either: "(i) demonstrate a legal duty separate from the duty to perform under the contract; or (ii) demonstrate a fraudulent misrepresentation collateral or extraneous to the contract; or (iii) seek special damages that are caused by the misrepresentations and unrecoverable as contract damages."

Plaintiff's (fraud) claim meets none of these requirements. First, no (fiduciary) duty, according to the Agreement, existed between LOA and Defendants apart from the duty to perform pursuant to the Agreement as reflected in the pleadings. Second, each of the misrepresentations alleged in the Complaint

is based upon the Securities Purchase Agreement. Plaintiff's conclusory assertion that "Defendants fail[ed] to disclose information concerning Defendants'
true intent," without more, does not adequately specify the requisite fraudulent
conduct. *See* Fed.R.Civ.P. 9(b).

D.   BREACH OF CONTRACT

LOA asserts that "Defendants are in material breach of the ['Investment
Purpose' and 'Restriction on Short Sales'] provisions contained in the Securities
Purchase Agreement." Defendants counter that: (i) Plaintiff has failed to allege
breach; and (ii) Plaintiff has failed to allege its own performance.

To state a breach of contract claim under New York law, a complaint must
allege "(1) the existence of an agreement, (2) adequate performance of the
contract by the plaintiff, (3) breach of contract by the defendant, and
(4) damages." For the reasons already discussed *supra*, the Court finds that
Plaintiff has failed sufficiently to plead that Defendants' alleged conduct
breached the provision(s) of the Agreement.

F.   DECLARATORY RELIEF AND RESCISSION

Plaintiff seeks declarations under both Section 29(b) of the 1934 Act, 15
U.S.C. §78cc(b), and the Declaratory Judgment Act, 28 U.S.C. §2201 that,
because of Defendants' alleged fraudulent conduct, Plaintiff is relieved of its
obligations and liabilities under the Transaction Documents. "By reason of the
fraud, illegality and manipulative conduct . . . LOA is entitled to a declaration
that . . . it is relieved of its obligations and liabilities under the [Transaction
Documents] and that the Defendants have no right to have their Convertible
Preferred Stock exchanged for LOA common stock." Plaintiff also seeks rescission of the Securities Purchase Agreement "by reason of the fraud, illegality and
manipulative conduct. . . ." Defendants assert that declaratory relief is unwarranted because the claims "are premised upon inadequate allegations of fraud,
breach of contract and Sections 13(d) and 16(b) violations." Defendants also
contend that the claim for rescission must be dismissed because Plaintiff has not
alleged actionable (securities) fraud.

To establish a violation under Section 29(b) of the 1934 Act, a plaintiff must
"show that (1) the contract involved a prohibited transaction, (2) he is in contractual privity with the defendant, and (3) he is in the class of persons the
[1934] Act was designed to protect." The Court finds that Plaintiff has not
adequately pled these requirements. Specifically, because the underlying claims
have been dismissed, Plaintiff has not (sufficiently) alleged that the Agreement
involved a "prohibited transaction."

IV.   CONCLUSION

For the foregoing reasons, Defendants' motion to dismiss is granted as to all
claims without prejudice.

PROBLEM SET 17.4

1. How, precisely, do the short selling allegations connect with the "death spiral convertibles?"
2. Why did LOA enter into this agreement in the first instance?
3. Why do convertibles exist at all? How might convertible debt different from straight debt of comparable maturities? Would you pay more or less for the conversion feature? *See* William A. Klien, *The Convertible Bond: A Peculiar Package*, 123 U. Pa. L. Rev. 547, 555–561 (1975).

18

DERIVATIVES

Derivatives are considered inherently complex instruments, and recent events have done nothing to change that perception. But derivatives remain in widespread use, not only among financial institutions, but also by corporations. Indeed, virtually every corporation of any noteworthy size will have some derivatives on its balance sheet.[1] It is important to remember that, at heart, all derivatives are contracts. Try to keep that in mind if you begin to feel overwhelmed.

Although there is no universal definition of *derivative*, it can be broadly defined as an instrument that derives its value from some other asset or measure, like an index. That primary asset or reference point is referred to as the underlying or the reference asset. For example, the reference asset of an S&P 500 futures contract (described later) is the S&P 500 index.

You have already seen derivatives in Chapter 17, as options clearly meet the definition. Other types of derivatives, like forwards and futures, have been around for more than a century and were designed to allow farmers and merchants to hedge risk stemming from uncertainty and instability of future commodity prices. Exchanges were eventually established to provide a marketplace with standardized contract terms and open price discovery.

The exchanges also created clearinghouses that act as buyer for every contract seller and as seller to every contract buyer, thereby limiting counterparty risk for market participants. The clearinghouse essentially becomes a hub in the middle of all transactions.

The clearinghouse protects itself from the risk of nonperformance by requiring market participants to maintain deposits, called margin. Like a bank that requires a customer to maintain a savings account before obtaining a loan, margin accounts provide a source of recovery for the clearinghouse if a market participant defaults.

But margin is small relative to the size of the trades that market participants are allowed to undertake, which represents one key aspect of the leverage inherent in most derivative trades. We come back to this point in Section 4.

---

1. *See generally* Kimberly D. Krawiec, *Derivatives, Corporate Hedging, and Shareholder Wealth: Modigliani-Miller Forty Years Later*, 1998 U. Ill. L. Rev. 1039 (1998).

In the 1970s, exchanges such as the Chicago Mercantile Exchange, New York Mercantile Exchange, and Chicago Board of Trade expanded beyond their commodity-based instruments to trade derivative contracts based on financial markets, including futures and options on securities indexes and foreign currencies. S&P 500 futures started trading on the Chicago Mercantile Exchange in 1982 and soon their trading volume exceeded that of physical shares.

Advances in computer technology also facilitated rapid expansion of over-the-counter (OTC) derivative markets. OTC derivatives are negotiated between the parties, without an exchange as the intermediary. Unlike exchange-traded derivatives, OTC contracts are not guaranteed by a clearinghouse and involve potentially significant counterparty risk, an issue that came to the fore in the recent financial crisis. In addition, OTC instruments can be more complicated to liquidate, and might require approval from the counterparty in the event of a proposed sale or transfer (called a "novation" in the industry).

Historically OTC swap markets were opaque and transactions were dominated by banks and brokers, who were parties to most trades. But the recently enacted Dodd-Frank Act might change that. In particular, Dodd-Frank does the following:

- Requires as many OTC derivative products as possible to be centrally cleared and traded on exchanges or other trading facilities.
- Subjects OTC swap dealers and major OTC swap participants to registration with either the Commodity Futures Trading Commission (CFTC) or SEC.
- Imposes capital, margin and reporting requirements on OTC swap dealers and large OTC swap participants.
- Requires public reporting of transaction and pricing data on both cleared and uncleared swaps.

Generally, Dodd-Frank contemplates transforming the OTC market for swaps into a market that will bear a strong resemblance to the futures markets, including standardized terms and daily "mark to market" adjustment to cash margin balances.

Following Dodd-Frank, regulation of the OTC derivatives market is divided between the CFTC and the SEC, with the CFTC having jurisdiction over "swaps," and the SEC having jurisdiction over "security-based swaps." A swap is defined to include most types of OTC derivatives, except "security-based swaps" and certain other specified exceptions.[2] A *security-based swap* is defined as a swap that references a security index or a single security or loan.[3]

Although OTC contracts are theoretically customized, most are based on standardized agreements (e.g., the International Swaps and Derivatives Association, Inc. [ISDA] Master Agreement), with individual trade confirmations that provide the customized specifics to the agreement. The basic terms of most deals thus tend to be quite similar.

---

2. 7 U.S.C. §1a(47)(A).
3. 15 U.S.C. §78c(a)(68).

1. FORWARDS AND FUTURES

A *forward* is a contract that obligates each party to the contract to trade an underlying asset at a specified price at a specified date upcoming. In some respects, most of your first-year Contracts class was devoted to forwards — although I bet the professor never used that word. But a contract signed today to buy wheat or widgets in the future, at a price set today, is a forward.

For example, a foreign exchange (FX) forward involves the exchange of one currency for another, on a future date and at a forward price established today. The winners and losers in this deal will be determined by the actual market exchange rate on the future date.

A *future*, which is a specialized kind of forward, is a standardized contract to purchase or sell an underlying asset in the future at a specified price and date. A futures contract is an agreement between two parties: a short position — the party who agrees to sell a commodity — and a long position — the party who agrees to buy a commodity.

Unlike forwards, futures are exchange-traded derivatives. That means that all trades go through the central clearinghouse, which stands in as the short party on one leg of the transaction, and the long party on the other leg of the transaction. If one party fails to perform, the clearinghouse's central position means the other party does not face any counterparty risk. As already noted, when you trade futures contracts you are required to post some margin to back up your performance on the contracts, which reduces the risk to the clearinghouse.

When you hear about trading in gold, rice, pork bellies, oranges, and so on, it is often in the futures market, where everyone trades the exact same contracts. Like a forward, a future involves agreeing to buy or sell something in the future at a price you are fixing today. Unlike a forward, however, physical delivery of that thing is not typically contemplated with a future.

Rather, futures contracts are "cash settled," in that the party on the wrong side of the bet makes a cash payment to make the other party whole, almost like expectation damages in first-year contract law. Unlike the stock market, where you don't really know how much you've gained or lost until you sell, futures positions are settled on a daily basis, which means that gains and losses from a day's market fluctuations are deducted or credited to each side's account every day. That reduces the chance that the "out of the money" party will have to make a massive payment when the future matures.

PROBLEM SET 18.1

1. What benefits are there to standardizing futures contracts?
2. A derivative can provide some information about broader sentiment, which might in turn influence trading in the underlying. Dow Jones Industrial Average futures contracts begin trading on the Chicago Board of Trade at 8:20 a.m. EST, and S&P 500 and Nasdaq 100 futures both open at 8:30 a.m. EST and trade on the Chicago Mercantile Exchange. In all cases this means the futures have been trading for at

least an hour before the NYSE opens. If you have access to international markets, trading in S&P 500 futures begins in Tokyo the evening before the market opens in the United States.

3. There two basic uses for derivatives: hedging and speculating. A hedger faces some sort of exposure to the underlying asset. For example, a farmer might use futures to hedge against changes in the value of her crop, particularly to avoid the risk of large price drops. What type of future position would she take? Of course by doing so, she gives up some of the potential upside if prices rise. A speculator is somebody who is betting on the price of the crop, without any exposure to the underlying. For example, people in $3,000 suits in Chicago and New York typically do not have large fields of growing crops, but they still might buy and sell futures tied to agricultural commodities. There is a vigorous policy debate about whether such traders (a) provide valuable liquidity to derivatives markets or (b) induce excess volatility in commodities markets, which effects food, fuel and other consumer prices. *See http://goo.gl/18KNp*

2. SWAPS

STEPHEN J. LUBBEN, *CREDIT DERIVATIVES AND THE FUTURE OF CHAPTER 11*
81 Am. Bankr. L.J. 405, 408–417 (2007)

A. DERIVATIVES GENERALLY

Financial derivatives are contracts that derive their value from interest rates, the outcome of specific events, or the price of underlying assets such as debt or equities. These contracts have no value in seclusion, but rather derive their value from movements in the value of other more substantive matter. Options, futures, and forwards are all long-recognized types of derivatives.

The heart of the modern derivatives markets was born in the early 1980s with the advent of swap agreements.[4] A swap is a contract between two parties to exchange cash flows at specified intervals. Unlike securities or futures contracts, which are standardized for easy trading on national exchanges, swaps are party-specific bilateral contracts and are thus traded over the counter.

One of the most common swaps is an interest rate swap, where the parties (or "counterparties") agree to exchange a fixed rate cash flow for a floating rate cash flow. The amount of the cash flows is determined by reference to a hypothetical or "notional" amount of money that is never actually exchanged between the parties.

---

4. *See* Bank One Corp. v. Comm'r, 120 T.C. 174, 186 (2003) ("The origin of the swaps market is generally traced to a currency swap negotiated between the World Bank and IBM in 1981. That transaction involved an exchange of payments in Swiss francs for payments in deutschmarks. The first interest rate swap was negotiated with the Student Loan Marketing Association in 1982.").

For example, assume two parties swap a fixed 4% payment for the three-month London Interbank Offered Rate (LIBOR)[5] plus 150 basis points,[6] based on a $100 million notional amount.[7] If LIBOR starts at 2.5% and rises to 5%, the cash flows on this swap look like this:

FIXED owes FLOATING $4 million
FLOATING owes FIXED $6.5 million
FLOATING pays FIXED $2.5 million[8]

By entering into this swap, the fixed rate payer has essentially replaced its interest rate risk with the credit risk of the floating rate payer, perhaps because it has a corresponding $100 million floating rate loan obligation. If the credit exposure issues appear acute, the risks of default are often balanced by posting collateral [i.e., margin], typically in the form of government securities. ISDA estimated that about $1.34 trillion of collateral was in use at the end of 2006.

B. CREDIT DERIVATIVES

Credit derivatives are a class of privately negotiated contracts designed with the express purpose of transferring credit risk from one party to another. As with other derivatives, credit derivatives do not themselves involve a credit relationship, but rather look to the credit consequences of other financial instruments or conditions to find their value.

In June of 2001, the first time the trade group ISDA conducted surveys of credit derivatives, the outstanding notional amount of credit derivatives was just over $631 billion. By June 2005, only four years later, the notional amount of outstanding credit default swaps, the key credit derivative instrument, stood at more than $12 trillion — almost a twenty-fold increase. About forty percent of outstanding credit derivatives are held by national banks, whose holdings are equally split between buyer and seller positions. Emerging market credit derivatives, the newest segment of the market, are expected to exceed $650 billion by this year.

The speedy growth of the credit derivatives market can be seen as a further extension of a larger, ongoing trend toward disaggregation of financial obligations, albeit one that is just now approaching the level of development on the default side that has been seen in the interest rate swap markets for over a

---

5. This is the rate of interest at which banks can borrow funds from other banks in the London interbank market. It is commonly used as a reference floating interest rate in swaps.

6. 0.01% = 1 basis point. Because swaps typically have net present values equal to zero at inception — that is, the swap is balanced and no payment is owing in either direction — the example implies a LIBOR rate of 2.5%. *See* Linda M. Beale, *Book-Tax Conformity and the Corporate Tax Shelter Debate: Assessing the Proposed Section 475 Mark-To-Market Safe Harbor*, 24 Va. Tax Rev. 301, 389–90 (2004).

7. For simplicity, I assume all payments are made annually, but actual practice varies by jurisdiction. In the United States fixed payments are often made semi-annually and floating payments are made quarterly. The numbers in the example also do not take into account date conventions. For example, in the United States many swaps trade under an actual/360 day count convention.

8. Conversely, if the LIBOR rate fell below 2.5%, so that the floating payment was less than 4% in total, FIXED would make payments to FLOATING equal to the difference in the two rates.

decade. While syndication of loans and securitization of receivables have long provided ways for the initial lender to reduce their exposure to the debtor, the subsequent investor still acquires something more than pure credit or default risk, while the initial lender necessarily incurs a corresponding reduction in its claim against the debtor. Credit derivatives, on the other hand, allow for the sale of the default risk of a loan separate from any other element of ownership. In addition, the growth of credit markets has allowed for "shorting" of bonds, something that was often impossible before-hand due to the limited liquidity of the corporate bond markets. Credit derivatives also allow investors an opportunity to invest in debt that trades in foreign markets without bearing currency risk.

As noted, the most important credit derivative instrument is the credit default swap, also known as a single-name credit default swap. This type of swap is a contract covering the risk that a specified debtor defaults. One party (the "protection seller") acquires the credit risk associated with a debt or class of debts in exchange for an annual fee from the counterparty (the "protection buyer"). The debtor on the referenced obligation is not a party to the swap, and in most cases is unaware of the transaction.

If the reference obligation goes into default, the protection buyer receives a payment meant to compensate it for its losses.[9] More specifically, the protection seller's payment obligation is triggered by the occurrence of a "credit event" with regard to a specified class of obligations incurred by the reference entity. Commonly used credit events include "bankruptcy,"[10] "failure to pay,"[11] and "restructuring."[12] Swaps written on sovereign or emerging markets debt add provisions regarding repudiations or debt moratoriums.[13] In the North American and European corporate markets, these events typically must occur with respect to "borrowed money" — effectively any obligation owed to voluntary creditors of the reference entity or its subsidiaries, if the parent guaranteed the subsidiaries' obligations — in excess of the $1 million and $10 million limitations built into the definitions of failure to pay and restructuring, respectively.

[Sometimes] the swap will call for "physical settlement" upon the occurrence of a credit event, meaning that the buyer will deliver a defaulted bond to the

---

9. Whether a credit event has occurred is sometimes subject to dispute, as when Argentina announced a debt exchange in 2001. Eternity Global Master Fund Ltd. v. Morgan Guar. Trust Co., 375 F.3d 168 (2d Cir. 2004); *see also* Stephen J. Choi & G. Mitu Gulati, *Contract as Statute*, 104 Mich. L. Rev. 1129, 1142–44 (2006).

10. ISDA, 2003 ISDA Credit Derivatives Definitions §4.2.

11. *Id.* §4.5. "Failure to Pay" is defined, in part, as the failure of the reference entity to make "payments in an aggregate amount of not less than the Payment Requirement." "Payment Requirement" is a term that the parties can define, but otherwise defaults to obligations of at least $1 million. *Id.* §4.8(d).

12. *Id.* §4.7. The restructuring must relate to debt in excess of the "Default Requirement," which is set at $10 million unless the parties agree otherwise. *Id.* §4.8(a). The definition of restructuring is not uniform among jurisdictions; for example, in the North American corporate market the definition is usually modified — and thus referred to as "Modified Restructuring" — by electing additional limitations on the maturity and transferability of the debt that can be delivered under the swap. *Id.* §2.32; *see also* Frank Packer & Haibin Zhu, *Contractual Terms and CDS Pricing*, Bis Q. Rev. (Mar. 2005) *available at http:// www.bis.org/publ/qtrpdf/r_ qt0503.htm*

13. ISDA, 2003 ISDA Credit Derivatives Definitions §4.6.

seller in exchange for payment of the full face value of the bond. Unlike insurance, credit default swaps do not require proof of actual loss, so the buyer can purchase a bond post-default and deliver it to the seller.[14]

The types of obligations that can be delivered to settle the swap are typically set forth in the documentation, although market practice does tend to give the protection buyer a choice within a range of debt instruments. This gives rise to the so-called "cheapest to deliver" option in a triggered swap; namely, the ability of a buyer to maximize recovery under the swap by purchasing the least valuable debt instrument that will satisfy the contractual provisions of the swap. In the North American and European corporate markets, swaps regularly allow for the delivery of any bond or loan issued by the reference entity, provided that, among other things, the obligation is not subordinated, is not bearer paper, and does not mature more than thirty years from the settlement date.

In a credit default swap transaction, the protection buyer gives up the risk of default by the debtor and takes on the risk of concurrent default by both the protection seller and the underlying debtor. While the risk of mutual default is likely remote, especially given the strong credit quality of many swap dealers, it is not inconceivable that a major corporate default could cause one or two financial institutions severe financial distress. The protection seller takes on the default risk of the debtor, as if it had lent money to the debtor. For this reason, the seller is sometimes described as a "synthetic" lender, albeit a short term lender, as the duration of swaps tends to extend for no more than a few years; whereas, a bond could last twenty or more years.[15]

Because of General Motors' recent financial difficulties, pricing information for its credit default swaps has been readily available. Table 2 illustrates the information conveyed by this new market in a firm's credit prospects. Because prices for long-term coverage are lower than mid-term protection, the market apparently believes that General Motors faces the biggest challenges in the next three or four years, after which the risks apparently moderate. By early 2007, General Motors' prospects had substantially improved, at least in the market's eyes, and five-year CDS spreads had shrunk to just over 330 basis points.

---

14. INSOL International, Credit Derivatives in Restructurings 12 (2006). This might occur if the buyer used the credit default swap to hedge an illiquid debt, such as a bank loan with transfer restrictions, or simply because the buyer was making a speculative bet on the reference debtor's credit worthiness. *Cf.* N.Y. Ins. Law §3401 (McKinney 2007) ("No contract or policy of insurance on property made or issued in this state, or made or issued upon any property in this state, shall be enforceable except for the benefit of some person having an insurable interest in the property insured. In this article, 'insurable interest' shall include any lawful and substantial economic interest in the safety or preservation of property from loss, destruction or pecuniary damage.").

15. According to one industry source, "the most liquid CDS is the five-year contract, followed by the three-year. . . . The fact that a physical asset does not need to be sourced means that it is generally easier to transact in large round sizes with CDS." Dominic O'Kane, et al., Lehman Brothers, The Lehman Brothers Guide to Exotic Credit Derivatives 6 (2003), *available at http://investinginbonds.com/assets/files/LehmanExoticCredDerivs.pdf.*

TABLE 2
General Motors CDS Spreads

Spread Over Risk Free Rate; As of March 30, 2006

	1 Year	2 Year	3 Year	5 Year	7 Year	10 Year
Spread (in basis points)	967.24	1199.32	1145.15	1083.29	1040.54	1012.21

Source: *www.markit.com*

Credit default swaps are used for speculation, hedging credit risk, and as building blocks in creating more complex financial products. For example, a credit default swap can be used to construct a synthetic asset securitization, where the risk of loss is transferred to the special purpose vehicle but all other aspects of ownership remain with the originator.

More recently, credit default swaps have moved from simple, single-name products to swaps that look to groups of reference entities. One product — known as an "nth to default" swap — protects the buyer against the nth default to occur among a group of debtors and then terminates. Similarly, swaps written on indexes give the protection buyer a hedge against a pool of representative debtors with similar credit profiles.

For example, the Dow Jones CDX IG portfolio consists of 125 North American investment grade bond issuers, each equally weighted in the index. Assume a swap written on this index with notional amount of $100 million. Upon a default of a single index element, the protection buyer would deliver bonds with a par value of $800,000 to the protection seller in exchange for a payment of $800,000 in cash.[16] The transaction continues until a predetermined "roll date," when the index is adjusted and reissued with a revised group of 125 issuers. Similar products exist for the foreign and high-yield markets.

The sudden growth of the credit derivative market has exposed several areas of structural underdevelopment, at least two of which are important for present purposes. First, even when it works as described, this market is rather opaque and is arguably not truly a "market" in the conventional sense.

Consisting entirely of privately negotiated bilateral contracts, one of the oft cited benefits of the market is the ability of lenders to hedge or diversify their credit exposure without incurring any relationship costs with respect to the borrower. Recently, however, it has become widely known that many credit default swaps were assigned to new protection buyers without the prior consent of the seller. Under the terms of the ISDA Master Agreement,[17] the prior written

---

16. $800,000 = (1/125)($100 million).

17. Most of the derivatives in the global derivatives market are documented under ISDA documentation. The ISDA Master Agreement, the most current version of which is the 2002 ISDA Master Agreement, is a standard agreement, used in the industry, to provide a set of default terms for a series of derivative transactions between a set of counterparties. A "schedule" is attached to the Master Agreement to account for party-specific terms of the deal. The economic terms of individual derivative transactions are reflected in "confirmation" term sheets, which are deemed to be part of the single Master Agreement between the parties, somewhat like the schedules of equipment used in long-term equipment leases. Each confirmation will incorporate by reference a relevant set of ISDA definitions. In the credit derivatives context, this is typically the 2003 ISDA Credit Derivatives Definitions. Also commonly used are documents related to credit support, which are used when parties are of differing credit quality and provide for the

consent of the other party is required when its counterparty in a trade wishes to assign its position in a trade to a third party. However, this non-conforming practice has apparently been tolerated in the community. Thus, upon a chapter 11 filing, it may not be clear which creditors are protected from losses, even among the parties to swaps. ISDA has moved to address regulatory concerns regarding assignments, so the problem of unauthorized transfers should hopefully disappear from the market. The larger question of which creditors have bought or sold protection will loom large in chapter 11 cases in the future.

Second, the rapid growth of the credit derivatives market has recently led to supply and demand problems upon a default. After the recent chapter 11 filing of automotive parts manufacturer Delphi Automotive, $2 billion of bonds were said to be in circulation when it filed for bankruptcy. However, the notional amount of outstanding derivatives was more than $20 billion, which initially had the explicable, although still strange, effect of driving up the market prices of the bonds just as Delphi filed for chapter 11. ISDA has stepped in to mitigate this problem through a series of "protocols," which were successfully deployed in not only the Delphi case but also in connection with other recent chapter 11 cases. Essentially, these protocols use an auction mechanism to set a price for the debtor's bonds, and then use that price to allow settlement of index credit default swaps without need for actual delivery of bonds.[18] Removing index swaps from the mix reduces but does not eliminate the supply and demand effects on the bond markets.

In recent years most CDS contracts, of all types, have moved to cash settlement.

U.S. COMPANY CREDIT-DEFAULT SWAPS DECLINE AFTER BERNANKE SPEECH

By Mary Childs on August 31, 2012, businessweek.com[19]

A benchmark gauge of U.S. company credit risk fell the most in two weeks after Federal Reserve Chairman Ben S. Bernanke made the case for further monetary easing.

The Markit CDX North America Investment Grade Index[20] of credit-default swaps, which investors use to hedge against losses on corporate debt or to speculate on creditworthiness, eased 1.4 basis points to a mid-price of 101.5 basis

---

lower credit quality party to provide collateral to reduce the credit risk associated with the transaction. *See generally www.isda.org; see also* Ursa Minor Ltd. v. Aon Fin. Prods., Inc., No. 00 Civ. 2474 (AGS), 2000 U.S. Dist. LEXIS 10166, at *6–8 (S.D.N.Y. July 21, 2000).

18. While traditionally these settlement procedures have been used only in conjunction with index products, the process was recently extended to single name swaps. See Press Release, Creditex and Markit Announce Results of Dura Credit Event Fixing for Defaulted Bonds (Nov. 28, 2006), available at *http://www.creditex.com/press/dura.pdf.* [And more recent practice is to cash settle CDS contracts.]

19. Used with permission of Bloomberg L.P. © 2013. All rights reserved.

20. This is the current name of the Dow Jones index described in the Lubben excerpt above. — AUTHOR

points at 4:06 p.m. in New York, according to prices compiled by Bloomberg. That's the biggest decline since a 1.5 basis-point decrease on Aug. 17.

The swaps measure decreased after Bernanke emphasized that a new round of bond purchases is an option in a speech to central bankers and economists at an annual forum in Jackson Hole, Wyoming. Investors speculated steps to boost the economy may come as soon as next month. Any move by the U.S. central bank to purchase more bonds would curb concern that companies will struggle to make debt repayments amid a slowing economy.

The "Fed is essentially saying they are going to continue monetary easing for years, and in particular any time there is a slowdown in the economy," according to Jon Ruff, a portfolio manager and director of research in San Francisco for a unit of AllianceBernstein LP. "The market's response to the Fed announcement only proves the theory," as the U.S. dollar fell and commodities and stocks rallied, he said.

The swaps index, which typically falls as investor confidence improves and rises as it deteriorates, reached a 15-week low of 98.5 basis points on Aug. 20.

The contracts pay the buyer face value if a borrower fails to meet its obligations, less the value of the defaulted debt. A basis point equals $1,000 annually on a contract protecting $10 million of debt.

In addition to the two types of swaps described in the Lubben excerpt — interest rate and credit default swaps — currency swaps are another common type of swap, used by many businesses that operate internationally.

Like an FX forward, a cross-currency swap consists of the exchange of principal amounts (based on today's spot rate) and interest payments between counterparties. Unlike a forward, however, a cross-currency swap involves multiple exchanges of interest rather than a single exchange of interest at the end, as in an FX forward), as well as the exchange of principal at maturity. The final principal exchange reverses an initial principal exchange, which makes FX swaps unlike other swaps where the notional amount never changes hand.

For example, consider a firm that receives USD interest and pays EUR interest under a currency swap. The front and back exchanges of principal amounts are based on the current spot rate, which means the profit or loss on the transaction (assuming no counterparty default) turns on the intermediate cash flows. The Euro cash flows are economically equivalent to issuing a Euro bond (as those are paid out by the firm); the USD cash flows are equivalent to investing in a USD bond, as they are received by the firm.

If the firm has engaged in USD borrowing, the swap converts the USD loan into a EUR loan. The firm pays interest on its loan in USD, but receives a corresponding payment under the swap.

If the swap is paired with a EUR investment, it converts the EUR asset into a USD asset. The asset throws off cash flows in EUR, which the firm then uses to pay its obligations under the swap, while the firm receives the USD cash flows from the swap.

Of course, these swaps can be used for currency speculation, too.

3. EQUITY DERIVATIVES

Options, which we covered in Chapter 17, are the most common equity derivatives because they directly grant the holder the right to buy or sell equity at a predetermined value. More complex equity derivatives include equity index swaps, equity swaps (such as total return swaps), and others.

Equity derivatives are typically divided between "delta one" products and products that have an option like payoff structure, which can accelerate in a nonlinear manner. Delta one refers to derivatives in which a change in the value of the underlying asset results in a change of the same, or nearly the same, proportion in the value of the derivative.[21] Some examples of delta one derivatives include equity swaps, forwards, futures, contracts for difference (CFD), and total return swaps. They all exhibit a linear relationship with the underlying.

A CFD is in essence an agreement to exchange the difference in the current value of a share, currency, commodity, or index and its value at the end of the contract. If the difference is positive, the seller pays the buyer. If it is negative, the buyer is the one who loses money. They are quite similar to futures.

STEPHEN J. LUBBEN, *THE BANKRUPTCY CODE*
WITHOUT SAFE HARBORS

84 Am. Bankr. L.J. 123, 131–132 (2010)

[I]magine that Lehman Brothers has intermediated a total-return swap on a million shares of BOGARTCO stock where Party A receives and Lehman pays the BOGARTCO return. BOGARTCO shares are currently trading at $40. As the total return payer, Lehman makes payments to Party A equal to the cash flows (any dividend payments on the BOGARTCO stock) plus any appreciation on the reference asset (the BOGARTCO shares). The total return receiver pays a floating interest rate, generally one of the LIBOR rates plus some additional amount, termed a spread, and any depreciation on the reference asset. The total return payer (Lehman in the top transaction on Figure 2) realizes the same returns as if it had sold the reference asset short. Meanwhile, the total return receiver (Party A) realizes the same returns as if it owned the reference asset, and is said to be "long" in this transaction. But Party A never actually owns BOGARTCO shares in any legal sense.

Because it is obligated only to make a series of payments based on the return of BORGATO, and is not purchasing the underlying shares from Lehman, Party A's investment in BOGARTCO is leveraged. For example, if Party A pays the 3-month LIBOR rate plus 100 basis points, it has effectively purchased stock and simultaneously financed the investment in the BOGARTCO shares by borrowing at the 3-month LIBOR rate plus 1%.

---

21. Somewhere in the recesses of your mind, you might recall that the Greek letter delta (Δ) is often used to symbolize change or the slope of a line. A slope of one would indicate a one to one relationship between x and y.

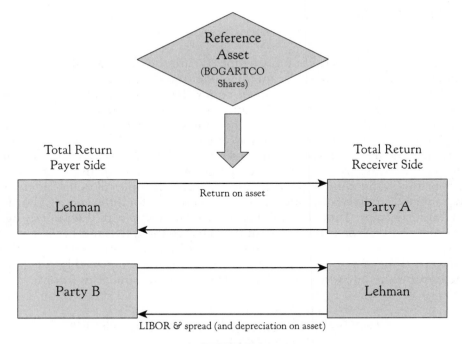

FIGURE 2
Total Return Swap Transaction

In the hypothetical, imagine that at the same time, Party B pays the return of BOGARTCO and Lehman receives the return of BOGARTCO for some period of time, during which Lehman pays Party B a floating interest rate payment, say LIBOR plus 50 basis points. Consequently, Lehman would earn 50 basis points, which is the difference in the spread between the two variable interest rate legs of these transactions.

One example of a non-delta one equity product is a prepaid variable share forward (PVSF). If an investor owns shares in a company, it can enter into a PVSF through a stock purchase agreement (SPA) with a counterparty. During the life of the SPA, the counterparty has the right to transfer and to vote the pledged shares but might be required to pay certain distributions received on the pledged shares to the investor.

In exchange for an up-front cash payment, which generally represents 75 percent to 85 percent of the current market value of the stock, the investor agrees to deliver a variable number of shares at maturity (typically three to five years), the precise number depending on the market price at maturity. The PVSF usually has a cash settlement option in lieu of delivering the underlying shares at maturity.

The professed benefits of the PVSF structure are said to be: (1) downside protection represented by the amount of the payment to the investor, (2) limited upside growth participation as reflected by the maximum share value price, (3) the potential for diversification by reinvesting the up-front cash advance, and (4) tax deferral of the gain to the maturity date of the PVSF, a point which the IRS has recently contested, arguing that the transfer to the counterparty counts as a sale.

4.   DERIVATIVES AND LEVERAGE

Unlike traditional securities, derivatives enable investors to purchase or sell exposure without committing cash in an amount equal to the economic exposure (the notional value) of the position. This should sound familiar, as it enables the same kind of magnification of exposure as we discussed with regard to debt-funded leverage.

For example, imagine you have $100 million. Don't linger on that bit too long. You could put your $100 million in the stock market, maybe buy an S&P 500 index fund. Then you would have $100 million of stock market exposure, and your net worth would rise and fall in lockstep with the market.

But what if you instead purchased S&P 500 futures contracts, which are traded on the Chicago Mercantile Exchange? These contracts run for a quarter of a year, with the first contract of any year expiring in March.

We will assume you're a positive sort, so you decide to go long the S&P 500. Each S&P 500 futures contract provides the equivalent to 250 times the current value of the index of exposure to the stock market. Thus, if you bought one contract when the index was at 1,000,[22] you would have gained $250,000 of exposure to the stock market. Because you are long, you will gain when the market goes up, and lose when the market goes down.

PROBLEM SET 18.2

1. How much exposure could you get to the stock market with your $100 million, if you purchase futures rather than actual securities? Remember that you will have to post margin in connection with the futures — assume that initially you post 5 percent and for this and the next problem, ignore any trading commissions you might pay.

2. What if you instead decided that you would like to obtain $100 million of exposure to the market and put the rest in a bank account. Assume that both your margin account and the bank account pay 4 percent per year. What would your cash flows look like if:

    a.   On the following day, the S&P 500 Index Level increases by 100 (from 1,000 to 1,100).

    b.   On the next day, the index level decreases by 200 (from 1,100 to 900). How would this compare to your cash flows if you had invested your $100 million directly into the index?

3. Return to the ProShares UltraPro S&P 500 (UPRO)[23] ETF from Chapter 10. Remember that it offered to provide investors with a return equal to three times the S&P 500, without using debt. How might that be? Look at

---

22. In reality, the index is currently (July 2013) at 1,687.71. But we'll keep using 1,000 to make the math easier.

23. *http://goo.gl/uXlIi*

its current holdings list.[24] Why so many total return swaps?[25] What is the drawback of having so many swaps that achieve the same ends?

5.   MARGIN AND TERMINATION

Because OTC derivatives only provided the desired hedge or speculation if the other side performs, OTC derivatives entail counterparty risk.[26]

The Dodd-Frank Act attempts to solve that problem by making swaps more like futures, where a central clearinghouse stands ready to perform despite the failure of one party to the swap. That works, so long as the clearinghouse does not fail.

More generally, the parties to swaps and other derivatives have developed two additional methods to reduce counterparty risk. These involve the posting of margin and the ability of parties to terminate trades on the occurrence of certain events.

Margin refers to the amount of cash or other collateral[27] deposited by a derivatives purchaser or seller. For exchange-traded derivatives, the collateral will be held by the broker or clearinghouse. For OTC derivatives, the terms of the collateral requirements will be specified in the ISDA documents between the parties to the transaction. Before the financial crisis, these documents often put big brokers in charge of holding margin. After the failure of Lehman, there has been some move to post margin with third parties.

Margin is subdivided into initial margin, which is the amount of margin set aside when the position is opened, and variation margin, which reflects daily adjustments to the initial margin to reflect movements in the value of the contract. In addition, if the parties of unequal credit quality, sometimes the lower quality party will have to post additional margin, which is called an "independent amount." Lehman Brothers, which had an investment grade credit rating until late 2008, held many hedge funds' independent amounts when it failed. Needless to say, there has been more skepticism about posting independent amounts in recent years.

It was the requirement to post margin that did in American International Group, Inc. ("AIG") during the financial crisis. AIG's London office had written many, many CDS contracts that referenced mortgaged backed securities (the subject of the next Chapter). AIG had a AAA credit rating, so it did not have to post much if any initial margin. But when these securities declined in value, and the probability of AIG having to pay out on the CDS contracts increased, and AIG had to post the variation margin. This obligation began to suck increasing amounts of cash out of the company.

---

24. *http://goo.gl/iwuxg*

25. Note that the S&P 500 E-Mini is a futures contract with 50 times the value of the index (versus 250 times the value, as discussed previously).

26. Of course, so do most securities, but with derivatives the risk is distinct from the overall performance of the investment.

27. U.S. government debt is often used, too.

In extreme cases, parties also have the right to terminate a derivative contract with a counterparty and replace it with a new one. The next case looks at these termination rights while also providing a nice overview of the ISDA documents that are used in most swap transactions, as well as the reality of the termination process.

LEHMAN BROTHERS INTERNATIONAL (EUROPE) (IN ADMINISTRATION), PLAINTIFF, v. AG FINANCIAL PRODUCTS, INC., DEFENDANT

Unreported Disposition
38 Misc.3d 1233(A)
Supreme Court, New York County, New York
No. 653284/2011 | March 12, 2013

Marcy S. FRIEDMAN, J.

This action arises out of a series of credit derivative transactions entered into between plaintiff Lehman Brothers International (Europe)(LBIE) and defendant AG Financial Products, Inc. (Assured Guaranty). Plaintiff alleges that defendant breached the contracts and the implied covenants of good faith and fair dealing by terminating nine transactions in December 2008 and 28 transactions in July 2009. Defendant moves, pursuant to CPLR 3211(a)(1) and (7), to dismiss the first and the third causes of action of the complaint, both for breach of the implied covenant.

FACTS

The facts, as alleged in the complaint, are undisputed unless otherwise stated. The parties, sophisticated commercial entities with the benefit of counsel, entered into 37 credit derivative transactions, each governed by three documents that form the contract for the transaction: a Master Agreement based on a 1992 template promulgated by the International Swaps and Derivatives Association; a negotiated Schedule to the Master Agreement; and a negotiated Confirmation for each transaction. The stated maturity date for each transaction is the maturity date of the underlying notes, referred to as the Reference Obligation.

As discussed below, the Master Agreement provides for termination of transactions upon "Event[s] of Default" which include bankruptcy, while the Confirmations for the transactions that were terminated in December 2008 enumerate "Additional Termination Events." The December 2008 terminations were based on the occurrence of an Additional Termination Event — namely, LBIE's failure to provide trustee reports for the underlying obligations. The July 2009 terminations were based on the occurrence of an Event of Default — namely, LBIE's entry into administration, the United Kingdom analogue of bankruptcy. The contractual methodologies for calculating the payments due upon termination differ significantly for these different grounds for termination.

DISCUSSION

It is well settled that on a motion to dismiss addressed to the face of the pleading, "the pleading is to be afforded a liberal construction . . ."

It is further settled that every contract contains an implied covenant of good faith and fair dealing. The implied covenant "embraces a pledge that neither party shall do anything which will have the effect of destroying or injuring the right of the other party to receive the fruits of the contract."

However, "the implied obligation is in aid and furtherance of other terms of the agreement of the parties. No obligation can be implied . . . which would be inconsistent with other terms of the contractual relationship." . . . As this Department explained in *Richbell Information Services, Inc. v. Jupiter Partners, L.P.* (309 A.D.2d 288, 302 [1st Dept 2003]), there is "tension between, on the one hand, the imposition of a good faith limitation on the exercise of a contract right and, on the other, the avoidance of using the implied covenant of good faith to create new duties that negate explicit rights under a contract." In the face of this tension, cases which uphold causes of action for breach of the implied covenant appear to fall into two main categories:

In the first, an implied covenant claim may be recognized where a contract provides for a party's exercise of discretion but does not expressly require that the discretion be exercised reasonably.

In the second, an implied covenant claim may be recognized where a party "exercise[s] a [contractual] right malevolently, for its own gain as part of a purposeful scheme to deprive plaintiffs of the benefits" of the contract. In support of the claim, a party may not merely assert that the opposing party should not be permitted to exercise an explicit contractual right or seek to "create new duties that negate specific rights under a contract" but, rather, must allege "bad faith targeted malevolence in the guise of business dealings." (*Richbell Info. Servs.*, 309 A.D.2d at 302 [denying motion to dismiss implied covenant claim where complaint alleged that defendant not only exercised contractual right to veto IPO that would have provided plaintiff with funds to repay note, but also entered into secret "bid rigging agreement" to orchestrate plaintiff's default on note, all for the purpose of enabling defendant to purchase plaintiff's stock at artificially low price]; *see also ABN AMRO Bank, N.V.*, 17 NY3d at 228–229 [denying motion to dismiss implied covenant claim by plaintiff-holders of financial guarantee insurance policies on structured finance products, based on allegation that defendants, by fraudulently transferring billions of dollars to subsidiary for no consideration, rendered defendant unable to meet its obligations under policies] . . .

A negotiated contract provision cannot, however, be nullified by a conclusory allegation that a defendant acted "unfairly" or "contrived" to deprive the opposing party of the benefits of the contract. Nor, where a contract contains an express covenant governing a subject, will the courts imply a covenant with respect to the same subject. *Staffenberg v. Fairfield Pagma Assocs, L.P.*, 95 AD3d 873, 875 [2d Dept 2012][on summary judgment motion, dismissing implied covenant claim where limited partnership agreement provided that client funds were to be invested with Madoff and "no other obligation to invest" could be implied under the agreement].)

DECEMBER 2008 TERMINATIONS

As noted above, the December 2008 terminations were based not on the Master Agreement but on the Confirmations which require that LBIE "obtain and provide [Assured Guaranty] with copies of all reports and other information relating to the Reference Obligation" that were required to be delivered to the holders of the Reference Obligation by any Reference Entity or its manager or servicer, or by a trustee. The Confirmations further provide that if LBIE fails to deliver the reports "promptly" or fails to cure within a 30–day period after written notice from Assured Guaranty, Assured Guaranty "may . . . declare an Additional Termination Event" and "designate an Early Termination Date" with respect to the subject transaction.

On November 13, 2008, Assured Guaranty sent LBIE nine "Notices of Failure to Deliver Reports," stating that LBIE had failed to provide Assured Guaranty with monthly trustee reports relating to the underlying Reference Obligations as required by Section 8(a)(ii) of the Confirmations. LBIE did not cure and, on December 23, 2008, Assured Guaranty sent Notices of Termination, designating December 24, 2008 as the Early Termination Date.

As the December 2008 terminations were based on an "Additional Termination Event," the Confirmations require LBIE to pay an Accrued Fixed Payment Amount. As pleaded in the complaint, and undisputed by defendant, the Accrued Fixed Payment Amount consists of the accrued and unpaid premiums that LBIE owed to Assured Guaranty as of the Early Termination Date. Upon the occurrence of an Additional Termination Event, "no amount (other than amounts due and not paid) is payable by either party in respect of the termination" of the transaction.[28] Both LBIE and Assured Guaranty refer to the Accrued Fixed Payment Amount as "walk-away money." On October 7, 2009, Assured Guaranty delivered a valuation statement, asserting that LBIE owed it an Accrued Fixed Payment Amount of $3,960,319.86.

LBIE argues that at the time of the terminations, the parties were engaged in settlement negotiations concerning possible novation of all 37 transactions, and that Assured Guaranty could have requested the reports from the negotiators or obtained them from other sources, including the trustee. LBIE acknowledges that Assured Guaranty had contractual authorization for the December 2008 terminations. However, LBIE contends that "act[s] consistent with a contract's express terms" do not bar a claim of breach of the implied covenant, and that the parties' "course of dealing" must be considered. Assured Guaranty, it claims, used the reports as a "pretext for termination" so that it could avail itself of the "more advantageous termination methodology" (the Accrued Fixed Payment Amount) available upon termination based on an Additional Termination Event.

Assured Guaranty contends that the implied covenant claim must be dismissed because it acted within its express contractual rights in terminating the transactions based on LBIE's failure to provide trustee reports. It further contends that in claiming a breach of the implied covenant, LBIE in effect

---

28. The Accrued Fixed Payment Amount is defined as follows: "[A]s of any Early Termination Date, the accrued and unpaid Fixed Payments under the Transaction for the period from and including the [premium payment date] immediately preceding the Early Termination Date to but excluding the Early Termination Date, plus any Unpaid Amounts payable to [Assured Guaranty] and outstanding on the Early Termination Date."

invites the court to rewrite the parties' respective contractual rights and obligations by requiring Assured Guaranty to provide oral notice of LBIE's failure to deliver the reports in addition to the written notice provided for by the Confirmations, or to undertake an additional obligation to obtain the reports from other sources. Assured Guaranty argues that such obligations are inconsistent with the terms of the contract.

The court holds that LBIE fails to state a claim for breach of the implied covenant based on the December 2008 terminations. It is undisputed that Assured Guaranty's right to terminate the transactions based on LBIE's failure to provide trustee reports was a bargained-for provision of the contract, and that the transactions were terminated in compliance with that provision. LBIE's conclusory assertion that Assured Guaranty terminated the transactions pursuant to the provision in order to avail itself of a favorable payment methodology falls far short of alleging the kind of fraudulent or malevolent scheme to deprive LBIE of the benefits of the contract that would support an implied covenant claim. Moreover, to hold that Assured Guaranty was required to have requested the reports from the parties engaged in settlement negotiations or to have obtained the reports on its own would, as Assured Guaranty correctly argues, impose obligations upon it additional to those imposed by the Confirmations, and therefore inconsistent with its right under the Confirmations to terminate the transactions upon LBIE's failure to provide the reports.

JULY 2009 TERMINATIONS

The July 2009 terminations were based on the Early Termination provision of the Master Agreement which provides in pertinent part: "If at any time an Event of Default with respect to a party (the Defaulting Party') has occurred and is then continuing, the other party (the Non-defaulting Party') may, by not more than 20 days notice to the Defaulting Party specifying the relevant Event of Default, designate a day not earlier than the day such notice is effective as an Early Termination Date in respect of all outstanding Transactions." Under the Master Agreement, the bankruptcy of a party constitutes an Event of Default.

On September 15, 2008, LBIE entered into administration in the United Kingdom. On July 23, 2009, Assured Guaranty gave notice terminating the remaining 28 Transactions based on LBIE's entrance into bankruptcy administration, and designated July 23, 2009 as the Early Termination Date.

As the termination of these transactions was based on an Event of Default, the Master Agreement provides for the early termination payment to be "determined by the Non-defaulting Party." The Schedule in turn provides that in calculating the payment, the Non-defaulting Party must first use the "Market Quotation" payment measure and "Second [payment] Method."

The Market Quotation methodology requires the Non-defaulting Party to obtain quotations from leading dealers in the relevant market, known as "Reference Market-makers," to "step into the shoes" of the Defaulting Party for a replacement transaction. Under the Master Agreement, if three quotations cannot be obtained, "it will be deemed that the Market Quotation in respect of such Terminated Transaction or group of Terminated Transactions cannot be determined." The alternative Loss methodology may be used to calculate the early termination payment if "a Market Quotation cannot be determined or would not (in the reasonable belief of the party making the determination) produce a commercially reasonable result." Loss is defined as "an amount that party reasonably determines in good faith to be its total losses and costs (or gain, in which case expressed as a negative number) in connection with . . . [the] group of Terminated Transactions . . ." The Loss methodology requires that a party "determine its Loss as of the relevant Early Termination Date, or, if that is not reasonably practicable, as of the earliest date thereafter as is reasonably practicable. A party may (but need not) determine its Loss by reference to quotations of relevant rates or prices from one or more leading dealers in the relevant markets."

According to plaintiff, Assured Guaranty represented that it could not obtain bids from at least three Reference Market-makers. Assured Guaranty therefore took the position that it could not use the Market Quotation method and instead applied the Loss method, determining that LBIE owed Assured Guaranty $24,799,972.85 for the July 2009 Terminations.

LBIE alleges that Assured Guaranty breached the implied covenant with respect to the July 2009 terminations by making the use of Market Quotation "impossible" in that it delayed its request for quotations "until well after the Early Termination Date," and then required the Reference Market-makers to agree to Assured Guaranty's onerous bidding procedures, including execution of a confidentiality agreement, thereby "effectively discouraging them from submitting bids." LBIE further contends that Assured Guaranty not only "bypass[ed]" the contractual requirement that the Market Quotation method be used, but also misapplied the Loss method. More particularly, LBIE claims that it is "accepted market practice to determine Loss by reference to the market price . . . for replacing the terminated transactions," but that Assured Guaranty instead determined Loss by "calculating the purported present value of all payments that [Assured Guaranty] expected to receive from LBIE during the entire term of each Transaction and subtracting from it the sum of all payments [Assured Guaranty] purportedly determined that it would likely have to pay to LBIE during the term of each Transaction. . . ." Further, LBIE alleges that Assured Guaranty used its "own undisclosed internal assumptions and models about the shortfalls that would occur on the underlying securities" to determine the present value and "ignored the then-market consensus as to the likelihood of defaults."

In moving to dismiss the implied covenant claim based on the July 2009 terminations, Assured Guaranty contends that it is duplicative of the second cause of action for breach of contract. Assured Guaranty points to allegations in the breach of contract cause of action that Assured Guaranty "bypass[ed] Market Quotation" and "improperly calculate[d] Loss without reference to any market information and in a manner that was commercially unreasonable."

A cause of action for breach of the implied covenant will be dismissed as duplicative of a breach of contract cause of action where both claims arise from the same facts and seek identical damages. (*Amcan Holding, Inc. v. Canadian Imperial Bank of Commerce*, 70 AD3d 423, 426 [1st Dept 2010]; *see MBIA Ins. Corp. v. Merrill Lynch*, 81 AD3d 419, 419–420 [1st Dept 2011].)

Here, the allegations of the breach of contract and implied covenant causes of action overlap in significant respects. As discussed above, both allege that

Assured Guaranty "bypassed" the contractually required Market Quotation and then applied the Loss methodology in an improper manner. The issue is therefore whether the implied covenant claim is maintainable based on the additional allegations, on which LBIE relies, that Assured Guaranty made the use of Market Quotation "impossible" by delaying its request for quotations and imposing unreasonable bidding procedures.

As to the allegation regarding delay, the Master Agreement contains a specific term requiring the party making the determination to request the Reference Market-makers to provide their quotations "to the extent reasonably practicable as of the same day and time . . . on or as soon as reasonably practicable after the relevant Early Termination Date," and further providing that "[t]he day and time on which those quotations are to be obtained will be selected in good faith." (Master Agreement, §14 "Market Quotation Definition.") The implied covenant cause of action, to the extent based on timing of the request for quotations, is thus duplicative of the contract cause of action.

As to the allegation regarding bidding, the Master Agreement imposes several requirements that the Market Quotation determination be made in good faith, including a requirement that the Replacement Transaction be "subject to such documentation as [the party making the calculation] and the Reference Market-maker may, in good faith, agree," and a requirement that the Reference Market-makers be selected "in good faith."

Significantly, the Master Agreement and other contract documents do not contain express directives as to the bidding procedures to be followed in obtaining the Market Quotations. Assured Guaranty has acknowledged that in making the determination of the Early Termination payment, it "had to act reasonably and in good faith subject to rights the contract specifically provided us." At this early juncture, however, the rights provided by the contract with respect to the bidding procedures are not settled.[29] The implied covenant claim, to the extent based on Assured Guaranty's conduct in the bidding process therefore cannot be said to be duplicative of the breach of contract cause of action. Moreover, LBIE's allegations regarding the bidding process, viewed in the light most favorable to LBIE, could rise to the level of deliberate conduct designed to deprive LBIE of the benefit of its bargain. Defendant's motion to dismiss will therefore be denied as to the implied covenant cause of action with respect to the July 2009 terminations.

It is accordingly hereby ORDERED that the motion of defendant AG Financial Products, Inc. to dismiss the first and third causes of action of the complaint is granted solely to the extent of dismissing the first cause of action.

If you have taken Bankruptcy, you might wonder why LBIE's administration proceeding did not stop AG Financial from terminating these agreements. The answer is *not* that UK insolvency law is markedly different: Indeed, the result would be no different under U.S. bankruptcy law.

---

29. Similarly, the Master Agreement does not set forth a detailed methodology for calculating Loss in the event a Market Quotation cannot be determined or would not produce a commercially reasonable result. (*See* Master Agreement, §14 "Loss" Definition.)

Under the Bankruptcy Code, clauses that allow parties to terminate a contract upon another party's bankruptcy or insolvency are unenforceable.[30] That is, that's the normal rule. Derivatives are subject to an alternative set of special rules.

STEPHEN J. LUBBEN, *THE BANKRUPTCY CODE WITHOUT SAFE HARBORS*
84 Am. Bankr. L.J. 123, 124–130 (2010)

A. THE SAFE HARBORS

The safe harbor provisions of the Code developed incrementally, growing from narrowly targeted provisions that addressed specific concerns about the interaction of bankruptcy and certain financial products, to the wide-open provisions enacted in 2005. Following the 2005 amendments to the Code, it is hard to envision a derivative that is not subject to special treatment.[31]

The safe harbors cover a wide range of contracts that might be considered derivatives, including securities contracts,[32] commodities contracts,[33] forward

---

30. 11 U.S.C. §365(e).

31. Michael Simkovic, *Secret Liens and the Financial Crisis of 2008*, 83 Am. Bankr. L.J. 253, 282 (2009).

32. The definition of "securities contract" in section 741(7) includes:

> a contract for the purchase, sale, or loan of a security, a certificate of deposit, a mortgage loan . . . or option on any of the foregoing, including an option to purchase or sell any such security, certificate of deposit, mortgage loan . . . including any repurchase or reverse repurchase transaction on any such security, certificate of deposit, mortgage loan . . .

The definition of "securities contract" was amended in 2005 to conform to the definition in the Federal Deposit Insurance Act. The term "security" is itself defined in §101(49).

33. 11 U.S.C. §781(4). As explained in *Collier's*:

> The meaning of the term "commodity contract" differs depending upon the type of commodity broker at issue. A commodity contract with respect to a futures commission merchant is a contract for the purchase or sale of a commodity for future delivery on, or subject to the rules of, a contract market or board of trade. Such a contract is known in the commodities trade as a "commodity futures contract." A commodity contract with respect to a foreign futures commission merchant is a foreign future, and with respect to a leverage transaction merchant is a leverage transaction. A commodity contract with respect to a clearing organization is either a commodity futures contract that is cleared by such clearing organization or is a commodity option traded on, or subject to the rules of, a contract market or a board of trade that is cleared by such clearing organization. A commodity contract with respect to a commodity options dealer is a commodity option.

Collier on Bankruptcy ¶761.05 (footnotes omitted). Commodity is defined in §761(8) through cross-reference to the Commodity Exchange Act ("CEA"). CEA §1a(4) defines "commodity" to include agricultural products "and all other goods and articles, except onions as provided in section 13-1 of this title, and all services, rights, and interests in which contracts for future delivery are presently or in the future dealt in." The origins of the amusing "onion" exception are detailed in *http://www.time.com/time/magazine/article/0,9171,891311,00.html* Several other parts of Code §761 also cross-reference the CEA. *See* Olympic Natural Gas, 294 F.3d 737, 740–41 (5th Cir. 2002) ("The term 'commodity contract' 'encompasses purchases and sales of commodities for future delivery on, or subject to the rules of, a contract market or board of trade . . . .' In contrast, 'forward contracts' are 'contracts for the future purchase or sale of commodities that are not subject to the rules of a contract market or board of trade.'").

contracts,[34] repurchase agreements,[35] and, most importantly, swap agreements.[36] The latter has become a kind of "catch-all" definition that covers the whole of the derivatives market, present and future.

A protected contract, that is one that falls within one of the foregoing categories, is only protected if the holder is also a protected person, as defined in the Bankruptcy Code. Financial participants[37] — essentially very large financial institutions — are always protected. And with regard to each class of protected derivative contract this is also a more specific class of protected parties.[38]

In some cases these latter categories have some real meaning. For example, forward contracts are only subject to the safe harbors with regard to financial participants and "forward contract merchants." A forward contract merchant means either a Federal Reserve Bank or an entity "whose business consists in whole or in part of entering into forward contracts."[39] On the other hand, the current definitions of "repo participant"[40] and "swap participant"[41] are essentially vacuous, requiring nothing more than the person in question be party to a repo or swap with the debtor. In short, anyone with standing to invoke the safe harbors is apt to be a protected person with regard to these contracts.

The safe harbors provide non-bankrupt counterparties with the ability to exercise contractual rights allowing liquidation, termination or acceleration of derivative contracts upon bankruptcy,[42] the right to set off or net derivative contracts free of the automatic stay,[43] and broad immunity from avoidance

34. Forward contract is defined in §101(25), to include contracts (other than commodity contracts, see *supra* note 32) for the purchase, sale, or transfer of a commodity at least two days in the future, and includes "a repurchase or reverse repurchase transaction . . . consignment, lease, swap, hedge transaction, deposit, loan, option, allocated transaction, unallocated transaction, or any other similar agreement."

35. 11 U.S.C. §101(47). A repurchase agreement or "repo," is essentially the sale of a financial instrument combined with a forward contract to repurchase the same. The initial "buyer" is compensated by the "seller" through a difference between the initial payment and the final payment. To qualify under the Code's definition, the repurchase obligation must occur within one year, but the definition expressly excludes a repurchase obligation under a participation in a commercial mortgage loan. Note, however, that these types of repos might constitute another type of protected contract, particularly a swap or securities contract. *See* In re Hamilton Taft & Co., 114 F.3d 991 (9th Cir. 1997).

36. 11 U.S.C. §101(53B). The definition includes not only obvious swaps, like CDS, interest rate swaps, and currency swaps, but also any instrument "of a type that has been, is presently, or in the future becomes, the subject of recurrent dealings in the swap markets" including "a forward, swap, future, option or spot transaction on one or more rates, currencies, commodities, equity securities, or other equity instruments, debt securities or other debt instruments, quantitative measures associated with an occurrence, extent of an occurrence, or contingency associated with a financial, commercial, or economic consequence, or economic or financial indices or measures of economic or financial risk or value." In short, every conceivable derivative contract.

37. 11 U.S.C. §101(22A) (defining "financial participant").

38. With regard to securities contracts with the debtor, the counterparty must be a "stockbroker," "financial institution," "financial participant" or "securities clearing agency."

39. 11 U.S.C. §101(26). *See also* In re Mirant Corp., 310 B.R. 548, 568 (Bankr. N.D. Tex. 2004).

40. 11 U.S.C. §101(46).

41. 11 U.S.C. §101(53C).

42. 11 U.S.C. §§555 (securities contracts), 556 (forward and commodities contracts), 559 (repurchase or "repo" agreements), 560 (swaps). The exceptions apply to a "contractual right," which includes rights provided for in a rule by various trade organizations or exchanges.

43. 11 U.S.C. §§362(b)(6) (securities contracts, forwards and commodity contracts), 362(b)(7) (repos), 362(b)(17) (swaps). *See also* 11 U.S.C. §§362(o) (exercise of rights under the forgoing provisions not subject to any stays), 556 (forwards and commodity contracts protected parties' right to margin payments under those contracts shall not be stayed, avoided or limited), 560 (under a swap right to offset or net-out any termination values or payment amounts shall not be stayed, avoided or limited).

actions.[44] These protections also extend to derivative transactions nestled under a master agreement, even if the master agreement aggregates disparate types of derivative contracts.[45] Security agreements and other credit enhancements are also encompassed within the definitions of protected contracts, and thus subject to the safe harbors.[46]

Many authors, especially those that come from a restructuring background, have expressed some skepticism about the safe harbor provisions,[47] and it is worth noting that the new Orderly Liquidation Authority, Dodd-Frank's special bankruptcy system for financial institutions, provides for a 24-hour stay on any termination of a derivative contract.

PROBLEM SET 18.3

1. The Lehman case above involved a "walkaway clause" that pays the non-defaulting party damages regardless of the underlying economic value of the swap. For example, Lehman might have been "in the money" on the swaps, but could have owed a payment to its counterparty nonetheless. Such clauses are not enforceable in bank receivership proceedings against the FDIC. Should they be enforceable in other contexts?

2. From the industry perspective, what benefits arise from the safe harboring of most swap agreements from the normal operation of the Bankruptcy Code? For example, how might the existence of the safe harbors influence the pricing of a swaps deal?

44. 11 U.S.C. §§546(e), (f), (g), (j), 548(d)(2)(B), (C), (D). The foregoing sections of section 546 prohibit the bringing of avoidance actions under sections 544, 545, 547, 548 (a)(1)(B), and 548 (b) of the Bankruptcy Code. The foregoing provisions of section 548 provide that a derivatives counterparty always takes for value, potentially complicating an attempt to recover a transfer as an actual fraudulent transfer. 11 U.S.C. §548(c).

This author is at a loss to explain how a derivative might be a statutory lien under section 545. These provisions do not seem to prohibit the lifting of the automatic stay to allow a creditor to bring an avoidance action under state or federal non-bankruptcy law, so long as the creditor did not bring such action on behalf of the estate. *Cf.* 11 U.S.C. §544(b)(1).

45. 11 U.S.C. §§362(b)(27) (allows setoffs and netting under master netting agreements) 561 (right to terminate, accelerate or liquidate, or to offset, or net termination values, payment amounts or other transfer obligations arising under or in connection with one or more securities contracts, commodity contracts, forward contracts, repurchase agreements, swap agreements or master netting agreements, shall not be stayed, avoided or limited by operation of the bankruptcy code or by order of a court or administrative agency). *See also* 11 U.S.C. §§101(38A) (definition of "master netting agreement"). The definitions of securities contracts, commodities, forward contracts, repurchase agreements, and swap agreements also include "a master agreement" that includes the defined contracts. Note the slight difference in terminology between "master agreement" and "master netting agreement."

46. *See, e.g.,* 11 U.S.C. §101(25)(E) (definition of "forward contract").

47. Frank Partnoy & David A. Skeel, Jr., *The Promise and Perils of Credit Derivatives,* 75 U. Cin. L. Rev. 1019, 1049 (2007) ("The first thing to note is that the standard explanation for the special treatment is not particularly compelling. It is far from clear that the exception reduces systemic risk; it may even increase this risk because it eliminates a possible curb on counter-parties' rush to close out their contracts in the event of a wave of failures.").

19

ASSET SECURITIZATION

If you followed the recent financial crisis at all, you probably heard about asset securitization—the famed mortgage-backed securities (MBS) that were at the center of many discussions of the crisis are one form of asset securitization.

Even before the financial crisis, asset securitization (briefly) entered mainstream discourse when David Bowie[1] securitized his music royalties from albums made before 1990 in exchange for $55 million from the Prudential insurance company.[2] Bowie essentially gave up ten years of royalty payments in exchange for a (very) large check.[3]

1. MOTIVATIONS

Securitization is a awkwardly named substitute for secured lending. In a basic secured loan, the borrower firm gives a bank a lien on an asset in exchange for cash. If the borrower fails to repay the loan, the bank can institute a foreclosure proceeding under state debtor-creditor law and take the asset. In the interim, there is some risk that the defaulting borrower will forestall this process by filing bankruptcy. Bankruptcy, as discussed in later chapters, allows a firm to renegotiate its loans from a position of greater strength than it would enjoy under state law.

The possibility of a bankruptcy filing means that a secured lender cannot count on being able to quickly obtain the collateral upon default. In many cases it probably does not really want the collateral, but getting the collateral beats not getting paid.[4] The delay associated with bankruptcy is thus a factor that

---

1. For those of you who are too young to know, David Bowie is a musician of great importance to some textbook authors who were in their youth in the 1970s and 1980s.

2. *http://en.wikipedia.org/wiki/Bowie_Bonds*

3. Teresa N. Kerr, Comment, *Bowie Bonding in the Music Biz: Will Music Royalty Securitization Be the Key to the Gold for Music Industry Participants?*, 7 UCLA Ent. L. Rev. 367 (2000).

4. Ronald J. Mann, *Strategy and Force in the Liquidation of Secured Debt*, 96 Mich. L. Rev. 159 (1997).

should influence the lender's expected return calculation, and thus the interest rate the debtor pays the lender on the loan.

Securitization involves the isolation of the asset in a way that—in theory— allows the lender to price the loan solely on the value of the asset, free from any risk of bankruptcy.

To return to the case of David Bowie, he might have gotten a bank loan secured by his royalties. One risk the bank would have faced was the possibility that David might have filed a personal bankruptcy case, and used the bankruptcy process to impose a new deal on the bank, perhaps paying off the loan over a longer term, while still retaining the rights to the royalties.

But when he securitized the royalties, they were moved into a separate legal entity, referred to as a Special Purpose Vehicle (SPV) or Entity (SPE), which did nothing but own the rights. The transfer would have been structured as a "true sale" that terminated David's rights in the royalties. A legal opinion would certify that some law firm really believes that this was actually a sale, and not simply a sham transaction (hence, the "true" sale).

The SPV paid David $55 million, and David gave the SPV the royalty rights. Where did the SPV get the $55 million? From Prudential. Why would Prudential give an SPV so much money? It's not because they're all Ziggy Stardust fanatics.

Prudential actually bought bonds issued by the SPV that promised to pay it a certain return, based on the expected payout that David Bowie's back catalog would generate over the course of ten years.

And who was the "owner" of the SPV? That would be David Bowie. When the transaction was completed, and Prudential was all paid back, he could do what he wanted with the rights. But if Prudential had not been paid during the interim, as a creditor of the SPV they could have taken the rights.

And David's own bankruptcy case would have had no effect on the operation of the SPV. Just like your own bankruptcy case would have no effect on Apple or Exxon, even if you owned shares in those companies. More formally, one expert explains the process thusly.

KENNETH C. KETTERING, *SECURITIZATION AND ITS DISCONTENTS: THE DYNAMICS OF FINANCIAL PRODUCT DEVELOPMENT*
29 Cardozo L. Rev. 1553 (2008)

The main purpose of this paper is to consider the process of innovation in financial and commercial products. It takes as its point of departure one of the major financial innovations of recent decades, namely the financing technique variously known as "securitization" or "structured finance." These terms are not well defined, but they have acquired a certain cachet in the marketplace, and so are often applied very loosely to transactions that have almost nothing in common. As used in this paper, "securitization" refers to a transaction that, in the first place, involves the issuance to financiers of debt instruments that are backed by a designated pool of assets — typically rights to payment owned by the firm that effects the transaction (referred to herein as the "Originator"). That description, by itself, would encompass a simple loan to the Originator secured by the asset pool. The distinctive feature of securitization is that the transaction also is structured to isolate the asset pool from the Originator in such a way that, if the Originator later becomes subject to an insolvency proceeding, the proceeding will not interrupt the continued receipt by the financiers of the payments due to them, as and when due, through realization on the asset pool. If that goal is achieved, the credit risk to the financiers will depend solely on the assets in the pool, and so will be independent of the creditworthiness of the Originator. For brevity that goal sometimes may be referred to as "bankruptcy isolation" of the securitized assets.

The term "securitization" is thus a misnomer insofar as it suggests that the issuance of securities is the heart of the matter. The debt instruments issued to the financiers in a securitization transaction might be securities issued into the capital markets, but they need not be; they might just as well be loan obligations owed to a syndicate of banks, involving no securities at all . . .

Securitization transactions, in the foregoing sense, were first employed in the late 1970s using asset pools comprised of mortgages. The first public transaction to securitize rights to payment other than mortgages (referred to as an "asset-backed" transaction, as opposed to a "mortgage-backed" transaction, in the somewhat illogical terminology conventional in the market) occurred in 1985. This infant was born under a lucky star, and from its birth it grew prodigiously: the volume of securities outstanding in securitization transactions at the end of 2006 aggregated $3.6 trillion. The growth of securitization indeed has been such as to move one scholar to predict the death of secured lending, as being hopelessly overshadowed by its more sophisticated relative.

This vast inverted pyramid of securitized debt is balanced uneasily on a pinpoint of legal doctrine: namely, that the structure employed for the purpose of isolating the pooled assets from the bankruptcy of the Originator will indeed achieve that purpose. From the beginning that doctrinal conclusion, or aspiration, was a shaky one. Even without detailed study the wobble is apparent from numerous outward signs. For example, in securitization transactions lawyers typically are asked to deliver opinions on the relevant points (or at least some of the relevant points) of bankruptcy doctrine. The opinion given is never a clean unqualified opinion that the structure works; rather, standard practice is to give a "reasoned" opinion, commonly dozens of pages long, which by its form and in its content signals substantial uncertainty about the result.

The dearth of case law is paralleled by the skimpiness of the academic literature casting a critical eye on the doctrinal foundations of the product. A vast amount has been written about securitization, understandably so because such transactions raise legal, tax, accounting, and other issues that are manifold, specialized, and arcane. But with few exceptions the literature is by and for practitioners, to assist in the doing of deals, and as such is naturally oriented toward cheerleading rather than skepticism.

I. THE PROTOTYPICAL SECURITIZATION, THE BANKRUPTCY TAX,
    AND BANKRUPTCY POLICY

Structures for securitization transactions, or at least for transactions that are advertised as securitizations, are many and varied. This paper focuses on the structure that is commonly viewed as being prototypical, and that indeed is used as the exemplar in the major law school textbook dedicated to teaching securitization. The doctrinal discussion in this paper is at a sufficiently high level of generality to be applicable to other securitization structures. Some of the terminology associated with the prototypical securitization was introduced earlier in this paper, but it is well to describe the transaction here even at the cost of some repetition.

In its simplest form, the prototypical securitization begins with the firm that wishes to procure financing against assets that it owns, which are typically rights to payment owed to it. Because that firm ordinarily (though not necessarily) will have originated those rights to payment by lending money to or providing property or services to the obligors, it is convenient to refer to that firm as the "Originator." The Originator forms a wholly-owned subsidiary conventionally referred to as a "special purpose entity," or "SPE," because it is formed for the purpose of the transaction and its operations are limited to those required in connection with the transaction. This SPE is (in further industry argot) "bankruptcy remote," in that it is created subject to an array of constraints designed to eliminate, to the extent possible, the risk that the SPE might in the future become subject to a proceeding under the Bankruptcy Code, whether involuntarily, voluntarily, or through the SPE being substantively consolidated with its Originator in the event of the Originator's bankruptcy. Thus, involuntary bankruptcy is countered by provisions in the SPE's organic documents authorizing it to engage only in activities necessary to the securitization transaction and by obtaining waivers of the right to file an involuntary petition against the SPE from third parties who deal with the SPE. Voluntary bankruptcy is countered by provisions in the SPE's organic documents requiring a unanimous vote of the SPE's board of directors to authorize the filing of a voluntary bankruptcy petition and requiring one or more members of the SPE's board to be independent of the Originator. Substantive consolidation[5] with the Originator is countered by covenants requiring the Originator and SPE to avoid acting in ways that would permit the invocation of any of the usual grounds for substantive consolidation, i.e., the SPE is to comply with proper corporate formalities, its assets are not to be commingled with those of the Originator, and so on.

After the SPE is formed, the Originator conveys the assets being securitized to the SPE. This conveyance, which is the key to the bankruptcy isolation that is sought for the securitized assets, is effected as a sale or a capital contribution. In the simplest structure, which might be referred to as "one tier," the securitization would then be completed by the SPE issuing debt instruments to financiers, secured by the securitized assets, and immediately passing the proceeds of the financing upstream to the Originator (by way of payment of the purchase price of the securitized assets or distribution on the SPE's equity, depending on how the conveyance of assets from the Originator to the SPE was effected). For accounting reasons, however, it is common to employ a slightly more elaborate structure referred to conventionally as "two tier." In the "two tier" structure, the SPE transfers the securitized assets to a second entity, typically a trust formed for

---

5. This is the bankruptcy counterpart of veil piercing, whereby a bankruptcy court can treat several related corporations as a single legal entity, pooling all assets and debts. — AUTHOR

the transaction ("SPE-2"), which issues the debt instruments to the financiers and passes the proceeds back to the SPE; the SPE is the residual beneficiary of SPE-2 and so is entitled to the residual value of the securitized assets after the financiers have been paid. In order to comply with the relevant accounting conventions the transfer of the assets from the SPE to SPE-2 need not be a sale for bankruptcy law purposes and it typically is not considered to be. Hence for purposes of bankruptcy analysis the "one tier" and "two tier" structures are practically identical, and for simplicity of exposition this paper will ignore SPE-2.

If the structure is respected, then the stream of payments to the financiers derived from collection of the securitized assets should not be affected by the subsequent bankruptcy of the Originator. Because the securitized assets are the property of the SPE, they will not be part of the Originator's bankruptcy estate. Moreover, the SPE should be practically immune from becoming the subject of a bankruptcy proceeding in its own right because of the bankruptcy remoteness conditions to which it is subject. The achievement of this "bankruptcy isolation" of the securitized assets is the purpose of the structure. The credit risk associated with the securitized debt issued to the financiers thus becomes independent of the creditworthiness of the Originator. The credit risk associated with the securitized debt is a function only of the amount and collectibility of the securitized assets and the amount of securitized debt issued against those assets.[6] The credit risk associated with the securitized debt when it is issued could be reduced as low as desired by providing a sufficiently high degree of overcollateralization.

That result is very much in contrast to the result if the Originator were to effect the financing as a simple secured debt — that is, if the Originator simply borrowed directly from the financiers, securing its obligation by granting a security interest in the same assets. In that event the assets, still owned by the Originator, would be part of the Originator's bankruptcy estate in the event of the filing of a petition under the Bankruptcy Code by or against the Originator. The Bankruptcy Code then would impair substantially the financiers' power to enforce their security interest in those assets — or, to make the same point from the perspective of the Originator and its unsecured creditors, the Bankruptcy Code would preserve for the benefit of the bankruptcy estate certain rights in those assets notwithstanding the financiers' security interest. In the first place, the automatic stay would prevent the financiers from exercising remedies against those assets.[7] As a result of the automatic stay, a secured creditor in a reorganization case is typically compelled to wait a long time before realizing

6. That bankruptcy isolation of the securitized assets causes the credit risk of the securitized debt to be independent of the creditworthiness of the Originator is a good first approximation, but it is subject to qualifications. For example, the transfer of the securitized assets by the Originator to the SPE is typically subject to representations and warranties by the Originator about the identity and nature of those assets, breach of which would implicate the creditworthiness of the Originator. Likewise, the Originator commonly acts as the servicer of the securitized assets (i.e., it administers and collects them), and its creditworthiness would be implicated if it were to reject its duties as servicer in a bankruptcy proceeding, commingle collections of the securitized assets with other funds, or otherwise breach its duties as servicer. Steps can be taken to mitigate these risks, such as building into the financing structure a servicing fee sufficient to discourage the Originator from rejecting its servicing duties in bankruptcy and to permit ready engagement of a substitute servicer.

7. Bankruptcy Code §362(a).

value on its secured claim. Although a secured creditor has the right to have the stay lifted if its interest is not adequately protected, adequate protection has not been construed to require the secured creditor to be paid interest by way of compensation for the delay in realization that the stay itself forces on the secured creditor. Other provisions of the Bankruptcy Code may entitle the secured creditor to postpetition interest to the extent he is overcollateralized, but a secured creditor who is undercollateralized, or who is not sufficiently overcollateralized to be entitled to postpetition interest for the duration of the bankruptcy proceeding, must suffer the delay in realization imposed by the stay without any compensation.

A second impairment imposed by the Bankruptcy Code on a financing structured as a secured loan to the Originator is that the bankruptcy estate would have the right to use the cash collections received on the collateral, so long as the secured creditor's interest is adequately protected. From the perspective of the debtor in possession, this is perhaps the most consequential of the rights it is granted by the Bankruptcy Code, for the bankruptcy estate typically is thirsty for cash and collections of such collateral can be used to slake that thirst, subject only to the constraint of providing the secured creditor adequate protection — which might be done by grant of a replacement lien on some illiquid substitute asset, or even by doing nothing at all, if there is a sufficient equity cushion in the collateral.

The Bankruptcy Code gives the bankruptcy estate numerous other rights in collateral that impair the nonbankruptcy rights of the secured creditor, but the two mentioned above are the most likely to be of importance to the bankruptcy estate in the case of assets of the type normally subjected to securitization. Borrowing from David Carlson, it is convenient to use the term "Bankruptcy Tax" to refer collectively to the rights that the Bankruptcy Code awards to the bankruptcy estate in collateral owned by the debtor that is subject to a security interest — or, if one prefers the view from the secured creditor's perspective, the collective set of impairments that the Bankruptcy Code imposes on the rights that the secured creditor has in the collateral under nonbankruptcy law. "Bankruptcy Tax" is useful both as a shorthand and as a metaphor that expresses an important truth: these impairments amount to a tax that the Bankruptcy Code levies on secured credit for the benefit of the bankruptcy estate as a whole. In a business bankruptcy, the main point of this Bankruptcy Tax is to improve the chances that a debtor that seeks to reorganize will be able to do so. The ultimate beneficiaries of the Bankruptcy Tax, therefore, are the unsecured creditors and other constituencies of the Originator that would benefit from a successful reorganization. Securitization thus can be viewed as a method of evading the Bankruptcy Tax.

The relief from the Bankruptcy Tax that securitization is designed to afford is securitization's reason for being. Because of this relief, securitized debt is rated by the credit rating agencies on the basis of the likelihood that the securitized assets will be sufficiently collectible to make the payments due under the securitized debt. The rating given to the securitized debt thus is independent of the credit rating of the Originator (that is, the rating that would be given to the Originator's ordinary unsecured debt). The securitized debt thus can achieve ratings much higher than the Originator's own credit rating. By contrast, simple secured debt issued by the Originator, even if so heavily overcollateralized that the secured creditor will eventually be paid in full, with interest, after a bankruptcy filing by the Originator, will not be rated much higher than the Originator's own credit rating. The reason is that a rating agency's rating of a debt instrument is predominantly a prediction of the likelihood that the debt will be paid in accordance with its terms. Ratings do give some weight to the amount of the recovery that the debtholder is likely to receive if the debt goes into default, but that weight is relatively modest. Payments on an Originator's secured debt will be interrupted by the Originator's bankruptcy filing, so no matter how well over-collateralized the debt may be, its rating will be based on the Originator's own rating, with only a modest bump upward, at best, to reflect the increased prob-ability of an eventual good recovery on the secured debt as compared to unse-cured debt. Neil Baron, the principal legal advisor to one of the two predominant rating agencies during the early days of securitization, stated the point as follows:

> A rating is a statement that payment will be made in accordance with the terms of an obligation. That means on time. A payment default on a triple-A rated bond is front page news. The fact that investors get paid fully at some later time makes page 11. Timeliness is an element rating agencies are obsessive about.

Substantially all of the benefits claimed for securitization are nothing more than consequences of the structure's purported avoidance of the Bankruptcy Tax, and the resulting willingness of the rating agencies to rate securitized debt on the assumption that payments thereon from collections of the securitized assets will not be interrupted by the bankruptcy of the Originator. The primary benefit claimed for securitization is that an Originator can use its securitizable assets to obtain financing at a substantially lower interest rate than the Origina-tor would have to pay on non-securitized debt. That is simply the result of the fact that, because of the bankruptcy avoidance to which securitized debt is pur-portedly entitled, securitized debt will receive a better rating than would debt incurred directly by the Originator secured by the same assets, and so financiers are content with a lower yield on the former than they would require on the latter.

Similarly, the product has been extolled on the ground that it promotes disintermediation — that is, it enables an Originator to issue debt securities and tap the capital markets directly, saving itself the middleman's fees that it would incur if it obtained financing by borrowing from a bank or other financial intermediary. That is at best a half truth. First, if the securitization structure works to avoid the Bankruptcy Tax when the debt issued by the SPE is in the form of securities, it works equally well when the debt issued by the SPE is an obliga-tion to repay a bank loan, and financing provided by banks and other traditional financial intermediaries today often is extended through securitization struc-tures when the Originator is of sufficient size to bear the transaction costs. More fundamentally, disintermediation was by no means impossible before securiti-zation structures came into use. An Originator owning assets that today it would securitize might instead issue into the capital markets its own debt securities, directly secured by those same assets. That is no more than a simple variation on a mortgage bond, familiar for more than a century and a half. Securitization structures did not make disintermediation possible; they merely made it more attractive to Originators, as a result of the rating benefit the structures afford. Disintermediation is not a separate benefit that securitization structures bestow upon Originators, but only another consequence of the avoidance of the Bankruptcy Tax.

The financing obtained by an Originator through the use of the prototypical securitization structure is economically equivalent to a nonrecourse loan by the financiers to the Originator that is secured by the assets used to support the financing. The only difference is that the securitization structure purports to be immune from the Bankruptcy Tax while the secured loan does not. In both transactions the Originator retains the residual value of the assets used to support the financing — that is, the value of the assets above what is necessary to pay the financiers their bargained-for return. In the case of the secured loan the Originator retains that residual value by its ownership of the assets. In the case of the prototypical securitization the Originator retains that residual value by its ownership of the equity of the SPE that holds the assets. In either transaction, as a result of the Originator's retaining the residual value of the assets, the risk of underperformance of the assets is borne by the Originator to the extent of that residual value. If, as is usual in a securitization transaction, the securitized debt is highly rated by a rating agency, that constitutes an evaluation by experts that it is extremely unlikely that the assets will underperform so far as to result in the financiers not receiving their bargained-for payment stream. In that event, all practical risk of the performance of the assets remains with the Originator and none is shifted to the financiers. Restated from a different perspective: not only is the prototypical securitization economically equivalent to a nonrecourse secured loan to the Originator, but in the usual case in which the securitized debt is highly rated, the financiers bear only a remote risk that the cash flow from the securitized assets will be insufficient to make the bargained-for payments to the financiers.

The economic equivalence of the prototypical securitization to a nonrecourse secured loan to the Originator is evident from comparison of the two structures, but the legal treatment that securitization seeks to achieve is dependent upon the securitization not being treated like a secured loan to the Originator by the Originator's future bankruptcy court. Hence securitization's advocates are apt to minimize or even deny the economic equivalence of the two transactions. For example, one scholar has asserted that the restrictive covenants in unsecured loan agreements "almost always" include a negative pledge covenant that restricts the debtor's ability to incur secured debt, but "rarely" restricts the debtor's ability to enter into securitization transactions. This assertion rests on slender anecdotal evidence, but even if true would merely reflect unsecured lenders' priorities in negotiating covenants. Credit analysts are not fooled. When credit analysts at rating agencies analyze the creditworthiness of an Originator that has previously done one or more securitization transactions, they treat those securitization transactions just like secured debt, adding the securitized assets and securitized debt back to the Originator's balance sheet if (as is almost invariably the case) the securitization does not transfer to the financiers any meaningful risk of performance of the securitized assets. As stated by Moody's, one of the two predominant rating agencies:

> Due to certain accounting rules established by FASB, a securitization may be considered off-balance-sheet under certain circumstances. However, most companies retain the subordinated interest in the transaction known as the equity tranche or "first-loss" piece, which is where all the risks associated with this asset pool resides. Consequently, should the asset not generate the expected amount of cash because losses have exceeded expectations, the holder of the "first-loss" position would be paid last. . . . [I]f a company retains most of the economic risk associated with its securitizations by retaining the "first-loss" piece, various financial ratios including leverage and cash flows are adjusted to account for securitization debt as the equivalent of on-balance-sheet secured borrowings.

Credit analysts at the other predominant rating agency, Standard & Poor's, are equally unblinkered.

The irony of the situation hardly requires emphasis. When analyzing the creditworthiness of an Originator, credit analysts at the predominant rating agencies steadfastly recognize that the Originator's securitized debt is economically equivalent to secured debt incurred by the Originator. Yet their colleagues at the same rating agencies who rate the securitized debt itself do so on the blithe assumption that it is quite different from secured debt incurred by the Originator.

As alluded to in the preceding discussion, accounting conventions have awarded to broad classes of securitization transactions the prize, much coveted by Originators, of off-balance-sheet treatment. That is, instead of being accounted for as if it were a secured loan (in which case, among other things, both the securitized assets and securitized debt would be shown on the Originator's consolidated balance sheet), the transaction is generally accounted for as if it were a sale of the securitized assets (and hence neither the securitized debt nor the securitized assets appear on the Originator's consolidated balance sheet). This is one attraction of securitization to Originators that, at least in principle, need not necessarily be a direct consequence of the avoidance of the Bankruptcy Tax. The accounting rules applicable to securitization have been revised repeatedly. Before 1996, avoidance of the Bankruptcy Tax was irrelevant to the accounting treatment of the transaction, but since then accounting rules have generally made avoidance of the Bankruptcy Tax a condition of off-balance-sheet treatment.

One might question the wisdom of accounting rules that permit off-balance-sheet treatment of such transactions when, as just noted, credit analysts treat them as if they were secured loans and promptly add the relevant assets and liabilities back to the balance sheet. The staff of the Securities and Exchange Commission has expressed marked skepticism about these accounting rules for that reason. Moreover, some Originators, desiring to bring their financial reporting in line with economic reality, are choosing to bring their securitizations back onto their balance sheets and accounting for them as secured debt. Whatever the attraction to other Originators of the beautification of their financial statements made possible by these accounting conventions, it cannot plausibly be claimed as a social benefit.

Naturally a securitization structure that varies from the prototypical would call for further analysis, but that does not affect the points just made. For instance, one scholar has suggested that the economic equivalence of securitization to a nonrecourse secured loan is undercut if the SPE to which the Originator conveys the securitized assets is not a subsidiary of the Originator but rather is a subsidiary of some other entity ("X"). That is by no means the case. As previously noted, the equity of the SPE in the prototypical structure represents the residual value of the assets that support the financing. A structure in which the equity of the SPE is owned by X, therefore, is simply the economic equivalent of a nonrecourse loan to the Originator secured by those assets, coupled with a conveyance of those assets to X subject to the security interest. Of course that residual interest will have significant value, as overcollateralization will have been necessary to afford the securitized debt a high rating, and the Originator will not simply give that value away to an unaffiliated X. Pricing that residual interest in a way that shifts the risk of its value to X is likely to be a problem. Losses from failure to collect any of the securitized assets will be borne by the holder of that residual interest, so its value will be very sensitive to small changes in the collectibility of the securitized assets; moreover, collection will be within the control of the Originator to some extent if, as is commonly the case, it acts as servicer of the securitized assets. This, no doubt, is why the rating agencies rarely see transactions that, like the foregoing, shift material risk of nonperformance of the securitized assets away from the Originator.

It is evident that securitization conflicts with the policy of the Bankruptcy Code as it currently stands. The Bankruptcy Code imposes the Bankruptcy Tax on secured transactions, and one of the central purposes for doing so is to promote reorganization by assuring that the debtor can use collateral, including cash collateral, during the reorganization process, subject to the adequate protection safeguard provided by the Code. A debtor who has engaged in a financing structured as the prototypical securitization has effected the economic equivalent of a secured transaction, but the structure, if respected, would prevent the debtor from using the cash generated by the securitized assets whether or not the financiers can be adequately protected. The whole purpose of the structure, and its only substantial effect, is to evade the Bankruptcy Tax, and thereby deprive the estate and other creditors of the benefits that follow from the Bankruptcy Tax — which, among other things, might make the difference between a successful reorganization and one that fails for want of cash.

The proposition that securitization conflicts with bankruptcy policy argues itself, and so is much less interesting than attempts to deny it. Steven Schwarcz advanced a rebuttal that is worth quoting in full:

> [T]he argument that securitization . . . undermines bankruptcy policy is a chimera. The originator, after all, freely makes the choice of its financing transactions. Securitization has a lower cost precisely due to bankruptcy remoteness. If, therefore, the originator chooses securitization in order to benefit from that lower cost, it should not have the right to later complain. Moreover, the very availability of securitization as a financing option, by providing liquidity to otherwise viable originators unable to borrow, has been shown to facilitate the fundamental bankruptcy policy of debtor rehabilitation. This sets forth two arguments, which

respectively implicate two long-running debates among scholars of bankruptcy and commercial law. Whatever the normative merits of these arguments, they are not consistent with the positive law of the Bankruptcy Code as it currently stands.

The final sentence of the quoted paragraph argues that avoidance of the Bankruptcy Tax provides liquidity for Originators who might be unable to borrow if their financiers had to suffer the Bankruptcy Tax (or, to make the point more generally, lower cost financing for all Originators who use the technique). That amounts to saying that the Bankruptcy Tax is bad policy—that debtors as a class, their unsecured creditors, and other affected constituencies are better off if debtors are allowed to do secured financing that is not subject to the Bankruptcy Tax (at least as to collateral of the type typically used to back securitizations). As a normative argument this is a special case of a more general decades-long academic debate as to the social utility of secured credit, played for lower stakes: the general debate considers the whole bundle of rights possessed by a secured creditor, while securitization involves only the relatively marginal increment of rights represented by the Bankruptcy Tax. The normative debate, though deeply interesting, is not to be confused with positive law. Congress has made its normative judgment on this point, and has ordained that secured creditors must bear the Bankruptcy Tax. A court adjudicating a challenge to a securitization transaction under the Bankruptcy Code as it currently stands is not at liberty to ignore that decision.

The other argument made by Schwarcz in the quoted paragraph is that an Originator who chooses to securitize, and thereby obtain the benefit of the lower-cost financing made available to it by the avoidance of the Bankruptcy Tax, should have no right after its bankruptcy to seek to impose the Bankruptcy Tax on the transaction. That amounts to saying that a debtor should have the power to enter into an enforceable prepetition waiver of the Bankruptcy Tax as to a secured financing (again, at least as to collateral of the type typically used to back securitizations), so long as the debtor receives consideration for the waiver. That argument implicates the long-running academic debate over "contract bankruptcy"—that is, the merits of replacing the current mandatory regime of bankruptcy rules with a regime that would allow each debtor to shape by contract in advance of its failure the rules that will apply to it following its failure . . .

Here too, Professor Schwarcz substitutes argument from a highly unsettled normative debate for positive law. The prototypical securitization is a structural substitute for an explicit prepetition waiver by a debtor of the Bankruptcy Tax that would otherwise apply to its secured financing, made by the debtor at the outset of the financing. Under current law, such an explicit waiver would not be enforceable . . .

To legal entrepreneurs seeking to avoid the Bankruptcy Tax on their secured financings, the pragmatic benefits of the securitization structure go beyond the obvious one of disguising the conflict with bankruptcy policy. It also shifts the burden of going forward in the event of the Originator's bankruptcy. In addition to its other defects, an express prepetition waiver of the Bankruptcy Tax given by the Originator to secured financiers would be of no avail to those financiers unless they place it before the bankruptcy judge and persuade him to enforce it. The securitization structure, by contrast, hums along without interruption after the Originator's bankruptcy . . .

PROBLEM SET 19.1

1. What are the benefits to the debtor of financing its operations by asset securitization? Who pays the costs?
2. The excerpt notes that the theory behind the securitization is to allow creditors to continue to collect cash flows from the assets, and maintain control over the assets, even after the originator's bankruptcy. But if the assets are central to the debtor-originator's business, what might the more likely outcome be?
3. One of the perceived benefits of securitization involved its accounting treatment — perhaps another example of the tension between reality and finance theory? The fundamental benefit involved the ability to leave SPEs (or SPVs) "unconsolidated" so that they did not show up on the balance sheet of the company. Following the recent financial crisis, GAAP has been further revised to require consolidation in more instances. See FASB Statement No. 166, FASB Statement No. 167.

2. UNDERSTANDING THE STRUCTURES

As the next case shows, the structures of asset securitizations have become increasingly complex.

BNY CORPORATE TRUSTEE SERVICES LIMITED AND OTHERS v. NEUBERGER BERMAN EUROPE LTD (ON BEHALF OF SEALINK FUNDING LTD) AND OTHERS

United Kingdom Supreme Court
Easter Term
[2013] UKSC 28
9 May 2013
Heard on 25 and 26 February 2013

LORD WALKER (with whom Lord Mance, Lord Sumption and Lord Carnwath agree)

INTRODUCTION

1. Sections (1) and (2) of section 123 of the Insolvency Act 1986 ("the 1986 Act") provide as follows:

"(1) A company is deemed unable to pay its debts — (a) [non-compliance with a statutory demand for a debt exceeding £750 presently due]

(b) to (d) [unsatisfied execution on judgment debt in terms appropriate to England and Wales, Scotland and Northern Ireland respectively]

(e) if it is proved to the satisfaction of the court that the company is unable to pay its debts as they fall due.

(2) A company is also deemed unable to pay its debts if it is proved to the satisfaction of the court that the value of the company's assets is less than the amount of its liabilities, taking into account its contingent and prospective liabilities."

A company in the situation described in subsection (1)(e) is often said to be "cash-flow" insolvent. A company in the situation described in subsection (2) is often said to be "balance-sheet" insolvent, but that expression is not to be taken literally. It is a convenient shorthand expression, but a company's statutory balance sheet, properly prepared in accordance with the requirements of company law, may omit some contingent assets or some contingent liabilities. There is no statutory provision which links section 123(2) of the 1986 Act to the detailed provisions of the Companies Act 2006 as to the form and contents of a company's financial statements. This appeal is concerned with the construction and effect of section 123(1)(e) and (2) as incorporated into the documentation of an issue of loan notes.

2. The statutory provisions were incorporated, with some small modifications, into the conditions applicable to loan notes issued in the course of a securitisation transaction comprising a portfolio of non-conforming mortgage loans secured on residential property in the United Kingdom. The issuer is Eurosail-UK 2007-3BL plc ("Eurosail"), one of many similar single purpose entities ("SPEs") set up by the Lehman Brothers group (but off the balance sheet of any of that group's companies) not long before its collapse. Eurosail is the principal respondent to this appeal, and it has a cross-appeal on a subsidiary issue. The other respondent appearing before this court, BNY Corporate Trustee Services Ltd ("the Trustee") is part of the BNY Mellon Group. It is the trustee for the holders ("Noteholders") of loan notes of various classes issued by Eurosail. It has adopted a neutral attitude in the proceedings (as explained in its written case), and has not appeared by counsel before this court. But it will, in the event that the appeal succeeds and the cross-appeal fails, have an important judgment to make as to material prejudice to the Noteholders' interests.

3. In 2007 Eurosail (described in the documentation as "the Issuer") acquired a portfolio of mortgage loans, secured on residential property in England and Scotland and denominated in sterling, to the principal amount of approximately £650m. Most of the mortgages were regarded as "non-conforming" in that they did not meet the lending requirements of building societies and banks. This purchase was funded by the issue on 16 July 2007 of loan notes in five principal classes (A, B, C, D and E) comprising 14 different subclasses, some denominated in sterling, some in US dollars and some in euros. In the designation of the classes "a" indicated that the loan was denominated in euros, "b" US dollars and "c" pounds sterling. The senior (class A) notes were divided into three sub-classes, denominated in one of the three currencies, designated and issued as follows:

A1b US$200,000,000
A1c £102,500,000
A2a € 64,500,000
A2b US$100,000,000
A2c £ 63,000,000
A3a €215,000,000
A3c £ 64,500,000

The B, C, D and E Notes were issued in smaller amounts, with variations in currency but no subclasses having different priorities as between themselves. There were also some notes designated as ETc "revenue-backed" notes. The total sum raised was just under £660,000,000. After payment of costs and expenses of the issue the initial surplus of assets over prospective liabilities (if taken at face value) was quite small.

4. The provisions of section 123(1) and (2) of the 1986 Act are incorporated into an important provision in the conditions of issue of the Notes ("the Conditions"). Condition 9(a) (events of default) provides that the Trustee may on the occurrence of any of five specified events (an "Event of Default") serve on Eurosail a written notice (an "Enforcement Notice") declaring the Notes to be due and repayable. In some circumstances the Trustee is obliged to serve such a notice. In the absence of an Event of Default the A1 Notes were repayable in 2027 at latest (in fact they have already been repaid, as have the revenue-backed notes). All the other Notes are repayable in 2045 at latest.

5. The Events of Default include (Condition 9(a)(iii)):

"The Issuer, otherwise than for the purposes of such amalgamation or reconstruction as is referred to in sub-paragraph (iv) below, ceasing or, through or consequent upon an official action of the Board of Directors of the Issuer, threatens to cease to carry on business or a substantial part of its business or being unable to pay its debts as and when they fall due or, within the meaning of section 123(1) or (2) (as if the words 'it is proved to the satisfaction of the court' did not appear in section 123(2) of the Insolvency Act 1986 (as that section may be amended from time to time), being deemed unable to pay its debts . . ."

Under a proviso to Condition 9(a), an occurrence falling within sub-paragraph (iii) counts as an Event of Default only if the Trustee certifies to Eurosail that it is, in the Trustee's sole opinion, materially prejudicial to the interests of the Noteholders.

6. The service of an Enforcement Notice would have immediate and far-reaching consequences for all the Noteholders (other than the A1 and ETc Noteholders, whose Notes have already been fully redeemed). As described in more detail below, an Enforcement Notice shifts their rights from the regime prescribed in Condition 2(g) (priority of payments prior to enforcement) to the regime prescribed in Condition 2(h) (priority of payments post-enforcement). Under the latter regime Noteholders of Class A3 ("A3 Noteholders") rank pari passu with Noteholders of Class A2 ("A2 Noteholders") for repayment of principal. That is in contrast with the present regime, under which A2 and A3 Noteholders rank pari passu for interest payments (clause 2(g)(vi)) but A2 Noteholders have priority over A3 Noteholders in receiving repayments of principal out of funds representing principal sums received on the redemption of mortgages in the portfolio (those funds being included in the definition of "Actual Redemption Funds" in the preamble to the Conditions).

7. It is in these circumstances that the construction of section 123(2) of the 1986 Act, as incorporated into Condition 9(a)(iii), has assumed such importance. Eurosail, together with those of the A2 Noteholders who appeared below, succeeded before Sir Andrew Morritt C [2010] EWHC 2005 (Ch), [2011] 1 WLR 1200, and the Court of Appeal [2011] EWCA Civ 227, [2011] 1 WLR 2524. The Court of Appeal considered that section 123(2) should be interpreted broadly and in line with standards of commercial probity:

"A balance has to be drawn between the right of an honest and prudent businessman, who is prepared to work hard, to continue to trade out of his difficulties if he can genuinely see a light at the end of the tunnel, and the corresponding obligation to 'put up the shutters,' when, by continuing to trade, he would be doing so at the expense of his creditors and in disregard of those business considerations which a reasonable businessman is expected to observe."

(That is a quotation from paragraph 216 of the *Report of the Review Committee on Insolvency Law and Practice* (1982) (Cmnd 8558), better known as the Cork Report, reflecting the view of Professor Goode; this passage is quoted in para 54 of the judgment of Lord Neuberger MR in the Court of Appeal). The appellant A3 Noteholders say that this passage is not in point. They have argued for a much stricter construction. They have emphasised that a company's inability to pay its debts is no more than a precondition to the exercise of the court's jurisdiction, which is discretionary, to make a winding up order or an administration order. The precondition to be satisfied should be, they have argued, transparent and certain, leaving scope for the exercise of discretion on the hearing of the petition. There has also been argument as to whether the statutory text (as incorporated in an amended form, and also allowing for possible future legislative amendment) must bear the same meaning as it would in actual winding-up proceedings, or whether it can and should, as incorporated, take account of the commercial context of the Conditions.

8. Those, in outline summary, are the positions of the opposing parties on the appeal. The cross-appeal, which is relevant only if the appeal is successful, is concerned with the so-called Post-Enforcement Call Option ("PECO") which is a subsidiary (but technically important) part of the securitisation transaction.

9. Before going further into the complexities of the appeal I would comment that the image invoked by Professor Goode of an honest and prudent trader working hard to turn his business round relates, as was pointed out by Mr Moss QC for the appellants, to the law of insolvency as it applies to individuals. Even if translated into corporate terms, it has very little bearing on the situation in which Eurosail now finds itself. Its present financial position and future prospects are not matters for which Eurosail and its managers merit either praise or criticism, since those matters are almost entirely out of their control. They depend on three imponderables: first, (since the currency and interest-rate hedging arrangements with the Lehman Brothers group have failed, leaving Eurosail with a claim in its insolvency) the movements of the US dollar and the euro relative to the pound sterling; secondly, movements in LIBOR or equivalent interest rates on loans denominated in those three currencies; and thirdly, the performance of the United Kingdom economy in general, and the United Kingdom residential property market in particular, as influencing the performance of the mortgage portfolio.

THE TRANSACTION DOCUMENTS

10. The legal documents relating to the securitisation issue are, as Lord Neuberger MR put it, regrettably and forbiddingly voluminous. Apart from the Conditions themselves there was a formal trust deed made between the Trustee and Eurosail, a Liquidity Facility Agreement, currency swaps agreements, a Fixed/Floating Swap Agreement, a BBR Swap Agreement and other agreements relating to administrative matters (there is a full list of "transaction documents" in the definition of that expression in the preamble to the Conditions). Several expressions used in the Conditions involve a paperchase to other documents in order to find their definitions. Mr Moss [the barrister representing the Appellant] opened the documents very lightly, moving rapidly from Condition 9(a)(iii) to concentrate his submissions on the construction of section 123(1) and (2) of the 1986 Act. Mr Dicker QC

(for Eurosail) went into the Conditions more fully to pave the way for his contextual arguments. Without pre-judging those arguments I think it is necessary, if only in order to appreciate the consequences of the opposing arguments, to have an outline understanding of how the SPE (which counsel concurred in describing as a "closed system" or "wrapper") operated before the collapse of Lehman Brothers, of how it operates now (after the collapse of Lehman Brothers but before any Enforcement Notice), and of how it would operate after the service of an Enforcement Notice.

11. Interest is payable on all unredeemed Notes quarterly in arrears, the first payment having been made on 13 September 2007. The annual rate of interest is linked to LIBOR or its dollar or euro equivalents, exceeding that rate by a margin which varies from 0.07% for A1b Notes to 4% for E Notes.

12. Mortgage interest received by Eurosail cascades down the metaphorical waterfall set out in the 24 sub-paragraphs of Condition 2(g). The first claims on the income stream are for remuneration, charges and expenses; then sums due to the Liquidity Facility Provider, and (sub-paragraph (v), but only until the collapse of Lehman Brothers) sums payable under or in connection with the Fixed/Floating Swap Agreement and the BBR Swap Agreement (but not any currency swaps). Payments to currency swaps counterparties were linked to interest payments to particular classes of Noteholders, so that payments to counterparties in respect of A Noteholders come into the provision for payment of interest to those Noteholders, which is made pari passu as between all the A sub-classes. The next priority was for payment-off of any A Principal Deficiency (another expression defined in the preamble), but in practice such a deficiency could arise only if all the junior classes of Notes had become valueless. Next in the waterfall come similar groups of provisions for payment of interest, sums due to the currency swaps counterparties (and any B Principal Deficiency) in respect of B Notes and so on for all the other classes.

13. On 15 September 2008 Lehman Brothers Holdings Inc ("LBHI"), the guarantor of the swaps counterparty, Lehman Brothers Special Financing Ltd ("LBSF") filed for Chapter 11 bankruptcy, as did LBSF on 3 October 2008. The swaps were terminated on 13 November 2009. Eurosail has made a claim against LBHI's and LBSF's bankrupt estates for about $221,000,000. At the time of the hearings below, the claim had not been admitted and no distribution has been made in respect of it. During the last three years sterling has depreciated significantly against both the euro and the dollar, but the prevailing low level of interest rates has resulted in a surplus ("excess spread") of mortgage interest received by Eurosail, which has enabled it to continue to pay in full the interest on all the outstanding Notes of every class.

14. In the meantime, both before and after the collapse of Lehman Brothers, Eurosail received principal sums from time to time as principal secured by the mortgages was repaid, either by way of partial or total redemption by mortgagors, or by enforcement of the security against mortgagors who were in default. These sums have been and are at present applied under Condition 5(b)(i) as "Actual Redemption Funds," on each date for payment of interest, in repaying the principal of the Notes in the order of priority A1 (now fully repaid), A2, A3, B, and so on. There is a proviso to Condition 5(b) under which the order of priority may be altered. The first possible variation (proviso (A)) applies if all the A1 and A2 Notes have been redeemed and other (favourable) specified conditions are satisfied: the A3 to E1c Notes then rank pari passu. Conversely, under the other variation (proviso (B)), which applies if there is an A Principal Deficiency, priority is granted to the A Notes as a single class ranking pari passu.

15. Events of default are regulated by Condition 9. The events specified in Condition 9(a) are, apart from that already set out (para 5 above): default in payment for three business days of any principal or interest due on any of the Notes; breach by Eurosail of any of its obligations and failure to remedy the breach (if remediable) for 14 days after notice of the breach given by the Trustee; the making of an order or resolution for the winding up of Eurosail, otherwise than for an approved amalgamation or reconstruction; and the initiation of insolvency or administration proceedings, or the levying of execution (subject to various qualifications which it is unnecessary to set out in detail).

16. If the Event of Default is an event under Condition 9(a)(iii) or a breach of Eurosail's obligations, there is a further requirement that the Trustee shall have certified to Eurosail "that such event is, in its sole opinion, materially prejudicial to the interests of the Noteholders." For this purpose the Trustee may under the trust deed "have regard only to (i) the interests of the A Noteholders if, in the Trustee's sole opinion, there is a conflict between the interests of the A Noteholders (or any Class thereof) and the interests of the B Noteholders, the C Noteholders, the D Noteholders and/or the E Noteholders." This provision does not indicate how the Trustee is to exercise its discretion in the event of a conflict (such as there now potentially is) between the interests of the A2 Noteholders and the A3 Noteholders. If there is an Event of Default (and, in the cases just mentioned, it is materially prejudicial) the Trustee may at its discretion serve an Enforcement Notice on Eurosail. Moreover it is obliged to do so if requested or directed (i) by holders of at least 25% of the outstanding "Most Senior Class of Notes" (defined as meaning the A Noteholders, rather than a subclass of them) or (ii) by an extraordinary resolution of the holders of that class. This court was not shown any evidence, and did not hear any submissions, as to whether either of those requirements would be likely to be satisfied in practice.

17. On service of the Enforcement Notice the Notes become immediately due and payable and the Noteholders' security becomes enforceable. Thereupon the order of priority shifts from that in Condition 2(g) to that in Condition 2(h). It is unnecessary to go through all the detail of Condition 2(h). The all-important change is that under Condition 2(h)(v) the available funds are applicable to pay "pari passu and pro rata (1) all amounts of interest and principal then due and payable on the A1c Notes, the A2c Notes and the A3c Notes and (2) [subject to provisions about currency swaps that have now lapsed] any interest and principal then due and payable on the A1b Notes, the A2a Notes, the A2b Notes and the A3a Notes, respectively." In practical terms, the A2 Notes would no longer have priority, in terms of principal, to the A3 Notes.

18. The opening words of condition 2(h) express the Trustee's obligation as being to make payments "to the extent of the funds available to [Eurosail] and from the proceeds of enforcement of the Security" (with exceptions that need not be detailed). The penultimate provision of Condition 2(h) provides: "The Noteholders have full recourse to [Eurosail] in respect of the payments prescribed above and accordingly are entitled to bring a claim under English law, subject to the Trust Deed, for the full amount of such payments in accordance with Condition 10 (Enforcement of Notes)." Mr Dicker did not challenge Mr Moss's submission that the opening words do not contradict the penultimate provision, and that seems to be correct. The opening words are directed to the Trustee's obligations, not to those of Eurosail.

19. Condition 5(j) contains the PECO (Post Enforcement Call Option) which is the subject of the cross-appeal. This option (which has been given effect to as a separate written agreement between the Trustee and a company named or

referred to as OptionCo) is regarded in the industry as a means of achieving the effect of limited recourse without the adverse tax consequences that would then have followed from a simple express non-recourse provision. The operative part of Clause 5(j) is as follows:

> "All of the Noteholders will, at the request of the holder of the Post Enforcement Call Option, sell all (but not some only) of their holdings of the Notes to the holder of the Post Enforcement Call Option, pursuant to the option granted to it by the Trustee (as agent for the Noteholders) to acquire all (but not some only) of the Notes (plus accrued interest thereon), for the consideration of one euro cent per Euro Note outstanding, one dollar cent per Dollar Note outstanding and one penny per Sterling Note outstanding (and for these purposes, each Global Note shall be one Note) in the event that the Security for the Notes is enforced, at any time after the date on which the Trustee determines that the proceeds of such enforcement are insufficient, after payment of all other claims ranking higher in priority to the Notes and pro rata payment of all claims ranking in equal priority to the Notes and after the application of any such proceeds to the Notes under the Deed of Charge, to pay any further principal and interest and any other amounts whatsoever due in respect of the Notes."

BANKRUPTCY REMOTENESS

20. "Bankruptcy remoteness" was the expression used by Standard & Poor's credit-rating agency, and generally in the industry, to describe one criterion for a SPE to obtain a satisfactory credit rating for its loan notes. This is not the place to consider either the reliability of the credit-rating agencies' judgments on Notes secured by sub-prime mortgages, or the influence that their judgments seem to have had in the market (caused, some have suggested, by the industry's general inability to comprehend the risks inherent in its own creations). But the notion of "bankruptcy remoteness," even if imperfectly understood, underlay many features of the Conditions and the arrangements of which they formed part.

21. In developing his contextual argument that this court should (if necessary) mould the meaning of section 123(1) and (2), as incorporated into Condition 9(a)(3) so as to take account of commercial realities, Mr Dicker [for the Respondents] drew particular attention to five features of the arrangements. They are set out and discussed in section B2 of Eurosail's case. Most of them have been mentioned already, at least in passing, but it may be helpful to bring them together in summary form. They are relevant not only (arguably) to the issue of construction but also (without room for argument) to determining the likely length of deferment of Eurosail's long-term liabilities under the Conditions, in the absence of an Event of Default which triggers an Enforcement Notice. These points are covered at some length in the witness statements of Mr Mark Filer, a director of Wilmington Trust SP Services (London) Ltd, Eurosail's corporate services provider.

22. The five salient features of the Conditions and the supporting documentation bearing on the likely deferment of Eurosail's obligations in respect of principal and interest are as follows:

> (1) Condition 2(g) defines Eurosail's obligations for payment of interest on the Notes (after remuneration, charges and expenses) in terms of the Available Revenue Fund (see para 12 above). If that source is insufficient for payment of interest on any of the Junior Notes (that is, those which are not A Notes) the obligation is deferred (while accruing interest) under Condition 6(i) and (j), if necessary until the final redemption date in 2045.

(2) Temporary shortages of income can be provided for by the Liquidity Facility (reimbursements to which have a high order of priority under Condition 2(g)(iv)).

(3) As to principal, redemption of Notes (other than the redeemed A1 Notes and the revenue-backed Notes) is not due until 2045. Until then redemption is limited to the Actual Redemption Funds (as defined in the preamble) which are applied in the appropriate order of priority under Condition 5(b) (see para 14 above).

(4) Any loss of principal resulting from default on mortgages is termed a 'Principal Deficiency' and is recorded in the Principal Deficiency Ledger (the detailed provisions as to this are found not in the Conditions but in Clauses 8 and 9 of the Cash/Bond Administration Agreement). If there is surplus income from the mortgage payments, the 'excess spread' can be used to reduce or eliminate any Principal Deficiency on whatever is the highest-ranking class of Notes with a deficiency. Recoupment of a Principal Deficiency takes priority to the payment of interest on lower-ranking Notes (see para 12 above).

(5) Finally there is the PECO, which is intended to produce the same, or a similar result as an express limited-recourse provision (see paras 18 and 19 above).

. . .

39. At first instance the Chancellor started with three propositions derived from the case law: that the assets to be valued are the present assets of the company; that "contingent and prospective liabilities" are not to be taken at their full face value; and that:

> "'Taking account of' must be recognised in the context of the overall question posed by the subsection, namely whether the company is to be deemed to be insolvent because the amount of its liabilities exceeds the value of its assets. This will involve consideration of the relevant facts of the case, including when the prospective liability falls due, whether it is payable in sterling or some other currency, what assets will be available to meet it and what if any provision is made for the allocation of losses in relation to those assets."

He then set out four reasons for concluding that the value of Eurosail's assets exceeded its liabilities, "having taken account of its contingent and prospective liabilities to such extent as appears to be necessary at this stage."

40. In the Court of Appeal Lord Neuberger MR did not disagree with anything in the Chancellor's judgment so far as it related to statutory construction. He did however go further in his detailed discussion of section 123(2). He observed:

> "In practical terms, it would be rather extraordinary if section 123(2) was satisfied every time a company's liabilities exceeded the value of its assets. Many companies which are solvent and successful, and many companies early on in their lives, would be deemed unable to pay their debts if this was the meaning of section 123(2). Indeed, the issuer is a good example of this: its assets only just exceeded its liabilities when it was formed, and it was more than possible that, even if things went well, it would fall from time to time within the ambit of section 123(2) if the appellants are right as to the meaning of that provision."

41. Lord Neuberger MR developed this at paras 47 to 49 of his judgment:

> "47. More generally, I find it hard to discern any conceivable policy reason why a company should be at risk of being wound up simply because the aggregate value (however calculated) of its liabilities exceeds that of its assets. Many companies in that position are successful and creditworthy, and cannot in any way be

characterised as 'unable to pay [their] debts.' Such a mechanistic, even artificial, reason for permitting a creditor to present a petition to wind up a company could, in my view, only be justified if the words of section 123(2) compelled that conclusion, and in my opinion they do not.

48. In my view, the purpose of section 123(2) has been accurately characterised by Professor Sir Roy Goode in *Principles of Corporate Insolvency Law*, 3rd ed (2005). Having referred to section 123(1)(e) as being the 'cash flow test' and to section 123(2) as being the 'balance sheet test,' he said this, at para 4–06: 'If the cash flow test were the only relevant test [for insolvency] then current and short-term creditors would in effect be paid at the expense of creditors to whom liabilities were incurred after the company had reached the point of no return because of an incurable deficiency in its assets.'

49. In my judgment, both the purpose and the applicable test of section 123(2) are accurately encapsulated in that brief passage."

42. Toulson LJ agreed with Lord Neuberger MR but expressed himself in a more guarded way. He agreed that Professor Sir Roy Goode had "rightly discerned the underlying policy" but added that Professor Goode's reference to a company having "reached the point of no return because of an incurable deficiency in its assets" illuminates the purpose of the subsection but does not purport to be a paraphrase of it. He continued:

"Essentially, section 123(2) requires the court to make a judgment whether it has been established that, looking at the company's assets and making proper allowance for its prospective and contingent liabilities, it cannot reasonably be expected to be able to meet those liabilities. If so, it will be deemed insolvent although it is currently able to pay its debts as they fall due. The more distant the liabilities, the harder this will be to establish."

I agree with what Toulson LJ said here, and with great respect to Lord Neuberger MR I consider that "the point of no return" should not pass into common usage as a paraphrase of the effect of section 123(2). But in the case of a company's liabilities that can as matters now stand be deferred for over 30 years, and where the company is (without any permanent increase in its borrowings) paying its debts as they fall due, the court should proceed with the greatest caution in deciding that the company is in a state of balance-sheet insolvency under section 123(2).

REASONING IN THE COURTS BELOW

43. Sir Andrew Morritt C, having set out some general propositions as to the effect of section 123 (1)(e) and (2), rejected the A3 Noteholders' submission that Eurosail was plainly insolvent for the purposes of section 123(2) as applied by Condition 9(a)(iii). He relied on four points, set out in paras 34 to 37 of his judgment. First, Eurosail's claims in the insolvencies of LBHI and LBSF, though not admitted, could not be ignored. The secondary market indicated that the claim was worth 35% to 37% of US$221m (that is, a value of the order of £60m). Second, a large part of the total deficiency that was claimed to exist was due to conversion into sterling at the prevailing spot rate of liabilities not due for payment until 2045. Third, the future liabilities were fully funded in the limited sense that deficiencies resulting from mortgage defaults reduced Eurosail's liability to the Noteholders through the operation of the Principal Deficiency Ledger. Fourth, the Chancellor was able to infer that a calculation of the then present values of assets and liabilities would not show a deficiency, since Eurosail was well able to pay its debts as they fell

due, there was no deficiency on the Principal Deficiency Ledger, and projected redemptions of each class of A Notes were in advance of the maturity dates.

44. In the Court of Appeal counsel appearing for the A2 Noteholders did not feel able to give complete support to the Chancellor's second point, and Lord Neuberger MR accepted the submission of counsel for the appellants:

> "As Mr Sheldon [then appearing for the A3 Noteholders] said, one has to value a future or contingent liability in a foreign currency at the present exchange rate. By definition, that is the present sterling market value of the liability."

I would also respectfully question the Chancellor's third point. The Chancellor had earlier in his judgment, at para 13, referred to clause 8 of the Cash/Bond Administration Agreement, which provides for the maintenance of Principal Deficiency Ledgers. That seems to be the basis of his point about liabilities being self-cancelling. But clause 8 seems to be concerned with no more than an accountancy exercise, not with a permanent extinction of liabilities. It operates to defer liabilities for principal until the final redemption date, if circumstances require, and provided that an Enforcement Notice is not given in the meantime. But Condition 2(h) provides for Eurosail to be liable on a full recourse basis post-enforcement, as already noted (para 18 above).

45. Lord Neuberger MR did not accept that a forecast deficiency based on then current exchange rates could be dismissed as entirely speculative. He started from Eurosail's audited accounts for the year ending 30 November 2009, which showed a net liability of £74.557m. He noted that this figure required two substantial amendments (one for the Lehman Brothers claim, and the other for the full recourse factor) "which, ironically and coincidentally, virtually cancel each other out." So his final discussion and conclusion starts with an assumed deficiency of the order of £75m.

46. Against that Lord Neuberger MR set three factors. The first was that a deficiency of £75m, with an aggregate principal sum of just over £420m outstanding on the mortgages, was less than 17% of the assets. Secondly, the deficit was largely based on the assumption that exchange rates would remain constant:

> "Of course, they are as likely to move in an adverse direction as they are to move in a favourable direction, but the volatility of those rates tell against the appellants given that they have to establish that the issuer has reached the point of no return."

Thirdly, the court was looking a long way ahead:

> "Not only do all the unredeemed notes have a final redemption date in 2045, but it appears from the evidence that the weighted average term of the remaining mortgages is in the region of 18 years, and the rate of early redemption has slowed significantly and is likely, according to expert assessment, to remain low for the time being."

47. Lord Neuberger MR accepted that there was a real possibility that, if no Enforcement Notice was served, events might turn out to the disadvantage of the A3 Noteholders:

> "However, as mentioned, a future or contingent creditor of a company can very often show that he would be better off if the company were wound up rather than being permitted to carry on business. In a commercially sensible legal system that cannot of itself justify the creditor seeking to wind up the company."

Toulson and Wilson LJJ agreed with this reasoning. Toulson LJ emphasised the importance of the liabilities being distant in time (para 119, quoted in para 42 above). The appeal was therefore dismissed, as was the cross-appeal.

CONCLUSIONS

48. The crucial issue, to my mind, is how far the Court of Appeal's conclusion depended on the "point of no return" test. For reasons already mentioned, I consider that that is not the correct test, if and in so far as it goes beyond the need for a petitioner to satisfy the court, on the balance of probabilities, that a company has insufficient assets to be able to meet all its liabilities, including prospective and contingent liabilities. If it means no more than that, it is unhelpful, except as illuminating (as Toulson LJ put it) the purpose of section 123(2).

49. In my view the Court of Appeal would have reached the same conclusion without reference to any "point of no return" test; and I would myself reach the same conclusion. Eurosail's ability or inability to pay all its debts, present or future, may not be finally determined until much closer to 2045, that is more than 30 years from now. The complex documentation under which the loan notes were issued contains several mechanisms (identified in para 22(1) to (4) above, the PECO being disregarded for present purposes) for ensuring that liabilities in respect of principal are, if necessary, deferred until the final redemption date, unless the post-enforcement regime comes into operation. The movements of currencies and interest rates in the meantime, if not entirely speculative, are incapable of prediction with any confidence. The court cannot be satisfied that there will eventually be a deficiency.

50. I would therefore dismiss the appeal. I would also dismiss the cross-appeal, for the same reasons as were given by the Chancellor and the Court of Appeal. It is not necessary to consider Mr Dicker's arguments based on supposed inconsistencies and commercial realities. . . . The loan notes documentation did indeed contain some provisions which are inconsistent with the post-enforcement regime being triggered by a temporary deficiency of assets. But the court might well have taken the view, on documents of such complexity, that the draftsman had simply failed to grasp all its many and various implications, and that it was not for the court to rewrite the documents for the parties.

LORD HOPE

51. I would dismiss the appeal for the reasons given by Lord Walker. I would also dismiss the cross-appeal, which concerns the effect of the PECO on the application of section 123(2) of the 1986 Act as incorporated into Condition 9(a)(iii). The question which it raises no longer needs to be answered as the Noteholders' appeal on the question whether Eurosail ("the Issuer") was unable to pay its debts was not successful. But Sir Andrew Morritt C [2011] 1 WLR 122 gave his view on it in paras 39–44 of his judgment, and so too did Lord Neuberger MR in the Court of Appeal [2011] 1 WLR 2524 in paras 84–100. A PECO is widely used in securitisation transactions of the kind that was entered into in this case, and we have been told that the question is of some importance to the securitisation market more generally. So it is appropriate that we should give our reasons for agreeing with the Chancellor and the Court of Appeal that it has no effect on the way the liability of the Issuer to the Noteholders for the purposes of the default provision in Condition 9(a)(iii) is to be calculated.

52. The Trustee entered into a PECO Agreement on behalf of the Noteholders on 16 July 2007, which is the same date as that on which the Notes were issued. By

Clause 3.1 it granted an option to a company called Eurosail Options Ltd (referred to in the Agreement as "OptionCo"):

"to acquire all (but not some only) of the Notes (plus accrued interest thereon) in the event that the Security for the Notes is enforced and the Trustee, after the payment of the proceeds of such enforcement, determines that the proceeds of such enforcement are insufficient, after payment of all claims ranking in priority to or pari passu with the Notes pursuant to the Deed of Charge, to pay in full all principal and/or interest and any other amounts whatsoever due in respect of the Notes. The Trustee shall promptly after the Security is enforced and the proceeds of such enforcement are paid, make a determination of whether or not there is such an insufficiency. If the Trustee determines that there is such an insufficiency the Trustee shall forthwith give notice (the 'Insufficiency Notice') of such determination to OptionCo and the Issuer."

53. Clause 3.1 has to be read together with Condition 5(j) (see para 19, above), which provides that each Noteholder will, on the exercise of the option conferred on OptionCo, sell to the company the whole of his holding of notes for the nominal consideration for which the PECO provides. It also has to be read together with the Event of Default described in Condition 9(a)(iii): see para 5, above. Under that provision a default occurs, among other things, in the event of the Issuer:

"being unable to pay its debts as and when they fall due or, within the meaning of section 123(1) or (2) (as if the words 'it is proved to the satisfaction of the court' did not appear in section 123(2)) of the Insolvency Act 1986 (as that section may be amended from time to time), being deemed unable to pay its debts."

54. The Prospectus at p 26 contains this explanation of the effect of these provisions, under the heading "Considerations related to the Instruments," for prospective purchasers:

"Although the Instruments will be full recourse obligations of the Issuer, upon enforcement of the security for the Instruments, the Trustee . . . will, in practice, have recourse only to the Loans and Collateral Security, and to any other assets of the Issuer then in existence as described in this document . . ."

55. The purpose of a PECO is to achieve bankruptcy remoteness for the issuer. Its aim is to prevent the issuer from being susceptible to insolvent winding up proceedings by ensuring so far as possible that, if its assets prove to be insufficient to meet its liabilities, a director of the issuer will not instigate bankruptcy proceedings in respect of it. Bankruptcy remoteness is one of the criteria used by the rating agencies which issuers of notes seek to satisfy so that their instruments will achieve the highest possible credit rating. That criterion is satisfied in other jurisdictions by provisions which limit the rights of noteholders against the issuer to the value of the issuer's assets. Until recent tax legislation altered the position, limited recourse provisions of that kind gave rise to UK stamp duty reserve tax at the rate of 1.5% of the amount subscribed for them. As the Chancellor explained in para 40, the PECO is designed to achieve the same result as limited recourse provisions, but without the adverse tax consequences.

56. The Issuer accepts that, as a matter of contract, the liabilities were unlimited in recourse. But it maintains that the commercial reality was that the liabilities alleged to be the debts that the issuer was unable to pay to the Noteholder were liabilities which it would never have to meet. In the event that the assets of the Issuer were exhausted, any claim that the Noteholder had against the Issuer would be assigned

to the option holder. That, it is said, would bring an end to the claim. So it would be wrong to treat the Issuer as falling within section 123(2) as incorporated into Condition 9(a)(iii) on the ground that it was unable to pay its debts, as in practice it was never intended or expected that the liabilities would be paid except out of the underlying assets available to the Issuer.

57. The soundness of this approach depends however on whether, in law, the PECO affects the liability of the Issuer to the Noteholder. In answering this question it is important to appreciate that the question is not whether the Issuer should actually be wound up on the grounds described in section 123(2), but whether its financial position is such that it falls within that subsection for the purposes of the default provision in Condition 9(a)(iii). The answer to that question is to be found by examining the wording of the Condition in the context of the provisions of the transaction documents as a whole. Does the PECO in any way alter the conclusion that would otherwise be drawn that the Issuer's assets were less than its liabilities and that it was unable to pay its debts?

58. The Chancellor based his judgment that it did not on the wording of section 123(2), as amended for the purposes of Condition 9(a)(iii). He held that if, in the application of that subsection the court concluded that the value of the company's assets was less than the amount of its liabilities, taking into account its contingent and prospective liabilities, the PECO had no effect on those liabilities at all: para 43. As he put it, the liabilities of the Issuer remain the same, whether or not there is a PECO or, if there is, whether or not the call option has been exercised. Unless and until the option holder releases the Issuer from all further liability, which it is under no obligation to do, the liability of the Issuer is unaffected.

59. Lord Neuberger reached the same conclusion, but for fuller reasons: see paras 92–97. He said that, reading the relevant provisions of the documents together, they established that the Issuer's liability to the Noteholders was to be treated as a liability of full recourse at least until the security was enforced and, arguably, until the option was exercised and the transfer to the option holder was completed. There was the statement in the Prospectus mentioned in para 54, above. It suggested a two-stage process, under which the Issuer's liability was treated initially as full recourse and liability would become limited recourse only on enforcement of the security. There was the closing part of clause 6.7 of the Deed of Charge which, having restricted the ability of the Trustee to enforce the Noteholders' rights on enforcement of the Security beyond the Issuer's assets, provided that this "shall not apply to and shall not limit the obligations of the Issuer to the [Noteholders] under the Instruments and this Deed." And there was the provision in Condition 2(h), which stated in terms that the Noteholders had full recourse to the Issuer in respect of payments due and that they were entitled to bring a claim under English law for the full amount of such payments.

60. Finally Lord Neuberger referred to the wording of Condition 9(a)(iii) itself. It was hard to see why any reference should be made in that Condition to section 123(2) if the Noteholders' rights against the Issuer were not to be treated as full recourse until the enforcement of the security. He also said that there was nothing commercially insensible in the conclusion that, for the purpose of Condition 9(a)(iii), the Noteholders' rights against the Issuer were treated as being of full recourse, notwithstanding the PECO: para 100.

61. The A3 Noteholders submit that the key operative provision is Clause 3.1 of the PECO itself. It makes it plain that it does not have the effect of limiting the liability of the Issuer in respect of the Notes to the value of the Issuer's assets. Its reference to there being an "insufficiency" of assets after enforcement to meet whatever is "due in respect of the Notes" is a clear indication that it contemplates that the amount of the liabilities that the Notes have created must be capable of exceeding

the value of the assets of the Issuer. Then there is the time at which the option is exercisable. It is not said to have any operative effect at all prior to enforcement of the security. So at all times prior to its exercise the Noteholders remain entitled to payment in accordance with the Conditions. And even when exercised all it does is provide a mechanism by which the right to be paid under the Notes is assigned to OptionCo.

62. As the Issuer relies on commercial reality rather than legal form, the legal effect of the documents is not really in dispute. The common intention of the parties is said by the Issuer to be quite different. Its argument is that, as inclusion of a PECO rather than a contractual limited recourse provision was done solely for tax reasons, it was not intended or understood to alter the commercial nature, effect and operation of the asset-backed securitisation. As a matter of contract the liabilities were unlimited in recourse. As a matter of commercial substance and in practice, they were the equivalent of a provision by which the rights of Noteholders were expressly limited. The Issuer's case is that its future obligations to pay principal under the Notes should be taken into account only to the extent that its assets were sufficient to pay for them. As Mr Dicker QC for the Issuer put it at the end of his argument, legal form should not triumph over commercial substance.

63. I do not think that it is possible to distinguish the intended commercial effect of these provisions from their legal effect in this way. The exercise that Condition 9(a)(iii) predicates is the quantification of the amount of the Issuers' assets and liabilities in order to determine whether there has been an Event of Default. The legal effect and the commercial effect of the PECO, on its true analysis, both point in the same direction. It has no effect, for the purpose of that quantification, on the amount of the Issuer's liabilities. To limit those liabilities as the Issuer contends would contradict the parties' clearly expressed commercial intention as found in the contractual documents. The fact that the economic result of the PECO may be the same as if the Noteholders' right of recourse had been limited to the Issuer's assets is beside the point. It can be expected to achieve bankruptcy remoteness as effectively. But it would not be in accordance with the true meaning of the documents to treat the two methods as if they had the same effect in law.

64. The ultimate aim in construing provisions of the kind that are in issue in this case, as it is when construing any contract, is to determine what the parties meant by the language that they have used. Commercial good sense has a role to play when the provisions are open to different interpretations. The court should adopt the more, rather than the less, commercial construction: *Rainy Sky SA v Kookmin Bank* [2011] UKSC 50, [2011] 1 WLR 2900. But, for the reasons given by the Chancellor and Lord Neuberger MR, the meaning to be given to the language that the parties used in this case is not open to doubt. The suggestion that to give effect to that meaning is to surrender to legal form over commercial substance amounts, in effect, to an invitation to depart from the settled role of commercial good sense. Its role is to find out what the parties meant when they entered into the arrangement, not to replace it with something which is not to be found in the language of the documents at all.

Be ready to describe and discuss the rather intricate Eurosail transaction in class. Why might Lehman have wanted to enter into this transaction? What was the purpose of issuing so many layers of debt? What role did the swaps play?

Lord Hope's concurrence makes clear that this transaction is one where bankruptcy and tax issues intersect. Be sure you understand precisely how that is so.

3. THE DRAWBACKS OF SECURITIZATION

The nature of securitization changed dramatically in the past decade. In particular, it moved away from traditional assets with specific terms such as mortgages, bank loans, or consumer loans (called self-liquidating assets).

Purportedly improved modeling and risk quantification as well as greater data availability encouraged issuers to consider a wider variety of asset types, including home equity loans, lease receivables, and small business loans, and, of course, royalty payments from rock stars. Soon, most of the world had claims against pools of American income generating assets. And then financial crisis hit.

The next case illustrates the myriad instruments involved, and the hidden problems. You also learn a vocabulary word.

IN RE CITIGROUP INC. SECURITIES LITIGATION

753 F.Supp.2d 206
United States District Court, S.D. New York
Nos. 09 md 2070 (SHS), 07 Civ. 9901 (SHS), 07 Civ. 10258 (SHS),
08 Civ. 135 (SHS), 08 Civ. 136 (SHS) | Nov. 9, 2010

Sidney H. STEIN, District Judge.

Plaintiffs bring these consolidated securities fraud actions on behalf of a proposed class of investors in Citigroup, Inc., against the company and fourteen of its officials alleging violations of Sections 10(b) and 20(a) of the Securities Exchange Act of 1934. Their claims span an array of Citigroup's business — from the mortgages it sold to consumers to the mortgage-backed securities it sold to institutional investors — but sound a similar note: Citigroup allegedly knowingly understated the risks it faced and overstated the value of the assets it possessed. In this way, plaintiffs claim, Citigroup materially misled investors about the company's financial health and caused them to suffer damages when the truth about Citigroup's assets was finally revealed.

Defendants move to dismiss plaintiffs' claims pursuant to Rule 12(b)(6) of the Federal Rules of Civil Procedure, arguing primarily that plaintiffs' complaint fails to satisfy the heightened pleading standards applicable in securities fraud actions.

The Court finds that plaintiffs have stated a claim to relief only with respect to alleged misstatements and omissions occurring between February 2007 and April 2008 concerning Citigroup's collateralized debt obligation holdings. Plaintiffs' remaining allegations do not adequately state a claim for relief. Accordingly, for the reasons set forth below, defendants' motion is granted in part and denied in part.

I. BACKGROUND

The Amended Consolidated Class Action Complaint ("Complaint"), filed on February 20, 2009, is 536 pages long, contains 1,265 paragraphs and weighs six pounds. The following facts are extracted from that tome and are presumed to be true for the purposes of this motion.

A. PARTIES

Plaintiffs are current or former Citigroup shareholders. Plaintiffs claim they purchased Citigroup common stock on the open market for a price that was inflated by defendants' alleged fraud. Plaintiffs purport to represent all persons who purchased Citigroup common stock between January 1, 2004 and January 15, 2009.

Citigroup is itself named as a defendant. Incorporated in Delaware with its principal place of business in New York, Citigroup is a financial services holding company operating in more than 100 countries. It employs over 300,000 people.

Plaintiffs also bring this action against several current and former directors and officers of Citigroup. The Complaint describes the individual defendants as follows:

- *Charles Prince* was Citigroup's Chief Executive Officer ("CEO") from 2003 to 2007 and Chairman of Citigroup's Board of Directors from 2006 to 2007. Plaintiffs allege that Prince was "forced to resign" on November 5, 2007 as a result of substantial losses Citigroup reported.
- *Robert Rubin* served as a Citigroup director beginning in 1999 and was named Chairman of the Board of Directors after Prince's departure.
- *Lewis Kaden,* starting in 2005, was Citigroup's Chief Administrative Officer ("CAO"), responsible for "audit and risk review" at Citigroup.
- *Sallie L. Krawcheck* was Citigroup's Chief Financial Officer ("CFO") from 2004 to 2007.
- *Gary Crittenden* replaced Krawcheck as CFO in March 2007.
- *Steven Freiberg* was the Chairman and CEO of Citigroup's Global Consumer Group and his responsibilities included consumer lending in the mortgage area.
- *Robert Druskin* was Citigroup's Chief Operating Officer from 2006 to 2007 and previously held other officer positions.
- *Todd S. Thomson* was Citigroup's CFO prior to 2004 and was the CEO of a Citigroup division between 2004 and 2007.
- *Thomas G. Maheras* held various officer positions with different Citigroup divisions, including the division responsible for Citigroup's collateralized debt obligation holdings.
- *Michael Stuart Klein,* like Maheras, held various officer positions with different Citigroup divisions, including the division responsible for Citigroup's collateralized debt obligation holdings.
- *David C. Bushnell* was Citigroup's Senior Risk Officer from 2003 to 2007 and served as CAO for two months in 2007.
- *John C. Gerspach* served as Citigroup's Chief Accounting Officer and Controller beginning in March 2005.
- *Stephen R. Volk* held various officer positions at Citigroup.
- *Vikram Pandit* became Citigroup's CEO following Prince's departure. He previously was the CEO of a Citigroup division.

Plaintiffs allege that many of the individual defendants sold large amounts of stock during the class period. Plaintiffs also allege that several individual defendants "signed and certified the accuracy of" Citigroup's SEC filings.

The theory of plaintiffs' case is that defendants materially misled them about the risks Citigroup was exposed to via various financial instruments, including CDOs, SIVs, Alt-A RMBS, CLOs and ARS. Understanding the allegations in this action requires understanding the nature of this gallimaufry of financial instruments. They are described in the Complaint as follows.

1.   Subprime and Alt–A Mortgages

A "conforming" mortgage is a mortgage that meets certain requirements designed to reduce the risk of default and to mitigate losses in the event of default. These include requiring the borrower to meet minimum standards of creditworthiness, to document his or her income and to make a down payment of at least 20% of the value of the home. In a conforming mortgage, the borrower's debt-to-income ratio does not exceed 35%. If the loan's interest rate is adjustable over time (for example, if the interest rate starts low but later increases), the borrower's debt-to-income ratio must be gauged at the "fully indexed" rate, which is the highest interest rate the loan will reach.

In the mid-2000s, banks increasingly issued "nonconforming" mortgages that departed from the requirements listed above. They issued mortgages to borrowers who were less creditworthy. They did not verify borrower income. They accepted lower down payments or eliminated the down-payment requirement altogether. This practice increased the loan-to-value ("LTV") ratio — the ratio of the loan amount to the home's value — which enhanced the risk of default and the size of the loss upon default. Banks issued mortgages when mortgage payments exceeded 35% of the borrower's income. In the case of "hybrid adjustable rate mortgages" or "hybrid ARMs," which featured a low teaser rate that lasted for two or three years that then ballooned higher, banks failed to measure debt-to-income ratios at the fully indexed rate.

These nonconforming mortgages included both "subprime" mortgages, which carried the highest risk of default, and "alternative A class" ("Alt-A") mortgages, which were riskier than conforming mortgages but not as risky as subprime mortgages.

2.   Residential-Mortgage-Backed Securities

Residential-mortgage-backed securities ("RMBS") are a type of asset-backed security. In RMBS, an underwriter buys a large quantity of residential mortgages — typically three to four thousand individual mortgages — and transfers the mortgages to a special purpose corporate entity. The entity's sole purpose is to receive those mortgages and issue securities — RMBS — that are collateralized by the mortgages the entity owns. An investor buys an RMBS and, over time, receives payments from the entity based on a "coupon" or interest rate. As homeowners make payments on their mortgages, the special purpose entity receives the income from the borrowers' payments and uses it to pay its investors, the RMBS owners. Thus, the entity's ability to continue making payments to the RMBS investor depends on the entity's continuing receipt of mortgage payments from the homeowners. If the mortgages are not paid, the entity's income stream decreases, undermining the entity's ability to pay the RMBS investors.

The risk of loss is not shared equally among all RMBS investors. Instead, the RMBS are divided into different "tranches" that carry different risks. The junior-most tranche absorbs the first losses until that tranche is completely wiped out, and is therefore the riskiest investment. Then the second-junior-most tranche begins to suffer losses. The senior-most tranche suffers losses only when all the other tranches have been eliminated. For example, if the junior-most tranche represents 4% of the RMBS securitization, and if mortgage defaults cause the securitization to lose four percent of its cash flow, then the junior-most tranche will suffer a complete loss. The other tranches, however, will suffer no loss whatsoever. The junior tranches thus protect the senior tranches by absorbing losses as mortgages default. Each RMBS tranche is assigned a credit rating (triple-A, double-A, single-A, triple-B, double-B, etc.) with the more senior, i.e. safer, tranches receiving higher ratings. The most senior RMBS tranche bears an AAA credit rating. (*Id.* at 32–33.) Tranches between the junior- and senior-most tranches are known as "mezzanine" tranches.

3. Collateralized Debt Obligations

Like RMBS, collateralized debt obligations ("CDOs") are a form of asset-backed security. An underwriter creates a CDO by purchasing a pool of assets and transferring those assets to a special purpose entity. The entity then issues debt securities whose interest payments are backed by the income stream generated by the entity's assets. Although RMBS and CDOs are similar in many ways, RMBS securitizations purchase mortgages and issue securities backed by those mortgages, whereas many CDOs purchase *other securities*—RMBS, for example—and issue securities backed by those.

RMBS and CDOs have different tranche structures. In an RMBS securitization, the senior-most tranche is the AAA-rated tranche. In contrast, CDOs split the AAA tranche into a junior AAA tranche and a "super senior" AAA tranche. This super senior tranche is the last to suffer losses, insulated by the junior AAA tranche and all the tranches below that. Since it is insulated by a tranche with an AAA rating (the junior AAA tranche), the super senior's credit rating is considered better than AAA. Because of this enhanced credit protection, the super senior tranche involves less risk and thus pays a lower interest rate. The money the CDO securitization saves by offering a lower yield to the super senior tranche is used to pay higher yields to the junior tranches. In a sense, yield is taken from the super senior tranche and added to the junior tranches. Because the super senior tranche is substantially larger than the junior tranches, a small yield decrease for the super senior tranche results in a substantial yield increase for the smaller junior tranches.

4. Structured Investment Vehicles

A structured investment vehicle ("SIV") is much like a CDO or RMBS securitization. The SIV is a special purpose corporate entity that invests in different kinds of long-term assets — for example, an SIV might invest in corporate bonds or RMBS. To finance its investments, the SIV issues securities in several tranches, with junior tranches absorbing the first losses and thus protecting more senior tranches.

SIVs finance their investments mostly by means of short-term securities: commercial paper and medium-term notes. As a result, an SIV earns profits through a form of arbitrage. The SIV invests in long-term securities with a certain yield. It finances those long-term securities with short-term debt securities that carry a lower yield. The SIV makes a profit that is equal to the difference between the higher "incoming" yield the SIV earns from its long-term assets and the lower "outgoing" yield the SIV must pay on its commercial paper and medium-term notes. Some of that "profit" goes to an equity tranche, and the rest of the profit is paid in the form of fees to the SIV's manager — here, Citigroup. In this way, a small "equity" investment in the SIV's junior tranches can be used to leverage substantial arbitrage gains resulting from the existence of large senior tranches of short-term debt.

Using short-term debt to purchase long-term assets creates "liquidity risk," a risk caused by the fact that an SIV must continually "roll-over" its short-term funding. An SIV's long-term assets generate income streams that are sufficient to pay the interest on the SIV's short-term debt. But when the short-term debt comes due — that is, when the SIV must return the principal of the commercial paper and medium-term notes — the SIV must issue *new* short-term debt to pay off the maturing short-term debt. This is called "rolling over" short-term debt. If an SIV were unable to roll-over its short-term debt, it would be forced to sell its long-term assets to pay its maturing short-term debt.

Losses stemming from liquidity risk can be substantial. If an SIV's long-term assets decline in value, the SIV will no longer be as safe an investment, and investors will become reluctant to purchase the SIV's short-term debt. The SIV will have to sell its long-term assets to meet the amount due on any short-term debt that is not rolled over. Because the assets have declined in value, however, the SIV will take losses on its asset sales. Thus, when the SIV's long-term assets lose value, the SIV is often forced to sell the assets immediately at a loss. A decline in asset value has the potential to cause the entire SIV to collapse.

SIVs typically employ two mechanisms in response to liquidity risk. First, SIV covenants often stipulate that, if the value of the SIV's assets falls so far that the SIV cannot meet its short-term-debt obligations, the SIV is declared in "defeasance" and must immediately liquidate its assets to pay senior debt investors. Second, SIVs often obtain "liquidity backstops" from banks, where the banks will purchase a limited amount of short-term debt from the SIV. Liquidity backstops allow SIVs to ensure that a limited amount of short-term financing will always be available.

5.   *Leveraged Loans and Collateralized Loan Obligations*

Leveraged loans are loans that banks arrange for companies, often in anticipation of mergers and acquisitions, leveraged buyouts, recapitalizations, or restructurings. Leveraged loans are typically made to companies with high debt-to-equity ratios, and thus leveraged loans garner a low credit rating and a high yield. In the mid-2000s, the market for leveraged loans boomed, and banks began arranging leveraged loans that were riskier than the leveraged loans arranged in the past.

Collateralized loan obligations (CLOs) are much like CDOs, except CLOs are collateralized primarily by corporate debt. In the mid–2000s, CLOs were increasingly collateralized by riskier leveraged loans.

C. CDO ALLEGATIONS

Plaintiffs allege that Citigroup made numerous material misstatements and omissions regarding its CDOs. Plaintiffs' principal grievance is that Citigroup did not disclose that it held tens of billions of dollars of super-senior CDOs until November 4, 2007. As described in greater detail below, plaintiffs allege that the market knew, at least by late 2006 or early 2007, that CDOs faced a substantial risk of losses.

Although the market knew that Citigroup had underwritten billions of dollars of CDOs, the market did not know who had purchased the CDOs that Citigroup had underwritten. In plaintiffs' view, defendants intentionally hid the truth: namely that billions of dollars of CDOs had not been purchased at all but had, instead, been retained by Citigroup. Plaintiffs further allege that defendants affirmatively misled investors by disclosing facts about Citigroup's CDO operations that were either half-truths or affirmatively misleading.

First, plaintiffs claim that defendants failed to give a full and truthful account of the extent of Citigroup's CDO exposure. Second, plaintiffs allege that defendants made misleading statements that failed to convey the subprime-related risks inherent in its CDO portfolio. Finally, plaintiffs take issue with Citigroup's accounting practices, claiming that the company's SEC filings violated accounting rules — and were thus misleading — because they failed to report Citigroup's CDO exposure and failed to value Citigroup's CDO holdings accurately . . .

In addition to withholding information about the extent of Citigroup's CDO holdings — or making only inadequate disclosures about those holdings — plaintiffs also allege that Citigroup's SEC filings affirmatively misled investors about the nature of the CDOs themselves: namely that defendants failed to convey in their statements the subprime related risks inherent in Citigroup's CDO portfolio.

Citigroup's SEC filings made the following statement regarding Citigroup's securitization of mortgages:

Mortgages and Other Assets

The Company provides a wide range of mortgage and other loan products to its customers. In addition to providing a source of liquidity and less expensive funding, securitizing these assets also reduces the Company's credit exposure to the borrowers.

The SEC filings also made the following statement:

The Company primarily securitizes credit card receivables and mortgages. . . . The Company's mortgage loan securitizations are primarily non-recourse, thereby effectively transferring the risk of future credit losses to the purchaser of the securities issued by the trust.

Plaintiffs claim that those statements were misleading because they suggested that Citigroup had, through securitization, reduced its exposure to losses from residential mortgage defaults. Plaintiffs maintain that, even if Citigroup had created RMBS from the mortgages it had originated, Citigroup then created CDOs of those and other RMBS and retained substantial CDO holdings. Thus, in plaintiffs' view, Citigroup's claim that securitization "reduces the Company's credit exposure to borrowers" was misleading in light of the fact that Citigroup's CDO operations exposed the company to billions of dollars of risk from mortgage defaults. Moreover, plaintiffs contend that Citigroup's claim that "loan securitizations . . . effectively transfer[ ] the risk of future credit losses to the purchaser of the securities" was misleading because Citigroup did not disclose that *Citigroup itself* was effectively "the purchaser" of billions of dollars of securities backed by loans.

Plaintiffs further allege that Citigroup's SEC filings misled investors about the extent to which Citigroup's CDO were backed by subprime mortgages. Plaintiffs claim that Citigroup's SEC filings were misleading because they presented Citigroup's underwriting of CDOs as distinct from Citigroup's securitizing of mortgages, giving a false impression that Citigroup's CDOs were backed by assets unrelated to mortgages.

In a section titled "Off-Balance Sheet Arrangements," Citigroup's August 3, 2007 Form 10-Q stated:

Mortgages and Other Assets

The Company provides a wide range of mortgage and other loan products to its customers. . . . The Company recognized gains related to the securitization of mortgages and other assets . . .

A later passage from the same section stated:

Creation of Other Investment and Financing Products

The Company packages and securitizes assets purchased in the financial markets in order to create new security offerings, including arbitrage collateralized debt obligations (CDOs) and synthetic CDOs for institutional clients and retail customers, which match the clients' investment needs and preferences.

Those statements were misleading, plaintiffs claim, because they placed Citigroup's "gains related to the securitization of mortgages" under a different heading from Citigroup's "new security offerings, including . . . CDOs." That, in plaintiffs view, falsely implied that Citigroup's CDOs did not involve assets tied to subprime mortgages.

Plaintiffs allege that Citigroup represented that its CDOs were assembled to diversify risk. Specifically, in portions of Citigroup's SEC filings describing CDOs, it stated, "Typically, these instruments diversify investors' risk to a pool of assets as compared with investments in an individual asset." This description was misleading, plaintiffs contend, because CDOs "were not based on diversified assets, but on a singular investment in subprime mortgages."

III. VALUING CDO HOLDINGS

Plaintiffs claim Citigroup, over a period stretching from March 2007 to April 2008, consistently over-valued its CDO holdings.

Citigroup first took a writedown on its CDO holdings on November 4, 2007. Plaintiffs contend that Citigroup's SEC filings should have reported a CDO-related writedown well before. The company stated that it "account[ed] for its CDO super senior subprime direct exposures and the underlying securities on a fair-value basis with all changes in fair value recorded in earnings." Plaintiffs allege that from through September 30, 2007, Citigroup valued its CDO holdings at par. They contend that had Citigroup actually undertaken a "fair value" assessment of its CDO holdings, it should have begun taking periodic writedowns on its impaired CDO holdings in March 2007. The failure to take these writedowns allegedly resulted in inflated revenue and income statements in Citigroup's periodic SEC filings. For example, "Had Citigroup valued its Mezzanine CDO[8] super senior holdings at fair value as of March 31, 2007, it would have had to take a writedown of $1.2 billion. This would have reduced Citigroup's reported revenues by $1.2 billion and pre-tax income by $1.2 billion."

2. November 4, 2007 and Later Statements

According to the Complaint, Citigroup on November 4, 2007 disclosed a net exposure to super-senior CDO tranches in the amount of $43 billion and estimated a writedown of $8 to $11 billion on those assets. Plaintiffs allege that the $43 billion figure was misleading. It did not include $10.5 billion worth of holdings that Citigroup had hedged by swapping the risk off to certain insurers. But according to plaintiffs, this insurance was effectively meaningless because the insurers could not honor it. The omission of these holdings from Citigroup's November 4 disclosure created the false impression that these hedged CDOs would not expose Citigroup to further losses. (*Id.*) Plaintiffs further allege that the writedowns Citigroup took on its CDOs on November 4 and thereafter were materially misleading because they did not reflect the actual value of those assets.

3. Allegations of Fraudulent Intent with Respect to CDO-Related Misstatements and Omissions

Plaintiffs also allege that defendants acted with fraudulent intent when they purportedly made material misstatements and omissions regarding CDOs. Plaintiffs contend that defendants knew that Citigroup's CDOs were risky investments and would suffer substantial losses if nationwide housing prices declined. Plaintiffs also allege that defendants knew that, once housing prices declined and the subprime mortgage market collapsed, Citigroup should have written

---

8. According to the complaint, Citigroup's Mezzanine CDOs invested primarily in the higher-risk RMBS junior tranches." In essence, they were a subprime RMBS BBB tranche writ large. These CDOs' extreme asset concentration in nonprime RMBS BBB tranches meant, ab initio, that a relatively small rise in underlying mortgage pool losses — sufficient to wipe out the thin, close-to-the-bottom BBB- and BBB tranches — would simultaneously destroy most of the collateral value of a Mezzanine CDO."

down the value of its CDO holdings — even if the CDOs' credit ratings had not yet been downgraded. Plaintiffs allege the following facts in support of their allegations that the defendants acted with fraudulent intent.

a.   Citigroup Underwrote the CDOs It Owned

Plaintiffs allege that defendants knew that Citigroup's CDO holdings were at risk of substantial losses by virtue of the fact that Citigroup had underwritten the very CDOs it owned. That is, Citigroup had selected assets for the CDOs and created the financial models to value them. As a result, plaintiffs allege that defendants knew that the CDOs involved concentrated, correlated risk and would suffer substantial losses if nationwide housing prices declined.

In particular, plaintiffs allege that Citigroup calculated the "expected loss" of its CDO tranches by assuming that housing prices would rise six percent per year. As a substantial player in the subprime mortgage market, moreover, Citigroup allegedly knew that subprime mortgages were viable only if housing priced continued to rise. Thus, according to plaintiffs, Citigroup knew that its CDOs — even the super-senior tranches — would suffer considerable losses if nationwide housing prices fell.

Plaintiffs point to Citigroup's mezzanine CDOs as an especially salient example of Citigroup's understanding that its CDOs were risky investments. Plaintiffs contend that, as underwriter for its mezzanine CDOs, Citigroup knew (1) that a nationwide fall in housing prices would cause an increased percentage of subprime mortgages to default; (2) that a high default rate would quickly wipe out the BB-rated junior tranches of all subprime-backed RMBS; (3) that once junior RMBS tranches were wiped out, the mezzanine RMBS tranches would begin to suffer losses; and (4) that once mezzanine RMBS tranches were impaired, even the super-senior tranches of Citigroup's mezzanine CDOs would suffer losses, as the mezzanine CDOs were collateralized almost *entirely* of mezzanine RMBS.

In other words, plaintiffs allege that Citigroup designed its AAA-rated mezzanine CDO tranches to be far riskier investments than their ratings reflected. Indeed, Citigroup must have known, plaintiffs contend, that its AAA-rated mezzanine CDO tranches were not much safer than BBB-rated mezzanine RMBS tranches, for if a nationwide housing decline wiped out all mezzanine RMBS tranches, AAA-rated mezzanine CDO super-senior tranches would likewise fail.

b.   The Market Believed that CDOs Were at Risk

Plaintiffs also allege that defendants knew that Citigroup's CDO holdings were at risk of substantial losses because there was a consensus in the market, at least by March 2007, that CDOs were at risk. Plaintiffs allege that, beginning in October 2006, the market began to suspect that CDOs were vulnerable. Plaintiffs base that allegation on the following facts:

- Financial analysts from late 2006 noted that subprime mortgages were defaulting at high rates and concluded, as a result, that RMBS and CDOs were likely to begin to take losses.

- Two indices — the ABX, which tracked the price of subprime RMBS, and the TABX, which tracked the price of mezzanine CDO tranches — began to decline.
- Newspaper articles reported on a possible decline in RMBS and CDO values.

Then, from March 2007 onward, plaintiffs allege that there was a "market consensus" that CDOs would suffer losses. Plaintiffs base that allegation on the conclusions of several financial analysts, many times reported in national newspapers, that "even investment grade rated CDOs [would] experience significant losses" that the "scenario where the BBB [-rated RMBS tranches] blow up [was] a reasonably possible scenario" that the credit ratings of CDO tranches were suspect, that there was the possibility of "severe" credit downgrades on CDOs, and that there had, in fact, already been "massive losses in the CDO market." In addition, plaintiffs allege that the ABX and TABX indices fell substantially in February and March 2007.

Thus, plaintiffs allege that defendants knew that Citigroup's disclosures were false and misleading because, at least after March 2007, there was a consensus that CDOs were vulnerable. Indeed, plaintiffs allege that defendants intentionally misled the market, which was keenly interested in learning which companies were exposed to CDO-related risk. According to plaintiffs, many in the market assumed that CDO underwriters had sold their CDOs to outside investors, thereby divesting themselves of any attendant risk. Defendants encouraged that misconception, plaintiffs claim, by failing to disclose Citigroup's allegedly massive CDO holdings.

c. Citigroup Analysts Express Concern About Subprime Mortgages and CDOs

In addition, plaintiffs cite three statements by Citigroup analysts showing, in plaintiffs' view, that Citigroup understood the weaknesses in the subprime mortgage market and Citigroup's CDO holdings:

- A report by Citigroup's "Fixed Income" division, issued in January 2007, concluded that the subprime mortgages originated in 2006 were the "worst vintage in subprime history."
- A report by Citigroup's "Quantitative Credit Strategy and Analysis Group," issued in March 2007, concluded that recent troubles in the subprime mortgage market were capable of causing widespread credit rating downgrades and resulting in losses even to senior CDO tranches. ("Translated into the CDO space, widespread downgrades [on the underlying ABS tranches] would, relatively speaking, be far worse for the senior tranches than for junior ones."). The report recommended that investors either sell their senior CDO tranches or hedge their risks through credit default swaps.
- At a Citigroup-sponsored conference in March 2007, Citigroup's "head of credit strategy" stated that the as for the "'near-term risk of further [subprime] market correction is concerned, it's at the top of the list' of worries." He went on to say that, in response to declines in the subprime market, some banks have engaged in a "'massive provisioning for losses.'" "'And to be honest,'" he said, "'that makes us deeply suspicious' of banks 'with exposures

in that space who have not declared anything like the same degree of provisioning.'" (quoting *Subprime Surprise for Europeans*, Wall. St. J., Mar. 9, 2007).

d.   Citigroup Creates CDOs to Buy Unwanted CDOs

Plaintiffs allege that, in late 2006 and early 2007, Citigroup found it increasingly difficult to find buyers for its CDOs. According to plaintiffs, Citigroup
created new CDOs and used those CDOs to purchase unwanted tranches of
old CDOs. That, in plaintiffs' view, shows that both (1) Citigroup realized
that its CDOs were overly risky and overvalued and (2) Citigroup intended to
create the appearance of CDO sales when, in reality, Citigroup was simply transferring assets between Citigroup-controlled entities.

e.   Citigroup Creates a Special Entity to Assume the Risks of Liquidity Puts

Citigroup sold $25 billion of CDO super-senior tranches with liquidity puts in
which Citigroup agreed to purchase back the CDOs from investors at full value.
In addition, plaintiffs allege that, in February 2007, Citigroup created a special
purpose entity called "Foraois Funding Ltd." for the purpose of engaging in a
"credit default swap" involving part of Citigroup's liquidity puts. That is,
Citigroup created Foraois and then paid Foraois a fee in order to assume
Citigroup's liabilities on $1.32 billion of Citigroup's liquidity puts. To finance
the Foraois entity, Foraois issued debt securities that were, in part, purchased by
a Citigroup-underwritten CDO. Plaintiffs claim that the Foraois transaction
shows that Citigroup was attempting to hide or dispose of its liability for liquidity
puts, demonstrating Citigroup's awareness that the liquidity puts would lead to
substantial losses.

f.   Citigroup Makes Collateral Demands on Mortgage Originators

Citigroup and other banks had an arrangement with subprime mortgage
originators in which Citigroup would extend so-called "warehouse lines of
credit." The originators would make loans to borrowers using the warehouse
credit, and then Citigroup would purchase the loans from the originator, reset-
ting the credit line.

According to plaintiffs, in March 2007, Citigroup and other banks began
pulling out of the warehouse credit arrangements by making large collateral
demands on the originators. In particular, plaintiffs allege that Citigroup's
collateral demands caused New Century Financial, one of the nation's largest
subprime mortgage originators, to file for bankruptcy protection. Citigroup's
collateral demands, plaintiffs claim, demonstrate Citigroup's awareness of the
weakness of the subprime mortgage market.

g.   Citigroup's CDO Prospectuses Warn of Risks

Plaintiffs allege that, beginning in April 2007, Citigroup CDO prospectuses
disclosed certain risk factors, including that:

* Defaults on subprime mortgages had increased, which had the possibility of
  "affect[ing] the performance of RMBS Securities."
* Adjustable-rate subprime mortgages were especially susceptible to default.

- A decline in housing prices had the possibility of leading to greater subprime mortgage defaults.
- Subprime mortgage originators had recently gone bankrupt, and the federal government had recently promulgated new rules for subprime mortgages, which had made it possible that subprime borrowers would have difficulty refinancing.

All of those risk factors, the prospectuses explained, could "reduce the cash flow which the [CDO] receives from RMBS Securities or CDO Securities held by the [CDO]" and "decrease the market value of such RMBS Securities and CDO Securities and increase the incidence and severity of credit events."

Plaintiffs allege that the new language in Citigroup's CDO prospectuses demonstrates that Citigroup understood that its CDOs faced substantial risks from the collapse of the subprime mortgage market.

h. Citigroup Purchases Insurance for Its CDO Holdings

Plaintiffs allege that, beginning in February 2007, Citigroup began to purchase insurance for its super-senior CDO holdings. That, in plaintiffs' view, shows that Citigroup understood that its super-senior CDO holdings faced a substantial risk of losses.

i. Citigroup Executives Hold Daily Risk Exposure Sessions

Plaintiffs allege that, according to news reports, defendant Rubin began in July 2007 to hold daily meetings regarding Citigroup's CDO exposures. That, in plaintiffs' view, demonstrates that Citigroup understood that its CDO holdings faced massive losses.

j. Citigroup Makes a Margin Call on Basis Capital Funds

Citigroup had lent money to several hedge funds called the Basis Capital Funds. Plaintiffs allege that, in mid-July 2007, Citigroup began making margin calls on Basis Capital on the understanding that a large portion of the collateral that Basis Capital had put up for the loans — CDOs tied to subprime mortgages — had declined in value and no longer provided sufficient security. That, in plaintiffs' view, shows that Citigroup understood that CDOs had, in general, become devalued.

D. ALT-A RMBS ALLEGATIONS

Plaintiffs allege that Citigroup's misled investors by failing to disclose Citigroup's Alt-A RMBS exposure and, once revealed, by failing to value those assets properly.

First, plaintiffs assert that Citigroup should have disclosed its Alt-A RMBS exposure prior to April 18, 2008, because plaintiffs claim that the market knew beginning in late 2007 that Alt-A RMBS holdings were impaired. Citigroup, plaintiffs claim, knew the risks facing Alt-A RMBS even better than the market because Citigroup, as the underwriter of the securities, "was in a uniquely advantageous position to observe the deteriorating performance of these assets before they became public knowledge."

Plaintiffs further allege that defendant Crittenden misled investors about the scope of Citigroup's Alt-A RMBS exposure in a January 22, 2008 earnings conference call. Crittenden stated that he did not "anticipate" that Citigroup's "Alt-A portfolio" would pose "a substantial risk." An analyst asked, "Is that a function of size or you just don't think that area is going to have the same deterioration we have seen in other credit buckets?" Crittenden responded, "It is a function of size." Plaintiffs claim that Crittenden's statement was misleading because, in fact, Citigroup's Alt-A RMBS holdings were massive — approximately $22 billion at the time of Crittenden's statement.

Finally, plaintiffs allege that, even when Citigroup announced its Alt-A RMBS exposure, Citigroup overvalued its Alt-A RMBS holdings. Plaintiffs claim that when Citigroup wrote down its Alt-A RMBS holdings to 66 cents on the dollar, other banks had written down their Alt-A RMBS holdings to between 35 and 50 cents on the dollar.

E.   SIV ALLEGATIONS

Plaintiffs' SIV allegations can be grouped into three categories.

First, plaintiffs contend that Citigroup misled investors by failing to disclose the SIV exposure it had on account of its "implicit guarantee" to provide liquidity support for its SIVs in the event they began to fail. According to plaintiffs, Citigroup's SIVs had sold $100 billion of securities to Citigroup customers, marketing them as safe investments. If the SIVs ever failed, Citigroup's reputation among its customers would be severely tarnished. To prevent that, plaintiffs claim that Citigroup implicitly guaranteed to provide liquidity backstops to its SIVs if they ever were to approach failure. Indeed, in December 2007, when Citigroup announced that it would bail out its SIVs with extensive liquidity backstops, Citigroup representatives allegedly stated that Citigroup's actions were an effort to prevent reputational damage. Although Citigroup insisted that it had no *contractual* obligation to bail out its SIVs, plaintiffs claim that the obligation nevertheless existed and the failure to disclose it was materially misleading.

Second, plaintiffs contend that Citigroup's failure to consolidate its SIVs on its balance sheet prior to December 2007 was intended to knowingly mislead investors. In conjunction with the announcement of its SIV bailout in December 2007, Citigroup said that, for the first time, it would consolidate the SIVs on its balance sheet. Plaintiffs claim that Citigroup should have consolidated its SIVs long before then and, as a result, that Citigroup's SEC filings prior to December 2007 were false and misleading.

Citigroup had classified its SIVs, like its CDOs, as VIEs governed by FIN-46(R). As discussed above, FIN-46(R) requires an enterprise to consolidate a VIE "if that enterprise has a variable interest . . . that will absorb a majority of the [VIE]'s expected losses." Plaintiffs claim that Citigroup had a variable interest in its SIVs because Citigroup had *implicitly* agreed, prior to the end of 2007, to provide liquidity backstops to the VIEs. Financial Accounting Standards Board, Staff Position No. FIN 46(R)-5 ("FSP FIN 46(R)-5") acknowledges that enterprises can have "implicit variable interests" and provides as an example "an implicit agreement to replace impaired assets held by a variable interest entity that protects holders of other interests in the entity from suffering losses."

Plaintiffs allege that Citigroup's implicit guarantee to provide liquidity back-stops to its SIVs was, effectively, an agreement to "replace impaired assets," and that the implicit agreement was meant to protect the SIV investors — Citigroup's customers — who were "holders of other interests in the entity." (*Id.*) Thus, although Citigroup had considered its SIVs to be "nonrecourse" — and thus not assets to be consolidated on Citigroup's balance sheet — plaintiffs allege that Citigroup always knew that it would have to bailout out its SIVs, which, in plaintiffs' view, amounted to an implicit variable interest pursuant to FSP FIN 46(R)-5, ¶6. Citigroup's failure to consolidate its SIVs prior to December 2007 allegedly misled investors by concealing this liability.

Third, plaintiffs claim Citigroup made material misstatements to investors even after it revealed it would provide liquidity support for its SIVs by stating that Citigroup's credit exposure on account of its SIVs was "substantially limited" due to the "high credit quality of the SIV assets." Such statements were materially misleading, plaintiffs allege, because Citigroup no longer had "limited involvement" because it had already begun providing liquidity support and because the assets underlying the SIVs were not, in fact, high quality.

F. MORTGAGE ALLEGATIONS

Plaintiffs allege that defendants made numerous material misstatements and omissions related to Citigroup's mortgage holdings. Plaintiffs also allege that Citigroup's financial statements violated GAAP by improperly accounting for Citigroup's mortgage holdings.

1. Alleged Mortgage–Related Misstatements

Plaintiffs allege that defendants misled investors by representing that Citigroup did not have exposure to risky mortgages that borrowers could not pay back. The following statements are illustrative of the basis of plaintiffs' claims:

- Bill Beckmann, COO of CitiMortgage, said in a 2006 magazine article: "[W]e're not going to make a loan on an affordability basis. We're going to make a loan because we believe it's right for a customer because we think they can pay it back."
- Defendant Freiberg said at an investor conference in 2006 that Citigroup's portfolio of first mortgages had a "high quality consumer profile (LTV and FICO), consistent over time."
- Citigroup represented in a 2006 magazine article that it "does not offer second-lien mortgages behind negative amortization first mortgages" and that its "average FICO Equity is a healthy 733, making it primarily a prime business."
- Freiberg said at a 2007 investor conference that "for the last, I would say, 12 to 15 months, we have been tightening criteria, we have been isolating whether [it's] channel, whether [it's] product or whether it is basically policy and/or criteria."
- Defendant Prince said in a 2007 investor conference: "I feel good about the composition of our portfolios, not only in the corporate and sovereign area

but especially in the U.S. mortgage area where we have avoided the riskier products at some cost to revenues in prior years."

Those statements, and others like them, were false or misleading, plaintiffs allege, because Citigroup's mortgage holdings were not safe mortgages that borrowers could repay. According to plaintiffs, Citigroup's mortgage holdings were riddled with fraudulent and nonconforming mortgages of various types. In addition, plaintiffs contend these misstatements were misleading because they discussed the standards that Citigroup used in its retail mortgage operations without disclosing the comparatively lax controls that Citigroup exerted over its correspondent channel mortgage operations.[9] Through the correspondent channels, plaintiffs assert, Citigroup purchased scores of risky, nonconforming mortgages, and thus information about the correspondent channels was necessary, in plaintiffs' view, to make defendants' statements about Citigroup's mortgage business accurate.

2. Alleged Mortgage-Related GAAP Violations

Plaintiffs allege that Citigroup violated GAAP by failing to report a sufficient "loan loss allowance" on Citigroup's financial statements. Several GAAP rules require mortgage originators to report a loan loss allowance that, for subprime mortgages, "should be sufficient to absorb at least all estimated credit losses on outstanding balances over the current operating cycle, typically 12 months." Citigroup did not, plaintiffs claim, properly account for the extent of fraudulent and worthless loans in Citigroup's mortgage holdings. As a result, Citigroup allegedly reported a loan loss allowance that was significantly lower than what GAAP required.

3. Allegations of Fraudulent Intent with Respect to Mortgage-Related Misstatements and Omissions

To show that defendants acted with fraudulent intent in making the mortgage-related statements addressed above, plaintiffs cite essentially two grounds on which defendants allegedly *knew* that Citigroup's mortgage portfolio contained fraudulent and risky mortgages and was overvalued in Citigroup's financial statements.

First, plaintiffs cite the testimony of confidential witnesses — as well as confidential internal Citigroup documents — that show, in plaintiffs' view, that Citigroup knew that its mortgage holdings were significantly impaired. Plaintiffs allege that "Citigroup management" was regularly informed of the status of Citigroup's mortgage holdings.

Second, plaintiffs allege that Citigroup knew that its mortgage holdings contained fraudulent and risky loans because Citigroup sued various mortgage originators in its correspondent channels. According to plaintiffs, Citigroup's court filings show that Citigroup was aware that the mortgages it had purchased from its correspondent channels contained fraudulent and impaired mortgages.

---

9. Correspondent channel loans are obtained through mortgage brokers, mortgage bankers, financial institutions, and homebuilders who sold previously funded mortgage loans to Citigroup at a previously negotiated price.

H. LEVERAGED LOAN AND CLO ALLEGATIONS

Plaintiffs cite an April 2004 conference call in which the "Company" stated: "Corporate loans . . . again, that's an area where we don't actually focus on growing that part of our business. . . . So that's not part of our growth strategy if you will." Plaintiffs also cite a July 2004 conference call in which the "Company" reiterated that "corporate loans" did not present "an area" where Citigroup intended to "look for a lot of growth." (Plaintiffs claim that those statements were misleading because they made it seem as if Citigroup's leveraged loan and CLO investments were conservative. In reality, plaintiffs assert that Citigroup's leveraged loan and CLO operations were risky and speculative, leading to the losses described above.

Plaintiffs also allege that Citigroup's financial statements contained material omissions because they did not disclose Citigroup's leveraged loan and CLO exposures. Plaintiffs further claim that, even when Citigroup did announce its leveraged loan and CLO exposures and losses, Citigroup's announcements still overvalued Citigroup's holdings and presented those holdings as less risky than they actually were.

I. SOLVENCY ALLEGATIONS

Plaintiffs allege that, from December 2007 through November 2008, Citigroup and defendant Pandit misled investors about the company's financial health in two ways: by overstating the strength of Citigroup's financial condition, and by overstating the value of Citigroup's assets in its quarterly and annual filings.

II. Discussion

Plaintiffs assert two causes of action. Count One alleges that all defendants committed securities fraud by violating Section 10(b) of the Securities Exchange Act, 15 U.S.C. §78j(b), and Rule 10b-5, 17 C.F.R. §240.10b-5, promulgated thereunder. Count Two alleges that the individual defendants are liable for securities fraud as controlling persons pursuant to Section 20(a) of the Securities Exchange Act, 15 U.S.C. §78t(a). Defendants have moved pursuant to Rule 12(b)(6) to dismiss the Complaint for failure to state a claim upon which relief may be granted.

For plaintiffs to state a claim against the individual defendants, they must plead scienter adequately for each. For defendants Krawcheck, Thomson, Pandit, Gerspach, Volk, Kaden and Freiberg, there are insufficient particularized allegations that they had knowledge of Citigroup's CDO operations, so there can be no finding of scienter as to these individuals. The CDO-related claims against them must be dismissed.

That leaves defendants Prince, Crittenden, Druskin, Maheras, Klein, Bushnell and Rubin. The Complaint alleges that all of these defendants attended meetings in the summer of 2007 that addressed Citigroup's CDO exposure. Although plaintiffs do not allege with specificity the matters discussed at these meetings, their mere existence is indicative of scienter: That defendants engaged in meetings concerning Citigroup's CDO risks is inconsistent with the company's public statements downplaying or concealing that risk. Accordingly, the court finds that plaintiffs have adequately alleged a strong inference of scienter for defendants Prince, Crittenden, Druskin, Maheras, Klein, Bushnell and Rubin . . .

For the reasons set forth above, defendants' motion to dismiss is **DENIED** with respect to 1) the Section 10(b) claims against Citigroup and the Section 10(b) and 20(a) claims against Prince, Crittenden, Druskin, Maheras, Klein, Bushnell and Rubin for the alleged misstatements and omissions relating to Citigroup's CDO exposure during the period from February 2007 through November 3, 2007; 2) the Section 10(b) claims against Citigroup and the Section 10(b) and 20(a) claims against Crittenden for the alleged CDO-related misstatements and omissions occurring in the period from November 4, 2007 to April 2008. Defendants' motion to dismiss the remainder of plaintiffs' claims is **GRANTED.**

Citigroup underwrote almost $42 billion of CDOs in 2007 alone. It ultimately settled the case, agreeing to pay the plaintiffs $590 million.[10]

PROBLEM SET 19.2

1. How could it be that a super senior tranche of a CDO that buys low-grade MBS earns the same credit rating as the governments of Switzerland or Norway?

2. The credit rating agencies note that until 2007, there had never been such a broad, steep decline in housing prices since the end of World War II. Why might that last qualification be important for utility of the improved models, discussed at the outset of this section?

3. Suppose you set up an SPV, and put a CDS contract in it. The CDS "reference entity," instead of being an operating company, could be an existing CDO or MBS. If the SPV were to then sell debt securities to investors, what might this look like? Are there any special risks to be concerned about here?

4. What if you take a bunch of CDOs that you own and put them into an SPV. If the SPV were to then sell debt securities to investors, what might this look like? What if instead of owning the CDOs, you own CDS contracts that reference the CDOs? What if you kept repeating this process (putting CDS contracts in SPVs that reference CDOs that are made up of CDS contracts that reference CDOs . . .)?

5. One of the key problems with asset securitization is that to work as advertised, the SPV must contain assets. It has been alleged in a recently settled whistleblower suit that Citibank was until very recently originating mortgages that ultimately made it into government-backed securitizations,

---

10. *http://goo.gl/NXfgj*

without following the proper procedures to ensure the loans were legally enforceable obligations not likely to default.[11]

6. Lest you think the case is quite remote from your near-term existence, what with high-level, oldish executives involved in boardroom drama, consider the case of Fabrice Tourre, a 28-year-old working for Goldman Sachs in New York, where he traded CDOs.[12] On the brink of the financial crisis in 2008, Tourre emailed friends that "The whole building is about to collapse anytime now . . . Only potential survivor the fabulous Fab[rice] . . . standing in the middle of all these complex, highly leveraged, exotic trades he created without necessarily understanding all of the implications of those monstruosities [sic]!!!" You'll be surprised to learn that he has "left" Goldman, and was recently found to have violated the securities laws in a civil suit brought by the SEC. But he's also pursuing a PhD in economics at the University of Chicago.

4. A NOTE ON COVERED BONDS

Covered bonds are bonds issued by banks and other financial institutions. They are quite common in Europe, and might become more common in North America if investors decide that securitization is not worth the risk. The "fabulous Fab" might have a role to play in that regard.

A covered bond is collateralized by a dedicated pool of mortgages, known as the cover pool. Unlike mortgages or other assets that are removed from the bank's balance sheet and moved into an SPV when securitized, the mortgages in the cover pool remain on the balance sheet, and the bank must hold capital against potential losses just like any other loan. Like securitization, the issuance of covered bonds converts illiquid assets into a funding source for the bank.

One of the key reasons why securitization became so popular in this country is because it enabled banks to remove loans from their balance sheets and to free up capital they would have had to hold in reserve.[13] Investors might have liked securitized assets because they provided a low-cost way of gaining some exposure to the real estate market without getting broader exposure to all the risks associated with a bank. This was probably especially true in the period between 2001 and 2007, when interest rates on traditional debt were quite low.

By contrast, covered bonds do not offer investors any exposure to the residential mortgage market even though they are backed by residential mortgages. There is no exposure because the interest and principal payments are the bank's obligation — they do not depend on the cash flows from mortgages in the pool.

---

11. *http://goo.gl/drzcT*
12. *http://goo.gl/VYOcm*
13. Banks operate with high degrees of leverage. To oversimplify, capital in this context is equity. The bank and its shareholders would like to operate with as little capital as possible, but capital provides a buffer against insolvency. Because the U.S. government insures bank deposits, it has some interest in making sure banks maintain adequate capital.

If a mortgage defaults or is prepaid, the bank has to replenish the cover pool with other mortgages on its balance sheet. If the bank becomes insolvent, the loans in the pool are separated from other assets and are used solely to repay the bank's obligation to covered bondholders. In other words, a covered bond is a secured debt obligation of the bank, for which the mortgages serve as collateral.

20

HEDGE FUNDS AND PRIVATE
EQUITY FUNDS

Hedge funds and private equity funds are unlike the other topics in this part of the text, in that they are types of investors rather than financial instruments.

Nonetheless, these funds are important users of many of the instruments previously discussed. For example, if a financial institution facilitates a company's desire to hedge its interest rate exposure by selling the company a swap, the financial institution might hedge its own exposure by selling a countervailing swap to a hedge fund.

As a review exercise, it bears considering what remaining risk the financial institution retains after selling two such mirror image swaps.

Hedge funds account for a large part of the trading volume in New York and London, and in some areas, like convertible debt, hedge fund trading dominates the market.

At a high level of abstraction, hedge funds are just like mutual funds. They pool money from investors and then invest that money. As a legal matter, a hedge fund or a mutual fund is just a legal entity—often a trust, in the case of mutual funds, or a limited partnership, in the case of hedge funds—whose business is investing.

As we shall see, hedge funds are expressly structured to avoid much of the regulation that mutual funds gladly accepted after the stock market crash in 1929.[1] Before then, however, it would have been possible for a mutual fund to do most everything a hedge fund at the time could do—if there were any hedge funds.

The first widely known hedge fund—there might have been earlier funds, especially before the crash—was established by Alfred W. Jones in 1949.[2] Jones combined normal stock picking with short sales to "hedge" against the risks of his portfolio, while also using some degree of leverage.[3] The growth of ever more

---

1. Steven M. Davidoff, *Black Market Capital*, 2008 Colum. Bus. L. Rev. 172, 201–216.
2. Sharon Reier, From Jones to LTCM: A Short (-Selling) History. *International Herald Tribune* (December 2, 2000).
3. *http://goo.gl/P7067*

complex financial products beginning in the 1970s — in parallel with the growth of computing — allowed future hedge fund managers to modify Jones's original idea in myriad ways.

Private equity funds are more recent, and the term *private equity fund* is more recent still. Before the term was widely used, firms like KKR and Forstmann Little essentially were private equity funds.[4] Structured similarly to hedge funds, the key distinction between hedge funds and private equity funds turns on their investment strategies.

Whereas hedge funds are somewhat like mutual funds, private equity funds are somewhat like merchant banks — financial institutions that take long-term stakes in a portfolio of companies.[5] The key innovation with private equity funds is that they typically leverage their investment, so that investors can gain exposure to potential large returns in exchange for comparatively modest principal investments.

Attorneys advise funds regarding compliance with laws governing securities offerings, regulation of investment companies, and regulation of investment managers. Fund attorneys also advise on permitted fund investments and other operations and changes to the management teams of funds.

1. STRUCTURAL ISSUES GENERALLY

At a sufficient level of generality, both types of funds discussed in this chapter are hedge funds. As a legal matter, a *hedge fund* is any professionally managed pool of investments exempt from the definition of "investment company" under the 1940 Investment Company Act and therefore not required to register with the Securities and Exchange Commission.

As a matter of corporate finance, the term hedge fund generally refers to an investment pool that is relatively liquid. On the other hand, private equity funds are investment pools that take longer term positions in companies and have more restrictions on investor withdrawal. Both types of funds can use leverage, but it is private equity funds that are most often associated with leveraged buy-outs of companies.

More generally, as a legal matter both private equity and hedge funds present an interesting package of tax, regulatory, and business associations law that make up their structure.[6] Beginning with the last issue first, we can note that typically these funds are structured as a group of related limited partnerships and limited liability companies.

---

4. Ronald J. Gilson & Charles K. Whitehead, *Deconstructing Equity: Public Ownership, Agency Costs, and Complete Capital Markets*, 108 Colum. L. Rev. 231 (2008); Brian Cheffins & John Armour, *The Eclipse Of Private Equity*, 33 Del. J. Corp. L. 1, 18 (2008).

5. *See* Arthur E. Wilmarth Jr., *The Dodd-Frank Act: A Flawed and Inadequate Response to the Too-Big-To-Fail Problem*, 89 Or. L. Rev. 951, 1045 (2011).

6. See Henry Ordower, *Demystifying Hedge Funds: A Design Primer*, 7 U.C. Davis Business L.J. 323 (2007).

GOLDENSON v. STEFFENS

802 F.Supp.2d 240
(D. Maine. 2011)
ORDER ON MOTION TO DISMISS

John A. WOODCOCK, Jr., Chief Judge.

On October 27, 2010, [the plaintiffs] filed a complaint against John L. Steffens; Gregory P. Ho; Spring Mountain Capital GP, LLC; Spring Mountain Capital LP; and Spring Mountain Capital, LLC, (Defendants) alleging under a variety of legal theories that the Defendants committed fraud against them by recommending that they invest their money in the Ascot Fund, a [formally unrelated] hedge fund with a complex proprietary strategy that stabilized investment returns and protected against market fluctuations when in fact, as the Defendants knew, the Ascot Fund was merely a feeder fund for the notorious Bernard Madoff, the infamous and now convicted perpetrator of the largest investment fraud in history. The Plaintiffs also claim that the Defendants committed a similar fraud by convincing them to invest in a Spring Mountain hedge fund called QP1 Fund, which itself was substantially invested in the Ascot Fund. The Defendants moved to dismiss the Complaint . . .

Spring Mountain Capital GP, LLC (SMCGP or with other Spring Mountain entities Spring Mountain) is a Delaware limited liability company and the general partner of the Spring Mountain Partners QP1, LP (QP1 Fund), a private investment instrument that functions as a so-called hedge fund. SMCGP has a principal place of business in the city of New York, state of New York. Spring Mountain Capital LP (SMCLP or collectively with other Spring Mountain entities Spring Mountain) is a Delaware limited partnership and the management company for QP1 Fund. Its principal place of business is in the city of New York, state of New York. Spring Mountain Capital, LLC (SM or collectively with other Spring Mountain entities Spring Mountain) is the general partner of the Management Company. Its principal place of business is in the city of New York, state of New York. SMCGP, SMCLP and SM were investment advisers within the meaning of the securities laws of the United States and the state of Maine.

John L. Steffens is the sole managing member of SMCGP, the Managing Director of SMCLP, and the sole managing member of SM. Id. He is a resident of the state of New Jersey and was an Investment Advisor (or was associated with an Investment Advisor) within the meaning of the securities laws of the United States and the state of Maine.

Gregory P. Ho is the President and Chief Operating Officer of SMCLP and is a resident of the city of New York, state of New York. Mr. Ho was an Investment Advisor (or was associated with an Investment Advisor) within the meaning of the securities laws of the United States and the state of Maine. The Plaintiffs claim that Mr. Steffens and Mr. Ho were the controlling persons of Spring Mountain. . . .

In the fall of 2001, the [Plaintiffs] learned about Mr. Steffens' Spring Mountain venture over dinner at a restaurant in Princeton, New Jersey. Mr. Steffens described Spring Mountain as a well-diversified "fund of funds" that employed numerous "sub-managers," who in turn used various investment strategies to generate earnings. Id. The [Plaintiffs] and Mr. Steffens met on a number of occasions and Mr. Steffens described how he and Spring Mountain carefully selected these sub-managers and monitored their trading strategies and performance. Mr. Steffens encouraged them to dispense with municipal bonds and invest instead in the QP1 Fund, a hedge fund. QP1 Fund has two components, a portfolio of underlying hedge funds and a private equity fund, collectively referred to as "Portfolio Funds" . . . Mr. Steffens encouraged them to invest in Spring Mountain because the QP1 Fund would simultaneously provide them with consistently superior rates of return and reduced risk.

On or about January 1, 2002, through SKG, the [Plaintiffs], acting on Mr. Steffens' advice, invested $2,000,000 in Spring Mountain's QP1 Fund.

PROBLEM SET 20.1

1. Diagram the relationships described in the foregoing case. Drawing on your knowledge of basic corporate law, what are some of the possible purposes for this structure?
2. In your introductory corporations class, you (hopefully) learned about limited liability. Given that, why does it matter that the individuals named in the case above controlled the legal entities in question? *See* Securities Exchange Act of 1934 §20.
3. The QP1 Fund is described as a "fund of funds." That is, it is a hedge fund that invests in other hedge funds. Often these funds have lower initial investment requirements, making them the primary way many individuals obtain entry into the more "exclusive" funds. Drawing on earlier discussions, including the discussion of portfolio theory, what might be the costs and benefits of investing in such a fund (beyond the risk that the manager outsources the entire investment to a Ponzi scheme)?
4. What do you make of the statement that "the QP1 Fund would simultaneously provide them with consistently superior rates of return and reduced risk"?

The key players in a hedge fund or private equity fund are the sponsor, the investment advisor, and, of course, the investors. The fund itself will normally be a limited partnership. The fund's general partner controls the fund, but usually is a pure holding company that has no employees. Quite often the entity or people who put together the fund in the first instance, the sponsors, own the general partner.

The sponsors are often also related to the investment advisor or management company, which provides the real people who make investment decisions and the physical office space that a layperson would associate with the fund.

Quite often the manager and the general partner are subsidiaries of an overarching holding company. Although they could be a single entity, fund managers based in New York City tend to bifurcate the general partner and the manager entities, for reasons of local tax law.[7]

---

7. In particular, it is preferable to have a separate entity receive the 20 percent "upside" payment discussed below to ensure it remains taxable as a capital gain, rather than as regular income or subject to the New York City unincorporated business tax.

The fund, the sponsor, and the manager are all bound together by a compensation scheme known as "2 and 20." The manager is paid an annual fee equal to 2 percent of assets under management, for which the manager not only provides management but also absorbs the "overhead" of the fund. The fund's general partner also receives a performance fee equal to 20 percent of the gains in the fund, referred to as the *carried interest*. Two and 20 are the standard terms, and of course variations might be negotiated by investors and the sponsor.[8]

GOLDMAN SAID TO PLAN BLACKSTONE CHALLENGE ON HEDGE-FUND STARTUPS

By Saijel Kishan and Katherine Burton, Bloomberg News[9]

May 16, 2011 (Bloomberg) — Goldman Sachs Group Inc. is seeking money to bankroll fledgling hedge funds, its second attempt since 2008 to break into a business now dominated by Blackstone Group LP, according to three people with knowledge of the plan.

The bank has spent the past year trying to attract clients for a seeding fund, which provides managers with startup investing capital in exchange for a cut of their fees, said the people, who asked not to be identified because the effort is private. Blackstone recently raised $2.4 billion for its second seeding fund, the industry's biggest.

Reservoir Capital Group, Larch Lane Advisors LLC and PineBridge Investments LLC also are marketing new funds, saying it's a good time to back startups because after the financial crisis investors are reluctant to trust even talented traders going out on their own. Goldman Sachs, based in New York, shut a fund in 2008, underscoring that betting on new managers can be tricky even for one of Wall Street's savviest firms.

"Seeding isn't an easy-money business," Alexis Graham, co-founder of Acceleration Capital Group, a New York-based firm that works with seed investors, said in a telephone interview. "There are only a small percentage of people out there who can consistently outperform, build a business and scale assets."

About half of the 100 or so firms that financed startups before 2008 have curtailed their investing or quit the industry, Graham said. Reasons for the shakeout include poor manager selection and hard-to-navigate financial markets.

SLICE OF FEES

Seeders generally invest $100 million to $150 million in a hedge fund, providing a pool of capital to help the manager begin trading. In return, the seeding fund gets 15 percent to 25 percent of the hedge fund's fees. Hedge-fund managers typically charge clients 2 percent of assets and take 20 percent of investment gains.

---

8. Large sovereign wealth funds and other important and very large investors often obtain preferential terms, including discounted management fees and carried interest.

9. Used with permission of Bloomberg L.P. © 2013. All rights reserved.

The seed money is often locked up in the hedge fund for three years, and seeders return initial capital to their investors after about five years. Seeding funds retain their ownership stake until it's bought out by the manager or a third party.

"If you have a 10-fund portfolio and three funds climb over $1 billion, then the economics work and you have a winner," said Eric Weinstein, who runs the $4 billion fund-of-fund business at Neuberger Berman Group LLC in New York. Seeders target annual returns of about 12 percent to 15 percent for their investors, he said.

BLACKSTONE'S RETURNS

Blackstone, the world's largest private-equity firm, jumped into seeding in 2007 with a $1.1 billion fund that took stakes in eight managers. While one of the hedge funds failed in 2008, the New York-based company's portfolio has returned about 50 percent since inception, according to investors. The remaining firms collectively manage $7 billion, and three have more than $1 billion, including Senrigan Capital Group Ltd., run by ex-Citadel LLC trader Nick Taylor in Hong Kong.

Often the fund documents prohibit the manager from collecting the 20 percent upside fee again until the investor's account value exceeds the level at which the fund previously accrued an incentive fee.[10] Imagine an investor with $1 million in a fund on January 1, whose account declines in value to $500,000 at the end of the year. If in the next year, the value of the account appreciates to $1.5 million, the hedge fund manager's performance fee would only be payable for the second year with respect to the $500,000 gain.

Managers themselves buy some of the limited partnership interests in the fund, a feature often referred to as *co-investment*. The 20 percent share of upside the manager gets can thus be seen as disproportionate allocation of profits, which gives the controlling party more than their pro rata share of the profits.[11]

Other investors consist primarily of insurance companies, pension funds, and other institutional investors, for reasons that will become clear after reading Section 4.[12] Regardless of the legal entity used, the fund itself is organized so that the partners, members, or shareholders are passive investors with little or no voting rights.

PROBLEM SET 20.2

1. What problems might arise from the fee structure just noted? In particular, what incentives might the fee structure give fund managers? What are the drawbacks of the "high water mark?"

---

10. This is known as a "high water mark."

11. Lee Sheppard, *News Analysis: Hedge Fund Managers' Tax Benefits Compared*, 119 Tax Notes 243 (2008).

12. The Volcker Rule provisions of the Dodd-Frank Act will largely prohibit certain financial institutions from owning, investing in, or sponsoring private equity and hedge funds.

2. Despite the increasing popularity of LLCs in other contexts, the most popular choice to structure the fund itself remains the limited partnership. Why might that be?

2. TAXES

Taxes drive many structural considerations, from both the investor and the manager perspective. At the most basic level, note that the entities used throughout much of the fund structure are "pass through" entities. This means the outside investors of the fund — the limited partners — will only pay tax, if at all, as if they had invested in the underlying securities in the fund, avoiding an entity level tax and permitting tax gains and losses to pass through to investors.[13] This allows the investors to realize investment tax subsidies built into the law: for example, long-term capital gains on securities held for more than one year and certain qualifying dividend income are taxed at a maximum rate of 15 percent, as compared with ordinary income that is currently taxed at a maximum rate of 35 percent.[14]

If the fund generates income that is connected with the conduct of a U.S. trade or business (Effectively Connected Income or (ECI)), the fund will be required to withhold U.S. income tax on the income that is attributable to the fund's non-U.S. investors, regardless of whether it is distributed.[15] In addition, all or a portion of the gain on the disposition by a non-U.S. investor of its interest in the fund can be taxed as ECI to the extent such gain is attributable to assets of the fund that generate ECI.

Moreover, a tax-exempt investor is subject to tax on some income earned from an entity treated as a partnership for tax purposes.[16] This type of tax is especially acute in private equity funds, given special rules for debt-funded investment income.[17]

Both of these issues lead many funds to structure themselves with parallel funds, incorporated at home and abroad, but utilizing the same basic investment style[18] For funds based in the United States, the Cayman Islands is the most frequently used jurisdiction for such parallel funds.

In mid-2013, the large role played by the Cayman Islands in the hedge fund industry became something of a mini controversy. Jeffrey Sachs, an economist at Columbia, wrote several letters to the *Financial Times* in which he noted that some residents of the Cayman Islands sit on hundreds of fund boards, while the Cayman financial system has $1.4 trillion in liabilities and assets. He termed

---

13. This status would be lost if the fund were publically traded. 27 U.S.C. §7704(b).

14. Various tax law proposals would change the tax treatment of the allocation of certain income and gain to the general partner, but have not been adopted as of the date of this writing.

15. *http://goo.gl/QqFI3*

16. Emily Cauble, *Harvard, Hedge Funds, and Tax Havens: Reforming the Tax Treatment of Investment Income Earned by Tax-Exempt Entities*, 29 Va. Tax Rev. 695 (2010).

17. Internal Revenue Code §514.

18. Summer A. LePree, *Taxation of United States Tax-Exempt Entities' Offshore Hedge Fund Investments: Application of the Section 514 Debt-Financed Rules to Leveraged Hedge Funds and Derivatives and the Case for Equalization*, 61 Tax Law. 807, 809–810 (2008).

the entire structure a "house of cards," a characterization that (unsurprisingly) representatives of the Cayman Islands financial industry dismissed.

In many cases, offshore funds use a master-feeder structure whereby offshore investors (and tax-exempt U.S. investors) invest in an offshore feeder, and U.S. taxable investors invest in either a domestic or foreign feeder that is taxed as a partnership, both of which are then aggregated into a single master investment pool.

3. REGULATION

As noted, a key consideration in constructing a hedge fund or a private equity fund involves securities regulation. In particular, these funds typically try to avoid the relevant securities law to the greatest extent possible, especially the laws that restrict the investment activities of mutual funds and the compensation of their managers.

PHILLIP GOLDSTEIN, ET AL., PETITIONERS v. SECURITIES AND EXCHANGE COMMISSION, RESPONDENT

451 F.3d 873

United States Court of Appeals, District of Columbia Circuit

No. 04-1434 | Argued Dec. 9, 2005 | Decided June 23, 2006

RANDOLPH, Circuit Judge. This is a petition for review of the Securities and Exchange Commission's regulation of "hedge funds" under the Investment Advisers Act of 1940, 15 U.S.C. §80b-1 et seq. See Registration Under the Advisers Act of Certain Hedge Fund Advisers, 69 Fed.Reg. 72,054 (Dec. 10, 2004) (codified at 17 C.F.R. pts. 275, 279) ("Hedge Fund Rule"). Previously exempt because they had "fewer than fifteen clients," 15 U.S.C. §80b-3(b)(3), most advisers to hedge funds must now register with the Commission if the funds they advise have fifteen or more "shareholders, limited partners, members, or beneficiaries." 17 C.F.R. §275.203(b)(3)-2(a). Petitioners Philip Goldstein, an investment advisory firm Goldstein co-owns (Kimball & Winthrop), and Opportunity Partners L.P., a hedge fund in which Kimball & Winthrop is the general partner and investment adviser (collectively "Goldstein") challenge the regulation's equation of "client" with "investor."

I.

"Hedge funds" are notoriously difficult to define. The term appears nowhere in the federal securities laws, and even industry participants do not agree upon a single definition . . . The term is commonly used as a catch-all for "any pooled investment vehicle that is privately organized, administered by professional investment managers, and not widely available to the public." President's

Working Group on Financial Markets, Hedge Funds, Leverage, and the Lessons of Long-Term Capital Management 1 (1999).

Exemption from regulation under the Investment Company Act allows hedge funds to engage in very different investing behavior than their mutual fund counterparts. While mutual funds, for example, must register with the Commission and disclose their investment positions and financial condition, id. §§80a-8, 80a-29, hedge funds typically remain secretive about their positions and strategies, even to their own investors. The Investment Company Act places significant restrictions on the types of transactions registered investment companies may undertake. Such companies are, for example, foreclosed from trading on margin or engaging in short sales, 15 U.S.C. §80a-12(a)(1), (3), and must secure shareholder approval to take on significant debt or invest in certain types of assets, such as real estate or commodities, id. §80a-13(a)(2). These transactions are all core elements of most hedge funds' trading strategies.

Another distinctive feature of hedge funds is their management structure. Unlike mutual funds, which must comply with detailed requirements for independent boards of directors, and whose shareholders must explicitly approve of certain actions, domestic hedge funds are usually structured as limited partnerships to achieve maximum separation of ownership and management. In the typical arrangement, the general partner manages the fund (or several funds) for a fixed fee and a percentage of the gross profits from the fund. The limited partners are passive investors and generally take no part in management activities.

Hedge fund advisers also had been exempt from regulation under the Investment Advisers Act of 1940, 15 U.S.C. §80b-1 et seq. ("Advisers Act"), a companion statute to the Investment Company Act, and the statute which primarily concerns us in this case. Enacted by Congress to "substitute a philosophy of full disclosure for the philosophy of caveat emptor" in the investment advisory profession, SEC v. Capital Gains Research Bureau, Inc., 375 U.S. 180, 186 (1963), the Advisers Act is mainly a registration and anti-fraud statute. Non-exempt "investment advisers" must register with the Commission, 15 U.S.C. §80b-3, and all advisers are prohibited from engaging in fraudulent or deceptive practices. By keeping a census of advisers, the Commission can better respond to, initiate, and take remedial action on complaints against fraudulent advisers.

Hedge fund general partners meet the definition of "investment adviser" in the Advisers Act. See 15 U.S.C. §80b-2(11). But they usually satisfy the "private adviser exemption" from registration in §203(b)(3) of the Act, 15 U.S.C. §80b-3(b)(3). That section exempts "any investment adviser who during the course of the preceding twelve months has had fewer than fifteen clients and who neither holds himself out generally to the public as an investment adviser nor acts as an investment adviser to any investment company registered under [the Investment Company Act]." Id. As applied to limited partnerships and other entities, the Commission had interpreted this provision to refer to the partnership or entity itself as the adviser's "client." See 17 C.F.R. §275.203(b)(3)-1. Even the largest hedge fund managers usually ran fewer than fifteen hedge funds and were therefore exempt.

Although the Commission has a history of interest in hedge funds . . . the current push for regulation had its origins in the failure of Long-Term Capital

Management, a Greenwich, Connecticut-based fund that had more than $125 billion in assets under management at its peak. In late 1998, the fund nearly collapsed. Almost all of the country's major financial institutions were put at risk due to their credit exposure to Long-Term, and the president of the Federal Reserve Bank of New York personally intervened to engineer a bailout of the fund in order to avoid a national financial crisis.

The Hedge Fund Rule first defines a "private fund" as an investment company that (a) is exempt from registration under the Investment Company Act by virtue of having fewer than one hundred investors or only qualified investors, see 15 U.S.C. §80a-3(c)(1), (7); (b) permits its investors to redeem their interests within two years of investing; and (c) markets itself on the basis of the "skills, ability or expertise of the investment adviser." 17 C.F.R. §275.203(b)(3)-1(d)(1). For these private funds, the rule then specifies that "[f]or purposes of section 203(b)(3) of the [Advisers] Act (15 U.S.C. §80b-3(b)(3)), you must count as clients the shareholders, limited partners, members, or beneficiaries . . . of [the] fund." Id. §275.203(b)(3)-2(a). The rule had the effect of requiring most hedge fund advisers to register by February 1, 2006.

II.

The Commission[] . . . argues that the Hedge Fund Rule amends only the method for counting clients under §203(b)(3), and that it does not "alter the duties or obligations owed by an investment adviser to its clients." 69 Fed.Reg. at 72,070. We ordinarily presume that the same words used in different parts of a statute have the same meaning. The Commission cannot explain why "client" should mean one thing when determining to whom fiduciary duties are owed, 15 U.S.C. §80b-6(1)-(3), and something else entirely when determining whether an investment adviser must register under the Act, id. §80b-3(b)(3).

The Commission also argues that the organizational form of most hedge funds is merely "legal artifice," to shield advisers who want to advise more than fifteen clients and remain exempt from registration. See Hedge Fund Rule, 69 Fed.Reg. at 72,068. But as the discussion above shows, form matters in this area of the law because it dictates to whom fiduciary duties are owed.

The Hedge Fund Rule might be more understandable if, over the years, the advisory relationship between hedge fund advisers and investors had changed. The Commission cited, as justification for its rule, a rise in the amount of hedge fund assets, indications that more pension funds and other institutions were investing in hedge funds, and an increase in fraud actions involving hedge funds. All of this may be true, although the dissenting Commissioners doubted it. But without any evidence that the role of fund advisers with respect to investors had undergone a transformation, there is a disconnect between the factors the Commission cited and the rule it promulgated. That the Commission wanted a hook on which to hang more comprehensive regulation of hedge funds may be understandable. But the Commission may not accomplish its objective by a manipulation of meaning.

The Commission has, in short, not adequately explained how the relationship between hedge fund investors and advisers justifies treating the former as clients of the latter. . . . The Commission points to its finding that a hedge fund adviser sometimes "may not treat all of its hedge fund investors the same." Hedge Fund Rule, 69 Fed.Reg. at 72,069–70 (citing different lock-up periods, greater access to information, lower fees, and "side pocket" arrangements). From this the Commission concludes that each account of a hedge fund investor "may bear many of the characteristics of separate investment accounts, which, of course, must be counted as separate clients." Id. at 72,070. But the Commission's conclusion does not follow from its premise. It may be that different classes of investors have different rights or privileges with respect to their investments. This reveals little, however, about the relationship between the investor and the adviser. Even if it did, the Commission has not justified treating all investors in hedge funds as clients for the purpose of the rule. If there are certain characteristics present in some investor-adviser relationships that mark a "client" relationship, then the Commission should have identified those characteristics and tailored its rule accordingly.

By painting with such a broad brush, the Commission has failed adequately to justify departing from its own prior interpretation of §203(b)(3). As we have discussed, in 1985 the Commission adopted a "safe harbor" for general partners of limited partnerships, enabling them to count the partnership as a single "client" for the purposes of §203 so long as they provided advice to a "collective investment vehicle" based on the investment objectives of the limited partners as a group. This "safe harbor" remains part of the Commission's rules and has since been expanded to include corporations, limited liability companies, and business trusts. The Hedge Fund Rule therefore appears to carve out an exception from this safe harbor solely for investment entities that have fewer than one hundred-one but more than fourteen investors. As discussed above, the Commission does not justify this exception by reference to any change in the nature of investment adviser-client relationships since the safe harbor was adopted. Absent such a justification, its choice appears completely arbitrary.

The petition for review is granted, and the Hedge Fund Rule is vacated and remanded.

So ordered.

Hedge and private equity funds avoid registering their shares under the 1933 Act because they structure their transactions to qualify for the private offering exemption from registration under Section 4(2) of the Securities Act and Regulation D adopted thereunder.[19]

They avoid reporting requirements under the 1934 Act by not listing on stock exchanges and by having fewer than 500 total investors.[20]

19. Regulation D requires that each investor in the fund be an accredited investor, which means individuals with a net worth of more than $1 million or income above $200,000 in the last two years and a reasonable expectation of reaching the same income level in the current year, and entities with more than US$5 million in assets. Under the Dodd-Frank Act, the accredited investor standard's net-worth test has been revised to exclude the value of the investor's primary residence from the calculation of the investor's total assets and the amount of any mortgage or other indebtedness secured by an investor's primary residence from the calculation of the investor's total liabilities, except to the extent the fair market value of the residence is less than the amount of such mortgage or other indebtedness. *See* 17 CFR 230.501-.508.

20. *See* Securities Exchange Act of 1934 §12(g); Rule 12g-1.

The Investment Company Act of 1940 generally requires "investment companies" to register as such with the SEC. Registered investment companies — commonly called mutual funds by humans (non-lawyers) — are subject to a complicated array of tax rules, investment restrictions, liquidity requirements and other constraints. Many of these rules are incompatible with typical hedge fund practices, as noted in *Goldstein*.

Hedge funds and private equity are exempt from the investment company definition under the 1940 Investment Company Act Section 3(c)(1), which exempts privately offered investment funds with up to 100 beneficial owners, and Section 3(c)(7), which exempts "qualified purchaser" funds.[21] Under a section 3(c)(1) structure, however, if the fund is to pay performance fees to its manager, all of the investors in the 3(c)(1) fund also must be "qualified clients."[22]

And both exclusions — 3(c)(1) and 3(c)(7) — require that the hedge fund not make a public offering of securities and that, with limited exceptions, all investors are "accredited investors" within the meaning of Rule 506 of Regulation D under the 1933 Act.

In short, depending on the particular fund structure used, the fund will have to make sure its investors are some combination of qualified purchasers, accredited investors, and qualified clients. Each investor in the fund will typically be required to represent that it is a qualified purchaser as defined in section 2(a)(51) of the 1940 Investment Company Act. In the event that not all of a private equity fund's investors are qualified purchasers, then the fund might still qualify for an exemption by limiting the number of investors to not more than 100 all of which must still be accredited investors. And in that case the fund will likely also want to make sure its investors are qualified clients.

If all of this has given you a headache, take some aspirin and then consider Table 20-1.

TABLE 20-1

	3(c)(1)	3(c)(7)
Accredited investor status — $1 million net worth requirement (or $200,000 per year of income for at least two years)	Applies	Applies
Public offering prohibition	Prohibited	Prohibited
Limitation on number of investors	Not more than 100 persons	No limitation
Qualified client status ($1 million/$2 million)	Applies	Applies
Qualified purchaser status ($5 million portfolio)	Not applicable	Applies

---

21. Qualified purchasers are investors who, in the case of individual investors, have at least $5 million net of debt in investments exclusive of the hedge fund in question.

22. The Dodd-Frank Act amended Section 205(e) of the Advisers Act to provide that, by July 21, 2011 and every five years thereafter, the SEC must adjust the dollar amount thresholds included in rules issued under Section 205(e) to account for inflation. Under the first such adjustment, qualified clients are now defined as individuals who had at least $1 million under management immediately after entering into the advisory contract or individuals who the adviser reasonably believed had a net worth of more than $2 million at the time the contract was entered into. Rule 205-3.

PROBLEM SET 20.3

1. It has been predicted that the section 3(c)(1) will become increasingly rare. Why might that be?
2. Alex Hamilton is the president of a large Gotham City bank, a job that pays him $1 million per year. He has $500,000 ready to invest in a hedge fund. Will he find a hedge fund to invest in?

That leaves the Investment Advisers Act of 1940, the subject of much of the *Goldstein* opinion reproduced earlier. This act generally requires investment advisors to register with the SEC. In 2004, the SEC estimated that just less than half of eligible investment advisers to hedge funds were registered under the Advisers Act.[23] Registration requires fund advisers to expand their disclosures, adopt compliance policies and procedures, appoint a Chief Compliance Officer and open their doors to the SEC for periodic inspections and examinations.[24]

Until recently, unregistered advisers generally relied on the private adviser exemption of Section 203(b)(3) in the 1940 Advisers Act. That section provided that an investment adviser would not have to register with the SEC if it (1) had fewer than 15 clients in the preceding 12 months, (2) did not hold itself out generally to the public as an investment adviser, and (3) did not act as an investment adviser to a registered investment company or business development company. An unregistered adviser also relied on Rule 203(b)(3)-1 that allowed it to count as clients the funds it advised, and not the number of actual investors in the fund. *Goldstein* halted the SEC's attempt to change that method of counting investors.

The Dodd-Frank Act repealed Section 203(b)(3), meaning that the SEC ultimately won the war, if not the battle.[25] With limited exceptions, most funds management companies will be registered with the SEC going forward.[26]

Similarly, in early 2012 the Commodities Futures Trading Commission adopted rule changes that rescind the exemption from commodity pool operator registration contained in its Rule 4.13(a)(4), which many hedge funds had used. As a result, unless an exemption is otherwise available, hedge funds will be required to register with the National Futures Association if the fund conducts more than a small amount of speculative trading in futures, commodity options, and other commodity interests. Note that it is the adviser or manager that registers, not the fund itself.

---

23. Inv. Adv. Act Release No. 2266 (July 20, 2004), 2004 WL 1636422, at *24; Inv. Adv. Act Release No. 2333 (Dec. 10, 2004), 2004 WL 2785492, at *6 n.62.
24. About 75 New York-based examiners are responsible for 2,000 advisers with $11 trillion under management, an SEC representative told a conference in November 2011.
25. William K. Sjostrom Jr., *A Brief History of Hedge Fund Adviser Registration and Its Consequences for Private Equity and Venture Capital Advisers*, Harvard Business L. Rev. (Feb. 1, 2011).
26. Rule 204(b)-1, recently adopted by the SEC, will require registered investment advisers with $150 million or more in private fund assets to file Form PF periodically with the SEC. Under Dodd-Frank, investment advisers who manage between $25 million and $100 million in assets under management, known as "mid-sized" investment advisers, will now be required to register with the state as opposed to the SEC.

Finally, under the Dodd-Frank Act, many hedge fund companies also will be subject to additional regulation by the SEC and the CFTC as "major swaps participants."

4. PUTTING IT ALL TOGETHER

IN RE MILLENNIUM GLOBAL EMERGING CREDIT MASTER FUND LIMITED, ET AL., DEBTORS IN FOREIGN PROCEEDINGS

458 B.R. 63

United States Bankruptcy Court, S.D. New York

No. 11-13171 | Aug. 26, 2011

Allan L. GROPPER, Bankruptcy Judge.

Before the Court are chapter 15 petitions filed by the joint liquidators (the "Liquidators" or "Petitioners") of Millennium Global Emerging Credit Master Fund Limited and Millennium Global Emerging Credit Fund Limited (respectively, the "Master Fund" and "Feeder Fund" and collectively the "Funds"), seeking recognition of Bermuda liquidation proceedings as foreign main proceedings or, alternatively, foreign nonmain proceedings. The Liquidators seek recognition in order to investigate the Funds' financial affairs, conduct discovery related to potential causes of action against parties in the United States, and ultimately provide for a distribution of recovered property to creditors. Recognition of the Bermuda proceedings is opposed by BCP Securities, LLC ("BCP" or "the Objectant") on the ground that Bermuda is not the Funds' center of main interests ("COMI") or a place of nontransitory economic activity of the Funds.

An evidentiary hearing regarding recognition was held on July 27, 2011, at which one of the Liquidators of the Funds, Michael Morrison, testified. By consent, the Petitioners' case was presented by admitting into evidence the verified petitions, the declarations in support of the petitions filed by Morrison and the Funds' Bermuda counsel, Robin J. Mayor, and the Offering Memorandum for the Feeder Fund ("Offering Memorandum"). *Declaration of Robert K. Dakis*, Ex. A., Dkt. No. 38. BCP cross-examined Morrison and introduced the confidential information memorandum of Millennium Global Emerging Credit Fund, L.P., a Delaware Limited Partnership (the "Delaware Fund").[27]

At the conclusion of the hearing, the Court informed the parties that it would enter an order recognizing the Bermuda proceedings as foreign main proceedings, with a written decision to follow.

---

27. The Delaware Fund was incorporated in Delaware to facilitate investments by qualified residents of the United States. It is not a debtor in these proceedings, and the Liquidators have not been appointed and do not seek relief with respect to that entity.

The Funds were incorporated in Bermuda for the purpose of creating an offshore investment fund that would invest in sovereign and corporate debt instruments from developing countries. The Feeder Fund was incorporated in Bermuda on October 12, 2006, and the Master Fund was incorporated in Bermuda on September 20, 2007. The Feeder Fund began operations in December 2006 as a Bermuda Institutional Scheme under the Bermuda Investment Funds Act of 2006. The Master Fund was incorporated in order to create a master-feeder structure that could facilitate investment from certain classes of foreign investors, and it operated under the Bermuda Investment Funds Act as a private fund with fewer than 20 participants. In fact, the Feeder Fund and the Delaware Fund were its only participants. At the time of the Master Fund's incorporation, the Feeder Fund transferred substantially all its assets to it in exchange for a 97% ownership interest in the Master Fund, with the other 3% held by the Delaware Fund, and all the service agreements of the Feeder Fund were novated in favor of the Master Fund.

The registered office of both Funds was in Bermuda at all times, at the address of their common administrator. As set forth in the Offering Memorandum, during the course of the Funds' operations they had no employees other than their three directors, Michael Collins, James Keyes, and Deborah Sebire, who each served on the boards of directors of both Funds. Collins and Keyes are both residents of Bermuda, and Sebire is said to be a resident of the Bailiwick of Guernsey (Channel Islands). Both funds retained the same administrator in Bermuda, Argonaut, Limited ("Argonaut"), a Bermuda company, as well as the same bank, Butterfield Trust (Bermuda) Limited, a subsidiary of Bank of NT Butterfield & Son Ltd. ("Butterfield Bank"). The Funds had approximately BD$900,000 on deposit at Butterfield Bank at the time of the opening of the Liquidation in 2008.

The Master Fund had a "manager," Millennium Asset Management Limited (the "Manager"), responsible for "management, administration, back office activities, marketing and investment activities"; it was said to be located in Guernsey. The Manager in turn appointed as investment manager Millennium Global Investments Limited, which was described as London-based. The Funds maintained prime brokerage accounts with Credit Suisse Securities (Europe) Limited and Citigroup, Inc., through which the investment manager conducted securities transactions. The Funds also conducted derivative and hedging transactions under standard ISDA contracts with various counterparties. The Offering Materials indicate that subscriptions of investors would be invested in the Master Fund, which was identified as a Bermuda entity, and that the Master Fund would set investment objectives for the Funds, exercise direct authority to oversee the investment manager's decisions, and replace the investment manager if necessary. The Offering Materials contain a directory that identifies the key parties involved in the management of the Funds, including: (i) the directors, located in Bermuda and Guernsey; (ii) the manager, located in Guernsey; (iii) the investment manager, apparently located in London; (iv) the administrator, located in Bermuda; (v) the prime broker, apparently located in London; (vi) the custodian, located in Bermuda; (vii) the auditors, located in Bermuda;

(viii) the valuation agents, located in the United States; (ix) the legal advisors, located in Bermuda, the United Kingdom, and the United States; and (x) the Feeder Fund's banker, located in Bermuda. The Offering Materials direct potential investors to direct subscription documents to the administrator in Bermuda and cash to Butterfield Bank in Bermuda.

The liquidation of the Funds commenced as a result of their inability to meet a margin call of the Master Fund's prime broker, Credit Suisse, on October 6, 2008. A default notice was issued by Credit Suisse on October 16, 2008, and on the same day the directors petitioned the Bermuda Court for an order directing the wind-up of the Funds. The Bermuda Court's order commencing the liquidation divested the directors of all authority over the Funds and caused the appointment of Michael W. Morrison, Charles Thresh, and Richard Heis, all of KPMG Advisory Ltd. or KPMG LLP, as provisional liquidators with full managerial authority over the Funds. The provisional liquidators were appointed as joint liquidators of the Master Fund on March 5, 2009 and of the Feeder Fund on April 16, 2009. Committees of inspection, which appear to be similar to the creditors' committee in a chapter 11 case, were formed by the Bermuda Court in both foreign proceedings.

As of the commencement of the liquidation, subscriptions to the Funds totaled $390 million, and the Liquidators estimate that as of September 30, 2008 the value of the Funds' portfolio was $738,209,753. However, subsequent to the closure of the prime brokerage accounts, the Funds' prime brokers asserted that there was a $170 million deficiency owed by the Funds. Although the prime brokers ultimately asserted claims against the Funds, there was an initial return of cash totaling $21.85 million, of which $10 million was allocated to the Feeder Fund and $11.85 million to the Master Fund. Approximately three years later, the Funds now have on hand close to $7 million held by the Feeder Fund and $7.5 million held by the Master Fund. Morrison testified that expenses to date have been exclusively for administration of the estates, including the fees of the Liquidators and for counsel in Bermuda, the United Kingdom, and the United States, and that all expenses have been subject to oversight by the committees of inspection and the Bermuda Court.

As a consequence of the decline in value of the Funds' portfolio, the Liquidators currently have at least one litigation pending in the United Kingdom and are pursuing an investigation of potential causes of action against parties in the United States. The filing of the chapter 15 petition on June 30, 2011 was authorized by the Feeder Fund Committee and approved by the Bermuda Court on June 22, 2011, with the stated purpose to pursue discovery against parties in the United States, commence litigation if indicated, and in the meantime, if possible, obtain relief from the expiration of any statutes of limitations.

The Objectant is one of the parties that was designated by the Liquidators in the Verified Petition as potentially affected by provisional relief, admittedly as a target of the Liquidators' investigation. On cross-examination of Morrison, the Objectant established that the administration of the Funds' liquidation proceedings in Bermuda has cost approximately $9 million to date, including about $5 million spent outside of Bermuda, predominantly on fees for counsel in the United Kingdom and United States. Morrison testified that the litigation that is currently pending or which may be commenced, all against parties outside of Bermuda, is likely to be the most valuable asset of the estates. It was also established that: (i) the Funds' investment manager was located in London and had an exclusive contractual right to invest the Funds' portfolio; (ii) the Funds' asset valuation agent, GlobeOp, operates out of multiple locations including the United States, the United Kingdom, and India; (iii) a majority of the Funds' investors were located outside Bermuda; (iv) substantially all of the Funds' assets were invested outside of Bermuda or committed to contracts (including derivatives such as swaps) with counterparties outside of Bermuda; (v) directors' meetings were customarily held with Collins and Keyes present in Bermuda and Sebire participating by telephone from Guernsey; (vi) meetings with the Funds' service providers prior to the liquidation were frequently held by telephone or in London; (vii) meetings with creditors required by Bermuda law as part of the liquidation have routinely been held in London for the convenience of creditors; (viii) claims have been submitted in the Bermuda liquidation but only for voting purposes, with no distributions having yet occurred; and (ix) none of the members of the Funds' committees of inspection is located in Bermuda. Morrison testified on redirect that all subscriptions and all requests for redemptions from the Funds were required to be directed to the Funds' administrator, Argonaut, in Bermuda, and that the investment manager in London was subject to dismissal by the Funds' directors, located in Bermuda and Guernsey.

The Objectant argued at the conclusion of the hearing that the Funds' COMI should be determined to be the United Kingdom based on the location of the investment manager, the location of many creditors and creditors' meetings, the location of the prime broker, Credit Suisse, and the fact that litigation is allegedly pending in London. The Petitioners argued that the record supported the conclusion that the Funds' COMI was in Bermuda prior to the commencement of the liquidation and had remained there or, in the alternative, had become lodged in Bermuda due to the control exercised by the Liquidators there and the fact that creditors look to the Bermuda proceedings for recoveries. Alternatively, the Petitioners argued that the Funds had an "establishment" in Bermuda and the foreign proceedings are entitled to recognition as foreign nonmain proceedings.

DISCUSSION

The principal issue in dispute with respect to this application for recognition under chapter 15 of the Bankruptcy Code is whether the Funds have their "center of main interests" or an "establishment" in Bermuda, entitling the Liquidators to recognition of the foreign proceedings as "foreign main" or "foreign nonmain" proceedings. BCP contends that the Bermuda liquidation proceedings in question, which have been pending in Bermuda for more than three years without any apparent objection by creditors or others affected by the proceedings and which have cost more than $9 million in fees and expenses, are not entitled to recognition as either main or nonmain proceedings because Bermuda is not the "center of main interests" ["COMI"] of either of the Funds and because they did not have an "establishment" in Bermuda, as required for nonmain recognition. If BCP is correct and the Bermuda proceedings are not recognized, the Liquidators may be unable to access the U.S. courts to investigate and prosecute possible claims against BCP and others, or they might have to start a new proceeding in some putative "center of main interests" and incur all the costs of duplicative liquidation proceedings. Chapter 15 of the Bankruptcy Code which is designed to foster cooperation with foreign proceedings, not to thwart them, does not mandate this result.

The appropriate date at which to determine COMI is on or about the date of the commencement of the foreign proceeding for which recognition is sought. The same date should be used to determine whether the foreign debtor has an "establishment" in the foreign nation. We therefore turn to the following questions: (i) the COMI of these debtors as of the date of the commencement of the liquidation in Bermuda in 2008; and (ii) whether they had an "establishment" in Bermuda at that time.

In this case, many of the factors that the courts have used in the COMI determination point toward Bermuda, and others point in various directions. Starting with those that point toward Bermuda, two of the Funds' three directors were located in Bermuda, and the directors had the right to replace all of the Funds' other agents, as well as the right to determine whether to place the Funds into an insolvency proceeding. Bermuda was also the location of the Funds' bank, their custodian, and their auditors. On the other hand, the day-to-day management of the Funds' investments did not take place in Bermuda. As the Offering Memorandum disclosed, the directors appointed as manager for the Funds an entity described as "Millennium Asset Management Limited, a Guernsey company." The manager had "responsibility for the Fund's management, administration, back-office activities, marketing and investment activities, all of which are subject to the overall control of the Directors." The Offering Memorandum further disclosed that the "manager" had appointed as "investment manager" a "London-based investment management company regulated by the Financial Services Authority of the United Kingdom" and also "registered with the SEC as an investment advisor." There is no evidence that any of the Funds' investors or other creditors resided in Bermuda, and the Funds did not invest in property in Bermuda.

A simple tally of the foregoing factors demonstrates that more point toward Bermuda than elsewhere. On the record of this case, this supports the finding that the COMI was Bermuda. In addition, there are two further reasons for finding that the Funds' COMI was in Bermuda as of the date of the wind-up order.

Most important, in the case at bar, the only center of main interests reasonably "ascertainable by third parties" was Bermuda. The Offering Memorandum for the Feeder Fund offered shares in "A Bermuda Exempted Company (Mutual Fund), classified as an Institutional Fund under the Investment Funds Act 2006 of Bermuda." The Offering Memorandum made it clear that the Funds were located in Bermuda and subject to the control of a Bermuda-based board of directors, and all investors were directed to send their cash to an account in Bermuda. The Funds' investors did not invest in a London hedge fund; they invested in an offshore fund, and if the daily investment decisions were made by a London-based adviser, the investment manager was subject to the ultimate control of the directors of the Funds. An investor could speculate as to the location of the manager (Guernsey, elsewhere?), and investors were informed that the investment manager was "London-based." Nevertheless, Bermuda was the only jurisdiction clearly identified with the Funds, and on this record it was the only jurisdiction reasonably "ascertainable by third parties."

Moreover, because the formation of the funds in Bermuda was clearly disclosed in the Offering Memorandum, investors could have reasonably expected that Bermuda was likely to be the venue of any proceeding to wind up or liquidate the Funds. Under Bermuda law, a Bermuda company is subject to being wound up, voluntarily or involuntarily, in a proceeding in Bermuda. It would have been pure speculation that the Funds would be liquidated or wound up in any other jurisdiction. One of the authors of the Model Law and of chapter 15 has suggested that the COMI determination should be affected by the likelihood that the COMI jurisdiction would have an acceptable substantive law. Although there are decisions that rigidly assert that equitable factors should play no role at the recognition phase of a chapter 15 case, it would seem that a determination relative to recognition and to the "center of main interests" of an enterprise should take into account the existence of a fair and impartial judicial system and a sophisticated body of law, as aspects of the *bona fides* of the proceedings. It bears noting, therefore, that Bermuda has a sophisticated, fair and impartial legal system that has been recognized and granted comity by our courts. *See, e.g., In re Board of Directors of Hopewell Int'l Ins. Ltd.*, 275 B.R. 699 (S.D.N.Y.2002), *aff'g.* 238 B.R. 25 (Bankr.S.D.N.Y.1999).

In addition to the fact that Bermuda was the only COMI reasonably ascertainable by third parties, there is insufficient evidence in this case that establishes the COMI in a location other than Bermuda. There was a manager, ostensibly in Guernsey, but even the Objectant does not contend that the Funds' COMI was Guernsey. The Funds' investment manager was said to be "London-based," but there is very little evidence of record as to where the investment manager actually was located; as a practical matter an investment manager can be anywhere he or she has access to a computer terminal to make a trade and to follow the market. The Funds' assets were securities issued in "emerging countries," probably represented by book entries in ledgers throughout the world. The location of the prime broker for the Funds, identified as Credit Suisse Securities (Europe) Limited, was disclosed in at least some of the offering materials as London, but testimony indicated that Citigroup, Inc. was also used as a prime broker, suggesting that at least some of the Funds' investments were subject to control from New York. Furthermore, there is evidence that the location of the prime broker could vary; a footnote in the Offering Memorandum states, "To the extent that assets of the Master Fund are treated as 'plan assets' under ERISA, the prime broker will be located in the United States." The record does not disclose where the Funds' investors were located, except that some were in the United Kingdom, some were in the United States, and some were themselves located in offshore jurisdictions. The evidence did disclose that post-liquidation meetings have been held in London for the convenience of creditors, but there is no evidence that the Funds' creditors were closely identified with any one jurisdiction.

On this record, the proof does not establish an alternative COMI. Since every entity has a center of main interests, *In re Chiang*, 437 B.R. at 403, the fact that the evidence does not disclose a COMI other than Bermuda operates in favor of granting recognition of the Bermuda proceedings as foreign main proceedings.

In conclusion, based on the record, assuming that the evidence is sufficient to rebut the §1516(c) presumption, the Liquidators satisfied their burden of establishing that the COMI of the Funds was in Bermuda as of the commencement of the liquidation in 2008. The foreign proceedings are entitled to recognition as foreign main proceedings.

The Liquidators are directed to settle an order consistent with this decision.

PROBLEM SET 20.4

1. Once again, diagram the related business entities at issue in the foregoing case. Which entity or entities are the funds? What assets do these funds own?

5. SEEKING ALPHA

We have already seen that an investment's return relative to the market can be measured by beta. But what of the return that is not measured by CAPM? We might add an error term to the CAPM equation, and call that "alpha," or if you prefer to be Mediterranean "α."

Hedge funds and private equity funds focus extensively on alpha. After all, why would you pay "2 and 20" to a manger who achieved the same return you could get from buying an index fund that charges 0.04 percent.[28]

This alpha could be return in addition to the stock market return, or return that is uncorrelated with the stock market.

Beta investing, as we have already discussed, involves taking on a degree of systematic risk for which the investor is compensated. For example, equity investments provide higher return than cash or safe government debt, because they involve higher expected risks.

The other way to make money through investing is by targeting alpha. Alpha investing involves an assumption that the investor is smarter or somehow better informed than other investors, and that this superior knowledge can be used to make excess returns.

As such, alpha investing involves a zero-sum game, where the investor (in this case the hedge fund manager) looks for assets that the current holder undervalues or does not fully understand.

In short, hedge funds seek return that is not explained by CAPM and the ECMH. Of course, the return not explained by CAPM might come from the manager's skill, but it might also come from other sources, too. Such as . . . (bet you'll be asked in class).

---

28. *https://www.schwabetfs.com/summary.asp*

6. FUND STRATEGIES

Hedge funds employ a variety of investment strategies, many far removed from the original Jones fund that gave "hedge funds" their name. For example, one common hedge fund strategy involves corporate governance activism — the fund takes a small but significant stake in a company, and pushes for improvements in the business. This really involves very little in the way of hedging.[29]

BRIAN R. CHEFFINS & JOHN ARMOUR, *THE PAST, PRESENT, AND FUTURE OF SHAREHOLDER ACTIVISM BY HEDGE FUNDS*
37 J. Corp. L. 51, 56–61 (2011)

Shareholder activism has been described as "the exercise and enforcement of rights by minority shareholders with the objective of enhancing shareholder value over the long term." While defining shareholder activism by reference to the use of shareholder rights to enhance shareholder value delineates the basic parameters of this corporate governance tactic, the formulation is too general in nature to distinguish hedge fund interventions from those carried out by mainstream institutional investors such as mutual funds and public pension funds. Law professors Marcel Kahan and Ed Rock have described the different approaches adopted as follows:

> Mutual fund and public-pension fund activism, if it occurs, tends to be incidental and ex post: when fund management notes that portfolio companies are underperforming, or that their governance regime is deficient, they will sometimes be active (footnote omitted). In contrast, hedge fund activism is strategic and ex ante: hedge fund managers first determine whether a company would benefit from activism, then take a position and become active.

Employing the adjectives "defensive" and "offensive" provides a convenient way to distinguish the sort of activism in which mainstream institutional shareholders engage from the sort for which hedge funds — private investment vehicles that do not necessarily hedge their positions but have historically taken advantage of exclusions and regulatory "safe harbors" to operate largely outside statutory rules on investment companies and investment advisers — have achieved notoriety. Defensive shareholder activism occurs when an investor with a pre-existing stake in a company becomes dissatisfied with corporate performance or corporate governance and reacts by lobbying for changes, whether "behind the scenes" or with a public challenge to management (e.g. proposing the election of directors the dissident supports). A shareholder acting in this sort of ex post fashion will not own enough shares to guarantee victory in a contest

---

29. Frank A. Partnoy, *Shapeshifting Corporations*, 76 U. Chi. L. Rev. 261, 266 (2009) ("Activist hedge funds purchase (or sell short) concentrated ownership positions in public companies. In the simplest case, one or more hedge funds acquire substantial (typically a" sweet spot "of 5 to 10 percent) equity stakes and then press for strategic change. Their involvement leads to immediate and dramatic changes in the shareholder base of a company, and typically also results in positive returns for shareholders.").

for boardroom control or to dictate corporate policy but potentially can use their stake as a departure point in garnering support for the changes they advocate. To the extent pension funds and mutual funds engage in shareholder activism, it will most often be of this reactive ex post sort, as they work "defensively" to protect the value of existing investments.

The key feature that makes activism "defensive" is that the shareholder or shareholders taking the initiative will have held a sizeable stake before stepping forward. This "initial endowment" is not a feature of offensive shareholder activism. What happens instead is that an investor lacking a meaningful stake in a company builds up one "offensively" on the presumption that the company is not currently maximizing shareholder returns and with the intention of agitating for change to unlock shareholder value should this be necessary. The investor crucially will plan ex ante to press for a fresh approach if management does not take the initiative. As the quote from Kahan and Rock indicates, this is precisely the sort of activism for which hedge funds have gained notoriety.

The adjective "offensive" potentially connotes an aggressive posture towards incumbent management. This form of activism does not necessarily imply, however, shareholder/executive antagonism. While hedge fund activists have gained notoriety for their confrontational approach, they often aim for a collegial, if firm, "hands on" approach with incumbent management. As Warren Lichtenstein, the founder of Steel Partners II, a prominent activist hedge fund, said in 2004, "The best situation is where we find a cheap stock with great management and a great business, and we can sit back and make money." Correspondingly, Lichtenstein found when Steel Partners II bought shares, "Many times managements are happy there's a long-term, supportive investor."

Lichtenstein's reference to the desirable properties of a "cheap stock" reveals an overlap in investment philosophies between activist hedge funds and the prototypical "value investor" who seeks through diligent analysis of corporate fundamentals to purchase shares trading at a bargain price, the proverbial dollar for 50 cents. Hedge funds that engage in offensive shareholder activism typically rely on the "value approach" when identifying targets, forming as such a subset of hedge funds that invests in equities in a manner akin to classic, value-oriented investors.

Managers of activist hedge funds correspondingly tend not to be experts in quantitative theories of finance — a typical attribute of a hedge fund manager — but are often former investment bankers or research analysts used to working hard to understand balance sheets and income statements. Activist hedge funds in turn often justify their investment strategy on the basis the companies they buy stakes in are undervalued, and the targets themselves, despite usually having sound operating cash flows and returns on assets, typically have a low share price relative to book value and low dividend payout ratios.

If an activist hedge fund identifies and invests in an "undervalued" company and the share price subsequently increases due to a belated reaction by the market rather than due to any prompting by the hedge fund, this will be relatively "easy money" for the hedge fund. The situation will be the same if management, on its own initiative, makes changes that serve to increase shareholder returns. Under such circumstances activist hedge funds who buy sizeable stakes in target companies merely need to wait to sell when the time is right and thus will be doing little more than.

The readiness to take a hands-on role to shake things up is the crucial additional dimension to hedge fund activism. Activist hedge funds, rather than merely adopting the passive approach that characterizes value investing and waiting for the market to self-correct — which may well never happen if a company's shares do not get noticed and instead drift lower — are prepared to take the initiative and accelerate matters by lobbying for changes calculated to boost shareholder returns. As a private equity fund manager said in 2007 of various prominent hedge fund activists, "I'd like to thank my friends Carl Icahn, Nelson Peltz, Jana Partners . . . for teeing up deals because . . . many times [activist targets] are being driven into some form of auction." Hence, despite Warren Lichtenstein characterizing Steel Partners II as a potentially "supportive investor," activist hedge funds do not give management a full-scale "vote of confidence" when they invest in companies.

. . .

The investment approach activist hedge funds employ is markedly different from the approach private equity adopts. Private equity firms believe that taking a "hands on" role with the management of companies they take private is necessary to set the stage for a profitable exit and thus are comfortable deploying sufficient capital to obtain outright voting control. Activist hedge funds rarely have any interest in going this far with the companies they target. Instead, they prefer not to tie up capital in the form of majority or sole ownership of companies and instead anticipate profiting as minority shareholders when shareholder returns improve due to changes management makes, in response to investor pressure if necessary. This is borne out by a 2009 article by economists Robin Greenwood and Michael Schor, who compiled a dataset of 784 instances between 1993 and 2006 where a hedge fund disclosed pursuant to federal securities law that it owned 5% or more of the shares of a publicly traded company and declared an intention to influence the management of the company. The hedge funds in question held, on average, 9.8% of the shares of the companies they targeted, far short of majority or sole ownership. Hedge fund activists do in some instances propose acquiring outright control of companies they focus upon. Only rarely, though, do they end up with a majority stake, with their bids either fading away as an engagement takes its course or being beaten out by a higher offer.

. . .

Hedge fund activists, when they opt to be proactive, will typically begin by sounding out management with a telephone call, letter, or e-mail pressing the incumbent board to make changes designed to increase shareholder value. Hedge funds often lobby for finance-oriented changes, such as having a target company squeeze value from the balance sheet by spinning off underperforming non-core assets and by using share buy-backs or a sizeable one-off dividend to distribute "excess" cash to shareholders. More radically, a hedge fund activist may advocate an outright sale of the target, either as a going concern or through divestiture of key operations. Hedge funds also sometimes lobby in favor of increased operational efficiency and reputedly began putting more emphasis on strategic changes when the tighter credit markets associated with the 2008 financial crisis made it more difficult for target companies to engage in financial engineering.

If a quiet approach fails to yield the desired results, an activist hedge fund can step up the pressure, perhaps by criticizing management in public or by threatening a lawsuit against the company's directors. A particularly forceful strategy is to threaten what Gilson and Schwartz term a "transfer by vote," this being the securing of managerial control by winning a proxy contest intended to determine who serves on the board. Activist investors say that because of the high costs involved they avoid proxy battles if possible. Moreover, the preference of hedge fund managers to avoid hands-on involvement in the running of target companies implies that securing board control will typically not be a high priority. Nevertheless, Alon Brav, Wei Jiang, Frank Partnoy, and Randall Thomas report in a widely cited study that in 13% of hedge fund activism incidents they uncovered through searches of filings under federal securities law the hedge fund was involved in a proxy contest to replace incumbent directors. A likely explanation for many of the proxy battles that do occur is that hedge funds use contests for board seats to signal to potential future targets that they are prepared to invest heavily in pursuing an activist campaign should this be required.

––––––––––––

Some big hedge funds invest across a wide variety of strategies. In these cases the only unifying theme is that the investments in question tend to be ones that individual investors are unable to implement themselves, due to either regulatory prohibitions or transaction costs.

OCH-ZIFF CAPITAL MANAGEMENT GROUP LLC
Form 10-K, For the Fiscal Year Ended December 31, 2010, 4–5

MULTI-STRATEGY APPROACH

Our funds invest across multiple strategies and geographies without any predetermined commitments. Portfolio composition is determined by evaluating what we believe are the best market opportunities, consistent with our goals of diversification and capital preservation. The primary investment strategies we employ in our funds include:

Convertible and derivative arbitrage, which takes advantage of price discrepancies between convertible and derivative securities and the underlying equity or other security. These investments may be made at multiple levels of an entity's capital structure to profit from valuation or other pricing discrepancies;

Credit, which includes a variety of credit-based strategies, such as high-yield debt investments in distressed businesses and investments in bank loans and senior secured debt. Credit also includes providing mezzanine financing and structuring creative capital solutions;

Long/short equity special situations, which consists of long/short and event-driven investing. Fundamental long/short investing involves analyzing companies and assets to profit where we believe mispricing or undervaluation exists. Event-driven investing attempts to realize gain from corporate events such as spin-offs, recapitalizations and other corporate restructurings, whether company specific or as a result of industry or economic conditions;

Merger arbitrage, which is an event-driven strategy involving multiple investments in entities contemplating a merger or similar business combination. This strategy seeks to realize a profit from pricing discrepancies among the securities of the entities involved in the event;

Private investments, which encompasses investments in a variety of special situations which seek to realize value through strategic sales or initial public offerings; and

Structured credit, which involves investments in residential and commercial mortgage-backed securities and other asset-backed securities. This strategy also includes investments in collateralized loan obligations (CLOs) and collateralized debt obligations (CDOs).

In all cases, consider how these strategies relate to some of the theories we have previously discussed, like the law of one price or the efficient capital markets hypothesis.

7. KEY HEDGE FUND RELATIONSHIPS

Hedge Funds enter into myriad contracts that form the basis of their business. While lawyers are rarely involved in the day to day trading operations at a hedge fund, they frequently advise funds with regard to these agreements, which include (i) ISDA agreements, (ii) futures agreements, (iii) repurchase agreements, (iv) stock loan agreements, (v) master netting agreements, (vi) debt prime brokerage agreements, (vii) derivatives intermediation agreements, and, most importantly, (viii) prime brokerage agreements.

This part of the chapter considers some of these key documents.

A. Prime Brokerage Agreements

1994 WL 808441 (S.E.C. NO — ACTION LETTER)
Publicly Available January 25, 1994

January 25, 1994
Mr. Jeffrey C. Bernstein
Prime Broker Committee
c/o Bear, Stearns & Co., Inc.
One Metrotech Center North
Brooklyn, NY 11201

Re: Prime Broker Committee Request

Dear Mr. Bernstein:

This is in response to your letter dated September 13, 1989 on behalf of the Prime Broker Committee in which you requested the views of the Division of

Market Regulation of the Securities and Exchange Commission ("Division") and the Division of Banking Supervision and Regulation of the Board of Governors of the Federal Reserve System ("FRS Division") regarding the applicability of Sections 7, 10, 11(d), 15(c)(3) and 17 of the Securities Exchange Act of 1934 ("Exchange Act") and Regulation T thereunder, and Rules 10a-1, 10b-10, 11d1-1, 15c3-1 and 15c3-3 under the Exchange Act to prime broker arrangements.

I.   BACKGROUND

On the basis of your letter, and subsequent conversations, we understand the facts to be the following.

Prime brokerage is a system developed by full-service firms to facilitate the clearance and settlement of securities trades for substantial retail and institutional investors who are active market participants. Prime brokerage involves three distinct parties: the prime broker, the executing broker, and the customer. The prime broker is a registered broker-dealer that clears and finances the customer trades executed by one or more other registered broker-dealers ("executing broker") at the behest of the customer. Each of the executing brokers receives a letter from the prime broker agreeing to clear and carry each trade placed by the customer with the executing broker where the customer directs delivery of money or securities to be made to or by the prime broker.

The customer maintains its funds and securities in an account with the prime broker. Orders placed with the executing broker are effected through an account with the executing broker in the name of the prime broker for the benefit of the customer. When a customer places a trade order ("trade date"), the executing broker buys or sells securities in accordance with the customer's instructions. On trade date, the customer notifies the prime broker of the trade performed by the executing broker. The transaction is recorded in the customer's cash or margin account with the prime broker. At the same time, the prime broker records the transaction in a "fail-to-receive/deliver" account with the executing broker.

The prime broker issues a confirmation or notification to the customer and computes all applicable credit and Regulation T amounts. The executing broker confirms the transaction with the prime broker through the Depository Trust Company's Institutional Delivery System. The prime broker then will affirm the trade if its information matches successfully with the information received from the executing broker. The trade may then be submitted to the National Securities Clearing Corporation for clearance and settlement following normal settlement procedures. The prime broker then settles with the customer in the normal way.

The prime broker issues a statement of account to its customer at least on a monthly basis. The statement includes all security transactions during that period and the resultant customer security positions and money balances.

The Prime Broker Committee believes that this arrangement is advantageous to prime brokerage customers because the prime broker acts as a clearing facility and accountant for all of the customer's security transactions wherever executed as well as a central custodian for the customer's securities and funds.

In addition to facilitating trading with multiple brokers, all from a single account, the prime broker typically acts a custodian for the fund, holding all of the fund's securities.

The prime broker also facilitates the fund's use of leverage in its trading strategies. First, the broker can provide the fund with typical margin credit. Moreover, because most prime brokers are part of larger financial institutions — Morgan Stanley and Goldman Sachs are said to dominate the business — the prime broker can arrange for an unregulated affiliate to provide additional financing to the fund.[30]

MORGAN STANLEY & CO. INCORPORATED, PLAINTIFF, v. PEAK RIDGE MASTER SPC LTD OBO THE PEAK RIDGE COMMODITIES VOLATILITY MASTER FUND SEGREGATED PORTFOLIO, DEFENDANT

United States District Court, S.D. New York
No. 10 CIV 8405
November 8, 2010

COMPLAINT

Plaintiff Morgan Stanley & Co. Incorporated ("Morgan Stanley" or "Plaintiff"), by and through its undersigned attorneys, for its complaint against defendant Peak Ridge Master SPC Ltd. obo the Peak Ridge Commodities Volatility Master Fund Segregated Portfolio ("Peak Ridge" or "Defendant"), alleges on knowledge for its own conduct and on information and belief as to all other matters as follows: —

NATURE OF THE ACTION

1. This is an action to recover damages resulting from Defendant's breach of the Commodity Futures Customer Agreement (the "Customer Agreement" between Morgan Stanley and Peak Ridge. In violation of its written Customer Agreement, Peak Ridge failed to, *inter alia*, meet and maintain agreed upon margins with respect to its futures trading account with Morgan Stanley.

2. Upon Defendant Peak Ridge's default, Morgan Stanley exercised its remedies pursuant to Section 4(b) of the Customer Agreement by limiting and eventually terminating Peak Ridge's right to the account, taking ownership of the account, and in its commercially reasonable discretion and for Morgan Stanley's own protection, managing Defendant Peak Ridge's positions.

---

30. Traditional margin lending by a regulated broker-dealer is subject to section 7 of the 1934 Exchange Act, and Regulations T and U, promulgated by the Federal Reserve Board. 12 C.F.R. §§220, 221.

3. In accordance with Section 4(b) of the Customer Agreement, Plaintiff Morgan Stanley hereby seeks damages, costs, losses, and fees incurred in connection with Defendant's breach of the Customer Agreement and Morgan Stanley's exercise of the remedies specified in the Customer Agreement.

THE PARTIES

4. Plaintiff Morgan Stanley is a global financial services firm incorporated under the laws of Delaware with its principal place of business in New York, New York. As part of its business, Morgan Stanley serves as a futures commission merchant ("FCM"), engaged in the business of executing and clearing commodity futures trades for customers. Morgan Stanley purchases and sells commodity futures contracts, options on futures, and other exchange-traded derivative instruments on behalf of and for the accounts of its customers.

5. Defendant Peak Ridge is a corporation organized under the laws of the Cayman Islands with its principal place of business in Hamilton, Bermuda. As described in detail below, Peak Ridge is a hedge fund that is focused on speculative trading in commodities and formerly had a commodities futures trading account with Morgan Stanley.

FACTS

9. On September 4, 2009, Peak Ridge sought to open a futures trading account with Morgan Stanley by executing a series of account documents, including the Customer Agreement (attached hereto as Exhibit 1). In the Customer Agreement, Peak Ridge agreed, among other things, that the Customer Agreement "shall govern the purchase and sale by Morgan Stanley of commodity futures contracts, options thereon, foreign futures and options thereon and interests therein . . . for the account of [Peak Ridge] through one or more accounts, including reactivated accounts, carried by Morgan Stanley or its affiliates on behalf of and in the name of Customer."

10. The Peak Ridge account at Morgan Stanley was opened and began trading in October 2009. In its Morgan Stanley account, Peak Ridge traded a variety of futures and derivatives in the natural gas markets, including futures and options on futures, including calendar spread options ("CSOs").

11. Each of the instruments purchased and sold by Peak Ridge in its Morgan Stanley account is a highly leveraged, risky, and speculative bet on the underlying natural gas markets. A futures contract is an exchange-traded agreement obligating the buyer to purchase an asset (or the seller to sell an asset) — in this case, a specific quantity of natural gas — at a predetermined future date and price. An option on a future is an agreement that gives the holder the right to buy or sell a futures contract at a

specified price by a stated expiration date. A calendar spread option is an option on futures contracts that gives the holder the right to buy (or sell) a future in one month and the corresponding right to sell (or buy) a similar future in a different month.

12. Morgan Stanley acted as an FCM on Peak Ridge's behalf, purchasing, selling, and/or clearing natural gas futures and options on futures, including calendar spread options contracts on various commodity exchanges in accordance with the trading instructions provided by Peak Ridge . . .

14. In order to protect clearing member FCMs and the futures exchanges against one party's default, exchange rules and the Morgan Stanley Customer Agreement required Peak Ridge to post "margin" in connection with the contracts purchased by Peak Ridge — minimum deposits to assure Peak Ridge's performance under the contracts. As an FCM, Morgan Stanley was permitted to establish greater margin requirements than those demanded by the exchange. Margin requirements serve both to cover intra-day market losses on positions and to protect against future daily fluctuations in the value of the contracts held in the Morgan Stanley account.

15. Pursuant to Section 6(e) of the Customer Agreement, Peak Ridge was required to ". . . make, or cause to be made, all applicable original margin, variation margin, intra-day margin and premium payments, in such amount, form and subject to such valuation mechanics, as may be required by Applicable Law or by Morgan Stanley."

16. Pursuant to Section 3 of the Customer Agreement, Peak Ridge was required to "pay Morgan Stanley upon demand . . . (d) the amount of any trading losses in the Account; (e) any debit balance or deficiency in the Account; . . . and (g) any other amounts owed by [Peak Ridge] to Morgan Stanley with respect to the Account or any transactions therein."

18. On Friday, June 4, 2010, the Peak Ridge account lost $9.8 million in a single day, reducing the account's NLV from approximately $25 million to approximately $15 million, and leaving Peak Ridge significantly below its required 4.5:1 minimum margin ratio.

21. Section 4(b) of the Customer Agreement provides that, upon the occurrence of an Event of Default, Morgan Stanley has the right to, among other things, "(i) buy, sell or otherwise liquidate any or all open Contracts held in or for the Account . . . ; (ii) apply any cash margin to any amount owed by Customer to Morgan Stanley; . . . or (vi) take such other or further actions Morgan Stanley, in its commercially reasonable discretion, deems necessary or appropriate for its protection, all without demand for margin and without notice . . . and to the full extent permitted under Applicable Law." Upon the occurrence of an Event of Default, Section 4(b) also gives Morgan Stanley the right to, "in its sole discretion and without prior notice to Customer" "in a commercially reasonable manner," "(C) close out positions in whole or in part, or limit and/or terminate the right of the Customer to trade in the

Account, other than for liquidation; (D) sell Contracts to itself or its affiliates . . . in arms-length transactions . . . ."

22. In violation of its Customer Agreement, at the close of business on Wednesday, June 9, Peak Ridge admittedly had not satisfied the 6:1 margin ratio. Before the start of trading on Thursday, June 10, Morgan Stanley received an email from Peak Ridge acknowledging that the margin ratio in the account as of the close of business on June 9, 2010 was just 5.3:1, and fell short of the 6:1 ratio required by Morgan Stanley and the Customer Agreement. Morgan Stanley confirmed this calculation.

23. On Thursday, June 10, 2010, Morgan Stanley declared Peak Ridge in default and sent Peak Ridge written notice of its default (attached hereto as Exhibit 3) under Section 4(a)(vi) of the Customer Agreement, notifying Peak Ridge that, effective immediately, Morgan Stanley shall have the right to, and shall exercise its remedies upon default as set forth in Section 4(b) of the Customer Agreement.

24. On Friday, June 11, 2010, Morgan Stanley sent Peak Ridge written notice (attached hereto as Exhibit 4), formally terminating Peak Ridge's access to the account and noting Morgan Stanley's intent to continue exercising its rights under Section 4(b) of the Customer Agreement.

25. From June 11, 2010 to June 23, 2010, in accordance with the Customer Agreement, Morgan Stanley entered into several transactions in the Peak Ridge account in order to reduce risk and stabilize the book in an orderly fashion consistent with the Customer Agreement and Morgan Stanley's duties as an FCM. In the course of these transactions, and as a result of the extreme risk in the existing positions bought and sold by Peak Ridge, Morgan Stanley incurred substantial losses in the Peak Ridge account due to, among other things, significant adverse market movements from June 10 to June 23, 2010. In addition to the losses on the positions, Morgan Stanley incurred losses on the account's hedges. Under the Customer Agreement, Peak Ridge is fully responsible for all of these losses, costs, and expenses.

26. On June 23, 2010, in accordance with Section 4(b) of the Customer Agreement, Morgan Stanley sold the account's remaining positions, its hedges placed up to that date, and its cash balance to a Morgan Stanley affiliate in an arms-length transaction.

27. On July 29, 2010, Morgan Stanley sent Peak Ridge a written demand for payment of approximately $40.6 million, the estimated amount then due and owing from Peak Ridge for losses incurred by Morgan Stanley arising out of or related to the positions established by Peak Ridge in its Morgan Stanley account. In breach of the Customer Agreement, Peak Ridge failed to pay these amounts rightfully due to Morgan Stanley under the Customer Agreement.

28. As a result of Peak Ridge's breaches of the Customer Agreement, Morgan Stanley has suffered substantial monetary losses, and incurred related fees, costs, and expenses, for which Peak Ridge is liable under the Customer Agreement.

NO. 10 CIV 8405 (VM)
November 29, 2010

ANSWER AND COUNTERCLAIM

COUNTERCLAIM

1. Defendant-counterclaim plaintiff Peak Ridge Master SPC Ltd. obo the Peak Ridge Commodities Volatility Master Fund Segregated Portfolio (the "Comm Vol Fund"), by its attorneys, Eiseman Levine Lehrhaupt & Kakoyiannis, P.C., avers for its counterclaim against plaintiff-counterclaim defendant Morgan Stanley & Co. Inc. ("Morgan Stanley"), upon knowledge with respect to its own acts and upon information and belief with respect to all other matters, as follows:

NATURE OF THE CASE

2. This counterclaim arises from Morgan Stanley's unwarranted and improper seizure of a commodity futures account of its customer, the Comm Vol Fund, an energy hedge fund, for allegedly failing to meet margin requirements, even though Morgan Stanley gave only four hours' notice of the purported change in margin requirements and never issued any margin call before seizing the account, and even though the account was in compliance with margin requirements at the time.

3. Over a three-day period in the first part of June 2010, Morgan Stanley (i) arbitrarily and capriciously imposed a new risk-weighted margin measure to manage portfolio risk; (ii) declared the Comm Vol Fund in default even though its account was in compliance with both the newly imposed and previous risk-weighted margin measures; (iii) while the account remained in compliance, seized the Comm Vol Fund's account without making a margin call (as it was required to do under the customer agreement governing the parties' relationship, applicable regulations, and industry standards); and (iv) denied the Comm Vol Fund all access to the account.

4. In the weeks following the improper seizure of the Comm Vol Fund account, without making any margin call, Morgan Stanley engaged in irresponsible and self-serving conduct that manifested an utter disregard for its obligations to liquidate the Comm Vol Fund account in a commercially reasonable manner. Incapable of managing the account itself, Morgan Stanley turned to Morgan Stanley Capital Group, Inc. ("MSCG"), an affiliate, to place trades into the Comm Vol Fund account. Morgan Stanley failed to use the services of an experienced energy trader and instead utilized Joel Stier, a former marketer who was not only inexperienced with trading the instruments in the Comm Vol Fund account but also hopelessly conflicted. Stier's regular position was with

Morgan Stanley's affiliate, MSCG, a direct competitor to the Comm Vol Fund in the trading markets and ultimately the buyer of the entire portfolio from Morgan Stanley. Stier, predictably, managed the account in a commercially unreasonable manner.

5. Morgan Stanley, through MSCG, grossly mishandled the Comm Vol Fund account and lost over $32 million. Among other problems, as it admitted in a letter after the liquidation, Morgan Stanley attempted to liquidate the Account's positions in an illiquid market. Ultimately, either always with the intent to transfer the account positions to its affiliate MSCG at a reduced price or out of gross negligence, Morgan Stanley wrongfully liquidated the Account entirely by selling all of its open positions to its affiliate, MSCG, at an enormous loss. Morgan Stanley later claimed that it, Morgan Stanley in its capacity as broker, was forced to take a $40 million loss by selling the open positions to its affiliate, despite the fact that at the time of the sale to MSCG, Morgan Stanley's affiliate MSCG made an immediate gain of over $23 million based on marks against settlement prices.

6. The contrived manner in which Morgan Stanley moved to change the margin measure, declare a default, seize the Comm Vol Fund's account, trade the account in a commercially unreasonable manner and then sell the account's open positions to its affiliate MSCG, demonstrates Morgan Stanley's eagerness to terminate the Comm Vol Fund account in furtherance of its own interests and contrary to the interests of the Comm Vol Fund in violation of the customer agreement.

7. Morgan Stanley's conduct breached its obligations under the customer agreement, regulatory requirements, the prior course of dealing between the parties, and the dictates of good faith, fair dealing, and commercial reasonableness. The Comm Vol Fund, therefore, asserts this counterclaim to recover damages of at least $30 million caused by Morgan Stanley's breach of its contractual and regulatory obligations.

PROBLEM SET 20.5

1. What risks does a hedge fund face with regard to its prime brokerage relationship? How might those risks be mitigated? What risks does the prime broker face?
2. When negotiating a prime brokerage agreement on behalf of a hedge fund client, what terms should be of special import?
3. Why might the fund want to execute trades with multiple brokers? That is, why not execute all trades with the brokerage that acts as prime broker?

B. ISDA Agreements

As noted in Chapter 18, most derivatives are traded under a set of model agreements published by ISDA. For hedge funds, which make wide use of the full range of derivative products, the agreements are of particular importance. The master agreement, which sets the tone for the relationship between the fund and large financial institution, is of special importance. But other, ancillary agreements are important, too.

CHARLES K. WHITEHEAD, *DESTRUCTIVE COORDINATION*
96 Cornell L. Rev. 323, 353–356 (2011)

Credit default swaps (CDS) transfer the risk of credit loss, usually in connection with a referenced asset or entity, from one swap counterparty to another. Under a typical CDS, the beneficiary pays a premium to the credit risk holder (the "protection seller") who agrees to pay the beneficiary an amount that reflects the decline in value of the referenced asset upon the occurrence of a credit event (such as a default or failure to pay).[31] CDS typically rely on ISDA documents, including the CSA [credit support annex].

Under the CSA, banks and other protection sellers are required to post collateral depending on their prospective payment obligations. For hedge funds, as pledgors, the typical requirement is that they post collateral for 100% of their potential obligation, and in some cases, the CSA may require that they post additional collateral as a buffer against the risk of future default.[32]

As it has for swaps generally, the use of standard language has reduced transaction costs and expanded the scope of the CDS market.[33] Likewise, the CSA lowered the cost to swaps dealers of entering into contracts with new counterparties. In 1994, when the CSA was introduced, the principal swaps dealers managed approximately $4.7 billion in collateral. Privately negotiated support arrangements involved significant time and expense to structure and negotiate. As a result, the major swaps dealers concentrated their business on firms that had investment-grade credit ratings. The CSA streamlined the credit process. At

---

31. See William K. Sjostrom, Jr., *The AIG Bailout*, 66 Wash. & Lee L. Rev. 943, 947–950 (2009).

32. The CSA requires the party with a swap payment obligation (the "pledgor") to transfer collateral to the counterparty with the net credit exposure (the "secured party") in order to minimize credit risk. Mechanically, the secured party must calculate the amount it is entitled to receive and then notify the pledgor by a pre-agreed time. The pledgor must then post the collateral with (or for the account of) the secured party by the close of business on the next business day. See CSA, *supra* note 55, at paras. 3, 4(b), 4(c), 13(c); see also Christian A. Johnson, *Derivatives and Rehypothecation Failure: It's 3:00 p.m., Do You Know Where Your Collateral Is?*, 39 Ariz. L. Rev. 949, 957–958 (1997) (describing various standardized documents prepared by ISDA for use in CDS transactions).

33. See Frank Partnoy, *Second-Order Benefits from Standards*, 48 B.C. L. Rev. 169, 184–188 (2007); Frank Partnoy & David A. Skeel, Jr., *The Promise and Perils of Credit Derivatives*, 75 U. Cin. L. Rev. 1019, 1025–1026 (2007). Perhaps the clearest example of coordination in the swaps markets is just beginning to become evident — namely, the fallout from litigation arising from the financial crisis. A court's interpretation of a CDS's terms in one jurisdiction may have market-wide impact due to their standardized and widespread use. Firms that were never parties to the original lawsuit but use the same CDS form may be directly affected. See Jeffrey B. Golden, *The Courts, The Financial Crisis and Systemic Risk*, 4 Capital Mkts. L.J. S141, S144–146 (2009). The U.S. federal courts have recognized a similar relationship in standard-form indenture provisions, noting that "[b]oilerplate provisions are thus not the consequence of the relationship of particular borrowers and lenders and do not depend upon particularized intentions of the parties to an indenture." Sharon Steel Corp. v. Chase Manhattan Bank, 691 F.2d 1039, 1048 (2d Cir. 1982), *cert. denied*, 460 U.S. 1012 (1983).

the end of 2008, collateral deposited under CSAs totaled about $4 trillion, an 850-fold increase over 1994—with approximately 65% of all derivatives being subject to CSAs or other collateral arrangements. Approximately 50% of CSAs involve hedge funds and institutional investors, followed by corporations, banks, and others.

A rise in the cost of a CDS above the protection seller's premium often indicates a greater probability that a credit event will occur, in turn requiring the protection seller to post additional collateral. CDS costs surged following the collapse of Lehman Brothers in September 2008, reflecting market-wide concern over the stability of other firms. The result was a significant increase in the amount of collateral that protection sellers were required to post. The CSA form leaves open how often a CDS is revalued and, reflecting any increase or decrease in value, how often collateral ("variation margin") is provided or returned (referred to as "marking-to-market"). CDS counterparties, however, typically agree that the seller's obligations will be marked-to-market on a daily basis, transferring collateral back and forth between them depending on the net increase or decrease in the value of the CDS. Following the Lehman Brothers collapse, protection sellers (many of them hedge funds) were required to post a significant amount of additional collateral within a single day, totaling $140 billion across the industry. To raise money, they sold other assets in unison, contributing to a substantial decline in securities prices around the world.

Protection sellers, in the absence of a CSA, would likely still have been required to post collateral. Creation of the CSA, however, significantly increased the amount of collateral used by market participants and . . . promoted uniformity in the derivatives markets. Standard provisions in the CSA caused protection sellers to react to the increase in CDS prices in the same way and at roughly the same time, simultaneously driving prices lower, which in turn required additional sales to raise further funds.

C. Liquidity Rights

Hedge funds often accept capital only at the beginning of calendar months and, if they determine that assets under management exceed their ability to effectively deploy such capital, they may temporarily close themselves to new investor contributions. On the other hand, hedge funds typically limit the ability of investors to withdraw capital or redeem from a fund, so that investors might only be able to exit at certain set points in time, upon tendering advance notice to the fund.

This differs distinctly from mutual funds, which offer daily liquidity to their investors. Liquidity, of course, simply means the ability to withdraw your investment at its present value—which might be much less than the amount you originally deposited with the fund.

Conversely, although the liquidity offered by mutual funds obviates the need for complex contractual provisions regarding exit from the fund, the lack of liquidity in a hedge fund makes such provisions all the more important.

ALKEK & WILLIAMS, LIMITED; ALBERT AND MARGARET ALKEK FOUNDATION, PLAINTIFFS–APPELLANTS v. TUCKERBROOK ALTERNATIVE INVESTMENTS, L.P.; TUCKERBROOK/SB GLOBAL SPECIAL SITUATIONS GP, L.L.C.; TUCKERBROOK/SB GLOBAL SPECIAL SITUATIONS FUND, L.P., DEFENDANTS–APPELLEES

419 Fed.Appx. 492
United States Court of Appeals, Fifth Circuit
No. 10-20395 | March 22, 2011

PER CURIAM: Plaintiffs–Appellants brought this breach of contract suit seeking to recover their capital accounts in Tuckerbrook/SB Global Special Situations Fund, L.P. as of May 31, 2008, the effective date of their alleged withdrawal from the partnership, together with fees and expenses allegedly wrongfully charged. The district court granted summary judgment in favor of Defendants–Appellees, reasoning that the event entitling Appellants to withdraw from the partnership as of May 31, 2008 had not occurred. We AFFIRM.

I. FACTUAL & PROCEDURAL BACKGROUND

This case is a dispute over the provisions of the Limited Partnership Agreement (the "Agreement") that governs Tuckerbrook/SB Global Special Situations Fund, L.P. ("GSS"), a Delaware limited partnership and investment fund specializing in distressed assets. Under the Agreement, the management of GSS is vested exclusively in Tuckerbrook/SB Global Special Situations Fund GP, L.L.C. ("GSS GP"), the general partner of GSS. Tuckerbrook Alternative Investments, L.P. ("Tuckerbrook") is a managing member of GSS GP with a fifty percent ownership interest and serves as the investment manager and management company of GSS GP.

Tuckerbrook hired Sumanta Banerjee to launch GSS and serve as its portfolio manager. As portfolio manager, Banerjee was responsible for the investment and management of GSS's capital. Banerjee was also a managing member with fifty percent ownership of GSS GP. GSS GP had no management agreement assigning management responsibilities between Banerjee and Tuckerbrook.

Plaintiffs–Appellants Alkek & Williams, Ltd. and the Albert and Margaret Alkek Foundation (collectively, "Alkek") are both limited partners in GSS and made capital contributions to GSS. One of the other limited partners in GSS was Tuckerbrook/SB Global Distressed Fund I, L.P. ("GDF"), a fund in which Tuckerbrook and Banerjee were also managing members. Under §5.03 of the Agreement, Alkek and the other limited partners had a right to withdraw from GSS if

> Sumanta Banerjee dies, becomes incompetent or disabled (*i.e.*, unable by reason of disease, illness or injury, to perform his functions as the managing member of the General Partner for 90 consecutive days), or ceases to be directly or indirectly involved in the activities of the General Partner.

On March 25, 2008, Tuckerbrook sent a letter to Alkek and the other limited partners in GSS notifying them that Banerjee had been terminated from his position as GSS's portfolio manager, but would continue to be a managing member of GSS GP. One month later, Alkek notified GSS that it was withdrawing from the partnership, stating that "Banerjee's lack of involvement in activities of [GSS GP]" had triggered its withdrawal rights under §5.03 of the Agreement. The other limited partners, including GDF, also filed withdrawal notices under §5.03. Defendants did not immediately act on these withdrawal notices, and Tuckerbrook ultimately declared GSS to be in dissolution in January 2009.

Shortly before Tuckerbrook declared GSS to be in dissolution, Alkek filed the instant lawsuit in federal district court on the basis of diversity jurisdiction. Alkek claimed that Defendants had breached the Agreement by failing to return Alkek's capital accounts in GSS after Alkek sent in its withdrawal notice and by charging Alkek management fees after its withdrawal from GSS became effective. Alkek also sought a declaratory judgment from the district court stating that it was entitled to withdraw from GSS effective May 31, 2008 (one month after it had tendered its withdrawal notice) and sought an accounting of the value of Alkek's capital accounts on that date.

Defendants filed a motion for summary judgment, arguing that Banerjee's removal from the position of portfolio manager did not trigger Alkek's withdrawal rights under §5.03. The district court denied this motion without prejudice to allow for additional discovery into whether Banerjee was involved in the activities of GSS GP after he was terminated from his position as portfolio manager of GSS. After discovery, Defendants filed a second motion for summary judgment on the same basis as the first. In response, Alkek argued there was a genuine dispute over whether Banerjee had remained involved in GSS GP for purposes of §5.03 of the Agreement. Alkek also argued that, under the doctrine of quasi-estoppel, Defendants could not dispute whether Banerjee's termination triggered §5.03 because Tuckerbrook itself submitted a §5.03 withdrawal notice in its capacity as a managing member of GDF after Banerjee was fired. Relatedly, Alkek argued that Defendants could not dispute the validity of the withdrawal notice because they did not explicitly reject Alkek's notice when it was tendered in April 2008.

IV. ANALYSIS

A. THE AGREEMENT'S WITHDRAWAL PROVISION

Under Delaware law, "[w]hen the contract is clear and unambiguous, [courts] will give effect to the plain-meaning of the contract's terms and provisions." *Osborn ex rel. Osborn v. Kemp*, 991 A.2d 1153, 1159–60 (Del.2010). As noted above, §5.03 of the Agreement gave the limited partners the right to withdraw from GSS if Banerjee "ceases to be directly or indirectly involved in the activities of [GSS GP]." The district court defined the term "involved" in this phrase to mean "to engage as a participant." This definition was proposed by Defendants and accepted by Alkek. Accordingly, summary judgment was inappropriate if there was a genuine dispute over whether Banerjee had ceased to directly or indirectly "engage as a participant" in the activities of GSS GP.

1. Banerjee's Involvement

The district court thoroughly documented Banerjee's participation in GSS GP immediately after his termination — and in the months that followed — and concluded that Banerjee "remained both directly and indirectly involved in the management of GSS GP." The record fully supports this conclusion. In its letter advising the limited partners of Banerjee's termination, Tuckerbrook noted that he would continue to be a managing member of GSS GP. Within days of his termination, Banerjee corresponded with the limited partners in GSS, counsel for GSS, GSS's administrator, and GSS's bank, stating that GSS GP could not act without his approval because he retained authority as a managing member and fifty percent owner of GSS GP. Shortly after this flurry of communication, GSS's administrator, Michael J. Liccar & Co., CPAs ("Liccar"), took the position that it could not make disbursements to Tuckerbrook or take other actions without Banerjee's approval.

Alkek argues that Tuckerbrook had successfully frozen Banerjee out of GSS GP by removing him from the position of portfolio manager, denying Banerjee access to GSS GP's books, reports and statements, unilaterally communicating with the limited partners, and attempting to execute separate investment management agreements with the limited partners and GSS GP that formalized Tuckerbrook's previous duties as investment manager. As the events of the months following Banerjee's termination demonstrate, however, these efforts to exclude Banerjee from participation were nugatory. Banerjee obtained a court order to resume access to GSS GP's books and records. Tuckerbrook was unable to collect management fees from Liccar without Banerjee's approval. Liccar required Banerjee's approval prior to releasing financial statements on behalf of GSS GP. Despite Tuckerbrook's directions to do so, Liccar refused to write off one of GSS's investments without Banerjee's approval. Banerjee also advised the limited partners on the proposed redemption of investments. All of this evidence competently demonstrates that, as the district court put it, "even to the extent that Tuckerbrook might not have wanted Banerjee to maintain any authority regarding GSS, Banerjee did in fact exert his influence." Thus, there is no genuine dispute over whether Banerjee remained directly and indirectly involved in the activities of GSS GP.

2. The Agreement's Ambiguity

Alkek also argues that the district court erred in granting summary judgment because §5.03 is ambiguous. "[A] contract is ambiguous only when the provisions in controversy are reasonably or fairly susceptible of different interpretations or may have two or more different meanings." *Rhone–Poulenc Basic Chems. Co. v. Am. Motorists Ins. Co.*, 616 A.2d 1192, 1196 (Del.1992). Alkek argues that summary judgment was inappropriate because the relevant portion of §5.03 could reasonably be read as allowing the limited partners to withdraw if Banerjee ceases to be either (1) directly involved in the activities of GSS GP as portfolio manager of GSS, or (2) indirectly involved in the activities of GSS GP as a managing member of GSS GP.

This interpretation is unnecessarily narrow. The language at issue in this appeal focuses Banerjee's involvement *vel non;* it does not hinge on his title as portfolio manager of GSS. If Banerjee's removal from the position of portfolio manager was to be sufficient to trigger the limited partners' withdrawal rights, such a term would have been stated in the Agreement.

Furthermore, Alkek's proposed reading incorrectly suggests that the portfolio manager is the only party that exerts direct control over the activities of GSS GP. Under the Agreement, both the portfolio manager and GSS GP (and therefore the managing members of GSS GP) exert authority over the activities of GSS GP. The Agreement vests the portfolio manager with the responsibility of allocating the amount of time GSS GP will spend on certain matters, but it does not diminish the enumerated powers of GSS GP. These enumerated powers include, among other things, providing investment strategies to the limited partners, making reports to the limited partners, collecting fees, and closing accounts, all of which are activities Banerjee participated in after his termination as portfolio manager.

Alkek has a further argument (which appeared only periodically in the district court) about the phrase "ceases to be directly or indirectly involved" in the activities of GSS GP that can only be described as strained. It is enough to say that the words "direct" and "indirect" are obviously intended to clarify that the word "involved" has a broad scope. Alkek's reading of §5.03 is unreasonable and does not create the type of contract ambiguity that requires reversal of the district court's order granting summary judgment.

B.   QUASI-ESTOPPEL

Alkek next argues that Tuckerbrook may not challenge whether §5.03 of the Agreement has been triggered because Tuckerbrook submitted a withdrawal notice on behalf of GDF and did not the reject the limited partners' withdrawal notices when they were filed. Citing *Personnel Decisions, Inc. v. Bus. Planning Sys., Inc.*, No. 3213-VCS, 2008 WL 1932404 (Del.Ch. May 5, 2008), among other cases, Alkek argues that the Delaware doctrine of quasi-estoppel precludes a party from taking a position in a lawsuit that is inconsistent with a prior position taken by that party and that resulted in either a benefit to that party or a disadvantage to the opposing party. The district court assumed, without deciding, that Tuckerbrook had taken inconsistent positions and concluded that Alkek had not proven either a benefit to Tuckerbrook or a detriment to Alkek.

Although Alkek claims Tuckerbrook benefitted from filing a withdrawal notice on GDF's behalf because it earned fees from managing GDF and risked being sued by GDF if it did not file the withdrawal notice, we agree with the district court. There is no evidence in the record to suggest that Tuckerbrook's management fees were contingent upon filing GDF's withdrawal notice, and, because the withdrawal notices were never honored, there is no evidence from which to conclude that Tuckerbrook would have been sued if it had not filed the withdrawal notice.

Alkek also argues that Tuckerbrook harmfully induced Alkek to rely on the validity of Alkek's withdrawal notice. As the district court correctly observed, however, Alkek could not have assumed its withdrawal notice was valid based on GDF's submission of a withdrawal notice because Alkek was not aware that GDF had submitted a withdrawal notice until after commencing the instant lawsuit. Alkek has not pointed to any other harm GDF's withdrawal notice could have caused. Nor did Tuckerbrook's failure explicitly to deny Alkek's withdrawal notice in its capacity as managing member of GSS GP damage Alkek. None of Tuckerbrook's communications to the limited partners stated that the withdrawal notices were valid. Assuming Alkek was entitled to rely on the validity of its withdrawal notice, Alkek has not elaborated on how such reliance was to its detriment.

Therefore, the district court correctly concluded that Defendants could not be estopped from challenging the validity of Alkek's withdrawal notice.

PROBLEM SET 20.6

1. Consider the historical context when the investors attempted to withdraw. Does that suggest another motive for the attempted withdrawal from the fund? How could the investors have better achieved this?
2. How do the liquidity rights discussed in this section interact with the regulatory issues discussed earlier in the chapter? In particular, does the nature of the investors in hedge funds suggest a different answer to the question of "why won't the fund give me my money back?"

8. PRIVATE EQUITY FUNDS

Private equity funds are essentially hedge funds that focus on illiquid securities or investment strategies with long-term investment horizons. That is, a private equity fund can be seen as a hedge fund with a specialized investment strategy.

Within the industry, private equity funds and hedge funds consider themselves quite distinct. The following excerpt provides some important background.

SUN CAPITAL PARTNERS III, LP; SUN CAPITAL PARTNERS III QP, LP; SUN CAPITAL PARTNERS IV, LP, PLAINTIFFS, APPELLEES, v. NEW ENGLAND TEAMSTERS & TRUCKING INDUSTRY PENSION FUND, DEFENDANT, THIRD PARTY PLAINTIFF, APPELLANT, SCOTT BRASS HOLDING CORP.; SUN SCOTT BRASS, LLC, THIRD PARTY DEFENDANTS.

United States Court of Appeals, First Circuit
2013 WL 3814984
No. 12–2312. | July 24, 2013.

LYNCH, Chief Judge.

This case presents important issues of first impression as to withdrawal liability for the pro rata share of unfunded vested benefits to a multiemployer pension fund of a bankrupt company, here, Scott Brass, Inc. (SBI). *See* Employee

Retirement Income Security Act of 1974 (ERISA), 29 U.S.C. §1001 *et seq., as amended by the* Multiemployer Pension Plan Amendment Act of 1980 (MPPAA), 29 U.S.C. §1381 *et seq.* This litigation considers the imposition of liability as to three groups: two private equity funds, which assert that they are mere passive investors that had indirectly controlled and tried to turn around SBI, a struggling portfolio company; the New England Teamsters and Trucking Industry Pension Fund (TPF), to which the bankrupt company had withdrawal pension obligations and which seeks to impose those obligations on the equity funds; and, ultimately, if the TPF becomes insolvent, the federal Pension Benefit Guaranty Corporation (PBGC), which insures multiemployer pension plans such as the one involved here. If the TPF becomes insolvent, then the benefits to the SBI workers are reduced to a PBGC guaranteed level. According to the PBGC's brief, at present, that level is about $12,870 for employees with 30 years of service.

The plaintiffs are the two private equity funds, which sought a declaratory judgment against the TPF. The TPF . . . has counterclaimed and sought payment of the withdrawal liability at issue. The TPF is supported on appeal by the PBGC, as amicus.

We conclude that at least one of the private equity funds which operated SBI, through layers of fund-related entities, was not merely a "passive" investor, but sufficiently operated, managed, and was advantaged by its relationship with its portfolio company, the now bankrupt SBI. We also conclude that further factual development is necessary as to the other equity fund. We decide that the district court erred in ending the potential claims against the equity funds by entering summary judgment for them under the "trades or businesses" aspect of the two-part "control group" test under 29 U.S.C. §1301(b)(1).

As a result, we remand for further factual development and for further proceedings under the second part of the "control group" test, that of "common control," in 29 U.S.C. §1301(b)(1). The district court was, however, correct to enter summary judgment in favor of the private equity funds on the TPF's claim of liability on the ground that the funds had engaged in a transaction to evade or avoid withdrawal liability.

I.

The material facts are undisputed.

A.   THE SUN FUNDS

Sun Capital Advisors, Inc. ("SCAI") is a private equity firm founded by its co-CEOs and sole shareholders, Marc Leder and Rodger Krouse. It is not a plaintiff or party in this case. SCAI and its affiliated entities find investors and create limited partnerships in which investor money is pooled, as in the private equity funds here. Moreover, SCAI finds and recommends investment opportunities for the equity funds, and negotiates, structures, and finalizes investment deals. SCAI also provides management services to portfolio companies, and employs about 123 professionals to provide these services.

The plaintiffs here are two of SCAI's private equity funds (collectively the "Sun Funds"), Sun Capital Partners III, LP ("Sun Fund III")[34] and Sun Capital Partners IV, LP ("Sun Fund IV"). They are organized as Delaware limited partnerships. SBI is one of their portfolio companies, and the two Sun Funds have other portfolio companies. The Sun Funds do not have any offices or employees; nor do they make or sell goods, or report income other than investment income on their tax returns. The stated purpose of the Sun Funds is to invest in underperforming but market-leading companies at below intrinsic value, with the aim of turning them around and selling them for a profit. As a result, the Sun Funds' controlling stakes in portfolio companies are used to implement restructuring and operational plans, build management teams, become intimately involved in company operations, and otherwise cause growth in the portfolio companies in which the Sun Funds invest. The intention of the Sun Funds is to then sell the hopefully successful portfolio company within two to five years. In fact, the Sun Funds have earned significant profits from sales of various portfolio companies.[35]

These private equity funds engaged in a particular type of investment approach, to be distinguished from mere stock holding or mutual fund investments. *See, e.g.,* S. Rosenthal, *Taxing Private Equity Funds as Corporate 'Developers'*, Tax Notes, Jan.21, 2013, at 361, 364 & n. 31 (explaining that private equity funds differ from mutual funds and hedge funds because they "assist and manage the business of the companies they invest in"). As one commentator puts it, "[i]t is one thing to manage one's investments in businesses. It is another to manage the businesses in which one invests." C. Sanchirico, *The Tax Advantage to Paying Private Equity Fund Managers with Profit Shares: What Is It? Why Is It Bad?*, 75 U. Chi. L.Rev. 1071, 1102 (2008).

The Sun Funds are overseen by general partners, Sun Capital Advisors III, LP and Sun Capital Advisors IV, LP. Leder and Krouse are each limited partners in the Sun Funds' general partners and, together with their spouses, are entitled to 64.74% of the aggregate profits of Sun Capital Advisors III, LP and 61.04% of such profits from Sun Capital Advisors IV, LP. The Sun Funds' limited partnership agreements vest their respective general partners with exclusive authority to manage the partnership. Part of this authority is the power to carry out all the objectives and purposes of the partnerships, which include investing in securities, managing and supervising any investments, and any other incidental activities the general partner deems necessary or advisable.

For these services, each general partner receives an annual fee of two percent of the total commitments (meaning the aggregate cash committed as capital to the partnership[36]) to the Sun Funds, paid by the limited partnership, and a percentage of the Sun Funds' profits from investments. The general partners also have a limited partnership agreement, which provides that for each general

---

34. Sun Fund III is technically two different funds, Sun Capital Partners III, LP and Sun Capital Partners III QP, LP. Like the district court, we consider them one fund for purposes of this opinion because they are "parallel funds" run by a single general partner and generally make the same investments in the same proportions.

35. For instance, Sun Fund IV, the larger of the Funds, reported total investment income of $17,353,533 in 2007, $57,072,025 in 2008, and $70,010,235 in 2009.

36. The aggregate capital commitment of Sun Fund IV was $1.5 billion, which the TPF asserts means the management fee at the 2% rate was $30 million.

partner a limited partner committee makes all material partnership decisions. Leder and Krouse are the sole members of the limited partner committees. Included in the powers of the limited partner committees is the authority to make decisions and determinations relating to "hiring, terminating and establishing the compensation of employees and agents of the [Sun] Fund or Portfolio Companies." The general partners also each have a subsidiary management company, Sun Capital Partners Management III, LLC and Sun Capital Partners Management IV, LLC, respectively. These management companies contract with the holding company that owns the acquired company to provide management services for a fee, and contract with SCAI to provide the employees and consultants. When portfolio companies pay fees to the management companies, the Sun Funds receive an offset to the fees owed to the general partner.

B.   THE ACQUISITION OF SCOTT BRASS, INC.

In 2006, the Sun Funds began to take steps to invest in SBI, the acquisition of which was completed in early 2007. Leder and Krouse made the decision to invest in SBI in their capacity as members of the limited partner committees.

SBI, a Rhode Island corporation, was an ongoing trade or business, and was closely held; its stock was not publicly traded. SBI was a leading producer of high quality brass, copper, and other metals "used in a variety of end markets, including electronics, automotive, hardware, fasteners, jewelry, and consumer products." In 2006, it shipped 40.2 million pounds of metal. SBI made contributions to the TPF on behalf of its employees pursuant to a collective bargaining agreement.

On November 28, 2006, a Sun Capital affiliated entity sent a letter of intent to SBI's outside financial advisor to purchase 100% of SBI. In December 2006, the Sun Funds formed Sun Scott Brass, LLC (SSB–LLC) as a vehicle to invest in SBI. Sun Fund III made a 30% investment ($900,000) and Sun Fund IV a 70% investment ($2.1 million) for a total equity investment of $3 million. This purchase price reflected a 25% discount because of SBI's known unfunded pension liability.[37] SSB–LLC, on December 15, 2006, formed a wholly-owned subsidiary, Scott Brass Holding Corp. (SBHC). SSB–LLC transferred the $3 million the Sun Funds invested in it to SBHC as $1 million in equity and $2 million in debt. *Id.* at 111. SBHC then purchased all of SBI's stock with the $3 million of cash on hand and $4.8 million in additional borrowed money. The stock purchase agreement to acquire SBI's stock was entered into on February 8, 2007.

On February 9, 2007, SBHC signed an agreement with the subsidiary of the general partner of Sun Fund IV to provide management services to SBHC and its subsidiaries, *i.e.,* SBI. Since 2001, that general partner's subsidiary had contracted with SCAI to provide it with advisory services. In essence, as the district court described, the management company acted as a middle-man, providing SBI with employees and consultants from SCAI.

---

37. The Sun Funds contend that they reduced the purchase price based on the expectation that a future buyer would pay less for a company with unfunded pension obligations, not because of a concern that they were incurring potential withdrawal liability.

Numerous individuals with affiliations to various Sun Capital entities, including Krouse and Leder, exerted substantial operational and managerial control over SBI, which at the time of the acquisition had 208 employees and continued as a trade or business manufacturing metal products. For instance, minutes of a March 5, 2007 meeting show that seven individuals from "SCP" attended a "Jump-start Meeting" at which the hiring of three SBI salesmen was approved, as was the hiring of a consultant to analyze a computer system upgrade project at a cost of $25,000. Other items discussed included possible acquisitions, capital expenditures, and the management of SBI's working capital. Further, Leder, Krouse, and Steven Liff, an SCAI employee, were involved in email chains discussing liquidity, possible mergers, dividend payouts, and concerns about how to drive revenue growth at SBI. Leder, Krouse, and other employees of SCAI received weekly flash reports from SBI that contained detailed information about SBI's revenue, key financial data, market activity, sales opportunities, meeting notes, and action items. According to the Sun Funds, SBI continued to meet its pension obligations to the TPF for more than a year and a half after the acquisition.

C.   SBI'S BANKRUPTCY AND THIS LITIGATION

In the fall of 2008, declining copper prices reduced the value of SBI's inventory, resulting in a breach of its loan covenants. Unable to get its lender to waive the violation of the covenants, SBI lost its ability to access credit and was unable to pay its bills.

In October 2008, SBI stopped making contributions to the TPF, and, in so doing, became liable for its proportionate share of the TPF's unfunded vested benefits. In November 2008, an involuntary Chapter 11 bankruptcy proceeding was brought against SBI. The Sun Funds assert that they lost the entire value of their investment in SBI as a result of the bankruptcy.

On December 19, 2008, the TPF sent a demand for payment of estimated withdrawal liability to SBI. The TPF also sent a notice and demand to the Sun Funds demanding payment from them of SBI's withdrawal liability, ultimately calculated as $4,516,539. The TPF asserted that the Sun Funds had entered into a partnership or joint venture in common control with SBI and were therefore jointly and severally liable for SBI's withdrawal liability under 29 U.S.C. §1301(b)(1).

On June 4, 2010, the Sun Funds filed a declaratory judgment action in federal district court in Massachusetts. The Sun Funds sought a declaration that they were not subject to withdrawal liability under §1301(b)(1) because: (1) the Sun Funds were not part of a joint venture or partnership and therefore did not meet the common control requirement; and (2) neither of the Funds was a "trade or business."

The TPF counterclaimed that the Sun Funds were jointly and severally liable for SBI's withdrawal liability in the amount of $4,516,539, and also that the Sun Funds had engaged in a transaction to evade or avoid liability under 29 U.S.C. §1392(c). The parties both filed cross-motions for summary judgment in September 2011.

The district court issued a Memorandum and Order on October 18, 2012, granting summary judgment to the Sun Funds. The district court did not reach the issue of common control, instead basing its decision on the "trade or business" portion of the two-part statutory test. It also decided the "evade or avoid" liability issue.

On the "trade or business" issue, the district court addressed the level of deference owed to a September 2007 PBGC appeals letter that found a private equity fund to be a "trade or business" in the single employer pension plan context. The appeals letter found the equity fund to be a "trade or business" because its controlling stake in the bankrupt company put it in a position to exercise control over that company through its general partner, which was compensated for its efforts.

The district court held that the appeals letter was owed deference only to the extent it could persuade. The district court found the letter unpersuasive for two reasons: (1) the appeals board purportedly incorrectly attributed activity of the general partner to the investment fund; and (2) the appeals board letter supposedly conflicted with governing Supreme Court tax precedent. Engaging in its own analysis, the court found that the Sun Funds were not "trades or businesses," relying on the fact that the Sun Funds did not have any offices or employees, and did not make or sell goods or report income other than investment income on their tax returns. Moreover, the Sun Funds were not engaged in the general partner's management activities.

As to its "evade or avoid" liability analysis, the district court stated that §1392(c) was not meant to apply to an outside investor structuring a transaction to avoid assuming a potential liability. The language of the statute suggested that "it is aimed at sellers, not investors," and imposing liability on investors for trying to avoid assumption of such liability would disincentivize investing in companies subject to multiemployer pension plan obligations, thereby undermining the aim of the MPPAA.

The TPF has timely appealed. It argues that the district court erred in finding that the Sun Funds were not "trades or businesses" and that the Sun Funds should be subject to "evade or avoid" liability under §1392(c). The PBGC has filed an amicus brief on appeal in support of reversal of the district court's "trades or businesses" decision, but has taken no position on the §1392(c) claim.

II.

B.   WITHDRAWAL LIABILITY UNDER THE MPPAA

The MPPAA was enacted by Congress to protect the viability of defined pension benefit plans, to create a disincentive for employers to withdraw from multiemployer plans, and also to provide a means of recouping a fund's unfunded liabilities. As such, the MPPAA requires employers withdrawing from a multiemployer plan to pay their proportionate share of the pension fund's vested but unfunded benefits. An employer withdraws when it permanently ceases its obligation to contribute or permanently ceases covered operations under the plan.

The MPPAA provides: "For purposes of this subchapter, under regulations prescribed by the [PBGC], all employees of trades or businesses (whether or not incorporated) which are under common control shall be treated as employed by a single employer and all such trades and businesses as a single employer." So, "[t]o impose withdrawal liability on an organization other than the one obligated to the [pension] Fund, two conditions must be satisfied: 1) the organization must be under 'common control' with the obligated organization, and 2) the organization must be a trade or business." The Act's broad definition of "employer" extends beyond the business entity withdrawing from the pension fund, thus imposing liability on related entities within the definition, which, in effect, pierces the corporate veil and disregards formal business structures.

While Congress in §1301(b)(1) authorizes the PBGC to prescribe regulations, those regulations "shall be consistent and coextensive with regulations prescribed for similar purposes by the Secretary of the Treasury under [26 U.S.C. §414(c)]" of the Internal Revenue Code. The PBGC has adopted regulations pertaining to the meaning of "common control," but has not adopted regulations defining or explaining the meaning of "trades or businesses."

The phrase "trades or businesses" as used in §1301(b)(1) is not defined in Treasury regulations and has not been given a definitive, uniform definition by the Supreme Court.

C. FAILING TO HAVE PROMULGATED REGULATIONS, THE PBGC NONETHELESS OFFERS GUIDANCE ON THE MEANING OF "TRADES OR BUSINESSES"

The only guidance we have from the PBGC is a 2007 appeals letter, defended in its amicus brief.

In a September 2007 response to an appeal, the PBGC, in a letter, applied a two-prong test it purported to derive from *Commissioner of Internal Revenue v. Groetzinger,* 480 U.S. 23, 107 S.Ct. 980, to determine if the private equity fund was a "trade or business" for purposes of the first part of the §1301(b)(1) requirement. The PBGC asked (1) whether the private equity fund was engaged in an activity with the primary purpose of income or profit and (2) whether it conducted that activity with continuity and regularity. *See id.* at 35, 107 S.Ct. 980 ("We accept . . . that to be engaged in a trade or business, the taxpayer must be involved in the activity with continuity and regularity and that the taxpayer's primary purpose for engaging in the activity must be for income or profit.").

The PBGC found that the private equity fund involved in that matter met the profit motive requirement. It also determined that the size of the fund, the size of its profits, and the management fees paid to the general partner established continuity and regularity. The PBGC also observed that the fund's agent provided management and advisory services, and received fees for those services. Indeed, the Appeals Board noted that the equity fund's agent, "N," received 20% of all net profits received in exchange for its services and that its acts were attributable to the fund as the fund's agent. In addition, the fund's controlling stake in the portfolio company put it in a position to exercise control through its general partner, consistent with its stated purpose. The approach taken by the PBGC has been dubbed an "investment plus" standard.

D. SUN FUND IV IS A "TRADE OR BUSINESS" UNDER §1301(B)(1), THE
    PBGC'S "INVESTMENT PLUS" APPROACH IS PERSUASIVE, AND THE SAME
    APPROACH WOULD BE EMPLOYED EVEN WITHOUT DEFERENCE

The Sun Funds argue that the "investment plus" test is incompatible with
Supreme Court tax precedent. Regardless, they argue, the Sun Funds cannot be
held responsible for the activities of other entities in the management and
operation of SBI. And even if the Sun Funds had engaged in those activities,
they argue, that would not be enough.

Where the MPPAA issue is one of whether there is mere passive investment to
defeat pension withdrawal liability, we are persuaded that some form of an
"investment plus" approach is appropriate when evaluating the "trade or business" prong of §1301(b)(1), depending on what the "plus" is. Further, even if
we were to ignore the PBGC's interpretation, we, like the Seventh Circuit, would
reach the same result through independent analysis. In *Central States, Southeast &
Southwest Areas Pension Fund v. Messina Products, LLC*, 706 F.3d 874, the Seventh
Circuit employed an "investment plus"-like analysis without reference to any
PBGC interpretation. We agree with that approach. We see no need to set
forth general guidelines for what the "plus" is, nor has the PBGC provided
guidance on this. We go no further than to say that on the undisputed facts of
this case, Sun Fund IV is a "trade or business" for purposes of §1301(b)(1).

In a very fact-specific approach, we take account of a number of factors,
cautioning that none is dispositive in and of itself. The Sun Funds make investments in portfolio companies with the principal purpose of making a profit.
Profits are made from the sale of stock at higher prices than the purchase price
and through dividends. But a mere investment made to make a profit, without
more, does not itself make an investor a trade or business.

Here, however, the Sun Funds have also undertaken activities as to the SBI
property. The Sun Funds' limited partnership agreements and private placement memos explain that the Funds are actively involved in the management
and operation of the companies in which they invest. Each Sun Fund agreement
states, for instance, that a "principal purpose" of the partnership is the "man-
ag[ement] and supervisi[on]" of its investments. The agreements also give the
general partner of each Sun Fund exclusive and wide-ranging management
authority.

In addition, the general partners are empowered through their own partnership agreements to make decisions about hiring, terminating, and compensating agents and employees of the Sun Funds and their portfolio companies. The
general partners receive a percentage of total commitments to the Sun Funds
and a percentage of profits as compensation — just like the general partner of
the equity fund in the PBGC appeals letter.

It is the purpose of the Sun Funds to seek out potential portfolio companies
that are in need of extensive intervention with respect to their management and
operations, to provide such intervention, and then to sell the companies. The
private placement memos explain that "[t]he Principals typically work to reduce
costs, improve margins, accelerate sales growth through new products and
market opportunities, implement or modify management information systems
and improve reporting and control functions." More specifically, those memos

represent that restructuring and operating plans are developed for a target portfolio company even before it is acquired and a management team is built specifically for the purchased company, with "[s]ignificant changes . . . typically made to portfolio companies in the first three to six months." The strategic plan developed initially is "consistently monitored and modified as necessary." Involvement can encompass even small details, including signing of all checks for its new portfolio companies and the holding of frequent meetings with senior staff to discuss operations, competition, new products and personnel.

Such actions are taken with the ultimate goal of selling the portfolio company for a profit. On this point, the placement memos explain that after implementing "significant operating improvements . . . during the first two years [,] . . . the Principals expect to exit investments in two to five years (or sooner under appropriate circumstances)."

Further, the Sun Funds' controlling stake in SBI placed them and their affiliated entities in a position where they were intimately involved in the management and operation of the company. Through a series of appointments, the Sun Funds were able to place SCAI employees in two of the three director positions at SBI, resulting in SCAI employees controlling the SBI board.

Through a series of service agreements described earlier, SCAI provided personnel to SBI for management and consulting services. Thereafter, individuals from those entities were immersed in details involving the management and operation of SBI, as discussed.

Moreover, the Sun Funds' active involvement in management under the agreements provided a direct economic benefit to at least Sun Fund IV that an ordinary, passive investor would not derive: an offset against the management fees it otherwise would have paid its general partner for managing the investment in SBI. Here, SBI made payments of more than $186,368.44 to Sun Fund IV's general partner, which were offset against the fees Sun Fund IV had to pay to its general partner. This offset was not from an ordinary investment activity, which in the Sun Funds' words "results solely in investment returns."

In our view, the sum of all of these factors satisfy the "plus" in the "investment plus" test.

The Sun Funds [argue] that because none of the relevant activities by agents and different business entities can be attributed to the Sun Funds themselves, withdrawal liability cannot be imposed upon them. We reject this argument as well. Without resolving the issue of the extent to which Congress intended in this area to honor corporate formalities, as have the parties we look to the Restatement of Agency. And, because the Sun Funds are Delaware limited partnerships, we also look to Delaware law.

Under Delaware law, a partner "is an agent of the partnership for the purpose of its business, purposes or activities," and an act of a partner "for apparently carrying on in the ordinary course the partnership's business, purposes or activities or business, purposes or activities of the kind carried on by the partnership binds the partnership." To determine what is "carrying on in the ordinary course" of the partnership's business, we may consider the partnership's stated purpose.

Here, the limited partnership agreements gave the Sun Funds' general partners the exclusive authority to act on behalf of the limited partnerships to effectuate their purposes. These purposes included managing and supervising investments in portfolio companies, as well as "other such activity incidental or ancillary thereto" as deemed advisable by the general partner. So, under Delaware law, it is clear that the general partner of Sun Fund IV, in providing management services to SBI, was acting as an agent of the Fund.

Moreover, even absent Delaware partnership law, the partnership agreements themselves grant actual authority for the general partner to provide management services to portfolio companies like SBI. And the general partners' own partnership agreements giving power to the limited partner committees to make determinations about hiring, terminating, and compensating agents and employees of the Sun Funds and their portfolio companies show the existence of such authority. Hence, the general partner was acting within the scope of its authority.

Even so, the Sun Funds argue that the general partner entered the management service contract with SBI on its own accord, not as an agent of the Sun Funds. The Sun Funds' own characterization is not dispositive.

The argument is unpersuasive for at least two reasons. First, it was within the general partner's scope of authority to provide management services to SBI. Second, providing management services was done on behalf of and for the benefit of the Sun Funds. The investment strategy of the Sun Funds could only be achieved by active management through an agent, since the Sun Funds themselves had no employees. Indeed, the management services agreement was entered into just one day after the execution of the stock purchase agreement. In addition, Sun Fund IV received an offset in the fees it owed to its general partner because of payments made from SBI to that general partner. That provided a benefit by reducing its expenses. The services paid for by SBI were the *same services* that the Sun Funds would otherwise have paid for themselves to implement and oversee an operating strategy at SBI.

The Sun Funds also make a policy argument that Congress never intended such a result in its §1301(b)(1) control group provision. They argue that the purpose of the provision is to prevent an employer "from circumventing ERISA obligations by divvying up its business operations into separate entities." It is *not*, they say, intended to reach owners of a business so as to require them to "dig into their own pockets" to pay withdrawal liability for a company they own.

These are fine lines. The various arrangements and entities meant precisely to shield the Sun Funds from liability may be viewed as an attempt to divvy up operations to avoid ERISA obligations. We recognize that Congress may wish to encourage investment in distressed companies by curtailing the risk to investors in such employers of acquiring ERISA withdrawal liability. If so, Congress has not been explicit, and it may prefer instead to rely on the usual pricing mechanism in the private market for assumption of risk.

We express our dismay that the PBGC has not given more and earlier guidance on this "trade or business" "investment plus" theory to the many parties affected. The PBGC has not engaged in notice and comment rulemaking or even issued guidance of any kind which was subject to prior public notice and comment. Moreover, its appeals letter that provides for the "investment plus" test leaves open many questions about exactly where the line should be drawn between a mere passive investor and one engaged in a "trade or business."

Because to be an "employer" under §1301(b)(1) the entity must both be a "trade or business" and be under common control, we reverse entry of summary judgment on the §1301(b)(1) claim in favor of Sun Fund IV and vacate the judgment in favor of Sun Fund III. We remand the §1301(b)(1) claim of liability to the district court to resolve whether Sun Fund III received any benefit from an offset from fees paid by SBI and for the district court to decide the issue of common control. We determine only that the "trade or business" requirement has been satisfied as to Sun Fund IV.

III.

We deny, for different reasons than the district court, the TPF's appeal from entry of summary judgment against its claim under 29 U.S.C. §1392(c). That provision of the MPPAA states "[i]f a principal purpose of any transaction is to evade or avoid liability under this part, this part shall be applied (and liability shall be determined and collected) *without regard to such transaction*." 29 U.S.C. §1392(c) (emphasis added).

The TPF argues that §1392(c) applies because the Sun Funds, during the acquisition, purposefully divided ownership of SSB–LLC into 70%/30% shares in order to avoid the 80% parent-subsidiary common control requirement of §1301(b)(1). Under Treasury regulations, to be in a parent-subsidiary group under common control, the parent must have an 80% interest in the subsidiary. 26 C.F.R. §1.414(c)–2(b)(2)(i). The TPF asserts that, because a Sun Fund representative testified that a principal purpose of the 70%/30% division was to avoid unfunded pension liability and because an email states that a reason ownership was divided was "due to [the] unfunded pension liability," liability can be imposed on the Sun Funds under §1392(c).

We hold that §1392(c) cannot serve as a basis to impose liability on the Sun Funds because, by applying the remedy specified by the statute, the TPF would still not be entitled to any payments from the Sun Funds for withdrawal liability.

The instruction requires courts to put the parties in the same situation as if the offending transaction never occurred; that is, to erase that transaction. It does not, by contrast, instruct or permit a court to take the affirmative step of writing in new terms to a transaction or to create a transaction that never existed. In order for the TPF to succeed, we would have to (improperly) do the latter because simply doing the former would not give the TPF any relief, but would only sever any ties between the Sun Funds and SBI.

Disregarding the agreement to divide SSB–LLC 70%/30% would not result in Sun Fund IV being the 100% owner of SBI. At the moment SSB–LLC was divided 70%/30%, the transaction to purchase SBI had not been completed. There is no way of knowing that the acquisition would have happened anyway if Sun Fund IV were to be a 100% owner, but it is doubtful.

The TPF argues that because Sun Fund IV had already signed a letter of intent to purchase 100% of SBI before the decision was made to divide ownership between the Sun Funds, we can rely on the letter of intent. The TPF claims that the decision to split ownership to avoid the automatic assumption of withdrawal liability at 80% ownership was made after a binding transaction was entered into through the letter of intent. That is not true. The letter of intent was so named because it was not a binding contract or any sort of purchase agreement. Rather, the letter explicitly contained a clause stating that:

> The first five captioned paragraphs of this letter ('Purchase Price', 'Purchase Agreement Terms', 'Financing', 'Timing & Process', and 'Due Diligence') represent only the intent of the parties, do not constitute a contract or agreement, are not binding, and shall not be enforceable against the Sellers, the Company, or Sun Capital . . . . [N]either party shall have any legally binding obligation to the other unless and until a definitive purchase agreement is executed.

This is simply not a case about an entity with a controlling stake of 80% or more under the MPPAA seeking to shed its controlling status to avoid withdrawal liability. As such, disregarding the agreement to divide ownership of SSB–LLC would *not* leave us with Sun Fund IV holding a controlling 80% stake in SBI.

The Sun Funds are not subject to liability pursuant to §1392(c) and the district court's conclusion that they are not is affirmed.

PROBLEM SET 20.7

1. As always, diagram the transaction and be ready to discuss.
2. Recall the discussion of taxation and ECI earlier in this chapter. Does this case present a problem for the common master-feeder structure?
3. Does the Court hold that the fund itself is engaged in a trade or business?
4. Marc Leder is also known for being the host of the private fund-raiser where the Republican presidential candidate Mitt Romney dismissed "47 percent" of Americans as dependent on the government.

9. UNDERSTANDING THE TERMS

Take a look at the sample term sheet available online. Be prepared to discuss the terms of an investment in the (purely hypothetical) Funk to Funky Capital XIV LP private equity fund.

10. CONTRAST WITH HEDGE FUNDS

Because a private equity fund obtains capital from its investors during the early years of the fund by making a series of capital calls based on each investor's capital commitment (as opposed to a hedge fund, which receives full payment when it issues shares or interests), there is the potential for a private equity fund investor to refuse or otherwise fail to meet a capital call. In these cases, the private equity fund documents usually provide a number of potential remedies against the defaulting investor. For example, some funds require a defaulting investor to forfeit its entire interest in the fund and thereafter offer the other investors the ability to purchase the forfeited interest. Alternatively, the manager may bring legal action against the defaulting investor.

And the investor in a private equity fund typically must stay invested for a longer period of time, too.

CARLYLE OFFERS CLIENTS OPTION TO EXIT FUND STAKES EARLY
Cristina Alesci & Sabrina Willmer, Bloomberg News, March 14, 2011[38]

Carlyle Group LP (CG), the private equity firm planning to go public this year, is making its next fund more liquid by offering to help investors exit their stakes early if they wish.

The firm, based in Washington, will give clients the chance twice a year to sell all or part of their stakes in Carlyle Partners VI LP, according to a private placement memorandum, a copy of which was obtained by Bloomberg News. The firm is attempting to raise $10 billion for the fund.

Investors in private equity, who typically agree to have their money locked up for 10 years or longer, are focusing more on liquidity since the 2008 global financial crisis froze credit markets. Stock market declines that year sent less-liquid private equity holdings over investors' target allocations, making it more difficult for them to meet capital calls from fund managers.

"Two big concerns of investors today are liquidity and management fees," said Rob Parkinson, an associate partner at Hewitt EnnisKnupp, a consulting firm in Chicago. Backers who put up $500 million or more for Carlyle Partners VI will pay a discounted management fee of 1.1 percent on committed capital, while smaller investors will be charged as much as 1.5 percent, depending on the size of their commitment. The life of Carlyle's sixth fund is 10 years.

Chris Ullman, a spokesman for Carlyle, declined to comment on fundraising.

SECONDARY BUYERS

Five secondary buyers, or firms that purchase existing private equity interests, have agreed to provide bids, according to Carlyle's sales material. They are Goldman Sachs Private Equity Group, Credit Suisse Group AG, Coller Capital Ltd., Landmark Partners and Partners Group AG. Carlyle may also purchase as much as 33 percent of each available interest, the firm said.

Many private equity firms don't get involved in their limited partners' use of the secondary market beyond making sure that any potential buyer is acceptable to them. A few firms, such as Sun Capital Partners Inc. and Bain Capital LLC, have offered qualified matching services to their limited partners, in which they

---

38. Used with permission of Bloomberg L.P. © 2013. All rights reserved.

pre-qualify potential buyers. Such services are usually more hands-off than Carlyle's approach.

The matching program will begin at least six months after the final close of the sixth fund, which officially started raising money in February.

MATCHING SYSTEM

Twice a year, Carlyle will come up with the final price on interests by taking the average weighted price of all bids required to meet the supply of available interests. The highest-priced bids will be matched first with the available interests to determine the final price.

The firm "cannot provide any assurance whatsoever" that it will be able to implement the program effectively, according to the memorandum. Secondary buyers can exit the program any time, and Carlyle can terminate it at any point, the firm said.

The matching program limits the amount of interests that can be sold in any six-month period to 5 percent of the fund's commitments. Buyers can hold no more than 15 percent of commitments to the fund, and sellers are required to pay an administrative fee to Carlyle.

11. STRATEGIES

Private equity funds, like hedge funds, have expanded into a variety of strategies. Common types include buyout funds, merchant banking funds, venture capital funds, mezzanine funds, "special situations" funds, real estate and other asset-backed funds, distressed debt funds, and infrastructure funds. A hedge fund heavily invested in illiquid assets or a private equity fund engaged in active trading become almost indistinguishable.

As noted, one key area for private equity fund activity involves takeovers of publicly traded firms, often by means of a leveraged buyout which turns the target company into a privately held firm. Approximately 25 percent of all global M&A volume during the first half of 2007 was attributable to such deals. Things changed dramatically with the failure of Lehman, and the lack of lending activity that followed.

Whether or not these funds provide real value to investors is the subject of some degree of debate, and whether any value they do provide is not simply the result of a wealth transfer from employees and creditors became the subject of much debate during the 2012 presidential election. Mitt Romney, you will recall, was the founder of a private equity firm, and his holdings in the Cayman Islands did little to help the industry's image as "rapacious asset-strippers who hide their ill-gotten gains in secret bank accounts."[39]

39. *http://goo.gl/yJNzn*

PROBLEM SET 20.8

1. Consider the following swap: Counterparty pays the investor a floating payment equal to the total return on a notional investment in a hedge fund. Investor makes an initial payment to the counterparty, periodic payments equal to a floating interest rate plus a spread on the notional amount less the initial payment, and any depreciation on the notional hedge fund investment. At the end of the term, counterparty returns the initial payment to investor. What type of swap is this? What is the economic equivalent of this investment? What are its risks?

2. What benefits do a private equity fund investor get that could not be obtained by buying a portfolio company's equity while it was still publicly traded?

3. Since the financial crisis many private equity and hedge funds have struggled to achieve returns in excess of those that could be had by investing in an S&P 500 index fund. Does this represent a threat to the "alternative investment" industry?

21

VENTURE CAPITAL FUNDS

Venture capital funds can be seen as a kind of specialized private equity fund, designed to invest in the early stages of businesses.

As part of the recently enacted Dodd-Frank legislation, the SEC adopted Rule 203(1)-1, which defines a venture capital fund as any private fund that

> (i) represents to investors and prospective investors that it pursues a venture capital strategy,
> (ii) immediately after the acquisition of any asset (other than qualifying investments or cash, cash equivalents, U.S. Treasury securities with a remaining maturity of 60 days or less and shares of an open-end management investment company registered under Section 8 of the Investment Company Act and regulated as a money market fund ("short-term holdings")), holds no more than 20% of the fund's aggregate capital contributions and uncalled capital commitments in assets (excluding short-term holdings) that are not qualifying investments, valued at cost or fair value, consistently applied by the fund,
> (iii) does not borrow, issue debt obligations, guarantee or otherwise incur leverage in excess of 15% of the private fund's aggregate capital contributions and uncalled committed capital, and any such permitted indebtedness or guarantee has a non-renewable term of no longer than 120 calendar days, except that any guarantee by the fund of a qualifying portfolio company's obligations up to the amount of the value of the fund's investment in the portfolio company is not subject to the 120 calendar day limit,
> (iv) does not offer its investors withdrawal, redemption, repurchase or other similar liquidity rights, except in extraordinary circumstances, and
> (v) is not registered under Section 8 of the Investment Company Act and has not elected to be treated as a business development company under Section 54 of the Investment Company Act.

This definition should immediately suggest at least one key difference between private equity and venture capital funds.

1. STRUCTURE OF THE FUND

If you understand the structure of hedge funds and private equity funds, the basic structure of venture capital funds should be easily understood, too. The following case involves an individual's tax dispute, which is, of course, not the subject of this class. But the opinion includes a rare, detailed description of the structure of actual venture capital funds so we read it on that basis.

TODD A. AND CAROLYN D. DAGRES, PETITIONERS v. COMMISSIONER OF INTERNAL REVENUE, RESPONDENT

136 T.C. 263
United States Tax Court
No. 15523-08 | March 28, 2011

GUSTAFSON, Judge:

On March 21, 2008, the Internal Revenue Service (IRS) issued to petitioners Todd and Carolyn Dagres a notice of deficiency pursuant to section 6212, determining a deficiency of $981,980 in income tax for 2003 and an accompanying accuracy-related penalty of $196,369 under section 6662(a). After Mr. Dagres's concession that the $30,000 of interest he received in 2003 constitutes taxable income, the issues for decision are whether: (1) Mr. Dagres is entitled to a $3,635,218 business bad debt deduction for 2003 pursuant to section 166(a); and (2) Mr. Dagres is liable for the accuracy-related penalty under section 6662(a).

On the facts proved at trial, we find that Mr. Dagres was in the trade or business of managing venture capital funds; and we hold that he suffered a bad debt loss in connection with that business in 2003, and that it was a business bad debt loss. As a result, he is entitled to deduct the loss under section 166(a). Because the bad debt deduction offsets all of Mr. Dagres's taxable income, he is not liable for the accuracy-related penalty.

In 1994 Mr. Dagres worked as an analyst for Montgomery Securities, an investment bank based in San Francisco, and he focused on the computer networking industry.

JOINING BATTERY VENTURES

In 1996 . . . Mr. Dagres left Montgomery Securities to engage in venture capital activities in Boston with a group of associated entities generally referred to as Battery Ventures. When Mr. Dagres joined Battery Ventures, four funds had already been established. Mr. Dagres stayed with Battery Ventures for 9 years (and at the time of trial in 2009 he worked at Spark Capital, another venture capital firm).

BATTERY VENTURES' ORGANIZATION

During the relevant years, Battery Ventures was a group of entities that consisted of the following three types:

(1) *Specific venture capital funds.* Each of Battery Ventures' venture capital funds was organized as a limited partnership, and each was governed by a limited partnership agreement. Important in the relevant period were funds named Battery Ventures IV, L.P. (organized in January 1997), Battery Ventures V, L.P. (organized in March 1999), and Battery Ventures VI, L.P. (apparently organized in 2000), which we refer to individually as Fund IV, Fund V, and Fund VI and collectively as the Venture Fund L.P.s. Funds IV, V, and VI were formed during Mr. Dagres's tenure at Battery Ventures. Each Venture Fund L.P. had limited partners (who were its principal investors) and a single general partner.

(2) *Limited liability companies* (L.L.C.s). Battery Ventures' L.L.C.s served as the general partners of the Venture Fund L.P.s, responsible for management and investment. Important in the relevant period were Battery Partners IV, L.L.C. (the general partner of Fund IV), Battery Partners V, L.L.C. (the general partner of Fund V), and Battery Partners VI, L.L.C. (the general partner of Fund VI), which we refer to individually as Partners IV, Partners V, and Partners VI and collectively as the General Partner L.L.C.s. The General Partner L.L.C.s were governed by limited liability company agreements that provided for several types of members ("Member Managers," "Special Members," and "Limited Members") and that set out the members' entitlement to share in the profits of the L.L.C. The members of the General Partner L.L.C.s were Battery Ventures personnel. Mr. Dagres was a Member Manager of Partners IV, V, and VI and was entitled to a 12–to 14–percent share of their profits.

(3) *Management companies.* The Battery Ventures management companies provided services to assist the operation of the Venture Fund L.P.s and their General Partner L.L.C.s. Relevant in this suit is Battery Management Co. (BMC), an S corporation that served as a management company in relevant years. Battery Ventures personnel, including Mr. Dagres, were salaried employees of BMC. BMC's shares were owned by the Member Managers of the General Partner L.L.C.s, including Mr. Dagres. At the end of each year, the management company paid unspent service fees to its shareholders, in proportion to their ownership interest in the management company (though the record does not show the fact or amount of actual payments in any particular year).

Mr. Dagres contends that, in addition to these specific entities, "'Battery Ventures' * * * likely constituted an oral partnership or partnership by estoppel under state law," and that this partnership was engaged in a venture capital business that should be attributed to him as a partner. It is true that Mr. Dagres held himself out as a "General Partner" of "Battery Ventures," and literature evidently published by Battery Ventures entities did the same. However, in view of our finding that the General Partner L.L.C.s were engaged in the business of managing venture capital funds, and our holding that this activity is attributed to Mr. Dagres as a Member Manager of those L.L.C.s, we need not and do not resolve the factual and legal issues prompted by this contention of partnership by estoppel.

SERVICES AND FEES

Under the limited partnership agreement of each Venture Fund L.P., its General Partner L.L.C. was responsible for managing the fund and making its investments, in return for a fee. The General Partner L.L.C. in turn entered into a service agreement with BMC, pursuant to which—in return for the General Partner L.L.C.'s promise of an equivalent fee to BMC—Mr. Dagres and other Battery Ventures personnel actually performed the necessary work of managing and investing for the Venture Fund L.P.

Under the service agreement, BMC assumed all the normal operating expenses of the General Partner L.L.C.s, including all routine expenses incident to serving the venture capital activities of the General Partner L.L.C.s. These included the expenses for investigating investment opportunities, compensating the officers and employees of BMC, paying the salaries of the Member Managers of the General Partner L.L.C.s, and paying the fees and expenses for administrative, accounting, bookkeeping, and legal services, office space, utilities, travel, liability insurance, and other related expenses. BMC provided the facilities and staff needed to perform the venture capital business of Battery Ventures, including staff who helped with identifying and researching potential investment targets, staff who helped perform due diligence on those prospects, staff who helped to manage the investments (by providing management assistance to the target companies themselves), and other support staff, such as receptionists, secretaries, accounting personnel, etc.

Each Venture Fund L.P. paid service fees annually of 2 to 2.5 percent of the partners' total committed capital in the fund. The limited partnership agreements obligated each Venture Fund L.P. to pay these service fees to its respective General Partner L.L.C., but each General Partner L.L.C. in turn agreed to reimburse BMC for organizational expenses incurred in setting up the General Partner L.L.C. and the Venture Fund L.P., and agreed to pay a service fee to BMC equal to the service fee described in the limited partnership agreement. Consequently, each Venture Fund L.P. remitted the service fees directly to BMC, by-passing the General Partner L.L.C. that was immediately obligated to perform the management services and entitled to receive the fees. Those service fees were the revenue source from which BMC paid salaries to its employees.

INVESTMENT AND RETURN

Each Venture Fund L.P. solicited investors to invest (as limited partners) in "developmental and emerging companies primarily in the software, communications and information systems industries primarily in the United States." The total maximum subscription or aggregate investment amount for Fund IV was $200 million, and the maximum for Fund V was $400 million. The aggregate investment amount is also called the amount of pledged funds or the "committed capital" of the fund. Each Venture Fund L.P. had a 10-year life, and each limited partnership agreement provided that the General Partner L.L.C. could not make additional calls for capital contributions by the limited partners after the fifth anniversary of the date of the agreement.[1]

The limited partner investors included insurance companies, pension funds, foundations, and high-net-worth individuals. Each limited partnership agreement required its General Partner L.L.C. to use its best efforts to conduct the partnership's affairs: (1) in a manner to avoid any classification for Federal income tax purposes that the partnership was engaged in the conduct of a trade or business, and (2) in a manner to avoid generating any unrelated business taxable income for any tax-exempt limited partner. The parties therefore agree that the activity of the Venture Fund L.P.s themselves was investment, and not the conduct of a trade or business.

The limited partners contributed 99 percent of each fund's capital. The remaining 1 percent of the funds in the Venture Fund L.P. came from the General Partner L.L.C. The members of that General Partner L.L.C. personally contributed the money to fund that 1 percent, presumably in proportion to their ownership interests in the General Partner L.L.C. (though the record does not show the proportions).

The General Partner L.L.C. was entitled to additional compensation for the management and investment services that it was obliged to provide (with support from the management company): Each Venture Fund L.P. granted a 20-percent profits interest to its General Partner L.L.C. This profits interest is called "carried interest" or "carry." As is explained above, this "carry" is an important feature of the venture capital arrangement. Though the venture capital firm makes only a relatively modest 1-percent contribution to the capital of the fund, it obtains an additional 20-percent interest in the profits. It therefore has a very substantial opportunity for gain — and, from the point of view of the other investors, it has a very substantial incentive to maximize the fund's success.[2]

---

1. The limited partnership agreements provided that Fund IV began on January 22, 1997, and would end December 31, 2007, and that Fund V began March 31, 1999, and would end December 31, 2009. At the end of that time, each Venture Fund L.P. was to be liquidated and its cash and securities distributed. Thus a capital call could occur for Fund IV as late as January 22, 2002, and for Fund V as late as March 31, 2004.

2. Strictly speaking, it appears that the General Partner L.L.C. obtains slightly less than 21 percent (20 percent plus 1 percent) of the profits. After the investors' capital has been returned to them, 20 percent of the profits is paid to the General Partner L.L.C. in its capacity as manager of the Venture Fund L.P., and then the remaining 80 percent of the profits is distributed to the investors in proportion to their investment. Since the General Partner L.L.C. invested 1 percent of the capital, it receives 1 percent of the investors' share — i.e., 1 — percent of 80 percent of the profits. Thus, the General Partner L.L.C. as a 1 percent investor receives 0.8 percent of the profits. For the sake of simplicity, we refer in this Opinion to the 20-percent and 1-percent interests without making this correction.

PROBLEM SET 21.1

1. Diagram the structure of the funds. What precisely do the general partner entities do?
2. What roles did Mr. Dagres play in the funds? In what ways did he receive cash flows from his various roles?
3. In a general sense, what was the cost of an investment in one of these funds? What was the potential return?

2.   STRUCTURE OF THE INVESTMENT

Venture capital funds typically invest in "early-stage" firms. "Early-stage" could mean almost anything from an entity with nothing more than an idea to a business that has operated for some time, but has yet to experience real growth.

Venture capital funds are generally considered to be the second of a three-stage finance process that begins with "angel" investors, who are the first outside investors in the firm, then venture capital investors, and then the public markets. A venture capital fund typically provides cash to its portfolio companies in exchange for preferred shares in the company. When additional capital is needed, additional preferred stock is purchased by the fund, with each new round of investment receiving specific rights.

RONALD J. GILSON, *ENGINEERING A VENTURE CAPITAL MARKET:*
LESSONS FROM THE AMERICAN EXPERIENCE
55 Stan. L. Rev. 1067, 1072 (2003)

The venture capital fund's equity investments in portfolio companies typically take the form of convertible preferred stock.[3] While not required by the formal legal documents, the fund is also expected to make important noncash contributions to the portfolio company. These contributions consist of management assistance, corresponding to that provided by management consultants; intensive monitoring of the portfolio company's performance which provides an objective view to the entrepreneur; and the use of the fund's reputation to give the portfolio company credibility with potential customers, suppliers, and employees. While each investment will have a "lead" investor who plays the primary role in monitoring and advising the portfolio company, commonly

---

3. Paul Gompers, Ownership and Control in Entrepreneurial Firms: An Examination of Convertible Securities in Venture Capital Investments 2, 314–15 (Harvard Business School, Working Paper, 1997) (on file with author); Sahlman, *supra* note 7, at 504. Steven Kaplan and Per Strömberg report that convertible preferred stock was used in 95% of a sample of 200 financing rounds in 118 portfolio companies made by 14 venture capital firms between 1996 and 1999. Steven N. Kaplan & Per Strömberg, Financial Contracting Theory Meets the Real World: An Empirical Analysis of Venture Capital Contracts 13 (Nat'l Bureau of Econ. Research, Working Paper 7660, 2000), available at *http://www.nber.org/papers/w7660*. Ronald Gilson and David Schizer argue that this consistency is driven by the tax efficiency of this capital structure in delivering high-powered incentives to management. Ronald J. Gilson & David M. Schizer, *Understanding Venture Capital Structure: A Tax Explanation for Convertible Preferred Stock*, 116 Harv. L. Rev. 874 (2003).

the overall investment is syndicated with other venture capital funds that invest in the portfolio company at the same time and on the same terms.

The initial venture capital investment usually will be insufficient to fund the portfolio company's entire business plan. Accordingly, investment will be "staged." A particular investment round will provide only the capital the business plan projects as necessary to achieve specified milestones set out in the business plan. While first round investors expect to participate in subsequent investment rounds,[4] often they are not contractually obligated to do so even if the business plan's milestones are met; the terms of later rounds of investment are negotiated at the time the milestones are met and the prior investment exhausted. Like the provision of noncapital contributions, an implicit, not explicit, contract typically governs the venture capital fund's right and obligation to provide additional rounds of financing if the portfolio company performs as expected. The venture capital fund's implicit right to participate in subsequent rounds — by contrast to its implicit obligation to participate — is protected by an explicit right of first refusal.[5]

The use of staged financing, with multiple rounds, has the potential to lead to the dilution of earlier investors. To protect against this, venture capital investors, as noted at the end of the excerpted article, retain a right to provide the next round of financing and thus maintain their relative ownership interest.

But venture capital investors also want to protect the conversion option in the preferred shares. This is particularly important to the investor if a subsequent round of financing results in a lower valuation of the startup company. This is commonly referred to as a "down round" financing.

The "*full-ratchet*" is the strongest form of protection against a down round. Under a "full ratchet," previous convertible preferred shares have their conversion ratio reset to the lowest subsequent conversion ratio.

For example, if the venture capital investor purchased 1 million shares of convertible preferred stock at $1 per share, and new capital is raised at 50 cents per share, then the venture capital investor's conversion price will be reduced to 50 cents, and the venture capital investor thus will be entitled to convert its preferred stock into 2 million shares instead of 1 million shares.

---

4. Sahlman reports that venture capital funds invest one third of their capital in new investments and two thirds in later round financing of companies already in their portfolios.

5. Kaplan and Strömberg report that some 15% of the financing rounds in their sample conditioned disbursement of a portion of the round on explicit contingencies. Many of these, however, are not inconsistent with the unconstrained option to abandon analysis in the text. First, in some number of these instances, subsequent financing was contingent on "no material deviation" from the business plan. Kaplan & Strömberg, *supra* note 14, at 59 tbl.6. While such a formulation does operate to make exercise of the option to abandon reviewable by a court, it hardly represents state contingent contracting and still leaves the venture capitalist with a great deal of discretion. Since material changes in a business plan are predictable given the nature of an early stage business, in most cases the material deviation contingency will collapse into a pure option to abandon. Second, contingencies are keyed to readily observable and verifiable events like the issuance of a patent, or the hiring of a chief executive officer, again instances when a specific uncertainty can be specified and its resolution observed. Finally, Kaplan and Strömberg do not suggest that the venture capitalists are committed to provide future financing rounds even in the minority of rounds where explicit contingencies are found. Taken as a whole, their data leave intact the general proposition that venture financing is staged, without binding future commitments by existing venture investors.

An alternative approach is referred to as the "weighted average" approach. Preexisting convertible preferred shares are adjusted based on a formula. There are a variety of ways to state the formula, but here is one of the simpler versions:

$$NCP = \frac{(X + Y)}{(Z)}$$

- NCP refers to the new conversion price.
- X equals the original issue price multiplied by the number of shares issued at that price.
- Y equals the new issue price multiplied by the number of shares issued at that price.
- Z equals the number of total number of shares outstanding after the new sale.

To give this some concreteness, use the numbers from before and assume a venture capital investor purchased 1 million shares of convertible preferred stock at $1 per share, and $1 million of new capital is raised at 50 cents per share. In all cases the preferred shares convert to common shares on a one for one basis.

X equals 1 million, Y equals 1 million. Two million divided by 3 million gets us the new conversion price of 66 cents per share, 16 cents more than under a full ratchet.

As a result, the original fund will be able to convert their preferred shares into just over 1.5 million common shares: more than their original 1 million, but again less than the 2 million shares they would have received under a full ratchet.

Typically the formula only adjusts the old conversion price if the new financing is a down round. Otherwise the holders of the old preferred shares are perfectly happy to have a discount conversion option.

Venture capital investors also have to be concerned about the same things that preferred shareholders of all types worry about.

BENCHMARK CAPITAL PARTNERS IV, L.P., PLAINTIFF, v. RICHARD VAGUE, JAMES STEWART, JOHN TOLLESON, DAVID MARSHALL, JOHN ORR, CHRISTINE CROUCHER, MOYA GREENE, RICHARD VENN, CHRISTOPHER GREENE, JUNIPER FINANCIAL CORP., CIBC DELAWARE HOLDINGS, INC. AND CANADIAN IMPERIAL BANK OF COMMERCE, DEFENDANTS

Court of Chancery of Delaware
No. Civ.A. 19719 | Submitted July 11, 2002 | Decided July 15, 2002
Memorandum Opinion

NOBLE, Vice Chancellor.

I. INTRODUCTION

This is another one of those cases in which sophisticated investors have negotiated protective provisions in a corporate charter to define the balance of power or certain economic rights as between the holders of junior preferred stock and senior preferred stock. These provisions tend to come in to play when additional financing becomes necessary. One side cannot or will not put up more money; the other side is willing to put up more money, but will not do so without obtaining additional control or other diminution of the rights of the other side. In short, these cases focus on the tension between minority rights established through the corporate charter and the corporation's need for additional capital.

In this case, Plaintiff Benchmark Capital Partners IV, L.P. ("Benchmark") invested in the first two series of the Defendant Juniper Financial Corp.'s ("Juniper") preferred stock. When additional capital was required, Defendant Canadian Imperial Bank of Commerce ("CIBC") was an able and somewhat willing investor.[6] As a result of that investment, Benchmark's holdings were relegated to the status of junior preferred stock and CIBC acquired a controlling interest in Juniper by virtue of ownership of senior preferred stock. The lot of a holder of junior preferred stock is not always a happy one. Juniper's Fifth Amendment and Restated Certificate of Incorporation (the "Certificate") contains several provisions to protect the holders of junior preferred stock from abuse by the holder of senior preferred stock. Two of those provisions are of particular importance here. The Certificate grants the junior preferred stockholders a series vote on corporate actions that would "[m]aterially adversely change the rights, preferences and privileges of the [series of junior preferred stock]." In addition, the junior preferred stockholders are entitled to a class vote before Juniper may "[a]uthorize or issue, or obligate itself to issue, any other equity security . . . senior to or on a parity with the [junior preferred stock]."

The Certificate provides that those provisions protecting the rights of the junior preferred stockholders may be waived by CIBC. CIBC may not, however, exercise this power "if such amendment, waiver or modification would . . . diminish or alter the liquidation preference or other financial or economic rights" of the junior preferred stockholders or would shelter breaches of fiduciary duties.

Juniper now must seek more capital in order to satisfy regulators and business requirements, and CIBC, and apparently only CIBC, is willing to provide the necessary funds. Juniper initially considered amending its charter to allow for the issuance of another series of senior preferred stock. When it recognized that the protective provisions of the Certificate could be invoked to thwart that strategy, it elected to structure a more complicated transaction that now consists principally of a merger and a sale of Series D Preferred Stock to CIBC. The merger is scheduled to occur on July 16, 2002 with a subsidiary merging with and into Juniper that will leave Juniper as the surviving corporation, but with a restated certificate of incorporation that will authorize the issuance of a new series of senior preferred stock and new junior preferred stock with a reduced liquidation preference and will cause a number of other adverse consequences or limitations to be suffered by the holders of the junior preferred. As part of this overall financing transaction, Juniper, after the merger, intends to issue a new

---

6. CIBC invested in Juniper through a subsidiary, Defendant CIBC Delaware Holdings, Inc. For purposes of this memorandum opinion, I do not distinguish between CIBC and its subsidiary.

series of preferred, the Series D Preferred Stock, to CIBC in exchange for a $50 million capital contribution. As the result of this sequence of events, the equity holdings of the junior preferred stockholders will be reduced from approximately 29% to 7%. Juniper will not obtain approval for these actions from the holders of the junior preferred stock. It contends that the protective provisions do not give the junior preferred stockholders a vote on these plans and, furthermore, in any event, that CIBC has the right to waive the protective provisions through the Series C Trump.[7]

Benchmark, on the other hand, asserts that the protective provisions preclude Juniper's and CIBC's heavy-handed conduct and brings this action to prevent the violation of the junior preferred stockholder's fundamental right to vote on these corporate actions as provided in the Certificate and to obtain interim protection from the planned evisceration of its equity interest in Juniper. Because of the imminence of the merger and the issuance of the new senior preferred stock, Benchmark has moved for a preliminary injunction to stop the proposed transaction. This is the Court's decision on that motion.

II.   THE PARTIES

Benchmark, a Delaware limited partnership based in Menlow Park, California, is a venture capital firm specializing in preferred stock investments. It manages more than $2 billion and has made approximately 50 preferred stock investments in the preceding 5 years.

Juniper is a Delaware corporation with its principal place of business in Wilmington, Delaware, where it has more than 300 employees. It is a financial services enterprise with the issuance of credit cards as its core business. Juniper Bank is Juniper's wholly-owned state-chartered banking subsidiary.

CIBC is a Canadian bank based in Toronto and controls Juniper through a subsidiary as the result of a $145 million investment in 2001.

The individual defendants are directors of Juniper. Defendants Richard Vague and James Stewart are founders and officers of Juniper. Defendant John Tolleson is a member of the special committee appointed by the board of Juniper to review the Series D Preferred financing.

III.   FACTUAL BACKGROUND

A.   BENCHMARK AND CIBC INVEST IN JUNIPER

Benchmark became the initial investor in Juniper when in June 2000, it invested $20 million and, in exchange, was issued Series A Preferred Shares. Juniper raised an additional $95.5 million in August 2000 by issuing its Series B Preferred Shares. Benchmark contributed $5 million in this effort. It soon became necessary for Juniper to obtain even more capital. Efforts to raise

---

7. Juniper concedes that CIBC does not have the power to waive any junior preferred stockholder's right to vote with respect to a diminished liquidation preference.

additional funds from existing investors and efforts to find new potential investors were unavailing until June 2001 when CIBC and Juniper agreed that CIBC would invest $27 million in Juniper through a mandatory convertible note while CIBC evaluated Juniper to assess whether it was interested in acquiring the company. CIBC also agreed to provide additional capital through a Series C financing in the event that it chose not to acquire Juniper and if Juniper's efforts to find other sources for the needed funding were unsuccessful.

In July 2001, CIBC advised Juniper that it would not seek to acquire Juniper. After reviewing its options for other financing, Juniper called upon CIBC to invest the additional capital. The terms of the Series C financing were negotiated during the latter half of the summer of 2001. A representative of Benchmark, J. William Gurley, and its attorney were active participants in these negotiations. Through the Series C Transaction, which closed on September 18, 2001, CIBC invested $145 million (including the $27 million already delivered to Juniper). With its resulting Series C Preferred holdings, CIBC obtained a majority of the voting power in Juniper on an as-converted basis and a majority of the voting power of Juniper's preferred stock. CIBC also acquired the right to select six of the eleven members of Juniper's board. As required by Juniper's then existing certificate of incorporation, the approval of the holders of Series A Preferred and Series B Preferred Stock, including Benchmark, was obtained in order to close the Series C Transaction.

B. THE CERTIFICATE'S PROTECTIVE PROVISIONS

In the course of obtaining that consent, CIBC had extensive negotiations regarding the provisions of Juniper's charter designed to protect the rights and interests of the holders of Series A Preferred and Series B Preferred Stock. For example, CIBC had sought the power to waive, modify or amend certain protective provisions held by the Series A Preferred and Series B Preferred stockholders. As the result of those discussions, the Certificate was adopted. CIBC obtained the right to waive certain protective voting provisions, but the right was not unlimited. A review of the Certificate's protective provisions directly involved in the pending dispute follows.

Juniper's Certificate protects the holders of Series A Preferred and Series B Preferred from risks associated with the issuance of any additional equity security that would be senior to those shares by requiring their prior approval through a separate class vote as prescribed in Section C.6.a(i):

So long as any shares of Series A Preferred Stock or Series B Preferred Stock remain outstanding, the Corporation shall not, without the vote or written consent by the holders of at least a majority of the then outstanding shares of the Series A Preferred Stock and Series B Preferred Stock, voting together as a single class; *provided, however,* that the foregoing may be amended, waived or modified pursuant to Section C.4.c: (i) Authorize or issue, or obligate itself to issue, any other equity security (including any security convertible into or exercisable for any equity security) senior to or on a parity with the Series A Preferred Stock or Series B Preferred Stock as to dividend rights or redemption rights, voting rights or liquidation preferences (other than the Series C Preferred Stock and Series C Prime Preferred

Stock sold pursuant to, or issued upon the conversion of the shares sold pursuant to, the Series C Preferred Stock Purchase Agreement . . .)

Under Section C.6.a(ii), Juniper also must provide the holders of the junior preferred stock with a class vote before it may proceed to dispose of all or substantially all of its assets or to "consolidate or merge into any other Corporation (other than a wholly-owned subsidiary Corporation)." Furthermore, this right to a class vote also applies to efforts to increase the number of Juniper's directors.

Because CIBC was investing a substantial sum in Juniper, it insisted upon greater control than it would have obtained if these voting provisions (and other comparable provisions) could be exercised without limitation by the holders of Series A Preferred and Series B Preferred shares as a class. Thus, it sought and obtained a concession from the Series A Preferred and Series B Preferred holders that it could amend, waive, or modify, *inter alia*, the protective provisions of Section C.6.a. The right of CIBC to waive the voting rights of the Series A Preferred and Series B Preferred holders was limited by excluding from the scope of the waiver authority any action that "would (a) diminish or alter the liquidation preference or other financial or economic rights, modify the registration rights, or increase the obligations, indemnities or liabilities, of the holders of Series A Preferred Stock, Series A Prime Preferred Stock or Series B Preferred Stock or (b) authorize, approve or waive any action so as to violate any fiduciary duties owed by such holders under Delaware law."

Another protection afforded the holders of both the Series A Preferred and Series B Preferred Stock was set forth in Sections C.6.c(ii) & C.6.d(ii) of the Certificate. Those provisions require a vote of the holders of each series, provided that the requirement for a series vote was not amended or waived by CIBC in accordance with Section C.4.c, if that corporate action would "[m]aterially adversely change the rights, preferences and privileges of the Series A Preferred [and Series B] Preferred Stock."

C.   ADDITIONAL FINANCING BECOMES NECESSARY

By early 2002, Juniper was advising its investors that even more capital would be necessary to sustain the venture. Because Juniper is in the banking business, the consequences of a capital shortage are not merely those of the typical business. Capital shortfall for a banking entity may carry the potential for significant and adverse regulatory action. Regulated not only by the Federal Reserve Board and the Federal Deposit Insurance Corporation but also by the Delaware Banking Commissioner, Juniper is required to maintain a "well-capitalized" status. Failure to maintain that standard (or to effect a prompt cure) may result in, among other things, regulatory action, conversion of the preferred stock into a "senior common stock" which could then be subjected to the imposition of additional security through the regulatory authorities, and the loss of the right to issue Visa cards and to have its customers serviced through the Visa card processing system.

Juniper, with the assistance of an investment banking firm, sought additional investors. The holders of the Series A Preferred and Series B Preferred Stock, including Benchmark, were also solicited. Those efforts failed, thus leaving CIBC as the only identified and viable participant available for the next round of financing, now known as the Series D Transaction.

D. THE SERIES D PREFERRED TRANSACTION

Thus, Juniper turned to consideration of CIBC's proposal, first submitted through a term sheet on March 15, 2002, to finance $50 million through the issuance of Series D Preferred Stock that would grant CIBC an additional 23% of Juniper on a fully-diluted basis and reduce the equity interests of the Series A Preferred and Series B Preferred holders from approximately 29% to 7%.

The board, in early April 2002, appointed a special committee to consider the CIBC proposal. As the result of the negotiations among Juniper, the special committee, and CIBC, the special committee was able to recommend the Series D Transaction with CIBC. The terms of the Series D Transaction are set forth in the "Juniper Financial Corp. Series D Preferred Stock Purchase Agreement" and the "Agreement and Plan of Merger and Reorganization by and Between Juniper Financial Corp. and Juniper Merger Corp."

In general terms, the Series D Transaction consists of the following three steps:

1. Juniper will carry out a 100–1 reverse stock split of its common stock.
2. Juniper Merger Corp., a subsidiary of Juniper established for these purposes, will be merged with and into Juniper which will be the surviving corporation. The certificate of incorporation will be revised as part of the merger.
3. Series D Preferred Stock will be issued to CIBC (and, at least in theory, those other holders of Series A, B and C Preferred who may exercise preemptive rights) for $50 million.

Each share of existing Series A Preferred and each share of existing Series B Preferred will be converted into one share of new Series A Preferred or Series B Preferred, respectively, and the holders of the existing junior preferred will also receive, for each share, a warrant to purchase a small fraction of a share of common stock in Juniper and a smaller fraction of a share of common stock in Juniper. A small amount of cash will also be paid. Juniper will receive no capital infusion as a direct result of the merger. Although the existing Series A Preferred and Series B Preferred shares will cease to exist and the differences between the new and distinct Series A Preferred and Series B Preferred shares will be significant, the resulting modification of Juniper's certificate of incorporation will not alter the class and series votes required by Section C.6. The changes to Juniper's charter as the result of the merger include, *inter alia*, authorization of the issuance of Series D Preferred Shares, which will be senior to the newly created Series A Preferred and Series B Preferred Stock with respect to, for example, liquidation preferences, dividends, and as applicable, redemption rights. Also the Series D Stock will be convertible into common stock at a higher ratio than the existing or newly created Series A Preferred and Series B Preferred Stock, thereby providing for a currently greater voting power. In general terms, the equity of the existing

Series A Preferred and Series B Preferred holders will be reduced from approximately 29% before the merger to approximately 7% after the Series D financing, and CIBC will hold more than 90% of Juniper's voting power.

Juniper intends to proceed with the merger on July 16, 2002 and to promptly thereafter consummate the Series D financing. It projects that, without the $50 million infusion from CIBC, it will not be able to satisfy the "well-capitalized" standard as of July 31, 2002. That will trigger, or so Juniper posits, the regulatory problems previously identified and business problems, such as the risk of losing key personnel and important business relationships. Indeed, Juniper predicts that liquidation would ensue and, in that event (and Benchmark does not seriously contest this), that the holders of Series A Preferred and Series B Preferred Stock would receive nothing (or essentially nothing) from such liquidation.

IV.   CONTENTIONS OF THE PARTIES

Benchmark begins its effort to earn a preliminary injunction by arguing that the junior preferred stockholders are entitled to a vote on the merger on a series basis under Sections C.6.c(ii) & C.6.d(ii) because the merger adversely affects, *inter alia*, their liquidation preference and dividend rights and on a class basis under Section C.6.a(i) because the merger, through changes to Juniper's capital structure as set forth in its revised certificate of incorporation, will authorize the issuance of a senior preferred security.[8] Benchmark also invokes its right to a class vote to challenge the Series D Purchase Agreement under Section C.6.a(i) because that agreement obligates Juniper to issue a senior preferred security. Similarly, Benchmark challenges the issuance of the new Series D Preferred Stock after the merger because it will be issued without a class vote by the holders of either the old or the new Series A Preferred Stock and the new Series B Preferred Stock.

In response, Juniper and CIBC argue that the junior preferred stockholders are not entitled to a class or series vote on any aspect of the Series D financing, particularly the merger. The adverse effects of the transaction arise from the merger and not from any separate amendment of the certificate of incorporation, which would have required the exercise of the junior preferred stockholders' voting rights.[9] Juniper and CIBC emphasize that none of the junior

---

8. While the Verified Complaint asserts general fiduciary duty and disclosure claims relating to the alleged scheme to dilute wrongfully the interests of the junior preferred stockholders, Benchmark has not relied upon these claims in pursuing its application for a preliminary injunction.

9. Juniper focuses on the separate statutory regimes for amendments of certificates of incorporation and for mergers. A corporation may amend its certificate of incorporation to reclassify its authorized stock, 8 *Del. C.* §242(a)(3), or to create a new class of stock with rights and preferences superior to other classes of stock, 8 *Del. C.* §242(a)(5). By 8 *Del. C.* §242(b)(2), "[t]he holders of the outstanding shares of a class shall be entitled to vote as a class upon a proposed amendment, whether or not entitled to vote thereon by the certificate of incorporation, if the amendment would increase or decrease the aggregate number of authorized shares of such class, increase or decrease the par value of the shares of such class, or alter or change the powers, preferences, or special rights of the shares of such class so as to affect them adversely." Mergers, by contrast, are accomplished in accordance with 8 *Del. C.* §251. A merger agreement, in accordance with 8 *Del. C.* §251(b)(3), and a certificate of merger, in accordance with 8 *Del. C.* §253(c)(4), shall state: "[I]n the case of a merger, such amendments or changes in the certificate of incorporation of the surviving corporation as are desired to be effected by the merger. . . ."

preferred stock protective provisions expressly applies to mergers. Finally, Juniper and CIBC assert that the Series C Trump allows for the waiver of all of the voting rights at issue (except for the diminishment of the liquidation preference accomplished by the merger). Benchmark, as one might expect, maintains that the exercise of the Series C Trump is precluded because the "economic or financial rights" of the holders of the junior preferred will be adversely affected and, therefore, the limitation on CIBC's right to exercise the Series C Trump is controlling.

Juniper and CIBC also vigorously contest the issuance of a preliminary injunction by arguing that a balancing of the equities (or balancing of the relative harms from granting or not granting the preliminary injunction) heavily counsels against its issuance. They point out that, in the absence of the proposed financing, Juniper would encounter severe regulatory and business problems, that liquidation would be likely, and that, with liquidation, Benchmark and the other junior preferred shareholders would receive little or nothing from their interests in Juniper.

V. ANALYSIS

A. PRELIMINARY INJUNCTION STANDARD

The familiar standard for a preliminary injunction places the burden on the movant to demonstrate "(1) a reasonable probability of success on the merits, (2) irreparable harm if the injunction is not granted, and (3) a balance of equities in favor of granting the relief." Because a preliminary injunction is an extraordinary remedy, such relief will not be granted "where the remedy sought is excessive in relation to, or unnecessary to prevent, the injury threatened."

. . .

Thus, there is no question as to Juniper's pressing need for capital. CIBC has come forward and is willing to invest an additional $50 million in the company. In light of Benchmark's failure to challenge effectively the evidence of Juniper's current critical need for additional capital, the lack of any alternate source for such funding, and the onerous consequences that failure to secure such capital will cause Juniper and its constituents, Benchmark's argument that Juniper's position is a mere gloom and doom one is unpersuasive. As such, this case may be distinguished from the one before this Court in *Sorrento* where "the record before the Court indicate[d] that [the company's need for additional cash was] not imminent and that [the defendant company] ha[d] the means to sustain itself well beyond any final determination of th[e challenged] action."

While loss of a shareholder's right to vote would certainly be a factor that must be given serious weight in this analysis, when viewed in light of the factual setting of this case, I am of the opinion that Benchmark's risks are minor when compared to those which would likely result from depriving Juniper of financing through the Series D Transaction. Considering that Benchmark would recover nothing (or almost nothing) if Juniper were forced into liquidation, my conclusion that the equities tip in favor of Juniper is bolstered even more. Accordingly, I find that the potential for harm caused by denying Juniper the much needed financing resulting from the Series D Transaction outweighs any potential harm attributable to any deprivation of Benchmark's class voting rights or dilution of its equity interest.

VI. CONCLUSION

Because Benchmark has failed to meet any of the three criteria which should be satisfied by an applicant for a preliminary injunction, denial of its motion should easily follow. I pause to note, however, that Benchmark has ably advocated several arguments that are not easily dismissed. In addition, Benchmark seeks to preserve its voting rights and the voting rights of other Series A Preferred and Series B Preferred shareholders. Its claims to a right to vote as part of a class implicate significant issues of corporate governance. Nonetheless, as I balance the various well-known factors as I must, I conclude that Benchmark has failed to justify issuance of a preliminary injunction.

Therefore, for the foregoing reasons, Benchmark's motion for a preliminary injunction is denied. An order will be entered in accordance with this memorandum opinion.

PROBLEM SET 21.2

1. Assume that the founder of a company holds all the common shares, and a first round venture capital fund holds convertible preferred shares. Would the founder prefer a full ratchet or weighted average term in the convertible shares? What concerns would the founder have with either?

2. And of course be ready to discuss the Juniper transaction, including the goals of each side as the deal was negotiated and how they might have better positioned themselves through changes in the documents.

3. A certificate of designation for a new class of convertible preferred shares has the following term in the initial draft:

> The holders shall be entitled to receive dividends in preference to any dividend on the Common Stock at the rate of _____ % of the Original Purchase Price per annum/$_____ per share, *when, as and if* declared by the Board of Directors except that if the preferred shares have not converted to common shares by [date], dividends shall begin to accumulate from that date and shall be due and payable quarterly in arrears.

What would you argue for if you were representing the founders? The venture capital funds?

3. GOVERNANCE AND EXIT

The goal of the venture capital fund is to sell all of its portfolio company investments by the end of the fund's life, typically ten years. Obviously the entire portfolio cannot be sold precisely at year ten, so the second half of the fund's life span is often spent in the gradual process of selling off investments, and returning capital to investors. This second step facilitates the sale of newly formed funds to existing investors.

During the duration of the investment, the fund will want to make sure its interests are represented in the governance of the portfolio company. That is, while the fund's investors are passive, the fund itself is far from a passive investor.

Convertible preferred stock issued in venture capital transactions typically has the same voting rights as existing common stock, even before conversion. In addition, the holders of convertible preferred stock, voting separately as a class, usually have the right to veto certain corporate transactions affecting the convertible preferred stock directly. Other voting rights may include a class vote for election of directors and rights to elect a majority of the board of directors upon a breach of the terms of the convertible preferred stock.

ROBERT P. BARTLETT, III, *VENTURE CAPITAL, AGENCY COSTS, AND THE FALSE DICHOTOMY OF THE CORPORATION*
54 UCLA L. Rev. 37, 71 (2006)

VC investors ordinarily seek to exit company investments through one of two principal methods: the sale of shares into the public equity markets after a company's IPO or the acquisition of a company for cash or publicly traded securities. In either case, differences in VC investors' stock ownership may create differences as to what constitutes an acceptable exit event for a company. As one prominent attorney in the industry notes, "[T]he actual exit strategy employed . . . may require cooperation from shareholders who will not (or may not) be in agreement with the timing, price or other terms as proposed by [a particular] VC."

The source of these differences arises from the potentially different investment returns each VC investor in a start-up company will receive on a proposed exit. In FormFactor [a venture-backed company that completed an IPO], for instance, investors who acquired shares of the company's Series G Preferred Stock at $15.00 per share would view less favorably a proposed IPO in January 2003 at $10.00 per share than would MDV [Mohr Davidow Ventures, an "early stage venture capital firm"], whose average price paid per share was $1.34. MDV would stand to realize at this price a total return on investment of almost 650 percent, or an annual internal rate of return (IRR) of approximately 37 percent. In contrast, a stockholder who only participated in the Series G financing would realize a total return on investment of −33 percent, or an annual IRR of approximately −27 percent.

The extent to which VC investors purchase their pro rata share in each stage of financing does little to mitigate the potential for divergent investment returns among VC investors . . .

The structure of the VC market encourages VC investors to focus on achieving positive returns for several reasons. As a general matter, venture capitalists must offer LPs the prospect of significant investment returns in order to compensate them for the limited liquidity and significant risks associated with start-up investments. Among early-stage venture capitalists, for instance, it is generally assumed that an investment portfolio should yield an IRR of approximately 30 to 50 percent. Moreover, because many of these investments will ultimately be written off, VC investors commonly make individual company investments with the expectation that each will produce a 40 to 50 percent projected IRR after accounting for the venture capitalist's fees and compensation.

VC fund structure further accentuates this concern with investment returns owing to the capital-time investment constraint and the investment return incentives. First, the intense pressure to raise successive VC funds can encourage a venture capitalist to time exit events so as to accelerate positive returns and to delay negative returns. By exiting an investment with a significant return, a VC investor locks in a gain that helps lift the IRR of a portfolio likely to contain several losing investments. For a VC investor in the process of raising another fund, these early "home runs" may be critical to attracting LPs. Moreover, under the prevailing industry valuation standards, VC investors generally carry a company investment at cost until an exit event or a subsequent financing. IRR calculations will therefore be higher the sooner a fund liquidates a successful investment. For similar reasons, a VC investor faced with a losing investment may present a healthier picture of its overall portfolio to its current and prospective LPs by delaying an exit given that an investment valued at cost looks better to LPs than an investment loss.

In addition to these marketing pressures, the carried interest also encourages venture capitalists to focus on accelerating positive returns and delaying negative returns. As noted above, the carried interest entitles a venture capitalist to receive a specified percentage (usually 20 percent) of the profits realized on a fund's start-up company investments. A corollary of the carry is the so-called "claw-back" provision, which ensures that the venture capitalist receives no more than her specified percentage of fund profits upon the termination of a fund. This result can occur where a VC fund initially liquidates profitable investments and later liquidates losing investments — a common pattern among VC funds. In such situations, the claw-back provision requires a venture capitalist to recontribute capital to the fund in order to avoid receiving excess compensation. Consequently, the ability of a venture capitalist to realize a profit rather than a loss on an investment may potentially mean the difference between receiving an incentive payment from the VC fund and having to recontribute capital to its LPs.

Thus, because of staged investment and investment syndication, a venture capitalist who invests in a start-up company faces a discernable risk that it may disagree at some point with the company's other VC investors concerning what constitutes a proper exit event. In the highly volatile start-up markets, investors holding higher-priced securities may simply be more willing than holders of lower-priced securities to postpone an exit event until the next "up" market. Moreover, the challenge of achieving investor consensus on this issue is made more complicated by the limited life of VC funds. Because of the ten-year term of most funds, an early investor who has held an investment for several years may face a structural incentive to exit at a time when a company's later investors are not subject to these pressures. A company's earlier investors may therefore be less willing to forego a low-value exit yielding a return on investment, even if the investors believe the company could obtain a higher valuation in the long term.

THE CONTRACTUAL RESPONSE

Given the risk that a company's VC investors may disagree over an acceptable exit event, an important aspect of VC contracting centers on mechanisms that contain this risk. The risk is especially acute for VC investors who have lost their original control rights in a company following multiple rounds of staged financing. Even where a new VC investor obtains significant control rights in a company, there can be no guarantee that an exit event will arise during the period in which the investor controls the company. For instance, the company may have to undergo additional rounds of financing before an exit event appears likely, by which time the investor's control may be significantly diminished through dilution. As a result, a VC investor will ordinarily seek specific contract rights that protect its preferences concerning the proper timing and amount of an exit regardless of the level of control it possesses as a result of its equity holdings. In the words of one leading VC lawyer, "[C]ontracts signed at the time of VC's initial investment will generally give VC certain future rights to control its exit strategy. This is especially important where VC will not (or may not) control [the] portfolio company at the back end when the exit strategy is executed."

In the context of an IPO, a VC investor will ordinarily obtain these special control rights by demanding a veto right over the completion of an IPO at an unacceptably low price per share. VC investors accomplish this by relying on the virtually universal practice among investment bankers that, prior to completing an IPO, all shares of a company's preferred stock must convert into common stock. Because of this industry practice, the preferred stock purchased by VC investors will generally have a provision requiring the automatic conversion of preferred stock upon either an IPO at a pre-specified price per share or the requisite vote of preferred stockholders. For many investors, a condition to making a company investment will be setting the automatic conversion price of its preferred stock to a price that equals or exceeds its purchase price. Likewise, with regard to an automatic conversion by means of a stockholder vote, VC investors commonly seek a special veto right with respect to the conversion of its shares of preferred stock. As a result of these two provisions, a VC investor can block the conversion of its preferred stock on an IPO — and thereby block the IPO entirely — if the offering price is less than the investor's purchase price.

An example of each of these techniques appears in FormFactor's charter. Under FormFactor's charter, shares of Series A, Series B, Series C, and Series D Preferred Stock would automatically convert into common stock at an IPO having a price per share of at least $6.90 — a price well in excess of the per-share purchase price of each series. For the higher-priced Series E, Series F, and Series G Preferred Stock, the minimum IPO price for automatic conversion of each series was set at exactly its per-share purchase price ($7.50, $11.00, and $15.00, respectively). To convert any series of FormFactor's preferred stock by means of a stockholder vote, it was necessary to obtain the approval of two-thirds of the outstanding shares of each series.

A VC investor will also seek to protect its particular economic preferences concerning the price and timing of a company acquisition. These protections may take the form of either special veto rights or special liquidation preferences. With regard to veto rights, a VC investor may seek specific class veto rights that guarantee it a blocking right over a company's acquisition. Alternatively, where existing investors already hold an approval right over an acquisition, a later-stage investor may seek to increase the voting threshold required for approving an acquisition to ensure that its vote is required.

In addition to veto rights, a new VC investor may seek to protect its preferences concerning an exit event through a senior liquidation preference. As noted above, a liquidation preference entitles a stockholder to a specified preferential return (ordinarily, an investor's purchase price) on its preferred shares prior to any common stock payments in the event of a company's acquisition. A senior liquidation preference entitles one VC investor to receive its liquidation preference in advance of other VC investors. According to one attorney in the industry:

> [L]ater investors typically want to be first in line to get their original investment (and hopefully their return on investment) out. By subordinating the liquidation preferences of earlier investors, later round investors ensure their priority directly behind creditors and ahead of other equity investors including those who invested in earlier rounds, as well as angel investors, founders and employees.

Unfortunately, the manner in which VC investors seek to protect their particular preferences regarding a company's exit strategy is not always easy to discern. The ability to identify how VC investors resolve potential conflicts over a company exit event requires an analysis of VC investor stock ownership, as well as an understanding of how voting rights and liquidation preferences can work in tandem to create a system of reciprocal veto rights. For instance, a straightforward analysis of FormFactor's charter might suggest its VC investors are generally aligned in their preference concerning the company's acquisition. Under its charter, the protective provisions provide merely that an acquisition of the company must be approved by the holders of a majority of the shares of Series B through Series G Preferred Stock. However, analysis of the VC investors' stock ownership reveals a more complicated story: This voting threshold ensured that no acquisition could occur without the collective approval of MDV, IVP, and MSVP [three venture funds].

The voting threshold clearly provided less protection to the Series E through Series G investors, as MDV, IVP, and MSVP could approve an acquisition without their consent. How did these investors protect against the risk that MDV, IVP, and MSVP would approve a low-value acquisition? The answer is in the liquidation preferences negotiated by these investors: The company's charter granted to the holders of Series D through Series G Preferred Stock a senior liquidation preference. This liquidation preference guaranteed that if MDV, IVP, and MSVP approved a low-value acquisition, no proceeds could be paid on their shares of Series B and Series C Preferred Stock until each share of Series D through Series G Preferred Stock had been distributed an amount equal to the share's original cost ($3.45, $7.50, $11.00, and $15.00, respectively). In other words, no VC investor was at risk that an acquisition would be approved against its will where the investor did not receive back at least its original investment cost.

As analysis of FormFactor's charter reveals, the common use among VC investors of series veto rights and liquidation preferences seeks to address a fundamental challenge of VC investment. It is a challenge unrelated to concerns about whether managers will act as good agents. Rather, it is a challenge arising from the potentially conflicting interests among VC investors concerning what constitutes a proper exit event for a start-up company.

PROBLEM SET 21.3

1. Some investment agreements provide that if the venture capital fund is unable to exit through the normal changes — sales, IPO, and so on — the portfolio company may be required to repurchase the fund's shares at a specified price. Such puts are often also triggered by certain events, such as a default on a bank loan. What are the limitations to this sort of a contractual term?

2. The venture capital investor's block of stock will usually come with the power to appoint at least one member to the board. Often this right of representation means that that fund has a disproportionate influence relative to the size of its stake (especially in early rounds). Based on your knowledge of corporate governance law from prior classes, what risks does this present for the fund?

III

MERGERS AND ACQUISITIONS

22

MERGERS

You might have covered the essentials of mergers in your Corporations or Business Associations class. The basic idea is that two corporations combine, and the target shareholders either become shareholders in the new, combined corporation or they are "cashed-out," which amounts to a forced sale of their shares. Consideration paid to the target shareholders can also consist of a mixture of cash, stock, and even debt.

The seminal duty of care case in the merger context is *Smith v. Van Gorkom*, 488 A.2d 858 (Del. 1985). In *Van Gorkom*, the Delaware Supreme Court held that directors can be personally liable for the difference between the consideration actually paid and a judicially determined "fair price" when the company agrees to a transaction without appropriate board consideration of whether it was in the best interests of shareholders.

The facts of *Van Gorkom* are rather extreme: The court found that the directors approved a deal after thinking about it for two hours, without prior notice, and with only a sketch of the proposed transaction available. And since the case, Delaware has enacted section 102(b)(7), which greatly limits duty of care claims.

Under the *Revlon* doctrine, the board of a company selling itself is obligated to seek the best value reasonably available for shareholders. But in 2009 the Delaware Supreme Court explained that "[n]o court can tell directors exactly how to accomplish that goal [of getting the best price in a sale], because they will be facing a unique combination of circumstances, many of which will be outside their control."[1]

Although management cannot entrench itself in a job for life, the Delaware court has also made it clear that it does not adhere to a strong form of the ECMH, explaining that "it is not a breach of faith for directors to determine that the present stock market price of shares is not representative of true value."[2]

The board is entitled to select the transaction that they believe provides shareholders the best long-term prospects with the least amount of downside risk;

---

1. Lyondell Chemical Corp. v. Ryan, 970 A.2d 235, 242 (Del. 2009). *See* William W. Bratton, *Lyondell: A Note of Approbation*, 55 N.Y.L. Sch. L. Rev. 561, 572 (2011).
2. Paramount Communications, Inc. v. Time Inc., 571 A.2d 1140, 1150 n.12 (Del. 1989).

the directors thus have substantial discretion. In its *Time* decision, the Delaware Supreme Court held that the directors' statutory mandate "includes a conferred authority to set a corporate course of action, including time frame, designed to enhance corporate profitability."[3]

Whereas your prior class mostly focused on the duties of the board, in this chapter we focus on the negotiation of the deal itself. Of course, part of that negotiation must involve the board exercising its duties.

1. MERGER AGREEMENTS

Business combinations are typically achieved by use of either a merger or stock purchase agreement. Stock purchase agreements are used when the target company's shares are concentrated among a few holders, which most often happens with smaller firms. Otherwise deals will typically be done by a merger agreement, which must be approved by the shareholders after the board consents to the deal.[4]

To paraphrase *Casablanca*,[5] a merger agreement is just like any other contract, only more so.[6]

One key thing to understand is that any corporate transaction is like buying a house. The contract is signed, but the actual exchange of assets for consideration does not happen until some later point called the "closing." Thus, the contract must not only set forth the terms of the underlying deal, but also account for the possible changes that might occur during the interregnum.

Moreover, during the interim period the parties will have a chance to investigate each other — much like you might have a house inspected before the closing — and regulators might have an ability to review the deal, depending on the size of the deal and particular industries involved.

The contract has to provide a mechanism for dealing with information learned during this process. For example, if the buyer learns that the target has some previously unknown problem, the buyer will want the right to renegotiate the price or even terminate the deal. If a regulator refuses to approve, or imposes conditions, what happens?

Moreover, the parties must agree on how the parties' confidential information will be treated before it is shared. Typically this is done by a separate contract ingeniously called a "confidentiality agreement."

In addition to the obligation to maintain information in confidence, the confidentiality agreement will limit the uses of the information. This provides protection against the recipient using confidential information to facilitate a hostile bid in the event discussions fall apart.

In addition to confidentiality provisions, confidentiality agreements sometimes contain provisions limiting the right of the buyer to try to hire away

---

3. 571 A.2d at 1150.
4. Del. Gen. Corp. Law §251(c).
5. *http://goo.gl/kODiO*
6. Claire A. Hill, *Bargaining in the Shadow of the Lawsuit: A Social Norms Theory of Incomplete Contracts*, 34 Del. J. Corp. L. 191, 203 (2009).

employees of the target that buyer representatives meet or become aware of during the diligence process. Also, confidentiality agreements sometimes contain standstill provisions, which limit the potential buyer's ability to acquire or control the target or any substantial portion of the target for some period of time, outside of the confines of a friendly transaction.

A. Market Risk

The delay between signing and closing, combined with the frequent use of stock as consideration in mergers, means that a deal is subject to pricing risks over a period of time between announcement and the closing.

For example, a drop in the price of an acquirer's stock between execution of the acquisition agreement and the closing of the transaction results in the seller's shareholders receiving less for their shares. This market risk can be dealt with by a pricing structure that uses a valuation formula instead of a fixed exchange ratio.

But that itself can have risks. For example, several years ago a company called Cendant signed a deal to acquire a target in which each target share would be converted into Cendant common stock. But then Cendant's share price declined tremendously. At the new price, Cendant would have had to issue about four times as many shares as it had anticipated, massively diluting its existing shareholders. Rather than proceed under these circumstances, Cendant paid $400 million to get out of the deal.[7]

This kind of risk is somewhat addressed with a collar, which provides for adjustment of the stock consideration within a specified range. A collar protects the acquirer by placing an upper limit on the amount of stock it will be required to issue in the event of a decline in the price of its stock between signing and closing, and protects the target shareholders by providing a floor on their compensation under the deal. Once the share price is outside the collar range, no further adjustments are made and the exchange ratio becomes fixed at its upper or lower limit.

Some transactions also include so-called "walk-away" provisions permitting unilateral termination by the seller-target in the event the acquirer's share price falls below a certain level, set either on an absolute basis or by reference to some index.

Cash consideration, of course, faces no such risk, at least if the buyer and seller are within the same jurisdiction. Buyers operating in different currencies face the exchange rate risk.[8]

B. Covenants, Reps and Warranties

Representations and warranties appear in many types of agreements, including acquisition, loan, and venture investment agreements, and loan agreements and bond indentures, which we have already discussed.

---

7. *http://goo.gl/u27xl*
8. The currency swaps you covered in Chapter 18 might have a role to play here.

A representation is simply a statement of fact. For example, "The target is properly incorporated in Delaware."

A warranty is a promise of indemnity if a statement of fact is false. The distinction between this and a representation is discussed in the following case.

CBS INC., APPELLANT, v. ZIFF-DAVIS PUBLISHING CO. ET AL., RESPONDENTS.

75 N.Y.2d 496, 553 N.E.2d 997, 554 N.Y.S.2d 449
Court of Appeals of New York
Argued February 8, 1990; decided April 3, 1990

HANCOCK, Jr., J.

A corporate buyer made a bid to purchase certain businesses based on financial information as to their profitability supplied by the seller. The bid was accepted and the parties entered into a binding bilateral contract for the sale which included, specifically, the seller's express warranties as to the truthfulness of the previously supplied financial information. Thereafter, pursuant to the purchase agreement, the buyer conducted its own investigation which led it to believe that the warranted information was untrue. The seller dismissed as meritless the buyer's expressions of disbelief in the validity of the financial information and insisted that the sale go through as agreed. The closing took place with the mutual understanding that it would not in any way affect the previously asserted position of either party. Did the buyer's manifested lack of belief in and reliance on the truth of the warranted information prior to the closing relieve the seller of its obligations under the warranties? This is the central question presented in the breach of express warranty claim brought by CBS Inc. (CBS) against Ziff-Davis Publishing Co. (Ziff-Davis). The courts below concluded that CBS's lack of reliance on the warranted information was fatal to its breach of warranty claim and, accordingly, dismissed that cause of action on motion under CPLR 3211 (a) (7). We granted leave to appeal and, for reasons stated hereinafter, disagree with this conclusion and hold that the warranty claim should be reinstated.

I

The essential facts pleaded — assumed to be true for the purpose of the dismissal motion — are these. In September 1984, Goldman Sachs & Co., acting as Ziff-Davis's investment banker and agent, solicited bids for the sale of the assets and businesses of 12 consumer magazines and 12 business publications. The offering circular, prepared by Goldman Sachs and Ziff-Davis, described Ziff-Davis's financial condition and included operating income statements for the fiscal year ending July 31, 1984 prepared by Ziff-Davis's accountant, Touche Ross & Co. Based on Ziff-Davis's representations in the offering circular, CBS, on November 9, 1984 submitted a bid limited to the purchase of the 12 consumer magazines in the amount of $362,500,000. This was the highest bid.

On November 19, 1984 CBS and Ziff-Davis entered into a binding bilateral purchase agreement for the sale of the consumer magazine businesses for the price of $362,500,000. Under section 3.5 of the purchase agreement, Ziff-Davis warranted that the audited income and expense report of the businesses for the 1984 fiscal year, which had been previously provided to CBS in the offering circular, had "been prepared in accordance with generally accepted accounting principles" (GAAP) and that the report "present[ed] fairly the items set forth." Ziff-Davis agreed to furnish an interim income and expense report (Stub Report) of the businesses covering the period after the end of the 1984 fiscal year, and it warranted under section 3.6 that from July 31, 1984 until the closing, there had "not been any material adverse change in Seller's business of publishing and distributing the Publications, taken as a whole." Section 6.1(a) provided that "all representations and warranties of Seller to Buyer shall be true and correct as of the time of the closing," and in section 8.1, the parties agreed that all "representations and warranties . . . shall survive the closing, notwithstanding any investigation made by or on behalf of the other party." In section 5.1 Ziff-Davis gave CBS permission to "make such investigation" of the magazine businesses being sold "as [it might] desire" and agreed to give CBS and its accountants reasonable access to the books and records pertaining thereto and to furnish such documents and information as might reasonably be requested.

Thereafter, on January 30, 1985 Ziff-Davis delivered the required Stub Report. In the interim, CBS, acting under section 5.1 of the purchase agreement, had performed its own "due diligence" examination of Ziff-Davis's financial condition. Based on this examination and on reports by its accountant, Coopers & Lybrand, CBS discovered information causing it to believe that Ziff-Davis's certified financial statements and other financial reports were not prepared according to GAAP and did not fairly depict Ziff-Davis's financial condition.

In a January 31, 1985 letter, CBS wrote Ziff-Davis that, "[b]ased on the information and analysis provided [to it, CBS was] of the view that there [were] material misrepresentations in the financial statements provided [to CBS] by Touche Ross & Co., Goldman, Sachs & Co. and Ziff-Davis." In response to this letter, Ziff-Davis advised CBS by letter dated February 4, 1985 that it "believe[d] that all conditions to the closing . . . were fulfilled," that "there [was] no merit to the position taken by CBS in its [Jan. 31, 1985] letter" and that the financial statements were properly prepared and fairly presented Ziff-Davis's financial condition. It also warned CBS that, since all conditions to closing were satisfied, closing was required to be held that day, February 4, 1985, and that, if it "should fail to consummate the transactions as provided . . . Ziff-Davis intend[ed] *to pursue all of its rights and remedies as provided by law.*" (Emphasis added.)

CBS responded to Ziff-Davis's February 4, 1985 letter with its own February 4 letter, which Ziff-Davis accepted and agreed to. In its February 4 letter, CBS acknowledged that "a clear dispute" existed between the parties. It stated that it had decided to proceed with the deal because it had "spent considerable time, effort and money in complying with [its] obligations . . . and recogniz[ed] that [Ziff-Davis had] considerably more information available." Accordingly, the parties agreed "to close [that day] on a mutual understanding that the decision to close, and the closing, [would] not *constitute a waiver of any rights or defenses either of us may have"* (emphasis added) under the purchase agreement. The deal was consummated on February 4.

CBS then brought this action claiming . . . that Ziff-Davis had breached the warranties made as to the magazines' profitability. Based on that breach, CBS alleged that "the price bid and the price paid by CBS were in excess of that which would have been bid and paid by CBS had Ziff-Davis not breached its representation and warranties." Supreme Court granted Ziff-Davis's motion to dismiss the breach of warranty cause of action because CBS alleged "it did not believe that the representations set forth in Paragraphs 3.5 and 3.6 of the contract of sale were true" and thus CBS did not satisfy "the law in New York [which] clearly requires that this reliance be alleged in a breach of warranty action." Supreme Court also dismissed CBS's fourth cause of action relating to an alleged breach of condition. The Appellate Division, First Department, unanimously affirmed for reasons stated by Supreme Court. There should be a modification so as to deny the dismissal motion with respect to the . . . cause of action for breach of warranties.

II

In addressing the central question whether the failure to plead reliance is fatal to CBS's claim for breach of express warranties, it is necessary to examine the exact nature of the missing element of reliance which Ziff-Davis contends is essential. This critical lack of reliance, according to Ziff-Davis, relates to CBS's disbelief in the truth of the warranted financial information which resulted from its investigation *after* the signing of the agreement and *prior to* the date of closing. The reliance in question, it must be emphasized, does not relate to whether CBS relied on the submitted financial information in making its bid or relied on Ziff-Davis's express warranties as to the validity of this information when CBS committed itself to buy the businesses by signing the purchase agreement containing the warranties.

Under Ziff-Davis's theory, the reliance which is a necessary element for a claim of breach of express warranty is essentially that required for a tort action based on fraud or misrepresentation — i.e., a belief in the truth of the representations made in the express warranty and a change of position in reliance on that belief. Thus, because, prior to the closing of the contract on February 4, 1985, CBS demonstrated its lack of belief in the truth of the warranted financial information, it cannot have closed in reliance on it and its breach of warranty claim must fail. This is so, Ziff-Davis maintains, despite its unequivocal rejection of CBS's expressions of its concern that the submitted financial reports contained errors, despite its insistence that the information it had submitted complied with the warranties and that there was "no merit" to CBS's position, and despite its warnings of legal action if CBS did not go ahead with the closing. Ziff-Davis's primary source for the proposition it urges — that a change of position in reliance on the truth of the warranted information is essential for a cause of action for breach of express warranty — is language found in older New York cases such as Crocker-Wheeler Elec. Co. v Johns-Pratt Co. (29 App Div 300, *affd* 164 NY 593).

CBS, on the other hand, maintains that the decisive question is whether it purchased the express warranties as bargained-for contractual terms that were part of the purchase agreement. It alleges that it did so and that, under these circumstances, the warranty provisions amounted to assurances of the existence of facts upon which CBS relied in committing itself to buy the consumer magazines. Ziff-Davis's assurances of these facts, CBS contends, were the equivalent of promises by Ziff-Davis to indemnify CBS if the assurances proved unfounded. Thus, as continuing promises to indemnify, the express contractual warranties did not lose their operative force when, prior to the closing, CBS formed a belief that the warranted financial information was in error. Indeed, CBS claims that it is precisely because of these warranties that it proceeded with the closing, despite its misgivings.

As authority for its position, CBS cites, *inter alia,* Ainger v Michigan Gen. Corp. and Judge Learned Hand's definition of warranty as "an assurance by one party to a contract of the existence of a fact upon which the other party may rely. It is intended precisely to relieve the promisee of any duty to ascertain the fact for himself; *it amounts to a promise to indemnify the promisee for any loss if the fact warranted proves untrue, for obviously the promisor cannot control what is already in the past.* " (Metropolitan Coal Co. v Howard, 155 F2d 780, 784 [2d Cir 1946] [emphasis added].

We believe that the analysis of the reliance requirement in actions for breach of express warranties adopted in Ainger v Michigan Gen. Corp. and urged by CBS here is correct. The critical question is not whether the buyer believed in the truth of the warranted information, as Ziff-Davis would have it, but "whether [it] believed [it] was purchasing the [seller's] promise [as to its truth]." This view of "reliance" — i.e., as requiring no more than reliance on the express warranty as being a part of the bargain between the parties — reflects the prevailing perception of an action for breach of express warranty as one that is no longer grounded in tort, but essentially in contract. The express warranty is as much a part of the contract as any other term. Once the express warranty is shown to have been relied on as part of the contract, the right to be indemnified in damages for its breach does not depend on proof that the buyer thereafter believed that the assurances of fact made in the warranty would be fulfilled. The right to indemnification depends only on establishing that the warranty was breached.

If, as is allegedly the case here, the buyer has purchased the seller's promise as to the existence of the warranted facts, the seller should not be relieved of responsibility because the buyer, after agreeing to make the purchase, forms doubts as to the existence of those facts. Stated otherwise, the fact that the buyer has questioned the seller's ability to perform as promised should not relieve the seller of his obligations under the express warranties when he thereafter undertakes to render the promised performance.

The cases which Ziff-Davis cites as authority for the application of its tort-action type of reliance requirement do not support the proposition it urges. None are similar to the case at bar where the warranties sued on are bargained-for terms in a binding bilateral purchase contract. In most, the basis for the decision was a factor other than the buyer's lack of reliance such as, for example, insufficient proof of the existence of the alleged express warranty or that the warranty sued upon was expressly excluded by terms of the contract or that there was insufficient proof that the express warranty had been breached; and some involve implied rather than express warranties . . .

Viewed as a contract action involving the claimed breach of certain bargained-for express warranties contained in the purchase agreement, the case may be summarized this way. CBS contracted to buy the consumer magazine businesses in consideration, among other things, of the reciprocal promises made by Ziff-Davis concerning the magazines' profitability. These reciprocal promises included the express warranties that the audited reports for the year ending July 31, 1984 made by Touche Ross had been prepared according to GAAP and that the items contained therein were fairly presented, that there had been no adverse material change in the business after July 31, 1984, and that all representations and warranties would "be true and correct as of the time of the closing" and would "survive the closing, notwithstanding any investigation" by CBS.

Unquestionably, the financial information pertaining to the income and expenses of the consumer magazines was relied on by CBS in forming its opinion as to the value of the businesses and in arriving at the amount of its bid; the warranties pertaining to the validity of this financial information were express terms of the bargain and part of what CBS contracted to purchase. CBS was not merely buying identified consumer magazine businesses. It was buying businesses which it believed to be of a certain value based on information furnished by the seller which the seller warranted to be true. The determinative question is this: should Ziff-Davis be relieved from any contractual obligation under these warranties, as it contends that it should, because, prior to the closing, CBS and its accountants questioned the accuracy of the financial information and because CBS, when it closed, did so without *believing in* or *relying on* the truth of the information?

We see no reason why Ziff-Davis should be absolved from its warranty obligations under these circumstances. A holding that it should because CBS questioned the truth of the facts warranted would have the effect of depriving the express warranties of their only value to CBS — i.e., as continuing promises by Ziff-Davis to indemnify CBS if the facts warranted proved to be untrue (*see*, Metropolitan Coal Co. v Howard, *supra*, at 784).

Ironically, if Ziff-Davis's position were adopted, it would have succeeded in pressing CBS to close despite CBS's misgivings and, at the same time, would have succeeded in *defeating* CBS's breach of warranties action because CBS harbored these *identical misgivings*.

Judges Simons, Alexander and Titone concur with Judge Hancock, Jr.; Judge Bellacosa dissents in part and votes to affirm in a separate opinion; Chief Judge Wachtler and Judge Kaye taking no part.

One way to shift risk in the representations or warranties is with materiality exceptions or qualifications. Depending on the degree of the qualification, a certain number of breaches will be nonactionable. That effectively means the other party bears the risk and costs with respect to any nonmaterial items. And then there are the covenants.

Some covenants apply from the signing of the agreement until the closing date and provide assurance that the proper actions are taken to facilitate the closing of the transaction and preserve the business pending the closing. For example, some of the covenants require the parties to obtain the necessary approvals from various governmental agencies and other third parties that are required for the consummation of the deal. The space between agreement and closing provides the parties with time to perform these covenants.

Other covenants survive the closing for a certain length of time, such as covenants requiring cooperation of the parties with respect to the post-closing operation of the business or sharing of facilities.

C. Conditions

A merger agreement becomes binding and the closing must happen only if any conditions to closing have been satisfied.[9] As noted earlier, a standard agreement will contain representations, warranties, and covenants (often qualified by materiality standards, as also described earlier).

The agreement will also provide that closing is conditional on the truth of the other party's representations and warranties, as well as either specific closing conditions. For example, if the other party made no effort to get a needed regulatory approval, that will breach a covenant and closing will be excused.

There will also be conditions in the form of bright line tests that must be met or a general closing condition tied to the nonoccurrence of a "material adverse change," or "material adverse event," which itself might be subject to various materiality exceptions.

That is a long way of saying that any breach of a covenant, representation, or warranty gives the other side an option to terminate the deal or, more likely, to renegotiate the price. But when such an option is triggered is not always clear, and the parties will typically negotiate a settlement in light of the relevant case law.

IN RE IBP, INC. SHAREHOLDERS LITIGATION
789 A.2d 14
Court of Chancery of Delaware, New Castle County
Submitted: June 3, 2001 | Decided: June 15, 2001

STRINE, Vice Chancellor.

This post-trial opinion addresses a demand for specific performance of a "Merger Agreement" by IBP, Inc., the nation's number one beef and number two pork distributor. By this action, IBP seeks to compel the "Merger" between itself and Tyson Foods, Inc., the nation's leading chicken distributor, in a transaction in which IBP stockholders will receive their choice of $30 a share in cash or Tyson stock, or a combination of the two.

The IBP-Tyson Merger Agreement resulted from a vigorous auction process that pitted Tyson against the nation's number one pork producer, Smithfield

---

9. Albert Choi & George Triantis, *Strategic Vagueness in Contract Design: The Case of Corporate Acquisitions*, 119 Yale L.J. 848, 863–864 (2010).

Foods. To say that Tyson was eager to win the auction is to slight its ardent desire to possess IBP. During the bidding process, Tyson was anxious to ensure that it would acquire IBP, and to make sure Smithfield did not. By succeeding, Tyson hoped to create the world's preeminent meat products company — a company that would dominate the meat cases of supermarkets in the United States and eventually throughout the globe.

During the auction process, Tyson was given a great deal of information that suggested that IBP was heading into a trough in the beef business. Even more, Tyson was alerted to serious problems at an IBP subsidiary, DFG, which had been victimized by accounting fraud to the tune of over $30 million in charges to earnings and which was the active subject of an asset impairment study. Not only that, Tyson knew that IBP was projected to fall seriously short of the fiscal year 2000 earnings predicted in projections prepared by IBP's Chief Financial Officer in August, 2000.

By the end of the auction process, Tyson had come to have great doubts about IBP's ability to project its future earnings, the credibility of IBP's management, and thought that the important business unit in which DFG was located — Foodbrands — was broken.

Yet, Tyson's ardor for IBP was such that Tyson raised its bid by a total of $4.00 a share after learning of these problems. Tyson also signed the Merger Agreement, which permitted IBP to recognize unlimited additional liabilities on account of the accounting improprieties at DFG. It did so without demanding any representation that IBP meet its projections for future earnings, or any escrow tied to those projections.

After the Merger Agreement was signed on January 1, 2001, Tyson trumpeted the value of the merger to its stockholders and the financial community, and indicated that it was fully aware of the risks that attended the cyclical nature of IBP's business. In early January, Tyson's stockholders ratified the merger agreement and authorized its management to take whatever action was needed to effectuate it.

During the winter and spring of 2001, Tyson's own business performance was dismal. Meanwhile, IBP was struggling through a poor first quarter. Both companies' problems were due in large measure to a severe winter, which adversely affected livestock supplies and vitality. As these struggles deepened, Tyson's desire to buy IBP weakened.

This cooling of affections first resulted in a slow-down by Tyson in the process of consummating a transaction, a slow-down that was attributed to IBP's on-going efforts to resolve issues that had been raised about its financial statements by the Securities and Exchange Commission ("SEC"). The most important of these issues was how to report the problems at DFG, which Tyson had been aware of at the time it signed the Merger Agreement. Indeed, all the key issues that the SEC raised with IBP were known by Tyson at the time it signed the Merger Agreement. The SEC first raised these issues in a faxed letter on December 29, 2000 to IBP's outside counsel. Neither IBP management nor Tyson learned of the letter until the second week of January, 2001. After learning of the letter, Tyson management put the Merger Agreement to a successful board and stockholder vote.

But the most important reason that Tyson slowed down the Merger process was different: it was having buyer's regret. Tyson wished it had paid less especially in view of its own compromised 2001 performance and IBP's slow 2001 results.

By March, Tyson's founder and controlling stockholder, Don Tyson, no longer wanted to go through with the Merger Agreement. He made the decision to abandon the Merger. His son, John Tyson, Tyson's Chief Executive Officer, and the other Tyson managers followed his instructions. Don Tyson abandoned the Merger because of IBP's and Tyson's poor results in 2001, and not because of DFG or the SEC issues IBP was dealing with. Indeed, Don Tyson told IBP management that he would blow DFG up if he were them.

After the business decision was made to terminate, Tyson's legal team swung into action. They fired off a letter terminating the Agreement at the same time as they filed suit accusing IBP of fraudulently inducing the Merger that Tyson had once so desperately desired.

This expedited litigation ensued, which involved massive amounts of discovery and two weeks of trial.

In this opinion, I address IBP's claim that Tyson had no legal basis to avoid its obligation to consummate the Merger Agreement, as well as Tyson's contrary arguments. The parties' extensive claims are too numerous to summarize adequately, as are the court's rulings.

THE BASIC CONTENTIONS OF THE PARTIES

The parties have each made numerous arguments that bear on the central question of whether Tyson properly terminated the Merger Agreement, which is understandable in view of the high stakes. The plethora of theories and nuanced arguments is somewhat daunting and difficult to summarize. But the fundamental contentions are as follows.

IBP argues that Tyson had no valid reason to terminate the contract on March 29, 2001 and that the Merger Agreement should be specifically enforced. In support of that position, IBP argues that it has not breached any of the contractual representations and warranties. In addition, IBP contends that Tyson improperly terminated the Cash Offer on February 28, 2001 because all closing conditions were met as of that date. In this regard, IBP says that Tyson did not need IBP to formally file its Restated Financials in order for Tyson to proceed with the Cash Offer. As a result, IBP says that §2.01(e) and (h) of the Agreement do not provide Tyson with a contractual safe harbor.

Tyson argues that its decision to terminate was proper for several reasons. First, Tyson contends that IBP breached its contractual representations regarding the Warranted Financials, as evidenced by the Restatements. Second, Tyson contends that the DFG Impairment Charge as well as IBP's disappointing first quarter 2001 performance are evidence of a Material Adverse Effect, which gave Tyson the right to terminate.

Finally, Tyson argues that the Merger Agreement should be rescinded because that Agreement (and related contracts) were fraudulently induced.

In this respect, Tyson contends that IBP's failure to disclose the Comment Letter and certain DFG-related documents before January 1, 2001 constitutes ground for rescission. Tyson says that the Agreement should also be rescinded because IBP management made oral statements regarding the Rawhide Projections that they knew to be false, on which Tyson reasonably relied to its detriment. For identical reasons, Tyson says that a letter agreement it signed in connection with the Merger Agreement should also be rescinded, thus entitling Tyson to a refund of a $66 million termination fee it paid to the Rawhide group on behalf of IBP.

The parties have chosen to accompany their basic contentions with a variety of subsidiary theories, all of which derive from the same factual issues.

Was Tyson's Termination Justified Because IBP Has Suffered a Material Adverse Effect?

Tyson argues that it was . . . permitted to terminate because IBP had breached §5.10 of the Agreement, which is a representation and warranty that IBP had not suffered a material adverse effect since the "Balance Sheet Date" of December 25, 1999, except as set forth in the Warranted Financials or Schedule 5.10 of the Agreement.

Under the contract, a material adverse effect (or "MAE") is defined as "any event, occurrence or development of a state of circumstances or facts which has had or reasonably could be expected to have a Material Adverse Effect" . . . "on the condition (financial or otherwise), business, assets, liabilities or results of operations of [IBP] and [its] Subsidiaries taken as whole. . . ."

Tyson asserts that the decline in IBP's performance in the last quarter of 2000 and the first quarter of 2001 evidences the existence of a Material Adverse Effect. It also contends that the DFG Impairment Charge constitutes a Material Adverse Effect. And taken together, Tyson claims that it is virtually indisputable that the combination of these factors amounts to a Material Adverse Effect.

In addressing these arguments, it is useful to be mindful that Tyson's publicly expressed reasons for terminating the Merger did not include an assertion that IBP had suffered a Material Adverse Effect. The post-hoc nature of Tyson's arguments bear on what it felt the contract meant when contracting, and suggests that a short-term drop in IBP's performance would not be sufficient to cause a MAE. To the extent the facts matter, it is also relevant that Tyson gave no weight to DFG in contracting.

The resolution of Tyson's Material Adverse Effect argument requires the court to engage in an exercise that is quite imprecise. The simplicity of §5.10's words is deceptive, because the application of those words is dauntingly complex. On its face, §5.10 is a capacious clause that puts IBP at risk for a variety of uncontrollable factors that might materially affect its overall business or results of operation as a whole. Although many merger contracts contain specific exclusions from MAE clauses that cover declines in the overall economy or the relevant industry sector, or adverse weather or market conditions, §5.10 is unqualified by such express exclusions.

IBP argues, however, that statements in the Warranted Financials that emphasize the risks IBP faces from swings in livestock supply act as an implicit carve-out, because a Material Adverse Effect under that section cannot include an Effect that is set forth in the Warranted Financials. I agree with Tyson, however, that these disclaimers were far too general to preclude industry-wide or general factors from constituting a Material Adverse Effect. Had IBP wished such an exclusion from the broad language of §5.10, IBP should have bargained for it. At the same time, the notion that §5.10 gave Tyson a right to walk away simply because of a downturn in cattle supply is equally untenable. Instead, Tyson would have to show that the event had the required materiality of effect.[10]

The difficulty of addressing that question is considerable, however, because §5.10 is fraught with temporal ambiguity. By its own terms, it refers to any Material Adverse Effect that has occurred to IBP since December 25, 1999 unless that Effect is covered by the Warranted Financials or Schedule 5.10. Moreover, Tyson's right to refuse to close because a Material Adverse Effect has occurred is also qualified by the other express disclosures in the Schedule, by virtue of (i) the language of the Annexes that permits Tyson to refuse to close for breach of a warranty unless that breach results from "actions specifically permitted" by the Agreement; and (ii) the language of the Agreement that makes all disclosure schedules apply to Schedule 5.10 where that is the reasonably apparent intent of the drafters. Taken together, these provisions can be read to require the court to examine whether a MAE has occurred against the December 25, 1999 condition of IBP as adjusted by the specific disclosures of the Warranted Financials and the Agreement itself. This approach makes commercial sense because it establishes a baseline that roughly reflects the status of IBP as Tyson indisputably knew it at the time of signing the Merger Agreement.

But describing this basic contractual approach is somewhat easier than applying it. For example, the original IBP 10-K for FY 1999 revealed the following five-year earnings from operations and earnings per share before extraordinary items:

		1999	1998	1997	1996	1995
Earnings from Operations (in thousands)	$	528,473	373,735	226,716	322,908	480,096
Net Earnings Per Share	$	3.39	2.21	1.26	2.10	2.96

The picture that is revealed from this data is of a company that is consistently profitable, but subject to strong swings in annual EBIT and net earnings. The averages that emerge from this data are of EBIT of approximately $386 million per year and net earnings of $2.38 per share. If this average is seen as weighting

---

10. *But see* Pittsburgh Coke & Chem. Co. v. Bollo, 421 F.Supp. 908, 930 (E.D.N.Y.1976) (where Material Adverse Condition ("MAC") clause applied to a company's "financial condition," "business," or "operations," court read that clause narrowly to exclude "technological and economic changes in the aviation industry which undoubtedly affected the business of all who had dealings with that industry").

the past too much, a three-year average generates EBIT of $376 million and net earnings of $2.29 per share.

The original Warranted Financials in FY 2000 also emphasize that swings in IBP's performance were a part of its business reality. For example, the trailing last twelve month's earnings from operations as of the end of third quarter of FY 2000 were $462 million, as compared to $528 million for full year 1999, as originally reported. In addition, the third quarter 10-Q showed that IBP's earnings from operations for the first 39 weeks of 2000 were lagging earnings from operations for the comparable period in 1999 by $40 million, after adjusting for the CFBA Charges.

The financial statements also indicate that Foodbrands was hardly a stable source of earnings, and was still much smaller in importance than IBP's fresh meat operations. Not only that, FY 2000 Foodbrands performance was lagging 1999, even accounting for the unusual, disclosed items.

The Rawhide Projections add another dimension to the meaning of §5.10. These Projections indicated that IBP would not reach the same level of profitability as originally reported *until FY 2004*. In FY 2001, IBP was expected to have earnings from operations of $446 and net profits of $1.93 a share, down from what was expected in FY 2000. This diminishment in expectations resulted from concern over an anticipated trough in the cattle cycle that would occur during years 2001 to 2003. Moreover, the performance projected for FY 2001 was a drop even from the reduced FY 2000 earnings that Tyson expected as of the time it signed the Merger Agreement.

These negotiating realities bear on the interpretation of §5.10 and suggest that the contractual language must be read in the larger context in which the parties were transacting. To a short-term speculator, the failure of a company to meet analysts' projected earnings for a quarter could be highly material. Such a failure is less important to an acquiror who seeks to purchase the company as part of a long-term strategy. To such an acquiror, the important thing is whether the company has suffered a Material Adverse Effect in its business or results of operations that is consequential to the company's earnings power over a commercially reasonable period, which one would think would be measured in years rather than months. It is odd to think that a strategic buyer would view a short-term blip in earnings as material, so long as the target's earnings-generating potential is not materially affected by that blip or the blip's cause.

In large measure, the resolution of the parties' arguments turns on a difficult policy question. In what direction does the burden of this sort of uncertainty fall: on an acquiror or on the seller? What little New York authority exists is not particularly helpful, and cuts in both directions. One New York case held a buyer to its bargain even when the seller suffered a very severe shock from an extraordinary event, reasoning that the seller realized that it was buying the stock of a sound company that was, however, susceptible to market swings.[11]

---

11. Bear Stearns Co. v. Jardine Strategic Holdings, No. 31371187, slip. op. (N.Y.Supr. June 17, 1988), *aff'd mem.*, 143 A.D.2d 1073, 533 N.Y.S.2d 167 (1988) (Tender offeror who was to purchase 20% of Bear Stearns could not rely on the MAC clause to avoid contract despite $100 million loss suffered by Bear Stearns on Black Monday, October 19, 19[8]7, and the fact that Bear Stearns suffered a $48 million quarterly loss, its first in history. The buyer knew that Bear Stearns was in a volatile cyclical business.).

Another case held that a Material Adverse Effect was evidenced by a short-term drop in sales, but in a commercial context where such a drop was arguably quite critical.[12] The non-New York authorities cited by the parties provide no firmer guidance.

Practical reasons lead me to conclude that a New York court would incline toward the view that a buyer ought to have to make a strong showing to invoke a Material Adverse Effect exception to its obligation to close. Merger contracts are heavily negotiated and cover a large number of specific risks explicitly. As a result, even where a Material Adverse Effect condition is as broadly written as the one in the Merger Agreement, that provision is best read as a backstop protecting the acquiror from the occurrence of unknown events that substantially threaten the overall earnings potential of the target in a durationally-significant manner.[13] A short-term hiccup in earnings should not suffice; rather the Material Adverse Effect should be material when viewed from the longer-term perspective of a reasonable acquiror. In this regard, it is worth noting that IBP never provided Tyson with *quarterly* projections.

When examined from this seller-friendly perspective, the question of whether IBP has suffered a Material Adverse Effect remains a close one. IBP had a very sub-par first quarter. The earnings per share of $.19 it reported exaggerate IBP's success, because part of those earnings were generated from a windfall generated by accounting for its stock option plan, a type of gain that is not likely to recur. On a normalized basis, IBP's first quarter of 2001 earnings from operations ran 64% behind the comparable period in 2000. If IBP had continued to perform on a straight-line basis using its first quarter 2001 performance, it would generate earnings from operations of around $200 million. This sort of annual performance would be consequential to a reasonable acquiror and would deviate materially from the range in which IBP had performed during the recent past.

Tyson says that this impact must also be coupled with the DFG Impairment Charge of $60.4 million. That Charge represents an indication that DFG is likely to generate far less cash flow than IBP had previously anticipated. At the very least, the Charge is worth between $.50 and $.60 cents per IBP share, which is not trivial. It is worth even more, says Tyson, if one realizes that the Rawhide Projections portrayed Foodbrands as the driver of increased profitability in an era of flat fresh meats profits. This deficiency must be considered in view of the overall poor performance of Foodbrands so far in FY 2001. The Rawhide Projections had targeted Foodbrands to earn $137 million in 2001. In a January 30, 2001 presentation to Tyson, Bond had presented an operating plan that hoped to achieve $145 million from Foodbrands. As of the end of the first quarter,

---

12. In Pan Am Corp. v. Delta Air Lines, 175 B.R. 438, 492-493 (S.D.N.Y.1994), Pan Am airlines suffered a sharp decline in bookings over a three-month period that was shocking to its management. The court held that a MAC had occurred. It did so, however, in a context where the party relying on the MAC clause was providing funding in a work-out situation, making any further deterioration of Pan Am's already compromised condition quite important.

13. A contrary rule will encourage the negotiation of extremely detailed "MAC" clauses with numerous carve-outs or qualifiers. An approach that reads broad clauses as addressing fundamental events that would materially affect the value of a target to a reasonable acquiror eliminates the need for drafting of that sort.

Foodbrands had earned only $2 million, and thus needed another $135 million in the succeeding three quarters to reach its Rawhide Projection. IBP's overall trailing last twelve month's earnings had declined from $488 million as of the end of the third quarter of 2000 to $330 million.

As a result of these problems, analysts following IBP issued sharply reduced earnings estimates for FY 2001. Originally, analysts were predicting that IBP would exceed the Rawhide Projections in 2001 by a wide margin. After IBP's poor first quarter, some analysts had reduced their estimate from $2.38 per share to $1.44 a share. *Even accounting for Tyson's attempts to manipulate the analyst community's perception of IBP*, this was a sharp drop.

Tyson contends that the logical inference to be drawn from the record evidence that is available is that IBP will likely have its worst year since 1997, a year which will be well below the company's average performance for all relevant periods. As important, the company's principal driver of growth is performing at markedly diminished levels, thus compromising the company's future results as it enters what is expected to be a tough few years in the fresh meats business.

IBP has several responses to Tyson's evidence. IBP initially notes that Tyson's arguments are unaccompanied by expert evidence that identifies the diminution in IBP's value or earnings potential as a result of its first quarter performance. The absence of such proof is significant. Even after Hankins generated extremely pessimistic projections for IBP in order to justify a lower deal price, Merrill Lynch still concluded that a purchase of IBP at $30 per share was still within the range of fairness and a great long-term value for Tyson. The Merrill Lynch analysis casts great doubt on Tyson's assertion that IBP has suffered a Material Adverse Effect.

IBP also emphasizes the cyclical nature of its businesses. It attributes its poor first quarter to an unexpectedly severe winter. This led ranchers to hold livestock back from market, causing a sharp increase in prices that hurt both the fresh meats business and Foodbrands. Once April was concluded, IBP began to perform more in line with its recent year results, because supplies were increasing and Foodbrands was able to begin to make up its winter margins. Bond testified at trial that he expects IBP to meet or exceed the Rawhide Projection of $1.93 a share in 2001, and the company has publicly indicated that it expects earnings of $1.80 to $2.20 a share. Peterson expressed the same view.

IBP also notes that any cyclical fall is subject to cure by the Agreement's termination date, which was May 15, 2001. By May 15, IBP had two weeks of strong earnings that signaled a strong quarter ahead. Moreover, by that time, cattle that had been held back from market were being sold, leading to plentiful supplies that were expected to last for most of the year.

Not only that, IBP notes that not all analyst reporting services had been as pessimistic as Tyson portrays. In March, Morningstar was reporting a mean analyst prediction of $1.70 per share for IBP in 2001. By May, this had grown to a mean of $1.74 a share. Throughout the same period, Morningstar's consensus prediction was an FY 2002 performance of $2.33 range in March, and $2.38 in May. Therefore, according to Morningstar, the analyst community was predicting that IBP would return to historically healthy earnings next year, and that earnings for this year would fall short of the Rawhide Projections by less than $.20 per share.

IBP also argues that the Impairment Charge does not approach materiality as a big picture item. That Charge is a one-time, non-cash charge, and IBP has taken large charges of that kind as recently as 1999. While IBP does not deny that its decision to buy DFG turned out disastrously, it reminds me that DFG is but a tiny fraction of IBP's overall business and that a total shut-down of DFG would likely have little effect on the future results of a combined Tyson/IBP. And as a narrow asset issue, the charge is insignificant to IBP as a whole.

I am confessedly torn about the correct outcome. As Tyson points out, IBP has only pointed to two weeks of truly healthy results in 2001 before the contract termination date of May 15. Even these results are suspect, Tyson contends, due to the fact that IBP expected markedly better results for the second week just days before the actual results come out. In view of IBP's demonstrated incapacity to accurately predict near-term results, Tyson says with some justification that I should be hesitant to give much weight to IBP's assurances that it will perform well for the rest of the year.

In the end, however, Tyson has not persuaded me that IBP has suffered a Material Adverse Effect. By its own arguments, Tyson has evinced more confidence in stock market analysts than I personally harbor. But its embrace of the analysts is illustrative of why I conclude that Tyson has not met its burden.

As of May 2001, analysts were predicting that IBP would earn between $1.50 to around $1.74 per share in 2001. The analysts were also predicting that IBP would earn between $2.33 and $2.42 per share in 2002. These members are based on reported "mean" or "consensus" analyst numbers. Even at the low end of this *consensus* range, IBP's earnings for the next two years would not be out of line with its historical performance during troughs in the beef cycle. As recently as years 1996–1998, IBP went through a period with a three year average earnings of $1.85 per share. At the high end of the analysts' consensus range, IBP's results would exceed this figure by $.21 per year.

This predicted range of performance from the source that Tyson vouches for suggests that no Material Adverse Effect has occurred. Rather, the analyst views support the conclusion that IBP remains what the baseline evidence suggests it was — a consistently but erratically profitable company struggling to implement a strategy that will reduce the cyclicality of its earnings. Although IBP may not be performing as well as it and Tyson had hoped, IBP's business appears to be in sound enough shape to deliver results of operations in line with the company's recent historical performance. Tyson's own investment banker still believes IBP is fairly priced at $30 per share. The fact that Foodbrands is not yet delivering on the promise of even better performance for IBP during beef troughs is unavailing to Tyson, since §5.10 focuses on IBP as a whole and IBP's performance as an entire company is in keeping with its baseline condition.

Therefore, I conclude that Tyson has not demonstrated a breach of §5.10. I admit to reaching this conclusion with less than the optimal amount of confidence. The record evidence is not of the type that permits certainty.

IBP IS ENTITLED TO AN AWARD OF SPECIFIC PERFORMANCE

Having determined that the Merger Agreement is a valid and enforceable contract that Tyson had no right to terminate, I now turn to the question of whether the Merger Agreement should be enforced by an order of specific performance. Although Tyson's voluminous post-trial briefs argue the merits fully, its briefs fail to argue that a remedy of specific performance is unwarranted in the event that its position on the merits is rejected.

This gap in the briefing is troubling. A compulsory order will require a merger of two public companies with thousands of employees working at facilities that are important to the communities in which they operate. The impact of a forced merger on constituencies beyond the stockholders and top managers of IBP and Tyson weighs heavily on my mind. The prosperity of IBP and Tyson means a great deal to these constituencies. I therefore approach this remedial issue quite cautiously and mindful of the interests of those who will be affected by my decision.

I start with a fundamental question: is this is a truly unique opportunity that cannot be adequately monetized? If the tables were turned and Tyson was seeking to enforce the contract, a great deal of precedent would indicate that the contract should be specifically enforced. In the more typical situation, an acquiror argues that it cannot be made whole unless it can specifically enforce the acquisition agreement, because the target company is unique and will yield value of an unquantifiable nature, once combined with the acquiring company. In this case, the sell-side of the transaction is able to make the same argument, because the Merger Agreement provides the IBP stockholders with a choice of cash or Tyson stock, or a combination of both. Through this choice, the IBP stockholders were offered a chance to share in the upside of what was touted by Tyson as a unique, synergistic combination. This court has not found, and Tyson has not advanced, any compelling reason why sellers in mergers and acquisitions transactions should have less of a right to demand specific performance than buyers, and none has independently come to my mind.

In addition, the determination of a cash damages award will be very difficult in this case. And the amount of any award could be staggeringly large. No doubt the parties would haggle over huge valuation questions, which (Tyson no doubt would argue) must take into account the possibility of a further auction for IBP or other business developments. A damages award can, of course, be shaped; it simply will lack any pretense to precision. An award of specific performance will, I anticipate, entirely eliminate the need for a speculative determination of damages.

Finally, there is no doubt that a remedy of specific performance is practicable. Tyson itself admits that the combination still makes strategic sense. At trial, John Tyson was asked by his own counsel to testify about whether it was fair that Tyson should enter any later auction for IBP hampered by its payment of the Rawhide Termination Fee. This testimony indicates that Tyson Foods is still interested in purchasing IBP, but wants to get its original purchase price back and then buy IBP off the day-old goods table. I consider John Tyson's testimony an admission of the feasibility of specific performance.[14]

Probably the concern that weighs heaviest on my mind is whether specific performance is the right remedy in view of the harsh words that have been said in the course of this litigation. Can these management teams work together?

14. It may also be Tyson's preference, if it has to suffer an adverse judgment. Any damages award will be huge and will result in no value to Tyson.

The answer is that I do not know. Peterson and Bond say they can. I am not convinced, although Tyson's top executives continue to respect the managerial acumen of Peterson and Bond, if not that of their financial subordinates.

What persuades me that specific performance is a workable remedy is that Tyson will have the power to decide all the key management questions itself. It can therefore hand-pick its own management team. While this may be unpleasant for the top level IBP managers who might be replaced, it was a possible risk of the Merger from the get-go and a reality of today's M & A market.

The impact on other constituencies of this ruling also seems tolerable. Tyson's own investment banker thinks the transaction makes sense for Tyson, and is still fairly priced at $30 per share. One would think the Tyson constituencies would be better served on the whole by a specific performance remedy, rather than a large damages award that did nothing but cost Tyson a large amount of money.

In view of these factors, I am persuaded that an award of specific performance is appropriate, regardless of what level of showing was required by IBP. That is, there is clear and convincing evidence to support this award. Such an award is decisively preferable to a vague and imprecise damages remedy that cannot adequately remedy the injury to IBP's stockholders.

CONCLUSION

For all the foregoing reasons, IBP's claim for specific performance is granted. Tyson's claims for relief are dismissed. The parties shall collaborate and present a conforming partial final order no later than June 27. In addition, the parties shall schedule an office conference with the court to occur later that same week.

Suffice to say, this case looms large in the minds of any potential acquirer who is thinking of invoking the MAC clause.

PROBLEM SET 22.1

1. What factors might go into the choice of pricing mechanisms in a merger agreement?
2. Consider the MAC clause from both sides of the deal. What considerations go into the negotiation? Should Tyson have bargained for an easier to implement clause?
3. Later cases have expanded on the holding in *Ziff-Davis*. For example, in Galli v. Metz, 973 F.2d 145 (2d Cir. 1992), the Second Circuit determined that "where a buyer closes on a contract in the full knowledge and acceptance of facts disclosed by the seller which would constitute a breach of warranty under the terms of the contract, the buyer should be foreclosed from later asserting the breach. In that situation, unless that buyer expressly preserves his rights under the warranties (as CBS did in *Ziff-Davis*), we think the buyer has waived the breach." Does this new gloss on Ziff-Davis represent a workable rule?

2. DEAL STRUCTURES

Companies that want to merge have a variety of choices. They could pursue the following options:

- A merger of the parent holding companies.
- A reverse triangular merger of a newly formed subsidiary of the acquirer into the target company where the target company survives as a subsidiary of the acquirer.
- A forward triangular merger where the target company is merged into a newly formed subsidiary of the acquirer and the merger subsidiary survives.
- The formation of a new holding company into which both companies are merged, either directly into the holding company or into separate subsidiaries of the holding company.

Tax and liability considerations tend to drive the choice of structure. The tax issues are summarized in the next section.

We discuss liability issues in more detail in connection with financial distress later in the course, but if there are liability issues in the deal that will push in the direction of using a triangular structure.

The basic rule is that a merger results in the pooling of assets and liabilities.[15] Thus, if one company acquires another and the target has potential tort liabilities (imagine a products liability case), a merger of the two will make the acquiring company's assets available to pay the target's tort creditors. Putting the target into a newly created subsidiary contains the liability, at least so long as there are no grounds for piercing the corporate veil.

If there are significant liability issues, such as a Superfund site or a massively unfunded pension, the deal might be restructured as an asset sale, where the buyer only takes the "good" assets of the target.[16] The normal rule, subject to some important exceptions discussed in later chapters, is that an asset buyer does not take any liabilities not expressly purchased.

If the lingering liabilities are extreme, a sale in bankruptcy becomes an option.[17] We cover that in another forthcoming chapter.[18]

There are other instances in which the form of the transaction will be driven by one party having certain attributes that the parties wish to maintain, regardless of which party is the nominal "acquirer." For example, a change of control provision in a contract or indenture might tilt the balance in favor of having one entity be the "survivor" of the transaction, even if that entity is immediately renamed to reflect the "true" acquiring company.

Quite often you will see deals done as "two-step" transactions. This involves a tender offer (the subject of Chapter 23) followed by a merger. The tender offer involves the purchase of the target's shares, and if sufficiently successful, can

---

15. Del. Gen. Corp. Law §259(a).
16. Del. Gen. Corp. Law §271. Asset sales are the subject of Chapter 24.
17. 11 U.S.C. §363(f).
18. Chapter 29.

allow the second step to be done by "short form" merger that requires no minority shareholder voting.[19]

3. TAXES AND MERGERS

The type of consideration paid in the deal can influence the taxation, and thus the form of the merger.

Forward cash out mergers will generally result in taxation at both the corporate and shareholder levels for the target.[20] The buyer then takes the target's assets at their current fair market value.

For this reason, cash out mergers are often structured as reverse triangular mergers. The target survives the transaction, which prevents taxation at the target level.[21] The target shareholders will still have to pay tax upon receipt of the proceeds, but at least the proceeds are not reduced by corporate tax.

If the consideration is at least partially in shares, there may be ways in which the parties can avoid incurring taxes at the time of the deal.

Direct mergers — where the target merges directly into the acquirer (or vice versa) — will generally be nontaxable to all concerned, namely the target, the acquirer, and the target shareholders. The shareholders must receive at least 40 percent of their total consideration in stock of the surviving corporation.

In the case of a forward triangular merger, there are two additional requirements before the deal will be tax-free. First, the acquiring subsidiary is not allowed to issue any stock in the transaction.

Thus, if the buyer wishes to assume the target's preferred stock, for example, it must be replaced with new stock from the parent company — the subsidiary that is the actual buyer must not assume the shares. Otherwise the stock must be redeemed before the closing.

Second, the subsidiary must acquire "substantially all" of the assets of target, generally 90 percent of net assets and 70 percent of gross assets.

In a reverse triangular merger, the acquirer must obtain at least 80 percent of all of target's voting stock and 80 percent of each other class of target stock in exchange for its voting stock. Thus, any preferred stock of Target must be given a vote and left outstanding at the target level, exchanged for acquirer voting stock or redeemed before the merger. In addition, the target must hold substantially all the assets of the new buyer subsidiary after the transaction is completed (which would normally be the case).

In Rev. Rul. 2001-26, the IRS made it clear that a two-step reverse triangular merger is permissible, provided that the two steps occur under an integrated plan. In 2001, the IRS also made it clear that the requirement that the target "hold" substantially all of its assets and substantially all of the subsidiary's assets

---

19. Del. Gen. Corp. Law §253.
20. *See, e.g.*, Rev. Rul. 69-6, 1969-1 C.B. 104 (ruling that the merger of target into acquirer, which failed to qualify as a tax-free reorganization, resulted in two levels of tax).
21. *See, e.g.*, Rev. Rul. 79-273, 1979-2 C.B. 125.

after the merger is not violated where target sells assets following the merger if the target retains the sales proceeds and does not, for example, distribute them to its new parent.

All of which is to say that you really should take the Corporate Tax class if you want to practice in this area.

4. BREAKUP FEES

Once the parties sign a deal, they often want to make sure that the deal happens.[22] This is especially true in friendly deals.

But the board has duties in most states—such as the *Revlon* duties in Delaware—that require the board to consider other offers, particularly when those offers value the company at a higher level than the preferred deal.

Moreover, there is the chance that a deal fails not because of a competing offer, but because one of the closing contingencies was not met. For example, maybe a regulator would not approve the deal. Or the buyer found out that some representation was breached and then exercised its right to cancel the closing. But in either case, the original buyer by that point has expended some degree of effort in making its offer. Management has considered the deal from the business side, while the buyer's lawyers have spent some time drafting an agreement, and probably the many letters that preceded the agreement. In addition to these out-of-pocket expenses, the buyer may have incurred less quantifiable costs resulting from the firm's expending time on the deal that could have been put toward other projects (i.e., opportunity costs).

The target can incur costs, too, and sometimes its choice of offers might be influenced by the risk that a deal will not close and the target will have incurred costs for nothing.[23]

The most common way to address these issues is through breakup fees, with fees paid to the target sometimes termed "reverse" breakup fees.[24]

SILVER LAKE BREAKUP RULES MAKE ENDING DELL BID COSTLY
By Peter Burrows and Jeffrey McCracken—April 22, 2013, Bloomberg.com[25]

Silver Lake Management LLC and Michael Dell attached such stringent conditions to their Dell Inc. (DELL) buyout proposal that they may have little choice but to stick with the deal even as the personal-computer industry contracts at a faster-than-predicted pace.

---

22. Marcel Kahan & Edward Rock, *How to Prevent Hard Cases from Making Bad Law: Bear Stearns, Delaware, and the Strategic Use of Comity*, 58 Emory L.J. 713, 726 (2009).
23. Steven M. Davidoff, *The Failure of Private Equity*, 82 S. Cal. L. Rev. 481, 518 (2009).
24. Afra Afsharipour, *Transforming the Allocation of Deal Risk Through Reverse Termination Fees*, 63 Vand. L. Rev. 1161, 1224 (2010).
25. Used with permission of Bloomberg L.P. © 2013. All rights reserved.

Walking away from the $24.4 billion leveraged buyout means the Silver Lake-led group would have to pay as much as $750 million to extricate itself, according to the merger agreement. The terms also let Dell sue the group to force it to complete the transaction.

Dell's stock fell below the original $13.65-a-share offer on April 19 amid speculation that the deal might unravel after Blackstone Group LP (BX) abandoned its counteroffer, citing "the rapidly eroding financial profile of Dell" and greater weakness in the PC market than the company is projecting. Still, the Silver Lake-led group will probably stick with its plan, rather than subject itself to financial penalties, said Erik Gordon, a professor at the Ross School of Business at the University of Michigan in Ann Arbor.

"Silver Lake is in a corner," Gordon said. The provision allowing the company to sue is "a gun to Silver Lake's head. If it wants to back out, it will have to negotiate a settlement that makes the company happy or close the deal," he said.

When CEO Dell and Silver Lake began buyout discussions last year, the PC maker predicted operating income of $5.6 billion for the fiscal year through January 2014, according to a March 29 filing. That forecast was reduced to $3 billion after three revisions and a record drop in PC shipments during the first quarter.

Deal Terms

Neither Silver Lake nor the banks financing the buyout — Barclays Plc, Bank of America Corp., Royal Bank of Canada and Credit Suisse Group AG — have expressed a desire to get out of the deal after Blackstone pulled out April 19, said a person with knowledge of the matter who declined to be identified because the information is private.

David Frink, a spokesman for Dell, declined to comment. A spokesman for Menlo Park, California-based Silver Lake had no immediate comment. Dell said in a filing April 19 that it continued to support the agreement with Silver Lake and expected the deal to close by the end of the fiscal second quarter, which ends in July.

Chief Executive Officer Michael Dell and Silver Lake agreed to the restrictions, which also included limits on their ability to match bids for Dell, in order to create a deal that would withstand shareholder scrutiny, people familiar with the matter said after the agreement was announced Feb. 5. The breakup fee is also higher than normal, said the people, who asked not to be identified because the talks were private.

Silver Lake

Under the terms, the Silver Lake-led group agreed to pay the company $250 million if it withdraws the offer because of changes in tax law, or if other legal obstacles emerge. The higher $750 million penalty applies if the group simply backs out, breaching the agreement.

Unforeseeable developments that would be considered a "material adverse effect," such as representations turning out not to be true, could also let Silver Lake and CEO Dell pull out of the agreement with fewer or no penalties. Any dispute taken to court would probably result in a deal, according to Barbara Black, a law professor at Columbia University in New York.

"A court could order Silver Lake to complete the deal rather than just forcing the private-equity fund to pay Dell damages," Black said in an interview.

Silver Lake came close to walking away in January, during a stalemate that wasn't resolved until it increased its final offer by 5 cents a share.

PC SLUMP

"If Silver Lake closes the deal, it has time to address its problems if the deal turns out to be a bad deal," Gordon said. "If Silver Lake balks, it has a problem, today, and probably kisses a couple of hundred million dollars goodbye."

Research firm IDC released data earlier this month showing that PC shipments plummeted 14 percent in the first quarter, a faster pace than its projection for a 7.7 percent decline, as demand dropped in every region of the world. The slump comes as consumers shun PCs in favor of smartphones and tablets to check e-mail, browse the Web and watch television and movies.

Blackstone had offered to pay at least $14.25 a share to current Dell investors with an option to hold onto some of their stake through a so-called equity stub.

LOGICAL INVESTOR

Blackstone pulled its offer after deciding that Dell's plan to expand share in the $3 trillion enterprise-computing market was still years away, a person familiar with the matter said last week. Profits from new products weren't going to be generated fast enough as the PC business deteriorated, said one of the people, who declined to be identified because the details were private.

"The PC problem is just the start of it," said Tripatinder Chowdhry, an analyst at Global Equities Research in San Francisco. "Enterprise servers are going to get hit, too."

Before Blackstone dropped its bid, the stock had been trading at a premium to the offer on speculation that a bidding war would erupt after Blackstone and billionaire investor Carl Icahn proposed higher offers. Dell's largest outside shareholders including Southeastern Asset Management and T. Rowe Price Group Inc. also opposed the original bid as being too low.

"Blackstone was viewed as a more logical investor to follow through with this deal, so with them gone, the prospect of a bidding war is also gone," said Rich Kugele, an analyst at Needham & Co. in Boston who has a hold rating on the shares.

ICAHN'S PROPOSAL

Blackstone's exit also followed reports that International Business Machines Corp. (IBM) is in talks to sell its low-end server division to Lenovo Group Ltd.

(992) Servers have been a bright spot for Dell, posting 18 percent sales growth in the latest quarter.

Dave Johnson, one of the Blackstone executives overseeing the firm's bid, joined the buyout group in January from Dell, where he led mergers and acquisitions for almost four years. Before that, he served in a similar role at IBM, making him uniquely qualified to assess the risks and rewards involved in a proposal to buy the PC maker.

Even if Silver Lake remains committed, Michael Dell and the private-equity firm will have to deflect a rival proposal by Icahn, who has offered to pay $15 a share in cash for as much as 58 percent of Dell's stock. The company has said that Icahn's proposed offer could be superior to the Silver Lake group's deal for all of the company.

PROXY FIGHT

Dell said April 16 that Icahn had agreed not to amass more than a 10 percent stake in the company, or to join with other shareholders to build more than a 15 percent holding.

Icahn said he's retaining the right to start a proxy fight and seek to replace Dell's directors with his own candidates. That's not likely to happen until after a vote by shareholders at an annual meeting, which hasn't yet been scheduled yet. A majority shareholder vote in favor of the deal, excluding Michael Dell's 15.6 percent stake, is required for approval of the joint offer with Silver Lake, according to the agreement.

The key issue with breakup fees and other deal protection is when is the breakup fee too high or the protection too strong? Both target and buyer would like to receive a very large fee, but Delaware case law makes clear that a breakup fee large enough to deter other bidders from showing up is unenforceable.

Moreover, Delaware case law also provides that directors must negotiate for a "fiduciary out." One noted Delaware scholar (and former judge) describes a fiduciary out as follows:

> Fiduciary outs are anomalous contract provisions that generally provide an escape hatch to a target corporation from performing some contractual undertaking meant to advance the closing of an acquisition agreement. Thus, after a target board has concluded a friendly merger negotiation, it will often approve the inclusion of terms in the merger agreement that limit its future options. Most commonly these provisions will: (i) restrict the target corporation's ability to shop for alternative transactions or to supply confidential information to alternative buyers until the shareholders have voted on this deal; (ii) require the board to submit this merger agreement and no other merger agreement to the shareholders for approval; and (iii) require the board to recommend to shareholders that they approve the agreement. One, of course, understands why a buyer might demand such terms in its contract . . .
>
> A fiduciary out typically provides that if some triggering event occurs (often the receipt of a defined "Superior Offer" and sometimes the receipt from the corporation's outside lawyers of an opinion to the effect that the board must *as a matter of*

fiduciary duty do an act that the contract forbids or must not do an act the contract requires), then the doing of that act (or the refraining from doing a required act) will not constitute a breach.[26]

5. DYNEGY MERGER AGREEMENT

With that background behind us, we are ready to look at a real merger agreement. The merger agreement is available on the course webpage, and relates to a merger between Dynegy and entities controlled by Carl Icahn, a well-known investor.[27] The Merger Agreement is attached to an 8-K that explains the deal. That's a good place to start reading.

In addition, take a look at the Dynegy 2010 annual report we looked at in connection with Chapter 1. Pages 2-3, F-24, F-72, and F-73 to F-74 are relevant here. Be prepared to discuss the merger agreement in light of the above reading.

---

26. William T. Allen, *Understanding Fiduciary Outs: The What and the Why of an Anomalous Concept*, 55 Bus. Law. 653 (2000).
    27. http://www.forbes.com/profile/carl-icahn/

23

TENDER OFFERS

A *tender offer* is an offer to buy shares from the market,[1] typically at a premium over the price that the shares traded at before the announcement of the offer.[2]

As noted in Chapter 22, quite often deals are done as two-step transactions, where a buyer purchases a majority position through a tender offer, and then proceeds to effectuate a merger with the target company that is now a subsidiary of the buyer. The merger changes the subsidiary into a wholly-owned subsidiary.

The other context in which tender offers are used is hostile deals. If the buyer cannot convince the target board to accept its offer, a tender offer that makes the buyer the majority shareholder is a key way around that deadlock. Given the power that most boards have, particularly with regard to poison pills as discussed later, a purely hostile takeover will often have to be combined with some sort of proxy contest, to change the composition of the board, or a litigation strategy that argues that the board is breaching its duties by not considering the proffered deal.

By and large, tender offers were unregulated until the late 1960s. State statutory corporate law has little to say about secondary market share purchases, and the federal securities laws originally did not address tender offers except in the general sense of prohibiting fraud in connection with the securities markets. That changed in 1968 when the Williams Act amended the '34 Act. We discuss the Williams Act later, which you might have also covered to some extent in your Business Associations class.

Initially state fiduciary duty law did not address tender offers either. This provided a strong incentive for deals to be done by tender offer, and if the tender offer obtained more than 90 percent of the outstanding shares, the second step merger could happen by way of a short form merger, thus avoiding the entire body of law that the Delaware courts had developed to address take-overs by controlling shareholders.[3]

---

1. We cover tender offers for debt, commonly called exchange offers, in Chapter 26.

2. In Wellman v. Dickinson, 475 F. Supp. 783, 823-824 (S.D.N.Y. 1979), *aff'd on other grounds*, 682 F.2d 355 (2d Cir. 1982), *cert. denied*, 460 U.S. 1069 (1983). *See* Rand v. Anaconda-Ericsson, Inc., 794 F.2d 843, 848-849 (2d Cir. 1986), *cert. denied*, 479 U.S. 987 (1986).

3. In a nutshell, this law requires controlling shareholders to show the deal's "entire fairness," unless an independent board committee approves the deal or a "majority of the minority" of shareholders

That has begun to change in recent years, although this case law comes from Delaware chancery (trial) courts, so it is hard to say if this development is permanent.

IN RE CNX GAS CORPORATION SHAREHOLDERS LITIGATION

4 A.3d 397, Court of Chancery of Delaware
C.A. No. 5377-VCL | Submitted: May 24, 2010 | Decided: May 25, 2010

LASTER, Vice Chancellor.

Representatives of a putative class of minority stockholders have challenged a controlling stockholder freeze-out structured as a first-step tender offer to be followed by second-step short-form merger. The plaintiffs have sued the controlling stockholder, its controlled subsidiary, and the four members of the subsidiary board. Three of the subsidiary directors are also directors of the controller. The fourth is an independent outsider and the sole member of the special committee formed to respond to the controller's tender offer. The plaintiffs have moved for a preliminary injunction against the transaction.

I apply the unified standard for reviewing controlling stockholder freeze-outs described in In re Cox Communications, Inc. Shareholders Litigation, 879 A.2d 604 (Del.Ch.2005). Under that standard, the business judgment rule applies when a freeze-out is conditioned on *both* the affirmative recommendation of a special committee *and* the approval of a majority of the unaffiliated stockholders. Because the special committee did not recommend in favor of the tender offer, the transaction at issue in this case will be reviewed for entire fairness. Although the lack of an affirmative recommendation is sufficient to trigger fairness review under *Cox Communications*, the plaintiffs also have shown that the special committee was not provided with the authority to bargain with the controller on an arms' length basis. The plaintiffs similarly have established a reasonable basis to question the effectiveness of the majority-of-the-minority tender condition.

Because a fairness standard applies to the challenged transaction, any harm to the putative class can be remedied through a post-closing damages action. There are no viable disclosure claims, and the tender offer is not coercive. I therefore decline to issue a preliminary injunction.

Did the plaintiffs win or lose here?

---

approves the deal, in which case the standard stays at entire fairness but the burden of proof shifts to the plaintiffs.

After a tender offer, the second step of a deal will involve a controlling shareholder. But the Delaware courts have held this law does not apply in short form mergers. Glassman v. Unocal Exploration Corp., 777 A.2d 242 (Del. 2001) (holding that absent fraud or illegality an appraisal is the exclusive remedy available to stockholders in a §253 short form merger, entire fairness doctrine does not apply, and no need for the target to use a special committee because there is no opportunity to "deal" with majority holder).

1. STRUCTURAL ISSUES

Why pick a tender offer or a two-step structure instead of just a merger? There are several reasons, beginning with the speed of tender offers. A merger requires a shareholder vote, and that usually requires SEC approval of a proxy statement and also a registration statement if stock is to be issued in the transaction.[4]

On the other hand, all-cash tender offers may be consummated quickly, subject only to a minimum offer period of 20 business days from commencement. This reduces the degree of market risk the buyer is exposed to in the period between contract and closing.

And then there is the more favorable standard of review, noted earlier. Recent case law imposes more procedural requirements, but once met the transaction is less likely to be challenged (or challenged successfully) after closing.

A tender offer also does not suffer from the so-called dead vote problem that arises in merger transactions when a substantial number of shareholders sell their shares after the record date and then do not vote, or do not change an outdated vote, after they have sold their economic interest. The only vote in a tender offer is the implicit one involved in taking the consideration offered.

However, a two-step structure involving a tender offer is not necessarily always preferable to a one-step merger. For example, in a deal that involves a regulatory approval process, the tender offer would have to remain open until the regulatory approval was obtained, because the buyer must condition the offer on authorization to buy the target. During that period the parties might have been able to obtain shareholders' votes on a straight merger.

Also tender offers can sometimes be difficult to finance if the buyer is reliant on outside funding. The most obvious source of collateral for the buyer is the target shares that it will be acquiring, but the Federal Reserve Board's margin rules restrict loans secured by public company stock to half of the shares' market value. In a merger, the buyer can have direct access to the target's assets and use those for collateral for the loan.

2. TOP-UP OPTIONS

JOANNE OLSON v. EV3, INC.

37 Del. J. Corp. L. 229, Court of Chancery of Delaware
C.A. No. 5583-VCL | Submitted: Jan. 28, 2011 | Decided: Feb. 21, 2011

LASTER, Vice Chancellor.
Plaintiff Joanne Olson challenged the use of a top-up option to facilitate a two-step acquisition. The parties agreed to a settlement that achieved everything the

4. *See* 15 U.S.C. §78n; 17 C.F.R §§240.14a-1 to-20 (rules for proxy solicitation); *id.* at §240.14a-101 (information required in proxy statement); *id.* at §239.25 (information "for the registration of securities issued in business combination transactions").

plaintiff could have hoped to accomplish through litigation. The parties then attempted without success to negotiate the amount of a fee award that the defendants would not oppose. On January 28, 2011, I approved the settlement. I now grant the plaintiff a fee award of $1.1 million, representing the full amount requested.

I. FACTUAL BACKGROUND

The facts are drawn from the record presented for settlement approval and the parties' briefing on the fee dispute.

A. THE DEVELOPMENT OF TOP-UP OPTIONS

A top-up option is a stock option designed to allow the holder to increase its stock ownership to at least 90 percent, the threshold needed to effect a short-form merger under Section 253 of the Delaware General Corporation Law (the "DGCL"), 8 *Del. C.* §253. A top-up option typically is granted to the acquirer to facilitate a two-step acquisition in which the acquirer agrees first to commence a tender offer for at least a majority of the target corporation's common stock, then to consummate a back-end merger at the tender offer price if the tender is successful.

The top-up option speeds deal closure if a majority of the target's stockholders have endorsed the acquisition by tendering their shares. Once the acquirer closes the first-step tender offer, it owns sufficient shares to approve a long-form merger pursuant to Section 251 of the DGCL, 8 *Del. C.* §251. Under the merger agreement governing the two-step acquisition, the parties contractually commit to complete the second-step merger. A long-form merger, however, requires a board resolution and recommendation and a subsequent stockholder vote, among other steps. *See id.* §251(b) & (c). When the deal involves a public company, holding the stockholder vote requires preparing a proxy or information statement in compliance with the federal securities law and clearing the Securities and Exchange Commission. This process can take two to three months and cost tens of thousands of dollars.

The top-up option accelerates closing by facilitating a short-form merger. Pursuant to Section 253, a parent corporation owning at least 90% of the outstanding shares of each class of stock of the subsidiary entitled to vote may consummate a short-form merger by a resolution of the parent board and subsequent filing of a certificate of ownership and merger with the Delaware Secretary of State. *See* 8 *Del. C.* §253(a). This simplified process requires neither subsidiary board action nor a stockholder vote.

In a third-party arm's-length transaction, the top-up option offers the constituent corporations what appears to be a win-win. The second step closes sooner, minimizing transaction risk for both sides. Target stockholders get the consideration faster, avoiding lost time value of money. The whole process costs less. Not surprisingly, given these advantages, top-up options have become ubiquitous in two-step acquisitions. They appeared in more than 93% of two-step deals during 2007, 100% of two-step deals during 2008, and more than 91% of two-step deals during 2009.

B. PRE-EV3 CHALLENGES TO TOP-UP OPTIONS

From time to time, plaintiffs have brought claims challenging top-up options. Prior to 2010, there were no written Delaware opinions addressing this deal feature. The only decisions were two transcript rulings, each ruling on a motion to expedite. *See* In re Gateway, Inc. S'holders Litig., C.A. No. 3219-VCN (Del. Ch. Sep. 14, 2007) (TRANSCRIPT); NECA–IBEW v. Prima Energy Corp., C.A. No. 522-VCL (Del. Ch. June 30, 2004) (TRANSCRIPT) . . .

As in *Prima Energy*, the *Gateway* plaintiffs sought an expedited hearing on a motion for preliminary injunction. Faced with *Prima Energy*, the *Gateway* plaintiffs did not claim interference with voting rights. They instead argued that the option impermissibly enabled the defendants to avoid fiduciary duty review because appraisal would be the stockholders' exclusive remedy under Glassman v. Unocal Exploration Corp., 777 A.2d 242 (Del.2001). Vice Chancellor Noble granted the motion to expedite without explicitly addressing the challenges to the top-up option. He generally described the plaintiffs' claims as "far from compelling," but scheduled an injunction hearing because the plaintiffs had demonstrated a minimally colorable claim based on a "confluence of many different factors."

The *Gateway* plaintiffs also argued that the top-up option coerced stockholders to tender because of the threat of "appraisal dilution." According to this theory, a top-up option threatens stockholders who might seek appraisal with the issuance of a significant number of shares at less than what the dissenting stockholder believes is fair value. Because the top-up shares will be outstanding at the time of the short-form merger, any remaining stockholders who might otherwise have sought appraisal would find their proportionate interest in the firm diluted by the issuance of what they regard as underpriced shares. The top-up option allegedly makes appraisal less attractive and thereby coerces stockholders who otherwise would seek appraisal into tendering for reasons unrelated to the economic merits of the transaction. The *Gateway* case settled after expedited discovery and briefing, with the settlement consideration consisting of supplemental disclosures and an agreement by the acquirer not to argue that any shares issued pursuant to the top-up option or any related consideration should be considered for purposes of appraisal.

C. THE MERGER AGREEMENT

At a time when *Prima Energy* and *Gateway* provided the only guidance on top-up options, defendant ev3, Inc. ("ev3" or the "Company") and Covidien Group S.a.r.1. ("Covidien") entered into an agreement and plan of merger (the "Merger Agreement" or "MA"). The Merger Agreement provided for Covidien to acquire ev3 via a standard two-step acquisition, facilitated by a top-up option if certain conditions were met. In the first step, Covidien's wholly owned acquisition subsidiary, COV Delaware Corporation ("COV"), would offer to purchase ev3's outstanding shares for $22.50 per share in cash (the "Tender Offer").

If COV owned a majority of ev3's outstanding shares after the Tender Offer, then the parties would effect a prompt second-step merger in which all remaining ev3 stockholders would receive the same consideration, subject to their right to seek appraisal (the "Merger"). So long as COV obtained a majority of ev3's shares in the first-step Tender Offer, then the parties were contractually obligated to complete the second-step Merger "as promptly as practicable." If COV acquired sufficient shares to do so, COV was required to close the second step via a short-form merger.

Section 1.4 of the Merger Agreement granted COV a top-up option. It stated:

Section 1.4 *Top-up Option.*

(a) *Grant and Availability of Top-Up Option.* Subject to the terms and conditions set forth herein, the Company hereby grants to the Purchaser an irrevocable option (the "*Top-Up Option*") to purchase, at a price per share equal to the Offer Price, that number of newly issued Shares (the "*Top-Up Option Shares*") equal to the lowest number of Shares that, when added to the number of Shares owned by the Purchaser, the Parent and their wholly owned Subsidiaries at the time of exercise of the Top-up Option (including all Shares validly tendered and not properly withdrawn in the Offer at the Share Acceptance Time but excluding Shares tendered pursuant to guaranteed delivery procedures that have not yet been delivered in settlement or satisfaction of such guarantee), constitutes one Share more than 90% of all outstanding Shares (assuming the issuance of the Top-up Option Shares). The Top-up Option shall only be exercised one time by the Purchaser in whole but not in part. The Top-up Option shall be exercised by the Purchaser (and the Parent shall cause the Purchaser to exercise the Top-up Option) promptly (but in no event later than one (1) Business Day) after the Share Acceptance Time or the expiration of a Subsequent Offering Period, as applicable, if (i) at the Share Acceptance Time or the expiration of any such Subsequent Offering Period, as applicable, the Parent, the Purchaser or any wholly owned Subsidiary own in the aggregate at least 75% of all Shares then outstanding (excluding Shares tendered pursuant to guaranteed delivery procedures that have not yet been delivered in settlement or satisfaction of such guarantee) and (ii) after giving effect to the exercise of the Top-up Option, the Parent, the Purchaser and any wholly owned Subsidiary of the Parent or the Purchaser would own in the aggregate one share more than 90% of the number of outstanding Shares (after giving effect to the issuance of the Top-up Option Shares but excluding Shares tendered pursuant to guaranteed delivery procedures that have not yet been delivered in settlement or satisfaction of such guarantee); *provided, however,* that the obligation of the Purchaser to exercise the Top-up Option and the obligation of the Company to deliver Top-up Option Shares upon the exercise of the Top-up Option is subject to the conditions, unless waived by the Company, that (x) no provision of any applicable Law and no applicable order, injunction or other judgment shall prohibit the exercise of the Top-up Option or the delivery of the Top-up Option Shares in respect of such exercise, (y) upon exercise of the Top-up Option, the number of Shares owned by the Parent or the Purchaser or any wholly owned Subsidiary of the Parent or the Purchaser (excluding Shares tendered pursuant to guaranteed delivery procedures that have not yet been delivered in settlement or satisfaction of such guarantee) constitutes one Share more than 90% of the number of Shares that will be outstanding immediately after the issuance of the Top-up Option Shares, and (z) the number of Top-up Option Shares issued pursuant to the

Top-up Option shall in no event exceed the number of authorized and unissued shares of Company Common Stock less the maximum number of shares of Company Common Stock potentially necessary for issuance with respect to all outstanding Company Stock Options, Company Restricted Stock, Company RSUs or other obligations of the Company. The parties shall cooperate to ensure that the issuance of the Top-up Option Shares is accomplished consistent with all applicable Laws, including compliance with an applicable exemption from registration of the Top-up Option Shares under the Securities Act; provided, further, that the Top-up Option shall terminate concurrently with the termination of this Agreement.

(b) *Exercise of Top-up Option.* Upon the exercise of the Top-up Option in accordance with *Section 1.4(a)*, the Parent shall so notify the Company and shall set forth in such notice (i) the number of Shares that are expected to be owned by the Parent, the Purchaser or any wholly owned Subsidiary of the Parent or the Purchaser immediately preceding the purchase of the Top-up Option Shares and (ii) a place and time for the closing of the purchase of the Top-up Option Shares (which, subject to applicable Law and any required regulatory approvals, shall be effected as promptly as practicable and not more than two (2) Business Days after date such notice is delivered to the Company). Such notice shall also include an undertaking signed by the Parent and the Purchaser that, as promptly as practicable following such exercise of the Top-up Option, the Purchaser shall, and the Parent shall cause the Purchaser to, as promptly as practicable after such exercise and the delivery by the Company of the Top-up Option Shares, consummate the Merger in accordance with the terms hereof. The Company shall, as soon as practicable following receipt of such notice, notify the Parent and the Purchaser of the number of Shares then outstanding and the number of Top-up Option Shares. At the closing of the purchase of the Top-up Option Shares, the Parent or the Purchaser, as the case may be, shall pay the Company the aggregate price required to be paid for the Top-up Option Shares, and the Company shall cause to be issued to the Parent or the Purchaser, as applicable, a certificate representing the Top-up Option Shares. The aggregate purchase price payable for the Top-up Option Shares may be paid by the Parent or the Purchaser (i) in cash or (ii) by executing and delivering to the Company a promissory note having a principal amount equal to the balance of the aggregate purchase price for the Top-up Option Shares, or some combination thereof. Any such promissory note shall be on terms as provided by the Parent or the Purchaser, which terms shall be reasonably satisfactory to the Company. Upon the delivery of the appropriate exercise notice and the tender of the consideration described above, the Purchaser shall, to the extent permitted by applicable Law, be deemed to be the holder of record of the Top-up Option Shares issuable upon that exercise, notwithstanding that certificates representing those Top-up Option Shares shall not then be actually delivered to the Purchaser or the Company shall have failed to [sic] refused to designate the account described above.

(c) *Accredited Investor Status.* The parties shall cooperate to ensure that the issuance of the Top-up Option Shares is accomplished consistent with all applicable Law. Consistent therewith, the Parent and the Purchaser acknowledge that the Top-up Option Shares that the Purchaser may acquire upon exercise of the Top-up Option will not be registered under the Securities Act of 1933, as amended (the "*Securities Act*"), and will be issued in reliance upon an exemption thereunder for transactions not involving a public offering. Each of the Parent and the Purchaser hereby represents and warrants to the Company that the Purchaser will be upon the purchase of the Top-up Option Shares an "accredited investor," as defined in

Rule 501 of Regulation D under the Securities Act. The Purchaser agrees that the Top-up Option and the Top-up Option Shares to be acquired upon exercise of the Top-up Option are being and will be acquired by the Purchaser for the purpose of investment and not with a view to, or for resale in connection with, any distribution thereof (within the meaning of the Securities Act).

Section 1.4(a) of the Merger Agreement thus provided COV with an irrevocable option to purchase, at a price per share equal to the Tender Offer price, a number of shares that when added to the shares owned by Covidien and its affiliates would constitute one share more than 90% of all outstanding shares. Section 1.4(b) of the Merger Agreement provided that COV could pay for the Top-up Option Shares in cash or by delivering a promissory note to ev3 with a principal amount equal to the purchase price of the Top-up Shares, *with the promissory note's terms to be set in the future and determined in the first instance by Covidien or COV.* MA §1.4(b) ("Any such promissory note shall be on terms as provided by the Parent or the Purchaser, which terms shall be reasonably satisfactory to the Company.").

The record reflects that the attorneys working on the Merger Agreement focused on the payment feature of the Top-up Option. ev3's counsel originally proposed terms for the promissory note. Covidien's counsel struck those terms and substituted the language contemplating a future determination, and ev3 accepted the change. I suspect the drafters saw little reason to dwell on the note's terms when they believed it would be outstanding for a matter of hours. If the Top-up Option were exercised, it would be for the purpose of effecting a short-form merger. The shares would be issued and the note outstanding only for the period of time required for COV to file a certificate of ownership and merger with the Delaware Secretary of State.

Nominally, however, the size of the promissory note and the number of shares issued would be prodigious. As of June 7, 2010, ev3 had (i) 300 million shares of common stock authorized, (ii) 114,792,961 shares issued and outstanding, (iii) 8,068,577 share of common stock issuable upon the exercise of outstanding options and (iv) 216,451 shares of common stock underlying restricted stock units. This left 176,922,011 shares of common stock authorized and available for issuance as Top-up Option Shares. COV would reach the 75% threshold if it acquired a total of approximately 86.1 million of ev3's approximately 114.8 million outstanding shares. To raise its ownership from 75% to 90%, COV would need approximately 172.2 million Top-up Option Shares, or one-and-a-half times ev3's pre-exercise capitalization. At $22.50 per share, the nominal cost to COV to exercise the Top-up Option and increase its ownership from 75% to 90% would be approximately $3.9 billion.

D. THE STOCKHOLDER LITIGATION

On June 18, 2010, Olson filed a detailed, 34-page complaint and sought a preliminary injunction blocking the transaction on the grounds that (i) the Top-up Option failed to comply with Sections 152, 153 and 157 of the DGCL, 8 *Del. C.* §§152, 153 & 157, (ii) the exercise of the Top-up Option would coerce stockholders to tender because of the threat of "appraisal dilution," (iii) the ev3 directors breached their fiduciary duties in granting the Top-up Option, and (iv) COV aided and abetted their breach. Olson simultaneously moved for an expedited hearing on her injunction application. On June 24, the defendants filed a lengthy and substantive opposition to the motion to expedite. Olson replied on June 25. A hearing on the motion to expedite took place later that day.

I granted the motion to expedite. Two factors weighed critically in that determination. First, Olson's complaint advanced a strong claim that the Top-up Option as granted in the Merger Agreement failed to comply with Sections 152, 153, and 157 of the DGCL. If COV effected the second-step Merger using shares received through the exercise of an invalid option, then the Merger itself would be subject to attack as *ultra vires* and void. Second, at the time of the hearing, *Prima Energy* and *Gateway* were the only extant Delaware authorities on top-up options. Neither addressed the creative notion of "appraisal dilution" . . . there is Delaware authority that can be cited in support of the post-exercise share calculation that underlies the theory. The "appraisal dilution" claim therefore was colorable, if barely so.

The Olson complaint also included disclosure claims on issues unrelated to the Top-up Option, such as the sufficiency of the description of the investment bankers' work. After reviewing the disclosures issued in connection with the Tender Offer, I held that the disclosure claims were not colorable and declined to expedite that aspect of the litigation.

At the conclusion of the hearing on the motion to expedite, I scheduled a hearing on the plaintiff's application for a preliminary injunction for July 8, 2010. Discovery was limited to the challenges to the Top-up Option. A flurry of litigation activity ensued. On June 29, the defendants produced approximately 6,000 pages of documents. On June 30, the plaintiff deposed ev3's Chief Financial Officer as the Rule 30(b)(6) designee. Later on June 30, the defendants produced approximately 1,500 additional pages of documents.

E. THE SETTLEMENT

One week after the hearing on the motion to expedite, the parties entered into a memorandum of understanding dated June 2, 2010 (the "MOU"). Although the settlement was reached quickly, it provided the plaintiff with all the relief she could have hoped to achieve on the merits.

The MOU called for comprehensive amendments to the Top-up Option and Merger Agreement to cure the statutory challenges. Section 1.4(b) of the Merger Agreement was amended to specify the consideration to be received for the Top-up Shares. The amended provision specified the material terms of the promissory note and mandated that the par value of the Top-up Shares be paid in cash. To ensure board-level compliance with the DGCL, the MOU required that the amendments to the Merger Agreement be approved by the ev3 board of directors at a meeting where the terms and operation of the Top-up Option were thoroughly reviewed and the necessary statutory determinations made. In addition, Section 9.1 of the Merger Agreement was supplemented to prevent any amendment of Section 1.4 in a manner that would adversely affect the rights of other ev3 stockholders after COV became a majority stockholder.

The MOU resolved any concern about "appraisal dilution" by providing that Top-up Option Shares and related consideration would not be considered for purposes of appraisal. The MOU also provided for supplemental disclosures describing the revised terms of the Top-up Option and how it would operate.

[The court then proceeded to consider the merits of the plaintiff's original claims as part of approving the settlement agreement, as the parties could not agree on how much attorney's fees the plaintiff's should recover.]

The theory of "appraisal dilution" . . . founders on the language of the appraisal statute and the real-world operation of the appraisal process. But assuming there remained some residual uncertainty from *Cavalier Oil*, the problem can be fixed with ease. As the settlements in *Gateway* and in this case demonstrate, a respondent corporation can agree not to count top-up shares and the related consideration in any appraisal proceeding arising out of the merger.

For all these reasons, I regard the settlement of the "appraisal dilution" claim as conferring at best a minimal benefit. It eliminated legal uncertainty that the constituent corporations could have addressed themselves by agreement in their disclosure documents. A fee award of $100,000 adequately compensates the plaintiff for this aspect of the settlement.

B.   THE BENEFITS CONFERRED BY REMEDYING THE STATUTORY INVALIDITY
     ISSUES

In contrast to the questionable benefit resulting from the elimination of "appraisal dilution," the litigation conferred a meaningful benefit on ev3 and its stockholders by addressing the statutory problems with the Top-up Option. As originally structured in the Merger Agreement, the Top-up Option and any shares issued upon its exercise likely were void. To the extent a short-form merger closed in reliance on the resulting shares, the validity of the Merger could be attacked. The invalidity of that transaction in turn could have called into question subsequent acts by the surviving corporation. By defusing a potential corporate landmine, Olson and her counsel conferred an unquantifiable but nevertheless significant corporate benefit on ev3 and its stockholders — and on Covidien and its stockholders as well.

Section 157 of the DGCL provides, in the pertinent part, as follows:

(b) The terms upon which, including the time or times which may be limited or unlimited in duration, at or within which, and the consideration (including a formula by which such consideration may be determined) for which any such shares may be acquired from the corporation upon the exercise of any such right or option, shall be such as shall be stated in the certificate of incorporation, or in a resolution adopted by the board of directors providing for the creation and issue of such rights or options, and, in every case, shall be set forth or incorporated by reference in the instrument or instruments evidencing such rights or options. In the absence of actual fraud in the transaction, the judgment of the directors as to the consideration for the issuance of such rights or options and the sufficiency thereof shall be conclusive.

(d) In case the shares of stock of the corporation to be issued upon the exercise of such rights or options shall be shares having a par value, the consideration so to be received therefor shall have a value not less than the par value thereof. In case the shares of stock so to be issued shall be shares of stock without par value, the consideration therefor shall be determined in the manner provided in §153 of this title.

8 *Del. C.* §157. Section 157(b) thus requires that the option terms, including the consideration to be provided for the shares, be set forth in the certificate of incorporation "or in a resolution adopted by the board of directors providing for the creation and issue of such rights or options, and, in every case, shall be set forth or incorporated by reference in the instrument or instruments evidencing such rights or options."

The Merger Agreement was the "instrument . . . evidencing" the Top-up Option. Olson had a strong argument that the instrument did not set forth the consideration to be paid for the shares or a formula by which the consideration could be determined. Section 1.4(b) of the Merger Agreement authorized the consideration for the Top-up Shares to be paid with a promissory note, but failed to set forth the material terms of the note, including the terms of repayment, provisions for interest, whether the note will be secured, negotiable or transferable, or other material terms. Section 1.4(b) expressly contemplated that the material terms would be set in the future "on terms as provided by the Parent or the Purchaser, which terms shall be reasonably satisfactory to the Company."

The lack of specificity in the Merger Agreement pointed to a second statutory flaw. Section 157(b) requires that the option terms be set forth in the certificate of incorporation or "in a resolution adopted by the board of directors providing for the creation and issue of such rights or options." 8 *Del. C.* §157(b). Because the Merger Agreement failed to set any terms for the promissory note, one could readily infer at the pleadings stage that there was no board resolution. Discovery revealed that was indeed the case.

In addition, Section 157(d) requires that the consideration to be received for shares with par value "have a value not less than the par value thereof." Section 153 imposes a similar requirement. 8 *Del C.* §153(a) ("Shares of stock with par value may be issued for such consideration, having a value not less than the par value thereof, as determined from time to time by the board of directors, or by the stockholders if the certificate of incorporation so provides."). Because the terms of the promissory note were not set at the time the ev3 board attempted to grant the Top-up Option, the board could not make this determination.

Finally, longstanding Delaware case law interpreting Section 152 and its statutory predecessors requires that the board of directors determine the sufficiency of the consideration received for shares. "[U]nder the Delaware statutes the directors of a Delaware corporation may not delegate, except in such manner as may be explicitly provided by statute, the duty to determine the value of the property acquired as consideration for the issuance of stock." Field v. Carlisle Corp., 68 A.2d 817, 820 (Del.Ch.1949) (Seitz, V.C.); *accord* Bowen v. Imperial Theatres, Inc., 115 A. 918, 920 (Del.Ch.1922).

The requirement of board approval for the issuance of stock is not limited to the act of transferring the shares of stock to the would-be stockholder, but includes an antecedent transaction that purports to bind the corporation to do so. As noted, Section 152 requires the directors to determine the "consideration . . . for subscriptions to, or the purchase of, the capital stock" of a corporation. Thus, director approval of the transaction fixing such consideration is required. Moreover, it is well established in the case law that directors must approve a sale of stock. This duty is considered so important that the directors cannot delegate it.

Directors are authorized to determine the form and manner of payment, such as with a note, but they actually must make those determinations. Under the original Merger Agreement, the directors did not make those determinations but rather left them to a future date, and the terms of the promissory note would be set in the first instance by Covidien and COV.

Cases interpreting Sections 151(a) and 251(b) of the DGCL reinforce the strength of the invalidity claim. Section 151(a) authorizes the terms of a class or series of stock to be "made dependent upon facts ascertainable outside the certificate of incorporation or of any amendment thereto, or outside the resolution or resolutions providing for the issue of such stock." 6 Section 251(b) authorizes the terms of a merger agreement to be "made dependent upon facts ascertainable outside of [the] agreement." This Court has held that a board abdicated its statutory duty under Section 251(b) when it delegated the determination of the merger consideration to an investment bank selected by the acquirer. Sections 152, 153, and 157 do not contain a similar grant of statutory authority to condition terms on "facts ascertainable" outside the governing instrument, indicating that those provisions should be read more narrowly than Sections 151(a) and 251(b).

The defendants have attempted to minimize the import of these statutory problems by suggesting that the directors understood the general nature of the Top-up Option, its efficacy in speeding deal closure, and the lack of any prejudice to minority stockholders. *Cf.* In re Cogent, Inc. S'holders Litig., 7 A.3d 487, 505 (Del.Ch.2010). That level of knowledge would be pertinent, as in *Cogent*, to a breach of fiduciary duty claim attacking the board's decision to approve the Top-up Option. *See id.* If the board actually made a determination about the sufficiency of the consideration received, that level of knowledge also would be pertinent to the "absence of actual fraud" standard found in Section 152 and Section 157. *See id.* at 506. Knowing about the generalities of the transaction structure does not satisfy the explicit statutory requirements of Sections 152, 153 and 157(b) and (d).

The defendants also have pointed out that if all worked as planned, the Top-up Option Shares would be issued and outstanding for only a brief period — as it happened, less than a day. A brief statutory violation is nonetheless a statutory violation. In *Waggoner*, the Delaware Supreme Court rejected a similar attempt to "trivialize" the requirements for issuing stock as "mere 'technicalities.'" 588 A.2d at 1136. "The issuance of corporate stock is an act of fundamental legal significance having a direct bearing upon questions of corporate governance, control and the capital structure of the enterprise. The law properly requires certainty in such matters."

Deep faults could have developed in the ev3 corporate structure if the Top-up Option Shares were found invalidly issued and the Merger invalidly consummated. The settlement administered a preventative cure. First, Section 1.4(b) was amended to specify the material terms of the promissory note. The amended section provided as follows:

> Any such promissory note shall be on terms as provided by the Parent or the Purchaser, which terms shall include the following: (i) the principal amount and accrued interest under the promissory note shall be payable upon the demand of the Company, (ii) the unpaid principal amount of the promissory note will accrue simple interest at the per annum rate of 3.0%, (iii) the promissory note may be prepaid in whole or in part at any time, without penalty or prior notice and (iv) the unpaid principal amount and accrued interest under the promissory note shall immediately become due and payable in the event that (x) Purchaser fails to make any payment of interest on the promissory note as provided therein and such failure continues for a period of 30 days or (y) Purchaser files or has filed against it any petition under any bankruptcy or insolvency law or makes a general assignment for the benefit of creditors.

By requiring that the Merger Agreement spell out the terms of the promissory note, the settlement ensured that the "instrument . . . evidencing" the Top-up Option set forth the consideration to be paid for the shares as required by Section 157(b).

Second, the settlement required that the ev3 board meet to approve the amended Merger Agreement and adopt an implementing resolution. This term ensured that the board would determine the consideration to be received for the Top-up Option Shares, as required by Sections 152, 153(a), and 157(d), and that a board resolution would exist that provided for the creation and issuance of the Top-up Option, as required by Section 157(b).

Third, Section 1.4(b) was amended to require that Covidien pay the par value of any Top-up Shares in cash. Prior to 2004, payment of the par value in cash was necessary to provide "constitutional consideration" for the shares. *See* Drexler, *supra*, §17.02, at 17-17 (describing the requirements of Del. Const. art. IX, §3 and Section 152 as they existed prior to the 2004 amendments). Section 152 now provides that consideration may consist of "cash, any tangible or intangible property or any benefit to the corporation, or any combination thereof." 8 *Del. C.* §152. Nevertheless, providing for payment of the par value in cash eliminates any conceivable debate over whether the value of the consideration received for the Top-up Option Shares might be less than the par value of those shares, as required by Section 153(a).

By pursuing this litigation and obtaining the settlement, Olson and her counsel prevented the seeds of a future legal crisis from germinating. The resulting benefit is non-quantifiable and immeasurable but in my view quite substantial. An award of $1 million is fair and reasonable compensation for a settlement that cured serious statutory flaws . . .

For the foregoing reasons, plaintiff's counsel is awarded fees and expenses of $1.1 million. **IT IS SO ORDERED.**

The *ev3* opinion, although rendered in the context of settlement hearing, is the clearest statement yet that the legality of a properly structured top-up option is well settled under Delaware law. The decision effectively "codifies" best practices in structuring a top-up option.

PROBLEM SET 23.1

1. Review D.G.C.L §157 in the statutory supplement. Given the terms of that provision, are the concerns over top-up options overstated? Why might a board decide to follow the rules set forth in the *ev3* opinion nonetheless?
2. A further refinement of the top-up option, the so-called Burger King structure, has been used in several deals, often involving private equity buyers. Under this approach, the minimum condition to the front-end tender offer is set at the percentage that, when added to the maximum available top-up option, will ensure that the buyer will cross the 90-percent short-form threshold; if the tender fails to meet that higher minimum condition (often much higher than 50 percent), the parties abandon the tender offer and proceed with a one-step merger using a proxy statement that is prepared and filed while the tender offer is pending. What are the drawbacks of this approach?
3. Note that use of a top-up option is checked in cases where there are insufficient authorized but unissued shares to allow the exercise of the option to carry the buyer offer over the 90-percent level. This is something to consider when drafting the certificate of incorporation in the first instance.

3.   THE WILLIAMS ACT

The Williams Act was passed in 1968 to protect shareholders in the course of takeovers and tender offers by granting the SEC and the courts the power to manage problems that arise. The Act added several provisions to the Securities Exchange Act of 1934.

Section 14(d)(1) of the '34 Act requires compliance with certain disclosure and filing requirement in connection with any tender offer for more than 5 percent of a class of equity security registered under Section 12 of the '34 Act, as well as certain securities of insurance and investment companies. The principal filing, dissemination, and disclosure requirements with respect to third-party tender offers are set forth in Regulation 14D.

All written communications from and including the first public announcement of the tender offer are filed on a Schedule TO no later than the date of the communication.

Under Rule 14e-1(a) a tender offer is required to remain open at least until midnight on the 20th business day from the date of commencement. For an offer to be "open," the bidder must be willing to accept shares for deposit each day during the 20 business-day period. In a hostile tender offer, the 20 business-day period begins on the date when the bidder files its Schedule TO and makes a request to the target under Rule 14d-5 to obtain a shareholder list and, in the case of an offer to exchange existing shares for new shares, files a registration statement with the SEC.

Rule 14e-1(b) requires a tender offer remain open at least 10 business days from the date there is an increase or decrease in the consideration offered, the percentage of securities sought in the tender offer (other than increases of 2 percent or less, a kind of de minimus exception), or the dealer's soliciting fee.

Under the "all holders rule," Rule 14d-10, a tender offer must be open to all shareholders of the class of securities subject to the tender offer. This represents a partial "overruling" of the Delaware Supreme Court's opinion in the famous *Unocal* decision, where the court held that a selective tender offer (that cut out a hostile bidder) did not violate state corporate law.

The tender offer rules also include a "best-price rule" in Rule 14d-10. This requires that the consideration paid to any security holder in a tender offer be the highest consideration paid to any other security holder in the offer. Amounts paid under an employment compensation, severance, or other employee benefits arrangement are exempted from the best-price rule if the amounts payable under the arrangement relate solely to past or future services or future services to be refrained from and are not based on the number of shares the employee owns or tenders.

4. POISON PILLS

In some cases, the target does not want to do a deal, or it only wants to do a deal at a much higher price. The most effective way to hold off an unwanted acquirer is through a shareholders' rights plan. These are commonly known as *poison pills.*

The key features of a rights plan are the "flip-in" and "flip-over" provisions, the effect of which is to impose unacceptable levels of share dilution on an acquirer. The rights are triggered when the stock ownership of a shareholder, or a group of shareholders acting in concert, exceeds some threshold — often 20 percent. The plan then gives all other shareholders the right to purchase either the target's stock (flip-in) or the acquirer's stock (flip-over) at a substantial discount, effectively diluting the acquirer's stock ownership.

Rights plans also generally provide that, once the triggering threshold is crossed, the target's board may exchange, in whole or in part, the rights of all holders other than the acquirer for shares of the company's common stock. This provision avoids the expense of requiring rights holders to exercise their flip-in rights and eliminates any uncertainty as to whether individual holders will in fact exercise the rights.

But before getting bogged down in the mechanics of the plan, understand that a rights plan is somewhat like a thermonuclear bomb: It's not really intended to be used; instead it is supposed to act as a deterrent. Hopefully the hostile bidder is rational, and will never trigger the plan.

Instead the plan forces the bidder to negotiate with the board, because the board retains the right to deactivate the pill.

With the basic legality of pills established by case law in the 1980s and early 1990s, almost all litigation now focuses on whether or not a board should be required to redeem the rights in response to a particular bid.[5]

AIR PRODUCTS AND CHEMICALS, INC., v. AIRGAS, INC., ET AL., DEFENDANTS
IN RE AIRGAS INC. SHAREHOLDER LITIGATION
16 A.3d 48, Court of Chancery of Delaware
| Submitted: Feb. 8, 2011 | Decided: Feb. 15, 2011

CHANDLER, Chancellor

This case poses the following fundamental question: Can a board of directors, acting in good faith and with a reasonable factual basis for its decision, when faced with a structurally non-coercive, all-cash, fully financed tender offer directed to the stockholders of the corporation, keep a poison pill in place so as to prevent the stockholders from making their own decision about whether they want to tender their shares — even after the incumbent board has lost one election contest, a full year has gone by since the offer was first made public, and the stockholders are fully informed as to the target board's views on the inadequacy of the offer? If so, does that effectively mean that a board can "just say never" to a hostile tender offer?

The answer to the latter question is "no." A board cannot "*just* say no" to a tender offer. Under Delaware law, it must first pass through two prongs of exacting judicial scrutiny by a judge who will evaluate the actions taken by, and the motives of, the board. Only a board of directors found to be acting in good faith, after reasonable investigation and reliance on the advice of outside advisors, which articulates and convinces the Court that a hostile tender offer poses a legitimate threat to the corporate enterprise, may address that perceived threat by blocking the tender offer and forcing the bidder to elect a board majority that supports its bid.

In essence, this case brings to the fore one of the most basic questions animating all of corporate law, which relates to the allocation of power between directors and stockholders. That is, "when, if ever, will a board's duty to 'the corporation and its shareholders' require [the board] to abandon concerns for 'long term' values (and other constituencies) and enter a current share value maximizing mode?" More to the point, in the context of a hostile tender offer, who gets to decide when and if the corporation is for sale?

Since the Shareholder Rights Plan (more commonly known as the "poison pill") was first conceived and throughout the development of Delaware corporate takeover jurisprudence during the twenty-five-plus years that followed, the debate over who ultimately decides whether a tender offer is adequate and should be accepted — the shareholders of the corporation or its board of directors — has raged on. Starting with Moran v. Household International, Inc.[6] in 1985, when

---

5. William B. Chandler III, *The Delaware Court of Chancery: An Insider's View of Change and Continuity*, 2012 Colum. Bus. L. Rev. 411, 413 (2012).

6. 490 A.2d 1059 (Del.Ch.1985).

the Delaware Supreme Court first upheld the adoption of the poison pill as a valid takeover defense, through the hostile takeover years of the 1980s, and in several recent decisions of the Court of Chancery and the Delaware Supreme Court, this fundamental question has engaged practitioners, academics, and members of the judiciary, but it has yet to be confronted head on.

For the reasons much more fully described in the remainder of this Opinion, I conclude that, as Delaware law currently stands, the answer must be that the power to defeat an inadequate hostile tender offer ultimately lies with the board of directors. As such, I find that the Airgas board has met its burden under *Unocal* to articulate a legally cognizable threat (the allegedly inadequate price of Air Products' offer, coupled with the fact that a majority of Airgas's stockholders would likely tender into that inadequate offer) and has taken defensive measures that fall within a range of reasonable responses proportionate to that threat. I thus rule in favor of defendants. Air Products' and the Shareholder Plaintiffs' requests for relief are denied, and all claims asserted against defendants are dismissed with prejudice.

INTRODUCTION

This is the Court's decision after trial, extensive post-trial briefing, and a supplemental evidentiary hearing in this long-running takeover battle between Air Products & Chemicals, Inc. ("Air Products") and Airgas, Inc. ("Airgas"). The now very public saga began quietly in mid-October 2009 when John McGlade, President and CEO of Air Products, privately approached Peter McCausland, founder and CEO of Airgas, about a potential acquisition or combination. After McGlade's private advances were rebuffed, Air Products went hostile in February 2010, launching a public tender offer for all outstanding Airgas shares.

Now, over a year since Air Products first announced its all-shares, all-cash tender offer, the terms of that offer (other than price) remain essentially unchanged. After several price bumps and extensions, the offer currently stands at $70 per share and is set to expire today, February 15, 2011 — Air Products' stated "best and final" offer. The Airgas board unanimously rejected that offer as being "clearly inadequate." The Airgas board has repeatedly expressed the view that Airgas is worth at least $78 per share in a sale transaction — and at any rate, far more than the $70 per share Air Products is offering.

So, we are at a crossroads. Air Products has made its "best and final" offer — apparently its offer to acquire Airgas has reached an end stage. Meanwhile, the Airgas board believes the offer is clearly inadequate and its value in a sale transaction is at least $78 per share. At this stage, it appears, neither side will budge. Airgas continues to maintain its defenses, blocking the bid and effectively denying shareholders the choice whether to tender their shares. Air Products and Shareholder Plaintiffs now ask this Court to order Airgas to redeem its poison pill and other defenses that are stopping Air Products from moving forward with its hostile offer, and to allow Airgas's stockholders to decide for themselves whether they want to tender into Air Products' (inadequate or not) $70 "best and final" offer.

A week-long trial in this case was held from October 4, 2010 through October 8, 2010. Hundreds of pages of post-trial memoranda were submitted by the parties. After trial, several legal, factual, and evidentiary questions remained to be answered. In ruling on certain outstanding evidentiary issues, I sent counsel a Letter Order on December 2, 2010 asking for answers to a number of questions to be addressed in supplemental post-trial briefing. On the eve of the parties' submissions to the Court in response to that Letter Order, Air Products raised its offer to the $70 "best and final" number . . .

Now, having thoroughly read, reviewed, and reflected upon all of the evidence presented to me, and having carefully considered the arguments made by counsel, I conclude that the Airgas board, in proceeding as it has since October 2009, has not breached its fiduciary duties owed to the Airgas stockholders. I find that the board has acted in good faith and in the honest belief that the Air Products offer, at $70 per share, is inadequate.

Although I have a hard time believing that inadequate price alone (according to the target's board) in the context of a non-discriminatory, all-cash, all-shares, fully financed offer poses any "threat" — particularly given the wealth of information available to Airgas's stockholders at this point in time — under existing Delaware law, it apparently does. Inadequate price has become a form of "substantive coercion" as that concept has been developed by the Delaware Supreme Court in its takeover jurisprudence. That is, the idea that Airgas's stockholders will disbelieve the board's views on value (or in the case of merger arbitrageurs who may have short-term profit goals in mind, they may simply ignore the board's recommendations), and so they may mistakenly tender into an inadequately priced offer. Substantive coercion has been clearly recognized by our Supreme Court as a valid threat.

Trial judges are not free to ignore or rewrite appellate court decisions. Thus, for reasons explained in detail below, I am constrained by Delaware Supreme Court precedent to conclude that defendants have met their burden under *Unocal* to articulate a sufficient threat that justifies the continued maintenance of Airgas's poison pill. That is, assuming defendants have met their burden to articulate a legally cognizable threat (prong 1), Airgas's defenses have been recognized by Delaware law as reasonable responses to the threat posed by an inadequate offer — even an all-shares, all-cash offer (prong 2).

In my personal view, Airgas's poison pill has served its legitimate purpose. Although the "best and final" $70 offer has been on the table for just over two months (since December 9, 2010), Air Products' advances have been ongoing for over sixteen months, and Airgas's use of its poison pill — particularly in combination with its staggered board — has given the Airgas board over a full year to inform its stockholders about its view of Airgas's intrinsic value and Airgas's value in a sale transaction. It has also given the Airgas board a full year to express its views to its stockholders on the purported opportunistic timing of Air Products' repeated advances and to educate its stockholders on the inadequacy of Air Products' offer. It has given Airgas *more time than any litigated poison pill in Delaware history* — enough time to show stockholders four quarters of improving financial results, demonstrating that Airgas is on track to meet its projected goals. And it has helped the Airgas board push Air Products to raise its bid by $10 per share from when it was first publicly announced to what Air

Products has now represented is its highest offer. The record at both the October trial and the January supplemental evidentiary hearing confirm that Airgas's stockholder base is sophisticated and well-informed, and that essentially all the information they would need to make an informed decision is available to them. In short, there seems to be no threat here — the stockholders know what they need to know (about both the offer and the Airgas board's opinion of the offer) to make an informed decision.

That being said, however, as I understand binding Delaware precedent, I may not substitute my business judgment for that of the Airgas board.[7] The Delaware Supreme Court has recognized inadequate price as a valid threat to corporate policy and effectiveness.[8] The Delaware Supreme Court has also made clear that the "selection of a time frame for achievement of corporate goals . . . may not be delegated to the stockholders." Furthermore, in powerful dictum, the Supreme Court has stated that "[d]irectors are not obliged to abandon a deliberately conceived corporate plan for a short-term shareholder profit unless there is clearly no basis to sustain the corporate strategy." Although I do not read that dictum as eliminating the applicability of heightened *Unocal* scrutiny to a board's decision to block a non-coercive bid as underpriced, I do read it, along with the actual holding in *Unitrin*, as indicating that a board that has a good faith, reasonable basis to believe a bid is inadequate may block that bid using a poison pill, irrespective of stockholders' desire to accept it.

Here, even using heightened scrutiny, the Airgas board has demonstrated that it has a reasonable basis for sustaining its long term corporate strategy — the Airgas board is independent, and has relied on the advice of three different outside independent financial advisors in concluding that Air Products' offer is inadequate. Air Products' *own three nominees* who were elected to the Airgas board in September 2010 have joined wholeheartedly in the Airgas board's determination, and when the Airgas board met to consider the $70 "best and final" offer in December 2010, it was one of those Air Products Nominees who said, "We have to protect the pill." Indeed, one of Air Products' *own directors* conceded at trial that the Airgas board members had acted within their fiduciary duties in their desire to "hold out for the proper price," and that "if an offer was made for Air Products that [he] considered to be unfair to the stockholders of Air Products . . . [he would likewise] use every legal mechanism available" to hold out for the proper price as well. Under Delaware law, the Airgas directors have complied with their fiduciary duties. Thus, as noted above, and for the reasons more fully described in the remainder of this Opinion, I am constrained to deny Air Products' and the Shareholder Plaintiffs' requests for relief.

---

7. Paramount Commc'ns, Inc. v. Time, Inc., 571 A.2d 1140, 1154 (Del.1990); *see* City Capital Assocs. Ltd. P'ship v. Interco, Inc., 551 A.2d 787 (Del.Ch.1988); Grand Metro. Pub. Ltd. Co. v. Pillsbury Co., 558 A.2d 1049 (Del.Ch.1988).

8. *See* Unitrin, Inc. v. Am. Gen. Corp., 651 A.2d 1361, 1384 (Del.1995) ("This Court has held that the 'inadequate value' of an all cash for all shares offer is a 'legally cognizable threat.'") (quoting Paramount Commc'ns, Inc. v. Time, Inc., 571 A.2d 1140, 1153 (Del.1990)).

A BRIEF POISON PILL PRIMER—*MORAN* AND ITS PROGENY

This case unavoidably highlights what former-Chancellor Allen has called "an anomaly" in our corporation law. The anomaly is that "[p]ublic tender offers are, or rather can be, change in control transactions that are functionally similar to merger transactions with respect to the critical question of control over the corporate enterprise." Both tender offers and mergers are "extraordinary" transactions that "threaten [ ] equivalent impacts upon the corporation and all of its constituencies including existing shareholders." But our corporation law statutorily views the two differently—under DGCL §251, board approval and recommendation is required before stockholders have the opportunity to vote on or even consider a merger proposal, while traditionally the board has been given no statutory role in responding to a public tender offer. The poison pill was born "as an attempt to address the flaw (as some would see it) in the corporation law" giving boards a critical role to play in the merger context but no role to play in tender offers.

These "functionally similar forms of change in control transactions," however, have received disparate legal treatment—on the one hand, a decision not to pursue a merger proposal (or even a decision not to engage in negotiations at all) is reviewed under the deferential business judgment standard, while on the other hand, a decision not to redeem a poison pill in the face of a hostile tender offer is reviewed under "intermediate scrutiny" and must be "reasonable in relation to the threat posed" by such offer . . .

In Moran v. Household International, Inc., written shortly after the *Unocal* decision in 1985, the Delaware Supreme Court first upheld the legality of the poison pill as a valid takeover defense. Specifically, in *Moran*, the Household board of directors "react[ed] to what it perceived to be the threat in the market place of coercive two-tier tender offers" by adopting a stockholder rights plan that would allow the corporation to protect stockholders by issuing securities as a way to ward off a hostile bidder presenting a structurally coercive offer. The *Moran* Court held that the *adoption* of such a rights plan was within the board's statutory authority and thus was not *per se* illegal under Delaware law. But the Supreme Court cabined the use of the rights plan as follows:

> [T]he Rights Plan is not absolute. When the Household Board of Directors is faced with a tender offer and a request to redeem rights, they will not be able to arbitrarily reject the offer. They will be held to the same fiduciary standards any other board of directors would be held to in deciding to adopt a defensive mechanism, the same standard they were held to in originally approving the Rights Plan.

The Court went on to say that "[t]he Board does not now have unfettered discretion in refusing to redeem the Rights. The Board has no more discretion in refusing to redeem the Rights than it does in enacting any defensive mechanism." Accordingly, while the Household board's adoption of the rights plan was deemed to be made in good faith, and the plan was found to be reasonable in relation to the threat posed by the "coercive acquisition techniques" that were prevalent at the time, the pill at that point was adopted merely as a preventive mechanism to ward off future advances. The "ultimate response to an actual takeover," though, would have to be judged by the directors' actions taken at that time, and the board's "use of the Plan [would] be evaluated when and if the issue [arose]."

In Paramount Communications, Inc. v. Time, Inc., however, the Delaware Supreme Court explicitly rejected an approach to *Unocal* analysis that "would involve the court in substituting its judgment as to what is a 'better' deal for that of a corporation's board of directors." Although not a "pill case," the Supreme Court in *Paramount* addressed the concept of substantive coercion head on in determining whether an all-cash, all-shares tender offer posed a legally cognizable threat to the target's stockholders.

As the Supreme Court put it, the case presented them with the following question: "Did Time's board, having developed a [long-term] strategic plan . . . come under a fiduciary duty to jettison its plan and put the corporation's future in the hands of its stockholders?" Key to the Supreme Court's ruling was the underlying pivotal question in their mind regarding the Time board's specific long-term plan—its proposed merger with Warner—and whether by entering into the proposed merger, Time had essentially "put itself up for sale." This was important because, so long as the company is *not* "for sale," then *Revlon* duties do not kick in and the board "is not under any *per se* duty to maximize shareholder value in the short term, even in the context of a takeover." The Supreme Court held that the Time board had not abandoned its long-term strategic plans; thus *Revlon* duties were not triggered and *Unocal* alone applied to the board's actions.

In evaluating the Time board's actions under *Unocal*, the Supreme Court embraced the concept of substantive coercion, agreeing with the Time board that its stockholders might have tendered into Paramount's offer "in ignorance or a mistaken belief of the strategic benefit which a business combination with Warner might produce." Stating in no uncertain terms that "in our view, precepts underlying the business judgment rule militate against a court's engaging in the process of attempting to appraise and evaluate the relative merits of a long-term versus a short-term investment goal for shareholders" (as to do so would be "a distortion of the *Unocal* process"), the Supreme Court held that Time's response was proportionate to the threat of Paramount's offer. Time's defensive actions were not aimed at "cramming down" a management-sponsored alternative to Paramount's offer, but instead, were simply aimed at furthering a pre-existing long-term corporate strategy. This, held the Supreme Court, comported with the board's valid exercise of its fiduciary duties under *Unocal*.

Five years later, the Supreme Court further applied the "substantive coercion" concept in Unitrin, Inc. v. American General Corp. There, a hostile acquirer (American General) wanted Unitrin (the target corporation) to be enjoined from implementing a stock repurchase and poison pill adopted in response to American General's "inadequate" all-cash offer. Recognizing that previous cases had held that "inadequate value" of an all-cash offer could be a valid threat (i.e. *Interco*), the Court also reiterated its conclusion in *Paramount* that inadequate value is not the only threat posed by a non-coercive, all-cash offer. The *Unitrin* Court recited that "the Time board of directors had reasonably determined that inadequate value was not the only threat that Paramount's all cash for all shares offer presented, but was *also* reasonably concerned that the Time stockholders might tender to Paramount in ignorance or based upon a mistaken belief, i.e., yield to substantive coercion."

Relying on that line of reasoning, the *Unitrin* Court determined that the Unitrin board "reasonably perceived risk of substantive coercion, i.e., that Unitrin's shareholders might accept American General's inadequate Offer because of 'ignorance or mistaken belief' regarding the Board's assessment of the long-term value of Unitrin's stock." Thus, perceiving a valid threat under *Unocal*, the Supreme Court then addressed whether the board of Unitrin's response was proportional to the threat.

Having determined that the Unitrin board reasonably perceived the American General offer to be inadequate, and Unitrin's poison pill adoption to be a proportionate response, the Court of Chancery had found that the Unitrin board's decision to authorize its stock repurchase program was disproportionate because it was "unnecessary" to protect the Unitrin stockholders from an inadequate bid since the board already had a pill in place. The Court of Chancery here was sensitive to how the stock buy back would make it extremely unlikely that American General could win a proxy contest. The Supreme Court, however, held that the Court of Chancery had "erred by substituting its judgment, that the Repurchase Program was unnecessary, for that of the board," and that such action, if not coercive or preclusive, could be valid if it fell within a range of reasonableness.

Under the first prong of *Unocal*, defendants bear the burden of showing that the Airgas board, "after a reasonable investigation . . . determined in good faith, that the [Air Products offer] presented a threat . . . that warranted a defensive response."

Although the Airgas board meets the threshold of showing good faith and reasonable investigation, the first part of *Unocal* review requires more than that; it requires the board to show that its good faith and reasonable investigation ultimately gave the board "grounds for concluding that a threat to the corporate enterprise existed." In the supplemental evidentiary hearing, Airgas (and its lawyers) attempted to identify numerous threats posed by Air Products' $70 offer: It is coercive. It is opportunistically timed. It presents the stockholders with a "prisoner's dilemma." It undervalues Airgas — it is a "clearly inadequate" price. The merger arbitrageurs who have bought into Airgas need to be "protected from themselves." The arbs are a "threat" to the minority. The list goes on.

The reality is that the Airgas board discussed essentially none of these alleged "threats" in its board meetings, or in its deliberations on whether to accept or reject Air Products' $70 offer, or in its consideration of whether to keep the pill in place. The board did not discuss "coercion" or the idea that Airgas's stockholders would be "coerced" into tendering. The board did not discuss the concept of a "prisoner's dilemma." The board did not discuss Air Products' offer in terms of any "danger" that it posed to the corporate enterprise. In the October trial, Airgas had likewise failed to identify threats other than that Air Products' offer undervalues Airgas. In fact, there has been no specific board discussion since the October trial over whether to keep the poison pill in place (other than Clancey's "protect the pill" line).

Airgas's board members testified that the concepts of coercion, threat, and the decision whether or not to redeem the pill were nonetheless "implicit" in the board's discussions due to their knowledge that a large percentage of Airgas's stock is held by merger arbitrageurs who have short-term interests and would be willing to tender into an inadequate offer. But the only threat that the board discussed — the threat that has been the central issue since the beginning of this case — is the inadequate price of Air Products' offer. Thus, inadequate price, coupled with the fact that a majority of Airgas's stock is held by merger arbitrageurs who might be willing to tender into such an inadequate offer, is the only real "threat" alleged. In fact, Airgas directors have admitted as much. Airgas's CEO van Roden testified:

> Q. [O]ther than the price being inadequate, is there anything else that you deem to be a threat?
> A. No.

In the end, it really is "All About Value." Airgas's directors and Airgas's financial advisors concede that the Airgas stockholder base is sophisticated and well-informed, and that they have all the information necessary to decide whether to tender into Air Products' offer.

PILLS, POLICY AND PROFESSORS (AND HYPOTHETICALS)

When the Supreme Court first upheld the use of a rights plan in *Moran*, it emphasized that "[t]he Board does not now have unfettered discretion in refusing to redeem the Rights." And in the most recent "pill case" decided just this past year, the Supreme Court reiterated its view that, "[a]s we held in *Moran*, the adoption of a Rights Plan is not absolute."[9] The poison pill's limits, however, still remain to be seen.

The merits of poison pills, the application of the standards of review that should apply to their adoption and continued maintenance, the limitations (if any) that should be imposed on their use, and the "anti-takeover effect" of the combination of classified boards plus poison pills have all been exhaustively written about in legal academia.[10] Two of the largest contributors to the

---

9. Versata Enters., Inc. v. Selectica, Inc., 5 A.3d 586, 607 (Del.2010) (citing *Moran*, 500 A.2d at 1354). Marty Lipton himself has written that "the pill was neither designed nor intended to be an absolute bar. It was always contemplated that the possibility of a proxy fight to replace the board would result in the board's taking shareholder desires into account, but that the delay and uncertainty as to the outcome of a proxy fight would give the board the negotiating position it needed to achieve the best possible deal for all the shareholders, which in appropriate cases could be the target's continuing as an independent company. . . . A board cannot say 'never,' but it can say 'no' in order to obtain the best deal for its shareholders." Martin Lipton, *Pills, Polls, and Professors Redux*, 69 U. Chi. L.Rev. 1037, 1054 (2002) (citing Marcel Kahan & Edward Rock, *How I Learned to Stop Worrying and Love the Pill: Adaptive Responses to Takeover Law*, 69 U. Chi. L.Rev. 871, 910 (2002) ("[T]he ultimate effect of the pill is akin to 'just say wait.'")). As it turns out, for companies with a "pill plus staggered board" combination, it might actually be that a target board can "just say wait . . . a very long time," because the Delaware Supreme Court has held that having to wait two years is not preclusive.

10. I will not cite them all here, but a sampling of just the early generation of articles includes: Martin Lipton, *Takeover Bids in the Target's Boardroom*, 35 Bus. Law. 101 (1979); Frank Easterbrook & Daniel

literature are Lucian Bebchuk (who famously takes the "shareholder choice" position that pills should be limited and that classified boards reduce firm value) on one side of the ring, and Marty Lipton (the founder of the poison pill, who continues to zealously defend its use) on the other.[11]

The contours of the debate have morphed slightly over the years, but the fundamental questions have remained. Can a board "just say no"? If so, when? How should the enhanced judicial standard of review be applied? What are the pill's limits? And the ultimate question: Can a board "just say never"? In a 2002 article entitled *Pills, Polls, and Professors Redux*, Lipton wrote the following:

> As the pill approaches its twentieth birthday, it is under attack from [various] groups of professors, each advocating a different form of shareholder poll, but each intended to eviscerate the protections afforded by the pill. . . . Upon reflection, I think it fair to conclude that the [ ] schools of academic opponents of the pill are not really opposed to the idea that the staggered board of the target of a hostile takeover bid may use the pill to "just say no." Rather, their *fundamental disagreement is with the theoretical possibility that the pill may enable a staggered board to "just say never."* However, as . . . almost every [situation] in which a takeover bid was combined with a proxy fight show, the incidence of a target's actually saying "never" is so rare as not to be a real-world problem. While [the various] professors' attempts to undermine the protections of the pill is argued with force and considerable logic, none of their arguments comes close to overcoming the cardinal rule of public policy — particularly applicable to corporate law and corporate finance — "If it ain't broke, don't fix it."

Well, in this case, the Airgas board has continued to say "no" even after one proxy fight. So what Lipton has called the "largely theoretical possibility of continued resistance after loss of a proxy fight" is now a real-world situation.

Conclusion

Vice Chancellor Strine recently suggested that:

> The passage of time has dulled many to the incredibly powerful and novel device that a so-called poison pill is. That device has no other purpose than to give the

---

Fischel, *Takeover Bids, Defensive Tactics, and Shareholders' Welfare*, 36 Bus. Law. 1733 (1981); Martin Lipton, *Takeover Bids in the Target's Boardroom: An Update After One Year*, 36 Bus. Law. 1017 (1981); Frank Easterbrook & Daniel Fischel, *The Proper Role of a Target's Management in Responding to a Tender Offer*, 94 Harv. L.Rev. 161 (1981); Martin Lipton, *Takeover Bids in the Target's Boardroom: A Response to Professors Easterbrook and Fischel*, 55 N.Y.U. L.Rev. 1231 (1980); Ronald J. Gilson, *A Structural Approach to Corporations: The Case Against Defensive Tactics in Tender Offers*, 33 Stan. L.Rev. 819 (1981); Lucian Arye Bebchuk, *The Case for Facilitating Competing Tender Offers*, 95 Harv. L.Rev. 1028 (1982).

11. In addition, Lipton often continues to argue that the deferential business judgment rule should be the standard of review that applies, despite the fact that that suggestion was squarely rejected in *Moran* and virtually every pill case since, which have consistently applied the *Unocal* analysis to defensive measures taken in response to hostile bids. Accordingly, although it is not the law in Delaware, Lipton's "continued defense of an undiluted application of the business judgment rule to defensive conduct" has been aptly termed "tenacious." Ronald Gilson & Reinier Kraakman, *Delaware's Intermediate Standard for Defensive Tactics: Is There Substance to Proportionality Review?*, 44 Bus. Law. 247, 247 n. 1 (1989).

board issuing the rights the leverage to prevent transactions it does not favor by diluting the buying proponent's interests.[12]

There is no question that poison pills act as potent anti-takeover drugs with the potential to be abused. Counsel for plaintiffs (both Air Products and Shareholder Plaintiffs) make compelling policy arguments in favor of redeeming the pill in this case — to do otherwise, they say, would essentially make all companies with staggered boards and poison pills "takeover proof." The argument is an excellent sound bite, but it is ultimately not the holding of this fact-specific case, although it does bring us one step closer to that result.

As this case demonstrates, in order to have any effectiveness, pills do not — and can not — have a set expiration date. To be clear, though, this case does not endorse "just say never." What it does endorse is Delaware's long-understood respect for reasonably exercised managerial discretion, so long as boards are found to be acting in good faith and in accordance with their fiduciary duties (after rigorous judicial fact-finding and enhanced scrutiny of their defensive actions). The Airgas board serves as a quintessential example.

Directors of a corporation still owe fiduciary duties to *all stockholders* — this undoubtedly includes short-term as well as long-term holders. At the same time, a board cannot be forced into *Revlon* mode any time a hostile bidder makes a tender offer that is at a premium to market value. The mechanisms in place to get around the poison pill — even a poison pill in combination with a staggered board, which no doubt makes the process prohibitively more difficult — have been in place since 1985, when the Delaware Supreme Court first decided to uphold the pill as a legal defense to an unwanted bid. That is the current state of Delaware law until the Supreme Court changes it.

For the foregoing reasons, Air Products' and the Shareholder Plaintiffs' requests for relief are denied, and all claims asserted against defendants are dismissed with prejudice. The parties shall bear their own costs.

Rights plans may also be used to protect a corporation's tax "assets." As we will discuss later in the course, a company with net operating losses (NOLs) can offset those losses against future income. But if the company experiences a change of control, generally a greater than 50 percent increase in ownership by 5-percent shareholders in any three-year period under Section 382 of the Internal Revenue Code, it could lose the right to use those NOLs. Some companies have adopted rights plans to prevent such a change of control which is a somewhat different thing than preventing a hostile takeover generally.

Please read pages 38 to 39 of the 2010 10-K regarding the Dynegy shareholders' rights plan, and the Dynegy pill available online, and be prepared to discuss in class. Also review DGCL §109 in the Statutory Supplement at the same time.

---

12. Hollinger Int'l, Inc. v. Black, 844 A.2d 1022, 1083 (Del.Ch.2004).

5. DYNEGY'S TENDER OFFER

Recall that the Dynegy merger agreement we looked at in Chapter 22 was the second part of a two-step transaction. Go back and look at the top-up option provisions and be prepared to discuss in class.

The Schedule TO for the tender offer describes the background to the tender offer thusly:

On August 13, 2010, the Company announced that it had entered into the Prior Merger Agreement pursuant to which it would be acquired by an affiliate of The Blackstone Group L.P. (the "*Blackstone Merger*"). On October 12, 2010, Icahn Partners, Icahn Master, Icahn Master II, Icahn Master III and High River (collectively, the "*Icahn Parties*") filed a Schedule 13D with the SEC (the "*13D*") disclosing an aggregate beneficial ownership of 12,000,000 Shares. The Icahn Parties stated in the 13D that they acquired the Shares believing them to be undervalued. In the 13D, the Icahn Parties also disclosed their belief that the $4.50 per share consideration agreed to in the Prior Merger Agreement was inadequate and disclosed that they may seek to have conversations with the Company to discuss the Blackstone Merger. On October 19, 2010, senior management of the Company and representatives from Greenhill & Co., LLC ("*Greenhill*"), the Company's financial advisor, met with Carl Icahn and other representatives of the Icahn Parties at the offices of the Icahn Parties. At this meeting, senior management of the Company expressed its support for the Blackstone Merger, explained why the Company's Board of Directors recommended it and indicated that the Icahn Parties should also consider supporting the Blackstone Merger.

On November 12, 2010, the Icahn Parties amended the 13D to disclose that they intended to vote against approval of the proposal to adopt the Prior Merger Agreement and would demand appraisal rights. In addition, and in response to concerns raised by the Company that if the Prior Merger Agreement was not approved, the Company would face potential liquidity issues, on November 12, 2010, Carl Icahn and other representatives of the Icahn Parties contacted Bruce Williamson, the Chairman, President and Chief Executive Officer of the Company, and informed Mr. Williamson that the Icahn Parties would consider offering a replacement credit facility if that would mitigate such liquidity concerns. Mr. Williamson and other members of the Company's management responded that the Company required a long-term solution rather than the solution provided by the replacement facility offered by the Icahn Parties.

On November 23, 2010, the Company announced that the Prior Merger Agreement failed to receive the necessary votes to be adopted, and as a result, the Prior Merger Agreement had been terminated. In addition, on November 23, 2010, the Company announced that it had adopted the Rights Agreement.

On November 30, 2010, Carl Icahn and other representatives of the Icahn Parties met with Mr. Williamson, the Company's Chairman and Chief Executive Officer, and other representatives of the Company, at the offices of the Icahn Parties. At that meeting, the parties discussed the Company's strategic options in light of the termination of the Prior Merger Agreement. The parties discussed entering into a confidentiality agreement that would permit the Icahn Parties to receive certain material non-public information concerning the Company. In the following days, representatives from the Icahn Parties and the Company and their respective advisors exchanged drafts of, but did not execute, a confidentiality agreement that also included a standstill agreement that, among other things, restricted the Icahn Parties' ability to buy or sell the Company's securities.

On December 7, 2010, the Icahn Parties and the Company discussed the possibility of entering into a negotiated merger agreement pursuant to which the Icahn Parties would agree to launch a tender offer, followed by a merger. In the following days, the Icahn Parties, the Company and their representatives negotiated such an agreement as well as the Stockholder Support Agreement and the Guarantee.

On December 15, 2010, the Offeror, Merger Sub and the Company entered into the Merger Agreement, pursuant to which Offeror agreed to launch the Offer, and, after the completion of the Offer and the satisfaction or waiver of all of the conditions applicable to the Merger, Merger Sub would be merged with and into the Company, and the Company would survive the Merger as a wholly-owned subsidiary of Offeror and an indirect wholly-owned subsidiary of IEH. In certain circumstances, the parties have agreed to consummate the Merger, without the prior completion of the Offer, after receipt of the vote of the holders of a majority of the issued and outstanding shares of Common Stock on a record date yet to be selected in favor of the adoption of the Merger Agreement. In that case, the consummation of the Merger would be subject to conditions similar to the conditions to the Offer, other than the addition of a condition that the holders of a majority of the issued and outstanding shares of Common Stock have adopted the Merger Agreement and the inapplicability of the Minimum Condition. Also on December 15 and simultaneously with the execution of the Merger Agreement, the Support Parties and the Company entered into a Stockholder Support Agreement, and IEH entered into the Guarantee in favor of the Company. Pursuant to the Stockholder Support Agreement, the Support Parties agreed, subject to the terms and conditions of such agreement, to, among other things, vote shares of Common Stock (and shares of Common Stock underlying call options to the extent exercised), constituting up to approximately 14.92% of the issued and outstanding shares of Common Stock entitled to vote thereon, in favor of the adoption of the Merger Agreement, if necessary. Pursuant to the Guarantee, IEH is guaranteeing the payment and other obligations of the Offeror and Merger Sub under the Merger Agreement and in connection with the Offer (other than certain obligations related to indemnification of directors and officers of the Company).

On December 16, 2010, Dynegy and Icahn Enterprises L.P. issued the following press release:

FOR IMMEDIATE RELEASE
DYNEGY ENTERS INTO AGREEMENT TO BE ACQUIRED BY ICAHN ENTERPRISES LP FOR $5.50 PER SHARE IN CASH
OPEN STRATEGIC ALTERNATIVES PROCESS TO CONTINUE IN
ORDER TO SOLICIT SUPERIOR ALTERNATIVE PROPOSALS

HOUSTON, DECEMBER 15, 2010—Dynegy Inc. (NYSE: DYN) today announced that its Board of Directors has unanimously approved a definitive agreement to be acquired by Icahn Enterprises LP (NYSE: IEP) in a tender offer followed by a merger for $5.50 per share in cash, or approximately $665 million in the aggregate. Dynegy has approximately $3.95 billion of outstanding debt, net of cash.

Under the terms of the agreement, Dynegy stockholders will receive $5.50 in cash for each outstanding share of Dynegy common stock they own, which is $0.50 per share or 10% higher than the previous offer and represents a 10% premium to Dynegy's average closing stock price over the last 30 trading days. In connection with today's announcement, it is expected that a wholly-owned subsidiary of IEP will commence a tender offer for all of the outstanding shares of Dynegy that they do not already own no later than December 22, 2010. IEP and its affiliates own approximately 9.9% of Dynegy's outstanding shares and have previously acquired options to purchase approximately 5% of Dynegy's outstanding shares. IEP has also agreed that, in certain circumstances, if a "superior" all cash offer is made and supported by Dynegy, and IEP does not wish to top the "superior" offer, it will support it.

As you will recall from Chapter 22, the tender offer failed and thus the merger was never consummated. The following information from the 2010 10-K, regarding Dynegy's shares may provide some insight into the failure of the tender offer:

COMMON SHARE DATA*

	2010	2009	2008
Earnings (loss) per diluted common share attributable to Dynergy Inc	$ (1.95)	$ (7.60)	$ 1.04
Annual cash divided per common share**	–	–	–
Market price at year end	5.62	9.05	10.00
Average common shares outstanding (in millions)			
Diluted	121	165	168
Basic	120	164	168

Of course, by Fall 2012 the Dynegy shares were trading at 2.5 cents per share. Does this suggest anything about the common assumption that shareholders behave rationally? Dynegy's largest shareholder after the Icahn entities was Seneca Capital, who argued that the Icahn offer undervalued Dynegy.[13]

---

13. *http://goo.gl/BsQQS*

24

ASSET SALES

Another way to sell or acquire a business is through an asset sale. This involves a sale of the target's assets to a buyer, or, more often, a newly formed buyer subsidiary, that pays cash or shares to the target. Typically the target then dissolves under state corporate law, using the sale consideration to pay off its obligations in a manner consistent with the absolute priority rule.

1. THE ASSET PURCHASE AGREEMENT

Having seen a merger agreement, an asset purchase agreement (APA) will be familiar stuff. But there are important differences. For example, and perhaps most obviously, an APA will also contain transfer provisions that differ from those found in a merger agreement or a stock purchase agreement.

The APA will usually provide for the "Acquired Assets" — capitalized to indicate it's a defined term — to be transferred at the closing. But because the law of asset transfers in the United States is largely dependent on the nature of the underlying assets, the parties need different documents to transfer different sorts of assets. Thus, there will be the following:

- A bill of sale covering all the tangible personal property.
- Deeds conveying each piece of real property.
- Assignments of lease rights.
- Assignments of other contractual rights.
- Assignments of intellectual property rights.

The APA will also likely provide for the "Assumed Liabilities" to be transferred at the closing.

Recall that only liabilities that are among the Assumed Liabilities transfer over to the buyer, unless one of the exceptions described in Section 3 below applies.

In all other cases, the creditor's rights remain against the seller corporation and the consideration the seller has just received.

As a result, the indemnification section of an APA will differ from that of a merger agreement or SPA. In addition to indemnifying buyer for breaches of representations and covenants, the target shareholders will typically indemnify the buyer for all excluded liabilities. What considerations go into negotiating the scope of this provision?

AIRBORNE HEALTH, INC. AND WEIL, GOTSHAL & MANGES LLP, v. SQUID SOAP, LP

984 A.2d 126, Court of Chancery of Delaware
C.A. No. 4410-VCL | Submitted: Nov. 13, 2009 | Decided: Nov. 23, 2009

LASTER, Vice Chancellor.

Plaintiffs Airborne Health, Inc. ("Airborne") and Weil, Gotshal & Manges LLP ("Weil") have moved for judgment on the pleadings against defendant Squid Soap, LP ("Squid Soap"). Except for two minor issues, I grant the motion.

I.   FACTUAL BACKGROUND

I assume the following facts to be true for purposes of the motion for judgment on the pleadings. The facts are drawn solely from the pleadings, which consist of Airborne and Weil's complaint, Squid Soap's first amended answer and counterclaims, and Airborne and Weil's replies to the counterclaims. I also have considered the Asset Purchase Agreement (the "Agreement" or the "APA"), which is incorporated by reference in all of the pleadings. Because this is a motion for judgment on the pleadings, I have assumed that all disputed factual allegations would be resolved in favor of Squid Soap, the non-movant. I likewise have given Squid Soap the benefit of all reasonable factual inferences.

A.   THE PARTIES.

Defendant Squid Soap is a Texas limited partnership with its principal place of business in Austin, Texas.

Plaintiff Airborne is a Delaware corporation with its principal place of business in Minneapolis, Minnesota. Effective as of June 15, 2007, Airborne and Squid Soap entered into an Asset Purchase Agreement by which Airborne acquired all of Squid Soap's assets, including certain intellectual property.

Plaintiff Weil is a New York limited liability partnership with its headquarters in New York, New York. Weil served as legal counsel to Airborne for purposes of drafting and negotiating the APA.

B. SQUID SOAP'S POTENTIAL.

In the early 1990s, John Lynn saw a business opportunity in society's growing awareness that thorough hand washing limits the spread of germs. Mr. Lynn believed that germ-focused parents, educators, and health professionals would embrace his invention. According to the counterclaims, he was right. Squid Soap received national attention. It was featured in magazines such as Redbook, Woman's Day, InStyle, and Parenting, and it appeared on television shows such as Good Morning America and the Fox Morning Show. Newspapers and websites praised it.

Buoyed by its unique attributes and the same favorable market trends that propelled sales of hand sanitizer and anti-bacterial wipes, Squid Soap became a hit. Retailers like Wal-Mart, Target, CVS, and Walgreen's stocked Squid Soap products. A consumer product paradise beckoned with high recurrent sales and patent-protected margins. All Squid Soap needed was a nationwide marketing platform and brand-name recognition.

C. SQUID SOAP TALKS WITH POTENTIAL STRATEGIC PARTNERS.

In early 2007, Mr. Lynn was approached by companies and investment groups seeking to capitalize on Squid Soap's potential. Each group expressed great interest in Squid Soap. The suitors included the consumer products powerhouse Procter & Gamble, a multibillion dollar hedge fund HBK Investments, and a publicly traded business development company Capital Southwest Corporation.

D. AIRBORNE'S STORY.

Like Squid Soap, Airborne started out as a small, single-product company focused on stopping the spread of germs. Airborne's initial product was a cocktail of various vitamins, herbs and other ingredients that Airborne marketed as preventing and even curing the common cold. Indeed, Airborne required vendors to place its product displays on their cough and cold remedy aisles.

Victoria Knight-McDowell founded Airborne in 1997. In 2005, Summit Partners acquired majority ownership of Airborne. Ms. Donahue became CEO, replacing Mrs. Knight-McDowell, who continued her role as a brand spokesperson and board member.

By 2006, propelled by celebrity endorsements and aggressive advertising, Airborne ranked at the top of a list of the fastest-growing privately held companies. It experienced furious growth and at one time projected $300 million in annual sales. Airborne was at the pinnacle of brand recognition. Its name was its product.

E. SQUID SOAP SELLS TO AIRBORNE.

Airborne's story charmed Mr. Lynn. The counterclaims allege that "[b]ased on Airborne's representations about, among other things, its brand name, sterling reputation, marketing prowess, and in particular its promises to leverage the Airborne name and marketing platform to fully maximize Squid Soap's potential, Squid Soap, relying on and induced by Airborne's representations and promises, re-focused its acquisition talks to Airborne, to the exclusion of its other suitors."

Squid Soap and Airborne eventually agreed on a transaction through which Airborne would purchase Squid Soap's assets (the "Asset Purchase"). The terms of the Asset Purchase are memorialized in the APA. The APA was an integrated contract, and in Section 10.3, the parties agreed that it reflected their compete agreement on the terms for the transaction.

Several aspects of the APA stand out. Most notably, Squid Soap agreed to sell its assets for $1 million in cash at closing, plus the potential for earn-out payments of up to $26.5 million if certain targets were achieved. Squid Soap asserts in the counterclaims that "[t]he high price tag was a reflection of Squid Soap's enormous market value." What an earn-out (and particularly a large one) typically reflects is disagreement over the value of the business that is bridged when the seller trades the certainty of less cash at closing for the prospect of more cash over time. In theory, the earn-out solves the disagreement over value by requiring the buyer to pay more only if the business proves that it is worth more. But since value is frequently debatable and the causes of underperformance equally so, an earn-out often converts today's disagreement over price into tomorrow's litigation over the outcome. Based on an earn-out of this magnitude (viewed in terms of the portion of total potential consideration), the plain inference is that Squid Soap believed that its business had tremendous value and was willing to bet heavily on that proposition.

Reinforcing this inference is a second notable feature of the APA. Airborne purchased Squid Soap's brand name, goodwill, and intellectual property, including the Patents, but the APA required that Airborne return the assets to Squid Soap if certain business targets were not met. Section 3.2 of the APA states:

> Notwithstanding anything herein to the contrary, in the event that (i) Purchaser does not incur at least $1,000,000 of marketing, account retail programs and/or advertising spending (including brand spending but excluding co-op fees, slotting fees and product discounts) specifically focused upon the [Squid Soap] Products within the first twelve months after Closing . . . , and (ii) Net Sales of the [Squid Soap] Products have not reached $5,000,000 within the first twelve months after Closing, then Purchaser shall transfer the Purchased Assets existing as of such date (other than inventory) back to Seller for the consideration of $10.00 and other valuable consideration of which the Purchaser and Seller both agree is valuable and adequate consideration. Upon such transfer, each person's obligations under this Agreement shall terminate except for obligations due and payable up through the date of termination.

Similarly, Section 3.2(g) provides:

> Notwithstanding anything herein to the contrary, in the event Purchaser ceases to market, advertise and sell [Squid Soap] Product(s) at any time prior to reaching aggregate Net Sales of $7,500,000 then Purchaser agrees to transfer the Purchased Assets existing as of such date (other than inventory) back to Seller for $10.00 and

other valuable consideration of which the Purchaser and Seller both agree is valuable and adequate consideration. Upon such transfer, each person's obligations under this Agreement shall terminate except for obligations due and payable up through the date of termination.

I will refer to these provisions as the "Asset Return Provisions."

The Asset Return Provisions establish a framework in which Airborne gets to take its shot at making Squid Soap a success, but if things do not work out, then Airborne has to return the assets. Section 3.2 is particularly instructive in this regard. It gives Airborne twelve months. After that point, if Airborne has not spent $1 million on marketing and achieved $5 million in Net Sales, then Airborne must return the assets to Squid Soap. Like the earn-out, this structure indicates that Squid Soap believed its product was a winner, that it was in demand, and that if Airborne could not make a go of it, then Squid Soap would get the assets back and could pursue a relationship with someone else.

A third noteworthy aspect of the APA is the absence of any specific commitments by Airborne regarding the level of efforts or resources that it would devote. Squid Soap alleges that "the APA required Airborne to spend a minimum of $1,000,000.00 on marketing specifically for Squid Soap's products within the first 12 months after the APA was signed." This is not what the APA provides. The $1 million figure appears in Section 3.2, one of the Asset Return Provisions, and establishes a requirement that Airborne must hit if it wants to retain the assets.

A mandatory commitment by Airborne to expend funds easily could have been drafted. All it needed to say was "Purchaser shall incur at least $1,000,000 of marketing, account retail programs and/or advertising spending (including brand spending but excluding co-op fees, slotting fees and product discounts) specifically focused upon the Squid Soap Products within the first twelve months after Closing." Squid Soap did not obtain a commitment of this nature.

A fourth noteworthy feature of the APA is the absence of detailed representations by Airborne regarding the issues that Squid Soap now claims were critically important. Squid Soap alleges:

> In entering the APA, Squid Soap relied on and was induced by Airborne's promises and representations regarding its positive brand name and image, its marketing power, as well as Airborne's intent and, importantly, its ability to market Squid Soap and to leverage Airborne's positive brand image. These representations by Airborne were at the core of Squid Soap's decision to sell to Airborne. Given their importance, Squid Soap relied upon Airborne's repeated assurances about its reputation and brand image and their effect on Airborne's ability to market and leverage that positive brand name.

Yet there are no contractual representations in the APA by Airborne regarding these matters.

The APA called for a simultaneous signing and closing, which took place on June 15, 2007.

F.   AIRBORNE SUFFERS SIGNIFICANT REVERSES.

According to the counterclaims, at the time Squid Soap entered into the APA, Squid Soap did not know that Airborne's product had been severely criticized by a special investigation conducted by ABC News and aired on Good Morning America. The special report found that the clinical study on which Airborne based its germ-fighting claims had been produced by a "two-man operation started up just to do the Airborne study." The news report led to intense scrutiny of Airborne's products, marketing, and claims.

Squid Soap also says it did not know then that there was a class action pending against Airborne in California state court, filed in May 2006, which asserted various claims for false or misleading advertising, consumer fraud, deceptive or unfair business practices, concealment, omission, and unfair competition (the "California Action"). The Center for Science in the Public Interest, a non-profit organization with significant expertise in litigation over product mislabeling, joined the California Action on the plaintiffs' side. The Center's litigation director called the case a "great opportunity for CSPI to participate in a major lawsuit against one of the biggest supplement frauds in the country."

Airborne's post-APA problems immediately became Squid Soap's problems because Airborne owned Squid Soap and because Squid Soap had been repackaged as "Squid Soap by Airborne." Squid Soap alleges that Airborne's difficulties "killed Squid Soap in its infancy."

G.   AIRBORNE RETURNS THE SQUID SOAP ASSETS.

Since its legal stumbles, Airborne has engaged in damage control. Mrs. Knight-McDowell reacquired Airborne and launched a highly publicized campaign to restore consumer confidence and rebuild the company. According to the counterclaims, Airborne has focused on its historic products and has done nothing to market or rehabilitate Squid Soap.

Under the Asset Return Provisions, Airborne was required to return Squid Soap's assets, including the Patents, to Airborne if the financial thresholds in those provisions were not met. It is undisputed that the thresholds were not met.

Squid Soap contends that because the thresholds were not met, the assets automatically reverted to Squid Soap on June 15, 2008, one year after the closing of the Asset Purchase. This is not what the Asset Return Provisions say. They obligate Airborne to return the assets, but title does not revert automatically.

Airborne attempted to return the assets to Squid Soap. In an email dated September 9, 2008, Mr. Rainone, President of Airborne's Squid Soap Division, advised Squid Soap that Airborne would be returning the assets. As quoted in the counterclaims, the email stated:

> We [Airborne] understand your need to transition [the Patents and other purchased assets back to Squid Soap] and will do whatever is necessary to make it a smooth one. . . . Our goal is to transition this to you in a way which will make it seamless for our customers. . . . [L]et's discuss a plan for a smooth transition.

It appears that at the same time, Airborne was in the process of securing financing from BNP Paribas, secured by Airborne assets that included the

Patents. On September 29, 2008, just three weeks after Mr. Rainone's email, Airborne entered into an agreement assigning an interest in the Patents to BNP Paribas. The interest was recorded the following day with the United States Patent and Trademark Office.

Squid Soap sees further perfidy in Airborne's actions, which it claims "prevent[ed] Squid Soap from marketing or selling Squid Soap to any would-be buyers after the reversion date [allegedly June 15, 2008] but before the onset of the current economic crisis that has solidly dead-stopped private investment into companies like Squid Soap." I take judicial notice of the indisputably troubled state of the financial markets prior to June 2008, including the shotgun acquisition of Bear Stearns by JPMorgan in March of that year. Squid Soap has not identified any potential buyer, interested party, or prospect that it could have pursued.

It is undisputed that Airborne continued to attempt to return the assets to Squid Soap. It is equally undisputed that Squid Soap has refused to accept them.

H.   SQUID SOAP SUES IN TEXAS, BUT THAT ACTION IS DISMISSED.

The APA contains a forum selection clause requiring all disputes arising out of or relating to the Agreement to be heard in this Court or any federal court in the State of Delaware. Section 10.4(b) states:

> All actions and proceedings arising out of or relating to this Agreement shall be heard and determined in the Chancery Court of the State of Delaware or any federal court sitting in the State of Delaware, and the parties hereto hereby irrevocably submit to the exclusive jurisdiction of such courts (and, in the case of appeals, appropriate appellate courts therefrom) in any such action or proceeding and irrevocably waive the defense of an inconvenient forum to the maintenance of any such action or proceeding.

Despite this provision, on December 3, 2008, Squid Soap filed suit in the United States District Court for the District of Texas against Airborne and BNP Paribas asserting various causes of action arising out of and relating to the APA, including conversion, fraud, negligent misrepresentation, breach of fiduciary duty, unjust enrichment, and conspiracy. On February 6, 2009, Squid Soap amended its complaint in the Texas action to drop BNP Paribas and add Weil. On May 14, 2009, the Texas court dismissed the Texas action without prejudice.

Meanwhile, on March 6, 2009, Airborne and Weil sought a declaratory judgment from this Court establishing that they were not liable under the APA. On June 30, Squid Soap amended it answer to assert counterclaims against Airborne and Weil. After Airborne and Weil replied to the counterclaims, they moved for judgment on the pleadings.

THE IMPLIED COVENANT OF GOOD FAITH AND FAIR DEALING

Squid Soap ultimately falls back to the implied covenant of fair dealing. This count recasts both of Squid Soap's basic complaints — Airborne's failure to disclose litigation risks and Airborne's failure to spend on marketing or achieve sales — as breaches of the implied covenant.

The implied covenant of good faith and fair dealing inheres in every contract governed by Delaware law and "requires a party in a contractual relationship to refrain from arbitrary or unreasonable conduct which has the effect of preventing the other party to the contract from receiving the fruits of the bargain." The implied covenant does not apply when "the subject at issue is expressly covered by the contract." At the same time, the covenant exists to fulfill the reasonable expectations of the parties, and thus the implied obligation must be consistent with the terms of the agreement as a whole. The doctrine thus operates only in that narrow band of cases where the contract as a whole speaks sufficiently to suggest an obligation and point to a result, but does not speak directly enough to provide an explicit answer. In the Venn diagram of contract cases, the area of overlap is quite small.

The test for the implied covenant depends on whether it is "clear from what was expressly agreed upon that the parties who negotiated the express terms of the contract would have agreed to proscribe the act later complained of as a breach of the implied covenant of good faith — had they thought to negotiate with respect to that matter." Katz v. Oak Indus., Inc., 508 A.2d 873, 880 (Del.Ch.1986) (Allen, C.). "[I]mplying obligations based on the covenant of good faith and fair dealing is a cautious enterprise." "[C]ourts should be most chary about implying a contractual protection when the contract easily could have been drafted to expressly provide for it."

Squid Soap's implied covenant claim based on litigation disclosure is easily addressed. The parties to the APA agreed upon a specific representation by Airborne relating to litigation in Section 6.3. Squid Soap could have insisted on a broader representation. With the benefit of hindsight, it should have. But the implied covenant is not a means to re-write agreements.

Squid Soap's arguments regarding Airborne's obligation to spend funds on marketing and to achieve sales have a tinge more color. Squid Soap understandably questions what it obtained under the APA if Airborne had no obligation actually to expend resources. The APA does not contain any language that specifically addresses the issue, either by requiring Airborne to expend resources or by saying explicitly that Airborne has no obligation to expend resources. The APA does, however, contain explicit financial targets on which the parties agreed. This allows Squid Soap to contend plausibly that this case falls within the narrow band of the implied covenant. The provision Squid Soap seeks to imply is that Airborne could not arbitrarily refuse to expend resources and thereby deprive Squid Soap of the prospects for the earn-out. In Squid Soap's view, Airborne at least had to make an honest go of it.

There is support in our law for this argument. When a contract confers discretion on one party, the implied covenant requires that the discretion be used reasonably and in good faith. Airborne thus could not have refused arbitrarily or in bad faith to pursue the Squid Soap business. But Squid Soap does not contend that Airborne failed to expend funds to make the business a success arbitrarily, in bad faith, or for no reason. Squid Soap's counterclaims quite clearly allege that Airborne suffered a corporate crisis in its core business and, at least in part as a result of that crisis, did not expend resources on Squid Soap. Squid Soap specifically recognizes that Airborne was "[u]ndoubtedly restrained by the legal and financial burdens of the settlement and systemic market damage." This as-pled scenario does not support a claim that Squid Soap exercised its contractual discretion in bad faith.

Squid Soap's position is also undercut by the ease with which Squid Soap could have insisted on specific contractual commitments from Airborne regard-ing the expenditure of resources, or some form of "efforts" obligation for Air-borne. These provisions are familiar to any transactional lawyer, and Squid Soap was a sophisticated party represented by able counsel. Moreover, Section 7.6, entitled "Obligations of Seller," provides that "[e]ach Selling Partner agrees to take all reasonable actions necessary to cause Seller to perform its obligations hereunder and to otherwise comply with the terms of this Agreement." Squid Soap could have insisted on a provision binding Airborne. Rather than holding out for these types of contractual protections, Squid Soap accepted earn-out provisions that are expressly phrased in conditional terms.

Importantly for purposes of the implied covenant, I do not think it irrational, or even unreasonable, that Squid Soap would have chosen this deal structure. The APA provides contractual downside protection, but in the different form of a requirement that Airborne return the assets so that Squid Soap could go elsewhere. Squid Soap alleges that it had a hot property, and thus the prospect of getting the assets back and linking up with a better partner could well have made sense. At the same time, Airborne had powerful incentives to want Squid Soap to succeed, and thus Squid Soap and Airborne's interests were largely aligned. Squid Soap made an understandable business decision, albeit one it now regrets.

This is not a case in which Squid Soap has been deprived of the fruit of its bargain arbitrarily or in a manner where the implied covenant of good faith and fair dealing should come into play. The price of the greater consideration that Squid Soap hoped to achieve through the earn-out was the risk that Airborne would fail. Unfortunately for Squid Soap, Airborne did not succeed, but that does not allow Squid Soap to rewrite the deal it cut in more optimistic days. I therefore enter judgment on the pleadings against Squid Soap and in favor of Airborne on Squid Soap's implied covenant claim.

E. THE CLAIMS AGAINST WEIL.

Squid Soap seeks to hold Weil liable under theories of aiding and abetting and conspiracy. These theories require an underlying wrong that Weil could have aided or abetted or conspired to effect. I have already held that there is no underlying wrong. I therefore enter judgment in Weil's favor and do not reach any of Weil's unique arguments.

F. AIRBORNE AND WEIL'S AFFIRMATIVE CLAIMS FOR RELIEF.

My analysis of Squid Soap's counterclaims largely disposes of all of the issues presented by the motion for judgment on the pleadings . . .

2. VOTING RIGHTS

Under the corporate law of most states, the buyer shareholders do not get to vote on an asset sale. And the target-seller shareholders only get to vote when the sale involves "all or substantially all" of the seller's assets.[1] Others may have contractual rights that are triggered in similar circumstances. But what does "all or substantially all" mean?

HOLLINGER INC., A CANADIAN CORPORATION, AND 504468 N.B. INC., A NEW BRUNSWICK CORPORATION, PLAINTIFFS, V. HOLLINGER INTERNATIONAL, INC., A DELAWARE CORPORATION, DEFENDANT

858 A.2d 342
Court of Chancery of Delaware, New Castle County
C.A. No. 543-N I Submitted: July 23, 2004 I Decided: July 29, 2004

STRINE, Vice Chancellor.

If the questions resolved in this lengthy opinion could be distilled to three, they would be as follows:

1. Has the judiciary transmogrified the words "substantially all" in §271 of the Delaware General Corporation Law into the words "approximately half"?

[The other questions are omitted.]

This opinion answers each question in the same way: no.

Hollinger Inc. (or "Inc.") seeks a preliminary injunction preventing Hollinger International, Inc. (or "International") from selling the *Telegraph* Group Ltd. (England) to Press Holdings International, an entity controlled by Frederick and David Barclay (hereinafter, the "Barclays"). The *Telegraph* Group is an indirect, wholly owned subsidiary of International and publishes the *Telegraph* newspaper and the *Spectator* magazine. The *Telegraph* newspaper is a leading one in the United Kingdom, both in terms of its circulation and its journalistic reputation.

The key question addressed in this decision is whether Inc. and the other International stockholders must be provided with the opportunity to vote on the sale of the *Telegraph* Group because that sale involves "substantially all" the assets of International within the meaning of 8 *Del.* C. §271. The sale of the *Telegraph* followed a lengthy auction process whereby International and all of Hollinger's operating assets were widely shopped to potential bidders.

As a practical matter, Inc.'s vote would be the only one that matters because although it now owns only 18% of International's total equity, it, through high-vote Class B shares, controls 68% of the voting power.

---

1. Del. Gen. Corp. Law §271.

Inc. argues that a preliminary injunction should issue because it is clear that the sale of the *Telegraph* satisfies the quantitative and qualitative test used to determine whether an asset sale involves substantially all of a corporation's assets. The *Telegraph* Group is one of the most profitable parts of International and is its most prestigious asset. After its sale, International will be transformed from a respected international publishing company controlling one of the world's major newspapers to a primarily American publishing company whose most valuable remaining asset, the *Chicago Sun-Times*, is the second leading newspaper in the Second City.

In response to these arguments, International makes several points.

Initially, it contends that the sale of the *Telegraph* Group does not trigger §271. However prestigious the *Telegraph* Group, International says its sale does not involve, either quantitatively or qualitatively, the sale of substantially all International's assets. Whether or not the *Chicago Sun-Times* is as prestigious as the *Daily Telegraph*, it remains a profitable newspaper in a major city. Along with a group of profitable Chicago-area community newspapers, the *Chicago Sun-Times* has made the "Chicago Group" International's most profitable operating segment in the last two years and its contribution to International's profits has been comparable to that of the *Telegraph* Group for many years. Moreover, International retains a number of smaller newspapers in Canada and the prestigious *Jerusalem Post*. After the sale of the *Telegraph* Group, International therefore will quantitatively retain a sizable percentage of its existing assets and will qualitatively remain in the same business line. Although the *Telegraph* sale is admittedly a major transaction, International stresses that §271 does not apply to every major transaction; it only applies to transactions that strike at the heart of a corporation's existence, which this transaction does not. Only by ignoring the statute's language, International argues, can this court determine that International will have sold substantially all its assets by divesting itself of the *Telegraph* Group.

As an alternative argument, International contends that §271 is inapplicable for another reason. International argues that none of *its* assets are being sold at all, because the *Telegraph* Group is held through a chain of wholly owned subsidiaries and it is only the last link in that chain which is actually being sold to the Barclays.

In this opinion, I conclude that Inc.'s motion for a preliminary injunction motion should be denied as neither its §271 nor its equitable claims have a reasonable probability of success.

I choose not to decide whether International's technical statutory defense has merit. It is common for public companies to hold all of their operating assets through indirect, wholly owned subsidiaries. International wants me to hold that a parent company board may unilaterally direct and control a process by which its indirect, wholly owned subsidiary sells assets that would, if held directly by the parent, possibly comprise substantially all of the parent's assets and by which the sale proceeds under a contract that the parent corporation itself negotiates, signs, and fully guarantees. In that circumstance, International says that §271 would have no application unless the selling subsidiary has no corporate dignity under the strict test for veil piercing. A ruling of that kind would, as a practical matter, render §271 an illusory check on unilateral board power at most public companies. And while that ruling would involve a rational reading of §271, it would not represent the only possible interpretation of that statute. Because this motion can be resolved on substantive economic grounds and because the policy implications of ruling on International's technical defense are important, prudence counsels in favor of deferring a necessarily hasty decision on the interesting question presented.

Instead, I address the economic merits of Inc.'s §271 claim and treat the *Telegraph* Group as if it were directly owned by International. An application of the governing test, which was originally articulated in Gimbel v. Signal Cos.,[2] to the facts demonstrates that the *Telegraph* Group does not come close to comprising "substantially all" of International's assets. Although the *Telegraph* Group is a very important asset of International's and is likely its most valuable asset, International possesses several other important assets. Prominent among these is its so-called Chicago Group, a valuable collection of publications that, by any objective standard approaches the *Telegraph* Group in economic importance to International. In fact, earlier this year, Inc. based its decision to try to sell itself to the Barclays on advice that the Chicago Group was worth more than the *Telegraph* Group. And the record is replete with evidence indicating that the Chicago Group's recent performance in outperforming the profitability of the *Telegraph* Group was not anomalous and that many reasoned observers — including Inc.'s controlling stockholder, Conrad Black — believe that the Chicago Group will continue to generate EBITDA at levels akin to those of the *Telegraph* Group.

Put simply, after the *Telegraph* Group is sold, International will retain considerable assets that are capable of generating substantial free cash flow. Section 271 does not require a vote when a major asset or trophy is sold; it requires a vote only when the assets to be sold, when considered quantitatively and qualitatively, amount to "substantially all" of the corporation's assets.

Inc.'s inability to meet this economically focused test has led it to place great weight on the greater journalistic reputation of the *Telegraph* newspaper when compared to the *Sun-Times* and the social importance of that newspaper in British life. The problem with this argument is that §271 is designed as a protection for rational owners of capital and its proper interpretation requires this court to focus on the economic importance of assets and not their aesthetic worth. The economic value of the *Telegraph's* prestige was reflected in the sales process for the *Telegraph* Group and in the cash flows projected for that Group. The Barclays' bid includes the economic value that bidders place on the *Telegraph's* social cachet and does not approach a price that puts the *Telegraph* Group close to being substantially all of International's assets. Nor does the sale of the *Telegraph* Group break any solemn promise to International stockholders. During its history, International has continually bought and sold publishing assets, and no rational investor would view the *Telegraph* Group as immune from the company's ongoing M & A activity.

A sale of all or substantially all of a company's assets might also trigger *Revlon* duties, although the case law on this point is sparse. Also remember that many

---

2. 316 A.2d 599 (Del.Ch.), *aff'd*, 316 A.2d 619 (Del.1974).

credit agreements and indentures contain covenants that restrict asset sales. The most significant case on this issue is *Sharon Steel Corp. v. The Chase Manhattan Bank, N.A.*, which hopefully is vaguely familiar.

Appraisal rights also vary based on the nature of the transaction structure. For example, Delaware law provides that shareholders who do not approve of a merger may exercise appraisal rights if they are dissatisfied with the consideration they receive in the merger. On the other hand, appraisal rights are not available in a stock purchase, either by tender or SPA. Some jurisdictions, but not Delaware, provide for appraisal rights in connection with certain asset sales.[3]

PROBLEM SET 24.1

1. California grants broader voting rights than Delaware in some assets sales, but not others. *See* Cal. Corp. Code. §§181, 1000, 1200, 1201. Why might they draw the distinction that they do? Is this approach preferable to the Delaware approach?

3. THE LIMITS OF ASSET SALES

DARREL FRANKLIN ET AL., PLAINTIFFS AND RESPONDENTS, v. USX CORPORATION, DEFENDANT AND APPELLANT

87 Cal.App.4th 615
Court of Appeal, First District, Division 3, California
No. A091473. March 2, 2001

WALKER, J.

Jeannette Franklin, now deceased, and her husband, Darrel Franklin (respondents), filed an action for personal injury, premises liability and loss of consortium against several defendants, including appellant USX Corporation (USX). Respondents contended that Jeannette had contracted mesothelioma, an asbestos-caused cancer, as a result of childhood exposure to second hand asbestos carried home by her parents, who worked at the Western Pipe & Steel Shipyard (WPS) in South San Francisco during World War II. Respondents sought to hold USX liable for their injuries on the theory that it was the successor in interest to WPS. By stipulation, the successor in interest issue was tried by the court on a statement of facts that were either agreed to or disputed, along with an agreed-upon documentary record; no testimony was presented in this phase of the trial. The trial court concluded that USX was the successor in interest to WPS, and was therefore liable for any damages caused by WPS. In a bifurcated proceeding, a jury decided the issues of liability and damages, and returned a verdict against USX in excess of $5 million.

---

3. N.Y. Bus. Corp. §910(a)(B).

USX appeals the trial court's conclusion that it was the successor in interest to WPS. It also appeals the jury verdict on several grounds. We hold that the trial court erred in finding USX liable as the successor in interest to WPS. Accordingly, we do not address the issues pertaining to the jury verdict.

General Background

Prior to the beginning of World War II, WPS owned a steel fabrication plant in South San Francisco, which had been used to build ships during World War I. When World War II broke out, WPS entered into a contract with the United States Maritime Commission to again build ships for use in the war. The contract required the use of ship building materials containing asbestos.

Jeannette Franklin was a child during World War II. Both of her parents worked at WPS from 1942 to 1945. Neither of her parents worked directly with asbestos-containing materials, but they both worked in areas where asbestos was present. At times, they were exposed to airborne dust during the mixing of mud, during insulation work, and when workers swept up debris. Franklin alleged that she was exposed to this asbestos-containing dust because her parents brought it home on their clothing and in their car. In 1996, Franklin was diagnosed with peritoneal mesothelioma, which she maintained was caused by her childhood second hand exposure to asbestos.

Corporate History

In December 1945, the assets of WPS were purchased by Consolidated Steel Corporation of California (Con Cal) for over $6.2 million in cash. In connection with the sale, Con Cal agreed to assume all of the liabilities, obligations and commitments of WPS.

On December 14, 1946, Con Cal and some of its affiliates entered into an agreement (the purchase agreement) to sell certain assets (the transfer assets) to Columbia Steel Company (Columbia), a division of U.S. Steel. Although the closing date was set for March 31, 1947, the filing of a Sherman Act antitrust action delayed the closing until the summer of 1948. In August 1948, Columbia assigned its rights under the purchase agreement to a newly formed corporation and subsidiary of U.S. Steel, Consolidated Western Steel Corporation of Delaware (Con Del). On August 31, 1948, Con Cal sold the transfer assets to Con Del for almost $8.3 million in cash, plus additional consideration that brought the total purchase price to over $17 million. Con Del was later merged into U.S. Steel, which thereafter changed its name to USX, the appellant here.[4] After August 31, 1948, Con Cal changed its name to Consolidated Liquidating Corporation, which dissolved on February 29, 1952. Alden G. Roach was Con Cal's president and chairman of the board at the time of the sale; after the sale

---

4. To avoid confusion, we will hereafter refer to the purchasing party as USX.

he continued as president of Con Del and Columbia, and was appointed chairman of Columbia's board.

DISCUSSION

It has been generally stated that "where one corporation sells or transfers all of its assets to another corporation, the latter is not liable for the debts and liabilities of the former unless (1) the purchaser expressly or impliedly agrees to such assumption, (2) the transaction amounts to a consolidation or merger of the two corporations, (3) the purchasing corporation is merely a continuation of the selling corporation, or (4) the transaction is entered into fraudulently to escape liability for debts." In addition, under certain limited circumstances an exception has been judicially created to provide a remedy against the successor when a person has been injured by the predecessor's product. This exception, first enunciated in Ray v. Alad, *supra*, 19 Cal.3d 22, 136 Cal.Rptr. 574, 560 P.2d 3, has become known as the "product line successor" rule. The trial court found USX liable for respondents' injuries under the first three general exceptions to non-liability, as well as under the product line successor exception. We consider each ground, and hold that USX cannot be found to be the successor in interest to Con Cal/WPS under any of the theories asserted.

USX DID NOT EXPRESSLY OR IMPLIEDLY ASSUME THE TORT LIABILITIES OF CON CAL/WPS

Based upon its interpretation of the 1946 purchase agreement and other extrinsic evidence, the trial court found that USX had expressly or impliedly assumed the tort liabilities of Con Cal/WPS. Because no issue of credibility was involved in the trial court's determination, we review the agreement and the extrinsic evidence de novo with an eye toward giving effect to the mutual intentions of the contracting parties. We first consider the language of the purchase agreement itself, which we conclude unambiguously shows that USX did not assume the tort liabilities of Con Cal/WPS. We further hold that, because the unambiguous contract was expressly integrated, it was improper to consider extrinsic evidence to vary or alter its terms. Finally, even if the extrinsic evidence is taken into account, it does not show the parties' intention that USX assume the liabilities at issue in this action.

Pursuant to the 1946 purchase agreement, the bulk of Con Cal's business assets were purchased by USX, with Con Cal retaining certain specified assets and certain existing contracts. With regard to USX's assumption of liabilities, the agreement provided: "The Buyer shall not, except as herein otherwise specifically provided, directly or indirectly, by virtue of any of the provisions of this agreement, become liable for any of the debts, obligations, liabilities, undertakings, agreements or commitments of the Sellers of any nature whatsoever. ...." It further provided that, while USX would assume responsibility for performing "all the obligations of the Sellers with respect to the uncompleted portion of [assumed] contracts, orders and subcontracts ... *in no event* shall the Buyer assume any obligations of the Sellers, or any of them, arising out of deliveries of goods, wares or merchandise made by the Sellers prior to the closing, including, but not limited to, any claims on account of any allegedly defective goods, wares or merchandise delivered by the Sellers pursuant to any such contract or order, or otherwise." (Italics added.)

The quoted language is clear and unambiguous; USX assumed only the liabilities specified in the purchase agreement, which did not include the assumption of contingent tort liabilities. It is equally clear that the purchase agreement was an integrated document. It provided that "[t]here are no agreements, contracts, promises, representations or statements between the parties hereto except as contained in this agreement, and this agreement shall constitute the entire and whole contract between the parties hereto."

Notwithstanding the quoted language of the integrated agreement, the trial court found the "contract documents" to be ambiguous, and considered documents extrinsic to the contract in order to resolve the perceived ambiguity. Based upon the purchase agreement provision rendering USX responsible for all unfilled sales orders and on an indemnity clause contained in a document entitled "Bill of Sale" entered into on August 31, 1948, the court found that the agreement between the parties regarding the assumption of liabilities was ambiguous. The indemnity clause in the bill of sale provided that the seller would use its best efforts to obtain written consent from "third parties to all assignments and transfers of leases, contracts, agreements, licenses, options and other property, assets and business assigned and transferred to the respective Buyers . . . in order to make effective as against said third parties any such assignment and transfer, it being understood that, if the respective Buyer shall assume all liabilities thereunder of the Seller to the third party or parties remaining unperformed at the time of such assignment, the Seller will save, defend and keep harmless the respective Buyer of, from and against such part of such unperformed liabilities as shall relate to the period to and including August 31, 1948."

This indemnity provision was itself clear, and did not render ambiguous the parties' intentions with regard to the assumption of tort liabilities, as it had nothing to do with those liabilities. The subject matter of this indemnity clause pertained only to unfinished contracts assumed by USX in the purchase, and to Con Cal's promise to indemnify USX for those parts of the contracts remaining unperformed before the closing date. While USX agreed to assume responsibility to complete those contracts after the closing date, it specifically disavowed responsibility and liability under the contracts to the extent these arose prior to the closing.

In addition, we note that the bill of sale contained specific and clear provisions relating to the buyer's general non-assumption of liability. It stated that "[t]he transfer of the Seller's business and certain of its property and assets to the Buyers is made without the assumption by the Buyers of any of the liabilities of the Seller except those specifically enumerated below, and the Seller hereby covenants and agrees at all times to save, defend and keep harmless the Buyers . . . from and against any and all claims . . . expenses and liabilities whatsoever, based upon, arising out of or in any way connected with the Seller's liabilities except those specifically enumerated. . . ." Those specifically enumerated exceptions were for liabilities on contracts, purchase orders, unfilled sales orders, performance bonds and indemnity contracts arising *after* August 31, 1948. This provision, as well as the indemnity provision relied upon by the trial court, comport completely with the clear and unambiguous terms of the purchase agreement, by which USX assumed no liabilities for the damages at issue in this lawsuit. We thus conclude that, because the contract language was unambiguous, and the parol evidence created no ambiguity and was consistent with the contract, the trial court erred in considering the extrinsic evidence to vary or modify the terms of the contract. (Pacific Gas & Electric v. G.W. Thomas Drayage Co. (1968) 69 Cal.2d 33, 37, 69 Cal.Rptr. 561, 442 P.2d 641.)

Nonetheless, by referring to extrinsic evidence, the court concluded that USX had, expressly or by implication, assumed liability for the personal injury claims asserted by the Franklins. In reaching its conclusion, the trial court looked to two other categories of extrinsic evidence.

First, it considered letters written by USX to third parties after the execution of the purchase agreement. In these letters, Con Cal's customers, vendors and subcontractors were informed of the sale of Con Cal's "business and operating properties" to Con Del, and were told that "[t]he change of ownership will not in any way affect the fulfillment of the contractual obligations of the selling company. All undelivered orders and uncompleted contracts of that company will be assumed by the acquiring company and will be performed by it in strict accordance with their terms." In similar letters, various governmental entities were informed of the sale, and advised that Con Del "will continue to operate the transferred facilities and business without material change in present personnel, management or business policies."

The trial court concluded that the "business policies" referred to in these letters "included, among others, Consolidated California's policy to assume WPS' debts and liabilities of any nature." The fundamental problem with this finding is that it finds absolutely no support in the record. These letters speak for themselves: they were written to inform the recipients of the change in ownership, and assure them that the change would have no effect on the fulfillment of the seller's contractual obligations. Based upon the evidence in the record, the letters were not susceptible to the trial court's interpretation.

The court also looked to a Navy contract that USX assumed as part of the purchase agreement. This contract was the one under which WPS had agreed to build ships during the war, resulting in the employment of Jeannette Franklin's parents. The trial court found that the Navy contract imposed on WPS the obligation to maintain and repair the premises at its South San Francisco shipyard, that "all of USX's potential liability in this premises liability case arises out of WPS' operation of the shipyard under this contract, and therefore arises directly out of the fulfillment of this contract that USX specifically assumed," and that "had WPS fulfilled all of its obligations under this contract, Jeannette Franklin's parents likely would not have endured the asbestos exposures at WPS' shipyard that are the subject of this lawsuit against USX." From this analysis, the trial court concluded that USX expressly assumed the tort liabilities of Con Cal/WPS. Again, our review of the document and of the evidence in the record does not support the trial court's conclusion.

The Navy contract in question imposed upon WPS the responsibility to maintain and repair the facilities prior to their transfer to the government. It made no mention of any obligations that could be interpreted as inuring to the benefit of shipyard employees and their safety. Thus, even if considered for the purpose of shedding light on the intent of the parties with respect to assumption of the seller's tort liabilities, the Navy contract contributed nothing. In addition, there was no evidence in the record to support the trial court's finding that WPS had not fulfilled its obligations under the Navy contract, or that had it done so Jeannette Franklin's parents "likely would not have endured the asbestos exposures."

THERE WAS NO DE FACTO MERGER OR MERE CONTINUATION

The trial court also found that USX could be deemed to have assumed the liabilities of Con Cal/WPS under the de facto merger theory and under the theory that USX was a "mere continuation" of Con Cal. Although these two theories have been traditionally considered as separate bases for imposing liability on a successor corporation, we perceive the second to be merely a subset of the first.[5] The crucial factor in determining whether a corporate acquisition constitutes either a de facto merger or a mere continuation is the same: whether adequate cash consideration was paid for the predecessor corporation's assets.

No California case we have found has imposed successor liability for personal injuries on a corporation that paid adequate cash consideration for the predecessor's assets. The trial court recognized this limitation to its holding, but found "no logical reason why the fact that the consideration for a purchase of corporate assets is cash (with an agreement to liquidate) rather than stock should in itself bar victims from recovering from the purchaser for the seller's tortious conduct." We, however, perceive a very sound reason for the rule of non-liability in adequate cash sales: predictability. "Predictability is vital in the corporate field. Unforeseeable alterations in successor liability principles complicate transfers and necessarily increase transaction costs. [Citations.] Major economic decisions, critical to society, are best made in a climate of relative certainty and reasonable predictability. The imposition of successor liability on a purchasing company long after the transfer of assets defeats the legitimate expectations the parties held during negotiation and sale. Another consequence that must be faced is that few opportunities would exist for the financially troubled company that wishes to cease business but has had its assets devalued by the extension of successor liability. In addition, of course, a sale for adequate cash consideration ensures that at the time of sale there are adequate means to satisfy any claims made against the predecessor corporation. (See Ray v. Alad, *supra*, 19 Cal.3d at p. 29, 136 Cal.Rptr. 574, 560 P.2d 3.)

In reaching its conclusion that the sale of Con Cal's assets to USX constituted a de facto merger, the trial court relied on Marks v. Minnesota Mining & Manufacturing Co. (1986) 187 Cal.App.3d 1429, 232 Cal.Rptr. 594 (*Marks*). In *Marks*, the court . . . noted: "The critical fact is that while there was more than one merger or reorganization, an analysis of each transaction discloses to

---

5. In fact, it appears to us that the mere continuation theory swallows up the de facto merger theory, because once the two mere continuation elements are satisfied there is no need to further consider the additional elements of the de facto merger theory in establishing successor liability.

us that its intrinsic structure and nature, *unlike a sale of assets for cash*, was of a type in which the corporate entity was continued and all liability was transferred."

Marks is not alone in recognizing the overriding significance of the type and adequacy of consideration paid in a corporate asset sale.

In discussing the mere continuation exception to the general rule of successor nonliability, the court in Ray v. Alad stated that liability has been imposed on a successor corporation "only upon a showing of *one or both* of the following factual elements: (1) no adequate consideration was given for the predecessor corporation's assets and made available for meeting the claims of its unsecured creditors; (2) one or more persons were officers, directors, or stockholders of both corporations. [Citations.]" (Ray v. Alad, 19 Cal.3d at p. 29, 136 Cal.Rptr. 574, 560 P.2d 3, italics added.) Respondents make much of the second prong enunciated by Ray v. Alad, asserting that the trial court properly found USX to be a mere continuation of Con Cal because Alden Roach was president and a board member of both the predecessor and the successor corporations. However, a review of the cases cited by the Ray v. Alad court to support its statement reveals that all of the cases involved the payment of inadequate cash consideration, and some also involved near complete identity of ownership, management or directorship after the transfer. None of these cases involved a situation such as the one before us, where the consideration paid was undisputedly adequate, and only a single person with minimal ownership interest in either entity remained as an officer and director.

Thus, although other factors are relevant to both the de facto merger and mere continuation exceptions, the common denominator, which must be present in order to avoid the general rule of successor non-liability, is the payment of inadequate consideration. The evidence presented showed that in 1948 Con Cal was paid in excess of $17 million for its business assets. As was the case in Ray v. Alad, no claim has been made that this consideration was inadequate, or that there were insufficient assets available *at the time of the predecessor's dissolution* to meet the claims of its creditors. Lacking the essential factor of inadequate consideration, there was no de facto merger, nor could USX be deemed a mere continuation of Con Cal.

THE PRODUCT LINE SUCCESSOR THEORY DOES NOT APPLY TO TORT CLAIMS

Finally, contrary to established California precedent, the trial court found that pursuant to Ray v. Alad, USX was liable as a product line successor in interest to Con Cal/WPS, even though respondents had asserted no claim for strict product liability.

In Ray v. Alad, *supra*, 19 Cal.3d 22, 136 Cal.Rptr. 574, 560 P.2d 3, the California Supreme Court imposed liability on Alad Corporation for the plaintiff's injury sustained in a fall from a defective ladder manufactured by Alad Corporation's predecessor. The injury occurred more than six months after Alad Corporation had acquired the assets of the dissolved ladder manufacturer. Although none of the traditional bases for imposing liability on Alad Corporation were present in the plaintiff's action against it for strict product liability, the court held that given the specific circumstances, the plaintiff should recover under a special exception to the general rule. The court explained that "'the paramount policy to be promoted by the [strict product liability] rule is the protection of otherwise defenseless victims of manufacturing defects and the spreading throughout society of the cost of compensating them.'" It held that imposition of strict liability against the successor to the manufacturer was justified where, as in the case before it, the plaintiff had no viable remedy against the then nonexistent manufacturer of the defective product, the successor to the manufacturer continued to manufacture the same product line as its predecessor, retained the same personnel, used the same designs and customer lists, gave no outward indication of the change in ownership and had opportunities to evaluate production risks and pass on the cost of meeting those risks almost identical to its predecessor's. The Ray v. Alad court presented a three-part rationale for imposing strict liability on the successor corporation: "(1) the virtual destruction of the plaintiff's remedies against the original manufacturer caused by the successor's acquisition of the business, (2) the successor's ability to assume the original manufacturer's risk-spreading role, and (3) the fairness of requiring the successor to assume a responsibility for defective products that was a burden necessarily attached to the original manufacturer's good will being enjoyed by the successor in the continued operation of the business."

The trial court here found that the Ray v. Alad product line successor exception should not be limited to product liability claims, but should extend to ordinary negligence actions. Respondents urge us to reach the same conclusion. In Monarch Bay II v. Professional Service Industries, Inc. (1999) 75 Cal.App.4th 1213, 89 Cal.Rptr.2d 778 (*Monarch Bay II*) and *Maloney, supra,* 207 Cal.App.3d 282, 255 Cal.Rptr. 1, this precise argument was presented and rejected. As did those two courts before us, we decline to expand the product line exception beyond the arena of product liability.

We concur with the court's comments in *Monarch Bay II:* "[Appellant] argues there is no significant difference between a plaintiff injured by a defective product and one harmed by corporate negligence and urges us to broaden the *Ray* exception. We agree that in many respects, the distinction is without a difference. But we see no policy reasons to extend *Ray's* holding beyond strict tort liability. The criticisms levied at the product line exception, which, of course, we are bound to follow under the principles of stare decisis, militate against eroding the traditional rule even further. . . . The trend in other jurisdictions appears to be away from expansion of successor liability. Although the product line exception was adopted by a number of courts following the *Ray* opinion, 'recent cases from a variety of states have rejected the product line exception in favor of retaining the traditional rule on non-liability.' The *Ray* court clearly intended the product line exception to be limited to the circumstances presented in that case, and we decline to extend the rationale to other circumstances." (*Monarch Bay II, supra,* 75 Cal.App.4th at pp. 1218–1219, 89 Cal.Rptr.2d 778.)

The court in *Monarch Bay II* also concluded, as we have in the context of de facto mergers, that an imposition of product line successor liability in non-product-liability cases would upset the predictability so vital to key economic decisions made in the corporate milieu. (*Monarch Bay II, supra,* 75 Cal.App.4th at p. 1218, 89 Cal.Rptr.2d 778.) We, too, view this predictability as crucial. There is no legal basis to support a conclusion that USX was a product line successor liable to respondents for their tort claims.

CONCLUSION AND DISPOSITION

The trial court found USX liable for the Franklins' injuries allegedly caused by WPS. We conclude that no such successor in interest liability attaches. The fully integrated purchase agreement between the predecessor of USX and Con Cal expressly and unambiguously provided that the buyer was not assuming the seller's liabilities except as specifically provided. The specific assumptions pertained only to business related obligations, and not to the liabilities at issue in this action. Because the purchase agreement was unambiguous and fully integrated, the trial court erred in considering extrinsic evidence to vary or alter the terms of the agreement. Even considering that evidence, however, the agreement was not reasonably susceptible to the court's interpretation. Since respondents have not asserted that the consideration for the sale of Con Cal's assets was inadequate or that there were insufficient assets to satisfy creditors' claims at the time of dissolution, USX was not liable as a successor in interest under the theories of de facto merger or mere continuation. Finally, we conclude that the product line successor rule applies only to product liability actions, and is therefore inapplicable to the present case. Based upon these holdings, we reverse the trial court's determination of the successor in interest issue, and do not address the remaining issues raised. The judgment entered against USX is reversed. Appellant shall recover its costs on appeal.

CORRIGAN, Acting P.J., and PARRILLI, J., concur.

Contractual solutions sometimes provide an answer to the question of how a deal can still proceed in the face of the risk of successor liability. But only if they are drafted very carefully, as the next case shows.

FINA, INC., v. ARCO, BP OIL COMPANY; SOHIO PIPE LINE COMPANY

200 F.3d 266
United States Court of Appeals, Fifth Circuit
No. 98-41021 | Jan. 4, 2000 | Rehearing and Rehearing En Banc Denied Feb. 17, 2000

WIENER, Circuit Judge:

In this case arising under the Comprehensive Environmental Response, Compensation, and Liability Act ("CERCLA"), 42 U.S.C. §§9601 *et seq.*, Plaintiff-Appellant Fina, Inc. ("Fina") appeals the district court's grant of summary judgment in favor of Defendants-Appellees BP Oil Company ("BP") and Atlantic Richfield Company ("ARCO"). Fina contends that the district court improperly applied Delaware law in holding that cross-indemnities running between the parties bar Fina's CERCLA claims against BP and ARCO. We hold that the indemnities are unenforceable with respect to the CERCLA liability in question, and accordingly reverse and remand for proceedings consistent with this opinion.

I.

FACTS AND PROCEEDINGS

BP acquired a refinery located in Port Arthur, Texas from ARCO in 1969. BP subsequently sold the refinery to Fina in 1973. The ARCO/BP and BP/Fina agreements of sale contain cross-indemnities that apportion responsibility between the contracting parties for liabilities arising from the operation of the refinery. The ARCO/BP agreement provides in relevant part that:

> BP shall indemnify, defend, and hold harmless ARCO . . . against all claims, actions, demands, losses or liabilities arising from the ownership or the operation of the Assets . . . and accruing from and after Closing . . . except to the extent that any such claim, action, demand, loss or liability shall arise from the gross negligence of ARCO.

The BP/Fina agreement provides in relevant part that:

> Fina shall indemnify, defend and hold harmless BP . . . against all claims, actions, demands, losses or liabilities arising from the use or the operation of the Assets . . . and accruing from and after closing.

In 1989, Fina conducted an environmental investigation covering all areas of the refinery. It found seven areas of the refinery contaminated with solid and hazardous wastes. Investigating the origins of the contamination, Fina unearthed evidence that the pollution was at least in part attributable to the activities of BP and ARCO.

Fina reported its discovery to the State of Texas. The Texas Natural Resource Conservation Commission ordered Fina to conduct several further investigations. Those investigations are still ongoing. Fina has already incurred over $14 million in investigatory and remedial response costs.

In 1996, Fina sued BP and ARCO seeking contribution and cost recovery under the Comprehensive Environmental Response, Compensation, and Liability Act ("CERCLA"), 42 U.S.C. §§9607 and 9613(f). BP filed a declaratory judgment counterclaim against Fina, arguing that Fina's claims are covered by the indemnity provision in the BP/Fina agreement of sale. ARCO filed a similar declaratory judgment cross-claim against BP.

All parties moved for summary judgment. The district court granted the motions of BP and ARCO, ruling that (1) Fina's claims against BP are covered by the BP/Fina indemnity provision, (2) Fina's claims against ARCO are covered by the ARCO/BP indemnity provision, and (3) because ARCO is indemnified by BP which in turn is indemnified by Fina, a "circuitous indemnity obligation" is owed by Fina to ARCO, which obligation covers Fina's claims against ARCO.

ISSUES

We are called on to interpret and determine the enforceability of two related yet distinctly different indemnity provisions. The BP/Fina and ARCO/BP indemnity provisions both allocate responsibility between the contracting parties for liabilities arising from the ownership or operation of the refinery. The two provisions differ, however, in two significant respects. First, whereas the BP/Fina agreement of sale includes a choice of law provision designating Delaware law as the governing law, the ARCO/BP agreement of sale does not contain a choice of law provision. Second, the ARCO/BP indemnity provision, unlike its BP/Fina counterpart, states that it covers all claims "except to the extent that any such claim . . . shall arise from the gross negligence of ARCO." We must therefore analyze the two indemnity provisions separately.

1. The BP/Fina Indemnity Provision

Fina contends that the BP/Fina indemnity provision does not indemnify BP for retroactive CERCLA liability. Under the indemnity provision, Fina's obligations to BP extend only to those liabilities that accrue after the closing date of the BP/Fina agreement of sale. Fina contends that, although CERCLA was not enacted until 1980, the CERCLA liability "accrued" at the time that BP and ARCO polluted the refinery grounds-well before the closing date of the BP/Fina agreement of sale. Fina argues in the alternative that, even if the BP/Fina indemnity provision does purport within its broad terms to cover the CERCLA liability in question, the provision is unenforceable with respect to that liability because governing Delaware law requires that, to indemnify a party for prospective strict liability claims, an indemnity provision must "clearly and unequivocally" state that it covers such claims. As we conclude that the indemnity provision is unenforceable under Delaware law with respect to the CERCLA liability at issue here, we need not reach the question whether the liability "accrued" prior to closing, within the meaning of the agreement.

Under Delaware law, contracts to indemnify a party against the consequences of its own negligence are strictly construed against the indemnitee. The purpose of this rule is to ensure that the indemnitor is fully cognizant of the extraordinary risk that it is assuming.

Delaware law thus requires that, to be enforceable, "the intent to indemnify must be clear and unequivocal" on the face of an indemnity provision. "To be enforceable, the provision must specifically focus attention on the fact that by the agreement the indemnitor was assuming liability for [the] indemnitee's own negligence." The Delaware courts have often stated that there are no particular words that must be used to render an indemnity provision enforceable. But "[n]o Delaware case has allowed indemnification of a party for its own negligence without making specific reference to negligence of the indemnified party."

The BP/Fina indemnity provision gives no indication that the parties considered the issue of indemnifying BP for the consequences of its own negligence: There is no reference in the indemnity to BP's own negligence, and its use of the phrase "all claims, actions, demands, losses or liabilities" is insufficient as a matter of Delaware law to satisfy the clear and unequivocal test. Thus, the BP/Fina indemnity provision is unenforceable as applied to the prospective CERCLA liability at issue in this case.

We hold, therefore, that (1) the BP/Fina indemnity provision is subject to the clear and unequivocal test under Delaware law as applied to Fina's CERCLA claims against BP; (2) the BP/Fina indemnity provision fails to satisfy the clear and unequivocal test; and (3) the indemnity provision consequently does not bar Fina's claims against BP.

The ARCO/BP agreement of sale does not contain a choice-of-law provision. ARCO and BP agree, however, that the contract is governed by Texas law. Since 1987, Texas has applied the "express negligence" test in lieu of the "clear and unequivocal" test. The "express negligence" test holds that "parties seeking to indemnify the indemnitee from the consequences of its own negligence must express that intent in specific terms." This rule is applicable to claims based on strict liability. And, because the rationale behind the Texas rule is the same as the rationale behind the Delaware rule, we are satisfied that Texas would apply the "express negligence" test to all claims that were merely prospective at the time the indemnity provision was signed.

The ARCO/BP provision indemnifies ARCO for "all claims . . . arising from the ownership or the operation of the Assets . . . and accruing from and after Closing . . . except to the extent that any such claim . . . shall arise from the gross negligence of ARCO." It makes no mention of claims based on BP's own negligence or on strict liability. The Texas Supreme Court has held that an indemnification provision is not enforceable as applied to claims based on strict liability unless that provision expressly states the indemnitor's intent to cover such claims. Even if the exclusion of gross negligence from the indemnity's coverage is interpreted as indicating that BP intended to indemnify ARCO for ordinary negligence, claims based on strict liability are of quite a different nature. Texas law requires that each type of claim be separately referenced by an indemnity provision: "Indemnification against strict liability is an exception to usual business practices in the same manner as indemnifying against someone else's negligence. . . . [F]airness dictates against imposing liability on an indemnitor unless the agreement clearly and specifically expresses the intent to encompass strict liability claims." Thus, the ARCO/BP indemnity provision is not enforceable under Texas law as applied to claims based on strict liability. Consequently, ARCO may not seek indemnification from BP for any amounts recovered against it by Fina based on strict liability.

For the reasons discussed above, the district court's grant of summary judgment is reversed and the case is remanded for further proceedings consistent with this opinion.

What are the other limits of these sorts of contractual solutions?

4. TAX MATTERS

As a general matter, the sale of all of the target's assets will result in a taxable event for the target to the extent it receives more for its assets than the current tax basis of those assets, and its shareholders will recognize gain on the distribution of any proceeds from the sale.

Thus, an asset sale results in two levels of tax on the seller side if proceeds are distributed, an unfavorable result for the seller and its shareholders if significant appreciation in target asset value exists. The parties must weigh this against the other factors that might suggest the need to proceed by APA.

And note that the corporate level tax will not be an issue if the target has sufficient NOLs to offset against any gains realized upon sale. The tax basis of the target's assets is increased at closing to the purchase price paid, which may be of some benefit to the buyer.

25

LEVERAGED BUYOUTS AND DISTRESSED ACQUISITIONS

According to one court, a *leveraged buyout* (LBO) is "a shorthand expression describing a business practice wherein a company is sold to a small number of investors, typically including members of the company's management, under financial arrangements in which there is a minimum amount of equity and a maximum amount of debt."[1] Although this definition is somewhat dated, it is still apt.

Today LBOs are strongly associated with private equity firms, who often use an LBO to move a publicly traded firm into the private equity firm's portfolio of companies. Distressed acquisitions, on the other hand, involve acquisition of a company that is already highly indebted, and perhaps experiencing or on the verge of financial distress.

Both types of transactions involve the M&A techniques discussed in earlier classes, but also invoke a special set of considerations examined in this chapter. As a general rule, leveraged buyouts tend to peak during good economic times, when banks are quite willing to lend to potential buyers.

Thus, following Lehman Brothers' chapter 11 filing in September 2011, JC Flowers & Co. LLC backed out of a $26 billion buyout of SLM Corp.; Goldman Sachs Capital Partners cancelled an $8 billion deal for Harman International Industries, Inc.; Bain Capital LLC, Carlyle Group, and Clayton, Dubilier & Rice, Inc.'s $10.3 billion buyout of Home Depot, Inc.'s H&D Supply, Inc. was reduced to $8.5 billion; and Thomas H. Lee Partners LP and Bain Capital's buyout of Clear Channel Communications, Inc., originally announced for $25 billion, was restructured to involve much less consideration. This represented a rather abrupt end to more than five years of frenzied LBO activity.

Distressed acquisitions can occur during any economic phase, although they obviously increase in volume when more potential sellers are distressed.

For the distressed seller, the choice of transaction structure will be driven by whether the assets sold constitute substantially all the assets of the company,

---

1. United States v. Tabor Court Realty Corp., 803 F.2d 1288 (3d Cir. 1986).

whether the sale proceeds can be maximized by separate assets sales to multiple buyers, and what is the best way to consummate a transaction given the seller's obligations to its creditors.[2] The reasons behind these considerations should be apparent from earlier classes.

In an LBO, the goal is typically to "cash out" the existing shareholders and replace them with the new owners, and quite often new management, too. LBOs come in a few different flavors. For example, a "bust up" LBO is based on the notion that that the whole is worth less than the sum of the parts.

More often recent LBO transactions have been based on an operational turnaround or a cyclical swing. Turnaround deals almost invariably involve the introduction of new management. Cyclical deals are based on a bet that the buyer is right about timing an industry cycle.

1. FINANCING LBOs

The typical LBO is financed with a combination of devices already seen earlier in this course. The next case examines the typical structure, and the conflicts of interest that can arise.

PARACOR FINANCE, INC., (FKA ELDERS FINANCE, INC.), v. GENERAL ELECTRIC CAPITAL CORPORATION

96 F.3d 1151
United States Court of Appeals, Ninth Circuit
No. 94-15633 | Argued and Submitted Aug. 14, 1995 | Decided March 13, 1996 | As Amended
on Denial of Rehearing and Rehearing En Banc Sept. 20, 1996

O'SCANNLAIN, Circuit Judge:
In reviewing this saga of a debenture offering turned sour, we must decide whether any of the supporting cast on the offeror's side have violated the securities laws. In particular, we must determine whether the lender in a financial transaction should be considered a "controlling person" of its borrower.

I

We begin with the facts that led up to the debenture offering at issue here as an appeal from a "Final Partial Judgment" under Federal Rule of Civil Procedure 54(b) which recapped a series of prior orders of the district court granting summary judgments. Jordan Schnitzer, a Portland businessman, hired Bear, Stearns & Co. to locate a profitable corporation which he could purchase and

---

2. It is generally accepted that the creditors of an insolvent company can enforce the fiduciary duties that you learned about in your basic Corporations or Business Associations class. N. Am. Catholic Educ. Programming Fund v. Gheewalla, 930 A.2d 92 (Del. 2007).

merge with an unprofitable corporation he owned in order to utilize his corporation's net operating loss carryforwards and obtain certain tax benefits. He was directed to Casablanca Industries, Inc., a California manufacturer of ceiling fans.

In December 1988, Schnitzer approached General Electric Capital Corp. ("GE Capital") for financing for a leveraged buyout of Casablanca. After undertaking its own due diligence, GE Capital agreed to provide a bridge loan for the acquisition. One condition of the bridge loan was that the acquired Casablanca would immediately sell $27 million in high-yield subordinated debentures (aka "junk bonds"), which would be used partially to pay down the loan. The bridge financing would then be replaced with permanent financing by GE Capital. A bridge loan of $53 million to Casablanca Acquisition Corp., a company formed by Schnitzer to make the acquisition, was eventually made in April 1989.

In March 1989, Shearson Lehman Brothers Inc. ("Shearson") was retained to place the subordinated debentures with investors. Shearson prepared a Private Placement Memorandum ("Placement Memorandum") for this purpose. The Placement Memorandum contained various representations about Casablanca including sales projections of $83.3 million and earnings of $8.5 million for fiscal year 1989. Shearson distributed the Placement Memorandum to various institutional investors active in the subordinated debt market.

Elders Finance, Inc. (now known as Paracor Finance, Inc.), Cargill Financial Services Corp., Lutheran Brotherhood, and Farm Bureau Life Insurance Co. (collectively "the Investors") received the Placement Memorandum. During the following weeks, analysts for the Investors performed their own due diligence on the offering. The analysts inspected Casablanca's books, met with its management, visited Casablanca's offices, and had occasional contacts with GE Capital (the substance of which forms part of this dispute). By early May, the Investors had decided to purchase the debentures. The closing of the deal was delayed until late June, however, by continuing negotiations over its terms.

By June, Schnitzer had successfully completed his tender offer and merged his corporation with Casablanca. In the interim, Casablanca's fortunes had been declining. Casablanca's April sales were only $7.88 million, compared with projections of $10.195 million. May and June sales were also below projections. During this time, Burton Burton was the CEO of Casablanca (though the extent of his involvement in its affairs is disputed), and Jerry Holland was the President.

A Debenture Purchase Agreement ("Purchase Agreement") was eventually negotiated between the Investors and Casablanca. In the Purchase Agreement, Casablanca represented that "[s]ince March 31, 1989, Casablanca has not suffered any Material Adverse Effect." The Investors represented that they "had access to the information [they] requested from [Casablanca]" and that they "made [their] own investment decision with respect to the purchase of the Debentures . . . without relying on any other Person." On June 17, 1989, the parties signed the deal documents. On June 23, the Investors wired $27 million to GE Capital as the escrow agent for the various parties to the transaction.

After its first payment of interest on the debentures in August, Casablanca defaulted. Casablanca filed for bankruptcy a little over a year later in November 1990. The Investors, needless to say, were upset.

In March 1991, the Investors filed suit against everyone involved in the transaction, including Casablanca, GE Capital and Schnitzer, Burton, and Holland (collectively "the defendants"). The Investors claimed (1) primary and secondary violations of section 10(b) and Rule 10b-5 of the Securities Exchange Act of 1934, (2) violations of Oregon Revised Statute §59.115 (the "Oregon Securities Law"), and (3) common-law torts of fraud and negligent misrepresentation. The Investors also brought a claim of unjust enrichment against GE Capital alone. The Investors' claims against Casablanca were subject to the bankruptcy stay.

II

The Investors contend that GE Capital and Burton are primarily liable for violations of section 10(b) and Rule 10b-5 for making affirmative misrepresentations and for failing to disclose material facts about Casablanca's sales. The heart of the Investors' claim is that they were not provided with the negative sales data for the three months immediately prior to the closing.

Rule 10b-5(b), enacted under section 10(b) of the Securities Exchange Act of 1934, 15 U.S.C. §78j(b), makes it unlawful "[t]o make any untrue statement of a material fact or to omit to state a material fact necessary in order to make the statements made, in the light of the circumstances under which they were made, not misleading." 17 C.F.R. §240.10b-5(b). The elements of a Rule 10b-5 claim are: (1) a misrepresentation or omission of a material fact, (2) reliance, (3) scienter, and (4) resulting damages. If one of these elements is missing, the Investors' claim fails.

A

Regarding GE Capital, both of the first two elements pose significant obstacles to the Investors' claims. As this is an appeal from summary judgment, we will look at the facts underlying these elements in the light most favorable to the Investors.

1

The heart of the Investors' Rule 10b-5 claim is that GE Capital knew of Casablanca's poor April-June quarter sales results and failed to disclose them. It takes more than mere knowledge, however, to amount to an actionable omission. "Rule 10b-5 is violated by nondisclosure only when there is a duty to disclose." "[T]he parties to an impersonal market transaction owe no duty of disclosure to one another absent a fiduciary or agency relationship, prior dealings, or circumstances such that one party has placed trust and confidence in the other." A number of factors are used to determine whether a party has a duty to disclose: (1) the relationship of the parties, (2) their relative access to information, (3) the benefit that the defendant derives from the relationship, (4) the defendant's awareness that the plaintiff was relying upon the relationship in making his investment decision, and (5) the defendant's activity in initiating the transaction.

Canvassing these factors, the relationship between GE Capital and the Investors did not rise to the level at which GE Capital assumed a duty to disclose. First, GE Capital had no relationship with the Investors prior to the debenture transaction. During the transaction, it had no contact whatsoever with two of the Investors (Lutheran Brotherhood and Farm Bureau Life Insurance), and its contact with the other two amounted to a couple of brief face-to-face meetings and a handful of telephone calls. Second, the Investors' access to information was comparable to GE Capital's. After GE Capital funded the bridge loan in April, Casablanca was required to provide daily "Open Sales Order" reports and weekly "Tuesday" reports. Although the Investors did not receive these reports, they had their own channels for information. The Investors, sophisticated institutions with competent analysts, conducted their own due diligence. They also signed representations that they were provided with all information that they requested, and conceded that such representations were accurate.

Third, GE Capital certainly benefitted from the Investors' purchase of the debentures by having their exposure on the $53 million unsecured bridge loan effectively reduced. Fourth, GE Capital informed Cargill Financial Services and Elders Finance on more than one occasion and in writing that they could not rely on GE Capital. When GE Capital did provide Elders Finance with a copy of its business survey of Casablanca, it insisted that Elders Finance state in writing that it was not relying on GE Capital. Finally, GE Capital effectively initiated the debenture transaction, because its bridge loan to Schnitzer was conditioned on the debenture offering being made.

Taken together, these factors show that GE Capital initiated a financial transaction from which it stood to benefit. They do not show, however, that GE Capital assumed a relationship of trust and confidence with the Investors.

According to the Investors, GE Capital's employees made several oral misrepresentations to employees of Elders Finance and Cargill Financial Services about Casablanca's performance. For example, at a late April meeting, GE Capital's Steve Read stated that Casablanca was "a good property, a good investment."

It is somewhat troubling that while GE Capital was smiling and nodding to the Investors it may have been grimacing in private. At the same time GE Capital's Bengtson was telling Elders Finance's Gerstel that Casablanca was performing in accordance with expectations, Bengtson had also sent a memo to her superior at GE Capital, Scott Lavie, informing him about Casablanca's declining sales. However, the Investors have not introduced evidence that GE Capital lacked at least a reasonable basis for their various representations, even though in hindsight they may now appear a little too rosy. GE Capital's Lavie stated that, as of the closing date, GE Capital was "aware that [Casablanca's fan division] itself [would] not attain its full projections, but we also realized on the twelve months year-to-date, the results were not significantly off what was projected."

The Investors were not novices in the financial markets; these statements, although hedged with reassurances, were sufficient to put them on notice that Casablanca's fan sales were not breezing along as usual. In light of all of the information available to them, and the generality of GE Capital's statements, the

Investors have failed to demonstrate an issue of material fact as to whether GE Capital made actionable misrepresentations.

2

Even if the Investors had succeeded in meeting the first element of a Rule 10b-5 claim, they would also have to demonstrate that they had relied on GE Capital. Justifiable reliance "is a limitation on a rule 10b-5 action which insures that there is a causal connection between the misrepresentation and the plaintiff's harm." Atari Corp. v. Ernst & Whinney, 981 F.2d 1025, 1030 (9th Cir.1992) (internal quotation marks omitted).

The Investors have failed to introduce an issue of material fact that they justifiably relied on GE Capital. Significantly, in Section 4.4 of the Purchase Agreement the Investors recited that they were given "access to the information [they have] requested from the Company" and that they "made [their] own investment decision with respect to the purchase of the Debentures . . . without relying on any other Person." Elders Finance's Thomas Goossens conceded that the representations in Section 4.4 were true as of the signing of the Purchase Agreement. These representations do much to defeat the Investors' claims of reliance on GE Capital.

Since the Investors fail to establish either of the first two elements of their Rule 10-b5 claim against GE Capital, we do not reach the remaining two.

III

The Investors claim that GE Capital and Burton are secondarily liable for Casablanca's alleged Rule 10b-5 violations because they were "controlling persons" of Casablanca under section 20(a) of the Securities Exchange Act of 1934, 15 U.S.C. §78t(a).

Section 20(a) provides:

> Every person who, directly or indirectly, controls any person liable under any provision of this chapter or of any rule or regulation thereunder shall also be liable jointly and severally with and to the same extent as such controlled person to any person to whom such controlled person is liable, unless the controlling person acted in good faith and did not directly or indirectly induce the act or acts constituting the violation or cause of action.

To establish "controlling person" liability, the plaintiff must show that a primary violation was committed and that the defendant "directly or indirectly" controlled the violator. The plaintiff need not show the controlling person's scienter or that they "culpably participated" in the alleged wrongdoing. If the plaintiff establishes that the defendant is a "controlling person," then the defendant bears the burden of proving he "acted in good faith and did not directly or indirectly induce the act or acts constituting the violation or cause of action." 15 U.S.C. §78t(a).

Here, a material issue of fact exists as to whether a primary violation was committed by Casablanca, through its President, Holland. The district court denied Holland's motion for summary judgment on the section 10(b) claims, stating: "He signed the no material adverse change certificate. It seems to me having done that, the remaining issues of liability are one of fact that can't be resolved on summary judgment motion." Whether Holland (and Casablanca) violated Rule 10b-5 is a pending issue in the district court. The question thus becomes whether there are issues of material fact as to GE Capital's or Burton's control over Casablanca.

A

Regarding GE Capital, the Investors have introduced evidence that it had a strong hand in Casablanca's debenture offering. GE Capital's bridge loan to Schnitzer was conditioned on the debenture offering taking place. GE Capital, along with Schnitzer, retained Shearson to market the debentures. GE Capital may have indirectly contributed to the Placement Memorandum by working with Casablanca's management to come up with "assumptions" for their long-term projections. GE Capital had the right to select the lead investor and exercised its right to select Elders Finance. Finally, GE Capital participated in the drafting and negotiating of the Purchase Agreement.

However, the Investors have not shown any of the traditional indicia of control of Casablanca in a broader sense. GE Capital had no prior lending relationship with Casablanca. GE Capital did not own stock in Casablanca prior to the closing and did not have a seat on its Board. GE Capital's bridge loan was unsecured by any of Casablanca's assets. In short, there is no evidence that GE Capital exercised any influence whatsoever over Casablanca on a day-to-day basis.

Other courts addressing this situation have been very reluctant to treat lenders as controlling persons of their borrowers . . .

GE Capital did not exercise control over the "management and policies" of Casablanca, nor did it direct its day-to-day affairs in any sense. As we hold that at least some indicia of such control is a necessary element of "controlling person" liability, the Investors cannot sustain a secondary liability claim against GE Capital.

PROBLEM SET 25.1

1. As illustrated in the case, leveraged buyouts are typically financed by a loan that is then replaced, in whole or in part, by bond financing. What are the risks of this structure? Why not simply use bonds from inception?
2. What were the loan's proceeds used for in this transaction? Should the law discourage the intentional creation of a company that is insolvent?
3. As noted in the opinion, the buyer purchased the target in this LBO to better utilize certain tax losses that the buyer had, but could not use. The issue of "NOLs" will be further considered in the subsequent class on exchange offers.
4. As we have previously noted, one advantage of financing a company with debt is that interest payments, unlike dividend payments, are typically tax

deductible by the corporation. In the late 1980s, following concerns about the growth of leveraged buyouts, Congress enacted rules that limit interest deductions on "applicable high-yield discount obligations" (AHYDO, as the tax lawyers like to call it). Generally, the rules provide that, if a debt obligation has a term of more than five years, has a yield at least equal to the risk-free rate plus 5 percent and has significant OID,[3] then the yield that exceeds the risk-free rate plus 6 percent is not deductible and the rest of the yield is only deductible when actual cash payments are made. What is the likely effect of this rule? Does it represent a sensible policy decision?

2.   FRAUDULENT TRANSFER LAWS

As discussed earlier in the text, corporate law (and corporate bankruptcy law) provides for the creditors of a company to be paid before the owners of the company: debt before equity. This is the absolute priority rule.[4]

Fraudulent transfer laws are intended to give the creditors of a company a tool to ensure that the indebtedness of the company is paid before the holders of the equity in the enterprise receive payments in respect of their equity interests.

Fraudulent transfer laws date back to at least Elizabethan England—most notably the Statute of 13 Elizabeth from 1571[5]—and thus came to the United States as part of the preindependence common law.[6] In present days, fraudulent transfers are addressed by state and federal law, and the occasional state still addresses fraudulent transfer via common law.

State law is more typically based on one of two uniform laws: the Uniform Fraudulent Conveyance Act ("UFCA") or the Uniform Fraudulent Transfer Act ("UFTA"). The UFCA was promulgated in 1918 by the National Conference of Commissioners on Uniform State Laws in an attempt to codify and clarify the common law of fraudulent conveyance. The UFCA remains in effect in three jurisdictions: Maryland, the US Virgin Islands, and, most important, New York.[7]

The UFTA was promulgated by the Commissioners in 1984 to work with the overall design and structure of the then recently enacted 1978 Federal Bankruptcy Code. Forty-four jurisdictions have adopted the UFTA, but some, like California, have made changes that reduce the statute's "uniformity."

Under the Bankruptcy Code, the trustee or the debtor will typically have the choice of bringing a fraudulent transfer action under either the applicable state

---

3. Original issue discount; recall the discussion of this in the bond unit.
4. *See* Chapter 3.
5. 13 Eliz 1, c 5 (1571).
6. Fraudulent transfer was initially a common law concept in colonial America, but a statutory concept in England.
7. In New York, a bill to enact the UFTA was before the Senate Judiciary Committee in 2007. However, the bill was not addressed during the 2007 or 2008 legislative sessions.

law or the fraudulent transfer provision in the Code. Section 544 of the Bankruptcy Code gives the trustee the right to avoid a transaction that might be avoided under applicable state law. Section 548 of the Bankruptcy Code sets forth the basic right of the "trustee" in bankruptcy (which for this purpose includes a debtor in chapter 11 reorganization case) to avoid any "obligation incurred" by a debtor or any "transfer" of property (including any payments or the grant of a lien) that constitutes a "fraudulent transfer" by the debtor.

A key distinction among all three statutes is the relevant statute of limitations: UFCA (six years), UFTA (four years), Bankruptcy Code §548 (two years).[8]

The statutes attack two types of fraudulent conveyances: the intentional fraudulent conveyance and the constructive fraudulent conveyance.

In the case of an *intentional* fraudulent conveyance or transfer, the debtor "conveys" or "transfers" property, or incurs an obligation, with the "actual intent to hinder, delay or defraud creditors." Giving your car, house, dog, and wallet to a friend right after entry of a big tort judgment would be an obvious example.

More often fraudulent intent is determined by reference to certain "badges of fraud" — a concept that also dates back to England. Indeed, the most famous badges of fraud case is *Twyne's Case*, a 1601 opinion from the Star Chamber.[9] Don't you just love a good, pre-*Mayflower*, Star Chamber opinion?

UFTA section 7, unlike the Bankruptcy Code or the UFCA, provides a list of "badges of fraud" that a court may consider in determining whether actual intent exists. The UFTA list includes (i) the transfer or obligation was to an insider; (ii) the debtor retained possession or control of the property transferred after the transfer; (iii) the transfer or obligation was concealed; (iv) before the transfer was made or obligation was incurred, the debtor had been sued or threatened with suit; (v) the transfer was of substantially all of the debtor's assets; (vi) the debtor absconded; (vii) the debtor removed or concealed assets; (viii) the debtor was insolvent or became insolvent shortly after the transfer was made or the obligation was incurred; (ix) the transfer occurred shortly before or shortly after a substantial debt was incurred; (x) the debtor transferred the essential assets of the business to a lienor who transferred the assets to an insider of the debtor.

The concept of a *constructive* fraudulent transfer arises in situations where fraud is presumed because the benefit of the transaction to the debtor is small and the harm to creditors is large. That is, transfers for less than "reasonably equivalent value" can be undone as constructively fraudulent transfers.

In an LBO situation, lenders have to worry that their loan might itself be a fraudulent transfer if the debtor grants a lien in exchange for the proceeds used to buy out the old shareholders. After all, what precisely does the corporation get in such a transaction? In the case of a distressed acquisition, the potential that the asset sale will be challenged after the fact looms large.

---

8. UFCA generally uses the time period applicable to fraud claims, which is six years in New York.
9. 3 Coke 806 (Star Chamber 1601).

IN RE JEVIC HOLDING CORPORATION, ET AL., DEBTORS.
OFFICIAL COMMITTEE OF UNSECURED CREDITORS,
PLAINTIFF, v. THE CIT GROUP/BUSINESS CREDIT, INC.,
IN ITS CAPACITY AS AGENT, SUN CAPITAL PARTNERS IV, LP,
SUN CAPITAL PARTNERS MANAGEMENT IV, LLC, AND SUN
CAPITAL PARTNERS, INC., DEFENDANTS

United States Bankruptcy Court, D. Delaware
2011 WL 4345204
Bankruptcy No. 08-11006 (BLS) | Adversary No. 08-51903 | Sept. 15, 2011

Brendan Linehan SHANNON, Bankruptcy Judge.

Before the Court is a motion to dismiss (the "Motion") filed by the CIT Group/
Business Credit, Inc. ("CIT"). By the Motion, CIT seeks the dismissal of all
claims in the complaint and objection to claims, as amended (the "Complaint")
filed by the Official Committee of Unsecured Creditors (the "Committee") of
Jevic Holding Corporation ("Jevic") that initiated this adversary proceeding.

I.   BACKGROUND

On May 20, 2008 (the "Petition Date"), Jevic and various of its affiliates
(collectively, the "Debtors") each filed voluntary petitions for relief under chapter 11 of title 11 of the United States Code (the "Bankruptcy Code") in the U.S.
Bankruptcy Court for the District of Delaware. Founded in 1981, Jevic was a
trucking company that provided regional and interregional transportation services across the United States and portions of Canada. In 2004, after years of
profitability, Jevic began experiencing a prolonged financial downturn from
which it never rebounded and which eventually led Jevic into bankruptcy.

Until 2006, Jevic was wholly owned by SCS Transportation, Inc. ("SCS").
Earlier that year, Jevic hired an investment banking firm to explore its financial
and strategic alternatives. On June 30, 2006, Sun Capital Partners IV, LP
("Sun") purchased Jevic from SCS for $77.4 million (the "Acquisition").[10]
To finance the Acquisition, Sun obtained a $90 million loan (the "Acquisition
Facility") from Bank of Montreal to cover the purchase price and transaction
costs. The Acquisition Facility was evidenced by a demand note, secured by all
assets of Jevic and JHC, and guaranteed by Sun.

Within a month of the Acquisition, Jevic entered into a credit agreement
administered by CIT to refinance the Acquisition Facility (the "Refinancing
Facility"). Under the Refinancing Facility, Jevic obtained a revolving line of
credit in the amount of $85 million (the "Revolver") and a $16.2 million
term loan (the "Term Loan"), for a total credit facility in the amount of
$101.2 million. The Refinancing Facility was secured by a first lien on all of
Jevic's assets including its accounts receivable and stock, but the Term Loan
was separately secured by two specific real estate properties owned by Jevic (the

---

10. For the sake of accuracy, the Court notes that Jevic was formally purchased by Jevic Holding
Corporation ("JHC"), Sun's wholly owned investment vehicle, but for the purpose of ruling upon the
Motion, the Court generally refers to Sun as the acquiring entity.

"Properties"). The proceeds of the Refinancing Facility were used to pay off the Acquisition Facility and to finance the transaction costs and fees.

Jevic was almost immediately in default of various provisions of the Refinancing Facility. In exchange for relaxing certain covenants, CIT obtained from Jevic various concessions and required Jevic to market the Properties and, upon their sale, to apply the sale proceeds of the Properties toward the outstanding principal of the Term Loan. Accordingly, within several months of the Acquisition, Jevic sold the Properties for approximately $20 million and delivered the proceeds to CIT. Jevic simultaneously entered into 20-year leases with the new owners of the Properties in order to continue to use the Properties for its ongoing business operations. The Committee refers to the sale of the Properties, the turnover of sale proceeds to CIT, and the execution of the leases in the aggregate as the "Sale–Leaseback." After the Sale–Leaseback, Jevic's obligations on the Refinancing Facility diminished: the Term Loan was paid in full and the Revolver was reduced to $55 million.

Notwithstanding these various transactions, Jevic's financial condition continued to deteriorate. Unable to meet its obligations under the Refinancing Facility, Jevic entered into a forbearance agreement with CIT, which was amended several times to extend the expiration date. The forbearance agreement finally expired without further extension on May 12, 2008. Eight days later, Jevic declared bankruptcy. Since the Petition Date, the Debtors have shut down their business operations and have liquidated their assets through a sale under 11 U.S.C. §363.[11]

As of the Petition Date, the Debtors' total liability on the Refinancing Facility was $50,417,204, and CIT has filed proofs of claim against the Debtors in this amount.

On December 31, 2008, the Committee timely objected to CIT's claims under the Refinancing Facility by filing a joint objection and complaint to initiate this adversary proceeding.

As it relates to CIT, the Complaint contains . . . claims for relief grounded in the following causes of action: constructively fraudulent transfers under 11 U.S.C. §§544 and 548, . . . aiding and abetting breach of fiduciary duty, and equitable subordination under §510. The Court addresses the sufficiency of the Committee's allegations with respect to each of these causes of action in turn.

A. FRAUDULENT TRANSFER CLAIMS (CLAIMS I THROUGH IV)

In Claims I and II, the Committee alleges that the Debtors' obligations on the Refinancing Facility, the liens on Jevic's assets which secure the Refinancing Facility, and the payments made on account of the Refinancing Facility, including the turnover of the proceeds from the sale of the Properties, are all constructively fraudulent transfers under 11 U.S.C. §544(b) and the Uniform Fraudulent Transfer Act ("UFTA"). In Claims III and IV, the Committee alleges that these same transfers and obligations are also voidable as fraudulent

---

11. 363 sales are the subject of Chapter 29. — AUTHOR

transfers under 11 U.S.C. §548(a). In support of its fraudulent transfer claims, the Committee argues that the Acquisition, the Acquisition Facility, the Refinancing Facility, and the Sale–Leaseback should all be viewed as component transactions that must be collapsed in a single integrated transaction, which in the aggregate comprise the leveraged buyout ("LBO") of Jevic by Sun. The Court first addresses the Committee's argument for collapsing these transactions and then considers whether the Committee has adequately alleged fraudulent transfer claims against CIT under §§548 or 544, or both.

1.   Collapsing the Transactions

The Third Circuit has recognized the propriety of collapsing multiple transactions and treating them as one integrated transaction for the purpose of assessing a defendant's fraudulent transfer liability. United States v. Tabor Court Realty Corp., 803 F.2d 1288, 1301-03 (3d Cir.1986), *cert. denied*, 483 U.S. 1005 (1987). In *Tabor*, the Third Circuit explained that where a series of transactions were all "part of one integrated transaction," a court could look "beyond the exchange of funds" in one transaction and consider the "*aggregate* transaction.*" An LBO is the classic context in which courts have collapsed multiple transactions for the purpose of assessing and finding fraudulent transfer liability. *See id.* at 1302; HBE Leasing Corp. v. Frank, 48 F.3d 623, 635 (2d Cir.1995) ("This [collapsing] approach finds its most frequent application to lenders who have financed leveraged buyouts of companies that subsequently become insolvent.").

To determine whether a series of transactions should be "collapsed" and viewed as a single integrated transaction, courts focus on the substance rather than on the form of the transactions and consider the overall intent and impact of the transactions. While the transactions that are sought to be collapsed may be structurally independent and distinct from one another, courts focus their analysis "not on the structure of the transaction but the knowledge and intent of the parties involved in the transaction."

The courts in this District have considered the following factors when assessing whether the parties to the transactions sought to be collapsed had the requisite knowledge and intent to warrant consideration of the asserted transactions in the aggregate: whether all parties involved in the individual transactions had knowledge of the other transactions; whether each transaction sought to be collapsed would have occurred on its own; and whether each transaction was dependent or conditioned on the other transactions.

Whether the relevant parties to the various transactions had notice of the overall scheme has been a central issue for courts that have applied the collapsing theory.

Whether the parties had the requisite intent can be ascertained by demonstrating that the transactions sought to be collapsed are interdependent because "[e]ach step of the [collapsed] [t]ransaction would not have occurred on its own, as each relied on additional steps to fulfill the parties' intent." The passage of some time between the various transactions sought to be collapsed is not fatal if they are sufficiently related. Boyer v. Crown Stock Distribution, Inc. *(In re Boyer)*, 587 F.3d 787, 795-96 (7th Cir. 2009). For example, in *Boyer*, the Seventh

Circuit collapsed transactions that were about three years apart, finding that they were all "an integral part of the LBO."

Ultimately, in the LBO context, courts will frequently collapse a series of transactions upon a showing that these transactions are part of "an overall scheme to defraud the estate and its creditors by depleting all the assets through the use of a leveraged buyout." Neither time nor transactional formalities can shield a party involved in such a series of transactions. With respect to lender liability specifically, the Third Circuit explained in *Tabor* that where a lender has been "intimately involved" with the overall transaction at issue, "[t]ry as they might to distance themselves from the transaction now, they cannot rewrite history."

Here, the Committee seeks to collapse the Acquisition, the Acquisition Facility, the Refinancing Facility, the liens on Jevic's assets to secure the Refinancing Facility, and the Sale-Leaseback into one integrated transaction which, in the aggregate, should be viewed as Sun's leveraged buyout of Jevic (the "Jevic LBO"). In support of its argument, the Committee alleges that the overall intent of the transacting parties, *viz.*, Sun, Bank of Montreal, CIT, and Jevic — was to enable, facilitate, and effectuate the Jevic LBO. The Committee further asserts that CIT was aware of Sun's intentions to acquire Jevic from the start, even though the Acquisition Facility was initially provided by another bank. According to the Committee, Sun "turned to CIT to provide a 'comprehensive financing solution'" to facilitate its acquisition of Jevic. The Complaint alleges that Sun and CIT negotiated for a June closing date months before the Acquisition occurred, but CIT was unable to close at that time. To avoid delaying the closing, the Committee alleges that Sun obtained the Acquisition Facility from Bank of Montreal to serve as a "bridge facility" for the purpose of effectuating the Acquisition "until CIT was prepared to move forward with what would then be permanent financing." By the end of July, CIT had refinanced the Acquisition Facility through the Refinancing Facility. The Committee contends that "Sun would not have caused [its subsidiary] to borrow $90 million under [the Acquisition Facility], and Sun would not have guaranteed . . . repayment of the [Acquisition Facility], if Sun was not all but certain that CIT would successfully complete the re-financing in a short period of time."

CIT argues that the Committee has failed to allege bad faith or an intent to defraud Jevic's creditors. However, the Court notes that the Complaint includes allegations of collusion between Sun and CIT to maximize the Refinancing Facility. The Committee argues that the Refinancing Facility, which exceeded the Acquisition Facility by more than $10 million, was the result of a collaborative and calculated effort by Sun and CIT to render unrealistically high asset valuations and revenue projections for Jevic with an eye towards obtaining the highest possible loan package. The Committee maintains that CIT would not have funded the Refinancing Facility — the Revolver and the Term Loan — without these allegedly excessive valuations and projections.

The Court is satisfied that the Committee has sufficiently pleaded that there is cause to collapse the series of transactions which are allegedly comprised in the Jevic LBO. Based on the Committee's allegations, the Court could conclude that CIT, Sun, Bank of Montreal, and Jevic were all apprised of the overall goal — Sun's acquisition of Jevic through a highly leveraged buyout — of each of these separate transactions in which the various parties were involved. Assuming the veracity of the Committee's assertions and making all reasonable inferences in its favor, the Committee could establish that CIT had sufficient knowledge and notice of the Jevic LBO. The Court also finds that the Committee has adequately alleged that the various transactions constituting the Jevic LBO would not have occurred independently of each other. Given the short time span within which these transactions occurred and their asserted relatedness, the Court concludes that the Committee has provided enough facts from which the Court could reasonably infer the common aim of these transactions.

CIT attempts to shield itself from liability with respect to the Jevic LBO by maintaining that "[it] did not play any role in the leveraged buyout whatsoever." While the Court acknowledges that the intervening role Bank of Montreal complicates the Committee's case and may ultimately prove fatal to the claims in the Complaint, the purpose of the integration doctrine is to enable a plaintiff to overcome precisely the type of argument against liability which CIT is now asserting. Despite CIT's detachment from the Acquisition Facility pursuant to which Sun initially acquired Jevic, the Court concludes that the Committee has sufficiently alleged that CIT was nonetheless "fully engaged," "actively pursuing the transaction," and intimately involved in the Jevic LBO. Accordingly, the Committee is entitled to develop and present evidence to corroborate its claims with respect to the propriety of collapsing the asserted transactions into Jevic LBO for the purpose of establishing CIT's fraudulent transfer liability.

2. *Constructively Fraudulent Transfer Claims under §548 (Claims III and IV)*

Section §548(a)(1) of the Bankruptcy Code grants a trustee the power to avoid any transfer made or obligation incurred by a debtor of an interest in property, made no more than two years before the debtor files for bankruptcy relief, if the transfer or obligation is deemed to be actually or constructively fraudulent. Here, the Committee has alleged that the Refinancing Facility, and its attendant liens and loan payments by Jevic, are voidable as constructively fraudulent transfers. A transfer or an obligation is deemed constructively fraudulent and thus voidable if the debtor received less than reasonably equivalent value in exchange for such transfer or obligation, and (i) the debtor was insolvent when such transfer was made or obligation was incurred, or became insolvent as a result thereof, (ii) the debtor retained unreasonably small capital to operate its business when the transfer was made or obligation was incurred, or (iii) the debtor made the transfer or incurred the obligation when it was already unable to service its debts. Thus, to survive this Motion with respect to §548(a)(1), the Complaint must include facts sufficient to show that Jevic did not receive reasonably equivalent value in exchange for the obligations it incurred and the attendant transfers it made. The Complaint must also include enough facts to show that Jevic was or became insolvent when these transactions occurred, or that it retained unreasonably small capital as a result thereof, or that it was unable to pay its debts when the transactions occurred.

a. *Reasonably Equivalent Value*

A transfer or obligation is avoidable under §548(a)(1)(B) only if the debtor "received less than a reasonably equivalent value in exchange for such transfer or obligation." The term "reasonably equivalent value" is not defined in the Bankruptcy Code and "courts have rejected the application of any fixed mathematical formula to determine reasonable equivalence." The Third Circuit has held that assessing whether a debtor received reasonably equivalent value in exchange for a transfer or obligation requires a two-step approach. First, "a court must consider whether, 'based on the circumstances that existed at the time' of the transfer, it was 'legitimate and reasonable' to expect some value accruing to the debtor."

Second, if the court finds that the debtor received any value, the court must engage in a fact-driven comparison between such value and the transfer or obligation sought to be avoided to determine "whether the debtor got roughly the value it gave." To assess the reasonable equivalence of the transfer or obligation and the value received by the debtor, a court should "look to the 'totality of the circumstances,' including (1) the 'fair market value' of the benefit received as a result of the transfer, (2) 'the existence of an arm's-length relationship between the debtor and the transferee,' and (3) the transferee's good faith." Courts have previously upheld the reasonable equivalence of indirect value as well.

In the LBO context, courts assess the value transferred to and from the debtor in the aggregate when the plaintiff in an avoidance action — typically the debtor or the trustee — has established that the various transactions which compose the LBO should be collapsed and assessed collectively. The debtor may be deemed to have received reasonably equivalent value in exchange for a transfer or obligation when one of a series of transactions is viewed in isolation and apart from the others. However, when the collapsed transactions are analyzed in the aggregate, courts have often found that the total value accruing to the debtor is not reasonably equivalent to the total value of the transfers made or obligations incurred by the debtor. *See, e.g., Tabor*, 803 F.2d at 1302. For instance, the *Tabor* court found that certain funds which were alleged to have provided the debtor with reasonably equivalent value in fact merely passed through the debtor when the relevant transactions were integrated and viewed in the aggregate, prompting the court to find that the debtor did not receive reasonably equivalent value after all. *Id.*

Here, the Committee alleges that Jevic did not receive reasonably equivalent value in exchange for its obligation with respect to the Refinancing Facility, the liens that secure it, and the various payments made on account thereof. CIT argues that in exchange for Jevic's obligation on the Refinancing Facility and the liens on Jevic's assets, CIT provided value to Jevic in the form of the loan proceeds. CIT also asserts that in exchange for certain payments on account of the Refinancing Facility — specifically, to pay off the Term Loan using the proceeds from the sale of the Properties — CIT gave value via forbearance. However, CIT's argument does not take into account the Committee's argument that when the transactions relating to the Jevic LBO are collapsed, the aggregate value of the obligation incurred and the transfers made by Jevic exceeds and is therefore not reasonably equivalent to the aggregate value that CIT provided to Jevic in return. The Committee alleges that the loan proceeds relating to the Refinancing Facility were used to pay off the Acquisition Facility, on which Sun's wholly owned affiliate was the obligor and Sun the guarantor. Considering all allegations and reasonable inferences in favor of the Committee, the Court concludes that the Complaint contains sufficient allegations that, if true, could support a finding that the loan proceeds received by Jevic merely passed through Jevic and thus failed to provide reasonably equivalent value to Jevic in exchange for the accumulated value Jevic transferred to CIT. While the Committee will still need to marshal evidence to refute CIT's charge that Jevic received reasonably equivalent value, the Court finds that the Committee has adequately alleged the absence of such value at this stage and is entitled to further pursue its claims.

b. Insolvency

The Bankruptcy Code defines insolvency as the "financial condition such that the sum of [an] entity's debts is greater than all of such entity's property." 11 U.S.C. §101(32)(A). When determining liability under §548, a court measures a debtor's solvency "at the time the debtor transferred value, not at some later or earlier time." Here, the Committee alleges that Jevic was "insolvent or would be rendered insolvent by the transactions undertaken in connection with the [Jevic] LBO, the [Refinancing Facility], and Sale-Lease Back." The Court concludes that these allegations are sufficient to survive this motion.

c. Unreasonably Small Capital

Like insolvency, the Bankruptcy Code does not define what constitutes unreasonably small capital. In the context of an LBO, the Third Circuit has held that "the test for unreasonably small capital is reasonable foreseeability. "The problem universal to all LBOs — transactions characterized by their high debt relative to equity interest — is that they are less able to weather temporary financial storms because debt demands are less flexible than equity interest." When determining whether the LBO-related transactions sought to be collapsed and unwound left the target — now the debtor entity — with unreasonably small capital, the court should determine whether the projections for the LBO target, which forecast that the debtor would retain sufficient cash or credit to operate and sustain its business, were reasonable. In other words, "[the court's] task in determining whether a company had sufficient working capital as evidenced by cash flow projections was not to examine what happened to the company but whether the projections employed prior to the LBO were prudent."

The Court finds it significant that the Third Circuit has stated that "leveraged buyouts present great potential for abuse." In a typical LBO, the target company alone — not the buyer — becomes obligated on the LBO debt that is secured by the target company's assets. The target company's capital structure is radically altered as a result of the LBO because its equity is substituted for highly leveraged debt for the benefit of the parties who are driving the LBO deal and to the detriment of the target company and its creditors. The risk of the LBO is thereby externalized to unsecured creditors and away from the parties to the LBO deal. For this reason, "[a]n LBO may be attractive to the buyer, seller, and lender because the structure of the transaction could allow all parties to the buyout to shift most of the risk of loss to other creditors of the corporation if the provisions of section 548(a)(2) were not applied."

Here, the Committee alleges that the transactions related to the Jevic LBO left Jevic with unreasonably small capital. In support of this allegation, the Committee asserts that following the Jevic LBO, Jevic's equity was reduced from $46 million to $1 million while its debt rose from $55 million to $101.2 million. The Committee further alleges that the projections underlying which the Refinancing Facility, allegedly prepared by Sun and approved by CIT, were unrealistic and highly unreasonable, but were made for the purpose of maximizing the Refinancing Facility. Assuming the truth of the Committee's allegations, the Court concludes that the Committee could establish that Jevic was left with unreasonably small capital within the meaning of §548.

3. Fraudulent Transfer Claims under §544 (Claims I and II)

Under §544(b), a debtor may avoid any transfer of an interest in the debtor's property that is voidable under applicable state law by a creditor holding an allowable unsecured claim. Here, the Committee invokes the Uniform Fraudulent Transfer Act ("UFTA") but has failed to allege the state-specific UFTA law upon which such claim is grounded. As a general matter, UFTA allows a debtor's creditors to recover property that was transferred by a debtor who did not receive reasonably equivalent value for it and who was insolvent when the transfer occurred or became insolvent as a result thereof. Because UFTA generally tracks 11 U.S.C. §548, the Committee's success on a §544(b) action will likely mirror its success on a §548 action that is based upon the same facts. Here, however, the Committee's failure to identify the state-specific UFTA upon which its claims are based leads the Court to conclude that the Committee has failed to put CIT on sufficient notice of the grounds upon which the cause of action against it are based. In light of *Twombly* and *Iqbal* especially, case law provides that such inadequate notice necessitates dismissal of the Committee's §544 claim for failure to state a claim upon which relief can be granted.

D. AIDING AND ABETTING BREACH OF FIDUCIARY DUTY (CLAIM VI)

In Claim VI, the Committee alleges that CIT aided and abetted Jevic's officers and directors in the breach of their fiduciary duties. The Committee asserts that the officers and directors of Jevic breached their fiduciary duties by supporting and approving the Acquisition, the Refinancing Facility, the transfer of liens on Jevic's assets to CIT, the Sale-Leaseback, the transfer of the proceeds from the sale of the Properties to CIT, and the payments made by Jevic on account of the Refinancing Facility. The Committee also contends that CIT knew the officers and directors and knew that they breached their fiduciary duties by supporting and approving these transactions. The Committee maintains that notwithstanding this knowledge, "CIT directed, encouraged, assisted, facilitated and/or participated" in the conduct that has given rise to the directors' and officers' alleged breach of their fiduciary duties. According to the Committee, by aiding and abetting such conduct, CIT directly and proximately harmed Jevic by diminishing its estate, reducing its ability to operate its business, and increasing the likelihood that its creditors would not be paid in the event that Jevic declared bankruptcy.

Under the internal affairs doctrine, only one state has the authority to regulate a corporation's internal affairs, which include matters peculiar to relationships among or between the corporation and its current officers, directors, and shareholders. Edgar v. MITE Corp., 457 U.S. 624, 645 (1982). The Supreme Court has held that the state under which the corporation is chartered has this authority. *Id.* Courts have long recognized that few, if any, claims are more central to a corporation's internal affairs than those relating to an alleged breach of a fiduciary duty by a corporation's directors and officers.

Here, because Jevic is a Delaware corporation, Delaware law governs the Committee's claim for aiding and abetting the breach of a fiduciary duty. As with a claim for the breach of a fiduciary duty, the internal affairs doctrine compels the Court to also apply Delaware law to a claim for aiding and abetting the breach of a fiduciary duty asserted against CIT.

Delaware courts have articulated four elements that must be proven to establish a claim for aiding and abetting the breach of a fiduciary duty: (1) the existence of a fiduciary relationship; (2) the breach of a duty by the fiduciary; (3) the knowing participation in the breach by the defendant, who is not a fiduciary; and (4) damages to the plaintiff resulting from the concerted action of the fiduciary and the nonfiduciary. Proof of scienter is the crux of a successful claim. "In order to be found liable for aiding and abetting a breach of a fiduciary duty, one must demonstrate that the party knew that the other's conduct constituted a breach of a fiduciary duty and gave substantial assistance or encouragement to the other in committing that breach." A plaintiff must demonstrate the defendant's "knowing participation" with specific facts.

Here, the Committees fails to plead specific facts in support of its allegation that CIT knowingly participated in the breach of a fiduciary duty. The Complaint merely states in general terms that CIT knew the directors and officers of Jevic who breached their fiduciary duties, knew that their conduct amounted to such breach, and directed, encouraged, and assisted such conduct.

E.   EQUITABLE SUBORDINATION UNDER §510(C) (CLAIM VII)

Finally, in Claim VII, the Committee alleges that there is a sufficient factual predicate in support of its request for the equitable subordination under 11 U.S.C. §510(c) of CIT's claims against the estate in the amount of approximately $50.4 million. The Committee asserts that CIT's conduct resulted in injury to the Debtors, conferred an unfair advantage to CIT, or both.

The Bankruptcy Code provides that a court may "under principles of equitable subordination, subordinate for purposes of distribution all or part of an allowed claim to all or part of another allowed claim." Proof of three elements is required to establish equitable subordination: (1) the defendant engaged in some type of inequitable conduct; (2) the misconduct caused injury to the creditors or conferred an unfair advantage on the defendant; and (3) equitable subordination of the claim is consistent with bankruptcy law. Benjamin v. Diamond (In re Mobile Steel Co.), 563 F.2d 692, 699-705 (5th Cir.1977).

See also United States v. Noland, 517 U.S. 535, 538-39 (1996) (adopting the *Mobile Steel* test for equitable subordination). Courts differentiate between insiders and outsiders when analyzing whether conduct was inequitable. "The most important factor in determining if a claimant has engaged in inequitable conduct for the purposes of equitable subordination is whether the claimant was an insider or outsider in relation to the debtor at the time of the act." In re Mid–Am. Waste Sys., Inc., 284 B.R. 53, 69 (Bankr.D.Del.2002). If a defendant is not an insider, then evidence of more egregious conduct such as fraud, spoliation or overreaching is necessary."

Here, the Committee has alleged only that CIT's conduct, as it is described in the Committee's preceding claims, warrants the equitable subordination of CIT's claims against the Debtors.. Based on such sparse allegations, however, the Court cannot conclude that the Committee has sufficiently alleged a claim for equitable subordination against CIT and will therefore dismiss this claim.

As you will see in Chapter 27, our old friend Dynegy also had some fraudulent transfer problems after the Icahn deal fell through. But they did not involve an LBO, so we leave them for the bankruptcy chapters.

PROBLEM SET 25.2

1. Why not leave fraudulent transfer issues to contract and the terms of bond indentures and loan agreements? What are the risks fraudulent transfer laws?
2. And of course, diagram the transaction in the case and be prepared to discuss its motivations in class. In particular, who benefits? Who was hurt?

3. BULK SALES (UCC ARTICLE 6)

If an acquisition is structured as the sale of the assets of the target company, the sale may be subject to the bulk transfer laws contained in Article 6 of the Uniform Commercial Code, if Article 6 is in effect in the jurisdictions that might be applicable to the transaction. Under the bulk sales laws, "bulk transfers" of assets are ineffective against creditors of the seller unless there is compliance with the special procedures of Article 6 that provide notice to the target's creditors. What justifications might exist for such a statute?

Article 6 is a fading statute, still in force in but a handful of states.[12] New York repealed its version of the statute in 2001. Nonetheless, it remains a concern when dealing with a multistate business.

----

12. *http://www.lawrev.state.nj.us/rpts/ucc6.pdf*

4.   A NOTE ON ALTERNATIVE ACQUISITION STRUCTURES

Most commonly distressed acquisitions take the form of asset sales that are structured (as best as possible) to show the payment of "reasonably equivalent value." The buyer hopes to avoid both fraudulent transfer and successor liability as a result.

But a distressed company's assets might also be acquired through the state law foreclosure system. In general, liens on personal property are governed by the Uniform Commercial Code, which authorizes both private and public foreclosure sales. Liens on interests in real estate, or mortgages, are governed by more complex state real property law and the foreclosure procedures will vary from state to state.

A potential purchaser could wait until the secured party exercises its remedies under state law and then buy the assets at the foreclosure sale. Or the buyer could acquire the secured party's debt, which will allow the purchaser to control the foreclosure process and acquire the assets at the foreclosure sale through a credit bid.[13]

As opposed to an asset sale under state corporate law, the foreclosure process has the advantage that the sale may not be challenged as a fraudulent transfer in a subsequent bankruptcy case.[14]

Another state law procedure that can be useful in acquiring assets is known as the assignment for the benefit of creditors. This statutory procedure allows a distressed company to assign all of its assets to a representative who then liquidates the assets and distributes the proceeds to the creditors. In some sense this can be seen as a state law bankruptcy process — although the states are limited by the Contract Clause in the Constitution in their ability to provide full bankruptcy relief.[15]

5.   WORKER ADJUSTMENT AND RETRAINING NOTIFICATION ACT ("WARN")

IN THE MATTER OF FLEXIBLE FLYER LIQUIDATING TRUST, DEBTOR. DAVID D. ANGLES; GRADY BARCLAY; MEGAN BIBBS; PEARLY BILLUPS; ROMELL BLACK; ET AL, APPELLANTS v. FLEXIBLE FLYER LIQUIDATING TRUST, FORMERLY KNOWN AS FF ACQUISITION CORPORATION, DOING BUSINESS AS FLEXIBLE–FLYER, APPELLEE

511 Fed.Appx. 369, 2013 WL 586823 | Feb. 11, 2013

PER CURIAM:

This appeal addresses an employer's duty to notify employees of a plant closing and mass layoff under the Worker Adjustment and Retraining Notification Act

---

13. Credit bids are discussed in the bankruptcy materials, but essentially involve the lender "bidding" part of its debt at the auction — in place of cash.

14. BFP v. Resolution Trust Corp., 511 U.S. 531, 545 (1994).

15. *See* Stephen J. Lubben, *The Bankruptcy Clause*, 64 Case W. Res. L. Rev. — (forthcoming 2014).

("WARN Act"), where lenders suddenly and without advance notice completely terminated the company's financing. The question presented is whether such circumstance satisfies the WARN Act exception for "unforeseeable business circumstances." The case largely turns on the factual findings of the bankruptcy court. Because the findings are not clearly erroneous, we AFFIRM.

I.

Cerberus Capital Management Corp. ("Cerberus"), a private equity hedge fund, formed the now bankrupt Flexible Flyer in 1997 to purchase the assets of a bankrupt company. Flexible Flyer manufactured swing sets, hobby horses, go-carts, utility vehicles, and fitness equipment. These products were sold to a variety of retailers, including Wal-Mart, Toys-R-Us, K-Mart, and Sam's Club.

Flexible Flyer never made a profit—indeed it constantly lost money—but hope and a few good signs kept it going. Until late 2000, Flexible Flyer was funded entirely by its parent company, Cerberus. During this time, Cerberus infused Flexible Flyer with $85 million in capital. In late 2000, Flexible Flyer obtained an additional source of operating capital when it entered into a factoring arrangement with CIT Group Commercial Systems, LLC ("CIT"). Under this arrangement, Flexible Flyer assigned its eligible accounts receivables to CIT, and CIT advanced Flexible Flyer 80% of the receivables that it acquired. The factoring arrangement with CIT and occasional capital infusions from Cerberus were Flexible Flyer's primary sources of operating funds during its struggling existence.

CIT and Cerberus closely monitored Flexible Flyer's financial performance, because, as we have indicated, Flexible Flyer consistently operated at a deficit. Each year, Cerberus told Flexible Flyer that it would shut Flexible Flyer down if it did not become profitable within a year. But, despite the failure to make a profit and despite issuing these warnings year after year, Cerberus never took the steps to close Flexible Flyer. Cerberus continued to provide capital and did not refuse Flexible Flyer's requests for additional funding when Flexible Flyer indicated that more funding was essential for its continued operation.

In 2005, Flexible Flyer's situation became even more tenuous. It experienced a number of financial problems, and the company notified its employees in April of possible layoffs in the go-cart section. Two months later, Flexible Flyer was forced to recall 10,000 go-carts because of defective parts. Around this same time, Wal-Mart, K-Mart, and Toys-R-Us notified Flexible Flyer that they would be deferring the purchase of approximately $5 million in swing sets until the next year. Another customer, Tractor Supply Company, withheld $300,000 in payments for merchandise that had already been shipped.

Michael Earrey, Flexible Flyer's Chief Financial Officer, took a number of actions attempting to address these problems. In August 2005, he convinced Wal-Mart to pay its invoices sooner, and several vendors agreed to defer payments due from Flexible Flyer. Earrey was less successful, however, in convincing some customers, most notably Wal-Mart, to provide written commitments regarding projected delivery dates or future orders. Despite the lack of written commitments, Earrey testified that he remained optimistic Flexible Flyer could weather the storm. During this time, Flexible Flyer's primary domestic competitor had filed for bankruptcy protection, leaving Flexible Flyer as the only U.S. manufacturer of swing sets. Fewer competitors gave Earrey a reason to be encouraged about Flexible Flyer's future.

Recognizing that it needed additional funds to operate, Flexible Flyer consulted with an attorney in August 2005 to explore all of its options. Among those options were exiting the go-cart business completely, selling the fitness equipment business, or possibly filing for Chapter 11 bankruptcy protection. Before Flexible Flyer decided on which course of action to take, however, CIT reduced its credit line. Instead of continuing to advance Flexible Flyer 80% of its receivables, CIT cut the amount to 50%. Earrey believed that Flexible Flyer could continue to operate at the 50% rate, but two weeks after the initial cut, CIT informed Flexible Flyer that it would no longer be advancing credit at all. Earrey attempted to get funding from Cerberus, but this time, Cerberus refused. With no cash to operate, Flexible Flyer was forced to file for bankruptcy on September 9, 2005, two days after CIT terminated all funding. That same day, Flexible Flyer notified its employees that it would be terminating business operations, resulting in company-wide layoffs.

A group of over 100 former Flexible Flyer employees filed an adversary action in Flexible Flyer's bankruptcy proceeding, alleging that Flexible Flyer was liable under the WARN Act for failing to give them the required sixty-day layoff notice. Both parties agreed that there were more than 100 employees involved, that Flexible Flyer had failed to give the sixty-day notice, and that consequently the WARN Act applied. After a bench trial, the bankruptcy court determined, however, that Flexible Flyer was excused from providing advance notice because it had established that the shutdown was the result of an unforeseeable business circumstance. The court credited Earrey's testimony, finding that the abrupt unavailability of operating funds caused the layoffs and that the sudden lack of funds was completely unanticipated. The court concluded that "[t]he shutdown of Flexible Flyer and the mass layoffs were not planned, proposed, or foreseeable" and found that Flexible Flyer had provided WARN Act notice at "the earliest practical date that such a notice could be provided."

The employees appealed to the district court, which held that "the factual determinations made by the [bankruptcy] court were not clearly erroneous, and the legal conclusions were thorough and correct." This timely appeal from the district court's judgment followed.

III.

The WARN Act, 29 U.S.C. §§2101–2109, requires covered employers who are planning a plant closing or mass layoff to give affected employees sixty days notice of such action. 20 C.F.R. §639.2. Advance notice is meant to provide "workers and their families some transition time to adjust to the prospective loss of employment, to seek and obtain alternative jobs and, if necessary, to enter skill training or retraining." There are exceptions, however, that excuse employers who fail to provide the required notice. If a WARN Act exception applies, employers are required to give only "as much notice as is practicable."

The unforeseeable business circumstance exception applies when the closing or layoff was "caused by business circumstances that were not reasonably foreseeable as of the time that notice would have been required." Closings and layoffs are not foreseeable when "caused by some sudden, dramatic, and unexpected action or condition outside the employer's control." In assessing the foreseeability of business circumstances, our focus is "on an employer's business judgment. An employer is required only to "exercise such commercially reasonable business judgment as would a similarly situated employer in predicting the demands of its particular market."

We previously have stated that where it only is possible that the business circumstance at issue may occur, such circumstances are not reasonably foreseeable. Rather, "it is the probability of occurrence that makes a business circumstance 'reasonably foreseeable' and thereby forecloses use of the [unforeseeable business circumstances] exception."

Here, the bankruptcy court was the finder of fact. It determined that the September 9, 2005 closing of Flexible Flyer's business was not reasonably foreseeable. The record showed that sixty days before the shutdown, Flexible Flyer was undisputedly experiencing financial difficulties. But, even so, there was no indication that a company shutdown was imminent. Indeed, the bankruptcy court credited Earrey's testimony that, until almost the last moment, he had been working tirelessly to turn the company around and was considering a number of cost-saving measures designed to keep the company operating for as long as possible. Moreover, Flexible Flyer's position in the market had improved as a result of its competitor's demise, and Earrey had presented Wal-Mart with projections for Flexible Flyer's 2006 operations, demonstrating his belief that the company would continue operations into the new year. Earrey also testified that he was considering options for "an orderly downsizing of the business over time, not an immediate shutdown." All of the evidence proffered thus shows that the focus of Flexible Flyer's management was on saving the company, not planning for an upcoming shutdown. Based on Earrey's testimony, the bankruptcy court found that, "Earrey's exercise of his business judgment, in keeping Flexible Flyer going and in anticipating that Flexible Flyer would continue operations into 2006, was completely reasonable." We cannot say that the bankruptcy court clearly erred in crediting Earrey's testimony or in concluding that his exercise of business judgment was reasonable under the circumstances.

The holdings of the bankruptcy and district courts are further supported by the showing that during the time period immediately preceding the closure, Flexible Flyer still had financing in place from CIT, as well as back-up funding from Cerberus, who had never refused Flexible Flyer's previous requests for additional capital. It was only when CIT and Cerberus both decided to cut off funding completely, and did so almost simultaneously without warning, that the shutdown became inevitable. Earrey testified that he had "no clue" that CIT was going to cut funding, and Cerberus's refusal to provide capital was a sudden departure from its prior actions in response to Flexible Flyer's funding requests. Again crediting Earrey's testimony, the bankruptcy court concluded that the "abrupt unavailability of operating funds" caused the layoffs, and that CIT and Cerberus's actions were "completely unanticipated." Nothing in the record suggests that these findings and conclusions were clearly erroneous.

The arguments of the former employees suggest that the sixty days notice should have been issued sometime following the June 2005 go-cart recall. Contrary to the contention of the former employees, Flexible Flyer's financial difficulties in July and in the ensuing weeks do not establish the foreseeability of a complete withdrawal of funding; nor consequently, the company's sudden closure on September 9, 2005. As noted above, the bankruptcy court credited Earrey's testimony that CIT and Cerberus's decision to cut all funding was an unanticipated event taking place two days before the shutdown. Under [case law] and the WARN Act regulations, the focus of the analysis of this appeal must be on the probability that the plant closure and subsequent layoffs would occur, and the employer's exercise of business judgment. It is true that Flexible Flyer's financial condition was perilous for much of its eight-year existence. But it is also true that encouraging events continued to renew probabilities that better days may be ahead. The WARN Act allows good faith, well-grounded hope, and reasonable expectations. Its regulations protect the employer's exercise of business judgment and are intended to encourage employers to take all reasonable actions to preserve the company and the jobs. Holding Flexible Flyer liable for a WARN Act violation on the facts found by the bankruptcy court would serve only to encourage employers to abandon companies even when there is some probability of some success.

Thus, we hold that the bankruptcy court did not err in finding Earrey's testimony credible; based on his testimony, he pursued numerous options to save Flexible Flyer up until the sudden termination of all funding by CIT and Cerberus. Termination of outside funding may have always been possible, but it cannot be said on the record before us that Flexible Flyer probably knew during or before July 2005 that it would be stripped of funding, causing an immediate shutdown. This case presents a convincing example of an event that meets the unforeseeable business circumstance exception. The bankruptcy court correctly concluded that the exception applied in this case. The district court's judgment therefore is AFFIRMED.

The responsibility to notify employees whose employment will be terminated as a result of a sale remains with the seller up to and including the effective date of the transaction, and thereafter is assumed by the buyer.[16]

What transitional considerations does the WARN Act raise in the context of a leveraged buyout or distressed acquisitions?

6. BANKRUPTCY RISKS OF DISTRESSED ACQUISITIONS

Bankruptcy will be discussed in subsequent chapters, but it bears noting at this point that if a financially distressed company does file for bankruptcy

16. 29 U.S.C. §2101 (b)(1).

protection after the signing but before the closing of the transaction, the buyer is subject to risk that the now-bankrupt target will exercise its rights under section 365 of the Bankruptcy Code to reject the sale agreement. Alternatively, the target might use its powers under the Bankruptcy Code to attempt to renegotiate the terms of the sale by threatening rejection. Moreover, the representations, warranties and indemnities contained in the asset purchase agreement might not be worth very much after the target's bankruptcy filing. In short, because of the risk of future bankruptcy cases, the acquirer has strong incentives to close the transaction quickly.

IV

FINANCIAL DISTRESS

26

EXCHANGE OFFERS AND WORKOUTS

This chapter begins the fourth and final section of the course. The fourth unit deals with corporate finance in the context of financial distress. Just as these chapters are the beginning of the end of your course, these topics are often the beginning of the end of the firm. But not always.

The most obvious way to deal with financial distress is through bankruptcy. But this chapter examines the ways in which a firm can try to solve its problems outside of bankruptcy.

It is generally thought that these sorts of out-of-court processes involve less cost, as bankruptcy is a court-driven process that requires lots of pleadings to be drafted, even when there is general consensus among the firm and its claimants.

At a basic level a workout is simply an agreement between the debtor firm and its creditors. That presupposes the firm knows who its creditors are — the advent of distressed debt investors and derivatives might make this more complicated than it would appear.

STEPHEN J. LUBBEN & RAJESH P. NARAYANAN, *CDS AND THE RESOLUTION OF FINANCIAL DISTRESS*
24 J. Applied Corp. Fin. 129 (2012)

The ownership of debt conveys to the creditor a bundled set of rights — cash flow rights to principal and interest payments, and control rights to protect and recover these promised payments through the ability to vote on covenant waivers, reorganization plans and liquidation decisions. Hedging in the CDS markets immunizes the creditor to the debtor's financial condition and thus functionally unbundles the cash flow rights from the control rights embodied in the debt contract.

The potential for this unbundling to cause problems in restructurings was first identified by Lubben (2007), and then given the moniker the "empty creditor problem" by Hu and Black (2008a, 2008b). In short, the issue relates to how the altered incentives of hedged creditors result in unexpected behavior after the onset of financial distress.

While it is normally assumed that creditors are interested in keeping a solvent but financially distressed firm out of bankruptcy and hence willing to renegotiate out-of-court, a hedged creditor will lack the incentive to participate in an out of court workout — such as an exchange offer. In extreme cases, the creditor might have incentives to thwart workouts and file involuntary bankruptcy cases, all with an eye toward triggering their CDS contract. This problem could be especially extreme in North America, where, for historical reasons, "restructuring" is often not included as a credit event in standard CDS contracts.

It is also possible that the holder of a large, speculative CDS position could acquire a position in a distressed firm's traded debt to block a potential workout. After the onset of financial distress, it could be that the cost of such a blocking position on the distressed debt markets would be justified given a sufficiently large CDS position. Indeed, if the CDS market is made up of mostly speculators, the prior scenario, or something like it, might be the most plausible. After all, it is unclear how many CDS buyers actually use such swaps to hedge ordinary bonds.

Similarly, it should be noted that such a blocking strategy would not necessarily involve buying debt at the same level in the capital structure as referenced by the investor's CDS contracts. Indeed, it would typically be more effective to purchase senior secured debt, which would result in a higher return upon bankruptcy and facilitate greater blocking power. For example, many syndicated loan agreements require super majority votes to waive defaults. And in chapter 11, secured creditors are separately classified, resulting in greater voting power.

CDS may also place artificial time limits on restructuring negotiations, given that most contracts run for five years, and will presumably have been purchased before financial distress made the cost prohibitive. Credit default swaps expire without value to the protection buyer if no credit event occurs before maturity. Thus, as maturity dates approach on outstanding credit default swaps, protected creditors will have an increasing disincentive to work with the debtor on the terms of a restructuring arrangement that might not be announced or consummated until after the creditors' swaps have terminated. More generally, the protection buyer faces the risk that any workout could extend the underlying debt obligation beyond the duration of the swap.

Even the more extreme cases, such as creditors filing involuntary bankruptcy petitions to manufacture a credit event, are not apt to be easily detected, so long as the creditor has other, more traditional grounds for filing the petition. At present, there is no legal obligation for a petitioning creditor to disclose whether it has hedged its position.

Identifying these problems in actual cases of financial distress is quite difficult. Most workouts require the creditor to balance what they are offered in the workout with what they would receive in a hypothetical chapter 11 or chapter 7 case of the same debtor. CDSs do not change this analysis, but rather places a thumb on the bankruptcy side of the scale. That is, CDSs result in a marginal change of incentives, rather than an absolute change. Detecting such a shift, separate from the underlying attractiveness of the competing offers in the workout, requires subtle analysis.

Press reports on the difficulties facing debtors attempting to reorganize in the presence of hedged creditors first began to appear in connection with British telecom company Marconi's renegotiations with its lenders in 2001–2002. Since then, press coverage on problems with hedged creditors has accompanied the bankruptcies of Mirant, Lyondell-Basell, General Growth Properties, Six Flags, Abitibi-Bowater, featuring most prominently in the 2009 bankruptcies of General Motors and Chrysler.

In 2009, ISDA examined whether the ability to hedge using CDSs made out-of-court restructurings less likely than bankruptcy filings. Positing that "*the correlation between number of defaults and restructurings as percent of defaults should be lower when credit default swaps are available that when they are not,*" it reported "*the correlation between number of defaults in a given year and restructurings relative to defaults in the same year is about 9 percent over the entire sample period. But restricting attention to the period of liquid credit default swap markets, which arguably began in 2003 with the publication of the 2003 ISDA Credit Derivative Definitions and the subsequent initiation of trading in the CDX and iTraxx credit indexes, the correlation jumps to 90 percent. While correlations within small data sets should be interpreted carefully, the correlation statistics presented here would not appear to support the empty creditor hypothesis, according to which the availability of credit default swaps would make restructurings less likely.*

Further evidence comes from the list of restructurings that occurred during 2008 and the first half of 2009. During that time, twenty-one firms underwent out-of-court restructurings; credit default swap protection was available on eleven of them (52 percent). And of the restructurings that occurred during that period, four subsequently filed for Chapter 11 bankruptcy; of those four, two had liquid CDS available and two did not. Again, the evidence thus far does not appear to support the empty creditor hypothesis." (Mengle, pp. 8–9)

More generally, exchange offers often fail because of holdout problems associated with disparate creditors. Bedendo, Cathcart, El-Jahel (2010) account for this possibility and attempt to discern whether the failure of exchange offers is due to hedged creditors. They find that "... the outcome of the debt renegotiation process seems to be driven by essentially the same variables in both reference and non-reference entities" (pp. 3) and is not linked to hedged creditors.

To get at the issue more directly, Danis (2012) examines whether creditor participation rates in exchange offers vary with the ability to hedge in the CDS markets. He finds that average participation rates are lower in exchange offers conducted by reference entities compared to non-reference entities which suggests that hedged creditors may make it more difficult for firms to restructure debt out-of-court.

Debtors may respond by structuring their exchange offers to circumvent hedged creditors. Typically, the reference obligation underlying the CDS is senior unsecured debt. Narayanan and Uzmanoglu (2012) posit that debtors target junior debt in the exchange offer as a way to alleviate distress. They provide evidence that, relative to non-reference entities, reference entities disproportionately restructure junior debt by offering creditors greater concession to tender in the exchange.

Debtors may find it useful to use a coercive exchange offer, to force the "true" stakeholders of a firm to reveal themselves. Of course, this move might also further encourage involuntary bankruptcy petitions, with the attendant risk of an unplanned filing in an unfavorable jurisdiction.

There is some indirect evidence associated with hedged creditors increasing the cost of distress resolution. Subrahmanyam, Tang and Wang (2011) find that both the probability of future credit downgrade and the probability of filing for bankruptcy increase after the introduction of CDS trading on a firm, leading them to state that the "the reluctance of (CDS protected lenders) to restructure is the most likely cause of the increase in credit risk." (pp. 1)

More broadly, growth of credit derivatives could well impede the negotiation of workouts, as well as prenegotiated or prepackaged bankruptcy plans, inasmuch as the party with the real risk of loss will often be unknown. Creditors may no longer behave in predictable ways; previously unknown creditors may appear on the scene, demanding a voice in the proceedings, and the debtor's true stakeholders may be subject to dispute.

In short, negotiations on the eve of bankruptcy can be expected to become increasingly complex and opaque (Skeel and Partnoy 2007). In large part this is the result of the design of the credit protection markets, which expressly seek to allow banks and other lenders the ability to offload credit risk without alerting their customers of this fact and incurring the resulting reputation costs. However, this lack of transparency creates obvious and severe information asymmetries that may hinder pre-bankruptcy negotiation and planning, a serious problem after the 2005 amendments to the Bankruptcy Code make it increasingly difficult for a debtor to enter chapter 11 without such planning.

1.   EXCHANGE OFFERS

The most common method for effectuating a workout is through an exchange offer. The firm negotiates a deal for the refinancing of its debt with a group of large creditors, and then it commences a tender offer for its outstanding debt.

The tender offer it institutes is an "exchange offer" in that it typically offers new, longer dated (and perhaps lower couponed) debt in exchange for the existing debt.

NEWS RELEASE

Media Contact:
Grace Platon
800.365.8957

VERTIS HOLDINGS COMMENCES COMPREHENSIVE REFINANCING PLAN

Improved Capital Structure Expected to Reduce Overall Debt by More Than $250 Million, Extend Debt Maturities and Decrease Interest Expense

BALTIMORE—April 16, 2010 – Vertis Holdings, Inc. ("Holdings") announced today that its principal operating subsidiary, Vertis, Inc. ("Vertis"), has commenced (i) a private exchange offer, a tender offer and a consent solicitation relating to its outstanding $13^1/_2$ percent Senior Pay-in-Kind Notes due 2014 (the "Senior Notes"), and (ii) a private exchange offer and a consent solicitation relating to its $18^1/_2$ percent Senior Secured Second Lien Notes due 2012 (the "Existing Second Lien Notes" and, together with the Senior Notes, the "Notes") held by eligible holders (collectively, the "Offers").

The Offers represent elements of a comprehensive $1.1 billion refinancing of substantially all of Vertis' outstanding secured and unsecured indebtedness. Upon completion of the planned transactions, Vertis will have significantly reduced its outstanding indebtedness and related interest expense and extended its debt maturity profile. In addition to the Offers, the refinancing (collectively, the "Refinancing Transactions") is expected to include:

- the refinancing of Vertis' existing $225 million revolving credit facility with the proceeds of a new senior secured asset-based revolving credit facility of up to $200 million;

- the incurrence of approximately $600 million of new first lien indebtedness, the proceeds of which will be used to refinance Vertis' existing term loan and to fund the cash consideration for the Second Lien Notes Exchange Offer;

- the issuance to Avenue Capital of approximately $113 million of new 13/15 percent PIK-Option Senior Secured Notes due 2016 in a private exchange for amounts owed to Avenue Capital under Vertis' existing term loan; and

- the exchange of approximately $74 million aggregate principal amount of Existing Second Lien Notes held by Avenue Capital for shares of $13^1/_2$ percent exchangeable pay-in-kind preferred stock of Holdings.

The purpose of the Refinancing Transactions is to improve Vertis' capital structure by reducing its overall debt by more than $250 million, reducing its annual interest expense and extending its debt maturity profile. Vertis believes consummation of the Refinancing Transactions will better position Vertis to mitigate future refinancing risks and provide it with greater flexibility in making decisions to accomplish its business objectives and investing in its future. In addition, Vertis believes consummation of the Refinancing Transactions will provide customers, employees, suppliers and stakeholders with more confidence in Vertis as a result of an improved capital structure.

Prior to the date hereof, certain eligible holders of the Notes executed support agreements whereby they agreed to validly tender approximately 70 percent of the Senior Notes and more than 75 percent of the Existing Second Lien Notes (excluding Existing Second Lien Notes held by Avenue Capital) in the applicable Offer at or prior to the applicable Consent Time (as defined below).

NICHOLAS P. SAGGESE, ET AL., *A PRACTITIONER'S GUIDE TO EXCHANGE OFFERS AND CONSENT SOLICITATIONS*
24 Loy. L.A. L. Rev. 527 (1991)

The general purpose of restructuring transactions is to preserve the going concern value of a financially troubled corporation by modifying its capital structure to reduce interest or dividend expense, or to eliminate or modify covenants in the corporation's existing securities that restrict or prohibit a restructuring, or that the corporation can no longer satisfy.[1]

A corporation can effect a restructuring in a number of ways. One often-used technique involves the consensual exchange (Exchange Offer) of new securities of the corporation (New Securities) for certain of its then outstanding securities (Target Securities).

In addition, a corporation contemplating an out-of-court restructuring may choose to solicit security holders' consents to modify Target Securities (Consent Solicitation), reclassify equity securities pursuant to an amendment to the corporation's charter (Reclassification) or repurchase Target Securities for cash. A financially troubled corporation may also utilize a "pre-packaged" plan of bankruptcy (Prepackaged Bankruptcy) to avoid protracted chapter 11 proceedings. This Article, however, focuses on issues related to out-of-court restructurings generally as well as certain issues unique to Exchange Offers that involve an exchange or a series of exchanges of New Securities for Target Securities pursuant to section 3(a)(9) of the Securities Act of 1933, as amended (the Securities Act).

The issuance of New Securities in exchange for Target Securities requires registration of the offering of the New Securities with the Securities and Exchange Commission (the SEC), unless an exemption is available. Section 3(a)(9) of the Securities Act (Section 3(a)(9)) provides such an exemption and is often relied upon in the context of out-of-court restructurings. This exemption, often called the "exchange exemption," applies when New Securities are exchanged, except in a case under title 11 of the United States Code, "by the issuer with its existing security holders exclusively where no commission or other remuneration is paid or given directly or indirectly for soliciting such exchange."

A restructuring conducted as an exchange of securities pursuant to Section 3(a)(9) (Section 3(a)(9) Exchange) offers a distinct advantage over alternative forms of restructurings — by avoiding the delay associated with the registration of securities with the SEC, a Section 3(a)(9) Exchange can be commenced relatively quickly and relatively inexpensively. A Section 3(a)(9) Exchange, however, also has one significant disadvantage to the corporation — the corporation cannot retain paid agents to solicit the participation of the holders of Target Securities in the proposed exchange. If a corporation believes that professional solicitation efforts are essential to the success of its restructuring, the corporation must either conduct the exchange within the parameters of another Securities Act exemption, or it must register the sale of New Securities offered in the exchange by filing a registration statement with the SEC (Registered Exchange).

---

1. For example, a corporation may offer shares of its common stock to holders of its debt securities to eliminate interest expense or to preferred stockholders to eliminate dividend requirements. *See, e.g.*, Bally Manufacturing Corp., Offering Circular (May 30, 1990); Financial Corporation Of Santa Barbara, Prospectus (Nov. 7, 1989) (amended by three supplements, the last of which was dated Jan. 3, 1990) (common stock for one series of preferred stock and two series of debt). Obviously, the reduction of interest expense and dividend obligations would be attractive to non-financially troubled corporations, as well. Non-financially troubled corporations have, in fact, used some of the techniques described in this Article to accomplish these goals. *See, e.g.*, Occidental Petroleum Corporation, Offering Circular (Sept. 23, 1987) (offering common stock for senior notes); Occidental Petroleum Corporation, Offering Circular (July 2, 1987) (offering common stock for preferred stock that was exchangeable into debt securities).

From a legal standpoint, Exchange Offers may involve a plethora of regulations and issues, including the following:

- the elements of Section 3(a)(9), if applicable;
- if there is a concurrent Consent Solicitation, the proxy rules . . . promulgated under the Securities Exchange Act of 1934, as amended (the Exchange Act);
- the tender offer and "going private" rules promulgated under the Williams Act, as amended;
- if the New Security is a qualifying debt security, the requirements of the Trust Indenture Act of 1939, as amended (the TIA) and the rules promulgated thereunder;
- the continuing concern about the proper timing of public disclosure about the restructuring and related issues from the conception to consummation of the restructuring;
- the laws governing fiduciary duties and contractual obligations owed to various classes of security holders;
- state blue sky and securities laws;
- the rules of securities exchanges;
- the rules of the National Association of Securities Dealers, Inc. (the NASD) [In 2007, the NASD merged with the New York Stock Exchange's regulation committee to form the Financial Industry Regulatory Authority, or FINRA.]; and
- tax and debtor/creditor considerations.

Ultimately, the process of selecting and executing a particular Exchange Offer requires extensive cross-disciplinary legal analyses and guidance.

II. CERTAIN PRELIMINARY CONSIDERATIONS

Several significant factors impact how and whether a corporation should attempt an out-of-court restructuring by means of an Exchange Offer. Though many of the issues raised in this section are discussed more thoroughly elsewhere, it is important to set them out initially to provide a framework for this Article.

A. TIME

The passage of time is almost always an enemy of the financially troubled corporation. As time passes, suppliers may tighten credit and customers may question orders, both of which further damage a corporation's cash flow. Employees may question the security of their positions, possibly depriving the corporation of valuable human resources. Rating agencies may downgrade existing securities. All of these factors can directly or indirectly decrease a corporation's access to capital and thereby exacerbate its difficulties. Consequently, the more quickly a corporation can successfully restructure, the better its future prospects tend to be. Section 3(a)(9) Exchanges generally can be commenced more quickly than most other types of out-of-court restructurings, in some cases within a few weeks. Consequently, time pressures by themselves might dictate the use of a Section 3(a)(9) Exchange.

B.   DEVELOPMENT OF INCENTIVES FOR EXISTING SECURITY HOLDERS TO
     PARTICIPATE IN AN EXCHANGE OFFER AND THE ISSUE OF "HOLDOUTS"

Corporations have long sought to create both positive and negative incentives for existing investors to participate in Exchange Offers. The positive incentives have included inserting terms in the New Securities that are intended to make them trade at a premium over the current market price of the Target Securities, such as a higher interest or dividend rate than the Target Securities, a shorter maturity, a ranking senior to the Target Securities (with the New Securities possibly being secured), protective covenants not included in the Target Securities, or other attributes that might benefit the New Securities relative to the Target Securities.

A common negative incentive is the possibility of bankruptcy if the Exchange Offer is not completed. Additionally, nonexchanging holders often run the risk that if the exchange succeeds, their Target Securities will be contractually subordinated to the New Securities. To create another negative incentive, some corporations have sought to amend or eliminate certain covenants in Target Securities that remain outstanding after the Exchange Offer through a Consent Solicitation of the holders of the Target Securities (including those participating in the Exchange Offer) that is conducted concurrently with the Exchange Offer.

From the corporation's perspective, a continuing issue that can inhibit the success of an Exchange Offer is the issue of "holdouts," *i.e.*, holders of Target Securities who do not participate in the exchange. Some holders of Target Securities choose to hold out in hopes of negotiating a better deal. Others may simply believe retaining their Target Securities is better than owning the New Securities. In other cases, entities — often called "debt raiders" or "vulture capitalists" — buy strategic layers of a corporation's securities at distressed prices with the hope of taking control of the corporation or at least the negotiation process.

Corporations employ a variety of techniques, including the incentives and disincentives discussed above, to discourage holdouts. Another important technique frequently used to reduce the number of holdouts is to include a high minimum acceptance condition in the Exchange Offer, such as requiring the tender of at least a specified percentage (often eighty percent or higher) of the aggregate outstanding principal amount or number of shares of the Target Securities.

If the particular circumstances permit, some other forms of restructuring can eliminate holdouts. For example, Prepackaged Bankruptcies are increasing in popularity largely because all holders of Target Securities are bound if the Prepackaged Bankruptcy is approved by more than two-thirds in amount and more than one-half in number of the allowed claims casting a vote. In addition, reclassifications will bind all stockholders of the Target Securities upon the receipt of the requisite stockholder vote.

C.   COMPOSITION OF, AND NEGOTIATION WITH, SECURITY HOLDERS AND
     THEIR COMMITTEES

An important factor in the success, and therefore the advisability, of an Exchange Offer is the composition of the holders of prospective Target Securities. Depending on the number of such holders, as well as the complexity of the restructuring proposal, a corporation may determine that a form of restructuring that permits the retention of paid solicitors (*e.g.*, Registered Exchanges) may be preferable to a Section 3(a)(9) Exchange; or, it may decide that it should merely hire an information agent to help distribute offering materials or run tombstone advertisements or both in order to inform holders of Target Securities about the transaction. The key to this decision is whether a corporation believes that its regular employees can effectively solicit the proposed exchange.

A corporation should also consider the mix of recent purchasers of the Target Securities and long-time holders of Target Securities, who already may have incurred large losses. This mix may indicate the different motives of the holders of the Target Securities and, thereby, how best to structure the terms of the New Securities to be offered in the Exchange Offer.

Another important factor is the now common practice of certain holders of Target Securities' organizing committees (committees) that negotiate on behalf of holders of Target Securities. Committees, often represented by legal counsel and financial advisors, can form a unified front, enhancing the likelihood of the consummation of the Exchange Offer. On the other hand, the differing motives of committee members and disagreements amongst committees of different security holders can delay or even prevent the completion of the restructuring . . .

In any event, all participants in any restructuring, including a Section 3(a)(9) Exchange, should realize at the outset that most restructurings involve a process of negotiation. Most holders and committees expect that the corporation's first offer will not be its best offer. The ability of a corporation and its advisors to commence and conduct negotiations, however, is often limited by regulations applicable to the proposed restructuring. Ultimately, in many troubled-company situations, holders must be convinced that the offer on the table is the last offer, and potentially the last hope for the corporation short of bankruptcy.

D.   FIDUCIARY DUTIES OWED TO DIFFERENT SECURITY HOLDERS

Courts in Delaware clearly and repeatedly have concluded that, except in "special circumstances," neither a corporation, its directors nor its controlling stockholders owe a fiduciary duty to holders of convertible or non-convertible debt securities or, in certain instances, preferred stock. The basic rationale for this conclusion is that rights of debtholders and the preferential rights of preferred stockholders are derived from contract law, while those of common equity holders are based upon the trust relationship between the board of directors of a corporation and its common stockholders. Contracting parties generally are limited in seeking redress of alleged wrongs to the remedies provided or implied within the four corners of the document. As a result, a corporation should proceed with a restructuring plan on the basis of what is in the best interests of the common stockholders, unless one of the special circumstances arises.

Insolvency and bankruptcy are among the "special circumstances" that can create a fiduciary duty in a contractual relationship. In these circumstances, the class of beneficiaries to whom directors of a corporation owe fiduciary duties is enlarged, if not shifted, to include the corporation's creditors. This metamorphosis creates an enormous practical problem for the directors of a troubled company and its advisors. If a corporation is solvent, the directors' relationship with bondholders and, in certain instances, preferred stockholders, is at arm's length and commercial in nature. In a transaction between a corporation and its bondholders, directors have a fiduciary duty to negotiate with bondholders to obtain the best possible result for the corporation and its common stockholders. If, however, the corporation is insolvent, the directors risk liability to creditors for failing to protect the best interests of creditors. Therefore, if there is any doubt about the "solvency" of a corporation, directors of the troubled corporation are well advised to establish a record that demonstrates that they did their best to attempt to resolve matters on a basis that is "fair" to all constituencies of security holders — common stockholders, preferred stockholders and debtholders.

E.   LIABILITIES AND DISCLOSURE OBLIGATIONS UNDER SECURITIES LAWS

There is always a tension between the obligation of a public corporation to disclose information to the public in certain situations and the practical difficulty of trying to conduct business in a fishbowl. The securities laws recognize that, in many circumstances, a corporation may lawfully choose to keep information confidential, particularly where premature disclosure would be harmful to the corporation and its stockholders.

This tension is particularly acute for a financially troubled corporation. For example, although an announcement that the corporation is having preliminary discussions with its bank group regarding the restructuring of its senior debt may be desirable from a full disclosure point of view, it may also cause suppliers to withhold normal trade credit and customers to delay ordinary course payments, all exacerbating a downward spiral for the corporation. Even if such an announcement is deemed to be unnecessary, the troublesome issue of selective disclosure remains. This problem typically arises when a corporation conducts discussions with one or more of its creditors in an attempt to determine the feasibility of a restructuring before turning to its other creditors and security holders generally. Rumors and leaks about the corporation's financial position may creep into the market following such meetings, possibly forcing the corporation to issue a press release disclosing its troubled financial situation to the world.

F.   THE BANKRUPTCY ALTERNATIVE

Bankruptcy is often the only alternative (other than a Section 3(a)(10) Settlement Exchange) for a financially troubled corporation that is not able to restructure successfully out of court. As such, it may provide the strongest incentive for security holders to participate in an out-of-court restructuring, such as a Section 3(a)(9) Exchange, or at least to reach an agreement on a Prepackaged Bankruptcy.

While a reorganization under chapter 11 of the Bankruptcy Code offers its own unique advantages, it also presents significant disadvantages to the ongoing operations of a financially troubled corporation and to its security holders. The financially troubled corporation must balance the advantages and disadvantages of a chapter 11 reorganization against other restructuring alternatives in selecting the best course of action.

PROBLEM SET 26.1

1. Review section 3(a)(9) and section 4(2) in your statutory supplement and be prepared to discuss in class. What are the practical limitations of using these sections to reduce a firm's fixed costs?
2. How might you address the issue discussed in the Lubben-Narayanan article? Have the authors identified a real problem?

2. EXIT CONSENTS

As you will recall from Chapter 14, the Trust Indenture Act prohibits changes to certain fundamental provisions of an indenture without unanimous bondholder consent.[2] But a majority of the bondholders—unless the indenture provides otherwise—can consent to changes in other terms of the indenture. This grant of "exit consents"—given right before the holder exits into a new security under an exchange offer—is both controversial and useful, at least from the firm's perspective.

MOISE KATZ v. OAK INDUSTRIES INC.

508 A.2d 873

Court of Chancery of Delaware, New Castle County

Submitted: March 7, 1986 | Decided: March 10, 1986

ALLEN, Chancellor.

A commonly used word—seemingly specific and concrete when used in everyday speech—may mask troubling ambiguities that upon close examination are seen to derive not simply from casual use but from more fundamental epistemological problems. Few words more perfectly illustrate the deceptive dependability of language than the term "coercion" which is at the heart of the theory advanced by plaintiff as entitling him to a preliminary injunction in this case.

Plaintiff is the owner of long-term debt securities issued by Oak Industries, Inc. ("Oak"), a Delaware corporation; in this class action he seeks to enjoin the consummation of an exchange offer and consent solicitation made by Oak to holders of various classes of its long-term debt. As detailed below that offer is an integral part of a series of transactions that together would effect a major reorganization and recapitalization of Oak. The claim asserted is in essence, that the

---

2. 15 U.S.C. §§77aaa, 77ddd(a); *see also* George W. Shuster, Jr., *The Trust Indenture Act and International Debt Restructurings*, 14 Am. Bankr. Inst. L. Rev. 431, 437 (2006).

exchange offer is a coercive device and, in the circumstances, constitutes a breach of contract. This is the Court's opinion on plaintiff's pending application for a preliminary injunction.

I.

The background facts are involved even when set forth in the abbreviated form the decision within the time period currently available requires.

Through its domestic and foreign subsidiaries and affiliated entities, Oak manufactures and markets component equipments used in consumer, industrial and military products (the "Components Segment"); produces communications equipment for use in cable television systems and satellite television systems (the "Communications Segment") and manufactures and markets laminates and other materials used in printed circuit board applications (the "Materials Segment"). During 1985, the Company has terminated certain other unrelated businesses. As detailed below, it has now entered into an agreement with Allied-Signal, Inc. for the sale of the Materials Segment of its business and is currently seeking a buyer for its Communications Segment.

Even a casual review of Oak's financial results over the last several years shows it unmistakably to be a company in deep trouble. During the period from January 1, 1982 through September 30, 1985, the Company has experienced unremitting losses from operations; on net sales of approximately $1.26 billion during that period it has lost over $335 million. As a result its total stockholders' equity has first shriveled (from $260 million on 12/31/81 to $85 million on 12/31/83) and then disappeared completely (as of 9/30/85 there was a $62 million deficit in its stockholders' equity accounts). Financial markets, of course, reflected this gloomy history.[3]

Unless Oak can be made profitable within some reasonably short time it will not continue as an operating company. Oak's board of directors, comprised almost entirely of outside directors, has authorized steps to buy the company time. In February, 1985, in order to reduce a burdensome annual cash interest obligation on its $230 million of then outstanding debentures, the Company offered to exchange such debentures for a combination of notes, common stock and warrants. As a result, approximately $180 million principal amount of the then outstanding debentures were exchanged. Since interest on certain of the notes issued in that exchange offer is payable in common stock, the effect of the 1985 exchange offer was to reduce to some extent the cash drain on the Company caused by its significant debt.

About the same time that the 1985 exchange offer was made, the Company announced its intention to discontinue certain of its operations and sell certain of its properties. Taking these steps, while effective to stave off a default and to reduce to some extent the immediate cash drain, did not address Oak's longer-range problems. Therefore, also during 1985 representatives of the Company

3. The price of the company's common stock has fallen from over $30 per share on December 31, 1981 to approximately $2 per share recently. (p. 38). The debt securities that are the subject of the exchange offer here involved . . . have traded at substantial discounts.

held informal discussions with several interested parties exploring the possibility of an investment from, combination with or acquisition by another company. As a result of these discussions, the Company and Allied-Signal, Inc. entered into two agreements. The first, the Acquisition Agreement, contemplates the sale to Allied-Signal of the Materials Segment for $160 million in cash. The second agreement, the Stock Purchase Agreement, provides for the purchase by Allied-Signal for $15 million cash of 10 million shares of the Company's common stock together with warrants to purchase additional common stock.

The Stock Purchase Agreement provides as a condition to Allied-Signal's obligation that at least 85% of the aggregate principal amount of all of the Company's debt securities shall have tendered and accepted the exchange offers that are the subject of this lawsuit. Oak has six classes of such long term debt.[4] If less than 85% of the aggregate principal amount of such debt accepts the offer, Allied-Signal has an option, but no obligation, to purchase the common stock and warrants contemplated by the Stock Purchase Agreement. An additional condition for the closing of the Stock Purchase Agreement is that the sale of the Company's Materials Segment contemplated by the Acquisition Agreement shall have been concluded.

Thus, as part of the restructuring and recapitalization contemplated by the Acquisition Agreement and the Stock Purchase Agreement, the Company has extended an exchange offer to each of the holders of the six classes of its long-term debt securities. These pending exchange offers include a Common Stock Exchange Offer (available only to holders of the $9^5/8\%$ convertible notes) and the Payment Certificate Exchange Offers (available to holders of all six classes of Oak's long-term debt securities). The Common Stock Exchange Offer currently provides for the payment to each tendering noteholder of 407 shares of the Company's common stock in exchange for each $1,000 $9^5/8\%$ note accepted. The offer is limited to $38.6 million principal amount of notes (out of approximately $83.9 million outstanding).

The Payment Certificate Exchange Offer is an any and all offer. Under its terms, a payment certificate, payable in cash five days after the closing of the sale of the Materials Segment to Allied-Signal, is offered in exchange for debt securities. The cash value of the Payment Certificate will vary depending upon the particular security tendered. In each instance, however, that payment will be less than the face amount of the obligation. The cash payments range in amount, per $1,000 of principal, from $918 to $655. These cash values however appear to represent a premium over the market prices for the Company's debentures as of the time the terms of the transaction were set.

The Payment Certificate Exchange Offer is subject to certain important conditions before Oak has an obligation to accept tenders under it. First, it is necessary that a minimum amount ($38.6 million principal amount out of $83.9 total outstanding principal amount) of the $9^5/8\%$ notes be tendered

4. The three classes of debentures are: 13.65% debentures due April 1, 2001, $10^1/2\%$ convertible subordinated debentures due February 1, 2002, and $11^7/8\%$ subordinated debentures due May 15, 1998. In addition, as a result of the 1985 exchange offer the company has three classes of notes which were issued in exchange for debentures that were tendered in that offer. Those are: 13.5% senior notes due May 15, 1990, $9^5/8\%$ convertible notes due September 15, 1991 and $11^5/8\%$ notes due September 15, 1990.

pursuant to the Common Stock Exchange Offer. Secondly, it is necessary that certain minimum amounts of each class of debt securities be tendered, together with consents to amendments to the underlying indentures.[5] Indeed, under the offer one may not tender securities unless at the same time one consents to the proposed amendments to the relevant indentures.

The condition of the offer that tendering security holders must consent to amendments in the indentures governing the securities gives rise to plaintiff's claim of breach of contract in this case. Those amendments would, if implemented, have the effect of removing significant negotiated protections to holders of the Company's long-term debt including the deletion of all financial covenants. Such modification may have adverse consequences to debt holders who elect not to tender pursuant to either exchange offer.

Allied-Signal apparently was unwilling to commit to the $15 million cash infusion contemplated by the Stock Purchase Agreement, unless Oak's long-term debt is reduced by 85% (at least that is a condition of their obligation to close on that contract). Mathematically, such a reduction may not occur without the Company reducing the principal amount of outstanding debentures (that is the three classes outstanding notes constitute less than 85% of all long-term debt). But existing indenture covenants (See Offering Circular, pp. 38–39) prohibit the Company, so long as any of its long-term notes are outstanding, from issuing any obligation (including the Payment Certificates) in exchange for any of the debentures. Thus, in this respect, amendment to the indentures is required in order to close the Stock Purchase Agreement as presently structured.

Restrictive covenants in the indentures would appear to interfere with effectuation of the recapitalization in another way. Section 4.07 of the 13.50% Indenture provides that the Company may not "acquire" for value any of the $9^5/8$% Notes or $11^5/8$% Notes unless it concurrently "redeems" a proportionate amount of the 13.50% Notes. This covenant, if unamended, would prohibit the disproportionate acquisition of the $9^5/8$% Notes that may well occur as a result of the Exchange Offers; in addition, it would appear to require the payment of the "redemption" price for the 13.50% Notes rather than the lower, market price offered in the exchange offer.

In sum, the failure to obtain the requisite consents to the proposed amendments would permit Allied-Signal to decline to consummate both the Acquisition Agreement and the Stock Purchase Agreement.

As to timing of the proposed transactions, the Exchange Offer requires the Company (subject to the conditions stated therein) to accept any and all tenders received by 5:00 p.m. March 11, 1986. A meeting of stockholders of the Company has been called for March 14, 1986 at which time the Company's stockholders will be asked to approve the Acquisition Agreement and the Stock Purchase Agreement as well as certain deferred compensation arrangements for key employees. Closing of the Acquisition Agreement may occur on

5. The holders of more than 50% of the principal amount of each of the 13.5% notes, the $9^5/8$% notes and the $11^5/8$% notes and at least $66^2/3$% of the principal amount of the 13.65% debentures, $10^1/2$% debentures, and $11^7/8$% debentures, must validly tender such securities and consent to certain proposed amendments to the indentures governing those securities.

March 14, 1986, or as late as June 20, 1986 under the terms of that Agreement. Closing of the Stock Purchase Agreement must await the closing of the Acquisition Agreement and the successful completion of the Exchange Offers.

The Exchange Offers are dated February 14, 1986. This suit seeking to enjoin consummation of those offers was filed on February 27. Argument on the current application was held on March 7.

II.

Plaintiff's claim that the Exchange Offers and Consent Solicitation constitutes a threatened wrong to him and other holders of Oak's debt securities[6] appear to be summarized in paragraph 16 of his Complaint:

> The purpose and effect of the Exchange Offers is [1] to benefit Oak's common stockholders at the expense of the Holders of its debt securities, [2] to force the exchange of its debt instruments at unfair price and at less than face value of the debt instruments [3] pursuant to a rigged vote in which debt Holders who exchange, and who therefore have no interest in the vote, *must* consent to the elimination of protective covenants for debt Holders who do not wish to exchange.

As amplified in briefing on the pending motion, plaintiff's claim is that no free choice is provided to bondholders by the exchange offer and consent solicitation. Under its terms, a rational bondholder is "forced" to tender and consent. Failure to do so would face a bondholder with the risk of owning a security stripped of all financial covenant protections and for which it is likely that there would be no ready market. A reasonable bondholder, it is suggested, cannot possibly accept those risks and thus such a bondholder is coerced to tender and thus to consent to the proposed indenture amendments.

It is urged this linking of the offer and the consent solicitation constitutes a breach of a contractual obligation that Oak owes to its bondholders to act in good faith. Specifically, plaintiff points to three contractual provisions from which it can be seen that the structuring of the current offer constitutes a breach of good faith. Those provisions (1) establish a requirement that no modification in the term of the various indentures may be effectuated without the consent of a stated percentage of bondholders; (2) restrict Oak from exercising the power to grant such consent with respect to any securities it may hold in its treasury; and (3) establish the price at which and manner in which Oak may force bondholders to submit their securities for redemption.

---

6. It is worthy of note that a very high percentage of the principal value of Oak's debt securities are owned in substantial amounts by a handful of large financial institutions. Almost 85% of the value of the 13.50% Notes is owned by four such institutions (one investment banker owns 55% of that issue); 69.1% of the 9 5/8% Notes are owned by four financial institutions (the same investment banker owning 25% of that issue) and 85% of the 11 5/8% Notes are owned by five such institutions. Of the debentures, 89% of the 13.65% debentures are owned by four large banks; and approximately 45% of the two remaining issues is owned by two banks.

III.

In order to demonstrate an entitlement to the provisional remedy of a preliminary injunction it is essential that a plaintiff show that it is probable that his claim will be upheld after final hearing; that he faces a risk of irreparable injury before final judgment will be reached in the regular course; and that in balancing the equities and competing hardships that preliminary judicial action may cause or prevent, the balance favors plaintiff.

I turn first to an evaluation of the probability of plaintiff's ultimate success on the merits of his claim. I begin that analysis with two preliminary points. The first concerns what is not involved in this case. To focus briefly on this clears away much of the corporation law case law of this jurisdiction upon which plaintiff in part relies. This case does not involve the measurement of corporate or directorial conduct against that high standard of fidelity required of fiduciaries when they act with respect to the interests of the beneficiaries of their trust. Under our law — and the law generally — the relationship between a corporation and the holders of its debt securities, even convertible debt securities, is contractual in nature. Arrangements among a corporation, the underwriters of its debt, trustees under its indentures and sometimes ultimate investors are typically thoroughly negotiated and massively documented. The rights and obligations of the various parties are or should be spelled out in that documentation. The terms of the contractual relationship agreed to and not broad concepts such as fairness define the corporation's obligation to its bondholders.

Thus, the first aspect of the pending Exchange Offers about which plaintiff complains — that "the purpose and effect of the Exchange Offers is to benefit Oak's common stockholders at the expense of the Holders of its debt" — does not itself appear to allege a cognizable legal wrong. It is the obligation of directors to attempt, within the law, to maximize the long-run interests of the corporation's stockholders; that they may sometimes do so "at the expense" of others (even assuming that a transaction which one may refuse to enter into can meaningfully be said to be at his expense) does not for that reason constitute a breach of duty. It seems likely that corporate restructurings designed to maximize shareholder values may in some instances have the effect of requiring bondholders to bear greater risk of loss and thus in effect transfer economic value from bondholders to stockholders. But if courts are to provide protection against such enhanced risk, they will require either legislative direction to do so or the negotiation of indenture provisions designed to afford such protection.

The second preliminary point concerns the limited analytical utility, at least in this context, of the word "coercive" which is central to plaintiff's own articulation of his theory of recovery. If, *pro arguendo*, we are to extend the meaning of the word coercion beyond its core meaning — dealing with the utilization of physical force to overcome the will of another — to reach instances in which the claimed coercion arises from an act designed to affect the will of another party by offering inducements to the act sought to be encouraged or by arranging unpleasant consequences for an alternative sought to be discouraged, then — in order to make the term legally meaningful at all — we must acknowledge that some further refinement is essential. Clearly some "coercion" of this kind is legally unproblematic. Parents may "coerce" a child to study with the threat of withholding an allowance; employers may "coerce" regular attendance at work by either docking wages for time absent or by rewarding with a bonus such regular attendance. Other "coercion" so defined clearly would be legally relevant (to encourage regular attendance by corporal punishment, for example). Thus, for purposes of legal analysis, the term "coercion" itself — covering a multitude of situations — is not very meaningful. For the word to have much meaning for purposes of legal analysis, it is necessary in each case that a normative judgment be attached to the concept ("inappropriately coercive" or "wrongfully coercive," etc.). But, it is then readily seen that what is legally relevant is not the conclusory term "coercion" itself but rather the norm that leads to the adverb modifying it.

In this instance, assuming that the Exchange Offers and Consent Solicitation can meaningfully be regarded as "coercive" (in the sense that Oak has structured it in a way designed — and I assume effectively so — to "force" rational bondholders to tender), the relevant legal norm that will support the judgment whether such "coercion" is wrongful or not will, for the reasons mentioned above, be derived from the law of contracts. I turn then to that subject to determine the appropriate legal test or rule.

Modern contract law has generally recognized an implied covenant to the effect that each party to a contract will act with good faith towards the other with respect to the subject matter of the contract. The contractual theory for this implied obligation is well stated in a leading treatise:

> If the purpose of contract law is to enforce the reasonable expectations of parties induced by promises, then at some point it becomes necessary for courts to look to the substance rather than to the form of the agreement, and to hold that substance controls over form. What courts are doing here, whether calling the process "implication" of promises, or interpreting the requirements of "good faith," as the current fashion may be, is but a recognition that the parties occasionally have understandings or expectations that were so fundamental that they did not need to negotiate about those expectations. When the court "implies a promise" or holds that "good faith" requires a party not to violate those expectations, it is recognizing that sometimes silence says more than words, and it is understanding its duty to the spirit of the bargain is higher than its duty to the technicalities of the language. *Corbin on Contracts* (Kaufman Supp.1984), §570.

It is this obligation to act in good faith and to deal fairly that plaintiff claims is breached by the structure of Oak's coercive exchange offer. Because it is an implied *contractual* obligation that is asserted as the basis for the relief sought, the appropriate legal test is not difficult to deduce. It is this: is it clear from what was expressly agreed upon that the parties who negotiated the express terms of the contract would have agreed to proscribe the act later complained of as a breach of the implied covenant of good faith — had they thought to negotiate with respect to that matter. If the answer to this question is yes, then, in my opinion, a court is justified in concluding that such act constitutes a breach of the implied covenant of good faith.

With this test in mind, I turn now to a review of the specific provisions of the various indentures from which one may be best able to infer whether it is apparent that the contracting parties — had they negotiated with the exchange offer and consent solicitation in mind — would have expressly agreed to prohibit contractually the linking of the giving of consent with the purchase and sale of the security.

IV.

Applying the foregoing standard to the exchange offer and consent solicitation, I find first that there is nothing in the indenture provisions granting bondholders power to veto proposed modifications in the relevant indenture that implies that Oak may not offer an inducement to bondholders to consent to such amendments. Such an implication, at least where, as here, the inducement is offered on the same terms to each holder of an affected security, would be wholly inconsistent with the strictly commercial nature of the relationship.

Nor does the second pertinent contractual provision supply a ground to conclude that defendant's conduct violates the reasonable expectations of those who negotiated the indentures on behalf of the bondholders. Under that provision Oak may not vote debt securities held in its treasury. Plaintiff urges that Oak's conditioning of its offer to purchase debt on the giving of consents has the effect of subverting the purpose of that provision; it permits Oak to "dictate" the vote on securities which it could not itself vote.

The evident purpose of the restriction on the voting of treasury securities is to afford protection against the issuer voting as a bondholder in favor of modifications that would benefit it as issuer, even though such changes would be detrimental to bondholders. But the linking of the exchange offer and the consent solicitation does not involve the risk that bondholder interests will be affected by a vote involving anyone with a financial interest in the subject of the vote other than a bondholder's interest. That the consent is to be given concurrently with the transfer of the bond to the issuer does not in any sense create the kind of conflict of interest that the indenture's prohibition on voting treasury securities contemplates. Not only will the proposed consents be granted or withheld only by those with a financial interest to maximize the return on their investment in Oak's bonds, but the incentive to consent is equally available to all members of each class of bondholders. Thus the "vote" implied by the consent solicitation is not affected in any sense by those with a financial conflict of interest.

In these circumstances, while it is clear that Oak has fashioned the exchange offer and consent solicitation in a way designed to encourage consents, I cannot conclude that the offer violates the intendment of any of the express contractual provisions considered or, applying the test set out above, that its structure and timing breaches an implied obligation of good faith and fair dealing.

One further set of contractual provisions should be touched upon: Those granting to Oak a power to redeem the securities here treated at a price set by the relevant indentures. Plaintiff asserts that the attempt to force all bondholders to tender their securities at less than the redemption price constitutes, if not a breach of the redemption provision itself, at least a breach of an implied covenant of good faith and fair dealing associated with it. The flaw, or at least one fatal flaw, in this argument is that the present offer is not the functional equivalent of a redemption which is, of course, an act that the issuer may take unilaterally. In this instance it may happen that Oak will get tenders of a large percentage of its outstanding long-term debt securities. If it does, that fact will, in my judgment, be in major part a function of the merits of the offer (i.e., the price offered in light of the Company's financial position and the market value of its debt). To answer plaintiff's contention that the *structure* of the offer "forces" debt holders to tender, one only has to imagine what response this offer would receive if the price offered did not reflect a premium over market but rather was, for example, ten percent of market value. The exchange offer's success ultimately depends upon the ability and willingness of the issuer to extend an offer that will be a financially attractive alternative to holders. This process is hardly the functional equivalent of the unilateral election of redemption and thus cannot be said in any sense to constitute a subversion by Oak of the negotiated provisions dealing with redemption of its debt.

Accordingly, I conclude that plaintiff has failed to demonstrate a probability of ultimate success on the theory of liability asserted.

V.

An independent ground for the decision to deny the pending motion is supplied by the requirement that a court of equity will not issue the extraordinary remedy of preliminary injunction where to do so threatens the party sought to be enjoined with irreparable injury that, in the circumstances, seems greater than the injury that plaintiff seeks to avoid. Eastern Shore Natural Gas Co. v. Stauffer Chemical Co., Del.Supr., 298 A.2d 322 (1972). That principal has application here.

Oak is in a weak state financially. Its board, comprised of persons of experience and, in some instances, distinction, have approved the complex and interrelated transactions outlined above. It is not unreasonable to accord weight to the claims of Oak that the reorganization and recapitalization of which the exchange offer is a part may present the last good chance to regain vitality for this enterprise. I have not discussed plaintiff's claim of irreparable injury, although I have considered it. I am satisfied simply to note my conclusion that it is far outweighed by the harm that an improvidently granted injunction would threaten to Oak.

For the foregoing reasons plaintiff's application for a preliminary injunction shall be denied.

As you will recall, most indentures contain either a New York or English choice of law clause. In contrast to New York law-governed debt, where debt is exchanged in a tender offer, English law-governed bonds and notes typically would be amended by a vote of holders at a meeting of the holders.

ASSÉNAGON ASSET MANAGEMENT S.A. v. IRISH BANK RESOLUTION CORPORATION LIMITED (FORMERLY ANGLO IRISH BANK CORPORATION LIMITED)

Case No: HC11C01320 [2012] EWHC 2090 (Ch)
In the High Court of Justice Chancery Division Royal Courts of Justice Strand,
London, WC2A 2LL
27/07/2012

Mr Justice BRIGGS:

INTRODUCTION

1. This part 8 Claim test, for the first time, the legality under English law of a technique used by the issuers of corporate bonds which has acquired the label "exit consent." The technique may be summarised thus. The issuer wishes to persuade all the holders of a particular bond issue to accept an exchange of their bonds for replacement bonds on different terms. The holders are all invited to offer their bonds for exchange, but on terms that they are required to commit themselves irrevocably to vote at a bondholders' meeting for a resolution amending the terms of the existing bonds so as seriously to damage or, as in the present case substantially destroy, the value of the rights arising from those existing bonds. The resolution is what has become labelled the exit consent.

2. The exit consent has no adverse effect in itself upon a holder who both offers his bonds for exchange and votes for the resolution. That is either because the issuer nonetheless fails to attract the majority needed to pass the resolution (in which case both the resolution and the proposed exchange do not happen) or simply because, if the requisite majority is obtained, his bonds are exchanged for new bonds and cancelled by the issuer. By contrast, a holder who fails to offer his bonds for exchange and either votes against the resolution or abstains takes the risk, if the resolution is passed, that his bonds will be either devalued by the resolution or, as in this case, destroyed by being redeemed for a nominal consideration. This is in part because the efficacy of the technique depends upon the deadline for exchange being set before the bondholders' meeting so that, if the resolution is then passed, the dissenting holder gets no *locus poenitentiae* during which to exchange his bonds on the terms offered, and accepted in time, by the majority.

3. It is readily apparent, and not seriously in dispute, that the purpose of the attachment of the exit consent to the exchange proposal is to impose a dissuasive constraint upon bondholders from opposing the exchange, even if they take the view that the proffered new bonds are (ignoring the exit consent) less attractive than the existing bonds. The constraint arises from the risk facing any individual bondholder that a sufficient majority of his fellow holders will participate in the exchange and

therefore (as required to do) vote for the resolution. The constraint is variously described in textbooks on both sides of the Atlantic as encouraging, inducing, coercing or even forcing the bondholders to accept the exchange.

4. The technique depends for its persuasive effect upon the difficulties faced by bondholders in organising themselves within the time allowed by the issuer in such a way as to find out before the deadline for accepting the exchange whether there is a sufficient number (usually more than 25% by value) determined to prevent the exchange going ahead by voting against the resolution. They were described in argument as facing a variant of the well-known prisoner's dilemma.

5. Exit consents of this type (but falling short of expropriation) have survived judicial scrutiny in the USA, in the face of challenge by minority bondholders. In *Katz v Oak Industries Inc.* (1986) 508 A.2d 873 the attachment of an exit consent designed to devalue the existing bonds in the hands of dissenting holders who declined an associated exchange offer was challenged in the Delaware Chancery Court as amounting to a breach of the contractual obligation of good faith by the issuer, as against the bondholders. It was not suggested that the participation in the process by the majority bondholders (by committing themselves to vote for the proposed amendment devaluing the existing bonds) constituted an abuse by them of their rights under the terms of the bond issue to bind the minority to a variation of those terms. Chancellor Allen concluded that the particular exit consent in that case, (which included the removal of significant negotiated protections to the bondholders, and the deletion of all financial covenants), did not despite its coercive effect amount to a breach of the contractual obligation of good faith between issuer and bondholders in what he evidently regarded as an ordinary commercial arms-length contract.

6. By contrast, the challenge made in the present case to the exit consent technique is mainly based upon an alleged abuse by the majority bondholders of their power to bind the minority, albeit at the invitation of the issuer. The challenge is based upon the well recognised constraint upon the exercise of that power by a majority, namely that it must be exercised *bona fide* in the best interests of the class of bondholders as a whole, and not in a manner which is oppressive or otherwise unfair to the minority sought to be bound. Such limited published professional comment as there is upon the use of this technique within an English law context appears to assume that, provided the exchange offer and associated exit consent proposal is made and fairly disclosed to all relevant bondholders, no question of oppression or unfairness can arise. I was told (although it is impossible for the court to know for sure) that this technique has been put into significant, if not yet widespread, use within the context of bonds structured under English law, in particular in connection with the affairs of banks and other lending institutions requiring to be re-structured as a result of the 2008 credit crunch, so that a decision on this point of principle may be of much wider consequence than merely

the amount at issue between the parties to this claim, which relates to subordinated notes in the company then known as Anglo Irish Bank Corporation Limited ("the Bank") acquired by the claimant Assenagon Asset Management S.A. in tranches between September 2009 and April 2010, for an aggregate of just over £17m.

THE FACTS

7. There is no dispute about the primary facts, which consist of the terms of the relevant bonds, the circumstances in which the exchange proposal was launched, succeeded and concluded, so far as affects the claimant, by redemption of its £17m Notes for a payment by the Bank of a mere £170.

8. There is by contrast not a complete unanimity as to background facts. The parties' differences related more to the relevance of parts of the background, and no request was made by either side for cross-examination. As will appear, I have not found it necessary to resolve any disputes as to fact and little of the background was of significant assistance in resolving the issues which I have to decide. These concern construction (including for that purpose implied terms), together with the allegation of infringement of the constraint upon the exercise of the power by a majority to bind a minority to which I have referred.

9. The bond issue to which this dispute relates consists of the Bank's subordinated floating rate notes due 2017 ("the 2017 Notes") issued by the Bank on 15 June 2007 pursuant to the terms of a trust deed dated 15 August 2001 between the Bank and Deutsche Bank Trustee Co. Limited ("the Trustee") as subsequently amended and supplemented by six supplemental trust deeds. I shall refer to the re-stated form of the trust deed applicable to the 2017 Notes as "the Trust Deed." Terms particular to the 2017 Notes are also contained in written Final Terms dated 15 June 2007 ("the Final Terms"). The commercial terms of the 2017 Notes may be summarised as follows:

> i) They were to mature in 2017, for redemption at par, unless redeemed earlier at the Bank's election (also at par) on any interest payment date after 19 June 2012.
> ii) In the meantime they carried a floating rate of interest at 0.25% above three months Euribor until 2012 and 0.75% above three months Euribor thereafter.
> iii) The Notes were subordinated, so as to be prioritised for payment in an insolvency after all secured and unsecured creditors (including the Bank's depositors) and ahead only of equity shareholders. They were wholly unsecured.

10. The 2017 Notes were issued as part of the Bank's Euro Medium Term Note Programme. The Bank issued, in addition, subordinated notes due

2014 and 2016 ("the 2014 and 2016 Notes"). The nominal amount of the 2017 Notes was £750m. I am invited to assume that, for the most part, holders of the 2017 Notes were, at the time of the exchange offer, sophisticated professional investors.

11.   It is necessary to focus in some detail upon the provisions in the Trust Deed providing what counsel called "note-holder democracy," namely the calling of note-holders' meetings, the extent of the powers of the majority to bind the minority, the requisite quorum and voting majorities, together with a particular voting disability prayed in aid by the claimant.

12.   The 2017 Notes were issued in the form of a single global note to a depository, such that investors recorded as holding proportions of the aggregate nominal amount in the books of the depository were to be treated for all purposes under the Trust Deed as note-holders: see the definition of Noteholders (Trust Deed page 5), clause 8 of the Trust Deed and paragraph 1 of Schedule 1 thereto (incorporating terms and conditions of the Notes pursuant to the definition of Conditions on page 2 of the Trust Deed).

13.   Clause 38 of the Trust Deed provided for it to be governed by English law, subject to certain irrelevant exceptions, and clause 39 contained a sufficient submission to the jurisdiction of the English courts for the purposes of these proceedings.

14.   Paragraph 14 (i) of the First Schedule to the Trust Deed contained provisions as to the quorum for Noteholders' meetings. It is unnecessary to set it out, because it is replicated, with added detail, in paragraph 5 of Schedule 3, headed Provisions for Meetings of Noteholders, incorporated by clause 9 of the Trust Deed. Paragraph 2 of Schedule 3 permits the Issuer (the Bank) or the Trustee at any time to call a Noteholders' meeting, and required the Issuer to do so upon a requisition signed by the holders of not less than one-tenth in nominal amount of the Notes.

15.   Paragraph 5 of Schedule 3 set out three successively stringent quorum requirements. In relation to an ordinary resolution it was one-twentieth of the nominal amount of the Notes. For an Extraordinary Resolution (defined below) it was a clear majority in nominal amount of the Notes. Finally, for seven specified types of Extraordinary Resolution the quorum was two-thirds of the nominal amount of the Notes. Paragraph 5(b) identified "reduction or cancellation of the principal payable on the Notes or the exchange or conversion thereof or the minimum rate of interest payable thereon" as one of the seven types of Extraordinary Resolution calling for a two-thirds quorum.

16.   Paragraph 13 of Schedule 3 contained provision as to who might attend or speak at Noteholders' meetings, but continued:

> "Neither the Issuer nor any Subsidiary shall be entitled to vote at any meeting in respect of Notes beneficially held by it or for its account."

17. Paragraph 18 of Schedule 3 set out in detail the powers capable of being exercised by a majority of Noteholders by Extraordinary Resolution. They included:

> "(a) Power to sanction any compromise or arrangement proposed to be made between the Issuer and the Noteholders. . . .
> (b) Power to sanction any abrogation, modification, compromise or arrangement in respect of the rights of the Noteholders . . . against the Issuer or against any of its property whether such rights shall arise under these presents or otherwise.
> (c) Power to assent to any modification of the provisions contained in these presents which shall be proposed by the Issuer or the Trustee."

18. Paragraph 20 provided that an Extraordinary Resolution required a three-fourths majority of persons voting. Paragraph 19 provided that a resolution duly passed at a Noteholders' meeting would be binding upon all Noteholders whether present or absent, voting or abstaining.

19. By September 2008 the Bank had become the third largest bank in the Irish domestic market with £101 billion of gross assets on its balance-sheet, representing about 50% of Irish GDP. It had a particular focus on commercial property lending, and as a result of the 2008 financial crisis, with a linked rapid decline in commercial property values, the Bank faced a liquidity crisis which, unless it was rescued by the Irish Government, would have forced it into insolvent liquidation. Nonetheless, being regarded as of systemic importance to the maintenance of the stability of the Irish financial system, it was indeed rescued by the Irish government by a series of steps, which I shall briefly summarise. The first consisted of a guarantee by the Irish government of certain liabilities of Irish financial institutions, including the 2017 Notes, for the period from 30 September 2008 to 29 September 2010 pursuant to the Credit Institutions (Financial Support) Scheme 2008. The Scheme prohibited any call on that guarantee after 29 September 2010.

20. Secondly, in December 2009 the Irish government guaranteed certain eligible liabilities of participating institutions, including the Bank, pursuant to the Credit Institutions (Eligible Liabilities Guarantee) Scheme 2009. Those liabilities did not include the 2017 Notes, because they were subordinated.

21. On 21 January 2009 the Bank was nationalised, because of its systemic importance to the maintenance of the stability of the Irish financial system, pursuant to the Anglo Irish Bank Corporation Act 2009.

22. On 7 April 2009 the Minister for Finance announced the creation of the National Asset Management Agency ("NAMA") formed to purchase certain distressed loans from banks carrying on in business in Ireland. This had no direct effect upon the 2017 Notes.

23. On 29 May 2009, in view of the continued deterioration in the Bank's financial position following nationalisation, the Irish government announced its intention to make urgent provision of up to £4 billion of capital to the Bank through the purchase of new ordinary shares. This

support (but not the earlier nationalisation) required approval from the European Commission which was granted on 26 June 2009. The Commission required to be satisfied that financial support by a member state to a domestic bank was provided on terms that minimised the amount of state aid to that necessary to protect the wider financial system in Ireland and, to that end, the Bank proposed to increase its Core Tier 1 capital by engaging in a "Liability Management Exercise" under which it intended to buy back subordinated loans, at a premium above the prevailing market rates no higher than "necessary only to ensure a participation rate sufficient to make the Liability Management Exercise worthwhile."

24. By December 2009 the Bank had incurred an aggregate loss of some £12.7 billion. In March, May and August 2010 the Irish government increased its support to the Bank by amounts of £8.3 billion, £2 billion and £8.58 billion respectively.

25. On 8 September 2010, just before the expiry of the October 2008 guarantee, the Minister of Finance made an announcement about the proposed re-structuring of the Bank, which contemplated its being split into a depositors' bank and an asset management entity. In the event this did not proceed. By 30 September, the day after expiry of the October 2008 guarantee, the Irish government had provided a total of £22.88 billion of capital to the Bank by way of share subscription and promissory notes, and NAMA had purchased £6.5 billion worth of distressed loans.

26. It was during the staged rescue of the Bank which I have summarised, and the currency of the October 2008 guarantee of (inter alia) the 2017 Notes, that the claimant acquired its holding of 2017 Notes in the market, at prices ranging between 0.418 and 0.420 per nominal Euro, between 23 September 2009 and 1 April 2010. The substantial discount at which the Notes were trading in the market no doubt reflected a perception that the 2008 guarantee was unlikely to be extended indefinitely, and that holders of subordinated debt could not expect to be treated with the same sympathy as the Bank's retail customers. The claimant acquired its holding as manager of two Luxembourg funds. It may safely be inferred that it did so on behalf of sophisticated investors.

27. On 30 September 2010 (immediately after the expiry of the 2008 guarantee) the Minister of Finance made a statement on the banking system in Ireland which, while stating an intention to respect all senior debt obligations in the Bank, continued:

"The principle of appropriate burden sharing by holders of subordinated debt, however, is one with which I agree. As can be seen from the figures outlined above, the losses in the bank are substantial and it is right that the holders of Anglo's subordinated debt should share the costs which have arisen.

In keeping with this approach, my Department in conjunction with the Attorney General is working on resolution and re-organisation legislation, which will enable the implementation re-organisation measures specific to

Anglo Irish Bank and Irish Nationwide Building Society which will address
the issue of burden-sharing by subordinated bondholders. The legislation
will be consistent with the requirements for the measures to be recognised
as a re-organisation under the relevant EU Directive in other EU Member
States.
I expect the subordinated debt holders to make a significant contribution
towards meeting the costs of Anglo.''

28.   This announcement contemplated a two stage approach. The first was to
pursue a voluntary re-structuring of subordinated debt, if possible, by
agreement with Noteholders (or a qualifying majority of them). The
second was to complete the process, if necessary, by legislation, capable
of being enforced in relation to an English law regulated note issue in
the English courts, pursuant to the EU Directive referred to in the
announcement. The exchange proposal to the 2017 Notes was part of
the first of those two stages.

THE 2010 EXCHANGE OFFER

29.   On 21 October 2010 the Bank announced exchange offers in respect of
certain series of its Notes, including the 2017 Notes (as well as the 2014
and 2016 Notes). The Bank issued three documents, the first two of
which substantially overlap in terms of content:

i) The Announcement
ii) The Exchange Offer Memorandum
iii) A Notice of a Noteholders' meeting in respect of the 2017 Notes

30.   The Announcement and the Memorandum both began (more or less
identically) by proposing to Noteholders an exchange of (inter alia) the
2017 Notes for new Notes ("the New Notes") in the exchange ratio 0.20
i.e. an offer of a holding of 20 cents New Notes for every one Euro of
2017 Notes. The New Notes were not to be subordinated. They were to
carry a coupon of three month Euribor plus 3.75 per cent, to be
guaranteed by the Irish government and to mature in December
2011. The Announcement continued as follows:

"In connection with the Exchange Offers, the Bank is also convening
(at the times specified in the . . . Memorandum) separate meetings inviting
the Holders of each Series of Existing Notes (*a definition which included the
2017 Notes*) to approve, by separate Extraordinary Resolution in respect of
each Series, proposed amendments to the terms and conditions of each
Series including giving the Bank the right to redeem all, but not some only,
of the Existing Notes of each Series at an amount equal to £0.01 per £1000
in principal amount of Existing Notes at any time after the relevant Settlement Date . . .
The Bank will announce its decision whether to accept valid offers of Existing Notes for exchange pursuant to each Exchange Offer together with the

final aggregate principal amount of the Existing Notes of each Series accepted for exchange and the aggregate principal amount of the New Notes to be issued as soon as reasonably practical after the Expiration Deadline applicable to the relevant Series. Each Exchange Offer begins on 21 October 2010 and will expire at (i) 4.00 p.m. London time on 19 November 2010 in respect of the 2017 Notes . . . unless extended, re-opened or terminated as provided in the . . . Memorandum. The expected Settlement Date for the Exchange Offers is (i) 24 November 2010 in respect of the 2017 Notes Exchange Offer . . ."

Under the heading Accrued Interest the Bank undertook to pay interest due on the Existing Notes up and until the Settlement Date.

31. At pages 4-6 of the Announcement the Bank provided an intended timetable for the Exchange Offer Process in relation to each Series. The timetable for 2017 Notes was as follows:

"Commencement of Exchange Offers,
Notice of Meeting   21 October 2010
2017 Notes Expiration Deadline   4 pm 19 November 2010
2017 Notes Results Announcement
(namely whether the Bank intended to accept
the offers, and the amount of 2017 Notes
accepted for Exchange)   22 November 2010
2017 Notes Meeting   10am 23 November 2010
Announcement Results of 2017 Notes Meeting   23 November 2010
2017 Notes Settlement Date   24 November 2010"

That timetable was followed by a warning that it was subject to the right of the Bank to extend, re-open, amend and/or terminate each Exchange Offer.

32. The Memorandum had annexed to it the notice of Meeting for the 2017 Notes, describing the terms of the Extraordinary Resolution. It is unnecessary to describe it in detail. It provided for the insertion into the Final Terms of a right for the Bank to redeem the 2017 Notes on any date after the Settlement Date (i.e. 24 November 2010, unless amended) upon payment at a rate of £0.01 per £1000. By contrast with the exchange ratio of 0.20 in the Exchange Offer this amounted to a payment ratio of 0.00001.

33. In addition to replicating most of the provisions of the Announcement, the Memorandum contained the following additional provisions, the first paragraph of which (quoted below) is set out in capital letters and heavy type.

"By offering to exchange its Existing Notes, a holder will be deemed to have given instructions for the appointment of the exchange and tabulation agent (or its agent) as its proxy to vote in favour of the relevant Extraordinary Resolution in respect of all Existing Notes of the relevant series offered for exchange by such holder and which are accepted by the Bank at the . . . 2017 Notes Meeting . . .

It will not be possible for Holders of a Series of Existing Notes to validly offer to exchange Existing Notes pursuant to the Exchange Offer without at the same time appointing the Exchange Tabulation Agent (or its agent) as their proxy to vote in favour of the Extraordinary Resolution in respect of the relevant Series as described above. If a Holder does not offer to exchange its Existing Notes, or if its offer to exchange Existing Notes is not accepted by the Bank, such Holder may (subject to meeting certain deadlines for making such arrangements — see '*Risk Factors and other Considerations — Deadlines for making arrangements to vote at Meetings if Exchange Instruction is rejected*') separately arrange to be represented, and vote such Holder's Existing Notes, at the relevant Meetings.''

34. Under the heading Risk Factors and Other Considerations, the Memorandum provided (inter alia) as follows:

"If an Extraordinary Resolution is passed in respect of any Series of Existing Notes and the approved amendments are implemented by the Bank by way of publication (expected to be part of the announcement confirming the results of the relevant Meeting) of amendments to the Final Terms of the relevant Series, the amendments shall be binding on all Holders of Existing Notes of such Series, whether or not those Holders attended or were otherwise represented at the relevant Meeting and/or voted in favour of the relevant Proposal.

(*heavy type*) If the Bank chooses to exercise such call right (which the Bank currently intends to do shortly after the relevant Settlement Date, although the Bank is under no obligation to do so), the redemption amounts payable to a Holder of Existing Notes (being £0.01 per £1000 in principle amount of Existing Notes) will be significantly less than the principal amount of the New Notes such Holder would have received had such Existing Notes been exchanged pursuant to the relevant Exchange Offer.

The Risk Factors statement continued with a reference to the burden sharing legislation then proposed by the Irish government, including the passage from the ministerial statement of 30 September 2010, which I have quoted above.

35. Under the sub-heading "Deadlines for making arrangements to vote at Meetings if Exchange Instruction is rejected" the Memorandum continued:

"If a Holder's offer to exchange Existing Notes is not accepted by the Bank at the relevant Expiration Deadline and such Holder nevertheless wishes to vote at the . . . 2017 Notes Meeting . . . , such Holder must either validly request a voting certificate, or otherwise appoint the Exchange Tabulation and Agent (or its agent) as its proxy to vote in favour of or against the relevant Extraordinary Resolution at the relevant Meeting . . . , such request to be submitted to the Exchange and Tabulation Agent through the Clearing Systems. Holders must request a voting certificate or appoint the Exchange and Tabulation Agent (or its agent) as proxy not later than 48 hours before the relevant Meeting. (*heavy type*) The indicative timetable for the Exchange Offers is such that, if a Holder's offer to exchange Existing Notes is rejected at or after the relevant Expiration Deadline, such

Holder may not have the opportunity — or may have a very limited period of time in which — to make separate voting arrangements in respect of the relevant Meeting, and accordingly may not be able to vote at the relevant Meeting."

When it is borne in mind that the timetable set out both in the Announcement and the Memorandum contemplated that the Bank would announce its decision whether, and how far, to accept Exchange Offers only one day before the 2017 Notes Meeting, that last warning was, if anything, an understatement.

36. The exchange ratio of 0.20 in the Exchange Offer broadly reflected the price at which the 2017 Notes were then trading in the market, although there is some dispute, which I need not resolve, about the then liquidity of that market. No premium over the then market price for the 2017 Notes was added as an incentive, but the combined effect of the exchange offer and the disincentive to rejecting it constituted by the linked resolution to permit the Bank to redeem the 2017 Notes (if not exchanged) for 0.00001 of their face value was sufficient to ensure that 92.03 per cent of the 2017 Noteholders by value offered their notes for exchange and conditionally bound themselves to vote in favour of the Resolution by the stated deadline of 4 pm on 19 November 2010.

37. The Bank notified acceptance of all notes offered for exchange on 22 November and the Resolution was therefore duly passed by at least the same majority at the 2017 Noteholders' meeting held on the following day. Settlement of the exchange of Existing Notes for New Notes duly then occurred in accordance with the advertised timetable and, on 30 November 2010, the Bank exercised its newly acquired right to redeem the remaining 2017 Notes at the nominal price of £0.01 per £1000 face value pursuant to which the claimant received £170 for its £17 million face value of 2017 Notes.

38. The claimant did not attend, or vote by proxy at, the 2017 Noteholders' meeting. It first complained about what had occurred on 30 November. This claim was issued on 15 April 2011.

THE CLAIMANT'S CASE

39. In their skeleton argument and in oral submissions, Mr Richard Snowden QC and Mr Ben Griffiths put the claimant's case for a declaration that the resolution purportedly passed at the 2017 Noteholders' meeting on 24 November 2010 was invalid on three independent but related grounds:

(1) The Resolution constituted, in substance, the conferral of a power on the Bank to expropriate the 2017 Notes for no more than a nominal consideration. It was therefore ultra vires the power of the majority under paragraph 18 of Schedule 3 to the Trust Deed.

(2) At the time of the Noteholders' meeting on 23 November, all those noteholders whose votes were counted in support of the Resolution held their Notes beneficially, or for the account of, the Bank. Accordingly, all those votes are to be disregarded pursuant to paragraph 13 of Schedule 3 to the Trust Deed.

(3) Even if ultra vires, the Resolution constituted an abuse of the power of the voting majority because:

> (i) It conferred no conceivable benefit or advantage upon the 2017 Noteholders as a class; and,
>
> (ii) It affected, and could by then only have affected, the Notes of that minority which had not coupled an offer of their Notes for exchange with a commitment to vote in favour of the resolution. Accordingly it was both oppressive and unfair as against that minority.

48.   [E]ven in provisions conferring wide powers, the parties may include bespoke restrictions designed to avoid its exercise otherwise than for the benefit of the relevant class. It is common ground in the present case that the disenfranchisement of Notes beneficially held by or for the account of the Issuer or any Subsidiary was designed with that objective in mind, because of the likelihood that any such Notes would be voted so as to serve the interests of the Bank rather than the Noteholders.

49.   [And] a statute may also intervene. There is in England and Wales the statutory remedy for unfairly prejudicial conduct now to be found in Part 30 of the Companies Act 2006. In the USA, the US Trust Indenture Act of 1939 provides at s.316 (b) a general prohibition against the modification of payment terms without the unanimous consent of all the holders of securities issued and registered with the SEC under the US Securities Act of 1933. There are however no statutory safeguards against abuse of power by a majority of the 2017 Noteholders in the present context.

ABUSE OF POWER

69.   [After finding for the bondholders on their second argument, the court continues:] My conclusions thus far are sufficient to determine this case in favour of the claimant. Nonetheless, since its success thus far depends upon my decision on a point of construction in relation to which I have acknowledged there are arguments to the contrary of real substance, I shall nonetheless address this third limb of the claimant's case, upon the hypothesis that the paragraph 13 prohibition does not apply, not least because the issue as to abuse of power has been fully argued and raises the question of wide importance within the bond market. In that context Mr Snowden eventually acknowledged that if his submissions were correct (at least in their original form), they could prima facie apply to any form of exit consent which imposed less favourable consequences upon those who declined to participate in the associated exchange offer,

even if not amounting in substance, as they do in the present case, to a complete expropriation of the relevant securities from the dissentient minority.

70. I have already outlined the claimant's case under this heading. In slightly more detail, it is that, viewed as at the date of the Noteholders' meeting, the only effect of the Resolution was to impose upon a by then defined minority of Noteholders (namely those who had not offered or had accepted their Notes for exchange by the Bank) the expropriation of their Notes in circumstances where the majority had by then the benefit of contracts for their exchange for New Notes of substantial value. The Resolution could not therefore be described as being of any conceivable benefit to Noteholders, and was both oppressive and unfairly prejudicial to that minority. I have already referred to the settled authority upon the basis of which it is therefore claimed that the passing of the Resolution was an abuse of power, not by the Bank, but by those Noteholders who, albeit entirely unaffected by it, voted for it.

71. For the Bank Mr Dicker QC submitted that this was an entirely misconceived approach to the matter. He submitted that the true analysis of the Bank's proposal was as follows. First, that it proposed a Resolution applicable equally to all Noteholders, but coupled (in the form of the associated exchange proposal) with a proffered inducement made openly rather than covertly, offered to all Noteholders who wished to accept it, with full and fair disclosure of the consequences of not doing so. He said that it left each recipient Noteholder free to decide in his (or its) best interests whether to accept the proposal by offering his Notes for exchange, and that the proposal, taken as a whole, could not possibly be said to be incapable of being for the Noteholders' benefit. Taking into account the exchange offer, it proffered real value for the 2017 Notes in the form of the proposed New Notes, as part of a voluntary process which, if it were not to succeed, would be likely to be followed by legislation from the Irish government forcing subordinated bondholders to bear their share of the burden arising from the Bank's predicament. He pointed to the undoubted fact that in excess of 90 per cent of the 2017 Noteholders in fact accepted the proposal by proffering their Notes for exchange.

72. I must turn to the authorities upon which that submission was based . . .

73. Those authorities do not in my judgment constitute a statement of the whole of the abuse principle, so that wherever there is a disclosed inducement a challenge must fail.

82. . . . It is just possible to characterise the offer of the New Notes as a financial inducement to vote in favour of the Resolution. Nonetheless I consider that characterisation to be flawed. The reality is the other way round. The Resolution is used as a negative inducement to deter Noteholders from refusing the proffered exchange.

83. More generally the differences between the two cases substantially outweigh their similarities. First and foremost, the resolutions to postpone the interest payments in the *Azevedo* case were the substance of that

which the issuer (and in the event the majority of noteholders) wished to achieve, whereas in the present case the substance of the Bank's plan was to substitute New Notes for the Existing Notes by way of a contractual exchange. The Resolution in the present case was no more than a negative inducement to deter Noteholders from refusing the proffered exchange. Secondly it was the issuer in *Azevedo* which proffered the inducement, whereas here it is the majority of the Noteholders which (albeit at the issuer's request) wields the negative inducement constituted by the Resolution. Thirdly the postponements sought by the resolutions in *Azevedo* were plainly capable of being beneficial to noteholders, since they were designed to facilitate a reconstruction of the issuer, beneficial to all its stakeholders. Here the Resolution was designed in substance to destroy rather than to enhance the value of the Notes and was, on its own, of no conceivable benefit to Noteholders. Fourthly, no case of oppression or unfairness was advanced in *Azevedo*, only a case of bribery. Here by contrast the case is centred on alleged oppression, and bribery is not alleged at all.

84. After some hesitation, I have concluded that Mr Snowden arrived eventually at the correct question, which is whether it can be lawful for the majority to lend its aid to the coercion of a minority by voting for a resolution which expropriates the minority's rights under their bonds for a nominal consideration. In my judgment the correct answer to it is in the negative. My reasons derive essentially from my understanding of the purpose of the exit consent technique, as described at the beginning of this judgment. It is not that the issuer positively wishes to obtain securities by expropriation, rather than by the contractual exchange for value which it invites the bondholders to agree. On the contrary, the higher percentage of those accepting, generally the happier the issuer will be. Furthermore, the operation of the exit consent (here the Bank's new right to redeem for a nominal consideration) is not the method by which the issuer seeks to achieve the reconstruction constituted by the replacement of existing securities with new. The exit consent is, quite simply, a coercive threat which the issuer invites the majority to levy against the minority, nothing more or less. Its only function is the intimidation of a potential minority, based upon the fear of any individual member of the class that, by rejecting the exchange and voting against the resolution, he (or it) will be left out in the cold.

85. This form of coercion is in my judgment entirely at variance with the purposes for which majorities in a class are given power to bind minorities, and it is no answer for them to say that it is the issuer which has required or invited them to do so. True it is that, at the moment when any individual member of the class is required (by the imposition of the pre-meeting deadline) to make up his mind, there is at that point in time no defined minority against which the exit consent is aimed. But it is inevitable that there will be a defined (if any) minority by the time when the exit consent is implemented by being voted upon, and its only purpose is to prey upon the apprehension of each member of the class (aggravated by his relative inability to find out the views of his fellow

class members in advance) that he will, if he decides to vote against, be
part of that expropriated minority if the scheme goes ahead.

86. Putting it as succinctly as I can, oppression of a minority is of the essence
of exit consents of this kind, and it is precisely that at which the principles restraining the abusive exercise of powers to bind minorities are
aimed.

CONCLUSIONS

87. The claimant therefore fails on the first limb of its case, but succeeds on
the second and third. The claimant is therefore entitled to the substance
of the declaration sought in paragraph 2 of the Claim Form. I will hear
submissions, in the absence of agreement, as to the precise form which
those declarations should take.

The decision was appealed to the UK Court of Appeal, but the appeal was
withdrawn, so the High Court decision remains the last word in this particular
case.

PROBLEM SET 26.2

1. Be prepared to discuss the merits of the U.S. and English approaches in
class. Would the exchange offer in this last case have been permissible
under U.S. law?
2. How might a bondholder protect against the use of exit consents?

3. WORKOUTS, NOLs, AND COD

No, this section does not involve the Gloucester fisherman. It involves taxes.
Again.

To greatly oversimplify the matter — again, you really must take Corporate
Tax — the company undergoing the workout faces two key tax issues. First, these
sorts of firms often have net operating losses (NOLs). Often lots and lots of
NOLs.

Section 382 of the Tax Code limits the firm's ability to use its NOLs if the firm
experiences a change of control.[7] For most firms, NOLs can be offset against
future income and income earned in the prior three years. But for a firm that
experiences a change of control, section 382 severely limits the ability to use the
NOLs.

If the firm does not continue in the same line of business, NOLs disappear
altogether. This prevents trafficking in old corporate shells. Even if the old line
of business is continued, the amount of losses that can be used each year

---

7. 26 U.S.C. §§382(b) & 382(e)(1), I.R.C. §§382(b) & 382(e)(1).

becomes a function of value of the firm's shares immediately before the ownership change.

In general, a change occurs if the percentage of stock owned by 5 percent shareholders increases by more than 50 percent over the lowest percentage of stock owned by any individual shareholder during a specified period (usually three years).

In the workout context, if a creditor owns no shares of a corporation but then receives 10 percent of the firm's shares in exchange for its bonds, a potential change of control has occurred (the 5 percent shareholder stake has increased from zero to 10 percent with regard to this creditor).

A partial exemption from the change in control limitation is available in a formal bankruptcy case, so long as the historic shareholders and "qualified creditors" of the debtor corporation own at least 50 percent of the value and voting power of the firm's shares after the restructuring. Thus, tax issues may influence the choice of structure in financial distress, just as they did in the merger context.

In addition, when old debt is exchanged for new debt it may give rise to cancellation of debt ("COD") income on the old debt.[8] Similarly, section 108(e)(10) provides that when stock is issued in exchange for outstanding debt, COD income is recognized to the extent that the principal of the debt exceeds the value of the stock.

In short, when a borrower borrows, the borrower is not taxed on those funds because the borrower has an obligation to repay them. If that obligation goes away, then the borrower has taxable income in an amount equal to the forgiven amount of the loan.[9]

If the firm has sufficient NOLs, it can offset those against the COD income, subject to certain limits. Otherwise an exchange offer could result in a substantial tax bill for the distressed company—something most distressed firms are not in a position to deal with. Giving the creditors ample shares in the firm is a way around the COD problem, but is apt to trigger a change of control.

COD income is not includible as income on the firm's tax return if the release of indebtedness occurs in a bankruptcy case. Instead the debtor firm simply reduces its "tax attributes," essentially the firm's basis, by the amount of COD income avoided. This defers the tax on the COD income until such point as the firm is sold.

This bankruptcy treatment again can influence the choice between an out-of-court workout and a formal bankruptcy filing.

---

8. *See* 26 U.S.C. §61(a)(12), §61(a)(12); §1273(a), §1273(a).
9. 26 C.F.R. §1.61-12, Treas. Reg. §1.61-12.

27

PREPACKAGED CHAPTER 11
CASES

It is commonly believed, at least among bankruptcy attorneys, that exchange offers often fail because the only way to ensure sufficient "buy in" to the offer is to offer terms that a financially distressed firm cannot afford to offer.

As we noted in the prior chapter, only those bondholders that consent to the exchange offer will have their securities exchanged. Those that "hold out" will continue to hold old securities and will be entitled to full payments in accordance with the terms of their existing debt instruments. If exit consents are used those securities might be less valuable than before the exchange offer, but they still might return more than the new securities given in exchange.

Because of this, most exchange offers provide that the company will only consummate the exchange if a certain percentage of holders agree to the exchange (generally at least 75 percent). This is another reason exchange offers often fail.

The common solution to the holdout problem is a prepackaged bankruptcy case. This is a chapter 11 case where the firm has solicited votes on the reorganization plan before filing for bankruptcy. Often this solicitation will be combined with the solicitation for an exchange offer: If the exchange offer gets sufficient "buy in," that is implemented, but if not, then the debtor firm proceeds with the bankruptcy case. An example of such a two-prong offer is shown in Figure 27-1.

At one time, it was common to make this structure somewhat coercive. For example, bondholders would be offered new securities in the exchange offer that provided somewhat better treatment than they would receive under the proposed bankruptcy plan. This difference was spelled out in the solicitation documents.

More recently, the prepackaged bankruptcy case is simply a way to implement the proffered exchange offer. As you will see, bankruptcy allows a majority to bind the minority to a plan under certain conditions. This solves the holdout problem.

Moreover, discharging debt in a formal bankruptcy proceeding receives favorable tax treatment as compared to out-of-court workouts.

Stacked against these considerations are the reputational and out-of-pocket costs associated with filing for bankruptcy. Of course, it could be that the reputational issues are diminishing: Do you avoid flying on United, Delta, or American Airlines simply because they are or were in chapter 11?

FIGURE 27-1
Example of a Combined Exchange Offer/Prepack Solicitation

AMENDED AND RESTATED OFFERING MEMORANDUM, CONSENT SOLICITATION STATEMENT AND DISCLOSURE STATEMENT SOLICITING ACCEPTANCES OF A PREPACKAGED PLAN OF REORGANIZATION

CENTRAL EUROPEAN DISTRIBUTION CORPORATION
CEDC FINANCE CORPORATION INTERNATIONAL, INC.

Offer to exchange (the "*CEDC Exchange Offer*") all of the outstanding 3.00% Convertible Senior Notes due 2013 (collectively, the "*Existing 2013 Notes*") issued by Central European Distribution Corporation for new shares of common stock of Central European Distribution Corporation ("*New Common Stock*")

and

Offer to exchange (the "*CEDC FinCo Exchange Offer*" and, together with the CEDC Exchange Offer, the "*Exchange Offers*") all of the outstanding 9.125% Senior Secured Notes due 2016 (the "*9.125% Existing 2016 Notes*") and the 8.875% Senior Secured Notes due 2016 (the "*8.875% Existing 2016 Notes*" and, together with the 9.125% Existing 2016 Notes, the "*Existing 2016 Notes*" and, together with the Existing 2013 Notes, the "*Existing Notes*") issued by CEDC Finance Corporation International, Inc. for (i) cash consideration and/or (ii) new Senior Secured Notes due 2018 (the "*New Secured Notes*") and new Convertible Secured PIK Toggle Notes due 2018 (the "*New Convertible Secured Notes*" and, together with the New Secured Notes, the "*New Notes*")

and

Solicitation of consents to amendments to the indenture governing the Existing 2016 Notes

and

Solicitation of acceptances of a prepackaged plan of reorganization

The New Secured Notes offered in the CEDC FinCo Exchange Offer will bear interest, payable semi-annually, at an initial rate per annum of 8.0% with a 1.0% step-up per annum to a maximum rate per annum of 10.0% and will mature on April 30, 2018. The New Convertible Secured Notes offered in the CEDC FinCo Exchange Offer will bear interest, payable in cash or in kind, at a fixed rate per annum, payable semi-annually, equal to 10.0% and will mature on April 30, 2018. The New Convertible Secured Notes will be convertible into New Common Stock initially equal to 20% of CEDC's outstanding common stock, and increasing up to 35% depending on the conversion time. Interest on the New Notes will be payable on April 30 and October 31 of each year, commencing October 31, 2013.

> **THE EXCHANGE OFFERS WILL EXPIRE AT 11:59 P.M., NEW YORK CITY TIME, ON MARCH 22, 2013 UNLESS EXTENDED OR EARLIER TERMINATED BY US (SUCH DATE AND TIME, AS THE SAME MAY BE EXTENDED OR EARLIER TERMINATED, THE "*EXPIRATION TIME*"). IN ORDER TO RECEIVE THE CONSIDERATION (AS HEREINAFTER DEFINED) APPLICABLE TO THE EXISTING NOTES, NOTEHOLDERS (AS HEREINAFTER DEFINED) MUST VALIDLY TENDER AND NOT WITHDRAW THEIR EXISTING NOTES, AT OR PRIOR TO THE EXPIRATION TIME. HOLDERS OF EXISTING NOTES MAY TENDER THEIR NOTES IN THE EXCHANGE OFFERS WITHOUT DELIVERING ACCEPTANCES TO THE PLAN OF REORGANIZATION OR DELIVERING THEIR CONSENTS (AS HEREINAFTER DEFINED), AS APPLICABLE. HOLDERS OF EXISTING 2016 NOTES MAY DELIVER THEIR CONSENTS WITHOUT TENDERING THEIR EXISTING 2016 NOTES IN THE EXCHANGES OFFERS OR DELIVERING THEIR ACCEPTANCES TO THE PLAN OF REORGANIZATION. HOLDERS OF EXISTING NOTES MAY DELIVER ACCEPTANCES TO THE PREPACKAGED PLAN OF REORGANIZATION WITHOUT TENDERING THEIR NOTES IN THE EXCHANGE OFFERS BUT MUST DELIVER THEIR CONSENTS, AS APPLICABLE.**
>
> **TENDERS OF EXISTING 2013 NOTES AND ACCEPTANCES OF THE PLAN OF REORGANIZATION MAY BE WITHDRAWN AT ANY TIME PRIOR TO THE EXPIRATION TIME. TENDERS OF EXISTING 2016 NOTES AND CONSENTS TO AMENDMENTS TO THE EXISTING 2016 NOTES INDENTURE MAY BE WITHDRAWN AT ANY TIME PRIOR TO THE EARLIER OF (A) THE DATE AND TIME THAT CEDC FINCO NOTIFIES THE TRUSTEE UNDER THE EXISTING 2016 NOTES INDENTURE THAT CEDC FINCO HAS RECEIVED THE REQUISITE CONSENTS (AS DEFINED BELOW), AND (B) 5:00 PM NEW YORK CITY TIME ON MARCH 14, 2013 (THE "*CONSENT TIME*"). HOLDERS OF EXISTING 2016 NOTES WHO VOTE TO ACCEPT THE PLAN OF REORGANIZATION PRIOR TO THE CONSENT FEE DEADLINE (AS DEFINED) BELOW MAY MODIFY THEIR VOTES AT ANY TIME PRIOR TO THE CONSENT TIME. HOLDERS OF EXISTING 2016 NOTES WHO VOTE TO ACCEPT THE PLAN OF REORGANIZATION AFTER THE CONSENT FEE DEADLINE OR WHO VOTE TO REJECT THE PLAN OF REORGANIZATION MAY MODIFY THEIR VOTES AT ANY TIME PRIOR TO THE VOTING DEADLINE (AS DEFINED BELOW).**
>
> **NOTEHOLDERS SHOULD REFER TO THE SECTIONS HEREIN ENTITLED "THE EXCHANGE OFFERS AND CONSENT SOLICITATION" AND "PROCEDURES FOR VOTING ON THE PLAN OF REORGANIZATION" FOR INSTRUCTIONS ON HOW TO TENDER NOTES, CONSENT TO THE AMENDMENTS TO THE INDENTURE GOVERNING THE EXISTING 2016 NOTES AND VOTE ON THE PLAN OF REORGANIZATION.**

Upon the terms and subject to the conditions set forth in this offering memorandum and consent solicitation statement (as it may be amended from time to time, the "*Offering Memorandum*"), disclosure statement soliciting acceptances of the Plan of Reorganization (as hereinafter defined) (as it may be amended from time to time, the "*Disclosure Statement*" and, together with the Offering Memorandum, this "*Offering Memorandum and Disclosure Statement*") and the ballot ("*Ballot*") for accepting or rejecting the Plan of Reorganization.

- Central European Distribution Corporation, a Delaware corporation ("*CEDC*"), is (i) offering to exchange any and all of its outstanding Existing 2013 Notes for the consideration set forth below, and (ii) soliciting acceptances from all holders of Existing 2013 Notes of the prepackaged plan of reorganization attached hereto as Appendix A (the "*Plan of Reorganization*"); and

- CEDC Finance Corporation International Inc., a Delaware corporation ("*CEDC FinCo*") is (i) offering to exchange any and all of its outstanding Existing 2016 Notes for the consideration set forth below; (ii) soliciting consents (the "*Consent Solicitation*") to amendments to the indenture governing the Existing 2016 Notes (the "*Existing 2016 Notes Indenture*" and, together with the indenture governing the Existing 2013 Notes, the "*Indentures*"); and (iii) soliciting acceptances from all holders of Existing 2016 Notes of the Plan of Reorganization.

Each holder of Existing 2016 Notes who delivers Consents with respect to its Existing 2016 Notes by 5:00 PM, New York City time on March 14, 2013 (the "*Consent Fee Deadline*"), and does not validly withdraw such Consents, will receive a cash payment equal to 0.50% of the principal amount of the Existing 2016 Notes for which Consents were delivered and not withdrawn (the "*Consent Fee*") promptly after the Consent Fee Deadline (the "*Consent Fee Payment Date*"), assuming all of the conditions to the payment of the Consent Fee are met. Holders of Existing 2016 Notes that deliver Consents after the Consent Fee Deadline will not be entitled to a Consent Fee. The Consent Fee will be payable in U.S. dollars. Payments of the Consent Fee in respect of Consents from holders of 8.875% Existing 2016 Notes will be paid based upon the prevailing euro/US dollar exchange rate in effect at the time of payment. The Consent Fee will only be payable if the Collateral and Guarantee Amendments are approved by or before the Consent Fee Deadline.

This Offering Memorandum and Disclosure Statement includes a solicitation of acceptances of the Plan of Reorganization from holders of the Existing Notes ("*Noteholders*", and each a "*Noteholder*"). You should rely only on the information contained herein and in the related Ballot, as applicable, in making your decision to participate in the Exchange Offers, to participate in the Consent Solicitation, and/or to vote to accept the Plan of Reorganization. Holders of Existing 2016 Notes may tender their Existing 2016 Notes in the Exchange Offers without delivering acceptances to the Plan of Reorganization or delivering their Consents, as applicable. Holders of Existing 2016 Notes may deliver their Consents without tendering their Existing 2016 Notes in the Exchange Offers or delivering acceptances to the Plan of Reorganization. Holders of Existing 2016 Notes may deliver their acceptances to the Plan of Reorganization without tendering their Existing 2016 Notes in the Exchange Offers but must deliver their Consents.

NEITHER THE SECURITIES AND EXCHANGE COMMISSION (THE "*SEC*") NOR ANY STATE SECURITIES COMMISSION HAS APPROVED OR DISAPPROVED OF THIS TRANSACTION OR THESE SECURITIES, PASSED UPON THE MERITS OR FAIRNESS OF THE TRANSACTION OR DETERMINED IF THIS OFFERING MEMORANDUM IS TRUTHFUL OR COMPLETE. ANY REPRESENTATION TO THE CONTRARY IS A CRIMINAL OFFENSE.

The Exchange Offers are intended to be exempt from the federal registration requirements of the U.S. Securities Act of 1933 (the "*Securities Act*") pursuant to the exemption from such registration contained in Section 3(a)(9) thereof, and, therefore, considered a federal "covered security" by Section 18(b)(4)(D) (formerly, Section 18(b)(4)(C)), of the Securities Act. The Exchange Offers are exempt from state securities registration by virtue of the preemption as a covered security under Section 18(b)(4)(D) and/or the preemption for "listed securities" under Section 18(b)(1) of the Securities Act.

The date of this Offering Memorandum and Disclosure Statement is March 8, 2013.

1. DEAL STRUCTURE

IN RE: METRO-GOLDWYN-MAYER STUDIOS INC., ET AL.

United States Bankruptcy Court, S.D. New York
No. 10BK15774
October 7, 2010

Metro-Goldwyn-Mayer Studios Inc. and certain of its affiliates (collectively, the *"Debtors"*) are sending you this disclosure statement (the *"Disclosure Statement"*) because you may be a creditor entitled to vote on the Joint Prepackaged Plan of Reorganization of Metro-Goldwyn-Mayer Studios Inc. and certain of its Affiliates (the *"Plan"*). This solicitation (the *"Solicitation"*) of votes is being conducted to obtain sufficient acceptances of the Plan *prior* to the filing of voluntary cases under chapter 11 of title 11 of the United States Code (the *"Bankruptcy Code"*). If sufficient votes to obtain confirmation of the Plan are received and certain other conditions are met, the Debtors intend to file voluntary cases under chapter 11 of the Bankruptcy Code to implement the Plan. Because no chapter 11 cases have yet been commenced, this Disclosure Statement has not been approved by any Bankruptcy Court as containing "adequate information" within the meaning of section 1125(a) of the Bankruptcy Code. Following the commencement of their chapter 11 cases, the Debtors expect to seek promptly an order of the Bankruptcy Court (1) approving (a) this Disclosure Statement as having contained "adequate information" and (b) the Solicitation as having been in compliance with Section 1125(b) of the Bankruptcy Code, and (2) confirming the Plan described herein.

DISCLOSURE STATEMENT DATED OCTOBER 7, 2010 PREPETITION SOLICITATION OF VOTES WITH RESPECT TO JOINT PREPACKAGED PLAN OF REORGANIZATION OF METRO-GOLDWYN-MAYER STUDIOS INC. AND CERTAIN OF ITS AFFILIATES SPECIAL NOTICE REGARDING FEDERAL AND STATE SECURITIES LAWS

Neither this Disclosure Statement nor the Plan has been filed with or reviewed by the Bankruptcy Court, and the securities to be issued on or after the Effective Date (as defined below) are not the subject of a registration statement filed with the United States Securities and Exchange Commission (the *"SEC"*) under the United States Securities Act of 1933, as amended (the *"Securities Act"*), or any securities regulatory authority of any state under any state securities law (*"Blue Sky Law"*). The Debtors are relying on section 4(2) of the Securities Act and similar provisions of state securities law, as well as, to the extent applicable, the exemption from the Securities Act and equivalent state law registration requirements provided by section 1145(a)(1) of the Bankruptcy Code, to exempt from registration under the Securities Act and Blue Sky Law the offer and sale of new securities in connection with the Solicitation and the Plan.

Each holder of a Credit Agreement Claim (as defined in the Plan) or authorized signatory for the beneficial owner of a Credit Agreement Claim will be required to certify on its Ballot whether such holder or beneficial owner is an Accredited Investor, as that term is defined by Rule 501 of Regulation D of the Securities Act.

The Plan has not been approved or disapproved by the SEC or any state securities commission and neither the SEC nor any state securities commission has passed upon the accuracy or adequacy of the information contained herein. Any representation to the contrary is a criminal offense. Neither the Solicitation nor this Disclosure Statement constitutes an offer to sell, or the solicitation of an offer to buy securities in any state or jurisdiction in which such offer or solicitation is not authorized.

This Disclosure Statement and the information set forth herein are confidential. This Disclosure Statement contains material non-public information concerning the Debtors, their subsidiaries, and their respective securities. Each recipient hereby acknowledges that it (a) is aware that the federal securities laws of the United States prohibit any person who has material non-public information about a company, which is obtained from the company or its representatives, from purchasing or selling securities of such company or from communicating the information to any other person under circumstances in which it is reasonably foreseeable that such person is likely to purchase or sell such securities and (b) is familiar with the United States Securities Exchange Act of 1934, as amended (the *"Securities Exchange Act"*), and the rules and regulations promulgated thereunder, and agrees that it will not use or communicate to any person, under circumstances where it is reasonably likely that such person is likely to use or cause any person to use, any confidential information in contravention of the Securities Exchange Act or any of its rules and regulations, including Rule 10b-5.

THE VOTING DEADLINE TO ACCEPT OR REJECT THE JOINT PREPACKAGED PLAN OF REORGANIZATION OF METRO-GOLDWYN-MAYER STUDIOS INC. AND CERTAIN OF ITS AFFILIATES IS 5:00 P.M. PREVAILING EASTERN TIME ON OCTOBER 22, 2010, UNLESS EXTENDED BY THE DEBTORS (THE *"VOTING DEADLINE"*). THE RECORD DATE FOR DETERMINING WHETHER A HOLDER OF AN IMPAIRED CLAIM IS ENTITLED TO VOTE ON THE PLAN IS OCTOBER 4, 2010 (THE *"VOTING RECORD DATE"*).

THE DEBTORS ARE FURNISHING THIS DISCLOSURE STATEMENT TO EACH MEMBER OF AN IMPAIRED CLASS UNDER THE JOINT PREPACKAGED PLAN OF REORGANIZATION OF METRO-GOLDWYN-MAYER STUDIOS INC. AND CERTAIN OF ITS AFFILIATES. THIS DISCLOSURE STATEMENT IS TO BE USED BY EACH RECIPIENT SOLELY IN CONNECTION WITH HIS, HER, OR ITS EVALUATION OF THE PLAN, AND USE OF THIS DISCLOSURE STATEMENT FOR ANY OTHER PURPOSE IS NOT AUTHORIZED. WITHOUT THE PRIOR WRITTEN CONSENT OF THE DEBTORS, THIS DISCLOSURE STATEMENT MAY NOT BE REPRODUCED OR PROVIDED TO OTHERS (OTHER THAN THOSE ADVISORS OF ANY RECIPIENT OF THIS DISCLOSURE STATEMENT WHO MAY REVIEW THE INFORMATION CONTAINED HEREIN TO ASSIST SUCH RECIPIENT IN HIS, HER, OR ITS EVALUATION OF THE PLAN).

INTRODUCTION AND DISCLAIMER

Metro-Goldwyn-Mayer Studios Inc. (*"MGM Studios"*) and its affiliated Debtors (collectively, together with their non-Debtor affiliates the *"Company"* or *"MGM"*) submit this Disclosure Statement to certain holders of claims against the Debtors in connection with the Solicitation of acceptances of the proposed Joint Pre-packaged Plan of Reorganization of Metro-Goldwyn-Mayer Studios Inc. and Certain of Its Affiliates, dated as of October 7, 2010 (a copy of which is annexed hereto as *Appendix A*). The Debtors are soliciting such acceptances from holders of secured obligations under the Credit Agreement.

I. OVERVIEW OF THE COMPANY

This Disclosure Statement contains, among other things, descriptions and summaries of provisions of the Plan. Unless otherwise defined herein, all capitalized terms contained herein have the meanings ascribed to them in the Plan.

A. CORPORATE STRUCTURE OF THE COMPANY

MGM Holdings Inc. (*"Holdings"*) is the ultimate parent of the MGM family of companies. Holdings owns MGM Holdings II Inc. which, in turn, owns Metro-Goldwyn-Mayer Inc. Metro-Goldwyn-Mayer Inc. owns, directly or indirectly, a number of subsidiaries, including various non-Debtor entities. Metro-Goldwyn-Mayer Inc.'s principal direct and indirect subsidiaries are MGM Studios, United Artists Corporation, United Artists Films Inc. and Orion Pictures Corporation.

A list of the Debtors is attached as *Exhibit B* to the Plan. Generally, the Debtors include all the wholly owned domestic subsidiaries of Holdings other than certain special purpose subsidiaries whose organizational documents contain bankruptcy remote provisions.

The Company's executive offices are located at 10250 Constellation Boulevard, Los Angeles, California 90067–6241. The Company's telephone number is (310) 449–3000. The Company's internet address is *www.mgm.com*. Attached hereto as *Appendices D* and *E*, respectively, is the Company's audited financial statement for the fiscal year ending March, 2009, and unaudited financial statement for the fiscal year ending March, 2010 (collectively, the *"Financial Statements"*).

B. OVERVIEW OF BUSINESS OPERATIONS

MGM is a film entertainment company, with one of the world's largest film and television libraries and a group of important content franchises. The Company is engaged primarily in the development, production and worldwide distribution of feature films, television programming, interactive media, music, and licensed merchandise. The Company's film and television library (the *"MGM Library"*) contains approximately 4,100 theatrically released feature film titles and approximately 10,800 television episodes, and is one of the largest collections of post-1948 feature films in the world. Films in the MGM Library have won over 200 Academy Awards, including fifteen Best Picture Awards. The MGM Library also contains rights to many iconic film and television franchises. More specifically, assets comprising the MGM Library include: (i) MGM (post-1985)/United Artists film library which consists of more than 2,100 MGM, United Artists and Cannon Group titles, including the *James Bond, Pink Panther*, and *Rocky* franchises as well as *Legally Blonde, Hannibal, Rain Man*, and *A Fish Called Wanda;* (ii) the Orion Pictures film library which consists of more than 1,300 titles, including *Silence of the Lambs* and *Dances With Wolves;* (iii) the Polygram film library which consists of more than 700 titles, including *When Harry Met Sally* and *Four Weddings and a Funeral;* and (iv) the television programs library which includes approximately 10,800 episodes of programming, including *Stargate SG-1*, the longest running science fiction series in U.S. television history. The Company also co-owns the rights to produce two films based on *The Hobbit*, a book which has sold more than 100 million copies worldwide.

C.   CORPORATE HISTORY

The Metro-Goldwyn-Mayer brand was established in 1924 when Metro Pictures Corporation (founded in 1916), the Goldwyn Picture Corporation (founded in 1917), and Louis B. Mayer Pictures Corporation (founded in 1918) were joined together by Marcus Loew, the owner of a large theatre chain, Loew's Theatres. During the 1930s and 1940s, Metro-Goldwyn-Mayer was the most dominant motion picture studio in Hollywood and since that time has remained one of the most recognizable worldwide film studios. Following a series of corporate transactions, MGM currently owns one of the largest modern (post-1948) collections of feature films in the world, comprised of the post-1985 MGM library, and the historic United Artists, Orion Pictures, and Polygram film libraries. The following timeline notes key events since 1996.

In July 10, 1996, Metro-Goldwyn-Mayer Inc., a Delaware corporation, was formed specifically to acquire from an indirect wholly-owned subsidiary of Consortium de Realisation all of the outstanding capital stock of MGM Studios and its subsidiaries. Metro-Goldwyn-Mayer Inc. was majority owned by an investor group including Kirk Kerkorian, Tracinda Corporation, a corporation that is principally owned by Mr. Kerkorian, and certain current and former executive officers of MGM Studios. On October 10, 1996, Metro-Goldwyn-Mayer Inc. purchased MGM Studios for an aggregate consideration of $1.3 billion.

In July 1997, Metro-Goldwyn-Mayer Inc. acquired all of the outstanding capital stock of Orion Pictures Corporation and its subsidiaries, including the entity formerly known as The Samuel Goldwyn Company and now known as Orion Film Classics Company, from Metromedia International Group, Inc. In connection with the Orion Pictures Corporation acquisition, Metro-Goldwyn-Mayer Inc. obtained the film and television libraries of Orion Pictures Corporation companies consisting of approximately 1,900 film titles and 3,000 television episodes. In January 7, 1999, Metro-Goldwyn-Mayer Inc. acquired certain film libraries, including 1,300 feature films, and film-related rights that were previously owned by PolyGram N.V. and its subsidiaries.

In November 1997, Metro-Goldwyn-Mayer Inc. completed an initial public offering, whereby it issued and sold 9,000,000 new shares of common stock at a price per share of $20.00 for net proceeds of $165 million. Concurrently with the consummation of the initial public offering, Tracinda Corporation purchased 3,978,780 shares of the common stock for an aggregate purchase price of $75 million. From 1998 to 2003, Metro-Goldwyn-Mayer Inc. made subsequent securities offerings, including public offerings and private placements.

On April 8, 2005, Metro-Goldwyn-Mayer Inc. was acquired by Holdings, a Delaware corporation owned by a consortium comprised of Sony Corporation of America, Providence Equity Partners, Texas Pacific Group, Comcast Corporation and DLJ Merchant Banking Partners (the *"Acquisition"*). The consortium acquired Metro-Goldwyn-Mayer Inc. for a total price of $4.9 billion, consisting of $3.0 billion in cash and $1.9 billion in assumed debt. Subsequent to the Acquisition, Metro-Goldwyn-Mayer Inc.'s shares were de-listed from the New York Stock Exchange and Metro-Goldwyn-Mayer Inc. became privately held. In 2007, Quadrangle Capital Partners purchased a small stake in Holdings from Providence Equity Partners.

D. CAPITAL STRUCTURE

1. MGM Credit Facility

In connection with the Acquisition, the Debtors entered into a credit agreement, dated as of April 8, 2005, by and among MGM Holdings II Inc. (*"Holdings II"*), Metro-Goldwyn-Mayer Inc., as Borrower, Bank of America, N.A., Citicorp USA, Inc. and The Royal Bank of Scotland PLC, as Documentation Agents, Credit Suisse, as Syndication Agent, JPMorgan Chase Bank, N.A., as Administrative Agent, and the lenders from time to time party thereto (as amended, the *"Credit Agreement"*). The Credit Agreement provided the Company with a credit facility (the *"MGM Credit Facility"*) consisting of a five-year $250 million revolving credit facility (*"Revolving Facility"*), a six-year $1.05 billion term loan (*"Term Loan A"*) and a seven-year $2.7 billion term loan (*"Term Loan B"*). The proceeds of Term Loan A and Term Loan B were used to finance a portion of the Acquisition and to pay related fees and expenses. The proceeds of the Revolving Facility were used to finance the working capital needs and general corporate purposes of MGM and its subsidiaries.

Holdings II and several of its direct and indirect subsidiaries guarantee the MGM Credit Facility (collectively, the *"Guarantors"*). The MGM Credit Facility is secured by substantially all of the assets of Metro-Goldwyn-Mayer Inc. and the Guarantors, including perfected first-priority security interests in the capital stock and, subject to certain exceptions, substantially all other tangible and intangible assets of MGM and the Guarantors.

On March 9, 2007, Holdings II and Metro-Goldwyn-Mayer Inc. entered into the second amendment to the Credit Agreement which replaced Term Loan A with a five-year $1.1 billion term loan (*"Term Loan B-1"*) that incorporated the same loan amortization payment requirements of Term Loan B. Both Term Loan B and Term Loan B-1 mature on April 8, 2012, while the Revolving Facility maturity date remained April 8, 2010. On September 30, 2009, the parties entered into a Third Amendment to the Credit Agreement, Amendment To Swap Agreements and Forbearance Agreement (the *"Initial Forbearance Agreement"*) extending until December 15, 2009 the time for payment of interest, letter of credit participation fees and swap termination payments that otherwise would be due and payable from and including September 30, 2009 through December 15, 2009. On November 13, 2009, the parties entered into a Fourth Amendment To Credit Agreement, Amendment To Swap Agreements and Second Forbearance Agreement extending the forbearance period to January 31, 2010. On January 31, 2010, the parties entered into a Fifth Amendment To Credit Agreement, Amendment To Swap Agreements and Third Forbearance Agreement extending the forbearance period to March 31, 2010. On March 31, 2010, the parties entered into a Sixth Amendment To Credit Agreement, Amendment To Swap Agreements and Fourth Forbearance Agreement extending the forbearance period to May 14, 2010. On May 14, 2010, the parties entered into a Seventh Amendment To Credit Agreement, Amendment To Swap Agreements and Fifth Forbearance Agreement extending the forbearance period to July 14, 2010. On July 14, 2010, the parties entered into an Eighth Amendment To Credit Agreement, Amendment To Swap Agreements and Sixth Forbearance Agreement extending the forbearance period to September 15, 2010. On September 15, 2010, the parties entered into a Ninth Amendment To Credit Agreement, Amendment To Swap Agreements and Seventh Forbearance Agreement extending the forbearance period to October 28, 2010.

As of the date hereof, the aggregate amount of the outstanding obligations under the Credit Agreement is approximately $4.737 billion plus an additional $152 million outstanding obligations on account of certain interest rate protection arrangements entered into in connection with the Credit Agreement.

2. *Print and Advertising Facility*

On September 19, 2006, MGM Studios and certain of its distribution subsidiaries entered into an Amended and Restated Revenue Participation Agreement with Domestic Distribution Inc. (*"DDI"*) (as amended, the *"P&A Facility"*). Under the P&A Facility, MGM Studios committed to offer to sell to DDI revenue participations in certain qualifying pictures in exchange for a purchase price that is tied to MGM Studio's domestic print and advertising costs for such picture. DDI, in turn, committed to pay the purchase price for such revenue participations, however such commitment was limited to DDI's availability under the DDI Credit Agreement (as defined below).

DDI's revenue participation is secured by a first priority security interest in (i) an interest in a cash collateral account of up to $20 million funded by MGM Studios from receipts generated from exploitation of certain television and home video rights with respect to qualifying pictures, (ii) certain domestic distribution agreements pursuant to which MGM Studios distributes qualifying pictures, (iii) any collateral granted to MGM Studios with respect to such qualifying pictures, and (iv) subject to certain limitations, any interest in the underlying copyright in, and physical materials relating to, such qualifying picture solely to the extent necessary to exercise certain distribution rights for such qualifying picture.

DDI is a non-Debtor special purpose entity that was formed for the sole purpose of providing financing to the Company under the P&A Facility. DDI funded its obligations under the P&A Facility by borrowings under a credit agreement among DDI, as borrower, JP Morgan Chase Bank, N.A., as administrative agent, and the lenders from time to time party thereto (as amended, the *"DDI Credit Agreement"*). The DDI Credit Agreement provided DDI with a $175 million revolving credit facility, the proceeds of which were to be used by DDI to purchase revenue participations under the P&A Facility. The DDI Credit Agreement is secured by all of the assets of DDI, including all of DDI's rights in and to the P&A Facility as well as a collateral assignment of the security interest in the qualified pictures granted by the Company to DDI in the P&A Facility. The failure to pay principal under the Credit Agreement at the April 8, 2010 maturity date triggered a cross-default under the P&A Facility.

As of the date hereof, the aggregate principal amount of the Debtors' obligations under the P&A Facility is approximately $52 million.

3. United Artists Entertainment Credit Facility

As set forth above, MGM Studios is a majority owner of United Artists Entertainment. New United Artists was formed to develop and create new theatrically released films under the New United Artists banner.

On August 16, 2007, United Artists Entertainment, through its wholly-owned subsidiary, UAPF, entered into (i) a Credit and Security Agreement (the *"UAPF Credit Agreement"*) with certain lenders and others, and (ii) a Note Purchase and Security Agreement (the *"UAPF Note Purchase Agreement"*) with certain lenders and others.

The UAPF Credit Agreement provided United Artists Entertainment with a $250 million senior credit facility (the *"UAPF Facility"*). In addition, under the UAPF Note Purchase Agreement, United Artists Entertainment sold mezzanine promissory notes totaling $75 million (the *"Mezzanine Notes"*). The proceeds of this financing were designed to support the production or acquisition by New United Artists of up to 18 films to be produced under the New United Artists banner and distributed by MGM under the Master Distribution Agreement. Obligations under the UAPF Facility and UAPF Note Purchase Agreement are guaranteed by UAPF's domestic subsidiaries and are secured by substantially all of UAPF's and its domestic subsidiaries' assets, including the certain intellectual property rights related to the films produced and developed by New United Artists. To secure MGM Studios' performance of certain obligations under the Master Distribution Agreement, including its obligations to make payments to UAPF, MGM Studios and certain of its subsidiaries granted UAPF a security interest in their rights, title, and interest in and to certain collateral relating to licensed pictures. A "Stop Funding Event" has occurred under the UAPF Facility. Therefore the lenders under the UAPF Facility are not required to make additional loans to UAPF for new films.

Neither United Artists Entertainment nor UAPF are expected to be debtors in the Debtors' Chapter 11 cases.

E.   EVENTS LEADING TO CHAPTER 11 CASES

The Revolving Facility under the Credit Agreement matured in April 2010 and material amortization of Term Loan B and Term Loan B-1 is scheduled to begin in June 2011. Through a combination of industry-wide pressures and Company-specific issues, it became evident to the Debtors' board in the Spring of 2009 that the value of the Company might not support a re-financing or re-payment of the Revolving Facility at maturity. Subsequently, the Company's board determined that a balance sheet restructuring was the only viable alternative for the Company to continue to operate as a going concern post-maturation of the Revolving Facility. The industry-wide factors include a precip-itous decline in home video sales and the worldwide economic downturn which has reduced consumer spending on discretionary items, such as entertainment, and has chilled the capital markets for new financial accommodations. The Company has also suffered because it has not had sufficient resources to support new production and thereby maximize the value of the MGM Library by main-taining an optimal level of new production.

1.   Industry-Wide Factors

The greatest macroeconomic factor affecting the Company is the dramatic decline in consumer spending which directly affected the home entertainment business. Due to the economic downturn, consumer spending on discretionary items such as home video has decreased significantly, and remains dormant. Similarly, many consumers are delaying new Blu-ray disc purchases until Blu-ray players become more affordable, and those that do purchase Blu-ray discs are generally selecting new titles. The economic downturn has also caused many retailers to stop selling new DVDs as loss-leaders to drive store traffic. Compe-titors' aggressive pricing strategy on new releases has also affected the sale of older MGM Library titles.

In addition to the foregoing, the home video market has experienced an overall decline due to consumer shifts to cable-based and Internet-based on demand service providers which allow consumers to view movies and other programming without the need for DVDs or similar physical media. Likewise, consumer shifts toward subscription-based rental services, such as Netflix, have led to a decrease in home video sales.

The economic downtown has also resulted in lower advertising spending, which has negatively affected television broadcasting revenues. This decline directly impacts advertising sales on MGM-owned channels as well as third-party owned channels that license MGM Library content.

2.   Lack of New Production

After the Acquisition in April, 2005, the Company sought to implement a business plan that attempted to exploit the MGM Library with limited new production. Limiting new production failed to maximize the value of the MGM Library and allowed the MGM Library to become stale. Therefore, the Company determined that a more robust new production slate was necessary to refresh and replenish the MGM Library, drive sales of MGM Library product, and otherwise preserve the inherent value of the MGM Library. To that end, as set forth above, in August, 2007, the Company established New United Artists with its joint venture partners. Thereafter, in March, 2008, Ms. Mary Parent, an executive with extensive entertainment industry and financial management experience, was appointed Chairperson of the Company's Worldwide Motion Picture Group.

The current credit crisis has also restricted the Company's ability to procure third-party production financing. Because a substantial portion of cash flow generated from the MGM Library has been dedicated to debt service requirements, the Company has had insufficient liquidity to fund new production at levels that the Company believes is necessary to maximize the value of the MGM Library.

3. *Evaluation of Restructuring Alternatives*

Due to the approaching April 2010 maturity of the Revolving Facility and the issues identified above, in April 2009 the Company retained Moelis & Company (*"Moelis"*), as financial advisor, to assist it in exploring strategic alternatives. Shortly thereafter, a steering committee (the *"Steering Committee"*) of certain lenders under the Credit Agreement was formed in connection with a potential restructuring of the Debtors' obligations under the Credit Agreement, and the Company and the Steering Committee commenced discussions regarding potential alternatives. On August 18, 2009, the Company hired restructuring expert Mr. Stephen Cooper (co-founder and former chairman of the restructuring firm Zolfo Cooper), who was appointed to the newly created office of the Chief Executive Officer together with Mary Parent (Chairperson for Worldwide Motion Picture Group), and Bedi A. Singh (President, Finance and Administration & Chief Financial Officer).

In September 2009 the Company requested, among other things, an extension under the Credit Agreement of the time for payment of interest, letter of credit participation fees and swap termination payments that otherwise would be due and payable from and including September 30, 2009 to December 15, 2009. On September 30, 2009, the parties to the Credit Agreement entered into the Initial Forbearance Agreement, granting such extensions. As set forth in Section I.D.1. hereof, the Company requested and continued to receive additional extensions of the forbearance period from time to time.

Starting in September 2009, the Debtors, by and through a Capital Structure Committee of Holdings' Board of Directors (*"CSC"*), collaborated with Moelis to draft a confidential information memorandum (*"CIM"*) regarding a potential sale of the Company. In this regard, the Debtors, along with Moelis (in consultation with the Steering Committee's advisors), prepared a potential buyers list and Moelis reached out to numerous potential parties to gauge interest. Beginning in December 2009, Moelis began delivering CIMs to eighteen potential buyers and their respective advisors following execution of confidentiality agreements. These potential buyers and their advisors were also granted access to a virtual data room.

In January 2010, the Debtors received non-binding indications of interest from eight parties. Following such indications of interest, the Debtors, working with Moelis and the Steering Committee's advisors, invited six of these parties to participate in a second round of bidding. The parties' indications of interests were evaluated primarily on long term value to the Company's stakeholders, proposed structure, the perceived ability of each party to consummate a transaction on a timely basis, and the ability to obtain the requisite Secured Lender support for the transaction.

During the second round, bidders were granted access to both physical and virtual data rooms. The Debtors also invited the bidders to management presentations to discuss the Company's business. Bidders were later invited to follow-up diligence sessions with the Company's management to address questions following the management presentation as well as questions resulting from the review of documents in the data rooms.

Following the second round, three parties submitted non-binding bid letters by the end of March, 2010, subject to, among other things, continued due diligence and the negotiation of definitive documents. The Steering Committee determined that such bids were inadequate, and informed the Debtors that its members would not support a plan of reorganization embodying a transaction based upon these bids, and as a result, the Debtors did not accept any of the bids. The Steering Committee then requested that the Debtors present their business plan that assumed a stand-alone plan of reorganization. In April 2010, the Steering Committee, with the Company's consent, elected to meet with certain industry experts to inform their perspectives of such standalone plan and formed an informal committee of certain members of the Steering Committee (the *"Subcommittee"*) to do so and to consider additional alternatives. During April and May, 2010, the Subcommittee met with numerous industry experts and potential partners to discuss their perspectives on MGM and potential alternatives for a reorganization of the Company. During the months of June and July, 2010, the discussions narrowed to Spyglass and handful of other parties.

Ultimately, the Subcommittee, in consultation with the Steering Committee and, separately, the Debtors, negotiated a non-binding letter of intent with Spyglass and the C/G Stockholders, which was presented to the Debtors for their consideration. The Steering Committee advised the Debtors that it supported moving forward with a proposal with Spyglass and the C/G Stockholders. After analyzing the proposed transaction, and considering the viability of any other alternatives, the Debtors, after consultation with their advisors, determined that under the circumstances the Spyglass transaction was the best alternative available to the Debtors at which point the Company, Spyglass and the C/G Stockholders negotiated and signed a non-binding letter of intent.

F.   THE PROPOSED PLAN

After several months of considering their strategic alternatives, the Debtors and the Steering Committee negotiated the terms of the Plan, the Investment Agreement, and related documents with Spyglass and the C/G Stockholders. The Plan is a prepackaged plan of reorganization. The overall purpose of the Plan is to provide for a restructuring of the Debtors' liabilities in a manner designed to maximize value to all stakeholders and to enhance the financial viability of the reorganized Debtors. Generally, the Plan provides for a balance sheet restructuring whereby (i) existing equity in Holdings will be cancelled,

(ii) approximately \$4.75 billion of claims under the Credit Agreement will be converted into approximately 95.3% of the equity in Reorganized Holdings, (iii) Spyglass will contribute certain assets to the Reorganized Company in exchange for 0.52% of the equity in Reorganized Holdings, and (iv) Cypress and Garoge will merge with and into a special purpose direct limited liability company subsidiary of Reorganized Holdings, with the Debtor affiliate as the surviving entity and the C/G Stockholders receiving approximately 4.17% of the equity in Reorganized Holdings. All other classes of claims are unimpaired under the Plan. Furthermore, all equity interests in Subsidiary Debtors will be reinstated.

In furtherance of the implementation of the Plan, the Debtors have entered into (or will be entering into) the Transaction Documents, which include the Investment Agreement, the Stockholders Agreement, and the Registration Rights Agreement as well as related documents, including the Stock Incentive Plan. Set forth below in Section I.H. are summaries of the terms of such Investment Agreement, Stockholders Agreement, Registration Rights Agreement, and Stock Incentive Plan. The Plan also contemplates that the Reorganized Debtors will enter into a New Credit Facility on the Effective Date. The New Credit Facility is contemplated to be a \$500 million credit facility to be entered into between the Reorganized Debtors and the lenders party thereto, which shall have terms substantially as set forth in the commitment letter or term sheet attached to the Plan as *Exhibit A*, which will be filed with the Bankruptcy Court at least five business days prior to the deadline that the Bankruptcy Court sets for parties in interest to file objections to confirmation of the Plan.

The Debtors believe that their businesses and assets have significant value that would not be maximized in a liquidation. Further in connection with the Debtors' decision to pursue the Plan, the Debtors' financial advisors have prepared and delivered a going concern valuation of the business. The Steering Committee has advised the Debtors that its financial advisors have also prepared a going concern valuation. Moreover, the Debtors believe that any alternative to confirmation of the Plan, such as an out-of-court restructuring or attempts by another party in interest to file a plan of reorganization, would result in significant delays, litigation, and additional costs, and ultimately would lower the recoveries for Holders of Allowed Claims. Additionally, based upon feedback during the course of this restructuring from both the Subcommittee and the Steering Committee, the Company concluded that as a practical matter no other plan of reorganization could be proposed that would garner the support of the Secured Lenders, whose support is essential to the success of any plan. *Accordingly, the Debtors strongly recommend that you vote to accept the Plan, if you are entitled to vote.*

The Debtors have been advised that the Subcommittee and the Administrative Agent also support the Plan and will recommend that Holders of Credit Agreement Claims vote in favor of the Plan.

G. SPYGLASS, CYPRESS AND GAROGE

Spyglass is a film and television production company, co-founded by Gary Barber and Roger Birnbaum. Cypress and Garoge (together, *"Cypress/Garoge"*) are affiliates of Messrs. Barber and Birnbaum that own and exploit a library of films. Collectively, these films have grossed over $5 billion in worldwide box office. They enjoyed instant success with the blockbuster *The Sixth Sense* and have produced a slate of successful films including, among others, *Bruce Almighty, Seabiscuit, Memoirs of a Geisha, 27 Dresses,* and *Invictus.* Spyglass and Cypress/Garoge films have amassed over 34 Oscar nominations, including three wins. Spyglass also co-financed the 2009 blockbusters *Star Trek* and *GI Joe: The Rise of Cobra.*

Under the Plan, Messrs. Barber and Birnbaum will be appointed as co-chairmen and co-chief executive officers of Reorganized Holdings. Reorganized Holdings will enter into identical employment agreements with each of Messrs. Barber and Birnbaum, which will be effective as of the Effective Date and have a 5 year term, subject to the terms and conditions of such agreements. Messrs. Barber and Birnbaum will also be issued options for stock in Reorganized Holdings at a strike price equal to or greater than the value of the stock of Reorganized Holdings at the Effective Date, which options will be subject to vesting.

Messrs. Barber and Birnbaum will be subject to noncompetition and nonsolicitation restrictions while employed by Reorganized Holdings for certain periods following a termination of their respective employment. Messrs. Barber and Birnbaum will also continue to act as directors of Spyglass, and under the terms of the Investment Agreement and their employment agreements, they will be subject to restrictions on the scope of activities they may perform in that capacity. Spyglass will remain a separate entity, subject to restrictions on its activities pursuant to the Investment Agreement, and will receive 0.52% of the New Common Stock in Reorganized Holdings in consideration of the contribution of certain assets under the Investment Agreement. The C/G Stockholders (which include the trusts of Messrs. Barber and Birnbaum) will receive 4.17% of the New Common Stock issued under the Plan in connection with the mergers.

II. SUMMARY OF TREATMENT OF CLAIMS AND INTERESTS UNDER THE PLAN

The table set forth below summarizes the classification and treatment of the prepetition Claims and Interests under the Plan.

The Debtors intend to pursue consummation of the Plan and to cause the Effective Date to occur immediately after all conditions to the Effective Date are satisfied or waived. There can be no assurance, however, as to when or whether the Effective Date will occur. *See* Section VI — "Risk Factors To Be Considered" for a further discussion of certain factors that could delay or prevent the occurrence of the Effective Date.

The Debtors believe that the distributions contemplated by the Plan reflect an appropriate resolution of the Claims, taking into account the differing nature and priority of such Claims.

Description And Amount Of Claims Or Interests	*Summary Of Treatment*
Administrative Claims	On, or as soon as reasonably practicable after, the later of (a) the Effective Date, (b) the date on which an Administrative Claim becomes an Allowed Administrative Claim, or (c) the date on which an Allowed Administrative Claim becomes payable under any agreement relating thereto, each Holder of such Allowed Administrative Claim shall receive, in full and final satisfaction, settlement, release, and discharge of, and in exchange for, such Allowed Administrative Claim, Cash equal to the unpaid portion of such Allowed Administrative Claim. Notwithstanding the foregoing, (y) any Allowed Administrative Claim based on a liability incurred by a Debtor in the ordinary course of business during the Chapter 11 Cases may be paid in the ordinary course of business in accordance with the terms and conditions of any agreement relating thereto and (z) any Allowed Administrative Claim may be paid on such other terms as may be agreed to between the Holder of such Claim and the Debtors or the Reorganized Debtors.
Priority Tax Claims	On, or as soon as reasonably practicable after, the later of (a) the Effective Date or (b) the date on which a Priority Tax Claim becomes an Allowed Priority Tax Claim each Holder of an Allowed Priority Tax Claim shall receive, in full and final satisfaction, settlement, release, and discharge of, and in exchange for, such Allowed Priority Tax Claim, in the sole discretion of the Debtors, (i) Cash equal to the unpaid portion of such Holder's Allowed Priority Tax Claim, (ii) treatment in any other manner such that such Holder's Allowed Priority Tax Claim shall not be impaired pursuant to section 1124 of the Bankruptcy Code, including payment in accordance with the provisions of section 1129(a)(9)(C) of the Bankruptcy Code over a period of not later than five years from the Petition Date, or (iii) such other treatment as to which the Debtors or the Reorganized Debtors and such Holder shall have agreed upon in writing.
Class 1 — Non-Tax Priority Claims	Except to the extent that the Holder of an Allowed Non-Tax Priority Claim has agreed

to a less favorable treatment of such Claim, on, or as soon as reasonably practicable after the latest of (a) the Effective Date, (b) the date on which such Non-Tax Priority Claim becomes an Allowed Non-Tax Priority Claim, (c) the date on which such Allowed Non-Tax Priority Claim is otherwise due and payable and (d) such other date as mutually may be agreed to by and between the Debtors and the Holder of such Non-Tax Priority Claim, each Holder of an Allowed Non-Tax Priority Claim shall receive, in full and final satisfaction, release, and discharge of, and in exchange for, such Allowed Non-Tax Priority Claim, Cash equal to the unpaid portion of such Allowed Non-Tax Priority Claim.

Class 1 is an Unimpaired Class, and the Holders of Allowed Class 1 Non-Tax Priority Claims are conclusively deemed to have accepted the Plan pursuant to section 1 126(f) of the Bankruptcy Code. Therefore, the Holders of Class 1 Non-Tax Priority Claims are not entitled to vote to accept or reject the Plan.

Class 2 — Other Secured Claims

On the Effective Date, or as soon thereafter as is reasonably practicable, each Holder of an Allowed Class 2 Other Secured Claim shall, in the sole discretion of the applicable Debtor, be entitled to the treatment set forth below in option A, B, C, or D. The Debtors and the Reorganized Debtors specifically reserve the right to challenge the validity, nature and perfection of, and to avoid pursuant to the provisions of the Bankruptcy Code and other applicable law, any purported Liens relating to the Other Secured Claims.

Option A: Allowed Other Secured Claims with respect to which the applicable Debtor elects option A shall be Reinstated. The failure of the Debtors to file an objection, prior to the Effective Date, with respect to any Other Secured Claim that is Reinstated hereunder shall be without prejudice to the rights of the Reorganized Debtors to contest or otherwise defend against such Claim in an appropriate forum (including the Bankruptcy Court in accordance with Article X of the Plan) when and if such Claim is sought to be enforced. Any cure amount that the Debtors may be required to pay pursuant to section 1124(2) of the Bank-ruptcy Code on account of any such Reinstated Other Secured Claim shall be paid on, or as soon as practicable after, the latest of (a) the Effective Date, (b) the date on which such Other Secured Claim becomes Allowed, or (c) such other date as mutually may be agreed to by and between such Holder and the Debtors or Reorga-nized Debtors.

Option B: Allowed Other Secured Claims with respect to which the applicable Debtor elects option B shall be paid in Cash, in full, including any amounts owed under section 506 of the Bankruptcy Code, on, or as soon as reasonably practicable after, the latest of (a) the Effective Date, (b) the date on which such Other Secured Claim becomes an Allowed Other Secured Claim, (c) the date on which such Other Secured Claim is otherwise due and payable and (d) such other date as mutually may be agreed to by and between such Holder and the Debtors or Reorganized Debtors.

Option C: Allowed Other Secured Claims with respect to which the applicable Debtor elects option C shall be satisfied by the surrender to the Holder of the Claim of the collateral securing the applicable Other Secured Claim.

Option D: Allowed Other Secured Claims with respect to which the applicable Debtor elects option D shall be satisfied in accor-dance with such other terms and condi-tions as may be agreed upon by the applicable Debtor or Reorganized Debtors and the Holder of such Allowed Other Secured Claim.

The applicable Debtor shall be deemed to have elected option A with respect to all Allowed Other Secured Claims except those with respect to which the applicable Debtor elects another option in writing prior to the Confirmation Hearing.

Class 2 is an Unimpaired Class, and the Holders of Allowed Class 2 Other Secured Claims are conclusively deemed to have accepted the Plan pursuant to section 1 126(f) of the Bankruptcy Code. Therefore, the Holders of Class 2 Other Secured Claims are not entitled to vote to accept or reject the Plan.

Class 3 — Credit Agreement Claims

Each Holder of an Allowed Credit Agreement Claim shall receive, in full and final satisfaction, release, and discharge of, and in exchange for, such Allowed Credit Agreement Claim, its pro rata share of 95.3% of the New Common Stock to be issued and outstanding on the Effective Date, subject to dilution by the Equity Incentive Plan, plus the consideration described in the paragraph immediately below. Distributions on account of Credit Agreement Claims shall be made on the Effective Date to each Holder of an Allowed Credit Agreement Claim in accordance with Section 6.2 of the Plan. As set forth in Section 5.4 of the Plan, the New Common Stock will be subject to the Stockholders Agreement. For the purpose of the Plan all Class 3 Claims shall be deemed Allowed in an amount not less than $4,888,053,018.00 in accordance with the terms of the Credit Agreement and the Loan Documents and shall not be subject to defense, offset, counterclaim or reduction.

With respect to each of the Letters of Credit outstanding on the Effective Date (if any), the Debtors will, at their discretion and in consultation with the Administrative Agent, (i) return such Letter of Credit to the issuing bank undrawn and marked "cancelled," (ii) "roll" such Letters of Credit into the New Credit Facility in a manner and pursuant to documentation reasonably satisfactory to the applicable issuing lenders of such Letters of Credit, or (iii) cash collateralize Claims in respect of their obligations under such Letters of Credit in an amount acceptable to the Administrative Agent that is intended to insure as much as is practicable a recovery on such Claims that is ratable with other Class 3 Claim recoveries. As of the date hereof, there are approximately $78,000 principal amount of letters of credit issued and outstanding under the Credit Agreement.

All fees, costs and expenses of the Administrative Agent as well as reasonable professional fees and expenses for the Administrative Agent and also for the Steering Committee payable shall be paid in full and in cash on the Effective Date or as soon thereafter as is practicable.

	Class 3 is Impaired. Pursuant to section 1126 of the Bankruptcy Code, each Holder of an Allowed Class 3 Credit Agreement Claim is entitled to vote to accept or reject the Plan.
Class 4 — P&A Facility Claims	Holders of Class 4 P&A Facility Claims shall have such Claims Reinstated on the Effective Date.
	Class 4 is an Unimpaired Class, and the Holders of Allowed Class 4 P&A Facility Claims are conclusively deemed to have accepted the Plan pursuant to section 1126(f) of the Bankruptcy Code. Therefore, the Holders of Class 4 P&A Facility Claims are not entitled to vote to accept or reject the Plan.
Class 5 — General Unsecured Claims	On the latest of (a) the Effective Date, (b) the date on which such General Unsecured Claim becomes Allowed, and (c) such other date as mutually may be agreed to by and between the Debtors or Reorganized Debtors and the Holder of such General Unsecured Claim, or, in each case, as soon thereafter as practicable, each Holder of an Allowed General Unsecured Claim in Class 5 shall be paid in Cash the amount of such Allowed General Unsecured Claim, in full and final satisfaction of such Holder's Allowed General Unsecured Claim; *provided, however*, a General Unsecured Claim that is not due and payable on or before the Effective Date shall be paid thereafter (i) in the ordinary course of business in accordance with the terms of any agreement governing, or other documents relating to, such General Unsecured Claim or (ii) in accordance with the course of practice between the Debtors and such Holder with respect to such General Unsecured Claim.
	Class 5 is an Unimpaired Class, and the Holders of Allowed Class 5 General Unsecured Claims are conclusively deemed to have accepted the Plan pursuant to section 1126(f) of the Bankruptcy Code. Therefore, the Holders of Class 5 General Unsecured Claims are not entitled to vote to accept or reject the Plan.
Class 6 — Interests in Subsidiary Debtors	Holders of Allowed Class 6 Interests in Subsidiary Debtors shall have such Interests Reinstated on the Effective Date.
	Class 6 is an Unimpaired Class, and the Holders of Allowed Class 6 Interests are

	conclusively deemed to have accepted the Plan pursuant to section 1126(f) of the Bankruptcy Code. Therefore, the Holders of Class 6 Interests are not entitled to vote to accept or reject the Plan.
Class 7 — Interests in Holdings	All Interests in Holdings shall be cancelled, and each Holder of Allowed Interests in Holdings shall not receive or retain any property on account thereof.
	Holders of Allowed Interests in Holdings are conclusively deemed to have rejected the Plan pursuant to section 1126(g) of the Bankruptcy Code. Therefore, the Holders of Class 7 Interests in Holdings are not entitled to vote to accept or reject the Plan.

THE PLAN IS A SINGLE PLAN OF REORGANIZATION FOR THE JOINTLY ADMINISTERED CHAPTER 11 CASES, BUT DOES NOT CONSTITUTE A SUBSTANTIVE CONSOLIDATION OF THE DEBTORS' ESTATES.

III.   PLAN VOTING INSTRUCTIONS AND PROCEDURES

A.   NOTICE TO HOLDERS OF CLAIMS

This Disclosure Statement will be transmitted to Holders of Claims that are entitled under the Bankruptcy Code to vote on the Plan. Holders of Claims in Class 3 are the only Holders of Claims that are entitled to vote on the Plan. The purpose of this Disclosure Statement is to provide adequate information to enable such Holders to make a reasonably informed decision with respect to the Plan prior to exercising their right to vote to accept or reject the Plan. With the exception of Class 7 Equity Interests in Holdings, all other Classes are Unimpaired under the Plan and the Holders of Claims and Interests in such classes are deemed to have accepted the Plan.

ALL HOLDERS OF CLAIMS IN CLASS 3 ARE ENCOURAGED TO READ THIS DISCLOSURE STATEMENT AND ITS APPENDICES CAREFULLY AND IN THEIR ENTIRETY BEFORE DECIDING TO VOTE TO ACCEPT OR REJECT THE PLAN. This Disclosure Statement contains important information about the Plan and important considerations pertinent to acceptance or rejection of the Plan.

THIS DISCLOSURE STATEMENT, THE PLAN, AND BALLOTS ARE THE ONLY DOCUMENTS TO BE USED IN CONNECTION WITH THE SOLICITATION OF VOTES ON THE PLAN. No person has been authorized to distribute any information concerning the Company relating to the Solicitation other than the information contained herein.

B.   SOLICITATION PACKAGE

In soliciting votes for the Plan pursuant to this Disclosure Statement from the Holders of Claims in Class 3, the Debtors also will send copies of the Plan (attached hereto as *Appendix A*) and one or more Ballots to be used by Holders of Claims in such Class to vote to accept or reject the Plan.

C. VOTING PROCEDURES AND BALLOTS AND VOTING DEADLINE

After carefully reviewing the Plan, this Disclosure Statement, and the detailed instructions accompanying your Ballot, please indicate your acceptance or rejection of the Plan by voting in favor of or against the Plan on the enclosed Ballot. Please complete and sign your Ballot and return your Ballot to Donlin, Recano & Company, Inc. (the *"Voting Agent"*) either by first class mail, or by hand delivery, or overnight courier to the address set forth below, so that it is received by the Voting Deadline.

THE VOTING DEADLINE IS 5:00 P.M. PREVAILING EASTERN TIME ON OCTOBER 22, 2010, UNLESS EXTENDED BY THE DEBTORS.

The Voting Record Date for determining whether a Holder of an Impaired Claim is entitled to vote on the Plan is October 4, 2010.

FOR YOUR VOTE TO BE COUNTED, YOUR BALLOT MUST BE PROPERLY COMPLETED AS SET FORTH ABOVE AND IN ACCORDANCE WITH THE VOTING INSTRUCTIONS ON THE BALLOT AND RECEIVED NO LATER THAN THE VOTING DEADLINE BY THE VOTING AGENT BY FIRST CLASS MAIL, HAND DELIVERY, OR OVERNIGHT COURIER AT THE ADDRESS SET FORTH BELOW.

PROBLEM SET 27.1

1. What was the structure of the original acquisition of MGM? What did the lenders who facilitated that transaction receive in exchange for their loans?
2. What is the structure of the reorganization of MGM? What times of transactions that you have seen before do you recognize in the reorganization?

2. SOLICITATION ISSUES

STEPHEN J. LUBBEN, *THE DIRECT COSTS OF CORPORATE REORGANIZATION: AN EMPIRICAL EXAMINATION OF PROFESSIONAL FEES IN LARGE CHAPTER 11 CASES*

74 Am. Bankr. L.J. 509, 516 (2000)

A true prepack involves a prepetition solicitation of votes on a plan. A partial prepack involves both a prepetition solicitation (e.g., of bondholders) and a postpetition solicitation (e.g., of equity). Partial prepacks are usually done to avoid having to conduct a "registered prepack," which is subject to review and comment by the SEC, and takes substantially longer than a nonregistered prepack. A prearranged or prenegotiated case involves no prepetition solicitation, and thus is little different from a traditional Chapter 11 case, save for the fact that a proposed plan and disclosure statement are fully drafted on the first day of the case.

Which type of prepack is the MGM plan? Why would an equity solicitation require registration with the SEC? The next case provides some further indication of why registered prepacks are often avoided.

IN RE ZENITH ELECTRONICS CORPORATION, A DELAWARE CORPORATION, DEBTOR

241 B.R. 92
United States Bankruptcy Court, D. Delaware
Bankruptcy No. 99-2911 (MFW) | Nov. 2, 1999

Mary F. WALRATH, Bankruptcy Judge.

This case is before the Court on the request of Zenith Electronics Corporation ("Zenith") for approval of its Disclosure Statement and confirmation of its Pre-Packaged Plan of Reorganization filed August 24, 1999 ("the Plan"). The Plan is supported by Zenith's largest shareholder and creditor, LG Electronics, Inc. ("LGE"), and the holders of a majority of the debentures issued by Zenith pre-petition ("the Bondholders").[1] The Plan is opposed by the Official Committee of Equity Security Holders ("the Equity Committee") and numerous shareholders, including Nordhoff Investments, Inc. ("Nordhoff") (collectively, "the Objectors"). For the reasons set forth below, we overrule the objections, approve the Disclosure Statement and will confirm the Plan, if modified in accordance with this Opinion.

I.   FACTUAL BACKGROUND

Zenith has been in business for over 80 years. It was a leader in the design, manufacturing, and marketing of consumer electronics for many years. In recent years it has experienced substantial financial difficulties. It incurred losses in 12 of the last 13 years.

In 1995 Zenith persuaded one of its shareholders, LGE which held approximately 5% of its stock, to invest over $366 million in acquiring a total 57.7% stake in the company. Notwithstanding that investment, and loans and credit support in excess of $340 million provided subsequently by LGE, Zenith's financial condition continued to deteriorate. Zenith suffered net losses in 1996 of $178 million, in 1997 of $299 million and in 1998 of $275 million.

In late 1997, the Asian financial crisis and the continuing losses at Zenith, caused LGE (and Zenith) to question LGE's ability to continue to support

---

1. An ad hoc committee of the Bondholders was formed pre-petition which included Loomis Sayles & Company, L.P., Mariner Investment Group, Inc., and Caspian Capital Partners, L.L.P. ("the Bondholders' Committee").

Zenith and Zenith's need to reorganize. LGE retained McKinsey & Co. ("McKinsey") to evaluate its investment in Zenith and to suggest improvements Zenith could make in its operations and focus. Zenith hired an investment banking firm, Peter J. Solomon Company ("PJSC") in December, 1997, and a new CEO, Jeff Gannon, in January 1998. Under Mr. Gannon, Zenith made substantial operational changes, including a conversion from manufacturer to a marketing and distribution company which outsourced all manufacturing. Zenith's manufacturing facilities were sold or closed in 1998 and 1999. While those operational changes did have some effect on stemming the losses, they were insufficient to eliminate them. Contemporaneously, PJSC evaluated Zenith's assets on a liquidation and going concern basis.

In early 1998, Zenith also attempted to attract a strategic investor or purchaser of part or all of its business or assets. Because of its financial condition, Zenith was advised that it could not raise money through the issuance of more stock or debt instruments. Zenith's strategy was to identify companies which might have an interest and then to have Zenith's CEO approach the target's CEO to discuss the possibilities. Several meetings were conducted with such entities. No offers were received for a sale of substantial assets or business divisions; nor were any offers of equity investments received.

In April 1998, LGE proposed a possible restructuring of its debt and equity in Zenith, contingent on substantial reduction of the bond debt and elimination of the shareholder interests. Zenith appointed a Special Committee of its Board of Directors to evaluate the restructuring proposal and to conduct negotiations on behalf of Zenith. After agreement was reached with the Special Committee, negotiations proceeded with the Bondholders' Committee. Ultimately the restructuring proposal was reduced to a pre-packaged plan of reorganization.

A Disclosure Statement and Proxy Statement-Prospectus for the solicitation of votes on the Plan was prepared and reviewed by the SEC. Discussions with the SEC over the requirements of the Disclosure Statement started in August 1998. On July 15, 1999, after numerous revisions, the SEC declared the Disclosure Statement effective.

On July 20, 1999, Zenith mailed the Plan and Disclosure Statement to the Bondholders and others entitled to vote on the Plan. After voting was completed on August 20, 1999, the Bondholders had voted in favor of the Plan by 98.6% in amount and 97.01% in number of those voting. LGE and Citibank, a secured creditor, had also voted to accept the Plan. Zenith immediately filed its chapter 11 petition on August 24, 1999. At the same time, Zenith filed its Plan and Disclosure Statement and sought prompt approval of both. A combined Disclosure Statement and confirmation hearing was scheduled for September 27 and 28, 1999.

An ad hoc committee of minority shareholders sought a postponement of the confirmation hearing, which was denied. We did, however, grant its motion for appointment of an official committee of equity holders, over the objection of Zenith, LGE and the Bondholders' Committee. We did so to give the equity holders an opportunity to conduct discovery and present their arguments against confirmation of the Plan.

The combined Disclosure Statement and confirmation hearing was held on September 27 and 28, 1999. Post trial briefs were filed by the parties on October 4, 1999.

II. DISCUSSION

As an initial matter, the Equity Committee objects to the adequacy of the Disclosure Statement, asserting that it failed to advise those voting on the Plan of numerous "essential facts" including (1) that LGE had hired PJSC, thus tainting the valuation of Zenith done by PJSC, (2) that different entities had done different analyses of the value of Zenith, including McKinsey, and (3) that alternatives to the Plan had been analyzed but the results not revealed. Zenith, LGE and the Bondholders' Committee all dispute the Equity Committee's contentions.

A. APPROVAL OF THE DISCLOSURE STATEMENT

Typically, under chapter 11 of the Bankruptcy Code, the court approves the debtor's disclosure statement before it, and the plan of reorganization, are sent to creditors and others entitled to vote on the plan. Section 1125(b) provides:

> (b) An acceptance or rejection of a plan may not be solicited after the commencement of the case under this title from a holder of a claim or interest with respect to such claim or interest, unless, at the time of or before such solicitation, there is transmitted to such holder the plan or a summary of the plan, and a written disclosure statement approved, after notice and a hearing, by the court as containing adequate information.

11 U.S.C. §1125(b). *See also*, Fed. R. Bankr.P. 3017 & 3018.

However, Congress recognized the validity of votes solicited pre-bankruptcy (a practice which had developed under chapter X of the Bankruptcy Act). Section 1126(b) provides:

> (b) For the purposes of subsections (c) and (d) of this section, a holder of a claim or interest that has accepted or rejected the plan before the commencement of the case under this title is deemed to have accepted or rejected such plan, as the case may be, if —
> (1) the solicitation of such acceptance or rejection was in compliance with any applicable nonbankruptcy law, rule, or regulation governing the adequacy of disclosure in connection with such solicitation; or
> (2) if there is not any such law, rule, or regulation, such acceptance or rejection was solicited after disclosure to such holder of adequate information, as defined in section 1125(a) of this title.

11 U.S.C. §1126(b).

Zenith asserts that the Disclosure Statement meets both criteria. We agree.

1. Standing

Zenith asserts as a threshold issue that the Equity Committee does not have standing to object to the Disclosure Statement. Under the Plan, equity holders are receiving nothing. Therefore, the equity holders are conclusively presumed to have rejected the Plan and do not have the right to vote. 11 U.S.C. §1126(g).

Since the Disclosure Statement need only contain adequate information for those entitled to vote, some courts have concluded that non-voting classes have no standing to be heard on the issue.

However, the Equity Committee, as an official committee in this case, does have standing to appear and be heard on any issue in the case. 11 U.S.C. §1109(b). Thus, we conclude that it has standing to object to the Disclosure Statement.

2. Approval by the SEC

Zenith asserts that the adequacy of its Disclosure Statement is governed by section 1126(b), not section 1125. *See, e.g.,* In re The Southland Corp., 124 B.R. 211, 223 (Bankr.N.D.Tex.1991) (where votes are solicited pre-petition, section 1126(b) applies unless there is no applicable nonbankruptcy law dealing with the adequacy of disclosure issue).

In this case, the SEC was required to approve the Disclosure Statement because the Plan provides for the issuance of new securities to the Bondholders. The SEC did approve the Disclosure Statement on July 15, 1999, as containing adequate information (after 11 months of discussions and numerous amendments).

We conclude that the Disclosure Statement, having been approved by the SEC as containing adequate information, complies with the provisions of section 1126(b)(1).

3. Adequacy of Information

Even if it did not fit the provisions of section 1126(b)(1), the Disclosure Statement does contain sufficient information to comply with section 1126(b)(2) and 1125(a). The Disclosure Statement is almost 400 pages. It contains numerous financial statements and historical information about Zenith. It has lengthy descriptions of Zenith's efforts to restructure its operations and finances and alternatives to the proposed Plan. It describes LGE's relationship to Zenith. It provides valuation information and a liquidation analysis.

Further, Zenith is a public company. Consequently, substantial information about its finances and operations is publicly available. It files periodic statements with the SEC, and media attention to its plight has been intense.

In considering the adequacy of a disclosure statement, it is important to keep in mind the audience. Here, those entitled to vote on the Plan are sophisticated, institutional investors. They have competent professionals assisting them in analyzing and testing the information provided by Zenith. They have also been involved in negotiations with Zenith and LGE for over a year before voting on the Plan. Significant documents and information (in addition to the Disclosure Statement) were made available to the Bondholders' Committee and its professionals during that time.

Finally, there is no suggestion that the Disclosure Statement contains false information — only that certain additional information was not included. What the Equity Committee asserts is missing, however, is not uncontested, concrete facts, but rather the Equity Committee's interpretation of those facts or duplicative information. We do not believe that such "information" must be included in the Disclosure Statement.

Given the sophistication of the parties, the wealth of information contained in the Disclosure Statement and publicly available elsewhere, the approval by the SEC and the lack of objection by any party entitled to vote on the Plan, we readily conclude that the Disclosure Statement contains adequate information and the votes solicited by it are valid. The Disclosure Statement will be approved, pursuant to section 1126(b) and/or 1125(a).

. . .

III. Conclusion

For all the foregoing reasons, we conclude that the objections of the Equity Committee and Nordhoff to approval of the Disclosure Statement should be overruled. We further conclude that the Plan satisfies the requirements of sections 1123 and 1129 of the Bankruptcy Code and may be confirmed if modified in accordance with the comments . . . above. An appropriate Order is attached.

When soliciting votes on a prepacked plan, who you solicit matters. Sometimes you need to find them. For example, during the PennCentral bankruptcy in the 1970s, the bankruptcy attorneys had to find a large group of European bondholders. But the bonds were bearer bonds, so there was no record of who the current owners were. Newspaper advertisements were used to try to reach as many of the bondholders as possible.

In the United States, the complex ownership structure we discussed in Chapter 12 rears its head again in this context.

IN RE PIONEER FINANCE CORP., A NEVADA CORPORATION, DEBTOR IN RE PIONEER HOTEL, INC., A NEVADA CORPORATION, DEBTOR

246 B.R. 626
United States Bankruptcy Court, D. Nevada
Bankruptcy Nos. BK-S-99-11404-LBR, BK-S-99-12854-LBR | Jan. 21, 2000

Linda B. Riegle, Bankruptcy Judge.

A Chapter 11 debtor seeks confirmation of a proposed plan of reorganization pursuant to a prepetition offering made to record bondholders. In conjunction with its motion, the debtor seeks a determination that its offering qualifies as a valid prepetition solicitation under 11 U.S.C. §1126(b), and a finding that the consents of the record bondholders to the offering are binding obligations to support and vote for its proposed plan. The prepetition offering was in the form of a combined exchange offer and consent solicitation. The offering proposed to exchange new bonds for old bonds or, in the alternative, sought consent of the bondholders to (among other things) vote in favor of a plan of reorganization that complied with the terms of the offering. The offering was sent only to the record holders of the bonds. It was not sent to the beneficial holders.

The Court holds that under the wording of the offering, the bondholders consented only to agree to vote on a plan in the *future*, they did not vote on a present plan. The consents obtained are thus not sufficient to constitute acceptances of the plan which is now proposed. The Court further holds that for the purposes of confirmation of a plan under the Bankruptcy Code, there is insufficient notice and authority to constitute valid acceptances where, as here, a prepetition solicitation was sent only to record bondholders, but not to the beneficial bondholders, and no showing has been made that the record holders had the authority to vote on behalf of the beneficial holders.

FACTUAL SUMMARY

Pioneer Finance Corp. is a debtor-in-possession in the jointly administered Chapter 11 cases of Pioneer Finance Corp. ("PFC") and Pioneer Hotel Inc. ("PHI") (collectively the "Debtors").

PFC is a single purpose entity created to finance Santa Fe Gaming Corp.'s acquisition of the Pioneer Hotel, which is located in Laughlin, Nevada. PFC's sole asset is a Note and Deed of Trust on the assets of PHI. On December 1, 1988, PFC issued $120 million in "13.5% First Mortgage Bonds due December 1, 1998" (the "1988 Bonds"). PFC is the obligor on the 1988 Bonds. Santa Fe Gaming Corp. ("SFGC"), the parent of PHI and PFC, is the guarantor of PFC's obligations on the 1988 Bonds.

The 1988 Bonds were issued in accordance with an Indenture by and between PFC as issuer, Sahara Casino Partners, L.P. (predecessor-in-interest to SFGC) as guarantor, and Security Pacific National Bank, predecessor to IBJ Whitehall Bank & Trust Company ("IBJ") as indenture trustee (the "Indenture Trustee").

The 1988 Bonds and the PHI Note and Deed of Trust matured and came due on December 1, 1998. On that date, PHI did not make the principal and interest payments due at maturity of the PHI Note and Deed of Trust. In addition, PFC defaulted on its obligations on the 1988 Bonds and SFGC defaulted on its obligations on the guaranty.

THE OFFERING

Prior to the defaults which occurred on December 1, 1998, SFGC, PHI and PFC began negotiating with Foothill Capital Corp. ("Foothill") to restructure the bond obligation. Foothill then held approximately 26.50% of the face amounts of the outstanding 1988 Bonds.

After the negotiations, PFC issued an "Offer To Exchange All Outstanding $13\frac{1}{2}$% First Mortgage Bonds Due December 1, 1998 ($60,000,000 Principal Amount Outstanding) For $13\frac{1}{2}$% First Mortgage Notes Due 2006 and Consent Solicitation Statement" ("Exchange Offer and Consent Solicitation").

The Exchange Offer and Consent Solicitation was dated October 23, 1998. It was supplemented by an "Amended Offer To Exchange" which was dated November 14, 1998. (Both are collectively referred to as the "Offering").

The Offering proposed two alternatives. On the one hand it proposed to exchange the 1988 Bonds for new bonds with a later maturity date secured by a pledge of certain assets by the guarantor if 100% of the bondholders agreed and tendered their 1988 Bonds to PFC (the "Exchange Offer").

Alternatively, if less than 100% of bondholders agreed, PFC simultaneously sought the consent ("Consents") of holders of no less than $42,000,000 principal amount of the 1988 Bonds to, among other things: (1) forbear until December 15, 2000 against exercising any rights against PFC or SFGC in the event of PFC's default on the 1988 Bonds; (2) forbear until December 15, 2000 against exercising any rights in the event of PHI's default on the PHI Note; (3) "consent to and support a plan of reorganization" under Chapter 11 of the Bankruptcy Code which substantially complied with the Offering ("Consent Solicitation"). If the requisite consents were received, the Debtors agreed to repurchase from the Consenting Bondholders up to $6.5 million principal amount of the 1988 Bonds together with accrued interest. Upon receipt of the Consents, SFGC would pledge the common stock of certain of its affiliates for its guaranty.

The Offering was mailed to the registered holders of the 1988 Bonds ("Record Holders") utilizing the lists maintained by IBJ, who served as the exchange and solicitation agent for the Offering. IBJ maintained a list of Record Holders in its capacity as the Indenture Trustee. An information agent, D.F. King & Co., was hired to facilitate the dissemination of the Offering. The Debtors acknowledge that the Offering was transmitted "to the only parties known to them, the record owners of the 1998 Bonds." Each Record Holder was also mailed, among other documents, a form upon which to register its consent to the Offering ("Consent Form").

The Offering expired on November 24, 1998. Less than 100% of the bondholders agreed to the Exchange Offer alternative. Holders of $45,816,750 in principal amount of 1988 Bonds (approximately 76.4% of the outstanding bonds), however, did agree to the Consent Solicitation ("Consenting Bondholders"). Upon this acceptance, Consenting Bondholders received payments on account of the repurchase and SFGC caused the pledge of the assets.

PFC filed its Chapter 11 petition on February 23, 1999. PHI filed a Chapter 11 petition on April 12, 1999. PFC and PHI filed their first joint disclosure statement and their first plan on April 12, 1999. They filed a revised disclosure statement on June 4, 1999, which was approved on August 30, 1999. The Debtors filed their proposed "Second Amended Plan of Reorganization" in conjunction with the instant "Motion To Approve Prepetition Solicitation" ("Motion to Approve") on August 13, 1999.

In support of their revised disclosure statement, the Debtors at first argued that the Consent Solicitation was a pre-negotiated plan, not a pre-packaged plan. They argued that the Consent Solicitation did not have to comply with the notice provisions of the Bankruptcy Code because it was not a prepetition plan solicitation.

Now, in support of their Motion to Approve, the Debtors argue that the Consent Solicitation *does* qualify as a prepetition solicitation under §1126(b) and Bankruptcy Rule 3018(b), and that the Consents are votes in favor of the Second Amended Plan. They further contend that the disclosure requirements of §1125(a) do not apply because, under §1126(b)(1), they have complied with applicable nonbankruptcy law governing the adequacy of disclosure.

LEGAL ANALYSIS

PREPACKAGED REORGANIZATIONS

In a conventional Chapter 11 case, the debtor files a bankruptcy petition, then negotiates a reorganization plan and solicits votes after a disclosure statement has been approved.

With a "prepackaged" plan, however, which is authorized under 11 U.S.C. §1126(b), a plan proponent has negotiated a plan and solicited votes prior to the filing of a Chapter 11 petition and before there is a hearing to determine the adequacy of the disclosure. With prepackaged plans, the adequacy of the disclosure is evaluated under "applicable nonbankruptcy law, rule or regulation" or, if there is none, under the "adequate information" standard set forth in §1125(a)(1). In a "prenegotiated" plan, the details of a plan are negotiated prior to the filing of the petition. Solicitation, however, does not occur until after the filing.

Regardless of whether a plan is prepackaged or "prenegotiated," it must comply with the provisions of the Bankruptcy Code.

11 U.S.C. §1126 governs the acceptance and rejection of Chapter 11 reorganization plans, whether acceptance occurs before or after the commencement of the case. The adequacy of the Debtors' prepetition solicitation process is thus measured by this section, particularly §1126(b), which concerns acceptance of a plan before the commencement of case, and §1126(c), which defines "acceptance" of a plan.

ADEQUACY OF THE DEBTORS' SOLICITATION PROCESS

A.   The Consents Do Not Constitute Acceptance of the Second Amended Plan

Pursuant to 11 U.S.C. §1126(a) the "holder of a claim or interest" is entitled to accept or reject a plan. 11 U.S.C. §1126(c) states that "acceptance" occurs when "such plan has been accepted by creditors . . . that hold at least two-thirds in amount and more than one-half in number of the allowed claims. . . ." Under §1126(b), the holder of a claim or interest that has accepted or rejected "the plan" prepetition is deemed to have done so if the solicitation was in compliance with any applicable nonbankruptcy law or, if there is no such law, there was disclosure of "adequate information" under §1125(a).

In the instant case there has been no acceptance of "the plan" under §1126(b). Instead, under the language of the relevant documents, there has merely been an agreement to consent to some plan *in the future*. The Consenting Bondholders merely *agreed* to *agree* on a plan.

THE CONSENT FORM

Under the language of the Consent Form, a Consenting Bondholder merely *agreed* to *agree* on a future plan. The Consent Form stated the following, in pertinent part:

Part II — Consents
(To be completed by Holders who wish to consent to the Proposed Consents)

The undersigned is a Holder . . . of the [1988 Bonds]. As a Holder of such [1988 Bonds], *the undersigned hereby:*
Consents Does Not Consent
to the following in the event the Exchange Offer is not consummated (the "Proposed Consents"):

— — — — —

3. *To consent to and support a plan of reorganization under Chapter 11 of the United States Bankruptcy Code* which provides for treatment of the [1988 Bonds] in a bankruptcy case under Chapter 11 of the Bankruptcy Code that is substantially similar to the treatment of the [1988 Bonds] offered in the Exchange (the "Plan"). Such support shall include, without limitation, (i) voting to accept the Plan and making reasonable efforts to obtain confirmation of the Plan, even if the Plan involves a "cramdown" under Section 1129(b) of the Bankruptcy Code of classes of claims or equity interests other than the class that includes the [1988 Bonds], (ii) not agreeing to, consenting to or voting for any plan that contains terms inconsistent with the Plan and (iii) not objecting to or otherwise commencing any proceeding to oppose or alter the Plan or making any action that is inconsistent with, or that would delay solicitation, confirmation, effectiveness or substantial consummation of the Plan.

(Emphasis added).

THE EXCHANGE OFFER AND CONSENT SOLICITATION

The language of the Exchange Offer and Consent Solicitation also shows that the Consenting Bondholders merely *agreed* to *agree* on a future plan. That document states the following, at page 25:

> Concurrently with the Exchange Offer, [PFC] is seeking the Consents so that if the Minimum Condition or any other condition to the Exchange Offer is not satisfied and the Exchange Offer is not consummated, [PFC] will have the Consents of certain holders of [1988 Bonds] pursuant to which, among other things, the consenting Holders *agree to . . . vote to accept a plan of reorganization which provides for treatment of the [1988 Bonds] in a bankruptcy case under Chapter 11 of the Bankruptcy Code that is substantially similar to the treatment of the [1988 Bonds] offered in the Exchange (the "Plan").*

(Emphasis added).

THE AMENDED OFFER TO EXCHANGE

Similarly, the wording of the Amended Offer To Exchange is such that a Consenting Bondholder merely *agreed* to *agree* on a plan, and agreed to vote to accept *some plan in the future*. The Amended Offer To Exchange states the following, at page 11:

> *[PFC] is soliciting the consents* (the "Consents") of the Holders to the following (the "Proposed Consents"), which will be effective only if the Exchange Offer is not

consummated and valid consents are properly furnished by the Solicitation Expiration Date with respect to at least $42 million principal amount of [1988 Bonds]:

— — — — —

To consent to and support a plan of reorganization under Chapter 11 of the Bankruptcy Code which provides for treatment of the [1988 Bonds] in a bankruptcy case under Chapter 11 of the Bankruptcy Code that is substantially similar to the treatment of the [1988 Bonds] offered in the Exchange; provided that (1) the additional Event of Default described under "Modifications to the Exchange Offer and Terms of the New Notes to be Issued in the Exchange Offer" will occur if the events contemplated by paragraphs (a) or (b) thereof have not occurred by the later of December 31, 1999 or six months after the date of a plan of reorganization is confirmed in a Chapter 11 case and (2) the Excess Cash Redemption obligation will commence on the first June 30 or December 31 following the date on which a plan of reorganization is confirmed (the "Plan"). Such support shall include, without limitation, (i) voting to accept the Plan and making reasonable efforts to obtain confirmation of the Plan, even if the Plan involves a "cramdown" under Section 1129(b) of the Bankruptcy Code of classes of claims, including the class that includes the [1988 Bonds] or equity interests, (ii) not agreeing to, consenting to, recommending or voting for any plan that contains terms inconsistent with the Plan, and (iii) not objecting to or otherwise commencing any proceeding to oppose or alter the Plan or taking any action that is inconsistent with, or that would delay solicitation, confirmation, effectiveness or substantial consummation of the Plan. . . .

(Emphasis added).

While it may be argued that the terms of the proposed Second Amended Plan substantially conform to the Offering, the Offering sought only the consent of Record Holders to a *future plan*. The Consents do not constitute acceptance of "the plan" under §1126(b). Indeed, the Debtors themselves have acknowledged that they did not present a plan or disclosure statement to the 1988 bondholders prepetition, and that "1988 Bondholders were not asked to vote on a specific plan, only to agree to support and vote for a plan embodying the Consent Solicitation."

Even if the Consents were to a present plan, however, the Offering is inadequate because it was sent only to the Record Holders.

B. Disclosure To Record Holders v. Beneficial Holders

The Bankruptcy Code requires that a creditor receive adequate notice before its claim is impacted. In this regard, a prepetition solicitation process must be scrutinized to ensure that substantially all creditors who are affected by the plan receive notice. In this case, the Offering was sent only to the Record Holders. The Record Holders, however, may or may not be the "holder of the claim" which is based upon the 1988 Bonds.

Pursuant to §1126(a), it is only the "holder of a claim or interest" who is entitled to vote on a plan. Under the Code, a holder of a "claim" is one who has a "right to payment." 11 U.S.C. §101(5)(A). Plainly, it is the beneficial holder, not a holder of record, who has the "claim" and the "right to payment."

Although Fed.R.Bankr.P. 3018 makes reference to the acceptance of a plan by a "holder of record," such language is at odds with §1126, which provides that it is the "holder of a claim or interest" who may accept or reject a plan. Nowhere does §1126(b) refer to "record holders." Where a bankruptcy rule affects a substantive change in the Code, the Code must prevail. *See also*, In re Southland Corp., 124 B.R. 211 (Bankr.N.D.Tex.1991) (Bankruptcy Rule 3018 references to "holder of record" as entity who may accept or reject plan is attempted substantive change in Bankruptcy Code, and does not prevail over identification of "holder of claim" as entity who may accept plan under §1126(b)).

Rule 3018(c) ("Form of Acceptance or Rejection") provides that an acceptance or rejection of a Chapter 11 plan may be made by an "authorized agent." Such authority, however, must be established. Here, there has been no showing that the Beneficial Holders authorized the Record Holders to accept the Consent Solicitation.

In In re Southland Corp., 124 B.R. 211 (Bankr.N.D.Tex.1991) the debtor, relying on Fed.R.Bankr.P. 3018, solicited only the record holders of claims by mailing the solicitation materials to broker dealers, who held the securities in street name. The court required that the votes be re-solicited using procedures designed to identify and obtain the vote of the beneficial holders, because there was no evidence of the authority of the record holders to vote on the plan. The court held that if votes were cast by broker-dealers or other representatives, there had to be certification of the representative's authority to vote. *Id.* at 227. As the *Southland* court stated:

> If the record holder of a debt is not the owner of a claim, or a true creditor, he may not vote validly to accept or reject, unless he is an authorized agent of the creditor, and this authority is established under appropriate bankruptcy law and rules.

Southland, 124 B.R. 211, 227 (Bankr.N.D.Tex.1991).

It is true that Section 308 of the Indenture states that the person in whose name the 1988 Bond is registered is treated as the "owner" for all purposes, and that §101 of the Indenture defines "bondholder" and "holder" as "a person in whose name a bond is registered on the bond register." The Indenture, however, does not control who has the authority to vote for a plan of reorganization under the Bankruptcy Code. While record holders may vote on behalf of beneficial holders outside of bankruptcy under the federal securities laws, under §1126 of the Bankruptcy Code it is the "holder of a claim or interest" who is entitled to receive a plan solicitation package and to vote. Having made the decision to file bankruptcy in order to restructure a debt which could not otherwise be contractually restructured outside bankruptcy, the Debtors must comply with the provisions of the Bankruptcy Code. There is simply no indication in the Bankruptcy Code or Rules that the notice required during a Chapter 11 solicitation process is superceded by federal securities law practices.

Although record holders may vote shares pursuant to the instructions of the beneficial owners under the securities laws, that process is designed to facilitate the rapid trading and marketability of securities. The Bankruptcy Code, however, concerns itself with providing full disclosure to creditors so that those creditors can cast their ballots intelligently. The Bankruptcy Code and the federal securities laws are simply different sets of laws with different purposes. There is no suggestion in Rule 3017(e) or the Committee Notes that practices developed under the federal securities laws have binding application to the chapter 11 voting process.

Moreover, Fed.R.Bankr.P. 3017(e) requires that the beneficial holders of bonds, not merely the record holders, must receive the disclosure statement, plan and ballot.

Thus, a pre-petition solicitation process is invalid where there is no evidence that the solicitation has been sent to beneficial bondholders, and no showing has been made that record holders have been authorized by beneficial holders to vote on their behalf.

The Debtors argue that outside bankruptcy, brokers cannot disclose the names of their customers to third parties, citing SEC Rule 14b-1(c) and 17 CFR §240.14(b)-1(c). The Court appreciates that there might be obligations outside bankruptcy to keep the identities of beneficial holders confidential. In a bankruptcy proceeding, however, Fed. R. Bankr.3017(e) provides a bankruptcy court wide latitude to fashion procedures to protect the confidentiality of the beneficial bondholders. Rule 3017(e) empowers a bankruptcy court to "determine the adequacy of the procedures" for transmitting disclosure to beneficial holders and to "enter any orders the court deems appropriate." While such procedures will most likely vary according to the specific facts of a case, they might include requiring affidavits from record holders who attest that a solicitation was transmitted to the beneficial holders. Alternatively, a consent form could contain a place where a beneficial bondholder could indicate that he or she has seen the solicitation and either does or does not authorize the record holder to vote in its behalf.

Given the Court's holding that there has not been an acceptance of a plan as provided for under §1126(b), the Court need not reach the Debtors' argument that §1125(a) does not have to be satisfied because the debtors have complied with "applicable nonbankruptcy law" governing disclosure.

For the reasons set forth above, the motion is hereby denied.

It is often difficult to identify the beneficial holders of publicly held debt. As such, firms soliciting votes from beneficial holders must do so through the cooperation of the record holders, which will then pass the solicitation information down the chain to the beneficial holders and seek instructions on how to vote. The information must then be passed back up the chain to the debtor firm. The entire process must be documented and presented to the bankruptcy court to enable a finding that votes were properly solicited from the beneficial holders.

3. TAX ISSUES

Knowing you are already expert in the issue of tax and debt, here is the relevant tax discussion from the MGM disclosure statement:

A. Certain U.S. Federal Income Tax Consequences to the Debtors

1. Cancellation Of Indebtedness Income

In general, the discharge of a debt obligation in exchange for cash and other property having a fair market value (or, in the case of a new debt instrument, an "issue price") less than the "adjusted issue price" of the debt gives rise to cancellation of indebtedness ("*COD*") income to the debtor. However, COD income is not taxable to the debtor if the debt discharge occurs in a Title 11 bankruptcy case. Rather, under the Tax Code, such COD income instead will reduce certain of the Debtors' tax attributes, generally in the following order: (a) net operating losses ("*NOLs*") and NOL carryforwards; (b) general business credit carryforwards; (c) minimum tax credit carryforwards; (d) capital loss carry-forwards; (e) the tax basis of the Debtors' depreciable and nondepreciable assets (but not below the amount of its liabilities immediately after the discharge); and (f) foreign tax credit carryforwards. A debtor may elect to alter the preceding order of attribute reduction and, instead, first reduce the tax basis of its depreciable assets (and, possibly, the depreciable assets of its subsidiaries). Where the debtor joins in the filing of a consolidated U.S. federal income tax return, applicable Treasury Regulations require, in certain circumstances, that certain tax attributes of the consolidated subsidiaries of the debtor and other members of the group be reduced. The reduction in tax attributes occurs only after the tax for the year of the debt discharge has been determined (i.e., such attributes may be available to offset taxable income that accrues between the date of discharge and the end of the Debtors' tax year). Any excess COD income over the amount of available tax attributes is not subject to United States federal income tax and has no other United States federal income tax impact.

The Debtors expect to realize a substantial amount of COD income as a result of the discharge of obligations pursuant to the Plan, which, under the attribute reduction rules described above, is expected to result in the substantial reduction of the Debtors' NOLs, and of certain other U.S. federal income tax attributes of the Debtors, including basis in the assets (the "*Attribute Reduction*").

2. Net Operating Losses — Section 382

In 2005, the Debtors experienced an "ownership change" (within the meaning of Section 382 of the Tax Code) (the "*Ownership Change*") as a result of which the Debtors' ability to use any pre-Ownership Change NOLs and certain other tax attributes is subject to an annual limitation. The Debtors anticipate that they will experience a second "ownership change" on the Effective Date as a result of the issuance of the New Common Stock to the Holders of Claims, Spyglass, and the C/G Stockholders pursuant to the Plan. As a result, the Debtors' ability to use any pre-Effective Date NOLs or other tax attributes to offset their income in any post-Effective Date taxable year (and in the portion of the taxable year of the ownership change following the Effective Date) to which such a carryforward is made generally (subject to various exceptions and adjustments, some of which are described below) will be subject to a second annual limitation. Subject to the discussion below, the annual limitation under Section 382 of the Tax Code is generally equal to the product of (i) the "long-term tax exempt" (for example, 3.98% for ownership changes occurring during the month of October 2010) and (ii) the fair market value of the stock of the corporation immediately before the ownership change occurs. Under section 382 of the Tax Code, NOLs attributable to a period preceding an earlier ownership change are treated as pre-change losses with respect to later ownership changes with the result that such NOLs always will be subject to the smaller of the earlier annual limitation and any later annual limitations. Thus, the second ownership change may cause pre-Ownership Change NOLs which survive the Attribute Reduction, if any, to be more significantly limited than they currently are and will subject the use of NOLs generated following the earlier ownership change which survive Attribute Reduction, if any, to an annual limit. Section 382 of the Tax Code may also limit the Debtors' ability to use "net unrealized built-in losses" to offset future taxable income. Moreover, the Debtors' loss carryforwards will be subject to further limitations if the Debtors experience additional future ownership changes and could potentially be reduced to zero if they do not continue their business enterprise for at least two years following the Effective Date.

If the Debtors are qualified to use the special rules for corporations in bankruptcy provided in section 382(1)(5) of the Tax Code, and do not elect out of that provision, then, to the extent that the Debtors have post-Ownership Change NOLs that survive the Attribute Reduction, the application of section 382 of the Tax Code will be materially different from that just described. In that case, the Debtors' ability to utilize post-Ownership Change NOLs generated prior to the Effective Date would not be limited as described in the preceding paragraph. However, several other limitations would apply to the Debtors under section 382(1)(5) of the Tax Code, including (a) the Debtors' NOLs would be calculated without taking into account deductions for interest paid or accrued in the portion of the current tax year ending on the Effective Date and all other tax years ending during the three-year period prior to the current tax year with respect to the Claims that are exchanged for New Common Stock pursuant to the Plan, and (b) if the Debtors undergo another ownership change within two years after the Effective Date, the Debtors' section 382 limitation with respect to that ownership change will be zero. Even if section 382(1)(5) of the Tax Code is available, the Debtors could elect not to apply the special rules of section 382(1)(5).

If the Debtors do not qualify for, or elect not to apply, the special rule under section 382(1)(5) of the Tax Code for corporations in bankruptcy described above, then, to the extent that the Debtors have post-Ownership Change NOLs that survive the Attribute Reduction, a different rule under section 382(1)(6) of the Tax Code applicable to corporations under the jurisdiction of a bankruptcy court may apply in calculating the annual section 382 limitation applicable to post-Ownership Change NOLs generated prior to the Effective Date. Under this rule, the limitation will be calculated by reference to the lesser of the value of the company's new stock (with certain adjustments) immediately after the ownership change or the value of such company's assets (determined without regard to liabilities) immediately before the ownership change. Although such calculation may substantially increase the annual section 382 limitation, the Debtors' use of NOLs or other tax attributes remaining after implementation of the Plan, if any, may still be substantially limited after an ownership change.

Because Holders of Class 3 Claims will hold a significant equity position in Reorganized Holdings following the consummation of the Plan, disposition by such persons or entities of all or a significant amount of this position after the Effective Date, could cause the Reorganized Debtors to undergo a subsequent ownership change. This would generally further limit (or possibly eliminate) the Reorganized Debtors' ability to use NOLs and other tax attributes.

In the prior chapter it was indicated that reorganization under the Bankruptcy Code was generally preferable to an exchange offer from a tax standpoint. Why then does MGM's discussion appear so gloomy?

4. VENUE ISSUES

Very large chapter 11 cases tend to file in either the Southern District of New York or Delaware. Under current law, debtors can file in one of three places: (a) their state of incorporation, (b) their principal place of business, or (c) a district where a related bankruptcy case is already pending.

The first one helps Delaware attract cases, the second helps the SDNY, since many businesses can argue that they have a key corporate office in New York City, and the third helps corporate groups file in either New York or Delaware, as one company in the group is apt to qualify under either the first or second test. While in practice, your author more than once filed the bankruptcy petition for an obscure subsidiary, only to then hand over the "related" petition of a Fortune 500 parent company.

Because Delaware and New York are obvious locales for so many large chapter 11 cases, the judges have lots of corporate restructuring experience. This in turn brings yet more large chapter 11 cases, from bankruptcy attorneys who appreciate having a judge who "gets it."

Prepackaged chapter 11 cases are especially likely to file in one of these two jurisdictions, because having a judge who "gets it" is important to realizing the benefits of a prepackaged case. But it is generally indisputable that prepackaged cases have a much higher refiling rate than other, more traditional types of chapter 11 cases. That is, a debtor reorganized under a prepackaged case is apt to need to go through a traditional chapter 11 case nonetheless.

Not everyone thinks this forum shopping is ideal. Most notably, UCLA law professor Lynn LoPucki, often with various coauthors, has argued in a controversial book and several articles that this represents "corruption" of the bankruptcy system.[2] And he argues that cases that file in New York or Delaware more often "fail" — his word for refiling — because of these jurisdictions' desire to appease large New York law firms that bring interesting cases to their courts. That is, the courts go easy on debtors, leading to a higher refiling rate.

But not everyone agrees with professor LoPucki's characterization of the issue.[3] Nonetheless, there are some indications that the United States Trustee's Office, part of the Justice Department that monitors bankruptcy cases, is sensitive to suggestions that prepackaged cases, in particular, engage in forum shopping.

---

2. *E.g.*, Lynn M. LoPucki, *Courting Failure: How Competition for Big Cases Is Corrupting the Bankruptcy Courts* (2005); Lynn M. LoPucki & Joseph W. Doherty, *Delaware Bankruptcy: Failure in the Ascendancy*, 73 U. Chi. L. Rev. 1387, 1418-1419 (2006); Lynn M. LoPucki & Sarah D. Kalin, *The Failure of Public Company Bankruptcies in Delaware and New York: Empirical Evidence of a "Race to the Bottom,"* 54 Vand. L. Rev. 231, 271 (2001).

3. Melissa B. Jacoby, *Fast, Cheap, and Creditor-Controlled: Is Corporate Reorganization Failing?*, 54 Buff. L. Rev. 401 (2006); Stephen J. Lubben, *Delaware's Irrelevance*, 16 Am. Bankr. Inst. L. Rev. 267 (2008); Todd J. Zywicki, *Is Forum Shopping Corrupting America's Bankruptcy Courts?*, 94 Geo. L.J. 1141 (2006).

IN RE HOUGHTON MIFFLIN HARCOURT PUBLISHING
COMPANY, ET AL., DEBTORS

474 B.R. 122
United States Bankruptcy Court, S.D. New York
No. 12–12171 REG | June 22, 2012

Robert E. GERBER, Bankruptcy Judge.

In this contested matter in the jointly administered chapter 11 cases of debtor Houghton Mifflin Harcourt Publishing Company ("**Publishing**") and 24 affiliates, who filed these cases with a prepackaged plan of reorganization that secured the unanimous support of their creditors, the United States Trustee Program ("**UST**") moves, pursuant to 28 U.S.C. §1406 and Fed.R.Bankr.P. 1014(a)(2), to transfer the venue of these cases elsewhere.

The UST, over the objection of the Debtors and all of the creditors who have weighed in on the matter, contends that venue in this district never was proper, for failure to satisfy the requirements of the relevant statute, 28 U.S.C. §1408. Under these circumstances, the UST contends, dismissal or transfer is mandatory under §1406. The UST further contends that the fact that a transfer would be much more expensive and much less convenient for the Debtors' creditors — especially since we here have a prepack, where the case otherwise would be over in 30 days — does not matter.

For the latter reason, the UST's prosecution of this motion has been perplexing to the Court — not because it is in any way improper, but as a matter of prosecutorial discretion, since venue concerns can be waived, by creditors and the UST alike, and here any venue deficiencies were not a matter of concern to the Debtors' creditors. Venue objections of course should be raised, by the UST and creditors alike, when a debtor's venue choice is prejudicial to the creditor community. But here the venue choice was exactly what the creditors wanted; the case, if not slowed down by the UST's motion, would be over in 30 days; and the UST's motion was opposed by every party in the case with money on the line.

But with that said, the Court acts in accordance with the requirements of law. Once a §1406 motion has been filed, §1406 and its related caselaw leave the Court with no discretion. Here the Court must find, as a mixed question of fact and law, that the statutory requirements for venue in this district were not satisfied. The UST's motion having been filed, it thus must be granted, subject only to determining when and where to effect the transfer.

But while the Court has no discretion to retain the case, it still has the ability to reduce the prejudice to the creditors that an immediate transfer would entail. Venue, even if improper, is not jurisdictional. While §1406 mandates transfer or dismissal when statutory venue requirements have not been met, it does not dictate *when* the transfer must take place, nor does it foreclose steps in the interim to protect the creditors who might be harmed thereby.

Thus the Court will effect the transfer at a time that decreases the resulting prejudice to creditors, the Debtors, and the Debtors' employees. The case will be transferred on the first to occur of the Effective Date or three weeks from the date of entry of the confirmation order, if for some reason the Plan has not gone effective by then.

The Court's Findings of Fact, Conclusions of Law, and bases for the exercise of its discretion follow.

FACTS

1. BACKGROUND

The Debtors are in the publishing business, most significantly in textbooks used in elementary and secondary schools. Their enterprise is large. At the time of filing, the Debtors' combined assets (at book value) were reported to be $2.68 billion, and their total liabilities were said to be $3.54 billion. They had combined revenues of approximately $1.3 billion, and adjusted EBITDA of $238 million, in calendar year 2011. As described in their first day papers (and as unchallenged by the UST), the Debtors' financial difficulties were occasioned by excessive debt and a sharp decrease in demand for their product, particularly as a consequence of financial stress on their customers—state and municipal governments who were victims of the financial crisis of 2007-2008 and decreases in financial assistance from the federal government.

To address their difficulties, the Debtors engaged in prepetition discussions with their creditors to restructure their debt, leading to prepetition agreement on a consensual reorganization plan. Acceptances of a prepackaged plan of reorganization were sought and obtained before the filing of the Debtors' chapter 11 cases.

The prepackaged plan emerged from an agreement between the Debtors and an informal creditor group ("**Informal Creditor Group**") of holders of secured debt, which is one of the several parties that, along with the Debtors, oppose the UST's motion. The ultimately successful negotiations led to a plan support agreement (the "**Plan Support Agreement**") embodying the deal points that found their way into the ultimately accepted prepackaged plan. Though it is not relevant to matters that are purely questions of law (and is relevant only to matters of discretion, if that), the Plan Support Agreement *required* that the chapter 11 cases be filed in the Southern District of New York.[4]

In its simplest terms, the prepackaged plan provided for the conversion of billions of dollars of secured debt into equity. Significantly, the plan left general unsecured claims—most significantly, trade claims from the vendor community and tort claims—unimpaired. The idea, to be implemented by a confirmation hearing based on the plan acceptances that had been obtained prepetition, was to make the Debtors' chapter 11 cases as quick and painless for their creditors (especially their trade creditors) as possible. The plan was unanimously

---

4. Apart from choice of law issues that were articulated by Debtors' counsel in oral argument, the desire for a filing in New York is partly explained by a point made by the Informal Creditor Group. The latter notes that the agent for the DIP Credit Facility and proposed exit facility, Citibank, N.A. ("Citibank") (which likewise opposes the UST's motion), and substantially all of the senior creditors who are parties to the Plan Support Agreement are located in New York—as are the attorneys for each of the Debtors, the Informal Creditor Group, the first lien secured debt agents and the DIP lenders. The Informal Creditor Group points out that "transferring venue to a different district would appreciably increase professional fees and expenses in these cases." (Informal Creditor Group Br. at 4). That point is not disputed by the UST, but is argued to be irrelevant.

accepted by the Debtors' creditors. A confirmation hearing on the already-accepted plan was scheduled for a date only slightly after the earliest date permissible under the Federal Rules of Bankruptcy Procedure. Unless delayed as a consequence of the UST's motion, the case could be over in about 30 days.

While the UST was free to solicit membership in an official committee of unsecured creditors, no creditors' committee was formed, as there was insufficient interest in forming one. The unsecured creditors who, in another case, would form the natural constituency for such a creditors' committee here would be unimpaired.

2. THE DEBTORS' CHAPTER 11 FILINGS

On May 21, 2012, the 25 Debtors commenced these chapter 11 cases, one after another in quick succession. The first of the cases to be filed on the Court's docket (assuming that it matters) was Publishing, the Debtors' primary operating company. Publishing is a Delaware corporation, with its principal place of business in Boston, Massachusetts. The fourth of the Debtors to file was Houghton Mifflin Holding Company ("**HoldCo**"), also a Delaware corporation, the location of whose principal assets is a matter of dispute between the parties, but whose principal place of business is indisputably in Boston, Massachusetts. The Debtors assert that venue in New York was proper for each of Publishing and HoldCo, and thus that venue in New York for their debtor affiliates was proper as well.

To the extent that the principal places of business of the other Debtors are relevant (though the Court does not believe that they are), they are likewise in Massachusetts, or at least in places other than New York. None of the Debtors is organized under the laws of New York. Most of the Debtors (15 of the 25) are Delaware corporations.

To the extent that the "nerve center" of the entire corporate enterprise — as contrasted to that of any individual Debtor — is relevant (though again, given the underlying basis for the motion here, the Court does not believe that it is), the "nerve center" of the entire corporate enterprise is in Boston, Massachusetts — where "Houghton Mifflin Harcourt Publishing" (without being more specific as to what individual corporations were encompassed under that appellation) was identified by the Boston Redevelopment Authority as one of Boston's largest employers.

3. FACTS AS TO PUBLISHING AND HOLDCO

The first of the two key debtors, Publishing, has an office at 215 Park Avenue South in Manhattan, where Publishing leases the 12th floor and a portion of the 11th floor. At that office, Publishing employs 60 full-time employees; it also has 15 sales representatives associated with its New York office who work from their homes. That is enough for the Court to find that Publishing does business in the state of New York. But the Court does not understand the Debtors to argue, and in any event does not find, that such is sufficient for the Court to find that Publishing's principal place of business is in New York.

The second of the two key debtors, HoldCo, identified its basis for venue as the presence of its corporate affiliates when it first filed its petition on May 21. Eleven days later, HoldCo filed an amended petition, changing its stated basis for venue to its "domicile, residence, principal place of business or principal assets." HoldCo also changed the location of its principal assets from "N/A" to an address in Manhattan. Later, in their brief in opposition to the motion, the Debtors made clear that HoldCo was relying on the "principal assets" basis, premised on leased and subleased space in New York City.

HoldCo premised its venue assertions on space it leased and then subleased — described on the lease as "Room 815, 1350 Avenue of the Americas" (the "**Sixth Avenue Space**") — in Manhattan. The Sixth Avenue Space formerly served as the domestic office of a previous parent company, Education Media and Publishing Group International. However, HoldCo does not currently conduct operations in the Sixth Avenue Space or otherwise occupy it. Instead, it "is currently subleased *entirely* to an outside, nonaffiliated entity."

HoldCo pays its lessor approximately $415,000 per year for the Sixth Avenue Space, while receiving only $220,000 per year from its sublessee. The prime lease is a net cash drain, which might nevertheless have value if benefits were being obtained from it, but there is no showing of benefits here. Based on the record before the Court, the Sixth Avenue Space is money losing on a cash flow basis. Nor does the Court have evidence from which it could find, if that were so, that the Sixth Avenue Space is at a below-market rate — and thus would have intrinsic economic value to HoldCo as a valuable asset to be retained or that could be put up for sale to a prospective purchaser. The Court can and does find that the lease and sublease are assets of the HoldCo estate, but it cannot find, on the record before it, that they have any material value.

Additionally, however, the Court is compelled to find that the Debtor's presentation of HoldCo's asset mix was, until corrected at oral argument, materially inaccurate. In the Debtors' objection, the Court was told that "[HoldCo] has no other assets besides its rights under the lease and sublease described herein." But the Court cannot find that to be true. Rather, the Court finds that HoldCo was called a "Holding Company" for a reason. It had 15 direct and indirect subsidiaries. When HoldCo filed, it owned the stock of a subsidiary, Houghton Mifflin, LLC ("**LLC Sub**"), a Delaware corporation that also is a debtor in this case. LLC Sub had two subsidiaries of its own, debtor Houghton Mifflin Finance, Inc. ("**Finance**"), a Delaware corporation, and debtor Houghton Mifflin Holdings, Inc. ("**Holdings**"), also a Delaware corporation. And while Finance had no lower level subsidiaries, Holdings did: HM Publishing Corp. ("**HM Publishing**"), which also is a debtor in this case.

Then, HM Publishing had two subsidiaries, debtor Publishing (the first company to file, as discussed above), and HM Receivables Co. II, LLC ("**Receivables**"), apparently a nondebtor.

Finally, but importantly, one of the two subsidiaries of HM Publishing — debtor Houghton Mifflin Harcourt Publishing Company (the same company that was defined above as "Publishing") — which was the first of the 25 debtors to file, and which was designated by the Debtors as the "lead" case (though such designation is of no significance on this motion), had *nine* subsidiaries (the "**Nine Subsidiaries**"), seven of which are debtors here. Unlike the other debtors,

Publishing showed very substantial assets on its petition. Publishing checked the "More than $1 billion" box for "Estimated Assets." More significantly, assets of $2.407 billion were reported for Publishing in the Debtors' Rule 1007-2 Declaration (though these were at book value, which for most businesses is not necessarily the same as market value), and Publishing was the source of the overwhelming bulk of the Debtors' $238 million in 2011 EBITDA, an important metric by which companies are valued.

All 12 of the direct and indirect subsidiaries of HoldCo that are debtors showed a street address in Boston. There was no argument here that the locale of any of the Debtors' stock should be found to be anywhere other than in Boston.

No evidence was introduced as to the value of the LLC Sub stock, or (as such might affect the value of LLC Sub stock) the value of the stock of LLC Sub's direct and indirect subsidiaries Finance, Holdings, HM Publishing, Receivables, Publishing, or the Nine Subsidiaries. Nor was evidence submitted as to the extent to which HoldCo had other contractual rights or intangible assets, like tax attributes, such as net operating losses ("**NOLs**"), though it appears that at least some of these subsidiaries, or their predecessors, at least once had business operations, and lost money, requiring a restructuring of their operations — facts that tend to telegraph the presence of NOLs, though of course any NOLs might belong to another entity. HoldCo reported "Estimated Assets" of "$100,001 to $500,000" on its amended petition (a change from "$0 to $50,000" on its original petition), but was otherwise silent as to their nature or value. However, since competent debtor counsel do not put entities into chapter 11 for no reason, the Court must infer, and finds, that one or more of LLC Sub, Finance, Holdings, HM Publishing, the Nine Subsidiaries, and, of course, Publishing had significant assets to protect. They generated nearly a quarter of a billion dollars in EBITDA.

In any event, the Court is not in a position to find, and cannot find, that HoldCo's money-losing contractual rights for the Sixth Avenue Space were worth more than its direct and indirect ownership of no less than 15 separate subsidiaries, one of which represented its assets as worth more than a billion dollars, and was the source of nearly all of the Debtors' $238 million in EBITDA.

4. PROCEDURAL MATTERS

During the first day hearings on May 22, the UST articulated venue as a concern. The UST's rights were reserved; findings in the proposed orders that venue was proper were removed; and the Debtors' first day motions were otherwise granted.

One of those motions was to set a date for the confirmation hearing with respect to the previously solicited, and unanimously accepted, plan. Another was a routine motion for joint administration of the Debtors' 25 separate chapter 11 cases. As the Debtors put it, "[Publishing] initially was selected by the Debtors as the lead-filing entity and the lead-captioned entity in the Debtors' motion for joint administration." As the UST put it, the joint administration motion was granted, "under the caption, 'In re Houghton Mifflin Publishing Company, *et al.;*' thus identifying the first-filed debtor, [Publishing], as the 'lead debtor' of these mega cases." Each statement is true, but irrelevant.

On May 30, with confirmation scheduled for June 21, the UST moved to transfer these cases. The UST sought to file its motion on shortened notice. By endorsed order, the Court denied the request for a shortening of time, stating, among other things, that "[t]his matter is too important to be heard without giving the stakeholders in this case, whose money is on the line, the normal opportunity to respond."

DISCUSSION

I.   STATUTORY & RULE PROVISIONS

Venue for cases—as contrasted to proceedings[5]—under the Bankruptcy Code is addressed under 28 U.S.C. §1408, one of the several provisions of chapter 87 of the Judicial Code (which starts with §1390 and goes on to §1413) that address venue for matters in the federal district courts.
Section 1408 provides:

> Except as provided in section 1410 of this title,[6]
> a case under title 11 may be commenced in the district court for the district—
> (1) in which the domicile, residence, principal place of business in the United States, or principal assets in the United States, of the person or entity that is the subject of such case have been located for the one hundred and eighty days immediately preceding such commencement, or for a longer portion of such one-hundred-and-eighty-day period than the domicile, residence, or principal place of business, in the United States, or principal assets in the United States, of such person were located in any other district; or
> (2) in which there is pending a case under title 11 concerning such person's affiliate, general partner, or partnership.

Thus a non-chapter 15 case under the Bankruptcy Code may properly be brought in a district passing muster under one of the four enumerated bases for venue set forth in §1408(1) (*i.e.*, domicile, residence, principal place of

---

5. As the Court has previously explained, *see, e.g.*, Buena Vista Television v. Adelphia Communications Corp. *(In re Adelphia Communications Corp.)*, 307 B.R. 404, 413 n. 22 (Bankr.S.D.N.Y.2004), "case" as used in bankruptcy parlance is a word of art—referring to that which is commenced by the filing for a petition for relief under the Bankruptcy Code, and refers to the umbrella case under which many individual proceedings—applications, motions, contested matters and adversary proceedings—are heard. "Case" is the modern way of referring to what was commonly referred to as a "proceeding" under the former Bankruptcy Act. Though many unfamiliar with bankruptcy practice still refer to a bankruptcy "proceeding" when they should be referring to a bankruptcy "case," it should be understood that a "proceeding" as used in the Judicial Code, 28 U.S.C., is a matter that comes up in a "case," or is a separate proceeding (like an adversary proceeding) brought in connection with a "case." The appropriate venue for "proceedings" under the Bankruptcy Code is governed by a different provision of the Judicial Code, 28 U.S.C. §1409.

6. The exception addressed in §1410 is for cases, in aid of foreign insolvency proceedings, that are brought under chapter 15 of the Bankruptcy Code.

business or principal assets), or under the fifth basis, set forth in §1408(2), a district "in which there is pending" a case "concerning such person's affiliate, general partner, or partnership."

From time to time, a case under the Bankruptcy Code may be filed in a district that passes muster under one of the five bases just noted, but is less convenient for parties or otherwise less than optimum in the interests of justice. Also, from time to time, a case under the Bankruptcy Code may be filed in a district where none of the five enumerated bases has been satisfied. Two of the Judicial Code's venue provisions deal with changes in the venue for bankruptcy cases under such circumstances—one plainly, and one under the bulk of the applicable authority.

Without doubt, 28 U.S.C. §1412 applies to transfers of cases (and also, though not relevant here, proceedings) under the Bankruptcy Code. It provides:

> A district court[7] may transfer a case or proceeding under title 11 to a district court for another district, in the interest of justice or for the convenience of the parties.

Notably, §1412 is permissive; it says that a district court "*may*" transfer a case "in the interest of justice or for the convenience of the parties." It does not say that the court *must* do so.

Nevertheless, the Court concludes, reluctantly, that it should follow the majority on this issue. The Court comes to that view not by counting noses, but by an amalgam of textual analysis; comparison of former §1477 with §1406 and §1412;36 Bankruptcy Rule 1014(a)'s 1987 Advisory Committee comment; and respect for precedent in the Southern District of New York.

Thus the Court concludes that §1406 applies, at least in the first instance, if the Court cannot find one of §1408's five bases for venue to have been satisfied.

II.   COMPLIANCE WITH §1408

Turning then to consideration of those prospective bases for venue, the Court is compelled to find that none here has been satisfied.

The Debtors base venue for the 25 cases in their corporate enterprise on an amalgam of §1408(2) (providing venue for corporate affiliates if venue is proper for any of them), and §1408(1) compliance by either Publishing or HoldCo. But the Court cannot find satisfaction of any of the four bases under §1408(1) for either of those two key Debtors.

III.   CONVENIENCE OF PARTIES AND INTERESTS OF JUSTICE

The Debtors and their creditors speak at length as to how transfer would be destructive to creditor interests, to the great expense and inconvenience of the

---

7. It will be remembered that bankruptcy courts are arms of the district court, with bankruptcy judges presiding over cases under the Bankruptcy Code under orders of reference from their respective district courts. Thus, as a practical matter, while district judges occasionally preside over bankruptcy cases and may be called upon to make like decisions when sitting as bankruptcy courts of original jurisdiction, most decisions under 28 U.S.C. §1412 are made by bankruptcy judges.

parties (especially creditors), and the exact opposite of the interests of justice. Their showing in that regard is overwhelming. They would win in a heartbeat if this were a motion under §1412.

But the problem is that this motion is under §1406. On a §1406 motion, the Court's hands are tied by statutory and case law when venue is unsupportable under §1408. That is the exact point of the majority in the split between the majority and minority courts construing §1406. The parties, and the Court, are ultimately subject to the good sense of parties who have standing to make §1406 motions, including the UST, which has the power to make a motion like this under section 307 of the Bankruptcy Code, and the ability, like any other party, to waive any deficiencies that might otherwise lie. The answer, to the extent there is an answer, is for the UST to exercise prosecutorial discretion in deciding when to make motions like this one, keeping in mind the interests of the creditors who would be affected by the motion's outcome.

IV.   TIMING OF TRANSFER

As is apparent from the foregoing, the Court acts in accordance with the requirements of law. With the UST having made this motion, and the Court having found insufficient compliance with §1408, the Court will order the requested transfer. But §1406 requires only that the Court dismiss or transfer. It does not say when, and does not tie the hands of a court in mitigating the resulting damage to the creditor community.

The UST has cited no case, nor is the Court aware of one, that has determined that the Court must effect any required dismissal or transfer under any particular timetable dictated by law. Undoubtedly, any required action cannot be pocket vetoed or delayed for an indefinite period, but everything in the venue jurisprudence emphasizes the goal, and ability, of judges to protect the creditors and other stakeholders in the cases on those judges' watch. The Court will implement the decision it is required to make under a timetable that minimizes (though it may not wholly eliminate) the harm to the creditors and other stakeholders that this motion engendered.

As it announced that it would at the conclusion of oral argument on the UST's motion, the Court went forward with the confirmation hearing that was scheduled for this week, denying a UST request (in its objection to confirmation) that the confirmation hearing not be held. Similarly, the Court believes that it should not stay the Plan's Effective Date by reason of the UST's venue concerns. Venue objections, even if valid, are not jurisdictional. *Collier* notes that "[a]s is true with respect to venue generally, venue of a case can be waived by express agreement or by conduct." And the venue statute upon which the UST moves, §1406, effectively says the same thing.

It was shown, without dispute by the UST, that delaying the confirmation hearing, or the Effective Date if the Plan were confirmed, would materially prejudice the creditors in this case (who, it will be recalled, unanimously approved the prepackaged plan) and the Debtors and their employees — whose understandable goal was, as Citibank notes, to achieve their reorganization quickly and without the resulting damage of a lengthy chapter 11 case.[8] Delaying that confirmation hearing would have been materially prejudicial to the interests of the creditors whose money here is on the line.

The case will be transferred on the first to occur of the Effective Date or three weeks from the date of entry of the confirmation order, if for some reason the Plan has not gone effective by then. The Court understands and will respect the desires of the stakeholders here to conclude this case quickly, but will have doubts as to their commitment to that goal if the Plan has not gone effective by that time.

V. FUTURE PROCEEDINGS

Though the Court has determined that it must transfer this case, another question remains: to where? The leading contender might well be Massachusetts. But any other district in which the cases could properly have been filed (as the Court now knows the facts, the Districts of Colorado, Delaware, New Hampshire or Wyoming, or one of the districts in California, Illinois or Texas) would also appear to be permissible.

The Debtors, the Informal Creditor Group, Citibank and the UST (if it cares) are to consult with each other to reach agreement, if possible, on the particular district to which these cases will be transferred. In the event of an inability to agree, they are to submit simultaneous letters to the Court, explaining the bases for their preferences, after which the Court will decide.

CONCLUSION

For the foregoing reasons, the Court determines that the requirements for venue in the Southern District of New York, as set forth in 28 U.S.C. §1408, were not satisfied. Though a transfer would here be prejudicial to the interests of creditors, the Court has sworn to comply with the law. The Court thus will transfer these cases to a district where venue would be proper under §1408.

The Court will, however, effect the transfer at a time that minimizes the resulting prejudice to creditors, the Debtors, and the Debtors' employees. The case will be transferred on the first to occur of (x) the Effective Date or (y) three weeks from the date of entry of the confirmation order, if for some reason the Plan has not gone effective by then.

Provisions consistent with the foregoing may appear in the confirmation order, if the Debtors desire, or in a separate order if they prefer. In either case, decretal language implementing this ruling must be submitted promptly. If the plan supporters and the UST cannot agree upon the form of the order or any implementing decretal provisions, either side may settle an order.

---

8. In its decision in *General Motors*, the Court noted, repeatedly, how debtors and their stakeholders can be grievously injured, and value can be destroyed, when chapter 11 cases are not concluded quickly. *See* In re General Motors Corp., 407 B.R. 463, 479, 480, 484, 485, 491, 493 (Bankr.S.D.N.Y.2009), *stay pending appeal denied*, 2009 WL 2033079 (S.D.N.Y.2009) (Kaplan, J.), *appeal dismissed and aff'd*, 428 B.R. 43 (S.D.N.Y.2010) (Buchwald, J.) and 430 B.R. 65 (S.D.N.Y.2010) (Sweet, J.), *appeal dismissed*, No. 10-4882-bk (2d Cir. Jul. 28, 2011). Those concerns are even more applicable with respect to prepacks, which are agreed to by creditors on the assumption that they will proceed through bankruptcy with the unusual speed for prepackaged plans for which the Bankruptcy Code provides.

28

INTRODUCTION TO
CHAPTER 11

1. A BRIEF INTRODUCTION TO BANKRUPTCY

Even if you have not taken Bankruptcy, the coming chapters should be easy because you've now completed a lot of corporate law classes. Chapter 11 is simply another type of corporate negotiation, although bankruptcy attorneys have a certain kind of mystique (a nerdy mystique, granted) because they understand "the Code." In this respect they are kind of like tax lawyers.

A truly good corporate lawyer has some understanding of bankruptcy because it helps you be a better transactional lawyer: You can anticipate future problems and deal with them up front in the deal documents. Moreover, from a self-interested perspective, knowing something about chapter 11 makes you more valuable in economic downturns.

JOHN D. AYER ET AL., *WELCOME TO THE JUNGLE*
Am. Bankr. Inst. J. 24 (July/August 2003)

The overwhelming majority of bankruptcy cases involve debtors who have no assets to distribute to creditors and who are filing just to get the discharge. There were about a million and a half such cases in the past year. These are important cases for the people involved, and they provide work for a lot of lawyers. But they aren't our department, and we won't spend a lot of time on them. Instead, we will spend most of our time on the cases where the debtor does have assets, and where the goal is to "reorganize" (whatever that may mean — of which more will be discussed later).

Bankruptcy law is federal. It is federal because the Constitution says that Congress shall have the power to make bankruptcy law. Congress exercised the power through the Bankruptcy Reform Act of 1978 (BRA), including the Bankruptcy Code, which is codified in Title 11 of the U.S. Code.

The BRA creates bankruptcy courts that operate as "a unit of" the U.S. district courts. Formally, the big distinction is in the power of the judge: The district judge exercises his judicial power under Article III of the Constitution and is a lifetime appointee, while the bankruptcy judge is a term appointee (14 years), deriving his or her power from the bankruptcy clause in Article I of the Constitution. Because the bankruptcy judges are "Article I" judges, case law holds that there must be limitations on the power of a bankruptcy judge in order for the bankruptcy system to be constitutional. As a result, Title 28 of the U.S. Code was amended to put the bankruptcy judge under the "supervision" of the district judge: Certain decisions by a bankruptcy judge must be reviewed by a district judge, and the district judge can withdraw matters that are pending before the bankruptcy judge and instead decide them herself. But practically speaking, the overwhelming majority of what happens in bankruptcy cases takes place in the bankruptcy court, under the supervision of the bankruptcy judge.

Who are the players in the bankruptcy game?

We have already mentioned the bankruptcy judge; he or she presides over the bankruptcy court. There are about 325 bankruptcy judges around the country, give or take. Some came to the bankruptcy bench with a lot of bankruptcy experience, some did not. But it may not make much difference: Lots of those without bankruptcy experience are fast learners, and some of them brought valuable experience from elsewhere — *e.g.*, good trial skills . . .

In the mass of ordinary bankruptcies (the "chapter 7 cases" discussed below), the case is administered by a trustee . . .

Chapter 11 is different. There is no trustee unless the judge orders the appointment of one. In lieu of a trustee, the debtor remains in control of its business and assets as debtor-in-possession (DIP). The DIP has most of the powers and responsibilities of a trustee. In the typical case, it is the debtor who initiates the bankruptcy case through its (pre-bankruptcy) lawyer. Once it has filed, the debtor — now DIP — seeks court approval to retain its former lawyer as counsel for the DIP. The DIP's counsel becomes a kind of "point person" in the chapter 11 case.

Another important player in the bankruptcy system is the Office of the U.S. Trustee, a division of the Department of Justice that is charged with oversight of the bankruptcy system. The U.S. Trustee appoints and supervises panel trustees, appoints official committees (see below), reviews and comments on applications to employ and compensate professionals, investigates bankruptcy fraud and abuse, and can be heard on any other issue in a bankruptcy case. The U.S. Trustee is often active in the very early stages of a chapter 11 case, although once the case is up and running, and particularly if there is active creditor participation, the U.S. Trustee often backs off a bit.

Another player well worth noting in a chapter 11 case (they are permitted in chapter 7 too, but it rarely happens) is the creditors' committee. The committee typically consists of the five or seven largest unsecured creditors that are willing to serve. It hires counsel (and sometimes financial advisors or other professionals) who are paid for by the debtor's estate. The committee has standing to be heard on any issue in a chapter 11 case, and its views tend to be taken seriously by the bankruptcy judges. An active and well-represented committee can play a major role in the outcome of the case. In some cases, other committees will also be appointed, such as equity-holder committees, retiree committees, bondholder committees, etc. Other important players include secured parties, especially banks that may have liens on substantially all of a debtor's assets, and counter-parties to executory contracts.

Now, a word about the structure of the Code. As we said above, the Bankruptcy Code is in Title 11 of the U.S. Code and is divided into chapters. Chapters 1, 3 and 5 are "general" chapters designed to govern all cases.

Chapter 1 contains definitions, delineates who can be a debtor, describes the courts' powers and contains some other general rules. Chapter 3 governs "administration of the case," including matters such as the filing of new cases, employment of professionals, the automatic stay, the use, sale and lease of estate assets, post-petition financing, executory contracts, the dismissal and closing of cases, and some other matters. Chapter 5 covers a wide variety of matters relating to the rights of debtors and creditors, including claims and priorities, matters relating to exemptions and discharge of debts, and the "avoidance" provisions, which permit a trustee or DIP to claw back certain transfers made prior to the petition date . . .

Chapter 11, entitled "reorganization," is the chapter that governs the small number of "big" cases that entail a lot of lawyer time and effort, and generate a lot of professional fees. If you ask a chapter 11 lawyer what it means to reorganize, he will likely say something like this: The reorganization case allows the debtor to preserve the business as a going concern, and thereby to maximize value for creditors, shareholders, employees and other stakeholders.

This is a beguiling picture and not entirely false. But there are all kinds of difficulties. The most obvious is that not all businesses are worth more as a going concern than they are in liquidation. A notorious example is the case of the Penn Central Railroad, one of the largest bankruptcies in American history. Penn Central went into bankruptcy as an unprofitable network of railroads, then emerged as a valuable real estate company.

A second difficulty is that chapter 11 specifically provides that a reorganization plan may provide for the liquidation of some or all of the debtor's assets — so chapter 11 is not only about reorganization, and the Code implicitly recognizes that in some cases value is maximized through liquidation. Third, the debtor does not need to choose chapter 11 if he wants the business to continue; the trustee may, with court approval, continue to operate the business in chapter 7 (although it is not often done). Finally, the distinction between "liquidation" and "going concern" may be less clear in practice than it is in theory. One can perfectly well "liquidate" a business by selling it as a going concern, in which case the distinction does not mean anything at all. Indeed, "going concern" sales — and the use of asset sales to circumvent the chapter 11 plan process — seem to be a popular trend these days.

Why this muddle? The point is that bankruptcy law conflates two concepts that are overlapping but fundamentally quite different. One is the notion of maximizing the value of the assets. The other is the notion of saving the residual stake of the pre-bankruptcy owners. This confusion is apparent in the classic chapter 11 case. The old residual owners (equity-holders), still in control of the enterprise, will file the petition. They will remain in control (as DIP) and will propose "a plan" to "save the going concern." If all goes well, the effect will be to maximize the payout to creditors and to leave something on the table for the owners (while preserving jobs, generating future tax revenues and serving other social goods that are often touted as benefits of reorganization).

Such a scenario appears to be a self-evident win-win situation. The interests of creditors and equity appear to be allied. But it is rarely that simple. "Saving the going concern" means continuing the business, which means continuing to bear risk. Where the business is insolvent, equity always gains from taking risks: Liquidate today, and they get nothing; keep the business going, and they may have a chance. Creditors are correspondingly risk-averse: Liquidate today, and they get paid. Take a gamble, and the rewards go to equity, while the creditors bear the risk of loss. The point is not that creditors always favor liquidation — clearly, they don't — but the risk-reward calculation is different for creditors than it is for equity-holders.

There can be no doubt that chapter 11 obscures, rather than resolves, this tension — almost as if deliberately to allow the court to choose, from case to case and even from time to time within a case, whether "assets" or "equity" will dominate.

A chapter 11 case may be commenced on a voluntary or involuntary basis. Most are voluntary, especially with regard to big firms.[1]

As we noted with regard to prepacks, many of the largest cases are filed in either the Southern District of New York or the District of Delaware. Figure 28-1 provides an answer to how GM managed to file in New York, despite being a Delaware corporation headquartered in Detroit. Remember that each corporate entity within a "firm" files its own bankruptcy case, unless you want to concede grounds for piercing the corporate veil or its bankruptcy counterpart, substantive consolidation. When the firm has international subsidiaries, the choices become more complex.

Filing a bankruptcy petition creates something called the "bankruptcy estate."[2] In individual chapter 7 cases the estate is easy to understand: It is comprised of all the debtor's nonexempt assets; that is, all assets the creditor can get at state law. The trustee takes charge of the estate and liquidates the assets therein for the benefit of creditors. Essentially the debtor trades his or her assets for relief from creditors.

In chapter 11 the estate is a bit more abstract because the DIP remains "in possession" of its estate. Thus the estate is created, but it looks remarkably just like the pre-bankruptcy debtor.

To keep creditors from pulling the estate apart, and allow time for a reorganization plan to come together, the Code provides for an "automatic stay."[3] Think of it as a statutory, no-notice injunction that prevents creditors from using the remedies available under state and federal debtor-creditor law, like getting the marshal to sell the debtor's stuff to pay off the debts.

---

1. 11 U.S.C. §301. These Code provisions are in your statutory supplement, of course.
2. 11 U.S.C. §541.
3. 11 U.S.C. §362.

United States Bankruptcy Court Southern District of New York	Voluntary Petition

Name of Debtor (if individual, enter Last, First, Middle): **GENERAL MOTORS CORPORATION**	Name of Joint Debtor (Spouse) (Last, First, Middle): **N/A**
All Other Names used by the Debtor in the last 8 years (include married, maiden, and trade names): **See Schedule 1 Attached**	All Other Names used by the Joint Debtor in the last 8 years (include married, maiden, and trade names): **N/A**
Last four digits of Soc. Sec. or Individual-Taxpayer I.D. (ITIN) No./Complete EIN (if more than one, state all): **38-0572515**	Last four digits of Soc. Sec. or Individual-Taxpayer I.D. (ITIN) No./Complete EIN (if more than one, state all): **N/A**
Street Address of Debtor (No. and Street, City, and State): **300 Renaissance Center**	Street Address of Joint Debtor (No. and Street, City, and State): **N/A**
Detroit, Michigan ZIP CODE **48265-3000**	ZIP CODE
County of Residence or of the Principal Place of Business: **Wayne County**	County of Residence or of the Principal Place of Business: **N/A**
Mailing Address of Debtor (if different from street address): ZIP CODE	Mailing Address of Joint Debtor (if different from street address): **N/A** ZIP CODE
Location of Principal Assets of Business Debtor (if different from street address above): **767 Fifth Avenue, New York, New York**	ZIP CODE **10153**

Type of Debtor (Form of Organization) (Check **one** box.)
- ☐ Individual (includes Joint Debtors) *See Exhibit D on page 2 of this form.*
- ☒ Corporation (includes LLC and LLP)
- ☐ Partnership
- ☐ Other (If debtor is not one of the above entities, check this box and state type of entity below.)

Nature of Business (Check **one** box.)
- ☐ Health Care Business
- ☐ Single Asset Real Estate as defined in 11 U.S.C. § 101 (51B)
- ☐ Railroad
- ☐ Stockbroker
- ☐ Commodity Broker
- ☐ Clearing Bank
- ☒ Other

Automotive Manufacturing

Tax-Exempt Entity (Check box, if applicable.)
- ☐ Debtor is a tax-exempt organization under Title 26 of the United States Code (the Internal Revenue Code).

Chapter of Bankruptcy Code Under Which the Petition is Filed (Check one box)
- ☐ Chapter 7
- ☐ Chapter 9
- ☒ Chapter 11
- ☐ Chapter 12
- ☐ Chapter 13
- ☐ Chapter 15 Petition for Recognition of a Foreign Main Proceeding
- ☐ Chapter 15 Petition for Recognition of a Foreign Nonmain Proceeding

Nature of Debts (Check one box)
- ☐ Debts are primarily consumer debts, defined in 11 U.S.C. § 101(8) as "incurred by an individual primarily for a personal, family, or household purpose."
- ☒ Debts are primarily business debts.

Filing Fee (Check one box)
- ☒ Full Filing Fee attached
- ☐ Filing Fee to be paid in installments (applicable to individuals only). Must attach signed application for the court's consideration certifying that the debtor is unable to pay fee except in installments. Rule 1006(b). See Official Form 3A.
- ☐ Filing Fee waiver requested (applicable to chapter 7 individuals only). Must attach signed application for the court's consideration. See Official Form 3B.

Chapter 11 Debtors

Check one box:
- ☐ Debtor is a small business debtor as defined in 11 U.S.C. § 101(51D).
- ☒ Debtor is not a small business debtor as defined in 11 U.S.C. § 101(51D).

Check if:
- ☐ Debtor's aggregate noncontingent liquidated debts (excluding debts owed to insiders or affiliates) are less than $2,190,000.

Check all applicable boxes:
- ☐ A plan is being filed with this petition.
- ☐ Acceptances of the plan were solicited prepetition from one or more classes of creditors, in accordance with 11 U.S.C. § 1126(B).

Statistical/Administrative Information
- ☒ Debtor estimates that funds will be available for distribution to unsecured creditors.
- ☐ Debtor estimates that, after any exempt property is excluded and administrative expenses paid, there will be no funds available for distribution to unsecured creditors.

THIS SPACE IS FOR COURT USE ONLY

Estimated Number of Creditors (on a Consolidated Basis)

☐ 1-49	☐ 50-99	☐ 100-199	☐ 200-999	☐ 1,000-5,000	☐ 5,001-10,000	☐ 10,001-25,000	☐ 25,001-50,000	☐ 50,001-100,000	☒ Over 100,000

Estimated Assets (on a Consolidated Basis)

☐ $0 to $50,000	☐ $50,001 to $100,000	☐ $100,001 to $500,000	☐ $500,001 to $1 million	☐ $1,000,001 to $10 million	☐ $10,000,001 to $50 million	☐ $50,000,001 to $100 million	☐ $100,000,001 to $500 million	☐ $500,000,001 to $1 billion	☒ More than $1 billion

Estimated Liabilities (on a Consolidated Basis)

☐ $0 to $50,000	☐ $50,001 to $100,000	☐ $100,001 to $500,000	☐ $500,001 to $1 million	☐ $1,000,001 to $10 million	☐ $10,000,001 to $50 million	☐ $50,000,001 to $100 million	☐ $100,000,001 to $500 million	☐ $500,000,001 to $1 billion	☒ More than $1 billion

NY2:\1991951\11\16_ZZ11!.DOC\72240.0635

FIGURE 28-1
Pages from General Motors Bankruptcy Petition.

In chapter 11, the stay protects the debtor's estate, but not anyone else like officers or shareholders. Sometimes the debtor will ask the bankruptcy court to enter a regular injunction to protect these parties—and sometimes the court

09-50026-reg   Doc 1   Filed 06/01/09   Entered 06/01/09 07:57:51   Main Document
Pg 2 of 24

(Official Form 1) (1/08)		FORM B1, Page 2

Voluntary Petition
(This page must be completed and filed in every case)

Name of Debtor(s):
GENERAL MOTORS CORPORATION

All Prior Bankruptcy Case Filed Within Last 8 Years (If more than two, attach additional sheet.)

Location Where Filed: **N/A**	Case Number: **N/A**	Date Filed: **N/A**
Location Where Filed: **N/A**	Case Number: **N/A**	Date Filed: **N/A**

Pending Bankruptcy Case Filed by any Spouse, Partner or Affiliate of this Debtor (If more than one, attach additional sheet.)

Name of Debtor: **Chevrolet-Saturn of Harlem, Inc.**	Case Number: **As filed**	Date Filed: **June 1, 2009**
District: **Southern District of New York**	Relationship: **Wholly-Owned Direct Subsidiary of General Motors Corporation**	Judge: **Undetermined**

Exhibit A	**Exhibit B**
(To be completed if debtor is required to file periodic reports (e.g., forms 10K and 10Q) with the Securities and Exchange Commission pursuant to Section 13 or 15(d) of the Securities Exchange Act of 1934 and is requesting relief under chapter 11.)	(To be completed if debtor is an individual whose debts are primarily consumer debts.) I, the attorney for the petitioner named in the foregoing petition, declare that I have informed the petitioner that [he or she] may proceed under chapter 7, 11, 12, or 13 of title 11, United States Code, and have explained the relief available under each such chapter. I further certify that I have delivered to the debtor the notice required by § 342(b).
☒ Exhibit A is attached and made a part of this petition.	X_____ Signature of Attorney for Debtor(s) Date

Exhibit C

Does the debtor own or have possession of any property that poses or is alleged to pose a threat of imminent and identifiable harm to public health or safety?

☐ Yes, and Exhibit C is attached and made a part of this petition.

☒ No.

Exhibit D

(To be completed by every individual debtor. If a joint petition is filed, each spouse must complete and attach a separate Exhibit D.)

☐   Exhibit D completed and signed by the debtor is attached and made a part of this petition.

If this is a joint petition:

☐   Exhibit D also completed and signed by the joint debtor is attached and made a part of this petition.

Information Regarding the Debtor - Venue
(Check any applicable box.)

☐   Debtor has been domiciled or has had a residence, principal place of business, or principal assets in this District for 180 days immediately preceding the date of this petition or for a longer part of such 180 days than in any other District.]

☒   There is a bankruptcy case concerning debtor's affiliate, general partner, or partnership pending in this District.

☐   Debtor is a debtor in a foreign proceeding and has its principal place of business or principal assets in the United States in this District, or has no principal place of business or assets in the United States but is a defendant in an action or proceeding [in a federal or state court] in this District, or the interests of the parties will be served in regard to the relief sought in this District.

Certification by a Debtor Who Resides as a Tenant of Residential Property
(*Check all applicable boxes*)

☐   Landlord has a judgment against the debtor for possession of debtor's residence. (If box checked, complete the following.)

_____
(Name of landlord that obtained judgment)

_____
(Address of landlord)

☐   Debtor claims that under applicable nonbankruptcy law, there are circumstances under which the debtor would be permitted to cure the entire monetary default that gave rise to the judgment for possession, after the judgment for possession was entered, and

☐   Debtor has included with this petition the deposit with the court of any rent that would become due during the 30-day period after the filing of the petition.

☐   Debtor certifies that he/she has served the Landlord with this certification. (11 U.S.C. § 362(1)).

NY2:\1991951\1 1\16_ZZ11!.DOC\72240.0635

FIGURE 28-1 Continued.

will do so, but not as often as most debtors would probably like (keep in mind who it is that gets the debtor-firm to make the request in the first place).

The Code also expressly carves out a number of exceptions to the scope of the automatic stay, which are listed in section 362(b) of the Code. And a creditor may seek relief from the automatic stay, as provided in section 362(d).

The stability of the case in the early days is also protected by giving the debtor and only the debtor the first crack at coming up with a plan. But that is the subject of a future chapter.

2. MORE ON THE DIP

If you read sections 1101 and 1107 of the Code, you will begin to understand the concept of the DIP. The basic idea is that management of the debtor stays in place, without a trustee, but acts with the duties and powers of a bankruptcy trustee.

MICHELLE M. HARNER, *THE SEARCH FOR AN UNBIASED FIDUCIARY IN CORPORATE REORGANIZATIONS*
86 Notre Dame L. Rev. 469 (2011)

The primary goals of Chapter 11 are to rehabilitate corporate debtors and maximize recoveries to creditors. The Bankruptcy Code also generally seeks to level the playing field among a debtor's stakeholders, thereby providing a more equitable distribution. Achieving one or more of the Bankruptcy Code's objectives is difficult in any individual or business bankruptcy case. That task is even more onerous in a Chapter 11 case because the corporate debtor and its various stakeholders often have their own, competing agendas.

Creditors are not benevolent by nature. Rather, they endeavor to maximize their individual returns. If other creditors also benefit, that result typically is inadvertent and of secondary concern.

Early U.S. bankruptcy law did not address corporate reorganization. The laws primarily focused on merchants and "straight" bankruptcy (i.e., liquidation). Troubled corporations thus were left to their own devices, negotiating workouts with their major creditors in a largely unsupervised forum. The Great Depression of the 1930s produced the first federal bankruptcy laws covering corporate reorganizations, and aspects of those laws continue under the U.S. Bankruptcy Code. An understanding of the law's development is helpful in analyzing control contests and conflicts in bankruptcy and the role that DIPs and statutory committees do or should play.

In the late nineteenth century, creative lawyers and federal judges crafted a procedure to fill a void in U.S. bankruptcy laws and address the financial distress of the country's railroads. The procedure, commonly referred to as an equity receivership, allowed a troubled railroad—with the assistance of its major creditors—to invoke the jurisdiction of the federal courts to achieve a restructuring of its debt. Technically, the railroad's creditors would petition the court to appoint a receiver and the receiver would take title to the railroad's assets. The receiver's primary task was to find a buyer for the assets and to continue the railroad's operations until the time of the sale.

Although the basic description of an equity receivership leaves the impression that the railroad, its management and its creditors turned over control of the restructuring to a receiver, that result did not occur in most cases. Rather, management typically encouraged friendly creditors to petition for the appointment of a receiver, and then management and those creditors would negotiate a restructuring plan. Those creditors were sometimes referred to as a protective committee or a reorganization committee. Those creditors also were frequently the only (and therefore successful) bidders at the sale of the railroad's assets. Consequently, in most cases, the receiver played an insignificant role.

Other troubled corporations soon adopted equity receivership procedures similar to those invoked by the railroads. The process not only provided a structured forum in which corporations could reorganize, but it also facilitated a quick restructuring with little interference from outsiders, such as the court, the receiver, and the Securities and Exchange Commission (SEC). Corporate management thus frequently favored the process.

The insular nature of equity receiverships, however, lent the process to abuse and generated substantial criticism. The most notable critic was William O. Douglas. As discussed below, Justice Douglas launched his campaign against equity receiverships after the process was codified by Congress in 1934. He asserted that management and those creditors aligned with management controlled most aspects of the equity receivership process, providing no representation for, and frequently small returns to, other creditors. In fact, creditors not participating in the reorganization committee's plan could be cashed out for a fraction of their debt holdings.

Equity receivership was the preferred means of corporate reorganization well into the 1930s. Congress even adopted key features of equity receiverships in the first U.S. corporate reorganization laws, enacted in 1934 as section 77B of the 1898 Bankruptcy Act. Congress enacted section 77B in response to the Great Depression.

The codification of equity receiverships generated substantial criticism from the SEC and others. The result was a substantial overhaul of corporate reorganization laws, culminating in the Chandler Act of 1938. What equity receiverships and section 77B gave management and key creditors' groups, the Chandler Act essentially took away, at least with respect to public corporations.

The Chandler Act of 1938 established two business reorganization options — Chapter X for public companies and Chapter XI for small businesses. Chapter X stood in stark contrast to equity receiverships and section 77B. For example, it mandated the appointment of an independent bankruptcy trustee, SEC involvement in the plan process and significantly increased court involvement in the solicitation of votes on, and approval of, the plan of reorganization.

Not surprisingly, public corporations resisted filings under Chapter X. Managers and large creditors disliked the loss of control and corresponding uncertainty. Consequently, many corporations first tried to qualify for Chapter XI or negotiate a restructuring outside of the formal process. They viewed Chapter X as a last resort.

A sharp rise in consumer bankruptcy in the 1960s energized bankruptcy reform efforts that produced the Bankruptcy Code of 1978. Corporate reorganization received substantial attention in the reform process as well. The

Bankruptcy Code consolidated the business reorganization chapters into one chapter (i.e., Chapter 11) and eliminated what corporations found most offensive about Chapter X: the mandatory trustee and SEC participation.

Notably, the two key proposals set forth during the bankruptcy reform process did not directly recommend the elimination of trustees and the SEC's involvement in the plan process. For example, the proposal by the National Bankruptcy Review Commission contemplated a presumption in favor of a trustee in large cases and the appointment of a bankruptcy administrator to perform the tasks assigned to the SEC under Chapter X. Similarly, the proposal by the National Conference of Bankruptcy Judges maintained the role of the trustee and SEC in public corporation cases. The bankruptcy bar was, however, a strong proponent of a presumption that a trustee would not be appointed, leaving a corporation's restructuring in management's hands.

Chapter 11 of the Bankruptcy Code adopted much of the flexibility built into Chapter XI. Debtors (as DIPs) remain in possession of their assets and can operate their businesses and pursue their restructurings with oversight primarily from a creditors' committee. The Bankruptcy Code also created the U.S. trustee program, which serves some of the administrative functions assigned to the SEC under Chapter X. The U.S. trustee oversees both individual and business bankruptcies and rarely plays a substantive oversight role in any particular case. In addition, Chapter 11 permits the appointment of a trustee or examiner under certain circumstances.

Overall, the Bankruptcy Code was largely viewed as prodebtor legislation at the time of its enactment. In early Chapter 11 cases, courts granted the debtor's management lengthy periods of exclusivity in which only the debtor could propose a plan of reorganization; allowed the debtor to defer decisions on the treatment of most all contracts and leases until plan confirmation; and enjoined most all actions against the debtor and sometimes its directors, officers and nondebtor affiliates. The debtor's control of the process has weakened, however, as creditors have become more sophisticated, lobbied for favorable legislative amendments and created control opportunities.

As discussed above, Chapter 11 allows a DIP and its management to lead the debtor's restructuring efforts and contemplates the appointment of a statutory committee to oversee those efforts. Sections 1101 and 1107 of the Bankruptcy Code facilitate the DIP's role by recognizing the existence of a DIP and granting it "all the rights . . . and powers, and [authority to perform] all the functions and duties . . . of a trustee serving in a case under" Chapter 11. Section 1102 in turn provides that, in all but a few excluded cases, "the United States trustee shall appoint a committee of creditors or . . . of equity security holders as the United States trustee deems appropriate." The committee's duties are listed in §1103 and include consulting with the DIP; investigating the DIP's prepetition and postpetition conduct and affairs; and participating in the plan process.

The Bankruptcy Code itself does not use the term "fiduciary" or expressly designate either the DIP or the committee as a fiduciary. Nevertheless, case law recognizes the fiduciary nature of both statutory representatives. Specifically, courts treat the DIP as a fiduciary for the bankruptcy estate, and the committee as a fiduciary for those it represents. Courts also have suggested in certain circumstances that the committee's efforts must generally benefit the bankruptcy estate.

A fiduciary relationship traditionally exists where "one party to a fiduciary relation (the entrustor) is dependent on the other (the fiduciary)." The role envisioned for the DIP and the committee under the Bankruptcy Code certainly satisfies this basic definition. The debtor's stakeholders—i.e., parties with economic interests in the bankruptcy estate—rely on the DIP to propose and confirm a plan that maximizes the estate's value. Likewise, creditors or equity holders represented by a committee expect the committee to act in their best interests.

The United States is the only country that allows management such freedom upon insolvency. In England management is replaced by administrators, employees of a large accounting firm. In Canada, reorganization involves the appointment of a monitor, a kind of neutral party that opines on the debtor's proposed actions during the reorganization. Most continental countries simply replace management with a trustee, which is only routinely done in chapter 7 liquidations in the United States

If the debtor's management is not to be trusted, a trustee can be appointed. Appointment of a trustee, however, is often associated with conversion to chapter 7.[4] A less draconian solution is to appoint an examiner under section 1104 (also the provision for appointment of a trustee).

An examiner investigates the debtor or some related party, and reports back. But they do not take over control of the debtor. We saw an example of an examiner's report in Chapter 1 regarding Lehman's use of certain, odd repo transactions. Here's another examiner's report.

IN RE: DYNEGY HOLDINGS, LLC, ET AL., DEBTORS

United States Bankruptcy Court, S.D. New York
No. 11-38111 (CGM)
March 9, 2012
Jointly Administered
Report of Susheel Kirpalani, Examiner

I.   EXECUTIVE SUMMARY OF THE EXAMINER'S CONCLUSIONS

     A.   EXAMINER APPOINTMENT AND MANDATE

On January 11, 2012, Tracy Hope Davis, the United States Trustee for Region 2, appointed Susheel Kirpalani as Chapter 11 Examiner in the bankruptcy cases of Dynegy Holdings, LLC and its debtor affiliates. On January 12, 2012, the Honorable Cecelia G. Morris of the United States Bankruptcy Court for the Southern District of New York approved the appointment. The Examiner was asked to complete an independent, unfettered investigation of certain issues relating to the Debtors' conduct in the months leading up to the bankruptcy

---

4. Oscar Couwenberg & Stephen J. Lubben, *The Costs of Chapter 11 in Context: American and Dutch Business Bankruptcy*, 85 Am. Bankr. L.J. 63 (2011).

filing, and to file a report containing his findings within 60 days. The Examiner was also charged to serve as a court-appointed mediator to attempt to forge a consensual Chapter 11 plan among the Debtors' various constituents.

B.   SUMMARY OF FINDINGS AND CONCLUSIONS

Dynegy Inc. is a publicly traded holding company whose stock is listed on the New York Stock Exchange. Before September 1, 2011, Dynegy Inc.'s only asset was ownership of 100% of the equity in Dynegy Holdings, which in turn owned, through a variety of subsidiaries, all of Dynegy's operations. Dynegy's debt was issued by Dynegy Holdings or its subsidiaries.

Dynegy Holdings and certain of its indirect subsidiaries filed for bankruptcy protection on November 7, 2011. In the three months prior to filing, Dynegy Holdings had transferred or authorized the transfer of billions of dollars of its assets (stock or other direct or indirect ownership interests of subsidiaries) as part of a multi-step plan to reorganize Dynegy's business segments and restructure Dynegy's debts. The first phase of the restructuring facilitated a refinancing of Dynegy Holdings's secured bank debt, which, in the absence of a refinancing, was in danger of a covenant breach. Once the crisis of the potential bank default was averted, Dynegy implemented the next phase of its restructuring plan. The goal of this second phase was to reduce the amount of Dynegy's unsecured debt, while simultaneously increasing value for stockholders. To those familiar with the basic tenets of corporate finance, this may seem paradoxical, as it is a bedrock principle that a company's creditors must be paid in full before its stockholders can receive or retain any value — unless, of course, creditors agree otherwise. Over the spring and summer of 2011, Dynegy devised and implemented a plan to move assets away from the reach of Dynegy Holdings's unsecured creditors in order to encourage, for lack of a better word, such creditors to accept less than full payment and at the same time permit a recovery for stockholders. This report examines whether the techniques that Dynegy employed were legally permissible.

The Bankruptcy Court directed the Examiner to investigate Dynegy's prebankruptcy transactions and to report on the conduct of the Debtors, the existence of any fraudulent transfers, and whether Dynegy Holdings is capable of confirming a Chapter 11 plan. In carrying out its restructuring strategy, Dynegy was principally concerned with whether it was violating any of the contractual prohibitions contained in Dynegy Holdings's debt agreements. If it did not violate the letter of the contracts, then Dynegy believed it was free to implement the strategy of moving assets and, potentially, control away from Dynegy Holdings in the hope of convincing creditors to accept less than full payment for their debt. Dynegy expected that creditors would challenge this strategy and, to maximize its defenses, Dynegy tried to structure its transfers of assets away from Dynegy Holdings in a manner that it could claim were transfers in exchange for fair value. Put simply, Dynegy believed that, even if Dynegy Holdings was insolvent, as long as it transferred assets in exchange for what the law considers "reasonably equivalent value," then creditors would have no legitimate cause to complain.

Dynegy's strategy was permissible with respect to the transfers relating to the first phase of the restructuring, *i.e.*, transfers incident to the creation of two distinct silos of assets, CoalCo and GasCo,[5] because those transfers did not injure creditors and were not, in and of themselves, intended to do so. Indeed, following these so-called "ring-fencing" transactions, both silos of assets continued ultimately to be owned (as they had been) by Dynegy Holdings. While it is true that as a result of the ring-fencing and attendant refinancing of pre-existing secured bank debt, unsecured creditors of Dynegy Holdings could look only to the residual equity value of CoalCo and GasCo, this was, as a practical matter, always the case for unsecured creditors of Dynegy Holdings, regardless of whether the silos were created.[6]

Dynegy's strategy was ill-conceived, however, with respect to the second phase of the restructuring, *i.e.*, the transfer or purported "sale" of CoalCo by Dynegy Holdings to Dynegy Inc. in exchange for a piece of paper that Dynegy actively avoided valuing. This transfer of CoalCo, which the board of Dynegy Inc. then valued at $1.25 billion, was made in exchange for an illiquid, unsecured, highly unusual financial instrument called an "undertaking." In addition, the undertaking had no covenants to protect the holder's value against other actions that might be taken by Dynegy Inc. The Examiner believes that this undertaking had a midpoint value at the time (even prior to its amendment in a manner adverse to Dynegy Holdings) of approximately $860 million. Immediately after Dynegy Inc. provided the undertaking, Dynegy Inc. and Dynegy Holdings agreed to amend it so Dynegy Inc. could reduce its payment obligations by $1.678 over the course of the payment stream (an amount apparently designed to mimic a dollar-for-dollar present value reduction) for each dollar face amount of Dynegy Holdings bonds that was acquired or otherwise retired by Dynegy Inc., even if such debt was acquired or retired at a discount to the face amount. Dynegy took the position that Dynegy Inc.'s future satisfaction of Dynegy Holdings's debt would constitute value, as a matter of law, measured by the face amount of such debt—no matter what Dynegy Inc. paid for such debt, and regardless of whether Dynegy Inc. paid for such debt by pledging the stock of its newly acquired direct subsidiary, CoalCo. In this way, Dynegy Holdings transferred to Dynegy Inc. not only CoalCo, but also the corporate opportunity to use CoalCo as a vehicle for exchanging its outstanding bonds for structurally senior bonds at a discount, or otherwise to control its own restructuring of

5. The terms "CoalCo" and "GasCo" are sometimes used for convenience in this report to refer to the holding companies that were newly formed as part of a "ring-fencing" strategy to hold coal and gas assets previously held by subsidiaries of Dynegy Holdings.

6. To be clear, the amount of refinancing indebtedness did exceed the aggregate amount of Dynegy's funded, secured bank debt and the Sithe Debentures, all of which were repaid with the proceeds of the refinancing. Excess net proceeds of more than $250 million were set aside for general corporate purposes within the CoalCo and GasCo chains. In addition, $400 million of excess net proceeds essentially replaced the same amount of cash previously residing at Dynegy Holdings, which had been used to repay funded, secured bank debt, and was also set aside for general corporate purposes. Those purposes did ultimately include aspects of the second phase of the restructuring, but the Examiner has not found that the lenders under the refinancing loans had clear knowledge that this second phase would definitely occur . . . or, if it did, what the precise terms would be or how it might impact Dynegy Holdings, which was not obligated under the new facilities. As such, this type of financing is distinguishable from those where "collapsing" a loan with the use of the proceeds of such loan (*e.g.*, leveraged buyouts) may well be appropriate to determine the economic substance of a transaction on the borrower.

indebtedness with its own assets. Moreover, the addition of the payment reduction mechanism into the amended undertaking rendered the undertaking unsalable to third-parties, and thereby further eroded the value of the undertaking to Dynegy Holdings.

In other words, if creditors of Dynegy Holdings had been willing to compromise their indebtedness at less than face value in exchange for new debt backed by a pledge of CoalCo stock (which was a Dynegy Holdings asset), absent Dynegy Holdings's transfer of CoalCo to Dynegy Inc., that reduction of indebtedness would have appropriately inured to the benefit of Dynegy Holdings, and not to Dynegy Inc. Reduced to its essence, the transaction transferred hundreds of millions of dollars away from Dynegy's creditors in favor of its stockholders.

The decision to "sell" CoalCo to Dynegy Inc. in exchange for an undertaking and amended undertaking was made and implemented by directors and officers of Dynegy Inc. The three senior-most Dynegy Inc. officers also served as board members of Dynegy Holdings and its newly formed shell subsidiary, Dynegy Gas Investments, LLC. The boards of Dynegy Holdings and DGI did not appreciate that what may be good for Dynegy's ultimate parent, Dynegy Inc., may not be good for Dynegy Inc.'s insolvent[7] subsidiary, Dynegy Holdings. The Examiner believes that these officers did not understand the distinction, from a corporate and fiduciary perspective, between Dynegy Holdings and Dynegy Inc. — a lapse perhaps caused by having the same professionals advise all entities within the consolidated Dynegy family of companies. Indeed, when authorizing the transfer of CoalCo away from Dynegy Holdings, they believed they were attempting to obtain creditor concessions for the benefit of the "company" or "enterprise" as a whole.

The same cannot be said, however, for the board members of Dynegy Inc. Certain members of the Dynegy Inc. board did not even understand the transfer that was being made, or why the CoalCo transfer was prudent or appropriate; others did not even know whether there was a separate Dynegy Holdings board. But other members knew exactly what was happening, and why the CoalCo transfer was being made. In reviewing the CoalCo transfer, the board of Dynegy Inc. relied on the recommendations of the Dynegy Inc. board's Finance and Restructuring Committee.[8] The Chair of the FRC is an experienced investor who is employed by Dynegy Inc.'s largest stockholder. Certain members of the FRC understood that the goal was to capture any value attainable by acquiring Dynegy Holdings's bonds at a discount for the benefit of Dynegy Inc. They did not believe this was inappropriate so long as it did not violate the contractual restrictions in Dynegy Holdings's debt agreements. Indeed, given certain other actions that the FRC Chair believed Dynegy Inc. could have lawfully accomplished in the first phase of the restructuring — such as taking on extensive additional debt in what others called an "extend and pretend" strategy — Dynegy Inc. was, in his

---

7. For the reasons given in the Examiner's Work Plan, filed with the Bankruptcy Court on January 24, 2012, the Examiner has assumed that Dynegy Holdings was insolvent throughout the relevant period. While a solvency analysis is outside the scope of this report, the Examiner believes that such an assumption is reasonable and has ample support in the record.

8. The members of the FRC installed themselves as the majority of the members of the board of Dynegy Holdings shortly before the commencement of these Chapter 11 Cases. As such, as of the date of this report, the Debtors are controlled by the FRC.

view, "entitled" to compensation from Dynegy Holdings's creditors for forgoing such options.

The Examiner concludes that the conveyance of CoalCo to Dynegy Inc. was an actual fraudulent transfer and, assuming that Dynegy Holdings was insolvent on the date of the transfer (approximately two months before the bankruptcy filing), a constructive fraudulent transfer, and a breach of fiduciary duty by the board of directors of Dynegy Holdings. Dynegy Inc., through its board of directors, used its power to control the affairs of Dynegy Holdings—an insolvent subsidiary whose property should have been maximized, or at least safeguarded, for the benefit of Dynegy Holding's creditors—to disadvantage Dynegy Holdings for the benefit of Dynegy Inc. Dynegy Inc.'s conduct provides a basis for disregarding the corporate separateness among Dynegy Inc., Dynegy Holdings, and Dynegy Holdings's newly formed shell subsidiary, DGI. As such, DGI should be considered the alter ego of Dynegy Holdings, and DGI's transfer of CoalCo should be deemed a transfer to Dynegy Inc. of an interest in property of Dynegy Holdings. In that event, Dynegy Holdings would have a claim against Dynegy Inc. for the fraudulent transfer of CoalCo. Alternatively, to remedy the injustice occasioned upon Dynegy Holdings and, derivatively, its creditors, CoalCo should be deemed property of Dynegy Holdings's bankruptcy estate. Finally, the breach of fiduciary duty by the board of directors of Dynegy Holdings should be equally attributed to the board of directors of Dynegy Inc.

Throughout the planning and execution of the Prepetition Restructuring, the Dynegy Inc. board favored paths that benefited Dynegy Inc. and its stockholders to the detriment of Dynegy Holdings and its creditors. Indeed, a key purpose of the Prepetition Restructuring, which was identified as early as spring 2011 and ultimately implemented on September 1, 2011, was to transfer value from Dynegy Holdings to and for the benefit of Dynegy Inc., cloaking the central transaction with the semblance of fair value. The Examiner concludes that the Bankruptcy Court could confirm a chapter 11 plan for Dynegy Holdings, but, in light of the conduct of all but one of the members of the board of Dynegy Inc. as of September 1, 2011, four of whom now constitute the majority of the board of Dynegy Holdings, any plan that provides for these individuals to continue as directors would not be consistent with the interests of creditors and with public policy. That being said, the Examiner does not believe the continued service by senior management of Dynegy Inc., even in director or officer capacities, would be contrary to creditor interests or public policy.

In this case, the United States Trustee read the examiner's report and on March 11 moved for the appointment of a trustee. Ultimately the issue was settled, as you will see in a coming chapter.

3.   STABILIZING THE BUSINESS

In the days and weeks before a chapter 11 filing, bankruptcy attorneys begin to understand the debtor's business and documents are prepared to ease the company into the chapter 11 with minimal disruption to its business. Ideally.

In Lehman, the bankruptcy attorneys reportedly had a few hours to prepare to file the biggest bankruptcy case ever.

This prebankruptcy preparation has to be done carefully and confidentially. Otherwise the debtor risks having an involuntary case filed against it, vendors may stop supplying the debtor, forcing an earlier filing than planned, and there is always the risk of insider trading. Remember the discussion of short selling from earlier chapters.

Beyond the petition, the debtor will usually file motions to retain their bankruptcy counsel, motions to approve new financing arrangements (the subject of the next section of this chapter), and a series of "first day" motions. For example, the Code generally prohibits a debtor from paying any prepetition debts, so a debtor might file a motion seeking permission to pay prepetition employee wages or prepetition claims of critical trade vendors — imagine the railroad that delivers coal to the debtor's power plant.

The idea is that despite what the Code might require, the debtor will lose value by not paying employees and critical trade vendors who have no legal obligation to continue to work with the debtor after bankruptcy. In the days when these motions were done in paper form, they typically comprised a large black, four-inch binder that had a partner binder with all of the petitions for the case.

Not everyone thinks that first day motions are a good idea.

IN THE MATTER OF: KMART CORPORATION, DEBTOR-APPELLANT ADDITIONAL INTERVENING APPELLANTS: KNIGHT-RIDDER, INC.; HANDLEMAN COMPANY; IRVING PULP & PAPER, LIMITED

359 F.3d 866

United States Court of Appeals, Seventh Circuit

Nos. 03-1956, 03-1999, 03-2000, 03-2001, 03-2035, 03-2262, 03-2346, 03-2347, 03-2348 |
Argued Jan. 22, 2004 | Decided Feb. 24, 2004 | Rehearing and Rehearing En Banc Denied
May 6, 2004

EASTERBROOK, Circuit Judge.

On the first day of its bankruptcy, Kmart sought permission to pay immediately, and in full, the pre-petition claims of all "critical vendors." (Technically there are 38 debtors: Kmart Corporation plus 37 of its affiliates and subsidiaries. We call them all Kmart.) The theory behind the request is that some suppliers may be unwilling to do business with a customer that is behind in payment, and, if it cannot obtain the merchandise that its own customers have come to expect, a firm such as Kmart may be unable to carry on, injuring all of its creditors. Full payment to critical vendors thus could in principle make even the disfavored creditors better off: they may not be paid in full, but they will receive a greater portion of their claims than they would if the critical vendors cut off supplies and the business shut down. Putting the proposition in this way implies, however, that the debtor must *prove*, and not just allege, two things: that, but for immediate full payment, vendors *would* cease dealing; and that the business will gain enough from continued transactions with the favored vendors to provide some residual benefit to the remaining, disfavored creditors, or at least leave them no worse off.

Bankruptcy Judge Sonderby entered a critical-vendors order just as Kmart proposed it, without notifying any disfavored creditors, without receiving any pertinent evidence (the record contains only some sketchy representations by counsel plus unhelpful testimony by Kmart's CEO, who could not speak for the vendors), and without making any finding of fact that the disfavored creditors would gain or come out even. The bankruptcy court's order declared that the relief Kmart requested — open-ended permission to pay any debt to any vendor it deemed "critical" in the exercise of unilateral discretion, provided that the vendor agreed to furnish goods on "customary trade terms" for the next two years — was "in the best interests of the Debtors, their estates and their creditors." The order did not explain why, nor did it contain any legal analysis, though it did cite 11 U.S.C. §105(a). (The bankruptcy court issued two companion orders covering international vendors and liquor vendors. Analysis of all three orders is the same, so we do not mention these two further.)

Kmart used its authority to pay in full the pre-petition debts to 2,330 suppliers, which collectively received about $300 million. This came from the $2 billion in new credit (debtor-in-possession or DIP financing) that the bankruptcy judge authorized, granting the lenders super-priority in post-petition assets and revenues. Another 2,000 or so vendors were not deemed "critical" and were not paid. They and 43,000 additional unsecured creditors eventually received about 10¢ on the dollar, mostly in stock of the reorganized Kmart. Capital Factors, Inc., appealed the critical-vendors order immediately after its entry on January 25, 2002. A little more than 14 months later, after all of the critical vendors had been paid and as Kmart's plan of reorganization was on the verge of approval, District Judge Grady reversed the order authorizing payment. 291 B.R. 818 (N.D.Ill.2003). He concluded that neither §105(a) nor a "doctrine of necessity" supports the orders.

Appellants insist that, by the time Judge Grady acted, it was too late. Money had changed hands and, we are told, cannot be refunded. But why not?

Thus we arrive at the merits. Section 105(a) allows a bankruptcy court to "issue any order, process, or judgment that is necessary or appropriate to carry out the provisions of" the Code. This does not create discretion to set aside the Code's rules about priority and distribution; the power conferred by §105(a) is one to implement rather than override. We agree with this view of §105. "The fact that a [bankruptcy] proceeding is equitable does not give the judge a free-floating discretion to redistribute rights in accordance with his personal views of justice and fairness, however enlightened those views may be." In re Chicago, Milwaukee, St. Paul & Pacific R.R., 791 F.2d 524, 528 (7th Cir.1986).

A "doctrine of necessity" is just a fancy name for a power to depart from the Code. Although courts in the days before bankruptcy law was codified wielded power to reorder priorities and pay particular creditors in the name of "necessity" — see Miltenberger v. Logansport Ry., 106 U.S. 286, 1 S.Ct. 140, 27 L.Ed. 117 (1882); Fosdick v. Schall, 99 U.S. 235, 25 L.Ed. 339 (1878) — today it is the Code rather than the norms of nineteenth century railroad reorganizations that must prevail. *Miltenberger* and *Fosdick* predate the first general effort at codification, the Bankruptcy Act of 1898. Today the Bankruptcy Code of 1978 supplies the rules. Congress did not in terms scuttle old common-law doctrines, because it did not need to; the Act curtailed, and then the Code replaced, the entire apparatus. Answers to contemporary issues must be found within the Code (or legislative halls). Older doctrines may survive as glosses on ambiguous language enacted in 1978 or later, but not as freestanding entitlements to trump the text.

So does the Code contain any grant of authority for debtors to prefer some vendors over others? Many sections require equal treatment or specify the details of priority when assets are insufficient to satisfy all claims. E.g., 11 U.S.C. §§507, 1122(a), 1123(a)(4). Appellants rely on 11 U.S.C. §§363(b), 364(b), and 503 as sources of authority for unequal treatment. Section 364(b) reads: "The court, after notice and a hearing, may authorize the trustee to obtain unsecured credit or to incur unsecured debt other than under subsection (a) of this section, allowable under section 503(b)(1) of this title as an administrative expense." This authorizes the debtor to obtain credit (as Kmart did) but has nothing to say about how the money will be disbursed or about priorities among creditors. To the extent that In re Payless Cashways, Inc., 268 B.R. 543 (Bankr.W.D.MO.2001), and similar decisions, hold otherwise, they are unpersuasive. Section 503, which deals with administrative expenses, likewise is irrelevant. Pre-filing debts are not administrative expenses; they are the antithesis of administrative expenses. Filing a petition for bankruptcy effectively creates two firms: the debts of the pre-filing entity may be written down so that the post-filing entity may reorganize and continue in business if it has a positive cash flow. Treating pre-filing debts as "administrative" claims against the post-filing entity would impair the ability of bankruptcy law to prevent old debts from sinking a viable firm.

That leaves §363(b)(1): "The trustee [or debtor in possession], after notice and a hearing, may use, sell, or lease, other than in the ordinary course of business, property of the estate." This is more promising, for satisfaction of a pre-petition debt in order to keep "critical" supplies flowing is a use of property other than in the ordinary course of administering an estate in bankruptcy. Capital Factors insists that §363(b)(1) should be limited to the commencement of capital projects, such as building a new plant, rather than payment of old debts — as paying vendors would be "in the ordinary course" but for the intervening bankruptcy petition. To read §363(b)(1) broadly, Capital Factors observes, would be to allow a judge to rearrange priorities among creditors (which is what a critical-vendors order effectively does), even though the Supreme Court has cautioned against such a step. Yet what these decisions principally say is that priorities do not change unless a statute supports that step; and if §363(b)(1) is such a statute, then there is no insuperable problem. If the language is too open-ended, that is a problem for the legislature. Nonetheless, it is prudent to read, and use, §363(b)(1) to do the least damage possible to priorities established by contract and by other parts of the Bankruptcy Code. We need not decide whether §363(b)(1) could support payment of some pre-petition debts, because *this* order was unsound no matter how one reads §363(b)(1).

The foundation of a critical-vendors order is the belief that vendors not paid for prior deliveries will refuse to make new ones. Without merchandise to sell, a retailer such as Kmart will fold. If paying the critical vendors would enable a successful reorganization and make even the disfavored creditors better off, then all creditors favor payment whether or not they are designated as "critical." This suggests a use of §363(b)(1) similar to the theory underlying a plan crammed down the throats of an impaired class of creditors: if the impaired class does at least as well as it would have under a Chapter 7 liquidation, then it has no legitimate objection and cannot block the reorganization. For the premise to hold true, however, it is necessary to show not only that the disfavored creditors *will* be as well off with reorganization as with liquidation — a demonstration never attempted in this proceeding — but also that the supposedly critical vendors would have ceased deliveries if old debts were left unpaid while the litigation continued. If vendors will deliver against a promise of current payment, then a reorganization can be achieved, and all unsecured creditors will obtain its benefit, without preferring any of the unsecured creditors.

Some supposedly critical vendors will continue to do business with the debtor because they must. They may, for example, have long term contracts, and the automatic stay prevents these vendors from walking away as long as the debtor pays for new deliveries. See 11 U.S.C. §362. Fleming Companies, which received the largest critical-vendors payment because it sold Kmart between $70 million and $100 million of groceries and related goods weekly, was one of these. No matter how much Fleming would have liked to dump Kmart, it had no right to do so. It was unnecessary to compensate Fleming for continuing to make deliveries that it was legally required to make. Nor was Fleming likely to walk away even if it had a legal right to do so. Each new delivery produced a profit; as long as Kmart continued to pay for new product, why would any vendor drop the account? That would be a self-inflicted wound. To abjure new profits because of old debts would be to commit the sunk-cost fallacy; well-managed businesses are unlikely to do this. Firms that disdain current profits because of old losses are unlikely to stay in business. They might as well burn money or drop it into the ocean. Again Fleming illustrates the point. When Kmart stopped buying its products after the contract expired, Fleming collapsed (Kmart had accounted for more than 50% of its business) and filed its own bankruptcy petition. Fleming was hardly likely to have quit selling of its own volition, only to expire the sooner.

Doubtless many suppliers fear the prospect of throwing good money after bad. It therefore may be vital to assure them that a debtor will pay for new deliveries on a current basis. Providing that assurance need not, however, entail payment for pre-petition transactions. Kmart could have paid cash or its equivalent. (Kmart's CEO told the bankruptcy judge that COD arrangements were not part of Kmart's business plan, as if a litigant's druthers could override the rights of third parties.) Cash on the barrelhead was not the most convenient way, however. Kmart secured a $2 billion line of credit when it entered bankruptcy. Some of that credit could have been used to assure vendors that payment would be forthcoming for all post-petition transactions. The easiest way to do that would have been to put some of the $2 billion behind a standby letter of credit on which the bankruptcy judge could authorize unpaid vendors to draw. That would not have changed the terms on which Kmart and any of its vendors did business; it just would have demonstrated the certainty of payment. If lenders are unwilling to issue such a letter of credit (or if they insist on a letter's short duration), that would be a compelling market signal that reorganization is a poor prospect and that the debtor should be liquidated post haste.

Yet the bankruptcy court did not explore the possibility of using a letter of credit to assure vendors of payment. The court did not find that any firm would have ceased doing business with Kmart if not paid for pre-petition deliveries, and the scant record would not have supported such a finding had one been made. The court did not find that discrimination among unsecured creditors was the only way to facilitate a reorganization. It did not find that the disfavored creditors were at least as well off as they would have been had the critical-vendors order not been entered. For all the millions at stake, this proceeding looks much like the Chapter 13 reorganization that produced *In re Crawford*, 324 F.3d 539 (7th Cir.2003). Crawford had wanted to classify his creditors in a way that would enable him to pay off those debts that would not be discharged, while stiffing the creditors whose debts were dischargeable. We replied that even though classification (and thus unequal treatment) is possible for Chapter 13 proceedings, see 11 U.S.C. §1322(b), the step would be proper only when the record shows that the classification would produce some benefit for the disfavored creditors. Just so here. Even if §362(b)(1) allows critical-vendors orders in principle, preferential payments to a class of creditors are proper only if the record shows the prospect of benefit to the other creditors. This record does not, so the critical-vendors order cannot stand.

For a while there were three common venues for filing big chapter 11 cases: New York, Wilmington, and Chicago. Now there are two.

PROBLEM SET 28.1

1. Think about how the Kmart attorneys could have avoided this problem in the first instance. In the interest of full disclosure, you might want to know that your author worked on the Kmart case — but not this issue.
2. The necessity of payment doctrine that undergirds most first day motions has its roots in the old railroad reorganization cases. As a matter of public policy, railroads were not allowed to liquidate, which gave the "critical" vendors extreme bargaining power. Should that influence the analysis today?

4. FINANCING THE BUSINESS

Many bankruptcy filings are caused by liquidity problems. And if the debtor did not have a liquidity problem before, after chapter 11 they likely will, as vendors demand cash upon delivery.

The Bankruptcy Code provides ways for the debtor to obtain new, post-bankruptcy financing.

ATP RECEIVE FINAL APPROVAL FOR NEW SENIOR FINANCING
By Bill Rochelle, September 24, 2012, Bloomberg.com[9]

ATP Oil & Gas Corp., a producer and developer of oil and gas wells mostly in the Gulf of Mexico, received final approval on Sept. 20 for secured financing that includes $250 million in new borrowing power plus conversion of about $365 million in pre-bankruptcy secured debt into a post-bankruptcy obligation.

ATP filed under Chapter 11 in August when cash was down to $10 million. The Houston-based company listed assets of $3.6 billion and $3.5 billion of liabilities on the March 31 balance sheet.

The new financing is being provided by some of the same lenders owed $365 million on a first-lien loan where **Credit Suisse AG** serves as agent. There is $1.5 billion on second-lien notes with **Bank of New York Mellon Trust Co.** as agent. The new loan comes in ahead of the existing second-lien debt.

ATP's other debt includes $35 million on convertible notes and $23.4 million owing to third parties for their shares of production revenue. Trade suppliers have claims for $147 million, ATP said in a court filing.

The second-lien notes traded on Sept. 21 for 22.25 cents on the dollar, according to Trace, the bond-price reporting system of the **Financial Industry Regulatory Authority**. The notes traded at 29.625 cents on Aug. 17, the day of the Chapter 11 filing in Houston.

ATP reported a net loss of $145.1 million in the first quarter on revenue of $146.6 million. Income from operations in the quarter was $11.8 million. For 2011, the net loss was $210.5 million on revenue of $687.2 million. The year's operating income was $152.7 million.

———————

This article gives you one clue as to why a lender might want to lend to a bankruptcy company. How much money did the debtor borrow exactly? How much did this loan help its liquidity issues?

Section 364 is the place to look with regard to post-bankruptcy financing. But you might first look at section 363 with regard to cash collateral. The normal rule in bankruptcy is that the debtor can continue to use its property, even property that secured a pre-bankruptcy loan, in the ordinary course of business.

There is one important exception for cash collateral, which is cash that a lender has a lien on or has a right to set off against. For example, if Chase makes a loan to Bogartco, and Bogartco has its bank account at Chase, the bank can set the two off if Bogartco defaults on the loan.

How might Bogartco avoid this threat to its continued operations?

To use cash collateral, a debtor must either get the consent of the secured party or court authorization. If the creditor does not consent to the use of its cash collateral, then the debtor must provide "adequate protection" to the lender — essentially, the debtor must compensate the creditor for any loss the creditor might experience from not being able to take the collateral back right now.

If the debtor has no cash whatsoever, then they will require a loan. Section 364 of the Bankruptcy Code permits a debtor to borrow funds and offers protections and priorities to induce lenders to make these loans, which are called "DIP loans."

Take a look at section 364 before reading the next case.

IN RE LOS ANGELES DODGERS LLC, ET AL., DEBTORS

457 B.R. 308

United States Bankruptcy Court, D. Delaware

No. 11-12010(KG) | Re: Dkt No. 13 | July 22, 2011

Kevin GROSS, Bankruptcy Judge.

On June 27, 2011, Los Angeles Dodgers LLC,[10] and affiliates, debtors and debtors in possession in the above-captioned cases (the "Debtors"), filed the Emergency Motion for Interim and Final Orders (I) Authorizing Debtors to Obtain Postpetition Financing pursuant to 11 U.S.C. §§105, 362, and 364, and (II) Scheduling a Final Hearing Pursuant to Bankruptcy Rule 4001(b) and (c) [D.I. 13] (the "Motion"). Debtors sought the Court's approval of proposed financing further described below.

The Debtors and objecting parties reached agreement on revised terms. The Court entered an order on June 28, 2011 [D.I. 52] (the "Interim DIP Order") that, among other things, approved the Motion on an interim basis on the terms set forth in the Interim DIP Order and scheduled and held an evidentiary hearing on July 20, 2011.

Debtors seek authority to obtain final approval of postpetition financing consisting of a superpriority delayed draw term loan facility in an aggregate principal amount of up to $150,000,000 (the "DIP Facility"). Debtors received an initial draw of $60 million upon entry of the Interim Order and the remaining $90 million would be available from time to time following entry of a final order.

The proposed lenders are a group in the Highbridge Senior Loan Fund II family of funds ("Highbridge"), with whom Debtors have entered into a Credit and Security Agreement on terms more fully described below (the "Highbridge Loan"). The Office of the Commissioner of Baseball (the "Commissioner"), doing business as Major League Baseball ("Baseball") has objected to the Motion and the terms of the Highbridge Loan and has proposed its own loan (the "Baseball Loan") which it characterizes as an unsecured loan. Debtors dispute the nature of the loan.

Baseball fairly counters that, to date, Debtors have flatly refused to negotiate its proposal. Baseball is prepared immediately to engage in good faith negotiations toward an unsecured loan on the terms placed on the record.

---

10. This entity owns the Los Angeles Dodgers Major League Baseball team (the "Dodgers") whose rich and successful history is of mythical proportions. Its great former players, managers and executives could justify their own hall of fame. Formerly the Brooklyn Dodgers, the team name is derived from fans who used to "dodge" that city's trolleys.

The essential terms of the Highbridge Loan are as follows:

Amount:	$150,000,000 multiple draw term loans (of which $60,000,000 has been funded)
Rate:	LIBOR plus 6.00% for LIBOR Loans with a LIBOR floor of 3.00%
Timing of Interest Payments:	Paid at the end of an Interest Period/monthly during term of the facility
Number of Borrowings:	Borrower may only specify up to two Borrowing Dates during any 30 day period
Fees:	Closing date fees paid per Fee Letter:

- Closing commitment payment: 3.5% of the DIP Loan Commitment ($5,250,000), which has already been paid

Agent fee: $50,000 (paid annually)

Additional Credit Agreement Fees:

- Delayed draw fee: 0.50% of undrawn commitment
- Deferred commitment fee: $4,500,000 upon earlier of repayment in full and maturity
- Audit and collateral monitoring fees

Maturity:	June 27, 2012 (before expiration of Fox Sports' right of first negotiation)
Security:	All Assets of the Loan Parties
Debt Priority:	Super-priority administrative expense claims under section 364(c), senior to all other administrative expense claims

The Court will decide the Motion on the narrowest grounds possible, i.e., applying the applicable section of the Bankruptcy Code to the dispute and leaving to a later, more appropriate day, the issues surrounding the underlying feud between the Commissioner and Debtors' principal, Frank McCourt ("Mr. McCourt")[11]. It is clear that Baseball needs and wants the Dodgers to succeed and the Debtors are best served by maintaining Baseball's good will and contributing to the important and profitable franchise group under the Commissioner's leadership.

---

11. Mr. McCourt blames the Commissioner for Debtors' woes while the Commissioner alleges Mr. McCourt's mismanagement and self-dealing are the cause. It appears that their dispute will shortly be before the Court. Their acrimonious relationship and Mr. McCourt's belief that the Commissioner is hostile toward him is an unhelpful distraction which obfuscates the uncontroverted testimony from Debtors' representative, Mr. Jeffrey Ingram, that Baseball is not hostile to the Debtors.

A comparison of the Highbridge Loan and the proposed Baseball Loan clearly shows the substantial economic superiority of the Baseball Loan, as follows:

	Highbridge DIP Facility	*MLB DIP Facility*
Fees:	0.50% Delayed Draw Fee $4.5 MM Deferred Comm Fee $5.25 MM Closing Comm Fee $50,000 Annual Agent Fee	None
Interest Rate:	LIBOR + 6% (3% Floor) Base Rate + 6.0%	LIBOR + 5.5% (1.5% Floor) Base Rate + 4.5%
Security:	All Estate Assets	Unsecured
Priority:	Super–Priority Administrative	Administrative
Events of Default:	Case Dismissal Trustee or Examiner Appointed Termination of Debtors' Rights under Baseball Agreement	No Onerous Events of Default
Maturity Date:	June 27, 2012 (Before Fox Sports' Right of First Negotiation)	November 30, 2012 (After Fox Sports' Right of First Negotiation)

The Court will deny the Motion, premised upon of Section 364(b) of the Bankruptcy Code, 11 U.S.C. §364(b), which explicitly precludes the Highbridge Loan where, as here, Debtors are unable to prove that they are "unable to obtain unsecured credit allowable under section 503(b)(1) . . . as an administrative expense." The opposite holds true, *viz.*, Baseball is ready, anxious and able to provide unsecured financing and has committed to do whatever it takes to do just that. The Court will insure that Baseball honors its commitment.

In seeking approval of the Highbridge Loan, the Debtors have the burden of proving that:

(1) They are unable to obtain unsecured credit per 11 U.S.C. §364(b), i.e., by allowing a lender only an administrative claim per 11 U.S.C. §503(b)(1)(A);

(2) The credit transaction is necessary to preserve the assets of the estate; and

(3) The terms of the transaction are fair, reasonable, and adequate, given the circumstances of the debtor-borrower and the proposed lender.

The Court "may not approve any credit transaction under subsection (c) [of Section 364] unless the debtor demonstrates that it has attempted, but failed, to obtain unsecured credit under section 364(a) or (b)." In re Ames Dep't Stores, Inc., 115 B.R. 34, 37 (Bankr.S.D.N.Y.1990).

Debtors not only failed to attempt to obtain unsecured financing, they refused to engage Baseball in negotiations because, they explained, Baseball has been hostile to Debtors.

Debtors correctly posit that courts will almost always defer to the business judgment of a debtor in the selection of the lender. The business judgment rule is a standard of judicial review designed to protect the wide latitude conferred on a board of directors in handling the affairs of the corporate enterprise. The rule refers to the judicial policy of deferring to the business judgment of corporate directors in the exercise of their broad discretion in making corporate decisions. Under the rule, courts will not second-guess a business decision, so long as corporate management exercised a minimum level of care in arriving at the decision. The business judgment rule under Delaware law and the law of numerous other jurisdictions establishes a presumption that in making a business decision, the directors of a corporation acted on an informed basis, in good faith, and in the honest belief that the action taken was in the best interests of the company.

Under this formulation, the business judgment rule governs unless the opposing party can show one of four elements: (1) the directors did not in fact make a decision, (2) the directors' decision was uninformed; (3) the directors were not disinterested or independent; or (4) the directors were grossly negligent. Baseball relies on the third exception to argue that the business judgment rule does not apply. Baseball says Mr. McCourt did not make a disinterested or independent decision.

The evidence shows that if Debtors, controlled by Mr. McCourt, did not seek court approval for the Highbridge Loan, Mr. McCourt would personally owe $5.25 million to Highbridge. Such potential personal liability clearly compromised Debtors'/McCourt's independent judgment. Therefore, Debtors' decision is not entitled to review using the business judgment standard. Instead, the Court must review Debtors' decision to accept the Highbridge Loan applying the entire fairness standard. This requires proof of fair dealing and fair price and terms. Moran v. Household Int'l, Inc., 500 A.2d 1346 (Del.Supr.1985). The Debtors did not establish that the terms of the Highbridge Loan are entirely fair, particularly given Baseball's competing terms.

Additionally, Debtors refused to negotiate terms with Baseball to obtain a better and unsecured loan because of Mr. McCourt's poor relationship with the Commissioner. In this case, the Debtors decision to select the Highbridge Loan and refuse to negotiate with Baseball arises from recent dealings which Debtors claim show clearly an unworkable relationship with Baseball which will be harmful to reorganization efforts.[12] Further, Debtors contend that Highbridge is motivated to lend for commercial purposes unlike Baseball which Debtors fear has a nefarious strategy, namely, to seize control of the Dodgers away from Mr. McCourt. The Court finds that the Baseball Loan is not a vehicle for Baseball to control Debtors. Had Debtors negotiated with Baseball, a more economically viable loan may have developed—but at a high cost to the

---

12. It is unclear to the Court how Debtors think they can successfully operate a team within the framework of Baseball if they are unwilling to sit with Baseball to consider and negotiate even more favorable loan terms while under the Court's protection.

Debtors' decision-maker, Mr. McCourt. The Court therefore concludes that Debtors' decision is not entitled to deference as a matter of business judgment. Consequently, Debtors had to prove the entire fairness of the Highbridge Loan — fair dealing and fair price. Baseball's willingness to extend unsecured credit on better terms and Debtors' refusal to negotiate with Baseball precludes a finding of entire fairness.

The Court is confident that Baseball will propose to Debtors a short form credit agreement that is genuinely unsecured in nature and contains minimal — if any — representations, covenants and warranties, no releases for prepetition actions and no default triggers for violations of Baseball's rules and regulations. The Baseball Loan must be independent of and uncoupled from Baseball's oversight and governance of the Dodgers under the Major League Baseball Constitution. The Court, if necessary and as always, will provide ready access to Debtors in the hopefully unlikely event that Baseball strays from its obligations to act in good faith as Debtors' lender.

At the same time, Debtors are directed to negotiate with Baseball cooperatively and in good faith. Debtors and Baseball are entitled to the other's full cooperation in finalizing and administering an unsecured loan facility.

Therefore, based foremost on Debtors' failure to satisfy the statutory predicate for the Highbridge Loan and, secondarily, for failure to prove the entire fairness of the Highbridge Loan, the Court hereby denies the Motion.

5. DYNEGY IN BANKRUPTCY

Available online is a package of Dynegy materials related to the commencement of its bankruptcy case. Review them and be prepared to discuss them in class. Consider the purpose of the various pleadings, and how you might respond to them if you were representing a large bondholder in the Dynegy case.

29

SELL AND LIQUIDATE
REORGANIZATIONS

Chapter 11 as drafted in the late 1970s was designed to facilitate the negotiation and implementation of a reorganization plan. But after a few notable missteps in the 1980s — including the ultimate liquidation of PanAm and Eastern, two major airlines, following lengthy chapter 11 cases — senior creditors began to look to new ways to use the bankruptcy process in ways that would increase their power. After all, these creditors were held at bay while these unsuccessful reorganization attempts took place.

The power of senior secured lenders, particularly lenders who have granted debtor-firms a lifeline in bankruptcy under section 364, became the obvious tool.

STEPHANIE BEN-ISHAI & STEPHEN J. LUBBEN, *INVOLUNTARY CREDITORS AND CORPORATE BANKRUPTCY*

45 UBC L.Rev. 253 (2012)

Traditional corporate reorganization involves the acceptance of a plan by creditors, with a concomitant reduction of the debtors fixed claims and realignment of its operations. In the U.S., this process is facilitated by an automatic stay of actions against the debtor, and a similar stay is typically entered in Canadian *CCAA [Companies' Creditors Arrangements Act]* proceedings. In chapter 11, unsecured creditors are typically represented by a committee, while in *CCAA* this role is taken up by the monitor. The debtor formulates a plan, and the creditors then vote on the same. After the creditors approve the plan, the court will consider the plan and, if it meets the provisions of the statute, sanction it and it becomes binding on all claimants.

This traditional form of corporate bankruptcy is increasingly rare in larger corporate insolvency cases.[1] Instead, debtors utilize their power to sell their assets first, and then proceed to formulate a plan that distributes the sale proceeds to creditors.

Take, for example, the well-known case of Lehman Brothers. The Lehman holding company filed under chapter 11 in New York on 15 September 2008 and then sold office buildings and the North American investment-banking business to Barclays one week later. It recently confirmed a plan that will distribute the proceeds of this and other asset sales to creditors over time.

This change in approach has been attributed to the growing power of secured lenders. This is particularly true in the U.S., where it is argued that secured lenders have learned the lessons of the Eastern Airlines case — a major airline case from the 1980s that is said to typify debtor control, and which ultimately resulted in the eventual liquidation of Eastern — and now understand how they can use their prebankruptcy power over the debtor's liquidity to control the chapter 11 process.

But this is more a story of how, than why. Aside from the implicit benefits of avoiding a lengthy reorganization process, the reasons for why this turn to quick sales has happened, and whether it benefits anyone besides the senior lenders, is still open to debate. And some argue that the trend is affirmatively harmful to the goal of maximizing the value of the debtor.

The nearest thing to a normative justification for quick sales has been Baird and Rasmussen's argument that current American chapter 11 debtors generally lack substantial debtor-specific value, and thus the sale of these assets is apt to realize as much as any reorganization of the same.[2] This "no harm, no foul" argument was very likely a product of the specific time when Baird and Rasmussen wrote their papers: during the early part of this century the American bankruptcy system was still dealing with the remnants of the "tech bubble" of the late 1990s, meaning that many debtors of that era had fewer fixed assets than before, and, as we now know all too well, there was also a simultaneous credit bubble that allowed for purchasers to easily finance the acquisition of distressed assets, which no doubt reduced the risk that quick sales would result in reduced prices.

In this paper we present a new justification for quick sales that turns on the presence of involuntary creditors, especially environmental claims. Particularly in the U.S. . . . the existing case law on environmental claims in reorganization proceedings strongly encourages the breakup of the firm: untainted assets are transferred to a new owner, while the old debtor liquidates the contaminated property along with a distribution of the sale proceeds.

In Canada a similar set of issues are at stake, although the law is less developed on this point — especially since the asset sale provision of the *CCAA* is relatively new, its current form only coming into being with the 2009 reforms to the *CCAA*. In the past, without any express provisions dealing with asset sales in the *CCAA*,

---

1. Stephanie Ben-Ishai & Stephen J Lubben, "Sales or Plans: A Comparative Account of the 'New'-Corporate Reorganization" (2011) 56:3 McGill LJ 591. See also *Re Chrysler LLC*, 576 F (3d) 108 at 115 (2d Cir 2009), rev'd on other grounds (2009), 130 S Ct 1015 (Mem 2009), citing Douglas G Baird & Robert K Rasmussen, "The End of Bankruptcy" (2002) 55:3 Stan L Rev 751 at 751–52.

2. Douglas G. Baird & Robert K. Rasmussen, "Chapter 11 at Twilight" (2003) 56:3 Stan L Rev 673.

Canadian courts relied on their powers to impose terms and conditions under a stay order.

The tendency to move towards sales as opposed to reorganization plans is driven by two related factors: the focus on environmental obligations status as "claims," and the development in both chapter 11 and the *CCAA* of a strong ability to sell assets free and clear of charges on those assets.

The question of whether an environmental obligation is a claim has been particularly significant in the U.S., but the apparent victory of environmental regulators on this point is apt to be hollow, as it depends on the debtor's continued operations postinsolvency. And the growing strength of sale orders, transferring assets free and clear of obligations, means that the debtor and its controlling creditors are increasingly unconcerned about the ability to obtain a discharge at the end of the reorganization process. As the discharge loses its significance, the power of involuntary creditors is apt to dwindle . . .

If a debtor stays largely intact during its reorganization, the scope of its discharge at the end of the *CCAA* or chapter 11 process is key. But if the debtor sells most of its assets, discharge wanes in importance. And if the debtor can create a new entity to buy its assets, then the distinction between "normal" reorganization and sale vanishes from an operational perspective, and the only question is which process better rids the assets of past errors, thus maximizing the value of the same.

Outside of reorganization, the general rule is that an asset sale does not result in a transfer of liabilities, unlike a merger. But several other doctrines limit the general rule. For example, in many jurisdictions in the U.S., courts have developed successor liability doctrines that lead to continued liability for a purchaser for product defects. Moreover, a buyer outside of reorganization takes subject to the risk that the transaction will be challenged *ex post* as a fraudulent transfer, if the debtor is deemed to have sold its assets "too cheap."

Thus, in the chapter 11 or *CCAA* sale context, the vital feature of reorganization law is the ability to sell assets free and clear of claims to the buyer. For example, section 363(f) of the *Bankruptcy Code* authorizes the trustee or a debtor in possession to sell property of a debtor "free and clear of any interest in such property." An interest in property includes claims that arise from the assets being sold.

Essentially, section 363(f) authorizes the bankruptcy court to grant relief similar to the discharge enjoyed by debtors under the Bankruptcy Code, exonerating a buyer from successor liability, including liability for the debtor's environmental claims that are unrelated to the purchased assets.

The excerpt foreshadows the discussion of successor liability and bankruptcy sales late in the chapter, but also suggests a reason to prefer a sale over a traditional plan.

Many large chapter 11 cases involve Canadian subsidiaries, or even Canadian parent companies; so learning a bit about the CCAA doesn't hurt either.

Asset purchase agreements used in chapter 11 mirror those used in normal corporate circumstances. The key difference is that the buyer knows they will inevitably have to subject their bid to an auction process, which essentially means that all asset sales in bankruptcy invoke something like the *Revlon* duties in the board. And the agreement will typically include detailed procedures for conducting the sale of the debtor.

1. THE AUCTION PROCESS

Before the sale can happen, the debtor needs to set up an auction process to prove that it is obtaining the highest possible value for its creditors. The Bankruptcy Code provides no guidance on how such an auction should be conducted, but over the years courts, particularly in New York and Delaware, have developed a series of routine procedures that are typically put in place before the auction.

IN RE INNKEEPERS USA TRUST, ET AL., DEBTORS

448 B.R. 131
United States Bankruptcy Court, S.D. New York
No. 10-13800 | April 1, 2011

Shelley C. CHAPMAN, Bankruptcy Judge.
Before the Court is the Motion of Innkeepers USA Trust and certain of its debtor affiliates (collectively, the "Debtors") for entry of an order (i) authorizing the Debtors to enter into a commitment letter (the "Commitment Letter") with Five Mile Capital II Pooling REIT LLC ("Five Mile"), Lehman ALI Inc. ("Lehman"), and Midland Loan Services, a division of PNC Bank, National Association, in its capacity as special servicer for the Debtors' fixed rate mortgage loan ("Midland"),[3] (ii) approving the New Party/Midland Commitment between the Debtors and Midland, (iii) approving bidding procedures (the "Bidding Procedures"), (iv) approving bid protections, (v) authorizing an expense reimbursement to "Bidder D," and (vi) modifying cash collateral order to increase expense reserve (the "Motion").

I.   BACKGROUND: EVENTS LEADING TO THE SELECTION OF THE STALKING HORSE
     BIDDER

In late September 2010, the Debtors began working with their advisors to discuss and develop restructuring alternatives which would maximize value. In October 2010, Moelis & Company LLC ("Moelis"), the Debtors' investment banker, proposed and the Board of Trustees of Innkeepers USA Trust (the "Board") approved a timeline for selecting a stalking horse bidder. During that period, the Debtors identified five stalking horse candidates, including

---

3. Midland is the special servicer for that certain secured loan in the amount of not less than $825,402,542 plus interest, costs, and fees (the "Fixed Rate Loan"), owed by certain of the Debtors (the "Fixed Rate Debtors").

Five Mile. On or before the November 23, 2010 deadline established by the Debtors, four of the five stalking horse candidates responded with proposals. After further discussions with the candidates, the Debtors were left with two proposals, one from Five Mile and Lehman (together, "Five Mile/Lehman") and one from the bidder known as "Bidder D."[4]

At a board meeting on December 3, 2010, the Board selected Bidder D as the stalking horse bidder, subject to certain continuing discussions between the parties regarding modifications to Bidder D's bid. On December 11, 2010, Five Mile/Lehman informed the Debtors that it had substantially improved its proposal and that commitment letters had been signed between (i) Five Mile and Lehman and (ii) Five Mile and Midland. After approximately ten days of negotiation between the Debtors and Five Mile/Lehman, including a weekend of "near around-the-clock" negotiations regarding modifications to certain terms of the proposed Commitment Letter, the Independent Committee of the Board and the Board selected Five Mile/Lehman as the stalking horse bidder. As set forth in the Declaration of Mr. William Q. Derrough of Moelis which was filed in support of the Motion, while the Debtors would have preferred the exclusion of certain provisions from the bid, the Debtors determined that the Five Mile/Lehman bid represented the most favorable economic proposal received by the Debtors and provided an opportunity to forge consensus among the Debtors' constituents.

A. THE MOTION

As originally filed with the Court on January 14, 2011, the Motion sought (among other things) authorization for the Debtors to enter into the Commitment Letter with Five Mile and Lehman, which contemplated an enterprise-level transaction involving the Debtors' entire portfolio of 71 hotels. In connection with this stalking horse proposal (the "Original Five Mile/Lehman Bid"), Midland agreed to provide "stapled financing" to fund the Original Five Mile/Lehman Bid or any other qualified bid at the auction which (i) contained a debt-to-capitalization ratio for the reorganized enterprise of not greater than 70% and (ii) provided for payment to Lehman of not less than $200.3 million in cash. Although the Original Five Mile/Lehman Bid was supported by Lehman (as holder of the Floating Loan[5]) and Midland (as special servicer for the Fixed Rate Loan), together comprising over $1 billion in principal amount of secured debt, the chorus of objections to the Motion remained loud and clear.

After the filing of the Motion, the Debtors and their advisors actively continued the marketing process. Moelis compiled a list of potential buyers and made contact with over 200 of these parties, sending teasers to nearly 120 of them. The Debtors also executed more than thirty non-disclosure agreements and responded to detailed diligence requests from approximately thirty

---

4. Due to the highly confidential nature of the bid process, the parties early on adopted the convention of referring to bidders by letter designation.

5. The "Floating Rate Loan" is comprised of (a) that certain senior secured loan in the face amount of $250,000,000, plus interest, costs and fees and (b) that certain junior mezzanine loan in the face amount of $118 million, plus interest, costs, and fees, owed by certain of the Debtors (the "Floating Rate Debtors").

potential investors. Moelis also contacted nine potential financing sources, four of which executed non-disclosure agreements.

On January 24, 2011, the Debtors circulated a more detailed and updated process letter to potential bidders (the "Revised Process Letter"). The Revised Process Letter, which was also filed with the Court, further reminded potential bidders that the Debtors were open to all types of proposals for the Debtors' assets; it stated that the Debtors were willing to consider, in addition to superior enterprise-based transactions, *all* value-maximizing restructuring proposals, including those for pools of assets or individual assets. That same day, the Debtors also issued a widely-publicized press release announcing the Original Five Mile/Lehman Bid and the related Motion and indicating the Debtors' willingness to consider any and all other bids.

To date, as a result of these efforts, the Debtors have received multiple competing bid proposals, which were described in the sealed pleadings filed with the Court. Indeed, it appears that, as late as March 10, 2011, the date on which the hearing on the Motion commenced, interested parties continued to contact the Debtors to express interest in the Debtors' assets. The number of bids and their varying structures (each of which was for less than the entire enterprise) are evidence that there was no confusion in the market as to the Debtors' desire to receive bids in varying forms.

On February 25, 2011, formal objections to the Motion were filed by (i) the Ad Hoc Committee of Preferred Shareholders (the "Ad Hoc Committee"), (ii) LNR Securities Holdings, LLC and the ML-CFC 2006-4 and CSFB 2007-C1 Trusts (collectively, "LNR"), (iii) TriMont Real Estate Advisors, Inc. ("TriMont"), (iv) Appaloosa Investment L.P. I, Palomino Fund Ltd., Thoroughbred Fund L.P., and Thoroughbred Master Ltd. (collectively, "Appaloosa"), (v) CWCapital Asset Management LLC and CIII Asset Management LLC (together, "CW"), and (vi) the Official Committee of Unsecured Creditors.

A statement in response to the objections was filed by Apollo Investment Corporation ("Apollo"). Midland, in its capacity as special servicer, filed (i) a Statement in Support of the Motion, (ii) an Omnibus Reply to the Objections to the Motion, and (iii) a Supplemental Statement in Support of the Motion. Five Mile also filed a Reply to Objections and Statement in Support of the Motion.

B.   THE REVISED FIVE MILE/LEHMAN BID AND THE FINAL FIVE MILE/LEHMAN BID

What happened next exemplifies a chapter 11 process at its best. The Original Five Mile/Lehman Bid was modified — not once, but twice. First, it was revised to remove the seven hotel properties that are secured by individual mortgages (commonly referred to by the parties as the "Seven Sisters"), leaving only the hotels covered by the Fixed Rate Loan and Floating Rate Loan in the revised proposed transaction (the "Revised Five Mile/Lehman Bid"). The Revised Five Mile/Lehman Bid was described for the first time in the Debtors' Omnibus Reply in Support of the Motion, which was filed on March 6, 2011. Drafts of the revised Commitment Letter and Bidding Procedures were served on the Court and the Debtors' key constituents on March 8, 2011, and the final forms of such documents were filed with the Court on March 10, 2011, the date on which the hearing on the Motion commenced. Prior to the continuation of the hearing on March 11, 2011, the Revised Five Mile/Lehman Bid was altered again, and the Debtors submitted further revised, final documents to the Court (the "Final Five Mile/Lehman Bid") which eliminated the payment of any break-up fee to Five Mile/Lehman. Simply put, the creditors and preferred shareholders spoke and the Debtors listened.

It is the Final Five Mile/Lehman Bid and related Bidding Procedures that are before the Court today. The Final Five Mile/Lehman Bid proposes the following significant terms:

- The Final Five Mile/Lehman Bid contemplates an enterprise transaction involving the Debtors identified in Exhibit A to the Commitment Letter (the "Fixed/Floating Debtors") and is valued at $970.7 million. The Final Five Mile/Lehman Bid is comprised of a capital structure that includes approximately $622.5 million of debt financing and approximately $348.2 million of equity.
- The bid covers only the properties securing the Fixed Rate Loan and the Floating Rate Loan, and the Debtors will continue to market the Seven Sisters independent of the Fixed/Floating Debtors.
- Midland will provide "stapled financing" for the Final Five Mile/Lehman Bid as more fully set forth in the Commitment Letter and its related exhibits.
- General unsecured creditors with claims against the Fixed/Floating Debtors will share in a distribution of up to $3.75 million, but not to exceed a recovery of 65% of the face amount of allowed general unsecured claims against such Debtors.
- Apollo will contribute $375,000, all of which will be included in the amounts distributed to general unsecured creditors of the Fixed/Floating Debtors. Apollo will retain whatever rights it may have with respect to Debtors and property that are not covered by the Final Five Mile/Lehman Bid.
- Nothing in the Final Five Mile/Lehman Bid will impact the rights of any person or entity with respect to the $7.4 million in cash that is currently held in a bank account of Debtor Innkeepers USA Limited Partnership, which is not subject to the Final Five Mile/Lehman Bid. No amount of the cash will be distributed in connection with the bid.
- Confirmation of the plan encompassing the Final Five Mile/Lehman Bid will not be tied to the confirmation of any plan related to the Seven Sisters' Debtors.
- Five Mile/Lehman will receive an expense reimbursement of up to $3.0 million.

C. OBJECTIONS TO THE FINAL FIVE MILE/LEHMAN BID

On March 9 and 10, 2011, each of the objecting parties filed a statement indicating to the Court whether or not it intended to pursue its objection to the Motion in light of the revisions to the Original Five Mile/Lehman Bid. Based on each of the statements and the representations made at the hearing held on March 10 and 11, 2011, only Appaloosa continues to object to the Motion. The bases for its objection can be summarized as follows. Appaloosa believes that the revised Bidding Procedures are an impediment to competitive bidding; it specifically asserts that the revised Bidding Procedures do not permit a non-enterprise bid to be "Qualified" for the purpose of an auction and that, along with the "Overbid Allocation," the Bidding Procedures restrict bidders' ability to separately value and bid on "pool assets." Appaloosa further contends that the Lehman "cash-out" provision is a further deterrent to competitive bidding and that the "fiduciary out" contained in the Bidding Procedures does not cure any of these shortcomings. Appaloosa further objects on the basis that the revised Bidding Procedures improperly mandate terms of a plan of reorganization.

II.   APPALOOSA'S STANDING TO BE HEARD

As a preliminary matter, the Court must address whether Appaloosa, as an owner of certificated interests in the Fixed Rate Loan serviced by Midland as special servicer, has standing to be heard and to object to the Motion—specifically, standing to object to the approval of the Final Five Mile/Lehman Bid which now covers only the Fixed/Floating Debtors.

Section 1109(b) of the Bankruptcy Code provides that "[a] party in interest, including the debtor, the trustee, a creditors' committee, an equity security holders' committee, a creditor, an equity security holder, or any indenture trustee, may raise and may appear and be heard on any issue in a case under this chapter." 11 U.S.C. §1109(b). Appaloosa asserts that it has standing in the Debtors' cases under section 1109(b) as a "party in interest." This court has held that a party in interest is one that has a sufficient interest in the outcome of the case that would require representation, or a pecuniary interest that will be directly affected by the case. Courts in this District, while generally interpreting section 1109(b) broadly, have limited "party in interest" standing where a party's interest in the proceeding is not a direct one.

While it appears to be the case that no court has specifically addressed CMBS/REMIC certificateholder standing in a chapter 11 case, several courts have come close . . . Appaloosa holds beneficial interests in the REMICS, the C-6 Trust and the C-7 Trust, that own the Fixed Rate Loan, making it merely an investor in a creditor.

This Court is unpersuaded by Appaloosa's argument that "shutting [it] out of the Bankruptcy Case inevitably will result in litigation in other venues, which ultimately will impede the implementation of a confirmable plan." In light of the consensus the Debtors have achieved in the week prior to the hearing on the Motion with respect to the Final Five Mile/Lehman Bid, it appears that the Debtors can and will propose a confirmable plan for the Fixed/Floating Debtors—and for the Excluded Debtors—in the very near term.

III.   DECISION ON THE MOTION

I will now turn to the ruling on the Motion before the Court. The standards applicable to a motion of this character appear in numerous decisions issued by courts in this Circuit, most significantly (i) the Second Circuit's decision in In re Lionel Corp., 722 F.2d 1063, 1071 (2d Cir.1983); (ii) the District Court's opinion in In re Integrated Resources, 147 B.R. 650 (S.D.N.Y.1992), and (iii) the Bankruptcy Court's decision in In re Global Crossing, 295 B.R. 726 (Bankr.S.D.N.Y.2003), in which Judge Gerber discussed the decisions in *Lionel* and *Integrated Resources*. In each of these decisions, the courts have applied a business judgment test to evaluate whether a sound business purpose justifies the use, sale, or lease of property under section 363 of the Bankruptcy Code.

In *Lionel*, the Court of Appeals for the Second Circuit held that a proposed sale under section 363(b) of the Bankruptcy Code outside of a plan of reorganization should only be approved if the proponents of the sale present "some articulated business justification, other than appeasement of major creditors." In *Integrated Resources*, Judge Mukasey concluded that business judgment rule's presumption shields corporate decision makers and their decisions from judicial second-guessing only when the following elements are present: (i) a business decision, (ii) disinterestedness, (iii) due care, (iv) good faith, and (v) according to some courts and commentators, no abuse of discretion or waste of corporate assets.

I note that today I evaluate only the Debtors' business decision in seeking approval of the stalking horse bid set forth in the final commitment letter, the Bidding Procedures, and the other relief requested in the Motion; plan confirmation issues are not before the Court and all parties' rights are reserved in that regard.

The Court finds that the Debtors have appropriately exercised their business judgment in determining to enter into the Final Five Mile/Lehman Bid and to propose the revised Bidding Procedures. The Debtors have successfully modified the initial stalking horse bid to achieve consensus among their stakeholders, and the Court has found that the only remaining objector, Appaloosa, does not have standing as a certificateholder to be heard on its objections to the Motion and the Final Five Mile/Lehman Bid. After reviewing the uncontroverted declarations of Mr. Ruisi, Mr. Derrough, and Mr. Beilinson, the Court find that the Debtors have a sound business justification for entering into the Final Five Mile/Lehman Bid. Since Five Mile submitted its initial proposal to the Debtors in August 2010, the Debtors have successfully negotiated four subsequent proposals from Five Mile or Five Mile/Lehman, generating approximately $100 million in additional enterprise value. After months of hard-fought negotiations among the parties, which continued through the hearing on the Motion, the Debtors have demonstrated that the Final Five Mile/Lehman Bid constitutes the best bid received to date for the assets of the Fixed/Floating Debtors. For the reasons set forth herein, the Court grants the Motion and authorizes the Debtors to enter into the commitment letter supporting the Final Five Mile/Lehman Bid.

Even if the Court had granted standing to Appaloosa to be heard as a certificateholder with respect to its objections to the Motion, or if the Court considers Appaloosa's objections to be properly asserted in its capacity as a preferred shareholder or a DIP lender, the Court finds each of those objections to be without merit, for the following reasons.

First, Appaloosa argues that the revised Bidding Procedures are improper. Specifically, Appaloosa criticizes (i) the "enterprise only" limitation on bids, which mandates that all bids be structured on terms comparable to the Final Five Mile/Lehman Bid and include a debt to capitalization ratio of not greater than 70%, (ii) the "Overbid Allocation" requiring competing bids to be allocated in the same manner as the Final Five Mile/Lehman Bid, and (iii) the Leman "cash-out" provision, which requires payment in cash to Lehman of at least $200.3 million. Appaloosa asserts that each of these provisions will improperly restrict bidders and "chill" bidding.

The Court disagrees. I note that while, ideally, there would be total flexibility on each of these points in the Debtors' Bidding Procedures, the evidence in the record reveals that the Debtors by all accounts tried but failed to remove the Lehman cash-out provision. Notwithstanding the Debtors' inability to remove this provision, the Debtors have demonstrated to the Court that the other benefits of the Final Five Mile/Lehman Bid, including the fact that it is supported by the two largest secured creditors of the affected Debtors, outweighed this concern. Even LNR's financial advisor, Mr. Ronen Bojmel of Miller Buckfire, testified at his deposition (which, I note, was taken during the period in which LNR strenuously objected to the Motion) that a serious bidder would not have an issue obtaining the leverage in the market to fund a cash portion of its bid as required by the Bidding Procedures.

Similarly, Mr. Greenspan's Declaration indicates that the "not greater than 70%" leverage ratio required for Qualified Bids under the final Bidding Procedures is, if anything, higher than what a buyer may receive in the market. According to Mr. Greenspan, typical financing for hospitality assets in the current marketplace is often limited to 60% or 65% of market value and is very unlikely to exceed the 70% being offered to overbidders by Midland. Based on the entirety of the record — including the fact that interested bidders continued to engage in discussions with the Debtors through the night before the hearing on the Motion — the Court declines to second-guess the business judgment of the Debtors in agreeing to these terms. Far from being "chilled," the bidding process appears to be quite heated.

Appaloosa also criticizes the marketing process through which the Final Five Mile/Lehman Bid was obtained as "flawed" due to the Debtors' "adherence" to an enterprise-level restructuring. While the Court does not believe the Debtors' marketing process was perfect — no such process is — it was not flawed. Without question, the process has continued over an extended period of time and substantial concerns of stakeholders have been addressed as the process evolved. The allegations that the Debtors sent "mixed messages" which confused potential bidders as to whether parties could submit non-enterprise bids are unsubstantiated. To the contrary, as Mr. Derrough states in his Second Supplemental Declaration, contrary to these assertions, he has seen no evidence to support a conclusion that the marketplace is confused. Mr. Derrough declares that

[P]otential buyers have communicated that they understand the flexibility of the Debtors' marketing process and many potential investors are taking advantage of that flexibility by working to formulate proposals either on an enterprise or non-enterprise basis. Further, the fact that the Debtors have received multiple bids for less than the entire enterprise indicates that potential investors were quite clear that the Debtors were, and continue to be, willing to accept bids in all forms.

The Court also notes that the Debtors' assets have been "in play" since September 1, 2010, the date on which the Court declined to approve the Debtors' Plan Support Agreement. Accordingly, for the past six months, the market has been keenly aware of the availability of these assets — as an enterprise, as pools, or individually. There is no evidence that a potential bidder has sat on the sidelines because of the limitations on what constitutes a "Qualified Bid," because it has not had enough time, because the Lehman cash-out provision is a "show-stopper," or because it is "confused" by the Bidding Procedures and Revised Process Letter.

Sophisticated investors and bankers who identify an asset that they believe is undervalued by the marketplace will not be shy about joining the fray here. Strategic and financial buyers who want these valuable hotel properties will step forward if they have not done so already. In that regard, should other bidders wish to come to the table and bid on all or a portion of the Debtors' assets, the Debtors still have a marketing period of forty-five days after the approval of the Motion. For now, the time has come to give the market and the Debtors the certainty and the "rules" that they need to complete the auction process and move on to plan confirmation.

Moreover, as in *Innkeepers I*, the Debtors urge that, in any event, there is a "fiduciary out" and that the Debtors may and will consider any and all bids whether they are "Qualified Bids" under the revised Bidding Procedures or not. Unlike in *Innkeepers I*, however, the "fiduciary out" contained in the current transaction trumps every other provision in the controlling documents. Contained in Section 11 of the revised Bidding Procedures, it provides that "[u]pon the determination by the Debtors' directors, trustees, or members, as applicable, and upon advice of counsel, no term or provision of the Term Sheet or the Commitment Letter shall prevent, amend, alter, or reduce the Debtors' ability to exercise their fiduciary duties under applicable law." In other words, if a competing bidder submits a bid that reflects a higher return to either the Debtor obligors under the Fixed Rate Loan, the Floating Rate Loan, or both, albeit comprised of a different mix of cash, debt, and equity than that in the Final Five Mile/Lehman Bid, the Debtors can and should exercise their fiduciary duty to give it their full consideration.

Finally, it is worth noting that the Debtors need not have pursued an auction process at all; they could simply have proceeded directly to a plan. They ought not to be faulted for attempting to create a framework for additional value to be realized for creditors. *See, e.g.*, In re Neff Corp., Case No. 10-12610(SCC) (Bankr.S.D.N.Y.2010) (debtors' use of "payout event procedures" in plan process resulted in increased return for stakeholders from original proposal).

In that regard, the Court notes that certain of the remaining objections asserted by Appaloosa (and previously asserted by LNR, the Ad Hoc Committee, TriMont, and CW) are best categorized as confirmation objections. For example, Appaloosa contends that (i) the Final Five Mile/Lehman Bid and the revised Bidding Procedures dictate plan terms that go beyond the scope of the investment terms encompassed by the bid, (ii) the Term Sheet requires that the negotiated terms apply to any successful overbid, and (iii) the release provisions are overly broad and should not be approved absent the consent of each releasing party.

The Court finds that these concerns need not be addressed at this time. The Debtors are asking the Court to approve Bidding Procedures and a stalking horse bid so that they may conduct an auction. The winner of the auction will gain the right to sponsor a plan of reorganization. The proposed plan will still be required to meet all confirmation requirements set forth in the Bankruptcy Code, and parties in interest will be afforded the right to make relevant objections in the event that they believe the proposed plan falls short of such requirements. Ultimately, the transaction contemplated in the Final Five Mile/Lehman Bid, or any other bid ultimately selected by the Debtors, will not be consummated absent confirmation of a plan. The rights of all parties in interest to object to confirmation at the appropriate time are reserved and preserved.

With respect to the issue of releases, while releases may be important to the ultimate success of a plan, it is impossible to properly analyze the releases that have been proposed in the Term Sheet. Deciding whether a release is appropriate before a plan has been formulated or filed has the potential to short-circuit negotiations among the Debtors and their creditors. It remains to be seen if the proposed releases, including the Special Servicer Release, the Apollo Release, and the Global Release (as each is defined in the relevant documents comprising the Final Five Mile/Lehman Bid) are appropriate. These issues will be considered if they are raised once a plan of reorganization is proposed.

Accordingly, for all of the foregoing reasons, the Motion is granted.

Do you see any similarities between the standing issue here and the complaints that arose in *Chrysler*? Refer back to Chapter 16.

2.   CREDIT BIDDING

What stops the debtor from selling its assets to insiders at some lowball price? Extreme cases are apt to be checked by the court, but what if the price is low, but not so low as to be ridiculous? The Code, in section 363(k), provides an answer.

IN RE: SUBMICRON SYSTEMS CORPORATION, ET AL.

432 F.3d 448
United States Court of Appeals, Third Circuit
No. 03-2102 | Argued Sept. 14, 2004 | Jan. 6, 2006

AMBRO, Circuit Judge.

Appellant Howard S. Cohen ("Cohen"), as Plan Administrator for the bankruptcy estates of SubMicron Systems Corporation, SubMicron Systems, Inc.,

SubMicron Wet Process Stations, Inc. and SubMicron Systems Holdings I, Inc. (jointly and severally, "SubMicron"), challenges the sale to an entity created by Sunrise Capital Partners, LP ("Sunrise") of SubMicron's assets under 11 U.S.C. §363(b), which authorizes court-approved sales of assets "other than in the ordinary course of business." Sunrise negotiated directly with several—but not all—of SubMicron's creditors before presenting its bid to the District Court. These creditors—The KB Mezzanine Fund II, LP ("KB"), Equinox Investment Partners, LLC ("Equinox"),[6] and Celerity Silicon, LLC ("Celerity") (collectively, the "Lenders")—agreed to contribute toward the purchase of SubMicron's assets new capital along with all of their claims in bankruptcy against SubMicron in exchange for equity in the entity formed by Sunrise to acquire the assets—Akrion LLC ("Akrion"). Akrion in turn "credit bid" the full value of the Lenders' secured claims contributed to it as part of its bid for SubMicron's assets pursuant to 11 U.S.C. §363(k). The District Court approved the sale.[7]

Cohen, seeking as Plan Administrator of the SubMicron estates to aid unsecured creditors "cut out of the deal" by the Lenders and Sunrise, attacks the sale on several fronts. First, he argues that the purportedly secured debt investments made by the Lenders and contributed to Akrion should have been recharacterized by the District Court as equity investments. In the alternative, if the District Court did not err in declining to recharacterize the investments as equity, Cohen contends that it erred by failing to conclude that the debt was unsecured. Even if the District Court properly considered the debt secured, Cohen challenges the propriety of the District Court's allowance of the credit bid portion of Akrion's offer. As a last option, Cohen asserts that the District Court erred by declining to equitably subordinate the Lenders' secured claims to those of creditors with inferior claims. For the reasons discussed below, we reject these arguments and affirm the judgment of the District Court.

I. FACTS AND PROCEDURAL POSTURE

A. SUBMICRON'S FINANCING

Before its sale in bankruptcy, SubMicron designed, manufactured and marketed "wet benches"[8] for use in the semiconductor industry. By 1997, it was experiencing significant financial and operational difficulties. To sustain its operations in the late 1990s, SubMicron secured financing from several financial and/or investment institutions. On November 25, 1997, it entered into a $15 million working capital facility with Greyrock Business Credit ("Greyrock"), granting Greyrock first priority liens on all of its inventory, equipment,

---

6. Equinox was formed in 1996 to manage KB after it was acquired by Dresdner Bank. For the sake of simplicity, we shall refer to both entities simply as "KB/Equinox."

7. This bankruptcy case is before the District Court because it withdrew, pursuant to 28 U.S.C. §157(d), the reference of the case to the Bankruptcy Court for the District of Delaware.

8. Wet benches are automatic process tools used for cleaning and etching operations in semiconductor processing. *See http://www.semiconductorglos sary.com/default.asp?searchterm=wet+bench* (last visited Dec. 27, 2005).

receivables and general intangibles. The next day, SubMicron raised another $20 million through the issuance of senior subordinated 12% notes (the "1997 Notes") to KB/Equinox (for $16 million) and Celerity (for $4 million) secured by liens behind Greyrock on substantially all of SubMicron's assets. Submicron subsequently issued a third set of notes in 1997 (the "Junior 1997 Notes") for $13.7 million, comprising $8.7 million of 8% notes and a $5 million note to The BOC Group, Inc. The Junior 1997 Notes were secured but junior to the security for the 1997 Notes. Despite this capital influx, SubMicron incurred a net loss of $47.6 million for the 1997 fiscal year.

A steep downturn in the semiconductor industry made 1998 a similarly difficult year for SubMicron. By August of that year, it was paying substantially all of the interest due on the 1997 Notes as paid-in-kind senior subordinated notes. On December 2, 1998, SubMicron and Greyrock agreed to renew the Greyrock line of credit, reducing the maximum funds available from $15 to $10 million and including a $2 million overadvance conditioned on SubMicron's securing an additional $4 million in financing. To satisfy this condition, on December 3, SubMicron issued Series B 12% notes (the "1998 Notes") to KB/Equinox (for $3.2 million) and Celerity (for $800,000). The 1998 Notes ranked *pari passu* with the 1997 Notes and the interest was deferred until October 1, 1999. SubMicron incurred a net loss of $21.9 million for the 1998 fiscal year, and at year's end its liabilities exceeded its assets by $4.2 million.

SubMicron's financial health did not improve in 1999. By March of that year, its management determined that additional financing would be required to meet the company's immediate critical working capital needs. To this end, between March 10, 1999 and June 6, 1999, SubMicron issued a total of eighteen Series 1999 12% notes (the "1999 Tranche One Notes") for a total of $7,035,154 (comprising nine notes to KB/Equinox totaling $5,888,123 and nine notes to Celerity totaling $1,147,031). The 1999 Tranche One Notes proved insufficient to keep SubMicron afloat. As a result, between July 8, 1999 and August 31, 1999, KB/Equinox and Celerity made periodic payments to SubMicron (the "1999 Tranche Two Funding") totaling $3,982,031 and $147,969, respectively. No notes were issued in exchange for the 1999 Tranche Two Funding. Between the 1999 Tranche One Notes and the 1999 Tranche Two Funding (collectively, the "1999 Fundings"), KB/Equinox and Celerity advanced SubMicron a total of $9,870,154 and $1,295,000, respectively. (The 1999 Fundings were recorded as secured debt on SubMicron's 10-Q filing with the Securities and Exchange Commission.) Despite the cash infusions, during the first half of 1999 SubMicron incurred a net loss of $9.9 million. On June 30, 1999, SubMicron's liabilities exceeded its assets by $3.1 million.

By January 1999, KB/Equinox had appointed three members to SubMicron's Board of Directors. All appointees were either principals or employees of KB/Equinox. By June 1999, following resignations of various SubMicron Board members, KB/Equinox employees Bonaparte Liu and Robert Wickey, and Celerity employee Mark Benham, represented three-quarters of the Board, with SubMicron CEO David Ferran the lone Board member not employed by KB/Equinox or Celerity.

B. THE ACQUISITION

SubMicron began acquisition discussions with Sunrise in July of 1999. By all accounts, it was generally understood that if SubMicron failed to reach a deal with Sunrise, it would be forced to liquidate, leaving secured creditors-with the exception of Greyrock-with pennies on the dollar and unsecured creditors and shareholders with nothing. KB/Equinox, not SubMicron's management, conducted negotiations with Sunrise, developing and agreeing on the terms and financial structure of an acquisition to occur in the context of a prepackaged bankruptcy.

On August 31, 1999, SubMicron entered into an asset purchase agreement with Akrion, the entity created by Sunrise to function as the acquisition vehicle. The following day, SubMicron filed a Chapter 11 bankruptcy petition and an associated motion seeking approval of the sale of its assets to Sunrise outside the ordinary course of business pursuant to §363(b) of the Bankruptcy Code.

The asset purchase agreement reiterated, *inter alia*, that KB/Equinox and Celerity would contribute their secured claims (*i.e.*, the 1997 Notes, the 1998 Notes and the 1999 Fundings) in order for Akrion to credit bid these claims under §363 of the Bankruptcy Code — but only contingent on the closing of the sale. The agreement also required SubMicron, at the closing of the sale, to pay $5,500,000 immediately to the holders of the 1999 Fundings. In return, KB/Equinox and Celerity would receive a 31.475% interest in Akrion (KB/Equinox received a 30% interest and Celerity received a 1.475% interest). The Court and Official Committee of Unsecured Creditors (the "Creditors' Committee") were apprised of the terms of this agreement prior to the sale.

At the sale hearing Akrion submitted a bid of $55,507,587 for SubMicron. The cash component of the bid totaled $10,202,000 and included $5,500,000 in cash from Akrion, $3,382,000 to pay pre- and post-petition Greyrock secured debt, and $850,000 to cover administrative claims. The credit portion of the bid consisted of the $38,721,637 outstanding for the 1997 Notes, the 1998 Notes, and the 1999 Fundings (all of which KB/Equinox and Celerity had contributed to Akrion), plus $1,324,138 in individual secured claims, for a total of $40,045,775. Finally, the bid included SubMicron's liabilities that would be assumed by Akrion — $681,346 in lease obligations and $4,578,466 in other assumed liabilities for a total of $5,259,812. No other bid for SubMicron's assets was made, SubMicron's Board and the Court both approved Akrion's bid over the objection of the Creditors' Committee, and on October 15, 1999, the asset sale closed.

On April 18, 2000, the Creditors' Committee brought against the Lenders, among others, an adversary proceeding in which it made the claims before us on appeal. (Cohen was subsequently substituted for the Creditors' Committee.) After a bench trial before Judge Sue Robinson in late July/early August 2001, she ruled against Cohen, setting out her reasoning in a comprehensive opinion. Cohen appeals.

III.   Recharacterization as Equity

Cohen argues that the District Court erred by failing to recharacterize the infusion of the 1999 Fundings as an equity investment. To succeed with this argument, he must demonstrate that the District Court abused its discretionary authority or premised its determination on clearly erroneous findings of fact. Because he has failed to do so, we affirm the District Court's recharacterization holding . . .

V.   Propriety of §363 Credit Bid

Having determined that the 1999 Fundings represented an extension of secured debt, we turn to Cohen's argument that the §363(k) credit bid was improper because the Lenders did not (and could not) demonstrate that some portion of their claims remained secured by collateral as defined in Bankruptcy Code §506(a). The District Court determined that "there was no collateral available to actually secure the 1999 fundings." As a result, Cohen argues that, because the secured debt had no actual (or economic) value, it could not be credit bid under §363(k). Because that section empowers creditors to bid the total *face* value of their claims—it does not limit bids to claims' economic value—we disagree and hold that the District Court did not err in allowing the Lenders to credit bid their claims.

It is well settled among district and bankruptcy courts that creditors can bid the full face value of their secured claims under §363(k).

In fact, logic demands that §363(k) be interpreted in this way; interpreting it to cap credit bids at the economic value of the underlying collateral is theoretically nonsensical.

A hypothetical is illustrative.

> Assume that Debtor has a single asset: a truck, T. Lender is a secured creditor that has loaned Debtor $15, taking a security interest in T. Debtor is in Chapter 11 bankruptcy and has filed a §363 motion to sell T to Bidder for $10. Debtor argues that Lender can only credit bid $10 for T and must bid any excess in cash if it wishes to outbid B.

This hypothetical reveals the logical problem with an actual value bid cap. If Lender bids $12 for T, by definition $12 *becomes* the value of Lender's security interest in T. In this way, until Lender is paid in full, Lender can always overbid Bidder. (Naturally, Lender will not outbid Bidder unless Lender believes it could generate a greater return on T than the return for Lender represented by Bidder's offer.) As Lender holds a security interest in T, any amount bid for it up to the value of Lender's full claim becomes the secured portion of Lender's claim by definition. Given the weight of reason's demand that "it must be so," we see no reason to catalog the myriad other arguments that have been advanced to support this "interpretation."

Cohen is not out of plausible arguments, however, as he claims that because the Lenders were not *partially* undersecured but *completely* undersecured — that is, because the collateral was found to have no economic value — this case is different. Yet nothing about the logic of allowing credit bids up to the full face value of the collateral changes if the collateral has no actual value. Because the Lenders had a valid security interest in essentially all the assets sold, by definition they were entitled to the satisfaction of their claims from available proceeds of any sale of those underlying assets. Their credit bid did nothing more than preserve their right to the proceeds, as credit bids do under §363(k).

Unable squarely to rest this argument on a theoretically sound construction of the Bankruptcy Code's credit bidding provisions, Cohen enlists the aid of 11 U.S.C. §506(a), which provides for the splitting of partially secured claims into their secured claim and unsecured claim components. Yet §506(a) is inapplicable. As one member of the Supreme Court has explained, "[w]hen . . . the Bankruptcy Code means to refer to a secured party's entire allowed claim, *i.e.*, to both the 'secured' and 'unsecured' portions under §506(a), it uses the term *'allowed claim' — as in 11 U.S.C. §363(k). . . .*" Dewsnup v. Timm, 502 U.S. 410, 422, 112 S.Ct. 773, 116 L.Ed.2d 903 (1992) (Scalia, J., dissenting) (first emphasis in original). That is, §363(k) speaks to the full face value of a secured creditor's claim, not to the portion of that claim that is actually collateralized as described in §506.

Moreover, as a practical matter, no §506 valuation is required before a §363 sale of the underlying collateral can be approved. Section 363 attempts to *avoid* the complexities and inefficiencies of valuing collateral altogether by substituting the theoretically preferable mechanism of a free market sale to set the price. The provision is premised on the notion that the market's reaction to a sale best reflects the economic realities of assets' worth. Naturally, then, courts are not required first to determine the assets' worth before approving such a market sale. This would contravene the basis for the provision's very existence.

For these reasons, we conclude that the District Court properly allowed the Lenders to contribute their credit bids under the §363 sale.

PROBLEM SET 29.1

1. Some argue that credit bidding distorts an auction, because the lender does not have to bid actual cash. What do you make of this?
2. The ultimate effect of section 363(k) is that if the debtor's assets will not sell for more than the secured debt, the secured lender takes the assets if it wants them. That amounts to a foreclosure, but in this case the foreclosure is done in federal court. Should the bankruptcy courts be used for this purpose?
3. In the prior section we noted the tendency to adopt bidding procedures that include restrictions on who can become an actual participant in the 363 sale. Why?

3. SUCCESSOR LIABILITY AND 363 SALES

In Chapter 24 we noted that the normal rule was that an asset sale does not transfer any liabilities, unless certain exceptions applied. These exceptions are lumped under the general category of successor liability.

Now read section 363(f) of the Code:

(f) The trustee [or DIP] may sell property under subsection (b) or (c) of this section free and clear of any interest in such property of an entity other than the estate, only if—

(1) applicable nonbankruptcy law permits sale of such property free and clear of such interest;

(2) such entity consents;

(3) such interest is a lien and the price at which such property is to be sold is greater than the aggregate value of all liens on such property;

(4) such interest is in bona fide dispute; or

(5) such entity could be compelled, in a legal or equitable proceeding, to accept a money satisfaction of such interest.

Does this provision allow assets sales that happen under the Bankruptcy Code to rid assets of successor liability claims? Is a successor liability claim an "interest," and if so, can it be detached from the debtor's assets via bankruptcy?

JUSTIN LEFEVER, PLAINTIFF–RESPONDENT, v. K.P. HOVNANIAN ENTERPRISES, INC.

160 N.J. 307
Supreme Court of New Jersey
Argued Jan. 21, 1999 | Decided July 29, 1999

O'HERN, J.

This appeal concerns the meaning of the product-line exception in Ramirez v. Amsted Industries Inc., 86 N.J. 332, 431 A.2d 811 (1981), when a successor corporation acquires the predecessor's product line through a bankruptcy sale.

The general rule of corporate-successor liability is that when a company sells its assets to another company, the acquiring company is not liable for the debts and liabilities of the selling company simply because it has succeeded to the ownership of the assets of the seller. Traditionally, there have been only four exceptions: (1) the successor expressly or impliedly assumes the predecessor's liabilities; (2) there is an actual or *de facto* consolidation or merger of the seller and the purchaser; (3) the purchasing company is a mere continuation of the seller; or (4) the transaction is entered into fraudulently to escape liability. 15 William & Fletcher, *Cyclopedia of the Law of Corporations* §7122, nn. 9-15 (1990).

New Jersey, along with several other jurisdictions, has adopted a product-line exception to the general rule. Under that doctrine, by purchasing a substantial part of the manufacturer's assets and continuing to market goods in the same product line, a corporation may be exposed to strict liability in tort for defects in the predecessor's products. The question in this appeal is whether the product-line exception is applicable when the successor has purchased the predecessor's assets at a bankruptcy sale. Our task is made easier in this case because the bankrupt was not the manufacturer of the defective product, but rather an intermediary owner of the product line against whom no claim had been made by the injured party.

I

The facts of this case are more fully set forth in the reported opinion of the Appellate Division, 311 *N.J.Super.* 1, 709 *A.2d* 253 (1998). For convenience, we shall eliminate reference to certain intermediate business entities used by the parties. Conceptually, there were three distributors of the product line. Plaintiff, Justin Lefever, was injured in 1989 when a forklift he was operating tipped over and caused him to suffer crushing injuries. The Lull Engineering Corporation, Inc., whom we shall refer to as "Lull I," had manufactured and distributed the forklift. Through a series of transfers, Lull I's assets were acquired in 1986 by Lull Corporation ("Lull II"). In 1992, Lull II went into bankruptcy. In November 1993, the trustee in the bankruptcy proceedings conveyed to Lull Industries Inc. ("Lull III"), interests in substantially all of Lull II's assets.

On September 24, 1990, plaintiff sued "Lull Engineering Co., Inc." in the Superior Court, Law Division, Middlesex County.[9] Plaintiff never sued Lull II. During the course of discovery, plaintiff learned that Lull II had acquired the assets of Lull I, and that Lull II had transferred its assets to Lull III through a bankruptcy sale. Plaintiff joined Lull III as a party defendant. Lull III moved to dismiss plaintiff's claim on the basis that the bankruptcy sale was free and clear of any interests in the property, including any successor-liability claims. The trial court granted Lull III's motion.

On appeal, the Appellate Division reversed.

II

After analyzing the differences between the continuity exception formulated by the Michigan Supreme Court in *Turner* and the product-line exception [adopted by the California Supreme Court] in *Ray*, the *Ramirez* Court adopted the rule of *Ray* with its focus on the product causing the injury. Concerning its own justifications for the "product line" exception, the Court in *Ramirez* emphasized the two latter justifications of spreading the risk and enjoyment of the predecessor manufacturer's good will.

---

9. Although plaintiff in fact named as defendant a company that purchased Lull I's assets and later sold them to Lull II, it appears that plaintiff intended to sue Lull I, whose name is virtually identical to the name of its immediate successor. The named defendant has been a dormant corporation with no assets since 1986.

III

Does the supremacy of federal bankruptcy law prevent the application of state common law to claims against a successor business enterprise that has acquired its assets through a bankruptcy sale?

The short answer to this question is "yes," but only if the federal bankruptcy court has "dealt with" the claim. The long answer requires us to examine the function of a bankruptcy sale and to determine what effect a bankruptcy sale may have on other principles of law affecting the liability of a successor business enterprise. For purposes of this analysis, we will draw essentially on a summary of the law of bankruptcy sales set forth by Michael H. Reed in *Successor Liability and Bankruptcy Sales*, 51 Bus.Law. 653 (1996). This recital is not intended to be a digest of bankruptcy law but only a brief outline of what we understand to be the governing principles that apply in federal courts.

There are essentially two ways [in which] a bankruptcy trustee or debtor-in-possession can sell assets: (i) a sale pursuant to section 363 of the Code; or (ii) a sale pursuant to a confirmed Chapter 11 plan of reorganization.

A.   DOES A SECTION 363 SALE CUT OFF PRODUCT LIABILITY CLAIMS?

Section 363(f) of the Bankruptcy Code (the Code), 11 U.S.C.A. §363(f) (1978), authorizes the trustee or debtor-in-possession to sell property of the estate "free and clear of the 'interest' of another entity in such property . . . ." The primary purpose of that provision is "to permit the sale of property free and clear of the liens of secured creditors."

Some courts have held that notwithstanding the use of the term "interest" in section 363(f), the bankruptcy court has "the power to convey assets free and clear of not only property interests, such as liens and encumbrances, but also preconveyance claims, or in personam liabilities of the transferor

"Other courts, however, have held that, because the plain language of section 363(f) speaks only of 'interests' and makes no mention of 'claims,' it does not provide authority for a sale free and clear of preconveyance claims because claims, as distinguished from 'liens' and 'encumbrances,' are not property interests." Again, the author explains:

[I]t is difficult to quarrel with these [latter] decisions. The term "interest," while undefined, clearly connotes some form of property interest as it is utilized throughout the Code. It includes the property interest of an equity security holder . . . as well as the property interest of a lienholder. . . . Creditor-held interests clearly include not only "liens" but also "charges."

There is nothing in the Code, however, to suggest that the term "interest" was intended to embrace rights to payment, which are the substantive nuclei of bankruptcy "claims." *See* . . . §101(5) [of the Code]; *see also* Fairchild Aircraft, Inc. v. Campbell (In re Fairchild Aircraft Corp.) [discussed *infra* at 318, 734 A.2d at 296], wherein Judge Clark explained: "Section 363(f) does not authorize sales free and clear of any interest, but rather of any interest in such property. . . . The sorts of interests impacted by a sale free and clear are *in rem* interests which have attached to the property." *Id.* at 917–18.

That a Chapter 11 sale will resolve the question of successor liability is thus by no means clear. Courts analyzing the scope of the power of bankruptcy courts to sell property free and clear of claims reason that the breadth of such power is coextensive with the courts' power to discharge claims under the Code.

Thus, a claimant asserting successor liability would argue that even if, as a general proposition, the bankruptcy court has the power to convey assets free and clear of "claims," it does not have the power to cut off obligations or rights, such as environmental agency injunctions or future products liability claims, which are not cognizable as claims for dischargeability purposes. Such claims could not be divested, regardless of whether the sale is made within or outside of a plan of reorganization.

Although the asset purchase agreement between the trustee and the buyer at the bankruptcy sale expressly recites that the purchaser "will not assume, undertake, accept or be bound by or responsible for . . . any liabilities or obligations of Lull or Erickson or their affiliates that arise or have arisen prior to the Closing Date," such disclaimers are ineffective in insulating the buyer from successor liability when other principles of law require the imposition of liability.

Congress appears to have recognized the foregoing limitation on the scope of a bankruptcy discharge by expressly providing that in the case of debtors liable for personal injury due to asbestos-containing products, bankruptcy courts shall have the authority to insulate a successor from liability "with respect to any claim or demand made against such entity by reason of its becoming such a transferee or successor." In *Fairchild Aircraft, supra,* 184 *B.R.* at 931–33, which involved personal injury claims arising out of an airplane crash that occurred after a bankruptcy sale, the court refused to cut off those claims because of (1) insufficient or impossible notice to the putative successor liability claimants, (2) insufficient representation of the interests of such claimants, and (3) absence of any provision for such claimants under the plan of reorganization. Thus, even if a bankruptcy court were to seek to "deal with" preconfirmation conduct, at a minimum there probably should be notice to the class of claimants who would be subject to the claims, and some provision for such claimants should be made under the plan of reorganization. For example, in the silicone breast-implant cases, one of the manufacturers, Dow Corning, entered Chapter 11 and then sought to reach a settlement with its comprehensive general liability insurers. Although the court approving the settlement held that third parties injured as the alleged result of the defendant's silicone breast implants did not have an interest in the insurance policies, the court noted that "competing claims to the insufficient assets [would] be settled through the reorganization process . . ."

Justin Lefever's claim was simply not dealt with in the bankruptcy proceedings. Plaintiff was not a creditor of the bankrupt. He filed no claim in the bankruptcy proceedings. In addition, the sale here was under Section 363 and Lefever had no "interest" in the sense of a lien or encumbrance on the property. In fact, the bankruptcy trustee specifically authorized plaintiff to proceed with his suit against Lull III because the suit was not against the bankrupt. *But see* In re All Am. of Ashburn, Inc., 56 B.R. 186 Bankr.N.D.Ga.1986) (enjoining claim against successor because bankruptcy sale of assets was free and clear of all claims). The most that can be said is that the debtor, Lull II, listed plaintiff's claim in its schedule of affairs, but there was no attempt to "deal with it."

IV

If federal law permits it, should the principles of Ramirez call for successor liability after bankruptcy sales?

This is by far the harder of the two main issues in the case. Respected commentators find the "policies behind the 'product line' exception inapplicable to the purchase of assets at a bankruptcy sale. Not only does this extension of strict liability violate basic principles of tort law, but it also contradicts the fundamental goals of the Bankruptcy Code. . . ." David R. Kott & Walter A. Effross, *Forgive Us Our Predecessors: Bankruptcy Sales and the Product Line Exception,* 4 Prod.Liab.L.J. 123, 123 (May 1993). They argue that imposing successor liability amounts to creating a lien on the assets in favor of future products liability claimants and thereby decreases the sale price and effectively minimizes the assets available for the debtors. Future products liability claimants will have "jumped the line" to come out ahead of the debtor's current creditors who may be deprived of compensation for the claims. Although the argument is appealing, it has equal application to that wide variety of other contexts in which liability may be imposed on a successor. *See Chicago Truck Drivers, supra,* 59 F.3d at 51. For example, a purchaser of contaminated assets will be responsible for environmental cleanup costs even though the property has been acquired at a bankruptcy sale free and clear of liens. James B. Holden & Debora D. Jones, *Representing Purchasers of Assets from Bankruptcy Estates,* 20 Colo.Law. 2259, 2261 (1991). Liability also may be imposed on transferees in other contexts. *See, e.g.,* Upholsterers' Int'l Union Pension Fund v. Artistic Furniture of Pontiac, 920 F.2d 1323 (7th Cir.1990) (delinquent pension fund contributions); Klegerman v. F.G. Apparel, Inc., No. 85C7887, 1986 WL 2531 (N.D.Ill. Feb. 11, 1986) (considering successor's liability for age-discrimination claims despite acquisition of assets at bankruptcy sale).

We acknowledge that California, the jurisdiction that initiated the product-line exception, has declined to apply the exception to the acquisition of a product line through a bankruptcy sale. In Stewart v. Telex Communications, Inc., 1 Cal.App.4th 190, 1 Cal.Rptr.2d 669, 675 (1991), the California Court of Appeals adopted the reasoning of the Washington Supreme Court in Hall v. Armstrong Cork, Inc., 103 Wash.2d 258, 692 P.2d 787, 792 (1984), that "'[t]he traditional corporate rule of nonliability is . . . counterbalanced by the policies of strict liability [only] when acquisition by the successor, and not some [other] event or act, virtually destroys the ability of the plaintiff to seek redress from the manufacturer of the defective product.'" We believe, however, that the California court has focused on the first justification for the product-line exception, specifically, that strict liability is appropriate when the successor's acquisition of the business has virtually destroyed the plaintiff's remedies, to the exclusion of the more dominant themes.

We must first remember that in *Ramirez* the defendant did not cause the destruction of the plaintiff's remedies against the original manufacturer. On the same day that the Court decided *Ramirez,* the Court decided *Nieves, supra,* 86 N.J. 361, 431 A.2d 826. In that case, an intermediate producer of the product line argued that an essential justification for the imposition of liability was missing, namely, the nonavailability of a functioning manufacturer of the product line. The intermediate manufacturer argued that the first prong of the *Ray* doctrine is concerned solely with finding one viable extant corporate defendant that had succeeded to the manufacturing operation and that it was not such a defendant. The Court disagreed. In its view, "the imposition on [the intermediary] of potential liability for injuries . . . is justified as a fair and equitable burden necessarily attached to the substantial benefit that [the intermediary] enjoyed in the 'deliberate, albeit legitimate, exploitation of [the manufacturer's] established reputation as a going concern producing a specific product line.'" *Nieves, supra,* 86 N.J. at 369, 431 A.2d 826 (quoting *Ray, supra,* 136 Cal.Rptr. 574, 560 P.2d at 11). Both the intermediary and the final successor had the ability to assume the original manufacturer's risk-spreading and cost-avoidance roles.

One may fairly assume that a prudent purchaser of assets makes the cost-benefit analysis that renders the acquisition profitable. The *Ramirez* doctrine rests on principles of justice and fairness. "[T]he legal limitation on the scope of [products] liability is associated with policy — with our more or less inadequately expressed ideas of what justice demands, or of what is administratively possible and convenient."

Ultimately, the question is whether the imposition of a duty on the successor to respond to the complaints of its predecessor's customers is fair, when the successor trades on the loyalty of those customers.

In these circumstances, we do not consider it unfair to impose liability on the successor manufacturers of the Lull forklift.

The judgment of the Appellate Division is affirmed.

POLLOCK, J., dissenting.

With limited exceptions, successor corporations are not liable for harm caused by defective products made or distributed by a predecessor. *Restatement (Third) of Torts* sec. 12 (1997). Contrary to the rule in most jurisdictions, this Court recognizes the "product-line" exception . . .

The product-line exception represents our perception of the appropriate balance in the ordinary case between compensating injured parties and the uninhibited transfer of assets.

This appeal questions the weight to be placed in striking that balance when the selling corporation at the time of sale is in bankruptcy. The majority holds that the bankruptcy is of no weight. I believe, however, that when an injury occurs before bankruptcy and the injured party had the opportunity to file a claim in the bankruptcy proceeding, a court should weigh the bankruptcy when striking the balance of interests in the "product line" exception.

To place the matter in perspective, some facts in addition to those set forth in the majority opinion may help. Plaintiff, Justin Lefever, was injured in 1989 in an employment-related accident arising out of the operation of a forklift that had been manufactured by the corporation identified by the majority as "Lull I." Previously, in 1973, Lull I had sold its manufacturing assets to "Lull II," which assumed responsibility for product liability claims such as plaintiff's. Initially, plaintiff sued "Lull Engineering Co., Inc.," for manufacturing and design defects in producing the forklift. Plaintiff also joined as defendants Giles & Ransome, the distributor of the forklift, and K.P. Hovananian Enterprises, the owner of the work site where the accident occurred. Thereafter, plaintiff settled his claims against Giles and Ransome and K.P. Hovananian.

On March 3, 1992, nearly twenty years after acquiring Lull I's assets, Lull II filed a petition for a Chapter 11 bankruptcy. The trustee in bankruptcy promptly notified plaintiff of the bankruptcy, but plaintiff decided not to file a claim. In 1993, Badger R. Bazen (Badger) bought Lull II's assets "free and clear of all interests pursuant to Sections 363(b), 363(f) of the Bankruptcy Code" and with an express disclaimer of any of Lull II's liability for products manufactured or sold before the closing date. The bankruptcy court approved the sale. Also in 1993, Badger sold the assets to the corporation identified by the majority as Lull III.

The bankruptcy court stayed all actions against the debtor. In January 1995, however, the trustee sent plaintiff's counsel a letter stating that the stay did not apply because the present action is not against the debtor, Lull II. On November 14, 1996, plaintiff joined Lull III as a defendant.

One justification for the product line exception when the original manufacturer no longer exists at the time of the injury is that an injured party may be left without a remedy. *Mettinger, supra*, 153 N.J. at 383, 709 A.2d 779. When, however, the injured party has recourse against the original manufacturer, that consideration should yield to the unfairness of imposing liability on an innocent successor. The scale could tilt back toward the imposition of liability, if the successor agreed to assume liability in the asset-purchase agreement or if it knowingly participated in a fraudulent asset transfer. Here, the purchaser of Lull II's assets expressly disclaimed liability. Plaintiff, moreover, does not allege that Lull III participated in a fraudulent asset transfer or engaged in a sham transaction.

Significantly, plaintiff had recourse against Lull II, which had assumed contractually the liability of the manufacturer, Lull I. Admittedly, Lull II's bankruptcy could affect the amount paid on plaintiff's claim, but no more so than it would affect the claims of other creditors.

As the Third Circuit Court of Appeals stated, "If a remedy against the original manufacturer was available . . . the consumer has not been obliged to bear the risk and the justification for imposing successor liability evaporates." Conway v. White Trucks, 885 F.2d 90, 95 (1989). To the same effect, the Seventh Circuit Court of Appeals has written:

> Had the [plaintiffs] been parties to the bankruptcy proceeding, they would have had no possible basis for a suit against [the successor] . . . because the successorship doctrine on which they rely is inapplicable if the plaintiff had a chance to obtain a legal remedy against the predecessor, even so limited a remedy as that afforded by the filing of a claim in bankruptcy. [Zerand-Bernal, Inc. v. Cox, 23 F.3d 159, 163 (7th Cir.1994) (Posner, J.)].

The majority suggests that plaintiff should be permitted to proceed with his suit against Lull III because his claim was not "dealt with" in the bankruptcy proceedings. Continuing, the majority remarks that "even if a bankruptcy court were to seek to 'deal' with preconfirmation conduct, at a minimum there probably should be notice to the class of claimants . . . and some provision for such claimants should be made under the plan of reorganization." *See ante* at 320-21, 734 A.2d at 298. Plaintiff's claim was not "dealt with," however, only because he failed to file a claim in the bankruptcy proceedings, not because he had no notice of the bankruptcy.

The majority opinion limits the power of the bankruptcy court by denying it the power to permit the sale of the debtor's assets free of liability for tort claims. Section 363(f) of the Bankruptcy Code provides, however, that the bankruptcy court shall have the power to sell assets "free and clear of any interest in . . . property." 11 U.S.C. 363(f). Indeed, the sale of Lull II's assets, as approved by the bankruptcy court, so provided. A question remains whether such a sale is free and clear of tort claims that arise after the sale. No case, however, has ever held a successor corporation liable for a tort claim that arose before court approval of the sale.

When a tort occurs before bankruptcy, courts have treated a tort claimant like all other claimants. In that context, a sale of assets "free and clear" does not result in the imposition of liability on the successor corporation. To impose successor liability would frustrate "the orderly scheme of the bankruptcy law by allowing some unsecured creditors to recover without regard to the priority order of the bankruptcy proceedings." A bankruptcy court's authority to sell assets free and clear of existing tort claims is "implicit in the court's general equitable powers and its duty to distribute debtor's assets." The effect of subjecting the successor to the risk of liability is to diminish the value of the assets to the extent of the cost of that risk.

That diminution in value will redound to the detriment of all other creditors who seek to participate in the distribution of the bankruptcy estate. Permitting a tort claimant to pursue a successor after a bankruptcy sale would grant that claimant a priority over other claimants who were paid in accordance with the Bankruptcy Code and would produce a negative impact on the trustee's ability to sell assets of the estate at a fair price. Those considerations should tip the scale back toward the general rule of not imposing liability on a successor when a claimant has been injured before the bankruptcy proceedings and provided with notice and the opportunity to participate in the proceedings. In sum, the imposition of liability on the purchaser of assets from a bankrupt estate "free and clear of any interests in property" skews the balance of interests in the product line exception.

I respectfully dissent. Justices GARIBALDI and COLEMAN join in this opinion.

Does it seem odd to you that a state court doctrine could trump the federal Bankruptcy Code? How might the buyer have better addressed this issue?

IN RE GENERAL MOTORS CORP., ET AL., DEBTORS

407 B.R. 463
United States Bankruptcy Court, S.D. New York
No. 09–50026 (REG) | July 5, 2009

Robert E. GERBER, Bankruptcy Judge.
In this contested matter in the jointly administered chapter 11 cases of Debtors General Motors Corporation and certain of its subsidiaries (together, "**GM**"),

the Debtors move for an order, pursuant to section 363 of the Bankruptcy Code, approving GM's sale of the bulk of its assets (the "**363 Transaction**"), pursuant to a "Master Sale and Purchase Agreement" and related documents (the "**MPA**"), to Vehicle Acquisitions Holdings LLC (the "**Purchaser**")[10] — a purchaser sponsored by the U.S. Department of the Treasury (the "**U.S. Treasury**") — free and clear of liens, claims, encumbrances, and other interests. The Debtors also seek approval of the assumption and assignment of the executory contracts that would be needed by the Purchaser, and of a settlement with the United Auto Workers ("**UAW**") pursuant to an agreement (the "**UAW Settlement Agreement**") under which GM would satisfy obligations to an estimated 500,000 retirees.

GM's motion is supported by the Creditors' Committee; the U.S. Government (which has advanced approximately $50 billion to GM, and is GM's largest pre- and post-petition creditor); the Governments of Canada and Ontario (which ultimately will have advanced about $9.1 billion); the UAW (an affiliate of which is GM's single largest unsecured creditor); the indenture trustees for GM's approximately $27 billion in unsecured bonds; and an ad hoc committee representing holders of a majority of those bonds.

But the motion has engendered many objections and limited objections, by a variety of others. The objectors include, among others, a minority of the holders of GM's unsecured bonds (most significantly, an ad hoc committee of three of them (the "**F & D Bondholders Committee**"), holding approximately .01% of GM's bonds),[11] who contend, among other things, that GM's assets can be sold only under a chapter 11 plan, and that the proposed section 363 sale amounts to an impermissible "*sub rosa*" plan.

Objectors and limited objectors also include tort litigants who object to provisions in the approval order limiting successor liability claims against the Purchaser; asbestos litigants with similar concerns, along with concerns as to asbestos ailments that have not yet been discovered; and non-UAW unions ("**Splinter Unions**") speaking for their retirees, concerned that the Purchaser does not plan to treat their retirees as well as the UAW's retirees.

On the most basic issue, whether a 363 sale is proper, GM contends that this is exactly the kind of case where a section 363 sale is appropriate and indeed essential — and where under the several rulings of the Second Circuit and the Supreme Court in this area, GM's business can be sold, and its value preserved, before the company dies. The Court agrees. GM cannot survive with its continuing losses and associated loss of liquidity, and without the governmental funding that will expire in a matter of days. And there are no options to this sale — especially any premised on the notion that the company could survive the

---

10. When discussing the mechanics of the 363 Transaction, the existing GM will be referred to as "**Old GM**," and the Purchaser will be referred to as "**New GM.**"

11. When it filed its objection, the F & D Bondholders Committee, identifying itself as the "Family & Dissident" Bondholders Committee, said it was "representing the interests of" 1,500 bondholders, with bond holdings "believed to exceed $400 million." (F & D Bondholder Comm. Obj. at 1). But even after it filed the second of its Fed.R.Bankr.P.2019 statements, it identified no other bondholders for whom it was speaking, or provide the holdings, purchases and sales information for any others that Rule 2019 requires. Under these circumstances, the Court must consider that the committee speaks for just those three bondholders.

process of negotiations and litigation that characterizes the plan confirmation process.

As nobody can seriously dispute, the only alternative to an immediate sale is liquidation — a disastrous result for GM's creditors, its employees, the suppliers who depend on GM for their own existence, and the communities in which GM operates. In the event of a liquidation, creditors now trying to increase their incremental recoveries would get nothing.

Neither the Code, nor the caselaw — especially the caselaw in the Second Circuit — requires waiting for the plan confirmation process to take its course when the inevitable consequence would be liquidation. Bankruptcy courts have the power to authorize sales of assets at a time when there still is value to preserve — to prevent the death of the patient on the operating table.

Nor can the Court accept various objectors' contention that there here is a *sub rosa* plan. GM's assets simply are being sold, with the consideration to GM to be hereafter distributed to stakeholders, consistent with their statutory priorities, under a subsequent plan. Arrangements that will be made by the Purchaser do not affect the distribution of the *Debtor's* property, and will address wholly different needs and concerns — arrangements that the Purchaser needs to create a new GM that will be lean and healthy enough to survive.

Issues as to how any approval order should address *successor liability* are the only truly debatable issues in this case. And while textual analysis is ultimately inconclusive and caselaw on a nationwide basis is not uniform, the Court believes in *stare decisis;* it follows the caselaw in this Circuit and District in holding that to the extent the Purchaser has not voluntarily agreed to accept successor liability, GM's property — like that of Chrysler, just a few weeks ago — may be sold free and clear of claims.

Those and other issues are addressed below. GM's motion is granted.

10. SPECIFICS OF THE TRANSACTION

The sale transaction, as embodied in the MPA and related documents, is complex. Its "deal points" can be summarized as follows:

(A)   ACQUIRED AND EXCLUDED ASSETS

Under the Sale, New GM will acquire all of Old GM's assets, with the exception of certain assets expressly excluded under the MPA (respectively, the "**Purchased Assets**" and the "**Excluded Assets**"). The Excluded Assets chiefly consist of:

  (i) $1.175 billion in cash or cash equivalents;
  (ii)   equity interests in certain Saturn and other entities;
  (iii)   certain real and personal property;
  (iv)   bankruptcy avoidance actions;
  (v)   certain employee benefit plans; and
  (vi)   certain restricted cash and receivables.

(B)   ASSUMED AND EXCLUDED LIABILITIES

Old GM will retain all liabilities except those defined in the MPA as "**Assumed Liabilities.**" The Assumed Liabilities include:

(i)   product liability claims arising out of products delivered at or after the Sale transaction closes (the "*Closing*");

(ii)   the warranty and recall obligations of both Old GM and New GM;

(iii)   all employment-related obligations and liabilities under any assumed employee benefit plan relating to employees that are or were covered by the UAW collective bargaining agreement; and — by reason of an important change that was made in the MPA after the filing of the motion —

(iv)   broadening the first category substantially, *all* product liability claims arising from accidents or other discrete incidents arising from operation of GM vehicles occurring subsequent to the closing of the 363 Transaction, *regardless of when the product was purchased.*

The liabilities being retained by Old GM include:

(i)   product liability claims arising out of products delivered prior to the Closing (to the extent they weren't assumed by reason of the change in the MPA after the filing of objections);

(ii)   liabilities for claims arising out of exposure to asbestos;

(iii)   liabilities to third parties for claims based upon "[c]ontract, tort or any other basis";

(iv)   liabilities related to any implied warranty or other implied obligation arising under statutory or common law; and

(v)   employment-related obligations not otherwise assumed, including, among other obligations, those arising out of the employment, potential employment, or termination of any individual (other than an employee covered by the UAW collective bargaining agreement) prior to or at the Closing.

(C)   CONSIDERATION

Old GM is to receive consideration estimated to be worth approximately $45 billion, plus the value of equity interests that it will receive in New GM. It will come in the following forms:

(i)   a credit bid by the U.S. Treasury and EDC, who will credit bid the majority of the indebtedness outstanding under their DIP facility and the Treasury Prepetition Loan;

(ii)   the assumption by New GM of approximately $6.7 billion of indebtedness under the DIP facilities, plus an additional $1.175 billion to be advanced by the U.S. Treasury under a new DIP facility (the "**Wind**

Down Facility") whose proceeds will be used by Old GM to wind down its affairs;

(iii)   the surrender of the warrant that had been issued by Old GM to Treasury in connection with the Treasury Prepetition Loan;

(iv)   10% of the post-closing outstanding shares of New GM, plus an additional 2% if the estimated amount of allowed prepetition general unsecured claims against Old GM exceeds $35 billion;

(v)   two warrants, each to purchase 7.5% of the post-closing outstanding shares of New GM, with an exercise price based on a $15 billion equity valuation and a $30 billion equity valuation, respectively; and

(vi)   the assumption of liabilities, including those noted above.

(D)   OWNERSHIP OF NEW GM

Under the terms of the Sale, New GM will be owned by four entities.

(i)   Treasury will own 60.8% of New GM's common stock on an undiluted basis. It also will own $2.1 billion of New GM Series A Preferred Stock;

(ii)   EDC will own 11.7% of New GM's common stock on an undiluted basis. It also will own $400 million of New GM Series A Preferred Stock;

(iii)   A New Employees' Beneficiary Association Trust ("**New VEBA**") will own 17.5% of New GM's common stock on an undiluted basis. It also will own $6.5 billion of New GM's Series A Preferred Stock, and a 6-year warrant to acquire 2.5% of New GM's common stock, with an exercise price based on $75 billion total equity value; and

(iv)   Finally, if a chapter 11 plan is implemented as contemplated under the structure of the Sale transaction, Old GM will own 10% of New GM's common stock on an undiluted basis. In addition, if the allowed prepetition general unsecured claims against Old GM exceed $35 billion, Old GM will be issued an additional 10 million shares, amounting to approximately 2% of New GM's common stock. Old GM will also own the two warrants mentioned above.

(E)   OTHER ASPECTS OF TRANSACTION

New GM will make an offer of employment to all of the Sellers' non-unionized employees and unionized employees represented by the UAW. Substantially all of old GM's executory contracts with direct suppliers are likely to be assumed and assigned to New GM.

After the Closing, New GM will assume all liabilities arising under express written emission and limited warranties delivered in connection with the sale of new vehicles or parts manufactured or sold by Old GM.

One of the requirements of the U.S. Treasury, imposed when the Treasury Prepetition Loan was put in place, was the need to negotiate a new collective bargaining agreement which would allow GM to be fully competitive, and "equitize" — *i.e.*, convert to equity — at least one half of the obligation GM had to the UAW VEBA. Ultimately GM did so. New GM will make future contributions to the New VEBA that will provide retiree health and welfare benefits to former UAW employees and their spouses. Also, as part of the 363 Transaction, New GM will be the assignee of revised collective bargaining agreements with the UAW, the terms of which were recently ratified—though contingent upon the approval of the entirety of these motions.

(F)   THE PROPOSED SALE ORDER

Though GM's request has been narrowed, as noted above, to provide that New GM will assume liability for product liability claims arising from operation of GM vehicles occurring after the closing of the 363 Transaction (regardless of when the product was purchased), GM asks this Court, as in the *Chrysler* case, to authorize the Sale free and clear of all other "liens, claims, encumbrances and other interests," including, specifically, "all successor liability claims."

To effectuate this result, GM has submitted a proposed order to the Court (the "**Proposed Sale Order**") that contains provisions directed at cutting off successor liability except in the respects where successor liability was contractually assumed.

First, the Proposed Sale Order contains a finding—and a decretal provision to similar effect—that the Debtors may sell the Purchased Assets free and clear of all liens, claims, encumbrances, and other interests, including rights or claims based on any successor or transferee liability.

Second, the Proposed Sale Order would enjoin all persons (including "litigation claimants") holding liens, claims, encumbrances, and other interests, including rights or claims based on any successor or transferee liability, from asserting them against New GM or the Purchased Assets.

2.   SUCCESSOR LIABILITY ISSUES

Many objectors—including the Ad Hoc Committee of Consumer Victims (the "**Consumer Victims Committee**"), individual accident litigants ("the **Individual Accident Litigants**"), and attorneys for asbestos victim litigants (collectively, "the **Asbestos Litigants**") object to provisions in the proposed sale order that would limit any "successor liability" that New GM might have. Successor liability claims normally are for money damages—as, for example, the claims by the Individual Accident Litigants are. If permitted, such claims would be asserted against the successor in ownership of property that was transferred from the entity whose alleged wrongful acts gave rise to the claim.

"As a general rule, a purchaser of assets does not assume the liabilities of the seller unless the purchaser expressly agrees to do so or an exception to the rule exists." Successor liability is an equitable exception to that general rule. Successor liability depends on state law, and the doctrines vary from state to state, but generally successor liability will not attach unless particular requirements imposed by that state have been satisfied.

If a buyer cannot obtain protection against successor liability, "it may pay less for the assets because of the risk."[12] When the transfer of property takes place in a 363 sale, and the buyer has sought and obtained agreement from the debtor that the sale will be free and clear, the bankruptcy court is invariably asked to provide, in its approval order, that the transferee does not assume liability for the debtor's pre-sale conduct.

Such a request was likewise made here. Under the proposed order, in its latest form, New GM would voluntarily assume liability for warranty claims, and for product liability claims asserted by those injured after the 363 Transaction — even if the vehicle was manufactured before the 363 Transaction. But New GM would not assume any Old GM liabilities for injuries or illnesses that arose before the 363 Transaction. And the proposed order has a number of provisions making explicit findings that New GM is not subject to successor liability for such matters, and that claims against New GM of that character are enjoined.[13]

The issues as to the successor liability provisions in the approval order are the most debatable of the issues now before the Court. Textual analysis is ultimately inconclusive as to the extent to which a 363 order can bar successor liability claims premised upon the transfer of property, and cases on a nationwide basis are split. But principles of *stare decisis* dictate that under the caselaw in this Circuit and District, the Court should, and indeed must, rule that property can be sold free and clear of successor liability claims.

(A) TEXTUAL ANALYSIS

As before, the Court starts with textual analysis

Application of section 363(f)'s authority to issue a "free and clear" order with respect to a successor liability claim turns, at least in the first instance, on whether such a claim is an "interest in property." But while "claim" is defined in the Code, neither "interest" nor "interest in property" is likewise defined.

So in the absence of statutory definitions of either "interest" or "interest in property," what can we discern from the text of the Code as to what those words mean?

---

12. Whether the U.S. and Canadian Governments would have lent and ultimately bid a lesser amount here is doubtful, but this consideration provides the context for deciding legal issues that presumably will extend beyond this case.

13. The principal provisions in the proposed order provide, in relevant part:

> Except for the Assumed Liabilities, pursuant to sections 105(a) and 363(f) of the Bankruptcy Code, the Purchased Assets shall be transferred to the Purchaser in accordance with the MPA, and, upon the Closing, shall be free and clear of all liens, claims, encumbrances, and other interests of any kind or nature whatsoever . . . including rights or claims based on any successor or transferee liability. . . .
>
> . . . [A]ll persons and entities . . . holding liens, claims, encumbrances, and other interests of any kind or nature whatsoever, including rights or claims based on any successor or transferee liability, against or in a Seller or the Purchased Assets (whether legal or equitable, secured or unsecured, matured or unmatured, contingent or noncontingent, senior or subordinated), arising under or out of, in connection with, or in any way relating to, the Sellers, the Purchased Assets, the operation of the Purchased Assets prior to the Closing, or the 363 Transaction, are forever barred, estopped, and permanently enjoined from asserting against the Purchaser, its successors or assigns, its property, or the Purchased Assets, such persons' or entities' liens, claims, encumbrances, and other interests, including rights or claims based on any successor or transferee liability.

First, we know that "interest" includes more than just a lien. Subsection (f)(3) makes clear that "interest" is broader, as there otherwise would be no reason for (f)(3) to deal with the subset of interests where "such interest is a lien."

Second, we know that an "interest" is something that may accompany the transfer of the underlying property, and where bankruptcy policy, as implemented by the drafters of the Code, requires specific provisions to ensure that it *will not* follow the transfer.

The Individual Accident Litigants contend that here the Court should presume that "equivalent words have equivalent meaning when repeated in the same statute." But while that is often a useful aid to construction, we cannot do so here. That is because "interest" has wholly different meanings as used in various places in the Code,[14] and assumptions that they mean the same thing here are unfounded.

Thus, those in the bankruptcy community know, upon considering the usage of "interest" in any particular place in the Code, that "interest" means wholly different things in different contexts:

(i)   a nondebtor's *collateral*—as used, for example, in consideration of adequate protection of an interest under sections 361 and 362(d)(1), use of cash collateral under section 363(c)(2), or in many 363(f) situations, such as where a creditor has a lien;

(ii)   *a legal or equitable ownership of property*—as used, for example, in section 541 of the Code, or in other section 363(f) situations, where a nondebtor asserts competing ownership, a right to specific performance, or the like—or, quite differently,

(iii) *stock* or other equity in the debtor, *as contrasted to debt*—as used, for example, in section 1111 ("[a] proof of claim or interest is deemed filed under section 501"), or where a reorganization plan is to establish classes of claims and interests, under sections 1122 and 1123.

The Individual Accident Litigants place particular emphasis on section 1141(c) of the Code, asking this Court to compare and contrast it. They argue that

> In contrast, §1141(c) of the Bankruptcy Code provides that "property dealt with by the plan is free and clear of all *claims and interests . . . in* the debtor." (Emphasis added). Section 363 and 1141(c) are two mechanisms for transfer of estate property (one through a sale, the other through a plan). The difference between the words chosen by Congress in these two closely related sections shows that Congress did not intend a sale under §363(f) to be free and clear of "*claims,*" but only of "*interests in* such property" because "'it is generally presumed that Congress

---

14. *See* Postings of Stephen Lubben, Professor at Seton Hall Law School, to Credit Slips, *http://www. creditslips.org/creditslips/2009/06/claim-or-interest.html* (June 13, 2009, 8:25 PM EST); and *http://www.creditslips. org/creditslips/2009/06/claim-or-interest-part-2.html* (June 14, 2009, 6:42 PM EST). Blogs are a fairly recent phenomenon in the law, providing a useful forum for interchanges of ideas. While comments in blogs lack the editing and peer review characteristics of law journals, and probably should be considered judiciously, they may nevertheless be quite useful, especially as food for thought, and may be regarded as simply another kind of secondary authority, whose value simply turns on the rigor of the analysis in the underlying ideas they express.

actions intentionally and purposely' when it 'includes particular language in one section of a statute but omits it in another.'"

But this is not an apt comparison, since when "interests" is used in section 1141(c), it is used with the wholly different definition of (iii) above—*i.e.*, as stock or another type of equity—in contrast to the very different definitions in (i) and (ii) above, which are ways by which "interests in property" may be used in section 363(f).

Thus, as Lubben suggests, and the Court agrees, in section 1141 "interest" matches up with "equity," and "claim" matches up with debt.[15] Section 1141 is of no assistance in determining whether litigation rights transmitted through transfers of property fall within the meaning of "interests in property." Section 1141 does not provide a yardstick by which section 363(f)'s meaning can be judged.

So where does textual analysis leave us? It tells us that "interest" means more than a lien, but it does not tell us how much more. Textual analysis does not support or foreclose the possibility that an "interest in property" covers a right that exists against a new party solely by reason of a transfer of property to that party. Nor does textual analysis support or foreclose the idea that an "interest" is a right that travels with the property—or that it would do so unless the Code cut it off. Ultimately textual analysis is inconclusive. Neither the Code nor interpretive aids tells us how broadly or narrowly—in the particular context of section 363(f)—"interest in property" should be deemed to be defined.[16]

---

15. *See* Posting of Stephen Lubben, Professor at Seton Hall Law School, to Credit Slips, *http://www. creditslips.org/creditslips/2009/06/claim-or-interest.html* (June 13, 2009, 8:25 PM EST).

16. The Individual Accident Litigants also place heavy reliance on Butner v. United States, 440 U.S. 48, 99 S.Ct. 914, 59 L.Ed.2d 136 (1979), *see* Indiv. Accident Litigants Br. 8, suggesting that *Butner* requires deference to state law that might impose successor liability and that this would require excluding successor liability damages claims from any definition of "interest." But the Court cannot agree. First, when quoted in full, *Butner* (whose bottom line was that the issue of whether a security interest extended to rents derived from the property was governed by state law) stated:

> The Bankruptcy Act does include provisions invalidating certain security interests as fraudulent, or as improper preferences over general creditors. Apart from these provisions, however, Congress has generally left the determination of property rights in the assets of a bankrupt's estate to state law.

440 U.S. at 54, 99 S.Ct. 914. *Butner* further stated (in language the Individual Accident Litigants did not quote):

> Unless some federal interest requires a different result, there is no reason why such interests should be analyzed differently simply because an interested party is involved in a bankruptcy proceeding.

Id. at 55, 99 S.Ct. 914. But the *Butner* court laid out principles by which we determine what is property of the estate; it did not address the different issue of whether a state may impose liability on a transferee of estate property by reason of something the debtor did before the transfer. Moreover, *Butner* noted that provisions of the Code can and do sometimes trump state law. And section 363(f), for as much or as little as it covers, is exactly such a provision. In fact, 363(f) is a classic example of an instance where a "federal interest requires a different result." *Butner* neither supports nor defeats either party's position here.

Therefore, once again — as in the Court's earlier consideration of *Lionel* and its progeny and the cases establishing the judge-made law of *sub rosa* plans — the Court must go beyond the words of the Code to the applicable caselaw.

Viewed nationally, the caselaw is split in this area, both at the Circuit Court level and in the bankruptcy Courts. Some courts have held that section 363(f) provides a basis for selling free and clear of successor liability claims,[17] and others have held that it does not.[18]

But the caselaw is *not* split in this Circuit and District. In *Chrysler*, Judge Gonzalez expressly considered and rejected the efforts to impose successor liability. And more importantly, the Second Circuit, after hearing extensive argument on this issue along with others, affirmed Judge Gonzalez's *Chrysler* order for substantially the reasons Judge Gonzalez set forth in his *Chrysler* decision.

This Court has previously noted how *Chrysler* is so closely on point, and this issue is no exception. Judge Gonzalez expressly considered it. In material reliance on the Third Circuit's decision in *TWA*, "the leading case on this issue," Judge Gonzalez held that *TWA:*

> makes clear that such tort claims are interests in property such that they are extinguished by a free and clear sale under section 363(f)(5) and are therefore extinguished by the Sale Transaction. The Court follows *TWA* and overrules the objections premised on this argument. . . . [I]n personam claims, including any potential state successor or transferee liability claims against New Chrysler, as well as in rem interests, are encompassed by section 363(f) and are therefore extinguished by the Sale Transaction.

This Court has already noted its view of the importance of *stare decisis* in this district, and feels no differently with respect to this issue. This Court follows the decisions of its fellow bankruptcy judges in this district, in the absence of plain error, because the interests of predictability in commercial bankruptcy cases are of such great importance. Apart from the underlying reasons that have caused *stare decisis* to be embedded in American decisional law, *stare decisis* is particularly important in commercial bankruptcy cases because of the expense and trauma of any commercial bankruptcy, and the need to deal with foreseeable events, by pre-bankruptcy planning, to the extent they can be addressed. Likewise, litigation, while a fact of life in commercial bankruptcy cases, takes money directly out of the pockets of creditors, and predictability fosters settlements, since with predictability, parties will have an informed sense as to how any disputed legal issues will be decided.

17. *See, e.g., Chrysler*, 405 B.R. at 111; In re Trans World Airlines, Inc., 322 F.3d 283, 288-90 (3d Cir.2003) ("*TWA*"); *United Mine Workers of Am.1992 Benefit Plan v. Leckie Smokeless Coal Co. (In re Leckie Smokeless Coal Co.)*, 99 F.3d 573, 581-82 (4th Cir.1996).

18. *See, e.g.*, Michigan Empl. Sec. Comm. v. Wolverine Radio Co., Inc. (In re Wolverine Radio Co.), 930 F.2d 1132, 1147-48 (6th Cir.1991); Precision Indus., Inc. v. Qualitech Steel SBQ, LLC (In re Qualitech Steel Corp.), 327 F.3d 537, 545-46 (7th Cir.2003); Fairchild Aircraft Corp. v. Cambell (In re Fairchild Aircraft Corp.), 184 B.R. 910, 918 (Bankr.W.D.Tex.1995), *vacated as moot on equitable grounds*, 220 B.R. 909 (Bkrtcy.W.D.Tex.1998). *See also* Volvo White Truck Corp. v. Chambersburg Beverage, Inc. (In re White Motor Credit Corp.), 75 B.R. 944, 948 (Bankr.N.D.Ohio 1987) (concluding that 363(f) could not be utilized, but that section 105(a) could be used to effect 363 sale free and clear of claims).

Though for all of these reasons, this Court would have followed *Chrysler* even if that case had no subsequent history, we here have a hugely important additional fact. The Circuit affirmed *Chrysler, and* for "substantially for the reasons stated in the opinion below."

This Court fully understands the circumstances of tort victims, and the fact that if they prevail in litigation and cannot look to New GM as an additional source of recovery, they may recover only modest amounts on any allowed claims — if, as is possible, they do not have other defendants who can also pay. But the law in this Circuit and District is clear; the Court will permit GM's assets to pass to the purchaser free and clear of successor liability claims, and in that connection, will issue the requested findings and associated injunction.

PROBLEM SET 29.2

1. What steps did the buyer take in *GM* that the buyer in *Lefever* did not? Will these steps matter?
2. The appellants in the *Chrysler* case sought review in the Supreme Court following the Second Circuit's decision. The Supreme Court dismissed the appeal as moot — the Chrysler sale had already closed by that point — but also instructed the Circuit to dismiss its opinion on the same basis. Thus, Judge Gerber's opinion stands simply on the basis of his deference to the prior decision of his colleague in *Chrysler*, which is largely based on the Third Circuit's opinion in *TWA*. *See In re* Trans World Airlines, Inc., 322 F.3d 283, 288-90, 293 (3d Cir. 2003).
3. Should section 363(f) overcome state law successor liability claims? Is a successor liability claim an "interest" in the debtor's property at the time of the sale?
4. How does a 363 sale facilitate "reorganization"?

30

CHAPTER 11 PLANS

The traditional end of chapter 11 is confirmation of a plan. That plan often will be a reorganization plan, but sometimes it will be a liquidation plan. The latter is especially true if the debtor previously sold most of its assets under section 363. A chapter 11 plan can be seen as a contract. But unlike most contracts, this one can be imposed on dissenting parties. Namely, if the plan meets certain requirements that we talk about in this chapter, it becomes binding on all of the debtor's creditors and shareholders, regardless of whether they voted for the plan or participated in the chapter 11 case.

Moreover, the bankruptcy court has nationwide jurisdiction, so the binding effects of the plan are enforceable on any creditor that has minimum contacts with the United States. This means that large financial institutions, even if based in a foreign country, will typically be bound by a plan, since the financial institution will often have a presence in New York City.

1. EXCLUSIVITY, PLAN SOLICITATION, DISCLOSURE STATEMENTS, AND VOTING

The debtor-in-possession enjoys the exclusive right to file a plan for the first 120 days of a chapter 11 bankruptcy case.[1] The debtor's exclusive period ends

- upon the appointment of a Chapter 11 trustee,
- if the debtor has not filed a plan before the expiration of the 120-day period, or
- if the debtor has not filed a plan that has been accepted by each impaired class of claims or interests within the first 180 days of the bankruptcy case.[2]

---

1. 11 U.S.C. §1121(b).
2. 11 U.S.C. §1121(c).

Before 2005, courts could and routinely did extend the exclusive period for "cause." Competing plans were rare, especially in big cases.

Since 2005, bankruptcy courts are not permitted to extend the date for filing a plan beyond 18 months and the date for acceptance beyond 20 months. Both are measured from the date of filing.

After exclusivity lapses, any party in interest may propose a plan. In such cases, the court, and perhaps voting creditors, may have multiple plans to choose from. In all cases, creditors considering a plan must be provided with a disclosure statement that explains the plan. You saw examples of prepetition disclosure statements in Chapter 27.

IN RE OXFORD HOMES, INC., DEBTOR

204 B.R. 264
United States Bankruptcy Court, D. Maine
Bankruptcy No. 94–20135 | Jan. 6, 1997

James B. HAINES, Jr., Bankruptcy Judge.
Invoking §503(b)(3)(D) and §503(b)(4), Peter N. Connell, a former shareholder and prepetition creditor of Oxford Homes, Inc., seeks administrative expense treatment for $85,085.00 in counsel fees and $1,830.17 in counsel's expenses that he incurred in connection with Oxford's successful reorganization. For the reasons set forth below, I conclude that Connell's request will not be granted. To do so would subvert the disclosure statement and plan confirmation process and would be fundamentally unfair to Oxford's creditors, who voted to accept Oxford's reorganization plan with no inkling that Connell would request administrative treatment for any portion of his counsel's fees.

PROCEDURAL HISTORY

Oxford filed its voluntary Chapter 11 petition on February 22, 1994. After a rocky beginning, during which the case nearly converted to Chapter 7, the reorganization proceeded under the supervision of a Chapter 11 trustee. Along the way, the trustee's efforts were assisted mightily by Connell. Connell and the trustee jointly devised and proposed Oxford's reorganization plan. After a series of amendments and modifications, the joint plan was confirmed on December 23, 1994.

FACTS

1.   WHAT CONNELL AND HIS COUNSEL DID.

No party in interest disputes that Connell's active alliance with the Chapter 11 trustee fostered, indeed fathered, Oxford's reorganization. From a point soon after the trustee's appointment, Connell drew upon the assistance of Steven E.

Cope, Esq., of Cope & Cope, a Portland, Maine, law firm specializing in bankruptcy matters. Cope provided comprehensive legal services to Connell, working to negotiate and structure Oxford's reorganization. Cope authored and reportedly revised the plan and disclosure statement that Connell and the trustee proposed.

Cope asserts that his activities on Connell's behalf substantially contributed to Oxford's reorganization; reasonably required 486.2 hours of his time, billed at $175.00 per hour; and entailed reasonable expenses and disbursements amounting to $1,830.17. Cope performed additional services for Connell, generating approximately 50 hours of billable legal work, for which Connell does not seek administrative allowance.

The original disclosure statement, and each ensuing version, described in detail the administrative claims category and the Connell claims class. Nowhere did they advert to the possibility that Connell might seek to have his attorney's fees paid "off the top" through the plan as an administrative expense.

Notwithstanding the plan trustee's concession that as much as half of the $85,085.00 fee application is properly allowable as an administrative expense, and notwithstanding the absence of objection from any other quarter, I must review Connell's request by my own lights. "The bankruptcy judge has an independent duty to examine the propriety and reasonableness of fees, even if no party in interest objects to the application."

Although I am convinced of the necessity, reasonableness, and value of Cope's work, I am unconvinced of the *propriety* of *any* administrative fee award in this instance.

3. WHY THE APPLICATION MUST BE DISALLOWED.

A plan of reorganization may not be submitted to a debtor's creditors unless and until a disclosure statement has been approved by the court as containing "adequate information." 11 U.S.C. §1125(b). Adequate information is defined in the Code as:

> information of a kind, and in sufficient detail, as far as is reasonably practicable in light of the nature and history of the debtor and the condition of the debtor's books and records, that would enable a hypothetical reasonable investor typical of holders of claims or interests of the relevant class to make an informed judgment about the plan . . . ;

11 U.S.C. §1125(a)(1). As the Third Circuit recently observed:

> [D]isclosure requirements are crucial to the effective functioning of the federal bankruptcy system. Because creditors and the bankruptcy court rely heavily on the debtor's disclosure statement in determining whether to approve a proposed reorganization plan, the importance of full and honest disclosure cannot be overstated.

Ryan Operations G.P. v. Santiam–Midwest Lumber Co., 81 F.3d 355, 362 (3rd Cir.1996). The precise contours of "adequate information" were vaguely drawn by Congress so that bankruptcy courts might exercise their discretion to limn them in view of each case's peculiar circumstances.[3]

Although what constitutes "adequate information" will vary from case to case, a good faith estimate of administrative expenses, incurred and upcoming, is a virtual constant. Creditors deserve to be fairly informed of the transaction costs entailed in the reorganization plan they are being asked to back.

As a plan proponent whose counsel was intimately involved in drafting Oxford's disclosure statement[s] and plan[s], it was incumbent on Connell to reveal any intention he entertained to seek administrative payment of his legal expenses. This he failed to do.

At each stage of their evolution, the plan and disclosure statement not only neglected to reveal the possibility that Connell would seek administrative payment of 90% of his attorney's fees, their comprehensive explanation of the scope of administrative claims and the extent of Connell's claims seemingly ruled out such a possibility. Connell, who asked creditors to support the plan on that record, may not now ask them to pay his fees before realizing their plan distributions.

The result I reach is based on the need to honor the trust creditors are entitled to repose in the disclosure, solicitation, and confirmation processes that are at the heart of Chapter 11. Because Connell, through Cope, authored the disclosure statement and plan, it is only fair that he be bound by them. To the extent that the principle upon which I base my decision need be further defined, it represents a form of judicial estoppel.

Administrative allowance of Connell's attorney's fees was not an immaterial point when the disclosure statement was approved or at confirmation. It is not today.

---

3. Categories of information that ought to be considered for inclusion in a disclosure statement include:

1. The circumstances that gave rise to the filing of the bankruptcy petition;
2. A complete description of the available assets and their value;
3. The anticipated future of the debtor, with accompanying financial projections;
4. The source of the information provided in the disclosure statement;
5. The condition and performance of the debtor while in chapter 11;
6. Information regarding claims against the estate, including those allowed, disputed, and estimated;
7. A liquidation analysis setting forth the estimated return that creditors would receive under chapter 7;
8. The accounting and valuation methods used to produce the financial information in the disclosure statement;
9. Information regarding the future management of the debtor, including the amount of compensation to be paid to any insiders, directors, and/or officers of the debtor;
10. A summary of the plan of reorganization;
11. An estimate of all administrative expenses, including attorneys' fees and accountants' fees;
12. The collectibility of any accounts receivable;
13. Any financial information, valuations or *pro forma* projections that would be relevant to creditors' determinations of whether to accept or reject the plan;
14. Information relevant to the risks being taken by the creditors and interest holders;
15. The actual or projected value that can be obtained from avoidable transfers;
16. The existence, likelihood and possible success of nonbankruptcy litigation;
17. The tax consequences of the plan;
18. The relationship of the debtor with affiliates.

Moreover, the fees being sought today were more than just "foreseeable." As of the date the disclosure statement was finally approved, the lion's share of them had already accrued.

A class entitled to vote on a plan is deemed to accept a plan if creditors holding at least two-thirds in amount and more than one-half in number of the allowed claims in the class accept the plan.[4]

But certain classes have votes presumed for them. Unimpaired classes are conclusively presumed to have accepted the plan, making solicitation from the holders of claims or interests in such classes unnecessary.[5]

Conversely, a class is deemed to have rejected a plan if the plan provides that the holders of the claims or interests in such class will not receive or retain any property under the plan on account of such claims or interests.[6]

PROBLEM SET 30.1

1. Monkey Industries has recently filed a chapter 11 petition and begun to work on a plan. Hugo Capital Investors has its doubts about the management of the debtor, and has begun sending a memorandum with the outlines of an alternative plan to other large creditors to gauge their support. Does this present any problems under the Bankruptcy Code?
2. Disclosure statements tend to be almost as long as the form 10-Ks filed with the SEC. And then it is typical to attach a 10-K to the disclosure statement as well. Is this what is meant by "adequate information" in §1125(b) of the Bankruptcy Code? Why not write a shorter disclosure statement and incorporate the 10-K by reference?

2. CHAPTER 11 PLANS

Section 1123 provides what a plan must do, and also provides some examples of what it could do. But the permissive parts of 1123 are quite open ended, which leaves the parties open to negotiation of almost any creative solution they might imagine, so long as it does not violate some affirmative provision of the Code.

In the prior section we discussed the voting requirements for particular classes to approve a plan. But how are the classes constructed?

The Code is maddeningly vague on this point. Section 1123 requires classification "subject to section 1122." Section 1122(a) provides that "a plan may place a claim or an interest in a particular class only if such claim or interest is substantially similar to the other claims or interests of such class." That, of course, begs the question of what "substantially similar" means.

---

4. 11 U.S.C. §1126(c).
5. 11 U.S.C. §1126(f).
6. 11 U.S.C. §1126(g).

<u>IN RE TRIBUNE COMPANY, ET AL.,[7] DEBTORS</u>

476 B.R. 843, 228 F.3d 224
United States Bankruptcy Court, D. Delaware
No. 08-13141 (KJC) July 13, 2012

Kevin J. CAREY, Bankruptcy Judge.

Before the Court for consideration is the Fourth Amended Joint Plan of Reorganization for Tribune Company and Its Subsidiaries Proposed by the Debtors, the Official Committee of Unsecured Creditors, Oaktree Capital Management, L.P., Angelo Gordon & Co., L.P., and JPMorgan Chase Bank, as revised (the "Fourth Amended Plan"). The DCL Plan Proponents seek confirmation of the Fourth Amended Plan, but objections to confirmation filed by the following parties remained unresolved: (i) Aurelius Capital Management, L.P. ("Aurelius") (docket nos. 11664 and 11753), (ii) Law Debenture Trust Company of New York ("Law Debenture") (docket no. 11668), (iii) Deutsche Bank Trust Company of Americas ("Deutsche Bank") (docket no. 11667), (iv) Wilmington Trust Company ("WTC") (docket no. 11666), (v) Citadel Equity Fund Ltd. and Camden Asset Management LP (together, "Citadel Camden") (docket no. 11659), (vi) EGI-TRB LLC ("EGI") (docket no. 11658), (vii) certain former directors and officers of the Debtors (the "D & Os") (docket no. 11657), and (viii) F. Ashley Allen, Catherine M. Hertz, Michael D. Slason, and Louis J. Stancampiano ("Certain Former Employees") (docket no. 11661).

The DCL Plan Proponents responded to the objections to confirmation of the Fourth Amended Plan by filing the Memorandum of Law in Support of Confirmation and Omnibus Reply to Objections to Confirmation (docket no. 11746). Other parties weighed in by filing replies to some of the objections, including (i) the Statement of Robert R. McCormick Tribune Foundation (the "McCormick Foundation") and Cantigny Foundation in Response to Objection of Aurelius Capital Management, LP (docket no. 11725), (ii) the D & Os' Reply to the Objection of Aurelius Capital Management, LP (docket no. 11739), (iii) the D & Os' Joinder to the Statement of the Robert R. McCormick Tribune and Cantigny Foundations (docket no. 11740), and (iv) the Bridge Agent's Reply, and Joinder to the DCL Plan Proponents' Reply, to the Objection of Aurelius Capital Management, LP (docket no. 11748).

A hearing to consider confirmation of the Fourth Amended Plan was held on June 7 and 8, 2012, and continued via conference call on June 11, 2012 (together, the "Fourth Amended Plan Confirmation Hearing").

On June 18, 2012, the DCL Plan Proponents filed the revised Fourth Amended Plan (docket no. 11836) to incorporate modifications that resolved a number of objections to confirmation. On the same date, the DCL Plan

---

7. The chapter 11 case filed by Tribune Media Services, Inc. (Bky. Case No. 08-13236) is jointly administered with the Tribune Company bankruptcy case and 109 additional affiliated debtors pursuant to the Order dated December 10, 2008 (docket no. 43). An additional debtor, Tribune CNLBC, LLC (formerly known as Chicago National League Baseball Club, LLC) filed a voluntary petition for relief under chapter 11 of the Bankruptcy Code on October 12, 2009 (Bky. Case No. 09-13496), and is also jointly administered with the Tribune Company bankruptcy case pursuant to this Court's Order dated October 14, 2009 (docket no. 2333). The debtors in the jointly administered cases are referred to herein as the "Debtors."

Proponents also filed revised exhibits and other documents related to the Fourth Amended Plan, including (i) Plan Exhibit 13.1 — the Litigation Trust Agreement, the Litigation Trust Loan Agreement, the proposed Agreement Respecting Transfer of Documents, Information, and Privileges from Debtors and Reorganized Debtors (the "Debtors' LT Agreement"), the proposed Agreement Respecting Transfer of Documents, Information, and Privileges from the Official Committee of Unsecured Creditors (the "Committee's LT Agreement").

On June 20, 2012, Aurelius filed a letter objection with the Court (docket no. 11856) arguing that changes made to the proposed Committee's LT Agreement regarding the Litigation Trustee's discovery rights with respect to the Creditors' Committee did not address its concerns. The Creditors' Committee filed a letter in response (docket no. 11867) and a telephonic hearing was held on June 21, 2012 to discuss the issue.

On July 11, 2012, a further hearing was held to address the Certain Former Employees' objection and Aurelius' objection to the Committee's LT Agreement. After colloquy with counsel at the July 11, 2012 hearing, the objection by the Certain Former Employees was withdrawn. At the July 11, 2012 hearing, the Court also suggested language to address Aurelius' objection to provisions in the proposed Committee's LT Agreement concerning certain discovery rights of the Litigation Trustee vis-a-vis the Creditors' Committee (including its retained professionals). The parties discussed the Court's proposed language and agreed to make further revisions to the affected paragraphs. However, Aurelius requested one additional change to which the Creditors' Committee did not agree. The revised language as otherwise agreed to by the parties at the July 11, 2012 hearing (without Aurelius' final change), was submitted under Certification on July 12, 2012 (docket no. 12001). The proposed Committee's LT Agreement, as revised, fairly addresses Aurelius' concerns. Accordingly, Aurelius' last remaining request is denied.

For the reasons set forth herein, the remaining objections by Aurelius, Law Debenture, Deutsche Bank, WTC, EGI, Citadel Camden, the McCormick Foundation, and the D & Os will be overruled. Subject to submission of final revisions to the Fourth Amended Plan consistent with various resolutions that have been made, by agreement and consistent with this Memorandum, the Fourth Amended Plan will be confirmed.

BACKGROUND

The arduous journey for confirmation of a plan is chronicled in three previous decisions . . . . A detailed description of the Debtors (including an overview of the Debtors' business, their pre-petition debt structure, the 2007 leveraged buy-out (the "LBO")), and the chapter 11 proceedings (including the appointment of and investigation by the Examiner, plan mediation efforts, and the filing of four competing plans of reorganization) can be found in the Confirmation Opinion. *Tribune I*, 464 B.R. at 136-46, [the relevant parts of which are reproduced below:]

A.   OVERVIEW OF THE DEBTORS' BUSINESS

Tribune Company is a Delaware corporation with its principal place of business in Chicago, Illinois. Tribune Company directly or indirectly owns all (or substantially all) of the equity in 128 subsidiaries (the "Tribune Entities"), of which 110 are Debtors. The Tribune Entities are a leading media and entertainment conglomerate reaching more than eighty percent (80%) of households in the United States through their newspapers, other publications and websites, their television and radio stations, and their other news and entertainment offerings.

The Tribune Entities' operations are divided into two primary industry segments: the "Publishing Segment" and the "Broadcasting Segment." The Publishing Segment accounted for seventy percent (70%) of the Tribune Entities' consolidated revenues in 2009. The Publishing Segment includes operation of eight major-market daily newspapers: *The Los Angeles Times, Chicago Tribune, South Florida Sun–Sentinel, Orlando Sentinel, The Sun, Hartford Courant, The Morning Call,* and *The Daily Press. (Id.).*

The Broadcasting Segment accounted for thirty percent (30%) of the Tribune Entities' consolidated operating revenues in 2009 and includes 23 television stations in 19 markets. Various Tribune entities also have investments (typically minority equity interests) in a number of private corporations, limited liability companies, and partnerships, including CareerBuilder, Classified Ventures, TV Food Network, Homefinder, Topix, quadrantONE and Metromix.

In September 2006, the Tribune board of directors (the "Board") created a Special Committee to oversee a formal process of exploring strategic alternatives for Tribune, including a sale of all Tribune Entities, a leveraged recapitalization of Tribune, the sale of the Broadcasting Segment, a spin-off of the Broadcasting Segment, and a split-off of the Publishing Segment. As a result of that process, on April 1, 2007, based on the recommendation of the Special Committee, the Board approved a series of transactions with a newly formed Tribune Employee Stock Ownership Plan (the "ESOP"), EGI-TRB, LLC, a Delaware limited liability company wholly owned by Sam Investment Trust, a trust established for the benefit of Samuel Zell and his family ("EGI" or the "Zell Entity") and Samuel Zell ("Zell"). (DCL Ex. 1389, at TRB0430839). This Leveraged ESOP Transaction (also referred to as the "2007 Leveraged Buy-out" or the "LBO") was consummated in two principal steps, commonly referred to as "Step One" and "Step Two."

In Step One, the newly formed ESOP purchased 8,928,571 shares of Tribune common stock at $28 per share. The Zell Entity also made an initial investment of $250 million in Tribune in exchange for 1,470,588 shares of Tribune's common stock at a price of $34 per share and an unsecured subordinated exchangeable promissory note of Tribune in the principal amount of $200 million.

Thereafter, Tribune commenced a cash tender offer (at a price of $34 per share) to repurchase approximately 52% of its outstanding common stock. Tribune retired the repurchased shares on June 4, 2007. To finance the tender offer, Tribune entered into the $8.028 billion senior secured credit agreement (the "Senior Loan Agreement"). A number of Tribune's domestic subsidiaries (the "Guarantor Subsidiaries") provided unsecured guarantees of indebtedness under the Senior Loan Agreement. The proceeds from the Senior Loan Agreement were also used to refinance Tribune's 2006 Credit Facility and 2006 Bridge Credit Facility.

In Step Two, consummated in December 2007, Tribune merged with a Delaware corporation wholly owned by the ESOP, with Tribune surviving the merger. Upon completion of the merger, all issued and outstanding shares of Tribune's common stock (other than shares held by Tribune or the ESOP) were cancelled and Tribune became wholly owned by the ESOP. The merger was financed through additional borrowings of $2.1 billion under the Senior Loan Agreement (known as the "Incremental Facility") and $1.6 billion under the Bridge Loan Agreement. Incremental Facility and the Bridge Loan Facility are unsecured but guaranteed by the Guarantor Subsidiaries. The proceeds of the additional borrowings were used for, among other things, the consummation of the merger, the repurchase of outstanding Tribune shares not held by the ESOP at $34 per share, and the Step Two financing fees, costs and expenses.

As of the Petition Date, Tribune's pre-LBO indebtedness and LBO indebtedness, totaled approximately $12.706 billion in principal amount.]

The Confirmation Opinion addressed two proposed competing plans of reorganization for the Debtors: (i) the Second Amended Joint Plan of Reorganization for Tribune Company and Its Subsidiaries (the "Debtor/Committee/Lender Plan" or the "DCL Plan") proposed by the Debtors, the Creditors' Committee, Oaktree, Angelo Gordon, and JPM, and (ii) the Joint Plan of Reorganization for Tribune Company and Its Subsidiaries (the "Noteholder Plan") proposed by Aurelius, Deutsche Bank, Law Debenture and WTC. After a confirmation hearing spanning more than two weeks, followed by post-hearing briefing and closing arguments, I determined that both plans failed to meet the requirements of Bankruptcy Code §1129, for the reasons detailed in the Confirmation Opinion, and I denied confirmation of both plans.

However, the Confirmation Opinion contained detailed analyses and determined a number of disputed issues related to confirmation, including, among other things, the Debtors' valuation, and the reasonableness of the Settlements proposed in the DCL Plan. The Confirmation Opinion also analyzed the competing plans under §1129(c) and decided that, assuming the proponents of the competing plans could correct the flaws that prevented confirmation under §1129, and then refiled the corrected plans with substantially similar terms and similar voting results, then the DCL Plan would have the edge for confirmation.

On November 18, 2011, the DCL Plan Proponents filed the Third Amended Joint Plan of Reorganization for Tribune Company and Its Subsidiaries (docket no. 10273) (the "Third Amended Plan"). The Third Amended Plan included an "Allocation Dispute Protocol" which proposed to establish reserves for distributions to holders of allowed claims in certain classes that would be impacted by unresolved disputes regarding inter-creditor priorities, particularly with respect to the PHONES Notes and the EGI-TRB LLC Notes (the "EGI Notes"). Third Amended Plan, §5.18 and Exhibit 5.18. Upon the request of certain parties, I agreed to resolve the "Allocation Disputes," as defined in the Order dated

January 24, 2012 (docket no. 10692) before parties were required to vote on or object to confirmation of the Third Amended Plan. On April 9, 2012, I issued the Allocation Decision which, among other things, determined the applicability of subordination provisions and the order of priority of distributions under the DCL Plan Proponents' amended plan, contingent upon and subject to confirmation of a plan substantially in the form of the Third Amended Plan.

On April 17, 2012, the DCL Plan Proponents filed the Fourth Amended Plan, which incorporated the previously-approved DCL Plan Settlement, as well as Third Amended Plan modifications that addressed the issues raised in the Confirmation Opinion. Further, in light of the Allocation Decision, the Fourth Amended Plan eliminated the Allocation Dispute Protocol and provided for the allocation of distributions that had been proposed under the DCL Plan and Third Amended Plan (which, the DCL Plan Proponents assert, was upheld by the Allocation Decision).

On April 17, 2012, the DCL Plan Proponents also filed the Supplemental Disclosure Document relating to the Fourth Amended Plan. Following a hearing on the adequacy of the Supplemental Disclosure Document, the Court entered the DCL Plan Solicitation Order which, among other things, (i) approved the Supplemental Disclosure Document pursuant to section 1125 of the Bankruptcy Code, (ii) established procedures for the solicitation and tabulation of votes to accept or reject the Fourth Amended Plan, and (iii) scheduling the Confirmation Hearing and related deadlines.

The DCL Plan Proponents solicited votes to accept or reject the Fourth Amended Plan from the Revoting Classes in accordance with the DCL Plan Solicitation Order. As summarized in the Epiq Voting Declaration (DCL Ex. 3005), the Fourth Amended Plan was accepted by most Holders of Claims in the Revoting Classes, as follows:

Classes	Number of Voting Creditors	% Number Accepting	Amount Voted	% Amount Accepting	Result
Class 1C: Senior Loan Claims against Tribune Company	352	99.72%	$8,275,396,770.39	99.97%	Accept
Class 1D: Bridge Loan Claims against Tribune Company	30	100%	$1,600,000,000.00	100%	Accept
Class 1E: Senior Noteholder Claims against Tribune Company	196	85.20%	$1,143,639,844.07	9.95%	Reject
Class 1F: Other Parent Claims against Tribune Company	278	98.92%	$ 286,027,485.95	91.57%	Accept
Class 1I: EGI-TRB LLC Notes Claims against Tribune Company	1	0%	$ 167,047,531.55	0%	Reject

Classes	Number of Voting Creditors	% Number Accepting	Amount Voted	% Amount Accepting	Result
Class 1J: PHONES Notes Claims against Tribune Company	23	4.35%	$ 734,994,736.40	0.45%	Reject
Classes 2E, 4E–7E, 10E, 12E–15E, 18E–20E, 22E–29E, 31E38E, 40E, 42E, 43E and 46E–49E: General Unsecured Claims against Filed Subsidiary Debtors	1	100%	$ 1.00	100%	Accept
Classes 50C–111C: Senior Guaranty Claims	358	99.72%	$8,426,345,592.39	99.97%	Accept

Prior to the Confirmation Hearing for the Fourth Amended Plan, the DCL Plan Proponents negotiated with objecting parties and resolved a number of the objections. The remaining unresolved objections are discussed in detail below.

OBJECTIONS TO CONFIRMATION OF THE FOURTH AMENDED PLAN

A.   OBJECTIONS CHALLENGING THIS COURT'S PRIOR RULINGS

To preserve their rights on appeal, six parties (specifically, (i) Aurelius, (ii) WTC, (iii) Law Debenture, (iv) Deutsche Bank, (v) EGI, and (vi) the D & Os) filed objections to the Fourth Amended Plan that are reiterations of previously raised objections to the DCL Plan and the Third Amended Plan, including objections to the reasonableness of the DCL Plan Settlement, allocation of distributions under the DCL Plan, unfair discrimination, the establishment of the Litigation Trust, the proposed Bar Order, and other issues that were ruled upon in the Confirmation Opinion, the Reconsideration Decision, and the Allocation Decision. To the extent that the same objections are reasserted in opposition to the Fourth Amended Plan, they will be overruled for the same reasons as set forth in the Confirmation Opinion, Reconsideration Decision and/or the Allocation Decision. The objecting parties have not demonstrated a basis for reconsideration of those prior rulings.

C.   OBJECTION TO THE FOURTH AMENDED PLAN'S CLASSIFICATION OF THE
     SENIOR NOTES INDENTURE TRUSTEE ATTORNEY FEES CLAIM

Deutsche Bank, in its capacity as successor indenture trustee under the DBTCA Indentures, and Law Debenture, in its capacity as successor indenture trustee under the 1996 Indenture, each objected to the Fourth Amended Plan's classification of their claims based upon their asserted contractual rights to recover fees, costs and other amounts due in connection with their roles as indenture trustees under the DBTCA Indentures and the 1996 Indenture, respectively (collectively, the "Indenture Trustee Expense Claims").

The Fourth Amended Plan classifies the Indenture Trustee Expense Claims as Senior Noteholder Claims in Class 1E. "Senior Noteholder Claims" are defined as "all Claims arising under or evidenced by the Senior Notes Indentures and related documents and any Claim of the Senior Noteholders arising under the Pledge Agreement."

Deutsche Bank and Law Debenture argue that the Indenture Trustee Expense Claims are contractual obligations under the Senior Notes Indentures and are separate from the claims for payment of principal and interest owed to the Senior Noteholders. They argue that Bankruptcy Code §1122(a) requires claims within a class to be "substantially similar" and, therefore, contend that the Indenture Trustee Expense Claims should be classified as "Other Parent Claims" in Class 1F, which includes "General Unsecured Claims against Tribune and the Swap Claim (and for the avoidance of doubt includes all Claims against Tribune under Non-Qualified Former Employee Benefit Plans, but does not include Convenience Claims)." The definition of General Unsecured Claims also includes any allowed claim by WTC for fees and expenses arising under the PHONES Notes Indenture.

The DCL Plan Proponents respond that the Indenture Trustee Expense Claims are properly classified because (i) the claims arise under the Senior Notes Indentures, (ii) the claims are asserted against the same entity (Tribune Company), (iii) the claims have the same priority against Tribune, and (iv) the claims are asserted in the same proofs of claim that were filed for the other Senior Noteholder Claims for principal and interest due on the Senior Notes.

Section 1122(a) of the Bankruptcy Code provides that "a plan may place a claim or an interest in a particular class only if such claim or interest is substantially similar to the other claims or interests of such class." 11 U.S.C. §1122(a). Section 1122(a) is mandatory in one respect: only substantially similar claims may be classified together. Yet, Section 1122(a) is permissive is this respect: it does *not* provide that *all* similar claims must be placed in the same class. *See* In re AOV Indus., Inc., 792 F.2d 1140, 1150 (D.C.Cir.1986). *See also* In re Jersey City Med. Ctr., 817 F.2d 1055, 1061 (3d Cir.1987) ("[W]e agree with the general view which permits the grouping of similar claims in different classes.").

Although plan proponents have discretion to classify claims, the Third Circuit has recognized that the Code does not allow a plan proponent complete freedom to place substantially similar claims in separate classes. John Hancock Mut. Life Ins. Co. v. Route 37 Bus. Park Assocs. (In re Route 37 Bus. Park Assocs.), 987 F.2d 154, 158 (3d Cir.1993). Instead, a classification scheme must be reasonable. *Id.* The *John Hancock* Court wrote:

> [When] the sole purpose and effect of creating multiple classes is to mold the outcome of plan voting, it follows that the classification scheme must provide a reasonable method for counting votes. In a "cram down" case, this means that each class must represent a voting interest that is sufficiently distinct and weighty to merit a separate voice in the decision whether the proposed reorganization should proceed. Otherwise, the classification scheme would simply constitute a method for circumventing the requirement set out in 11 U.S.C. §1129(a)(10).

Id. at 159. *See also* Phoenix Mutual Life Ins. Co. v. Greystone III Joint Venture (In re Greystone III Joint Venture), 995 F.2d 1274, 1279 (5th Cir.1991) ("thou shalt not classify similar claims differently in order to gerrymander an affirmative vote on a reorganization plan."); In re W.R. Grace & Co., 2012 WL 2130981 at *37 (D.Del. June 11, 2012) ("It is a well-recognized principle that the classification of claims or interests must be 'reasonable,' and cannot be grouped together for arbitrary or fraudulent purposes.")

The threshold issue is whether the claims are "substantially similar" and presents two questions: first, are the claims within Class 1E (*i.e.*, the Indenture Trustee Expense Claims and the Senior Notes Claims) substantially similar, and, second, are the Indenture Trustee Expense Claims and the Other Parent Claims in Class 1F substantially similar?

Courts in this Circuit have interpreted "substantially similar" as a reflection of the "legal attributes of the claims, not who holds them." This analysis focuses on how the "legal character of [a] claim relates to the assets of the debtor" and whether the claims "exhibit a similar effect on the debtor's bankruptcy estate." For example, in *AOV*, the Court determined that a plan may classify all unsecured creditors in a single class, rejecting the argument that an unsecured claim with a third-party guaranty should be classified separately, writing:

> The existence of a third-party guarantor does not change the nature of a claim vis-a-vis the bankruptcy estate and, therefore, is irrelevant to a determination of whether claims are "substantially similar" for classification purposes.

AOV, 792 F.2d at 1151.

Deutsche Bank and Law Debenture argue that the claims in Class 1E are of different character and effect because the Indenture Trustee Expense Claims are contractual obligations to reimburse fees and expenses, while the Senior Notes Claims seek to recover principal and interest under the Notes. However, both types of claims are contractual claims arising from the Senior Notes Indentures. More importantly, as the DCL Plan Proponents point out, the Indenture Trustee Expense Claims and the Senior Notes Claims have the same priority as unsecured claims and are asserted against Tribune. Therefore, the Indenture Trustee Expense Claims and the Senior Notes Claims are substantially similar as to their rights against the Debtors' assets and may be placed within the same class.

Employing the reasoning above, I also conclude that the Indenture Trustee Expense Claims are substantially similar to the Other Parent Claims in Class 1F because all are unsecured claims asserted against Tribune. Is the Fourth Amended Plan's classification of the Indenture Trustee Expense Claims with the Senior Notes Claims, and separate from the Other Parent Claims, reasonable?

The parties have not alleged — and there is no evidence to indicate — that the Fourth Amended Plan's classification scheme was intended to gerrymander votes. Nor is there any indication that the Indenture Trustee Expense Claims were included in Class 1E with the Senior Notes Claims arbitrarily or for a fraudulent purpose.

In *Coram*, the Court noted that separate classification was reasonable when it determined that a group of unsecured noteholders represented a voting interest that was sufficiently distinct from the trade creditors to merit a separate voice in the reorganization. *Coram*, 315 B.R. at 350-51. *See also In re Armstrong World Indus., Inc.*, 348 B.R. 136, 159 (D.Del.2006) (holding that it was reasonable to separately classify personal injury claims and general unsecured claims despite their equal priority status). The Senior Noteholders merit a separate voice in this bankruptcy case and, therefore, the Fourth Amended Plan reasonably classifies the Senior Noteholder Claims separately from the Other Parent Claims. Moreover, throughout this bankruptcy case, the Indenture Trustees have represented the interests of their respective noteholders. Accordingly, the interests of the Indenture Trustees align with Senior Noteholders and the Plan reasonably includes the Indenture Trustees Expense Claims within Class 1E. The classification objections by Deutsche Bank and Law Debenture will be overruled.

3.   CONFIRMATION

The bankruptcy court will confirm a plan if the requirements of section 1129(a) are met. Review the provisions of 1129(a) before reading the next case, and be sure to review the specific sections of the Code discussed in the case.

IN RE PWS HOLDING CORPORATION

United States Court of Appeals, Third Circuit
Nos. 00-5042, 00-5074
Argued March 10, 2000
Filed Sept. 18, 2000

BECKER, Chief Judge.

W.R. Huff Asset Management Co., L.L.C. ("Huff"), and HSBC Bank USA ("HSBC") appeal from the order of the District Court confirming a reorganization plan for Bruno's, Inc., (Bruno's), and several affiliates. Bruno's is based in Alabama and operates a chain of supermarkets in the southeastern United States. Huff was the holder of $290 million in Bruno's subordinated notes; HSBC was the indenture trustee for the subordinated notes (we refer to them together as Huff). They argue that the District Court should not have confirmed the plan for a host of reasons.

Three separate interests have appeared to defend the plan: the debtors and debtors-in-possession (referred to throughout as the Debtors); the Chase Manhattan Bank, representing the group of banks (the Banks) that were the senior lenders to Bruno's before the reorganization; and the Official Unsecured Creditors' Committee.

Huff's . . . challenges to confirmation include that the plan should not have been confirmed because the District Court erred in determining that it was proposed in good faith as required by 11 U.S.C. §1129(a)(3). Huff has not offered anything but innuendo to support its contention that the Debtors violated this portion of the Code, and we find no error in the District Court's conclusion that the plan was proposed in good faith.

Additionally, Huff contends that the plan should not have been confirmed because it violates the following sections of the Bankruptcy Code: 11 U.S.C. §510(a), which provides that a "subordination agreement is enforceable in a case under this title to the same extent that such agreement is enforceable under applicable nonbankruptcy law;" 11 U.S.C. §524(e), which provides that "[e]xcept as provided in subsection (a)(3) of this section, discharge of a debt of the debtor does not affect the liability of any other entity on, or the property of any other entity for, such debt;" 11 U.S.C. §363, which governs the sale of assets outside of the reorganization plan; 11 U.S.C. §1129(a)(2), which provides that a court shall confirm a plan only if "[t]he proponent of the plan complies with the applicable provisions of this Title;" and 11 U.S.C. §1129(a)(7), which provides that a court shall confirm a plan only if the debtor demonstrated at the Confirmation Hearing that creditors rejecting the plan would not receive a greater recovery in a Chapter 7 liquidation.

We reject Huff's argument under §510(a) because the subordinated noteholders' rights under the agreement do not arise until the senior indebtedness is paid in full, which has not happened under the plan. We reject the §524(e) argument because we conclude that the limited release in Paragraph 58 of the plan does not come within the meaning of §524(e) and is consistent with the standard of liability under the Code. We reject Huff's §363 argument because we do not agree with the contention that the Plan triggered a duty to fully market the company. We conclude that Huff does not have standing to raise the challenge under §1129(a)(2) because third-party standing is limited on appeal in bankruptcy cases and Huff cannot show that it was personally aggrieved by any alleged failure of disclosure. Finally, because we are satisfied that the Debtors met the §1129(a)(7) burden of demonstrating that the creditors would not receive a greater recovery under Chapter 7, we reject the challenge under this section as well. We will therefore affirm the order of the District Court confirming the plan.

I. FACTUAL & PROCEDURAL BACKGROUND

As of the commencement date of the Chapter 11 cases, Bruno's was a chain of about 200 supermarkets operating in the southeastern United States (principally in Alabama). In 1995, affiliates of KKR acquired an 83.33% interest in Bruno's in a leveraged recapitalization. As part of this transaction, then existing shareholders of Bruno's were bought out for approximately $880 million. The leveraged recapitalization was financed by a revolving credit and term loan facility provided by the Banks, an equity contribution of $250 million by KKR through Crimson Associates LLP, and the issuance by Bruno's of $400 million in notes due in 2005 pursuant to an indenture. Section 9 of the indenture contains a subordination clause that provides that the noteholders' claims are fully subordinated to the payment in full (including interest) of the claims of the senior lenders (the Banks).

For at least two years following the leveraged recapitalization, Bruno's paid all of its debts as they matured (including $97.5 million in interest payments on the subordinated notes). In the summer of 1997, the Debtors were able to refinance the Bank debt relating to the recapitalization at a lower interest rate and on terms more favorable than the original terms. But by the second half of 1997, as a result of either mismanagement by the directors selected by KKR and a controversial change in pricing policy (according to Huff), or as a result of a greatly increased level of competition in the market (according to the Debtors), Bruno's began to falter. Bruno's had difficulty in meeting payment obligations from the recapitalization and in paying its suppliers and other creditors. On February 2, 1998, it filed a voluntary petition for relief under Chapter 11 of the Bankruptcy Code. Since the filing date, the Debtors have remained in possession.

As of the filing date, Bruno's owed approximately $462 million to the Banks, $135 million to trade vendors, suppliers, and other unsecured creditors, and $421 million on the subordinated notes. In the 90 days prior to filing for relief, it made payments to a variety of creditors and suppliers amounting to more than $600 million, including to firms that provided professional services to the Debtors.[8] However, the only preference action [under section 547 of the Code] the Debtors pursued was an action against the Banks seeking to avoid liens granted to the prepetition lenders in December 1997.

In February 1998, the Bankruptcy Trustee appointed a nine member "Official Unsecured Creditor's Committee" (the Committee). Huff, holder of $290 million in subordinated notes, was the largest creditor of the estate and was elected co-chair of the Committee. The other members of the Committee included four representatives of the Banks, three representatives from the trade, and one representative of the other subordinated noteholders. A representative from the United Food and Commercial Workers Union, which represented supermarket employees of Bruno's, was appointed to serve on the Committee from March 1998 to April 1999.

In October 1998, the Debtors presented a business plan to the Committee. The Committee rejected this plan and then appointed a subcommittee, the "Strategic Alternatives Committee," to work with the Debtors to develop a new plan. This Subcommittee conducted a test marketing of the enterprise and sent out a summary information package to two different sets of potential buyers (neither of which included financial buyers). The Subcommittee did not believe that there would be interest in purchasing the enterprise, and indeed none of the companies contacted expressed an interest. By January 1999, the Debtors concluded that no potential buyers had an interest in the acquisition.

Throughout the spring of 1999, the Committee and subgroups of the Committee convened several times to develop a reorganization plan. Huff asserts that it was excluded from these meetings and that many of the conferees pursued some interest other than maximizing the size of the bankruptcy estate. In March 1999, the Debtors' law firm determined that legal claims arising out of the

8. For example, payments to suppliers included approximately $19 million to Kraft Foods, $4.1 million to Frito-Lay, and $750,000 to Pillsbury. Payments to providers of professional services included $225,551.69 to Cravath, Swaine & Moore, $1.2 million to KKR, and $232,838.71 to Wasserstein Perella & Co.

leveraged recapitalization (primarily fraudulent transfer claims) were not worth pursuing because they believed that the claims were unlikely to succeed and that litigation would be expensive, time consuming, complicated, protracted and vigorously defended, and likely would delay the confirmation of the reorganization plan. In April 1999, the Committee voted to deny funds to pursue the claims, while preserving the claims for further consideration. In response, Huff successfully moved for the appointment of an independent examiner to evaluate the claims. The Debtors presented the first version of the new plan in May 1999. It was revised several times between May and December 1999.

As a part of the negotiations regarding reorganization, three independent entities (Wasserstein Perella & Co. (for the Debtors), PricewaterhouseCoopers (for the Committee), and Chilmark Partners (for the Banks)) conducted assessments of the Debtors and reported current value estimations ranging between $260 and $315 million. Huff's expert argued for a valuation at $580 million, but this valuation was rejected by the District Court, and Huff appears to have abandoned any argument for it on appeal. HSBC still appears to contend that the reorganized enterprise was "significantly undervalued by the Debtors and the Bank Group." HSBC does not, however, argue that the District Court committed clear error in determining that the reorganization value of the Debtors was "substantially below the amount necessary to allow for the satisfaction in full of the Bank claims" and thus that Huff and the other holders of subordinated notes were substantially out of the money (by about $300 million). The interests of the holders of the subordinated notes, including Huff and HSBC, were thus wiped out and, by operation of the Code, 11 U.S.C. §1126(g), the holders are deemed to have rejected the plan.

D.

The District Court confirmed the Debtors' reorganization plan after a three day hearing.

IV. GOOD FAITH

Huff contends that the plan should not have been confirmed because the District Court erred in determining that it was proposed in good faith. Section 1129(a)(3) provides that the court shall confirm a plan only if "[t]he plan has been proposed in good faith and not by any means forbidden by law." 11 U.S.C. §1129(a)(3). "[F]or purposes of determining good faith under section 1129(a)(3) . . . the important point of inquiry is the plan itself and whether such a plan will fairly achieve a result consistent with the objectives and purposes of the Bankruptcy Code." In re Abbotts Dairies of Pennsylvania, Inc., 788 F.2d 143, 150 n. 5 (3d Cir.1986) (quoting In re Madison Hotel Assocs., 749 F.2d 410, 425 (7th Cir.1984)) (alteration in original). The District Court's determinations of fact pertaining to good faith are reviewed for clear error.

Huff contends that the plan was not proposed in good faith because the releases from any claims arising out of the recapitalization were made in a collusive quid pro quo for the waiver of preferences. Huff's theory of bad faith is that KKR orchestrated the reorganization and controlled the Debtors throughout the reorganization in order to avoid potential liability arising out of the leveraged recapitalization, and that it persuaded the other creditors to agree to the reorganization plan by including the waiver of preferences.

As the District Court found, however, the timing of the releases belies this argument; there is scant evidence tying the release of the claims arising out of the recapitalization to the waiver of preferences. The Debtors decided not to pursue the preferences on March 17, 1999. One month later, the Committee passed a resolution preserving the claims arising out of the recapitalization until further information could be gathered about them. This shows that a month after the Debtors decided not to pursue the preferences, the Committee had not decided whether to release the claims arising out of the recapitalization plans.

At the confirmation hearing, Ms. Schirmang, co-chair of the Committee, testified that the Debtors did not release the claims arising out of the leveraged recapitalization in a quid pro quo deal for the preference claims. She testified that, when the Committee decided to release the claims in May 1999, it did so "in the interest of getting the plan into the hands of creditors and hopefully getting a distribution as soon as possible and getting the Debtor out of bankruptcy." Ms. Schirmang also testified that the preference waivers were intended to maintain and rehabilitate post-petition relationships within the trade, and that there was nothing unusual about the waiver of preferences: "to be honest with you, I have never seen a reorganized debtor pursuing preference actions." The trade creditors who benefitted from the waivers included key suppliers to the business. Huff has not presented anything but innuendo in support of its argument that the Debtors failed to act in good faith. Given the record evidence, we conclude that the District Court's finding that the plan was proposed in good faith was not in error.

V.   Conformity to Applicable Provision of Title II of the Code

Section 1129(a)(1) provides that the court shall confirm a plan if it "complies with the applicable provisions of this title." 11 U.S.C. §1129(a)(1). This requires that the plan conform to the applicable provisions of Title II. Huff argues that the plan should not have been confirmed because it violates several provisions of Title II.

A.   section 510(a)

Section 510(a) provides that a "subordination agreement is enforceable in a case under this title to the same extent that such agreement is enforceable under applicable nonbankruptcy law." Huff argues that it had subrogation rights under the indenture which are violated by the terms of the plan. The relevant provision of the indenture provides that

[a]fter all senior indebtedness has been paid in full. . . . Holders shall be subrogated . . . to the rights of holder of Senior Indebtedness to receive distributions [from the debtors] applicable to Senior Indebtedness to the extent that

distributions otherwise payable to the Holders have been applied to the payment of Senior Indebtedness. No payments or distributions to the holders of Senior Indebtedness to which the Holders of the Securities or the Trustee would be entitled except for the provisions of this Article . . . shall, as between the Company, its creditors other than holders of the Senior Indebtedness and the Holders of the Securities, be deemed to be a payment by the Company to or on account of Senior Indebtedness.

The subordination agreement is an intercreditor arrangement between the Banks (the senior indebtedness) and the subordinated noteholders. It does not relieve the Debtors of their payment obligations on the subordinated notes. But the subordinated noteholders' subrogation rights under the indenture described in these provisions never arose because the Banks' claims were not paid in full under the plan. There is no question that the Banks were not paid in full under the reorganization plan, because the reorganized entity was worth at most $340 million, whereas the Banks had claims of $421 million.

Huff argues that the subordinated noteholders had a right under this provision to subrogation. More specifically, Huff argues that it should be awarded warrants to purchase common stock if and when the reorganized company reaches a value of $421 million. But the bankruptcy estate is evaluated and distributions made at the time of the effective date of the reorganization plan. After that date, there are no remaining claims under which Huff could assert subrogation rights. This contention therefore fails.

Huff also argues that under an additional clause, the so-called X clause, the subordinated noteholders should get securities in the new entity subordinated to the Banks' interests to the same extent that they had an interest in the old entity. The clause states that

[u]ntil all Obligations with respect to Senior Indebtedness (as provided in Subsection above) are paid in full in cash or cash equivalent, any distribution to which holders would be entitled but for this article shall be made to holders of Senior Indebtedness (except that Holder may receive (i) securities that are subordinated to at least the same extent as the Securities to (a) Senior Indebtedness and (b) any securities issue in exchange for Senior Indebtedness), as their interests may appear.

This clause does not apply to the current situation. The clause requires that, if the Debtors distribute securities to the subordinated noteholders, the general obligation to turn over distributions to Senior Indebtedness is waived so long as the new securities are subordinated "to the same extent as" the existing subordinated debt.

As the Seventh Circuit has explained, these clauses are quite common, and are intended to avoid a procedure of requiring junior creditors to turn over securities and then receive them back once senior creditors are paid in full:

[s]uch clauses are common in bond debentures, although there is no standard wording. Without the clause, the subordination agreement that it qualifies would require the junior creditors to turn over to the senior creditors any securities that they had received as a distribution in the reorganization, unless the senior

creditors had been paid in full. Then, presumably, if the senior creditors obtained full payment by liquidating some of the securities that had been turned over, the remaining securities would be turned back over to the junior creditors. The X Clause shortcuts this cumbersome procedure and enhances the marketability of the securities received by the junior creditors, since their right to possess (as distinct from pocket the proceeds of) the securities is uninterrupted.

In the Matter of Envirodyne Indus., Inc., 29 F.3d 301, 306 (7th Cir.1994). We agree. The clause is not a requirement that the Debtors distribute to the subordinated noteholders subordinated securities, or warrants to purchase securities, if the reorganized entity does well in the future so that the Banks (the Senior Indebtedness) make back their losses, in proportion to any securities distributed to Senior Indebtedness.

Huff makes one final argument under this section — that the provision of the indenture that states that "nothing in the indenture shall impair, as between the Company and the holders, the obligation of the Company, which is absolute and unconditional, to pay principal of and interest on the Securities in accordance with their terms," requires the Debtors to preserve a recovery for the noteholders with the issuance of securities junior to the common stock. This is a misreading of the provision, which simply provides that the subordination agreement is an intercreditor arrangement, i.e., an arrangement between the Banks (the senior indebtedness) and the subordinated noteholders, and does not relieve the Debtors of their payment obligations on the subordinated notes.

B.   SECTION 524(E)

Section 524(e) provides that "[e]xcept as provided in subsection (a)(3) of this section, discharge of a debt of the debtor does not affect the liability of any other entity on, or the property of any other entity for, such debt." 11 U.S.C. §524(e). Huff argues that the release in Paragraph 58 of the confirmation order violates §524(e), because it affects the liability of the members of the Committee and professionals who provided services to the Debtors to third parties. However, we believe that Paragraph 58, which is apparently a commonplace provision in Chapter 11 plans, does not affect the liability of these parties, but rather states the standard of liability under the Code, and thus does not come within the meaning of §524(e).[9]

Section 524(e) "makes clear that the bankruptcy discharge of the debtor, by itself, does not operate to relieve non-debtors of their liabilities." In re Continental Airlines, 203 F.3d 203, 211 (3d Cir.2000) (*Continental II*) (citations omitted). Section 524(e), by its terms, only provides that a discharge of the debtor does not affect the liability of non-debtors on claims by third parties against

---

9. HSBC argues more generally that "[t]he most obvious defect of the Plan is that it incorporates releases and provides for extinction of causes of action against non debtor third parties for no consideration." It argues that under In re Continental Airlines, 203 F.3d 203, 211 (3d Cir.2000), a plan with releases is unconfirmable as a matter of law. HSBC reads §524(e) and *Continental II* too broadly. Section 524(e) provides that the bankruptcy discharge of the debtor does not operate to relieve non-debtors of their liabilities, but by its terms it does not govern provisions in a plan by which a debtor releases its own claims against third parties.

them for the debt discharged in bankruptcy. Thus, for example, §524(e) makes clear that a discharge in bankruptcy does not extinguish claims by third parties against guarantors or directors and officers of the debtor for the debt discharged in bankruptcy. Indeed, *Continental II* held that a plan that enjoined plaintiffs' actions against the debtor's directors and officers who "ha[d] not formally availed themselves of the benefits and burdens of the bankruptcy process," violated §524(e). The injunction in that plan protected directors and officers from actions taken prior to bankruptcy that allegedly violated the securities laws and thus abrogated the liability of third parties.

Paragraph 58 does not similarly affect the liability of third parties. Paragraph 58 provides that

> [n]one of the Debtors, the Reorganized Debtors, New Bruno's, the Creditor Representative, the Committee or any of their respective members, officers, directors, employees, advisors, professionals or agents shall have or incur any liability to any holder of a Claim or Equity Interest for any act or omission in connection with, related to, or arising out of, the Chapter 11 Cases, the pursuit of confirmation of the Plan, the consummation of the Plan or the Administration of the Plan or the property to be distributed under the Plan, except for willful misconduct or gross negligence, and, in all respects, the Debtors, the Reorganized Debtors, New Bruno's, the Creditor Representative, the Committee and each of their respective members, officers, directors, employees, advisors, professionals and agents shall be entitled to rely upon the advice of counsel with respect to their duties and responsibilities under the plan.

Under Paragraph 58, members of the Committee and professionals who provided services to the Debtors remain liable for willful misconduct or gross negligence. Because we conclude that this standard of liability is the standard that already applies in this situation, we believe that Paragraph 58 affects no change in liability.

Section 1103(c) of the Bankruptcy Code, which grants to the Committee broad authority to formulate a plan and perform "such other services as are in the interest of those represented," 11 U.S.C. §1103(c), has been interpreted to imply both a fiduciary duty to committee constituents and a limited grant of immunity to committee members.

This immunity covers committee members for actions within the scope of their duties. The committee members and the debtor are entitled to retain professional services to assist in the reorganization. In Pan Am Corp. v. Delta Air Lines, Inc., 175 B.R. 438, 514 (S.D.N.Y.1994), it was held that committee members and those professionals who provide services to the debtor with respect to reorganization, or to the committee members in their capacity as committee members, however, do remain liable for willful misconduct or *ultra vires* acts.

We agree with this interpretation of §1103(c) and hold that it limits liability of a committee to willful misconduct or *ultra vires* acts. The release in Paragraph 58 sets forth the appropriate standard for liability that would apply to actions against the committee members and the entities that provided services to the Committee in the event that they were sued for their participation in the reorganization. It does not affect the liability of another entity on a debt of the debtor within the meaning of §524(e).

Nothing in our recent opinion in *Continental II* is to the contrary. In that case, we held that a plan that enjoined plaintiffs' 7D actions against Continental's directors and officers violated §524(e). The release in question here differs from that in *Continental II* in a fundamental way: it sets forth the applicable standard of liability under §1103(c) rather than eliminating it altogether. In *Continental II*, we concluded that it was clear under any rule that the court might adopt that the releases at issue were impermissible because "the hallmarks of permissible non-consensual releases — fairness, necessity to the reorganization, and specific factual findings to support these conclusions-are all absent here." We did not treat §524(e) as a per se rule barring any provision in a reorganization plan limiting the liability of third parties. Because of the differences between the releases in the two cases, *Continental II* does not compel the conclusion that this release is impermissible. Indeed, because this release does not affect the liability of third parties, but rather sets forth the appropriate standard of liability, we believe that this release is outside the scope of §524(e).

C.   SECTIONS 363 AND 1123

Section 363 governs the sale of assets outside of the reorganization plan. It permits the trustee (or the debtor-in-possession), after notice and a hearing, to use, sell, or lease property of the estate outside of the ordinary course of business. . . . Huff characterizes the reorganization plan as involving a sale of assets and tries to transform these two sections of the Bankruptcy Code into a general duty to fully market the company, similar to the duty recognized by the Delaware Supreme Court in the context of corporate change in control transactions. *See* Paramount Communications v. QVC Network, 637 A.2d 34, 43 (Del.1994); Revlon, Inc. v. MacAndrews & Forbes Holdings, 506 A.2d 173, 182 (Del.1986).

This argument fails because these provisions of the Code, even if they do impose a duty to fully market assets in some circumstances (a question we do not address), are simply inapplicable to this situation. The plan wiped out old equity and issued new stock to the creditors. For tax purposes, this transaction was accomplished by transferring substantially all of the assets of the Debtors to a creditors' representative and immediately thereafter to the newly created Bruno's Supermarkets, a corporation whose equity is owned by the senior lenders. But just because a transaction is a sale or exchange for tax purposes does not mean that it is a sale within the meaning of the Code. In a similar case, Major's Furniture Mart, Inc. v. Castle Credit Corp., 602 F.2d 538, 546 (3d Cir.1979), we stated that

> [i]t is apparent to us that on this record none of the risks present in a true sale is present here. Nor has the custom of the parties or their relationship, as found by the district court, given rise to more than a debtor/creditor relationship in which Major's' debt was secured by a transfer of Major's' customer accounts to Castle. . . . Accordingly, we hold that on this record the district court did not err in determining that the true nature of the transaction between Major's and Castle was a secured loan, not a sale.

That the assets passed though the hands of a creditors' representative before being returned to the reorganized Debtors does not transform this plan from a stand-alone, internally generated plan of reorganization to a sale of assets to a third party. To hold otherwise would be to read §1129 of the Code as characterizing the many reorganizations involving the transfer of control from a corporation's old equity to its creditors as involving a sale, a position without support in our jurisprudence.

D.   SECTION 1129(A)(2)

Section 1129(a)(2) provides that the court shall confirm a plan only if "[t]he proponent of the plan complies with the applicable provisions of this Title." 11 U.S.C. §1129(a)(2). We agree with the District Court's conclusion that §1129(a)(2) requires that the plan proponent comply with the adequate disclosure requirements of §1125. Title 11 U.S.C. §1125(b) mandates the filing of a disclosure statement containing "adequate information." Huff argues that the plan proponents failed to comply with the disclosure requirements by failing to provide adequate information regarding the release of the preferences. The Debtors respond that Huff does not have standing to raise this argument.

Appellate standing in bankruptcy cases is more limited than standing under Article III or the prudential requirements associated therewith. "Generally, litigants in federal court are barred from asserting the constitutional rights of others." Kane v. Johns-Manville Corp., 843 F.2d 636, 643 (2d Cir.1988) (citing Warth v. Seldin, 422 U.S. 490, 499, 509, 95 S.Ct. 2197, 45 L.Ed.2d 343 (1975)). The court in *Kane* explained why limits on third-party standing are particularly relevant to appellate standing in bankruptcy proceedings:

> Bankruptcy proceedings regularly involve numerous parties, each of whom might find it personally expedient to assert the rights of another party even though that other party is present in the proceedings and is capable of representing himself. Third-party standing is of special concern in the bankruptcy context where, as here, one constituency before the court seeks to disturb a plan of reorganization based on the rights of third parties who apparently favor the plan. In this context, the courts have been understandably skeptical of the litigant's motives and have often denied standing as to any claim that asserts only third-party rights.

Id. at 644; *see also* Travelers Ins. Co. v. H.K. Porter Co., Inc., 45 F.3d 737, 741 (3d Cir.1995) (adopting the reasoning of *Kane*).

Title 11 U.S.C. §1109(b) — which provides that "[a] party in interest, including the debtor, the trustee, a creditors' committee, an equity security holders' committee, a creditor, an equity security holder, or any indenture trustee, may raise and may appear and be heard on any issue in a case under this chapter" — confers broad standing at the trial level. However, courts do not extend that provision to appellate standing:

> This rule of appellate standing is derived from former section 39(c) of the Bankruptcy Act of 1898, which permitted only a "person aggrieved" to appeal an order of the bankruptcy court. 11 U.S.C. §67(c) (1976) (repealed 1978). Although the present Bankruptcy Code does not contain any express restrictions on appellate

standing, courts have uniformly held that the "person aggrieved" standard is applicable to cases under the Code.

Kane, 843 F.2d at 641-42.

Since Huff cannot show that it was personally aggrieved by any failure to disclose, we conclude that Huff does not have standing to raise this claim.

We do not foreclose the possibility that, in another case, a creditor objecting to a plan for lack of disclosure that actually had the information it complains is missing from the disclosure might nevertheless have standing if it could show that there is a possibility that other creditors would have acted differently (thus benefitting the protesting creditor) if they had had the same information. But in this case, because Huff itself made the information available to the other creditors, it has not made such a showing. The chance that the other creditors would have acted differently is simply too speculative to be a basis for third party standing here.

E. SECTION 1129(A)(7)

Section 1129(a)(7) provides that a court shall confirm a plan only if

> With respect to each impaired class of claims or interests —
>   (A) each holder of a claim or interest of such class —
>   (i) has accepted the plan; or
>   (ii) will receive or retain under the plan on account of such claim or interest property of a value, as of the effective date of the plan, that is not less than the amount that such holder would so receive or retain if the debtor were liquidated under chapter 7 of this title on such date; or
>   (B) if section 1111(b)(2) of this title applies to the claims of such class, each holder of a claim of such class will receive or retain under the plan on account of such claim property of a value, as of the effective date of the plan, that is not less than the value of such holder's interest in the estate's interest in the property that secures such claims.

11 U.S.C. §1129(a)(7). The District Court found that the Debtors have demonstrated at the Confirmation Hearing that creditors rejecting the plan would not receive a greater recovery in a Chapter 7 liquidation. We review this factual finding for clear error.

Huff failed to challenge the Debtors' liquidation analysis. Huff also did not introduce evidence to demonstrate that the recapitalization claims have significant value or that it was in the best interests of the estate to pursue the preference claims. And as noted above, the Examiner's District Court findings to the contrary are well supported. Accordingly, the District Court did not commit clear error in holding that the Debtors met their burden under §1129(a)(7).

VI. CONCLUSION

For the foregoing reasons, the Order of the District Court confirming the Debtor's Second Amended Joint Plan of Reorganization under Chapter 11 of the Bankruptcy Code will be affirmed.

Section 1129(a)(7) is known as the "best interests of creditors" test in the restructuring community. Be sure to take a look at section 1111, referenced in 1129(a)(7). It is an important provision — although 1111(b) might be the most confusing (nontax) statutory provision you have ever read.

4. CRAMDOWN

A plan need not satisfy the absolute priority rule so long as any class affected by the deviation from absolute priority has accepted the plan. That is, deviations from absolute priority must be consensual — although consent is measured at the class level.

A plan also can be confirmed even if not every class has accepted it. This is the so-called cramdown power. Colorful term, no? You will find it in section 1129(b).

Indeed, this is quite common because, as we have already discussed, classes that receive no recovery under a plan are automatically deemed to reject the plan. Thus, if the old shares are cancelled and new shares issued to creditors, the shareholders will be deemed to have rejected the plan.

In such a case, at least one impaired class must have accepted the plan (not counting the votes of any insider) and the plan must be fair and equitable, which includes satisfying the absolute priority rule as to the nonaccepting class. It also must not unfairly discriminate against the dissenting class.

You know what the absolute priority rule requires. The next case looks at unfair discrimination.

IN RE ARMSTRONG WORLD INDUSTRIES, INC., ET AL., DEBTORS

348 B.R. 111
United States District Court, D. Delaware
No. 00-4471 | Aug. 14, 2006

Eduardo C. Robreno, District Judge.

I. Introduction

Before the Court is Armstrong World Industries, Inc.'s Fourth Amended Plan of Reorganization, as modified. The sole objection to the Fourth Amended Plan of Reorganization, as modified (the "Plan") is asserted by the Unsecured Creditors' Committee (the "UCC"), Class 6, which claims that the Plan unfairly discriminates against the Unsecured Creditors in favor of the Asbestos Personal Injury Claimants (the "Asbestos PI Claimants"), Class 7. Therefore, the UCC argues, the Plan does not comply with Section 1129(b) of the Bankruptcy Code. The Court must determine whether to confirm the Plan despite this objection.

The Court has considered the comprehensive submissions of Armstrong World Industries, Inc. ("AWI"), the Asbestos PI Claimants, and the Legal Representative for Future Asbestos Claimants (the "Plan Supporters" or

"Plan Proponents"), and those of the UCC (the "Plan Opponents"), as well as the evidence presented in a three-day hearing and oral argument.

This is the second time this Plan has been before the Court; in February 2005 the Court denied confirmation of the Plan based on its violation of the absolute priority rule embodied in Section 1129(b) of the Bankruptcy Code, and the Third Circuit affirmed this decision on December 29, 2005. The Plan has since been modified to address the violation, thereby leaving only the UCC's present objection for resolution.

The Plan provides for Available Cash, Plan Notes, and Common Stock of AWI, amounting to approximately $2.8 billion, to be distributed to the Unsecured Creditors and the Asbestos PI Claimants. The Unsecured Creditors will receive approximately $982 million. This allocation allows for each holder of an Allowed Unsecured Claim to receive approximately 59.5% of its allowed claim, based on an undisputed estimate of an upper limit of $1.651 billion for the Unsecured Creditors' claims. The remaining Available Cash, Plan Notes, and Common Stock, amounting to approximately $1.8 billion, will be distributed to an Asbestos PI Trust, which will assume and manage liability for all present and future Asbestos PI Claims.

The UCC asserts that the allocation of $1.8 billion to the Asbestos PI Trust amounts to a 91.3% recovery for the Asbestos PI Claimants, based on an upper limit of $1.96 billion for the asbestos PI claims, and therefore unfairly discriminates against the Unsecured Creditors, who will only receive approximately 59.5% of their claims. The Plan Proponents respond that the asbestos PI claims will amount to at least $3.1 billion, thereby fixing the Asbestos PI Claimants' recovery at 59.5% or less. In addition, the Plan Proponents state that the allocated value must be used for the costs of administering the Trust, and a part of the value will be reserved for an undetermined number of future personal injury claimants. Therefore, recovery for the personal injury claimants will be lower than for the Unsecured Creditors.

If the liability for the asbestos PI claims amounts to less than $3.1 billion, then the $1.8 billion allocated to the asbestos PI trust amounts to a higher recovery for the Asbestos PI Claimants than for the Unsecured Creditors. The Court must therefore determine whether this is, in fact, the case. If the recoveries to be received are different, the Court must decide whether the difference amounts to discrimination, and if so, whether the discrimination is unfair.

Of course, the Court's inquiry is complicated by the fact that AWI's liability for asbestos PI claims is an uncertain number; the trust to which the money is allocated is responsible for future claims as well as pending claims. Although there is no dearth of well-compensated experts willing to assume the task of predicting the future asbestos personal injury liability of companies emerging from bankruptcy — this Court heard from three very able estimation experts — the number of possible variables makes any pretense to certainty illusory. The best the Court can do is to consider the expert reports, "make reasonable adjustments based on the record created at trial and embrace the methodology it finds more reliable, while remaining vigilant to the potential bias that a party's expert may have on his or her estimation figures."

The Court concludes that a reasonable approximation of AWI's liability for its present and future asbestos personal injury claims is at least $3.1 billion. The

Court therefore finds that the Plan does not discriminate against the Unsecured Creditors, in that their percentage recovery under the Plan is not materially less than that of the Asbestos PI Claimants.

II. Factual and Procedural History

A. Overview

Armstrong World Industries, Inc.'s Chapter 11 bankruptcy and attempts at reorganization take place within the exhaustively depicted and much analyzed realm of asbestos litigation. Although the Court need not comprehensively rehearse this history, it is important to outline the environment from which this case arises. The resolution of the issue before the Court depends heavily on an understanding of the ways in which asbestos cases have historically moved through the courts.

The harmful effects of asbestos and the litigation that followed have greatly impacted public health, the legal system, and the economy of the United States for decades. The numbers are staggering: total corporate liability is expected to surpass $200 billion, approximately 20 million workers suffered occupational exposure in the United States, approximately 250,000 people have died from the exposure, and hundreds of thousands more have exposure-based illnesses. Samuel Issacharoff & John Fabian Witt, *The Inevitability of Aggregate Settlement: An Institutional Account of American Tort Law*, 57 Vand. L.Rev. 1571, 1619 (2004) (collecting data).

Courts and counsel, both plaintiffs' and defendants,' have struggled to create mechanisms to contain the asbestos litigation that has swamped the legal system — with varying degrees of success. *See* In re Combustion Engineering, Inc., 391 F.3d 190, 200-01 (3d Cir.2004) (stating that global settlement class actions have not succeeded); Issacharoff & Witt, *Aggregate Settlement*, 57 Vand. L.Rev. at 1620-31 (discussing concentration and specialization of claims). Given the inability of the courts to cope with the large number of claims filed, Congress has for years been contemplating the enactment of a scheme to resolve asbestos claims on a nationwide scale. Numerous corporations have filed for bankruptcy. *See* Issacharoff & Witt, *Aggregate Settlement*, 57 Vand. L.Rev. at 1619 (citing Deborah H. Hensler, *As Time Goes By*, 80 Tex. L.Rev. 1899, 1899 (2001) ("As a result of [asbestos litigation], more than forty corporations have filed for insolvency or reorganization")).

The environment of asbestos litigation is on the cusp of major change. Although there is much disagreement about the quantity of liability that asbestos corporations will face in the future, there is widespread acknowledgment that the legal landscape has altered since the 1990s. This shift is due to many factors, including the aging of the exposed asbestos population, state tort reform, the recognition of problems with the mechanisms used to resolve large numbers of asbestos cases through the 1990s, the discovery of widespread fraud in the medical diagnoses of silicosis, and the development of new litigation strategies by corporations beginning to emerge from bankruptcy.

Although there are clear signs that the flood of asbestos litigation may be abating, the questions of how fast and how much remain. *See* Issacharoff & Witt,

Aggregate Settlement, 57 Vand. L.Rev. at 1621 ("An estimated 10,000 Americans still die each year from asbestos-related diseases, a number that is expected to hold constant for the next decade.").

Standing on the surface of these shifting sands, the Court is asked to assess AWI's present and future asbestos-related personal injury liability.

B.   AWI AND ASBESTOS PERSONAL INJURY LITIGATION

Armstrong was founded in 1860 as a cork cutting business, and was incorporated in 1891. The company expanded to encompass products in addition to cork, such as brick, linoleum, and fiberboard. Armstrong was involved in insulation contracting since the early twentieth century. Most of the asbestos personal injury claims asserted against AWI derive from AWI's involvement in the installation of high temperature insulation. In 1958, AWI spun off its contracting business, which encompassed the insulation installation, into a wholly owned subsidiary named Armstrong Contracting and Supply Corporation ("Armstrong Contracting"). In 1969, AWI sold Armstrong Contracting, which became ACandS, Inc. AWI assigned certain trade names to ACandS in connection with the sale.

The first asbestos-related personal injury suit against AWI was filed in 1969. Claims against AWI in the next few decades included claims holding AWI responsible for the contracting activities of Armstrong Contracting, although Armstrong Contracting was a legally distinct subsidiary after 1958, and a completely separate company after 1969. For a variety of reasons, AWI was unsuccessful using the defense that it was not liable for the post-1958 activities of Armstrong Contracting.

C.   AWI'S BANKRUPTCY

AWI filed a voluntary Chapter 11 bankruptcy petition on December 6, 2000, in the United States Bankruptcy Court for the District of Delaware. Although AWI's primary place of business is Pennsylvania, it is incorporated in Delaware and therefore eligible to file for bankruptcy protection in the district of Delaware.

The case was originally assigned to the Honorable Joseph J. Farnan, Jr., of the United States District Court for the District of Delaware. At the time of the filing, the district court had withdrawn the reference for all Chapter 11 cases filed in the district. In the fourth quarter of 2001, the Third Circuit named the Honorable Alfred M. Wolin of the United States District Court for the District of New Jersey to sit by designation on the case, as well as on four other asbestos bankruptcies also pending in the district of Delaware. In turn, Judge Wolin referred the case to the Honorable Randall J. Newsome of the United States Bankruptcy Court for the Northern District of California, also sitting by designation. On June 16, 2004, the case was assigned to the undersigned.

After considerable legal maneuvering, AWI filed its Fourth Amended Plan of Reorganization on May 23, 2003. The UCC filed timely objections to the Plan, arguing that: (1) the Plan should not be approved until Congress resolved the

Fairness in Asbestos Injury Resolution Act ("FAIR"); and (2) the Plan violated Section 1129(b) and the "best interests" test of Section 1129(a)(7) of the Bankruptcy Code. The Bankruptcy Court held a confirmation hearing on November 17 and 18, 2003. On December 19, 2003, the Bankruptcy Court issued Proposed Findings of Fact and Conclusions of Law and a Proposed Confirmation Order. The UCC filed timely objections, and AWI, the Asbestos PI Claimants, and the Future Claimants' Representative filed a joint response.

On December 15, 2004, this Court held a hearing to consider the objections, and on February 23, 2005, issued a decision denying confirmation of the Plan.

E. THE MODIFIED FOURTH AMENDED PLAN OF REORGANIZATION

On February 21, 2006, in accordance with the Court's Case Management Order, entered February 8, 2006, AWI filed a Modified Plan with the Bankruptcy Court. The Modified Plan (hereinafter the "Plan") addressed the Court's denial of confirmation by eliminating the issuance of warrants to the class of Equity Interest Holders. The only outstanding objection to the Plan is the UCC's objection that the Plan unfairly discriminates pursuant to 11 U.S.C. §1129(b).

III. LEGAL STANDARDS

B. CONFIRMATION OF A REORGANIZATION PLAN UNDER 11 U.S.C. §1129

To confirm the Plan, the Court must determine whether it meets the specific requirements of Section 1129. The Plan Opponents assert that it does not. To satisfy the requirements of §1129(a), all impaired classes must accept the Plan. Section 1129(b) allows the confirmation of a plan over the objection of an impaired class if the "plan does not discriminate unfairly, and is fair and equitable, with respect to each class of claims or interests that is impaired under, and has not accepted, the plan." 11 U.S.C. §1129(b)(1).

A reorganization plan confirmed pursuant to §1129(b) is referred to as a "cramdown." A cramdown may be necessary under certain circumstances to foreclose the possibility that a small minority would prevent confirmation of the plan.

Unfair discrimination is not defined in the Bankruptcy Code, nor does the statute's legislative history provide guidance as to its interpretation. In the Matter of Johns–Manville Corp., 68 B.R. 618, 636 (Bankr.S.D.N.Y.1986). "Generally speaking, this standard ensures that a dissenting class will receive relative value equal to the value given to all other similarly situated classes." *Id.* The pertinent inquiry is not whether the plan discriminates, but whether the proposed discrimination is "unfair."

Courts have developed several methods to determine whether a proposed plan unfairly discriminates against a dissenting class. "The hallmarks of the various tests have been whether there is a reasonable basis for the discrimination, and whether the debtor can confirm and consummate a plan without the proposed discrimination."

Traditionally, courts applied a four-factor test to determine unfair discrimination. The factors considered are:

(1) whether the discrimination is supported by a reasonable basis;
(2) whether the debtor could consummate the plan without the discrimination;
(3) whether the discrimination is proposed in good faith; and
(4) the relationship between the discrimination and its basis or rationale.

In re Ambanc La Mesa Limited Partnership, 115 F.3d 650, 656 (9th Cir.1997); In re Dow Corning Corp., 244 B.R. 696, 700 n. 3 (Bankr.E.D.Mich.1999) (listing cases applying four-factor test). In *Dow Corning*, the bankruptcy court in the Eastern District of Michigan noted that some courts had pared the four-factor test down to two factors: (1) whether the discrimination is supported by a legally acceptable rationale; and (2) whether the discrimination is necessary "in light of the rationale." 244 B.R. at 701 n. 5 (internal citation omitted).

More recently, several courts have replaced the four-factor test with a rebuttable presumption test, first proposed in an article by Professor Bruce A. Markell in the American Bankruptcy Law Journal. *See Dow Corning*, 244 B.R. at 701 (citing Bruce A. Markell, *A New Perspective on Unfair Discrimination in Chapter 11*, 72 Am. Bankr.L.J. 227 (1998)). In this analysis, a rebuttable presumption of unfair discrimination arises when there is:

(1) a dissenting class; (2) another class of the same priority; and (3) a difference in the plan's treatment of the two classes that results in either (a) a materially lower percentage recovery for the dissenting class (measured in terms of the net present value of all payments), or (b) regardless of percentage recovery, an allocation under the plan of materially greater risk to the dissenting class in connection with its proposed distribution.

Dow Corning, 244 B.R. at 702.

If there is an allegation of a materially lower percentage recovery, the presumption can be rebutted "by showing that, outside of bankruptcy, the dissenting class would similarly receive less than the class receiving a greater recovery, or that the alleged preferred class had infused new value into the reorganization which offset its gain." A demonstration that the risk allocation was similar to the risk assumed by the parties prior to bankruptcy can rebut the presumption that a discriminatory risk allocation was unfair.

The bankruptcy court in *Dow Corning* found Professor Markell's test to more effectively target unfair discrimination than did the four-factor test, and therefore adopted and applied the rebuttable presumption standard.

Although the Third Circuit has not yet discussed what standard should apply when assessing unfair discrimination, the parties agree the Markell test should be applied in the instant case. The Court agrees and will apply the Markell test.

Applying the Markell test to this case, the Plan Proponents bear the burden of establishing that the Plan comports with §1129's requirements by a preponderance of the evidence. The UCC, as dissenters, bear the burden of producing evidence to support their objection. The UCC has timely raised its objection to the Plan. Consequently, the Plan Proponents must now prove, by a preponderance of the evidence, that the Plan does not unfairly discriminate.

The Court need only reach the question of whether the discrimination is unfair and utilize the rebuttable presumption test if it first finds that the Plan discriminates at all. A finding that all classes of the same priority will receive the identical amount under the proposed Plan is not necessary to find that the Plan does not discriminate. And under the Markell test, the presumption of unfair discrimination only arises if the dissenting class would receive a "materially lower" percentage recovery or will have a "materially greater risk" in connection with the distribution.

Under the circumstances of this case, the Court must decide whether the amount designated for the Unsecured Creditors is a materially lower recovery than that designated for the Asbestos PI Claimants. If the Court finds that $3.1 billion is a reasonable approximation of the liability for present and future personal injury claims, then the Unsecured Creditors, receiving an approximate 59.5% recovery for each claim, are not receiving a materially lower percentage recovery than the Asbestos PI Claimants. If the Court finds the liability for present and future personal injury claims is less than $3.1 billion, a rebuttable presumption of unfair discrimination arises. The Court must then assess whether the Plan Proponents have rebutted this presumption of unfairness.

The Court must compare the proposed allocations to the Asbestos PI Claimants and the Unsecured Creditors to determine whether the Plan unfairly discriminates against the UCC. The Court need not "pick a number," as in an estimation hearing, to make such a comparison. However, because the Court must determine whether $3.1 billion is a reasonable estimate of the asbestos personal injury liability to make this comparison, the Court's inquiry must be informed by the principles of estimation.

The Court has thoroughly considered the parties' criticisms of all of the expert analyses, and finds none of the methodologies to be flawless. However, as explained above, the Court need not choose an exact number for AWI's liability in order to confirm or deny confirmation of the Plan. Presented with three estimates of AWI's pending and future asbestos personal injury liability — $1.9 billion, $4.5 billion, and $6 billion — the Court agrees with the Plan Proponents, and finds that $3.1 billion is a reasonable prediction of the amount of liability AWI will face.

Both the Plan Proponents and the Plan Opponents attempt to correct the other party's expert predictions for what they see as flawed assumptions and methodology. Not surprisingly, each side is able to make the other side's expert prediction approximate their own. The Court will not engage in such calculations. Instead, the Court notes that it has found the expert estimations of the Plan Proponents to be more persuasive, and that Drs. Peterson and Florence adequately incorporate the changed litigation environment into their estimations.

The Court has looked at the experts' estimations, and has found the estimations of the Plan Proponents' experts to be more reliable and persuasive than that of Dr. Chambers, the Plan Opponents' expert. Even when Dr. Peterson's and Dr. Florence's higher estimates, of $6 billion and $4.5 billion, are corrected for flaws in their methodology or excesses of calculation, $3.1 billion is still a reasonable prediction. And when criticisms of Dr. Chambers' methodology are incorporated, her estimate rises close enough to the $3.1 billion to, again, demonstrate it to be a reasonable approximation of AWI's present and future liability.

[T]he Court stands on shifting sands. What may appear reasonable today may well, in a few years, with the benefit of hindsight, turn out to have been incorrect. Nevertheless, the role of the Court is to decide disputes based on the data available as to the present, while making sensible predictions as to the future. It is not to search for mathematical precision, nor ultimate certainty. The Court is not clairvoyant, not the holder of a crystal ball. Rather, it seeks to reach an informed judgment based on an assessment of past experience and current circumstances.

The Court finds, on balance, $3.1 billion to be a reasonable approximation of the debtor's present and future liability for asbestos-related personal injury claims. Thus, the Plan does not discriminate against the UCC, and the UCC's objection is overruled. An appropriate Order follows.

5. DISCHARGE AND EXIT

Typically a chapter 11 plan will not become "effective" upon confirmation. Instead, the plan usually specifies an effective date, which is often contingent on a variety of events happening first. In this way the plan is like other important corporate transactions that "close" some point after the deal is actually signed.

Upon confirmation, section 1141(d) provides that the provisions of a confirmed plan bind the debtor, any entity issuing securities or acquiring property under the plan, and creditors, and the equity security holders. Except as provided in the plan or in the confirmation order, property of the estate vests in the debtor and the property dealt with by the plan vests free and clear of all claims and interests of creditors, and equity security holders.

All claims that were or could have been filed against the debtor are discharged, and the creditors are prohibited by operation of federal law from attempting to collect such claims.

AUGUST 29, 2012, 10:47 AM
IN EXIT, DYNEGY SHAREHOLDERS LOOK TO EKE OUT SOMETHING
By Stephen J. Lubben, *New York Times Dealbook*[10]

Dynegy's controlling shareholders, led by Carl C. Icahn, entered Chapter 11 with a roar, but they are about to leave rather meekly.

Still, they may have covered their tails. Maybe.

Dynegy's original Chapter 11 plan was all about saving the shareholders. Before its bankruptcy, the company engaged in a series of transactions that moved value from a Dynegy unit upstream to the parent company, which was not part of the original bankruptcy filing. The goal was to reorder the normal priorities of bankruptcy, and thus save a position for the shareholders after a series of failed attempts to solve Dynegy's problems out of court.

But then a court-appointed examiner found it all to be a fraudulent transfer. While the existing research on the topic shows that examiners can be quite expensive, this may be an example where the process worked out well.

Next Wednesday, the Federal Bankruptcy Court in Poughkeepsie. N.Y., will begin hearings to consider confirmation of the revised Dynegy plan. While we started out with a "save the shareholders plan," the current plan calls for creditors to own 99 percent of the company when all is said and done.

That's more like it.

But before concluding that the shareholders wasted their time, keep in mind they are getting to keep 1 percent of the company, with warrants to potentially acquire more. And most important, if the plan as currently drafted is approved, the shareholders, directors and management would be released from all liability in connection with their prebankruptcy activities.

In an odd twist, it is another group of shareholders (along with the United States government) that is objecting to the releases in the plan. These shareholders are the lead plaintiffs in a pending class action, whose class comprises those who bought Dynegy shares after the fraudulent transfer, but before it was revealed as such by the examiner.

There may have been some willful blindness here — the fraudulent transfer issue was being litigated in state court before the bankruptcy case — yet this group may have a point.

The question of giving nondebtors releases in plans is largely a matter of case law. The bankruptcy code specifically talks about such releases only in the context of asbestos cases, and even that provision essentially codifies case law that was developed during the pathbreaking Johns Manville bankruptcy case.

But what case law there is suggests that bankruptcy courts should not be too casual about granting what amounts to a limited bankruptcy discharge to parties that have not themselves filed for bankruptcy.

It will be interesting to see how the bankruptcy court approaches this issue. But if it were to grant the release, I think you can count on an appeal. If the bankruptcy court takes out the releases, then the controlling shareholders spent a lot of money on professional fees to get 1 percent of the company, plus warrants.

They probably could have gotten that deal in 2011.

The plan "went effective" with the full releases. Dynegy's shareholders were found to have consented to the release despite receiving nothing under the plan, and thus not being entitled to vote, and having to write a letter to the voting agent to opt out of the release.

In May 2013, Bloomberg reported that Dynegy had sold new debt, but had been compelled to pay an "abuse premium" of 42 basis points.

TABLE OF CASES

Italics indicate principal cases.

INDEX